Mike Holt's Illustrated Guide to

UNDERSTANDING THE NATIONAL ELECTRICAL CODE®

Volume 2 Articles 500 - 820

BASED ON THE
2020 NEC®

MikeHolt.com • 888.NEC.CODE (632.2633)

NOTICE TO THE READER

The text and commentary in this book is the author's interpretation of the 2020 Edition of NFPA 70®, the *National Electrical Code*®. It shall not be considered an endorsement of or the official position of the NFPA® or any of its committees, nor relied upon as a formal interpretation of the meaning or intent of any specific provision or provisions of the 2020 edition of NFPA 70, *National Electrical Code*.

The publisher does not warrant or guarantee any of the products described herein or perform any independent analysis in connection with any of the product information contained herein. The publisher does not assume, and expressly disclaims, any obligation to obtain and include information other than that provided to it by the manufacturer.

The reader is expressly warned to consider and adopt all safety precautions and applicable federal, state, and local laws and regulations. By following the instructions contained herein, the reader willingly assumes all risks in connection with such instructions.

Mike Holt Enterprises disclaims liability for any personal injury, property or other damages of any nature whatsoever, whether special, indirect, consequential or compensatory, directly or indirectly resulting from the use of this material. The reader is responsible for relying on his or her personal independent judgment in determining safety and appropriate actions in all circumstances.

The publisher makes no representation or warranties of any kind, including but not limited to, the warranties of fitness for particular purpose or merchantability, nor are any such representations implied with respect to the material set forth herein, and the publisher takes no responsibility with respect to such material. The publisher shall not be liable for any special, consequential, or exemplary damages resulting, in whole or part, from the reader's use of, or reliance upon, this material.

Mike Holt's Illustrated Guide to Understanding the National Electrical Code®, Volume 2, based on the 2020 NEC®

First Printing: July 2020

Author: Mike Holt
Technical Illustrator: Mike Culbreath
Cover Design: Bryan Burch
Layout Design and Typesetting: Cathleen Kwas

COPYRIGHT © 2020 Charles Michael Holt
ISBN 978-1-950431-08-3

Produced and Printed in the USA

All rights reserved. No part of this work covered by the copyright hereon may be reproduced or used in any form or by any means graphic, electronic, or mechanical, including photocopying, recording, taping, or information storage and retrieval systems without the written permission of the publisher. You can request permission to use material from this text by e-mailing Info@MikeHolt.com.

For more information, call 888.NEC.CODE (632.2633), or e-mail Info@MikeHolt.com.

NEC®, NFPA 70®, NFPA 70E® and *National Electrical Code*® are registered trademarks of the National Fire Protection Association.

 This logo is a registered trademark of Mike Holt Enterprises, Inc.

If you are an instructor and would like to request an examination copy of this or other Mike Holt Publications:

Call: 888.NEC.CODE (632.2633) • Fax: 352.360.0983

E-mail: Info@MikeHolt.com • Visit: www.MikeHolt.com/Instructors

You can download a sample PDF of all our publications by visiting www.MikeHolt.com/products.

I dedicate this book to the
Lord Jesus Christ, *my mentor and teacher.*
Proverbs 16:3

 "For All Your Electrical Training Needs"

www.MikeHolt.com

We Care...

Since the day we started our business over 40 years ago, we have been working hard to produce products that get results, and to help individuals in their pursuit of learning how to be successful in this exciting industry. I have built my business on the idea that customers come first, and that everyone on my team will do everything they possibly can to take care of you. I want you to know that we value you, and are honored that you have chosen us to be your partner in electrical training.

I believe that you are the future of this industry and that it is you who will make the difference in years to come. My goal is to share with you everything that I know and to encourage you to pursue your education on a continuous basis. I hope that not only will you learn theory, code, calculations or how to pass an exam, but that in the process you will become the expert in the field and the person who others know to trust.

We are dedicated to providing quality electrical training that will help you take your skills to the next level and we genuinely care about you. Thanks for choosing Mike Holt Enterprises for your electrical training needs.

God bless and much success,

Exam Preparation | Continuing Education | Apprenticeship Products | In-House Training | & more

"...as for me and my house, we will serve the Lord." [Joshua 24:15]

TABLE OF CONTENTS

About This Textbook..xiii

Additional Products to Help You Learn.................................xvi

How to Use the National Electrical Code................................. 1

Article 90—Introduction to the *National Electrical Code* 7
- 90.1 Purpose of the *NEC* 7
- 90.2 Scope of the *NEC* 8
- 90.3 *Code* Arrangement 10
- 90.4 Enforcement 11
- 90.5 Mandatory Requirements and Explanatory Material 13
- 90.7 Examination of Equipment for Product Safety 13

Article 90—Practice Questions 15

CHAPTER 1—GENERAL RULES 19

Article 100—Definitions 21
- 100 Definitions 21

Article 110—Requirements for Electrical Installations .. 65
- Part I. General Requirements 65
- 110.1 Scope 65
- 110.2 Approval of Conductors and Equipment 65
- 110.3 Use and Product Listing (Certification) of Equipment 66
- 110.4 Voltage Rating of Electrical Equipment 66
- 110.5 Conductor Material 66
- 110.6 Conductor Sizes 67
- 110.7 Wiring Integrity 67
- 110.8 Suitable Wiring Methods 67
- 110.9 Interrupting Rating (Overcurrent Protective Devices)....68
- 110.10 Equipment Short-Circuit Current Rating 68
- 110.11 Deteriorating Agents 69
- 110.12 Mechanical Execution of Work 70
- 110.13 Mounting and Cooling of Equipment 72
- 110.14 Conductor Termination and Splicing 72
- 110.15 High-Leg Conductor Identification 79
- 110.16 Arc Flash Hazard Warning 80
- 110.21 Markings 81
- 110.22 Identification of Disconnecting Means 82
- 110.24 Available Fault Current 83
- 110.25 Lockable Disconnecting Means 83
- Part II. 1,000V, Nominal, or Less 84
- 110.26 Spaces About Electrical Equipment 84
- 110.28 Enclosure Types 92

Chapter 1—Practice Questions 95

CHAPTER 5—SPECIAL OCCUPANCIES 101

Article 500—Hazardous (Classified) Locations 103
- 500.1 Scope—Articles 500 Through 503 104
- 500.3 Other Articles 104
- 500.4 Documentation 104
- 500.5 Classifications of Hazardous Locations 105
- 500.6 Material Groups 107
- 500.7 Protection Techniques 107
- 500.8 Equipment 109

Article 501—Class I Hazardous (Classified) Locations 111
- Part I. General 111
- 501.1 Scope 111
- Part II. Wiring 111
- 501.10 Wiring Methods 111
- 501.15 Raceway and Cable Seals 113
- 501.30 Grounding and Bonding 119
- Part III. Equipment 120
- 501.115 Enclosures Containing Make-and-Break Contact Devices 120
- 501.125 Motors and Generators 121
- 501.130 Luminaires 121
- 501.135 Utilization Equipment 122
- 501.140 Flexible Cords, Class I, Divisions 1 and 2 122
- 501.145 Receptacles and Attachment Plugs 123
- 501.150 Limited-Energy and Communications Systems 124

Article 502—Class II Hazardous (Classified) Locations 125
- Part I. General 125
- 502.1 Scope 125
- 502.5 Explosionproof Equipment 125

Article 503 | Table of Contents

Part II. Wiring 125
502.10 Wiring Methods 125
502.15 Sealing 127
502.30 Grounding and Bonding 128

Part III. Equipment 129
502.115 Enclosures Containing Make-and-Break Contacts 129
502.125 Motors and Generators 130
502.130 Luminaires 130
502.140 Flexible Cords 131
502.145 Receptacles and Attachment Plugs 132
502.150 Limited-Energy and Communications Systems 132

Article 503—Class III Hazardous (Classified) Locations 133

Part I. General 133
503.1 Scope 133

Part II. Wiring 133
503.10 Wiring Methods 133
503.30 Grounding and Bonding 134

Part III. Equipment 135
503.115 Enclosures Containing Make-and-Break Contacts 135
503.125 Motors and Generators 135
503.130 Luminaires 135
503.140 Flexible Cords 136
503.145 Receptacles and Attachment plugs 136
503.150 Limited-Energy and Communications Systems 136

Article 511—Commercial Garages, Repair and Storage 137
511.1 Scope 137
511.3 Classification of Hazardous Areas 137
511.7 Wiring and Equipment Above Hazardous (Classified) Locations 138
511.8 Underground Wiring Below Class I Locations 139
511.9 Seals 139
511.10 Special Equipment 140
511.12 GFCI-Protected Receptacles 140

Article 514—Motor Fuel Dispensing Facilities 141
514.1 Scope 141
514.3 Classification of Locations 141
514.4 Wiring and Equipment Within Class I Locations 142
514.7 Wiring and Equipment Above Class I Locations 142
514.8 Underground Wiring 142
514.9 Conduit Seal 143
514.16 Grounding and Bonding 144

Article 517—Health Care Facilities 145

Part I. General 145
517.1 Scope 145
517.2 Definitions 145

Part II. Wiring and Protection 147
517.10 Applicability 147
517.12 Wiring Methods 147
517.13 Equipment Grounding Conductor for Receptacles and Fixed Electrical Equipment in Patient Care Spaces 147
517.16 Isolated Ground Receptacles 150
517.18 General Care Spaces 151

Article 518—Assembly Occupancies 153
518.1 Scope 153
518.2 General Classifications 153
518.3 Other Articles 154
518.4 Wiring Methods 154
518.6 Illumination 154

Article 525—Carnivals, Circuses, Fairs, and Similar Events 157

Part I. General Requirements 157
525.1 Scope 157
525.2 Definitions 157
525.5 Overhead Conductor Clearances 157
525.6 Protection of Electrical Equipment 158

Part III. Wiring Methods 158
525.20 Wiring Methods 158
525.21 Rides, Tents, and Concessions 159
525.22 Outdoor Portable Distribution or Termination Boxes 159
525.23 GFCI-Protected Receptacles and Equipment 160

Part IV. Grounding and Bonding 160
525.31 Equipment Grounding 160
525.32 Portable Equipment Grounding Conductor Continuity 160

Article 547—Agricultural Buildings 161
547.1 Scope 161
547.2 Definitions 161
547.5 Wiring Methods 162
547.8 Luminaires 163
547.10 Equipotential Planes 163

Article 550—Mobile Homes, Manufactured Homes, and Mobile Home Parks 165

Part I. General 165
550.1 Scope 165
550.2 Definitions 165
550.4 General Requirements 166

Part II. Mobile and Manufactured Homes	166
550.13	Receptacle Outlets	166
550.15	Wiring Methods and Materials	166
550.25	AFCI Protection	167

Part III. Services and Feeders 167
550.32	Mobile and Manufactured Home Service Disconnect	167
550.33	Feeder	167

Article 555—Marinas, Boatyards, and Docking Facilities 169

Part I. General 169
555.1	Scope	169
555.2	Definitions	169
555.3	Electrical Datum Plane Distances	171
555.4	Location of Service Equipment	172
555.5	Maximum Voltage	172
555.6	Load Calculations for Service and Feeder Conductors	172
555.7	Transformers	172
555.9	Boat Hoists	173
555.10	Electric Shock Hazard Signage	173
555.11	Motor Fuel Dispensing Stations—Hazardous (Classified) Locations	173
555.12	Repair Facilities—Hazardous (Classified) Locations	174
555.13	Bonding of Noncurrent-Carrying Metal Parts	174

Part II. Marinas, Boatyards, and Docking Facilities 174
555.30	Electrical Connections	174
555.33	Receptacles	175
555.34	Wiring Methods and Installation	175
555.35	Ground-Fault Protection of Equipment (GFPE) and Ground-Fault Circuit-Interrupter (GFCI) Protection	176
555.36	Boat Receptacle Disconnecting Means	177
555.37	Equipment Grounding Conductor	177

Article 590—Temporary Installations 179
590.1	Scope	179
590.2	All Wiring Installations	179
590.3	Time Constraints	179
590.4	General	180
590.5	Listing of Decorative Lighting	182
590.6	GFCI Protection for Personnel	182
590.8	Overcurrent Protective Devices	183

Chapter 5—Practice Questions 185

CHAPTER 6—SPECIAL EQUIPMENT 209

Article 600—Electric Signs and Outline Lighting 211
Part I. General 211
600.1	Scope	211
600.2	Definitions	212
600.3	Listing	212
600.4	Markings	213
600.5	Branch Circuits	213
600.6	Disconnecting Means	214
600.7	Grounding and Bonding	216
600.9	Location	218
600.21	Ballasts, Transformers, Class 2 Power Sources, and Electronic Power Supplies	218
600.24	Class 2 Power Sources	218

Part II. Field-Installed Skeleton Tubing, Outline Lightning, and Secondary Wiring 219
600.34	Photovoltaic (PV) Powered Sign	219
600.35	Retrofit Kits	219

Article 604—Manufactured Wiring Systems 221
604.1	Scope	221
604.2	Definition	221
604.6	Listing Requirements	221
604.7	Installation—Securing and Supporting	222
604.10	Uses Permitted	222

Article 620—Elevators, Escalators, and Moving Walks 223
Part I. General 223
620.1	Scope	223
620.6	GFCI-Protected Receptacles	223

Part II. Conductors 224
620.13	Feeder and Branch-Circuit Conductors	224
620.16	Short-Circuit Current Rating	224

Part III. Wiring 224
620.22	Branch Circuits for Elevator Car(s)	224
620.23	Branch Circuits for Machine Room/Machinery Space	225
620.24	Branch Circuit for Hoistway Pit Lighting and Receptacles	225

Part IV. Installation of Conductors 226
620.37	Wiring in Elevator Hoistways, Control, and Machine Rooms/Spaces	226

Part VI. Disconnecting Means and Control 226
620.51	Disconnecting Means	226

Article 625—Electric Vehicle Power Transfer System 227
Part I. General 227
625.1	Scope	227
625.2	Definitions	227
625.5	Listed	228

Part III. Installation 228
625.40	Electric Vehicle Branch Circuit	228
625.41	Overcurrent Protection	228
625.42	Rating	229
625.43	Disconnecting Means	229

Article 630 | Table of Contents

625.48	Interactive Systems	229
625.50	Location	229
625.52	Ventilation	229
625.54	Ground-Fault Circuit-Interrupter Protection for Personnel	230
625.60	Alternating-Current Electric Vehicle Power Export (EVPE) Receptacles	230

Article 630—Electric Welders 231
Part I. General 231
| 630.1 | Scope | 231 |
| 630.6 | Listing | 231 |

Part II. Arc Welders 231
630.11	Ampacity of Supply Conductors	231
630.12	Overcurrent Protection	234
630.13	Disconnecting Means	234

Part III. Resistance Welders 234
630.31	Ampacity of Supply Conductor	234
630.32	Overcurrent Protection	236
630.33	Disconnecting Means	236

Article 640—Audio Signal Amplification and Reproduction Equipment 237
Part I. General 237
640.1	Scope	237
640.2	Definitions	237
640.3	Locations and Other Articles	238
640.4	Protection of Electrical Equipment	238
640.6	Mechanical Execution of Work	238
640.9	Wiring Methods	239
640.10	Audio Systems Near Bodies of Water	239

Part II. Permanent Audio System Installations 240
| 640.21 | Use of Flexible Cords and Flexible Cables | 240 |
| 640.23 | Conduit or Tubing | 240 |

Article 645—Information Technology Equipment (ITE) 241
645.1	Scope	241
645.2	Definitions	241
645.3	Other Articles	241
645.4	Special Requirements	242
645.5	Supply Circuits and Interconnecting Cables	242
645.10	Disconnecting Means	245
645.15	Equipment Grounding and Bonding	245

Article 680—Swimming Pools, Spas, Hot Tubs, Fountains, and Similar Installations 247
Part I. General Requirements for Pools, Spas, Hot Tubs, and Fountains 247
680.1	Scope	247
680.2	Definitions	248
680.3	Approval of Equipment	251
680.4	Inspections After Installation	251
680.5	Ground-Fault Circuit Interrupters	251
680.6	Bonding and Equipment Grounding	251
680.7	Bonding and Equipment Grounding Terminals	251
680.9	Overhead Conductor Clearance	251
680.10	Electric Water Heaters	252
680.11	Underground Wiring	253
680.12	Equipment Rooms and Pits	253
680.13	Maintenance Disconnecting Means	253
680.14	Wiring Methods in Corrosive Environment	254

Part II. Permanently Installed Pools 254
680.20	General	254
680.21	Pool Motors	254
680.22	Receptacles, Luminaires, and Switches	255
680.23	Underwater Pool Luminaires	257
680.24	Junction Box, Transformer, or GFCI Enclosure	261
680.25	Feeders	262
680.26	Equipotential Bonding	262
680.27	Specialized Equipment	267
680.28	Gas-Fired Water Heaters	267

Part III. Storable Pools, Spas, Hot Tubs, and Immersion Pools 267
680.30	General	267
680.31	Pumps	267
680.32	GFCI Protection	267
680.34	Receptacle Locations	268
680.35	Storable and Portable Immersion Pools	268

Part IV. Spas and Hot Tubs, and Permanently Installed Immersion Pools 268
680.40	General	268
680.41	Emergency Switch for Spas and Hot Tubs	268
680.42	Outdoor Installations	269
680.43	Indoor Installations	269
680.44	GFCI Protection	270
680.45	Permanently Installed Immersion Pools	270

Part V. Fountains 271
680.50	General	271
680.51	Luminaires and Submersible Equipment	271
680.54	Connection to an Equipment Grounding Conductor	272
680.55	Methods of Equipment Grounding	272
680.56	Cord-and-Plug-Connected Equipment	272
680.57	Electric Signs in or Adjacent to Fountains	272
680.58	GFCI Protection for Adjacent Receptacles	273
680.59	GFCI Protection for Permanently Installed Nonsubmersible Pumps	273

Part VII. Hydromassage Bathtubs 273
680.70	General	273
680.71	GFCI Protection	273
680.73	Accessibility	273
680.74	Equipotential Bonding	274

Part VIII. Electrically Powered Pool Lifts................................274	691.5	Equipment 314
680.80	General 274	691.6	Engineered Design 314
680.81	Equipment Approval 274	691.7	Conformance of Construction to Engineered Design..............314
680.82	Protection..275	691.8	Direct-Current Operating Voltage 314
680.83	Bonding 275	691.9	Disconnect for Isolating Photovoltaic Equipment 314
680.84	Switching Devices and Receptacles 275	691.10	Arc-Fault Mitigation 314
		691.11	Fence Bonding and Grounding 314

Article 690—Solar Photovoltaic (PV) Systems 277

Part I. General 277

690.1	Scope 277
690.2	Definitions 278
690.4	General Requirements...282
690.6	Alternating-Current Modules and Systems 283

Part II. Circuit Requirements 284

690.7	Maximum PV System Direct-Current Circuit Voltage 284
690.8	Circuit Current and Conductor Sizing........................288
690.9	Overcurrent Protection 293
690.10	Stand-Alone Systems 295
690.11	Arc-Fault Circuit Protection 295
690.12	Rapid Shutdown 295

Part III. Disconnect 297

690.13	PV System Disconnect 297
690.15	PV Equipment Disconnecting Means to Isolate PV Equipment..298

Part IV. Wiring Methods 300

690.31	Wiring Methods 300
690.32	Component Interconnections 305
690.33	Connectors (Mating)..305
690.34	Access to Boxes 306

Part V. Grounding and Bonding 306

690.43	Equipment Grounding and Bonding 306
690.45	Size of Equipment Grounding Conductors 308
690.47	Grounding Electrode System 308

Part VI. Markings and Labels 309

690.53	Direct-Current PV Circuit Label 309
690.54	Interactive System Point of Interconnection 310
690.55	Energy Storage 310
690.56	Identification of Power Sources.................................310

Part VII. Connections to Other Sources 311

690.59	Connection to Other Power Sources 311

Part VIII. Energy Storage Systems 311

690.71	Energy Storage Systems 311
690.72	Self-Regulated PV Charge Control 312

Article 691—Large-Scale Photovoltaic (PV) Electric Supply Stations 313

691.1	Scope 313
691.4	Special Requirements for Large-Scale PV Electric Supply Stations 313

Article 695—Fire Pumps 315

695.1	Scope 315
695.3	Electric Power Source(s)...316
695.4	Continuity of Power 316
695.5	Transformers 317
695.6	Power Wiring 318
695.7	Voltage Drop 319
695.10	Listed Equipment 320
695.14	Control Wiring 320
695.15	Surge Protection 320

Chapter 6—Practice Questions..321

CHAPTER 7—SPECIAL CONDITIONS 343

Article 700—Emergency Systems 345

Part I. General 345

700.1	Scope 345
700.2	Definitions 346
700.3	Tests and Maintenance 346
700.4	Capacity and Rating..346
700.5	Transfer Equipment 346
700.7	Signs..347
700.8	Surge Protection 347

Part II. Circuit Wiring..348

700.10	Wiring 348

Part III. Sources of Power 349

700.12	General Requirements...349

Part IV. Emergency System Circuits for Lighting and Power............351

700.15	Loads on Emergency Branch Circuits.......................351
700.16	Emergency Illumination 351
700.19	Multiwire Branch Circuits 352

Part VI. Overcurrent Protection 352

700.30	Accessibility...352
700.32	Selective Coordination...352

Article 701—Legally Required Standby Systems 353

Part I. General 353

701.1	Scope 353
701.2	Definition 353
701.3	Tests and Maintenance 354

701.4	Capacity and Rating	354
701.5	Transfer Equipment	354
701.6	Signals	355
701.7	Signs	355
Part II. Circuit Wiring		355
701.10	Wiring	355
Part III. Sources of Power		355
701.12	General Requirements	355
Part IV. Overcurrent Protection		356
701.30	Accessibility	356
701.32	Selective Coordination	357

Article 702—Optional Standby Systems 359

Part I. General		359
702.1	Scope	359
702.2	Definition	360
702.4	Capacity and Rating	360
702.5	Transfer Equipment	361
702.6	Signals	362
702.7	Signs	362
Part II. Circuit Wiring		362
702.10	Wiring	362
702.11	Portable Generator Grounding	363
702.12	Outdoor Generator Sets	363

Article 705—Interconnected Electric Power Production Sources 365

Part I. General		365
705.1	Scope	365
705.2	Definitions	365
705.6	Equipment Approval	366
705.8	System Installation	366
705.10	Identification of Power Sources	366
705.11	Supply-Side Source Connections	367
705.12	Load-Side Source Connections	369
705.13	Power Control Systems	375
705.16	Interrupting and Short-Circuit Current Rating	376
705.20	Disconnect	376
705.25	Wiring Methods	376
705.28	Circuit Sizing and Current	377
705.30	Overcurrent Protection	377
705.32	Ground-Fault Protection	378
705.40	Loss of Utility Power	378
705.45	Unbalanced Interconnections	379
Part II. Microgrid Systems		380
705.50	System Operation	380
705.60	Primary Power Source Connection	380

Article 706—Energy Storage Systems 381

Part I. General		381
706.1	Scope	381
706.2	Definitions	382
706.3	Qualified Personnel	382
706.4	System Requirements	382
706.5	Listing	383
706.6	Multiple Systems	383
706.8	Storage Batteries	383
706.9	Maximum Voltage	383
Part II. Disconnect		383
706.15	Disconnect	383
Part III. Installation Requirements		384
706.20	General	384
706.21	Directory (Identification of Power Sources)	385
Part IV. Circuit Requirements		385
706.30	Circuit Sizing and Current	385
706.31	Overcurrent Protection	386
706.33	Charge Control	386
Part V. Flow Battery Energy Storage Systems		387

Article 710—Stand-Alone Systems 389

710.1	Scope	389
710.6	Equipment Approval	389
710.10	Identification of Power Sources	390
710.12	Stand-Alone Inverter Input Circuit Current	390
710.15	General	390

Article 725—Remote-Control, Signaling, and Power-Limited Circuits 393

Part I. General		393
725.1	Scope	393
725.2	Definitions	394
725.3	Other Articles	394
725.21	Electrical Equipment Behind Access Panels	398
725.24	Mechanical Execution of Work	398
725.25	Abandoned Cable	399
725.31	Safety-Control Equipment	400
725.35	Circuit Requirements	400
Part II. Class 1 Circuit Requirements		400
725.41	Class 1 Circuit Classifications and Requirements	400
725.43	Class 1 Circuit Overcurrent Protection	401
725.45	Class 1 Circuit Overcurrent Protective Device Location	401
725.46	Class 1 Circuit Wiring Methods	401
725.48	Conductors of Different Circuits in Same Cable, Cable Tray, Enclosure, or Raceway	401
725.49	Class 1 Circuit Conductors	402
725.51	Number of Conductors in a Raceway	402

Part III. Class 2 Circuit Requirements 402
- 725.121 Power Sources for Class 2 Circuits 402
- 725.124 Circuit Marking 403
- 725.127 Wiring Methods on Supply Side of the Class 2 Power Source 403
- 725.130 Wiring Methods on Load Side of the Class 2 Power Source 404
- 725.135 Installation of Class 2 Cables 404
- 725.136 Separation from Power Conductors 405
- 725.139 Conductors of Different Circuits in Same Cable, Enclosure, Cable Tray, Raceway, or Cable Routing Assembly 407
- 725.143 Support 408
- 725.144 Transmission of Power and Data 408
- 725.154 Applications of Class 2 Cables 410

Part IV. Listing Requirements 410
- 725.170 Listing and Marking of Equipment for Power and Data Transmission 410
- 725.179 Listing and Marking of Class 2 Cables 410

Article 760—Fire Alarm Systems 413

Part I. General 413
- 760.1 Scope 413
- 760.2 Definitions 413
- 760.3 Other Articles 414
- 760.21 Access to Electrical Equipment Behind Panels Designed to Allow Access 416
- 760.24 Mechanical Execution of Work 416
- 760.25 Abandoned Cables 417
- 760.30 Fire Alarm Circuit Identification 418
- 760.35 Fire Alarm Circuit Requirements 418

Part III. Power-Limited Fire Alarm (PLFA) Circuits 418
- 760.121 Power Sources for Power-Limited Fire Alarm Circuits 418
- 760.124 Marking 419
- 760.127 Wiring Methods on Supply Side of the Power-Limited Fire Alarm Source 419
- 760.130 Wiring Methods on Load Side of the Power-Limited Fire Alarm Power Source 419
- 760.135 Installation of PLFA Cables in Buildings 420
- 760.136 Separation from Power Conductors 421
- 760.143 Support of PLFA Cables 421
- 760.154 Applications of Power-Limited Fire Alarm Cables (PLFA) 421

Part IV. Listing Requirements 422
- 760.179 Listing and Marking of Power-Limited Fire Alarm Cables (PLFA) 422

Article 770—Optical Fiber Cables 423

Part I. General 423
- 770.1 Scope 423
- 770.2 Definitions 423
- 770.3 Other Articles 424
- 770.21 Access to Electrical Equipment Behind Panels Designed to Allow Access 424
- 770.24 Mechanical Execution of Work 424
- 770.25 Abandoned Cable 425
- 770.26 Spread of Fire or Products of Combustion 426

Part V. Installation Methods Within Buildings 426
- 770.110 Raceways and Cable Routing Assemblies, and Cable Trays for Optical Fiber Cables 426
- 770.113 Installation of Optical Fiber Cables 427
- 770.114 Grounding 428
- 770.133 Installation of Optical Fiber Cables and Electrical Conductors 428
- 770.154 Applications of Listed Optical Fiber Cables 428

Chapter 7—Practice Questions 429

CHAPTER 8—COMMUNICATIONS SYSTEMS 449

Article 800—General Requirements for Communications Systems 451

Part I. General 451
- 800.1 Scope 451
- 800.2 Definitions 451
- 800.3 Other Articles 452
- 800.21 Access to Electrical Equipment Behind Panels Designed to Allow Access 453
- 800.24 Mechanical Execution of Work 453
- 800.25 Abandoned Cable 454
- 800.26 Spread of Fire or Products of Combustion 454

Part II. Wires and Cables Outside and Entering Buildings 456
- 800.49 Metal Entrance Conduit Bonding 456
- 800.53 Separation from Lightning Conductors 456

Part III. Bonding Methods 456
- 800.100 Cable and Primary Protector Bonding 456

Part IV. Installation Methods Within Buildings 458
- 800.110 Raceways and Cable Routing Assemblies 458
- 800.113 Installation of Communications Wires, Cables, Raceways, and Cable Routing Assemblies 459
- 800.154 Applications of Listed Communications Wires, Cables, and Raceways, and Listed Cable Routing Assemblies 460
- 800.179 Plenum, Riser, General-Purpose, and Limited Use Cables 460

Article 805—General Requirements for Communications Circuits 461

Part I. General 461
- 805.1 Scope 461
- 805.2 Definitions 461
- 805.18 Installation of Equipment 461

Article 810 | Table of Contents

Part III. Protection..462
805.90 Primary Protection 462
805.93 Bonding or Interruption 462

Part IV. Installation Methods Within Buildings........................462
805.133 Installation of Communications Wires, Cables, and Equipment 462
805.154 Communications Cable(s) Substitutions 463
805.156 Dwelling Unit Communications Outlet 463

Article 810—Radio and Television Antenna Equipment 465

Part I. General 465
810.1 Scope 465
810.4 Community Television Antenna 466

Part II. Receiving Equipment—Antenna Systems......................466
810.12 Supports 466
810.13 Avoid Contact with Conductors of Other Systems 466
810.15 Metal Antenna Supports—Bonding 467
810.18 Clearances 467
810.20 Antenna Discharge Unit 467
810.21 Bonding Conductors and Grounding Electrode Conductors 468

Part III. Amateur and Citizen Band Transmitting and Receiving Stations—Antenna Systems 470
810.51 Other Sections 470
810.57 Antenna Discharge Units—Transmitting Stations 470
810.58 Bonding Conductors and Grounding Electrode Conductors—Amateur and Citizen Band Transmitting and Receiving Stations 470

Article 820—Community Antenna Television (CATV) and Radio Distribution Systems (Coaxial Cable) 471

Part I. General 471
820.1 Scope 471

Part III. Protection..471
820.93 Grounding of the Outer Conductive Shield of Coaxial Cables 471

Part IV. Grounding Methods 472
820.100 Bonding and Grounding Methods 472

Part V. Installation Methods Within Buildings 472
820.133 Installation of Coaxial Cables and Equipment 472

Chapter 8—Practice Questions 475

Final Exam A—Straight Order 481

Final Exam B—Random Order 491

INDEX 501

About the Author 509

About the Illustrator 510

About the Mike Holt Team 511

ABOUT THIS TEXTBOOK

Mike Holt's Illustrated Guide to Understanding the National Electrical Code®, Volume 2, based on the 2020 NEC®

Mike Holt's Illustrated Guide to Understanding the National Electrical Code®, Volume 2, based on the 2020 NEC® textbook provides you with the tools necessary to understand the technical requirements of the National Electrical Code (NEC), Articles 500 through 820, and is the second volume of a 2-part program.

This textbook is easy to use because of Mike's practical and informative writing style. Just like all of Mike Holt textbooks, this one is built around hundreds of full-color illustrations and photographs that show the requirements of the National Electrical Code in practical use. The images provide a visual representation of the information being discussed, helping you to better understand just how the Code rules are applied.

This textbook explains tips on proper electrical installations, warnings, or dangers related to improper electrical installations, and points out possible conflicts or confusing NEC requirements. Sometimes a rule seems confusing or it may be difficult to understand its actual application. Where this may be the case, you will find additional content to help you to better interpret the rule. Our goal is to help the industry understand the current NEC, point out areas that may need refinement, and encourage all Code users to be a part of the change process that helps create a better NEC for the future.

Chapters 5 through 8 of the NEC are specialized and technical, and require a complete understanding of the Code rules and requirements in Chapters 1 through 4. We recommend that you complete the Volume 1 textbook before moving on to Volume 2. In addition, we highly recommend that you use both books along with the accompanying videos. They contain additional Code insights and explanations from a panel of industry experts that provide further understanding of the intricacies of the Code rules and their application.

Keeping up with the requirements of the Code should be the goal of everyone involved in electrical safety—whether you are an installer, contractor, inspector, engineer, or instructor. This textbook is a great tool to help you get there.

The Scope of This Textbook

This textbook, Mike Holt's Illustrated Guide to Understanding the National Electrical Code, Volume 2, based on the 2020 NEC, covers the general installation requirements contained in the NEC from Articles 500 through 820 (NEC Chapters 5 through 8) along with relevant content from Chapter 1.

This program is based on 120/208V, 120/240V, or 277/480V, single-phase and three-phase solidly grounded alternating-current systems, using 90°C insulated copper conductors sized to 60°C rated terminals for 100A and less rated circuits, and with 75°C rated terminals for over 100A rated circuits, unless otherwise indicated in the text.

How to Use This Textbook

This textbook is intended to be used along with the NEC and not as a replacement for it. Be sure to have a copy of the 2020 National Electrical Code to reference as you study. You will notice that we have paraphrased a great deal of the wording, and some of the article and section titles appear different than those in the actual Code book. We believe doing so makes it easier to understand the content of the rule, so keep that in mind when comparing this textbook to the NEC.

Always compare what is being explained in this textbook to what the Code book says. Get with others who are knowledgeable about the NEC to discuss any topics you find difficult to understand or join our free Code Forum at www.MikeHolt.com/forum to post your question.

Format. This textbook follows the Code format, but it does not cover every requirement. For example, it does not include every article, section, subsection, exception, or Informational Note. So, do not be concerned if you see that the textbook contains Exception 1 and Exception 3, but not Exception 2.

Cross-References. Many NEC rules refer to requirements located in other sections of the Code. This textbook does the same with the intention of helping you develop a better understanding of how the NEC rules relate to one another. These cross-references are indicated by Code section numbers in brackets, an example of which is "[90.4]."

Informational Notes. Informational Notes contained in the *NEC* will be identified in this textbook as "Note."

Exceptions. Exceptions contained in this textbook will be identified as "Ex" and not spelled out.

As you read through this text, allow yourself enough time to review the outstanding graphics and examples to give yourself the opportunity for a deeper understanding of the *Code*. Be sure to take advantage of the practice questions to test your knowledge and don't be afraid to go back and review the text multiple times to further your understanding of an answer.

Technical Questions

As you progress through this textbook, you might find that you don't understand every explanation, example, calculation, or comment. Don't become frustrated, and don't get down on yourself. Remember, this is the *National Electrical Code*, and sometimes the best attempt to explain a concept isn't enough to make it perfectly clear. If you're still confused, visit www.MikeHolt.com/forum, and post your question on our free *Code* Forum. The forum is a moderated community of electrical professionals.

Textbook Corrections

We're committed to providing you with the finest product with the fewest errors and take great care to ensure our textbooks are correct. But we're realistic and know that errors might be found after printing. The last thing we want is for you to have problems finding, communicating, or accessing this information, so any adjustments to the text are listed on our website.

To check for known errors, visit www.MikeHolt.com/corrections.

If you believe that there's an error of any kind (typographical, grammatical, technical, etc.) in this textbook or in the Answer Key, and it's not listed on the website, send an e-mail that includes the textbook title, page numbers, print date, and any other pertinent information to corrections@MikeHolt.com.

Key Features

The layout and design of this textbook incorporate special features and symbols designed to help you navigate easily through the material, and to enhance your understanding.

QR Code

 Scan this **QR Code** with a smartphone app to take you to the web page that features sample video clips of Mike and his video panel from the recording of this title— www.MikeHolt.com/20UN2videos. For a complete list of all the videos that accompany this product, call 888.632.2633.

Caution, Warning, and Danger Icons

These icons highlight areas of concern.

 Caution: An explanation of possible damage to property or equipment.

 Warning: An explanation of possible severe property damage or personal injury.

 Danger: An explanation of possible severe injury or death.

Formulas

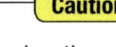

$P = I \times E$

Formulas are easily identifiable in green text on a gray bar.

About This Textbook | **Key Features**

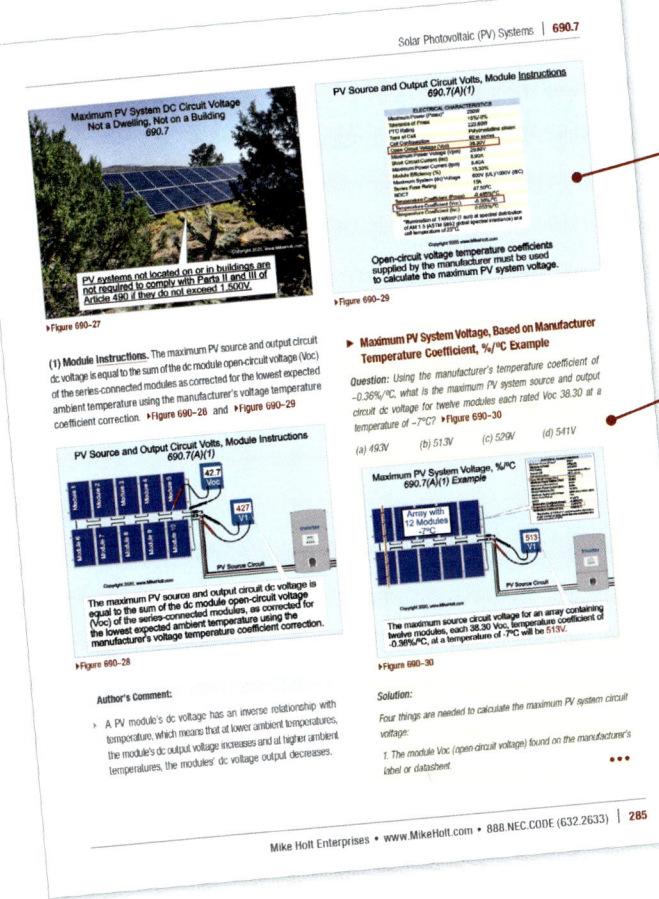

Full-Color, Detailed Educational Graphics. Industry-leading graphics help you visualize the sometimes complex language of the *NEC*, and illustrate the rule in real-world application(s). This is a great aid to reinforce learning.

Examples. These practical application questions and answers are contained in framed yellow boxes.

If you see an ellipsis (● ● ●) at the bottom of the example, it is continued on the following page.

***Code* Change text.** Underlined text denotes changes to the *Code* for the 2020 *NEC*.

***Code* Rule Headers.** The *Code* rule being taught is identified with a chapter color bar and white text. Chapters are color-coded and modular to make it easy to navigate through each section of the textbook.

Author's Comments. These comments provide additional information to help you understand the context.

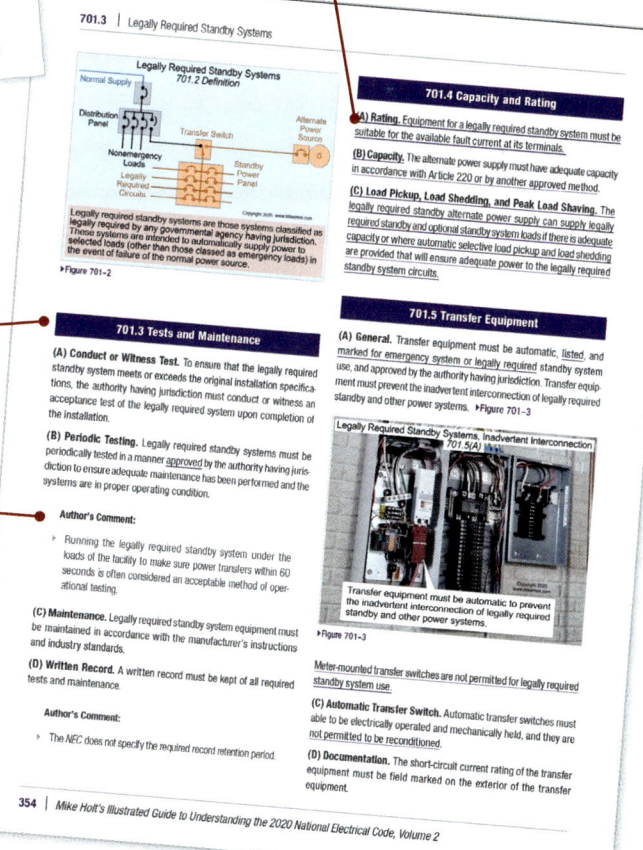

Mike Holt Enterprises • www.MikeHolt.com • 888.NEC.CODE (632.2633) | XV

ADDITIONAL PRODUCTS TO HELP YOU LEARN

Understanding the 2020 *National Electrical Code, Volume 2* Videos

One of the best ways to get the most out of this textbook is to use it in conjunction with the corresponding videos. Mike Holt's videos provide a 360° view of each topic with specialized commentary from Mike and his panel of industry experts. Whether you're a visual or an auditory learner, watching the videos will enhance your knowledge and understanding. The videos include:

- *Special Occupancies and Special Equipment*
- *Limited Energy and Communications Systems*

If you're interested in adding the videos that accompany this textbook, call our office at 888.632.2633 or e-mail info@MikeHolt.com.

Understanding the 2020 National Electrical Code, *Volume 1* Training Program

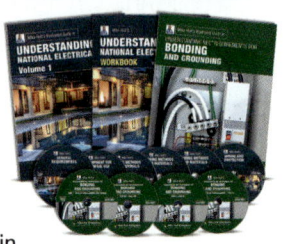

Our best-selling Understanding the *NEC* Volume 1 program has helped thousands of electricians learn the *Code* in an easy to use format. Volume 1 covers Articles 90 through 480. Mike guides students through the most utilized rules and breaks them down in a complete and thorough way. The full-color instructional graphics in the textbooks help students visualize and understand the concepts being taught; the videos provide additional reinforcement with Mike and the panel discussing each article, its meaning and its application in the real-world. When you need to know the *Code,* this program is the best tool you can use to start building your knowledge—there's no other product quite like it. This program includes:

Understanding the NEC—Volume 1 textbook
Understanding the NEC Workbook, Articles 90-480
Bonding and Grounding textbook

- *General Requirements* DVD
- *Wiring and Protection* DVD
- *Bonding and Grounding* DVDs (4)
- *Wiring Methods and Materials* DVDs (3)
- *Equipment for General Use* DVD

To order, visit www.MikeHolt.com/Code.

Solar Photovoltaic Systems Training Program

When you think of solar photovoltaic systems and the *Code*, you typically think of Article 690. But there are many supporting articles related to solar photovoltaic systems in the *NEC*. While Article 690 covers the rules related to the wiring at the array, it doesn't cover how to connect the array to the rest of the equipment and to the grid. The 2020 *Code* revisions resulted in a major rewrite of key articles and many additions and changes to rules that relate to PV systems throughout the *NEC*. Even if you're a seasoned expert, you'll need to know these changes.

Mike Holt's Understanding NEC Requirements for Solar Photovoltaic and Energy Storage Systems is required reading for anyone who designs, installs, services, and or inspects solar photovoltaic and energy storage systems. It not only includes the 2020 changes related to Articles 690 and 691, but also provides a complete review of the major rules that cover the installation of the related equipment, wiring, and connection to utility power.

The program includes:

Understanding NEC Requirements for Solar Photovoltaic and Energy Storage Systems textbook

- *Understanding NEC Requirements for Solar Photovoltaic and Energy Storage Systems* DVDs (3)

For more information visit www.MikeHolt.com/Solar.

HOW TO USE THE *NATIONAL ELECTRICAL CODE*

The original *NEC* document was developed in 1897 as a result of the united efforts of various insurance, electrical, architectural, and other cooperative interests. The National Fire Protection Association (NFPA) has sponsored the *National Electrical Code* since 1911.

The purpose of the *Code* is the practical safeguarding of persons and property from hazards arising from the use of electricity. It isn't intended as a design specification or an instruction manual for untrained persons. It is, in fact, a standard that contains the minimum requirements for an electrical installation that's essentially free from hazard. Learning to understand and use the *Code* is critical to you working safely; whether you're training to become an electrician, or are already an electrician, electrical contractor, inspector, engineer, designer, or instructor.

The *NEC* was written for qualified persons; those who understand electrical terms, theory, safety procedures, and electrical trade practices. Learning to use the *Code* is a lengthy process and can be frustrating if you don't approach it the right way. First, you'll need to understand electrical theory and if you don't have theory as a background when you get into the *NEC*, you're going to struggle. Take one step back if necessary and learn electrical theory. You must also understand the concepts and terms in the *Code* and know grammar and punctuation in order to understand the complex structure of the rules and their intended purpose(s). The *NEC* is written in a formal outline which many of us haven't seen or used since high school or college so it's important for you to pay particular attention to this format. Our goal for the next few pages is to give you some guidelines and suggestions on using your *Code* book to help you understand that standard, and assist you in what you're trying to accomplish and, ultimately, your personal success as an electrical professional!

Language Considerations for the *NEC*

Terms and Concepts

The *NEC* contains many technical terms, and it's crucial for *Code* users to understand their meanings and applications. If you don't understand a term used in a rule, it will be impossible to properly apply the *NEC* requirement. Article 100 defines those that are used generally in two or more articles throughout the *Code*; for example, the term "Dwelling Unit" is found in many articles. If you don't know the *NEC* definition for a "dwelling unit" you can't properly identify its *Code* requirements. Another example worth mentioning is the term "Outlet." For many people it has always meant a receptacle—not so in the *NEC*!

Many *Code* articles use terms unique to that specific article, and the definitions of those terms only apply to that given article. Definitions for them are usually found in the beginning of the article. For example, Section 250.2 contains the definitions of terms that only apply to Article 250—Grounding and Bonding. Whether definitions are unique to a specific article, or apply throughout the *NEC*, is indicated at the beginning of the definitions (xxx.2) section of the article. For example, Article 690 contains definitions (in 690.2) that apply ONLY to that article while Article 705 introduces definitions (in 705.2) that apply throughout the entire *Code*.

Small Words, Grammar, and Punctuation

Technical words aren't the only ones that require close attention. Even simple words can make a big difference to the application of a rule. Is there a comma? Does it use "or," "and," "other than," "greater than," or "smaller than"? The word "or" can imply alternate choices for wiring methods. A word like "or" gives us choices while the word "and" can mean an additional requirement must be met.

An example of the important role small words play in the *NEC* is found in 110.26(C)(2), where it says equipment containing overcurrent, switching, "or" control devices that are 1,200A or more "and" over 6 ft wide require a means of egress at each end of the working space. In this section, the word "or" clarifies that equipment containing any of the three types of devices listed must follow this rule. The word "and" clarifies that 110.26(C)(2) only applies if the equipment is both 1,200A or more and over 6 ft wide.

Mike Holt Enterprises • www.MikeHolt.com • 888.NEC.CODE (632.2633)

Grammar and punctuation play an important role in establishing the meaning of a rule. The location of a comma can dramatically change the requirement of a rule such as in 250.28(A), where it says a main bonding jumper shall be a wire, bus, screw, or similar suitable conductor. If the comma between "bus" and "screw" was removed, only a "bus screw" could be used. That comma makes a big change in the requirements of the rule.

Slang Terms or Technical Jargon

Trade-related professionals in different areas of the country often use local "slang" terms that aren't shared by all. This can make it difficult to communicate if it isn't clear what the meaning of those slang terms are. Use the proper terms by finding out what their definitions and applications are before you use them. For example, the term "pigtail" is often used to describe the short piece of conductor used to connect a device to a splice, but a "pigtail" is also used for a rubberized light socket with pre-terminated conductors. Although the term is the same, the meaning is very different and could cause confusion. The words "splice" and "tap" are examples of terms often interchanged in the field but are two entirely different things! The uniformity and consistency of the terminology used in the *Code*, makes it so everyone says and means the same thing regardless of geographical location.

NEC Style and Layout

It's important to understand the structure and writing style of the *Code* if you want to use it effectively. The *National Electrical Code* is organized using twelve major components.

1. Table of Contents
2. Chapters—Chapters 1 through 9 (major categories)
3. Articles—Chapter subdivisions that cover specific subjects
4. Parts—Divisions used to organize article subject matter
5. Sections—Divisions used to further organize article subject matter
6. Tables and Figures—Represent the mandatory requirements of a rule
7. Exceptions—Alternatives to the main *Code* rule
8. Informational Notes—Explanatory material for a specific rule (not a requirement)
9. Tables—Applicable as referenced in the *NEC*
10. Annexes—Additional explanatory information such as tables and references (not a requirement)
11. Index
12. Changes to the *Code* from the previous edition

1. Table of Contents. The Table of Contents displays the layout of the chapters, articles, and parts as well as the page numbers. It's an excellent resource and should be referred to periodically to observe the interrelationship of the various *NEC* components. When attempting to locate the rules for a specific situation, knowledgeable *Code* users often go first to the Table of Contents to quickly find the specific *NEC* rule that applies.

2. Chapters. There are nine chapters, each of which is divided into articles. The articles fall into one of four groupings: General Requirements (Chapters 1 through 4), Specific Requirements (Chapters 5 through 7), Communications Systems (Chapter 8), and Tables (Chapter 9).

Chapter 1—General
Chapter 2—Wiring and Protection
Chapter 3—Wiring Methods and Materials
Chapter 4—Equipment for General Use
Chapter 5—Special Occupancies
Chapter 6—Special Equipment
Chapter 7—Special Conditions
Chapter 8—Communications Systems (Telephone, Data, Satellite, Cable TV, and Broadband)
Chapter 9—Tables–Conductor and Raceway Specifications

3. Articles. The *NEC* contains approximately 140 articles, each of which covers a specific subject. It begins with Article 90, the introduction to the *Code* which contains the purpose of the *NEC*, what is covered and isn't covered, along with how the *Code* is arranged. It also gives information on enforcement, how mandatory and permissive rules are written, and how explanatory material is included. Article 90 also includes information on formal interpretations, examination of equipment for safety, wiring planning, and information about formatting units of measurement. Here are some other examples of articles you'll find in the *NEC*:

Article 110—Requirements for Electrical Installations
Article 250—Grounding and Bonding
Article 300—General Requirements for Wiring Methods and Materials
Article 430—Motors, Motor Circuits, and Motor Controllers
Article 500—Hazardous (Classified) Locations
Article 680—Swimming Pools, Fountains, and Similar Installations
Article 725—Remote-Control, Signaling, and Power-Limited Circuits
Article 800—General Requirements for Communications Systems

4. Parts. Larger articles are subdivided into parts. Because the parts of a *Code* article aren't included in the section numbers, we tend to forget to what "part" an *NEC* rule is relating. For example, Table 110.34(A) contains working space clearances for electrical equipment. If we aren't careful, we might think this table applies to all electrical installations, but Table 110.34(A) is in Part III, which only contains requirements for "Over 1,000 Volts, Nominal" installations. The rules for working clearances for electrical equipment for systems 1,000V, nominal, or less are contained in Table 110.26(A)(1), which is in Part II—1,000 Volts, Nominal, or Less.

5. Sections. Each *NEC* rule is called a "*Code* Section." A *Code* section may be broken down into subdivisions; first level subdivision will be in parentheses like (A), (B),..., the next will be second level subdivisions in parentheses like (1), (2),..., and third level subdivisions in lowercase letters such as (a), (b), and so on.

For example, the rule requiring all receptacles in a dwelling unit bathroom to be GFCI protected is contained in Section 210.8(A)(1) which is in Chapter 2, Article 210, Section 8, first level subdivision (A), and second level subdivision (1).

Note: According to the *NEC Style Manual*, first and second level subdivisions are required to have titles. A title for a third level subdivision is permitted but not required.

Many in the industry incorrectly use the term "Article" when referring to a *Code* section. For example, they say "Article 210.8," when they should say "Section 210.8." Section numbers in this textbook are shown without the word "Section," unless they're at the beginning of a sentence. For example, Section 210.8(A) is shown as simply 210.8(A).

6. Tables and Figures. Many *NEC* requirements are contained within tables, which are lists of *Code* rules placed in a systematic arrangement. The titles of the tables are extremely important; you must read them carefully in order to understand the contents, applications, and limitations of each one. Notes are often provided in or below a table; be sure to read them as well since they're also part of the requirement. For example, Note 1 for Table 300.5 explains how to measure the cover when burying cables and raceways and Note 5 explains what to do if solid rock is encountered.

7. Exceptions. Exceptions are *NEC* requirements or permissions that provide an alternative method to a specific rule. There are two types of exceptions—mandatory and permissive. When a rule has several exceptions, those exceptions with mandatory requirements are listed before the permissive exceptions.

Mandatory Exceptions. A mandatory exception uses the words "shall" or "shall not." The word "shall" in an exception means that if you're using the exception, you're required to do it in a specific way. The phrase "shall not" means it isn't permitted.

Permissive Exceptions. A permissive exception uses words such as "shall be permitted," which means it's acceptable (but not mandatory) to do it in this way.

8. Informational Notes. An Informational Note contains explanatory material intended to clarify a rule or give assistance, but it isn't a *Code* requirement.

9. Tables. Chapter 9 consists of tables applicable as referenced in the *NEC*. They're used to calculate raceway sizing, conductor fill, the radius of raceway bends, and conductor voltage drop.

10. Informative Annexes. Annexes aren't a part of the *Code* requirements and are included for informational purposes only.

Annex A. Product Safety Standards
Annex B. Application Information for Ampacity Calculation
Annex C. Raceway Fill Tables for Conductors and Fixture Wires of the Same Size
Annex D. Examples
Annex E. Types of Construction
Annex F. Critical Operations Power Systems (COPS)
Annex G. Supervisory Control and Data Acquisition (SCADA)
Annex H. Administration and Enforcement
Annex I. Recommended Tightening Torques
Annex J. ADA Standards for Accessible Design

11. Index. The Index at the back of the *NEC* is helpful in locating a specific rule using pertinent keywords to assist in your search.

12. Changes to the *Code*. Changes in the *NEC* are indicated as follows:

▸ Rules that were changed since the previous edition are identified by shading the revised text.

▸ New rules aren't shaded like a change, instead they have a shaded "N" in the margin to the left of the section number.

▸ Relocated rules are treated like new rules with a shaded "N" in the left margin by the section number.

▸ Deleted rules are indicated by a bullet symbol " • " located in the left margin where the rule was in the previous edition. Unlike older editions the bullet symbol is only used where one or more complete paragraphs have been deleted. There's no indication used where a word, group of words, or a sentence was deleted.

▸ A Δ represents text deletions and figure/table revisions.

How to Locate a Specific Requirement

How to go about finding what you're looking for in the *Code* book depends, to some degree, on your experience with the *NEC*. Experts typically know the requirements so well that they just go to the correct rule. Very experienced people might only need the Table of Contents to locate the requirement for which they're looking. On the other hand, average users should use all the tools at their disposal, including the Table of Contents, the Index, and the search feature on electronic versions of the *Code* book.

Let's work through a simple example: What *NEC* rule specifies the maximum number of disconnects permitted for a service?

Using the Table of Contents. If you're an experienced *Code* user, you might use the Table of Contents. You'll know Article 230 applies to "Services," and because this article is so large, it's divided up into multiple parts (eight parts to be exact). With this knowledge, you can quickly go to the Table of Contents and see it lists the Service Equipment Disconnecting Means requirements in Part VI.

> **Author's Comment:**
> ▸ The number "70" precedes all page numbers in this standard because the *NEC* is NFPA Standard Number 70.

Using the Index. If you use the Index (which lists subjects in alphabetical order) to look up the term "service disconnect," you'll see there's no listing. If you try "disconnecting means," then "services," you'll find that the Index indicates the rule is in Article 230, Part VI. Because the *NEC* doesn't give a page number in the Index, you'll need to use the Table of Contents to find it, or flip through the *Code* book to Article 230, then continue to flip through pages until you find Part VI.

Many people complain that the *NEC* only confuses them by taking them in circles. Once you gain experience in using the *Code* and deepen your understanding of words, terms, principles, and practices, you'll find it much easier to understand and use than you originally thought.

With enough exposure in the use of the *NEC*, you'll discover that some words and terms are often specific to certain articles. The word "solar" for example will immediately send experienced *Code* book users to Article 690—Solar Photovoltaic (PV) Systems. The word "marina" suggests what you seek might be in Article 555. There are times when a main article will send you to a specific requirement in another one in which compliance is required in which case it will say (for example), "in accordance with 230.xx." Don't think of these situations as a "circle," but rather a map directing you to exactly where you need to be.

Customizing Your *Code* Book

One way to increase your comfort level with your *Code* book is to customize it to meet your needs. You can do this by highlighting and underlining important *NEC* requirements. Preprinted adhesive tabs are also an excellent aid to quickly find important articles and sections that are regularly referenced. However, understand that if you're using your *Code* book to prepare to take an exam, some exam centers don't allow markings of any type. For more information about tabs for your *Code* book, visit www.MikeHolt.com/tabs.

Highlighting. As you read through or find answers to your questions, be sure you highlight those requirements in the *NEC* that are the most important or relevant to you. Use one color, like yellow, for general interest and a different one for important requirements you want to find quickly. Be sure to highlight terms in the Index and the Table of Contents as you use them.

Underlining. Underline or circle key words and phrases in the *Code* with a red or blue pen (not a lead pencil) using a short ruler or other straightedge to keep lines straight and neat. This is a very handy way to make important requirements stand out. A short ruler or other straightedge also comes in handy for locating the correct information in a table.

Interpretations

Industry professionals often enjoy the challenge of discussing, and at times debating, the *Code* requirements. These types of discussions are important to the process of better understanding the *NEC* requirements and applications. However, if you decide you're going to participate in one of these discussions, don't spout out what you think without having the actual *Code* book in your hand. The professional way of discussing a requirement is by referring to a specific section rather than talking in vague generalities. This will help everyone involved clearly understand the point and become better educated. In fact, you may become so well educated about the *NEC* that you might even decide to participate in the change process and help to make it even better!

Become Involved in the *NEC* Process

The actual process of changing the *Code* takes about two years and involves hundreds of individuals trying to make the *NEC* as current and accurate as possible. As you advance in your studies and understanding of the *Code*, you might begin to find it very interesting, enjoy it more, and realize that you can also be a part of the process. Rather than sitting back and allowing others to take the lead, you can participate by making proposals and being a part of its development. For the 2020 cycle, there were 3,730 Public Inputs and 1,930 comments. Hundreds of updates and five new articles were added to keep the *NEC* up to date with new technologies and pave the way to a safer and more efficient electrical future.

Here's how the process works:

STEP 1—Public Input Stage

Public Input. The revision cycle begins with the acceptance of Public Input (PI) which is the public notice asking for anyone interested to submit input on an existing standard or a committee-approved new draft standard. Following the closing date, the committee conducts a First Draft Meeting to respond to all Public Inputs.

First Draft Meeting. At the First Draft (FD) Meeting, the Technical Committee considers and provides a response to all Public Input. The Technical Committee may use the input to develop First Revisions to the standard. The First Draft documents consist of the initial meeting consensus of the committee by simple majority. However, the final position of the Technical Committee must be established by a ballot which follows.

Committee Ballot on First Draft. The First Draft developed at the First Draft Meeting is balloted. In order to appear in the First Draft, a revision must be approved by at least two-thirds of the Technical Committee.

First Draft Report Posted. First revisions which pass ballot are ultimately compiled and published as the First Draft Report on the document's NFPA web page. This report serves as documentation for the Input Stage and is published for review and comment. The public may review the First Draft Report to determine whether to submit Public Comments on the First Draft.

STEP 2—Public Comment Stage

Public Comment. Once the First Draft Report becomes available, there's a Public Comment period during which anyone can submit a Public Comment on the First Draft. After the Public Comment closing date, the Technical Committee conducts/holds their Second Draft Meeting.

Second Draft Meeting. After the Public Comment closing date, if Public Comments are received or the committee has additional proposed revisions, a Second Draft Meeting is held. At the Second Draft Meeting, the Technical Committee reviews the First Draft and may make additional revisions to the draft Standard. All Public Comments are considered, and the Technical Committee provides an action and response to each Public Comment. These actions result in the Second Draft.

Committee Ballot on Second Draft. The Second Revisions developed at the Second Draft Meeting are balloted. To appear in the Second Draft, a revision must be approved by at least two-thirds of the Technical Committee.

Second Draft Report Posted. Second Revisions which pass ballot are ultimately compiled and published as the Second Draft Report on the document's NFPA website. This report serves as documentation of the Comment Stage and is published for public review.

Once published, the public can review the Second Draft Report to decide whether to submit a Notice of Intent to Make a Motion (NITMAM) for further consideration.

STEP 3—NFPA Technical Meeting (Tech Session)

Following completion of the Public Input and Public Comment stages, there's further opportunity for debate and discussion of issues through the NFPA Technical Meeting that takes place at the NFPA Conference & Expo®. These motions are attempts to change the resulting final Standard from the committee's recommendations published as the Second Draft.

STEP 4—Council Appeals and Issuance of Standard

Issuance of Standards. When the Standards Council convenes to issue an NFPA standard, it also hears any related appeals. Appeals are an important part of assuring that all NFPA rules have been followed and that due process and fairness have continued throughout the standards development process. The Standards Council considers appeals based on the written record and by conducting live hearings during which all interested parties can participate. Appeals are decided on the entire record of the process, as well as all submissions and statements presented.

After deciding all appeals related to a standard, the Standards Council, if appropriate, proceeds to issue the Standard as an official NFPA Standard. The decision of the Standards Council is final subject only to limited review by the NFPA Board of Directors. The new NFPA standard becomes effective twenty days following the Standards Council's action of issuance.

Tentative Interim Amendment—(TIA)

Sometimes, a change to the *NEC* is of an emergency nature. Perhaps an editing mistake was made that can affect an electrical installation to the extent it may create a hazard. Maybe an occurrence in the field created a condition that needs to be addressed immediately and can't wait for the normal *Code* cycle and next edition of the standard. When these circumstances warrant it, a TIA or "Tentative Interim Amendment" can be submitted for consideration.

The NFPA defines a TIA as, "tentative because it has not been processed through the entire standards-making procedures. It is interim because it is effective only between editions of the standard. A TIA automatically becomes a Public Input of the proponent for the next edition of the standard; as such, it then is subject to all of the procedures of the standards-making process."

> **Author's Comment:**
>
> ▸ Proposals, comments, and TIAs can be submitted for consideration online at the NFPA website, www.nfpa.org. From the homepage, look for "Codes & Standards," then find "Standards Development," and click on "How the Process Works." If you'd like to see something changed in the *Code*, you're encouraged to participate in the process.

2020 *Code* Book and Tabs

The ideal way to use your *Code* book is to tab it for quick reference—Mike's best-selling tabs make organizing the *NEC* easy. If you're using your *Code* book for an exam, you'll need to confirm with your testing authority that a tabbed *Code* book is allowed into the exam room. In addition the newest version of our tabs are color-coded to match the chapters of this textbook—this allows you to easily cross-reference this textbook with the *NEC*.

Order your tabs today, at www.MikeHolt.com/tabs.

ARTICLE 90
INTRODUCTION TO THE *NATIONAL ELECTRICAL CODE*

Introduction to Article 90—Introduction to the *National Electrical Code*

Article 90 opens by saying the *National Electrical Code* (*NEC*/*Code*) is not intended as a design specification or instruction manual. It has one purpose only, and that is the "practical safeguarding of persons and property from hazards arising from the use of electricity." That does not necessarily mean the installation will be efficient, convenient, or able to accommodate future expansion; just safe. The necessity of carefully studying the *Code* rules cannot be overemphasized, and the step-by-step explanatory design of a textbook such as this is to help in that undertaking. Understanding where to find the requirements in the *NEC* that apply to the installation is invaluable. Rules in several different articles often apply to even a simple installation. You are not going to remember every section of every article of the *Code* but, hopefully, you will come away with knowing where to look after studying this textbook.

Article 90 then goes on to describe the scope and arrangement of the *NEC*. The balance of it provides the reader with information essential to understanding the *Code* rules.

Most electrical installations require you to understand the first four chapters of the *NEC* (which apply generally) and have a working knowledge of the Chapter 9 tables. That understanding begins with this article. Chapters 5, 6, and 7 make up a large portion of the *Code* book, but they apply to special occupancies, special equipment, or special conditions. They build on, modify, or amend the rules in the first four chapters. Chapter 8 contains the requirements for communications systems, such as radio and television equipment, satellite receivers, antenna systems, twisted pair conductors, and coaxial cable wiring. Communications systems are not subject to the general requirements of Chapters 1 through 4, or the special requirements of Chapters 5 through 7, unless there is a specific reference to a rule in the previous chapters.

90.1 Purpose of the *NEC*

(A) Practical Safeguarding. The purpose of the *National Electrical Code* is to ensure electrical systems are installed in a manner that protects people and property by minimizing the risks associated with the use of electricity. The *NEC* is not a design specification standard nor is it an instruction manual for the untrained and unqualified.
▶Figure 90–1

Author's Comment:

▶ The *Code* is intended to be used by those who are skilled and knowledgeable in electrical theory, electrical systems, building and electrical construction, and the installation and operation of electrical equipment.

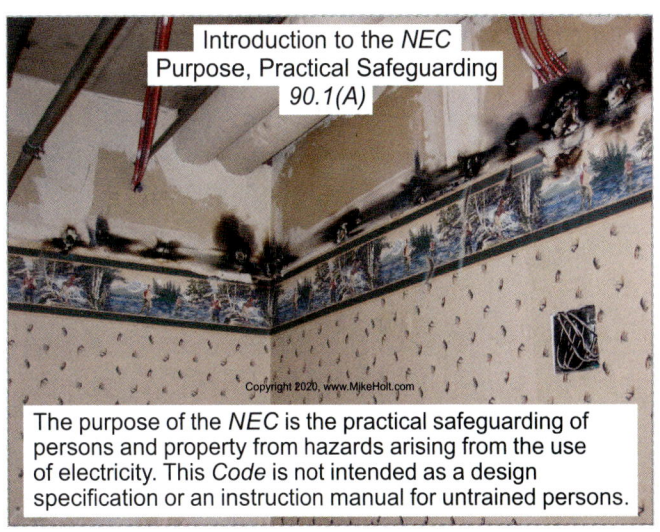

The purpose of the *NEC* is the practical safeguarding of persons and property from hazards arising from the use of electricity. This *Code* is not intended as a design specification or an instruction manual for untrained persons.

▶Figure 90–1

(B) Adequacy. The *NEC* contains the requirements considered necessary for a safe electrical installation. If one is installed in compliance with the *Code*, it is considered essentially free from electrical hazards.

The requirements contained in the *NEC* are not intended to ensure an electrical installation will be efficient, convenient, adequate for good service, or suitable for future expansion. ▶Figure 90–2

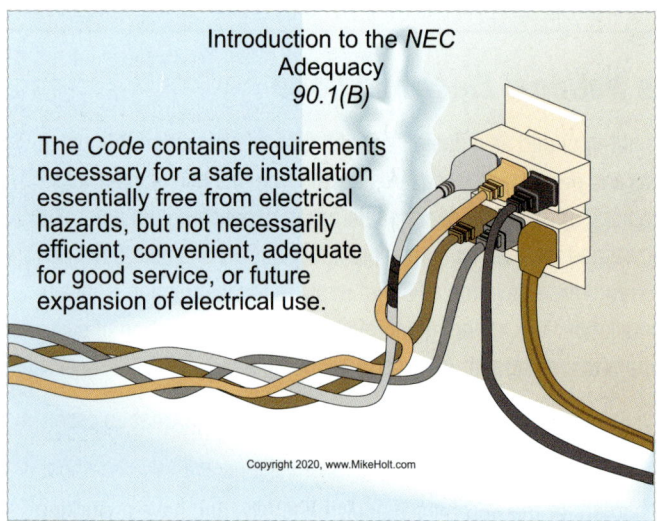

▶Figure 90–2

Author's Comment:

▸ Electrical energy management, equipment maintenance, power quality, or suitability for future loads are not issues within the scope of the *Code*.

Note: Hazards often occur because the initial wiring did not provide for increases in the use of electricity and therefore wiring systems become overloaded. ▶Figure 90–3

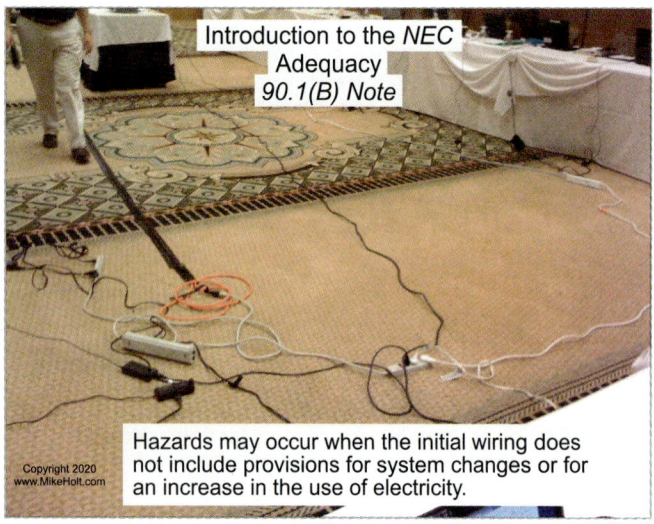

▶Figure 90–3

Author's Comment:

▸ The *NEC* does not require electrical systems to be designed or installed to accommodate future loads. However, the electrical designer (typically an electrical engineer) is concerned with not only ensuring electrical safety (*Code* compliance), but also that the electrical system meets the customers' needs, both for today and in the coming years. To satisfy their needs, electrical systems are often designed and installed above the minimum requirements contained in the *NEC*.

(C) Relation to International Standards. The requirements of the *Code* address the fundamental safety principles contained in the International Electrotechnical Commission (IEC) Standard.

Note: IEC 60364-1, Section 131, contains fundamental principles of protection for safety that encompass protection against electric shock, protection against thermal effects, protection against overcurrent, protection against fault currents, and protection against overvoltage. All of these potential hazards are addressed by the requirements in this *Code*. ▶Figure 90–4

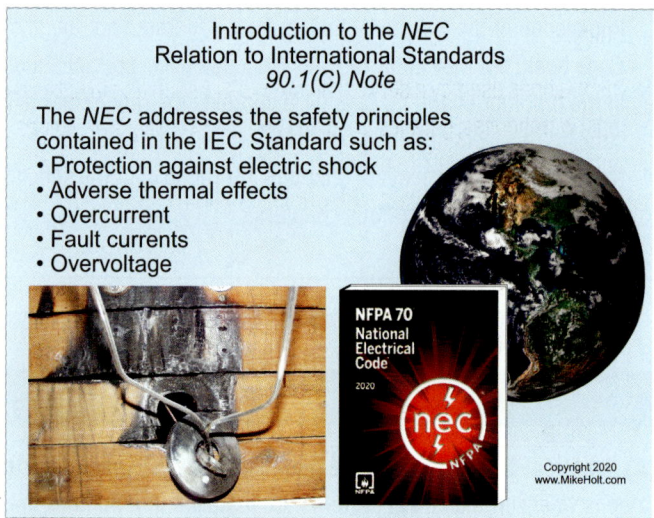

▶Figure 90–4

90.2 Scope of the *NEC*

(A) What is Covered by the *NEC*. The *NEC* covers the installation and removal of electrical conductors, equipment, and raceways; signaling and communications conductors, equipment, and raceways; and optical fiber cables and raceways for the following: ▶Figure 90–5

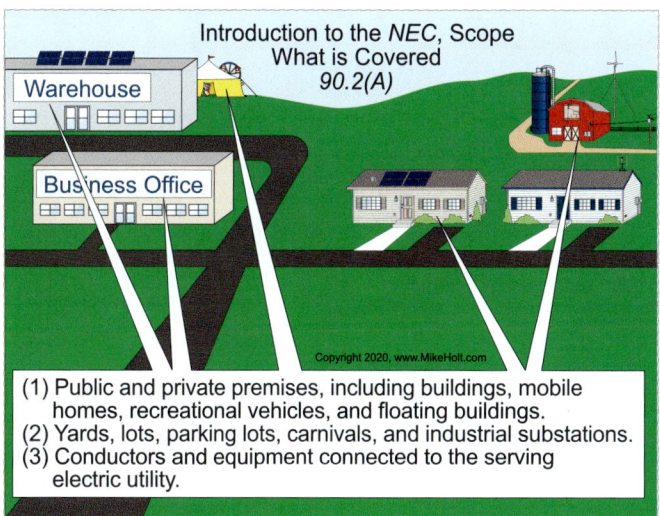
▶Figure 90–5

▶Figure 90–7

(1) Public and private premises including buildings, mobile homes, recreational vehicles, and floating buildings.

(2) Yards, lots, parking lots, carnivals, and industrial substations.

(3) Conductors and equipment connected to the serving electric utility.

(4) Installations used by a serving electric utility such as office buildings, warehouses, garages, machine shops, recreational buildings, and other electric utility buildings that are not an integral part of a utility's generating plant, substation, or control center. ▶Figure 90–6

Author's Comment:

▸ The new item in Article 90's scope, 90.2(A)(5), appears to include the power cable between the pedestal and the boat in the scope of the *NEC*, but there are no specific rules in Article 555 covering that power-supply cord.

▸ The text in 555.35(B) requires leakage detection equipment to detect leakage current from boats and applies to the load side of the supplying receptacle.

(6) Installations used to export electric power from vehicles to premises wiring or for bidirectional current flow ▶Figure 90–8

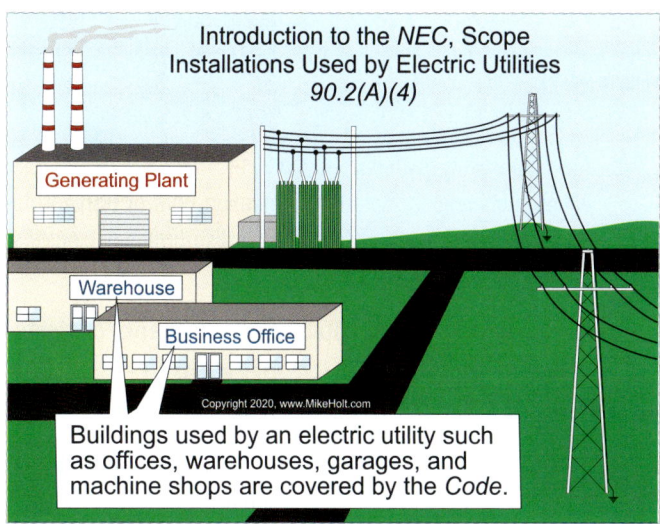
▶Figure 90–6

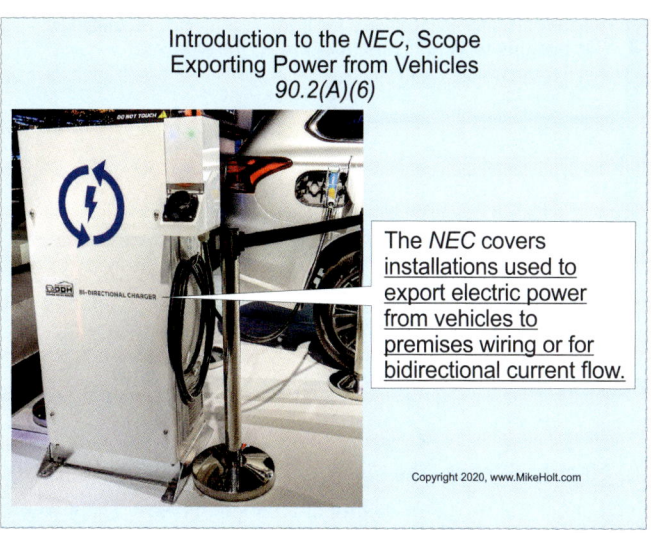
▶Figure 90–8

(5) Installations supplying shore power to watercraft in marinas and boatyards, including monitoring of leakage current. ▶Figure 90–7

90.3 | Introduction to the National Electrical Code

Author's Comment:

▸ The battery power supply of an electrical vehicle can be used "bidirectionally" which means it can be used as a backup or alternate power source to supply premises wiring circuits in the event of a power failure. The rules for this application can be found in Article 625.

(B) What is Not Covered by the NEC. The Code does not apply to the installation of electrical or communications systems for:

(1) Transportation Vehicles. The NEC does not apply to installations in ships and watercraft other than floating buildings, and automotive vehicles other than mobile homes and recreational vehicles.

(2) Mining Equipment. The Code does not apply to installations underground in mines, and in self-propelled mobile surface mining machinery and its attendant electrical trailing cables.

(3) Railways. The NEC does not apply to railway power, signaling, energy storage, and communications wiring.

(4) Communications Utilities. The Code does not apply to installations under the exclusive control of the communications utility located in building spaces used exclusively for these purposes or located outdoors. ▸Figure 90-9

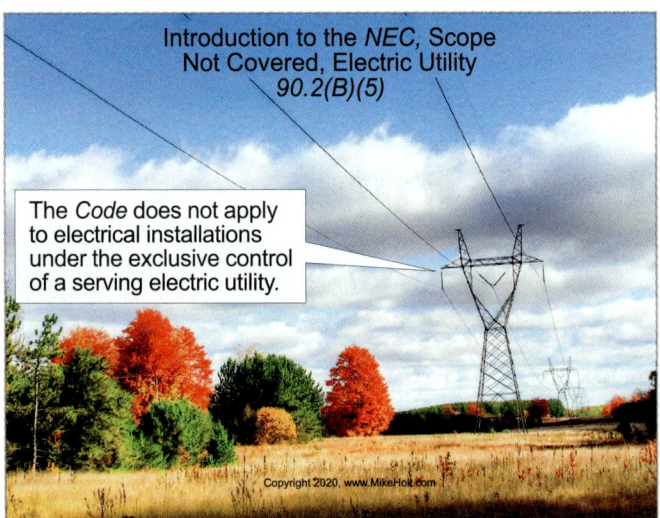

▸Figure 90-10

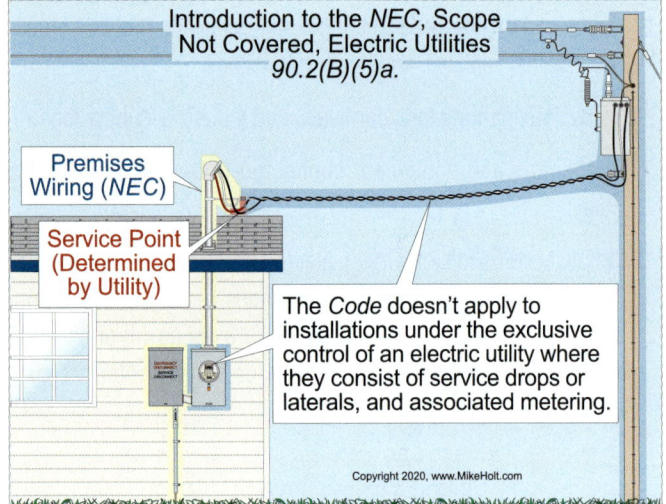

▸Figure 90-11

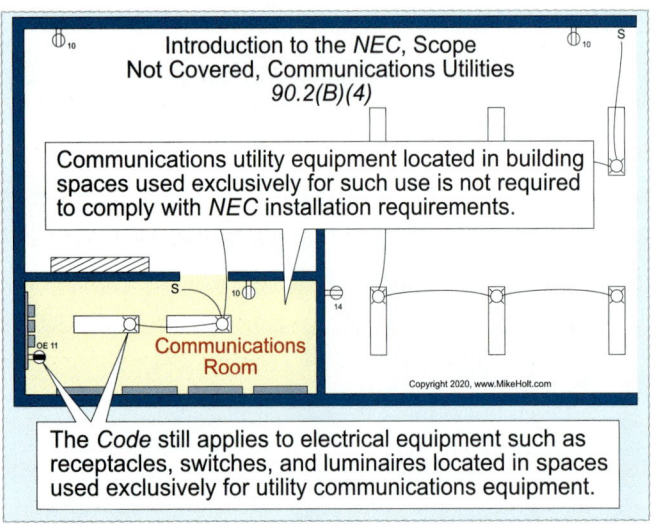

▸Figure 90-9

(5) Electric Utilities. The NEC does not apply to electrical installations under the exclusive control of a serving electric utility where such installations: ▸Figure 90-10

a. Consist of service drops or service laterals and associated metering, or ▸Figure 90-11

b. Are on property owned or leased by the utility for the purpose of communications, metering, generation, control, transformation, transmission, energy storage, or distribution of electrical energy, or ▸Figure 90-12

c. Are located in legally established easements or rights-of-way ▸Figure 90-13

90.3 Code Arrangement

General Requirements. The Code is divided into an introduction and nine chapters followed by informative annexes. Chapters 1, 2, 3, and 4 are general conditions. ▸Figure 90-14

Introduction to the *National Electrical Code* | 90.4

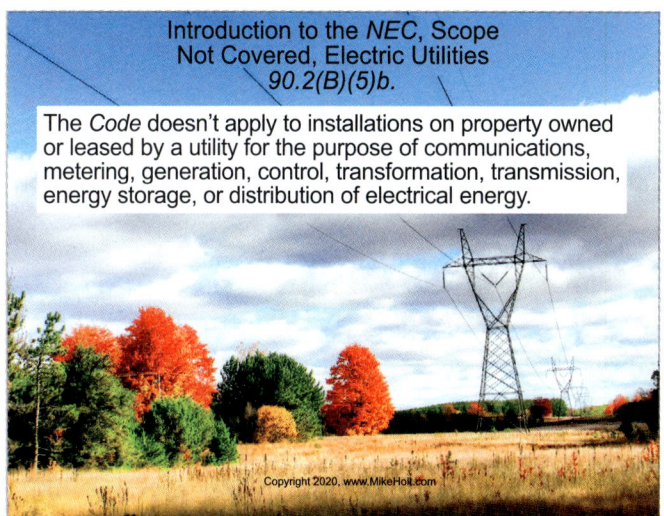
▶Figure 90–12

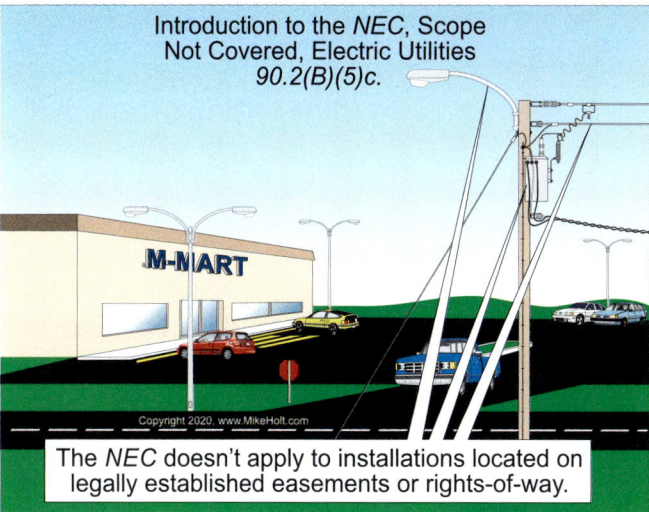
▶Figure 90–13

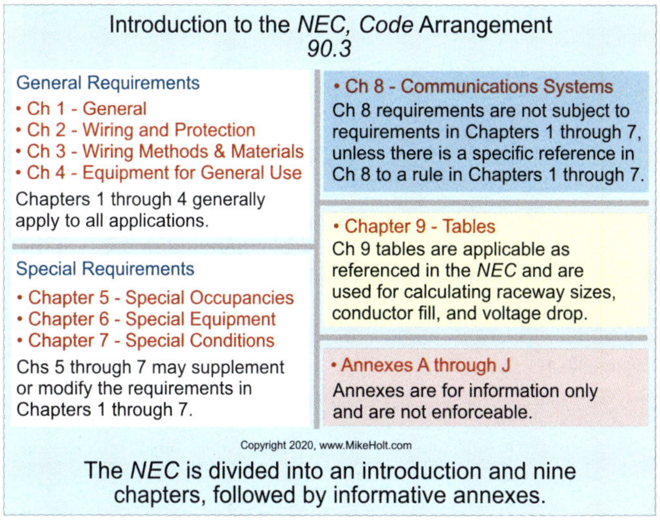

Introduction to the *NEC*, *Code* Arrangement 90.3

General Requirements
- Ch 1 - General
- Ch 2 - Wiring and Protection
- Ch 3 - Wiring Methods & Materials
- Ch 4 - Equipment for General Use

Chapters 1 through 4 generally apply to all applications.

Special Requirements
- Chapter 5 - Special Occupancies
- Chapter 6 - Special Equipment
- Chapter 7 - Special Conditions

Chs 5 through 7 may supplement or modify the requirements in Chapters 1 through 7.

• **Ch 8 - Communications Systems**
Ch 8 requirements are not subject to requirements in Chapters 1 through 7, unless there is a specific reference in Ch 8 to a rule in Chapters 1 through 7.

• **Chapter 9 - Tables**
Ch 9 tables are applicable as referenced in the *NEC* and are used for calculating raceway sizes, conductor fill, and voltage drop.

• **Annexes A through J**
Annexes are for information only and are not enforceable.

The *NEC* is divided into an introduction and nine chapters, followed by informative annexes.

▶Figure 90–14

The requirements contained in Chapters 5, 6, and 7 apply to special occupancies, special equipment, or other special conditions, which may supplement or modify the requirements contained in Chapters 1 through 7; but not Chapter 8.

Chapter 8 contains the requirements for communications systems (twisted wire, antennas, and coaxial cable) which are not subject to the general requirements of Chapters 1 through 4, or the special requirements of Chapters 5 through 7, unless a specific reference in Chapter 8 is made to a rule in Chapters 1 through 7.

Chapter 9 consists of tables applicable as referenced in the *NEC*. The tables are used to calculate raceway sizing, conductor fill, the radius of raceway bends, and conductor voltage drop.

Annexes are not part of the requirements of the *Code* but are included for informational purposes. There are ten annexes:

▸ Annex A. Product Safety Standards
▸ Annex B. Application Information for Ampacity Calculation
▸ Annex C. Raceway Fill Tables for Conductors and Fixture Wires of the Same Size
▸ Annex D. Examples
▸ Annex E. Types of Construction
▸ Annex F. Critical Operations Power Systems (COPS)
▸ Annex G. Supervisory Control and Data Acquisition (SCADA)
▸ Annex H. Administration and Enforcement
▸ Annex I. Recommended Tightening Torques
▸ Annex J. ADA Standards for Accessible Design

90.4 Enforcement

The *NEC* is intended to be suitable for enforcement by governmental bodies that exercise legal jurisdiction over electrical installations for power, lighting, signaling circuits, and communications systems such as: ▶Figure 90–15

Signaling circuits include:

▸ Article 725. Remote-Control, Signaling, and Power-Limited Circuits
▸ Article 760. Fire Alarm Systems
▸ Article 770. Optical Fiber Cables

Communications systems which include:

▸ Article 810. Radio and Television Equipment (Satellite Antenna)
▸ Article 820. Community Antenna Television and Radio Distribution Systems (Coaxial Cable)

90.4 | Introduction to the *National Electrical Code*

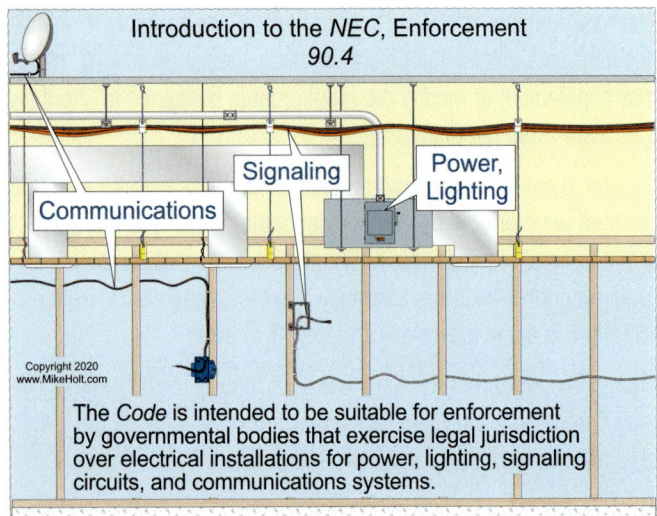
▶Figure 90–15

Author's Comment:

▸ Once adopted (in part, wholly, or amended), the *National Electrical Code* becomes statutory law for the adopting jurisdiction and is thereby considered a legal document.

Enforcement. The enforcement of the *NEC* is the responsibility of the authority having jurisdiction, who is responsible for interpreting requirements, approving equipment and materials, waiving *Code* requirements, and ensuring equipment is installed in accordance with listing instructions. ▶Figure 90–16

Author's Comment:

▸ "Authority Having Jurisdiction" is defined in Article 100 as the organization, office, or individual responsible for approving equipment, materials, an installation, or a procedure. See 90.4 and 90.7 for more information.

▸ "Approved" is defined in Article 100 as acceptable to the authority having jurisdiction; usually the electrical inspector.

Interpretation. The authority having jurisdiction is responsible for interpreting the *NEC*.

Author's Comment:

▸ The authority having jurisdiction's decisions must be based on a specific *Code* requirement. If an installation is rejected, the AHJ is legally responsible for informing the installer of the specific *NEC* rule that was violated.

▸ The art of getting along with the AHJ consists of doing good work and knowing what the *Code* says (as opposed to what you think it says). It is also useful to know how to choose your battles when the inevitable disagreement does occur.

Approval of Equipment and Materials. Only the authority having jurisdiction has the authority to approve the installation of equipment and materials. ▶Figure 90–17

▶Figure 90–16

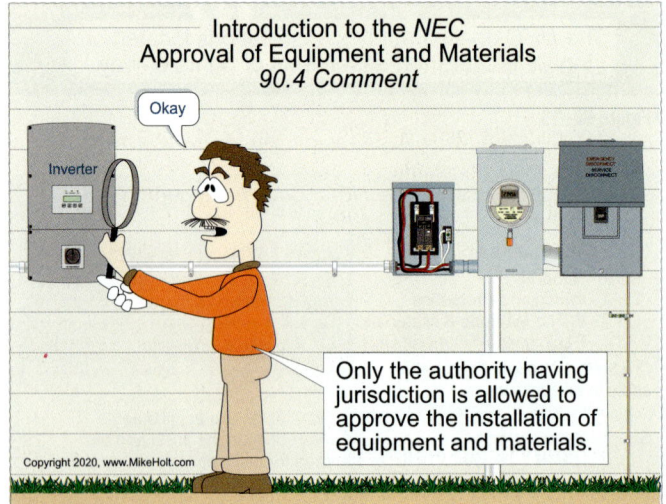
▶Figure 90–17

Introduction to the *National Electrical Code* | 90.7

Author's Comment:

▸ Typically, the AHJ will approve equipment listed by a product testing organization such as Underwriters Laboratories, Inc. (UL). The *NEC* does not require all equipment to be listed, but many state and local authorities having jurisdictions do. See 90.7, 110.2, and 110.3 and the definitions for "Approved," "Identified," "Labeled," and "Listed" in Article 100.

▸ According to the *Code*, the authority having jurisdiction determines the approval of equipment. This means he or she can reject an installation of listed equipment and can approve the use of unlisted equipment. Given our highly litigious society, approval of unlisted equipment is becoming increasingly difficult to obtain.

Approval of Alternate Means. By special permission, the authority having jurisdiction may approve alternate methods where it is assured equivalent safety can be achieved and maintained.

Author's Comment:

▸ "Special Permission" is defined in Article 100 as the written consent of the AHJ.

Waiver of Product Requirements. If the *Code* requires products, constructions, or materials that are not yet available at the time the *NEC* is adopted, the authority having jurisdiction can allow products that were acceptable in the previous *Code* to continue to be used.

Author's Comment:

▸ Sometimes it takes years for testing laboratories to establish product standards for new *NEC* product requirements; then it takes time before manufacturers can design, manufacture, and distribute those products to the marketplace.

90.5 Mandatory Requirements and Explanatory Material

(A) Mandatory Requirements. The words "shall" or "shall not" indicate a mandatory requirement.

Author's Comment:

▸ For greater ease in reading this textbook, we will use the word "must" instead of "shall," and "must not" will be used instead of "shall not."

(B) Permissive Requirements. When the *Code* uses "shall be permitted" it means the action is permitted, but not required. Permissive rules are often contained in exceptions to the general requirement.

Author's Comment:

▸ For greater ease in reading, the phrase "shall be permitted" (as used in the *NEC*) has been replaced in this textbook with "is permitted" or "are permitted."

(C) Explanatory Material. References to other standards or information related to a *Code* rule are included in the form of "Informational Notes." Such notes are for informational purposes only and are not enforceable as an *NEC* requirement.

For example, Informational Note No. 3 in 210.19(A)(1) recommends that the voltage drop of a circuit not exceed 3 percent; this is a recommendation—not a *Code* requirement.

Author's Comment:

▸ For convenience and ease in reading this textbook, "Informational Notes" will simply be identified as "Note."

> **Caution**
> Informational notes are not enforceable but notes to tables are. Within this textbook, we will call notes contained in a table a "Table Note."

(D) Informative Annexes. Informative annexes contained in the back of the *Code* book are for information only and are not enforceable as requirements of the *NEC*.

90.7 Examination of Equipment for Product Safety

Product evaluation for *Code* compliance, approval, and safety is typically performed by a nationally recognized testing laboratory in accordance with the listing standards.

Except to detect alterations or damage, listed factory-installed internal wiring of equipment that has been processed by a qualified testing laboratory does not need to be inspected for *NEC* compliance at the time of installation. ▸Figure 90–18

Note 1: The requirements contained in Article 300 do not apply to the integral parts of electrical equipment. See 110.3(B).

90.7 | Introduction to the *National Electrical Code*

▶Figure 90–18

Note 2: "Listed" is defined in Article 100 as equipment or materials included in a list published by a testing laboratory acceptable to the authority having jurisdiction. The listing organization must periodically inspect the production of listed equipment or material to ensure it meets appropriate designated standards and is suitable for a specified purpose.

ARTICLE 90 PRACTICE QUESTIONS

Please use the 2020 *Code* book to answer the following questions.

Article 90—Introduction to the *National Electrical Code*

1. The *NEC* is _____.

   (a) intended to be a design manual
   (b) meant to be used as an instruction guide for untrained persons
   (c) for the practical safeguarding of persons and property
   (d) published by the Bureau of Standards

2. Compliance with the *Code* and proper maintenance result in an installation that is essentially _____.

   (a) free from hazards
   (b) not efficient or convenient
   (c) not adequate for good service or future expansion
   (d) all of these

3. Compliance with the provisions of the *NEC* will result in _____.

   (a) good electrical service
   (b) an efficient electrical system
   (c) an electrical system essentially free from hazard
   (d) all of these

4. The *Code* contains provisions considered necessary for safety, which will not necessarily result in _____.

   (a) efficient use
   (b) convenience
   (c) good service or future expansion of electrical use
   (d) all of these

5. Electrical hazards often occur because the initial _____ did not provide for increases in the use of electricity and therefore wiring systems become overloaded.

   (a) inspection
   (b) owner
   (c) wiring
   (d) builder

6. Hazards often occur because of _____.

   (a) overloading of wiring systems by methods or usage not in conformity with the *NEC*
   (b) initial wiring not providing for increases in the use of electricity
   (c) manufacturing defects
   (d) overloading of wiring systems by methods or usage not in conformity with the *NEC* and initial wiring not providing for increases in the use of electricity

7. Which of the following systems shall be installed and removed in accordance with the *NEC* requirements?

   (a) Signaling conductors, equipment, and raceways
   (b) Communications conductors, equipment, and raceways
   (c) Electrical conductors, equipment, and raceways
   (d) all of these

8. The *NEC* applies to the installation of _____.

   (a) electrical conductors and equipment within or on public and private buildings
   (b) signaling and communication conductors
   (c) optical fiber cables
   (d) all of these

Article 90 | Practice Questions

9. This *Code* covers the installation of _____ for public and private premises, including buildings, structures, mobile homes, recreational vehicles, and floating buildings.

    (a) optical fiber cables
    (b) electrical equipment
    (c) raceways
    (d) all of these

10. Installations supplying _____ power to ships and watercraft in marinas and boatyards are covered by the *NEC*.

    (a) shore
    (b) primary
    (c) secondary
    (d) auxiliary

11. Installations used to export electric power from vehicles to premises wiring or for _____ current flow are covered by the *NEC*.

    (a) emergency
    (b) primary
    (c) bidirectional
    (d) secondary

12. The *NEC* does apply to installations in _____.

    (a) floating buildings
    (b) mobile homes
    (c) recreational vehicles
    (d) all of these

13. The *NEC* does not cover electrical installations in ships, watercraft, railway rolling stock, aircraft, or automotive vehicles.

    (a) True
    (b) False

14. The *Code* covers underground mine installations and self-propelled mobile surface mining machinery and its attendant electrical trailing cable.

    (a) True
    (b) False

15. The *Code* does not cover installations under the exclusive control of an electrical utility such as _____.

    (a) service drops and laterals
    (b) electric utility office buildings
    (c) electric utility warehouses
    (d) electric utility garages

16. Installations of communications equipment that are under the exclusive control of communications utilities and located outdoors or in building spaces used exclusively for such installations _____ covered by the *NEC*.

    (a) are
    (b) are sometimes
    (c) are not
    (d) may be

17. Chapters 1 through 4 of the *NEC* apply _____.

    (a) generally to all electrical installations
    (b) only to special occupancies and conditions
    (c) only to special equipment and material
    (d) all of these

18. Chapters 5, 6, and 7 apply to special occupancies, special equipment, or other special conditions and may supplement or modify the requirements in Chapters 1 through 7.

    (a) True
    (b) False

19. Chapters 5, 6, and 7 of the *NEC* apply to _____.

    (a) special occupancies
    (b) special equipment
    (c) special conditions
    (d) all of these

20. Communications wiring such as telephone, antenna, and CATV wiring within a building shall not be required to comply with the installation requirements of Chapters 1 through 7, except where specifically referenced in Chapter 8.

    (a) True
    (b) False

21. Installations shall comply with the material located in the *NEC* Annexes because they are part of the requirements of the *Code*.

    (a) True
    (b) False

22. The _____ has the responsibility for deciding on the approval of equipment and materials.

    (a) manufacturer
    (b) authority having jurisdiction
    (c) testing agency
    (d) the owner of the premises

23. The authority having jurisdiction has the responsibility for _____.

    (a) making interpretations of rules
    (b) deciding upon the approval of equipment and materials
    (c) waiving specific requirements in the *Code* and permitting alternate methods and material if safety is maintained
    (d) all of these

24. If the *NEC* requires new products that are not yet available at the time a new edition is adopted, the _____ may permit the use of the products that comply with the most recent previous edition of the *Code* adopted by that jurisdiction.

    (a) electrical engineer
    (b) master electrician
    (c) authority having jurisdiction
    (d) permit holder

25. In the *NEC*, the word(s) "_____" indicate a mandatory requirement.

    (a) shall
    (b) shall not
    (c) shall be permitted
    (d) shall or shall not

26. When the *Code* uses "_____," it means the identified actions are allowed but not required, and they may be options or alternative methods.

    (a) shall
    (b) shall not
    (c) shall be permitted
    (d) shall or shall not

27. Explanatory material, such as references to other standards, references to related sections of the *NEC*, or information related to a *Code* rule, are included in the form of Informational Notes.

    (a) True
    (b) False

28. Nonmandatory Informative Annexes contained in the back of the *Code* book are _____.

    (a) for information only
    (b) not enforceable as a requirement of the *Code*
    (c) enforceable as a requirement of the *Code*
    (d) for information only and not enforceable as a requirement of the *Code*

29. It is the intent of the *NEC* that factory-installed _____ wiring of listed equipment need not be inspected at the time of installation of the equipment, except to detect alterations or damage.

    (a) external
    (b) associated
    (c) internal
    (d) all of these

30. Factory-installed _____ wiring of listed equipment need not be inspected at the time of installation of the equipment, except to detect alterations or damage.

    (a) external
    (b) associated
    (c) internal
    (d) all of these

Notes

CHAPTER 1
GENERAL RULES

Introduction to Chapter 1—General Rules

Before you can make sense of the *NEC*, you must become familiar with its general rules, concepts, definitions, and requirements. Chapter 1 consists of two topics; Article 100 which provides definitions that help ensure consistency when *Code*-related matters are the topic of discussion, and Article 110 which supplies the general requirements needed to correctly apply the *NEC*.

After gaining an understanding of Chapter 1, some of the *Code* requirements that might be confusing to many, will become increasingly clear to you. *NEC* requirements will make more sense to you because you will have the foundation from which to build upon your understanding and application of the rules.

▶ **Article 100—Definitions.** Article 100 is organized into three parts. Part I contains the definitions of terms used throughout the *Code* for systems that operate at 1,000V, nominal, or less. The definitions of terms in Part II apply to systems that operate at over 1,000V, nominal, are not within the scope of this textbook. Part III contains definitions applicable to "Hazardous (Classified) Locations" found in Chapter 5 of the *NEC*.

This article overall, only contains terms used in more than one article. Definitions of standard terms, such as volt, voltage drop, ampere, impedance, and resistance, are not contained in Article 100. If the *NEC* does not define a term, then a dictionary or building code acceptable to the authority having jurisdiction should be consulted.

Definitions are sometimes located at the beginning of an article. When this occurs, those terms only apply to that given article. There is uniformity in the location of the definitions specific to an article in that the article number will be followed by ".2." For example, definitions specific to solar photovoltaic (PV) systems are found in 690.2.

▶ **Article 110—Requirements for Electrical Installations.** This article contains general requirements applicable to all electrical installations.

Notes

ARTICLE 100 DEFINITIONS

Introduction to Article 100—Definitions

Have you ever had a conversation with someone only to discover that what you said and what he or she heard were completely different? This often happens when people have different definitions or interpretations of the words being used, and that is why the definitions of key *NEC* terms are located at the beginning of the *Code* (Article 100), or at the beginning of each article. If we can all agree on important definitions, then we speak the same language and avoid misunderstandings. Words taken out of context have created more than their fair share of problems. Because the *NEC* exists to protect people and property, it is very important for you to be able to convey and comprehend the language used. Review and study Article 100 until you are confident you know the definitions presented.

100 Definitions

Scope. This article contains definitions essential to the application of this *Code*; it does not include general or technical terms from other *code*s and standards. In general, only those used in two or more articles are defined in Article 100.

Definitions are also found in the xxx.2 sections of other articles.

- Part I of this article contains definitions intended to apply wherever the terms are used throughout the *NEC*.
- Part III contains definitions applicable to Hazardous (Classified) Locations.

Accessible (as applied to equipment). Capable of being reached for operation, renewal, and inspection. ▶Figure 100–1

Accessible, Readily (Readily Accessible). Capable of being reached quickly for operation, renewal, or inspection without requiring those to whom ready access is necessary to use tools (other than keys), climb over or under obstructions, remove obstacles, resort to using portable ladders, and so forth. ▶Figure 100–2

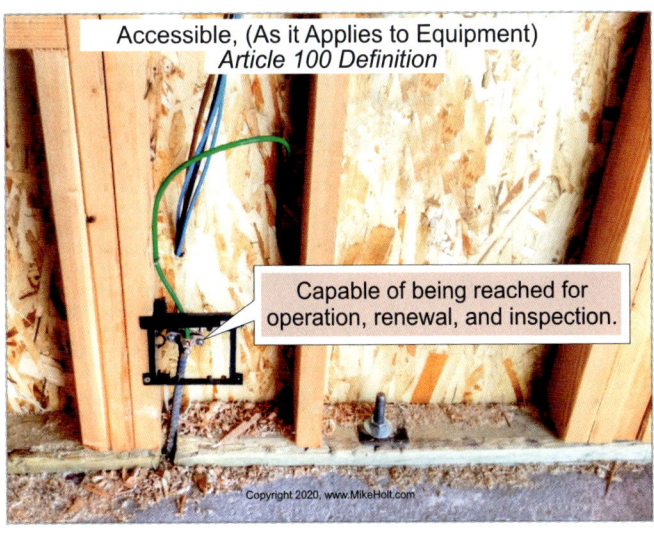

▶Figure 100–1

Note: The use of keys for locks on electrical equipment, and locked doors to electrical equipment rooms and vaults is a common practice and permitted by the *NEC*. ▶Figure 100–3

Adjustable-Speed Drive System. A combination of an adjustable speed drive, its associated motor(s), and any other equipment associated with the two.

100 | Definitions

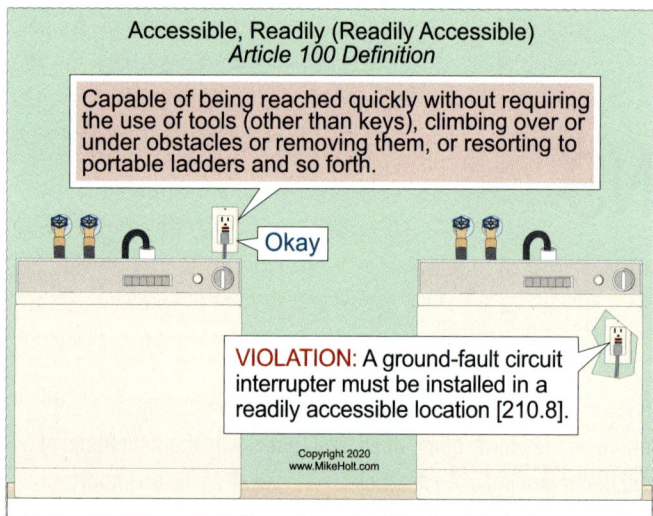
▶Figure 100–2

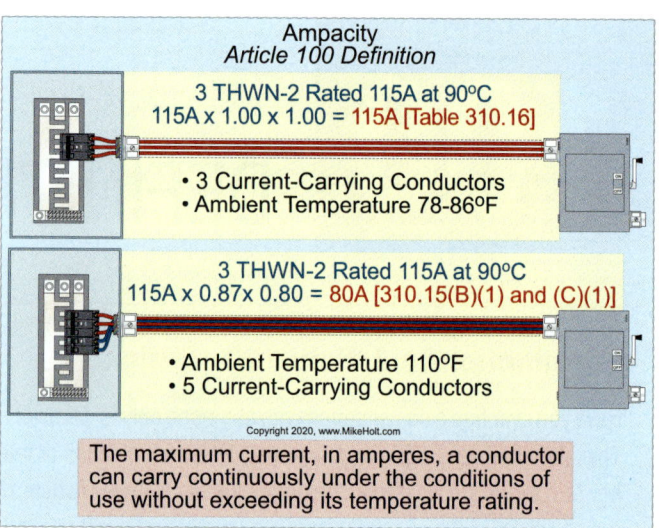
▶Figure 100–4

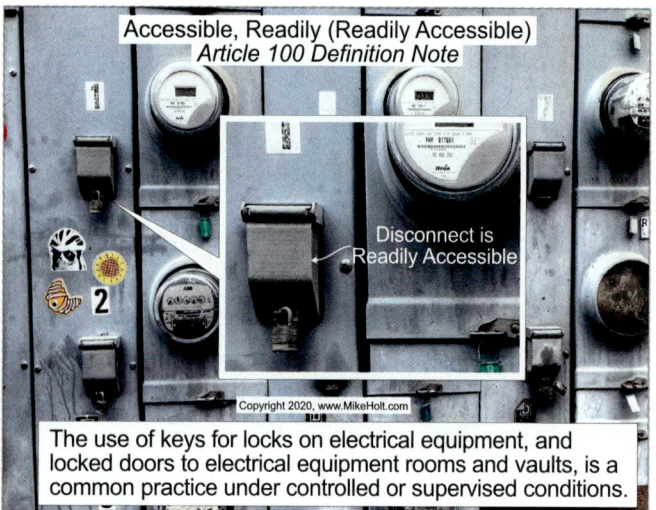
▶Figure 100–3

Author's Comment

▸ An adjustable-speed drive is a piece of equipment that provides a way to adjust the speed of an electric motor. Adjustable-speed drives are often referred to as "variable-speed drives" or "variable-frequency drives (VFDs)."

▸ A variable-frequency drive is a type of electronic adjustable-speed drive that controls the speed of an alternating-current motor by changing the frequency and voltage of the motor's power supply.

Ampacity. The current, in amperes, a conductor can carry continuously under its conditions of use without exceeding its temperature rating. ▶Figure 100–4

Author's Comment

▸ See 310.10 and 310.15 for details and examples.

Appliance [Article 422]. Electrical equipment, other than industrial equipment, built in standardized sizes. Examples of appliances are ranges, ovens, cooktops, refrigerators, drinking water coolers, and beverage dispensers.

Approved. Acceptable to the authority having jurisdiction; usually the electrical inspector. ▶Figure 100–5

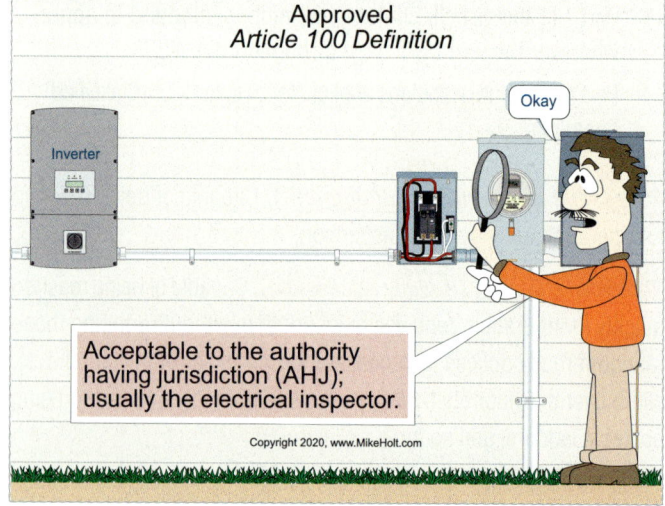
▶Figure 100–5

Author's Comment:

▸ Product listing does not mean the product is approved, but it can be a basis for approval. See 90.4, 90.7, and 110.2 and the definitions in this article for "Authority Having Jurisdiction," "Identified," "Labeled," and "Listed."

Arc-Fault Circuit Interrupter (AFCI). A device intended to de-energize the circuit when it detects the current waveform characteristics unique to an arcing fault. ▸Figure 100-6 and ▸Figure 100-7

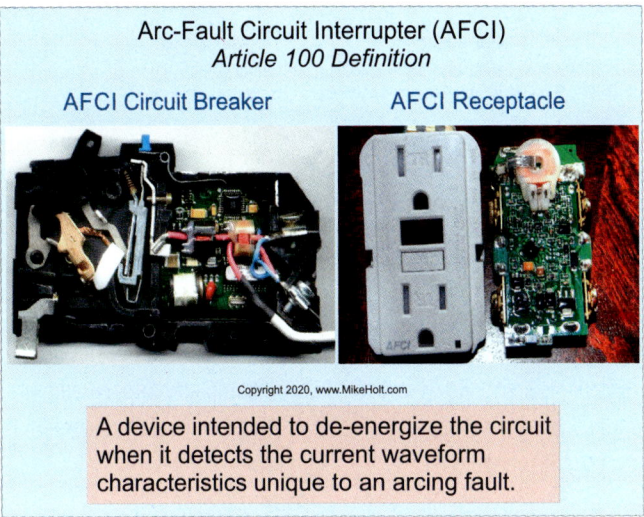
▸Figure 100-6

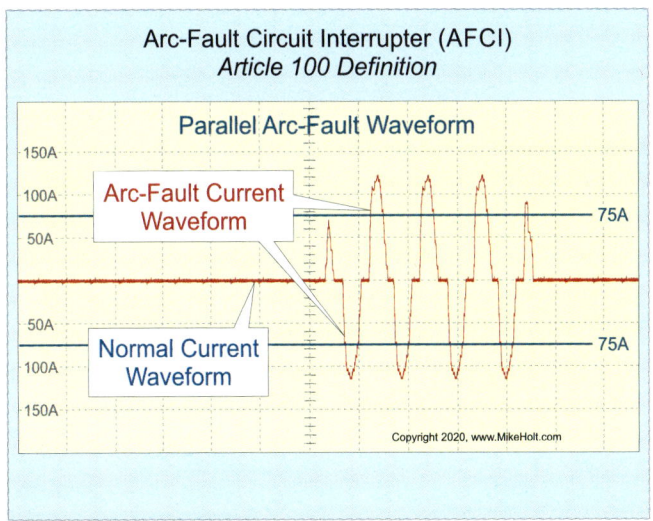
▸Figure 100-7

Attachment Fitting. A device that, by insertion into a locking support and mounting receptacle, establishes a connection between the conductors of the attached utilization equipment and the branch-circuit conductors connected to the locking support and mounting receptacle.

Note: An attachment fitting is different than an attachment plug, because no cord is associated with the fitting. An attachment fitting in combination with a locking support and mounting receptacle secures the associated utilization equipment in place and supports its weight.

Attachment Plug (Plug Cap), (Plug). A wiring device at the end of a flexible cord intended to be inserted into a receptacle in order to make an electrical connection. ▸Figure 100-8

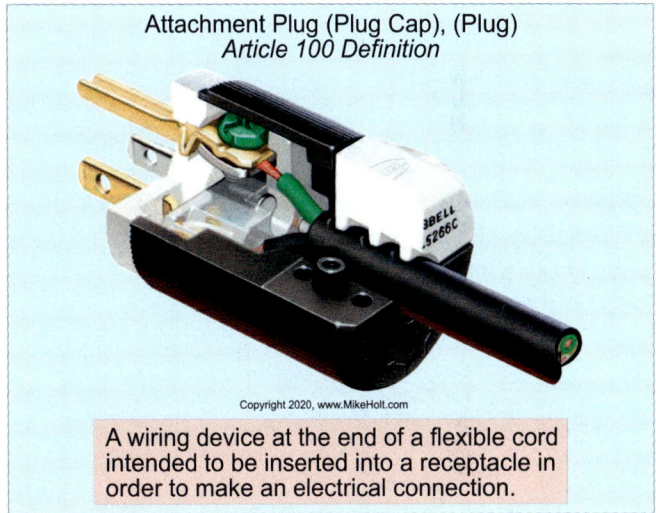
▸Figure 100-8

Authority Having Jurisdiction (AHJ). The organization, office, or individual responsible for approving equipment, materials, an installation, or a procedure. See 90.4 and 90.7 for more information.

Note: The authority having jurisdiction may be a federal, state, or local government department or individual such as a fire chief, fire marshal, chief of a fire prevention bureau, labor or health department, a building official, electrical inspector, or others having statutory authority. In some circumstances, the property owner or his or her agent assumes the role, and at government installations, the commanding officer or departmental official may be the authority having jurisdiction.

100 | Definitions

Author's Comment:

▸ The authority having jurisdiction is typically the electrical inspector who has legal statutory authority. In the absence of federal, state, or local regulations, the operator of the facility or his or her agent (such as an architect or engineer of the facility) can assume the role.

▸ Most expect the "authority having jurisdiction" to have at least some prior experience in the electrical field, such as having studied electrical engineering or having obtained an electrical contractor's license. In a few states this is a legal requirement. Memberships, certifications, and active participation in electrical organizations such as the International Association of Electrical Inspectors (IAEI) speak to an individual's qualifications. Visit www.IAEI.org for more information about that organization.

Automatic. Functioning without needing human intervention.

Bathroom. An area that includes a sink (basin) as well as one or more of the following: a toilet, urinal, tub, shower, bidet, or similar plumbing fixture. ▸Figure 100–9

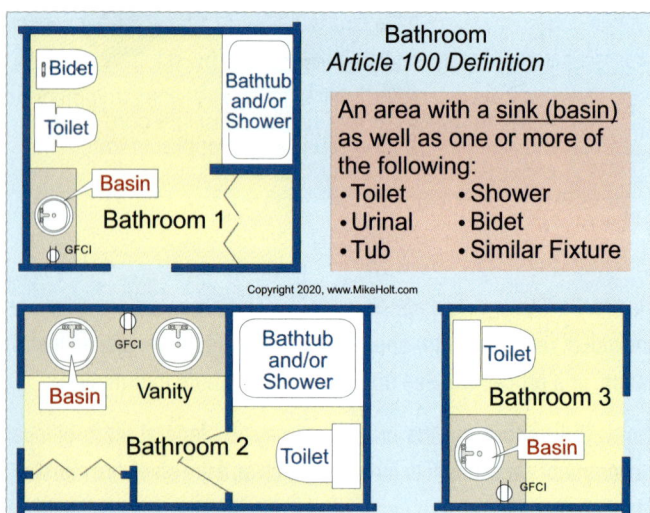
▸Figure 100–9

Battery System. An interconnection of one or more storage batteries and their chargers. It can also include converters, inverters, and other associated equipment. ▸Figure 100–10

Bonded (Bonding). Connected to establish electrical continuity and conductivity. ▸Figure 100–11 and ▸Figure 100–12

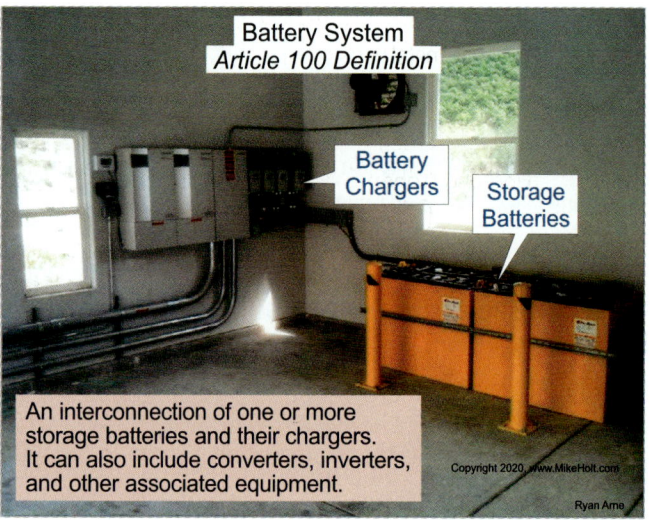
▸Figure 100–10

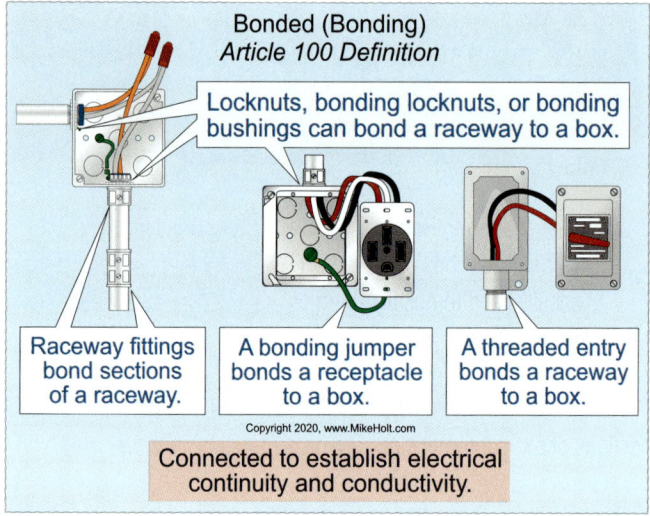
▸Figure 100–11

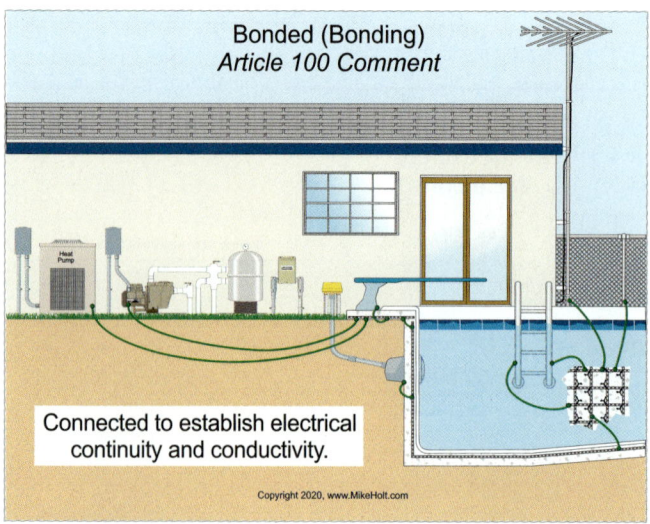
▸Figure 100–12

Definitions | **100**

Bonding Conductor or Jumper. A conductor that ensures electrical conductivity between metal parts of the electrical installation. ▶Figure 100–13

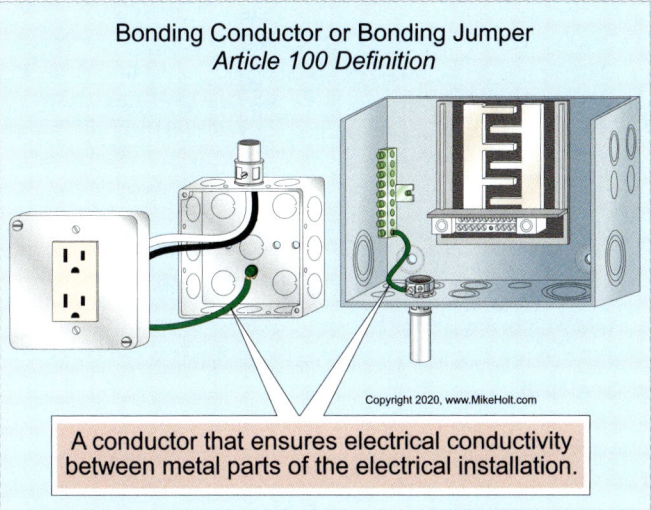

▶Figure 100–13

Author's Comment:

▸ Either the term "Bonding Conductor" or "Bonding Jumper" can be used. They can be short or several feet long and are typically used to ensure electrical conductivity between two metallic objects.

Bonding Jumper, Equipment. A connection between two or more portions of the equipment grounding conductor. ▶Figure 100–14

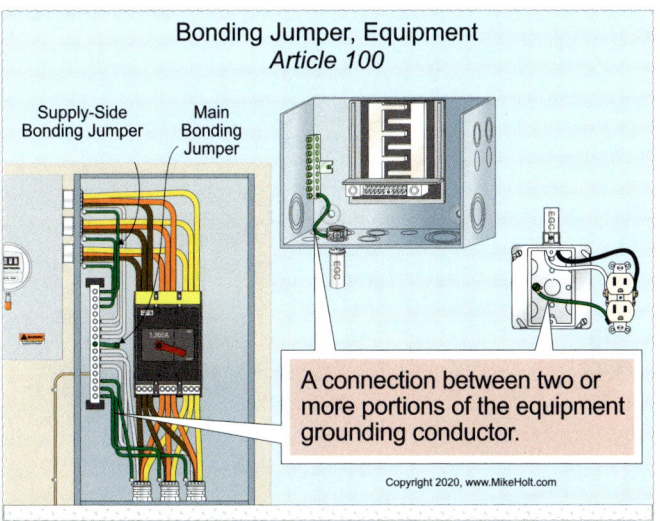

▶Figure 100–14

Author's Comment:

▸ Equipment bonding jumpers are used where the mechanical or electrical path for the effective ground-fault current path would be compromised or interrupted. ▶Figure 100–15

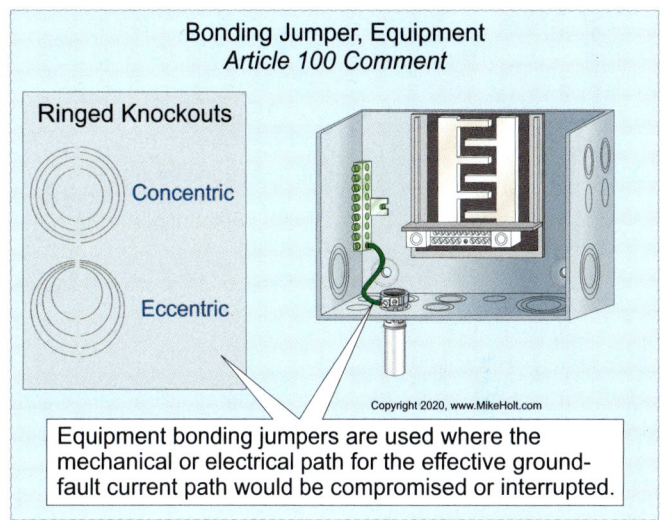

▶Figure 100–15

Bonding Jumper, Main. A conductor, screw, or strap used to connect the circuit equipment grounding conductor to the neutral conductor or to the supply-side bonding jumper at the service equipment in accordance with 250.24(B). ▶Figure 100–16 and ▶Figure 100–17

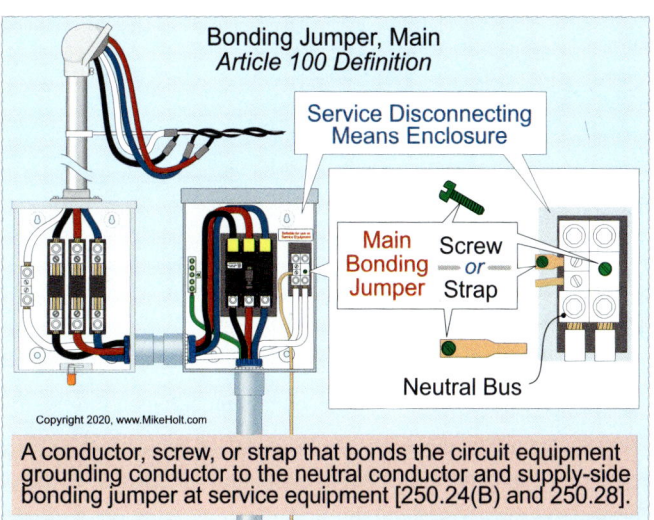

▶Figure 100–16

Mike Holt Enterprises • www.MikeHolt.com • 888.NEC.CODE (632.2633) | **25**

100 | Definitions

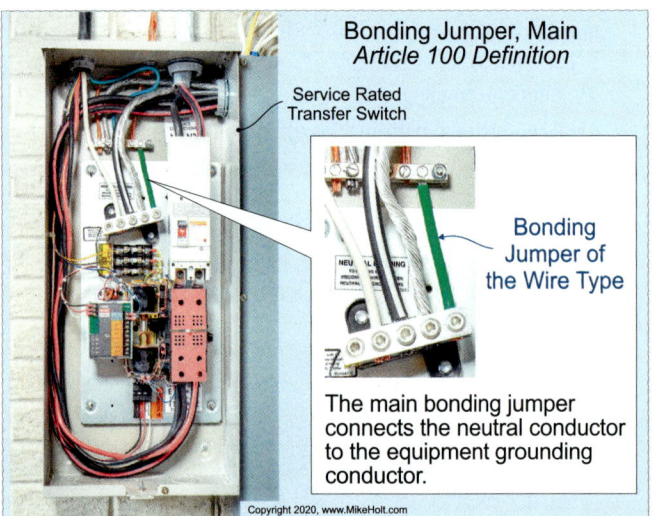
▶Figure 100-17

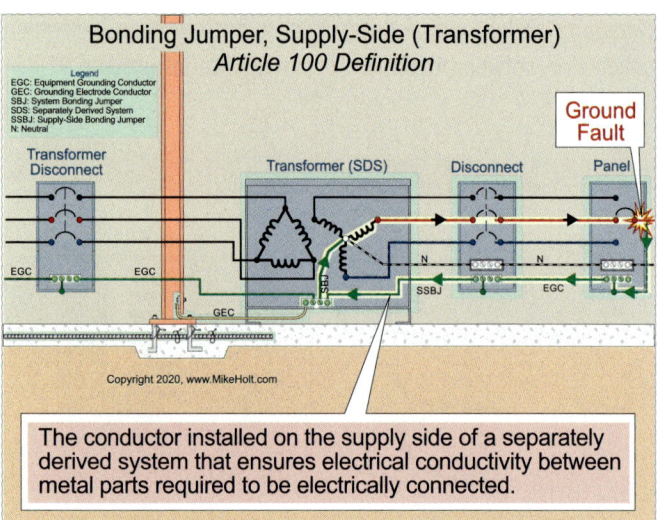
▶Figure 100-19

Bonding Jumper, Supply-Side. The conductor installed on the supply side of a service or separately derived system that ensures conductivity between metal parts required to be electrically connected. ▶Figure 100-18, ▶Figure 100-19, and ▶Figure 100-20

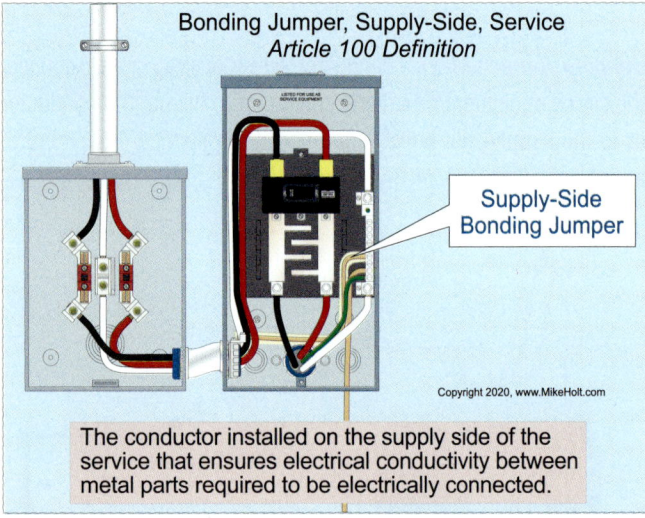
▶Figure 100-18

Bonding Jumper, System. The connection between the neutral conductor or grounded-phase conductor and the supply-side bonding jumper or equipment grounding conductor, or both, at a transformer. ▶Figure 100-21

Branch Circuit. The conductors between the final overcurrent device and the receptacle outlets, lighting outlets, or other outlets as defined in this article. ▶Figure 100-22

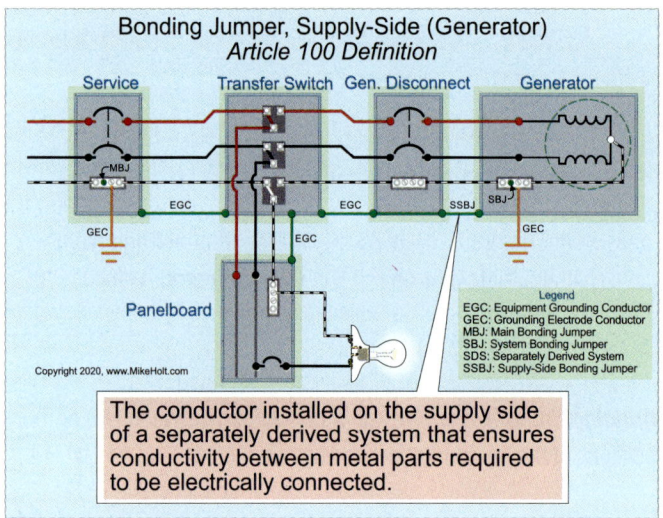
▶Figure 100-20

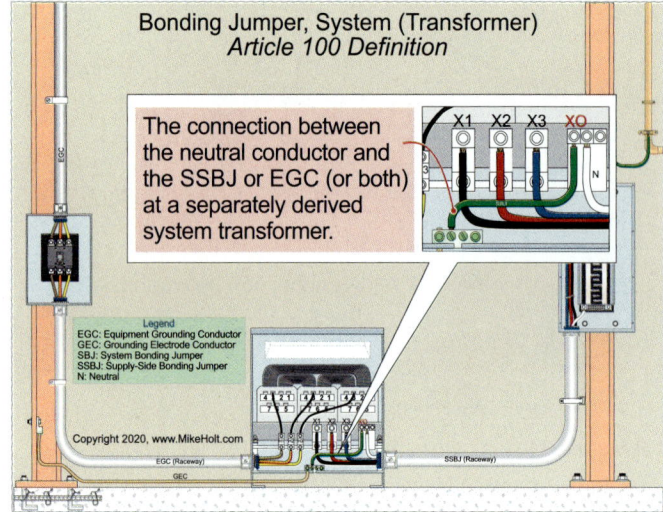
▶Figure 100-21

Definitions | 100

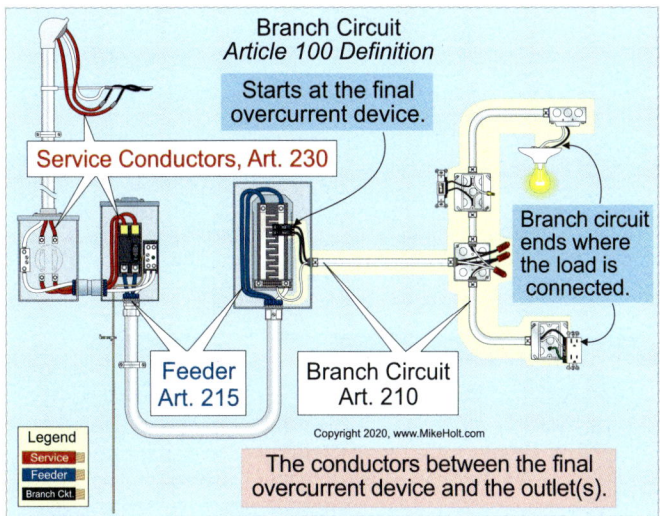
▶Figure 100–22

Branch Circuit, Individual (Individual Branch Circuit). A branch circuit that only supplies one load.

Branch Circuit, Multiwire (Multiwire Branch Circuit). A branch circuit consisting of two or more circuit phase conductors with a common neutral conductor. There must be a voltage between the phase conductors and an equal difference of voltage from each phase conductor to the common neutral conductor. ▶Figure 100–23

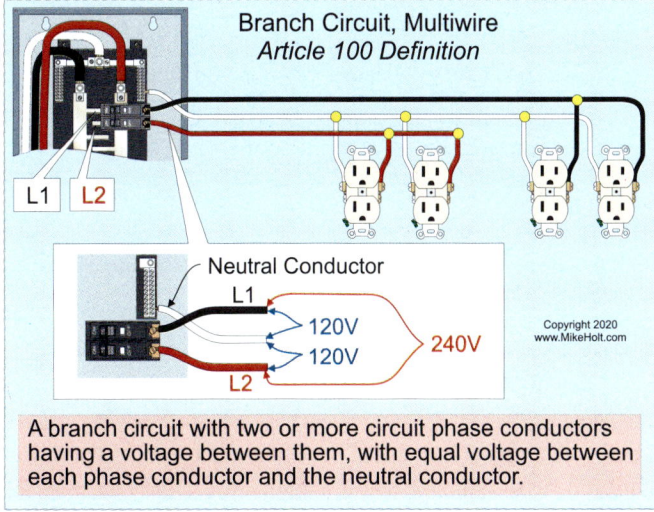
▶Figure 100–23

Author's Comment:

▸ Multiwire branch circuits offer the advantage of fewer conductors within a raceway which can result in smaller raceways, and reduced material and labor costs. In addition, multiwire branch circuits can reduce circuit voltage drop by as much as 50 percent. Because of the dangers associated with the use of multiwire branch circuits and the need for extra care, the *NEC* contains additional requirements to ensure a safe installation. See 210.4, 300.13(B), and 408.41 in this textbook for details.

▶ Hazard of an Open Neutral

Example: *A 3-wire, single-phase, 120/240V multiwire circuit supplies a 1,200W, 120V hair dryer and a 600W, 120V television.*
▶Figure 100–24

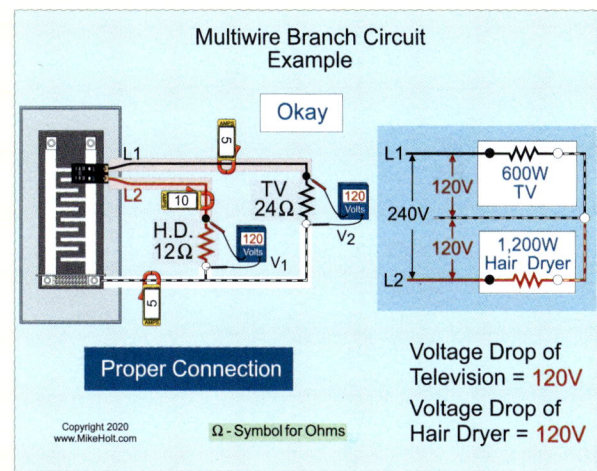
▶Figure 100–24

If the neutral conductor of the multiwire circuit is interrupted, it will cause the 120V television to operate at 160V and consume 1,067W of power (instead of 600W) for only a few seconds before it burns up. ▶Figure 100–25

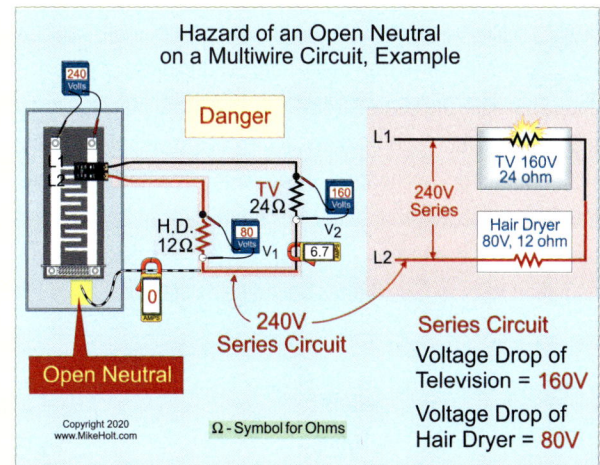
▶Figure 100–25

•••

Solution:

Step 1: Determine the resistance of each appliance.

$R = E^2/P$

R of the hair dryer = $120V^2/1{,}200W$
R of the hair dryer = 12 ohms

R of the television = $120V^2/600W$
R of the television = 24 ohms

Step 2: Determine the current of the circuit.

I = Volts/Resistance

Volts = 240V
R = 36 ohms (12 ohms + 24 ohms)
I = 240V/36 ohms
I = 6.70A

Step 3: Determine the operating voltage for each appliance.

Volts = I × R

I = 6.70A
R = 12 ohms for hair dryer and 24 ohms for TV

Voltage of hair dryer = 6.70A × 12 ohms
Voltage of hair dryer = 80V

Voltage of television = 6.70A × 24 ohms
Voltage of television = 160V

Answer: 160V

> **Warning**
>
> Failure to terminate the phase conductors to separate phases can cause the neutral conductor to become overloaded because the current from the phase conductors is additive and the insulation can be damaged or destroyed by excessive heat. Conductor overheating is known to decrease the service life of insulation, which creates the potential for arcing faults and can ultimately lead to fires. It is not known just how long conductor insulation lasts, but heat does decrease its life span.

Building. A structure that stands alone or is separated from adjoining structures by fire walls. ▶Figure 100-26

Cabinet. A surface-mounted or flush-mounted enclosure provided with a frame in which a door can be hung. ▶Figure 100-27

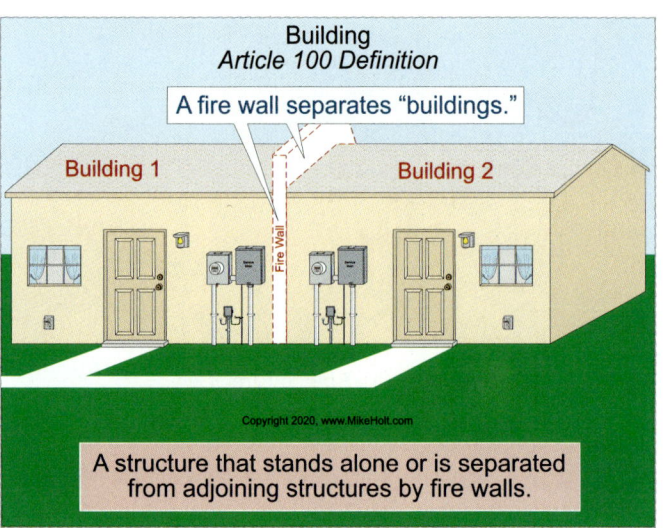

▶Figure 100-26

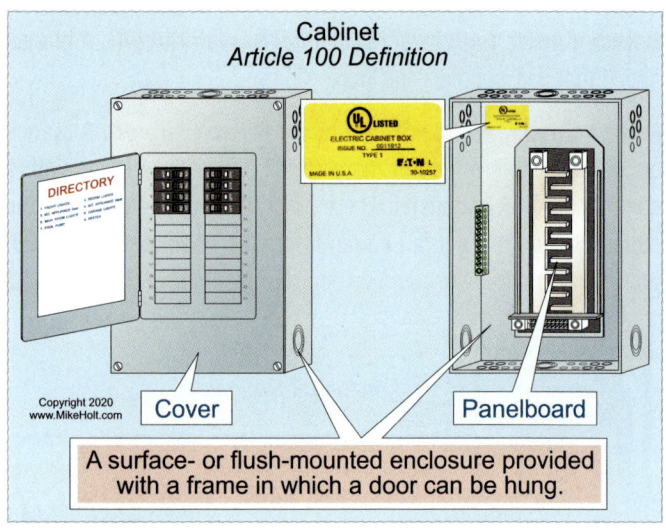

▶Figure 100-27

Author's Comment:

▶ Cabinets are used to enclose panelboards. See the definition of "Panelboard" in this article.

Cable, Coaxial. A cylindrical assembly containing a conductor centered inside a metallic shield, separated by a dielectric material, and covered by an insulating jacket. ▶Figure 100-28

Cable, Optical Fiber. An assembly of optical fibers. ▶Figure 100-29

Note: A field-assembled optical fiber cable is an assembly of one or more optical fibers within a jacket. The jacket is installed like a raceway into which the optical fibers are inserted.

Definitions | 100

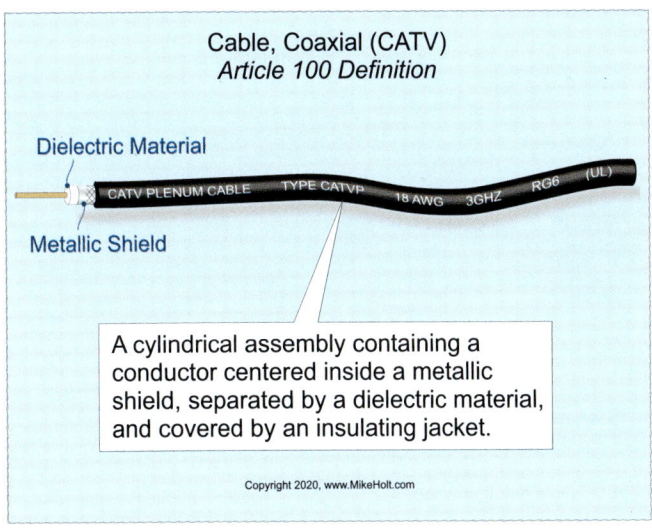
▶Figure 100-28

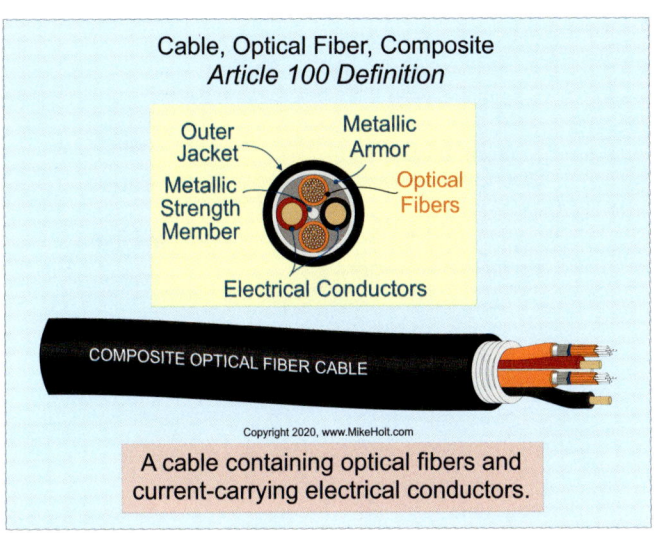
▶Figure 100-30

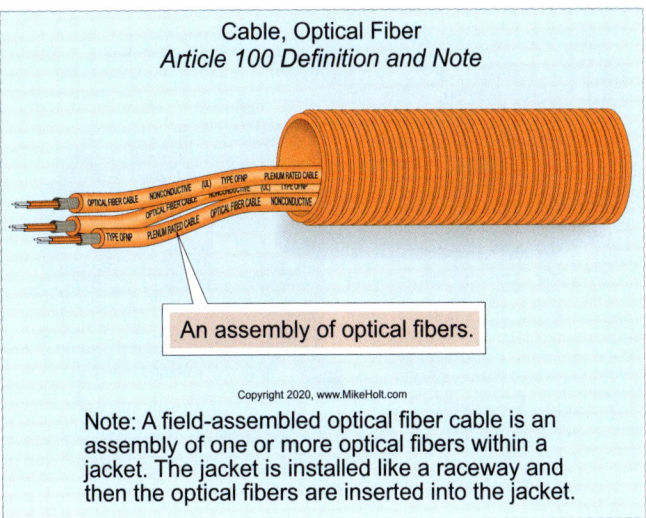
▶Figure 100-29

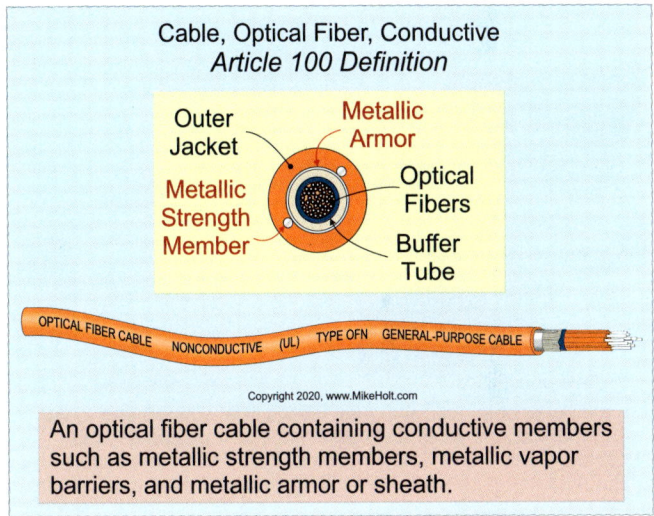
▶Figure 100-31

Cable, Optical Fiber, Composite. A cable containing optical fibers and current-carrying electrical conductors. ▶Figure 100-30

Author's Comment:

▸ Article 770 permits the use of composite optical fiber cables only where the optical fibers and current-carrying electrical conductors are functionally associated [770.133(A)].

Cable, Optical Fiber, Conductive. An optical fiber cable containing conductive members such as metallic strength members, metallic vapor barriers, or metallic armor or sheath. ▶Figure 100-31

Cable, Optical Fiber, Nonconductive. An optical fiber cable without any electrically conductive materials. ▶Figure 100-32

Cable Routing Assembly. A channel or channels (with their fittings) that support and route communications wires and cables, and optical fiber, data, Class 2, Type PLTC, and power-limited fire alarm cables in plenum, riser, and general-purpose applications. ▶Figure 100-33

Author's Comment:

▸ A cable routing assembly is typically a U-shaped trough (with or without covers) designed to hold cables. It is not a raceway.

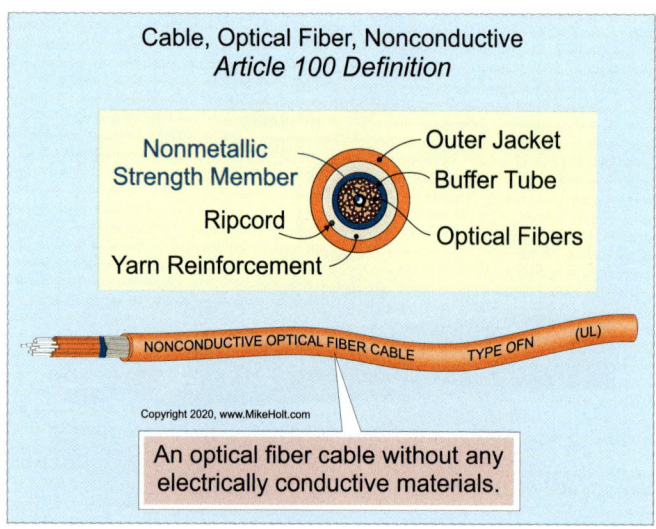

▶Figure 100-32

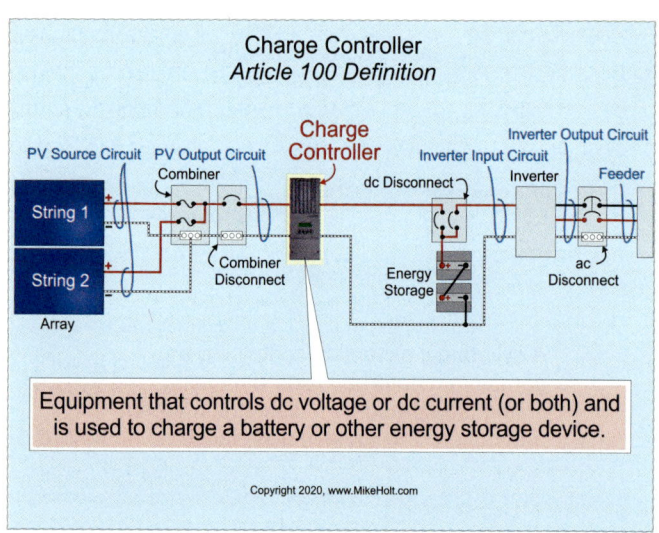

▶Figure 100-34

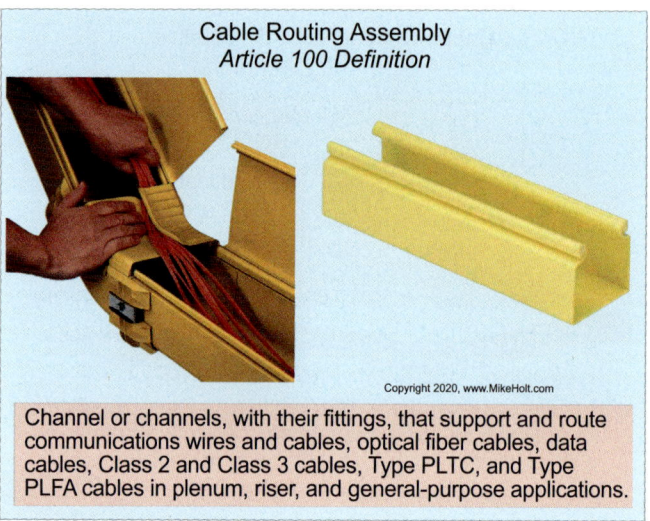

▶Figure 100-33

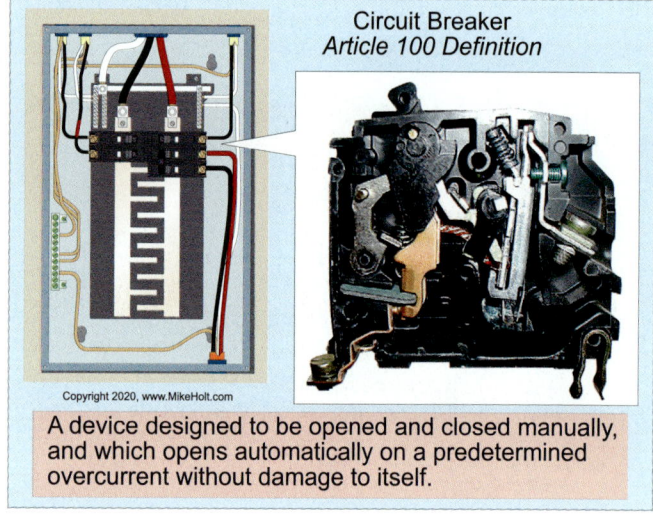

▶Figure 100-35

Charge Controller. Equipment that controls dc voltage or dc current, or both. It is used to charge a battery or other energy storage device. ▶Figure 100-34

Circuit Breaker. A device designed to be opened and closed manually and opens automatically at a preset overcurrent without damage to itself. Circuit breakers are available in different configurations such as adjustable trip (electronically controlled), instantaneous trip/motor-circuit protectors, and inverse time. ▶Figure 100-35

Circuit Breaker, Adjustable. Adjustable circuit breakers permit the circuit breaker to be set to trip at various values of current, time (or both), within a predetermined range.

Circuit Breaker, Instantaneous Trip. Instantaneous trip breakers only operate on the principle of electromagnetism and are used for motors. These devices are sometimes called "motor-circuit protectors." This type of overcurrent protective device does not provide overload protection. It only provides short-circuit and ground-fault protection; overload protection must be provided separately.

> **Author's Comment:**
>
> ▸ Instantaneous trip circuit breakers have no intentional time delay and are sensitive to current inrush, vibration, and shock. Consequently, they should not be used where these factors are known to exist.

Circuit Breaker, Inverse Time. This type of circuit breaker is purposely designed to delay its tripping action during an overcurrent condition. The intent is to compensate for the inrush of current during the normal start-up of equipment such as vacuum cleaners or air conditioners and helps avoid "nuisance tripping."

Author's Comment:

▸ Inverse time breakers operate on the principle that as the current increases, the time it takes for the devices to open decreases. They provide ordinary overcurrent protection during overload, short-circuit, or ground-fault conditions. This is the most common type of circuit breaker purchased over the counter.

Class 1 Circuit. The wiring system between the load side of a Class 1 circuit overcurrent protective device and the connected equipment.
▸Figure 100–36

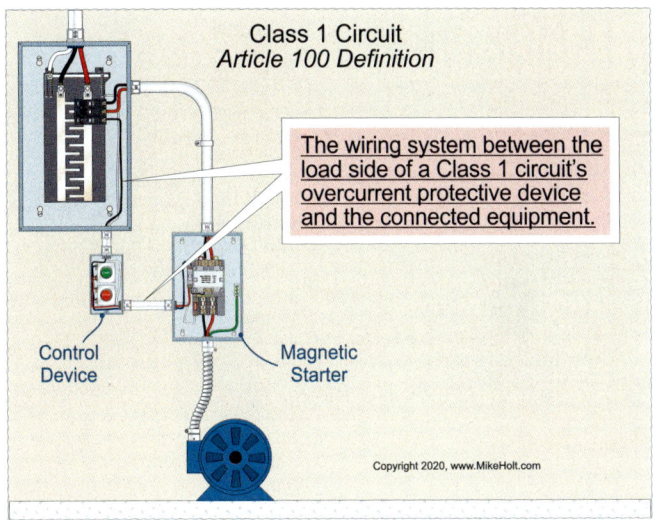
▸Figure 100–36

Note: See 725.41 for the voltage and power limitations of Class 1 circuits.

Class 2 Circuit. The portion of the wiring system between the load side of a Class 2 power supply and the connected Class 2 equipment.
▸Figure 100–37

Due to power the limitations of its power supply, a Class 2 circuit is considered safe from a fire initiation standpoint and provides acceptable electric shock protection.

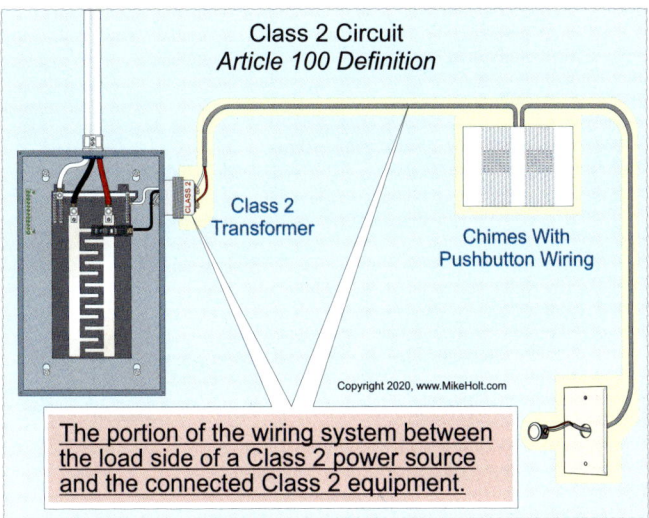
▸Figure 100–37

Author's Comment:

▸ Class 2 circuits are rendered safe by limiting the power supply to 100 VA for circuits operating at 30V or less, and the current to 5 mA for circuits over 30V [715.121(A) and Chapter 9, Table 11(A)].

▸ Class 2 circuits typically include wiring for low-energy, low-voltage loads such as thermostats, programmable controllers, burglar alarms, and security systems. This type of circuit also includes twisted-pair or coaxial cable that interconnects computers for local area networks (LANs), power over ethernet applications (POE), and programmable controller I/O circuits [725.121(A)(3) and 725.121(A)(4)].

Class 3 Circuit. The portion of the wiring system between the load side of a Class 3 power supply and the connected Class 3 equipment.
▸Figure 100–38

Author's Comment:

▸ Class 3 circuits are used when the power demand exceeds 30 VA but is not more than 100 VA [Chapter 9, Table 11(A)].

Clothes Closet. A nonhabitable room or space intended primarily for the storage of garments and apparel. ▸Figure 100–39

Author's Comment:

▸ The definition of a "Clothes Closet" provides clarification in the application of overcurrent protective devices [240.24(D)] and luminaires [410.16] in clothes closets.

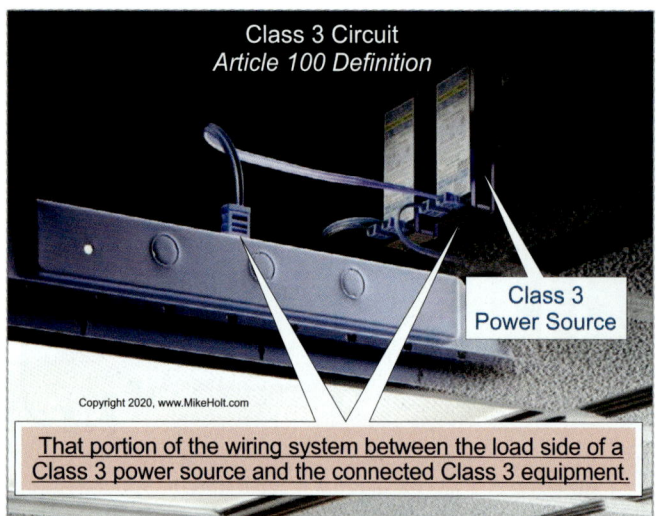
▶Figure 100-38

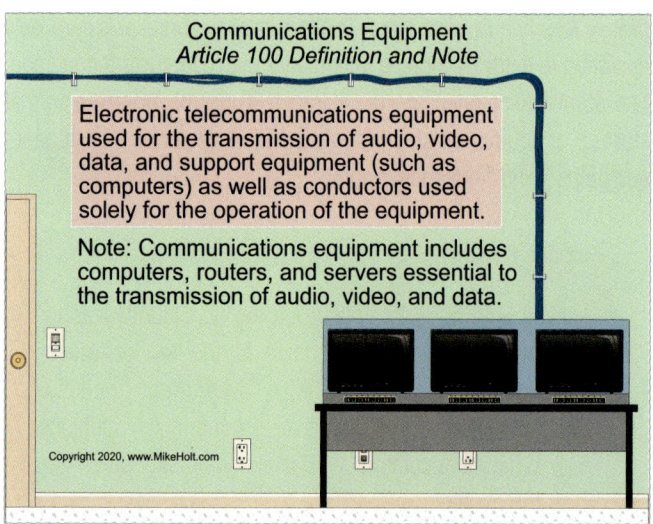
▶Figure 100-40

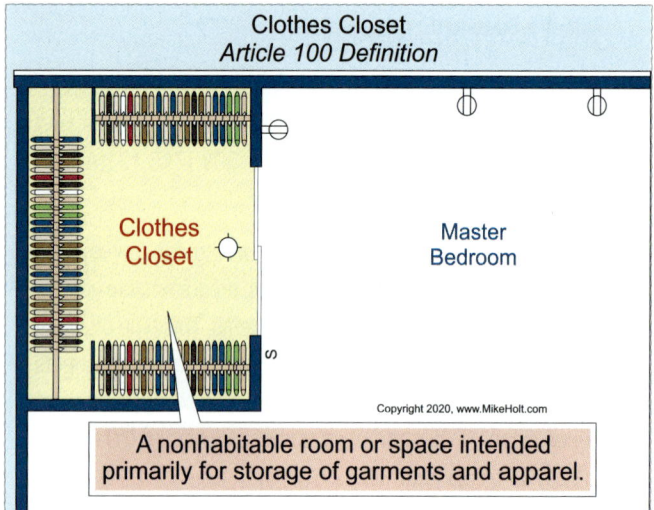
▶Figure 100-39

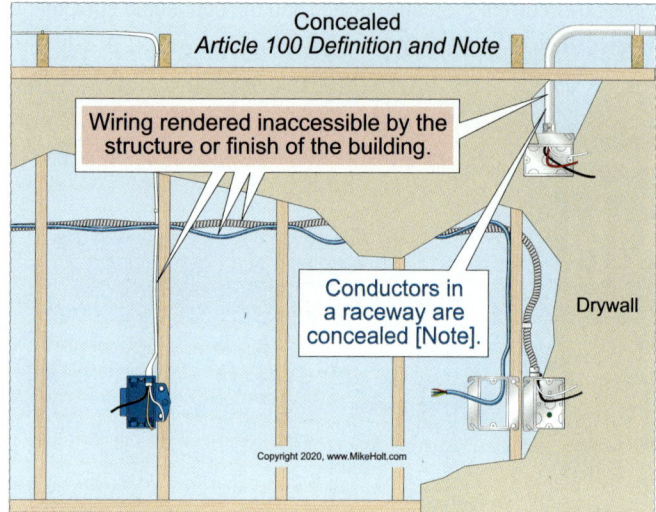
▶Figure 100-41

Communications Equipment. Electronic telecommunications equipment used for the transmission of audio, video, and data including support equipment (such as computers) and the conductors used solely for the operation of the equipment.

Note: Communications equipment includes the computers, routers, and servers essential to the transmission of audio, video, and data. ▶Figure 100-40

Concealed. Rendered inaccessible by the structure or finish of the building. ▶Figure 100-41

Note: Conductors in a concealed raceway are considered concealed even though they may be made accessible by withdrawing them from the raceway.

Author's Comment:

▸ Wiring behind panels designed to allow access, such as removable ceiling tile and wiring in accessible attics, is not considered concealed; it is considered exposed. See the definition of "Exposed (as applied to wiring methods)."

▸ Boxes are not permitted to be concealed by the finish of the building. ▶Figure 100-42

Conduit Body. A fitting installed in a conduit or tubing system that provides access to conductors through a removable cover. ▶Figure 100-43

Continuous Load. A load where the maximum current is expected to exist for 3 hours or more continuously such as in schools, office buildings, stores, or parking lot lighting.

Definitions | 100

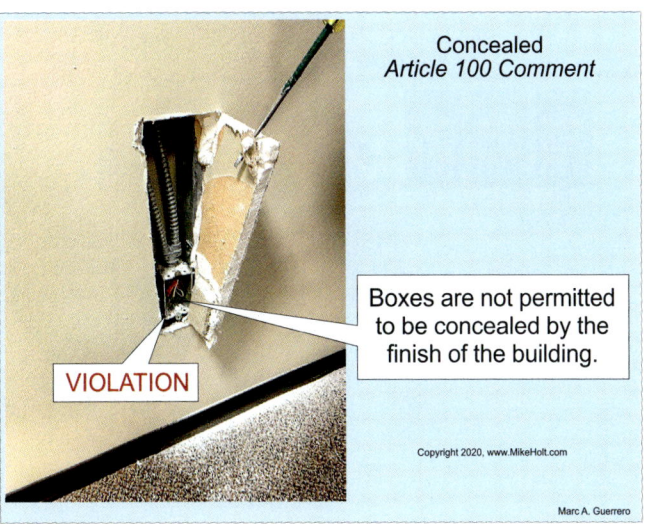
▶Figure 100-42

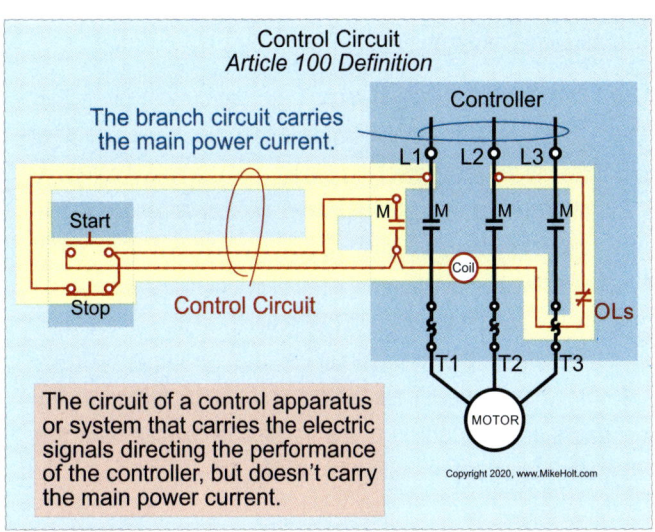
▶Figure 100-44

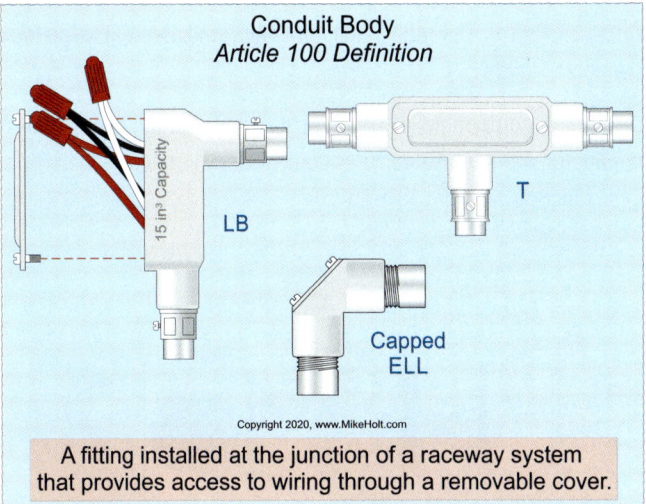
▶Figure 100-43

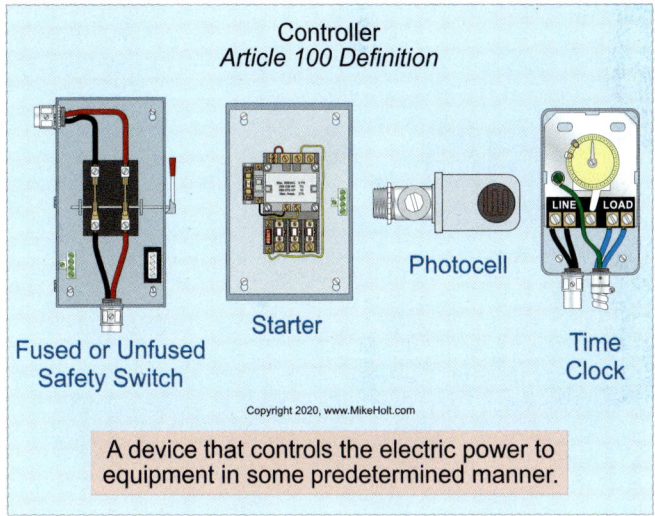
▶Figure 100-45

Control Circuit. The circuit of a control apparatus or system that carries the electric signals directing the performance of a controller but does not carry the main power current. ▶Figure 100-44

Controller. A device that controls the electric power delivered to electrical equipment in some predetermined manner. This includes time clocks, lighting contactors, photocells, and equipment with similar functions. ▶Figure 100-45

Coordination, Selective (Selective Coordination). Localization of an overcurrent condition to restrict outages to the circuit or equipment affected, accomplished by the choice of overcurrent protective devices. Selective coordination includes all currents from overloads, short circuits, or ground faults. ▶Figure 100-46

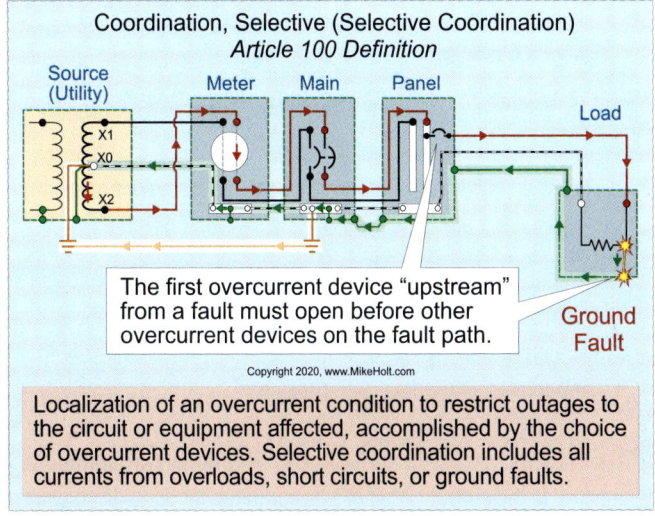
▶Figure 100-46

100 | Definitions

Author's Comment:

▸ Selective coordination means the overcurrent protection scheme confines the interruption to a specific circuit rather than to the entire electrical system. For example, if someone plugs in a space heater and raises the total demand on a 20A circuit to 25A, or if a short circuit or ground fault occurs with selective coordination, the only breaker or fuse that will open is the one protecting just that branch circuit. Coordinating overcurrent protection for an electrical system is especially important in healthcare facilities and data centers where the loss of power ahead of the troubled circuit can have dire consequences—including loss of life.

DC-to-DC Converter. A device that can provide an output dc voltage and current at a higher or lower value than the input dc voltage and current. ▸Figure 100-47

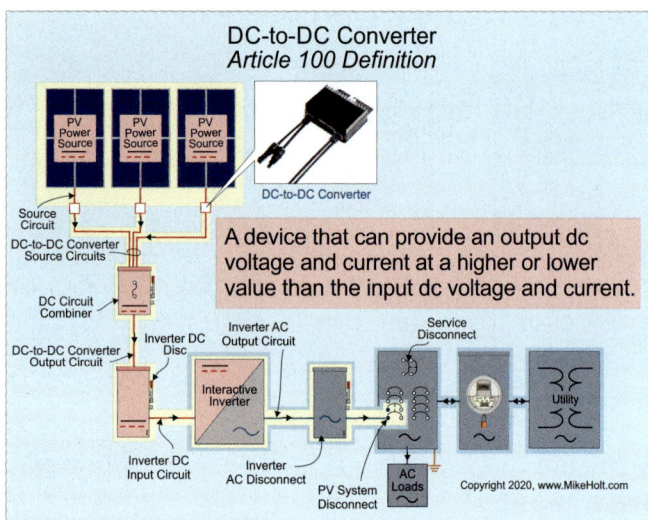

▸Figure 100-47

Author's Comment:

▸ DC-to-DC converters are intended to maximize the output of independent PV modules and reduce losses due to variances between modules' outputs. They are directly wired to each module and are bolted to the module frame or the PV rack.

▸ A dc-to-dc converter enables a PV inverter to automatically maintain a fixed circuit voltage, at the optimal point for dc/ac conversion by the inverter, regardless of circuit length and individual module performance.

DC-to-DC Converter Output Circuit. The dc circuit conductors connected to the output circuit of a dc combiner for dc-to-dc converter source circuits. ▸Figure 100-48

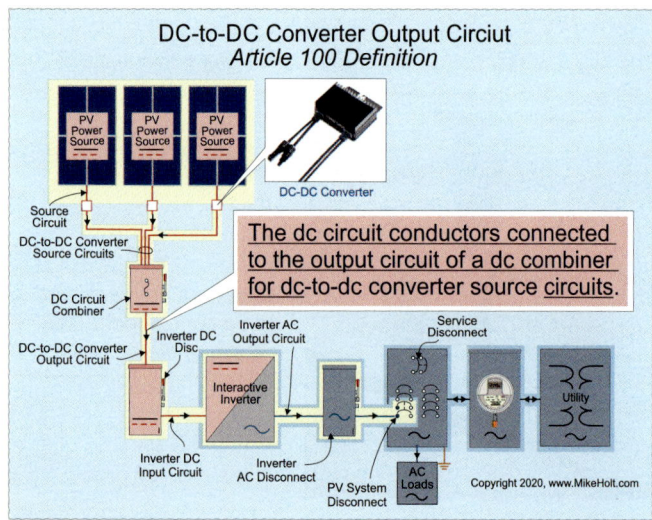

▸Figure 100-48

Demand Factor. The ratio of the maximum load demand to the total connected load.

Device. A component of an electrical installation, other than a conductor, intended to carry or control electric energy as its principal function. ▸Figure 100-49

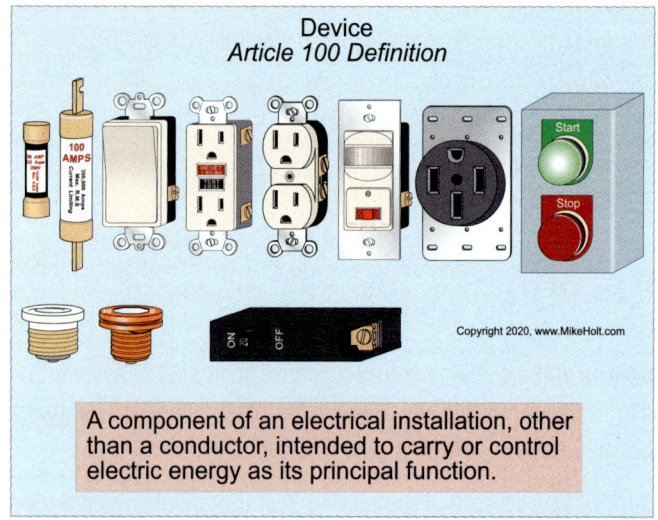

▸Figure 100-49

Author's Comment:

▸ Devices generally do not consume electric energy and include receptacles, switches, illuminated switches, circuit breakers, fuses, time clocks, controllers, attachment plugs, and so forth. Some (such as illuminated switches, contactors, or relays) consume very small amounts of energy and are still classified as a device based on their primary function.

Disconnecting Means (Disconnect). A device that disconnects the circuit conductors from their power source. Examples include switches, attachment plugs, and circuit breakers. ▶Figure 100-50

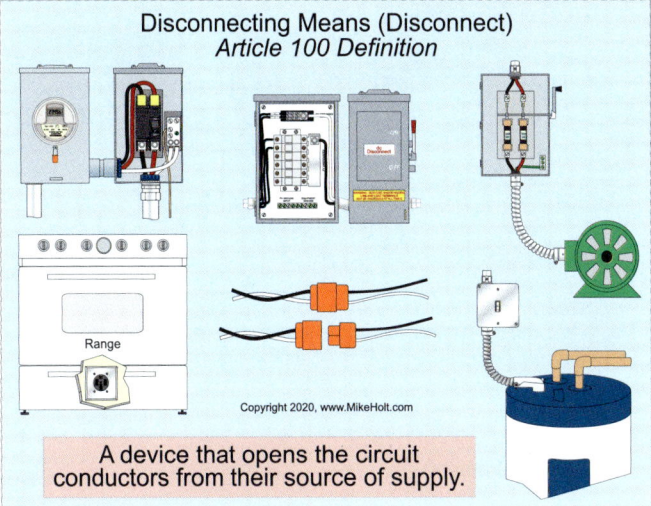

▶Figure 100-50

Dormitory Unit. A building or a space in a building in which group sleeping accommodations are provided in one room for more than 16 persons who are not members of the same family; or a series of closely associated rooms, under joint occupancy and single management, with or without meals, but without individual cooking facilities. ▶Figure 100-51

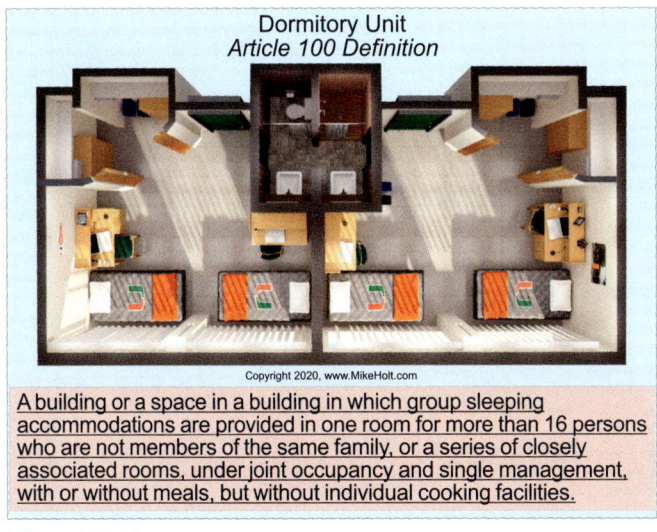

▶Figure 100-51

Duty, Continuous (Continuous Duty). Operation at a substantially constant load for an indefinite amount of time.

Duty, Varying (Varying Duty). Operation at loads, and for intervals of time, which may both be subject to wide variation.

Dwelling, One-Family (One-Family Dwelling). A building that consists solely of one dwelling unit.

Dwelling, Two-Family (Two-Family Dwelling). A building that consists solely of two dwelling units. ▶Figure 100-52

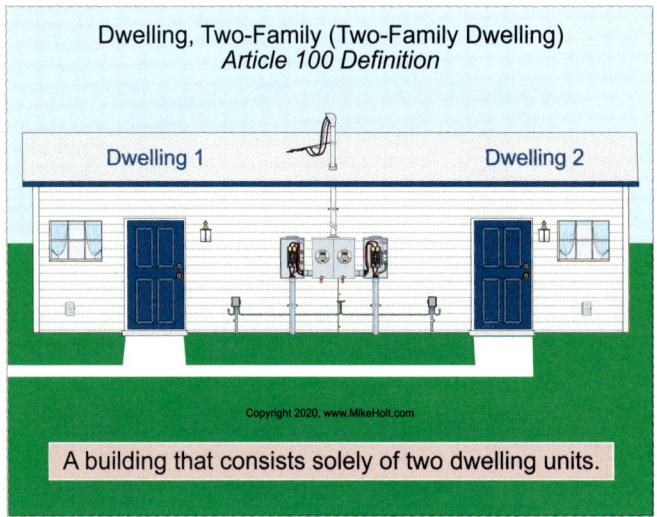

▶Figure 100-52

Dwelling, Multifamily (Multifamily Dwelling). A building that contains three or more dwelling units. ▶Figure 100-53

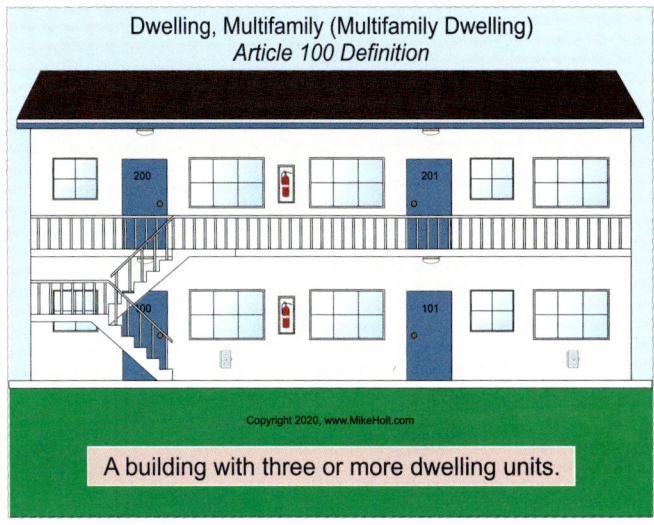

▶Figure 100-53

Dwelling Unit. A space that provides independent living facilities with space for eating, living, sleeping, and permanent provisions for cooking and sanitation. ▶Figure 100-54

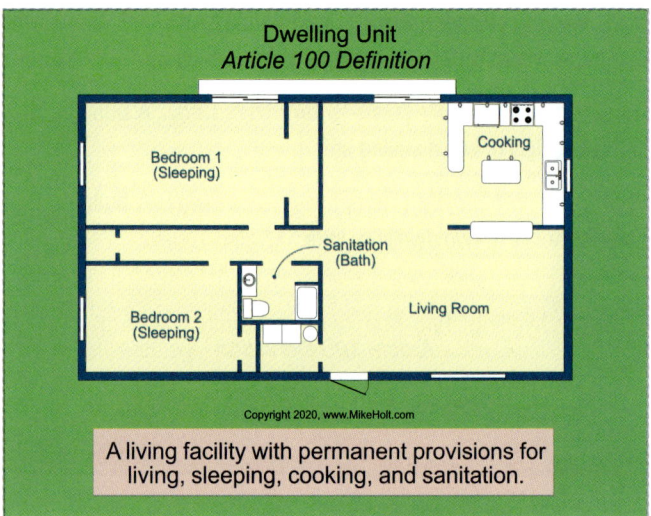
▶Figure 100-54

Effective Ground-Fault Current Path. An intentionally constructed low-impedance conductive path designed to carry ground-fault current from the point of a ground fault to the source for the purpose of opening the circuit overcurrent protective device. ▶Figure 100-55

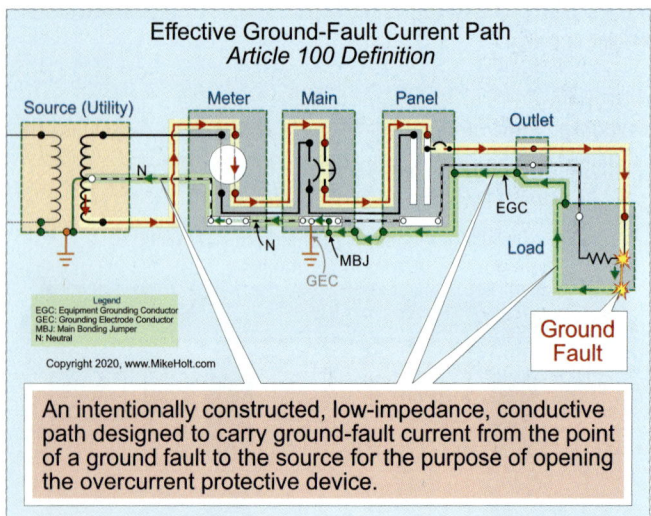
▶Figure 100-55

Author's Comment:

▸ The effective ground-fault current path is intended to help remove dangerous voltage from a ground fault by opening the circuit overcurrent protective device.

Electric Power Production and Distribution Network. A serving electric utility that is connected to premises wiring and is not controlled by an interactive system. ▶Figure 100-56

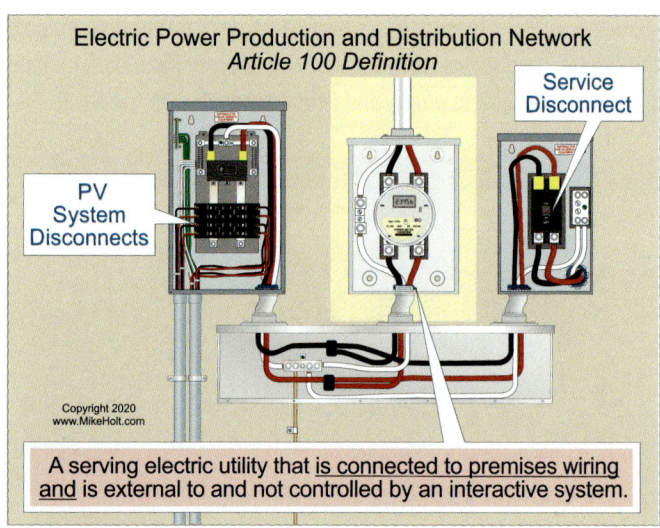
▶Figure 100-56

Author's Comment:

▸ An interactive system is an electric power production system that operates in parallel with, and may deliver power to, the serving electric utility. An example is a PV system interactively connected in parallel to the utility by an interactive inverter.

Electric Sign [Article 600]. A fixed, stationary, or portable self-contained, electrically operated and/or electrically illuminated piece of equipment with words or symbols designed to convey information or attract attention. ▶Figure 100-57

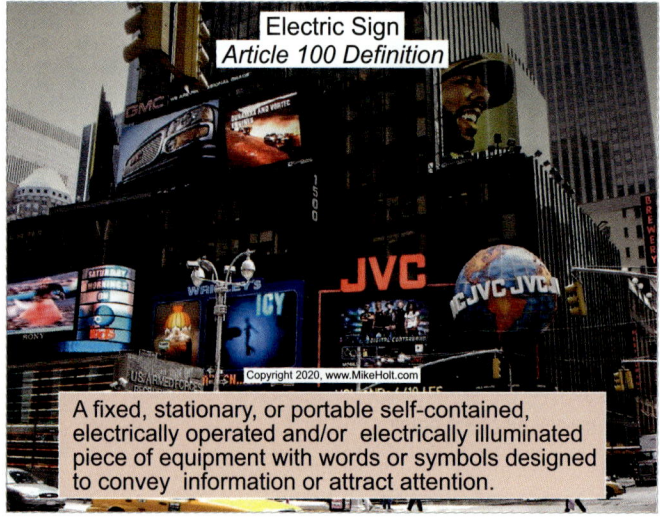
▶Figure 100-57

Electric-Discharge Lighting. Systems of illumination utilizing fluorescent lamps, high-intensity discharge (HID) lamps, or neon tubing. ▶Figure 100-58

Definitions | 100

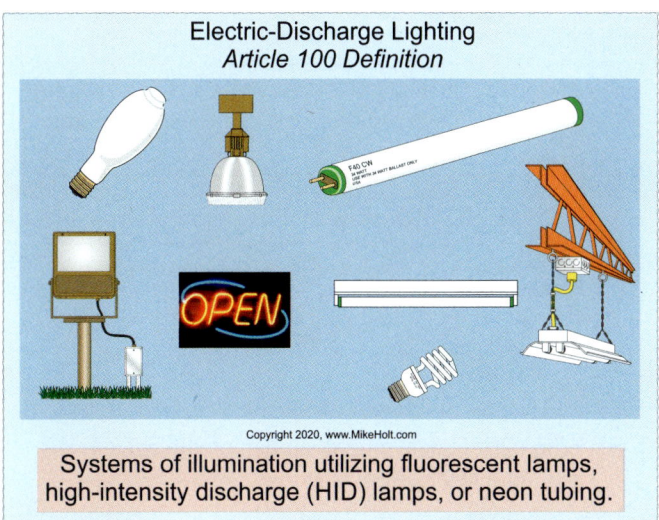
▶Figure 100–58

Electrical Datum Plane. A specified distance above a water level above which electrical equipment can be installed and electrical connections can be made.

> **Author's Comment:**
>
> ▸ This definition previously included the specific elevations of the electrical datum plane which acted as requirements. The detailed requirements in 682.5 appear as though they only apply within that article, and not to the others that also use the term.

Enclosed. Surrounded by a case, housing, fence, or wall(s) that prevents accidental contact with energized parts.

Energized. Electrically connected to a source of voltage.

Equipment. A general term including fittings, devices, appliances, luminaires, machinery, and the like as part of (or in connection with) an electrical installation. ▶Figure 100–60

Electric Vehicle. An on-road use automobile, bus, truck, van, neighborhood electric vehicle, or motorcycle primarily powered by an electric motor. ▶Figure 100–59

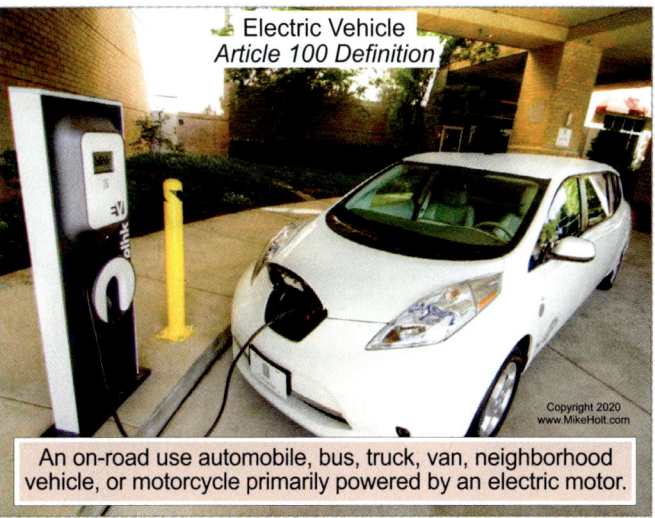
▶Figure 100–59

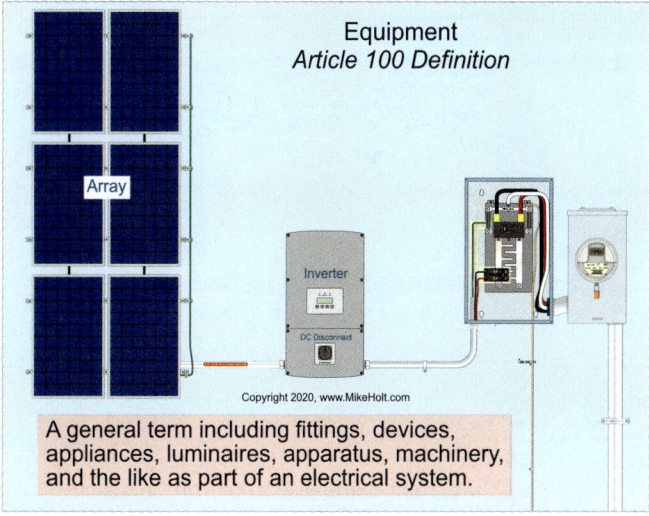
▶Figure 100–60

Off-road, self-propelled electric industrial trucks, hoists, lifts, transports, golf carts, airline ground support equipment, tractors, and boats are not electric vehicles.

> **Author's Comment:**
>
> ▸ The portion of plug-in hybrid type vehicles containing both an electric motor and a combustion engine that pertains to re-charging the electric motor is covered by Article 625.

Exposed (as applied to live parts). Capable of being accidentally touched or approached nearer than a safe distance. ▶Figure 100–61

Note: This term applies to parts that are not suitably guarded, isolated, or insulated for the condition such as line-side lugs in a meter socket or panelboard.

Exposed (as applied to wiring methods). On or attached to the surface of a building, or behind panels designed to allow access. ▶Figure 100–62

100 | Definitions

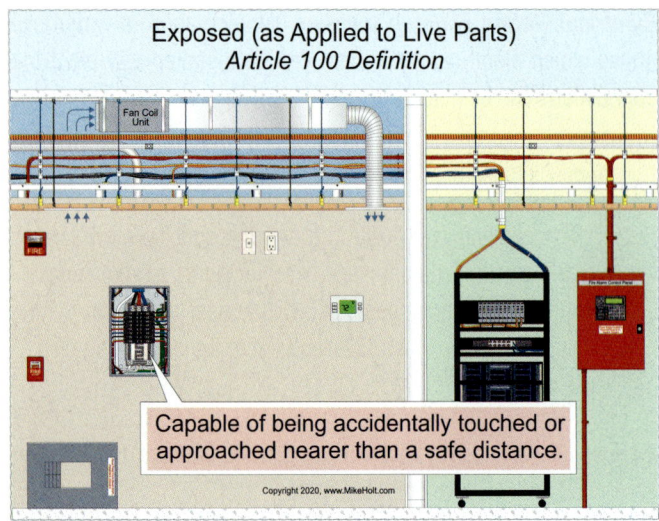
▶Figure 100-61

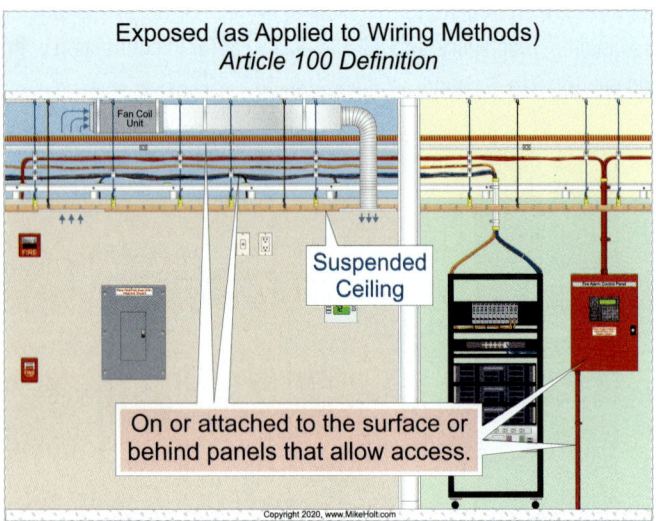
▶Figure 100-62

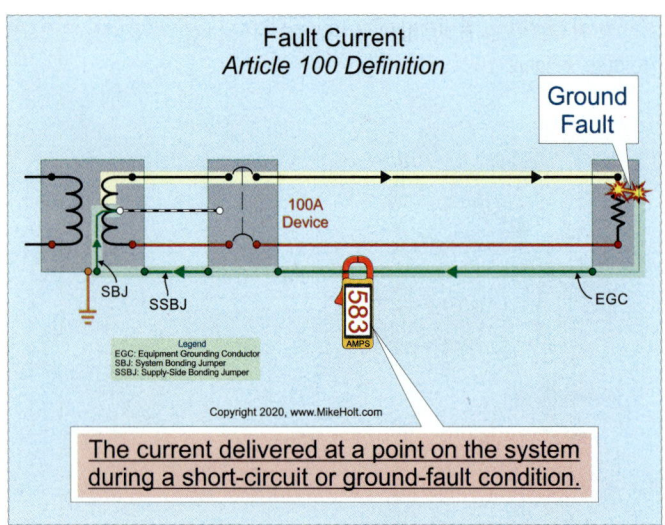
▶Figure 100-63

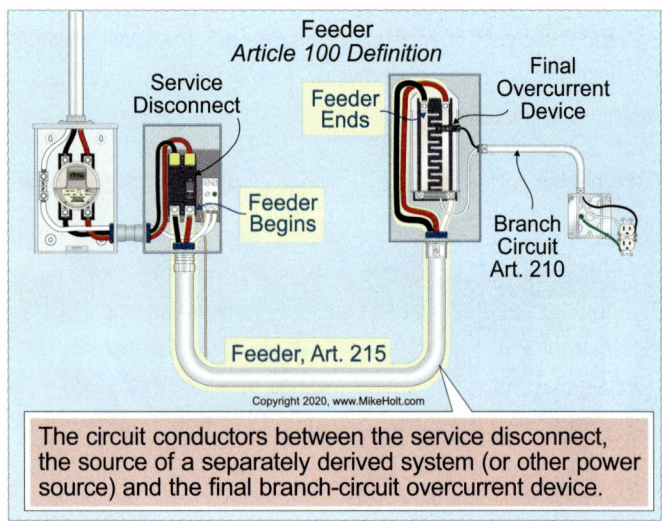
▶Figure 100-64

Fault Current. The current delivered at a point on the system during a short-circuit condition. ▶Figure 100-63

Note: A short circuit can occur during abnormal conditions such as a fault between circuit conductors or a ground fault.

Feeder. The conductors between the service disconnect, a separately derived system (typically a transformer), or other power-supply source and the final branch-circuit overcurrent device. ▶Figure 100-64

Author's Comment:

▸ An "other power-supply source" includes solar PV systems or conductors from generators. ▶Figure 100-65

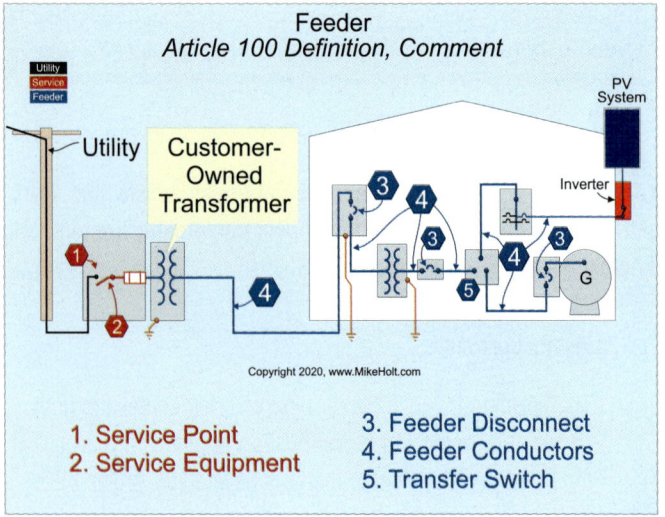
▶Figure 100-65

Festoon Lighting. A string of outdoor lights suspended between two points. ▶Figure 100-66

▶Figure 100-66

Field Evaluation Body (FEB). An organization or part of an organization that performs field evaluations of electrical equipment and materials.

Field Labeled (as applied to evaluated products). Equipment or materials which have a label, symbol, or other identifying mark of a field evaluation body (FEB) indicating the equipment or materials were evaluated and found to comply with the requirements described in the accompanying field evaluation report.

Fitting. An accessory such as a locknut, bushing, or other part of a wiring system that is primarily intended to perform a mechanical rather than an electrical function. ▶Figure 100-67

Free Air (as applied to conductors). An open or ventilated environment that allows for heat dissipation and air flow around a conductor. ▶Figure 100-68

Garage. A building or portion of a building where self-propelled vehicles can be kept.

Generating Capacity, Inverter. The sum of parallel-connected inverters' maximum continuous output power at 40°C in watts or kilowatts.

Ground. The Earth. ▶Figure 100-69

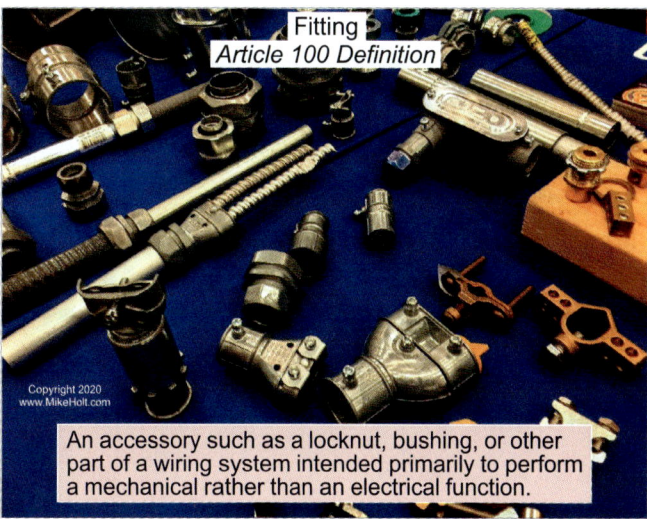
▶Figure 100-67

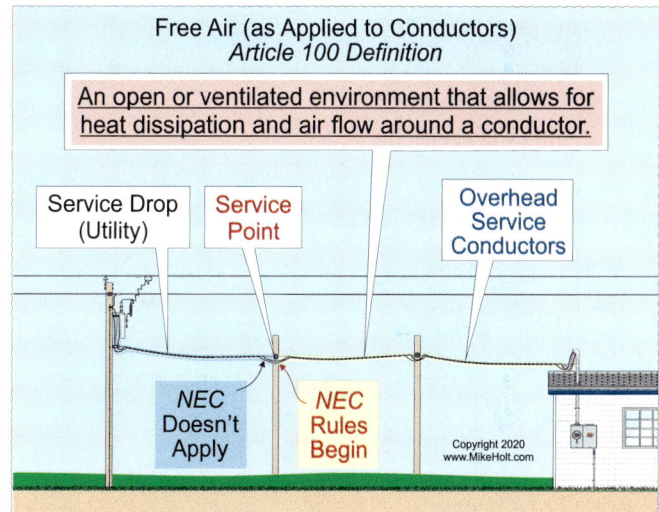
▶Figure 100-68

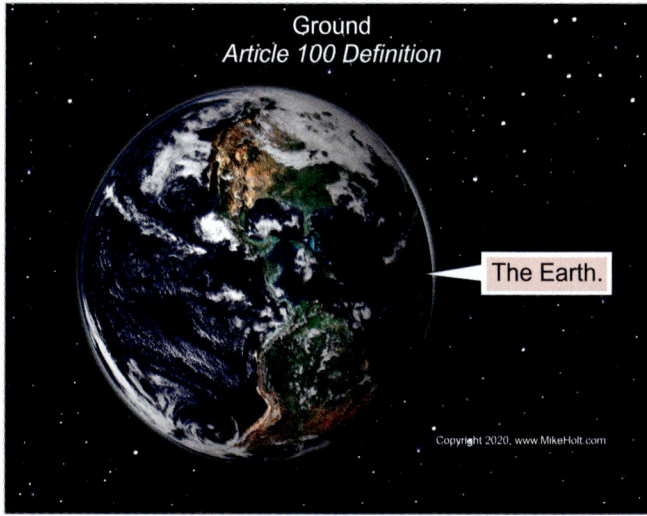
▶Figure 100-69

Ground Fault. An unintentional electrical connection between a phase conductor and normally noncurrent-carrying conductors, metal parts of enclosures, raceways, or equipment. ▶Figure 100-70

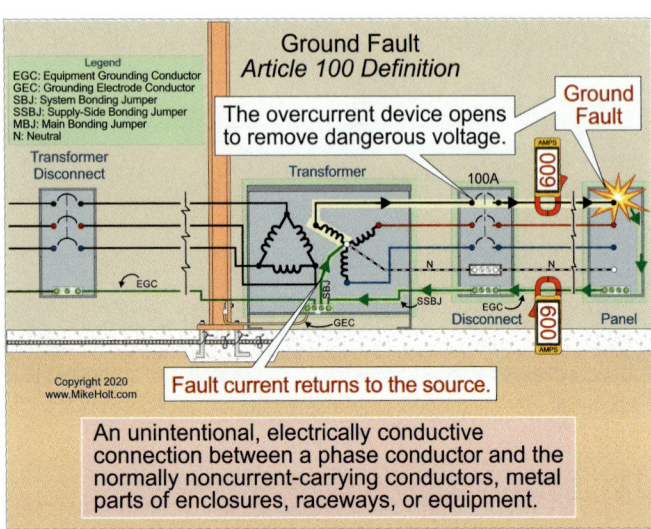
▶Figure 100-70

Grounded (Grounding). Connected to the Earth (ground) or to a conductive body that extends the Earth connection. ▶Figure 100-71

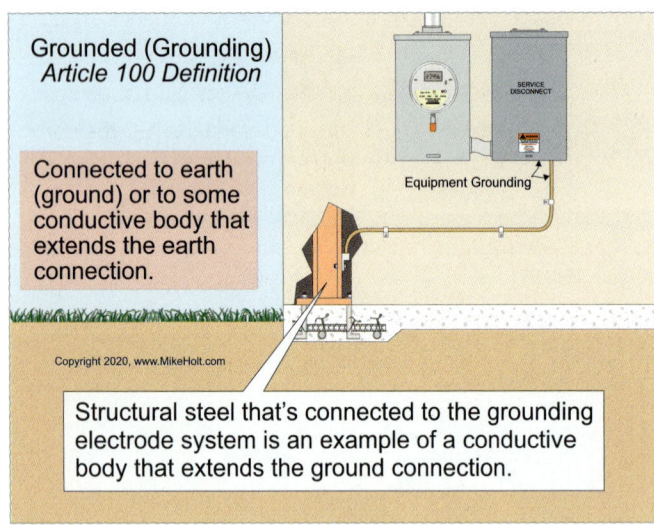
▶Figure 100-71

Author's Comment:

▸ An example of a "body that extends the ground (earth) connection" is a termination to structural steel that is connected to the Earth either directly or by the termination to another grounding electrode in accordance with 250.52.

Grounded Conductor. The system or circuit conductor that is intentionally connected to the Earth (ground). ▶Figure 100-72

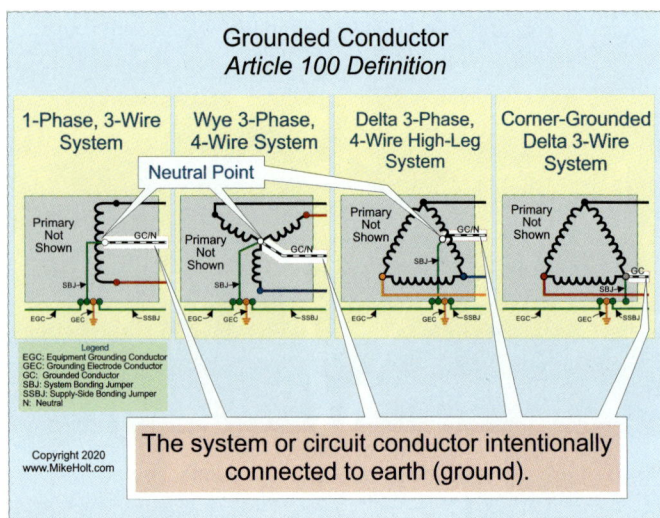
▶Figure 100-72

Note: Although an equipment grounding conductor is grounded, it is not considered a grounded conductor.

Author's Comment:

▸ There are two types of grounded conductors; neutral conductors and grounded-phase conductors. A system where the transformer secondary is wye connected with the neutral point grounded will have a neutral. ▶Figure 100-73

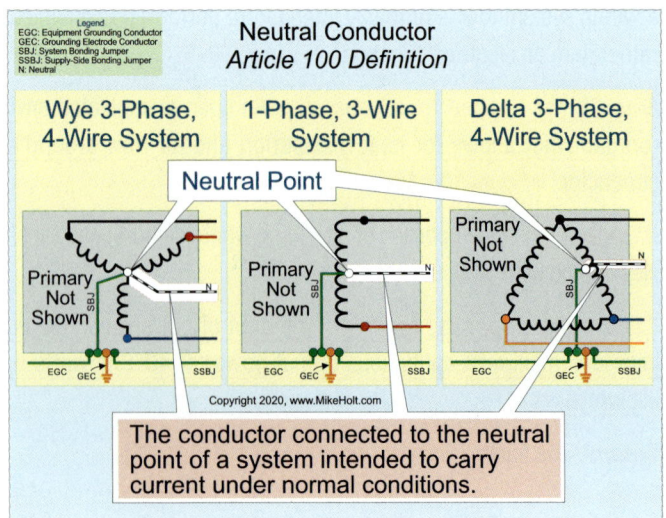
▶Figure 100-73

Author's Comment:

▸ A system where the transformer secondary is delta connected with one corner winding grounded will have a grounded-phase conductor. ▸Figure 100-74

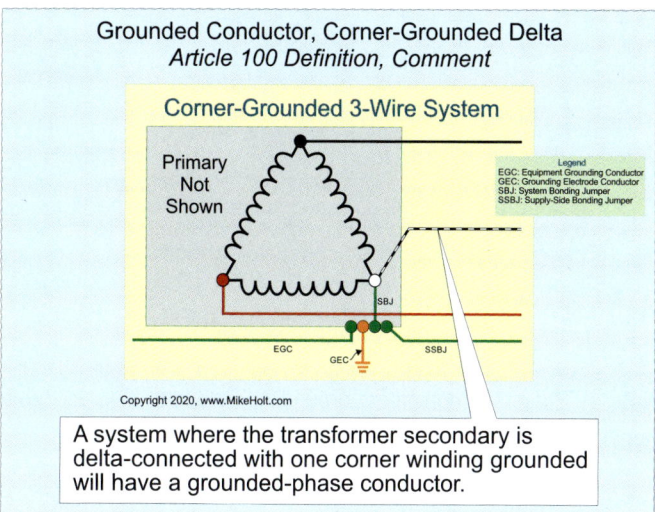
▸Figure 100-74

Grounded, Solidly (Solidly Grounded). Connected to ground (earth) without inserting any resistor or impedance device. ▸Figure 100-75

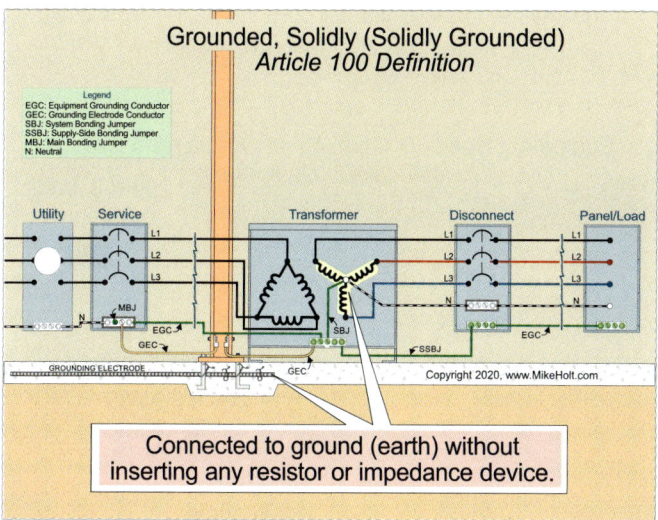
▸Figure 100-75

Ground-Fault Circuit Interrupter (GFCI). A device intended to protect people by de-energizing a circuit when ground-fault current exceeds the value established for a "Class A" device.

Note: A Class A ground-fault circuit interrupter opens the circuit when the ground-fault current is 6 mA or higher and does not trip when the ground-fault current is less than 4 mA. ▸Figure 100-76

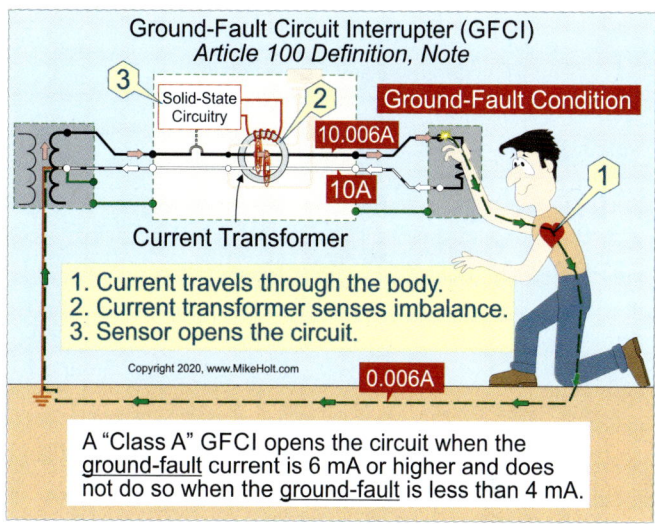
▸Figure 100-76

Author's Comment:

▸ A GFCI-protective device operates on the principle of monitoring the unbalanced current between the current-carrying circuit conductors. On a 120V circuit, the GFCI will monitor the unbalanced current between the phase and neutral conductors; on 240V circuits, monitoring is between all circuit conductors. Receptacles, circuit breakers, cord sets, and other types of devices that incorporate GFCI protection are commercially available. ▸Figure 100-77

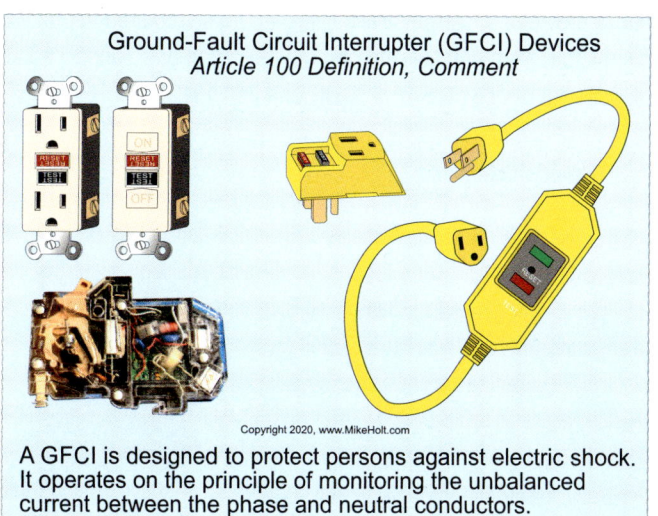
▸Figure 100-77

Ground-Fault Current Path. An electrically conductive path from the point of a ground fault on a wiring system through normally noncurrent-carrying conductors, neutral conductors, equipment, or the Earth to the electrical supply source. ▶Figure 100–78

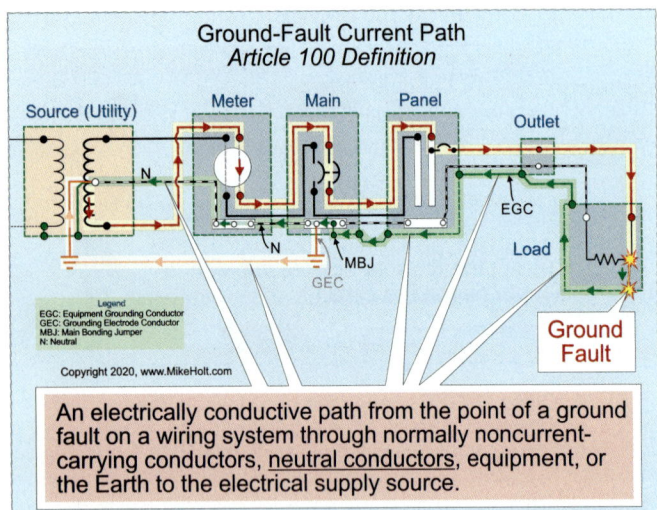

▶Figure 100–78

Note: Examples of ground-fault current paths are any combination of equipment grounding conductors, metallic raceways, metal cable sheaths, electrical equipment, and any other electrically conductive material such as metal, water, and gas piping; steel framing members; stucco mesh; metal ducting; reinforcing steel; shields of communications cables; neutral conductors; and the Earth itself.

Ground-Fault Protection of Equipment. A system intended to provide protection of equipment from damaging ground-fault currents by opening all phase conductors of the faulted circuit. This protection is provided at current levels less than those required to protect conductors from damage through the operation of a supply circuit overcurrent device [215.10, 230.95, and 240.13].

Author's Comment:

▸ This type of protective device is not intended to protect people since it trips (opens the circuit) at a higher current level than that of a "Class A" GFCI-protective device. It is typically referred to as ground-fault protection for equipment, or GFPE; but should never be called a GFCI.

Grounding Conductor, Equipment (Equipment Grounding Conductor). The conductive path(s) that is part of an effective ground-fault current path and connects metal parts of equipment to the system neutral conductor or grounded-phase conductor [250.110 through 250.126]. ▶Figure 100–79

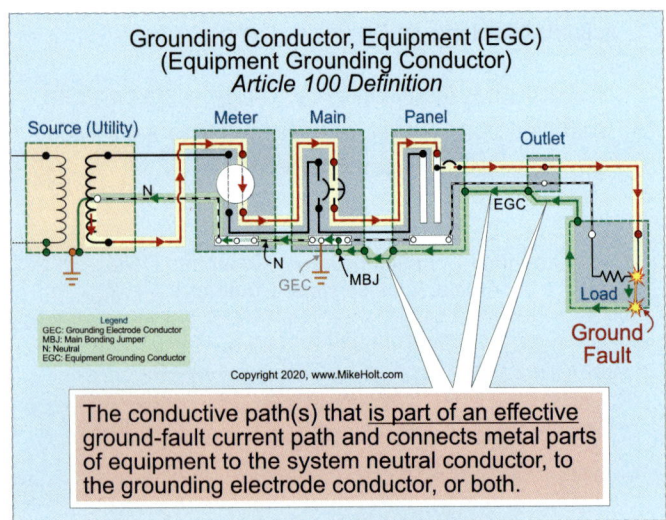

▶Figure 100–79

Note 1: The circuit equipment grounding conductor also performs bonding.

Author's Comment:

▸ To quickly remove dangerous touch voltage on metal parts from a ground fault, the equipment grounding conductor (EGC) must be connected to the system neutral conductor at the source and have low enough impedance so fault current will quickly rise to a level that will open the circuit's overcurrent protective device [250.4(A)(3)]. ▶Figure 100–80

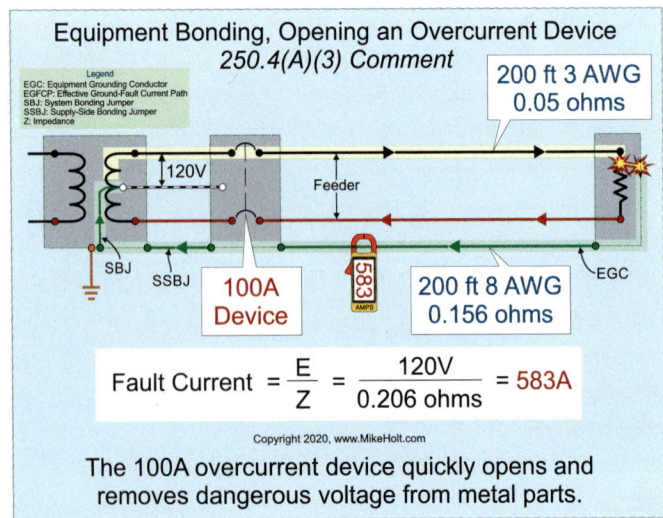

▶Figure 100–80

Note 2: An equipment grounding conductor can be any one or a combination of the types listed in 250.118. ▶Figure 100–81

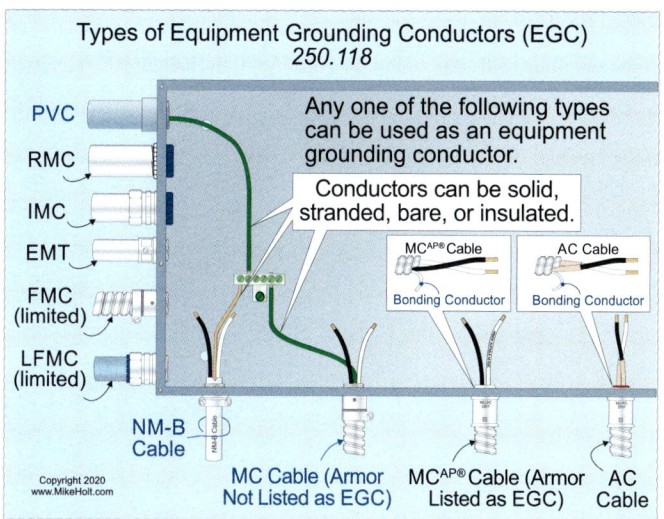
▶Figure 100-81

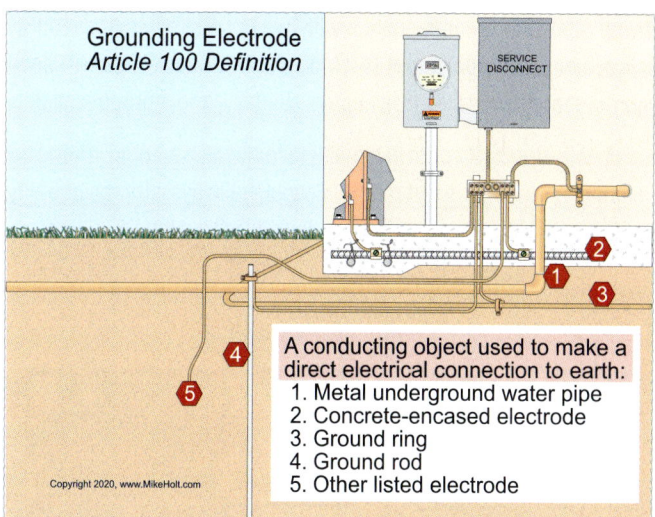
▶Figure 100-82

Author's Comment:

▸ Equipment grounding conductors include:

  ▸ A bare or insulated conductor
  ▸ Rigid metal conduit
  ▸ Intermediate metal conduit
  ▸ Electrical metallic tubing
  ▸ Listed flexible metal conduit as limited by 250.118(5)
  ▸ Listed liquidtight flexible metal conduit as limited by 250.118(6)
  ▸ Armored cable
  ▸ The copper metal sheath of mineral-insulated cable
  ▸ Metal-clad cable as limited by 250.118(10)
  ▸ Metal cable trays as limited by 250.118(11) and 392.60
  ▸ Electrically continuous metal raceways listed for grounding
  ▸ Surface metal raceways listed for grounding
  ▸ Metal enclosures

Grounding Electrode. A conducting object used to make a direct electrical connection to the Earth [250.50 through 250.70]. ▶Figure 100-82

Grounding Electrode Conductor. The conductor used to connect the system neutral conductor or grounded-phase conductor, or the equipment to the grounding electrode system. ▶Figure 100-83

Guest Room. An accommodation combining living, sleeping, sanitary, and storage facilities. ▶Figure 100-84

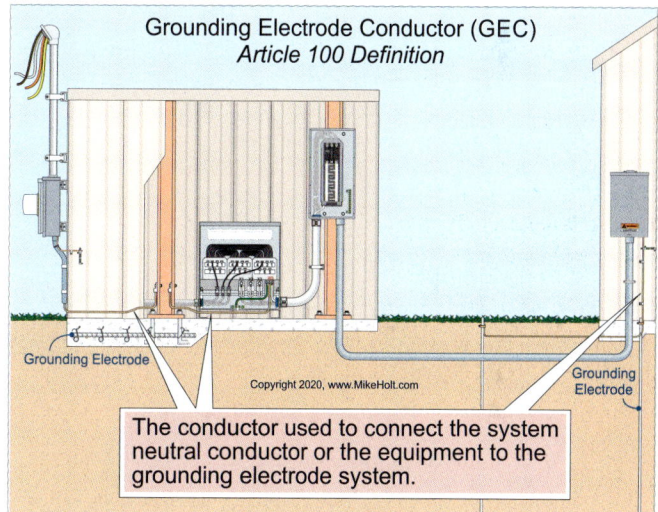
▶Figure 100-83

▶Figure 100-84

Guest Suite. An accommodation with two or more contiguous rooms comprising a compartment (with or without doors between such rooms) that provides living, sleeping, sanitary, and storage facilities.

Habitable Room. A room in a building for living, sleeping, eating, or cooking. Bathrooms, toilet rooms, closets, hallways, storage or utility spaces, and similar areas are excluded. ▶Figure 100-85

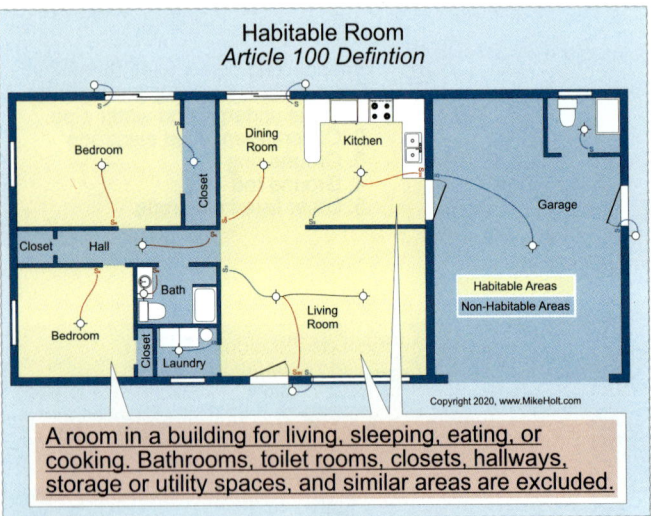

▶Figure 100-85

Handhole Enclosure. An underground enclosure with an open or closed bottom that is sized to allow personnel to reach into but not enter the enclosure. ▶Figure 100-86

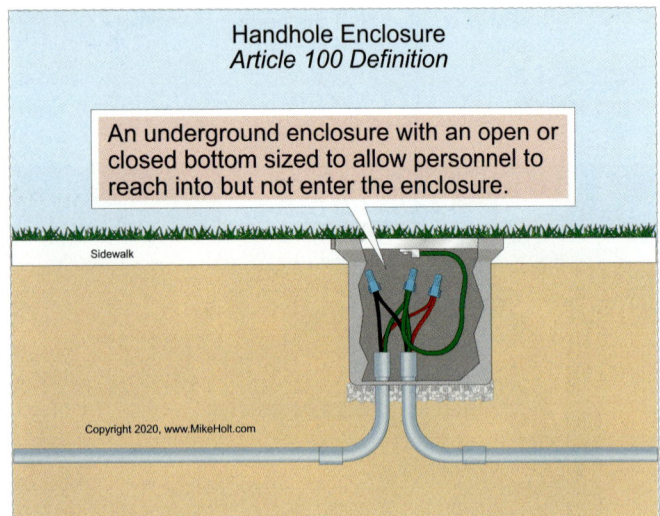

▶Figure 100-86

Author's Comment:

▸ See 314.30 for the installation requirements for handhole enclosures.

Hermetic Refrigerant Motor-Compressor. A compressor and motor enclosed in the same housing and operating in refrigerant.

Hoistway. A vertical opening or space in which an elevator or dumbwaiter is designed to operate. ▶Figure 100-87

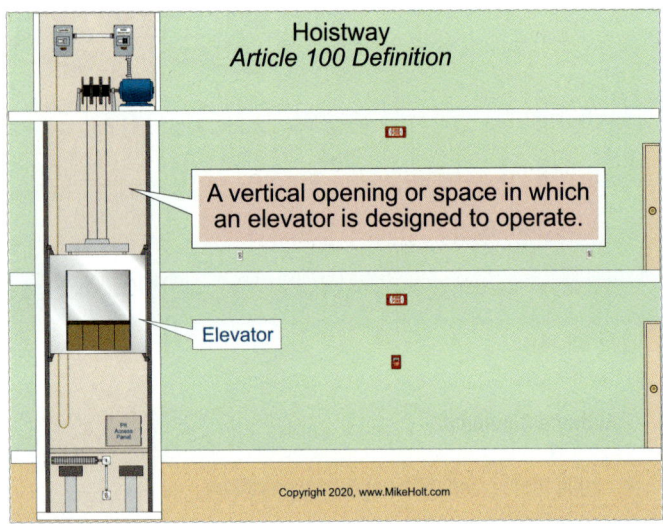

▶Figure 100-87

Hybrid System. A system comprised of multiple electric power sources such as photovoltaic, wind, micro-hydro generators, engine-driven generators, and others; but not the serving electric utility power system. ▶Figure 100-88

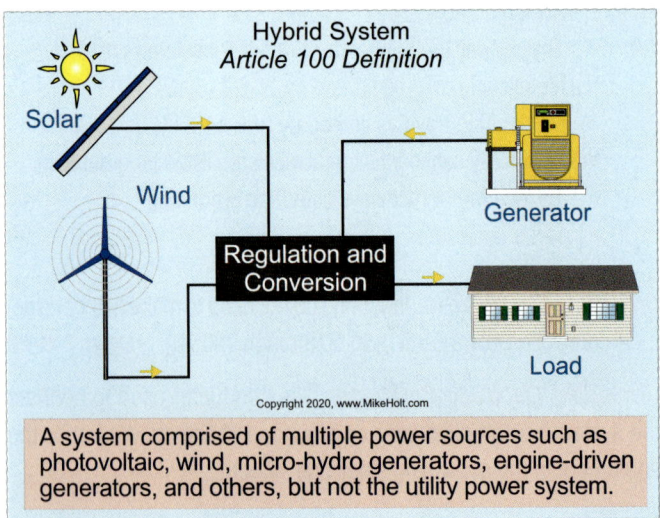

▶Figure 100-88

Identified (as applied to equipment). Recognized as suitable for a specific purpose, function, use, environment, or application where described in a *Code* requirement. ▶Figure 100-89

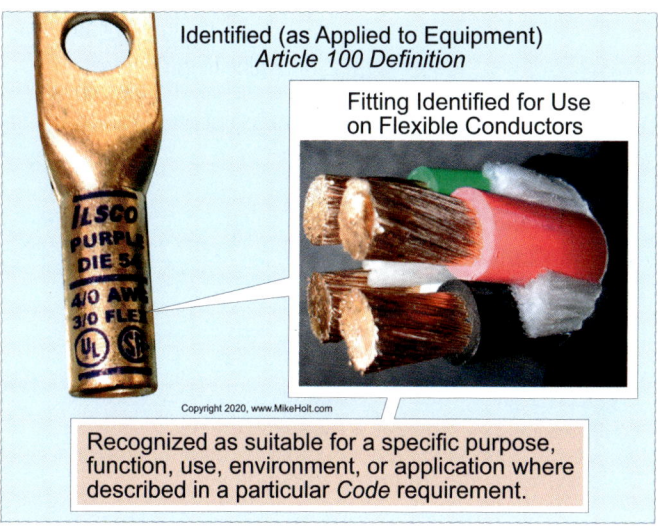

▶Figure 100-89

Author's Comment:

▸ See 90.4, 90.7, and 110.3(A)(1) and the definitions for "Approved," "Labeled," and "Listed" in this article.

Information Technology Equipment (ITE). Equipment used for the creation and manipulation of data, voice, and video. It does not include communications equipment. ▶Figure 100-90

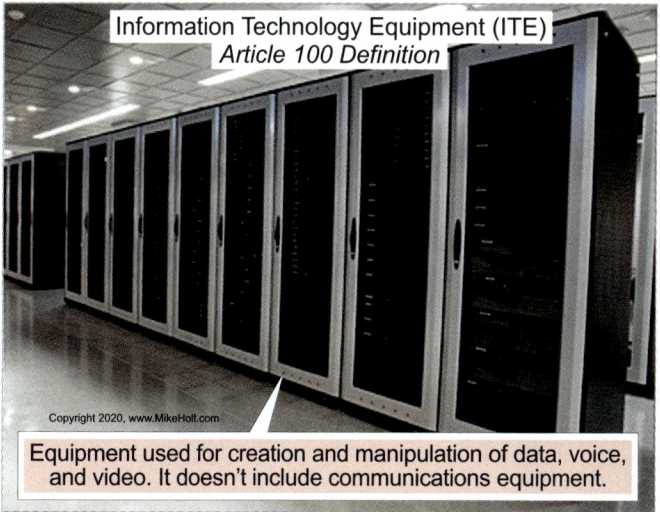

▶Figure 100-90

Innerduct. A nonmetallic raceway placed within a larger raceway. ▶Figure 100-91

In Sight From (Within Sight From). Visible and not more than 50 ft away from the equipment. ▶Figure 100-92

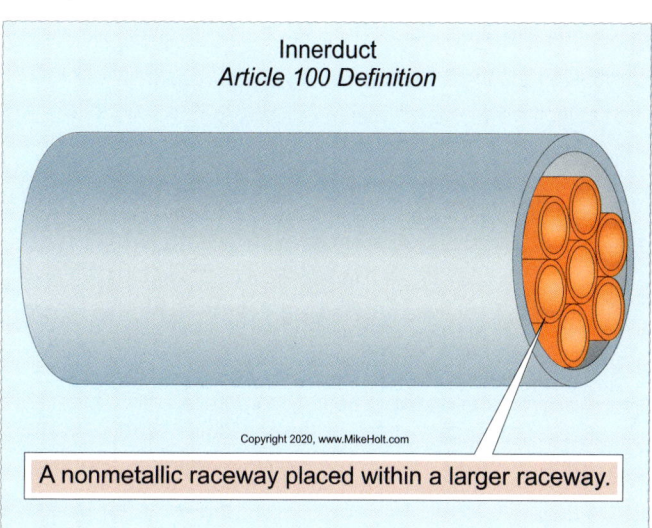

▶Figure 100-91

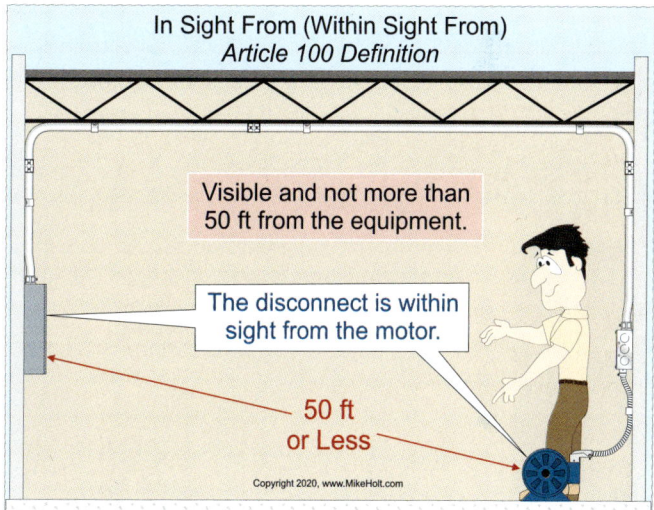

▶Figure 100-92

Interactive Inverter. An inverter intended to be used in parallel with a power source(s), such as the serving electric utility, to supply common loads and is capable of delivering power to the serving electric utility. ▶Figure 100-93

Author's Comment:

▸ A listed interactive inverter automatically stops exporting power upon loss of utility voltage and cannot be reconnected until the voltage has been restored. Interactive inverters can automatically or manually resume exporting power to the utility once the utility source is restored.

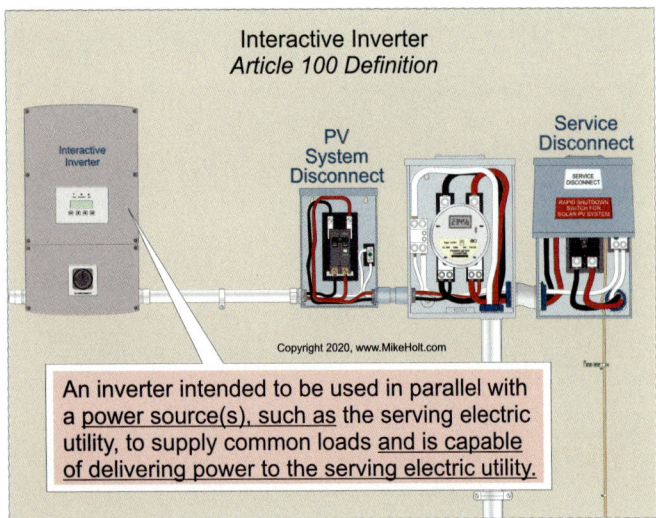

▶Figure 100–93

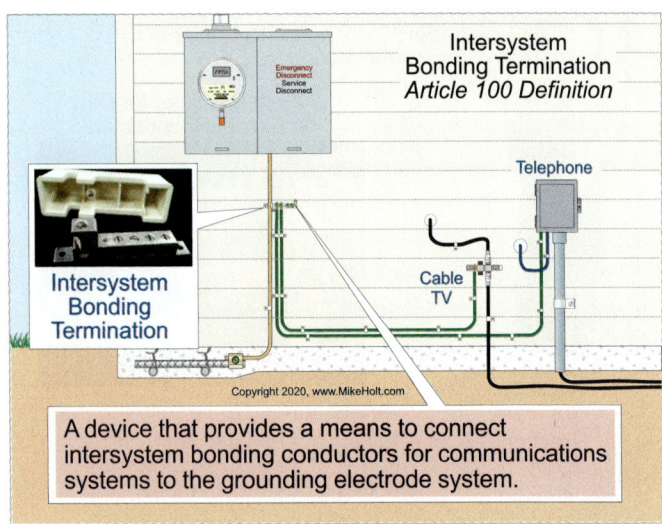

▶Figure 100–95

Interactive System. An electric power production system that operates in parallel with, and may deliver power to, the serving electric utility. ▶Figure 100–94

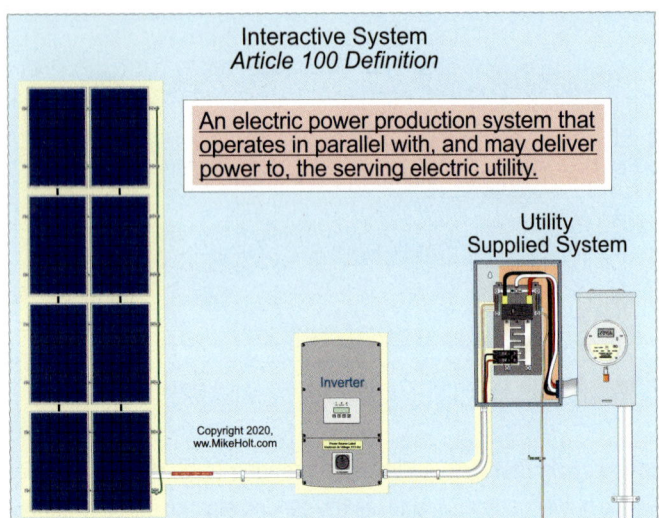

▶Figure 100–94

Interrupting Rating. The highest short-circuit current at rated voltage the device is identified to safely interrupt under standard test conditions.

Intersystem Bonding Termination. A device that provides a means to connect intersystem bonding conductors for communications systems (twisted wire, antennas, and coaxial cable) to the grounding electrode system, in accordance with 250.94. ▶Figure 100–95

Author's Comment:

▸ Overcurrent protective devices have two current ratings, "rated current" and "fault current." Rated current protects circuits under normal conditions and the rating is labeled on the handle of the circuit breaker. The fault current rating or "ampere interrupting capacity" (AIC) is the amount of current the device can safely handle during a ground fault or short circuit. Fault current ratings range up to the tens, or even hundreds, of thousands of amperes!

▸ For more information, see 110.9 in this textbook.

Inverter. Equipment that changes direct current to alternating current. ▶Figure 100–96

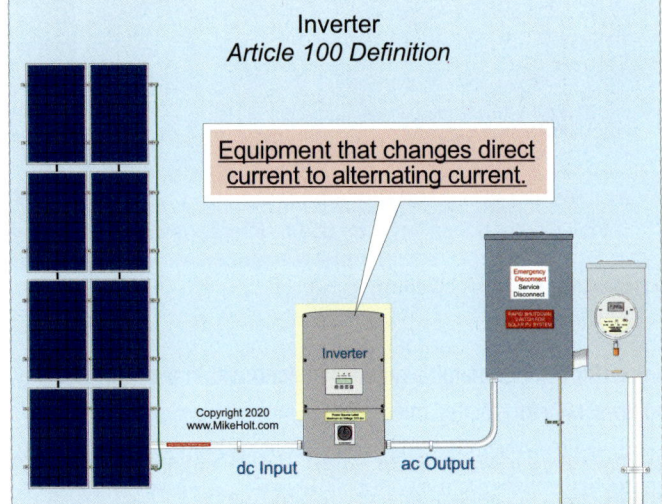

▶Figure 100–96

Definitions | 100

Inverter Input Circuit. Conductors connected to the direct-current input of an inverter. ▶Figure 100–97

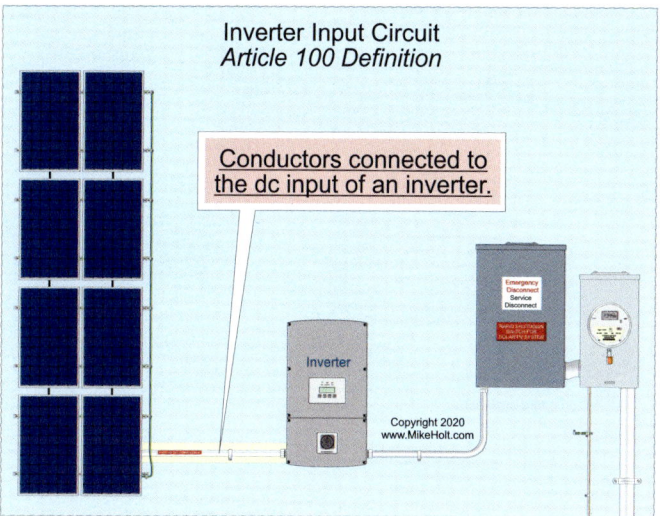
▶Figure 100–97

Inverter Output Circuit. The circuit conductors connected to the alternating-current output of an inverter. ▶Figure 100–98

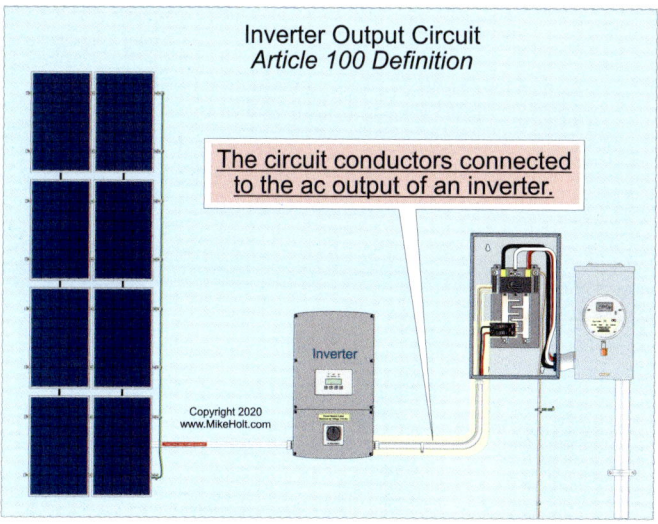
▶Figure 100–98

Inverter, Multimode. Equipment having the capabilities of both interactive and stand-alone inverters. ▶Figure 100–99

Island Mode. The operational mode for stand-alone power production equipment or an isolated microgrid (or for a multimode inverter or an interconnected microgrid) that is disconnected from an electric power production and distribution network or other primary power source.

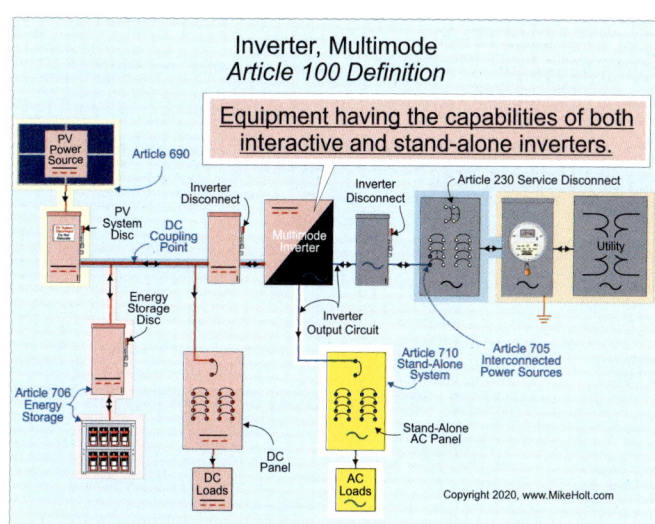
▶Figure 100–99

Isolated. Not readily accessible to persons unless special means for access are used.

Kitchen. An area with a sink and permanent provisions for food preparation and cooking. ▶Figure 100–100

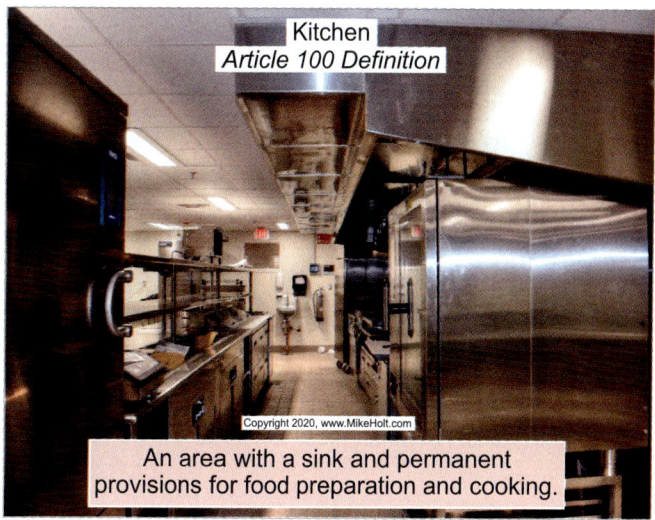
▶Figure 100–100

Author's Comment:

▶ An area like an employee break room with a sink and cord-and-plug-connected cooking appliance such as a microwave oven is not considered a kitchen.

100 | Definitions

Labeled. Equipment or materials that have a label, symbol, or other identifying mark in the form of a sticker, decal, printed label, or with the identifying mark molded or stamped into the product by a recognized testing laboratory acceptable to the authority having jurisdiction. ▶Figure 100–101

▶Figure 100–102

▶Figure 100–101

Author's Comment:

▸ Labeling and listing of equipment typically provides the basis for equipment approval by the authority having jurisdiction [90.4, 90.7, 110.2, and 110.3].

Note: When a listed product is of such a size, shape, material, or surface texture that it is not possible to legibly apply the complete label to the product, it may appear on the smallest unit container in which the product is packaged.

Laundry Area. An area containing (or designed to contain) a laundry tray, clothes washer, or clothes dryer. ▶Figure 100–102

Author's Comment:

▸ A "laundry tray" is a fixed laundry or utility sink with necessary plumbing connections most commonly installed near the washer and dryer. A "laundry area" is such by design regardless if the laundry equipment is in place or not.

Lighting Outlet. An outlet for connecting a luminaire. ▶Figure 100–103

Lighting Track (Track Lighting). A manufactured assembly designed to support and energize luminaires that can be readily repositioned on the track, and whose length may be altered by the addition or subtraction of sections of track. ▶Figure 100–104

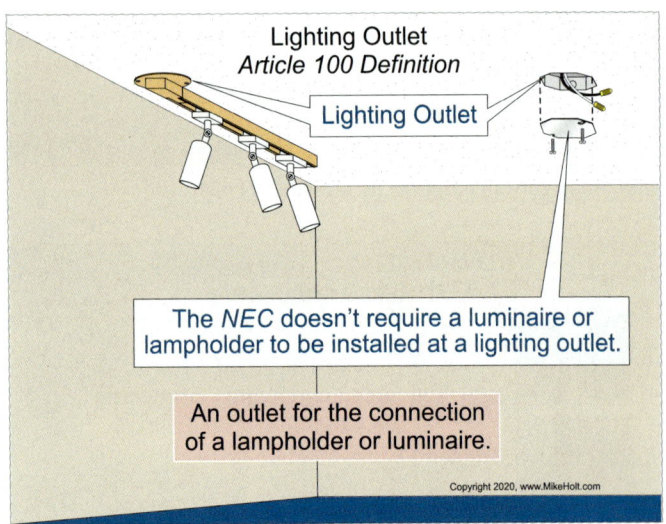
▶Figure 100–103

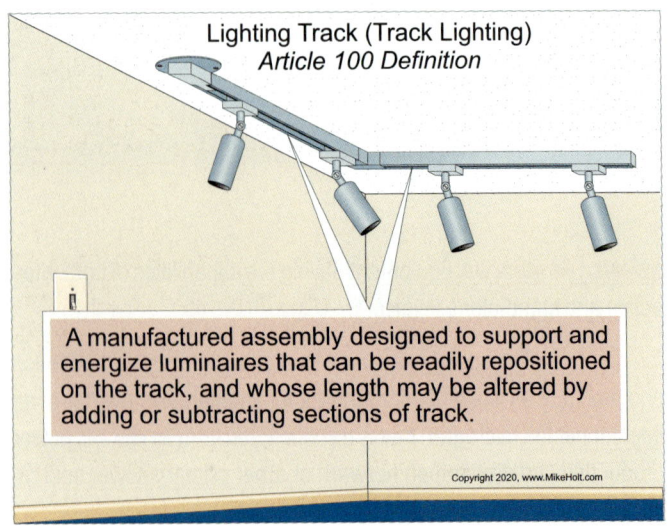
▶Figure 100–104

Listed. Equipment or materials included in a list published by a recognized testing laboratory acceptable to the authority having jurisdiction. The listing organization must periodically inspect the production of listed equipment or material to ensure they meet appropriate designated standards and are suitable for a specified purpose.

Note: Examples of nationally recognized testing laboratories (NRTLs) are Underwriters Laboratory (UL) and Canadian Standards Association (CSA). Both are accepted in either the United States or Canada and most electrical equipment is marked by both agencies. Always look for at least one of these seals and accept no imitations or counterfeits.

> **Author's Comment:**
>
> ▸ The *NEC* does not require all electrical equipment to be listed, but some *Code* requirements do specifically call for product listing. Organizations such as OSHA are increasingly requiring listed equipment to be used when such equipment is available [90.7, 110.2, and 110.3].

Location, Damp (Damp Location). Locations protected from weather and not subject to saturation with water or other liquids. ▸Figure 100–105

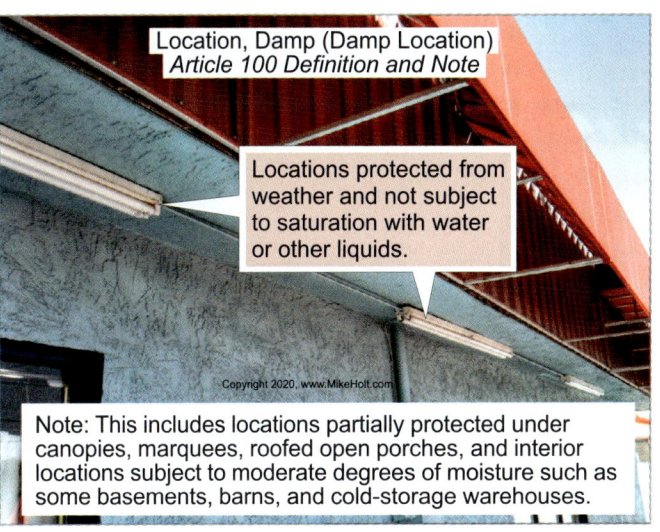

▸Figure 100–105

Note: This includes locations partially protected under canopies, marquees, roofed open porches, and interior locations subject to moderate degrees of moisture such as some basements, barns, and cold-storage warehouses.

Location, Dry (Dry Location). An area not normally subjected to dampness or wetness, but which may temporarily be subjected to dampness or wetness, such as a building under construction.

Location, Wet (Wet Location). An installation underground, in concrete slabs in direct contact with the Earth, areas subject to saturation with water, and unprotected locations exposed to weather. ▸Figure 100–106 and ▸Figure 100–107

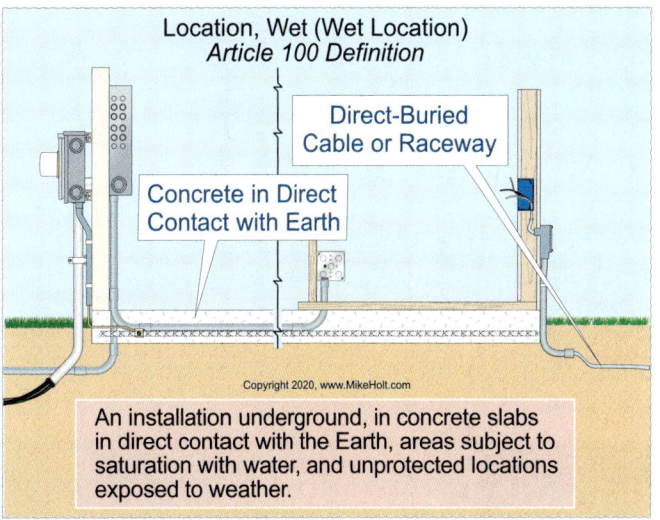

▸Figure 100–106

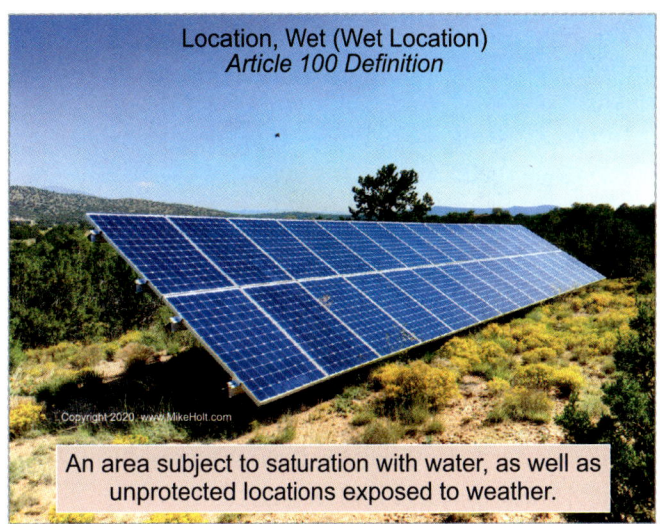

▸Figure 100–107

Luminaire. A complete lighting unit consisting of a light source with parts designed to position the light source and connect it to the power supply. It may also include parts to protect and distribute the light. ▸Figure 100–108

Messenger or Messenger Wire. A wire that is run along with, or integral to, a cable or conductor to provide mechanical support for the cable or conductor. ▸Figure 100–109

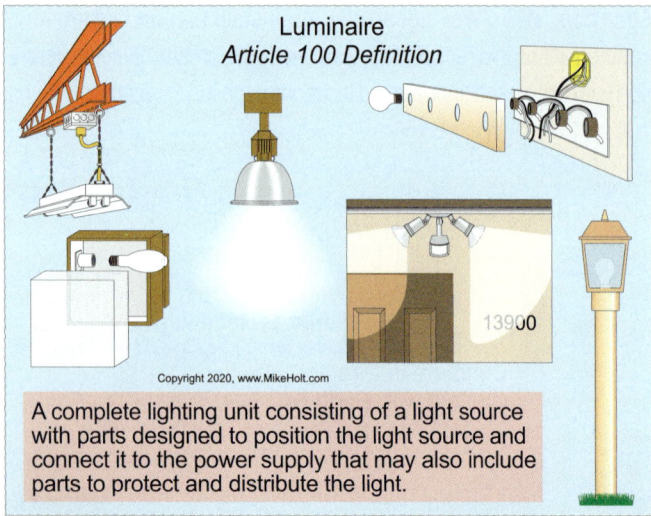

▶Figure 100-108

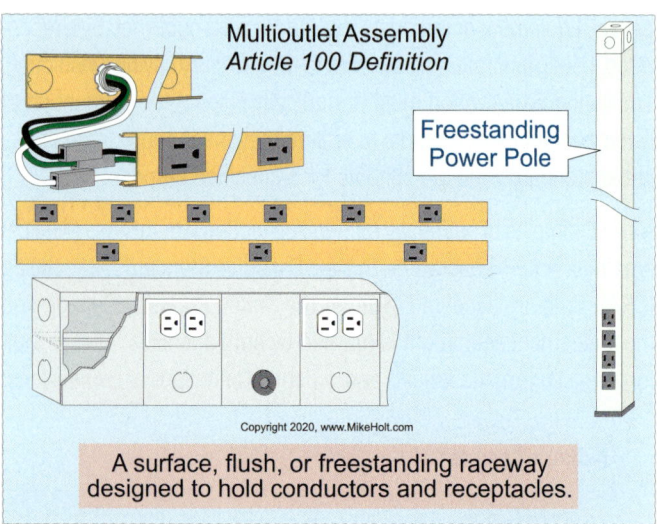

▶Figure 100-110

▶Figure 100-109

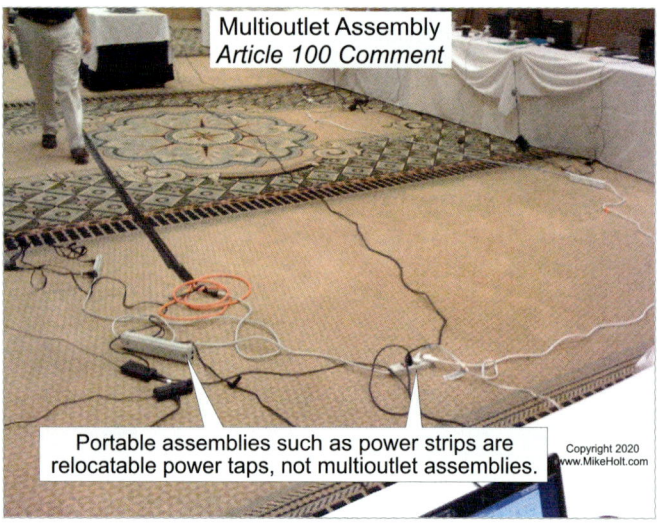

▶Figure 100-111

Multioutlet Assembly. A surface, flush, or freestanding raceway designed to hold conductors and receptacles. ▶Figure 100-110

Author's Comment:

▸ Portable assemblies such as power strips are relocatable power taps, not multioutlet assemblies. ▶Figure 100-111

Neutral Conductor. The conductor connected to the neutral point of a system that is intended to carry current under normal conditions. ▶Figure 100-112

Neutral Point. The common point of a 4-wire, three-phase, wye-connected system; the midpoint of a 3-wire, single-phase system; or the midpoint of the single-phase portion of a three-phase, delta-connected system. ▶Figure 100-113

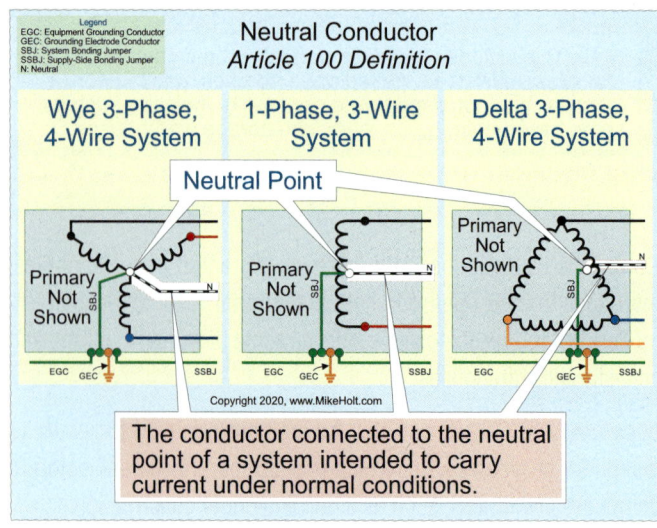

▶Figure 100-112

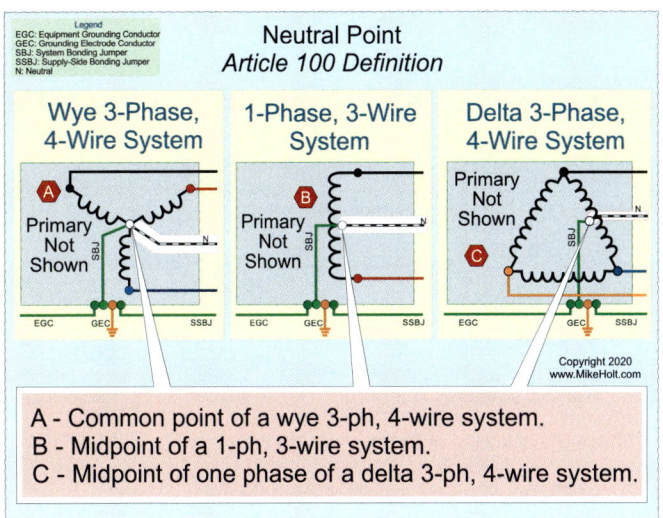

▶Figure 100–113

Nonautomatic. Requiring human intervention to perform a function.

Nonlinear Load. A load where the shape of the current waveform does not follow the shape of the applied sinusoidal voltage waveform. ▶Figure 100–114

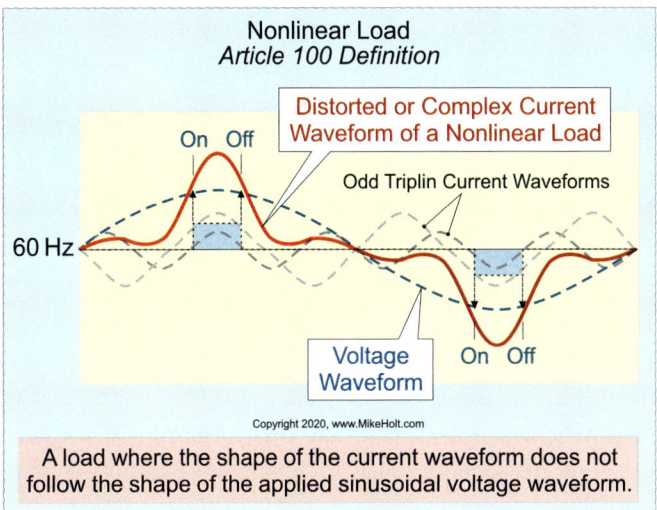

▶Figure 100–114

Note: Single-phase nonlinear loads include electronic equipment such as copy machines, laser printers, and electric-discharge lighting. Three-phase nonlinear loads include uninterruptible power supplies, induction motors, and electronic switching devices such as adjustable-speed drive systems. ▶Figure 100–115

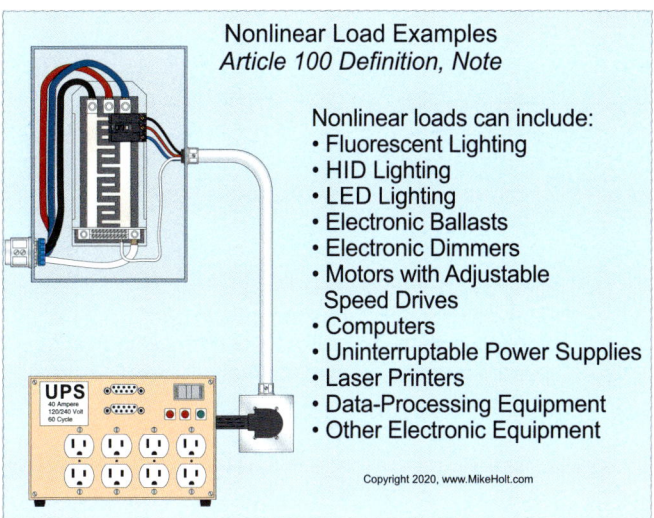

▶Figure 100–115

Author's Comment:

▸ The subject of nonlinear loads is beyond the scope of this textbook. For more information on this topic, visit www.MikeHolt.com, click on the "Technical" link, then on the "Power Quality" link.

Outlet. A point in the wiring system where electricity is made available to supply utilization equipment. ▶Figure 100–116

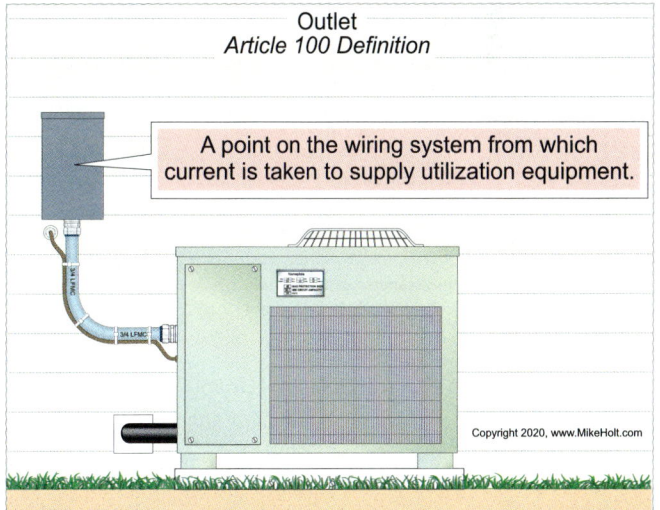

▶Figure 100–116

Author's Comment:

▸ This includes receptacle and lighting outlets, as well as those for ceiling paddle fans and smoke alarms. ▶Figure 100–117

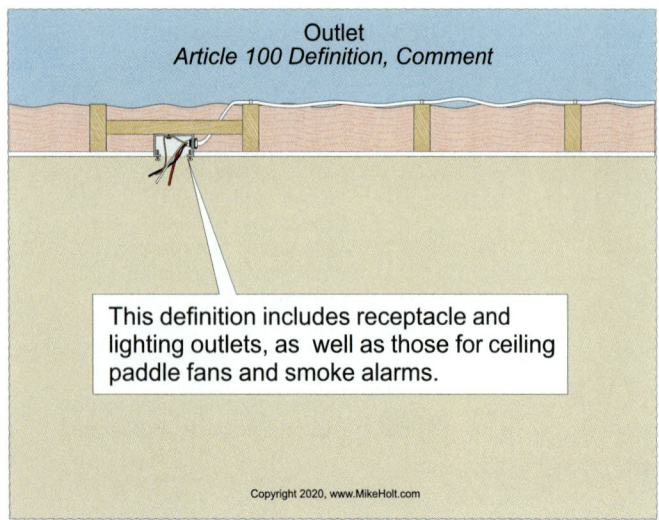
▶Figure 100–117

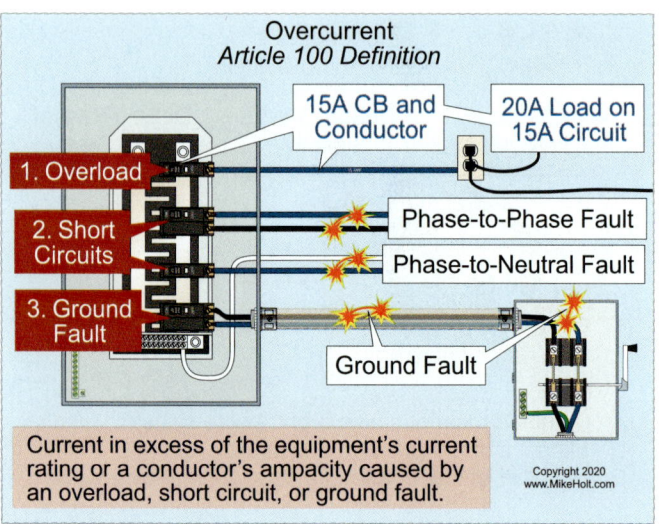
▶Figure 100–119

Outline Lighting. An arrangement of an electrically powered light source used to outline or call attention to building features such as the shape of a building or the decoration of a window. ▶Figure 100–118

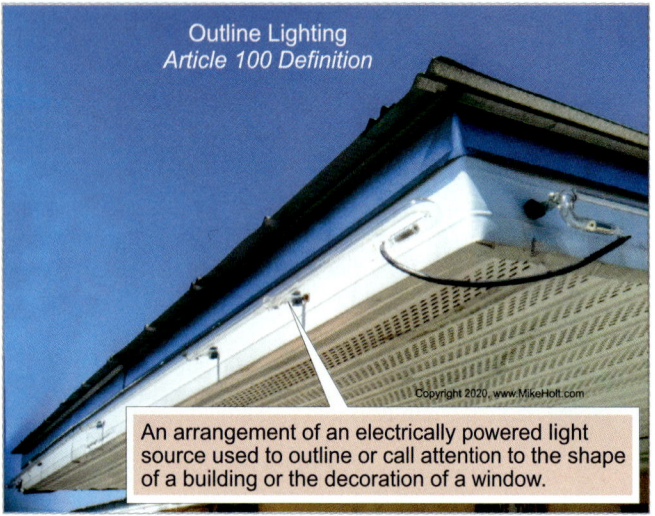
▶Figure 100–118

Overcurrent. Current in excess of the equipment's current rating or a conductor's ampacity caused by an overload, short circuit, or ground fault. ▶Figure 100–119

Overcurrent Protective Device, Branch Circuit. A device capable of providing protection from an overload, short circuit, or ground fault for service, feeder, and branch circuits.

Overcurrent Protective Device, Supplementary. A device intended to provide limited overcurrent protection for specific applications and utilization equipment, such as luminaires and appliances. This limited protection is in addition to the protection required and provided by the branch-circuit overcurrent protective device. ▶Figure 100–120

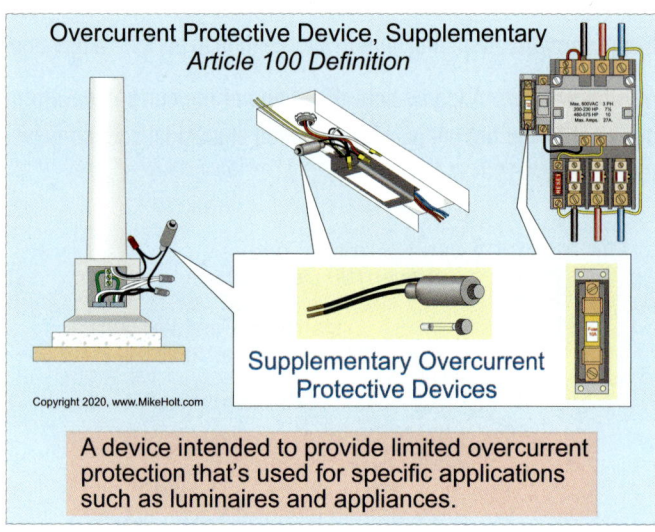
▶Figure 100–120

Overload. The operation of equipment above its current rating, or current in excess of a conductor's ampacity. If an overload condition persists long enough, the result can be equipment failure or a fire from damaging or dangerous overheating. A fault, such as a short circuit or ground fault, is not an overload. ▶Figure 100–121

Panelboard. An assembly designed for the distribution of light, heat, or power circuits with overcurrent devices and typically placed in a cabinet. ▶Figure 100–122

> **Author's Comment:**
>
> ▸ See the definition of "Cabinet" in this article.
>
> ▸ The slang term in the electrical field for a panelboard is "the guts." This is the interior of the panelboard assembly and is covered by Article 408, while the cabinet is covered by Article 312.

Definitions | 100

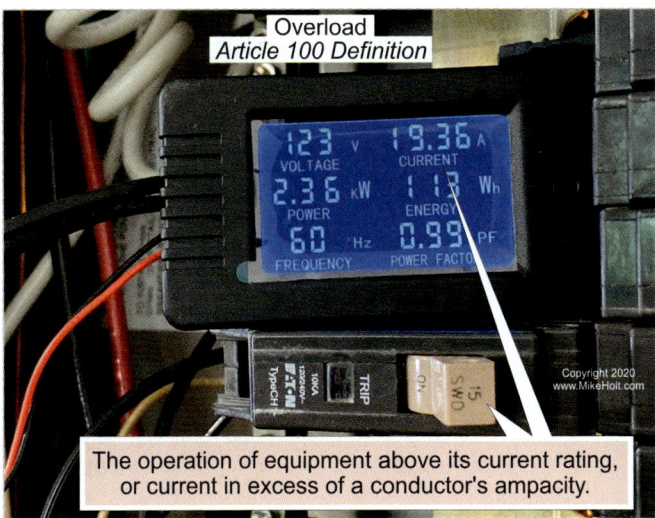
▶Figure 100–121

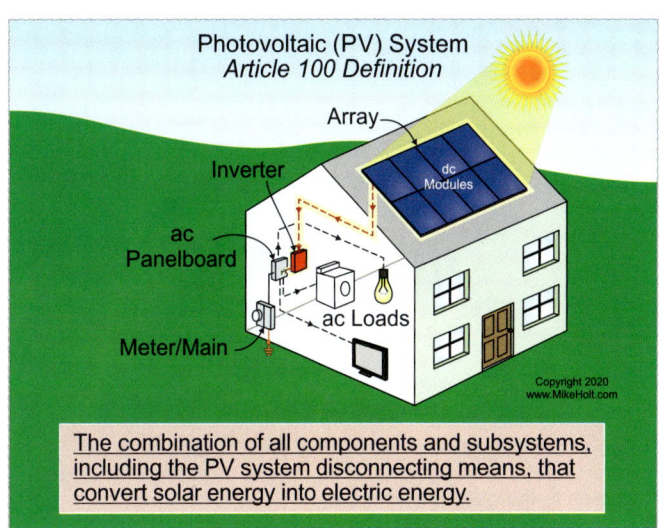
▶Figure 100–123

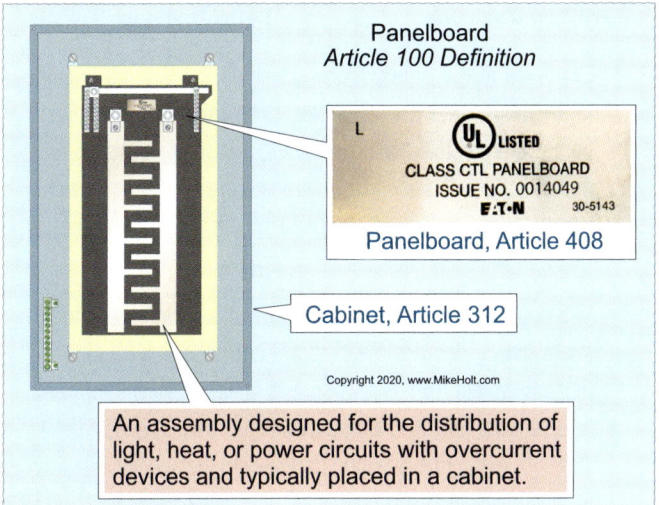
▶Figure 100–122

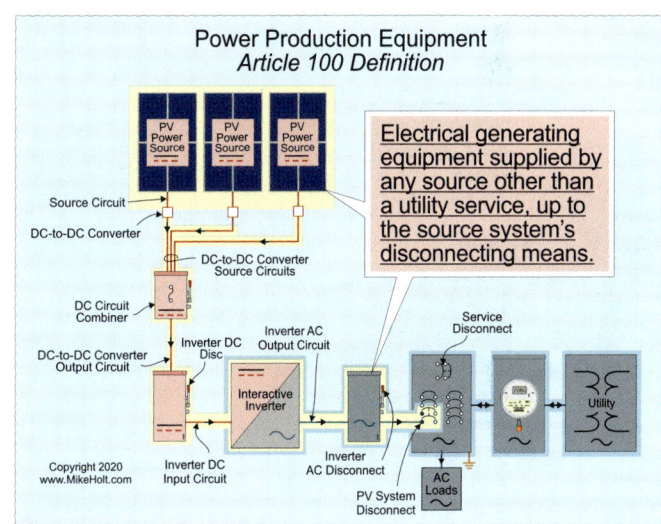
▶Figure 100–124

Photovoltaic (PV) System. The combination of all components and subsystems, including the PV system disconnecting means, that convert solar energy into electric energy for utilization loads. ▶Figure 100–123

Power Production Equipment. Electrical generating equipment supplied by any source other than a utility service, up to the source system's disconnecting means. ▶Figure 100–124

Note: Examples of power production equipment include such items as generators, solar photovoltaic systems, and fuel cell systems.

Premises Wiring. The interior and exterior wiring including power, lighting, control, and signaling circuits, and all associated hardware, fittings, and wiring devices. This includes permanently and temporarily installed wiring from the service point to the outlets. Where there is no service point, it is the wiring from and including the electric power source (such as a generator, transformer, or PV system) to the outlets. ▶Figure 100–125

Premises wiring does not include the internal wiring of electrical equipment and appliances such as luminaires, dishwashers, water heaters, motors, controllers, motor control centers, air-conditioning equipment, and so on [90.7 and 300.1(B)]. ▶Figure 100–126

100 | Definitions

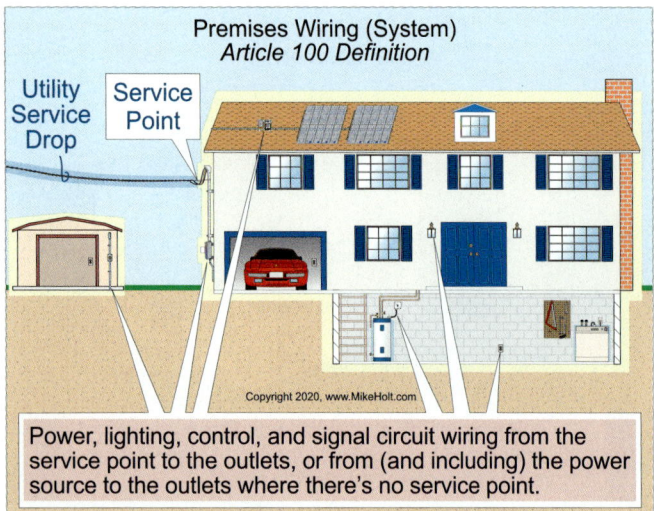
▶Figure 100-125

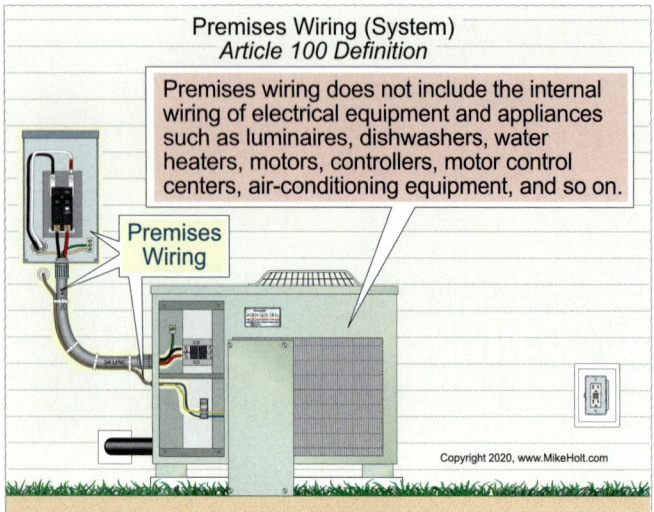
▶Figure 100-126

Note: Electric power sources include (but not limited to) interconnected or stand-alone batteries, PV systems, other distributed generation systems, and generators.

Prime Mover. The machine that supplies mechanical horsepower to a generator.

Qualified Person. A person who has the skill and knowledge related to the construction and operation of electrical equipment and its installation. This person must have received safety training to recognize and avoid the hazards involved with electrical systems. ▶Figure 100-127

Note: NFPA 70E, *Standard for Electrical Safety in the Workplace*, provides information on the safety training requirements expected of a "qualified person."

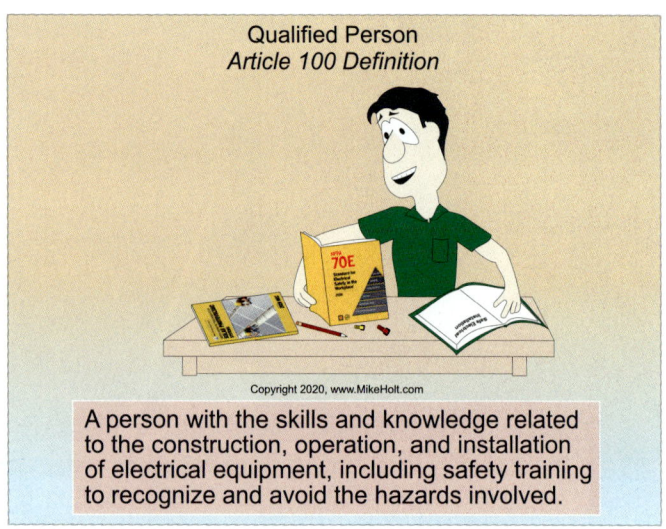
▶Figure 100-127

Author's Comment:

▸ Examples of this safety training include, but are not limited to, training in the use of special precautionary techniques, personal protective equipment (PPE), insulating and shielding materials, and the use of insulated tools and test equipment when working on or near exposed conductors or circuit parts that can become energized.

▸ In many parts of the United States, electricians, electrical contractors, electrical inspectors, and electrical engineers must complete from 6 to 24 hours of *NEC* review each year as a requirement to maintain licensing. This, in and of itself, does not make one qualified to deal with the specific hazards involved with electrical systems.

Raceway. A channel designed for the installation of conductors, cables, or busbars.

Author's Comment:

▸ A cable tray system is not a raceway; it is a support system for cables and raceways [392.2].

Raceway, Communications. An enclosed nonmetallic channel designed for holding communications wires and cables; optical fiber cables; data cables associated with information technology and communications equipment; Class 2, Type PLTC, and power-limited fire alarm cables in plenum spaces, risers, and general-purpose applications. ▶Figure 100-128

Rainproof. Constructed, protected, or treated to prevent rain from interfering with the successful operation of the apparatus under specified test conditions.

Definitions | 100

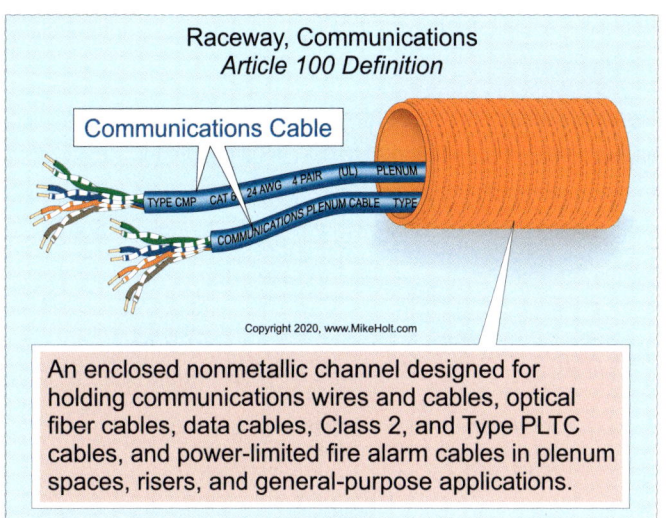
▶Figure 100–128

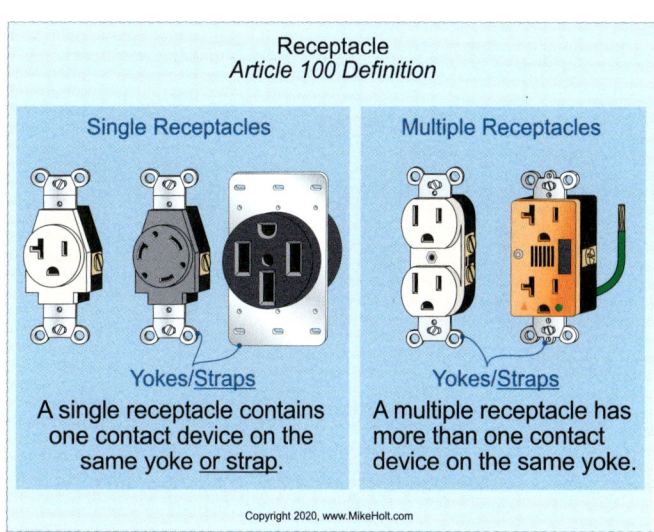
▶Figure 100–130

Raintight. Constructed or protected so exposure to a beating rain will not result in the entrance of water under specified test conditions.

Receptacle. A contact device installed at an outlet for the connection of an attachment plug, or for the direct connection of equipment designed to mate with the contact device (SQL receptacle). ▶Figure 100–129

Author's Comment:

▸ A yoke (also called a "strap") is the metal mounting structure for such items as receptacles, switches, switches with pilot lights, and switch/receptacles to name a few. ▶Figure 100–131 and ▶Figure 100–132

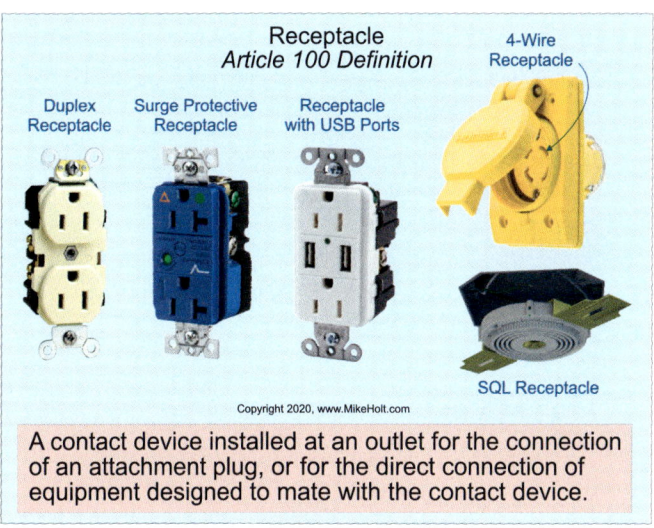
▶Figure 100–129

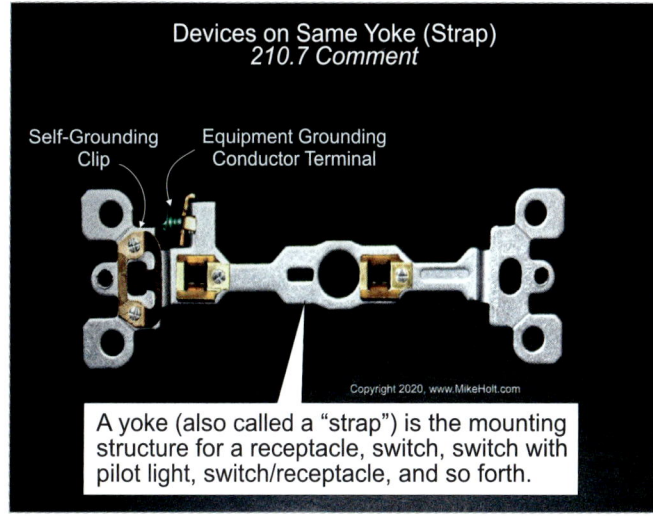
▶Figure 100–131

Author's Comment:

▸ For additional information about listed locking support and mounting receptacles, visit www.safetyquicklight.com.

A single receptacle contains one contact device on a yoke or strap; a multiple receptacle has more than one contact device on the same yoke or strap. ▶Figure 100–130

Note: A duplex receptacle is an example of a multiple receptacle with two receptacles on the same yoke or strap.

Receptacle Outlet. An opening in an outlet box where receptacles have been installed.

Mike Holt Enterprises • www.MikeHolt.com • 888.NEC.CODE (632.2633) | 55

100 | Definitions

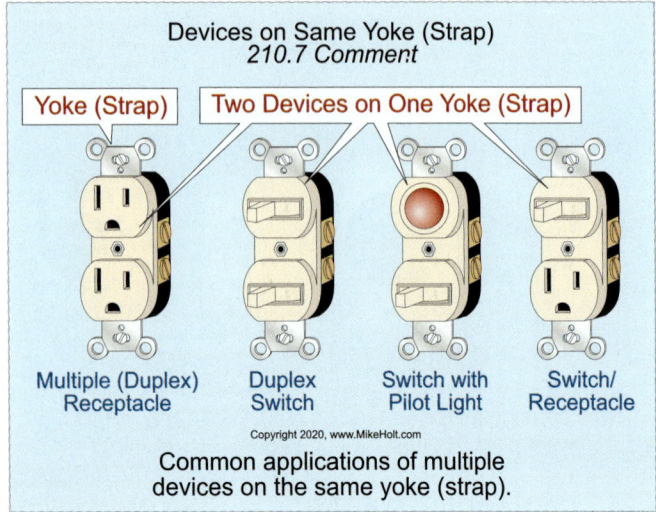
▶Figure 100–132

Reconditioned. Electromechanical systems, equipment, apparatus, or components that are restored to operating conditions. This process differs from normal servicing of equipment that remains within a facility, or replacement of listed equipment on a one-to-one basis.

Note: The term reconditioned is frequently referred to as rebuilt, refurbished, or remanufactured.

Remote-Control Circuit. An electric circuit that controls another circuit by a relay or equivalent device installed in accordance with Article 725. ▶Figure 100–133

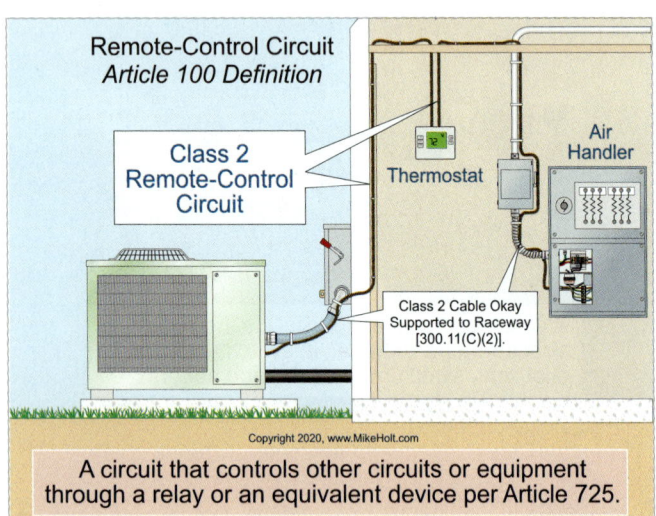
▶Figure 100–133

Retrofit Kit. An assembly of parts for the field conversion of utilization equipment.

Sealable Equipment. Equipment enclosed with a means of sealing or locking so live parts cannot be made accessible without opening the enclosure.

Note: The equipment may or may not be operable without opening the enclosure.

Separately Derived System. An electrical source, other than a service, having no direct connection(s) to the circuit conductors of any other electrical source other than those established by grounding and bonding connections. ▶Figure 100–134, ▶Figure 100–135, and ▶Figure 100–136

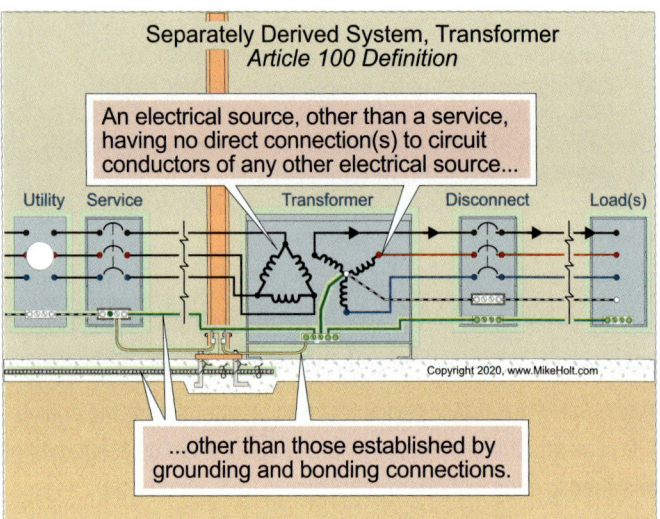
▶Figure 100–134

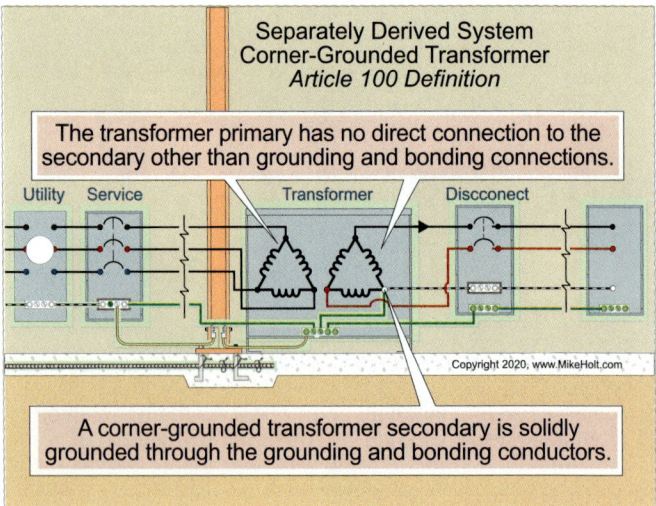
▶Figure 100–135

Author's Comment:

▶ A generator is not a separately derived system if the neutral conductor is solidly interconnected to a service-supplied system neutral conductor. An example is a generator provided with a transfer switch that includes a neutral conductor that is not switched. ▶Figure 100–137

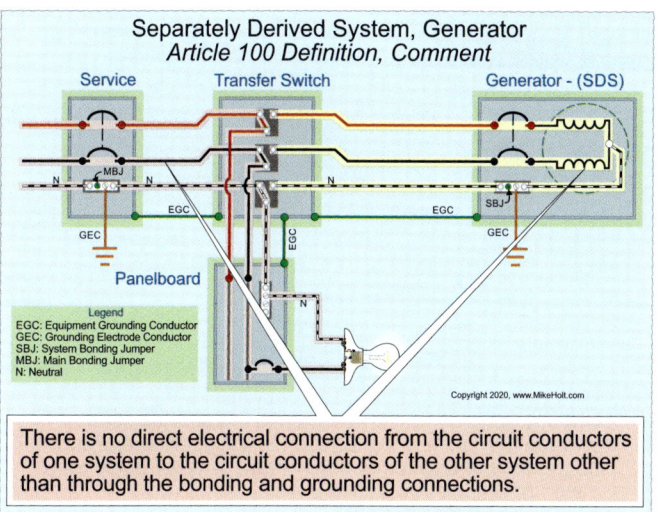
▶Figure 100-136

▶Figure 100-138

▸ Conductors from UPS systems, solar PV systems, generators, or transformers are not service conductors. See the definitions of "Feeder" and "Service Conductors" in this article.

Service Conductors. The conductors from the serving electric utility service point to the service disconnect. ▶Figure 100-139

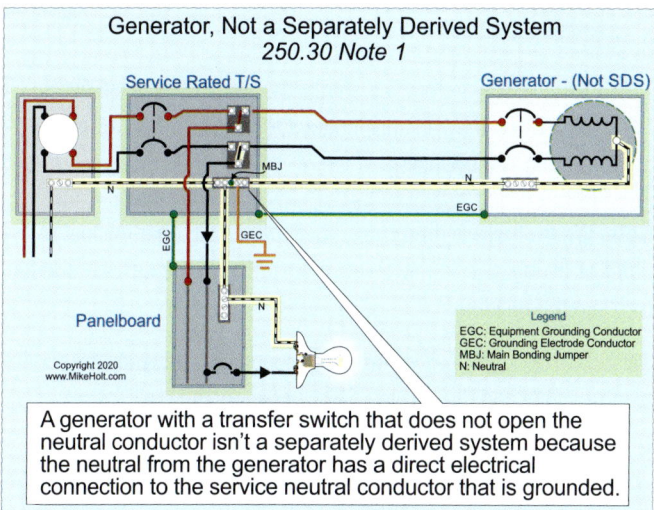
▶Figure 100-137

Author's Comment:

▸ Separately derived systems are much more complicated than the *Code*'s definition suggests and understanding them requires additional study. For more information, see 250.30.

Service [Article 230]. The conductors and equipment connecting the serving electric utility to the wiring system of the premises served. ▶Figure 100-138

Author's Comment:

▸ A service can only be supplied by the serving electric utility and is not covered by the *NEC*. If power is supplied by other than the serving electric utility, the conductors and equipment are part of a feeder and covered by the *Code*.

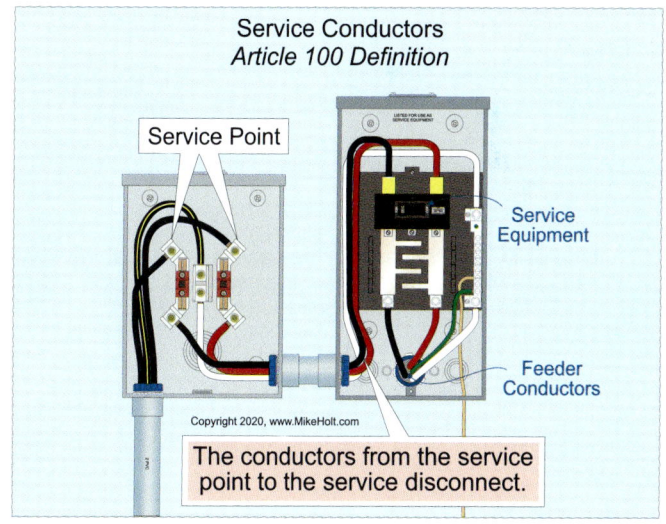
▶Figure 100-139

Author's Comment:

▸ Service conductors can include overhead service conductors, overhead service-entrance conductors, and underground service conductors. These conductors are not under the exclusive control of the serving electric utility, which means they are owned by the customer and are covered by the requirements in Article 230.

Service Conductors, Overhead (Overhead Service Conductors). Overhead conductors between the serving electric utility service point and the first point of connection to the service-entrance conductors at the building. ▶Figure 100–140

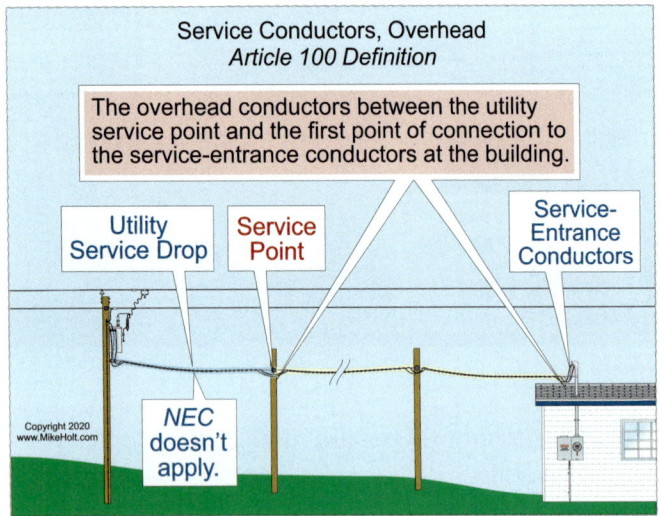
▶Figure 100–140

Author's Comment:

▶ The service point is typically determined by the serving electric utility. If the utility determines the service point is at the load side of their transformer, the overhead service conductors run to the service-entrance conductors. ▶Figure 100–141

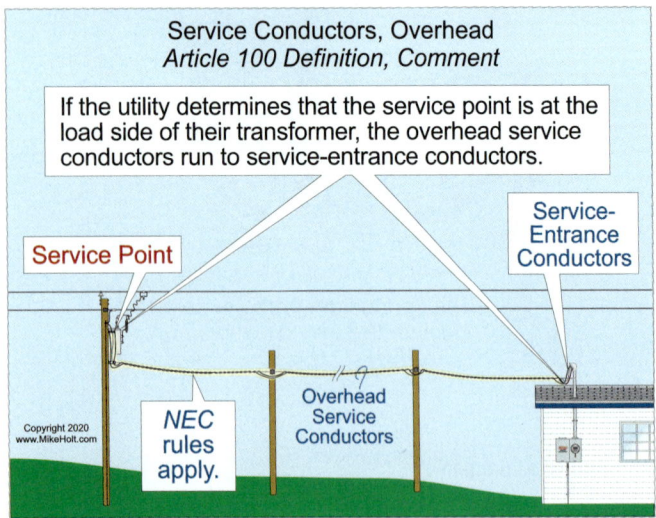
▶Figure 100–141

Service Conductors, Underground (Underground Service Conductors). Underground conductors between the service point and the first point of connection to the service-entrance conductors in a terminal box, meter, or other enclosure; inside or outside the building wall. ▶Figure 100–142

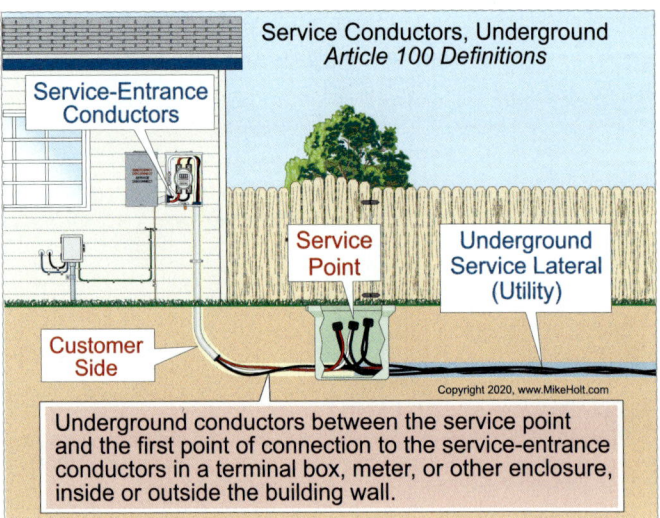
▶Figure 100–142

Author's Comment:

▶ Service conductors fall within the requirements of Article 230 since they are not under the exclusive control of the serving electric utility.

Note: Where there is no terminal box, meter, or other enclosure the point of connection is the point of entrance of the service conductors into the building.

Service Drop. Utility-owned overhead conductors between the serving electric utility and the service point. ▶Figure 100–143

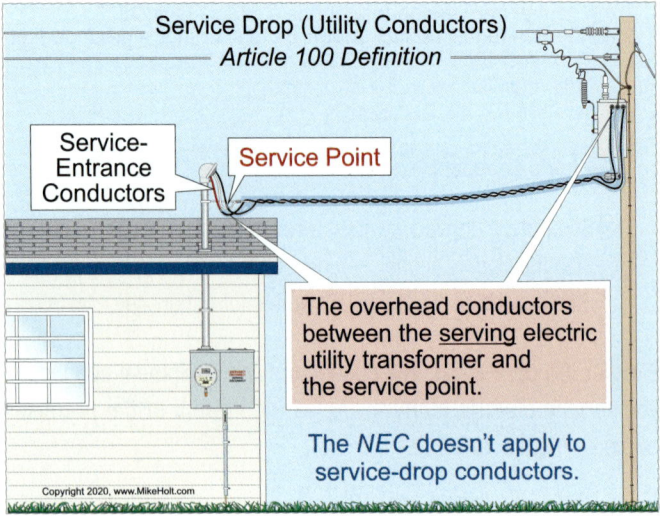
▶Figure 100–143

Author's Comment:

▶ The *NEC* does not apply to service drops.

Definitions | 100

Service-Entrance Conductors, Overhead (Overhead Service-Entrance Conductors). The conductors between the terminals of the service disconnect and service drop or overhead service conductors. ▶Figure 100–144

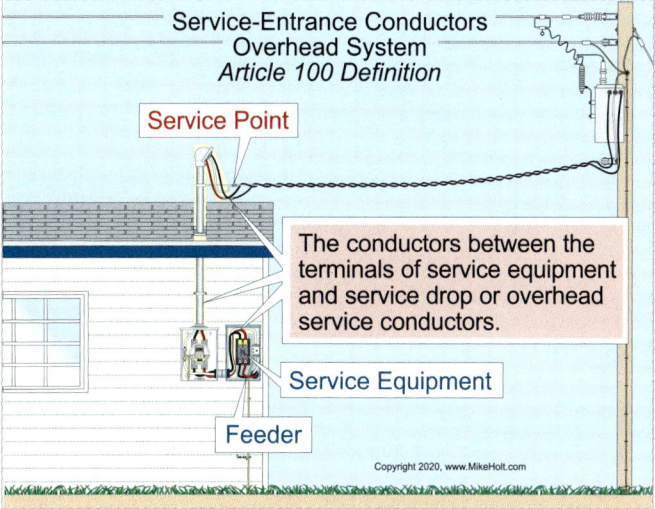
▶Figure 100–144

Author's Comment:

▶ Overhead service-entrance conductors are covered by the requirements of Article 230, since they are not under the exclusive control of the serving electric utility.

Service-Entrance Conductors, Underground (Underground Service-Entrance Conductors). The conductors between the terminals of the service disconnect and underground service point. ▶Figure 100–145

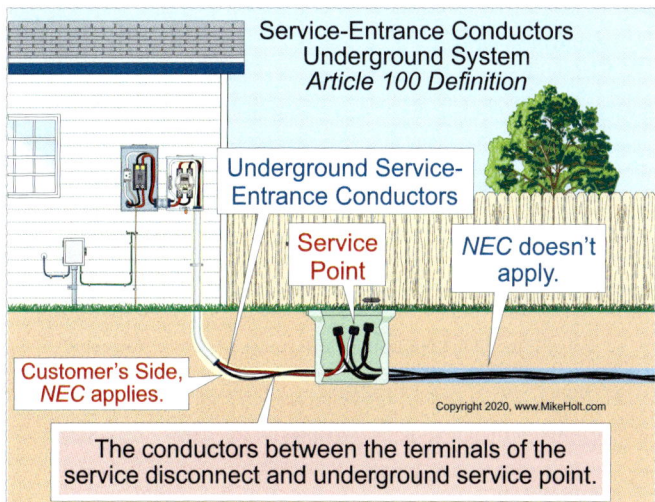
▶Figure 100–145

Author's Comment:

▶ Underground service-entrance conductors fall within the requirements of Article 230 since they are not under the exclusive control of the serving electric utility.

Service Equipment (Service Disconnect). Disconnects such as circuit breakers or switches connected to the serving electric utility, intended to control and disconnect the power from the serving electric utility. ▶Figure 100–146

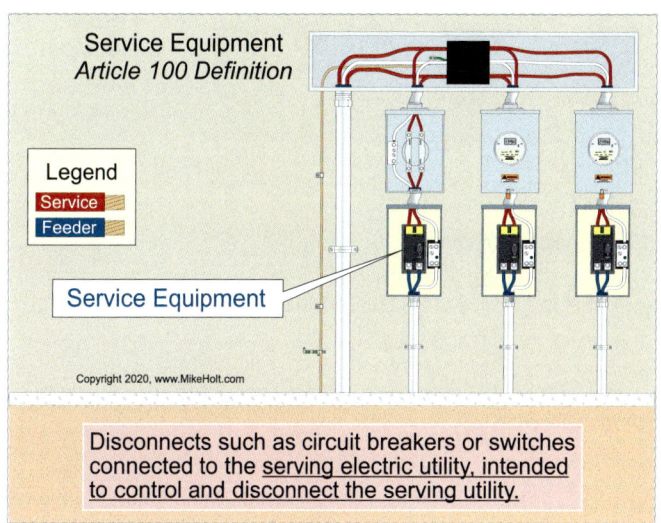
▶Figure 100–146

Author's Comment:

▶ It's important to know where a service begins and where it ends in order to properly apply the *Code* requirements. Sometimes the service ends before the metering equipment. ▶Figure 100–147 and ▶Figure 100–148

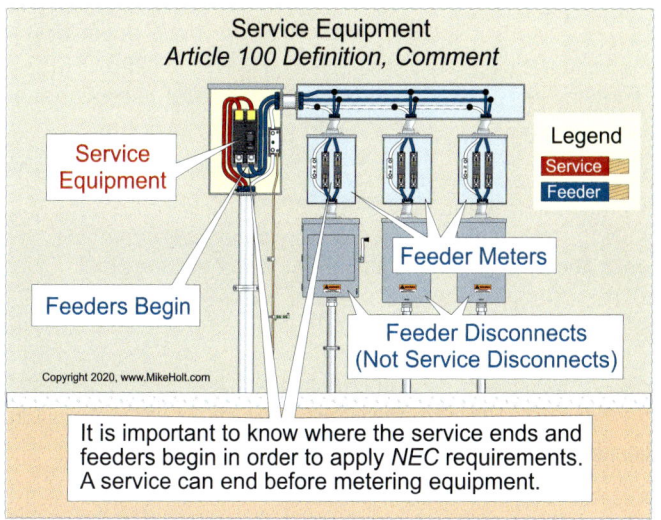
▶Figure 100–147

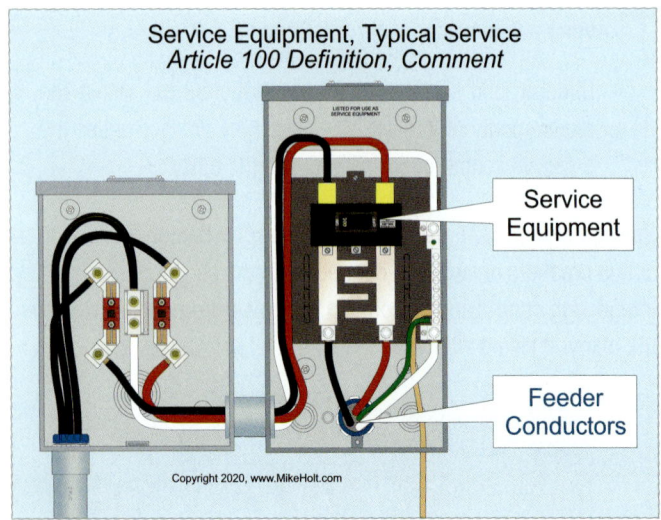
▶Figure 100–148

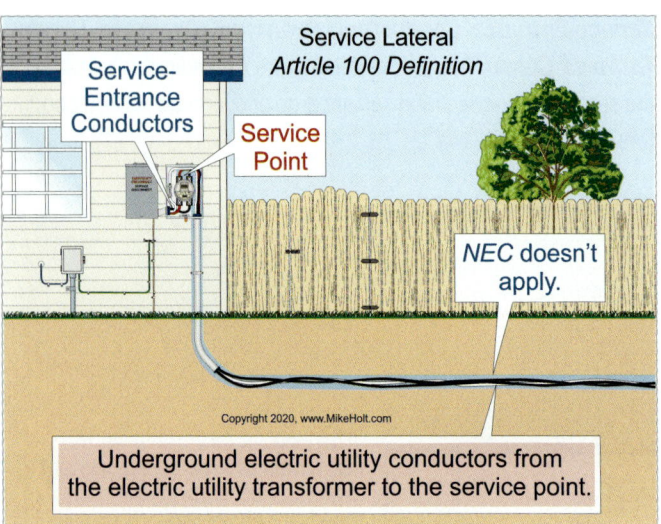
▶Figure 100–150

Author's Comment:

▸ Service equipment is often referred to as the "service disconnect" or "service main."

▸ Meter socket enclosures are not considered service equipment [230.66].

Service Lateral. Utility-owned underground conductors between the serving electric utility transformer and the service point. ▶Figure 100–149 and ▶Figure 100–150

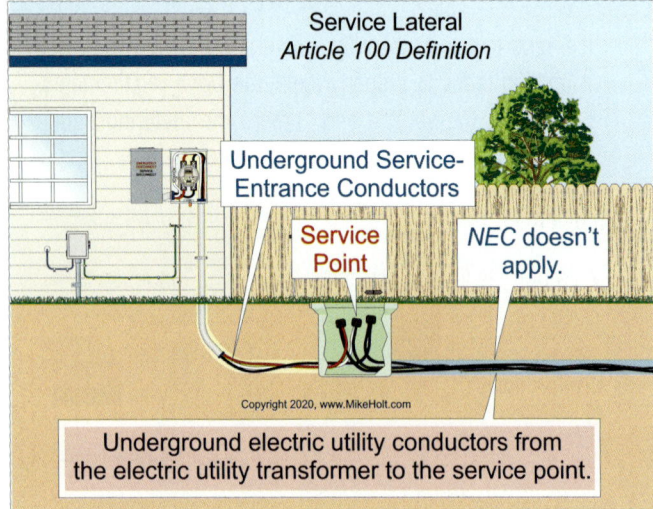
▶Figure 100–149

Service Point. The point where the serving electric utility conductors connect to customer-owned wiring. ▶Figure 100–151

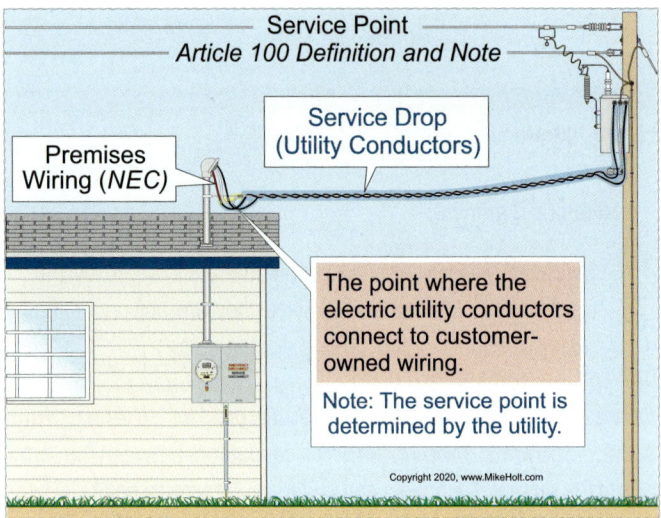
▶Figure 100–151

Author's Comment:

▸ The service point is typically determined by the serving electric utility and may vary with different utilities and different types of occupancies.

▸ For utility-owned transformers, the service point will be at the serving electric utility's transformer secondary terminals, at the service drop, or at the meter socket enclosure depending on where their conductors terminate. ▶Figure 100–152

▸ For customer-owned transformers, the service point will be at the termination of the serving electric utility's conductors; often at the utility's pole. ▶Figure 100–153

Definitions | 100

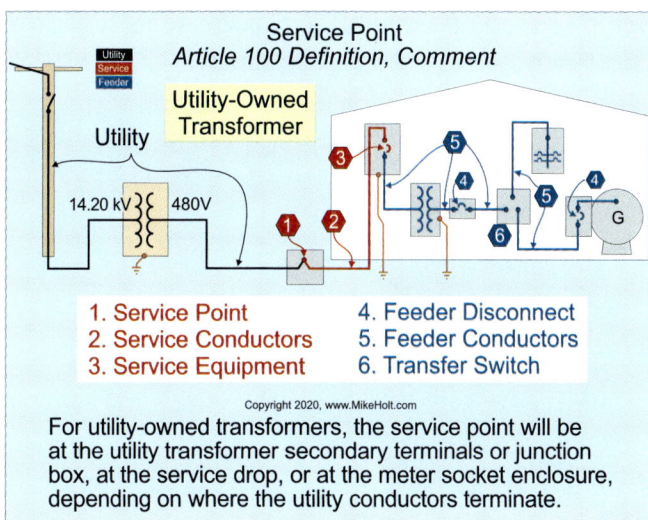
▶Figure 100-152

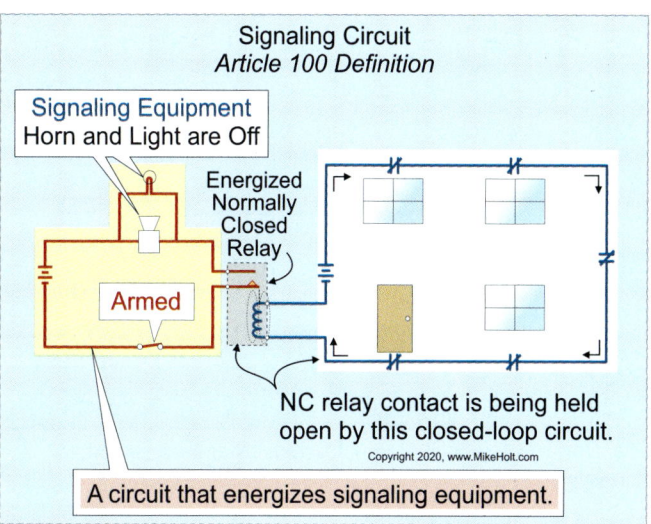
▶Figure 100-154

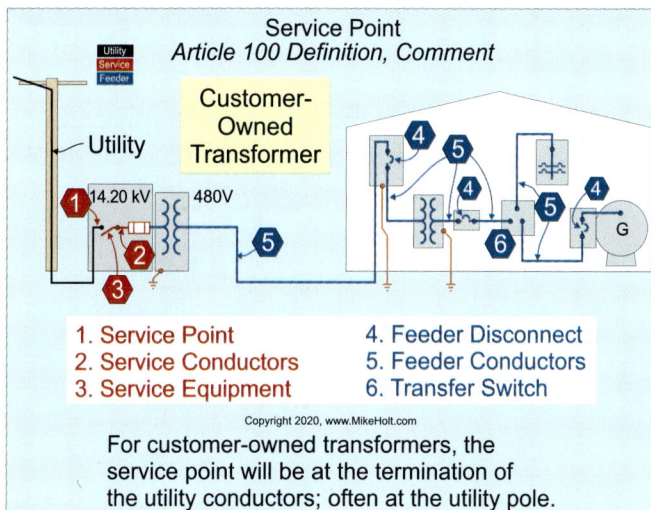
▶Figure 100-153

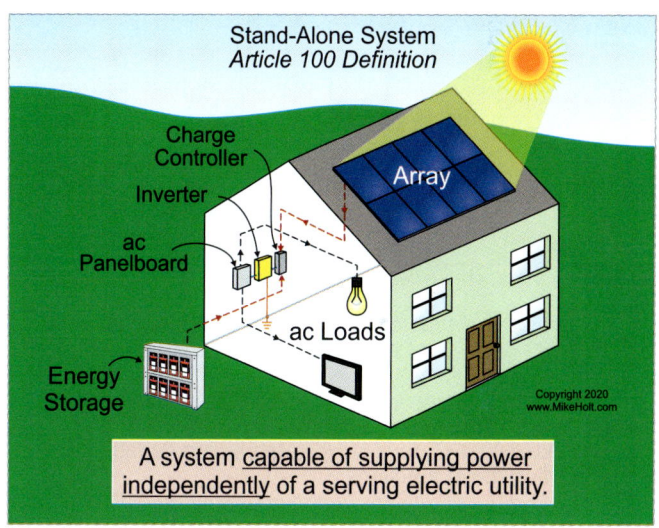
▶Figure 100-155

Short-Circuit Current Rating. The prospective symmetrical fault current at a nominal voltage to which electrical equipment can be connected without sustaining damage exceeding defined acceptance criteria.

Signaling Circuit [Article 725]. A circuit that energizes signaling equipment. ▶Figure 100-154

Special Permission. Written consent from the authority having jurisdiction.

> **Author's Comment:**
> ▸ See the definition of "Authority Having Jurisdiction."

Stand-Alone System. A system capable of supplying power independently of a serving electric utility. ▶Figure 100-155

> **Author's Comment:**
> ▸ Although stand-alone systems can operate independently of the serving electric utility, they may include a connection to the serving electric utility for use when not operating in stand-alone mode ("island mode").

Structure. That which is built or constructed, other than equipment. ▶Figure 100-156

Surge-Protective Device. A protective device intended to limit transient voltages by diverting or limiting surge current and preventing its continued flow while remaining capable of repeating these functions. ▶Figure 100-157 and ▶Figure 100-158

100 | Definitions

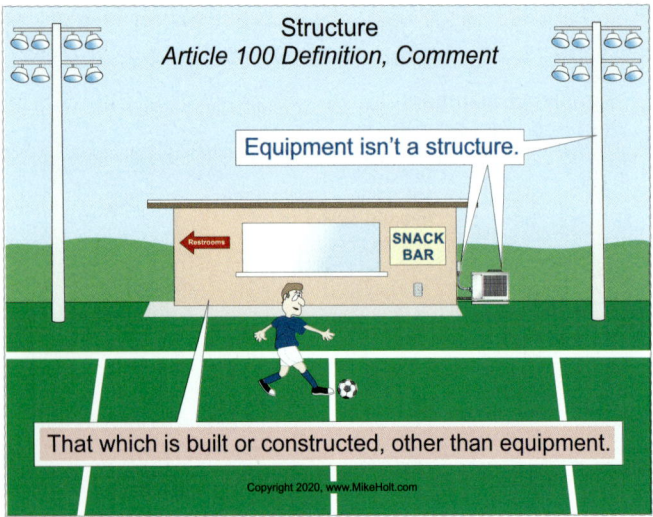
▶Figure 100-156

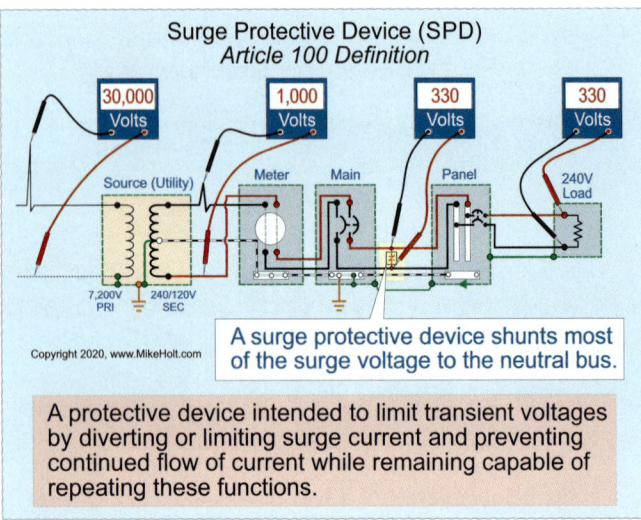
▶Figure 100-157

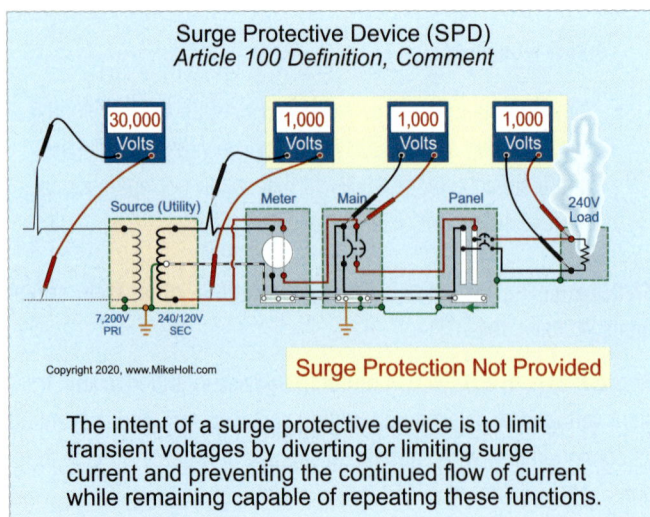
▶Figure 100-158

Type 1. A permanently connected surge protective device listed for installation at or ahead of the service disconnect. ▶Figure 100-159

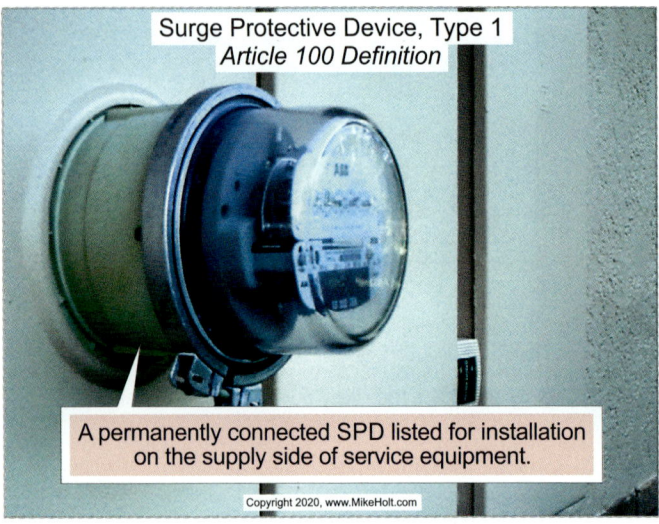
▶Figure 100-159

Type 2. A permanently connected surge protective device listed for installation on the load side of the service disconnect. ▶Figure 100-160

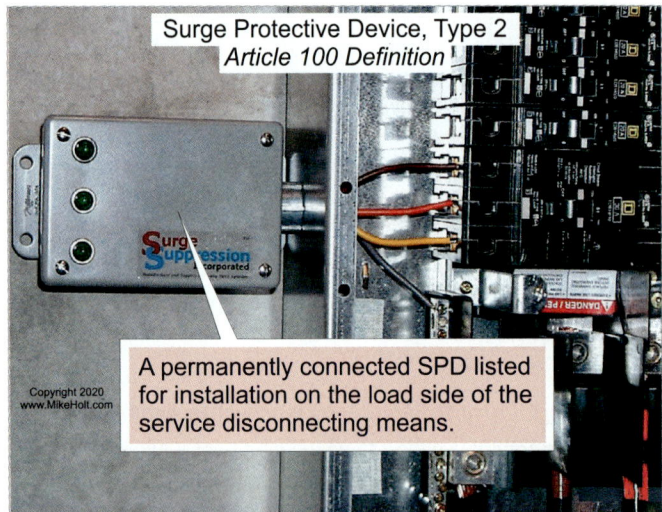
▶Figure 100-160

Type 3. A surge protective device listed for installation on branch circuits. ▶Figure 100-161

Author's Comment:

▸ Type 3 surge protective devices can be installed anywhere on the load side of branch-circuit overcurrent protection up to the equipment served, provided there is a conductor at least 30 ft long between the connection and the service or transformer [242.16].

Definitions | 100

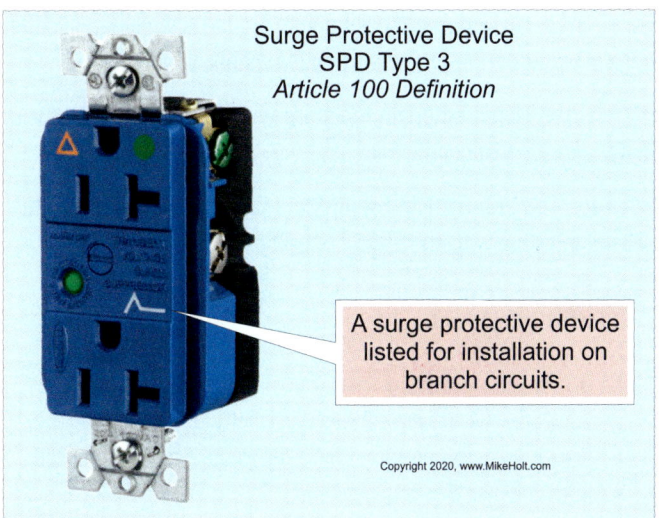
▶Figure 100–161

Type 4. A component surge protective device which includes those installed in receptacles and relocatable power taps (power strips).

Note: For further information, see UL 1449, *Standard for Surge Protective Devices.*

Switch, General-Use Snap (General-Use Snap Switch). A switch constructed to be installed in a device box or a box cover.

Ungrounded System. A power-supply system not connected to earth (ground). ▶Figure 100–162

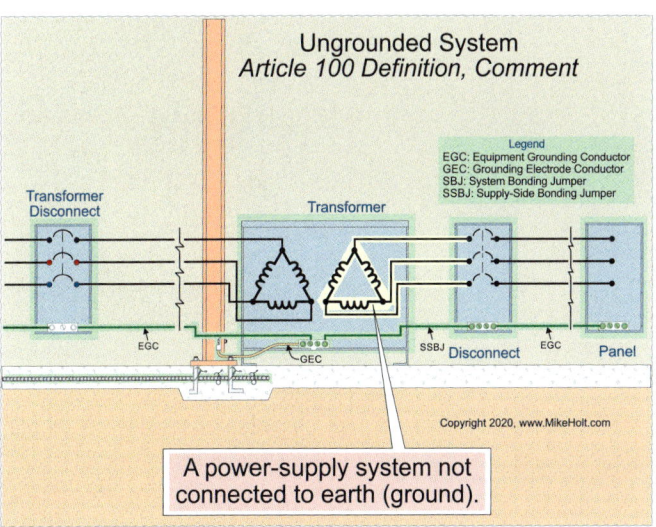
▶Figure 100–162

Author's Comment:

▸ An electrical system can be ungrounded, but the enclosure must still be connected to the Earth [250.4(B)].

Utilization Equipment. Equipment that utilizes electricity for electronic, electromechanical, chemical, heating, lighting, or similar purposes.

Voltage of a Circuit. The greatest effective root-mean-square (RMS) difference of voltage between any two conductors of the circuit. ▶Figure 100–163

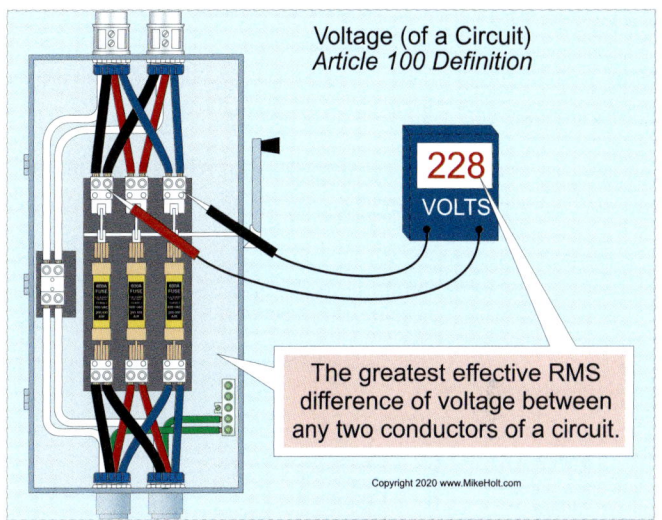
▶Figure 100–163

Voltage, Nominal (Nominal Voltage). A value assigned for conveniently designating voltage classes. Examples are 120/240V, 120/208V, or 277/480V [220.5(A)]. ▶Figure 100–164

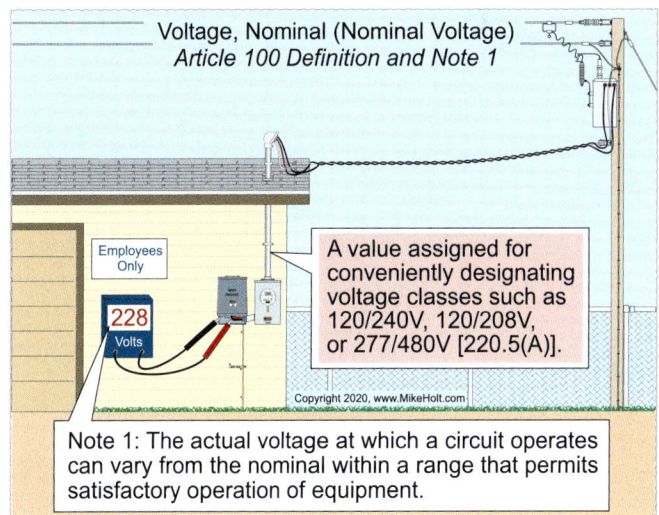
▶Figure 100–164

Note 1: The actual voltage at which a circuit operates can vary from the nominal within a range that permits satisfactory operation of equipment.

100 | Definitions

Author's Comment:

▸ Common voltage ratings of electrical equipment are 115V, 200V, 208V, 230V, and 460V. The electrical power supplied might be at the 240V, nominal, voltage but will be less at the equipment. Therefore, electrical equipment is rated at a value less than the nominal system voltage.

Note 3: Some battery units are rated 48V dc, nominal, even if they have a charging float voltage of up to 58V dc.

Voltage to Ground. For grounded systems, this is the voltage between a phase conductor and ground; typically, the neutral. ▸Figure 100–165

For ungrounded systems, the voltage to ground is the greatest difference of voltage (RMS) between any two phase conductor.

Watertight. Constructed so moisture will not enter the enclosure under specific test conditions.

Weatherproof. Constructed or protected so exposure to the weather will not interfere with successful operation.

Author's Comment:

▸ Article 100 now includes a "Part III" which contains definitions specific to Hazardous (Classified) Locations. While a few of the definitions are new to the *Code*, most were moved from Chapter 5 to this new part.

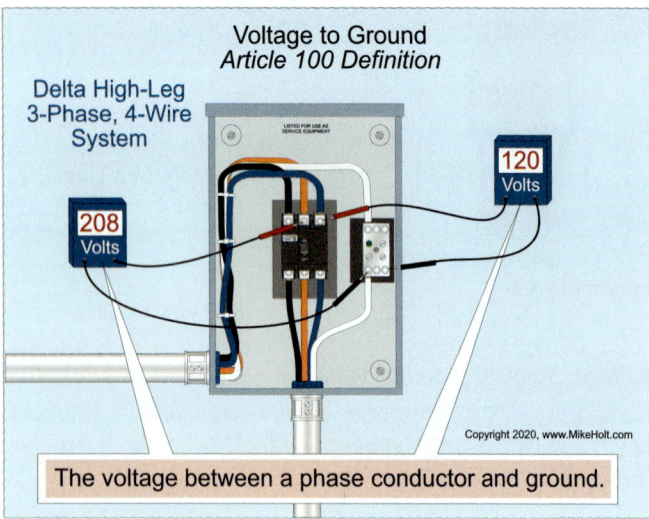
▸Figure 100–165

ARTICLE 110 — REQUIREMENTS FOR ELECTRICAL INSTALLATIONS

Introduction to Article 110—Requirements for Electrical Installations

Article 110 sets the stage for how the rest of the *NEC* is implemented. It is critical for you to completely understand all aspects of this article since it is the foundation for much of the *Code*. As you read and master Article 110, you are building your foundation for correctly applying the *NEC*. While the purpose of the *National Electrical Code* is to provide a safe installation, this article is perhaps focused a little more on providing an installation that is safe for the installer and maintenance electrician, so time spent here is a good investment.

Part I. General Requirements

110.1 Scope

Article 110 covers the general requirements for the examination and approval, installation and use, and access to spaces about electrical equipment. ▶Figure 110–1

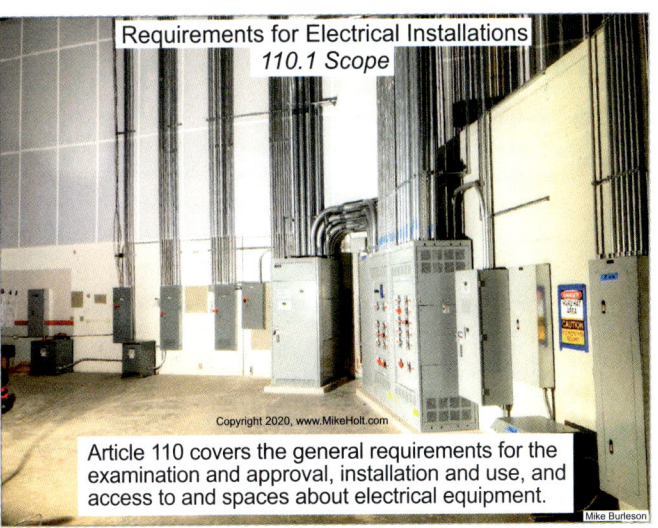
▶Figure 110–1

Note: See Annex J for information regarding ADA accessibility design.

Author's Comment:

▸ Requirements for people with disabilities include things like mounting heights for switches and receptacles, and requirements for the distance that objects (such as wall sconces) protrude from a wall.

110.2 Approval of Conductors and Equipment

The authority having jurisdiction must approve all electrical conductors and equipment. ▶Figure 110–2

▶Figure 110–2

110.3 | Requirements for Electrical Installations

Author's Comment:

▸ For a better understanding of product approval, review 90.4, 90.7, and 110.3 and the definitions for "Approved," "Identified," "Labeled," and "Listed" in Article 100.

110.3 Use and Product Listing (Certification) of Equipment

(A) Guidelines for Approval. The authority having jurisdiction must approve equipment. In doing so, consideration must be given to the following:

(1) Suitability for installation and use in accordance with the *NEC*

Note 1: Equipment may be new, reconditioned, refurbished, or remanufactured.

Note 2: Suitability of equipment use may be identified by a description marked on, or provided with, a product to identify the suitability of the product for a specific purpose, environment, or application. Special conditions of use or other limitations may be marked on the equipment, in the product instructions, or included in the appropriate listing and labeling information. Suitability of equipment may be evidenced by listing or labeling.

(2) Mechanical strength and durability

(3) Wire-bending and connection space

(4) Electrical insulation

(5) Heating effects under all conditions of use

(6) Arcing effects

(7) Classification by type, size, voltage, current capacity, and specific use

(8) Other factors contributing to the practical safeguarding of persons using or in contact with the equipment

(B) Installation and Use. Equipment that is listed, labeled, or both must be installed and used in accordance with any instructions included in the listing or labeling. ▸Figure 110-3

(C) Product Listing. Product testing, evaluation, and listing must be performed by a recognized qualified testing laboratory in accordance with standards that achieve effective safety to comply with the *NEC*.

Note: OSHA recognizes qualified electrical testing laboratories that provide product certification that meets their electrical standards.

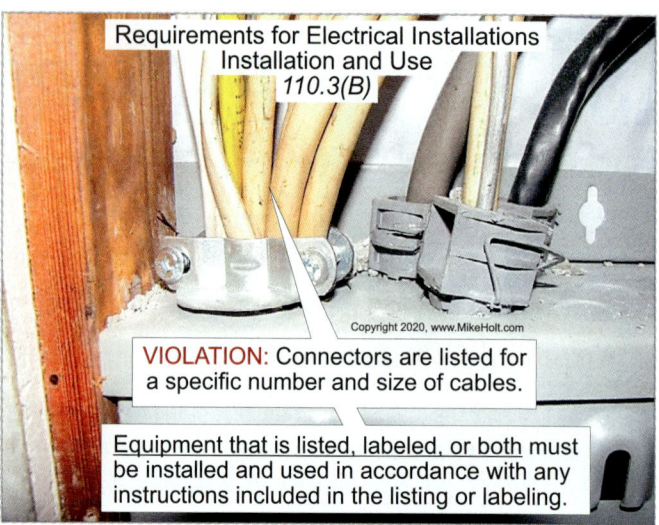

▸Figure 110-3

110.4 Voltage Rating of Electrical Equipment

The circuit nominal system voltage is not permitted to be greater than the rating of the equipment. ▸Figure 110-4

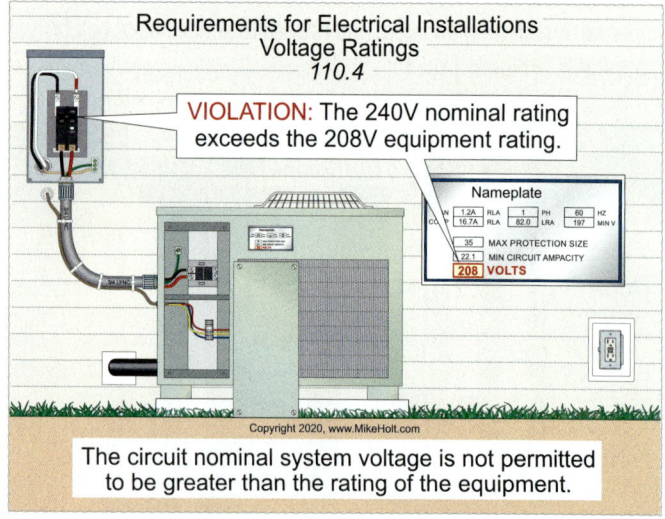

▸Figure 110-4

110.5 Conductor Material

Conductors must be copper, aluminum, or copper-clad aluminum unless otherwise provided in this *Code*; and when the conductor material is not specified in a rule, the sizes given in the *NEC* are based on a copper conductor. ▸Figure 110-5

Requirements for Electrical Installations | 110.8

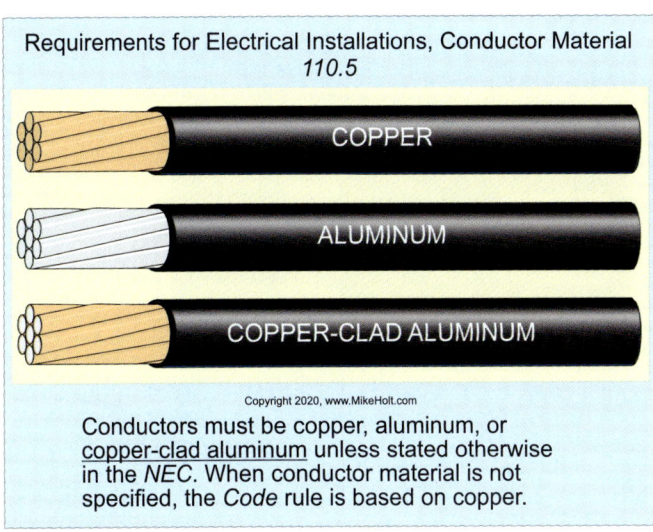
▶Figure 110–5

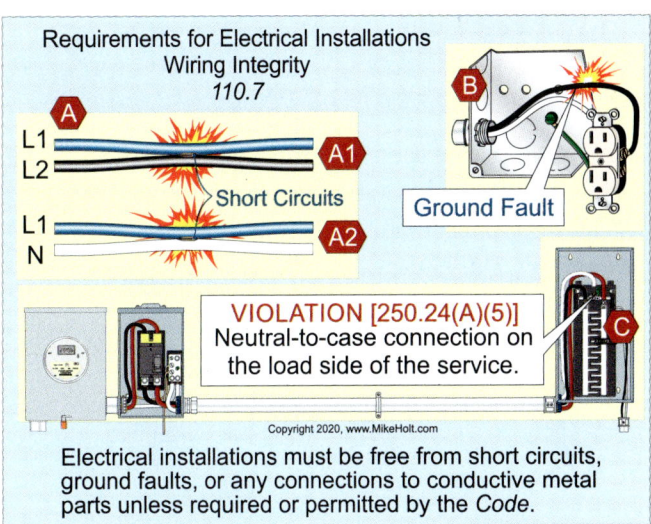
▶Figure 110–7

110.6 Conductor Sizes

Conductor sizes are expressed in American Wire Gage (AWG) or circular mils (cmil). ▶Figure 110–6

110.8 Suitable Wiring Methods

The only wiring methods permitted by the *NEC* are those included in the *Code*. ▶Figure 110–8

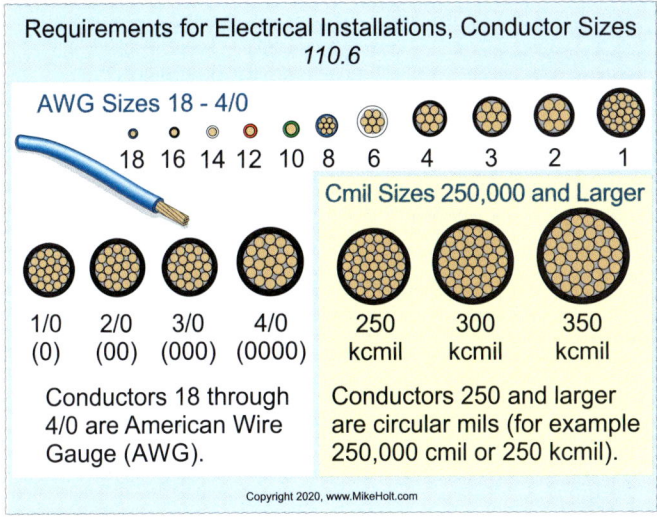
▶Figure 110–6

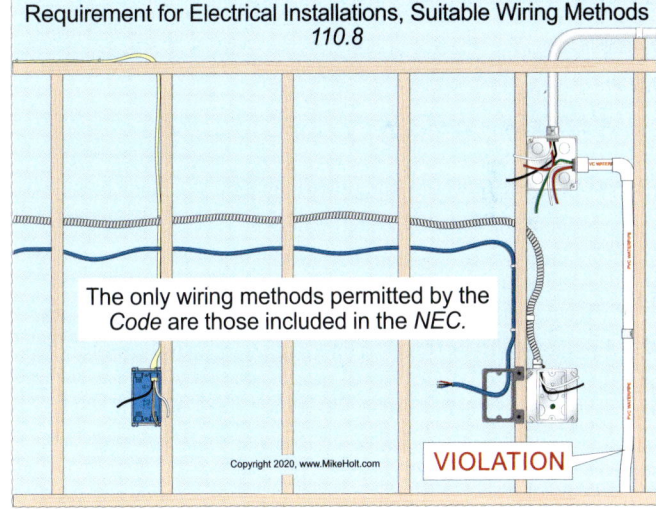
▶Figure 110–8

110.7 Wiring Integrity

Electrical installations must be free from short circuits, ground faults, or any connections to conductive metal parts unless required or permitted by the *Code*. ▶Figure 110–7

Author's Comment:

▸ See Chapter 3 for power and lighting wiring methods; Chapter 7 for signaling, remote-control, and power-limited circuit wiring methods; and Chapter 8 for communications circuits wiring methods.

110.9 Interrupting Rating (Overcurrent Protective Devices)

Overcurrent protective devices, such as circuit breakers and fuses, must have an interrupting rating capacity (AIC) equal to or greater than the fault current available at the line terminals of the equipment. ▸Figure 110–9

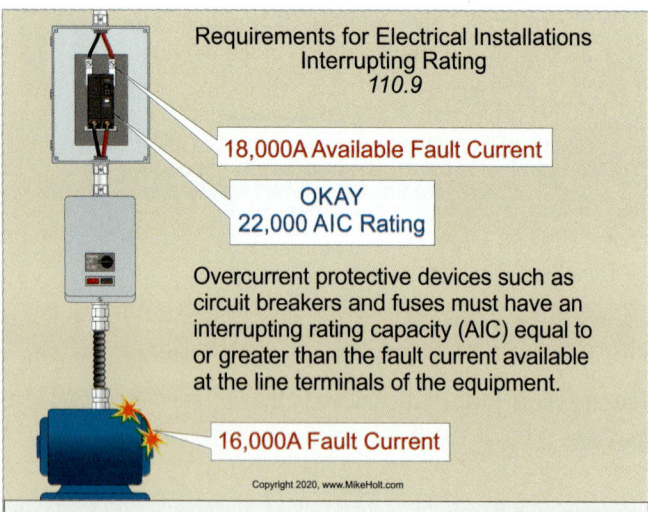
▸Figure 110–9

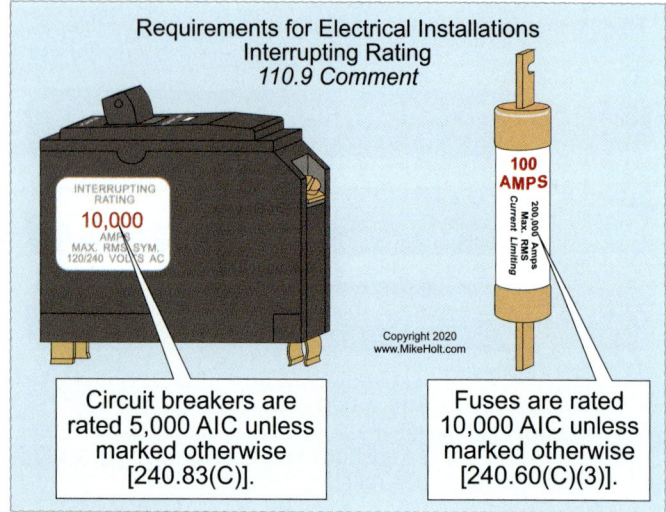
▸Figure 110–10

Author's Comment:

▸ According to Article 100, "Interrupting Rating" is the highest short-circuit current at rated voltage a device is identified to interrupt under standard test conditions.

▸ Interrupting ratings are often referred to as "Ampere Interrupting Rating" (AIR) or "Ampere Interrupting Capacity" (AIC).

▸ Unless marked otherwise, the ampere interrupting rating for circuit breakers is 5,000A [240.83(C)], and for fuses it is 10,000A [240.60(C)(3)]. ▸Figure 110–10

110.10 Equipment Short-Circuit Current Rating

Electrical equipment must have a short-circuit current rating that permits the circuit protective device to open due to a short circuit or ground fault without extensive damage to the electrical equipment. Listed equipment applied in accordance with its listing is considered to have met this requirement. ▸Figure 110–11 and ▸Figure 110–12

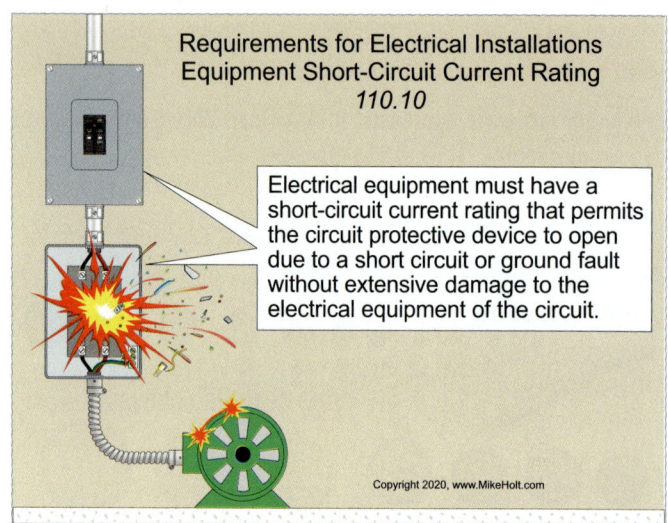
▸Figure 110–11

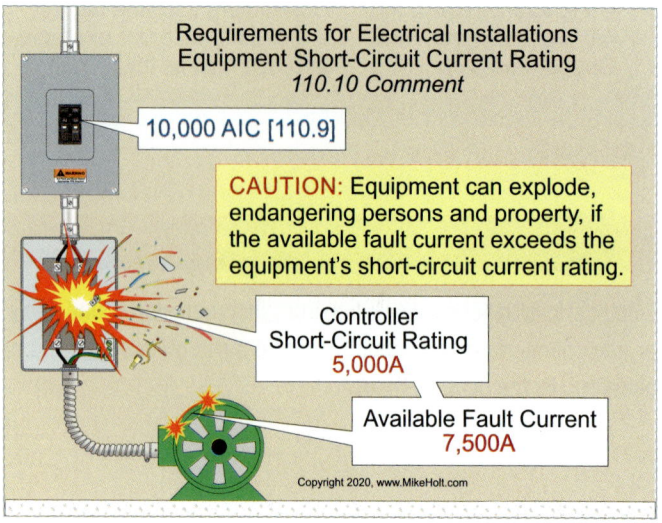
▸Figure 110–12

Available Short-Circuit Current

Sections 110.9 and 110.10 use similar sounding terms making it a bit challenging to understand the differences. Be careful not to confuse the term "interrupting rating" with "short-circuit rating."

Available short-circuit current is the current, in amperes, available at a given point in the electrical system. It is first determined at the secondary terminals of the serving electric utility transformer, as given by the serving electric utility's engineer. After that, it is calculated at the terminals of the service disconnect, then panelboards and other equipment as various connections are made downstream from the main service. Beginning at the serving electric utility transformer, the available short-circuit current decreases at each down-stream connection point of the electrical system.

The available short-circuit current at any point depends on the impedance of the circuit. As the circuit impedance increases, the available short-circuit current decreases. ▶Figure 110-13

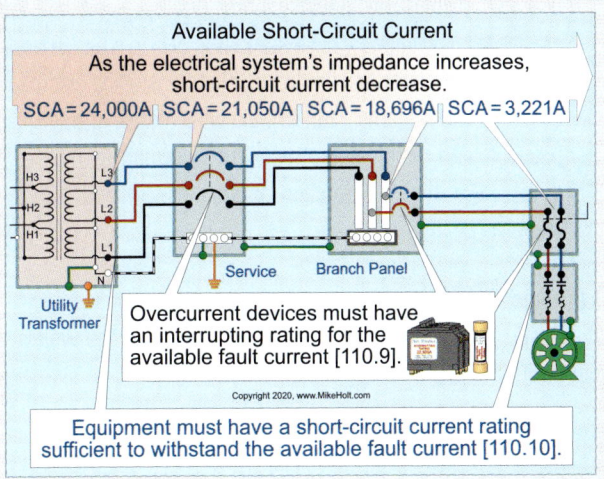

▶Figure 110-13

Factors that affect the available short-circuit current at the serving electric utility transformers are the system voltage, transformer kVA rating, and impedance. Properties that have an impact on the impedance of the circuit include the conductor material (copper versus aluminum), conductor size, conductor length, raceway type (metallic versus nonmetallic), ambient temperature, and motor loads.

Caution: Extremely high values of current flow caused by short circuits or ground faults produce tremendously destructive thermal and magnetic forces. If an overcurrent protective device is not rated to interrupt the current at the available fault values it can explode and literally vaporize metal components which can cause serious injury or death, as well as property damage and electrical system down time. ▶Figure 110-14

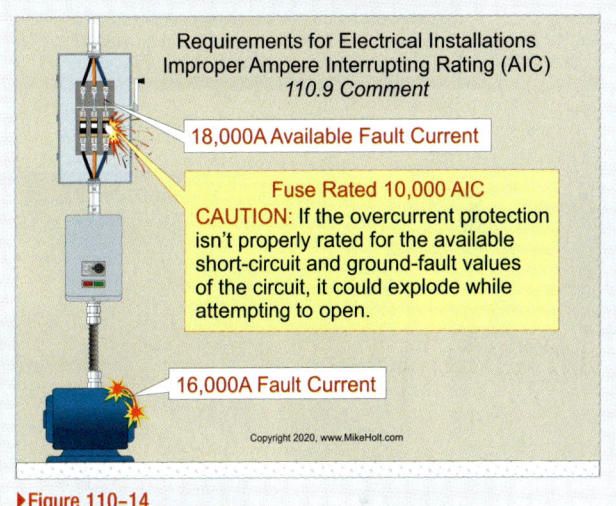

▶Figure 110-14

110.11 Deteriorating Agents

Electrical equipment and conductors must be suitable for the environment and the conditions for which they will be used. Consideration must also be given to the presence of corrosive gases, fumes, vapors, liquids, or other substances that can have a deteriorating effect on conductors and equipment. ▶Figure 110-15

Note 1: Raceways, cable trays, cablebus, cable armor, boxes, cable sheathing, cabinets, elbows, couplings, fittings, supports, and support hardware must be suitable for the environment; see 300.6. ▶Figure 110-16

Note 2: Some cleaning and lubricating compounds contain chemicals that can cause plastic to deteriorate.

Equipment identified for indoor use must be protected against damage from the weather during construction.

Note 3: See Table 110.28 for NEMA enclosure-type designations.

Note 4: For minimum flood provisions, see the *International Building Code (IBC)* and the *International Residential Code* (IRC).

110.12 | Requirements for Electrical Installations

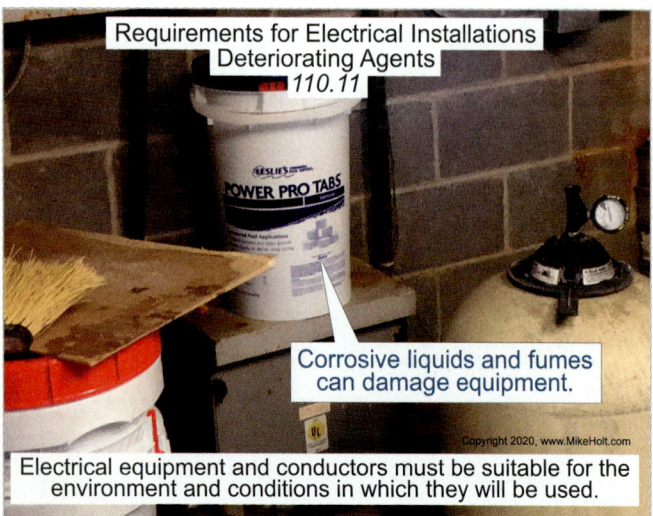
▶Figure 110–15

▶Figure 110–17

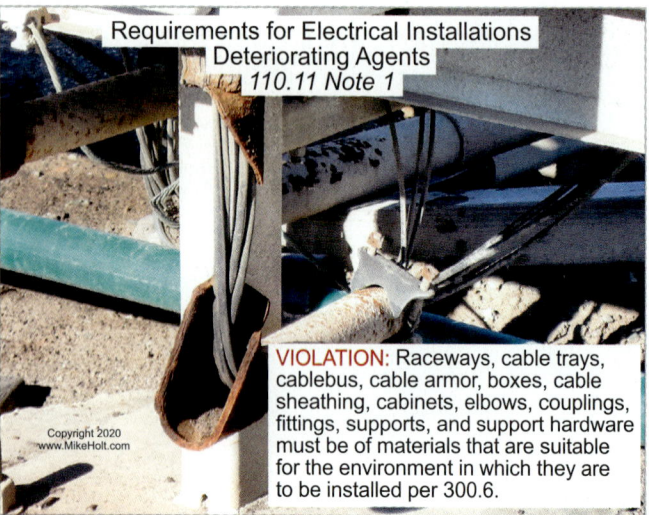
▶Figure 110–16

110.12 Mechanical Execution of Work

Electrical equipment must be installed in a neat and workmanlike manner. ▶Figure 110–17

Author's Comment:

▶ This rule is perhaps one of the most subjective of the entire *Code* and its application is still ultimately a judgment call made by the authority having jurisdiction.

Author's Comment:

▶ The National Electrical Contractors Association (*NEC*A) created a series of *National Electrical Installation Standards* (NEIS)® that established the industry's first quality guidelines for electrical installations. These standards define a benchmark (baseline) of quality and workmanship for installing electrical products and systems. They explain what installing electrical products and systems in a "neat and workmanlike manner" means. For more information about these standards, visit www.NECA-NEIS.org.

(A) Unused Openings. Unused openings must be closed by fittings that provide protection substantially equivalent to the wall of the equipment. ▶Figure 110–18

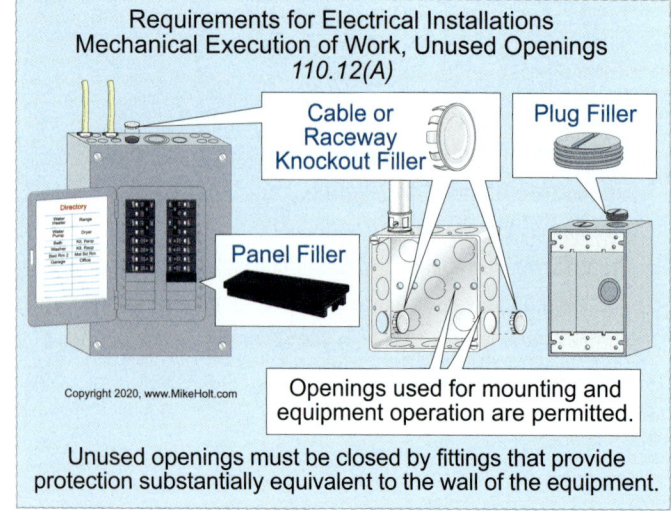
▶Figure 110–18

(B) Integrity of Electrical Equipment. Internal parts of electrical equipment must not be damaged or contaminated by foreign material, such as paint, plaster, cleaners, and so forth. ▶Figure 110–19

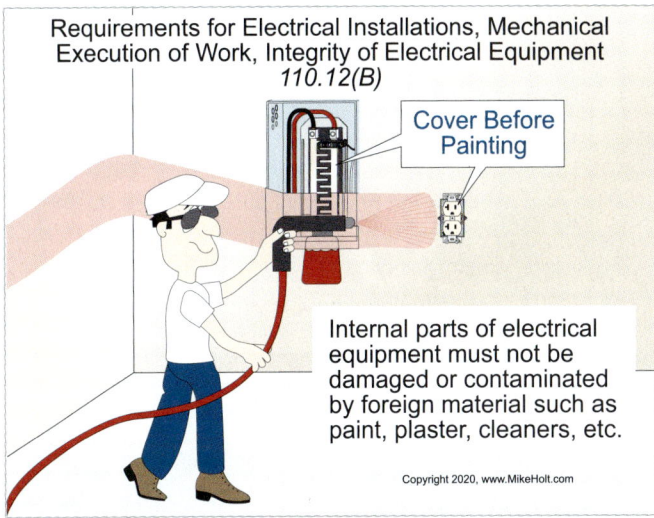
▶Figure 110–19

Author's Comment:

▸ Precautions must be taken to provide protection from contamination of the internal parts of panelboards and receptacles during building construction. Be sure the electrical equipment is properly masked and protected before sheetrock, painting, or other phases of the project that can contaminate or cause damage begins. ▶Figure 110–20

▶Figure 110–20

Electrical equipment containing damaged (such as items broken, bent, or cut) parts, or those that have been deteriorated by corrosion, chemical action, or overheating are not permitted to be installed. ▶Figure 110–21

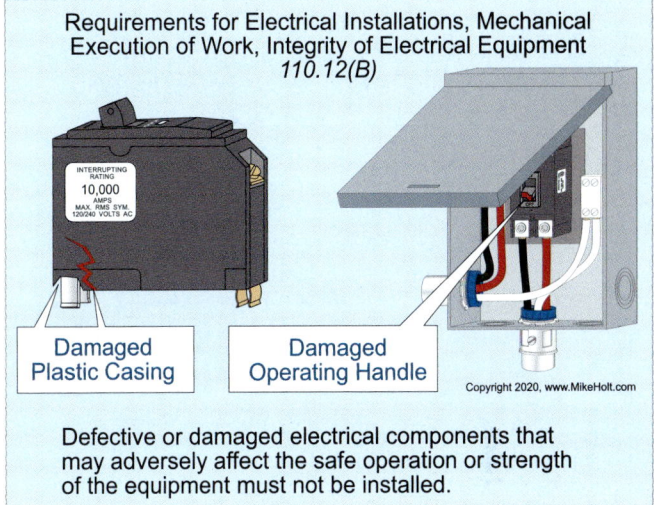
▶Figure 110–21

Author's Comment:

▸ Damaged parts include cracked insulators, arc shields not in place, overheated fuse clips, and damaged or missing switch handles or circuit-breaker handles.

(C) Cables and Conductors. Cables and conductors must be installed in a neat and workmanlike manner. ▶Figure 110–22

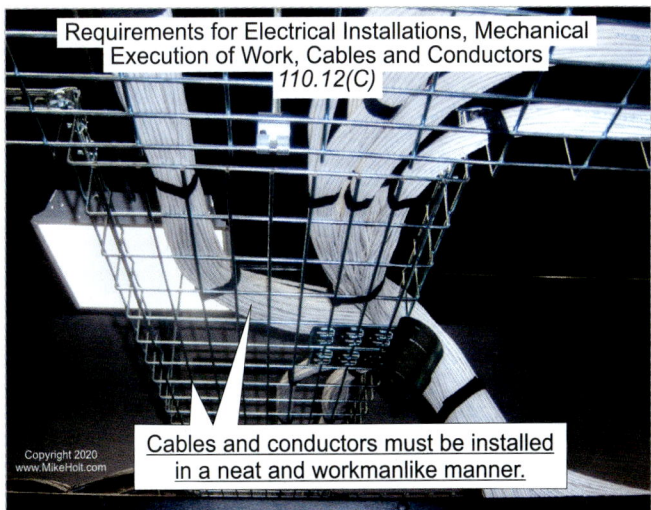
▶Figure 110–22

110.13 | Requirements for Electrical Installations

Exposed cables must be supported by the structural components of the building so they will not be damaged by normal building use. Support must be by straps, staples, hangers, cable ties, or similar fittings designed and installed in a manner that will not damage the cable. ▶Figure 110–23

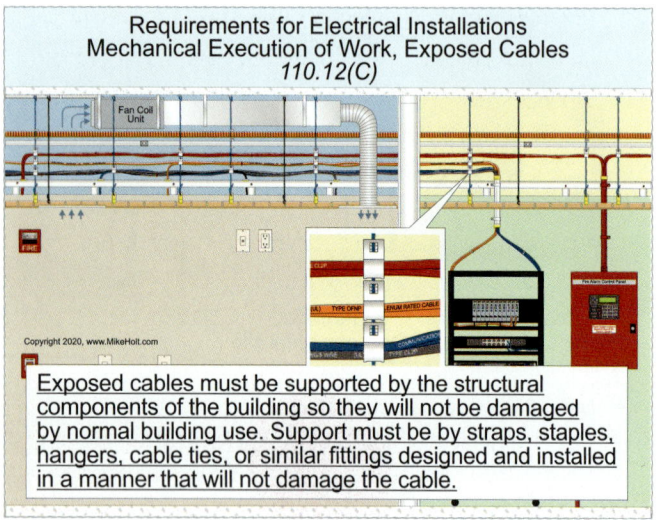

▶Figure 110–23

Note 1: Industry practices are described in ANSI/*NECA*/FOA 301, *Standard for Installing and Testing Fiber Optic Cables*, and other ANSI-approved installation standards.

Note 3: Paint, plaster, cleaners, abrasives, corrosive residues, or other contaminants can result in an undetermined alteration of optical fiber cable properties.

110.13 Mounting and Cooling of Equipment

(A) Mounting. Electrical equipment must be firmly secured to the surface on which it is mounted. ▶Figure 110–24

110.14 Conductor Termination and Splicing

Conductor terminal and splicing devices must be identified for the conductor material and must be properly installed and used in accordance with the manufacturer's instructions [110.3(B)]. ▶Figure 110–25

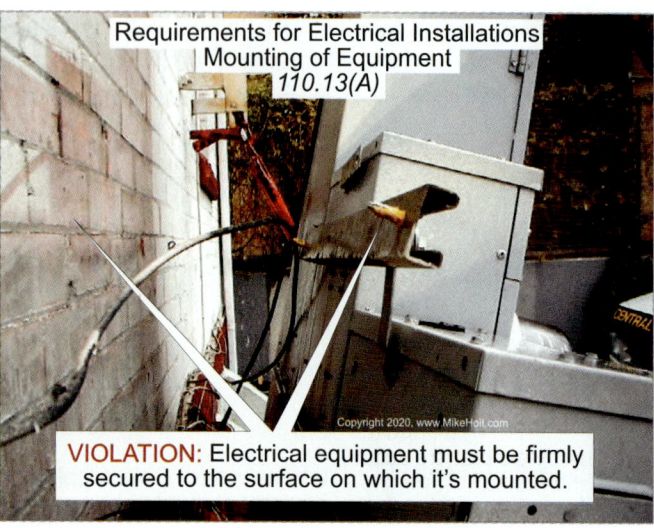

▶Figure 110–24

▶Figure 110–25

Author's Comment:

▶ Conductor terminals suitable for aluminum wire only will be marked "AL." Those acceptable for copper wire only will be marked "CU." Terminals suitable for both copper and aluminum will be marked "CU-AL" or "AL-CU." For 6 AWG and smaller, the markings can be printed on the container or on an information sheet inside the container. A "7" or "75" indicates a 75°C rated terminal, and a "9" or "90" indicates a 90°C rated terminal. If a terminal bears no marking, it can be used only with copper conductors. ▶Figure 110–26

Connectors and terminals for conductors more finely stranded than Class B and Class C must be identified for the use of finely stranded conductors. ▶Figure 110–27

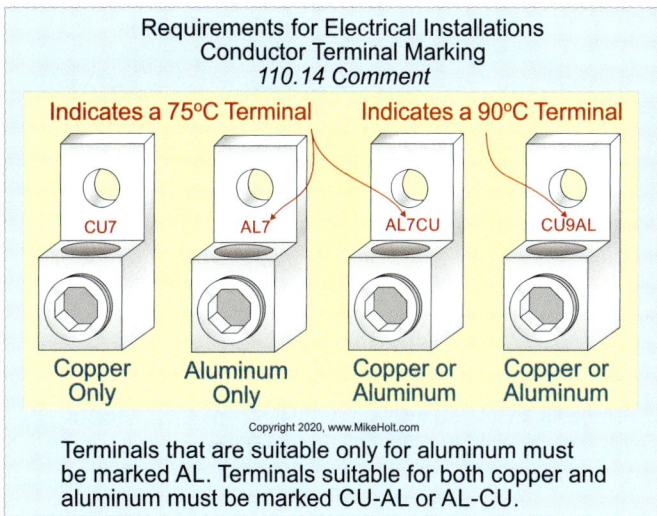
▶Figure 110-26

Copper and Aluminum Mixed. Copper and aluminum conductors (dissimilar metals) are not permitted to contact each other in a device unless the device is listed and identified for this purpose.

Author's Comment:

▸ Few terminations are listed for mixing aluminum and copper conductors, but if they are, that will be marked on the product package or terminal device. The reason copper and aluminum should not be in contact with each other is because corrosion develops between the two different metals due to galvanic action, resulting in increased contact resistance at the splicing device. This increased resistance can cause the splice to overheat and result in a fire.

(A) Conductor Terminations. Conductor terminals must ensure a good connection without damaging the conductors.

Terminals are listed for one conductor unless marked otherwise. Terminals for more than one conductor must be identified for this purpose, either within the equipment instructions or on the terminal itself. ▶Figure 110-28

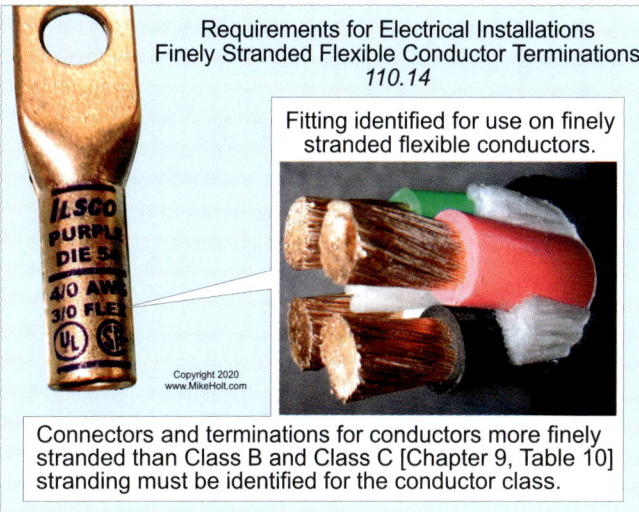
▶Figure 110-27

Author's Comment:

▸ According to Article 100, "Identified" means the item is recognized as suitable for a specific purpose, function, or environment by listing, labeling, or other means approved by the authority having jurisdiction.

▸ Conductor terminations must comply with the manufacturer's instructions as required by 110.3(B). For example, if the instructions for the device say, "Suitable for 18-12 AWG Stranded," then only stranded conductors can be used with the terminating device. If they say, "Suitable for 18-12 AWG Solid," then only solid conductors are permitted, and if the instructions say, "Suitable for 18-12 AWG," then either solid or stranded conductors can be used with the terminating device.

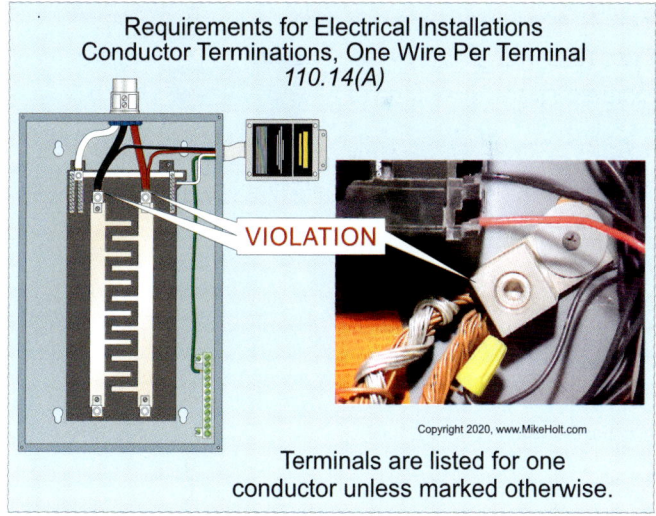
▶Figure 110-28

Author's Comment:

▸ Split-bolt connectors are commonly listed for only two conductors, although some are listed for three. However, it is a common industry practice to terminate as many conductors as possible within a split-bolt connector, even though this violates the *NEC*. ▶Figure 110-29

110.14 | Requirements for Electrical Installations

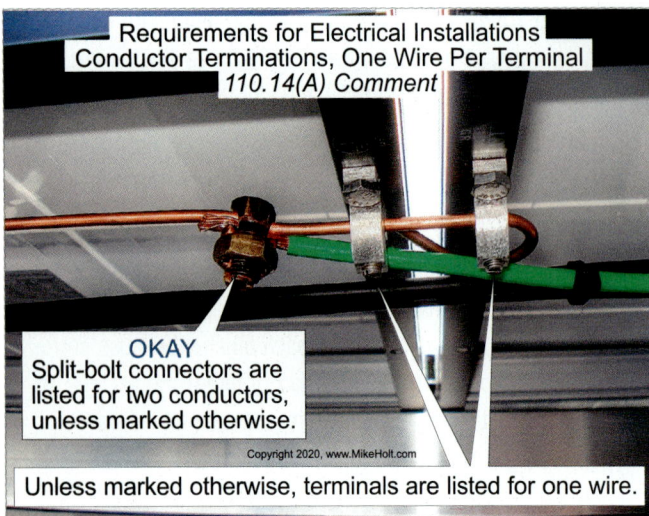
▶Figure 110–29

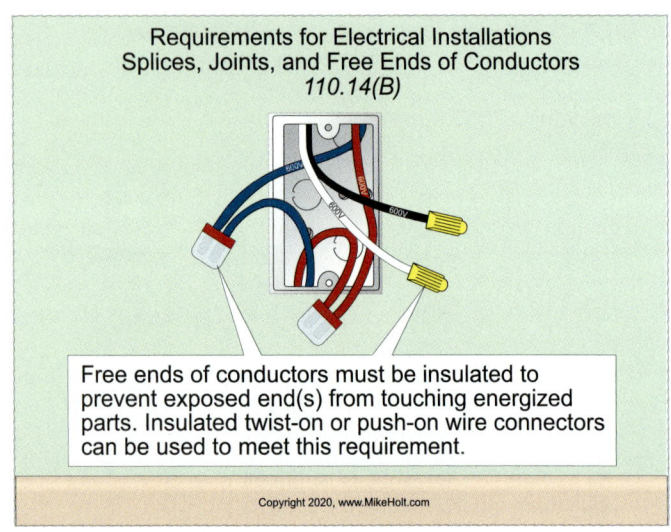
▶Figure 110–31

(B) Conductor Splices. Conductors must be spliced by a splicing device that is identified for the purpose. ▶Figure 110–30

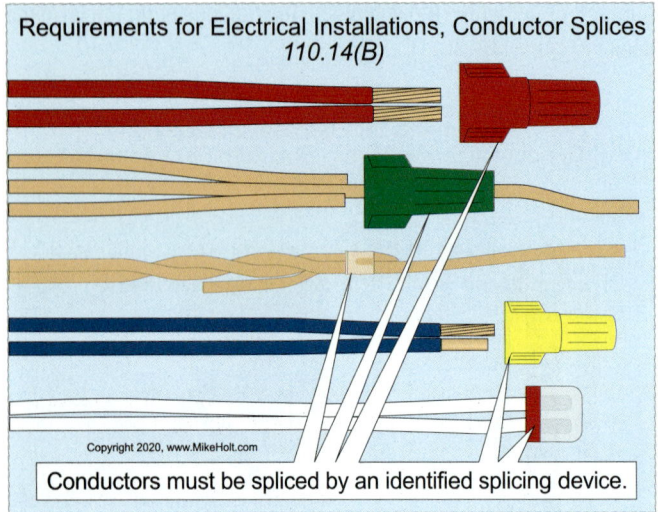
▶Figure 110–30

Unused circuit conductors are not required to be removed. However, to prevent an electrical hazard, the free ends of the conductors must be insulated to prevent the exposed end(s) from touching energized parts. This requirement can be met by using an insulated twist-on or push-on wire connector. ▶Figure 110–31

Author's Comment:

▸ According to Article 100, "Energized" means electrically connected to a source of voltage.

▸ Pre-twisting conductors before applying twist-on wire connectors has been a very common practice in the field for years. The question (and subsequent debate) has always been, "Is pre-twisting required?" The *NEC* does not require that practice and, in fact, Ideal® made a statement about their Wing-Nut® twist-on connectors which said, "Pre-twisting is acceptable, but not required." Always follow the manufacturer's instructions and there will be no question [110.3(B)].

▸ Reusing twist-on connectors seems to be another point of contention in the field. Should they be reused? Some say that they just never seem quite the same once they have been used, while others say they reuse them all the time. Defer to the manufacturer's instructions; Ideal® and 3M® both indicate in their information that it is perfectly fine to reuse their twist-on connectors. ▶Figure 110–32

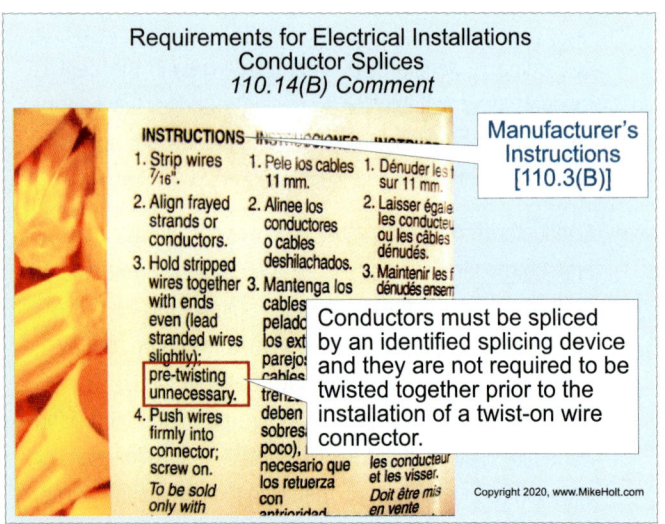
▶Figure 110–32

Underground Splices, Single Conductors. Single direct burial types UF or USE conductors can be spliced underground with a device listed for direct burial [300.5(E) and 300.15(G)]. ▶Figure 110–33

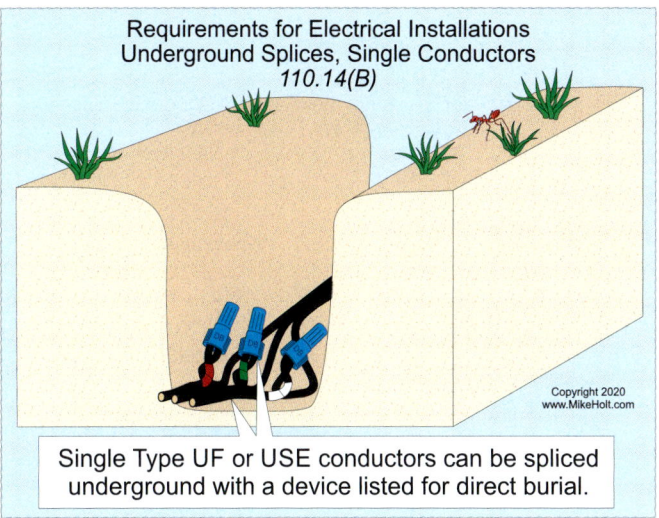

▶Figure 110–33

Underground Splices, Multiconductor Cable. The individual conductors of multiconductor UF or USE cable can be spliced underground with a listed splice kit that encapsulates the conductors and cable jacket.

Author's Comment:

▸ Electrical connection failures are the cause of many equipment and building fires. Improper terminations, poor workmanship, not following the manufacturer's instructions, and improper torqueing can all cause poor electrical connections. Improper electrical terminations can damage and melt conductor insulation resulting in short circuits and ground faults.

(C) Conductor Size to Terminal Temperature Rating. Conductors are sized in accordance with 110.14(C)(1) and (2).

(1) Equipment Terminals. Unless equipment is listed and marked otherwise, conductors are sized in accordance with (a) or (b) as follows:

(a) Equipment Rated 100A or Less

(2) Conductors with an insulation temperature rating greater than 60°C are permitted, but the conductor must be sized in accordance with the ampacities in the 60°C temperature column of Table 310.16. ▶Figure 110–34

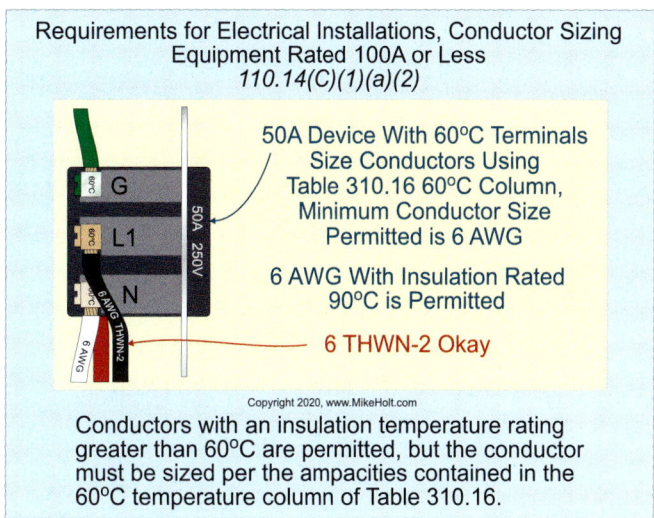

▶Figure 110–34

▶ **Example**

Question: According to Table 310.16, what size THWN-2 conductor is required for a circuit rated 50A?

(a) 10 AWG   (b) 8 AWG   (c) 6 AWG   (d) 4 AWG

Answer: (c) 6 AWG rated 55A at 60°C [110.14(C)(1)(a)(2) and Table 310.16]

(3) Conductors terminating on terminals rated 75°C can be sized in accordance with the ampacities in the 75°C temperature column of Table 310.16. ▶Figure 110–35

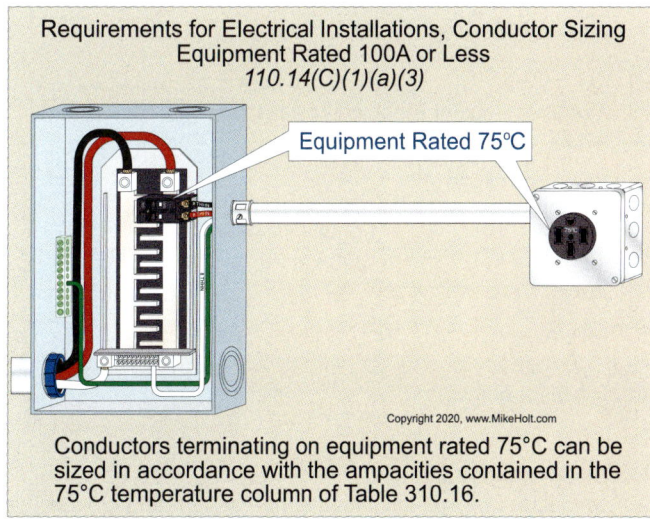

▶Figure 110–35

110.14 | Requirements for Electrical Installations

▶ **Example**

Question: *According to Table 310.16, what size THHN conductor is required for a 50A circuit where the equipment is listed for use at 75°C?* ▶Figure 110-36

(a) 10 AWG   (b) 8 AWG   (c) 6 AWG   (d) 4 AWG

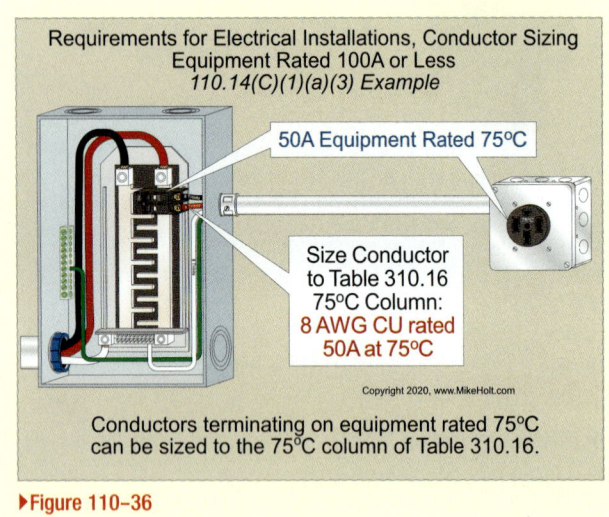

▶Figure 110-36

Answer: *(b) 8 AWG rated 50A at 75°C [110.14(C)(1)(a)(3) and Table 310.16]*

(b) Equipment Rated Over 100A

(2) Conductors with an insulation temperature rating greater than 75°C are permitted, but the conductor must be sized in accordance with the ampacities in the 75°C temperature column of Table 310.16. ▶Figure 110-37

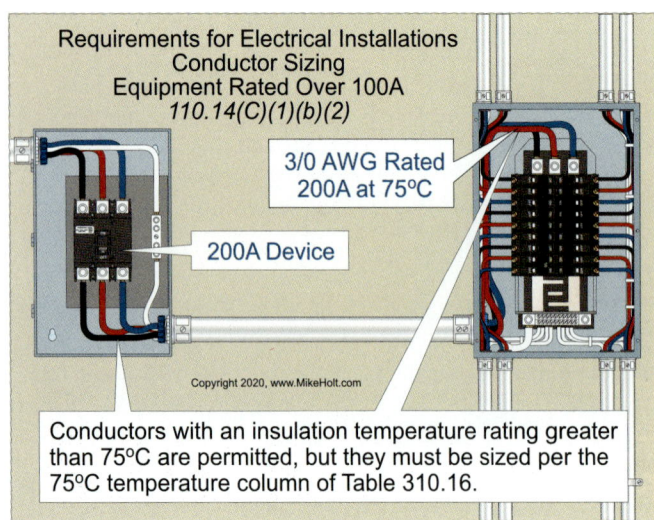

▶Figure 110-37

▶ **Example**

Question: *According to Table 310.16, what size THHN conductor is required to supply a 150A feeder?* ▶Figure 110-38

(a) 1/0 AWG   (b) 2/0 AWG   (c) 3/0 AWG   (d) 4/0 AWG

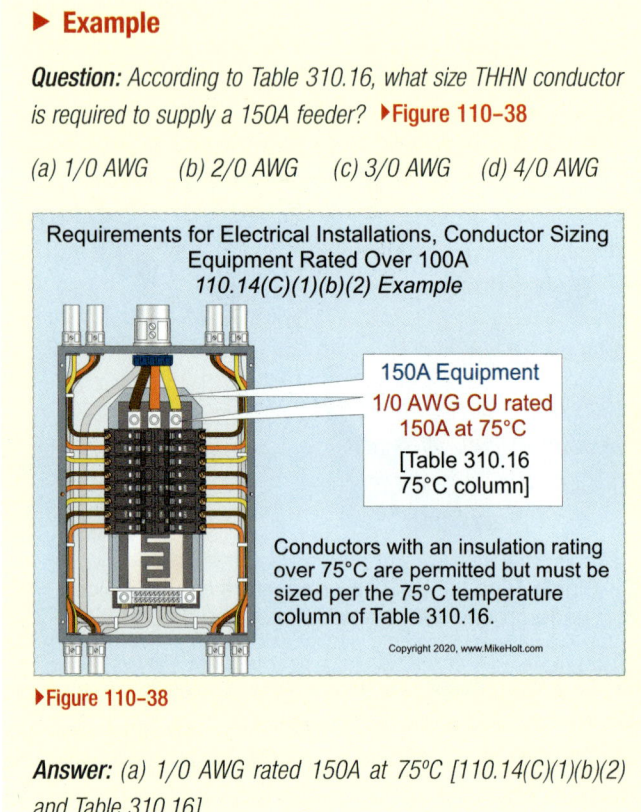

▶Figure 110-38

Answer: *(a) 1/0 AWG rated 150A at 75°C [110.14(C)(1)(b)(2) and Table 310.16]*

(2) Separate Connector. Splicing and terminating devices with terminals rated 90°C and not connected to electrical equipment can have the conductors sized in accordance with the ampacities in the 90°C temperature column of Table 310.16. ▶Figure 110-39

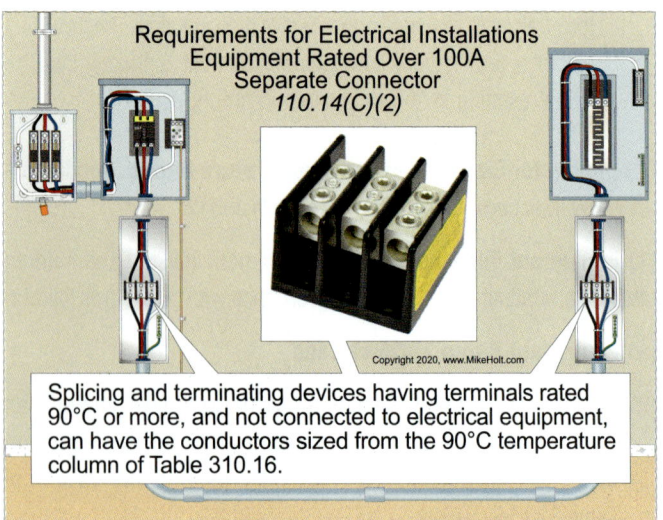

▶Figure 110-39

▶ Example 1

Question: According to Table 310.16, what size aluminum conductor can be used to interconnect busbars protected by a 200A overcurrent protective device if all terminals are rated 90ºC?

(a) 1/0 AWG   (b) 2/0 AWG   (c) 3/0 AWG   (d) 4/0 AWG

Answer: (d) 4/0 AWG aluminum rated 205A at 90ºC [Table 310.16]

▶ Example 2

Question: What size XHHW copper conductor can be used to interconnect 90°C rated power distribution blocks protected by a 400A overcurrent protective device serving a 320A continuous load? ▶Figure 110–40

(a) 250 kcmil   (b) 300 kcmil   (c) 350 kcmil   (d) 400 kcmil

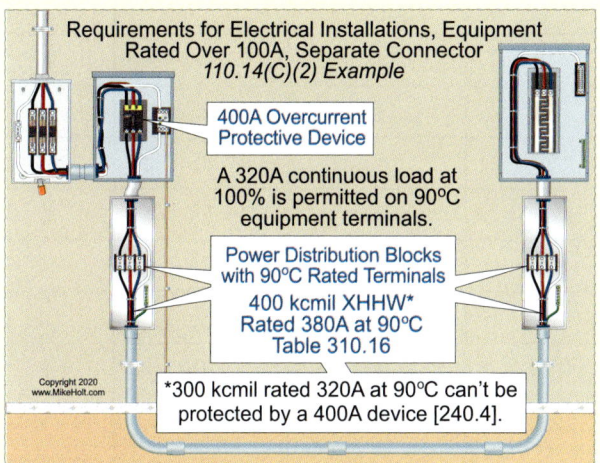

▶Figure 110–40

Note: 350 kcmil is rated 350A at 90°C; however, 350 kcmil cannot be used because it cannot be protected by a 400A overcurrent protective device [240.4].

Answer: (d) 400 kcmil rated 380A at 90ºC [Table 310.16]

▶ Example 3

Question: What size XHHW copper conductor can be used to interconnect 90°C rated power distribution blocks protected by a 400A overcurrent protective device serving a 375A continuous load? ▶Figure 110–41

(a) 250 kcmil   (b) 300 kcmil   (c) 350 kcmil   (d) 400 kcmil

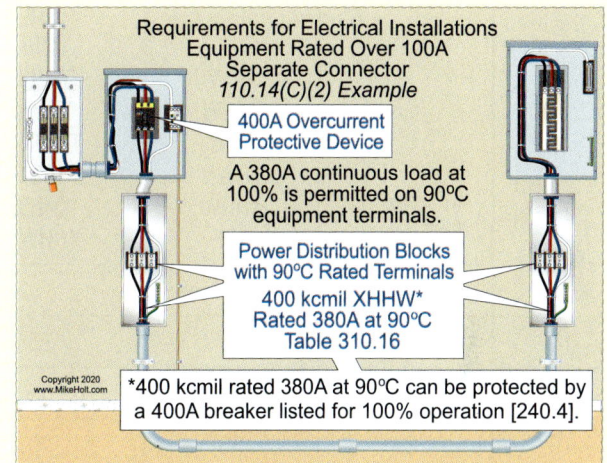

▶Figure 110–41

Answer: (d) 400 kcmil rated 380A at 90ºC [Table 310.16]

Table 310.16 Ampacities of Insulated Conductors
Based on Not More Than Three Current-Carrying Conductors and Ambient Temperature of 30°C (86°F)

Size	60°C (140°F)	75°C (167°F)	90°C (194°F)	60°C (140°F)	75°C (167°F)	90°C (194°F)	Size
		RHW THHW THW THWN XHHW USE	RHH RHW-2 THHN THHW THW-2 THWN-2 USE-2 XHHW XHHW-2		THW THWN XHHW	THHN THW-2 THWN-2 THHW XHHW XHHW-2	
AWG kcmil	TW UF			TW UF			AWG kcmil
	Copper			Aluminum/Copper-Clad Aluminum			
14	15	20	25				14
12	20	25	30	15	20	25	12
10	30	35	40	25	30	35	10
8	40	50	55	35	40	45	8
6	55	65	75	40	50	55	6
4	70	85	95	55	65	75	4
3	85	100	115	65	75	85	3
2	95	115	130	75	90	100	2
1	110	130	145	85	100	115	1
1/0	125	150	170	100	120	135	1/0
2/0	145	175	195	115	135	150	2/0
3/0	165	200	225	130	155	175	3/0
4/0	195	230	260	150	180	205	4/0
250	215	255	290	170	205	230	250
300	240	285	320	195	230	260	300
350	260	310	350	210	250	280	350
400	280	335	380	225	270	305	400
500	320	380	430	260	310	350	500

(D) Terminal Connection Torque. Tightening torque values for terminal connections must be as indicated on equipment or installation instructions. An approved means (a torque tool) must be used to achieve the indicated torque value. ▶Figure 110–42 and ▶Figure 110–43

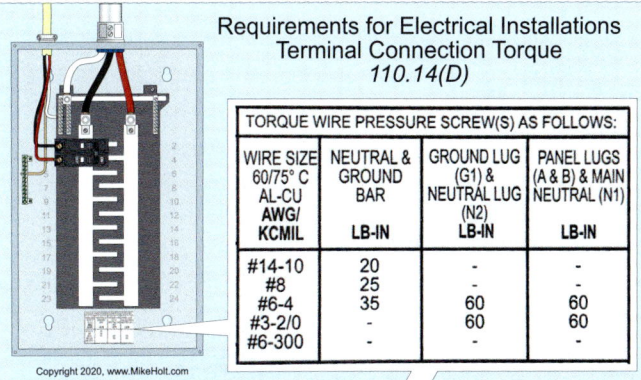

▶Figure 110–42

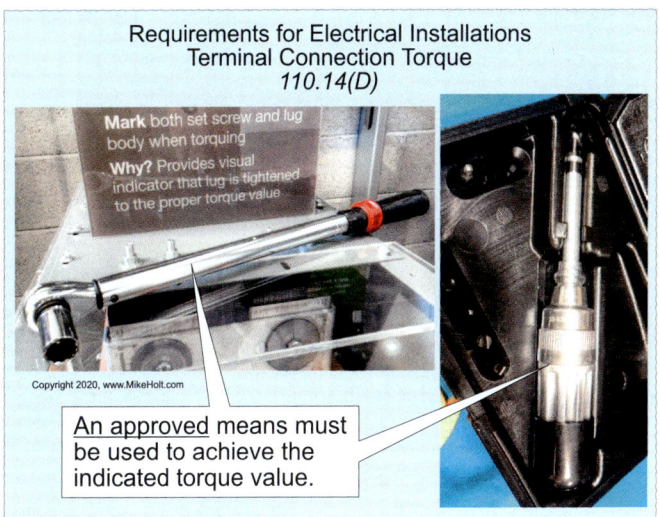

▶Figure 110–43

Author's Comment:

▸ Conductors must terminate in devices that have been properly tightened in accordance with the manufacturer's torque specifications included with equipment instructions. Failure to torque terminals properly can result in excessive heating of terminals or splicing devices due to a loose connection. A loose connection can also lead to arcing which increases the heating effect and may also lead to a short circuit or ground fault. Any of these can result in a fire or other failure, including an arc flash event. Improper torqueing is also a violation of 110.3(B), which requires all equipment to be installed in accordance with listing or labeling instructions.

Note 1: Examples of approved means of achieving the indicated torque values include the use of torque tools or devices such as shear bolts or breakaway-style devices with visual indicators that demonstrate the proper torque has been applied.

Note 2: The equipment manufacturer can be contacted if numeric torque values are not indicated on the equipment, or if the installation instructions are not available. Annex I of UL Standard 486A-486B, *Standard for Safety-Wire Connectors,* provides torque values in the absence of manufacturer's recommendations.

Note 3: Additional information for torqueing threaded connections and terminations can be found in Section 8.11 of NFPA 70B, *Recommended Practice for Electrical Equipment Maintenance.*

110.15 High-Leg Conductor Identification

On a 4-wire, delta-connected, three-phase system (where the midpoint of one phase winding of the secondary is grounded) the conductor with the resulting 208V to ground (high-leg) must be durably and permanently marked by an outer finish (insulation) that is orange in color or other effective means. Such identification must be placed at each point where a connection is made if the neutral conductor is present [230.56]. ▶Figure 110–44

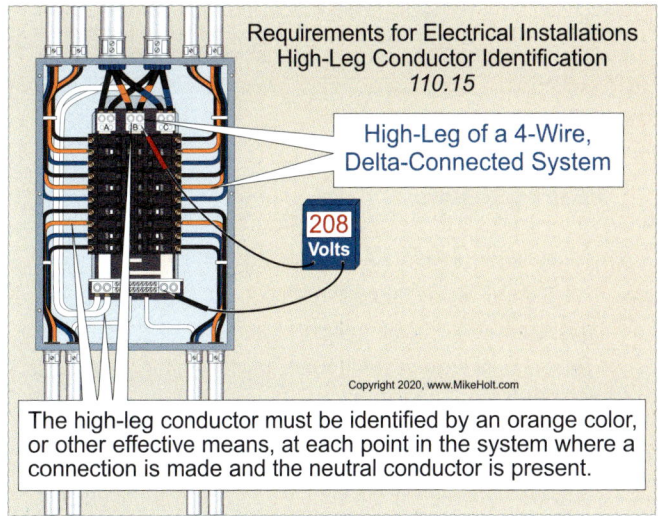

▶Figure 110–44

110.16 | Requirements for Electrical Installations

Author's Comment:

▸ The high-leg conductor is also called the "wild leg" or "stinger leg."

110.16 Arc Flash Hazard Warning

(A) Arc Flash Hazard Warning Label. In other than dwelling units, switchboards, switchgear, panelboards, industrial control panels, meter socket enclosures, and motor control centers must be marked to warn qualified persons of the danger associated with an arc flash resulting from a short circuit or ground fault. The arc flash hazard warning label must be permanently affixed, have sufficient durability to withstand the environment involved [110.21(B)], and be clearly visible to qualified persons before they examine, adjust, service, or perform maintenance on the equipment. ▸Figure 110–45

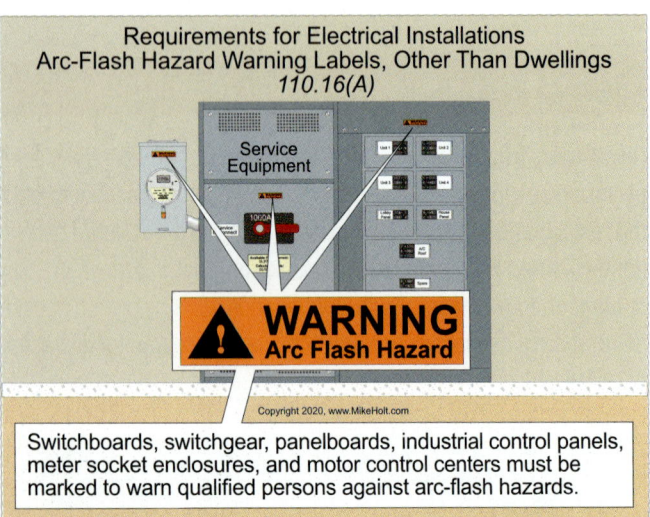

▸Figure 110–45

Author's Comment:

▸ According to Article 100, a "Qualified Person" is one who has the skill and knowledge related to the construction and operation of electrical equipment and its installation. This person must have received safety training to recognize and avoid the hazards involved with electrical systems.

▸ NFPA 70E, *Standard for Electrical Safety in the Workplace*, provides information on the safety training requirements expected of a "qualified person."

▸ Examples of this safety training include (but are not limited to) training in the use of special precautionary techniques, personal protective equipment (PPE), insulating and shielding materials, and in the use of insulated tools and test equipment when working on or near exposed conductors or circuit parts that can become energized.

▸ In many parts of the United States, electricians, electrical contractors, electrical inspectors, and electrical engineers must complete from 6 to 24 hours of *NEC* review each year as a requirement to maintain licensing. This does not necessarily make one qualified to deal with the specific hazards involved with electrical systems.

▸ This rule is intended to warn qualified persons who work on energized electrical systems that an arc flash hazard exists and to the level of danger present. They will then be able to select the necessary personal protective equipment (PPE) in accordance with industry accepted safe work practice standards. ▸Figure 110–46

▸Figure 110–46

(B) Service Disconnect. In addition to the requirements in 110.16(A), a service disconnect rated 1,200A or more must have a field or factory installed label containing the following details and have sufficient durability to withstand the environment: ▸Figure 110–47

(1) Nominal system voltage

(2) Available fault current at the line-side of the service overcurrent protective device

(3) Clearing time of the service overcurrent protective device

(4) Date the label was installed

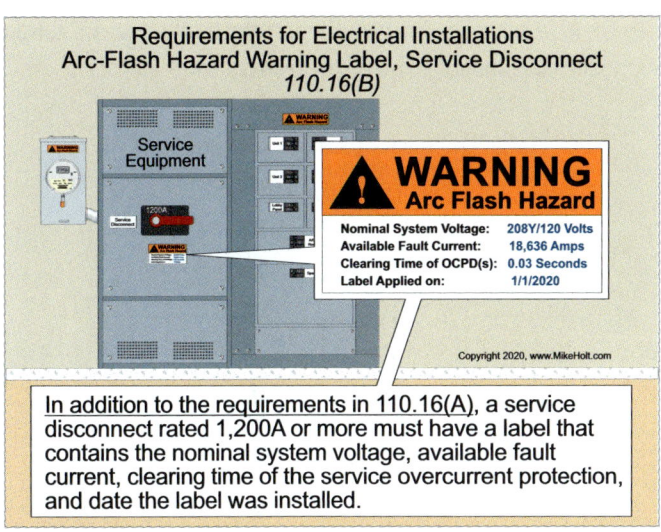

▶Figure 110-47

Author's Comment:

▸ Determining the available fault current on the line side of equipment terminals requires you to know the available fault current (provided by the electric utility), the conductor material, the length of the conductors, and the wiring method used to install the conductors. With this information, you can use an app or computer software to determine the available fault current at the line terminals.

Ex: Service disconnect fault current labeling is not required if an arc flash label in accordance with NFPA 70E, Standard for Electrical Safety in the Workplace, *is applied. See Note 3.* ▶Figure 110-48

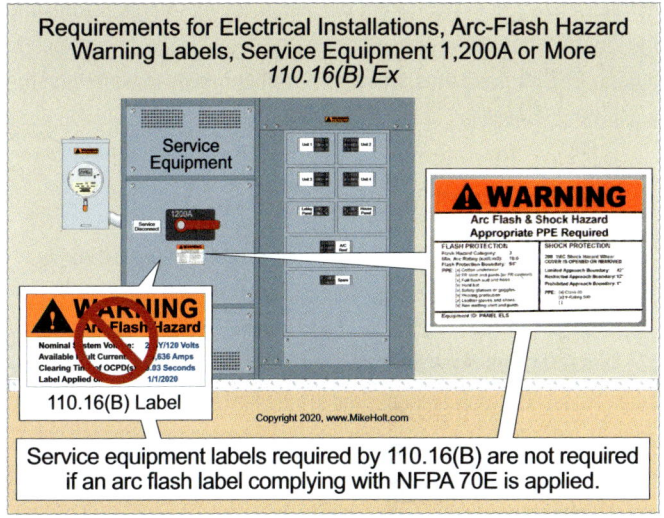

▶Figure 110-48

Note 1: NFPA 70E, *Standard for Electrical Safety in the Workplace,* provides guidance in determining the severity of potential exposure, planning safe work practices, arc flash labeling, and selecting personal protective equipment. ▶Figure 110-49

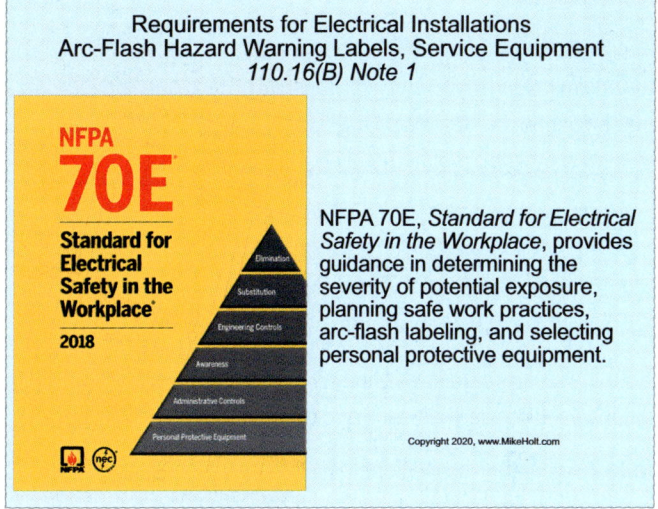

▶Figure 110-49

Note 3: NFPA 70E, *Standard for Electrical Safety in the Workplace* provides specific criteria for developing arc flash labels such as nominal system voltage, incident energy levels, arc flash boundaries, and selecting personal protective equipment.

Author's Comment:

▸ The information required by 110.16(B)(1), (2), and (3) is necessary in order to determine the incident energy and arc flash boundary distance by using of an app or computer software to ensure the label complies with NFPA 70E to increase safety during future work on service equipment.

110.21 Markings

(A) Equipment Markings

(1) General. The manufacturer's name, trademark, or other descriptive marking by which the organization responsible for the product can be identified must be placed on all electrical equipment. Other markings indicating voltage, current, wattage, or other ratings must be provided as specified elsewhere in this *Code*. The marking or label must be of sufficient durability to withstand the environment involved.

(2) Reconditioned Equipment

Reconditioned equipment must be marked with the name, trademark, or other descriptive marking by which the organization responsible for its reconditioning can be identified, along with the date of the reconditioning.

Reconditioned equipment must be identified as "reconditioned" and the original listing mark removed. Approval of the reconditioned equipment must not be based solely on the equipment's original listing.

Ex: In industrial occupancies, where conditions of maintenance and supervision ensure that only qualified persons service the equipment, the markings indicated in 110.21(A)(2) are not required for equipment that is reconditioned by the owner or operator as part of a regular equipment maintenance program.

Note 1: Industry standards are available for the application of reconditioned and refurbished equipment.

Note 2: The term "reconditioned" may be interchangeable with terms such as "rebuilt," "refurbished," or "remanufactured."

Note 3: The original listing mark may include the mark of the certifying body and not the entire equipment label.

(B) Field-Applied Hazard Markings. Where caution, warning, or danger labels are required, the labels must meet the following requirements:

(1) The markings must warn of the hazards using effective words, colors, symbols, or a combination of the three. ▶Figure 110–50

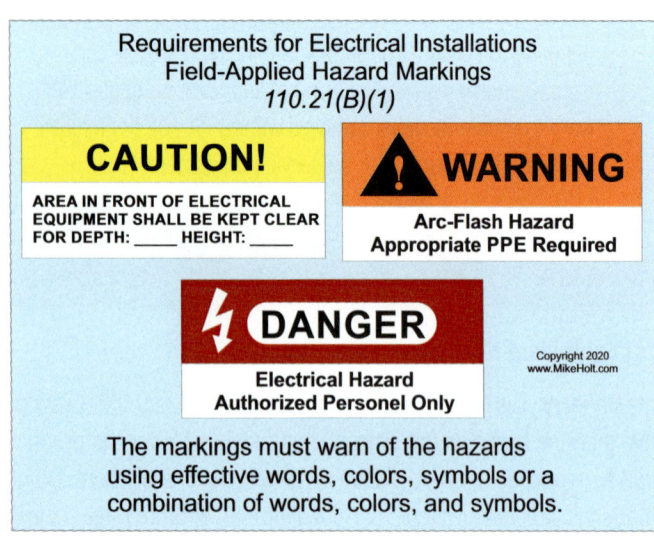

▶Figure 110–50

Note: ANSI Z535.4, *Product Safety Signs and Labels,* provides guidelines for the design and durability of signs and labels.

(2) The label cannot be handwritten and must be permanently affixed to the equipment. ▶Figure 110–51

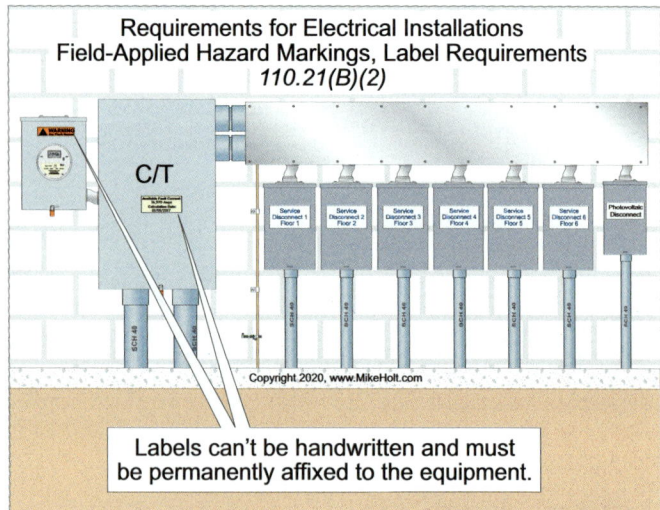

▶Figure 110–51

Ex: Labels containing information that is likely to change can be handwritten, if it is legible.

(3) The marking must be of sufficient durability to withstand the environment involved.

110.22 Identification of Disconnecting Means

(A) General. Each disconnect must be legibly marked to indicate its purpose unless located and arranged so the purpose is evident. In other than one- or two-family dwellings, the marking must include the identification of the circuit source that supplies the disconnecting means. The marking must be of sufficient durability to withstand the environment involved. ▶Figure 110–52

Author's Comment:

▸ See 408.4 for additional requirements for identification markings on circuit directories for switchboards and panelboards.

(C) Tested Series Combination Systems. Tested series-rated installations must be legibly field marked to indicate the equipment has been applied with a series combination rating in accordance with 240.86(B), be permanently affixed, and have sufficient durability to withstand the environment involved in accordance with 110.21(B) and state:

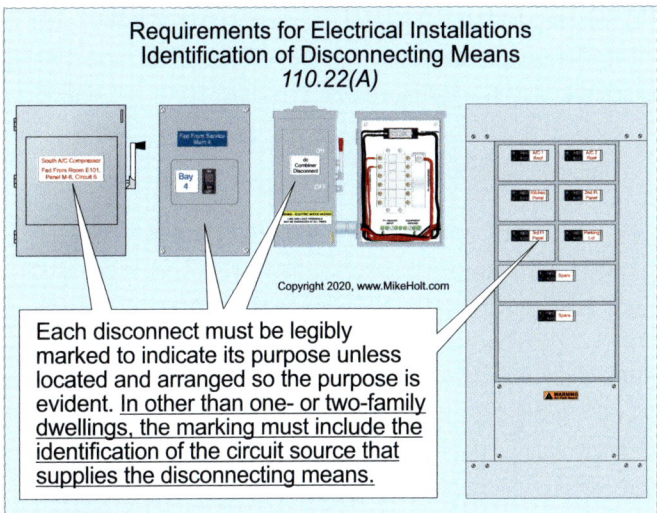
▶Figure 110-52

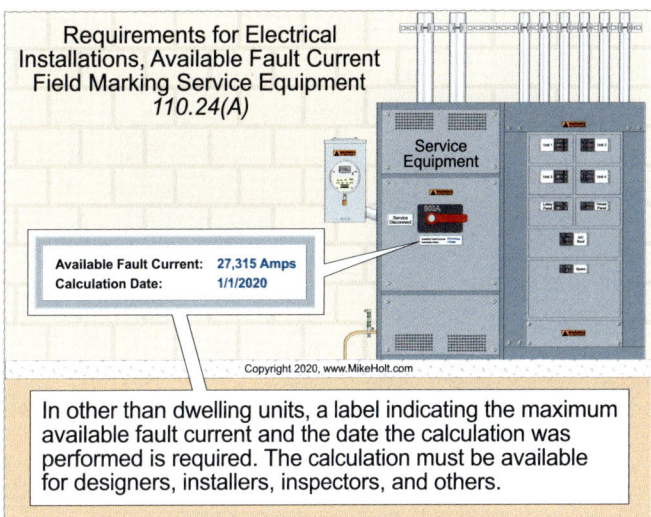
▶Figure 110-53

```
CAUTION—SERIES COMBINATION SYSTEM
RATED ____ AMPERES. IDENTIFIED REPLACEMENT
COMPONENTS REQUIRED
```

110.24 Available Fault Current

(A) Field Marking. In other than dwelling units, service disconnects must be field marked with the available fault current on the line side of the service disconnect, the date the fault current calculation was performed, and the marking must be of sufficient durability to withstand the environment present.

The available fault current calculation must be documented and available to those who are authorized to design, install, inspect, maintain, or operate the system. ▶Figure 110-53

Note 1: The available fault current markings required by this section are related to the short-circuit current and interrupting ratings of equipment required by 110.9 and 110.10. They are not intended to be used for arc flash analysis. Arc-flash hazard information is available in NFPA 70E, *Standard for Electrical Safety in the Workplace*.

Note 2: Values of available fault current for use in determining short-circuit current and interrupting ratings of service equipment are available from electric utilities in published or other forms.

(B) Modifications. When modifications to the electrical installation affect the available fault current at the service disconnect, the available fault current must be recalculated to ensure the short-circuit current ratings at the service disconnect is sufficient for the available fault current. The required field marking(s) in 110.24(A) must be adjusted to reflect the new level of available fault current.

Author's Comment:

▶ It is common for electrical systems to be modified to accommodate growth. When the capacity of the system increases, equipment is installed to increase efficiency or alternative energy systems are added to the existing installation. These factors can all influence the available fault current if the utility transformer is changed. This increase in available fault current could end up exceeding the short-circuit current ratings of equipment in violation of 110.9 and 110.10.

Ex: Field markings required in 110.24(A) and 110.24(B) are not required for industrial installations where conditions of maintenance and supervision ensure that only qualified persons service the equipment.

110.25 Lockable Disconnecting Means

If the *Code* requires a disconnect to be lockable in the open position, the provisions for locking must remain in place whether the lock is installed or not. ▶Figure 110-54

110.26 | Requirements for Electrical Installations

▶Figure 110–54

Part II. 1,000V, Nominal, or Less

110.26 Spaces About Electrical Equipment

For the purposes of safe operation and maintenance of equipment, access and working space must be provided around all electrical equipment. ▶Figure 110–55

▶Figure 110–55

Author's Comment:

▸ Spaces around electrical equipment (width, depth, and height) consist of working space for worker protection [110.26(A)] and dedicated space to provide access to, and protection of, equipment [110.26(E)].

(A) Working Space. Equipment that may need examination, adjustment, servicing, or maintenance while energized must have working space provided in accordance with 110.26(A)(1), (2), (3), and (4):

Author's Comment:

▸ The phrase "while energized" is the root of many debates. As always, check with the authority having jurisdiction to see what equipment he or she believes needs a clear working space.

Note: NFPA 70E, *Standard for Electrical Safety in the Workplace*, provides guidance in determining the severity of potential exposure, planning safe work practices including establishing an electrically safe work condition, arc flash labeling, and selecting personal protective equipment.

(1) Depth of Working Space. The depth of working space, which is measured from the enclosure front, cannot be less than the distances contained in Table 110.26(A)(1), which are dependent on voltage and three different conditions. ▶Figure 110–56

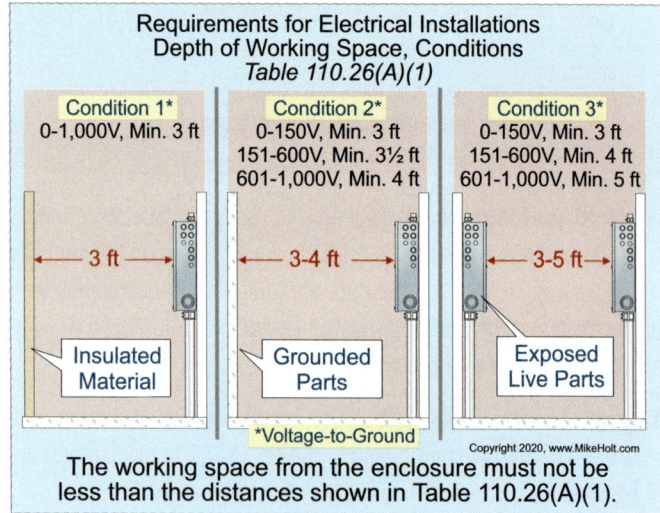

▶Figure 110–56

Author's Comment:

▸ Depth of working space must be measured from the enclosure front, not the live parts. ▶Figure 110–57

Requirements for Electrical Installations | 110.26

▶Figure 110-57

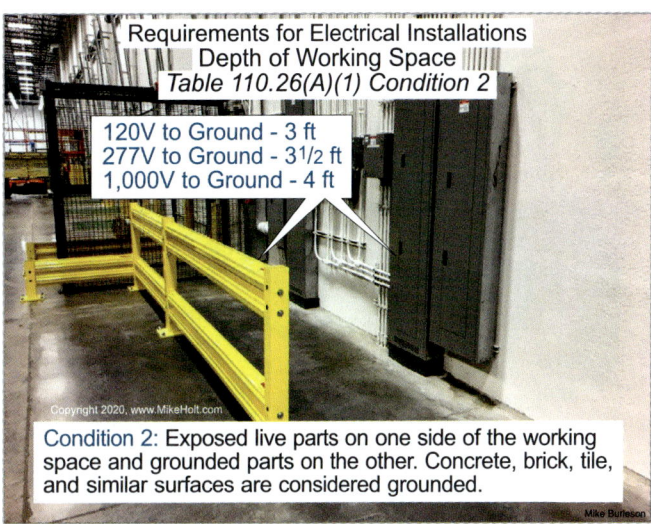
▶Figure 110-59

Table 110.26(A)(1) Working Space			
Voltage-to-Ground	Condition 1	Condition 2	Condition 3
0–150V	3 ft	3 ft	3 ft
151–600V	3 ft	3½ ft	4 ft
601–1,000V	3 ft	4 ft	5 ft

▶Figure 110-58, ▶Figure 110-59, and ▶Figure 110-60

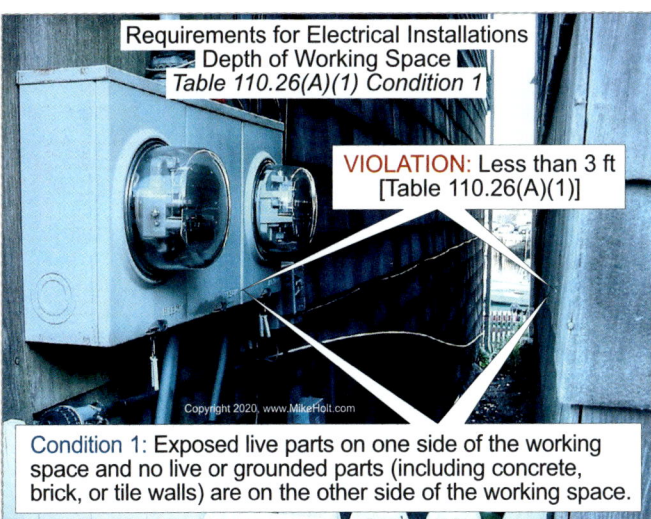
▶Figure 110-58

▶Figure 110-60

Author's Comment:

▸ If the working space is a platform, it must be sized to the working space requirements. ▶Figure 110-61

(a) Rear and Sides of Dead-Front Equipment. Working space is not required at the back or sides of equipment where all connections and all renewable, adjustable, or serviceable parts are accessible from the front. ▶Figure 110-62

Author's Comment:

▸ Sections of equipment that require rear or side access to make field connections must be marked by the manufacturer on the front of the equipment. See 408.18(C).

110.26 | Requirements for Electrical Installations

▶Figure 110–61

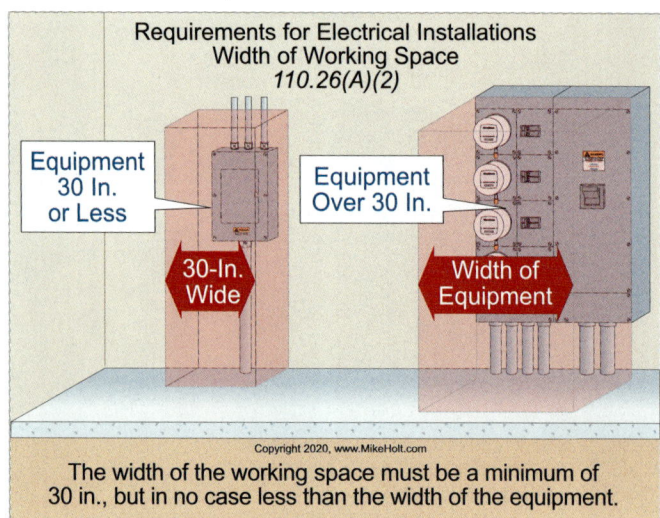
▶Figure 110–63

Author's Comment:

▸ The width of the working space can be measured from left-to-right, from right-to-left, or simply centered on the equipment and can overlap the working space for other electrical equipment. ▶Figure 110–64 and ▶Figure 110–65

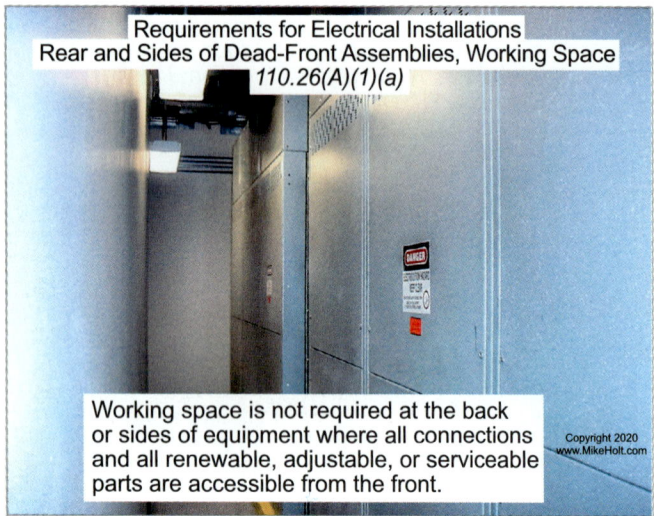
▶Figure 110–62

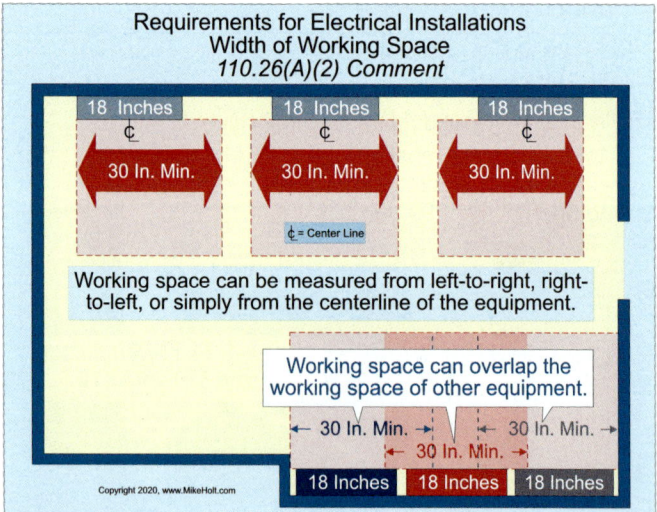
▶Figure 110–64

(c) Existing Buildings. If electrical equipment is being replaced, Condition 2 working space is permitted between dead-front switchboards, switchgear, panelboards, or motor control centers located across the aisle from each other where conditions of maintenance and supervision ensure that written procedures have been adopted to prohibit equipment on both sides of the aisle from being open at the same time, and only authorized, qualified persons will service the installation.

(2) Width of Working Space. The width of the working space must be a minimum of 30 in., but in no case less than the width of the equipment. ▶Figure 110–63

The working space must be of sufficient width, depth, and height to permit equipment doors to open at least 90 degrees. ▶Figure 110–66

(3) Height of Working Space. The height of the working space must be clear and extend from the grade, floor, or platform to a height of 6½ ft or the height of the equipment. ▶Figure 110–67

Requirements for Electrical Installations | 110.26

▶Figure 110-65

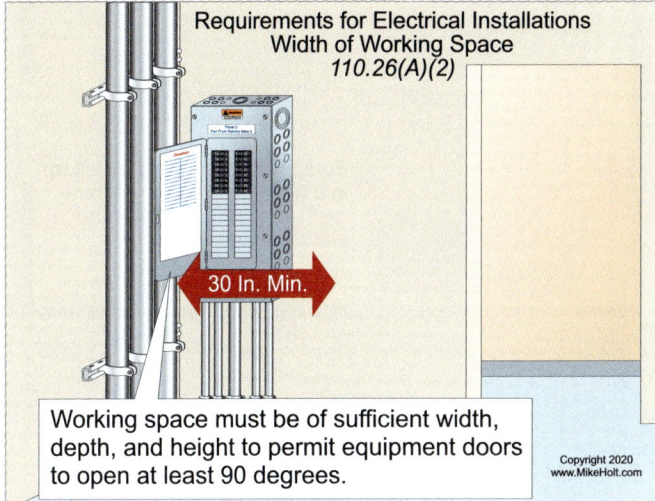

▶Figure 110-66

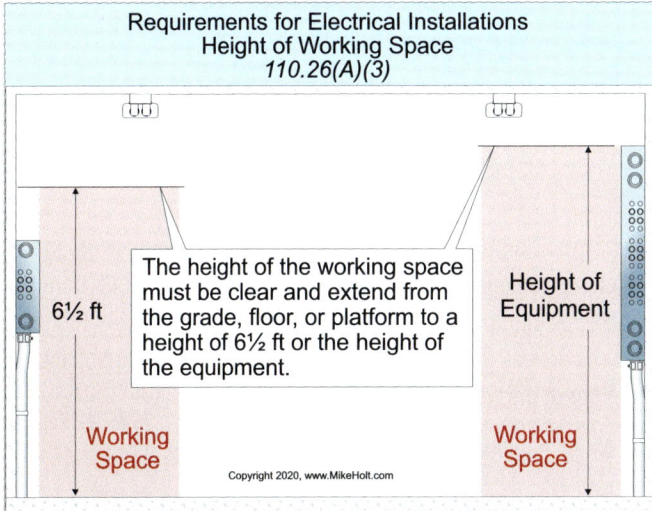

▶Figure 110-67

Electrical equipment such as raceways, cables, wireways, panelboards, or support structures (such as concrete pads) are permitted to extend not more than 6 in. beyond the front of the electrical equipment. ▶Figure 110-68 and ▶Figure 110-69

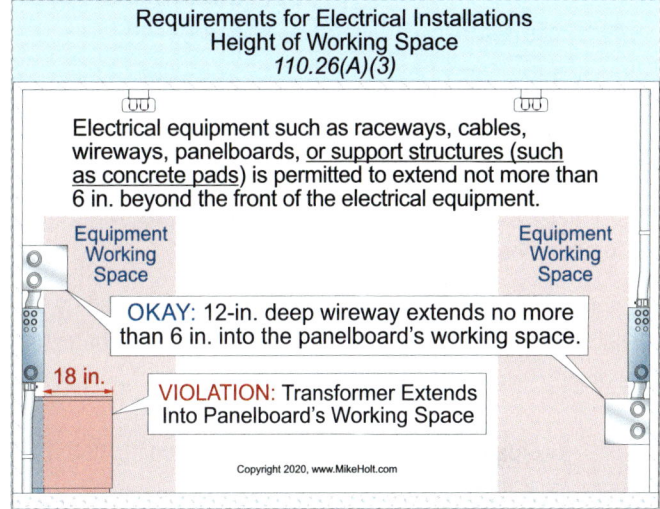

▶Figure 110-68

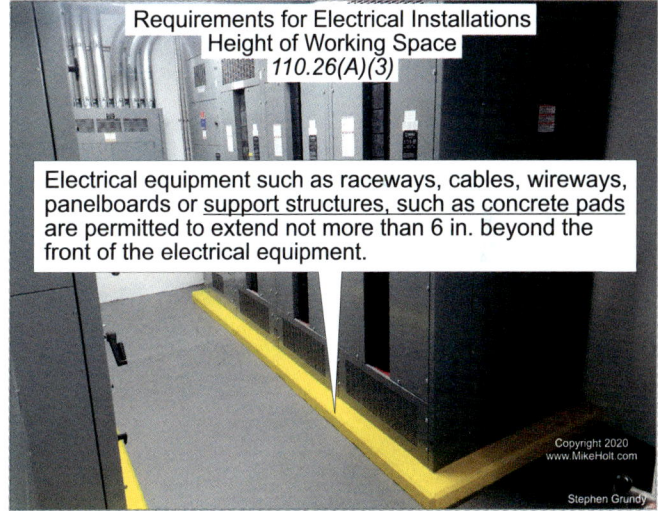

▶Figure 110-69

Ex 1: The minimum height of working space does not apply to a service disconnect or panelboards rated 200A or less located in an existing dwelling unit.

Ex 2: Meters are permitted in the working space.

(4) Limited Access. Where equipment is likely to require examination, adjustment, servicing, or maintenance while energized is located above a suspended ceiling or crawl space, all the following conditions apply:

(1) Equipment installed above a suspended ceiling must have an access opening not smaller than 22 in. × 22 in., and equipment installed in a crawl space must have an accessible opening not smaller than 22 in. × 30 in.

(2) The width of the working space must be a minimum of 30 in., but in no case less than the width of the equipment.

(3) The working space must permit equipment doors to open 90 degrees.

(4) The working space in front of equipment must comply with the depth requirements of Table 110.26(A)(1). Horizontal ceiling structural members are permitted in this space.

(B) Clear Working Space. The working space required by this section must always be clear; therefore, this space is not permitted for storage. ▶Figure 110-70

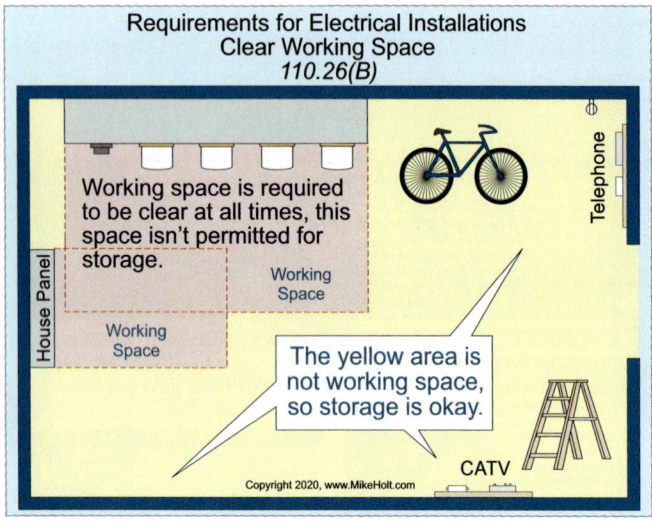

▶Figure 110-70

Caution

It is very dangerous to service energized parts in the first place, and unacceptable to be subjected to additional dangers by working around bicycles, boxes, crates, appliances, and other impediments.

When live parts are exposed for inspection or servicing, the working space (if in a passageway or open space) must be suitably guarded.

Author's Comment:

▸ When working in a passageway, the working space should be guarded from use by occupants. When working on electrical equipment in a passageway one must be mindful of a fire alarm. If one occurs, many people will need to be evacuated and will be congregating and moving through the area.

▸ Signaling and communications equipment are not permitted to be installed in a manner that encroaches on the working space of the electrical equipment. ▶Figure 110-71

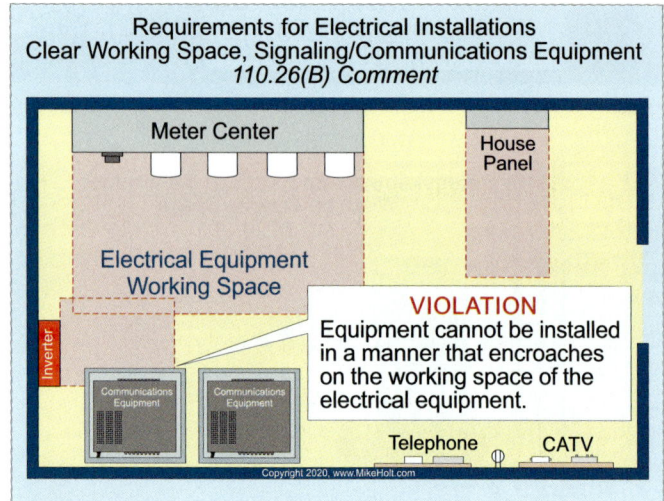

▶Figure 110-71

(C) Access to and Egress from Working Space

(1) Minimum Required. At least one entrance large enough to give access to and egress from the working space must be provided.

Author's Comment:

▸ Check to see what the authority having jurisdiction considers "large enough." Building *codes* contain minimum dimensions for doors and openings for personnel travel.

(2) Large Equipment. For large equipment containing overcurrent, switching, or control devices, an entrance to and egress from the required working space not less than 24 in. wide and 6½ ft high is required at each end of the working space. This requirement applies for either of the following conditions:

(1) Where equipment is over 6 ft wide rated 1,200A or more ▶Figure 110-72

Requirements for Electrical Installations | 110.26

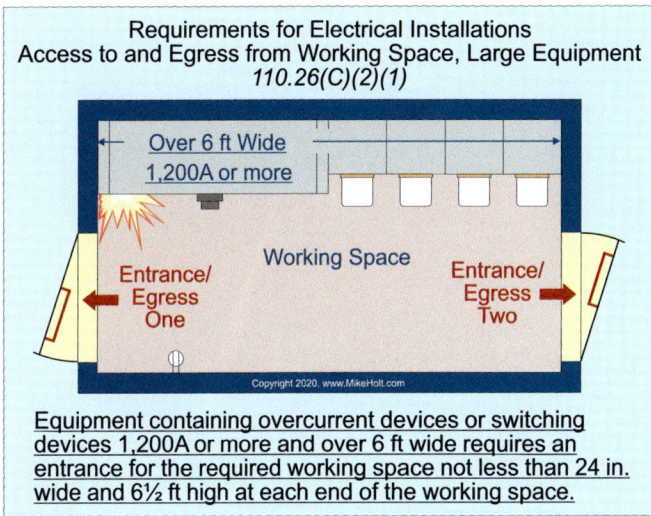
▶Figure 110-72

(2) Where the service disconnecting means installed in accordance with 230.71 has a combined rating of 1,200A or more and is over 6 ft wide ▶Figure 110-73

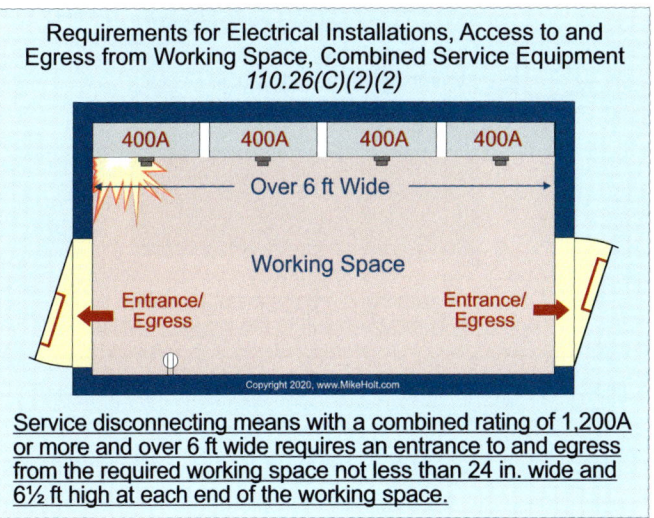
▶Figure 110-73

Open equipment doors must not impede the entry to or egress from the working space.

A single entrance for access to and egress from the required working space is permitted where either of the following conditions are met:

(a) **Unobstructed Egress.** Where the location permits a continuous and unobstructed way of egress travel. ▶Figure 110-74

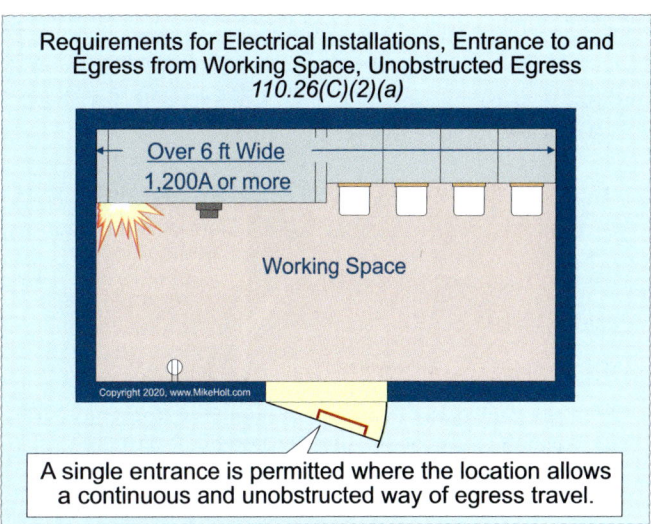
▶Figure 110-74

(b) **Double Working Space.** Where the required working space depth is doubled and the equipment is located so the edge of the entrance is no closer than the required working space distance. ▶Figure 110-75

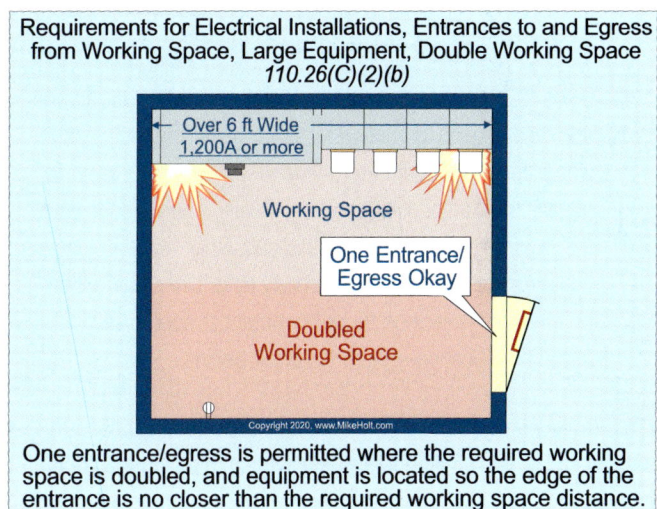
▶Figure 110-75

(3) **Fire Exit Hardware on Personnel Doors.** Where equipment rated 800A or more contains overcurrent, switching, or control devices is installed and there is a personnel door(s) intended for entrance to and egress from the working space less than 25 ft from the nearest edge of the working space, the door(s) are required to open in the direction of egress and be equipped with listed panic or listed fire exit hardware. ▶Figure 110-76

110.26 | Requirements for Electrical Installations

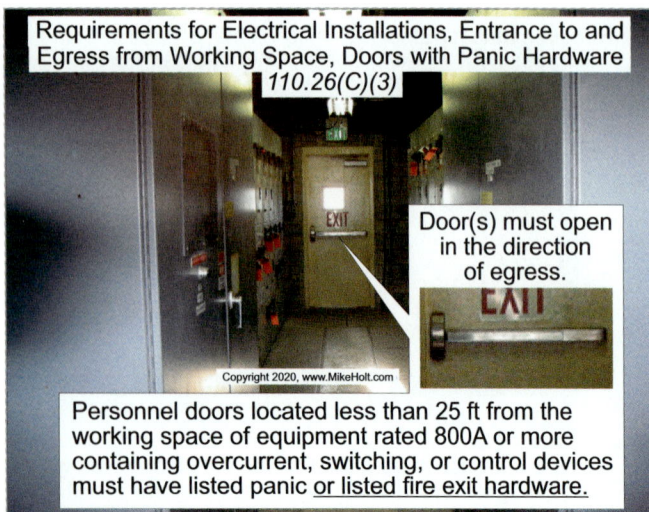
▶Figure 110–76

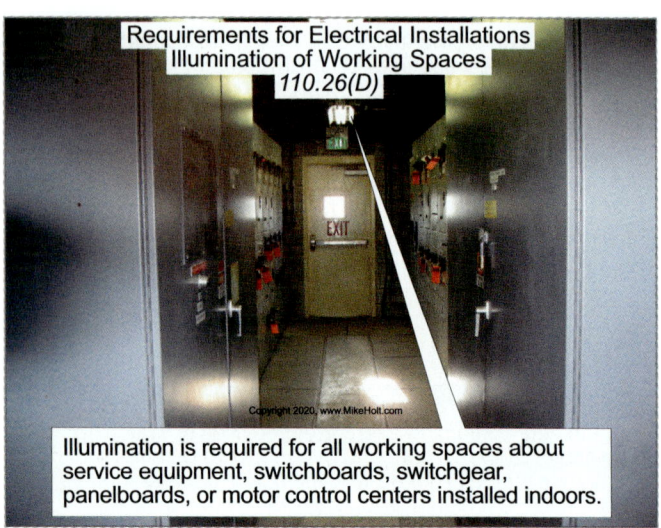
▶Figure 110–77

Author's Comment:

▸ History has shown that electricians who suffer burns on their hands in electrical arc flash or arc blast events often cannot open doors equipped with knobs that must be turned or doors that must be pulled open.

▸ Since this requirement is in the *NEC*, electrical contractors are responsible for ensuring panic hardware is installed where required. Some are offended at being held liable for nonelectrical responsibilities, but this rule is designed to save the lives of electricians. For this and other reasons, many construction professionals routinely hold "pre-construction" or "pre-con" meetings to review potential opportunities for miscommunication—before the work begins.

(D) Illumination. Illumination is required for all working spaces about service equipment, switchboards, switchgear, panelboards, or motor control centers installed indoors. Control by automatic means is not permitted to control all illumination within the working space. ▶Figure 110–77 and ▶Figure 110–78

Additional lighting outlets are not required where the working space is illuminated by an adjacent light source, or as permitted by 210.70(A)(1) Ex 1 for switched receptacles.

Author's Comment:

▸ The *Code* does not identify the minimum foot-candles required to provide proper illumination even though it is essential in electrical equipment rooms for the safety of those qualified to work on such equipment.

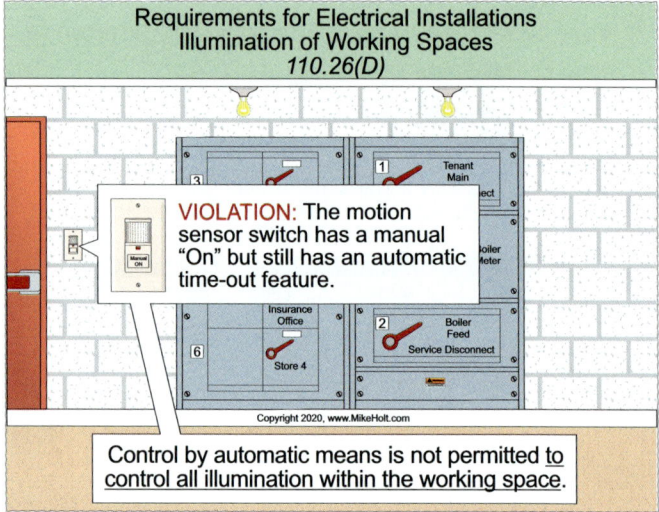
▶Figure 110–78

(E) Dedicated Electrical Equipment Space. Switchboards and panelboards must have dedicated equipment space and be protected from damage that could result from condensation, leaks, breaks in the foreign systems, and vehicular traffic as follows:

(1) Indoors. Switchboards and panelboards installed indoors must comply with the following:

(a) Equipment Space. The footprint space (width and depth of the equipment) extending from the floor to a height of 6 ft above the equipment or to the structural ceiling, whichever is lower, must be dedicated for electrical equipment. ▶Figure 110–79

No piping, ducts, or other equipment foreign to the electrical system can be installed in this dedicated electrical equipment space. ▶Figure 110–80

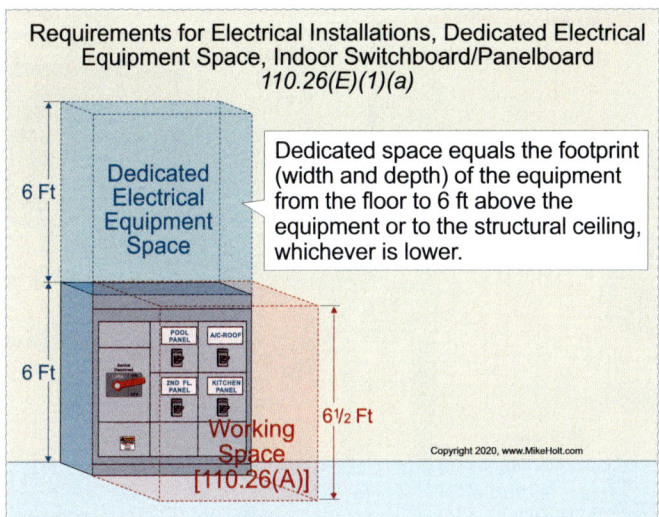
▶Figure 110-79

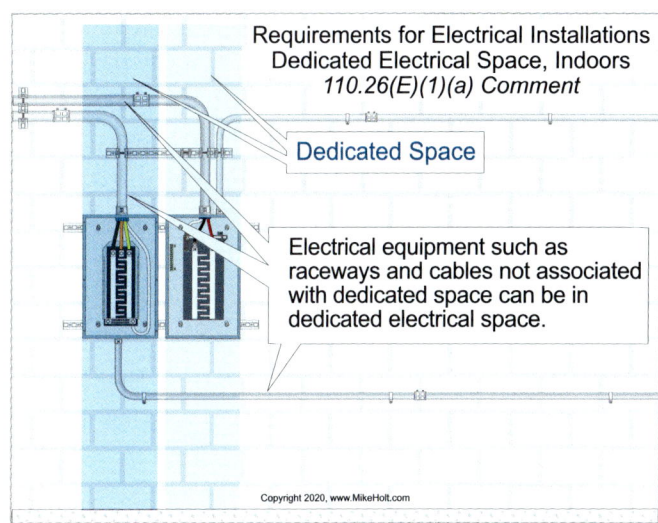
▶Figure 110-81

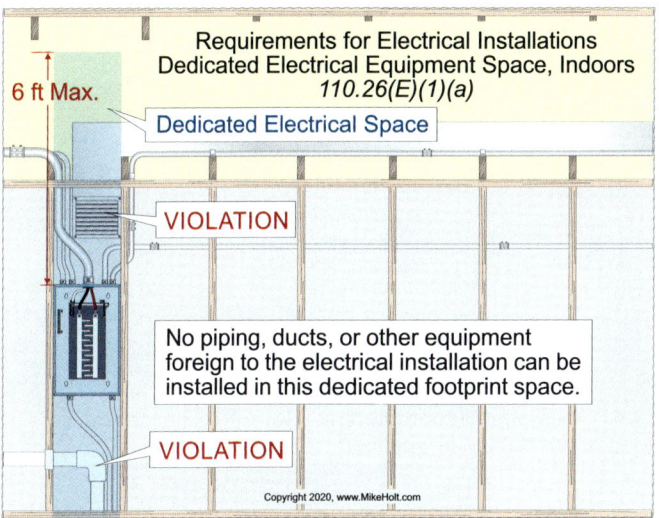
▶Figure 110-80

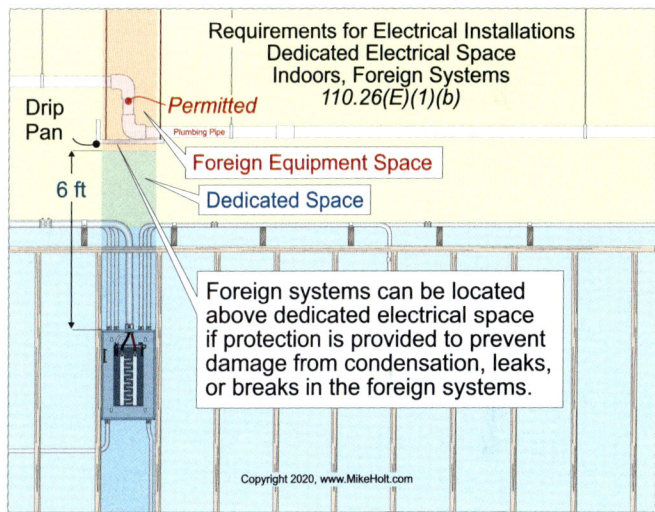
▶Figure 110-82

Author's Comment:

▸ Electrical equipment such as raceways and cables not associated with dedicated space can be in dedicated space. ▶Figure 110-81

Ex: Suspended ceilings with removable panels can be within the dedicated space [110.26(E)(1)(d)].

(b) Foreign Systems. Foreign systems can be located above the dedicated space if protection is installed to prevent damage to the electrical equipment from condensation, leaks, or breaks in the foreign systems. Such protection can be as simple as a drip-pan. ▶Figure 110-82

(c) Sprinkler Protection. Sprinkler protection piping is not permitted in the dedicated space, but the *NEC* does not prohibit sprinklers from spraying water on electrical equipment.

(d) Suspended Ceilings. A dropped, suspended, or similar ceiling is not considered a structural ceiling. ▶Figure 110-83

(2) Outdoor. Outdoor installations for switchboards and panelboard must comply with the following:

(a) Installation Requirements.

(1) Installed in identified enclosures

(2) Protected from accidental contact by unauthorized personnel or by vehicular traffic ▶Figure 110-84

110.28 | Requirements for Electrical Installations

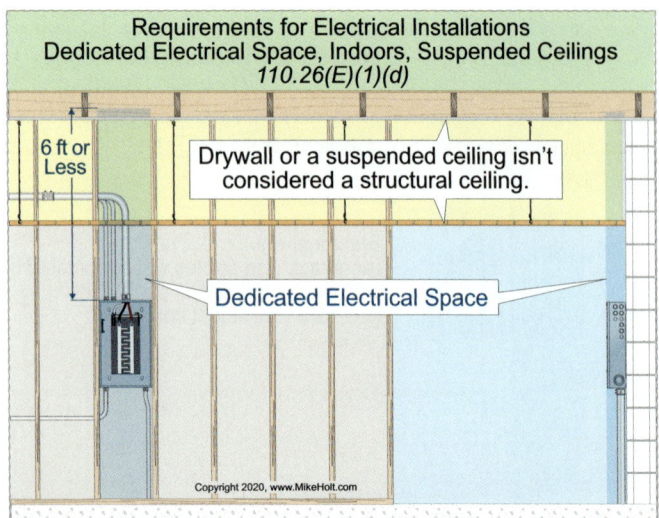
▶Figure 110–83

▶Figure 110–85

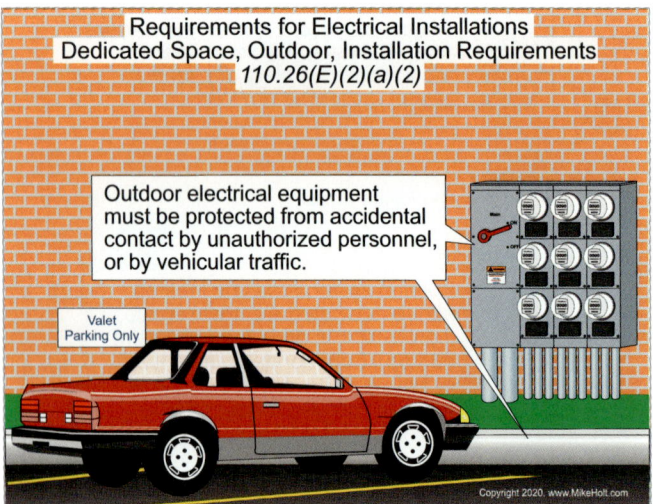
▶Figure 110–84

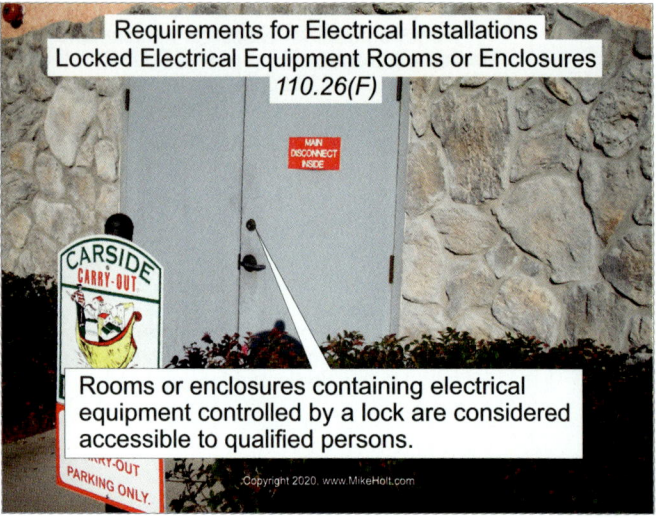
▶Figure 110–86

(3) Protected from accidental spillage or leakage from piping systems

(b) Working Space. The working clearance space includes the zone described in 110.26(A). Architectural appurtenances or other equipment are not permitted within this zone.

(c) Dedicated Equipment Space Outdoors. The footprint space (width and depth of the equipment) of the outdoor dedicated space extending from grade to a height of 6 ft above the equipment must be dedicated for electrical installations. No piping, ducts, or other equipment foreign to the electrical installation can be installed in this dedicated space. ▶Figure 110–85

(F) Locked Electrical Equipment Rooms or Enclosures. Rooms or enclosures containing electrical equipment controlled by a lock are considered accessible to qualified persons. ▶Figure 110–86

110.28 Enclosure Types

Enclosures must be marked with an enclosure-type number and be suitable for the location in accordance with Table 110.28. They are not intended to protect against condensation, icing, corrosion, or contamination that might occur within the enclosure or that enters via a raceway or unsealed openings. ▶Figure 110–87

Note 1: Raintight enclosures include Types 3, 3S, 3SX, 3X, 4, 4X, 6, and 6P; rainproof enclosures are Types 3R and 3RX; watertight enclosures are Types 4, 4X, 6, and 6P; driptight enclosures are Types 2, 5, 12, 12K, and 13; and dusttight enclosures are Types 3, 3S, 3SX, 3X, 5, 12, 12K, and 13.

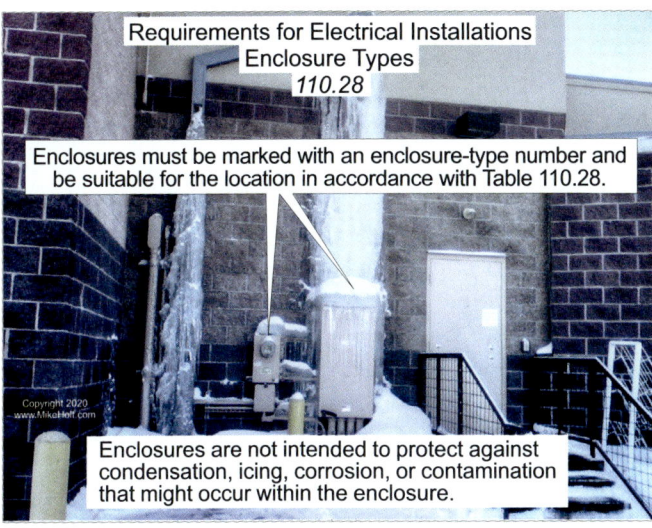
▶Figure 110–87

Note 3: Dusttight enclosures are suitable for use in hazardous locations in accordance with 502.10(B)(4), 503.10(A)(2), and 506.15(C)(9).

Note 4: Dusttight enclosures are suitable for use in unclassified locations and in Class II, Division 2; Class III; and Zone 22 hazardous (classified) locations.

Notes

CHAPTER 1

PRACTICE QUESTIONS

Please use the 2020 *Code* book to answer the following questions.

CHAPTER 1—GENERAL RULES

Article 100—Definitions

1. Part III of Article 100 contains definitions which are applicable to _____.

    (a) Solar (PV) Systems
    (b) Hazardous (Classified) Locations
    (c) Electrical Systems Over 1,000V
    (d) Healthcare Facilities

2. By definition, an attachment fitting is different from an attachment plug because no _____ is associated with the fitting.

    (a) cable
    (b) fixture wire
    (c) cord
    (d) wiring compartment

3. A battery system includes storage batteries and battery chargers, and can include inverters, converters, and associated electrical equipment.

    (a) True
    (b) False

4. A branch circuit that supplies only one utilization equipment is a(an) _____ branch circuit.

    (a) individual
    (b) general-purpose
    (c) isolated
    (d) special-purpose

5. A multiwire branch circuit consists of _____.

    (a) two or more ungrounded conductors that have a voltage between them
    (b) a grounded conductor that has equal voltage between it and each ungrounded conductor of the circuit
    (c) a grounded conductor connected to the neutral or grounded conductor of the system
    (d) all of these

6. Composite optical fiber cables contain optical fibers and _____.

    (a) strength members
    (b) vapor barriers
    (c) current-carrying electrical conductors
    (d) recycled plastic

7. Due to its power limitations, a Class 2 circuit considers safety from a fire initiation standpoint and provides acceptable protection from electric shock.

    (a) True
    (b) False

8. The _____ of any system is the ratio of the maximum demand of a system, or part of a system, to the total connected load of a system.

    (a) load
    (b) demand factor
    (c) minimum load
    (d) calculated factor

Article 100 | Practice Questions

9. Systems of illumination utilizing fluorescent lamps, high-intensity discharge (HID) lamps, or neon tubing are all types of _____ lighting.

   (a) area
   (b) flood
   (c) security
   (d) electric discharge

10. An effective ground-fault current path is an intentionally constructed, low-impedance electrically conductive path designed and intended to carry current during a ground-fault condition from the point of a ground fault on a wiring system to _____.

    (a) ground
    (b) earth
    (c) the electrical supply source
    (d) the grounding electrode

11. Surrounded by a case, housing, fence, or wall(s) that prevents persons from accidentally contacting energized parts is called "_____."

    (a) guarded
    (b) covered
    (c) protection
    (d) enclosed

12. Equipment or materials to which has been attached a(an) _____ of an FEB indicating the equipment or materials were evaluated and found to comply with requirements as described in an accompanying field evaluation report is known as "field labeled (as applied to evaluated products)."

    (a) symbol
    (b) label
    (c) other identifying mark
    (d) any of these

13. "Generating capacity, inverter" is defined as the sum of parallel-connected inverter maximum continuous output power at 40°C in _____.

    (a) amperes or kVA
    (b) volts or kV
    (c) watts or kW
    (d) a 24-hour period

14. Examples of ground-fault current paths include any combination of conductive materials including _____.

    (a) equipment grounding conductors
    (b) metallic raceways
    (c) metal water and gas piping
    (d) all of these

15. Connected (connecting) to ground or to a conductive body that extends the ground connection is called "_____."

    (a) equipment grounding
    (b) bonded
    (c) grounded
    (d) all of these

16. The installed conductive path(s) that is part of a ground-fault current path and connects normally noncurrent-carrying metal parts of equipment together and to the system grounded conductor or to the grounding electrode conductor, or both, is known as a(an) "_____ conductor."

    (a) grounding electrode
    (b) grounding
    (c) equipment grounding
    (d) neutral

17. A conducting object through which a direct connection to earth is established is a "_____."

    (a) bonding conductor
    (b) grounding conductor
    (c) grounding electrode
    (d) grounded conductor

18. A conductor used to connect the system grounded conductor, or the equipment to a grounding electrode or to a point on the grounding electrode system, is called the "_____ conductor."

    (a) main grounding
    (b) common main
    (c) equipment grounding
    (d) grounding electrode

19. A "_____" is an accommodation that combines living, sleeping, sanitary, and storage facilities within a compartment.

    (a) guest room
    (b) guest suite
    (c) dwelling unit
    (d) single-family dwelling

20. A hoistway is any _____ in which an elevator or dumbwaiter is designed to operate.
    (a) hatchway or well hole
    (b) vertical opening or space
    (c) shaftway
    (d) all of these

21. A hybrid system is comprised of multiple power sources, such as _____, but not the utility power system.
    (a) photovoltaic
    (b) wind
    (c) micro-hydro generators
    (d) all of these

22. Information technology equipment and systems are used for creation and manipulation of _____.
    (a) data
    (b) voice
    (c) video
    (d) all of these

23. "Within sight from" means visible and not more than _____ ft distant from the equipment.
    (a) 10
    (b) 20
    (c) 25
    (d) 50

24. The conductors connected to the direct-current input of an inverter for PV systems form the "_____."
    (a) branch circuit
    (b) feeder
    (c) inverter input circuit
    (d) inverter output circuit

25. The term "Luminaire" means a single individual lampholder by itself.
    (a) True
    (b) False

26. A wire that is run along with or integral with a cable or conductor to provide mechanical support for the cable or conductor is a "_____."
    (a) tension wire
    (b) messenger or messenger wire
    (c) guy wire
    (d) strain relief wire

27. "Nonautomatic" is defined as requiring _____ to perform a function.
    (a) protection from damage
    (b) human intervention
    (c) mechanical linkage
    (d) all of these

28. An overload is the same as a short circuit or ground fault.
    (a) True
    (b) False

29. NFPA 70E, *Standard for Electrical Safety in the Workplace*, provides information to help determine the electrical safety training requirements expected of a qualified person.
    (a) True
    (b) False

30. Any electrical circuit that controls any other circuit through a relay or an equivalent device is called a "_____."
    (a) primary circuit
    (b) remote-control circuit
    (c) signal circuit
    (d) controller

31. A "service drop" is defined as the overhead conductors between the utility electric supply system and the _____.
    (a) service equipment
    (b) service point
    (c) grounding electrode
    (d) equipment grounding conductor

32. The "_____" is the necessary equipment, usually consisting of a circuit breaker(s) or switch(es) and fuse(s) and their accessories, connected to the load end of service conductors, and intended to constitute the main control and cutoff of the supply.
    (a) service equipment
    (b) service
    (c) service disconnect
    (d) service overcurrent device

33. The underground conductors between the utility electric supply system and the service point are known as the "_____."
    (a) utility service
    (b) service lateral
    (c) service drop
    (d) main service conductors

34. A permanently connected surge-protective device (SPD) intended for installation on the load side of the service disconnect overcurrent device, including SPDs located at the branch panel, is a "Type _____ SPD."

    (a) 1
    (b) 2
    (c) 3
    (d) 4

Article 110—Requirements for Electrical Installations

1. In judging equipment for approval, considerations such as _____ shall be evaluated.

    (a) mechanical strength
    (b) wire-bending space
    (c) arcing effects
    (d) all of these

2. Listed or labeled equipment shall be installed and used in accordance with any instructions included in the listing or labeling.

    (a) True
    (b) False

3. All _____ shall be covered with an insulation equivalent to that of the conductors or with an identified insulating device.

    (a) splices
    (b) joints
    (c) free ends of conductors
    (d) all of these

4. Separately installed pressure connectors shall be used with conductors at the _____ not exceeding the ampacity at the listed and identified temperature rating of the connector.

    (a) voltages
    (b) temperatures
    (c) listings
    (d) ampacities

5. NFPA 70E, *Standard for Electrical Safety in the Workplace*, provides guidance, such as determining severity of potential exposure, planning safe work practices, arc-flash labeling, and selecting _____.

    (a) personal protective equipment
    (b) coordinated overcurrent protective devices
    (c) emergency egress plans
    (d) fire suppression systems

6. As applied to electrical equipment, the term "reconditioned" may be interchangeable with the term(s) "_____."

    (a) rebuilt
    (b) refurbished
    (c) remanufactured
    (d) any of these

7. Each disconnecting means shall be legibly marked to indicate its purpose unless located and arranged so _____.

    (a) it can be locked out and tagged
    (b) it is not readily accessible
    (c) the purpose is evident
    (d) it operates at less than 300 volts-to-ground

8. The *NEC* requires tested series-rated installations of circuit breakers or fuses to be legibly marked in the field to indicate the equipment has been applied with a series combination rating.

    (a) True
    (b) False

9. _____ at other than dwelling units shall be legibly field marked with the maximum available fault current, include the date the fault-current calculation was performed, and be of sufficient durability to withstand the environment involved.

    (a) Service equipment
    (b) Sub panels
    (c) Motor control centers
    (d) all of these

10. The required working space for access to live parts of equipment operating at 300 volts-to-ground, where there are exposed live parts on one side and grounded parts on the other side, is _____ ft.

    (a) 3
    (b) 3½
    (c) 4
    (d) 4½

11. The minimum working space on a circuit for equipment operating at 750 volts-to-ground, with exposed live parts on one side and grounded parts on the other side of the working space, is _____ ft.

    (a) 1
    (b) 3
    (c) 4
    (d) 6

12. The minimum height of working spaces about electrical equipment, switchboards, panelboards, or motor control centers operating at 1,000V, nominal, or less and likely to require examination, adjustment, servicing, or maintenance while energized shall be 6½ ft or the height of the equipment, whichever is greater, except for service equipment or panelboards in existing dwelling units that do not exceed 200A.

    (a) True
    (b) False

13. Working space shall not be used for _____.

    (a) storage
    (b) raceways
    (c) lighting
    (d) accessibility

14. For large equipment that contains service disconnecting means installed in accordance with 230.71 where the combined ampere rating is _____ or more and over 6 ft wide, there shall be one entrance to and egress from the required working space not less than 24 in. wide and 6½ ft high at each end of the working space

    (a) 800A
    (b) 1,000A
    (c) 1,200A
    (d) 2,000A

15. All switchboards, switchgear, panelboards, and motor control centers shall be located in dedicated spaces and protected from damage and the working clearance space for outdoor installations shall include the zone described in _____.

    (a) 110.26(A)
    (b) 110.26(B)
    (c) 110.26(C)
    (d) 110.26(D)

16. Electrical equipment rooms or enclosures housing electrical apparatus that are controlled by a lock(s) shall be considered _____ to qualified persons.

    (a) readily accessible
    (b) accessible
    (c) available
    (d) secured

Notes

CHAPTER 5
SPECIAL OCCUPANCIES

Introduction to Chapter 5—Special Occupancies

Chapter 5, which covers special occupancies, is the first of four *NEC* chapters that deal with special topics. Chapters 6 and 7 cover special equipment and special conditions, respectively. Chapter 8 covers communications systems, twisted pair and coaxial cable.

Remember, the first four chapters of the *Code* are sequential and form a foundation for each of the subsequent three which may (at times) modify or reference those foundational rules. Chapter 8 is not subject to the requirements of Chapters 1 through 7 except where the requirements are specifically referenced in Chapter 8 [90.3].

What exactly is a "Special Occupancy"? It is a location where a facility, or its use, creates specific conditions that require additional measures to ensure the "practical safeguarding of people and property," which is the purpose of the *NEC* as put forth in Article 90.

Many people struggle to understand the requirements for special occupancies (especially hazardous locations), mostly because of the narrowness of application. If you study the illustrations and explanations here, you will better understand them.

- **Article 500—Hazardous (Classified) Locations.** Article 500 contains general requirements applicable to all hazardous (classified) locations. A hazardous (classified) location is an area where the possibility of fire or explosion exists due to the presence of flammable or combustible liquid-produced vapors, flammable gases, combustible dusts, or easily ignitable fibers/flyings.

- **Article 501—Class I Hazardous (Classified) Locations.** A Class I hazardous (classified) location is an area where flammable or combustible liquid-produced vapors or flammable gases may present the hazard of a fire or explosion.

- **Article 502—Class II Hazardous (Classified) Locations.** A Class II hazardous (classified) location is an area where the possibility of fire or explosion may exist due to the presence of combustible dust.

- **Article 503—Class III Hazardous (Classified) Locations.** Class III hazardous (classified) locations are hazardous because fire or explosion risks may exist due to easily ignitible fibers/flyings. These include textile mills and clothing manufacturing plants which may produce fibers from materials such as cotton and rayon which are found in textile mills and clothing manufacturing plants. They can also include establishments and industries such as sawmills and woodworking plants.

- **Article 511—Commercial Garages, Repair and Storage.** These occupancies include locations used for service and repair operations in connection with self-propelled vehicles including (but not limited to) passenger automobiles, buses, trucks, and tractors in which flammable liquids or flammable gases are used for fuel or power.

- **Article 514—Motor Fuel Dispensing Facilities.** Article 514 covers gasoline dispensing and service stations where gasoline or other volatile liquids are transferred to the fuel tanks of self-propelled vehicles. Wiring and equipment in the area of service and repair rooms of service stations must comply with the installation requirements in Article 511.

...

Chapter 5 | Special Occupancies

▶ **Article 517—Health Care Facilities.** This article applies to electrical wiring in human health care facilities such as hospitals, nursing homes, limited care facilities, clinics, medical and dental offices, and ambulatory care—whether permanent or movable. It does not apply to animal veterinary facilities.

▶ **Article 518—Assembly Occupancies.** Article 518 covers buildings or portions of buildings specifically designed or intended for the assembly of 100 or more persons.

▶ **Article 525—Carnivals, Circuses, Fairs, and Similar Events.** This article covers the installation of portable wiring and equipment for temporary carnivals, circuses, exhibitions, fairs, traveling attractions, and similar functions including wiring in or on structures.

▶ **Article 547—Agricultural Buildings.** Article 547 covers agricultural buildings or those parts of buildings or adjacent areas where excessive dust or dust with water may accumulate, or where a corrosive atmosphere exists.

▶ **Article 550—Mobile Homes, Manufactured Homes, and Mobile Home Parks.** Article 550 covers electrical conductors and equipment within or on mobile and manufactured homes, conductors that connect mobile and manufactured homes to the electrical supply, and the installation of electrical wiring, luminaires, and electrical equipment in or on mobile and manufactured homes.

▶ **Article 555—Marinas, Boatyards, and Commercial and Noncommercial Docking Facilities.** This article covers the installation of wiring and equipment in the areas that comprise fixed or floating piers, wharves, docks, and other areas in marinas, boatyards, boat basins, boathouses, and similar locations used (or intended to be used) for the repair, berthing, launching, storing, or fueling of small craft and the mooring of floating buildings.

▶ **Article 590—Temporary Installations.** Article 590 covers temporary power and lighting for construction, remodeling, maintenance, repair, demolitions, and decorative lighting.

ARTICLE 500 — HAZARDOUS (CLASSIFIED) LOCATIONS

Introduction to Article 500—Hazardous (Classified) Locations

A hazardous (classified) location is an area where the possibility of fire or explosion can be created by the presence of flammable or combustible vapors, or flammable gasses, combustible dusts, or easily ignitable fibers/flyings. Electric arcs, sparks, and/or heated surfaces can serve as a source of ignition in such environments.

Article 500 provides the foundation for applying Article 501 (Class I Locations), Article 502 (Class II Locations), and Article 503 (Class III Locations). This article also provides a foundation for using Articles 510 through 516.

Before you apply any of the articles just mentioned you must understand and use Article 500, which is fairly long and detailed. You will notice when studying this article that there are many Informational Notes which you should review. Although Informational Notes are not *NEC* requirements [90.5(C)], they contain information that helps *Code* users better understand the related *NEC* rules.

A Fire Triangle (fuel, oxygen, and energy source) helps illustrate the concept of how combustion occurs. ▶Figure 500-1

- **Fuel.** Flammable gases or vapors, combustible dusts, and easily ignitable fibers/flyings.
- **Oxygen.** Air and oxidizing atmospheres.
- **Ignition Source (Heat).** Electric arcs or sparks, heat-producing equipment such as luminaires and motors, failure of transformers, coils, or solenoids, as well as sparks caused by metal tools dropping on metal surfaces.

Many of the graphics contained in Chapter 5 of this textbook and video use two shades of red to identify a Division location (darker red for Division 1 and lighter red to identify Division 2). In some cases, these color schemes are used as a background color to help you tell if the graphic applies to Division 1, Division 2, or both (split color background).

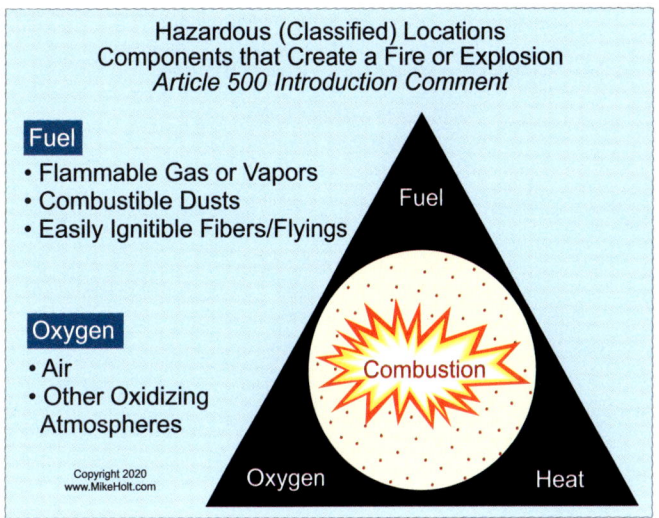

▶Figure 500-1

500.1 | Hazardous (Classified) Locations

500.1 Scope—Articles 500 Through 503

To help protect personnel from injury or death, or extensive damage to structures from fires or explosions, the *NEC* contains stringent requirements for equipment and its installation in hazardous (classified) locations where fire or explosion hazards may exist due to flammable gases, flammable liquid-produced vapors, combustible liquid-produced vapors, combustible dusts, or ignitible fibers/flyings. The specific requirements for electrical installations in hazardous (classified) locations are contained in: ▶Figure 500-2

- Article 501. Class I—Flammable or Combustible Liquid-Produced Vapors or Flammable Gases
- Article 502. Class II—Combustible Dust
- Article 503. Class III—Easily Ignitible Fibers/Flyings

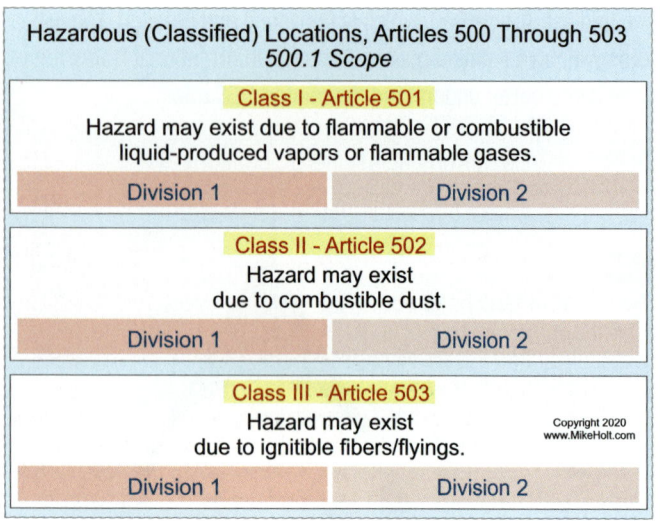

▶Figure 500-2

Author's Comment:

- Article 500 provides information related to the classifications [500.5], material groups [500.6], protection techniques [500.7], and equipment types [500.8] that are unique and required for Class I, Class II, and Class III locations. Articles 501, 502, and 503 cover the specific wiring requirements in hazardous (classified) areas.

Articles containing installation requirements for hazardous (classified) locations in special occupancies include:

- Article 511. Commercial Garages, Repair and Storage
- Article 513. Aircraft Hangars
- Article 514. Motor Fuel Dispensing Facilities
- Article 515. Bulk Storage Plants
- Article 516. Spray Application, Dipping, and Coating Processes
- Article 517. Health Care Facilities

500.3 Other Articles

Except as modified in Articles 500 through 503, all installation requirements contained in Chapters 1 through 4 of the *NEC* apply to electrical equipment and wiring installed in hazardous (classified) locations.

500.4 Documentation

All areas designated as hazardous (classified) locations must be properly documented. The documentation must be available to those who are authorized to design, install, inspect, maintain, or operate the electrical equipment.

Author's Comment:

- Proper documentation of hazardous areas assists the designer, installer, and authority having jurisdiction in ensuring adherence to the stringent requirements contained in Articles 501 through 517 of the *Code*.

- To assist in compliance with the above requirements, some authorities having jurisdiction require drawings that indicate hazardous (classified) location areas and their classification(s), material group properties such as auto ignition temperatures, and equipment construction suitability.

- Articles 511 through 517 do not classify locations as hazardous (classified) unless specifically identified as such in the articles. Determining the classification of a specific hazardous area is the responsibility of those who understand the dangers of the products being used such as the fire marshal, plant facility engineer, or insurance underwriter. It is not the responsibility of the electrical designer, electrical contractor, or electrical inspector. Before performing any wiring in or near a hazardous (classified) location, contact the plant facility and design engineer to ensure that proper installation methods and materials are used. Be sure to review 500.4(B) for additional standards that might need to be consulted.

Other Reference Standards. Important information related to topics covered in Chapter 5 may be found in other publications.

Note 1: For further information on the classification of locations, see:

- *Recommended Practice for the Classification of Flammable Liquids, Gases, or Vapors and of Hazardous (Classified) Locations for Electrical Installations in Chemical Process Areas,* NFPA 497
- *Standard for Dipping and Coating Processes Using Flammable or Combustible Liquids,* NFPA 34
- *Area Classification in Hazardous (Classified) Dust Locations,* ISA 12.10
- *Flammable and Combustible Liquids Code,* NFPA 30
- *Recommended Practice for Classification of Locations of Electrical Installations at Petroleum Facilities Classified as Class I, Division 1 and Division 2,* ANSI/API RP 500
- *Standard for Spray Application Using Flammable or Combustible Materials,* NFPA 33
- *Liquefied Petroleum Gas Code,* NFPA 58
- *Standard for Fire Overcurrent Protection in Wastewater Treatment and Collection Facilities,* NFPA 820

Note 2: For further information on protection against static electricity and lightning hazards in hazardous (classified) locations, see:

- *Standard for the Installation of Lightning Protection Systems,* NFPA 780
- *Recommended Practice on Static Electricity,* NFPA 77
- *Protection Against Ignitions Arising Out of Static Lightning and Stray Currents,* API RP 2003

500.5 Classifications of Hazardous Locations

(A) General. Locations are classified according to the properties of the flammable gases, flammable liquid-produced vapors, combustible liquid-produced vapors, combustible dusts, or easily ignitable fibers/flyings that may be present, and the likelihood that a flammable or combustible concentration will be present.

Each room, section, or area is considered individually in determining its classification. ▶Figure 500–3

Note 1: To reduce the need for expensive equipment and expensive wiring methods, locate as much electrical equipment as possible in an unclassified location.

(B) Identification of a Class I Location. A Class I location is an area where flammable gases, flammable liquid-produced vapors, or combustible liquid-produced vapors may be present in quantities sufficient to produce explosive or ignitible mixtures.

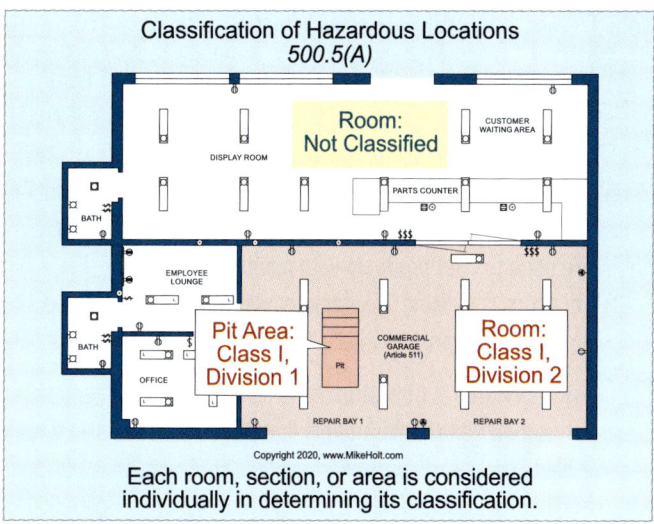

▶Figure 500–3

(1) Class I, Division 1 Location. A Class I, Division 1 location is a location in which: ▶Figure 500–4

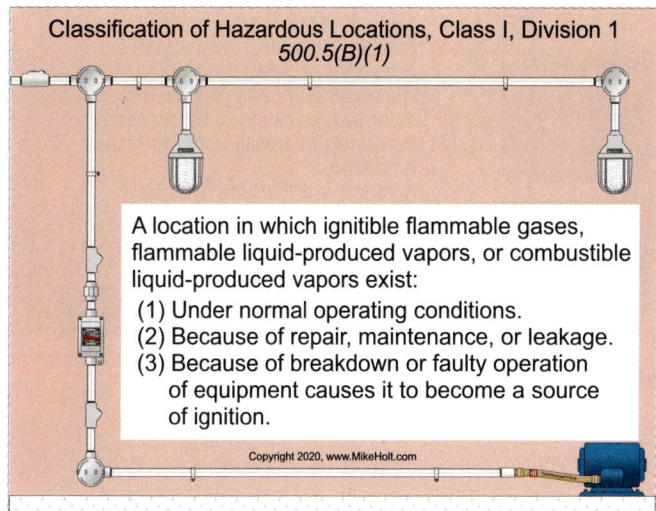

▶Figure 500–4

(1) Ignitible concentrations of flammable gases, flammable liquid-produced vapors, or combustible liquid-produced vapors may exist in the course of normal operations, or

(2) Ignitible concentrations of flammable gases, flammable liquid-produced vapors, or combustible liquids above their flash points may exist due to repair or maintenance operations or because of leakage, or

(3) Breakdown or faulty equipment releases ignitible concentrations of flammable gases, flammable liquid-produced vapors, or combustible liquid-produced vapors and the electrical equipment becomes a source of ignition.

Note 1: Class I, Division 1 locations include:

(1) Areas where volatile flammable liquids or liquefied flammable gases are transferred from one container to another, such as at gasoline storage and dispensing areas.
(2) Interiors of spray booths and areas in the vicinity of spraying and painting operations where volatile flammable solvents are used to coat products with paint or plastics.
(3) Locations containing open tanks or vats of volatile flammable liquids, or dip tanks for parts cleaning or other operations.

(2) Class I, Division 2 Location. An area where volatile flammable gases, or combustible or flammable liquid-produced vapors, would become hazardous only in case of an accident or of some unusual operating condition, or under any of the following conditions: ▶Figure 500–5

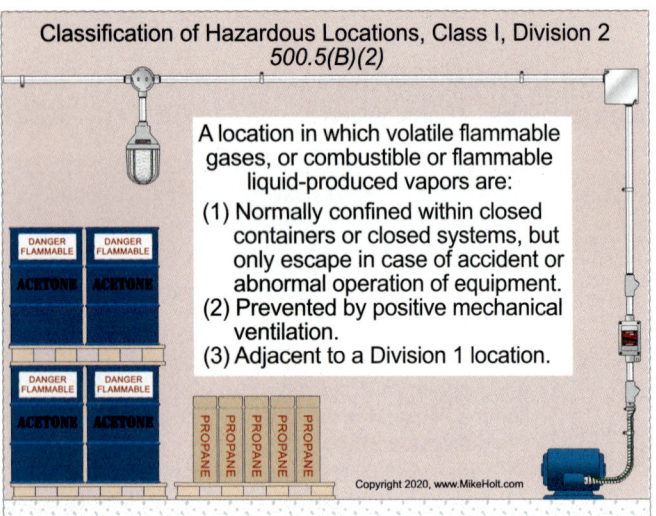
▶Figure 500–5

(1) If flammable gases, flammable liquid-produced vapors, or combustible liquid-produced vapors are handled, processed, or used, but are normally confined within closed containers and the gases would only escape in the case of accidental rupture or breakdown or in the case of abnormal operation of equipment.

(2) If ignitible concentrations of flammable gases, flammable liquid-produced vapors, or combustible liquid-produced vapors are normally prevented by positive mechanical ventilation but might become hazardous through failure or abnormal operation of the ventilating equipment.

(3) Areas adjacent to a Class I, Division 1 location and to where flammable gases, flammable liquid-produced vapors, or combustible liquid-produced vapors might occasionally be communicated unless prevented by adequate positive-pressure ventilation with effective safeguards against ventilation failure.

Note 1: The quantity of flammable gases, flammable liquid-produced vapors, or combustible liquid-produced vapors that might escape in case of accident, the adequacy of ventilating equipment, the total area involved, and the record of the industry with respect to explosions or fires are all factors that should be taken into consideration.

(C) Identification of a Class II Location. Class II locations are hazardous because of the presence of combustible dust. ▶Figure 500–6

▶Figure 500–6

(1) Class II, Division 1 Location. A Class II, Division 1 location is an area where combustible dust may exist under any of the following conditions:

(1) Under normal operating conditions combustible dust is continuously or periodically suspended in the air in sufficient quantities to produce mixtures that will ignite or explode, or

(2) If faulty equipment releases ignitible mixtures of dust and the equipment becomes a source of ignition, or

(3) In which Group E combustible dusts may be present in quantities sufficient to be hazardous in normal or abnormal operating conditions.

Note: Dusts containing magnesium or aluminum are particularly hazardous, and the use of extreme precaution is necessary to avoid ignition and explosion.

(2) Class II, Division 2 Location. An area where combustible dust would become hazardous under any of the following conditions:

(1) If combustible dust, due to abnormal operations, may be present in the air in quantities sufficient to produce explosive or ignitible mixtures, or

(2) If combustible dust accumulation is normally insufficient to interfere with the normal operation of electrical equipment, but where malfunctioning equipment may result in combustible dust being suspended in the air, or

(3) If combustible dust accumulations on, in, or near electrical equipment could be sufficient to interfere with the safe dissipation of heat from electrical equipment or could be ignitible by abnormal operation or failure of electrical equipment.

Note 1: The quantity of combustible dust that may be present and the adequacy of dust removal systems should be considered when determining the area classification.

(D) Identification of a Class III Location. A Class III location is an area where easily ignitible fibers or materials producing combustible flyings are handled, manufactured, or used and are not likely to be suspended in the air in quantities sufficient to produce ignitible mixtures.

(1) Class III, Division 1 Location. A Class III, Division 1 location is an area where easily ignitible fibers/flyings are manufactured, handled, or used.

Note 1: Such locations usually include some parts of rayon, cotton, and other textile mills or clothing manufacturing plants as well as facilities that create sawdust and flyings by pulverizing or cutting wood.

(2) Class III, Division 2 Location. A Class III, Division 2 location is an area where easily ignitible fibers/flyings are stored or handled other than in the manufacturing process.

500.6 Material Groups

For purposes of approval and area classification, air mixtures must be grouped in accordance with 500.6(A) and (B). ▶Figure 500–7

Author's Comment:

▸ Refer to 500.6(A) and (B) in the *NEC* to be certain that equipment is listed for the proper group.

▸ The Cooper Crouse-Hinds *Code Digest* contains a substantial list of different products and their group designations. It can be downloaded from www.coopercrouse-hinds.eu/en/service/brochures.html.

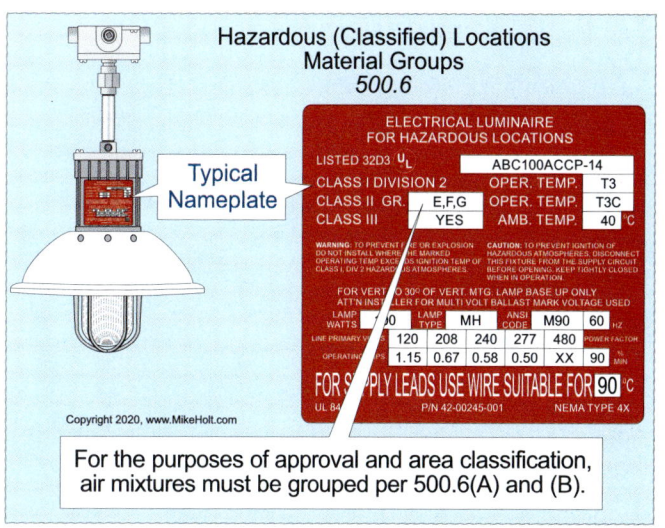

▶Figure 500–7

500.7 Protection Techniques

Electrical and electronic equipment in hazardous (classified) locations must be protected by one or more of the following techniques:

(A) Explosionproof Equipment. Explosionproof equipment is permitted in any Class 1 location for which it is identified. ▶Figure 500–8

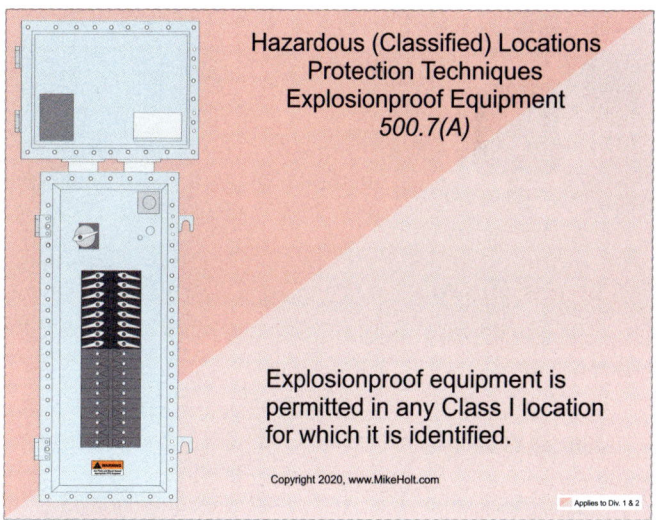

▶Figure 500–8

Author's Comment:

▸ Explosionproof equipment is designed to be capable of withstanding and containing the force of an internal explosion, and the hot gases within the enclosure cool as they escape [Article 100]. ▶Figure 500–9

500.7 | Hazardous (Classified) Locations

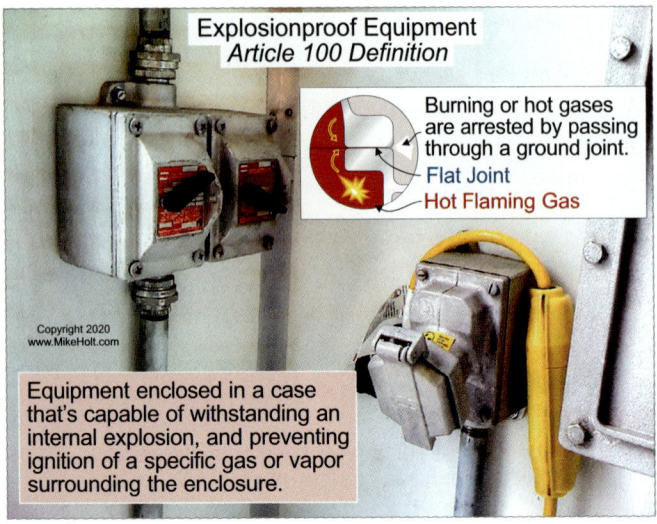
▶Figure 500–9

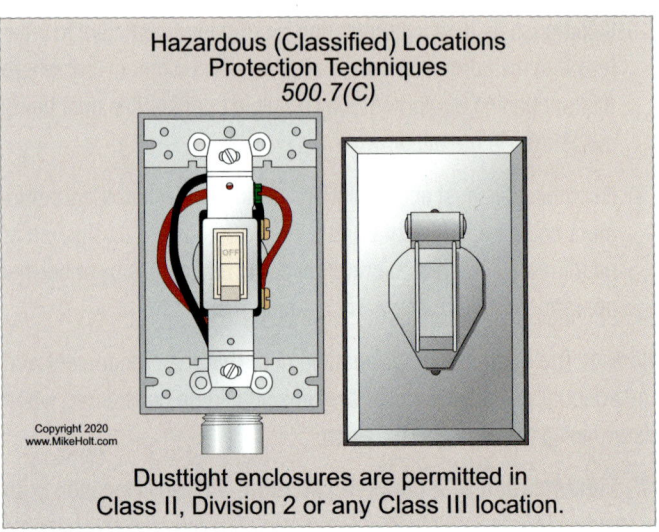
▶Figure 500–11

(B) Dust-Ignitionproof Enclosures. Dust-ignitionproof enclosures are permitted in any Class II location. ▶Figure 500–10

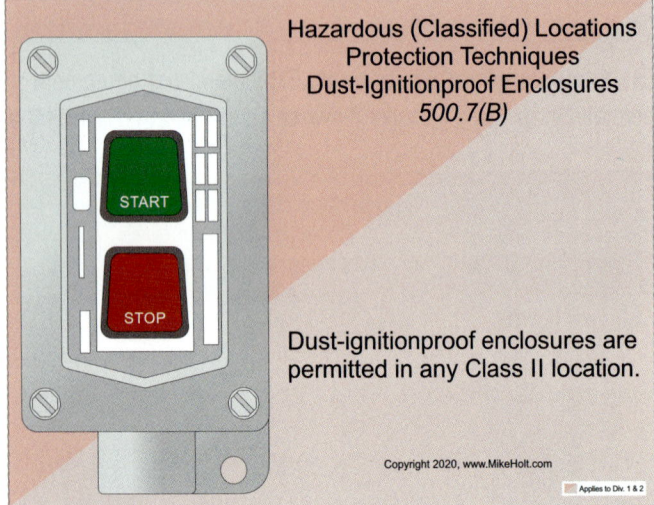
▶Figure 500–10

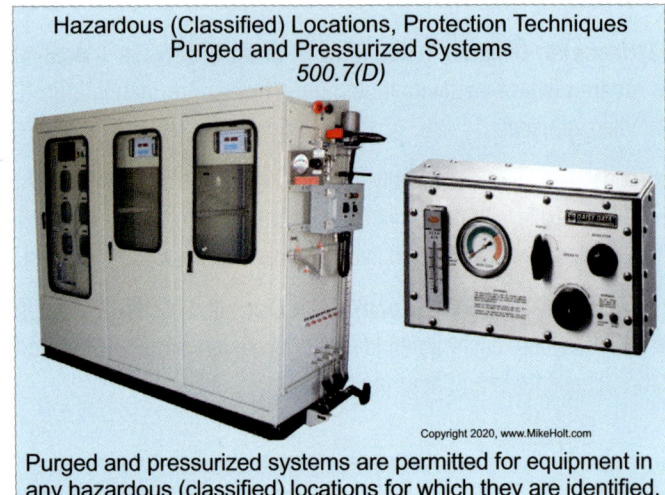
▶Figure 500–12

Author's Comment:

▶ Dust-ignitionproof enclosures are designed to exclude dusts and will not permit arcs, sparks, or heat within the enclosure to cause the ignition of exterior dust [Article 100].

(C) Dusttight Enclosures. Dusttight enclosures are permitted in Class II, Division 2 or any Class III location. ▶Figure 500–11

(D) Purged and Pressurized Systems. Purged and pressurized systems are permitted for equipment in any hazardous (classified) locations for which they are identified. ▶Figure 500–12

Author's Comment:

▶ "Purging" is supplying an enclosure with a safe gas at a flow and pressure to sufficiently reduce concentrations of flammable gases, flammable liquid-produced vapors, or combustible liquid-produced vapors to a safe level. "Pressurization" is supplying an enclosure with a safe gas, with or without a continuous flow, with enough pressure to prevent the entrance of combustible dust or ignitible fibers/flyings [Article 100].

(I) Oil-Immersed Contacts. Oil-immersed make-and-break contacts can be installed in a Class I, Division 2 location.

(J) Hermetically Sealed Contacts. Hermetically sealed contacts can be installed in Class I, Division 2; Class II, Division 2; or Class III locations.

Author's Comment:

▸ "Hermetically Sealed" is when equipment is sealed against the entrance of an external atmosphere where the seal is made by methods such as soldering, brazing, welding, or the fusion of glass to metal [Article 100].

(P) Other Protection Techniques. Other protection techniques used in equipment identified for use in hazardous (classified) locations are permitted.

500.8 Equipment

Articles 500 through 503 require equipment construction and installation that ensure safe performance under conditions of use and maintenance.

(A) Suitability of Equipment. Suitability of equipment must be determined by any of the following:

(1) Listing or labeling. ▸Figure 500-13

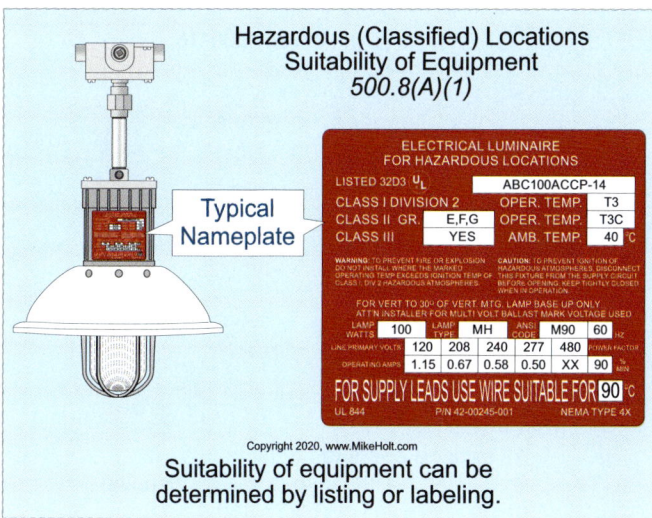

▸Figure 500-13

(2) Field evaluation by a qualified testing laboratory or inspection agency concerned with product evaluation.

(3) Evidence acceptable by the authority having jurisdiction such as a manufacturer's self-evaluation or an owner's engineering judgment.

Note: Additional documentation may include certificates demonstrating compliance with applicable equipment standards indicating special conditions of use and other pertinent information.

(B) Approval for Class and Properties.

(1) Identified for Use. Equipment installed in any hazardous (classified) location must be identified for the class and the explosive, combustible, or ignitible properties of the specific gas, vapor, dust, or fiber/flyings that will be present.

(3) A general-purpose enclosure without make-and-break contacts can be installed in Article 501, 502, and 503 Division 2 locations.
▸Figure 500-14

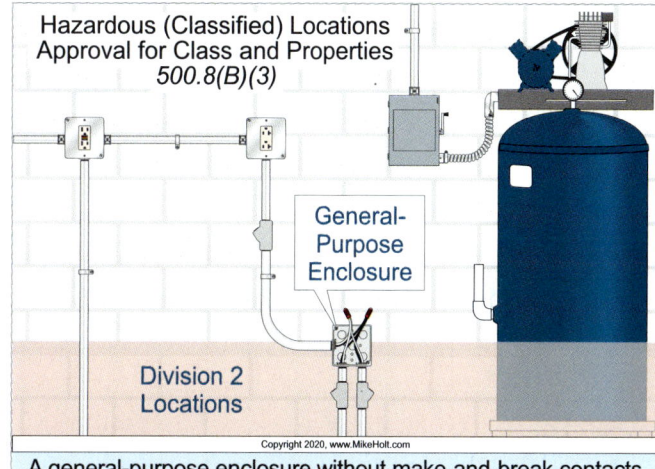

▸Figure 500-14

(D) Temperature.

(1) Class I Temperature. For Class I equipment, the Table 500.8(C) temperature marking must not exceed the autoignition temperature of the specific gas or vapor that may be encountered ▸Figure 500-15

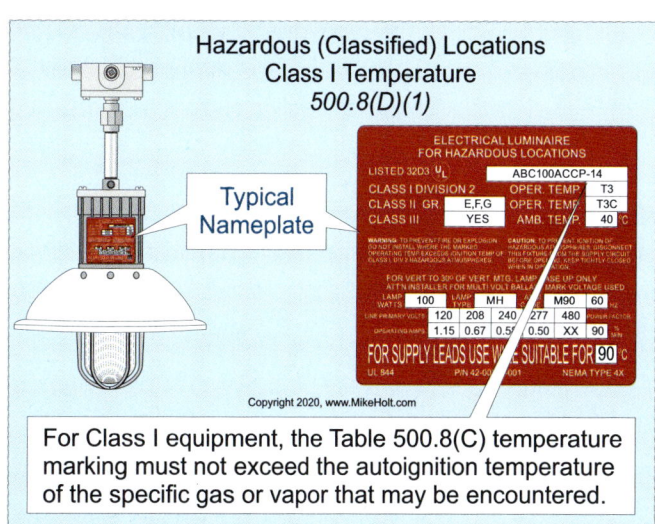

▸Figure 500-15

500.8 | Hazardous (Classified) Locations

Table 500.8(C) Classification of Maximum Surface Temperature

Maximum °C	Temperature °F	Temperature Class (T Code)
450	842	T1
300	572	T2
280	536	T2A
260	500	T2B
230	446	T2C
215	419	T2D
200	392	T3
180	356	T3A
165	329	T3B
160	320	T3C
135	275	T4
120	248	T4A
100	212	T5
85	185	T6

(2) Class II Temperature. Class II equipment must not have exposed surfaces operating at a temperature in excess of the autoignition temperature of the specific dust as contained in 500.8(C).

Author's Comment:

▸ This is accomplished by ensuring that the temperature marking on the equipment (especially luminaires and motors) does not exceed the autoignition temperature of the specific gases, vapors, or types of dust encountered.

(E) Threading. Threaded conduits must be made wrenchtight to prevent arcing when ground-fault current flows through the raceway system and to ensure the explosionproof or dust-ignitionproof integrity of the raceway system.

(1) Equipment with Threaded Entries. Threaded entries into explosionproof equipment must be made up with at least five threads fully engaged.

Ex: Listed explosionproof equipment with factory NPT entries must be made up with four and one-half threads fully engaged.

Author's Comment:

▸ This requirement ensures that if an explosion occurs within a raceway or enclosure, the expanding gas will sufficiently cool as it dissipates through the threads. This prevents hot flaming gases from igniting the surrounding atmosphere of a hazardous (classified) location.

▸ Remember that it is assumed the flammable atmosphere outside the raceway will seep into the raceway system over time. The goal of the *Code* is to contain any explosion that occurs inside the raceway so the event will not ignite the flammable mixture outside the raceway.

(3) Unused Openings. Unused raceway and cable openings must be closed with listed metal close-up plugs installed in accordance with 500.8(E)(1) or (E)(2) [110.12(A)]. ▸Figure 500–16

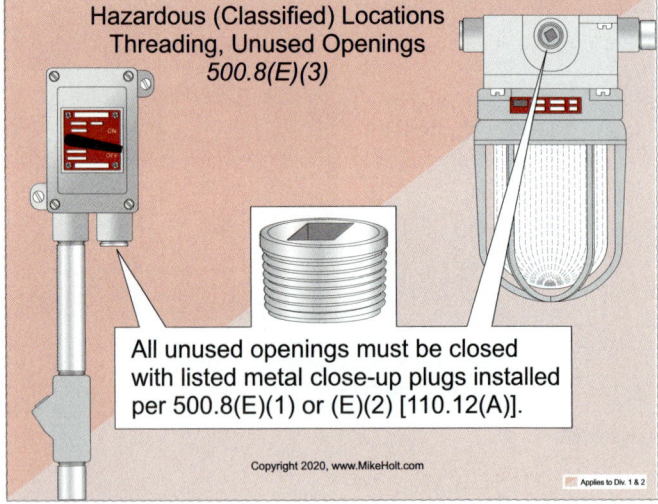

▸Figure 500–16

ARTICLE 501
CLASS I HAZARDOUS (CLASSIFIED) LOCATIONS

Introduction to Article 501—Class I Hazardous (Classified) Locations

If sufficient flammable or combustible gases, vapors, or liquids are (or may be) present to produce an explosive or ignitable mixture, you have a Class I location. Examples of such locations include some fuel storage areas, certain solvent storage areas, grain processing facilities (where hexane is used), plastic extrusion areas where oil removal is part of the process, refineries, and paint storage areas. Article 500 contained a general background on hazardous (classified) locations, described the differences between Class I, II, and III locations, and the differences between Division 1 and Division 2. Article 501 contains the actual Class I, Division 1 and Division 2 installation requirements, including wiring methods, seals, and specific equipment requirements.

Part I. General

501.1 Scope

Article 501 covers the electrical equipment and wiring for Class I, Division 1 and Division 2 locations where fire or explosion hazards may exist due to flammable gases or vapors or flammable liquids ▶Figure 501–1

▶Figure 501–1

Part II. Wiring

501.10 Wiring Methods

(A) Class I, Division 1.

(1) General. Only the following wiring methods are permitted within a Class I, Division 1 location.

(1) Threaded rigid metal conduit (Type RMC) or threaded intermediate metal conduit (Type IMC). ▶Figure 501–2

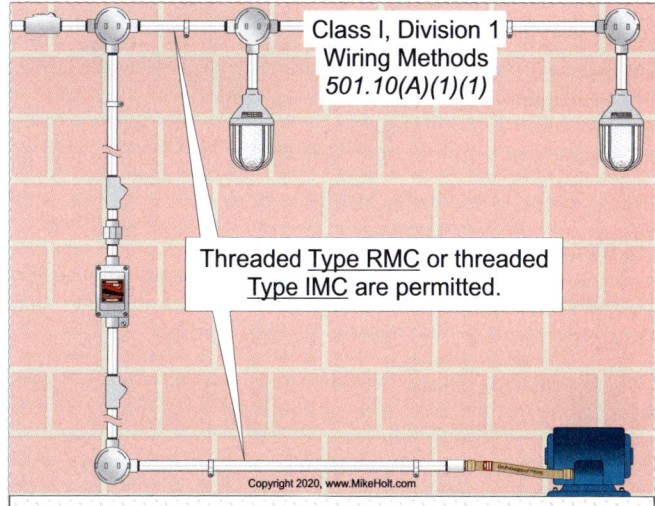

▶Figure 501–2

Mike Holt Enterprises • www.MikeHolt.com • 888.NEC.CODE (632.2633) | 111

501.10 | Class I Hazardous (Classified) Locations

Ex: Types PVC, RTRC, and HDPE conduit are permitted underground where encased in a minimum of 2 in. of concrete and a cover depth of not less than 24 in. measured from the top of the conduit to grade. Concrete encasement is not required when PVC, RTRC, or HDPE conduit is installed underground under fuel dispensers in accordance with 514.8 Ex 2.

(2) MI cable terminated with fittings that are listed for the location.

(2) Class 1, Division 1 Flexible Connections. When necessary for the presence of vibration or need for movement, the following are permitted: ▶Figure 501-3

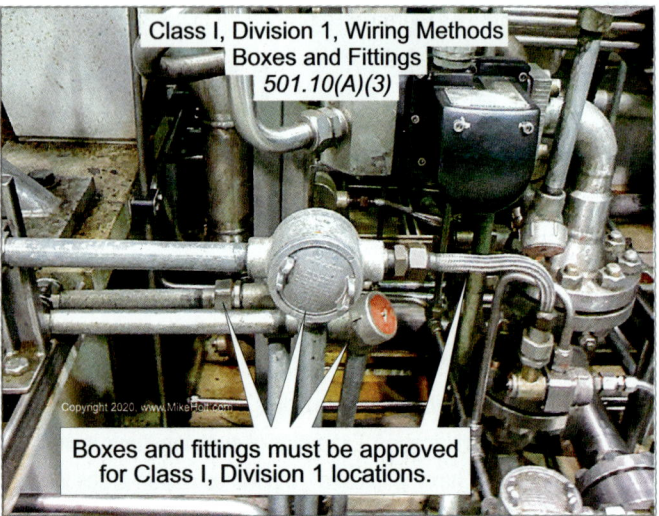

▶Figure 501-4

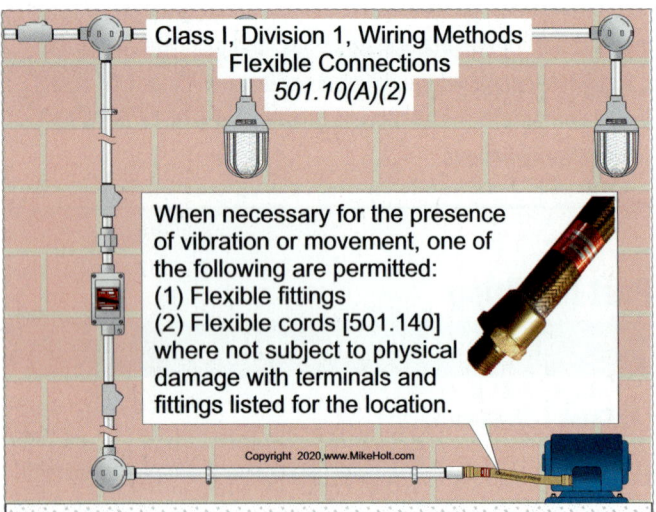

▶Figure 501-3

(1) Flexible fittings listed for the location.

(2) Flexible cords in accordance with 501.140, where the cable is not subject to physical damage and the cable terminates with fittings listed for the location.

(3) Boxes and Fittings. Boxes and fittings must be approved for Class I, Division 1 locations. ▶Figure 501-4

(B) Class I, Division 2.

(1) General. All wiring methods included in Class 1, Division 1 locations [501.10(A)] and the following wiring methods are permitted within a Class I, Division 2 location.

(1) Rigid and intermediate metal conduit with listed threaded or threadless fittings. ▶Figure 501-5

(2) Enclosed gasketed wireways.

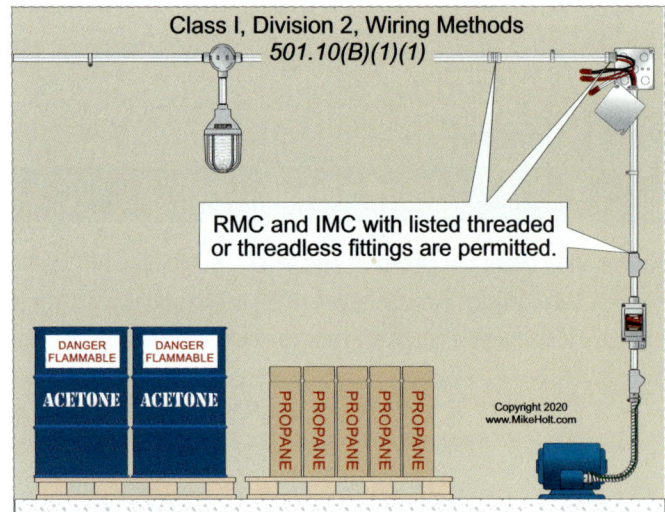

▶Figure 501-5

(3) Types PLTC and PLTC-ER cable terminated in accordance with Parts II and III of Article 725. Type PLTC-ER cable must include an equipment grounding conductor in addition to any drain wire that might be present.

(4) Types ITC and ITC-ER cable as permitted in 727.4. Type ITC-ER cable must include an equipment grounding conductor in addition to a drain wire.

(5) Types MC, MV, TC, or TC-ER cable terminated with listed fittings, including installation in cable tray systems. Type TC-ER cable must include an equipment grounding conductor in addition to any drain wire that might be present.

(6) Where metallic conduit does not provide sufficient corrosion resistance, any of the following wiring methods are permitted:

a. Listed reinforced thermosetting resin conduit (RTRC), factory elbows, and associated fittings, all marked with the suffix "-XW,"

b. PVC-coated rigid metal conduit (RMC), factory elbows, and associated fittings,

c. PVC-coated intermediate metal conduit (IMC), factory elbows, and associated fittings, or

d. In industrial establishments with restricted public access, where the conditions of maintenance and supervision ensure that only qualified persons service the installation, Schedule 80 PVC conduit, factory elbows, and associated fittings.

(7) Types OFNP, OFCP, OFNR, OFCR, OFNG, OFCG, OFN, and OFC optical fiber cables can be installed in cable trays or raceways [501.10(B)] and must be sealed in accordance with 501.15. ▶Figure 501-6

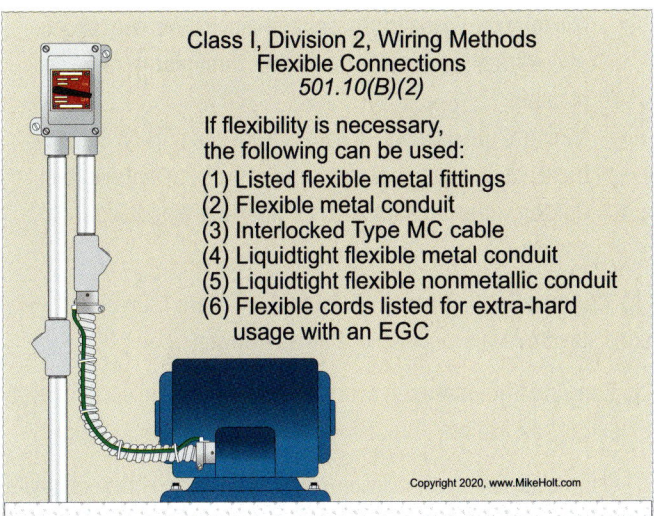
▶Figure 501-7

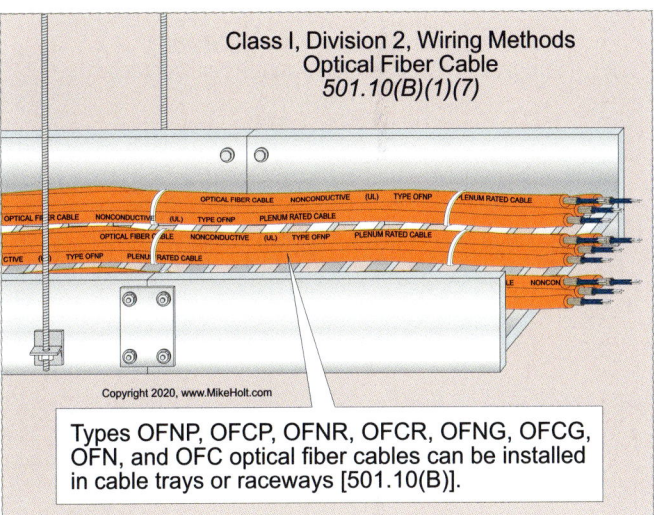
▶Figure 501-6

(8) Cablebus.

(2) Class 1, Division 2 Flexible Connections. If flexibility is necessary, the following are permitted: ▶Figure 501-7

(1) Listed flexible metal fittings.

(2) Flexible metal conduit with listed fittings.

(3) Interlocked Type MC cable with listed fittings.

(4) Liquidtight flexible metal conduit with listed fittings.

(5) Liquidtight flexible nonmetallic conduit with listed fittings.

(6) Flexible cords listed for extra-hard usage containing an equipment grounding conductor and terminated with listed fittings.

Author's Comment:

▶ If flexible cords are used, they must comply with 501.140.

(4) Boxes and Fittings. General-purpose enclosures and fittings in Class 1, Division 2 locations are permitted unless the enclosure contains make-and-break contacts.

501.15 Raceway and Cable Seals

Seals for raceway and cable systems must comply with 501.15(A) through (F).

Note 1: Raceway and cable seals must be installed to: ▶Figure 501-8

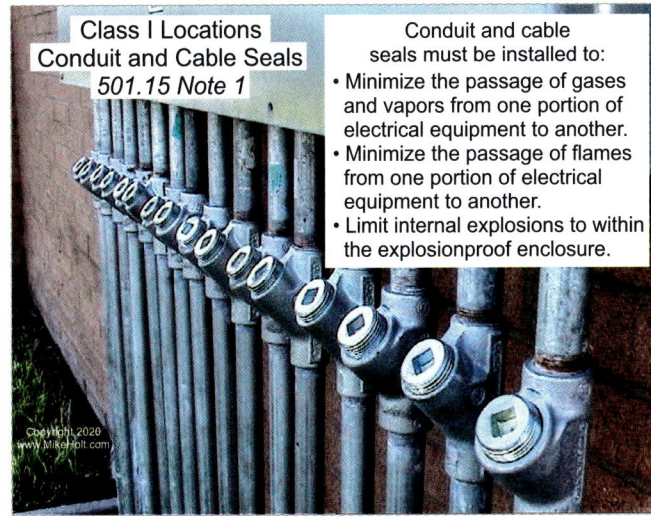
▶Figure 501-8

501.15 | Class I Hazardous (Classified) Locations

- Minimize the passage of gases and vapors from one portion of electrical equipment to another through the raceway or cable.
- Minimize the passage of flames from one portion of electrical equipment to another through the raceway or cable.
- Contain internal explosions within the explosionproof enclosure.

(A) Conduit Seal—Class I, Division 1. In Class I, Division 1 locations, conduit seals must be located as follows:

(1) Entering Enclosures. A conduit seal is required in each raceway that enters an explosionproof enclosure if either (1) or (2) apply:

(1) If the explosionproof enclosure contains make-and-break contacts.
▶Figure 501–9

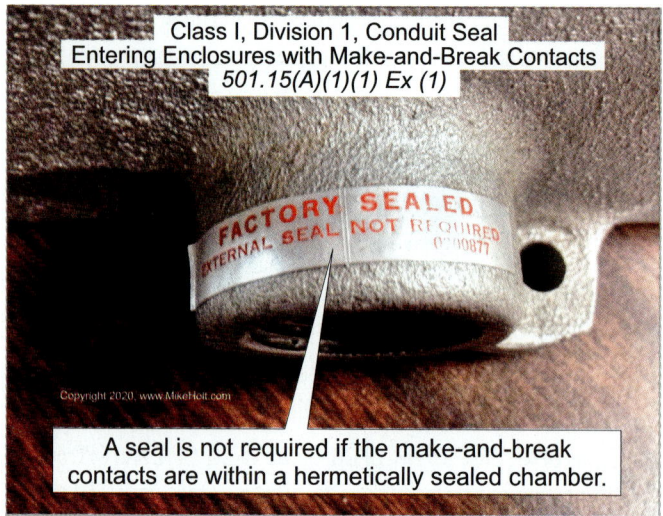
▶Figure 501–10

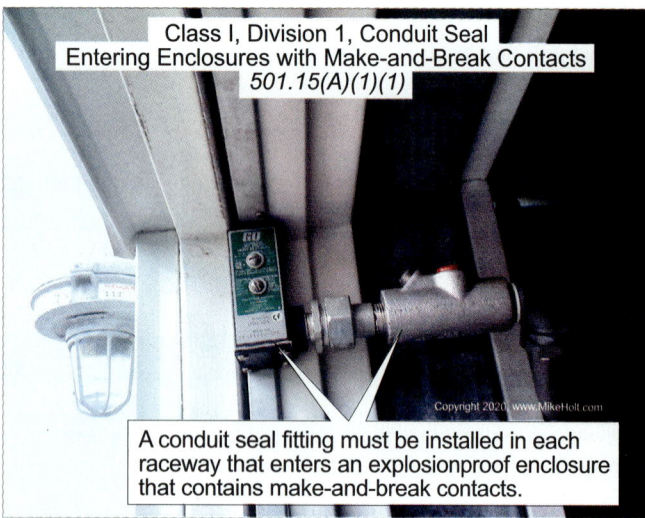
▶Figure 501–9

Ex: A conduit seal is not required if the make-and-break contacts are:

(1) Within a hermetically sealed chamber. ▶Figure 501–10

(2) Immersed in oil in accordance with 501.115(B)(1)(2).

(3) Contained within an enclosure that is marked "Leads Factory Sealed," "Factory Sealed," "Seal not Required," or the equivalent.

(2) If a trade size 2 or larger conduit enters any explosionproof enclosure without a make-and-break contact. ▶Figure 501–11

The conduit seal fitting must be installed within 18 in. of the explosionproof enclosure or as required by the enclosure markings. ▶Figure 501–12

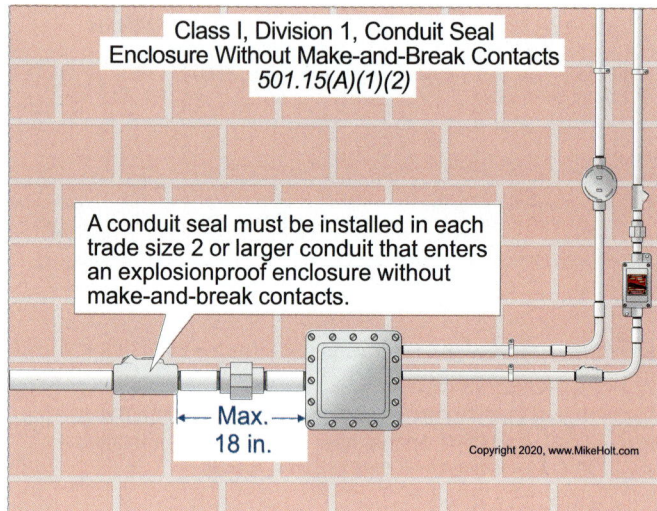
▶Figure 501–11

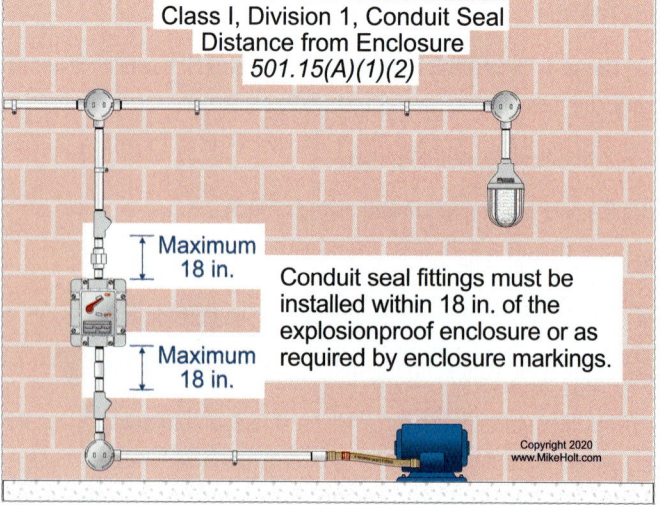
▶Figure 501–12

Only threaded couplings, or explosionproof fittings such as unions, reducers, elbows, and capped elbows are permitted between the conduit seal and the explosionproof enclosure. ▶Figure 501-13

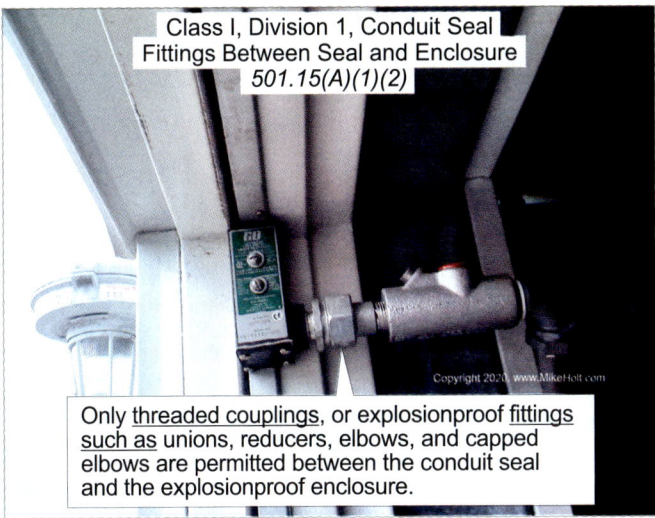
▶Figure 501-13

(2) Pressurized Enclosures. A conduit seal fitting must be installed in each conduit that is not pressurized where the conduit enters a pressurized enclosure. The conduit seal fitting must be installed within 18 in. of the pressurized enclosure.

(3) Between Explosionproof Enclosures. A single conduit seal fitting is permitted between two explosionproof enclosures if not more than 36 in. long containing make-and-break contacts if the conduit seal fitting is located not more than 18 in. from the explosionproof enclosures. ▶Figure 501-14

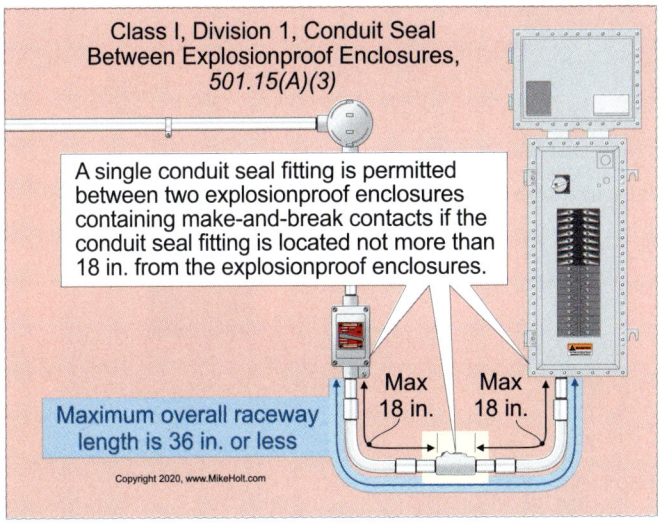
▶Figure 501-14

(4) Class I, Division 1 Boundary Seal. A conduit seal fitting must be installed in each conduit that leaves a Class I, Division 1 location within 10 ft of the Class I, Division 1 location on either side of the boundary. ▶Figure 501-15

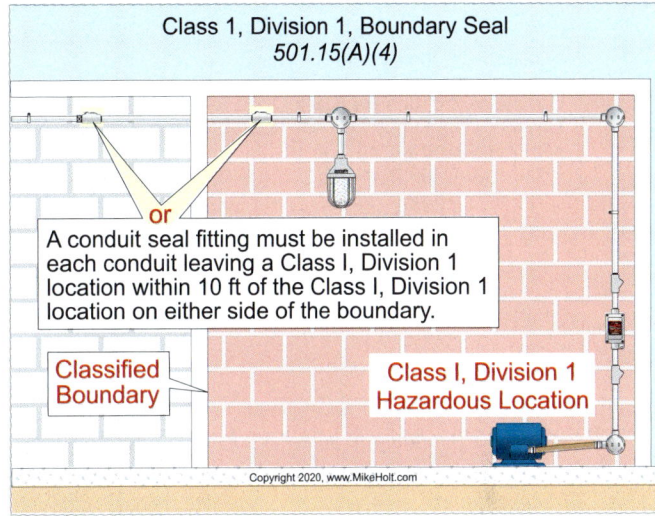
▶Figure 501-15

There must be no fitting, except for a listed explosionproof reducer installed at the conduit seal fitting, between the conduit seal fitting and the point at which the conduit leaves the Class I, Division 1 location. ▶Figure 501-16

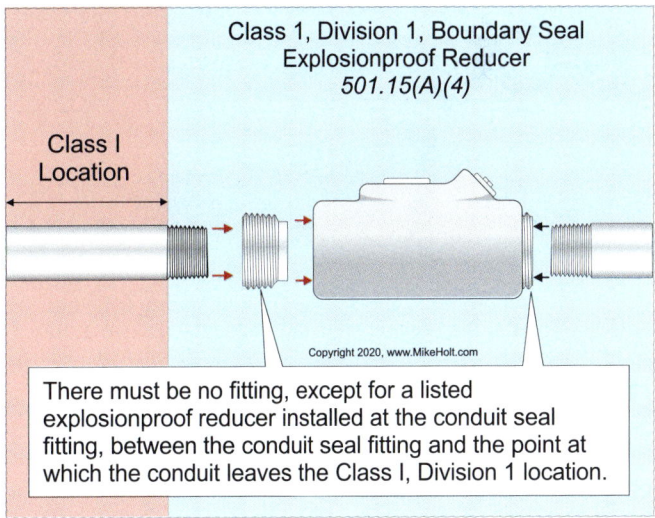
▶Figure 501-16

Ex 1: A conduit boundary seal fitting is not required for a conduit that passes completely through the Class I, Division 1 area unbroken with no fittings installed within 12 in. of either side of the boundary. ▶Figure 501-17

501.15 | Class I Hazardous (Classified) Locations

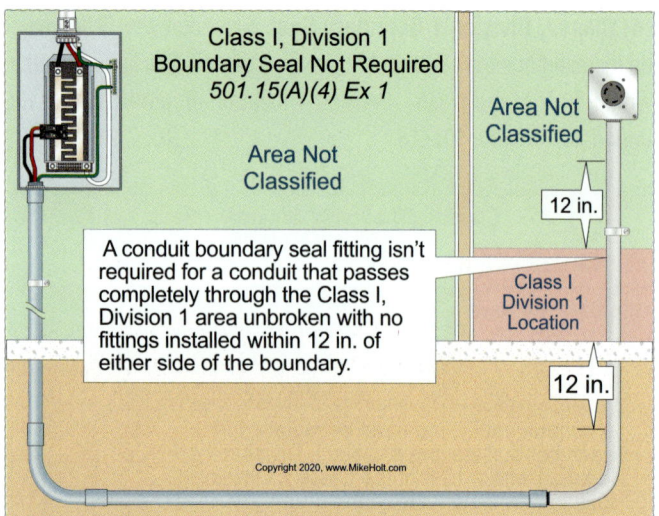

▶Figure 501–17

Ex 2: If the conduit boundary is below grade, the conduit seal can be located above grade. There must be no fitting, except for a listed explosionproof reducer installed at the conduit seal fitting, between the conduit seal fitting and the point at which the conduit emerges from below grade. ▶Figure 501–18

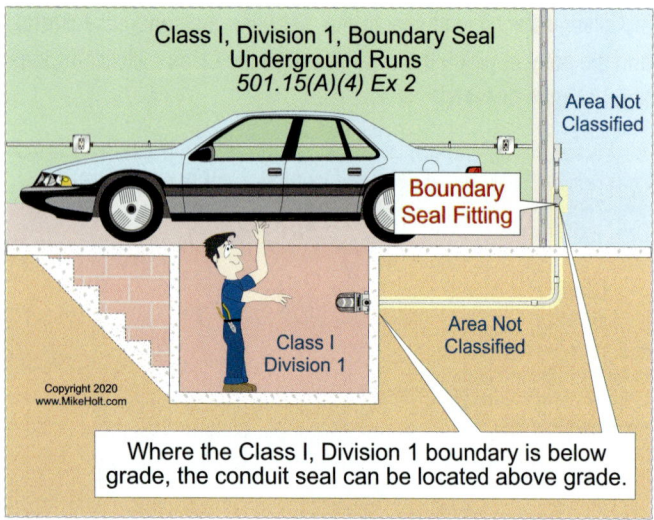

▶Figure 501–18

Author's Comment:

▶ The wiring method between the conduit seal fitting and the Class I, Division 1 boundary must be rigid metal conduit or intermediate metal conduit [501.10(A)(1)(1)].

(B) Conduit Seal, Class I, Division 2. In Class I, Division 2 locations, conduit seals must be located as follows:

(1) Enclosures with Make-and-Break Contacts. A conduit seal fitting must be installed in each raceway that enters an explosion-proof enclosure that contains make-and-break contacts. The seal fitting must be installed within 18 in. of the explosionproof enclosure [501.15(A)(1)(1) and (A)(3)]. The raceway between the seal and enclosure must be rigid or intermediate metal conduit in accordance with 501.10(A). ▶Figure 501–19

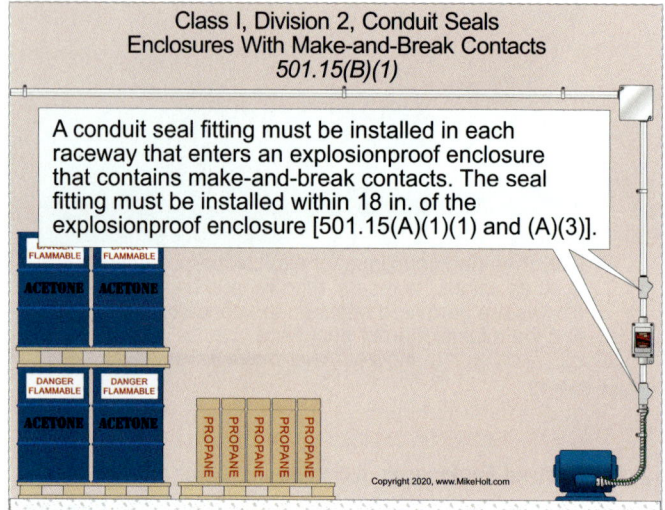

▶Figure 501–19

(2) Boundary Seal at Unclassified Location. A conduit seal fitting must be installed in each raceway that leaves a Class I, Division 2 location within 10 ft of the Class I, Division 2 location on either side of the boundary. ▶Figure 501–20

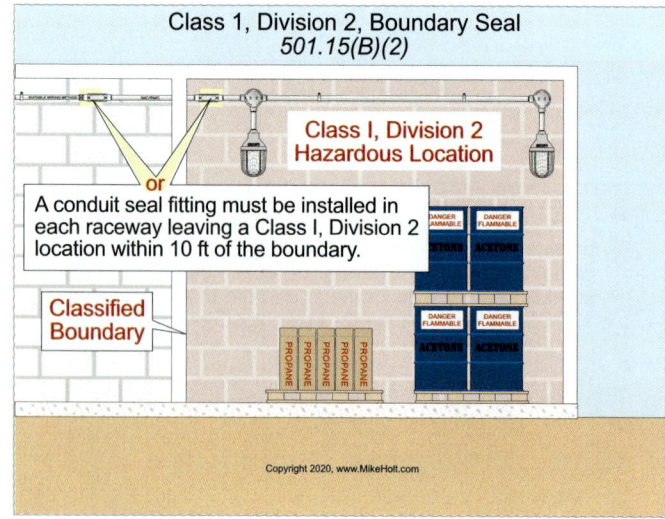

▶Figure 501–20

Rigid metal conduit or intermediate metal conduit must be installed between the sealing fitting and the point where the raceway leaves the Division 2 location, and the raceway must be threaded into the sealing fitting. ▶Figure 501–21

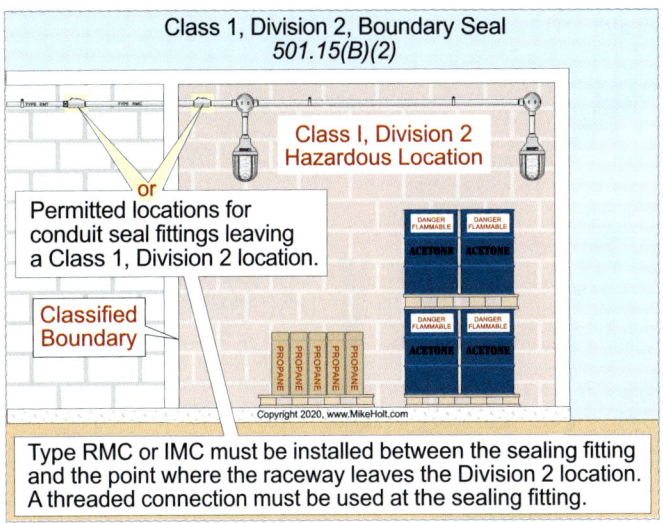

▶Figure 501–21

There must be no fitting, except for a listed explosionproof reducer installed at the conduit sealing fitting, between the conduit seal fitting and the point at which the raceway leaves the Class I, Division 2 location.

The Class 1, Division 2 boundary seal is not required to be explosionproof, but it must be identified to minimize the passage of gases under normal operating conditions and be accessible. ▶Figure 501–22

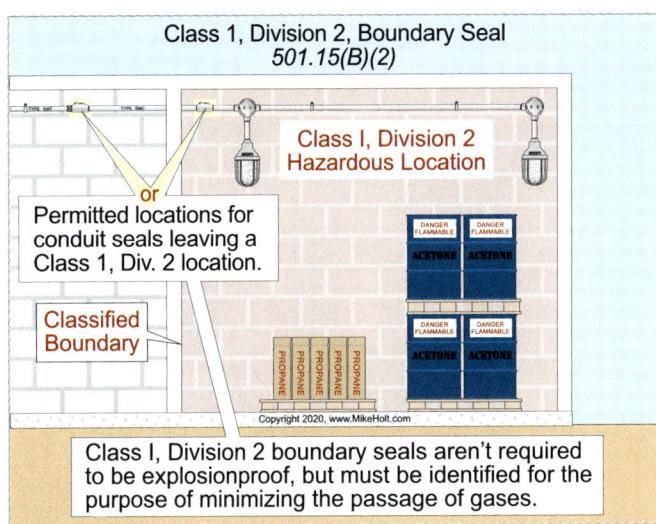

▶Figure 501–22

Author's Comment:

▸ The Class I, Division 2 boundary seal is not required to be listed for the Class 1, Division 2 use and an explosionproof seal off compound is not required, see 501.15(C) Ex.

▸ A type C conduit outlet body with the use of Polywater® FST™ Foam Duct Sealant meets the requirements of 501.15(B)(2).

Ex 1: A raceway boundary seal fitting is not required for a metal raceway that passes completely through the Class I, Division 2 area unbroken with no fittings installed within 12 in. of either side of the boundary.

Ex 2: A raceway boundary seal fitting is not required for raceways that terminate in an unclassified location where the metal conduit transitions to cable trays, cablebus, ventilated busways, MI cable, or open wiring if:

(1) The unclassified location is located outdoors or the unclassified location is indoors and the conduit system is entirely in one room.

(2) The raceways do not terminate at an enclosure containing an ignition source in normal operation.

Ex 3: A boundary seal fitting is not required for a raceway that passes from an enclosure or a room that is unclassified as a result of pressurization, into a Class I, Division 2 location.

(C) Conduit Seal, Installation Requirements. If explosionproof sealing fittings are required in Class I, Division 1 and 2 locations, they must comply with the following: ▶Figure 501–23

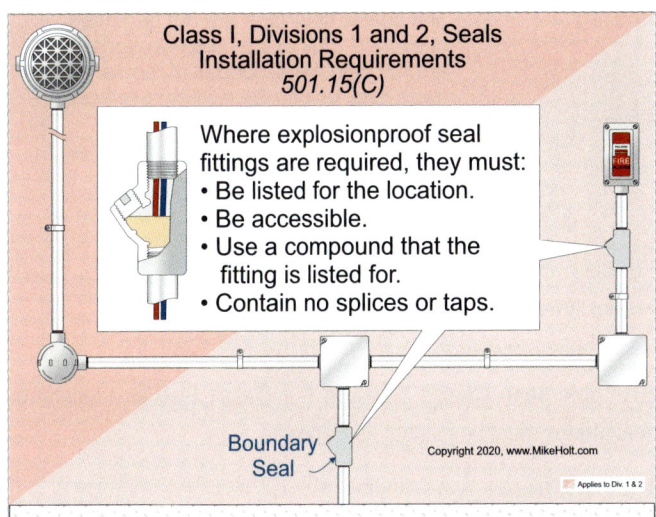

▶Figure 501–23

501.15 | Class I Hazardous (Classified) Locations

Ex: A Class 1, Division 2 boundary seal that is not required to be explosionproof in accordance with 501.15(B)(2) is not required to comply with the requirements of 501.15(C).

(1) Fittings. Conduit seal fittings must be listed for the location and for the specific sealing compounds and must be accessible.

(2) Compound. Seal off compound(s) must provide a seal, be applied so as to prohibit the passage of vapors and/or gases and be impervious to the surrounding environment with a melting point of not less than 93°C (200°F).

(3) Thickness of Compounds. Except for listed cable sealing fittings, the thickness of the conduit seal compound installed in completed seals cannot be less than the trade size of the seal fitting, and in no case less than ⅝ in.

(4) Splices and Taps. Splices and taps cannot be made within a conduit seal fitting.

(6) Number of Conductors or Optical Fiber Cables. The cross-sectional area of conductors and optical fiber tube are not permitted to exceed 25 percent of the cross-sectional area of rigid metal conduit of the same trade size, unless the seal is specifically identified for a higher percentage fill. ▶Figure 501–24

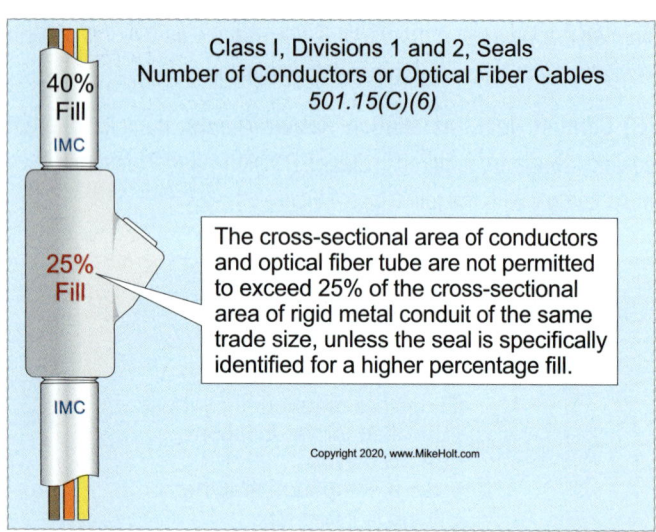

▶Figure 501–24

(D) Cable Seal—Class I, Division 1. In Class I, Division 1 locations, seal fittings must be located as follows:

(1) Terminations. Cables must be sealed with sealing fittings that comply with 501.15(C) at all terminations. While Type MC-HL cable is inherently gas/vaportight by the construction of the cable, termination fittings must permit the sealing compound to surround each individual insulated conductor to minimize the passage of gases or vapors. ▶Figure 501–25

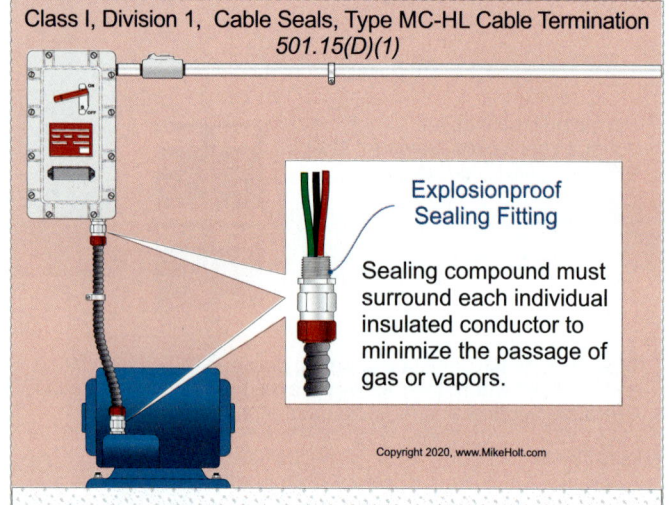

▶Figure 501–25

Seal fittings for cables entering enclosures must be installed within 18 in. of the enclosure or as required by the enclosure marking. Only explosionproof fittings such as unions, threaded couplings, reducers, elbows, and capped elbows can be installed between the cable seal fitting and the enclosure.

Ex: The removal of shielding material or the separation of the twisted pairs is not required within the seal fitting. ▶Figure 501–26

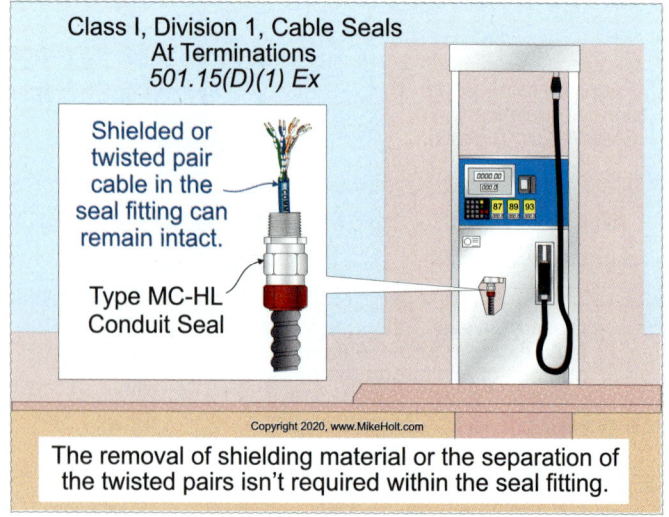

▶Figure 501–26

(2) Cables Capable of Transmitting Gases or Vapors in a Raceway. Raceways containing cables must be sealed after removing the jacket and any other coverings so that the sealing compound surrounds each individual insulated conductor or optical fiber tube in a manner that minimizes the passage of gases and vapors.

Ex: The removal of the outer sheathing of multiconductor cables is not required provided that the cable core is sealed within the conduit seal fitting. ▶Figure 501-27

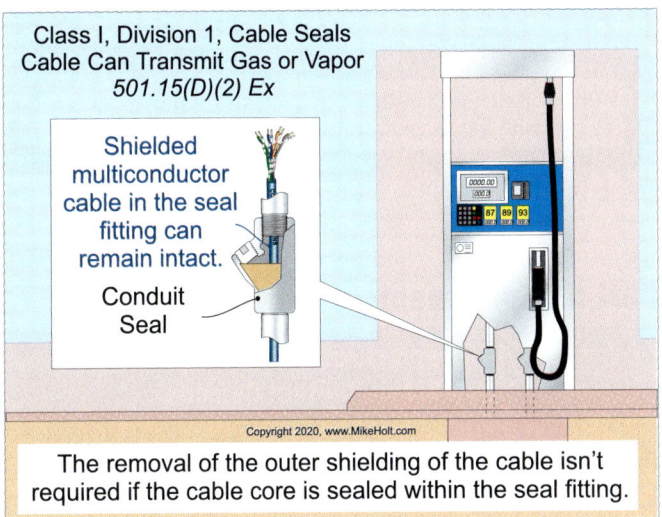

▶Figure 501-27

(3) Cables Not Capable of Transmitting Gases or Vapors in a Raceway. Each multiconductor cable installed within a raceway is considered to be a single conductor if the cable is incapable of transmitting gases or vapors through the cable core.

(E) Cable Seal, Class I, Division 2. In Class I, Division 2 locations, cable seals must be located as follows:

Ex: Seals are not required in a Class 1, Division 2 location if the cable passes through the location and has an unbroken gas or vaportight sheath.

(1) Multiconductor Cable. Multiconductor or optical fiber cables that enter an explosionproof enclosure must be sealed after removing the jacket and any other coverings so the sealing compound will surround each individual insulated conductor or optical fiber tube in a manner that minimizes the passage of gases and vapors.

Multiconductor cables or optical fiber cables installed within a raceway must be sealed in accordance with 501.15(D)(2) or (D)(3).

Ex 2: The removal of shielding material or the separation of the twisted pairs is not required within the conduit seal fitting.

(4) Cable Seal, Boundary. Cables without a gas/vaportight continuous sheath must be sealed at the boundary of the Class I, Division 2 location in a manner that minimizes the passage of gases or vapors into an unclassified location.

501.30 Grounding and Bonding

Because of the explosive conditions associated with electrical installations in hazardous (classified) locations [500.5], electrical continuity of metal parts of equipment and raceways must be ensured regardless of the voltage of the circuit.

(A) Bonding. Locknuts are not suitable for bonding purposes in hazardous (classified) locations; therefore, bonding jumpers or other approved means of bonding must be used for all intervening raceways, fittings, boxes, enclosures, and so forth between Class I locations and service equipment or separately derived systems. ▶Figure 501-28

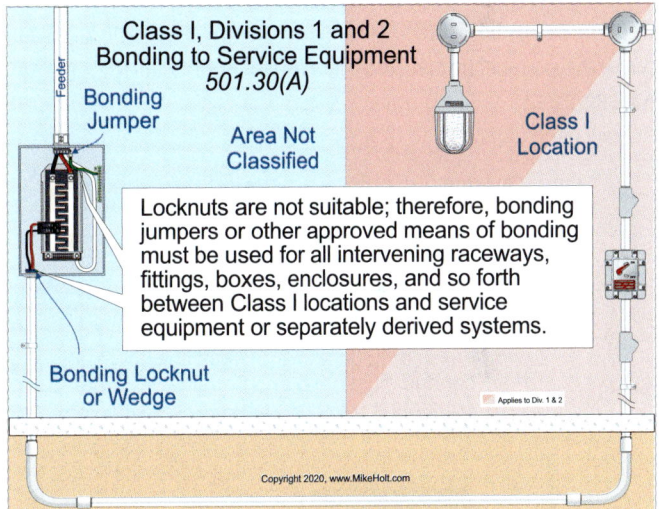

▶Figure 501-28

Author's Comment:

▸ Regardless of the circuit voltage, electrical continuity of metal parts of equipment and raceways in hazardous (classified) locations must be ensured by bonding-type locknuts, wedges, or bushings with bonding jumpers [250.92(B)(4)]; whether or not equipment grounding conductors of the wire type are installed in the raceway [250.100]. Locknuts alone are not sufficient to serve this purpose.

▸ A separate equipment grounding conductor is not required if a metal raceway is used for equipment grounding. Threaded couplings and hubs made up wrenchtight provide a suitable low-impedance fault current path [250.100]. ▶Figure 501-29

501.115 | Class I Hazardous (Classified) Locations

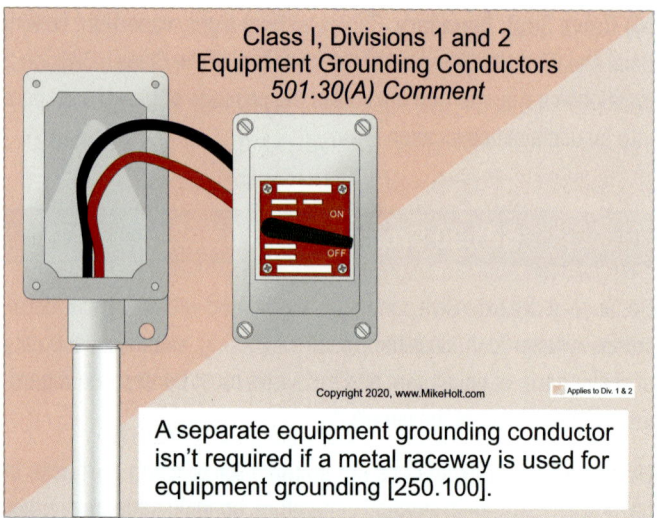
▶Figure 501–29

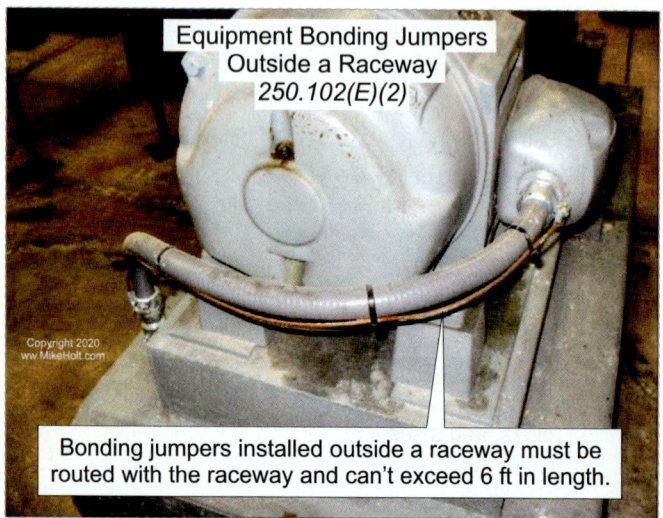
▶Figure 501–31

(B) Equipment Grounding Conductor, Flexible Raceway. Where flexible metal conduit or liquidtight flexible metal conduit is installed as permitted by 501.10(B)(2) or (4), an equipment bonding jumper of the wire type must be installed in accordance with 250.102. ▶Figure 501–30

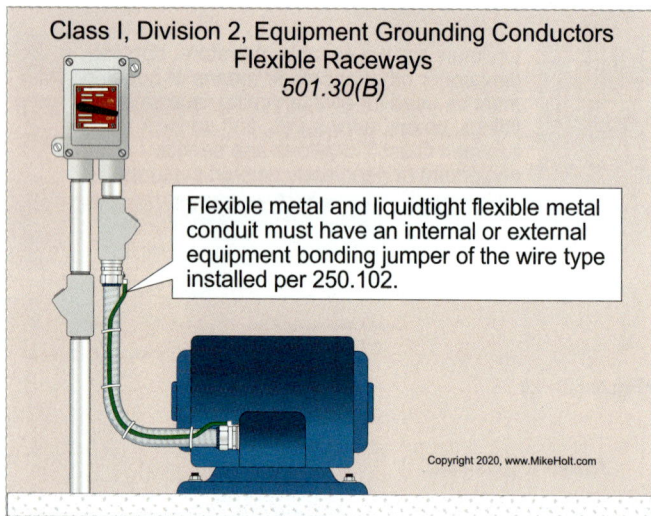
▶Figure 501–30

Author's Comment:

▸ Load side bonding jumpers are sized in accordance with Table 250.122 based on the rating of the overcurrent protective device [250.102(D)]. Where installed outside a raceway, the length of bonding jumpers is not permitted to exceed 6 ft and they must be routed with the raceway [250.102(E)(2)]. ▶Figure 501–31

Part III. Equipment

501.115 Enclosures Containing Make-and-Break Contact Devices

(A) Class I, Division 1. Enclosures containing switches, circuit breakers, motor controllers, and fuses (including pushbuttons, relays, and similar make-and-break contact devices) must be identified for use in a Class I, Division 1 location. ▶Figure 501–32

(B) Class I, Division 2.

(1) Type Required. Enclosures containing circuit breakers, motor controllers, fuses, pushbuttons, relays, and other make-and-break contact devices must be identified for use in a Class I, Division 1 location in accordance with 501.105(A). ▶Figure 501–33

Make-and-break contact devices can be installed in general-purpose enclosures if any of the following is provided:

(1) The interruption of current occurs within a hermetically sealed chamber.

(2) The make-and-break contacts are oil-immersed.

Class I Hazardous (Classified) Locations | 501.130

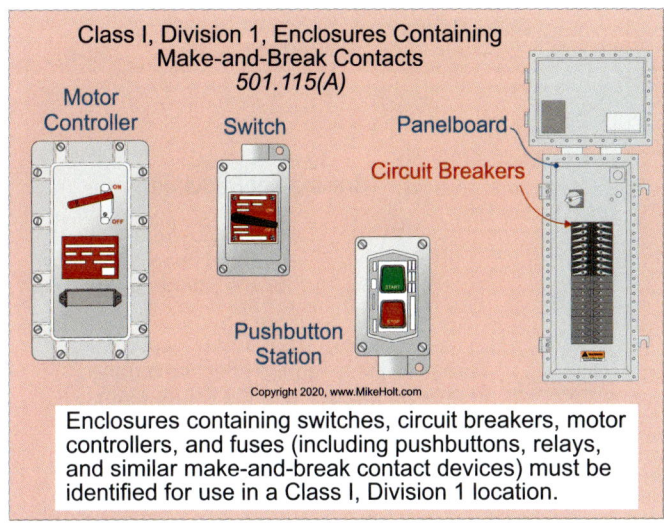
▶Figure 501–32

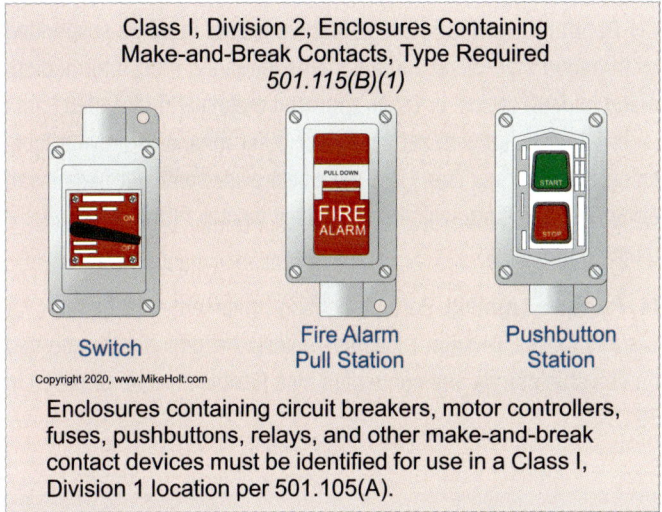
▶Figure 501–33

(3) The interruption of current occurs within an enclosure identified for the location and marked "Leads Factory Sealed," "Factory Sealed," "Seal not Required," or the equivalent.

501.125 Motors and Generators

(A) Class I, Division 1. Motors and generators installed in a Class I, Division 1 location must be:

(1) Identified for Class I, Division 1 locations, or be

(2) Of the totally enclosed type supplied with positive-pressure ventilation and arranged to automatically de-energize if the air supply fails.

(3) Of the totally enclosed inert gas-filled type and arranged to automatically de-energize if the gas supply fails.

(4) Submerged in a liquid flammable only when vaporized and mixed with air and arranged to automatically de-energize if the liquid is reduced to atmospheric pressure (vaporized).

Totally enclosed motors of the types specified in 501.125(A)(2) or (A)(3) must be designed so no external surface has an operating temperature in excess of 80 percent of the autoignition temperature of the gas or vapor involved. A device must be provided to de-energize the motor or sound an alarm if the temperature exceeds the designed limits.

(B) Class I, Division 2. Motors and generators installed in a Class I, Division 2 location must comply with the following:

(1) Be identified for Class I, Division 2 locations.

(2) Be identified for Class I, Division 1 locations where make-and-break contacts are present.

(3) If of the open or nonexplosionproof enclosed type, the motor must not contain any brushes, switching mechanisms, or similar arc-producing devices not identified for use in a Class I, Division 2 location, such as squirrel-cage induction motors without arcing devices. ▶Figure 501–34

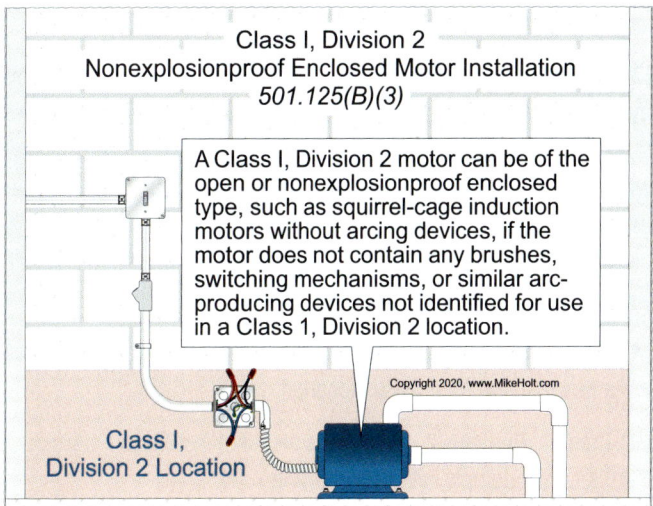
▶Figure 501–34

501.130 Luminaires

(A) Class I, Division 1. Luminaires installed in a Class I, Division 1 location must comply with the following:

(1) Luminaires. Luminaires must be identified for the Class I, Division 1 location. ▶Figure 501–35

501.135 | Class I Hazardous (Classified) Locations

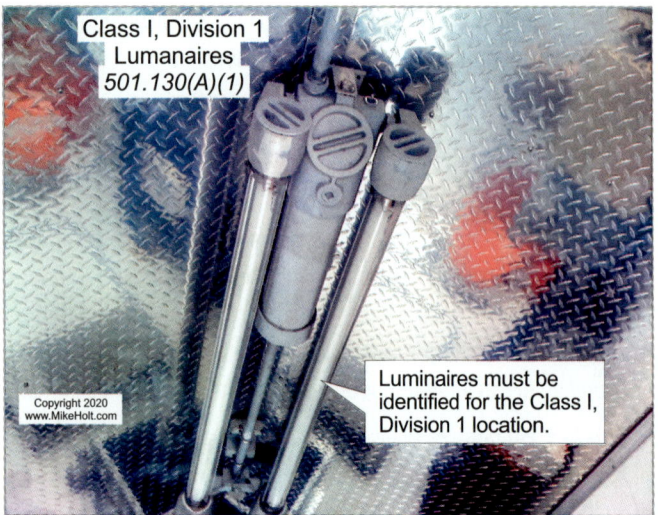

▶Figure 501-35

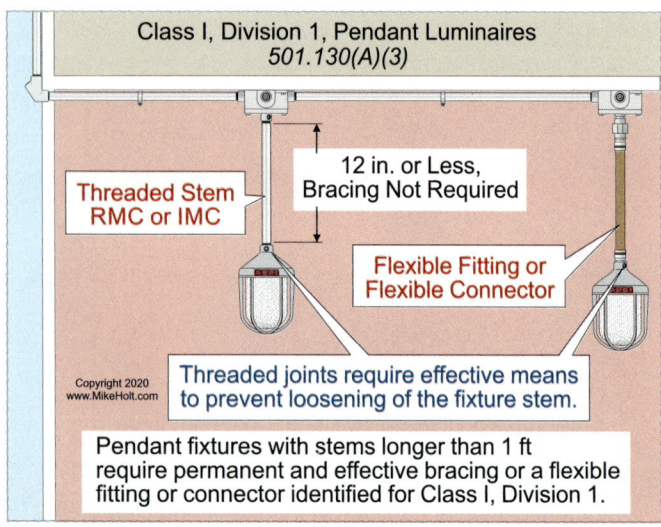

▶Figure 501-36

Author's Comment:

▸ Conduit seals are not required for listed Class I, Division 1 explosionproof luminaires because the lamp compartment is separated or sealed from the wiring compartment in accordance with the listing requirements.

(2) Physical Damage. Luminaires must be protected against physical damage by a suitable guard or by location.

(3) Pendant Luminaires. Pendant luminaires must be suspended by, and supplied through, threaded rigid metal conduit or threaded steel intermediate conduit stems. Threaded joints must be provided with set screws or other means to prevent loosening. Stems longer than 12 in. must be provided with permanent and effective lateral bracing, or with a flexible fitting or connector identified for the Class I, Division 1 location. ▶Figure 501-36

(4) Boxes and Fittings. Boxes or fittings used to support luminaires must be identified for a Class I location.

(B) Class I, Division 2. Luminaires installed in a Class I, Division 2 location must comply with the following:

(1) Luminaires. If the lamp temperature exceeds 80 percent of the autoignition temperature of the gas or vapor, luminaires must be identified for a Class I, Division 1 location.

(2) Physical Damage. Luminaires must be protected from physical damage by suitable guards or by location.

(3) Pendant Luminaires. Pendant luminaires must be suspended by threaded rigid metal conduit stems, threaded steel intermediate metal conduit stems, or other approved means and threaded joints must be provided with set screws or other means to prevent loosening. Stems longer than 12 in. must be provided with permanent and effective lateral bracing, or an identified flexible fitting or connector must be provided.

(4) Portable Lighting. Portable lighting equipment must be listed for use in a Class I, Division 1 location, unless the luminaire is mounted on movable stands and connected by a flexible cord as provided in 501.140.

501.135 Utilization Equipment

Utilization equipment such as heaters, motors, switches, circuit breakers, fuses, and such must comply with 501.135(A) and (B):

(A) Class I, Division 1. In Class I, Division 1 locations, all utilization equipment must be identified for use in Class I, Division 1 locations.

(B) Class I, Division 2. In Class I, Division 2 locations, all utilization equipment must be identified for use in Class I, Division 2 locations.

501.140 Flexible Cords, Class I, Divisions 1 and 2

(A) Permitted Uses. Flexible cord is permitted for:

Class I Hazardous (Classified) Locations | **501.145**

(1) Connection of portable lighting or portable utilization equipment. The flexible cord must be attached to the utilization equipment with a cord connector listed for the protection technique of the equipment wiring compartment. An attachment plug meeting the requirements of 501.140(B)(4) must also be used. ▶Figure 501–37

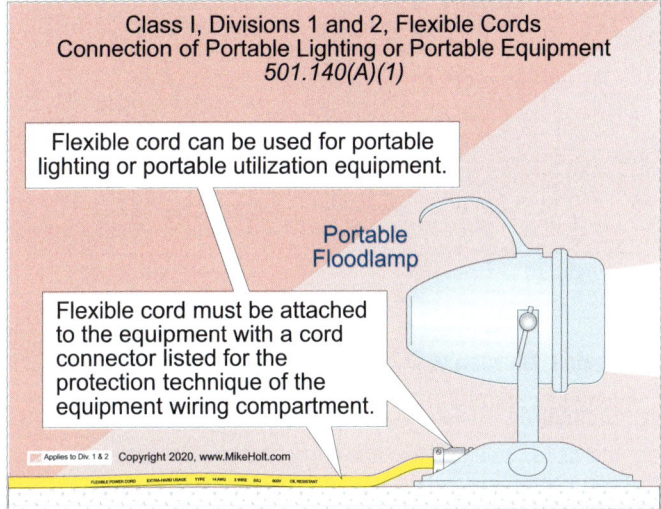

▶Figure 501–37

(2) In an industrial establishment where conditions of maintenance and engineering supervision ensure that only qualified persons install and service the installation, where the fixed wiring methods of 501.10(A) cannot provide the flexibility necessary or where necessary for mobile electrical equipment, and where the flexible cord is protected from damage by location or a suitable guard.

(3) Flexible cords for submersible pumps that can be removed without entering the wet-pit are permitted to be extended from the wet-pit to the power source within a suitable raceway.

(B) Installation. If flexible cords are used, the cords must:

(1) Be listed for extra-hard usage.

(2) Contain an equipment grounding conductor.

(3) Be supported so that no tension will be transmitted to the terminal connections.

(4) In Division 1 or Division 2 locations where the boxes, fittings, or enclosures must be explosionproof, the flexible cord must terminate with a flexible cord connector or attachment plug listed for the location, or a listed flexible cord connector installed with a seal that is listed for the location. In Division 2 locations where explosion-proof equipment is not required, the flexible cord must terminate with a listed flexible cord connector or listed attachment plug.

(5) Be of continuous length. Where 501.140(A)(5) is applied, cords must be of continuous length from the power source to the temporary portable assembly and from the temporary portable assembly to the utilization equipment.

501.145 Receptacles and Attachment Plugs

(A) Receptacles. Receptacles must be part of the premises wiring, unless they are part of a temporary portable assembly [501.140(A)(5)]. ▶Figure 501–38

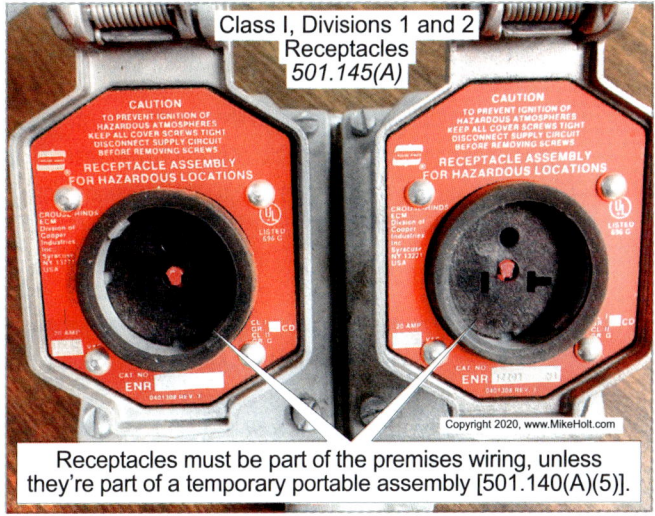

▶Figure 501–38

(B) Attachment Plugs. Attachment plugs must provide for the connection of an equipment grounding conductor of a permitted flexible cord and be identified for the class location. ▶Figure 501–39

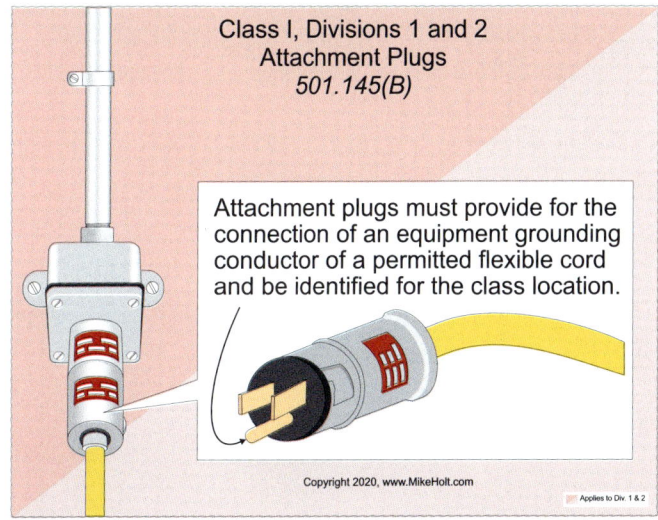

▶Figure 501–39

501.150 | Class I Hazardous (Classified) Locations

Author's Comment:

▸ See the definitions of "Attachment Plug" and "Receptacle" in Article 100.

▸ Receptacles listed for Class I locations can be any of the following types:

   ▸ **Interlocked Switch Receptacle.** This receptacle contains a built-in rotary switch interlocked with the attachment plug. The switch must be off before the attachment plug can be inserted or removed.

   ▸ **Manual Interlocked Receptacle.** The attachment plug is inserted into the receptacle and then rotated to operate the receptacle's switching contacts.

   ▸ **Delayed Action Receptacle.** This receptacle requires an attachment plug and receptacle constructed so that an electrical arc will be confined within the explosionproof chamber of the receptacle.

501.150 Limited-Energy and Communications Systems

(A) Class I, Division 1. Low-voltage, limited-energy, and communications systems (twisted pair and coaxial cable) in a Class I, Division 1 location must be installed in accordance with 501.10(A), 501.15(A), and 501.15(C).

Author's Comment:

▸ Wiring methods, enclosures, conduit seals, and other equipment used for limited-energy and communications systems, regardless of voltage, must be installed using the same techniques as those used for power conductors. ▸Figure 501–40

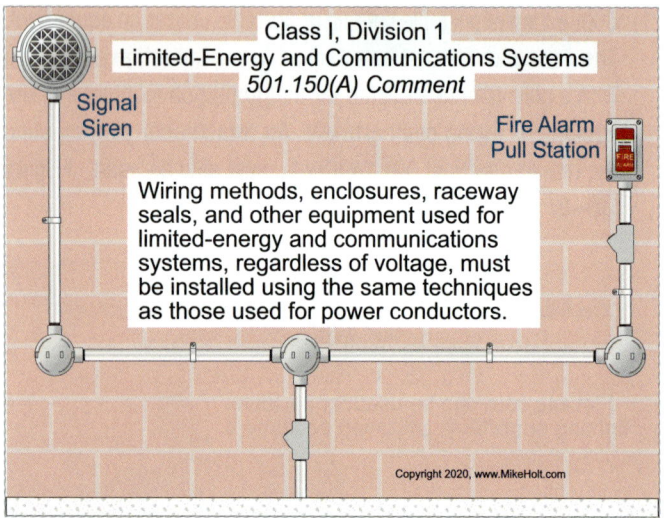

▸Figure 501–40

(B) Class I, Division 2.

(1) Enclosures. General-purpose enclosures are permitted, unless the enclosure contains make-and-break contacts. An enclosure identified for a Class I, Division 1 location must be used where the enclosure contains make-and-break contacts [501.105(A)].

Ex: General-purpose enclosures are permitted if the contacts are:

   (1) Immersed in oil.

   (2) Enclosed within a chamber hermetically sealed against the entrance of gases or vapors.

   (3) In nonincendive circuits.

   (4) Part of a listed nonincendive component.

(4) Wiring Methods and Seals. Wiring methods in a Class I, Division 2 location must be made with threaded rigid metal conduit, intermediate metal conduit, flexible metal conduit, or liquidtight flexible conduit with listed fittings. In addition, Types MI, MC, TC, ITC, and PLTC cables with fittings are permitted [501.10(B)]. Raceway and cable seals must be installed in accordance with 501.15(B) and 501.15(C).

ARTICLE 502 — CLASS II HAZARDOUS (CLASSIFIED) LOCATIONS

Introduction to Article 502—Class II Hazardous (Classified) Locations

If an area has combustible dust present, it is considered to be a Class II location. Examples of such locations include flour mills, grain silos, coal bins, wood pulp storage areas, and munitions plants.

Article 502 follows a logical arrangement similar to that of Article 501 and provides guidance in selecting equipment and wiring methods for Class II locations, including distinctions between Class II, Division 1 and Class II, Division 2 requirements.

Part I. General

502.1 Scope

Article 502 covers the requirements for electrical equipment and wiring in Class II, Division 1 and 2 locations where fire or explosion hazards may exist due to the presence of combustible dust. ▶Figure 502–1

▶Figure 502–1

Author's Comment:

- Examples of combustible dust include combustible metal dusts, coal, carbon black, charcoal, coke, flour, grain, wood, plastic, and chemicals in the air in quantities sufficient to produce explosive or ignitible mixtures [500.5(C) and 500.8]. See the Article 100 definition of "Combustible Dust."

502.5 Explosionproof Equipment

Explosionproof equipment cannot be installed in a Class II location, unless identified for a Class II location. ▶Figure 502–2

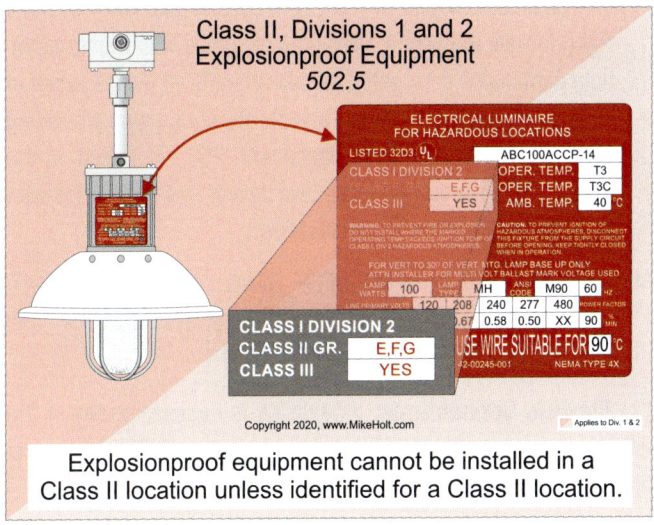

▶Figure 502–2

Part II. Wiring

502.10 Wiring Methods

(A) Class II, Division 1.

(1) General. The following wiring methods can be installed in a Class II, Division 1 location: ▶Figure 502–3

502.10 | Class II Hazardous (Classified) Locations

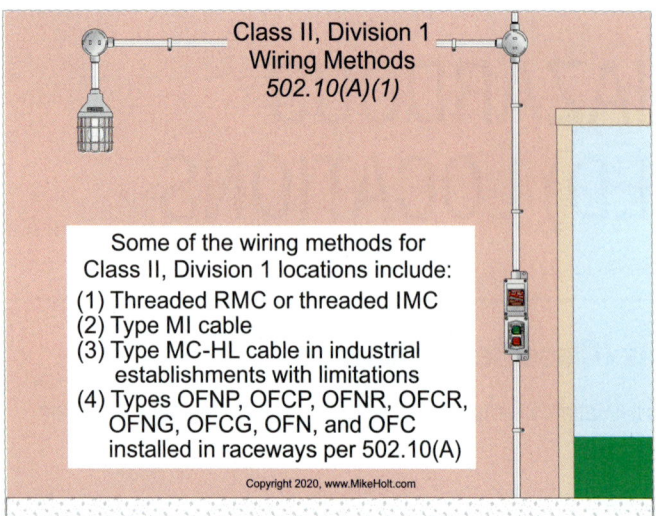
▶Figure 502–3

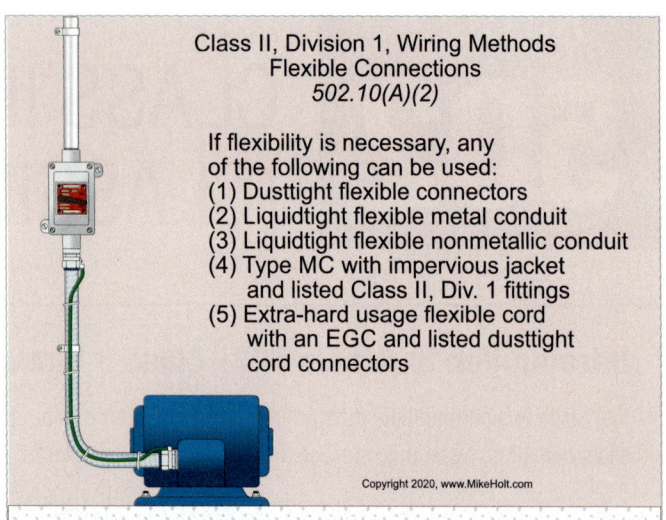
▶Figure 502–4

(1) Threaded rigid metal conduit or threaded intermediate metal conduit.

(2) Type MI cable terminated with fittings that are listed for the location.

(3) In industrial establishments with restricted public access where only qualified persons will service the installation, MC-HL cable listed for use in Class II, Division 1 locations with a gas/vapor-tight continuous corrugated metallic sheath, an overall jacket of suitable polymeric material, a separate equipment grounding conductor(s) sized in accordance with 250.122 based on the rating of the overcurrent protective device, and terminated with fittings that are listed for the location.

(4) Types OFNP, OFCP, OFNR, OFCR, OFNG, OFCG, OFN, and OFC optical fiber cable can be installed in raceways [502.10(A)] and must be sealed in accordance with 502.15.

(2) Flexible Connections. If flexibility is necessary, any of the following wiring methods are permitted in a Class II, Division 1 location: ▶Figure 502–4

(1) Dusttight flexible connectors.

(2) Liquidtight flexible metal conduit (Type LFMC) with listed fittings.

(3) Liquidtight flexible nonmetallic conduit (Type LFNC) with listed fittings.

(4) Interlocked armor Type MC cable with an impervious jacket and termination fittings listed for Class II, Division 1 locations.

(5) Flexible cords listed for extra-hard usage, containing an equipment grounding conductor and terminated with listed dusttight flexible cord connectors. The flexible cord must be installed in accordance with 502.140.

(3) Boxes and Fittings. Boxes and fittings must be provided with threaded bosses and must be dusttight. Boxes and fittings in which taps, joints, or terminal connections are made, or used in locations where dusts are of a combustible nature [500.6(B)(1) Group E], must be identified for Class II locations. ▶Figure 502–5

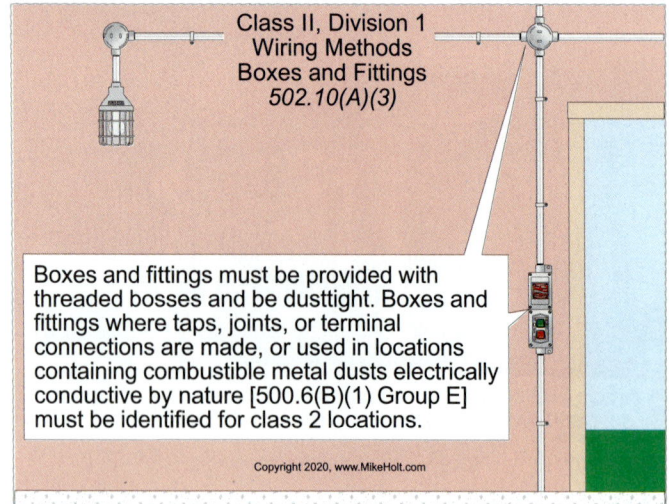
▶Figure 502–5

(B) Class II, Division 2.

(1) General. In Class II, Division 2 locations, the following wiring methods are permitted: ▶Figure 502–6

Class II Hazardous (Classified) Locations | **502.15**

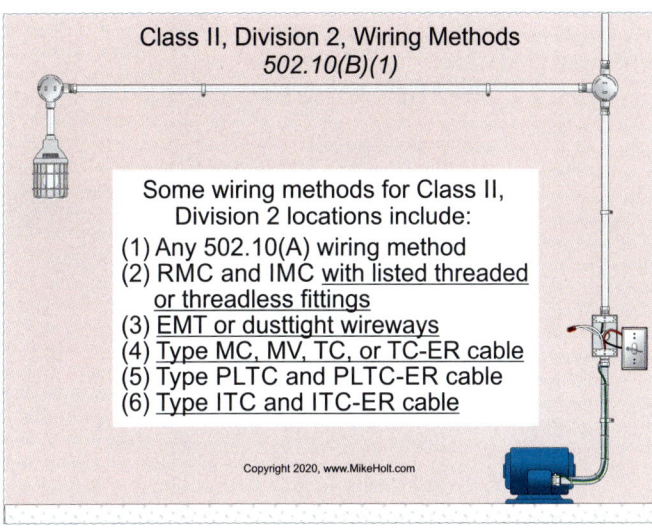

▶Figure 502–6

(1) Any of the wiring methods in 502.10(A).

(2) Rigid metal conduit (RMC) and intermediate metal conduit (IMC) with listed threaded or threadless fittings.

(3) Electrical metallic tubing (EMT) or dusttight wireways.

(4) Type MC, MV, TC, or TC-ER cable, including installation in cable tray systems. Type TC-ER cable must include an equipment grounding conductor in addition to any drain wire that might be present. The cable must be terminated with listed fittings.

(5) Type PLTC and PLTC-ER cable in accordance with Parts II and III of Article 725, including installation in cable tray systems. The cable must be terminated with listed fittings. Type PLTC-ER cable must include an equipment grounding conductor in addition to a drain wire that might be present.

(6) Type ITC and ITC-ER cable as permitted in 727.4 and terminated with listed fittings. Type ITC-ER cable must include an equipment grounding conductor in addition to a drain wire.

(7) Where metal conduit will not provide sufficient corrosion resistance, any of the following are permitted:

  a. Listed reinforced thermosetting resin conduit (RTRC), factory elbows, and associated fittings, all marked with the suffix "-XW"

  b. PVC-coated rigid metal conduit (RMC), factory elbows, and associated fittings

  c. PVC-coated intermediate metal conduit (IMC), factory elbows, and associated fittings

  d. In industrial establishments with restricted public access, where the conditions of maintenance and supervision ensure that only qualified persons service the installation, Schedule 80 PVC conduit, factory elbows, and associated fittings

(8) Types OFNP, OFCP, OFNR, OFCR, OFNG, OFCG, OFN, and OFC optical fiber cables can be installed in cable trays or raceways [502.10(B)] and must be sealed in accordance with 502.15. ▶Figure 502–7

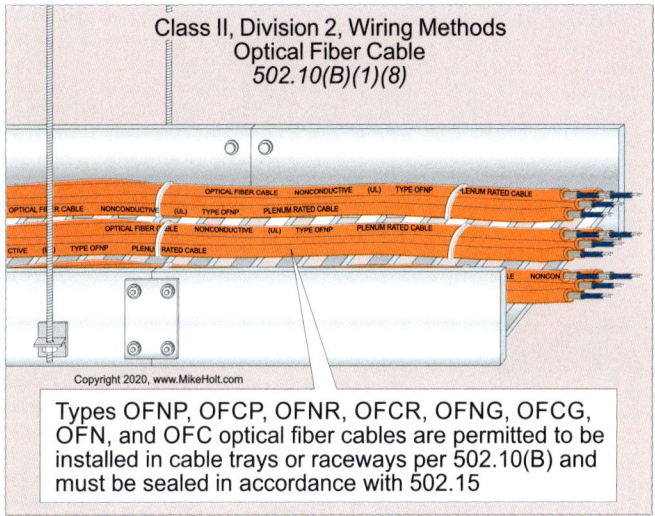

▶Figure 502–7

(2) Flexible Connections. If flexibility is required, wiring methods complying with 502.10(A)(2) are permitted in a Class II, Division 2 location.

(4) Boxes and Fittings. Boxes and fittings in Class II, Division 2 areas must be dusttight. ▶Figure 502–8

> **Author's Comment:**
>
> ▸ A standard weatherproof box with a cover and gasket meets this requirement.

502.15 Sealing

In Class II, Division 1 and 2 locations, dust must be prevented from entering the required dust-ignitionproof enclosure from a raceway by any of the following methods:

(1) A permanent and effective seal, such as sealing putty [502.15 Note].
▶Figure 502–9

502.30 | Class II Hazardous (Classified) Locations

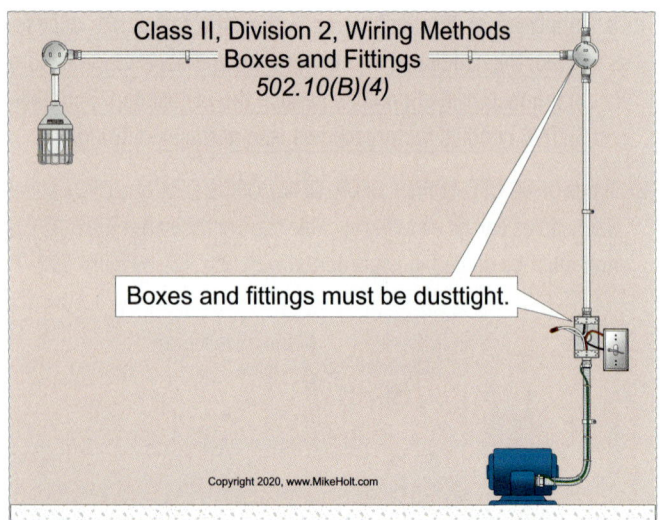

▶Figure 502–8

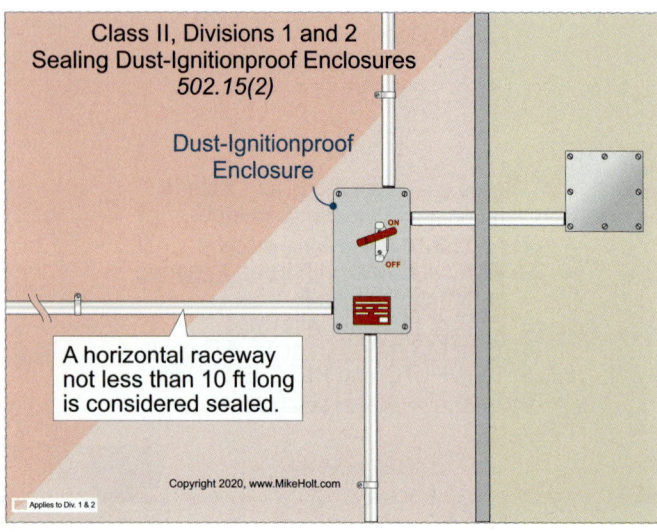

▶Figure 502–10

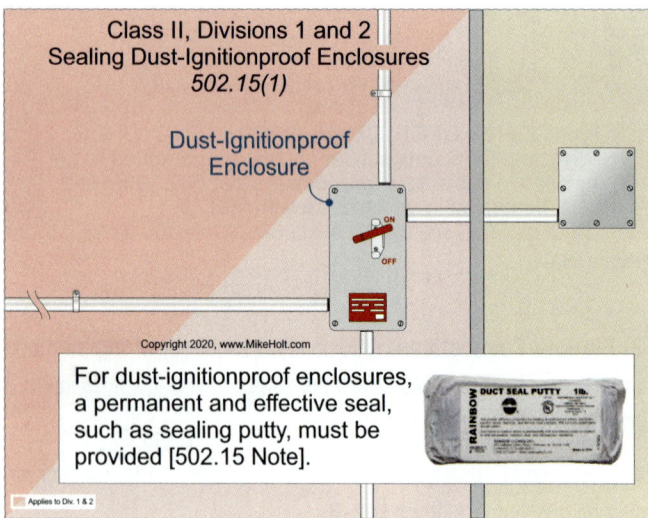

▶Figure 502–9

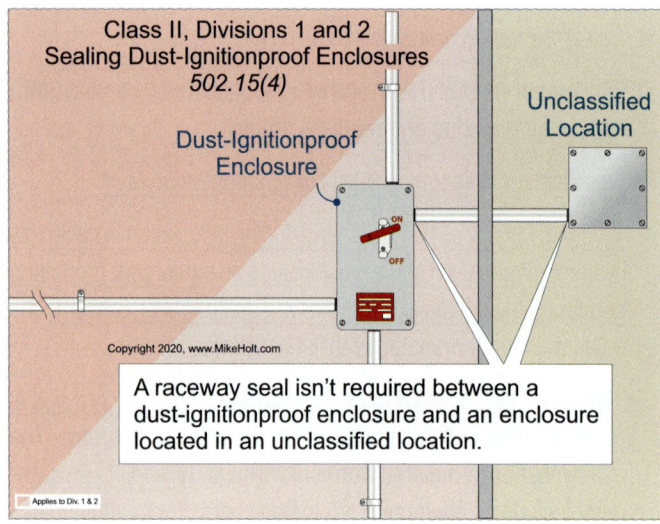

▶Figure 502–11

(2) A horizontal raceway not less than 10 ft long. ▶Figure 502–10

(3) A vertical raceway that extends downward for not less than 5 ft from the dust-ignitionproof enclosure.

(4) A raceway installed in a manner equivalent to (2) or (3) that extends only horizontally and downward from the dust-ignitionproof enclosure.

A conduit seal is not required between a dust-ignitionproof enclosure and an enclosure located in an unclassified location. ▶Figure 502–11

Sealing fittings for Class II locations must be accessible and are not required to be explosionproof.

Note: Electrical sealing putty is one method of sealing.

502.30 Grounding and Bonding

Because of the explosive conditions associated with electrical installations in hazardous (classified) locations [500.5], electrical continuity of the metal parts of equipment and raceways must be ensured regardless of the voltage of the circuit.

(A) Bonding. Locknuts are not suitable for bonding purposes in hazardous (classified) locations; therefore, bonding jumpers or other approved means of bonding must be used. Such means of bonding apply to all intervening raceways, fittings, boxes, enclosures, and so forth between Class II locations and service disconnects or the grounding point of a separately derived system. ▶Figure 502–12

Class II Hazardous (Classified) Locations | 502.115

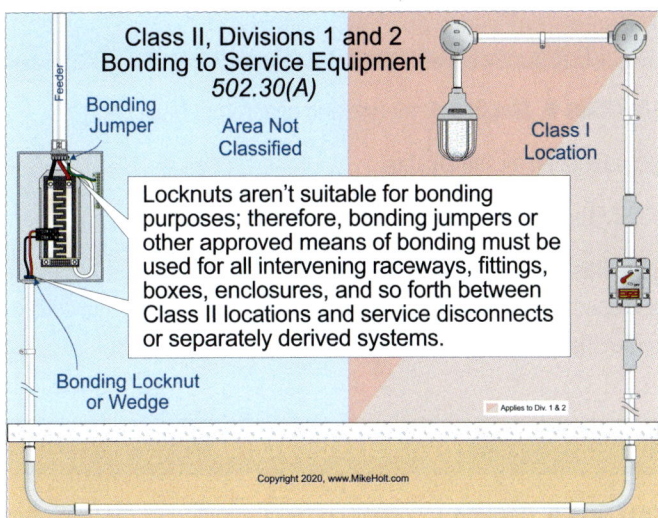

▶Figure 502-12

Author's Comment:

▶ A separate equipment grounding conductor is not required if a metal raceway is used for equipment grounding. Threaded couplings and hubs made up wrenchtight provide a suitable low-impedance ground-fault current path [250.100]. ▶Figure 502-13

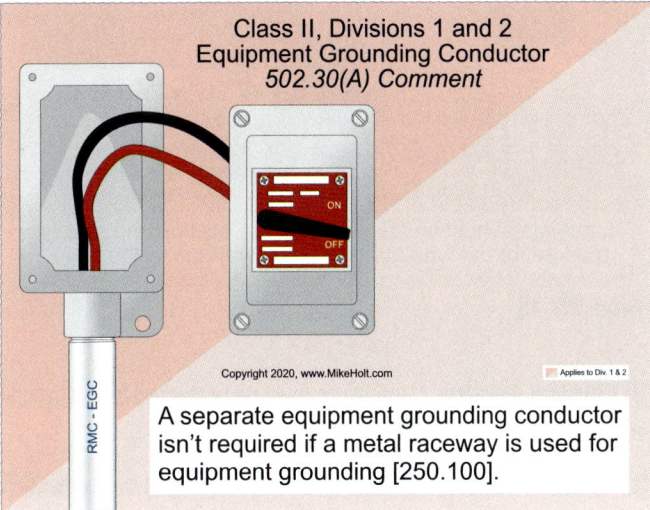

▶Figure 502-13

Author's Comment:

▶ The special bonding requirements for Class 2 locations are the same as those for 501.30(A) Class 1 locations. See 250.94(B)(4).

(B) Equipment Grounding Conductor, Type LFMC. Where liquidtight flexible metal conduit is installed as permitted by 502.10(A)(2), an equipment bonding jumper of the wire type must be installed in accordance with 250.102. ▶Figure 502-14

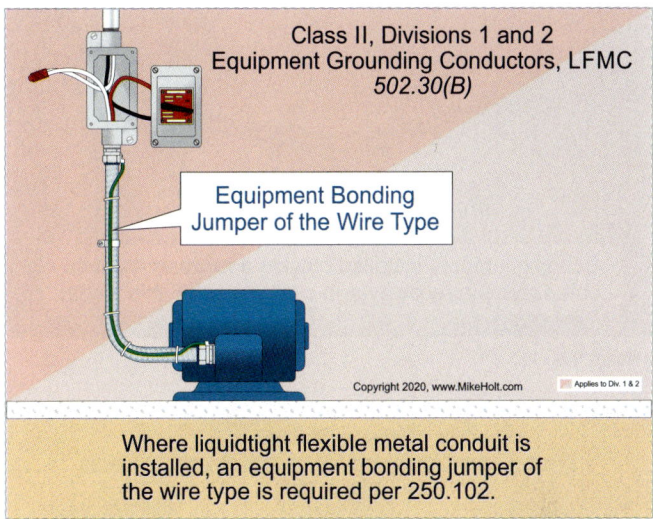

▶Figure 502-14

Author's Comment:

▶ Load side bonding jumpers must be sized in accordance with 250.122 based on the rating of the overcurrent protective device [250.102(D)], and where the bonding jumper is installed outside of a raceway, the length of the bonding jumpers are not permitted to exceed 6 ft and they must be routed with the raceway [250.102(E)(2)]. ▶Figure 502-15

Part III. Equipment

502.115 Enclosures Containing Make-and-Break Contacts

(A) Class II, Division 1. Enclosures for switches, circuit breakers, motor controllers, fuses, pushbuttons, relays, and similar devices must be identified for a Class II, Division 1 location. ▶Figure 502-16

(B) Class II, Division 2. Enclosures for fuses, switches, circuit breakers, and motor controllers (including pushbuttons, relays, and similar devices) must be dusttight or identified for a Class II, Division 2 location. ▶Figure 502-17

Author's Comment:

▶ A standard weatherproof box with a cover and gasket meets this requirement.

502.125 | Class II Hazardous (Classified) Locations

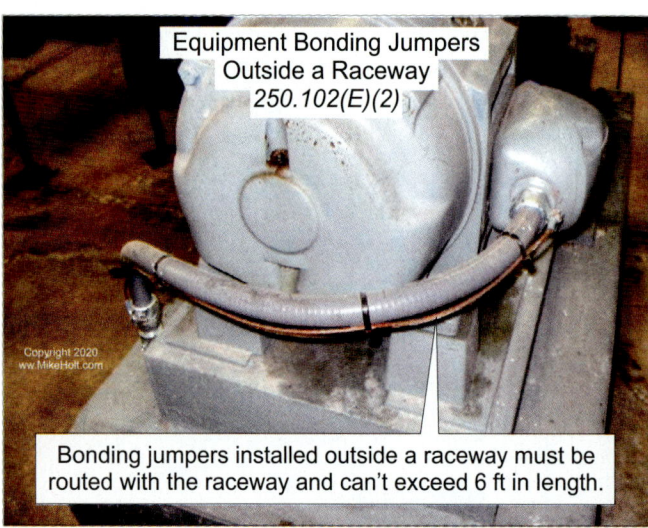

▶Figure 502–15

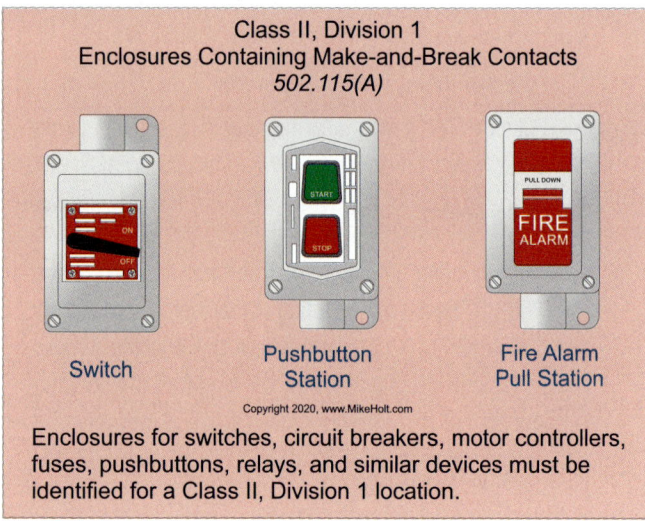

▶Figure 502–16

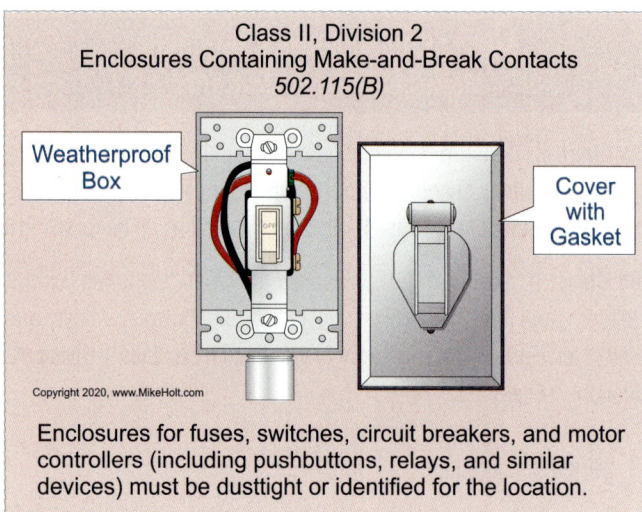

▶Figure 502–17

502.125 Motors and Generators

(A) Class II, Division 1. Motors and generators must be:

(1) Identified for the location.

(2) Of the totally enclosed pipe-ventilated type.

(B) Class II, Division 2. Motors and generators must be totally enclosed nonventilated, pipe-ventilated, water-air-cooled, fan-cooled, or be dust-ignitionproof.

502.130 Luminaires

(A) Class II, Division 1. Luminaires must comply with the following:

(1) Marking. Luminaires must be identified for the location and clearly marked for the type and maximum wattage of the lamp. ▶Figure 502–18

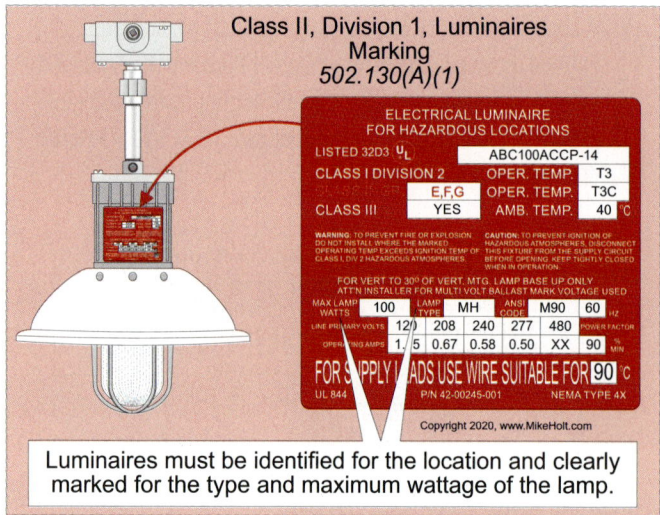

▶Figure 502–18

(2) Physical Damage. Luminaires must be protected from physical damage by suitable guards or by location. ▶Figure 502–19

(3) Pendant Luminaires. Pendant luminaires must be suspended by threaded rigid metal conduit stems, threaded steel intermediate metal conduit stems, by chains with approved fittings, or by other approved means. ▶Figure 502–20

Threaded joints must be provided with set screws or other effective means to prevent loosening. For stems longer than 1 ft, permanent, effective bracing, or a flexible fitting or connector listed for the Class II, Division 1 location must be provided not more than 1 ft from the point of attachment to the supporting box/fitting.

Class II Hazardous (Classified) Locations | 502.140

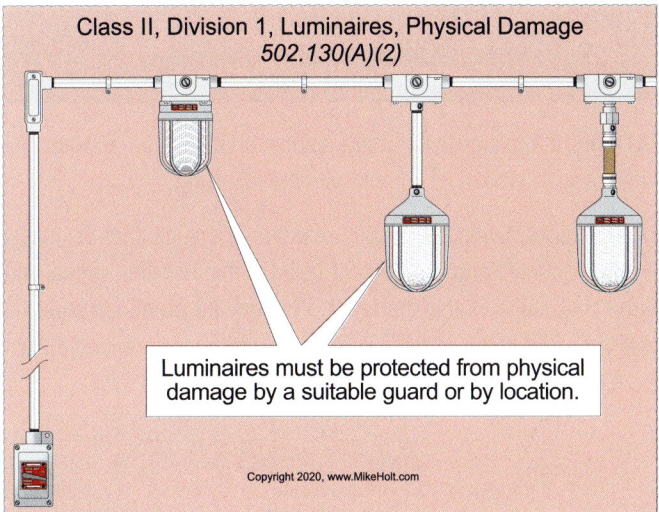
▶Figure 502–19

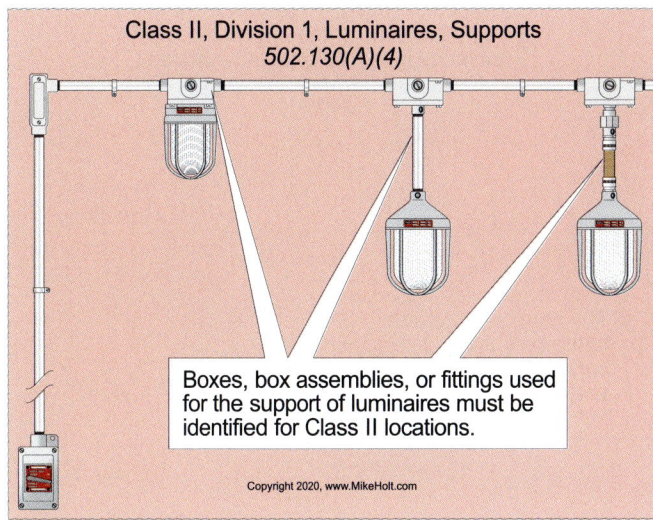
▶Figure 502–21

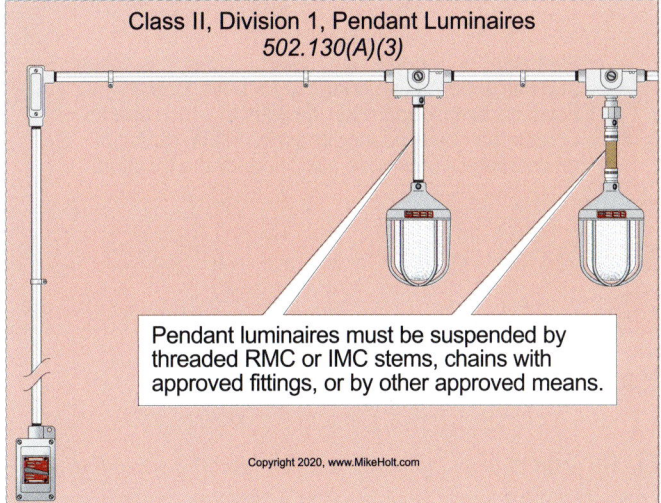
▶Figure 502–20

Flexible cord listed for hard usage is permitted as the wiring between an outlet box/fitting and a pendant luminaire when it contains an equipment grounding conductor and is terminated with fittings that are listed for the location in accordance with 502.10(A)(2)(5).

(4) Supports. Boxes, box assemblies, or fittings used for the support of luminaires must be identified for Class II locations. ▶Figure 502–21

(B) Class II, Division 2. Luminaires must comply with the following:

(1) Portable Lighting Equipment. Portable lighting equipment must be identified for the location.

(2) Fixed Lighting. Luminaires must be contained in enclosures that are dusttight or otherwise identified for the location.

(3) Physical Damage. Luminaires must be protected from physical damage by suitable guards or by location.

(4) Pendant Luminaires. Pendant luminaires must be suspended by threaded rigid metal conduit stems, threaded steel intermediate metal conduit stems, by chains with fittings approved by the authority having jurisdiction, or by other means approved by the authority having jurisdiction.

For stems longer than 1 ft, permanent, effective bracing, or a flexible fitting or connector must be provided not more than 1 ft from the point of attachment to the supporting box/fitting. Flexible cord listed for hard usage is permitted as the wiring between an outlet box/fitting and a pendant luminaire when it is terminated with a listed flexible cord connector that maintains the protection technique, but the flexible cord is not permitted to support the luminaire.

502.140 Flexible Cords

(A) Permitted Uses. Flexible cord is permitted for:

(1) Portable Lighting or Portable Utilization Equipment. The flexible cord must be attached to the equipment with a cord connector listed for the protection technique of the equipment wiring compartment, such as dust-ignitionproof. ▶Figure 502–22

An attachment plug of the grounding type that complies with 502.145 must also be used.

(B) Installation. Where flexible cords are used, the cords must comply with all of the following:

(1) Be of a type listed for extra-hard usage.

502.145 | Class II Hazardous (Classified) Locations

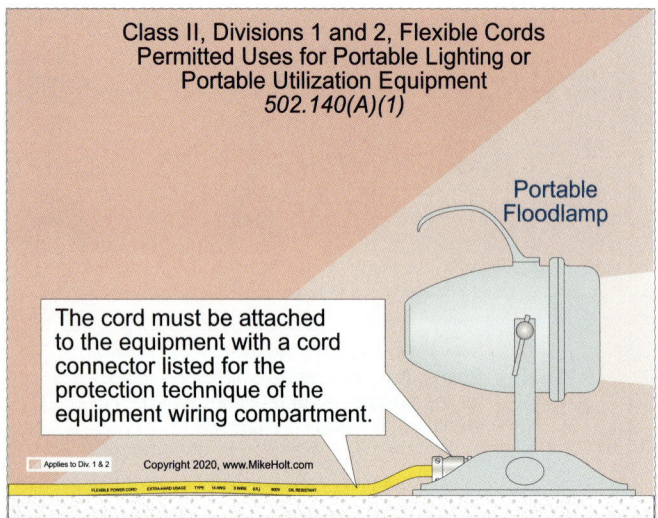

▶Figure 502-22

(2) Contain an equipment grounding conductor complying with 400.23.

(3) Be supported in such a manner that there will be no tension on the terminal connections.

(4) In Division 1 locations, the flexible cord must terminate with a flexible cord connector listed for the location or a listed flexible cord connector installed with a seal listed for the location. In Division 2 locations, the flexible cord must be terminated with a listed dusttight flexible cord connector.

502.145 Receptacles and Attachment Plugs

Receptacles and attachment plugs must be identified for the location.

(A) Class II, Division 1.

(1) Receptacles. In Class II, Division 1 locations, receptacles must be part of the premises wiring.

(2) Attachment Plugs. Attachment plugs must be of the type that provides for connection to the equipment grounding conductor of the flexible cord.

(B) Class II, Division 2.

(1) Receptacles. In Class II, Division 2 locations, receptacles must be part of the premises wiring.

(2) Attachment Plugs. Attachment plugs must be of the type that provides for connection to the equipment grounding conductor of the flexible cord.

502.150 Limited-Energy and Communications Systems

(A) Class II, Division 1. Signaling, alarm, remote-control, and communications systems must comply with the following:

(1) Contacts. Switches, circuit breakers, relays, contactors, fuses, and current-breaking contacts for bells, horns, howlers, sirens, and other devices in which sparks or arcs may be produced must be within enclosures that are dusttight or otherwise identified for the location. ▶Figure 502-23

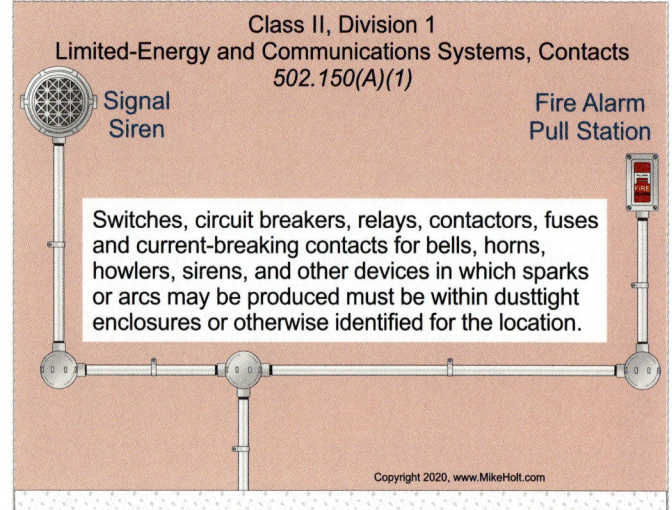

▶Figure 502-23

Ex: Enclosures of the general-purpose type are permitted if the contacts are immersed in oil or within a chamber sealed against the entrance of dust.

(B) Class II, Division 2. Signaling, alarm, remote-control, and communications systems must comply with the following:

(1) Contacts. Contacts must comply with 502.150(A)(1) or be installed in enclosures that are dusttight or otherwise identified for the location.

(2) Transformers. The windings and terminal connections of transformers must be provided with dusttight metal enclosures.

ARTICLE 503 — CLASS III HAZARDOUS (CLASSIFIED) LOCATIONS

Introduction to Article 503—Class III Hazardous (Classified) Locations

The Class III location scope can be a bit cumbersome, and some may have a hard time comprehending what it means. If you have easily ignitable fibers/flyings present, you may have a Class III location. Examples of such locations include sawmills, textile mills, and fiber processing plants. In many cases, the distinction between Class II and Class III locations may simply be the size of the particles. The definition of "Combustible Dust" in Article 100 defines it based on the size of the particles, so the same material (such as sawdust) may be subject to Article 503 if the predominant material is "larger" than the definition.

Author's Comment:

▸ Article 100 defines "Combustible Dust" as dust particles that are 500 microns in size or smaller. That is approximately $^2/_{100}$ of an inch!

Part I. General

503.1 Scope

Article 503 covers the requirements for electrical equipment and wiring for all voltages in Class III, Division 1 and 2 locations. These are areas where fire or explosion hazards might exist because easily ignitible fibers or materials producing combustible flyings are handled, manufactured, or used but are not likely to be suspended in the air in large enough quantities to produce ignitible mixtures [500.5(D)]. ▸Figure 503-1

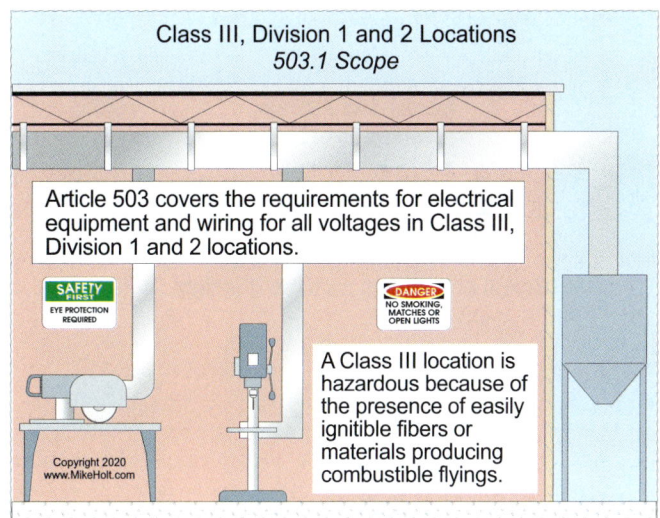

▸Figure 503-1

Part II. Wiring

503.10 Wiring Methods

The wiring methods permitted in Class III locations include:

(A) Class III, Division 1 Location.

(1) General. The following wiring methods can be installed in a Class III, Division 1 location: ▸Figure 503-2

(1) Rigid metal conduit (Type RMC), PVC conduit, RTRC conduit, intermediate metal conduit (Type IMC), electrical metallic tubing (EMT), dusttight wireways, or Types MC or MI cable terminated with fittings that are listed.

(2) Types PLTC and PLTC-ER cable terminated with listed fittings in accordance with Parts II and III of Article 725. Type PLTC-ER cable must include an equipment grounding conductor in addition to any drain wire that might be present.

(3) Type ITC and ITC-ER cable as permitted in 727.4 and terminated with listed fittings. Type ITC-ER cable must include an equipment grounding conductor in addition to a drain wire.

503.30 | Class III Hazardous (Classified) Locations

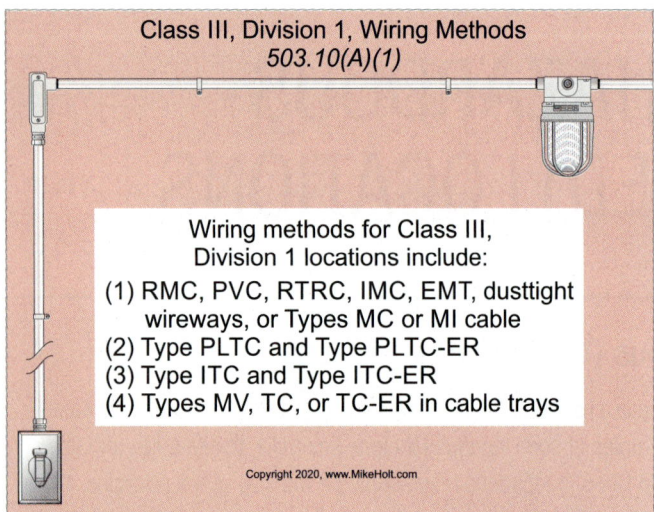

▶Figure 503-2

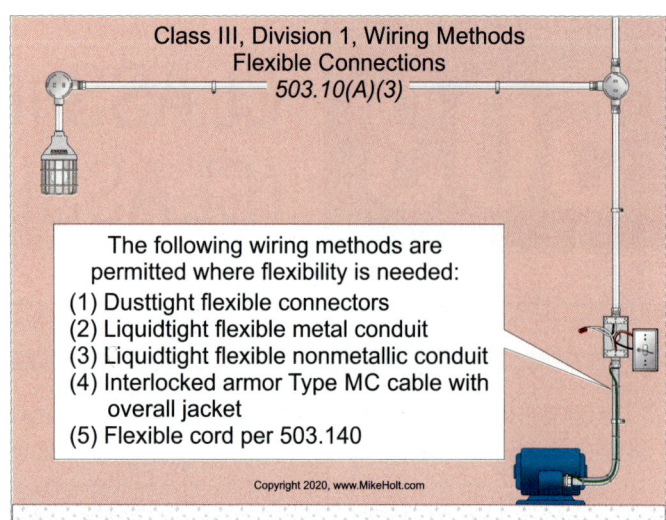

▶Figure 503-4

(4) Types MV, TC, or TC-ER cable including installation in cable tray systems. <u>Type TC-ER cable must include an equipment grounding conductor in addition to any drain wire that might be present.</u> The cable must be terminated with listed fittings.

(2) Boxes and Fittings. Boxes and fittings must be dusttight. ▶Figure 503-3

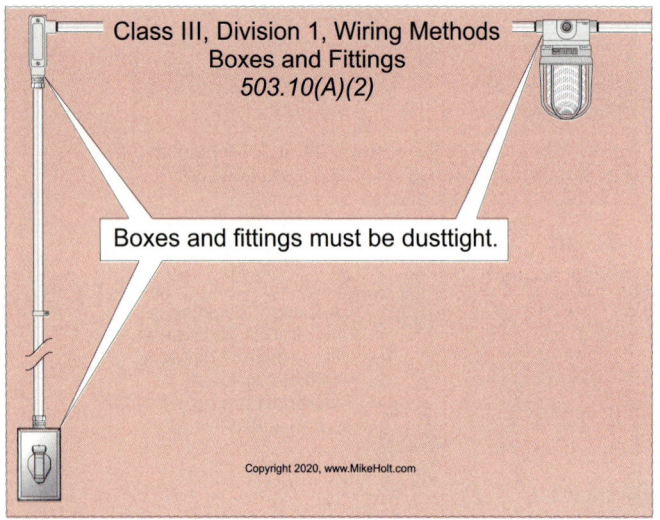

▶Figure 503-3

Author's Comment:

▸ A standard weatherproof box with a cover and gasket meets this requirement.

(3) Flexible Connections. Where flexibility is needed, the following can be used: ▶Figure 503-4

(1) Dusttight flexible connectors.

(2) Liquidtight flexible metal conduit (Type LFMC) with listed fittings.

(3) Liquidtight flexible nonmetallic conduit (Type LFNC) with listed fittings.

(4) Interlocked armor Type MC cable having an overall jacket of suitable polymeric material and installed with listed dusttight termination fittings.

(5) Flexible cord in accordance with 503.140.

(B) Class III, Division 2 Location. The wiring methods listed in 503.10(A) must be used in a Class III, Division 2 location.

503.30 Grounding and Bonding

Because of the explosive conditions associated with electrical installations in hazardous (classified) locations [500.5], electrical continuity of the metal parts of equipment and raceways must be ensured regardless of the voltage of the circuit.

(A) Bonding. Locknuts are not suitable for bonding purposes in hazardous (classified) locations; therefore, bonding jumpers or other approved means of bonding must be used. Such means of bonding apply to all intervening raceways, fittings, boxes, and enclosures between Class III locations and service disconnects.

(B) Type of Equipment Bonding Conductor. Where liquidtight flexible metal conduit is installed [503.10(A)(3)], an equipment bonding jumper of the wire type must be installed in accordance with 250.102. ▶Figure 503-5

Class III Hazardous (Classified) Locations | 503.130

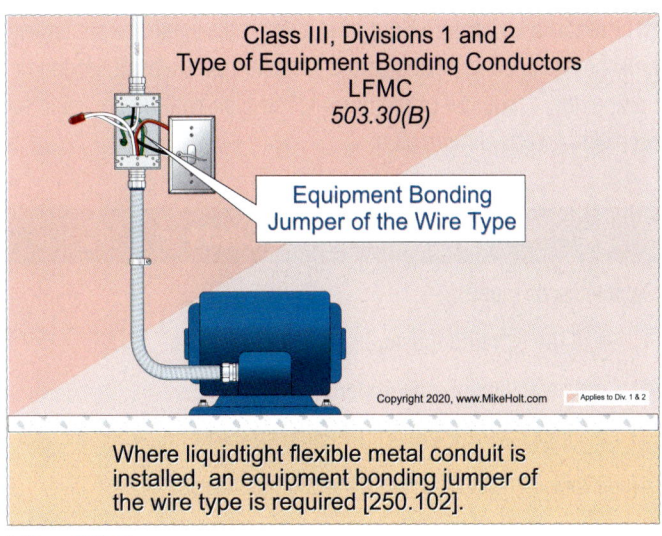

▶Figure 503-5

Author's Comment:

▶ Load side bonding jumpers must be sized in accordance with 250.122 based on the rating of the overcurrent protective device [250.102(D)]. Where bonding jumpers are installed outside a raceway, the length is not permitted to exceed 6 ft and they must be routed with the raceway [250.102(E)(2)].
▶Figure 503-6

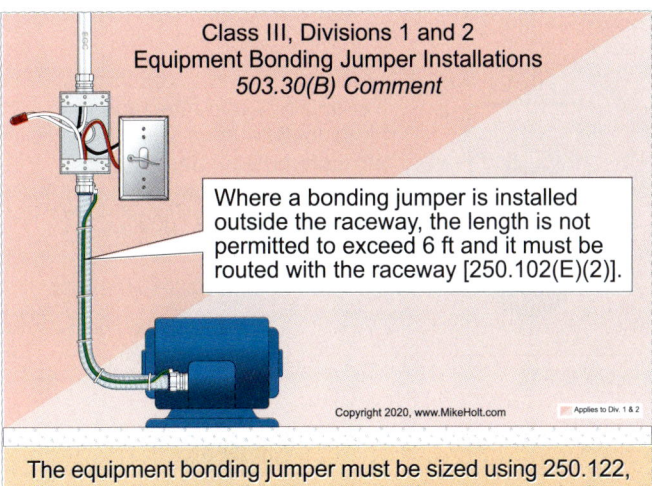

▶Figure 503-6

Part III. Equipment

503.115 Enclosures Containing Make-and-Break Contacts

Switches, circuit breakers, motor controllers, and fuses, including pushbuttons, relays, and similar devices intended to interrupt current during normal operation in Class III locations, must be installed in dusttight enclosures. ▶Figure 503-7

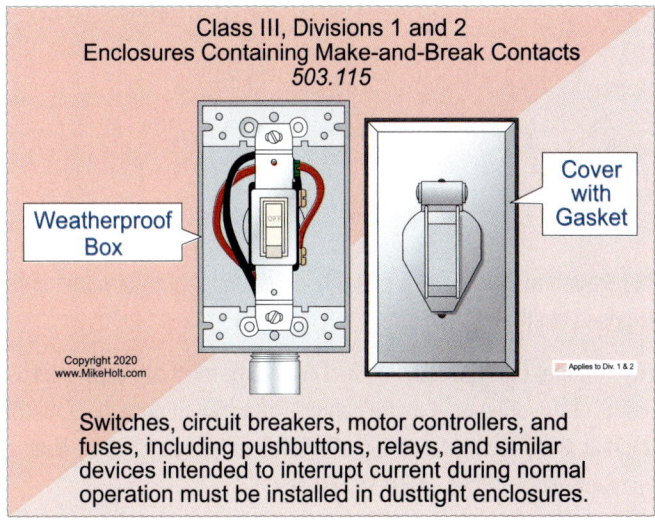

▶Figure 503-7

Author's Comment:

▶ A standard weatherproof box with a cover and gasket meets this requirement.

503.125 Motors and Generators

Motors and generators installed in Class III locations must be totally enclosed nonventilated, pipe ventilated, or fan cooled.

503.130 Luminaires

Luminaires installed in a Class III location must comply with the following:

(A) Fixed Lighting. Luminaires must be designed to minimize the entrance of fibers/flyings and to prevent the escape of sparks, burning material, or hot metal. ▶Figure 503-8

503.140 | Class III Hazardous (Classified) Locations

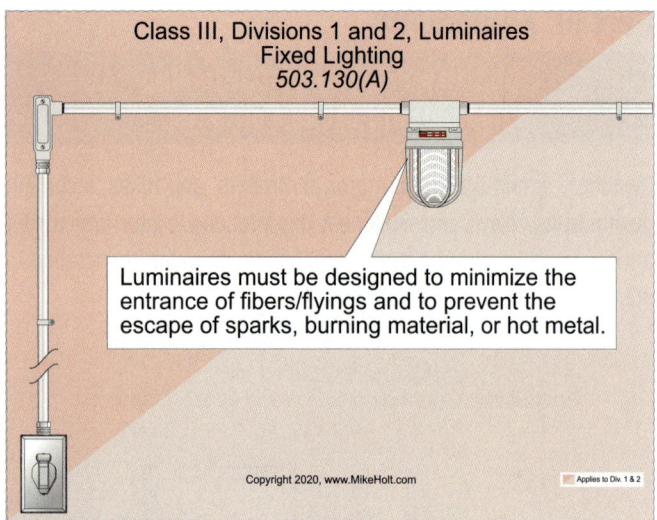

▶Figure 503-8

(B) Physical Damage. A suitable guard must protect luminaires exposed to physical damage.

(C) Pendant Luminaires. Pendant luminaires must be suspended by stems of threaded rigid metal conduit, threaded intermediate metal conduit, threaded metal tubing of equivalent thickness, or by chains with approved fittings. ▶Figure 503-9

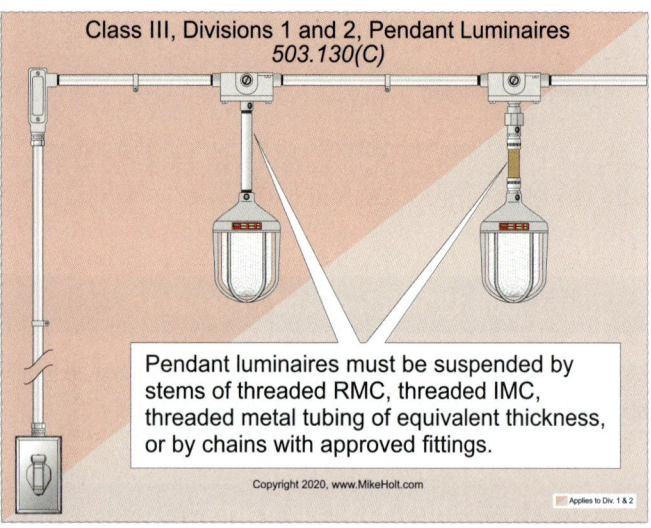

▶Figure 503-9

For stems longer than 1 ft, bracing against lateral movement is required at not more than 1 ft above the lower end of the stem, or flexibility in the form of an identified fitting or a flexible connector can be provided not more 1 ft from the point of attachment to the supporting box or fitting.

(D) Portable Luminaire Equipment. Portable luminaire equipment must be equipped with handles and protected with substantial guards. Lampholders must be of the unswitched type with no provision for receiving an attachment plug.

503.140 Flexible Cords

Flexible cords must:

(1) Be of the extra-hard usage type.

(2) Contain an equipment grounding conductor.

(3) Be supported so there is no tension on the terminal connections.

(4) Be terminated with a listed dusttight connector.

503.145 Receptacles and Attachment plugs

Receptacles and attachment plugs installed in a Class III location must be designed to minimize the accumulation or the entry of fibers/flyings. ▶Figure 503-10

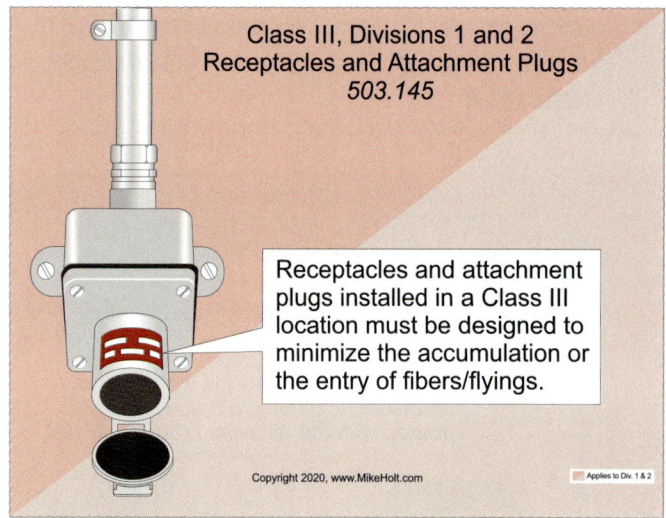

▶Figure 503-10

Ex: General-purpose grounding-type receptacles readily accessible for routine cleaning and mounted to minimize the entry of fibers/flyings can be used.

503.150 Limited-Energy and Communications Systems

Signaling, alarm, remote-control, and local loudspeaker systems must comply with Article 503 regarding wiring methods, switches, transformers, resistors, motors, luminaires, and related components.

ARTICLE 511 COMMERCIAL GARAGES, REPAIR AND STORAGE

Introduction to Article 511—Commercial Garages, Repair and Storage

Article 511 covers locations used for the service and repair of vehicles that use volatile flammable liquids or flammable gases for fuel.

First, it is essential to understand whether the facility is a major or minor repair garage. Pay careful attention to these definitions as you study this article. The next factor that makes a difference in the classification of a location is the presence or absence of a below-floor pit. Finally, mechanical ventilation is critical and can change the classification of a location. Read this material carefully, review the illustrations, and you will find that the Article 511 requirements are not very difficult.

511.1 Scope

Article 511 applies to areas used for the service and repair operations of self-propelled vehicles including passenger automobiles, buses, trucks, tractors, and so on, in which volatile flammable liquids or flammable gases are used for fuel or power. ▶Figure 511-1

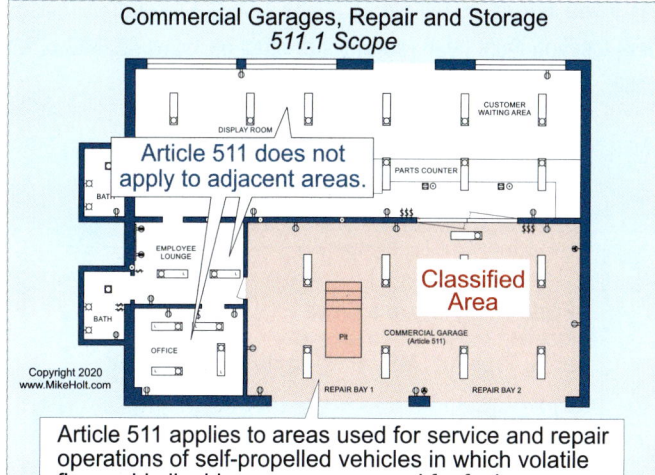

▶Figure 511-1

Author's Comment:

▸ Installations within the scope of Article 511 include automobile service/repair centers; service/repair garages for commercial vehicles such as trucks and tractors; service/repair garages for fleet vehicles such as cars, buses, and trucks; and shops that service motorcycles and all-terrain vehicles (ATVs).

▸ This article does not apply to garages used for diesel fueled or electric vehicle service.

▸ Definitions for this Article have been relocated to Part III of Article 100.

511.3 Classification of Hazardous Areas

General. Where flammable liquids or gaseous fuels are stored, handled, or transferred, electrical wiring and electrical utilization equipment must be designed in accordance with the requirements for Class I, Division 1 or 2 hazardous (classified) locations.

(A) Parking Garages. Parking or storage garages are not required to be classified.

(B) Repair Garages, With Dispensing. Major and minor repair garages that dispense motor fuels must have the dispensing functions classified in accordance with Table 514.3(B)(1).

511.7 | Commercial Garages, Repair and Storage

(C) Major and Minor Repair Garages. Where vehicles using flammable liquids or heavier-than-air gaseous fuels (such as LPG) are repaired, the hazardous area classification is contained in Table 511.3(C). ▶Figure 511-2

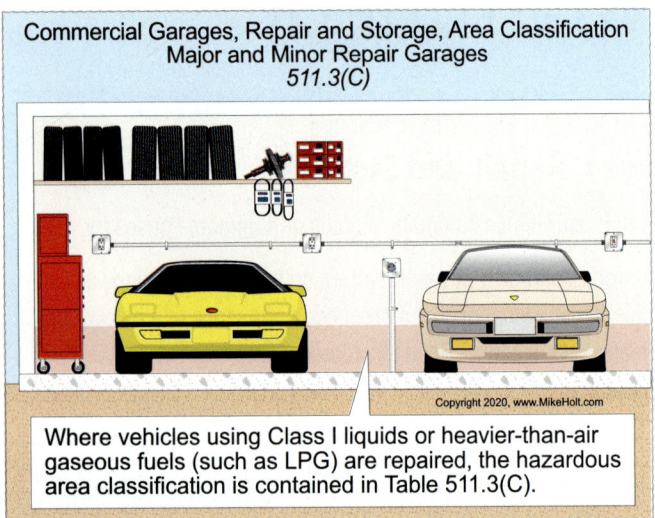

▶Figure 511-2

Author's Comment:

▶ NFPA 30A, *Code for Motor Fuel Dispensing Facilities and Repair Garages,* provides information for fire safety at motor fuel dispensing operations and motor vehicle repair facilities.

(D) Major Repair Garages. Where vehicles using lighter-than-air gaseous fuels (such as hydrogen and natural gas) are repaired or stored, hazardous area classification guidance is found in Table 511.3(D).

Author's Comment:

▶ Where vehicles using lighter-than-air gaseous fuels (such as hydrogen and natural gas) are repaired or stored in minor repair garages, the hazardous area classification guidance found in Table 511.3(D) is not applicable.

(E) Modifications to Classification.

(1) Classification of Adjacent Areas. Areas adjacent to classified locations are not classified if mechanically ventilated at a rate of four or more air changes per hour, or when walls or partitions effectively cut off the adjacent area. ▶Figure 511-3

(2) Alcohol-Based Windshield Washer Fluid. Areas used for the storage, handling, or dispensing into motor vehicles of alcohol-based windshield washer fluid in repair garages are unclassified unless otherwise classified by a provision of 511.3.

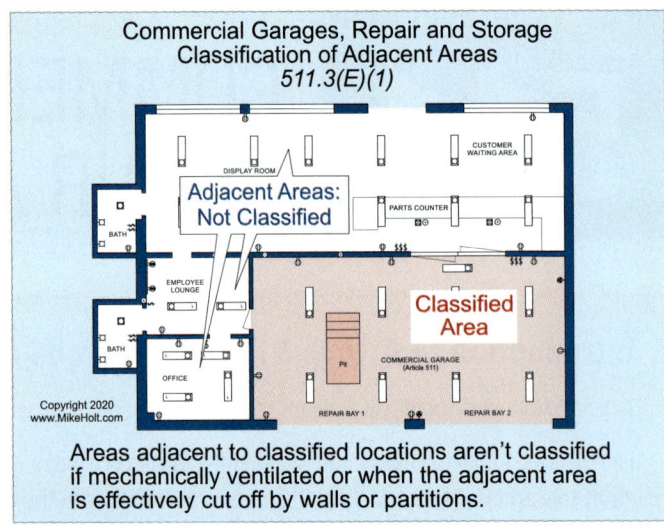

▶Figure 511-3

Author's Comment:

▶ Windshield washer fluid is not flammable.

511.7 Wiring and Equipment Above Hazardous (Classified) Locations

(A) Wiring Above Class I Locations.

(1) Fixed Wiring. Fixed wiring above a Class I hazardous (classified) location must be in raceways or must be Types AC, MC, or MI cable. ▶Figure 511-4

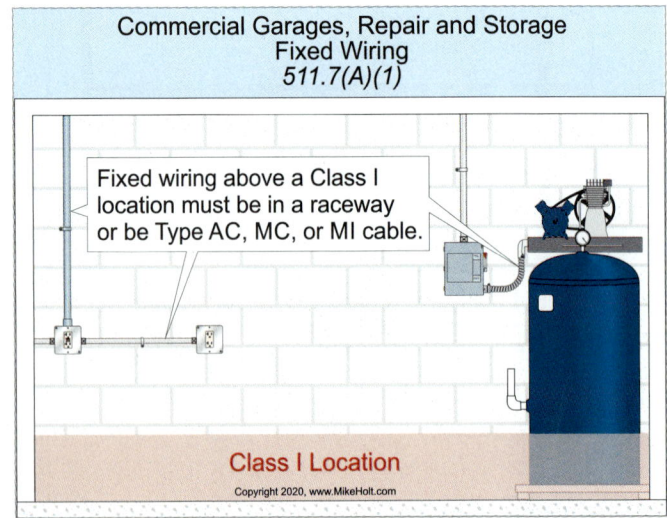

▶Figure 511-4

(2) Pendant (Drop-Cords). For pendants, flexible cord suitable for the type of service and listed for hard usage must be used.

(B) Equipment Above Class I Locations.

(1) Fixed Electrical Equipment. Electrical equipment in a fixed position must be located above the level of any defined Class I location or be identified for the location.

(a) Arcing Equipment. Equipment with make-and-break contacts installed less than 12 ft above the floor level must be of the totally enclosed type or constructed to prevent sparks or hot metal particles from escaping.

(b) Fixed Lighting. Lamps for fixed lighting over travel lanes or where exposed to physical damage must be located not less than 12 ft above the floor level, unless the luminaires are of the totally enclosed type or constructed to prevent sparks or hot metal particles from escaping. ▶Figure 511–5

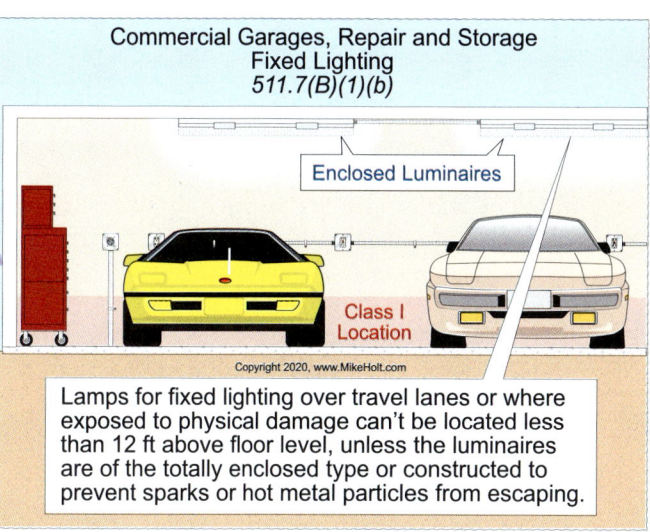

▶Figure 511–5

511.8 Underground Wiring Below Class I Locations

Wiring below a commercial garage must be threaded rigid metal conduit or intermediate metal conduit.

Ex: Type PVC conduit, Type RTRC conduit, and Type HDPE conduit can be installed below a commercial garage if buried under not less than 2 ft of cover. Threaded rigid metal conduit or threaded intermediate metal conduit must be used for the last 2 ft of the underground run. ▶Figure 511–6

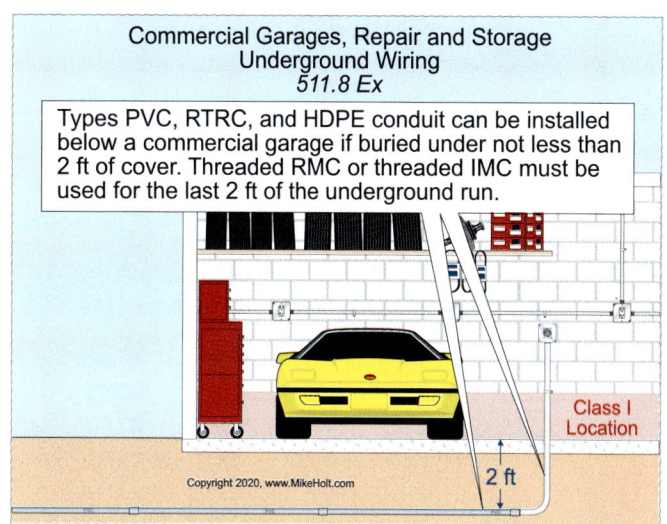

▶Figure 511–6

511.9 Seals

Raceway, cable, and boundary seals must be installed in accordance with 501.15 and apply to the horizontal as well as the vertical boundaries of the defined Class I locations.

Author's Comment:

▸ If the Class I, Division 1 boundary is beneath the ground, the conduit seal fitting can be installed after the raceway exits the ground. There can be no unions, couplings, boxes, or fittings (except explosionproof reducing bushings) between the seal fitting and the point where the raceway leaves the ground [501.15(A)(4) Ex 2]. ▶Figure 511–7

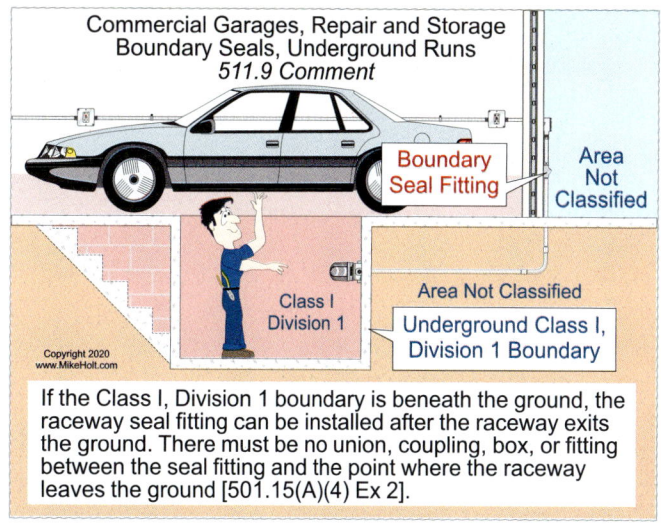

▶Figure 511–7

511.10 | Commercial Garages, Repair and Storage

511.10 Special Equipment

(A) Battery Charging Equipment. Battery chargers and batteries being charged are not permitted to be located within an area classified in accordance with 511.3(B).

511.12 GFCI-Protected Receptacles

GFCI protection is required in accordance with 210.8(B). ▶Figure 511–8

Author's Comment:

▸ GFCI protection is required for receptacles up to 50A, single-phase and receptacles up to 100A, three-phase supplied with circuits rated 150V to ground per 210.8(B).

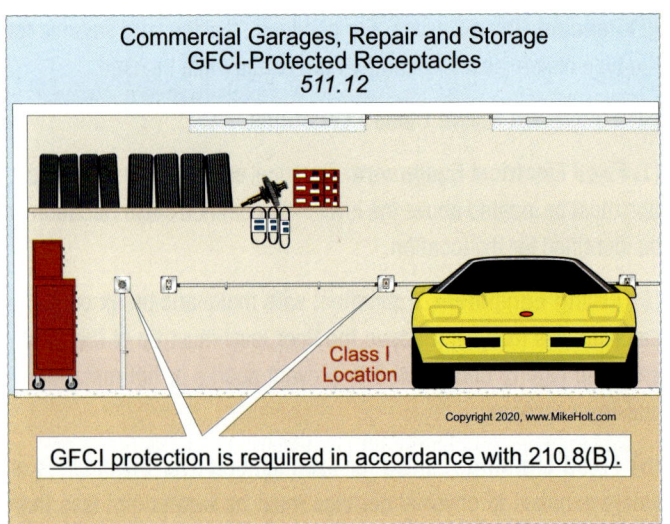

▶Figure 511–8

ARTICLE 514 — MOTOR FUEL DISPENSING FACILITIES

Introduction to Article 514—Motor Fuel Dispensing Facilities

The portion of a facility where fuel is stored and dispensed into the fuel tanks of motor vehicles and marine craft, or into approved containers, must comply with Article 514.

What is most striking is the large table that makes up about half of this article. It does not provide any electrical requirements, list any electrical specifications, or address any electrical equipment. What it does tell you is how to classify a motor fuel dispensing area. The rest of this article contains specific provisions and refers to other articles that must be applied.

Author's Comment:

▸ Diesel fuel is not a flammable liquid. Therefore, areas associated with diesel dispensing equipment and associated wiring are not required to comply with the hazardous (classified) location requirements of Article 514 [514.3(A)]. However, the other requirements in this article still apply.

514.1 Scope

Article 514 applies to motor fuel dispensing facilities, marine/motor fuel dispensing facilities, motor fuel dispensing facilities located inside buildings, and fleet vehicle motor fuel dispensing facilities. ▸Figure 514–1

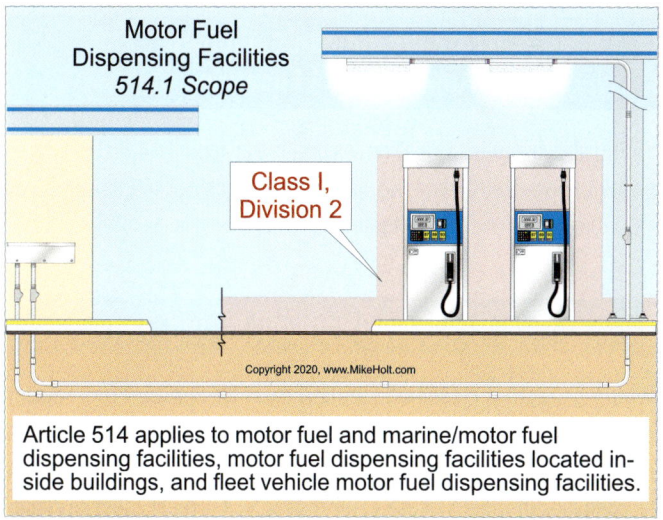

▸Figure 514–1

514.3 Classification of Locations

(A) Unclassified Locations. If the authority having jurisdiction is satisfied that flammable liquids having a flash point below 100°F (such as gasoline) will not be handled, such locations can be unclassified.

(B) Classified Locations.

(1) Class I Locations. Table 514.3(B)(1) must be used to classify motor fuel dispensing facilities and commercial garages as defined in 511.2 where a flammable liquid having a flash point below 100°F [Article 100 Volatile Flammable Liquid] is stored, handled, or dispensed.

A Class I location does not extend beyond an unpierced wall, roof, or other solid barrier.

Author's Comment:

▸ If conduit for a diesel dispenser passes through the Class I area around the gasoline dispenser, then the installation must comply with the sealing and wiring method requirement of Article 501. ▸Figure 514–2

514.4 | Motor Fuel Dispensing Facilities

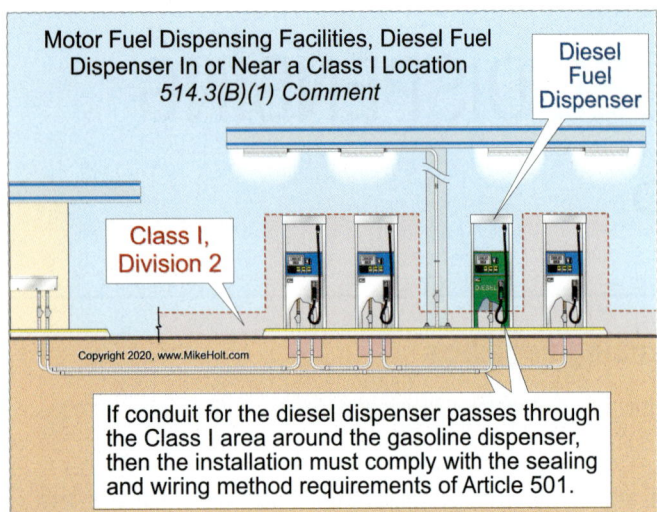

▶Figure 514-2

(1) The area 18 in. above the surface of the dock, pier, or wharf and extending 20 ft horizontally in all directions from the outside edge of the dispenser and down to the water level is considered a Class 1, Division 2 location. ▶Figure 514-4

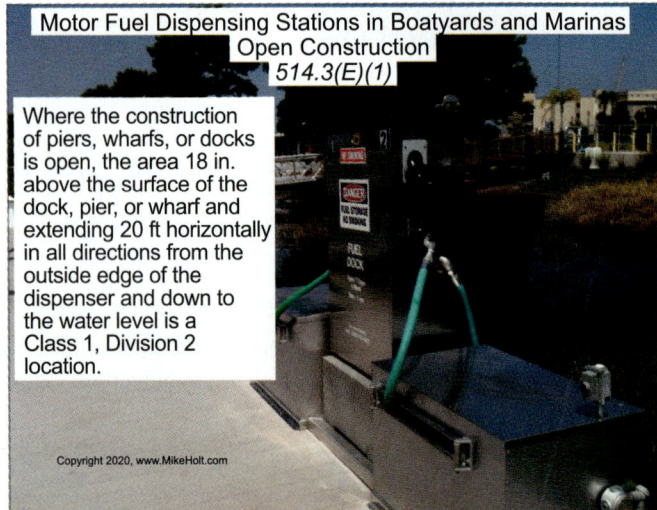

▶Figure 514-4

(C) Motor Fuel Dispensing Stations in Marinas and Boatyards.

(1) General. Electrical wiring and equipment serving motor fuel dispensing locations must be installed on the side of the wharf, pier, or dock opposite from the fuel piping system. ▶Figure 514-3

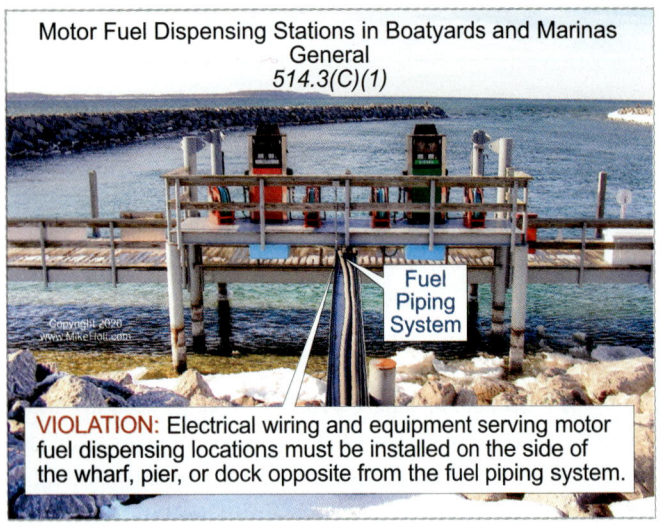

▶Figure 514-3

Author's Comment:

▸ Electrical wiring and equipment for motor fuel dispensing stations covered by Article 514 located in marinas, boatyards, and docking facilities must also comply with Article 555 [555.11].

(E) Open Construction. Where the construction of piers, wharfs, or docks is open, the following applies:

514.4 Wiring and Equipment Within Class I Locations

Electrical equipment and wiring within a Class I location, as defined in Table 514.3(B)(1), must comply with Article 501.

Ex: PVC conduit is permitted underground in accordance with 514.8 Ex 2.

514.7 Wiring and Equipment Above Class I Locations

Wiring above a Class I location, as defined in Table 514.3(B)(1), must be installed within a raceway or must be Types AC, MC, MI, PLTC, or TC cable [511.7(A)(1)]. ▶Figure 514-5

514.8 Underground Wiring

Wiring beneath a classified location must be installed in threaded rigid metal conduit or threaded intermediate metal conduit. Electrical conduits located below the surface of a Class I, Division 1 or 2 location, as contained in Table 514.3(B)(1) and Table 514.3(B)(2), must be sealed within 10 ft of the point of emergence above grade. ▶Figure 514-6

Motor Fuel Dispensing Facilities | 514.9

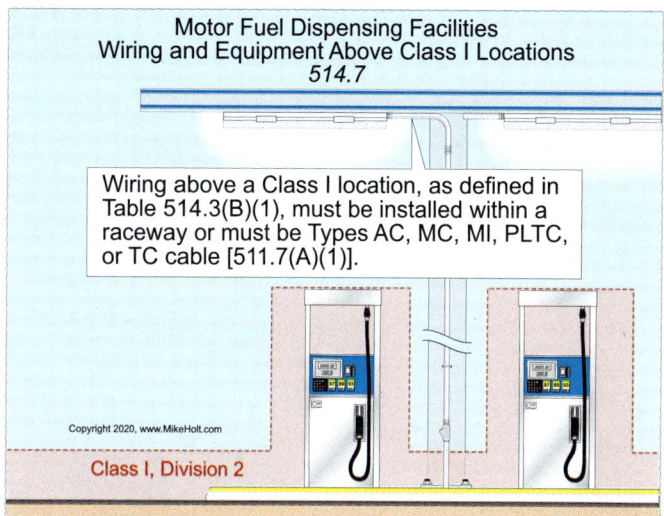
▶Figure 514-5

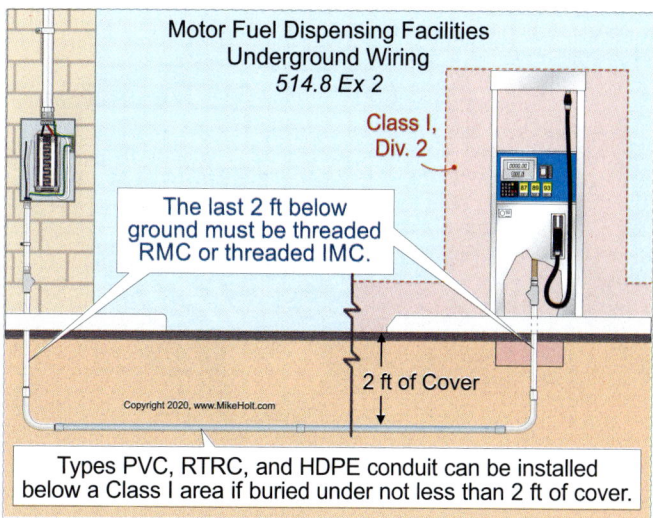
▶Figure 514-7

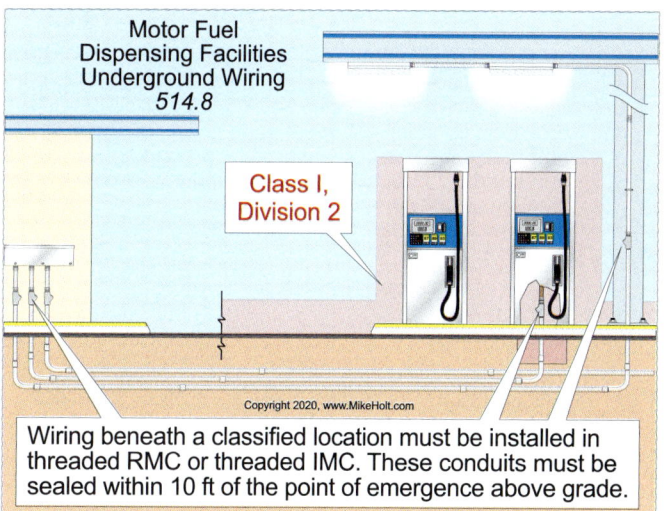
▶Figure 514-6

Except for listed explosionproof reducers at the conduit seal fitting, there must be no union, coupling, box, or fitting between the conduit seal fitting and the point of emergence above grade.

Ex 2: Type PVC conduit, Type RTRC conduit, and Type HDPE conduit can be installed below a classified location if buried under not less than 2 ft of cover. Threaded rigid metal conduit or threaded intermediate metal conduit must be used for the last 2 ft of the underground run.
▶Figure 514-7

Author's Comment:

▶ The underground area beneath dispensers is not a classified location, because there is not enough oxygen below ground to create ignition. There will be, however, a substantial amount of gasoline in the earth. Due to this, the *Code* includes requirements that act as though the underground area is classified, meaning that you must follow 514.8 even if you are just passing underneath the area without actually supplying equipment in the classified location.

514.9 Conduit Seal

(A) At Dispenser. A listed conduit seal fitting must be installed in each raceway run that enters or leaves a dispenser. The conduit seal fitting or listed explosionproof reducer at the seal must be the first fitting after the raceway emerges from the Earth's surface or concrete. ▶Figure 514-8

(B) At Boundary. An additional conduit seal fitting that complies with 501.15(A)(4) and (B)(2) must be installed in each raceway run that leaves a Class I location. ▶Figure 514-9

Author's Comment:

▶ If the boundary is beneath the ground, the sealing fitting can be installed after the raceway leaves the ground, but there must be no union, coupling, box, or fitting, other than listed explosionproof reducers at the sealing fitting in the raceway between the sealing fitting and the point at which the raceway leaves the Earth's surface [501.15(A)(4) Ex 2]. ▶Figure 514-10

514.16 | Motor Fuel Dispensing Facilities

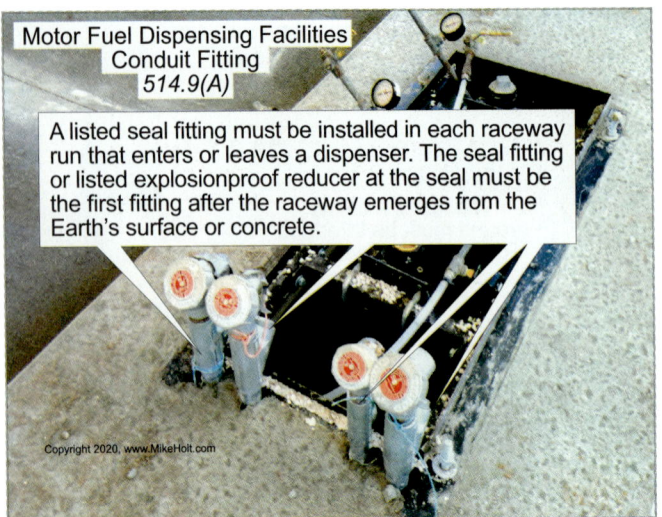
▶Figure 514-8

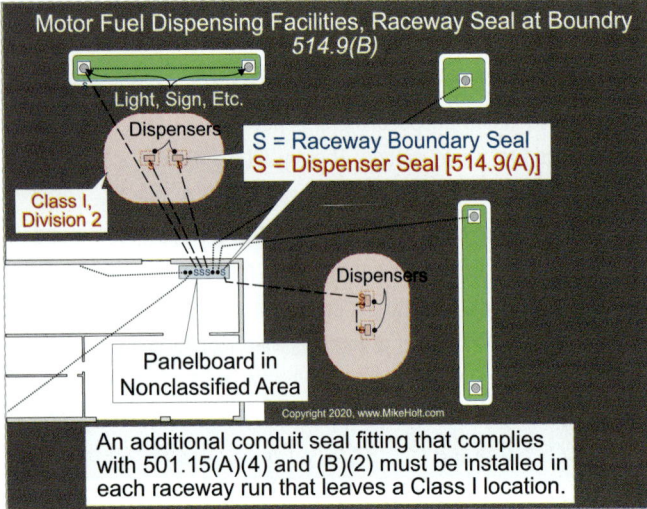
▶Figure 514-9

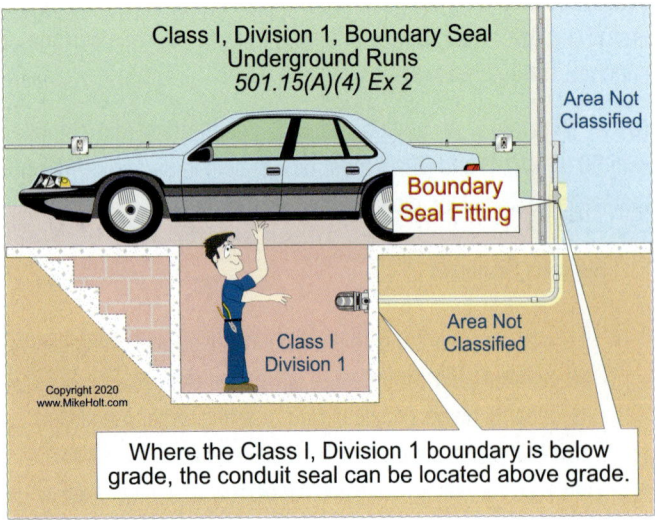
▶Figure 514-10

514.16 Grounding and Bonding

Because of the explosive conditions associated with electrical installations in hazardous (classified) locations [500.5], electrical continuity of metal parts of equipment and raceways must be ensured by grounding and bonding. Grounding and bonding in Class 1 locations must comply with 501.30. ▶Figure 514-11

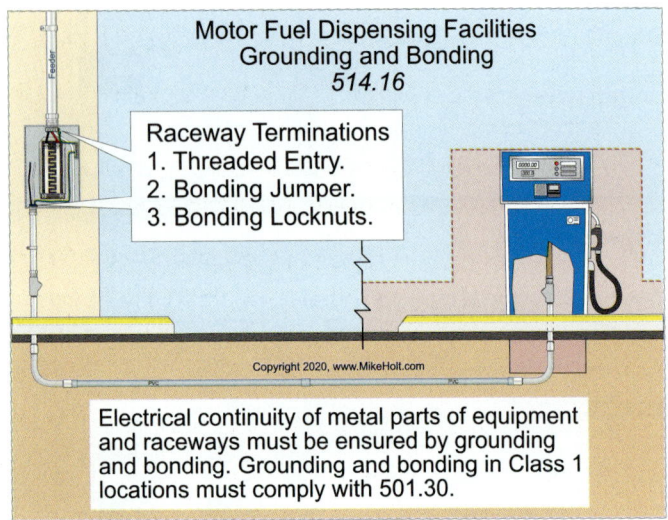
▶Figure 514-11

Author's Comment:

▶ Reference 250.100 for bonding at Class 1 locations as defined in 500.5 and use the method mentioned in 250.92(B)(4) whether the equipment grounding conductor of the wire type is installed or not.

ARTICLE 517
HEALTH CARE FACILITIES

Introduction to Article 517—Health Care Facilities

Health care facilities differ from other types of buildings in many important ways. Article 517 is primarily concerned with those parts of health care facilities where human patients are examined and treated. Whether those facilities are permanent or movable, they still fall under the scope of this article. However, Article 517 wiring and protection requirements do not apply to business offices or waiting rooms, and they do not apply to animal veterinary facilities.

This article contains many specialized definitions that only apply to health care facilities. While you do not need to be able to quote these definitions, you should have a clear understanding of what the terms mean. As you study Parts II and III, keep in mind the special requirements of hospitals and why they exist. The requirements in those parts are highly detailed and not intuitively obvious. Two of the main objectives of Article 517, Parts II and III are:

- Maximize the physical protection of wiring by requiring metal raceways.
- Minimize electrical hazards by keeping the voltage between patients' bodies and medical equipment low.

Part IV addresses gas anesthesia stations. The primary objective of this part is to prevent ignition.

Part V addresses X-ray installations and really has two main objectives:

- Provide adequate ampacity and overcurrent protection for the branch circuits.
- Address the safety issues inherent in high-voltage equipment installations.

Part VI provides requirements for low-voltage communications systems such as fire alarms and intercoms. The primary objective here is to prevent compromising those systems with inductive couplings or other sources of interference.

Part VII provides requirements for isolated power systems where the main objective is to keep them truly isolated.

Be aware that the *NEC* is just one of the standards that applies to health care facilities, and there may be additional requirements from other standards and special requirements for sophisticated equipment.

Part I. General

517.1 Scope

Article 517 applies to electrical wiring in health care facilities such as hospitals, nursing homes, limited care and supervisory care facilities, clinics, medical and dental offices, and ambulatory care facilities that provide services to human beings. ▶Figure 517–1

Author's Comment:

- This article does not apply to animal veterinary facilities.

- Areas of health care facilities not used for the treatment of patients (such as business offices and waiting rooms) are not required to comply with the provisions contained in Article 517.

517.2 Definitions

The definitions in this section apply only within this article.

Dental Office. A building or portion of a building in which the following occur:

517.2 | Health Care Facilities

▶Figure 517-1

(1) Examinations and minor treatments/procedures performed under the continuous supervision of a dental professional;

(2) Use of limited to minimal sedation and treatment or procedures that do not render the patient incapable of self-preservation under emergency conditions; and

(3) No overnight stays for patients or 24-hour operations.

Health Care Facilities. Buildings, portions of buildings, or mobile enclosures in which medical, dental, psychiatric, nursing, obstetrical, or surgical care is provided for humans.

Note: Examples of health care facilities include, but are not limited to, hospitals, nursing homes, limited care facilities, supervisory care facilities, clinics, medical and dental offices, and ambulatory care facilities.

Health Care Facility's Governing Body. The person or persons who have the overall legal responsibility for the operation of a health care facility.

Hospital. A building or an area of a building used for medical, psychiatric, obstetrical, or surgical care on a 24-hour basis of four or more inpatients.

Limited Care Facility. A building or an area of a building used for the housing, on a 24-hour basis, of four or more persons who are incapable of self-preservation because of age, physical limitations due to accident or illness, or limitations such as intellectual disability, developmental disability, mental illness, or chemical dependency.

Medical Office. A building or part thereof in which the following occur:

(1) Examinations and minor treatments/procedures are performed under the continuous supervision of a medical professional;

(2) The use of limited to minimal sedation and treatment or procedures that do not render the patient incapable of self-preservation under emergency conditions; and

(3) No overnight stays for patients or 24-hour operations.

Nursing Home. A building or an area of a building used for the lodging, boarding, and nursing care, on a 24-hour basis, of four or more persons who, because of mental or physical incapacity, may be unable to provide for their own needs and safety without the assistance of another person.

Patient Bed Location. The location of an inpatient sleeping bed.

Patient Care Space. Any space of a health care facility where patients are intended to be examined or treated. ▶Figure 517-2

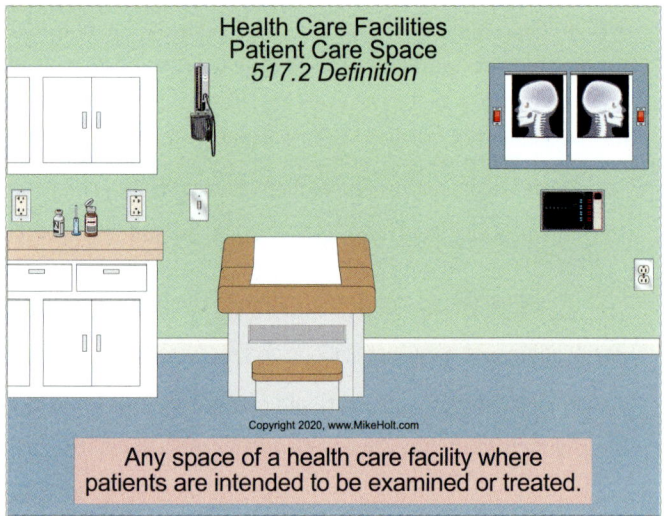

▶Figure 517-2

Note 2: Business offices, corridors, lounges, day rooms, dining rooms, or similar areas are not classified as patient care spaces.

Patient Care Vicinity. A space (within a location intended for the examination and treatment of patients) extending 6 ft beyond the normal location of the patient bed, chair, table, treadmill, or other device that supports the patient during examination and treatment and extending vertically to 7 ft 6 in. above the floor. ▶Figure 517-3

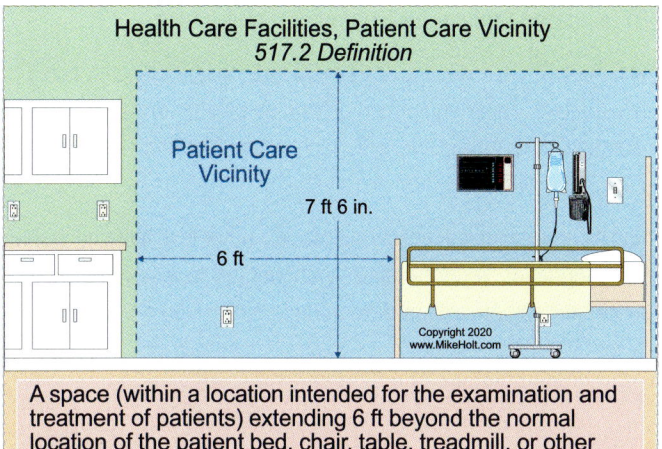

▶Figure 517-3

Part II. Wiring and Protection

517.10 Applicability

(A) Applicability. Part II applies to patient care spaces.

(B) Not Covered. The requirements contained in Part II of Article 517 do not apply to:

(1) Business offices, corridors, waiting rooms, or similar areas in clinics, medical and dental offices, and outpatient facilities.

(2) Areas of nursing homes and limited care facilities used exclusively for patient sleeping and wired in accordance with Chapters 1 through 4.

(3) Areas used exclusively for any of the following purposes:

   a. Intramuscular injections (immunizations)
   b. Psychiatry and psychotherapy
   c. Alternative medicine
   d. Optometry

517.12 Wiring Methods

Wiring methods must comply with the Chapter 1 through 4 provisions except as modified in this article.

517.13 Equipment Grounding Conductor for Receptacles and Fixed Electrical Equipment in Patient Care Spaces

Wiring in patient care spaces must comply with (A) and (B):

Author's Comment:

▸ Patient care spaces, as designated by the facility administrator, include patient rooms as well as examining rooms, therapy areas, treatment rooms, and some patient corridors. They do not include business offices, corridors, lounges, day rooms, dining rooms, or similar areas not classified as patient care spaces [517.2].

▸ Often referred to as redundancy, equipment grounding requirements in patient care spaces are based on the concept of two different types of equipment grounding conductors so if there is an installation error, the effective ground-fault current paths are not lost. One effective ground-fault current path is "mechanical" (the wiring method), and the other is of the "wire type." Section 517.13(A) requires the wiring method to be a metal raceway or metal cable that qualifies as an equipment grounding conductor in accordance with 250.118(8) and (10)(b), and Section 517.13(B) requires an insulated copper equipment grounding conductor of the wire type in accordance with 250.118(1).

(A) Wiring Methods. Branch-circuit conductors serving patient care spaces must be in a metal raceway or metal cable having a metal sheath that qualifies as an equipment grounding conductor in accordance with 250.118(10)(b). ▶Figure 517-4

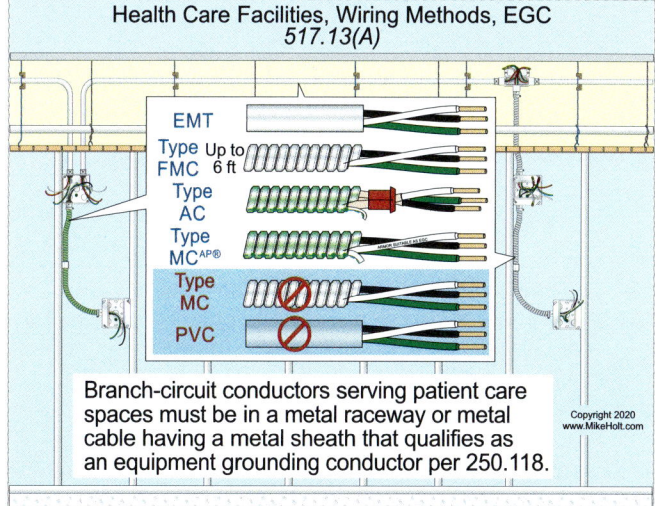

▶Figure 517-4

517.13 | Health Care Facilities

Author's Comment:

▸ The metal sheath of Type AC cable is identified as an equipment grounding conductor in 250.118(8) because it contains an internal bonding strip that is in direct contact with the metal sheath of the interlock cable. ▸Figure 517-5

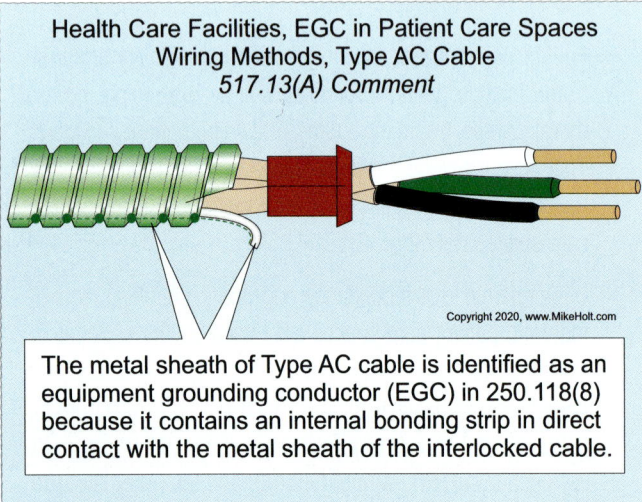

▸Figure 517-5

Author's Comment:

▸ The metal sheath of Type MC^{AP} (metal-clad all-purpose) cable is identified as an equipment grounding conductor in 250.118(10)(b) because it contains an internal bonding strip that is in direct contact with the metal sheath of the interlock cable. ▸Figure 517-6

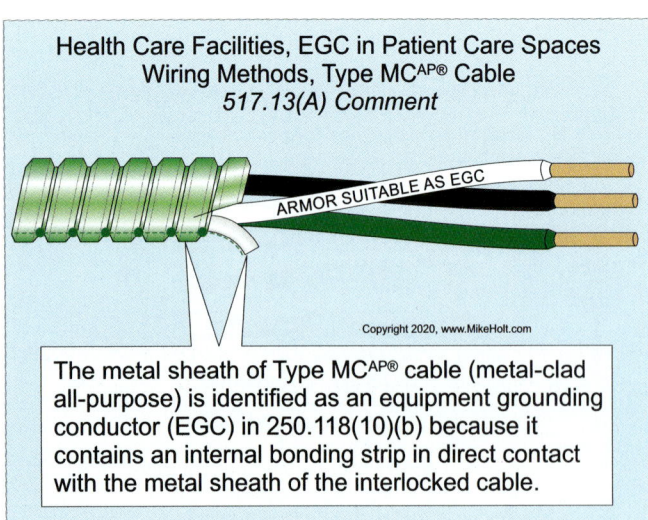

▸Figure 517-6

(B) Insulated Equipment Grounding Conductors.

(1) General. The following equipment must be directly connected to an insulated copper equipment grounding conductor that has green insulation along its entire length. Such conductors must be contained in a suitable wiring method as required in 517.13(A).

(1) The grounding contact of receptacles, other than isolated ground receptacles, must be directly connected to a green insulated copper equipment grounding conductor. ▸Figure 517-7

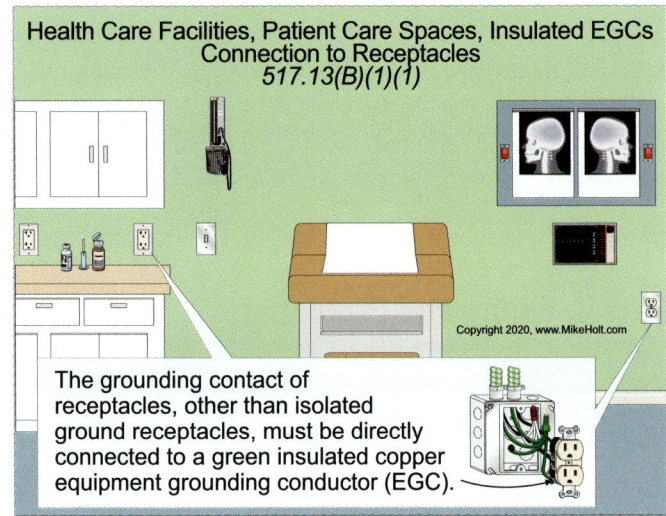

▸Figure 517-7

(2) Metal enclosures containing circuit conductors must be directly connected to a green insulated copper equipment grounding conductor. ▸Figure 517-8

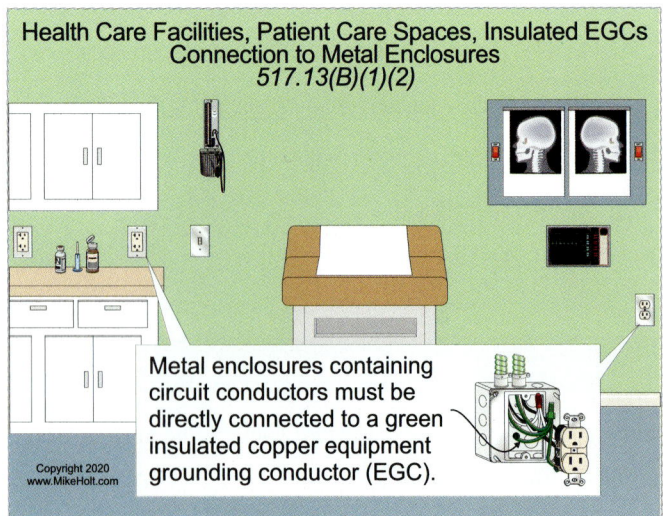

▸Figure 517-8

Health Care Facilities | 517.13

(3) Noncurrent-carrying metal parts of fixed electrical equipment operating at over 100V must be directly connected to an insulated copper equipment grounding conductor. ▶Figure 517–9

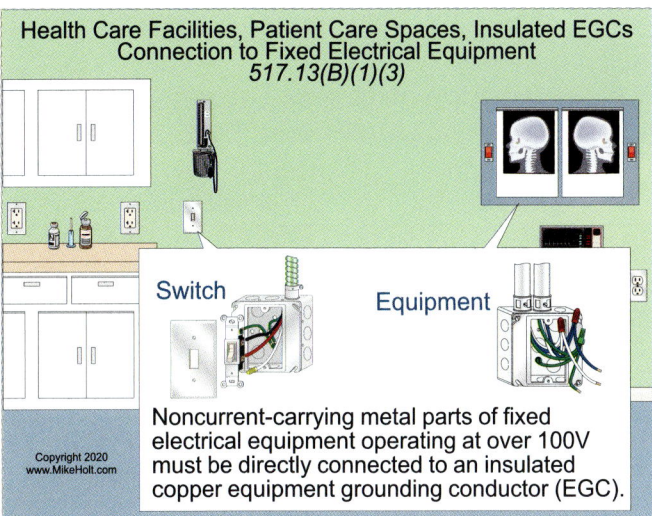
▶Figure 517–9

(4) Metal faceplates must be connected to the insulated cooper equipment grounding conductor by means of a metal mounting screw(s) securing the faceplate to a metal yoke or strap of a receptacle, or to a metal outlet box. ▶Figure 517–10

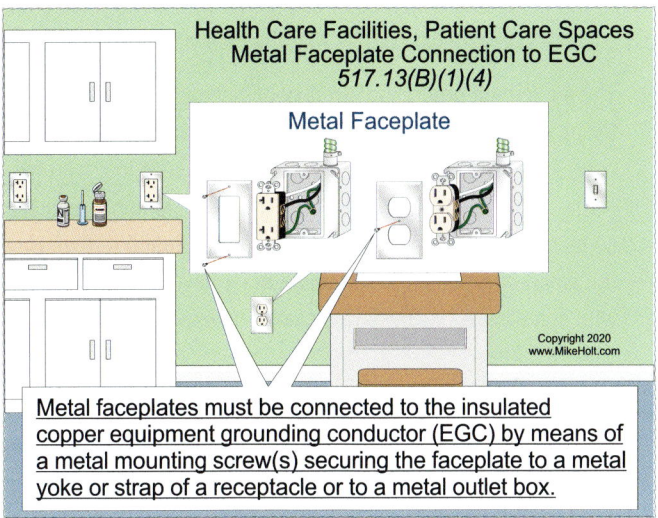
▶Figure 517–10

Ex 2: Circuits for luminaires located more than 7½ ft above the floor and switches located outside the patient care vicinity must be installed in a 517.13(A) wiring method; an equipment grounding conductor of the wire type is not required within the wiring method. ▶Figure 517–11

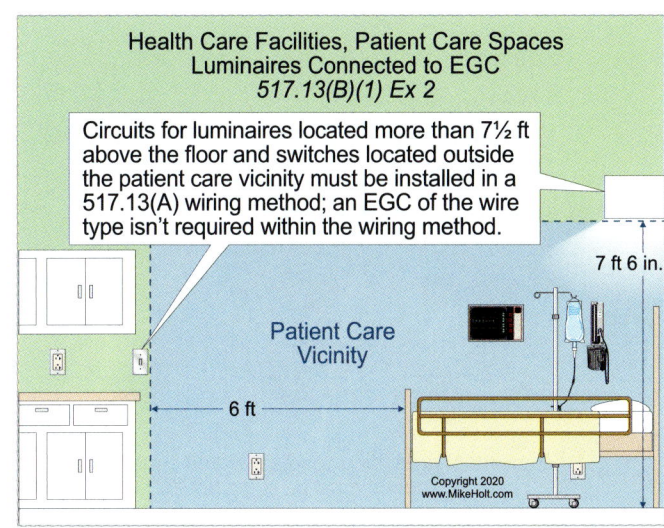
▶Figure 517–11

Author's Comment:

▸ The metal sheath of traditional Type MC interlocked cable does not qualify as an equipment grounding conductor [250.118(10)(a)], therefore this wiring method is not permitted to be used for circuits in patient care spaces. ▶Figure 517–12

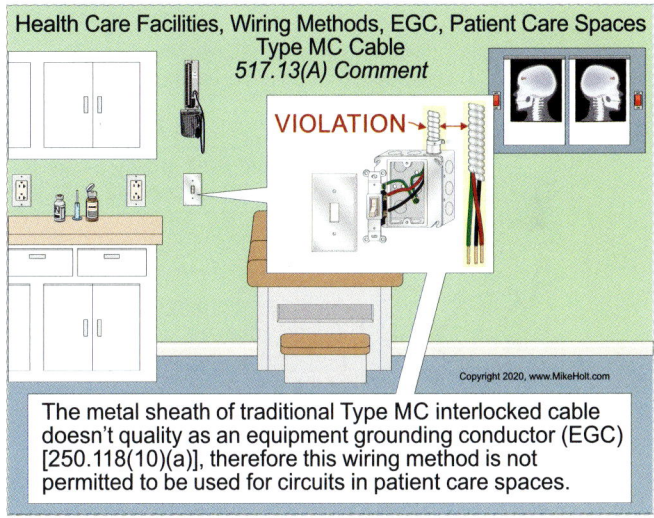
▶Figure 517–12

(2) Sizing. Equipment grounding conductors and equipment bonding jumpers must be sized in accordance with 250.122. ▶Figure 517–13

517.16 | Health Care Facilities

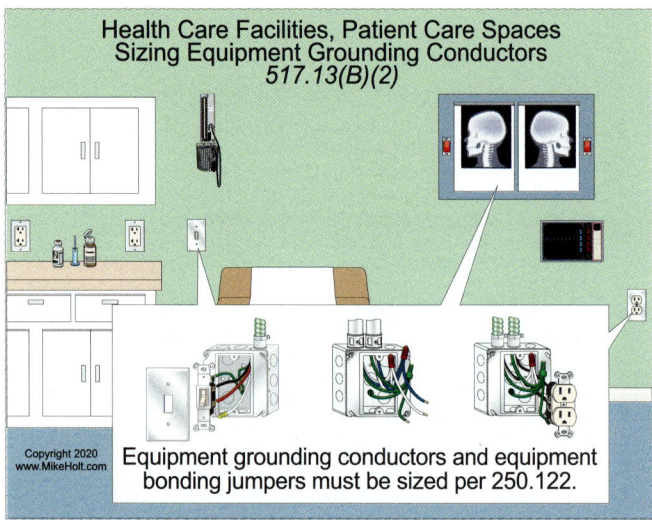
▶Figure 517-13

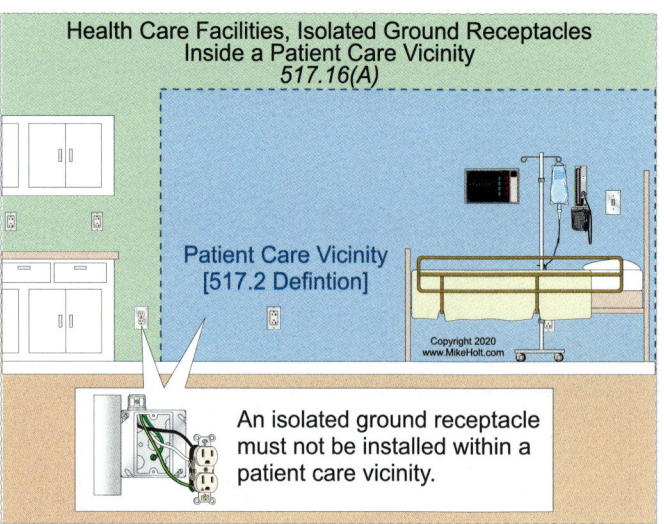
▶Figure 517-15

517.16 Isolated Ground Receptacles

An isolated ground receptacle, if used, must not defeat the purposes of the safety features of the grounding systems detailed in 517.13.
▶Figure 517-14

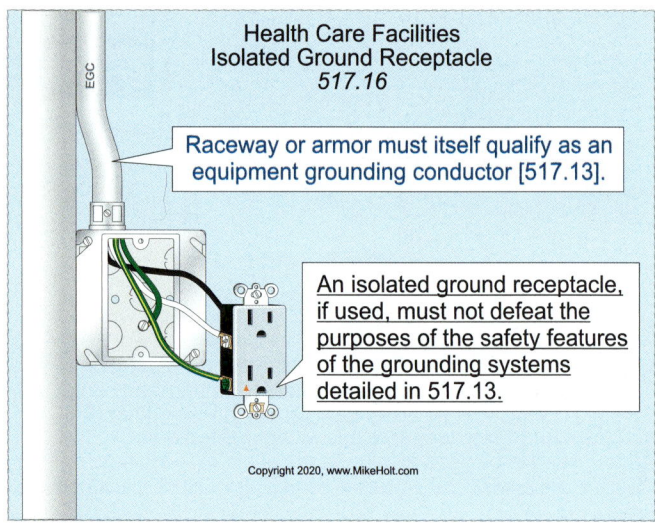
▶Figure 517-14

(A) Inside Patient Care Vicinity. An isolated ground receptacle must not be installed within a patient care vicinity. ▶Figure 517-15

Author's Comment:

▶ The patient care vicinity is a space extending 6 ft beyond the normal location of the patient bed, chair, table, treadmill, or other device that supports the patient during examination and treatment and extends vertically to 7 ft 6 in. above the floor [517.2 Definition].

(B) Outside Patient Care Vicinity. Isolated ground receptacle(s) within the patient care space (as defined in 517.2) but outside the patient care vicinity must comply with the following:

(1) The equipment grounding terminal of isolated grounding receptacles must be connected to an insulated equipment grounding conductor in accordance with 250.146(D) and installed in a wiring method described in 517.13(A). The equipment grounding conductor connected to the equipment grounding terminals of the isolated grounding receptacle must have green insulation with one or more yellow stripes along its entire length. ▶Figure 517-16

(2) The insulated equipment grounding conductor required by 517.13(B)(1) must be connected to the metal enclosure containing the isolated ground receptacle in accordance with 517.13(B)(1)(2).

Note 2: Care should be taken in specifying a system containing isolated ground receptacles because the impedance of the effective ground-fault current path is dependent on the equipment grounding conductor(s) and does not benefit from any conduit or building structure in parallel with the equipment grounding conductor.

Health Care Facilities | 517.18

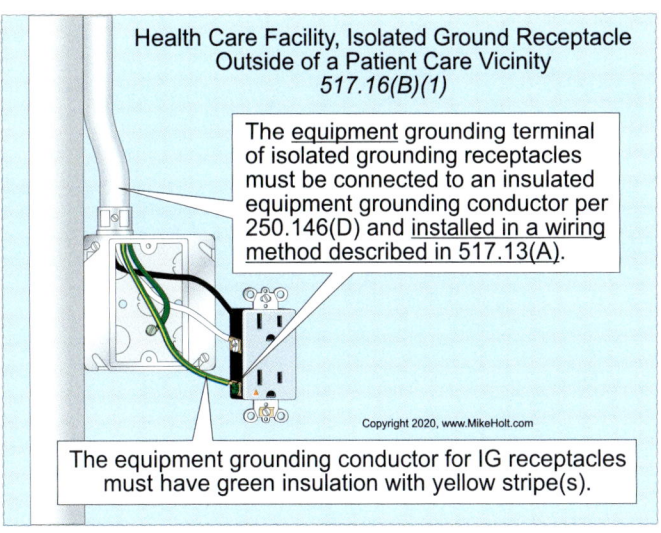

▶Figure 517-16

Author's Comment:

▶ Use of an isolated equipment grounding conductor does not relieve the requirement for connecting the raceway system and outlet box to an equipment grounding conductor to establish a low impedance effective ground fault path back to the supply source.

517.18 General Care Spaces

(B) Patient Bed Location Receptacles. At a location of a patient sleeping bed or the bed or procedure table of a critical care space, a minimum of eight listed and identified hospital grade receptacles must be provided. ▶Figure 517-17

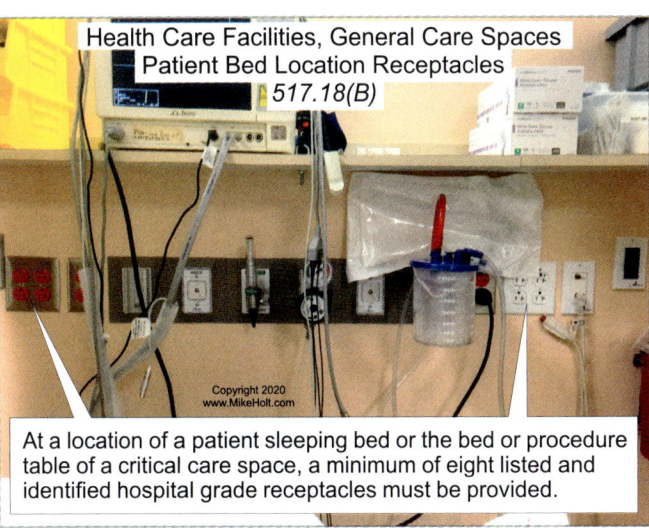

▶Figure 517-17

Author's Comment:

▶ Examples of general care spaces include, but are not limited to, inpatient bedrooms, dialysis rooms, in vitro fertilization rooms, procedural rooms, and similar rooms [514.2].

▶ Hospital grade receptacles are only required at the location of a patient sleeping bed or the bed or procedure table of a critical care space, not receptacles located in treatment rooms of clinics, medical or dental offices, or outpatient facilities.
▶Figure 517-18

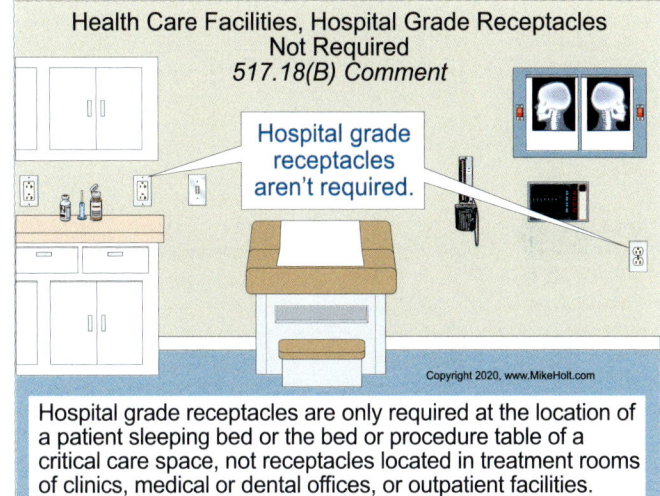

▶Figure 517-18

Mike Holt Enterprises • www.MikeHolt.com • 888.NEC.CODE (632.2633) | 151

Notes

ARTICLE 518 ASSEMBLY OCCUPANCIES

Introduction to Article 518—Assembly Occupancies

More commonly referred to as "Places of Occupancy," these are buildings or portions of buildings specifically designed or intended for the assembly of 100 or more people and fall under the requirements of Article 518. This article goes out of its way to eliminate any confusion about the types of occupancies to which it is intended to apply. See 518.2 for a list of occupancies.

518.1 Scope

Except for the assembly occupancies explicitly covered by 520.1, this article covers all buildings or portions of buildings or structures designed or intended for the gathering together of 100 or more persons for such purposes as deliberation, worship, entertainment, eating, drinking, amusement, awaiting transportation, or similar purposes. ▶Figure 518–1

▶Figure 518–1

Author's Comment:

▸ Occupancy capacity is determined in accordance with NFPA 101, *Life Safety Code*, or by the applicable building code.

518.2 General Classifications

(A) Examples. Assembly occupancies include, but are not limited to:

- Armories
- Assembly halls
- Auditoriums
- Bowling lanes
- Club rooms
- Conference rooms
- Courtrooms
- Dance halls
- Dining facilities
- Exhibition halls
- Gymnasiums
- Mortuary chapels
- Multipurpose rooms
- Museums
- Places awaiting transportation
- Pool rooms
- Places of religious worship
- Restaurants
- Skating rinks

(B) Multiple Occupancies. The requirements contained in Article 518 only apply to that portion(s) of any buildings specifically designed or intended for the assembly of 100 or more persons.

518.3 Other Articles

(B) Temporary Installations. Wiring for display booths in exhibit halls can be installed in accordance with Article 590. Approved flexible hard or extra-hard usage cords can be laid on the floor where protected from contact by the public. ▶Figure 518-2

▶Figure 518-2

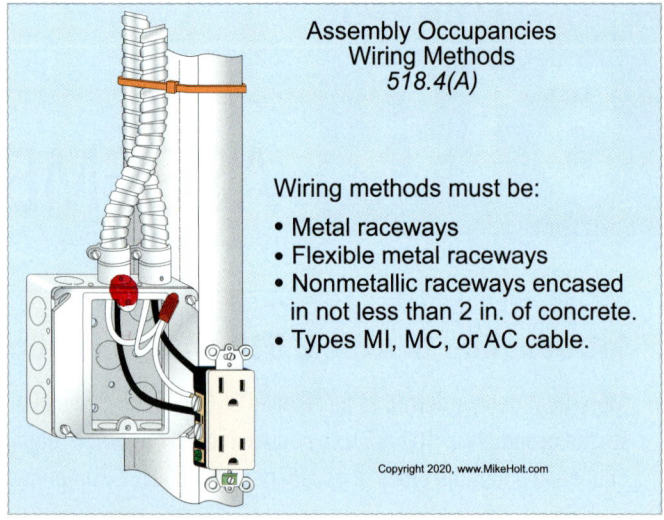

▶Figure 518-3

GFCI protection must be provided in accordance with 210.8(B) for receptacles where required by this *Code*, except for the temporary wiring requirements of 590.6.

Where GFCI protection is supplied by plug-and-cord-connection, the GFCI-protective device must provide a level of protection equivalent to a portable GFCI, whether assembled in the field or at the factory.

518.4 Wiring Methods

(A) General. The fixed wiring methods must be metal raceways, flexible metal raceways, nonmetallic conduits encased in not less than 2 in. of concrete or Types MI, MC, or AC cable. ▶Figure 518-3

The wiring method itself must qualify as an equipment grounding conductor in accordance with 250.118, or it must contain an equipment grounding conductor sized in accordance with Table 250.122.

Ex: Fixed wiring methods are permitted in the following:

(a) *Sound Systems—Article 640*

(b) *Communications Systems—Chapter 8*

(c) *Class 2 Remote-Control and Signaling Circuits—Article 725*

(d) *Fire Alarm Circuits—Article 760*

(B) Spaces of Nonrated Construction. In addition to the permitted 518.4(A) wiring methods, Type NM cable, electrical nonmetallic tubing, and PVC conduit can be installed in those portions of an assembly occupancy building that are not required to be of fire-rated construction.

Note: Fire-rated construction is the fire-resistive classification used in building codes.

(C) Spaces with Finish Ratings. Electrical nonmetallic tubing and PVC conduit can be installed in club rooms, conference and meeting rooms in hotels or motels, courtrooms, dining facilities, restaurants, mortuary chapels, museums, libraries, and places of religious worship where:

(1) Electrical nonmetallic tubing or Type PVC conduit is installed concealed within walls, floors, and ceilings that provide a thermal barrier with not less than a 15-minute finish rating. ▶Figure 518-4

(2) Electrical nonmetallic tubing or Type PVC conduit can be installed above nonplenum [300.22(C)] suspended ceilings where the suspended ceilings provide a thermal barrier with not less than a 15-minute finish rating.

518.6 Illumination

Illumination must be provided for all working spaces about fixed service equipment, switchboards, switchgear, panelboards, or motor control centers installed outdoors that serve assembly occupancies. Control by automatic means only is not permitted. Additional lighting outlets are not required where the workspace is illuminated by an adjacent light source. See 110.26(D).

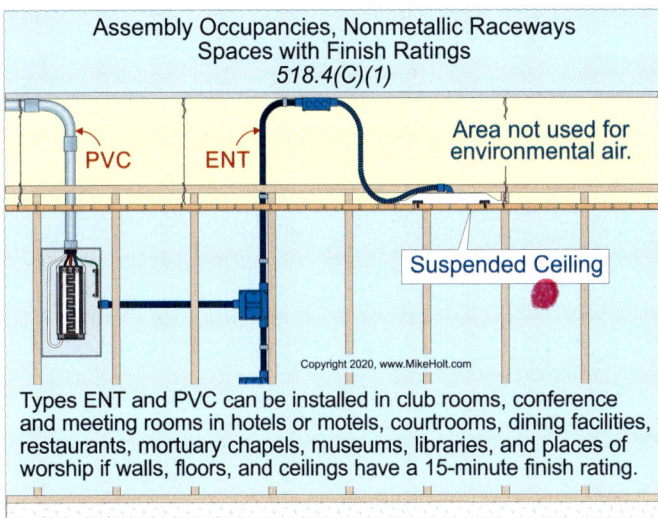
▶Figure 518-4

Notes

ARTICLE 525 CARNIVALS, CIRCUSES, FAIRS, AND SIMILAR EVENTS

Introduction to Article 525—Carnivals, Circuses, Fairs, and Similar Events

This article covers the installation of portable wiring and equipment for temporary carnivals, circuses, exhibitions, fairs, traveling attractions, and similar functions, including wiring in or on structures.

Part I. General Requirements

525.1 Scope

Article 525 covers the installation of portable wiring and equipment for carnivals, circuses, exhibitions, fairs, traveling attractions, and similar functions. ▶Figure 525–1

▶Figure 525–1

525.2 Definitions

The definitions in this section apply only within this article.

Operator. The individual responsible for starting, stopping, and controlling an amusement ride or supervising a concession. ▶Figure 525–2

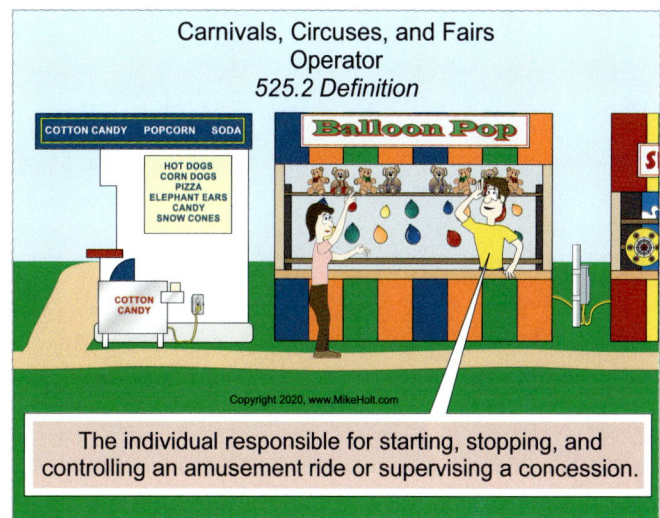

▶Figure 525–2

Portable Structures. Amusement rides, attractions, concessions, tents, trailers, and similar units designed to be moved. ▶Figure 525–3

525.5 Overhead Conductor Clearances

(A) Vertical Clearances. Overhead conductors installed outside tents and concession areas must have a vertical clearance to ground in accordance with 225.18. ▶Figure 525–4

525.6 | Carnivals, Circuses, Fairs, and Similar Events

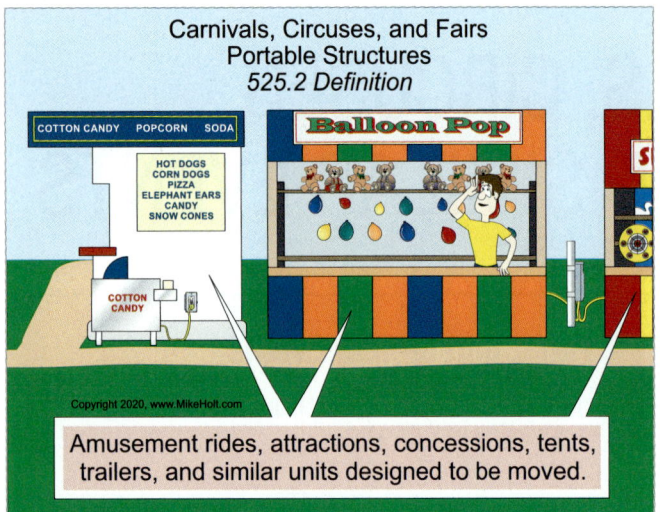
▶Figure 525–3

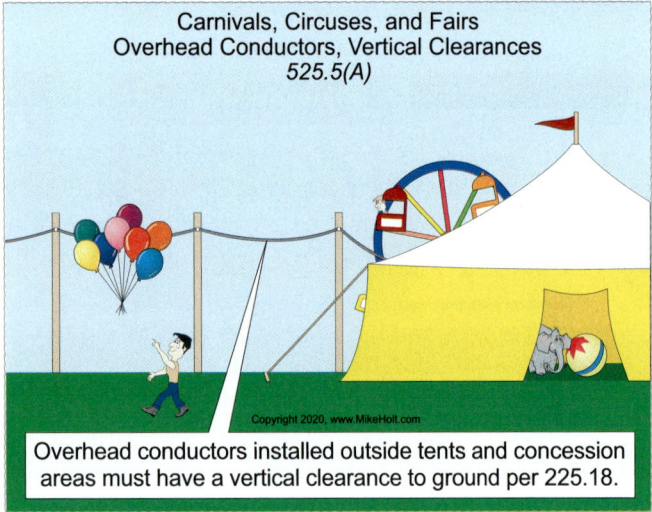
▶Figure 525–4

Author's Comment:

▶ Section 225.18 includes the following requirements:

  ▶ 10 ft above finished grade, sidewalks, platforms, or projections from which they might be accessible to pedestrians for 120V, 120/208V, 120/240V, or 240V circuits [225.18(1)].

  ▶ 12 ft above residential property and driveways, and those commercial areas not subject to truck traffic for 120V, 120/208V, 120/240V, 240V, 277V, 277/480V, or 480V circuits [225.18(2)].

  ▶ 18 ft over public streets, alleys, roads, parking areas subject to truck traffic, driveways on other than residential property, and other areas traversed by vehicles (such as those used for cultivation, grazing, forestry, and orchards) [225.18(4)].

(B) Clearance to Portable Structures.

(1) Overhead conductors, except for the conductors that supply the amusement ride or attractions, must have a clearance of 15 ft from portable amusement structures.

525.6 Protection of Electrical Equipment

Electrical equipment and wiring for portable structures must be provided with mechanical protection where subject to physical damage.

Part III. Wiring Methods

525.20 Wiring Methods

(A) Type. Flexible cords or flexible cables must be listed for extra-hard usage. Where used outdoors flexible cords and flexible cables must be listed for wet locations and be sunlight resistant. ▶Figure 525–5

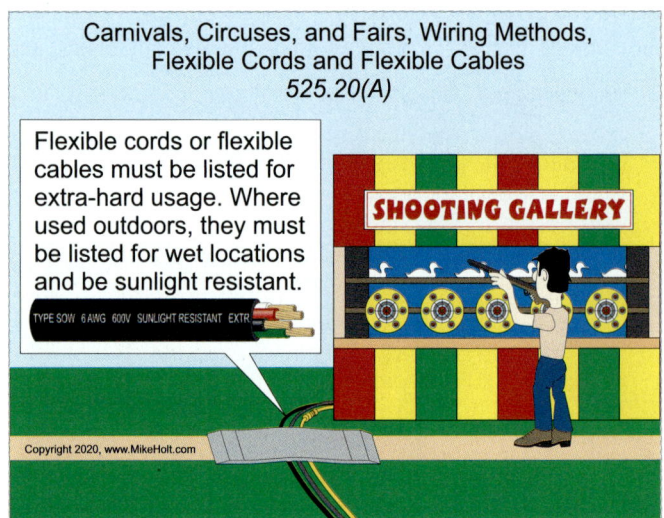
▶Figure 525–5

(B) Single Conductor. Single-conductor cable is permitted only in sizes 2 AWG and larger.

(C) Open Conductors. Open conductors are permitted as part of a listed assembly or part of festoon lighting installed in accordance with 225.6(B). ▶Figure 525–6

(D) Splices. Flexible cords or flexible cables must be continuous without splice or tap between boxes or fittings.

(E) Cord Connectors. Cord connectors laid on the ground must be listed for wet locations. Connectors and cable connections placed in audience traffic paths or areas accessible to the public must be guarded. ▶Figure 525–7

Carnivals, Circuses, Fairs, and Similar Events | 525.22

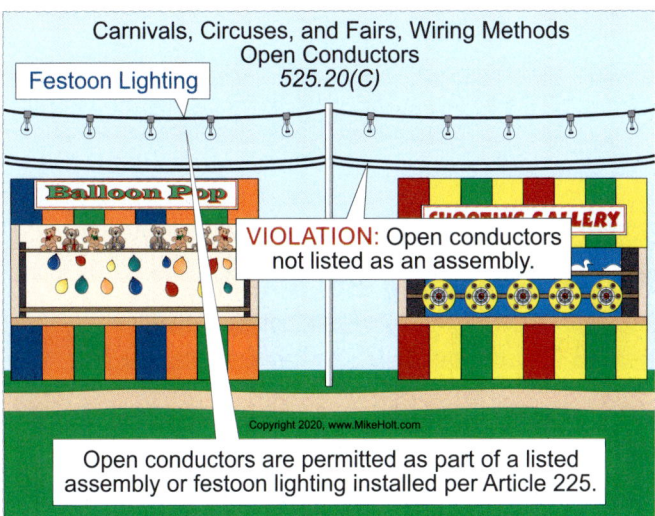
▶Figure 525-6

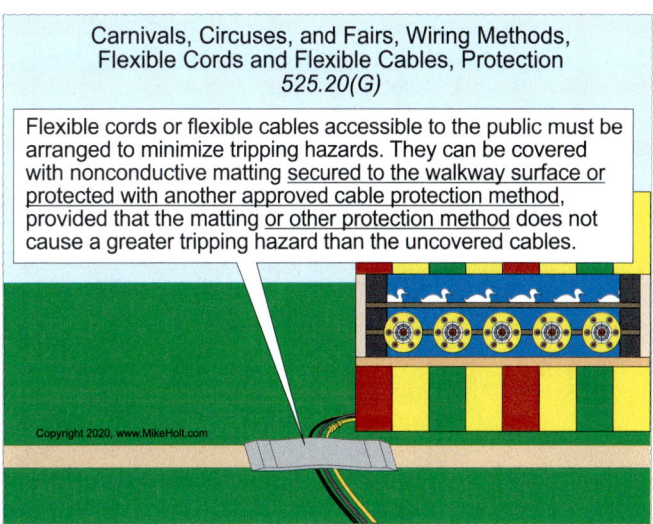
▶Figure 525-8

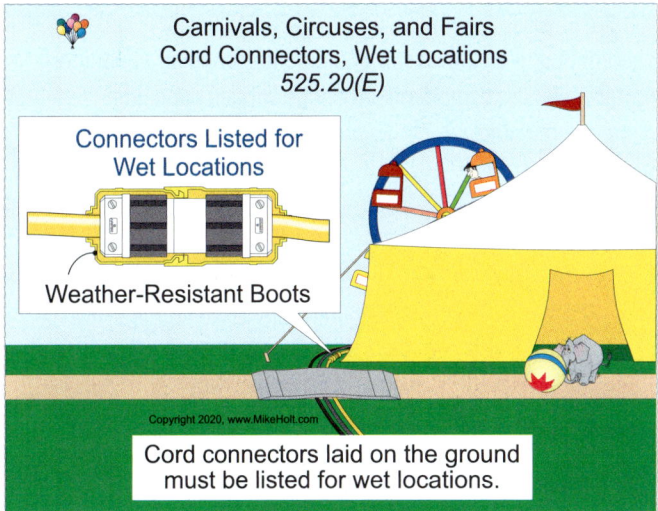
▶Figure 525-7

(G) Protection. Flexible cords or flexible cables accessible to the public must be arranged to minimize the tripping hazard. They can be covered with nonconductive matting secured to the walkway surface or protected with another approved cable protection method, provided that the matting or other protection method does not constitute a greater tripping hazard than the uncovered cables. ▶Figure 525-8

Burying cables is permitted and the burial depth requirements of 300.5 do not apply.

525.21 Rides, Tents, and Concessions

(A) Disconnecting Means. Each portable structure must have a disconnect that is within sight of, and within 6 ft of, the operator's station and readily accessible to the operator. Where accessible to unqualified persons, the disconnect must be lockable.

Author's Comment:

▸ According to Article 100, "Within Sight" means that it is visible and not more than 50 ft from the location of the equipment.

(B) Inside Tents and Concessions. Electrical wiring for lighting inside tents and concession areas must be securely installed. Where subject to physical damage, the wiring must be provided with mechanical protection [300.4] and lamps must be protected from accidental breakage by a suitable luminaire with a guard.

525.22 Outdoor Portable Distribution or Termination Boxes

(A) Terminal Boxes. Portable distribution and/or terminal boxes installed outdoors must be weatherproof, and the bottom of the enclosure must be not less than 6 in. above the ground.

525.23 GFCI-Protected Receptacles and Equipment

(A) GFCI Protection Required. In addition to the requirements of 210.8(B), GFCI protection must be provided for the following: ▶Figure 525-9

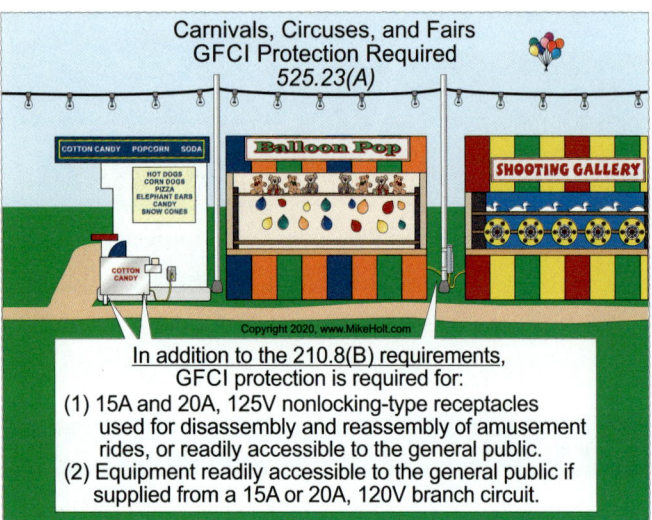

▶Figure 525-9

(1) 15A and 20A, 125V nonlocking-type receptacles used for disassembly and reassembly of amusement rides and attractions, or readily accessible to the general public.

(2) Equipment readily accessible to the general public if it is supplied from a 15A or 20A, 120V branch circuit.

GFCI protection can be integral with the attachment plug, located in the power-supply cord within 12 in. of the attachment plug, or a listed cord set incorporating GFCI protection.

(B) GFCI Protection Not Required. GFCI protection is not required for locking-type receptacles not accessible from grade level.

(C) GFCI Protection Not Permitted. GFCI protection is not permitted for egress lighting.

Author's Comment:

▸ The purpose of not permitting egress lighting to be GFCI protected is to ensure exit lighting remains energized and stays illuminated.

Part IV. Grounding and Bonding

525.31 Equipment Grounding

Metal parts of electrical equipment must be connected to an equipment grounding conductor of a type recognized by 250.118.

525.32 Portable Equipment Grounding Conductor Continuity

The continuity of the circuit equipment grounding conductors for portable electrical equipment must be verified each time the equipment is connected.

Author's Comment:

▸ Verification of circuit equipment grounding conductors is necessary to ensure electrical safety. This rule does not specify how it is verified, what circuits must be verified, how the verification is recorded, or who is required or qualified to perform the verification.

ARTICLE 547 AGRICULTURAL BUILDINGS

Introduction to Article 547—Agricultural Buildings

Three factors (dust, moisture, and an overall corrosive environment) have a tremendous influence on the lifespan of agricultural equipment.

Dust gets into mechanisms and causes premature wear. Add electricity to the mix, and dust adds two additional dangers: fire and explosion. Dust from hay, grain, and fertilizer is highly flammable. Litter materials, such as straw, are also highly flammable.

Another factor to consider in agricultural buildings is moisture which causes corrosion. Water is present for many reasons, including wash down.

Excrement from farm animals may cause corrosive vapors that eat at mechanical equipment and wiring methods and can cause electrical equipment to fail. For these reasons, Article 547 includes requirements for dealing with dust, moisture, and corrosion.

This article also has other rules. For example, you must install equipotential planes in all concrete floor confinement areas of livestock buildings containing metallic equipment accessible to animals and likely to become energized.

Livestock animals have a low tolerance to small voltage differences, which can cause loss of milk production and (at times) livestock fatality. As a result, the *NEC* contains specific requirements for an equipotential plane in buildings that house livestock.

547.1 Scope

Article 547 applies to agricultural buildings or to that part of a building (or adjacent areas of similar nature) as specified in (A) or (B). ▶Figure 547–1

Article 547 applies to agricultural buildings, or to that part of a building or adjacent areas of similar nature per (A) or (B).
(A) Buildings or areas where excessive dust and/or dust with water may accumulate.
(B) Buildings or areas where a corrosive atmosphere exists.

▶Figure 547–1

(A) Excessive Dust and Dust with Water. Buildings or areas where excessive dust and/or dust with water may accumulate such as areas of poultry, livestock, and fish confinement systems where litter or feed dust may accumulate.

(B) Corrosive Atmosphere. Buildings or areas where a corrosive atmosphere exists, and where the following conditions exist:

(1) Poultry and animal excrement.

(2) Corrosive particles that may combine with water.

(3) Areas made damp or wet by periodic washing.

547.2 Definitions

The definitions in this section apply only within this article.

Equipotential Plane (as applied to agricultural buildings). An area where conductive elements are embedded in or placed under concrete, bonded to all metal structures and nonelectrical equipment that could become energized, and connected to the electrical system to minimize voltage differences within the plane. ▶Figure 547–2

547.5 | Agricultural Buildings

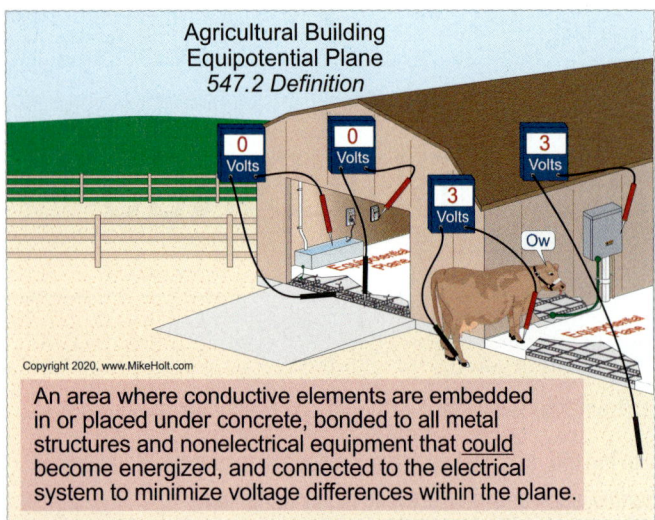
▶Figure 547–2

547.5 Wiring Methods

(A) Wiring Systems. Types UF, NMC, and SE cables with copper conductors, jacketed Type MC cable, PVC conduit, or liquidtight flexible nonmetallic conduit can be installed in agricultural building spaces.

(C) Equipment Enclosures, Boxes, Conduit Bodies, and Fittings.

(1) Excessive Dust. Equipment enclosures, boxes, conduit bodies, and fittings in areas of agricultural buildings where excessive dust may be present must be designed to minimize the entrance of dust. They must have no openings, such as holes for attachment screws, through which dust can enter the enclosure. ▶Figure 547–3

Author's Comment:

▸ Weatherproof boxes and covers can be used to meet this requirement.

(2) Damp or Wet Locations. In damp or wet locations of agricultural buildings, equipment enclosures, boxes, conduit bodies, and fittings must prevent moisture from entering or accumulating within. Boxes, conduit bodies, and fittings must be listed for use in wet locations and enclosures must be weatherproof.

(3) Corrosive Atmosphere. Where wet dust, excessive moisture, corrosive gases or vapors, or other corrosive conditions may be present in an agricultural building, equipment enclosures, boxes, conduit bodies, and fittings must have corrosion-resistant properties suitable for the conditions.

Note 1: See Table 110.28 for appropriate enclosures for the location.

(D) Flexible Connections. Where necessary for flexible connections, dusttight flexible connectors, liquidtight flexible metal conduit, liquidtight flexible nonmetallic conduit, or flexible cord listed for hard usage can be used.

(E) Physical Protection. Electrical wiring and equipment must be protected where subject to physical damage. See 300.4.

(F) Separate Equipment Grounding Conductor. Where the equipment grounding conductor is not part of a listed cable assembly, it must be insulated when installed underground. ▶Figure 547–4

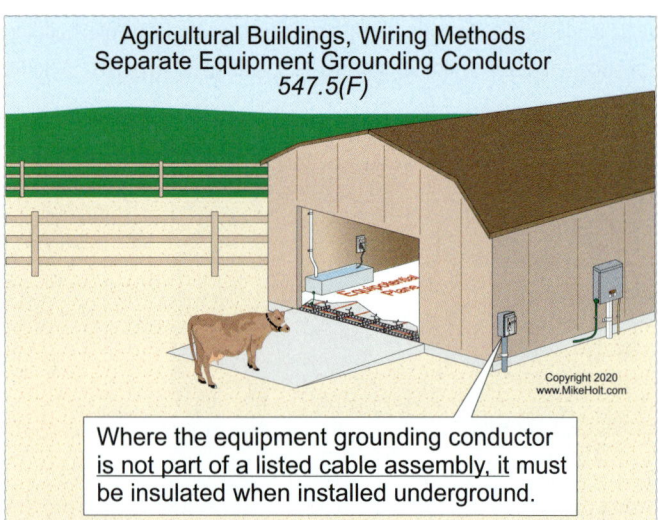
▶Figure 547–4

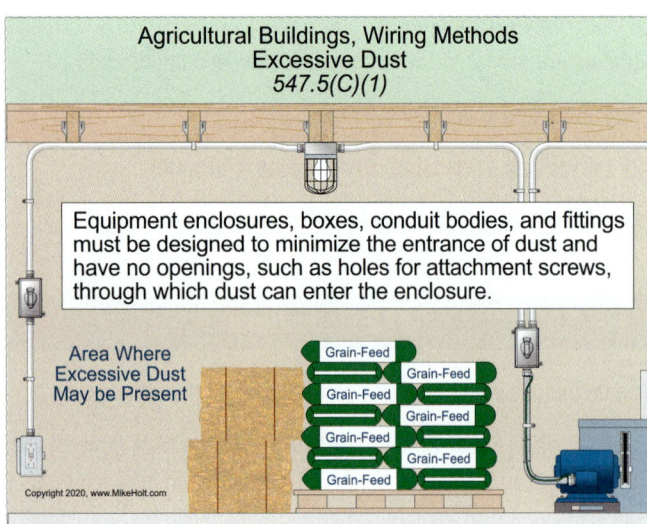
▶Figure 547–3

Agricultural Buildings | 547.10

(G) GFCI Protection of Receptacles. GFCI protection must be provided as required in 210.8(B). GFCI protection is not required for other than 125V, 15A and 20A receptacles installed within the following areas: ▶Figure 547-5

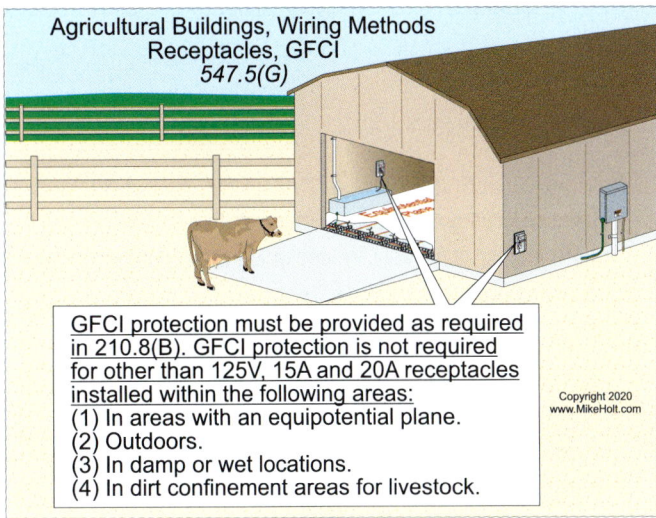
▶Figure 547-5

(1) In areas having an equipotential plane in accordance with 547.10(A).

(2) Outdoors.

(3) In damp or wet locations.

(4) In dirt confinement areas for livestock.

Author's Comment:

▸ See 210.8(B)(8) for GFCI protection of 250V, 30A and 50A receptacles installed in accessory buildings in adjacent agricultural areas used for storage or maintenance of farm equipment and supplies.

547.8 Luminaires

Luminaires must comply with the following:

(A) Minimize the Entrance of Dust. Luminaires must be installed to minimize the entrance of dust, foreign matter, moisture, and corrosive material.

(B) Exposed to Physical Damage. Luminaires must be protected against physical damage by a suitable guard.

(C) Exposed to Water. Luminaires exposed to water must be listed for use in wet locations.

547.10 Equipotential Planes

(A) Where Required. Equipotential planes must be installed as follows:

(1) Indoor Concrete Confinement Areas. An equipotential plane must be installed in indoor livestock confinement areas where metallic equipment accessible to livestock may become energized. ▶Figure 547-6

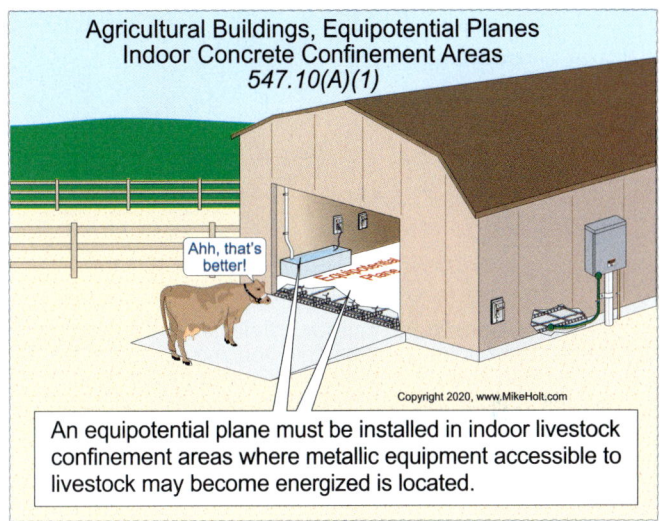
▶Figure 547-6

(2) Outdoor Concrete Confinement Areas. An equipotential plane must be installed in outdoor livestock confinement areas where metallic equipment accessible to livestock may become energized. ▶Figure 547-7

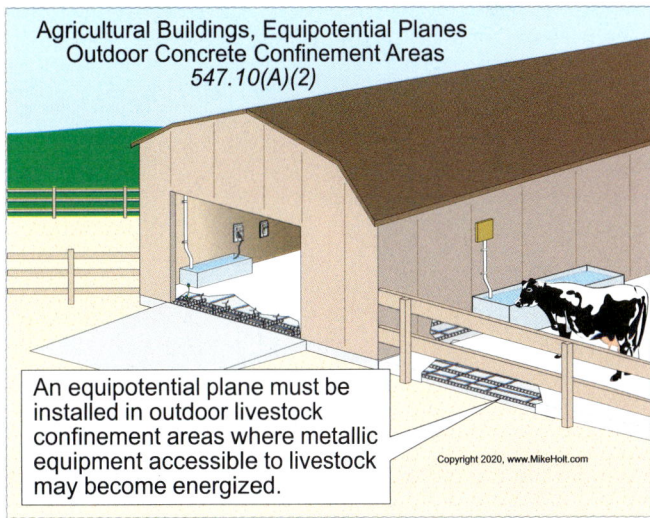
▶Figure 547-7

547.10 | Agricultural Buildings

(B) Bonding. The equipotential plane must be connected to the building electrical grounding system with a bonding conductor not smaller than an 8 AWG solid, insulated, or bare copper conductor using pressure connectors or clamps approved by the authority having jurisdiction. ▶Figure 547-8

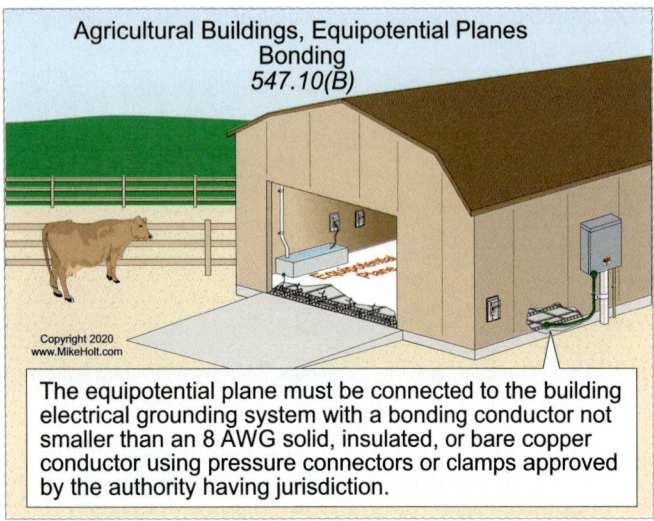

▶Figure 547-8

Note 1: ASABE Standard EP473.2, *Equipotential Planes in Animal Containment Areas*, provides the recommendation of a voltage gradient ramp at the entrances of agricultural buildings.

Note 2: See the American Society of Agricultural and Biological Engineers (ASABE) EP342.2, *Safety for Electrically Heated Livestock Waterers*.

Author's Comment:

▸ The bonding requirements contained in Article 547 are unique because of the sensitivity of livestock to small voltage differences, especially in wet or damp concrete animal confinement areas.

▸ In most instances the voltage difference between metal parts and the earth will be too low to present a shock hazard to people. However, livestock might detect the voltage difference if they come into contact with the metal parts. Although voltage differences may not be life threatening to the livestock, it has been reported that as little as 0.50V RMS can adversely affect milk production.

ARTICLE 550 — MOBILE HOMES, MANUFACTURED HOMES, AND MOBILE HOME PARKS

Introduction to Article 550—Mobile Homes, Manufactured Homes, and Mobile Home Parks

Among dwelling types, mobile homes have the highest rate of fire. Article 550 addresses some of the causes of those fires with the intent of reducing these statistics. This article recognizes that the same mobile or manufactured homes used as dwellings are also used for nondwelling purposes, such as construction offices or clinics [550.4(A)].

Mobile homes and manufactured homes are not covered by the same building codes as are site-built homes. They are covered by HUD standards instead. According to HUD, both are referred to as manufactured homes and the term "mobile home" has not been used for many years. This disparity between the NEC and industry practices can cause confusion, so read the Code carefully as you apply this article.

Part I. General

550.1 Scope

Article 550 covers electrical conductors and equipment installed within or on mobile and manufactured homes, conductors that connect mobile and manufactured homes to the electric supply, and the installation of electrical wiring, luminaires, and electrical equipment within mobile home parks. ▶Figure 550-1

In addition, this article applies to electrical equipment related to the mobile home feeder/service-entrance conductors and service disconnects as covered by Part III of this article.

550.2 Definitions

This definition applies within this article and throughout the Code.

Manufactured Home. A structure, in the travel mode, that is a minimum of 8 ft wide and 40 ft long built on a chassis and designed to be used as a dwelling unit with or without a permanent foundation. ▶Figure 550-2

> **Author's Comment:**
> ▸ See Article 100 for the definition of "Dwelling Unit."

This definition applies within this article and throughout the Code.

Mobile Home. A transportable structure built on a permanent chassis and designed to be used as a dwelling unit without a permanent foundation. In this article and unless otherwise indicated, the term "mobile home" includes manufactured homes.

This definition applies only within this article.

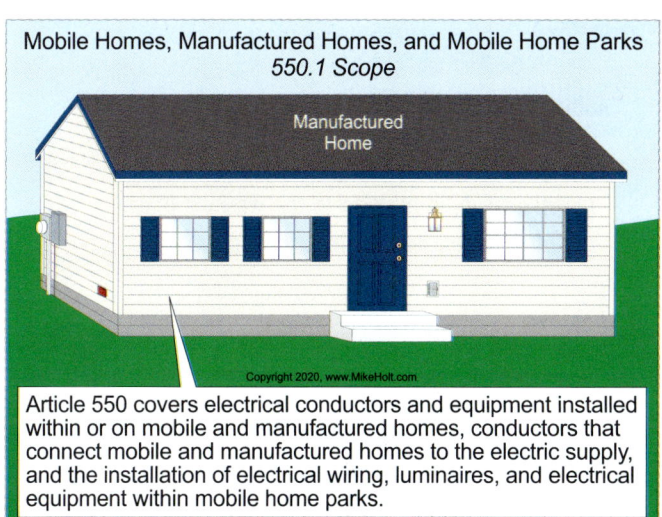
▶Figure 550-1

550.4 | Mobile Homes, Manufactured Homes, and Mobile Home Parks

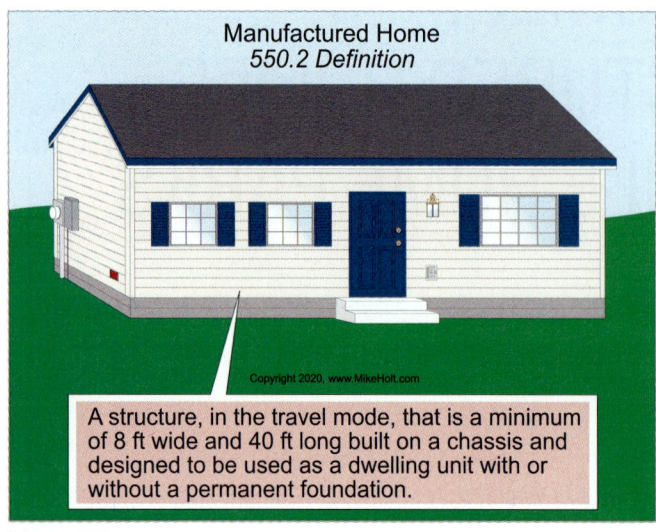

▶Figure 550-2

Mobile Home Accessory Building or Structure. Any awning, cabana, ramada, storage cabinet, carport, fence, windbreak, or porch established for the use of the occupant of the mobile home on a mobile home lot.

550.4 General Requirements

(B) Wiring System. Mobile homes must be connected to a 120/240V, nominal, grounded system.

Part II. Mobile and Manufactured Homes

550.13 Receptacle Outlets

(B) GFCI-Protected Receptacles. Ground-fault circuit-interrupter protection must be provided as required in 210.8(A). GFCI protection is not required for other than 125V, 15A and 20A receptacles installed within a mobile or manufactured home in the following areas:

(1) Compartments accessible from the outdoors.

(2) Bathroom areas.

(3) Kitchens, where receptacles are installed to serve countertop surfaces. ▶Figure 550-3

(4) Sinks, where within 6 ft from the top inside edge of the sink. ▶Figure 550-4

(5) Dishwashers. See 422.5(A)(7).

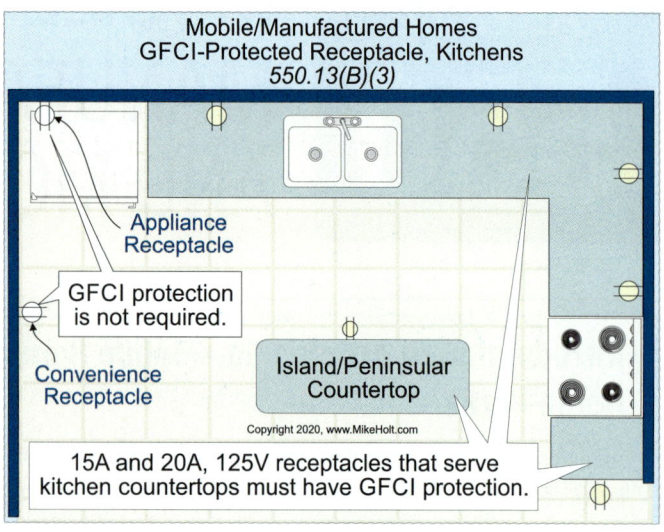

▶Figure 550-3

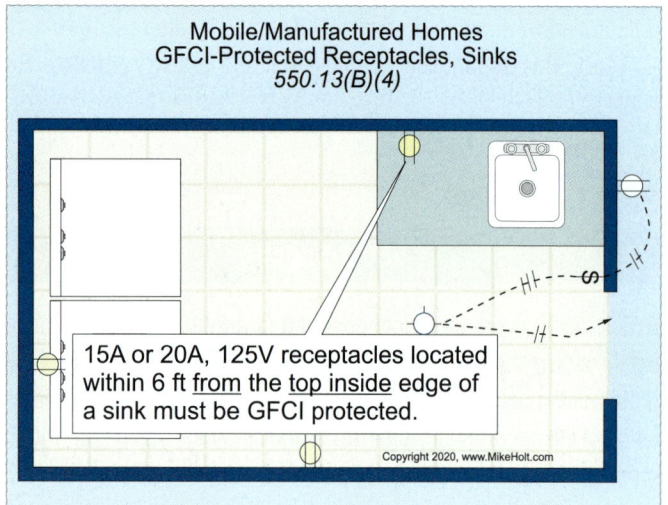

▶Figure 550-4

Author's Comment:

▶ See 210.8(A)(10) for mobile or manufactured homes with laundry areas; in addition to the washing machine, GFCI protection is required for the dryer receptacle.

550.15 Wiring Methods and Materials

(H) Under Chassis. Under-chassis line-voltage wiring (120V) must be installed in a raceway identified for wet locations.

ARTICLE 550 MOBILE HOMES, MANUFACTURED HOMES, AND MOBILE HOME PARKS

Introduction to Article 550—Mobile Homes, Manufactured Homes, and Mobile Home Parks

Among dwelling types, mobile homes have the highest rate of fire. Article 550 addresses some of the causes of those fires with the intent of reducing these statistics. This article recognizes that the same mobile or manufactured homes used as dwellings are also used for nondwelling purposes, such as construction offices or clinics [550.4(A)].

Mobile homes and manufactured homes are not covered by the same building codes as are site-built homes. They are covered by HUD standards instead. According to HUD, both are referred to as manufactured homes and the term "mobile home" has not been used for many years. This disparity between the *NEC* and industry practices can cause confusion, so read the *Code* carefully as you apply this article.

Part I. General

550.1 Scope

Article 550 covers electrical conductors and equipment installed within or on mobile and manufactured homes, conductors that connect mobile and manufactured homes to the electric supply, and the installation of electrical wiring, luminaires, and electrical equipment within mobile home parks. ▶Figure 550–1

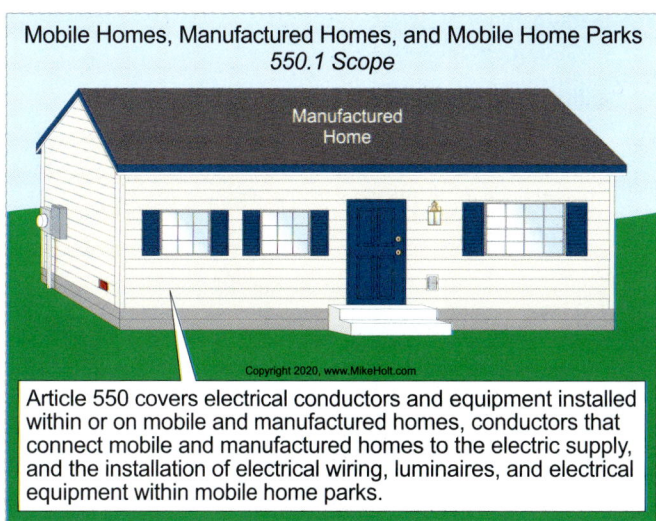

▶Figure 550–1

In addition, this article applies to electrical equipment related to the mobile home feeder/service-entrance conductors and service disconnects as covered by Part III of this article.

550.2 Definitions

This definition applies within this article and throughout the *Code*.

Manufactured Home. A structure, in the travel mode, that is a minimum of 8 ft wide and 40 ft long built on a chassis and designed to be used as a dwelling unit with or without a permanent foundation. ▶Figure 550–2

> **Author's Comment:**
> ▸ See Article 100 for the definition of "Dwelling Unit."

This definition applies within this article and throughout the *Code*.

Mobile Home. A transportable structure built on a permanent chassis and designed to be used as a dwelling unit without a permanent foundation. In this article and unless otherwise indicated, the term "mobile home" includes manufactured homes.

This definition applies only within this article.

550.4 | Mobile Homes, Manufactured Homes, and Mobile Home Parks

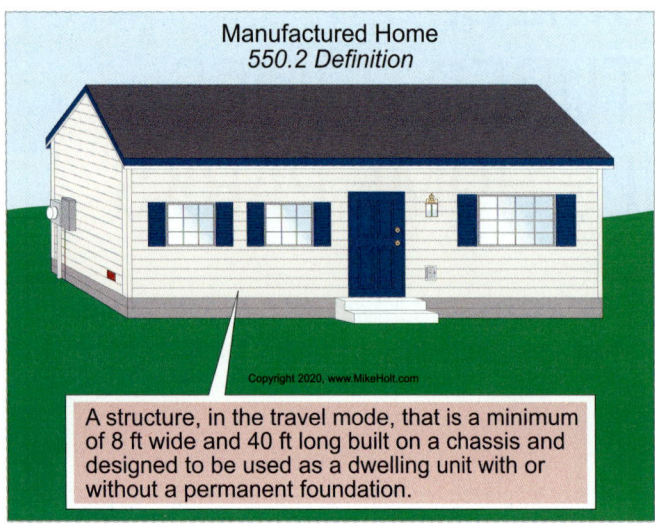

▶Figure 550–2

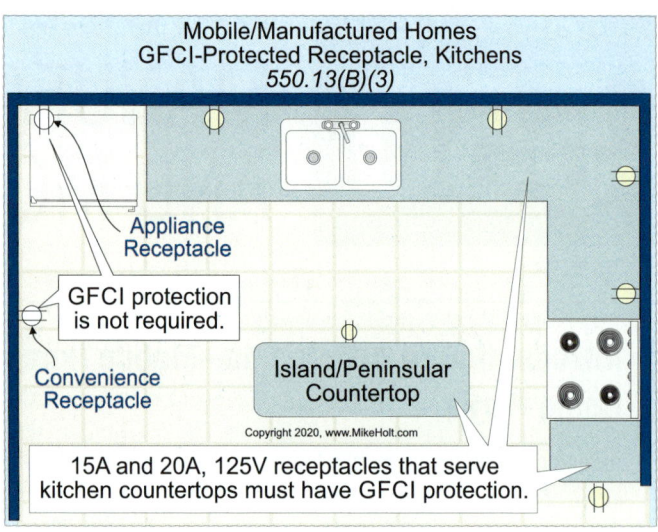

▶Figure 550–3

Mobile Home Accessory Building or Structure. Any awning, cabana, ramada, storage cabinet, carport, fence, windbreak, or porch established for the use of the occupant of the mobile home on a mobile home lot.

550.4 General Requirements

(B) Wiring System. Mobile homes must be connected to a 120/240V, nominal, grounded system.

Part II. Mobile and Manufactured Homes

550.13 Receptacle Outlets

(B) GFCI-Protected Receptacles. Ground-fault circuit-interrupter protection must be provided as required in 210.8(A). GFCI protection is not required for other than 125V, 15A and 20A receptacles installed within a mobile or manufactured home in the following areas:

(1) Compartments accessible from the outdoors.

(2) Bathroom areas.

(3) Kitchens, where receptacles are installed to serve countertop surfaces. ▶Figure 550–3

(4) Sinks, where within 6 ft from the top inside edge of the sink. ▶Figure 550–4

(5) Dishwashers. See 422.5(A)(7).

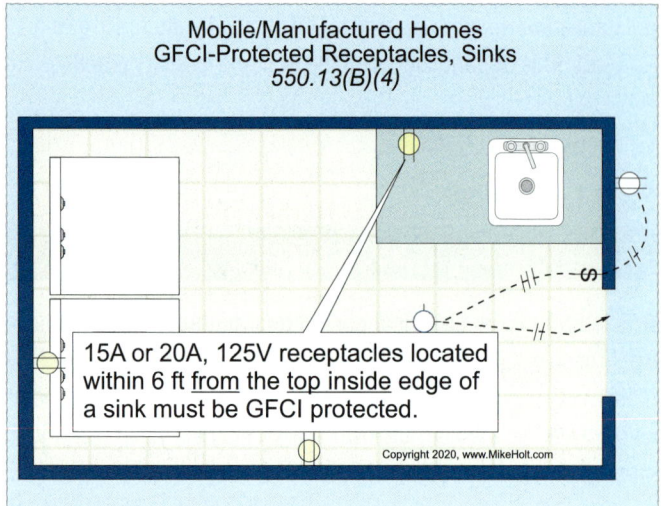

▶Figure 550–4

Author's Comment:

▸ See 210.8(A)(10) for mobile or manufactured homes with laundry areas; in addition to the washing machine, GFCI protection is required for the dryer receptacle.

550.15 Wiring Methods and Materials

(H) Under Chassis. Under-chassis line-voltage wiring (120V) must be installed in a raceway identified for wet locations.

Mobile Homes, Manufactured Homes, and Mobile Home Parks | 550.33

550.25 AFCI Protection

(B) Requirements. When a 15A or 20A, 120V, single-phase branch circuit supplying outlets or devices is installed by other than the manufacturer, the circuit must be AFCI protected in accordance with 210.12.

Part III. Services and Feeders

550.32 Mobile and Manufactured Home Service Disconnect

(A) Mobile Home Disconnect. The service disconnect for a mobile home must be located adjacent to but not mounted in or on the mobile home. The disconnect must be located within sight from, but not more than 30 ft from the exterior wall of the mobile home and be rated at not less than 100A [550.32(C)]. ▶Figure 550-5

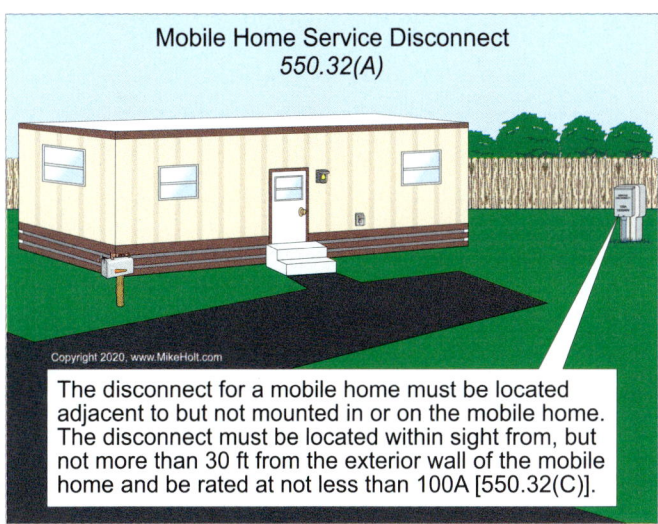
▶Figure 550-5

Author's Comment:

- According to Article 100, "Within Sight" means that it is visible and not more than 50 ft from the location of the equipment, but in this case one must comply with the maximum 30-ft requirement of this section.

(B) Manufactured Home Disconnect. The service disconnect can be located in or on a manufactured home. The manufacturer must include written installation instructions indicating that the home must be secured by an anchoring system or installed and secured to a permanent foundation [550.32(B)(1)]. ▶Figure 550-6

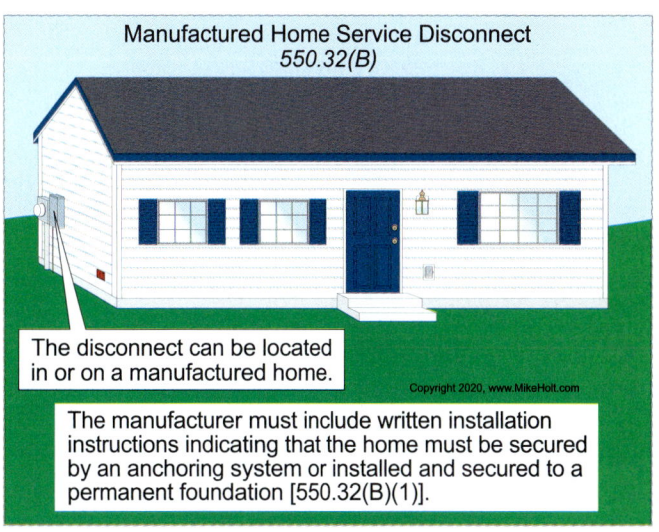
▶Figure 550-6

550.33 Feeder

(B) Feeder Capacity. The feeder for a mobile or manufactured home lot must have an ampacity of at least 100A at 120/240V and can be sized using 310.12 if feeder conductors supply the entire associated load. ▶Figure 550-7

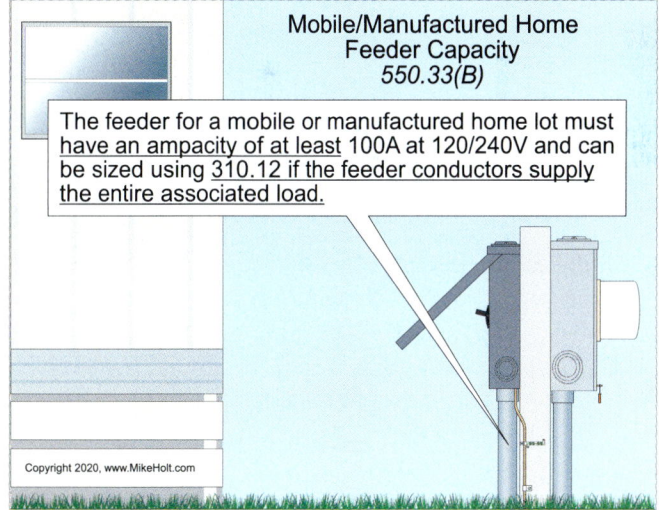
▶Figure 550-7

Notes

ARTICLE 555 — MARINAS, BOATYARDS, AND DOCKING FACILITIES

Introduction to Article 555—Marinas, Boatyards, and Docking Facilities

Water levels are not constant. Ocean tides rise and fall, while lakes and rivers vary in depth in response to rain. To provide power to a marina, boatyard, or docking facility, you must allow for these variations in water level between the point of use and the electric power source. Article 555 addresses this issue.

This article begins with the concept of the electrical datum plane. You might think of it as the border of a "demilitarized zone" for electrical equipment. Or, you can think of it as a line that marks the beginning of a "no man's land" where you simply do not place electrical equipment. Once you determine where this plane is, do not place transformers, connections, or receptacles below that line.

Because of recent ESD (electric shock drowning) incidents, installations supplying shore power in marinas and boatyards have increased electrical safety with the use of GFP (ground fault protection), leakage devices, and warning signs to raise awareness of hazardous voltage and currents present in the water of marinas, boatyards, and docking facilities.

Part I. General

555.1 Scope

Article 555 covers the installations in dwellings and commercial areas of wiring and equipment for fixed or floating piers, wharfs, docks, floating buildings, and other areas in marinas and boatyards. ▶Figure 555–1

▶Figure 555–1

555.2 Definitions

Author's Comment:

▸ Some of the definitions in this section of the text appear in Article 100 of the *Code*. They are included here as well for context and illustrative purposes.

Docking Facility. A covered or open, fixed or floating structure that provides access to the water and to which boats are secured.

Electrical Datum Plane. A specified distance above a water level (which may or may not be subject to tidal fluctuation) above which electrical equipment can be installed and electrical connections can be made. ▶Figure 555–2

Marina. A facility, generally on the waterfront, that stores and services boats in berths, on moorings, and in dry storage or dry stack storage. ▶Figure 555–3

Marine Power Outlet. An enclosed assembly that can include equipment such as receptacles, circuit breakers, watt-hour meters, and panelboards approved for marine use. ▶Figure 555–4

555.2 | Marinas, Boatyards, and Docking Facilities

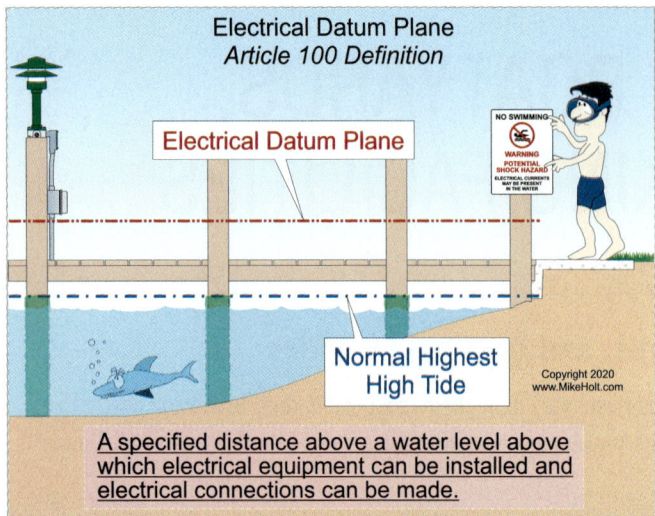

▶Figure 555–2

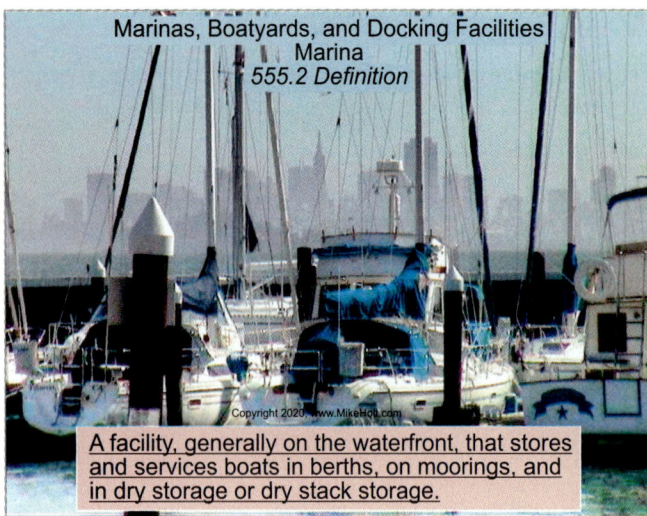

▶Figure 555–3

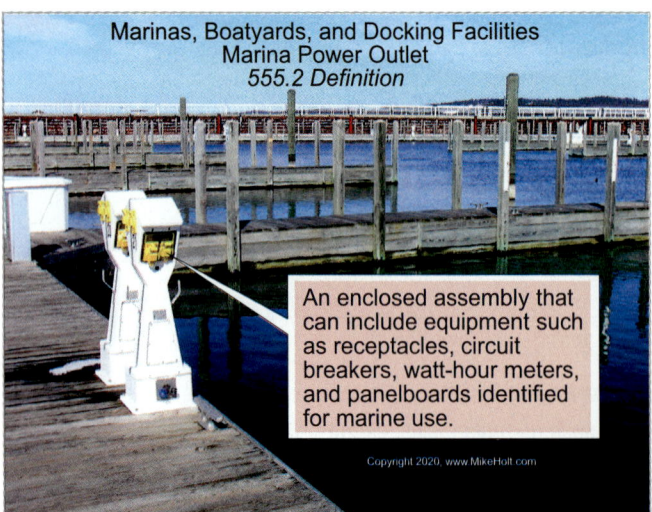

▶Figure 555–4

Pier. A structure extending over the water and supported on a fixed foundation (fixed pier), or on flotation (floating pier), that provides access to the water. ▶Figure 555–5

▶Figure 555–5

Pier, Fixed (Fixed Pier). A pier constructed on a permanent, fixed foundation (such as on piles) that permanently establishes the elevation of the structure's deck with respect to land. ▶Figure 555–6

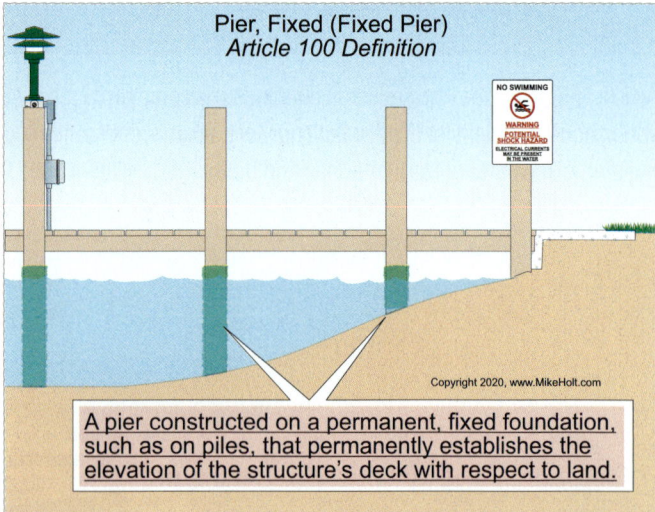

▶Figure 555–6

Pier, Floating (Floating Pier). A pier designed with inherent flotation capability that allows the structure to float on the water surface and rise and fall with water level changes. ▶Figure 555–7

Shore Power. The electrical equipment required to power a floating vessel including, but not limited to, the receptacle and cords. ▶Figure 555–8

Marinas, Boatyards, and Docking Facilities | 555.3

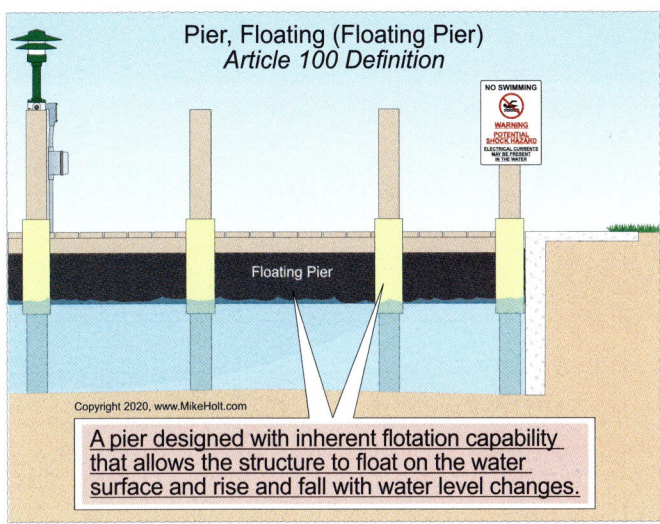
▶Figure 555-7

▶Figure 555-9

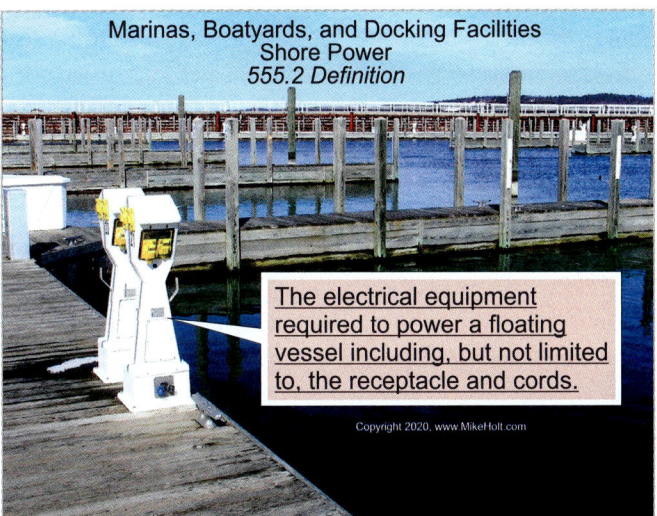
▶Figure 555-8

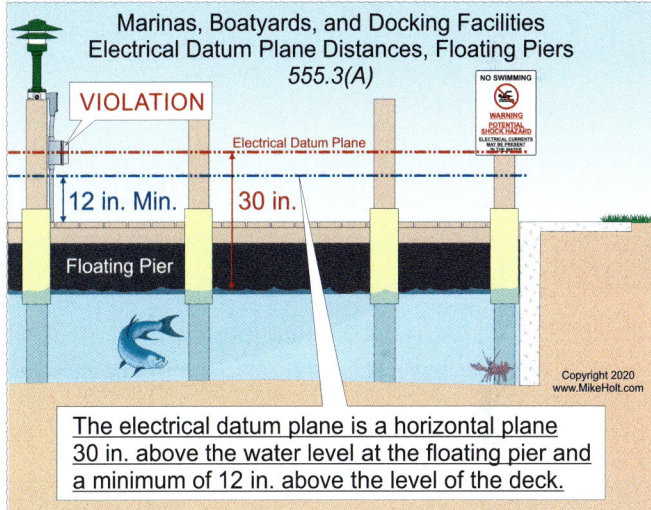
▶Figure 555-10

Slip. A berthing space between or adjacent to piers, wharves, or docks; the water areas associated with boat occupation. ▶Figure 555-9

555.3 Electrical Datum Plane Distances

(A) Floating Piers. The electrical datum plane for floating piers and boat landing stages is a horizontal plane 30 in. above the water level at the floating pier and a minimum of 12 in. above the level of the deck. ▶Figure 555-10

(B) Areas Subject to Tidal Fluctuations. In land areas subject to tidal fluctuation, the electrical datum plane is a horizontal plane 2 ft above the highest tide level for the area occurring under normal circumstances, based on the highest high tide. ▶Figure 555-11

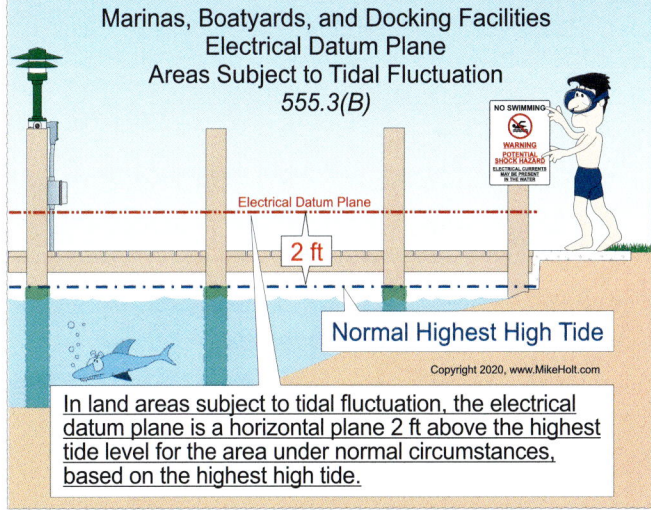
▶Figure 555-11

(C) Areas Not Subject to Tidal Fluctuations. In land areas not subject to tidal fluctuation, the electrical datum plane is a horizontal plane 2 ft above the highest water level for the area occurring under normal circumstances. ▶Figure 555-12

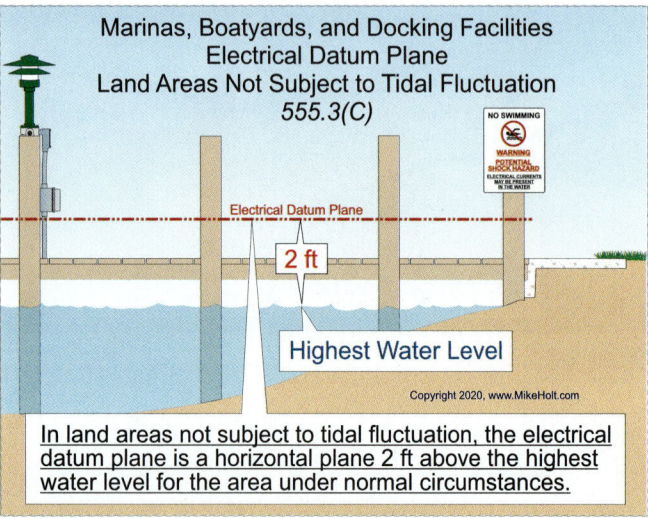

▶Figure 555-12

555.4 Location of Service Equipment

The service equipment for a floating building, dock, or marina must be located on land adjacent to the structure served, but not on or in the structure itself.

555.5 Maximum Voltage

Pier power distribution systems must not exceed 250V phase to phase. Pier power distribution systems, where qualified personnel service the equipment under engineering supervision, are permitted to exceed 250V but these systems must not exceed 600V.

555.6 Load Calculations for Service and Feeder Conductors

When calculating service and/or feeder ampacities, the demand factors shown in Table 555.6 can be applied.

Table 555.6 Demand Factors

Number of Shore Power Receptacles	Sum of the Rating of the Receptacles %
1–4	100
5–8	90
9–14	80
15–30	70
31–40	60
41–50	50
51–70	40
71 and Over	30

Note 1: Where shore power accommodations provide two receptacles specifically for an individual boat slip and these receptacles have different voltages (for example, one 30A, 125V and one 50A, 125/250V), only the receptacle with the larger kilowatt demand is required to be calculated. ▶Figure 555-13

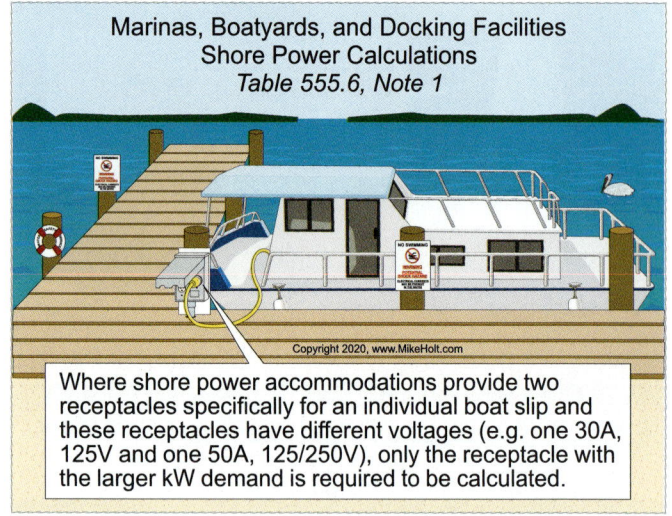

▶Figure 555-13

555.7 Transformers

(A) General. Transformers and enclosures must be identified for wet locations. The bottom of the transformer enclosure is not permitted to be located below the electrical datum plane. ▶Figure 555-14

Marinas, Boatyards, and Docking Facilities | 555.11

▶Figure 555-14

555.9 Boat Hoists

GFCI protection is required for a boat hoist not exceeding 240V installed at dwelling unit docking facilities. ▶Figure 555-15

▶Figure 555-15

Author's Comment:

▶ This section was previously covered in 210.8(C) but is now in Article 555 due to its scope now covering dwelling unit docking facilities.

555.10 Electric Shock Hazard Signage

A permanent safety sign is required to give notice of electrical shock hazard risks to persons using or swimming near a docking facility, boatyard, or marina. The safety sign must meet all of the following requirements: ▶Figure 555-16

▶Figure 555-16

(1) The sign must warn of the hazards using effective words, colors, or symbols (or a combination) in accordance with 110.21(B)(1) and be of sufficient durability to withstand the environment.

(2) The signs must be clearly visible from all approaches to a marina or boatyard facility.

(3) The signs must state:

> **WARNING—POTENTIAL SHOCK HAZARD—ELECTRICAL CURRENTS MAY BE PRESENT IN THE WATER.**

555.11 Motor Fuel Dispensing Stations— Hazardous (Classified) Locations

Electrical wiring and equipment located at or serving motor fuel dispensing locations must comply with Article 514 in addition to the requirements of this article. ▶Figure 555-17

555.12 | Marinas, Boatyards, and Docking Facilities

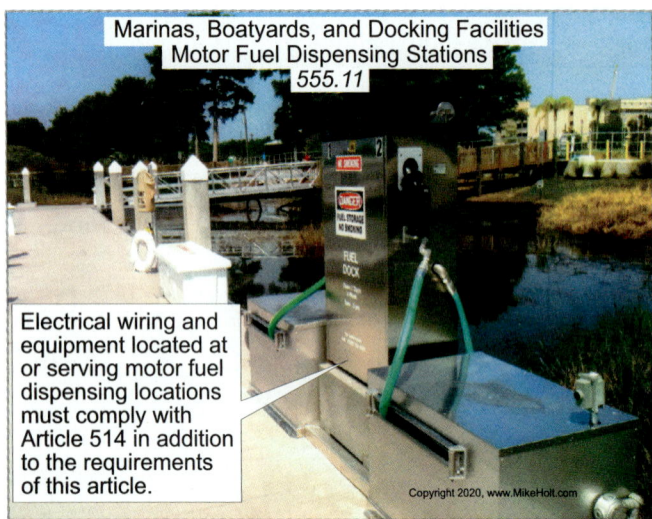

▶Figure 555–17

- 511.7—Wiring and Equipment Above Hazardous (Classified) Locations
- 511.9—Explosionproof Seals
- 511.12—GFCI-Protected Receptacles

555.13 Bonding of Noncurrent-Carrying Metal Parts

Metal parts in contact with the water, metal piping, and noncurrent-carrying metal parts likely to become energized must be connected to the grounding bus in the panelboard using a solid copper conductor that is insulated, covered, or bare and not smaller than 8 AWG. Connections must be made in accordance with 250.8.

Part II. Marinas, Boatyards, and Docking Facilities

555.30 Electrical Connections

(A) Floating Piers. Electrical connections must be located at least 12 in. above the deck of a floating pier. ▶Figure 555–19

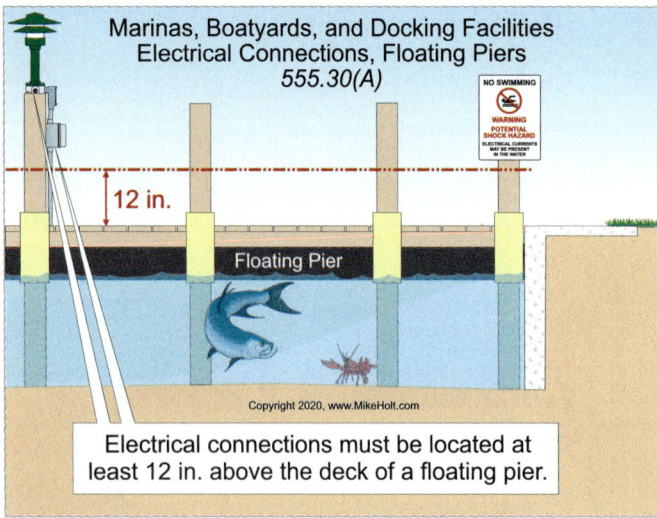

▶Figure 555–19

(B) Fixed Piers. Electrical connections must be located at least 12 in. above the deck of a fixed pier and not below the electrical datum plane. ▶Figure 555–20 and ▶Figure 555–21

555.12 Repair Facilities—Hazardous (Classified) Locations

Electrical wiring and equipment at marine craft repair facilities containing flammable or combustible liquids or gases must comply with Article 511 in addition to the requirements of this article. ▶Figure 555–18

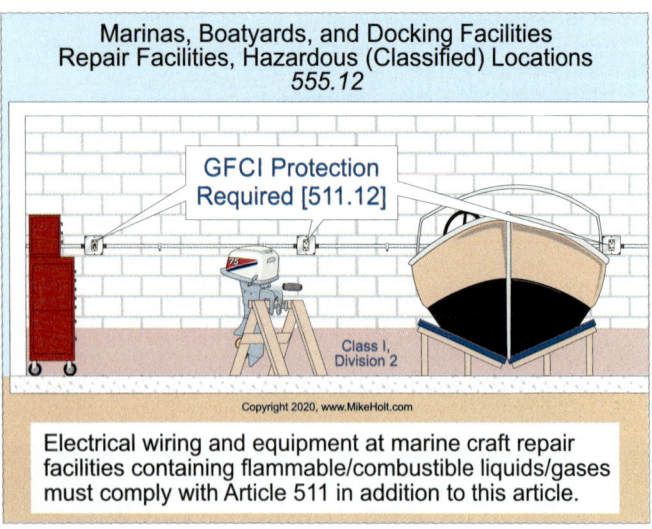

▶Figure 555–18

Author's Comment:

- Important rules in Article 511 to consider include:
  - 511.3—Classification of Hazardous Areas
  - 511.4—Wiring and Equipment in Hazardous (Classified) Locations

Marinas, Boatyards, and Docking Facilities | 555.34

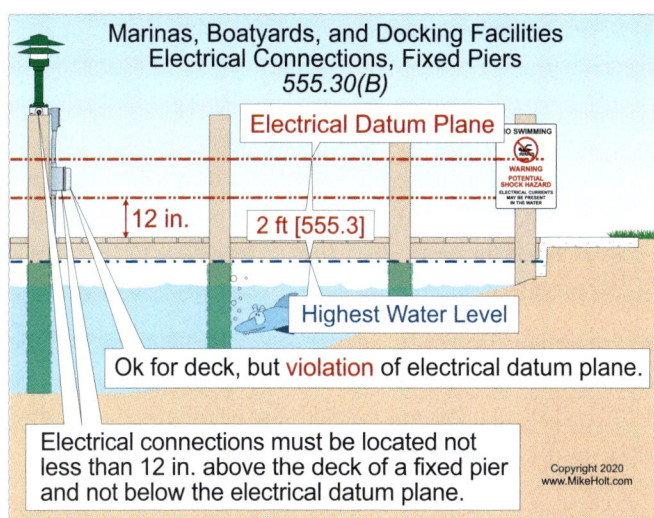
▶Figure 555-20

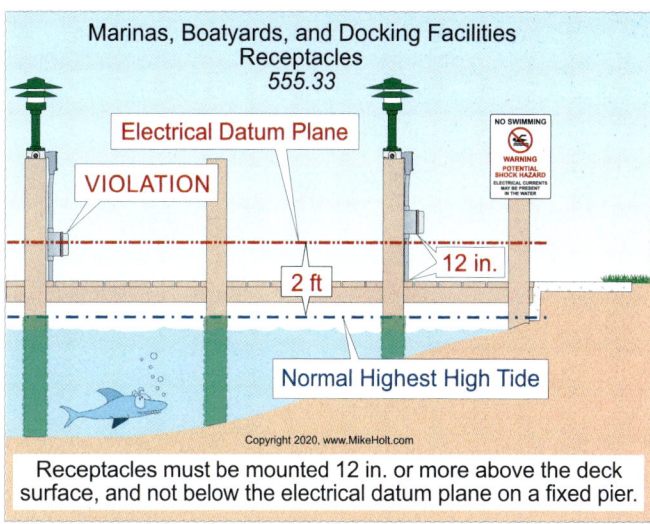
▶Figure 555-22

▶Figure 555-21

(C) Replacements. Replacement electrical connections for a floating pier must be located at least 12 in. above its deck. Conductor splices where located above the waterline but below the electrical datum plane for floating piers are required to be within junction boxes identified for wet locations, utilizing sealed wire connector systems listed and identified for submersion.

555.33 Receptacles

Receptacles must be mounted not less than 12 in. above the deck surface, and not below the electrical datum plane on a fixed pier.
▶Figure 555-22

(A) Shore Power Receptacles.

(1) Enclosures. Receptacles intended to supply shore power to boats must be part of a listed marina power outlet enclosure and be installed in listed enclosures protected from the weather or in listed weatherproof enclosures.

(4) Ratings. Receptacles that provide shore power for boats must be rated at least 30A and must be of the pin and sleeve type if rated 60A or higher.

> **Author's Comment:**
>
> ▶ The rating of the shore power receptacle does not depend on the length of the boat. The *Code* simply sets a minimum rating of 30A and leaves it up to the designer and/or owner to provide the receptacles they deem necessary based on the projected usage of the slips.

(B) Other Than Shore Power.

(1) GFCI Protection of Receptacles. Receptacles in other locations must be protected in accordance with 210.8. ▶Figure 555-23

(C) Replacement Receptacles. Replacement receptacles must comply with 555.33.

555.34 Wiring Methods and Installation

(A) Wiring Methods.

(1) General. Any Chapter 3 wiring method identified for wet locations is permitted.

555.35 | Marinas, Boatyards, and Docking Facilities

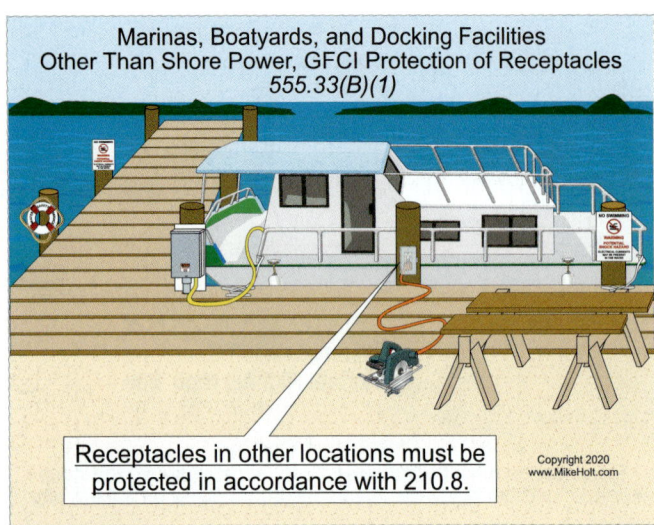
▶Figure 555–23

(2) Portable Power Cables. Sunlight resistant, extra-hard usage portable power cables listed for wet locations having an outer jacket resistant to temperature extremes (not less than 167°F), oil, gasoline, ozone, abrasion, acids, and chemicals are permitted as follows:

(1) As permanent wiring on the underside of piers (floating or fixed).

(2) Where flexibility is necessary as on piers composed of floating sections.

(3) Temporary Wiring. Temporary wiring, except as permitted by Article 590, must not be used to supply power to boats.

(B) Installation.

(2) Outdoor Branch Circuits and Feeders. Multiple feeders and branch circuits are permitted and clearances for overhead branch-circuit and feeder wiring in locations of the boatyard other than those described in 555.34(B)(1) must be not less than 18 ft above grade. Only Part I of Article 225 applies to marina installations.

(3) Portable Power Cables.

(a) Portable power cables permitted by 555.13(A)(2) must be:

(1) Properly supported.

(2) Located on the underside of the pier.

(3) Securely fastened by nonmetallic clips to structural members other than the deck planking.

(4) Not be subject to physical damage.

(5) Protected against chafing by a permanently installed oversized sleeve of nonmetallic material when cables pass through structural members.

(b) Where portable power cables are used, there must be a junction box of corrosion-resistant construction with permanently installed terminal blocks on each pier section to which the feeders are connected. A listed marina power outlet employing terminal blocks/bars is permitted in lieu of a junction box. Metal junction boxes and covers, and metal screws and parts that are exposed externally to the boxes, must be of corrosion-resistant materials or protected by material resistant to corrosion.

(4) Protection. Rigid metal conduit, reinforced thermosetting resin conduit (RTRC) listed for aboveground use, or rigid polyvinyl chloride (PVC) conduit suitable for the location must be used to protect wiring above the decks of piers and landing stages.

555.35 Ground-Fault Protection of Equipment (GFPE) and Ground-Fault Circuit-Interrupter (GFCI) Protection

(A) Ground-Fault Protection. For other than floating buildings, ground-fault protection for docking facilities must be provided in accordance with the following:

(1) GFPE Protection. Receptacles installed in accordance with 555.33(A) can have individual GFPEs set to open at currents not exceeding 30 mA.

(2) GFCI Protection. All 15A and 20A, 125V receptacles for other than shore power must be protected in accordance with 555.33(B)(1) and (B)(2).

(3) Feeder and Branch-Circuit Conductors with GFPE. Feeder and branch-circuit conductors that are installed on docking facilities must be provided with GFPEs set to open at currents not exceeding 100 mA. Coordination with the feeder GFPE overcurrent protective device is permitted.

Ex to (3): Transformer secondary conductors of a separately derived system that do not exceed 10 ft and are installed in a raceway are permitted to be installed without ground-fault protection. This exception also applies to the supply terminals of the equipment supplied by the transformer secondary conductors.

(B) Leakage Current Measurement Device. Where more than three receptacles supply shore power to boats, a leakage current measurement device must be available and be used to determine leakage current from each boat that will utilize shore power.

Note 1: Leakage current measurement will provide the capability to determine when an individual boat has defective wiring or other problems contributing to hazardous voltage and current. The use of this test device will allow the facility operator to identify a boat that is creating an electrical hazard. In some cases, a single boat may cause an upstream GFPE device protecting a feeder to trip even though multiple boats are supplied from the same feeder. The use of this test device will help the facility operator prevent a particular boat from contributing to hazardous voltage and current in the marina area.

Note 2: An annual test of each boat with the leakage current measurement device is a prudent step toward determining if a boat has defective wiring that may be contributing hazardous voltage and current. Where the leakage current measurement device reveals that a boat is contributing hazardous voltage and current, repairs should be made to the boat before it is permitted to utilize shore power.

555.36 Boat Receptacle Disconnecting Means

A disconnect must isolate each boat from its shore power receptacle.

(A) Type of Disconnecting Means. A circuit breaker or switch must be used as the required shore power receptacle disconnect and it must be identified as to which receptacle it controls. ▶Figure 555-24

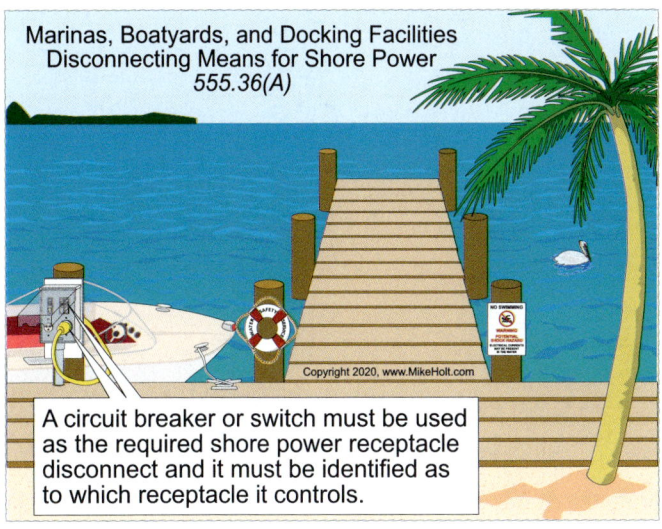
▶Figure 555-24

(B) Location. The disconnect for shore power receptacles must be readily accessible and located not more than 30 in. from the receptacle it controls. Circuit breakers or switches located in marina power outlets can be used for the shore power receptacle disconnect.
▶Figure 555-25

> **Author's Comment:**
> ▸ This shore power receptacle disconnect is intended to eliminate the hazard of someone engaging or disengaging the boat's shore power attachment plug with wet, slippery hands, and possibly contacting energized blades.

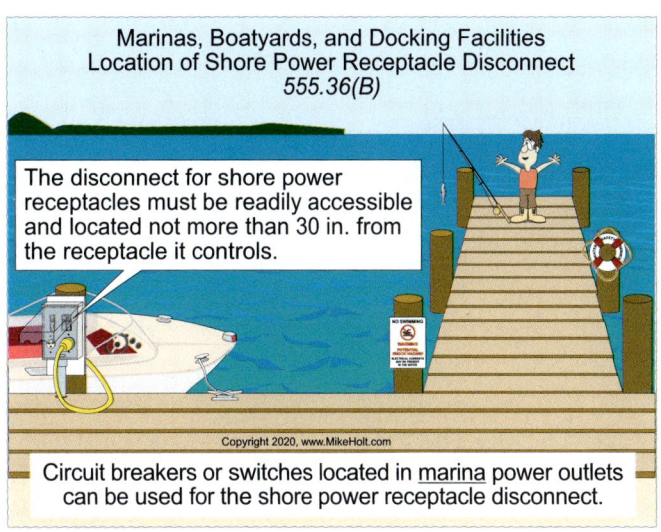
▶Figure 555-25

555.37 Equipment Grounding Conductor

(A) Equipment to be Connected to the Equipment Grounding Conductor. The following items must be connected to an equipment grounding conductor run with the circuit conductors in the same raceway, cable, or trench:

(1) Metal boxes, metal cabinets, and all other metal enclosures.

(2) Metal frames of utilization equipment.

(3) Grounding terminals of grounding-type receptacles.

(B) Type of Equipment Grounding Conductor. The equipment grounding conductor must be an insulated conductor with a continuous outer finish that is either green or green with one or more yellow stripes.

(C) Size of Equipment Grounding Conductor. The insulated equipment grounding conductor must be sized in accordance with 250.122, but not smaller than 12 AWG.

(D) Branch-Circuit Equipment Grounding Conductor. The insulated equipment grounding conductor for branch circuits must terminate at a grounding terminal in a remote panelboard or the grounding terminal in the main service equipment.

(E) Feeder Equipment Grounding Conductor. Where a feeder supplies a remote panelboard, an insulated equipment grounding conductor must extend from a grounding terminal in the service equipment to a grounding terminal in the remote panelboard.

Notes

ARTICLE 590 — TEMPORARY INSTALLATIONS

Introduction to Article 590—Temporary Installations

It is a common misconception that temporary wiring represents a lower standard of wiring than permanent wiring. In truth, it merely meets a different standard. The same rules of workmanship, ampacity, and overcurrent protection apply to temporary installations as to others.

So, how is a temporary installation different? You must remove a temporary installation upon completion of the purpose for which it was installed. If the temporary installation is for holiday displays, it cannot last more than 90 days.

Article 590 addresses the practicality and execution issues that are inherent in temporary installations, thereby making them less time consuming to install.

590.1 Scope

The requirements of Article 590 apply to temporary power and lighting installations and removals, including power for construction, remodeling, maintenance, repair, demolition, and decorative lighting.
▶Figure 590–1

Article 590 applies to temporary power and lighting installations and removals, including power for construction, remodeling, maintenance, repair, demolition, and decorative lighting.

▶Figure 590–1

This article also applies when temporary installations are necessary during emergencies or for tests and experiments [590.3(C)].

Author's Comment:

▶ Temporary wiring is only permitted for construction, remodeling, maintenance, repair, or demolition of buildings, structures, equipment, or similar activities or for emergencies and for tests, experiments, and developmental work. After the construction period, temporary wiring must be removed.

▶ Temporary installations for carnivals, circuses, fairs, and similar events must be installed in accordance with Article 525, not Article 590.

590.2 All Wiring Installations

(A) Other Articles. All *NEC* requirements apply to temporary installations unless specifically modified in this article. ▶Figure 590–2

(B) Approval. Temporary wiring methods are acceptable only if approved by the authority having jurisdiction based on the conditions of use and any special requirements of the temporary installation

590.3 Time Constraints

(A) Construction Period. Temporary electrical power and lighting installations are permitted during the period of construction, remodeling, maintenance, repair, or demolition of buildings, structures, equipment, or similar activities.

590.4 | Temporary Installations

▶Figure 590-2

▶Figure 590-4

(B) Decorative Lighting. Temporary electrical power for decorative holiday lighting and similar purposes is permitted for a period of up to 90 days. ▶Figure 590-3

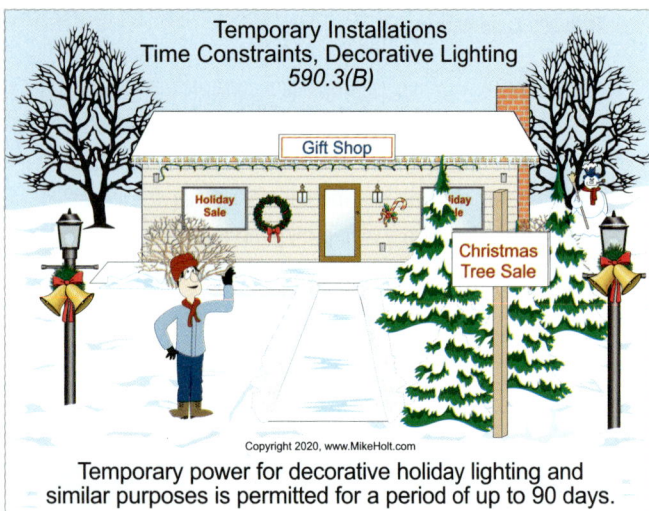
▶Figure 590-3

Author's Comment:

▸ Decorative lighting used for holiday lighting and similar purposes must be listed [590.5].

(C) Emergencies and Tests. Temporary electrical power and lighting installations are permitted for the duration necessary for emergencies or for tests and experiments.

(D) Removal. Temporary installations must be removed immediately upon the completion of the purpose for which they were installed. ▶Figure 590-4

590.4 General

(A) Services. Services must be installed in accordance with Parts I through VIII of Article 230 as applicable.

(B) Feeders. Overcurrent protection must be provided in accordance with 240.4 and 240.5. The following wiring methods are permitted:

(1) Type NM cable, Type SE cable, and flexible cords are permitted to be used in a building without height limitations or the type of construction. ▶Figure 590-5

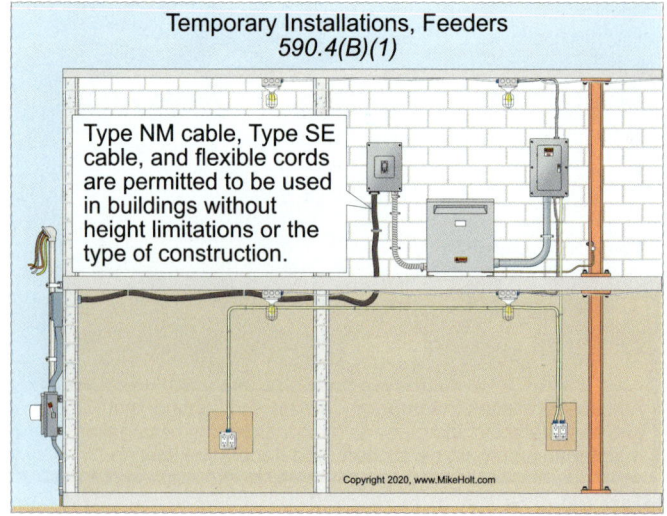
▶Figure 590-5

(2) Type SE cable may be installed in a raceway underground.

(C) Branch Circuits. Overcurrent protection must be provided in accordance with 240.4 and 240.5. The following wiring methods are permitted:

(1) Type NM cable, Type SE cable, and flexible cords are permitted to be used in a building without height limitations or the type of construction. ▶Figure 590–6

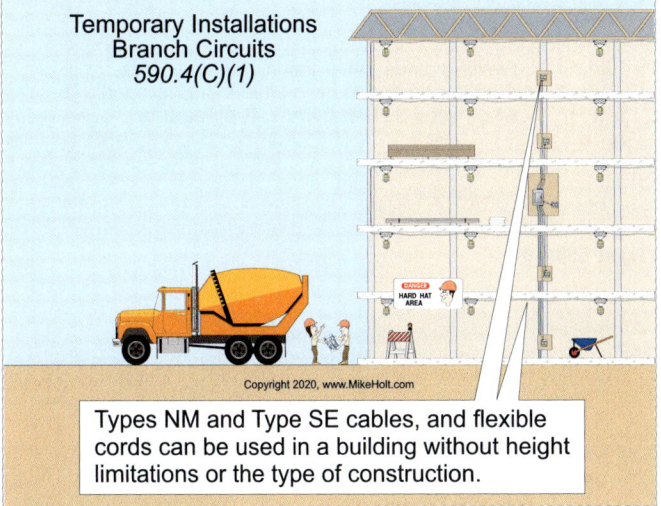

▶Figure 590–6

(2) Type SE cable may be installed in a raceway underground.

(D) Receptacles.

(1) Receptacles Not on Lighting Circuit. On a construction site, receptacles are not permitted on a branch circuit that supplies temporary lighting. ▶Figure 590–7

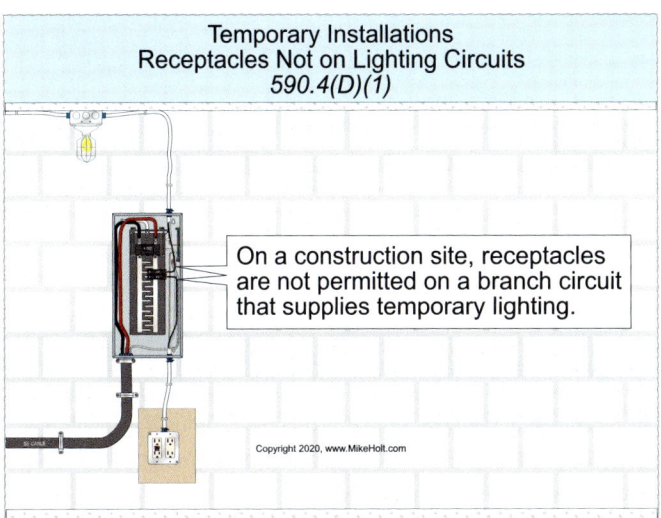

▶Figure 590–7

Author's Comment:

▸ This requirement is necessary so illumination is maintained, even when the receptacle's GFCI-protective device opens [590.6].

(2) Receptacles in Wet Locations. 15A and 20A receptacles installed in a wet location must be within an enclosure that is weatherproof when an attachment plug is inserted. ▶Figure 590–8

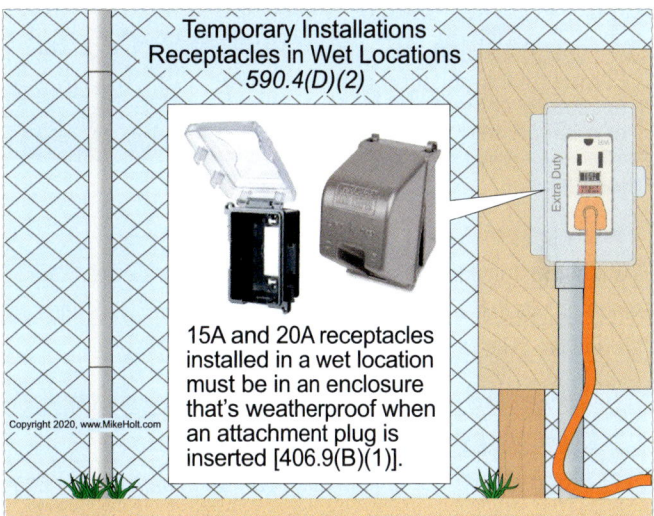

▶Figure 590–8

The outlet box hood must be listed for extra-duty use, and nonlocking-type receptacles in a wet location must be listed as weather resistant [406.9(B)(1)].

(F) Lamp Protection. Lamps (bulbs) must be protected from accidental contact by a suitable luminaire or lampholder with a guard. ▶Figure 590–9

(G) Splices. A box, conduit body, or other enclosure (with a cover installed) is required for all splices.

Ex 1: On construction sites, a box is not required if the conductors being spliced are from nonmetallic sheathed cables or cords, or metal-sheathed cable assemblies as long as the grounding continuity can be maintained without the box.

(1) The circuit conductors being spliced are all from nonmetallic multiconductor cord or cable assemblies, provided the equipment grounding continuity is maintained with or without the box.

(2) The circuit conductors being spliced are all from metal-sheathed cable assemblies terminated in listed fittings that mechanically secure the cable sheath to maintain effective electrical continuity.

590.5 | Temporary Installations

▶Figure 590-9

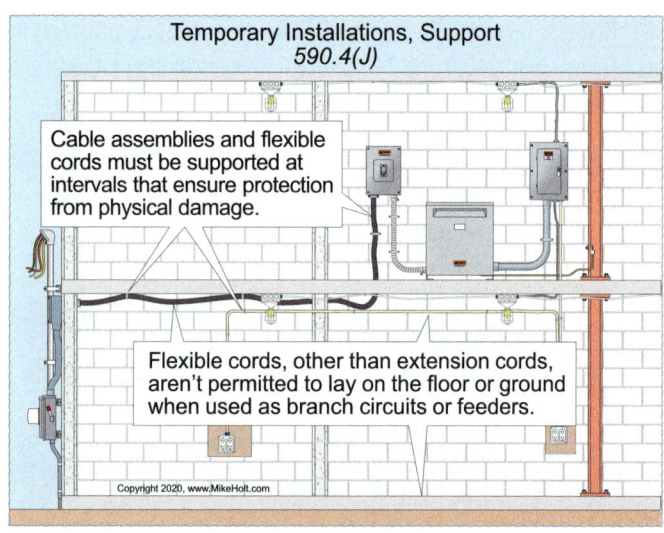
▶Figure 590-10

Ex 2: On construction sites a box is not required for GFCI-protected branch circuits that are permanently installed in framed walls and ceilings and are used to supply temporary power or lighting.

(1) A box cover is not required for splices installed completely inside of junction boxes with plaster rings.

(2) Listed pigtail-type lampholders can be installed in ceiling-mounted junction boxes with plaster rings.

(3) Finger safe devices are permitted for supplying and connecting devices.

(H) Protection from Accidental Damage. Cables and flexible cords must be protected from physical damage and from sharp corners and projections when the cables and flexible cords pass through doorways or other pinch points.

(J) Support. Cable assemblies and flexible cords must be supported at intervals that ensure protection from physical damage. Support must be in the form of staples, cable ties, straps, or other similar means designed not to damage the cable or flexible cord assembly. Flexible cords, other than extension cords, are not permitted to lay on the floor or the ground when used as branch circuits or feeders. ▶Figure 590-10

> **Author's Comment:**
>
> ▸ The support requirement for temporary cables is determined by the authority having jurisdiction based on the jobsite conditions [590.2(B)].

Vegetation is not permitted to be used for the support of overhead branch-circuit or feeder conductors. ▶Figure 590-11

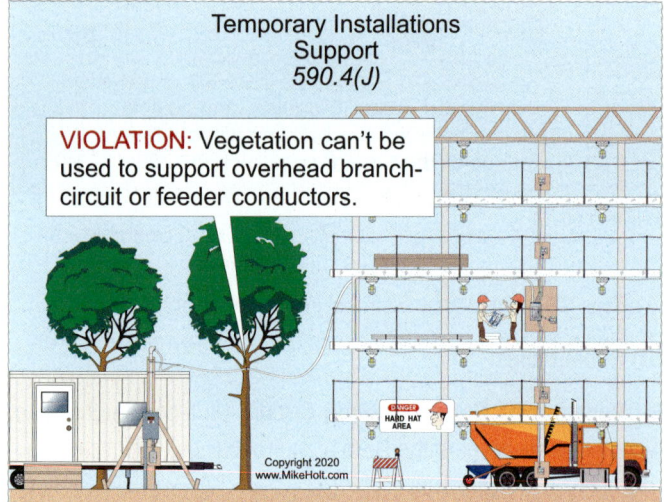
▶Figure 590-11

590.5 Listing of Decorative Lighting

Decorative lighting used during holidays and for similar purposes [590.3(B)] must be listed and labeled on the product.

590.6 GFCI Protection for Personnel

(A) Receptacle Outlets. GFCI protection is required for receptacles used for construction, remodeling, maintenance, repair, or demolition of buildings, structures, or equipment.

(1) Receptacles Not Part of Permanent Wiring. GFCI protection is required for 15A, 20A, and 30A receptacles that are not part of the permanent wiring of the building. ▶Figure 590-12

Temporary Installations | 590.8

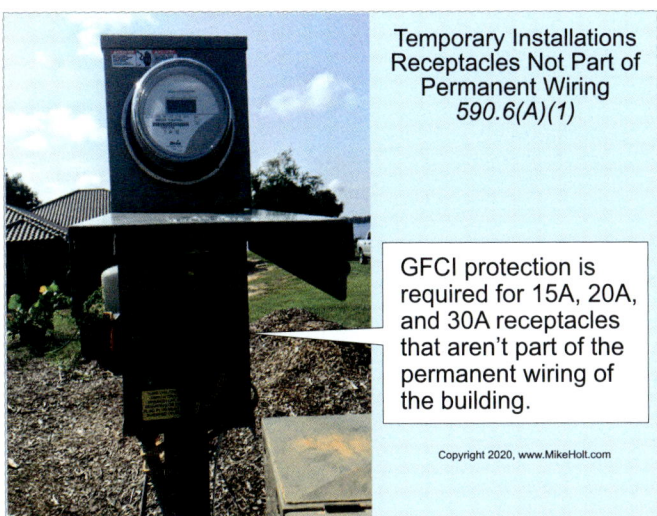

▶Figure 590–12

Author's Comment:

▸ Section 590.6(A) requires 125V and 125/250V, 15A, 20A, and 30A receptacles to have GFCI protection. Section 590.6(B) requires all other receptacles used on temporary installations to be GFCI protected. This simply means all 125V and 125/250V receptacles used for temporary power require GFCI protection.

(2) Receptacle Outlets Existing or Installed as Permanent Wiring. GFCI protection is required for 15A, 20A, and 30A receptacles that are being used as temporary power but are part of the permanent wiring of the building. Listed flexible cord sets or devices that incorporate listed GFCI protection can be used in addition to the required GFCI receptacles. ▶Figure 590–13

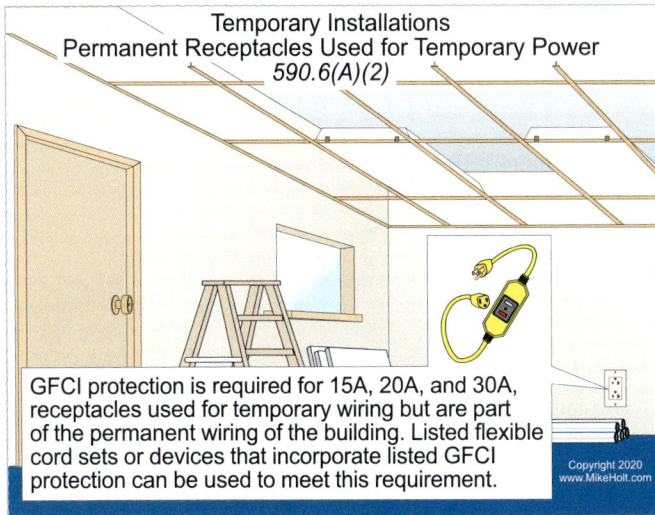

▶Figure 590–13

(3) Portable Generators 15 kW or Less. GFCI protection is required for 125V and 125/250V, 15A, 20A, and 30A receptacles that are part of a portable generator rated not greater than 15 kW. ▶Figure 590–14

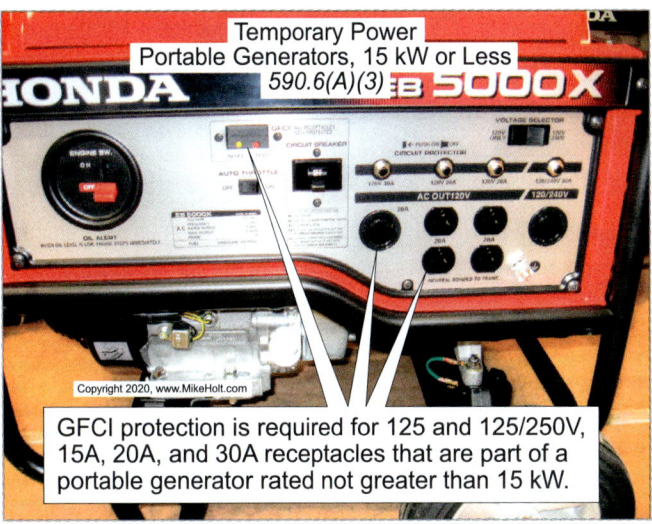

▶Figure 590–14

(B) Other Receptacle Outlets. Receptacles other than those covered by 590.6(A)(1) through (A)(3) that supply temporary power used by personnel during construction, remodeling, maintenance, repair, or demolition of buildings, structures, equipment, or similar activities must be GFCI protected.

590.8 Overcurrent Protective Devices

(A) Where Reused. Where overcurrent protective devices that have been previously used are installed in a temporary installation, they must be examined [110.3(A)] to ensure the devices have been properly installed, properly maintained, and there is no evidence of impending failure.

Note: The phrase "evidence of impending failure" means that there is evidence such as arcing, overheating, loose parts, bound equipment parts, visible damage, or deterioration. The phrase "properly maintained" means that the equipment has been maintained in accordance with the manufacturers' recommendations and applicable industry codes and standards.

References for manufacturers' recommendations and applicable industry codes and standards include but are not limited to NEMA AB 4, *Guidelines for Inspection and Preventative Maintenance of Molded-Case Circuit Breakers Used in Commercial and Industrial Applications*; NFPA 70B, *Recommended Practice for Electrical Equipment Maintenance*; NEMA GD, *Evaluating Water-Damaged Electrical Equipment*; and IEEE 1458, *IEEE Recommended Practice for the Selection, Field Testing, and Life Expectancy of Molded-Case Circuit Breakers for Industrial Applications*.

(B) Service Overcurrent Protective Devices. Overcurrent protective devices for 277/480V services must be of the current-limiting type.

CHAPTER 5
PRACTICE QUESTIONS

Please use the 2020 *Code* book to answer the following questions.

CHAPTER 5—SPECIAL OCCUPANCIES
Article 500—Hazardous (Classified) Locations

1. All areas designated as hazardous (classified) locations shall be properly _____ and shall be available to those authorized to design, install, inspect, maintain, or operate electrical equipment at these locations.

    (a) cleaned
    (b) documented
    (c) maintained
    (d) all of these

2. Hazardous (classified) locations shall be classified depending on the properties of the _____ that could be present, and the likelihood that a flammable or combustible concentration or quantity is present.

    (a) flammable liquid-produced vapors
    (b) flammable gases
    (c) combustible dusts
    (d) all of these

3. It is frequently possible to locate much of the equipment in less hazardous or unclassified locations and thus reduce the amount of special equipment required.

    (a) True
    (b) False

4. Class I, Division 1 locations are those in which ignitable concentrations of _____ can exist under normal operating conditions.

    (a) combustible dust
    (b) easily ignitable fibers or flyings
    (c) flammable gases or flammable liquid-produced vapors
    (d) pyrotechnics

5. An area that is adjacent to a Class I, Division 1 location, and to which ignitible concentrations of flammable gases, flammable liquid-produced vapors, or combustible liquid-produced vapors above their flash points might occasionally be communicated is a _____ location.

    (a) Class I, Division 1
    (b) Class II, Division 1
    (c) Class I, Division 2
    (d) Class II, Division 2

6. When determining a Class I, Division 2 location, the _____ is a factor that should be considered in determining the classification and extent of the location.

    (a) quantity of flammable material that might escape in case of an accident
    (b) adequacy of ventilating equipment
    (c) record of the industry or business with respect to explosions or fires
    (d) all of these

Article 500 | Practice Questions

7. Class II locations are those that are hazardous because of the presence of _____.

   (a) combustible dust
   (b) easily ignitible fibers/flyings
   (c) flammable gases or vapors
   (d) flammable liquids or gases

8. Locations in which combustible dust is in the air under normal operating conditions in quantities sufficient to produce explosive or ignitible mixtures are classified as _____.

   (a) Class I, Division 2
   (b) Class II, Division 1
   (c) Class II, Division 2
   (d) Class III, Division 1

9. A Class II, Division 2 location is a location _____.

   (a) in which combustible dust due to abnormal operations may be present in the air in quantities sufficient to produce explosive or ignitible mixtures
   (b) where combustible dust accumulations are present but are normally insufficient to interfere with the normal operation of electrical equipment, but could as a result of infrequent malfunctioning of handling or processing equipment become suspended in the air
   (c) in which combustible dust accumulations on, in, or in the vicinity of the electrical equipment could be sufficient to interfere with the safe dissipation of heat from electrical equipment
   (d) all of these

10. Class III locations are those that are hazardous because of the presence of _____.

    (a) combustible dust
    (b) easily ignitible fibers or materials producing combustible flyings
    (c) flammable gases or vapors
    (d) flammable liquids or gases

11. Class III, Division _____ locations include areas where easily ignitible fibers/flyings are handled, manufactured, or used.

    (a) 1
    (b) 2
    (c) 3
    (d) all of these

12. A Class III, Division _____ location is where easily ignitible fibers/flyings are stored or handled but not manufactured.

    (a) 1
    (b) 2
    (c) 3
    (d) all of these

13. Electrical and electronic equipment in hazardous (classified) locations shall be protected by a(an) _____ technique.

    (a) explosionproof
    (b) dust-ignitionproof
    (c) dusttight
    (d) any of these

14. Dusttight protection techniques shall be permitted for equipment in Class I, Division 2 locations.

    (a) True
    (b) False

15. Suitability of identified equipment for use in a hazardous (classified) location shall be determined by _____.

    (a) equipment listing or labeling
    (b) evidence of equipment evaluation from a qualified testing laboratory or inspection agency concerned with product evaluation
    (c) evidence acceptable to the authority having jurisdiction, such as a manufacturer's self-evaluation or an owner's engineering judgment
    (d) any of these

16. Equipment shall be identified not only for the class of hazardous (classified) location, but also for the explosive, combustible, or ignitible properties of the specific _____ present.

    (a) gas or vapor
    (b) dust
    (c) fibers/flyings
    (d) any of these

17. Threaded conduits or fittings installed in hazardous (classified) locations shall be made wrenchtight to _____.

    (a) prevent sparking when fault current flows through the conduit system
    (b) prevent seepage of gases or fumes
    (c) prevent sag in the conduit runs
    (d) maintain a workmanship like installation

Article 501—Class I Hazardous (Classified) Locations

1. Article 501 covers the requirements for electrical and electronic equipment and wiring for all voltages in Class I, Division 1 and 2 locations where fire or explosion hazards may exist due to flammable _____.

    (a) gases
    (b) vapors
    (c) liquids
    (d) any of these

2. Wiring methods and materials permitted in Class I, Division 1 locations include _____.

    (a) threaded rigid metal or threaded steel IMC
    (b) flexible fittings listed for Class I, Division 1 locations
    (c) boxes approved for Class I, Division 1 locations
    (d) all of these

3. Type PVC conduit, Type RTRC conduit, and Type HDPE conduit shall be permitted in Class I, Division 1 underground locations where encased in a concrete envelope a minimum of _____ in. thick and provided with not less than _____ in. of cover measured from the top of the conduit to grade.

    (a) 2, 12
    (b) 2, 24
    (c) 12, 2
    (d) 24, 2

4. MI cable terminated with fittings listed for the location is allowed in Class I, Division 1 locations.

    (a) True
    (b) False

5. In industrial establishments with restricted public access where only qualified persons will service the installation, MC-HL cable is allowed to be used in a Class I, Division 1 location if it _____ and terminated with fittings listed for the application. Such cable shall comply with Part II of Article 330.

    (a) is listed for use in Class I, Zone 1, or Division 1 locations
    (b) has a gas/vaportight continuous corrugated metallic sheath and an overall jacket of suitable polymeric material
    (c) has a separate equipment grounding conductor(s) in accordance with 250.122
    (d) all of these

6. In industrial establishments with restricted public access, where the conditions of maintenance and supervision ensure that only qualified persons service the installation, Type ITC-HL cable is allowed to be used in a Class I, Division 1 location if it _____ and installed in accordance with the provisions of Article 727.

    (a) is listed for use in Class I, Zone 1, or Division 1 locations
    (b) has a gas/vaportight continuous corrugated metallic sheath and an overall jacket of suitable polymeric material
    (c) is terminated with fittings listed for the application
    (d) all of these

7. When necessary to employ flexible connections in a Class I, Division 1 location, such as at motor terminals, flexible fittings listed for the location are permitted, or flexible cord in accordance with 501.140 is permitted if terminated with cord connectors listed for the location.

    (a) True
    (b) False

8. When necessary to employ flexible connections in a Class I, Division 1 location, such as at motor terminals, _____ shall be permitted.

    (a) flexible fittings listed for the location
    (b) flexible cord in accordance with the provisions of 501.140, terminated with cord connectors listed for the location
    (c) listed Type TC-ER-HL in industrial establishments with restricted public access, where the conditions of maintenance and supervision ensure that only qualified persons service the installation, and installed in accordance with 336.10
    (d) any of these

9. Wiring methods permitted in Class I, Division 1 locations are permitted in Class I, Division 2 locations.

    (a) True
    (b) False

Article 501 | Practice Questions

10. _____ is(are) among the wiring methods permitted within a Class I, Division 2 location.

    (a) Type MC, MV, TC, or TC-ER cable, including installation in cable tray systems and terminated with listed fittings
    (b) Optical fiber cable Types OFNP, OFCP, OFNR, OFCR, OFNG, OFCG, OFN, and OFC installed in cable trays or any other raceway in accordance with 501.10(B) and sealed in accordance with 501.15
    (c) Cablebus
    (d) all of these

11. In Class I, Division 2 locations, where metallic conduit does not provide sufficient corrosion resistance, reinforced thermosetting resin conduit (RTRC), factory elbow, and associated fittings all marked with the suffix "-XW" shall be permitted.

    (a) True
    (b) False

12. In Class 1, Division 2 locations, Schedule 80 PVC conduit shall be permitted _____.

    (a) where metal conduit does not provide sufficient corrosion resistance
    (b) where the conditions of maintenance and supervision ensure that only qualified persons service the installation
    (c) in industrial establishments with restricted public access
    (d) all of these

13. In a Class I, Division 2 location, if flexibility is necessary, _____ fittings are some of the wiring methods that are permitted.

    (a) listed flexible metal
    (b) flexible metal conduit, liquidtight flexible metal conduit, and liquidtight nonmetallic conduit, all with listed
    (c) interlocked armor Type MC cable with listed
    (d) all of these

14. When provisions for flexibility are necessary in Class I, Division 2 locations, FMC with listed fittings can be used.

    (a) True
    (b) False

15. In a Class I, Division 2 location, switches and circuit breakers shall be installed in explosionproof enclosures meeting the requirements for Class I, Division 1 locations.

    (a) True
    (b) False

16. General-purpose enclosures and fittings are permitted in Class I, Division 2 locations unless the enclosure contains make-and-break contacts for _____ as required by 501.105(B)(1), 501.115(B)(1), and 501.150(B)(1).

    (a) meters, instruments, and relays
    (b) circuit breakers or motor controllers
    (c) signaling, alarm, remote-control, and communications systems
    (d) all of these

17. In Class I hazardous (classified) locations, sealing compound shall be used in Type MI cable termination fittings to _____.

    (a) prevent the passage of gases or vapors
    (b) exclude moisture and other fluids from the cable insulation
    (c) limit a possible explosion
    (d) prevent the escape of powder

18. In Class I, Division 1 locations, seals shall not be required for conduit entering an enclosure if the switch, circuit breaker, fuse, relay, or resistor is _____.

    (a) enclosed within a chamber hermetically sealed against the entrance of gases or vapors
    (b) immersed in oil in accordance with 501.115(B)(1)(2)
    (c) enclosed within an enclosure, identified for the location, and marked "Leads Factory Sealed," or "Factory Sealed," "Seal not Required," or equivalent
    (d) any of these

19. Class I, Division 1 conduit seals shall be installed within _____ in. of the enclosure in each conduit entry into a pressurized enclosure where the conduit is not pressurized as part of the protection system.

    (a) 6
    (b) 12
    (c) 18
    (d) 24

20. In Class I, Division 1 locations, conduit seals entering pressurized enclosures, shall be installed within _____ in. from the enclosure or as required by the enclosure marking.

    (a) 12
    (b) 18
    (c) 20
    (d) 24

21. Where two or more explosionproof enclosures that require conduit seals are connected by nipples or runs of conduit not more than _____ in. long, a single conduit seal in each such nipple connection or run of conduit shall be considered sufficient if the seal is located not more than 18 in. from either enclosure.

    (a) 12
    (b) 18
    (c) 24
    (d) 36

22. A conduit run between a conduit seal and the point at which the conduit leaves a Class I, Division 1 location shall contain no union, coupling, box, or other fitting except for a listed _____ reducer installed at the conduit seal.

    (a) explosionproof
    (b) fireproof
    (c) vaportight
    (d) dusttight

23. A sealing fitting shall be permitted to be installed within _____ ft of either side of the boundary where a conduit leaves a Class I, Division 1 location.

    (a) 5
    (b) 6
    (c) 8
    (d) 10

24. Where the Class I, Division 1 location boundary is below grade, a sealing fitting shall be permitted to be installed _____, and there shall not be any unions, couplings, boxes, or fittings between the sealing fitting and the grade, other than listed explosionproof reducers.

    (a) after the conduit emerges from grade
    (b) before the conduit emerges from grade
    (c) within 10 ft of where the conduit emerges from grade
    (d) if the raceway type is RMC or PVC conduit

25. A conduit seal shall be required in each conduit run leaving a Class I, Division 2 location. The conduit sealing fitting shall be installed on either side of the boundary within _____ ft of the boundary.

    (a) 1
    (b) 3
    (c) 5
    (d) 10

26. A sealing fitting shall not be required if a metal conduit passes completely through a Class I, Division 2 location if the termination points of the unbroken conduit are located in unclassified locations and it has no fittings less than _____ in. of either side of the boundary of the hazardous (classified) location.

    (a) 6
    (b) 12
    (c) 18
    (d) 24

27. When sealing fittings are required for Class I locations, they shall comply with which of the following rule(s)?

    (a) They shall be listed for Class I locations and shall be accessible.
    (b) The minimum thickness of the sealing compound shall not be less than the trade size of the sealing fitting and, in no case, shall the thickness of the compound be less than 5/8 in.
    (c) Splices and taps shall not be made in the conduit seal.
    (d) all of these

28. The minimum thickness of sealing compound in Class I locations shall not be less than the trade size of the conduit or sealing fitting and, in no case, shall the thickness of the compound be less than _____ in.

    (a) 1/8
    (b) 1/4
    (c) 3/8
    (d) 5/8

29. In Class I, Division and 1 and Division 2 locations, the cross-sectional area of the conductors or optical fiber tubes (metallic or nonmetallic) permitted in a seal shall not exceed _____ percent of the cross-sectional area of a RMC of the same trade size unless the seal is specifically identified for a higher percentage of fill.

    (a) 25
    (b) 50
    (c) 100
    (d) 125

Article 501 | Practice Questions

30. In Class I, Division 1 locations, seals for cables at all terminations, shall be installed within _____ in. of the enclosure or as required by the enclosure marking.

    (a) 6
    (b) 12
    (c) 18
    (d) 20

31. In Class I, Division 1 locations, only threaded couplings, or explosionproof fittings such as unions, reducers, elbows, and capped elbows that are not larger than the _____ of the conduit shall be permitted between the sealing fitting and the enclosure.

    (a) cross-sectional area
    (b) trade size
    (c) volume
    (d) any of these

32. When installing shield cables and twisted-pair cables in conduit in a Class I, Division 1 hazardous (classified) location, the removal of shielding material or the separation of the twisted pairs of shielded cables and twisted pair cables is not required within the conduit seal fitting.

    (a) True
    (b) False

33. Each multiconductor cable installed in conduit in a Class I, Division 1 location shall be considered as a single conductor if the cable is incapable of transmitting _____ through the cable core.

    (a) gases or vapors
    (b) dust
    (c) flyings
    (d) any of these

34. The removal of shielding material or the separation of the twisted pairs of shielded cables and twisted pair cables is not required within the conduit seal fitting in a Class I, Division 2 hazardous (classified) location provided the termination is by an approved means to minimize the entrance of gases or vapors and prevent flame propagation.

    (a) True
    (b) False

35. In Class I locations, the locknut-bushing and double-locknut types of contacts shall not be depended on for bonding purposes.

    (a) True
    (b) False

36. When FMC or LFMC is used as permitted in Class I, Division 2 locations, it shall include an equipment bonding jumper of the wire type in compliance with 250.102.

    (a) True
    (b) False

37. Circuit breakers in Class I, Division 2 locations that are not hermetically sealed or oil-immersed shall be installed in a Class I, Division 1 enclosure.

    (a) True
    (b) False

38. Motors, generators, or other rotating electrical machinery identified for Class I, Division 2 locations can be used in Class I, Division 1 locations.

    (a) True
    (b) False

39. Totally enclosed motors of the types specified in 501.125(A)(2) or (A)(3) shall have a device to detect and automatically de-energize the motor or provide an adequate alarm if there is any increase in temperature of the motor beyond designed limits when operating in Class I, Division 1 locations.

    (a) True
    (b) False

40. Luminaires installed in Class I, Division 1 locations shall be identified as a complete assembly for the Class I, Division 1 location and shall be clearly marked to indicate the _____ for which it is identified.

    (a) maximum wattage of lamps
    (b) minimum conductor size
    (c) maximum overcurrent protection permitted
    (d) all of these

41. Luminaires installed in Class I, Division 1 locations shall be protected from physical damage by a suitable _____.

    (a) warning label
    (b) pendant
    (c) guard or by location
    (d) all of these

42. Pendant luminaires in a Class I, Division 1 location shall be suspended by and supplied through threaded rigid metal conduit stems or threaded steel intermediate conduit stems, and threaded joints shall be provided with _____ or other effective means to prevent loosening.

    (a) set-screws
    (b) welded joints
    (c) expansion joints
    (d) explosionproof flex

43. Boxes, box assemblies, or fittings used to support luminaires in Class I, Division 1 locations shall be identified for Class I locations.

    (a) True
    (b) False

44. Luminaires installed in Class I, Division 2 locations shall be protected from physical damage by a suitable _____.

    (a) warning label
    (b) pendant
    (c) guard or by location
    (d) all of these

45. In Class I, Division 1 locations, all utilization equipment shall be _____ for use in a Class I, Division 1 location.

    (a) identified
    (b) approved
    (c) marked
    (d) listed

46. Flexible cords are not permitted in Class I locations.

    (a) True
    (b) False

47. Flexible cords in Class I hazardous (classified) locations shall _____.

    (a) be listed as extra-hard usage
    (b) contain an equipment grounding conductor
    (c) be supported by clamps or other suitable means to avoid tension on the terminals
    (d) all of these

48. In Class I, Division 1 or Division 2 locations where the boxes, fittings, or enclosures are required to be explosionproof, if a flexible cord is used it shall terminate with a cord connector or attachment plug listed for the location, or a listed cord connector installed with a seal that is listed for the location. In Division 2 locations where explosionproof equipment is not required, the cord shall terminate _____.

    (a) with irreversible connections
    (b) with a listed receptacle
    (c) in a splice of any manner
    (d) with a listed cord connector or listed attachment plug

49. For Class I locations where 501.140(A)(5) is applied, flexible cords shall be _____ from the power source to the temporary portable assembly and from the temporary portable assembly to the utilization equipment.

    (a) permitted to be spliced
    (b) of continuous length
    (c) installed in a metal raceway
    (d) spliced only using listed splicing kits

50. In Class I locations, attachment plugs shall be of the type providing for _____ a permitted flexible cord and shall be identified for the location.

    (a) sealing compound around
    (b) quick connection to
    (c) connection to the equipment grounding conductor of
    (d) interlocking

51. In Class I, Division 1 locations, all apparatus and equipment of signaling, alarm, remote-control, and communications systems _____ shall be identified for Class I, Division 1 locations.

    (a) over 50V
    (b) over 100 volts-to-ground
    (c) regardless of voltage
    (d) except those operating at less than 24V

Article 502—Class II Hazardous (Classified) Locations

1. Article 502 covers the requirements for electrical and electronic equipment and wiring in Class II, Division 1 and 2 locations where fire or explosion hazards may exist due to _____.

    (a) gases or vapors
    (b) fibers/flyings
    (c) combustible dust
    (d) all of these

Article 502 | Practice Questions

2. Raceways permitted as a wiring method in Class II, Division 1 locations include _____.

   (a) threaded RMC and steel IMC
   (b) PVC conduit
   (c) electrical metallic tubing
   (d) any of these

3. Where flexibility is required, _____ are permitted in a Class II, Division 1 location.

   (a) dusttight flexible connectors
   (b) liquidtight flexible metal conduit with listed fittings
   (c) flexible cords listed for extra-hard usage with listed dust-tight cord connectors
   (d) any of these

4. Boxes and fittings used for taps, joints, or terminal connections shall be _____ where installed in Class II, Division 1 locations.

   (a) explosionproof
   (b) identified for Class II locations
   (c) dusttight
   (d) weatherproof

5. Rigid metal conduit and IMC shall not be required to be threaded when used in Class II, Division 2 locations.

   (a) True
   (b) False

6. In Class II, Division 2 locations, where provision must be made for flexibility, _____ shall apply.

   (a) 502.10(A)(2)
   (b) 502.10(A)(3)
   (c) 502.10(B)(1)
   (d) 502.10(B)(4)

7. In Class II locations, dust shall be prevented from entering the required dust-ignitionproof enclosure through a raceway by which of the following method(s)?

   (a) a permanent and effective seal
   (b) a horizontal raceway not less than 10 ft long
   (c) a vertical raceway that extends downward for not less than 5 ft
   (d) any of these

8. Seals in Class II hazardous (classified) locations shall be explosionproof.

   (a) True
   (b) False

9. In Class II locations, a permitted method of bonding is the use of bonding jumpers with proper fittings.

   (a) True
   (b) False

10. Where LFMC is used in a Class II, Division 1 location, it shall _____ in compliance with 250.102.

    (a) not be unsupported
    (b) not exceed 6 ft in length
    (c) include an equipment bonding jumper of the wire type
    (d) be listed for use in Class I locations

11. In Class II, Division 1 locations, switches, circuit breakers, motor controllers, and fuses, including pushbuttons, relays, and similar devices shall be provided with enclosures that are _____.

    (a) explosionproof
    (b) identified for the location
    (c) dusttight
    (d) weatherproof

12. In Class II, Division 2 locations, enclosures for fuses, switches, circuit breakers, and motor controllers, including pushbuttons, relays, and similar devices shall be _____.

    (a) dusttight or otherwise identified for the location
    (b) raintight
    (c) rated as Class I, Division 1 explosionproof
    (d) general duty

13. In Class II, Division 1 locations, motors, generators, and other rotating electrical machinery shall be _____.

    (a) listed for the environment
    (b) explosionproof
    (c) general duty
    (d) identified for the location or totally enclosed pipe-ventilated

14. In Class II, Division 2 locations, motors, generators, and other rotating electrical equipment shall be _____.

    (a) totally enclosed nonventilated or pipe-ventilated
    (b) totally enclosed water-air-cooled or fan-cooled
    (c) dust-ignitionproof
    (d) any of these

15. Luminaires installed in Class II, Division 1 locations shall be identified for the location and shall be clearly marked to indicate the _____.

    (a) maximum wattage and type of lamps for which they are designed
    (b) minimum conductor size
    (c) maximum overcurrent protection permitted
    (d) all of these

16. Luminaires installed in Class II, Division 1 locations shall be protected from physical damage by a suitable _____.

    (a) warning label
    (b) pendant
    (c) guard or by location
    (d) all of these

17. Pendant luminaires installed in Class II, Division 1 locations shall be suspended by threaded RMC or steel IMC conduit stems, by chains with approved fittings, or by other approved means. Stems shall be provided with _____ or other effective means to prevent loosening.

    (a) set-screws
    (b) welded joints
    (c) expansion joints
    (d) explosionproof flex

18. Luminaires for fixed lighting in Class II, Division 2 locations shall be equipped with enclosures that are _____ or otherwise identified for the location.

    (a) dust-ignitionproof
    (b) dusttight
    (c) dustproof
    (d) explosionproof

19. Luminaires for fixed lighting installed in Class II, Division 2 locations shall be protected from physical damage by a suitable _____.

    (a) warning label
    (b) pendant
    (c) guard or by location
    (d) all of these

20. In Class II, Division 2 locations, flexible cord can serve as the supporting means for a pendant luminaire.

    (a) True
    (b) False

21. Flexible cords used in Class II, Division 1 or 2 locations shall _____.

    (a) be listed for hard usage
    (b) be listed for extra-hard usage
    (c) not be permitted
    (d) be Type SJOT or SJOWT

22. Signaling, alarm, remote-control, and communications system circuits containing contacts installed in Class II, Division 2 locations shall be in enclosures that are _____ or otherwise identified for the location.

    (a) dust-ignitionproof
    (b) dusttight
    (c) dustproof
    (d) explosionproof

Article 503—Class III Hazardous (Classified) Locations

1. Article 503 covers the requirements for electrical and electronic equipment and wiring in Class III locations where fire or explosion hazards may exist due to ignitible _____.

    (a) gases or vapors
    (b) fibers/flyings
    (c) dust
    (d) all of these

2. Raceways permitted in a Class III, Division 1 location include _____.

    (a) RMC and IMC
    (b) Type MC cable with listed termination fittings
    (c) electrical metallic tubing
    (d) any of these

3. Boxes and fittings shall be _____ where installed in a Class III location.

    (a) explosionproof
    (b) dust-ignitionproof
    (c) dusttight
    (d) weatherproof

4. In Class III locations, locknut-bushing and double-locknut types of fittings may be depended on for bonding purposes.

    (a) True
    (b) False

Article 511 | Practice Questions

5. Where LFMC is used in a Class III location, it shall _____.
   (a) not be unsupported
   (b) not exceed 6 ft in length
   (c) include an equipment bonding jumper of the wire type in compliance with 250.102
   (d) be listed for use in a Class I hazardous (classified) location

6. In Class III locations, switches, circuit breakers, motor controllers, and fuses, including pushbuttons, relays, and similar devices, shall be provided with _____.
   (a) Class I enclosures
   (b) general duty enclosures
   (c) dusttight enclosures
   (d) seals at each enclosure

7. In Class III locations, motors, generators, and other rotating machinery shall be totally enclosed _____.
   (a) nonventilated
   (b) pipe ventilated
   (c) fan cooled
   (d) any of these

8. Luminaires for fixed lighting in Class III locations shall have enclosures for lamps and lampholders that are designed to prevent the escape of _____.
   (a) sparks
   (b) burning material
   (c) hot metal
   (d) all of these

9. Luminaires in Class III locations exposed to physical damage shall be protected by a(an) _____ guard.
   (a) plastic
   (b) metal
   (c) suitable
   (d) explosionproof

10. In a Class III location, pendant luminaires suspended by stems longer than _____ in. shall be provided with a fitting or flexible connector identified for the location or shall be provided with effective bracing.
    (a) 12
    (b) 18
    (c) 24
    (d) 30

11. In Class III locations, portable lighting equipment shall be equipped with handles and protected with substantial guards. Lampholders shall be of the unswitched type with no provision for _____.
    (a) receiving attachment plugs
    (b) grounding connections
    (c) lamp installation
    (d) hooks or hangers

12. In Class III locations, flexible cords shall _____.
    (a) be listed as extra-hard usage
    (b) contain an equipment grounding conductor
    (c) terminate with a listed dusttight cord connector
    (d) all of these

13. In Class III locations, receptacles and attachment plugs shall be of the grounding type, shall be designed so as to minimize the accumulation or the entry of _____, and shall prevent the escape of sparks or molten particles.
    (a) gases or vapors
    (b) particles of combustion
    (c) fibers/flyings
    (d) flammable liquids

Article 511—Commercial Garages, Repair and Storage

1. Article _____ contains the wiring requirements for service and repair operations in connection with self-propelled vehicles in which volatile flammable liquids or flammable gases are used for fuel or power.
   (a) 500
   (b) 501
   (c) 511
   (d) 514

2. Parking garages used for parking or storage shall be permitted to be unclassified locations.
   (a) True
   (b) False

3. In major and minor repair garages, where vehicles using Class _____ liquids or heavier-than-air gaseous fuels (such as LPG) are repaired, hazardous area classification guidance is found in Table 511.3(C).

   (a) I
   (b) II
   (c) III
   (d) all of these

4. In major repair garages where ventilation is not provided, any pit or depression below floor level shall be a Class I, Division _____ location.

   (a) 1
   (b) 2
   (c) 1 or Division 2
   (d) 1 and Division 2

5. For each floor area inside a major repair garage where ventilation is not provided and Class I liquids or gaseous fuels are not transferred or dispensed, the entire area up to a level of _____ in. above the floor is considered to be a Class I, Division 2 location.

   (a) 6
   (b) 12
   (c) 18
   (d) 24

6. Any pit for which ventilation is not provided below a minor repair garage floor level of a lubrication or service room is considered to be a Class I, Division _____ location.

   (a) 1
   (b) 2
   (c) 1 or Division 2
   (d) 1 and Division 2

7. Where Class I liquids or gaseous fuels will not be transferred in a minor repair garage, such location is considered to be a(an) _____ location, provided the entire floor area has mechanical ventilation providing a minimum of four air changes per hour or one cubic foot per minute of exchanged air for each square foot of floor area.

   (a) Class I, Division 1
   (b) Class I, Division 2
   (c) Class II, Division 1
   (d) unclassified

8. In major repair garages where vehicles using lighter-than-air gaseous fuels (such as hydrogen and natural gas) are _____, hazardous area classification guidance is found in Table 511.3(D).

   (a) salvaged for parts
   (b) assembled
   (c) sold to the public
   (d) repaired or stored

9. In major repair garages where lighter-than-air gaseous fueled vehicles, such as vehicles fueled by natural gas or hydrogen, are repaired or stored, the area within _____ in. of the ceiling is classified as Class I, Division 2 unless otherwise indicated in the Table footnotes.

   (a) 6
   (b) 12
   (c) 18
   (d) 24

10. The area used for _____ of alcohol-based windshield washer fluid in repair garages shall be unclassified.

    (a) storage
    (b) handling
    (c) dispensing into motor vehicles
    (d) any of these

11. Type NM cable can be installed above a Class I location in a commercial garage.

    (a) True
    (b) False

12. Fixed electrical equipment installed in spaces above a Class I location in a commercial garage shall be _____.

    (a) well ventilated
    (b) GFPE protected
    (c) GFCI protected
    (d) located above the level of any defined Class I location or identified for the location

13. A permanently mounted luminaire in a commercial garage, located over lanes on which vehicles are commonly driven, shall be located not less than _____ ft above floor level.

    (a) 10
    (b) 12
    (c) 14
    (d) 16

Article 514 | Practice Questions

14. Underground wiring below Class I locations in a commercial garage shall be installed in _____.

    (a) threaded rigid or intermediate metal conduit
    (b) Schedule 40 PVC conduit
    (c) Schedule 80 PVC conduit
    (d) coated EMT

15. In commercial garages, Type PVC conduit, Type RTRC conduit, and Type HDPE conduit shall be permitted where buried under not less than _____ ft of cover.

    (a) 1
    (b) 2
    (c) 2½
    (d) 3

16. Battery chargers and the batteries being charged can be located in any area of a commercial garage.

    (a) True
    (b) False

17. In commercial garages, GFCI protection for personnel shall be provided as required in 210.(B).

    (a) True
    (b) False

Article 514—Motor Fuel Dispensing Facilities

1. Article 514 applies to motor fuel dispensing facilities, marine/motor fuel dispensing facilities, motor fuel dispensing facilities located inside buildings, and _____ vehicle motor fuel dispensing facilities.

    (a) commercial
    (b) hybrid
    (c) military
    (d) fleet

2. In motor fuel dispensing facilities, where the authority having jurisdiction can satisfactorily determine that flammable liquids having a flash point _____, such as gasoline, will not be handled such location shall not be required to be classified.

    (a) above 100°F
    (b) below 100°F
    (c) below 86°F
    (d) above 86°F

3. Underground wiring to motor fuel dispensers shall be installed (or shall be permitted to be installed) in _____.

    (a) threaded rigid metal conduit
    (b) threaded steel IMC
    (c) PVC conduit, Type RTRC conduit, and HDPE conduit when buried under not less than 2 ft of cover
    (d) any of these

4. A listed seal for motor fuel dispensers shall be provided in each conduit run _____.

    (a) adjacent to a dispenser
    (b) within 36 in. of a dispenser
    (c) inside the dispenser equipment
    (d) entering or leaving a dispenser

5. The sealing fitting or listed explosionproof reducer at the seal for motor fuel dispensers shall be the _____ fitting after the conduit emerges from the earth or concrete.

    (a) first
    (b) second
    (c) third
    (d) fourth

6. In motor fuel dispensing facilities, all metal raceways, the metal armor or metallic sheath on cables, and all noncurrent-carrying metal parts of fixed and portable electrical equipment _____ shall be grounded and bonded.

    (a) operating at under 600V
    (b) regardless of voltage
    (c) over 300V
    (d) under 50V

Article 517—Health Care Facilities

1. Article 517 applies to electrical construction and installation criteria in health care facilities that provide services to _____.

    (a) human beings
    (b) animals
    (c) children only
    (d) intellectually challenged persons

2. A "Dental Office" is a building or part thereof in which _____ occur.

   (a) examinations and minor treatments or procedures are performed under the continuous supervision of a dental professional
   (b) use of limited to minimal sedation and treatment or procedures that do not render the patient incapable of self-preservation under emergency conditions
   (c) there are no overnight stays for patients or 24-hour operations
   (d) all of these

3. "Health care facilities" are defined as buildings or portions of buildings, or mobile enclosures in which human medical, dental, _____, or surgical care are provided.

   (a) psychiatric
   (b) nursing
   (c) obstetrical
   (d) any of these

4. The person or persons who have the overall _____ responsibility for the operation of a health care facility is known as the "governing body."

   (a) financial
   (b) legal
   (c) moral
   (d) all of these

5. A "hospital" is a building or portion thereof used for the medical, psychiatric, obstetrical, or surgical care, on a 24-hour basis, of _____ or more inpatients.

   (a) two
   (b) three
   (c) four
   (d) five

6. A "limited care facility" is defined as a building or portion thereof used on a(an) _____ basis for the housing of four or more persons who are incapable of self-preservation because of age; physical limitation due to accident or illness; or limitations such as intellectual disability/developmental disability, mental illness, or chemical dependency.

   (a) occasional
   (b) 10-hour or less per day
   (c) 24-hour
   (d) temporary

7. A "nursing home" is a building or portion of a building used for the housing and nursing care, on a 24-hour basis, of _____ or more persons who, because of mental or physical incapacity, might be unable to provide for their own needs and safety without the assistance of another person.

   (a) two
   (b) three
   (c) four
   (d) five

8. A "patient _____" is the location of an inpatient sleeping bed, or the bed or procedure table of a Category 1 (critical care) space.

   (a) bed location
   (b) care area
   (c) observation area
   (d) sterile area

9. The "patient care space" is any space within a health care facility where patients are intended to be _____.

   (a) admitted
   (b) evaluated
   (c) registered
   (d) examined or treated

10. Wiring methods in healthcare facilities shall comply with Chapters 1 through 4 of the *NEC* except as modified in Article _____.

    (a) 511
    (b) 516
    (c) 517
    (d) 518

11. In health care facilities, the _____ for branch circuits serving patient care spaces, shall itself qualify as an equipment grounding conductor in accordance with 250.118.

    (a) metal raceway system
    (b) metallic cable armor
    (c) sheath assembly
    (d) all of these

Article 517 | Practice Questions

12. In patient care spaces, an insulated equipment bonding jumper that directly connects to the equipment grounding conductor is permitted to connect the box and receptacle(s) to the equipment grounding conductor for other than _____ receptacles.

    (a) AFCI-protected
    (b) GFCI-protected
    (c) isolated ground
    (d) all of these

13. In patient care spaces, luminaires more than _____ ft above the floor and switches located outside of the patient care vicinity shall be permitted to be connected to an equipment grounding return path complying with 517.13(A) or (B).

    (a) 7
    (b) 7½
    (c) 7¾
    (d) 8

14. In patient care spaces, metal faceplates shall be directly connected to an insulated copper equipment grounding conductor by means of _____ securing the faceplate to a metal yoke or strap of a receptacle or to a metal outlet box.

    (a) ground clips
    (b) rivets
    (c) metal mounting screws
    (d) a spot weld

15. In health care facilities, isolated ground receptacles shall be installed in a patient care vicinity.

    (a) True
    (b) False

16. In health care facilities, _____ ground receptacle(s) installed in patient care spaces outside of a patient care vicinity(s) shall comply with 517.16(B)(1) and (B)(2).

    (a) AFCI-protected
    (b) GFCI-protected
    (c) isolated
    (d) all of these

17. Outside of patient care vicinities, the equipment grounding terminals of isolated ground receptacles installed in branch circuits for patient care _____ shall be connected to an insulated equipment grounding conductor in accordance with 250.146(D) installed in a wiring method described in 517.13(A).

    (a) vicinities
    (b) spaces
    (c) bathrooms
    (d) vicinities or spaces

18. Outside of patient care vicinities, the equipment grounding conductor connected to the equipment grounding terminals of isolated ground receptacles in patient care spaces, shall be clearly _____ along the equipment grounding conductor's entire length by green insulation with one or more yellow stripes.

    (a) listed
    (b) labeled
    (c) identified
    (d) approved

19. Outside of patient care vicinities, the insulated equipment grounding conductor required in 517.13(B)(1) shall be clearly _____ along its entire length by green insulation, with no yellow stripes, and shall not be connected to the grounding terminals of isolated equipment ground receptacles but shall be connected to the box or enclosure indicated in 517.13(B)(1)(2) and to noncurrent-carrying conductive surfaces of fixed electrical equipment indicated in 517.13(B)(1)(3).

    (a) listed
    (b) labeled
    (c) identified
    (d) approved

20. Outside of patient care vicinities, care should be taken in specifying a system containing isolated ground receptacles, because the _____ of the effective ground-fault current path is dependent upon the equipment grounding conductor(s) and does not benefit from any conduit or building structure in parallel with the equipment grounding conductor.

    (a) ampacity
    (b) resistance
    (c) effectiveness
    (d) impedance

Article 518—Assembly Occupancies

1. Except for the assembly occupancies explicitly covered by 520.1, Article 518 covers all buildings or portions of buildings or structures designed or intended for the gathering together of _____ or more persons.

    (a) 16
    (b) 50
    (c) 100
    (d) 125

2. Examples of assembly occupancies include _____.

    (a) restaurants
    (b) conference rooms
    (c) pool rooms
    (d) all of these

3. Temporary wiring in exhibition halls for display booths in assembly occupancies is permitted to be installed in accordance with Article 590, except _____.

    (a) GFCI requirements of 590.6 shall not apply
    (b) flexible cords and cables approved for hard or extra-hard usage shall be permitted to be laid on floors where protected from contact with the general public
    (c) GFCI protection shall be provided where required by the NEC except for the 590.6 requirements
    (d) all of these

4. Where ground-fault circuit interrupter protection for personnel is supplied by plug-and-cord-connection to the branch circuit or to the feeder, the ground-fault circuit interrupter protection shall be listed as _____ ground-fault circuit interrupter protection.

    (a) suitable
    (b) acceptable
    (c) accessible
    (d) portable

5. Which of the following wiring methods are permitted in an assembly occupancy?

    (a) Metal raceways
    (b) Type MC cable
    (c) Type AC cable
    (d) all of these

6. Nonmetallic raceways encased in not less than _____ in. of concrete shall be permitted in assembly occupancies.

    (a) 1
    (b) 2
    (c) 3
    (d) 4

7. In assembly occupancies, Type NM cable, ENT, and PVC conduit shall be permitted to be installed in those portions of buildings not required to be of _____ construction by the applicable building code.

    (a) Class I, Division 1
    (b) fire-rated
    (c) occupancy-rated
    (d) aboveground

Article 525—Carnivals, Circuses, Fairs, and Similar Events

1. Article(s) _____ cover(s) the installation of portable wiring and equipment for carnivals, circuses, fairs, and similar functions.

    (a) 518
    (b) 525
    (c) 590
    (d) all of these

2. The individual responsible for starting, stopping, and controlling an amusement ride or supervising a concession is known as the "_____."

    (a) operator
    (b) director
    (c) manager
    (d) facilitator

3. Overhead wiring outside of tents and concession areas of carnivals and circuses which are accessible to pedestrians shall maintain a vertical clearance of _____ ft above finished grade, sidewalks, or from platforms, projections, or surfaces from which the wiring might be reached.

    (a) 3
    (b) 6
    (c) 8
    (d) 10

Article 525 | Practice Questions

4. Portable carnival or circus structures shall be maintained not less than _____ ft in any direction from overhead conductors operating at 600V or less.

    (a) 7½
    (b) 10
    (c) 12½
    (d) 15

5. Electrical equipment and wiring methods in or on portable structures for carnivals, circuses, fairs, and similar events shall have mechanical protection where subject to _____.

    (a) public access
    (b) physical damage
    (c) exposure to the weather
    (d) operator access

6. When installed indoors for carnivals, circuses, and fairs, flexible cords and flexible cables shall be listed for wet locations and shall be sunlight resistant.

    (a) True
    (b) False

7. Cord connectors for carnivals, circuses, and fairs can be laid on the ground when the connectors are _____ for a wet location.

    (a) listed
    (b) labeled
    (c) approved
    (d) identified

8. Flexible cords and cables accessible to the public at carnivals or circuses shall be permitted to be buried and subject to the requirements of 300.5.

    (a) True
    (b) False

9. Each portable structure at a carnival, circus, or fair shall be provided with a means to disconnect it from all ungrounded conductors within sight of and within _____ ft of the operator's station.

    (a) 3
    (b) 6
    (c) 8
    (d) 10

10. Wiring for lighting located inside tents and concession areas at carnivals, circuses, and fairs, where subject to physical damage shall be provided with mechanical protection.

    (a) True
    (b) False

11. Portable distribution and termination boxes installed outdoors at carnivals, circuses, or fairs shall be weatherproof and mounted so the bottom of the enclosure is not less than _____ in. above the ground.

    (a) 6
    (b) 8
    (c) 10
    (d) 12

12. GFCI protection for personnel shall be provided at carnivals, circuses, and fairs for all 15A and 20A, 125V nonlocking-type receptacles that are readily accessible to the general public.

    (a) True
    (b) False

13. For carnivals and fairs, receptacles of the locking type not accessible from grade level that only facilitate quick disconnecting and reconnecting of electrical equipment shall not be required to be provided with GFCI protection.

    (a) True
    (b) False

14. GFCI protection is not permitted at carnivals, circuses, and fairs for _____.

    (a) portable structures
    (b) egress lighting
    (c) nighttime operation lighting
    (d) amusement lighting

15. At circuses and carnivals, all equipment to be grounded shall be connected to a(an) _____ conductor of a type recognized by 250.118.

    (a) equipment grounding
    (b) grounded
    (c) grounding electrode
    (d) ungrounded

16. The continuity of the equipment grounding conductors at carnivals, circuses, fairs, and similar events shall be verified each time that portable electrical equipment is connected.

    (a) True
    (b) False

Article 547—Agricultural Buildings

1. Agricultural buildings where excessive dust and dust with water may accumulate, including all areas of _____ confinement systems where litter dust or feed dust may accumulate shall comply with Article 547.

    (a) poultry
    (b) livestock
    (c) fish
    (d) all of these

2. Agricultural buildings where corrosive atmospheres exist include areas where _____ conditions exist(s).

    (a) poultry and animal excrement
    (b) corrosive particles which may combine with water
    (c) areas of periodic washing with water and cleansing agents
    (d) all of these

3. An "equipotential plane" is an area where wire mesh or other conductive elements are embedded in or placed under concrete and bonded to _____.

    (a) all metal structures
    (b) fixed nonelectrical equipment that could become energized
    (c) the electrical grounding system
    (d) all of these

4. Type NM cable shall be permitted in agricultural buildings.

    (a) True
    (b) False

5. Enclosures and fittings installed in areas of agricultural buildings where excessive dust may be present shall be designed to minimize the entrance of dust and shall have no openings through which dust can enter the enclosure.

    (a) True
    (b) False

6. In damp or wet locations of agricultural buildings, equipment enclosures and fittings shall be located or equipped to prevent moisture from _____ within the enclosure, box, conduit body, or fitting.

    (a) entering and accumulating
    (b) draining from
    (c) creating a short-circuit
    (d) causing damage

7. Where _____ may be present in an agricultural building, enclosures and fittings shall have corrosion-resistance properties suitable for the conditions.

    (a) wet dust or excessive moisture
    (b) corrosive gases or vapors
    (c) other corrosive conditions
    (d) any of these

8. Where an equipment grounding conductor is installed underground within an agricultural building, it shall be _____.

    (a) insulated
    (b) copper
    (c) bare
    (d) covered

9. All 15A and 20A, 125V, single-phase receptacles installed _____ of agricultural buildings shall be GFCI protected.

    (a) in areas having an equipotential plane
    (b) outdoors
    (c) in dirt confinement areas for livestock
    (d) any of these

10. Luminaires used in agricultural buildings shall _____.

    (a) minimize the entrance of dust, foreign matter, moisture, and corrosive material
    (b) be protected by a suitable guard if exposed to physical damage
    (c) be listed for use in wet locations when exposed to water
    (d) all of these

11. An equipotential plane shall be installed in all concrete floor confinement areas of livestock buildings, and all outdoor confinement areas with a concrete slab that contains metallic equipment accessible to livestock and that may become energized.

    (a) True
    (b) False

Article 550 | Practice Questions

12. The equipotential plane in an agricultural building shall be connected to the electrical grounding system with a solid copper, insulated, covered, or bare conductor and not smaller than _____ AWG.

    (a) 10
    (b) 8
    (c) 6
    (d) 4

Article 550—Mobile Homes, Manufactured Homes, and Mobile Home Parks

1. Article _____ covers the electrical conductors and equipment installed within or on mobile and manufactured homes and the conductors that connect mobile and manufactured homes to a supply of electricity.

    (a) 550
    (b) 551
    (c) 555
    (d) 590

2. A "_____" is a structure transportable in one or more sections that is built on a permanent chassis and designed to be used as a dwelling, with or without a permanent foundation, whether or not connected to the utilities, and includes plumbing, heating, air conditioning, and electrical systems contained therein.

    (a) manufactured home
    (b) mobile home
    (c) dwelling unit
    (d) manufactured or mobile home

3. The term "mobile home" includes manufactured homes, unless otherwise indicated.

    (a) True
    (b) False

4. GFCI protection in a mobile home shall be provided for _____.

    (a) receptacle outlets installed outdoors and in compartments accessible from outside
    (b) receptacles within 6 ft of a wet bar sink, dishwasher outlets, and where installed to serve countertop surfaces
    (c) all receptacles in bathrooms including receptacles in luminaires
    (d) all of these

5. Where outdoor or under-chassis line-voltage (120V, nominal, or higher) mobile home wiring is exposed, it shall be protected by a conduit or raceway identified for use in wet locations. The conductors shall be listed for use in _____ locations.

    (a) hazardous
    (b) damp
    (c) wet
    (d) corrosive

6. In mobile and manufactured homes, all 120V branch circuits that supply 15A and 20A outlets shall have _____ protection in accordance with 210.12.

    (a) AFCI
    (b) GFCI
    (c) AFCI and GFCI
    (d) adequate

7. Mobile home service equipment shall be located adjacent to the mobile home and located in sight from but not more than _____ ft from the exterior wall of the mobile home it serves.

    (a) 15
    (b) 20
    (c) 30
    (d) 40

8. Mobile home and manufactured home feeder circuit conductors shall have a capacity not less than the loads supplied and have an ampacity of not less than _____.

    (a) 50A
    (b) 60A
    (c) 100A
    (d) 200A

9. Mobile home and manufactured home feeder circuit conductors shall have a capacity not less than the loads supplied, shall have an ampacity of not less than 100A, and shall be permitted to be sized in accordance with 310.12.

    (a) True
    (b) False

Article 555—Marinas, Boatyards, and Docking Facilities

1. Article 555 covers marinas, boatyards, docking facilities but not floating buildings.

    (a) True
    (b) False

2. Article 555 covers the installation of wiring and equipment in the areas comprising _____ and other areas in marinas, boatyards.

   (a) fixed or floating piers
   (b) floating buildings
   (c) wharves and docks
   (d) all of these

3. A "marine _____" is an enclosed assembly that can include receptacles, circuit breakers, fused switches, fuses, watt-hour meter(s), panelboards, and monitoring means identified for marina use.

   (a) power receptacle
   (b) source outlet
   (c) power outlet
   (d) any of these

4. The electrical equipment required to power a floating vessel including, but not limited to, the receptacle and cords is known as "_____."

   (a) a marina service
   (b) dock power
   (c) shore power
   (d) ship power

5. The electrical datum plane for floating piers and boat landing stages shall be a horizontal plane 30 in. above the water level at the floating pier or boat landing stage and a minimum of _____ in. above the level of the deck.

   (a) 12
   (b) 18
   (c) 24
   (d) 30

6. The electrical datum plane for floating piers and boat landing stages, shall be a horizontal plane _____ in. above the water level at the floating pier or boat landing stage and a minimum of 12 in. above the level of the deck.

   (a) 12
   (b) 18
   (c) 24
   (d) 30

7. In land areas subject to tidal fluctuation, the electrical datum plane shall be a horizontal plane that is _____ ft above the highest tide level for the area occurring under normal circumstances, based on the highest high tide.

   (a) 1
   (b) 1½
   (c) 2
   (d) 2½

8. In land areas not subject to tidal fluctuation, the electrical datum plane shall be a horizontal plane that is _____ ft above the highest tide level for the area occurring under normal circumstances, based on the highest high tide.

   (a) 1
   (b) 1½
   (c) 2
   (d) 2½

9. Service equipment for floating docks or marinas shall be located _____ the floating structure.

   (a) on land adjacent to
   (b) on
   (c) in
   (d) any of these

10. The demand factor for marina load calculations of 45 shore power receptacles is _____ percent.

    (a) 40
    (b) 50
    (c) 60
    (d) 70

11. Where shore power accommodations provide two receptacles specifically for an individual boat slip, and these receptacles have different voltages, only the receptacle with the _____ shall be required to be calculated.

    (a) smaller kW demand
    (b) larger kW demand
    (c) higher voltage
    (d) nominal voltage

Article 555 | Practice Questions

12. In marinas, boatyards, and commercial and noncommercial docking facilities, the bottom of enclosures for transformers shall not be located below _____.

    (a) 2 ft above the dock
    (b) 18 in. above the electrical datum plane
    (c) the electrical datum plane
    (d) a dock

13. Permanent safety signs shall be installed to give notice of electrical shock hazard risks to persons using or swimming near a boat dock or marina and shall _____.

    (a) comply with 110.21(B)(1) and be of sufficient durability to withstand the environment
    (b) be clearly visible from all approaches to a marina, docking facility, or boatyard facility
    (c) state "WARNING—POTENTIAL SHOCK HAZARD—ELECTRICAL CURRENTS MAY BE PRESENT IN THE WATER"
    (d) all of these

14. In marinas, boatyards, and commercial and noncommercial docking facilities, all metal parts in contact with the water, all metal piping, and all noncurrent-carrying metal parts shall be connected to the grounding bus in the panelboard using solid copper conductors; insulated, covered, or bare; not smaller than _____ AWG.

    (a) 12
    (b) 10
    (c) 8
    (d) 6

15. Electrical connections shall be located at least _____ in. above the deck of a floating pier.

    (a) 12
    (b) 18
    (c) 24
    (d) 30

16. Conductor splices, within junction boxes identified for wet locations, utilizing sealed wire connector systems listed and identified for submersion shall be required for floating piers where located above the electrical datum plane for floating piers.

    (a) True
    (b) False

17. Electrical connections in marinas, boatyards, and commercial and noncommercial docking facilities shall be located _____ pier unless the conductor splices for floating piers are contained within sealed wire connector systems listed and identified for submersion.

    (a) at least 12 in. above the deck of a floating
    (b) at least 12 in. above the deck of a fixed
    (c) not below the electrical datum plane of a fixed
    (d) all of these

18. All electrical connections shall be located at least _____ in. above the deck of a fixed pier but shall not be located below the electrical datum plane.

    (a) 12
    (b) 18
    (c) 24
    (d) 30

19. Replacement electrical connections shall be located at least _____ in. above the deck of a floating pier.

    (a) 12
    (b) 18
    (c) 24
    (d) 30

20. Receptacles that provide shore power for boats shall be rated not less than _____.

    (a) 15A
    (b) 20A
    (c) 30A
    (d) 60A

21. All receptacles installed for other than shore power shall be protected in accordance with _____.

    (a) 110.11
    (b) 200.3
    (c) 210.8
    (d) 250.62

22. Shore power receptacles installed in accordance with 555.33(A) shall have individual GFPE set to open at currents not exceeding _____ milliamperes.

    (a) 6
    (b) 30
    (c) 75
    (d) 100

23. All _____, 15A and 20A receptacles for other than shore power shall be protected in accordance with 555.33(B)(1) and (B)(2).

    (a) 125V, single-phase
    (b) 250V, single-phase
    (c) single or three-phase
    (d) 125V, single-phase or 250V, single-phase

24. Feeder and branch-circuit conductors that are installed on docking facilities shall be provided with GFPE set to open at currents not exceeding _____ milliamperes.

    (a) 6
    (b) 30
    (c) 75
    (d) 100

25. Where more than _____ receptacles supply shore power to boats, a leakage current measurement device shall be available and be used to determine leakage current from each boat that will utilize shore power.

    (a) two
    (b) three
    (c) four
    (d) six

26. Leakage current measurement devices will provide the capability to determine when an individual boat has defective wiring or other problems contributing to hazardous voltage and current and will help the facility operator prevent a particular boat from contributing to hazardous voltage and current in the marina area.

    (a) True
    (b) False

27. A(an) _____ test of each boat with the leakage current measurement device is a prudent step toward determining if a boat has defective wiring that may be contributing hazardous voltage and current in the marina area.

    (a) monthly
    (b) quarterly
    (c) bi-annual
    (d) annual

28. Disconnecting means shall be provided to _____ each boat from its supply connection(s).

    (a) isolate
    (b) separate
    (c) guard
    (d) control

29. A _____ shall be used to serve as the required shore power receptacle disconnecting means, and it shall be identified as to which receptacle it controls.

    (a) circuit breaker
    (b) switch
    (c) circuit breaker or fused knife switch
    (d) circuit breaker, switch, or both

30. In marinas, boatyards, and commercial and noncommercial docking facilities, the disconnecting means shall be _____, located not more than 30 in. from the receptacle it controls, and shall be located in the supply circuit ahead of the receptacle.

    (a) accessible
    (b) readily accessible
    (c) remote
    (d) any of these

31. The disconnecting means for a shore power connection shall be not more than _____ in. from the receptacle it controls.

    (a) 12
    (b) 24
    (c) 30
    (d) 36

32. Marina or dock items shall be connected to an equipment grounding conductor run with the circuit conductors in the same raceway, cable, or trench. These items include metal boxes, metal cabinets, and all other metal enclosures; metal frames of utilization equipment; and _____.

    (a) metal fencing
    (b) wood rails of piers and docks
    (c) metal rails of piers and docks
    (d) grounding terminals of grounding-type receptacles

33. The equipment grounding conductor at a marina is required to be an insulated conductor for all circuits.

    (a) True
    (b) False

Article 590 | Practice Questions

34. Where a shore power feeder supplies a remote panelboard, an insulated _____ shall extend from a grounding terminal in the service equipment to a grounding terminal in the remote panelboard.

    (a) bonding jumper
    (b) equipment grounding conductor
    (c) grounding electrode conductor
    (d) copper conductor

Article 590—Temporary Installations

1. The provisions of Article _____ apply to temporary electric power and lighting installations.

    (a) 480
    (b) 555
    (c) 590
    (d) 600

2. Temporary wiring methods shall be acceptable only if _____ based on the conditions of use and any special requirements of the temporary installation.

    (a) listed
    (b) identified
    (c) approved
    (d) any of these

3. Temporary electrical power and lighting installations shall be permitted for a period not to exceed 90 days for _____ decorative lighting and similar purposes.

    (a) Christmas
    (b) New Year's
    (c) July 4th
    (d) holiday

4. Temporary electrical power and lighting shall be permitted during emergencies and for _____.

    (a) tests
    (b) experiments
    (c) developmental work
    (d) all of these

5. Temporary wiring shall be _____ immediately upon the completion of construction or purpose for which the wiring was installed.

    (a) disconnected
    (b) removed
    (c) de-energized
    (d) any of these

6. Types NM, NMC, and SE cables can be used for feeder temporary installations without height limitation and without concealment.

    (a) True
    (b) False

7. Type _____ cable shall be permitted to be installed in a feeder raceway in a temporary underground installation.

    (a) NM
    (b) NMC
    (c) SE
    (d) any of these

8. Types NM, NMC, and SE cables can be used for branch circuits for temporary installations without height limitation and without concealment.

    (a) True
    (b) False

9. Type _____ cable shall be permitted to be installed in a branch-circuit raceway in a temporary underground installation.

    (a) NM
    (b) NMC
    (c) SE
    (d) any of these

10. Receptacles on construction sites shall not be installed on _____ that supplies temporary lighting.

    (a) any branch circuit
    (b) the same feeder
    (c) any branch circuit or the same feeder
    (d) a cord or cable

11. For temporary installations, lamps for general illumination shall be protected from accidental contact or breakage by a suitable _____ or by the use of a lampholder with a guard.

    (a) globe
    (b) luminaire
    (c) fitting
    (d) porcelain fitting

12. For temporary installations, a box, conduit body, or other enclosure, with a cover installed, shall be required for all splices except where the circuit conductors being spliced are all from nonmetallic multiconductor _____ assemblies, provided that the equipment grounding continuity is maintained with or without the box.

    (a) listed
    (b) identified
    (c) cord or cable
    (d) feeder and service conductor

13. Flexible cords and flexible cables used for temporary wiring shall _____.

    (a) be protected from accidental damage
    (b) be protected where passing through doorways
    (c) avoid sharp corners and projections
    (d) all of these

14. For temporary installations, cable assemblies, flexible cords, and flexible cables shall be supported by _____ or similar fittings so as not to damage the wiring.

    (a) staples
    (b) cable ties
    (c) straps
    (d) any of these

15. Vegetation shall not be used to support overhead conductor spans of _____ for temporary installations.

    (a) luminaires
    (b) receptacles
    (c) branch circuits or feeders
    (d) lighting conductors

16. Ground-fault protection for personnel is required for all temporary wiring used for construction, remodeling, maintenance, repair, or demolition of buildings, structures, or equipment, from power derived from a(an) _____ or from an on-site-generated power source.

    (a) electric utility company
    (b) cable or cord
    (c) feeder
    (d) separately derived system

17. All _____, 125V receptacle outlets that are not part of the permanent wiring of the building or structure and are used by personnel for temporary power shall be GFCI protected.

    (a) 15A
    (b) 20A
    (c) 30A
    (d) all of these

18. GFCI protection is required for 15A, 20A, and 30A, 125V receptacle outlets that are installed or existing as part of the permanent wiring of the building/structure when used during construction or remodeling. Listed cord sets or adapters that incorporate listed GFCI protection for portable use can be used to meet this requirement.

    (a) True
    (b) False

19. For temporary power outlets existing or installed as permanent wiring, GFCI protection can be incorporated into a listed _____.

    (a) circuit breaker
    (b) receptacle
    (c) cord set
    (d) any of these

20. GFCI protection is required for 15A, 20A, and 30A, 125V and 125/250V receptacles that are part of a portable generator used for temporary wiring rated not greater than _____.

    (a) 5 kW
    (b) 7.50 kW
    (c) 10 kW
    (d) 15 kW

21. Receptacles rated other than 125V, single-phase, 15A, 20A, and 30A for temporary installations shall be protected by _____.

    (a) GFCI protection for personnel
    (b) SPGFCI protection for personnel
    (c) GFPE protection for equipment
    (d) a surge protective device (SPD)

Article 590 | Practice Questions

22. Where overcurrent protective devices that have been previously used are installed in a temporary installation, these overcurrent protective devices shall be examined to ensure these devices _____.

    (a) have been properly installed
    (b) have been properly maintained
    (c) show no evidence of impending failure
    (d) all of these

23. Where overcurrent protective devices that have been previously used are installed in a temporary installation, the phrase "evidence of impending failure" means that there is evidence such as _____.

    (a) arcing or overheating
    (b) loose or bound equipment parts
    (c) visible damage or deterioration
    (d) any of these

24. Where overcurrent protective devices that have been previously used are installed in a temporary installation, the phrase "properly maintained" means that the equipment has been maintained in accordance with the _____.

    (a) product listing
    (b) manufacturer's recommendations and applicable industry codes and standards
    (c) field evaluator's recommendations
    (d) any of these

CHAPTER 6

SPECIAL EQUIPMENT

Introduction to Chapter 6—Special Equipment

The first four chapters of the *Code* are sequential and form a foundation for each of the subsequent four. Chapter 6, which covers special equipment, is the second of the four *NEC* chapters that deal with special topics. Chapters 5 and 7 focus on special occupancies and special conditions respectively, while Chapter 8 covers communications systems.

What exactly is "Special Equipment"? It is equipment that, by the nature of its use, construction, or by its unique nature creates a need for additional measures to ensure the "safeguarding of people and property" mission of the *NEC*, as stated in Article 90. The *Code* groups the articles in this chapter logically, as you might expect.

- **Article 600—Electric Signs and Outline Lighting.** This article covers the installation of conductors and equipment for electric signs and outline lighting as defined in Article 100. They include all products and installations that utilize neon tubing, such as signs, decorative elements, skeleton tubing, or art forms.

- **Article 604—Manufactured Wiring Systems.** Article 604 covers field-installed manufactured wiring systems used for branch circuits, remote-control circuits, signaling circuits, and communications circuits in accessible areas. The components of a listed manufactured wiring system can be assembled at the jobsite.

- **Article 620—Elevators, Escalators, and Moving Walks.** This article covers electrical equipment and wiring used in connection with elevators, dumbwaiters, escalators, moving walks, wheelchair lifts, and stairway chair lifts.

- **Article 625—Electric Vehicle Power Transfer System.** An electrically powered vehicle needs a dedicated charging circuit and that is where Article 625 comes in. It provides the requirements for the electrical equipment needed to charge automotive-type electric and hybrid vehicles including cars, bikes, and buses.

- **Article 630—Electric Welders.** Electric welding equipment does its job either by creating an electric arc between two surfaces or by heating a rod that melts from overcurrent. Either way results in a hefty momentary current draw. Welding machines come in many shapes and sizes. This article covers electric arc welding and resistance welding apparatus, and other similar welding equipment connected to an electric supply system.

- **Article 640—Audio Signal Amplification and Reproduction Equipment.** Article 640 covers equipment and wiring for audio signal generation, recording, processing, amplification and reproduction, distribution of sound, public address, speech input systems, temporary audio system installations, and electronic musical instruments such as electric organs, electric guitars, and electronic drums/percussion.

- **Article 645—Information Technology Equipment.** This article applies to equipment, power-supply wiring, equipment interconnecting wiring, and grounding of information technology equipment and systems including terminal units in an information technology equipment room.

•••

Chapter 6 | Special Equipment

- **Article 680—Swimming Pools, Spas, Hot Tubs, Fountains, and Similar Installations.** Article 680 covers the installation of bonding and grounding devices for these installations, and the electric wiring and equipment that supply swimming, wading, therapeutic and decorative pools, fountains, hot tubs, spas, hydromassage bathtubs, and powered pool lifts whether permanently installed or storable.

- **Article 690—Solar Photovoltaic (PV) Systems.** This article focuses on reducing the electrical hazards that may arise from installing and operating a solar PV system, to the point where it can be considered safe for property and people. The requirements of the *NEC* Chapters 1 through 4 apply to these installations, except as specifically modified here.

- **Article 691—Large-Scale Solar Photovoltaic (PV) Electric Supply Stations.** Article 691 covers large-scale PV electric supply stations with a generating capacity of 5,000 kW or more and not under exclusive utility control.

- **Article 695—Fire Pumps.** This article covers the electric power sources and interconnecting circuits for electric motor-driven fire pumps. It also covers switching and control equipment dedicated to fire pump drivers. Article 695 does not apply to sprinkler system pumps in one- and two-family dwellings or to pressure maintenance (jockey) pumps.

ARTICLE 600 — ELECTRIC SIGNS AND OUTLINE LIGHTING

Introduction to Article 600—Electric Signs and Outline Lighting

One of the first things you will notice when entering a strip mall is that there is a sign for every store. Every commercial occupancy needs a form of identification, and the standard method is the electric sign; thus, 600.5 requires a sign outlet for the entrance of each tenant location. Section 600.6 requires a disconnect within sight of a sign unless it can be locked in the open position.

Author's Comment:

▸ Article 100 defines an electric sign as any "fixed, stationary, or portable self-contained, electrically illuminated utilization equipment with words or symbols designed to convey information or attract attention."

Freestanding signs, such as those that might be erected in a parking lot, must be located at least 14 ft above vehicle areas unless they are protected from physical damage [600.9(A)].

Neon art forms or decorative elements are subsets of electric signs and outline lighting. If installed and not attached to an enclosure or sign body, they are considered skeleton tubing for the purpose of applying the requirements of Article 600. However, if that neon tubing is attached to an enclosure or sign body, which may be a simple support frame, it is considered a sign or outline lighting subject to all the provisions that apply to signs and outline lighting such as 600.3 which requires the product to be listed.

Part I. General

600.1 Scope

Article 600 covers the installation of conductors, equipment, and field wiring for electric signs, retrofit kits, and outline lighting. It also covers installations and equipment using neon tubing such as signs, decorative elements, skeleton tubing, or art forms. ▸Figure 600-1

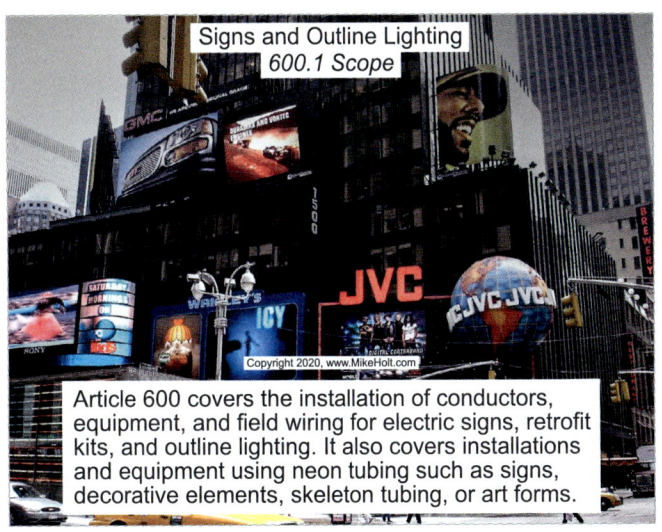

▸Figure 600-1

Author's Comment:

▸ Outline lighting is an arrangement of incandescent lamps or electric-discharge lighting to outline or call attention to certain features, such as the shape of a building or the decoration of a window [Article 100]. ▸Figure 600-2

Note: Sign and outline lighting systems can include cold cathode neon tubing, high-intensity discharge lamps (HID), fluorescent or incandescent lamps, light emitting diodes (LEDs), and electroluminescent and inductance lighting.

600.2 | Electric Signs and Outline Lighting

▶Figure 600–2

600.2 Definitions

The definitions in this section apply only within this article.

Neon Tubing. Electric-discharge luminous tubing, including cold cathode luminous tubing, that is made into shapes to illuminate signs, form letters, parts of letters, skeleton tubing, outline lighting, or other decorative elements, or art forms and filled with various inert gases.

Photovoltaic (PV) Powered Sign. A sign powered by a solar PV system. ▶Figure 600–3

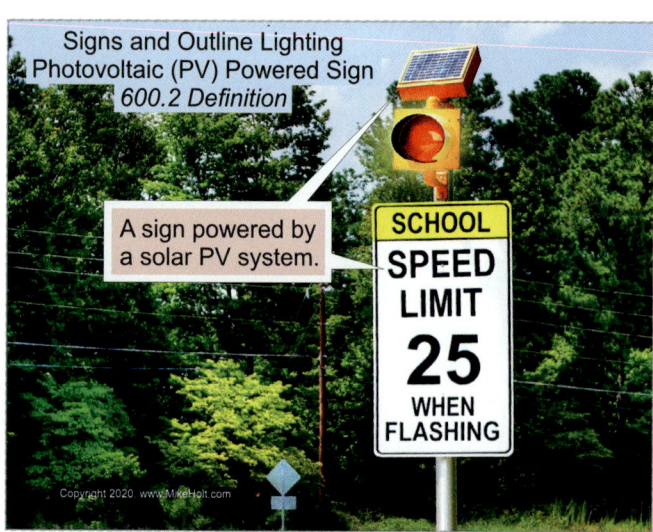

▶Figure 600–3

Host Sign. A sign or outline lighting system already installed in the field that is designated for field conversion of the illumination system with a retrofit kit.

Retrofit Kit, General Use. A kit consisting of primary parts, which does not include all the parts for a complete subassembly but includes a list of required parts and installation instructions to complete the subassembly in the field.

Retrofit Kit, Sign Specific. A kit consisting of the necessary parts and hardware to allow for field installation in a host sign, based on the included installation instructions.

> **Author's Comment:**
> ▶ Of the two "retrofit kit" definitions, the general use retrofit kit will likely be the most commonly used.

Section Sign. A sign or outline lighting system that requires field-installed wiring between the subassemblies which can be physically joined or installed as separate remote parts of an overall sign. ▶Figure 600–4

▶Figure 600–4

Skeleton Tubing. Neon tubing serving as a sign or outline lighting when not attached to an enclosure or sign body. ▶Figure 600–5

Subassembly. Component parts or a segment of a sign, retrofit kit, or outline lighting system that, when assembled, forms a complete unit or product.

600.3 Listing

Fixed, mobile, or portable electric signs, section signs, outline lighting, PV powered signs, and retrofit kits must be listed and labeled, and installed in accordance with their installation instructions.

Electric Signs and Outline Lighting | 600.5

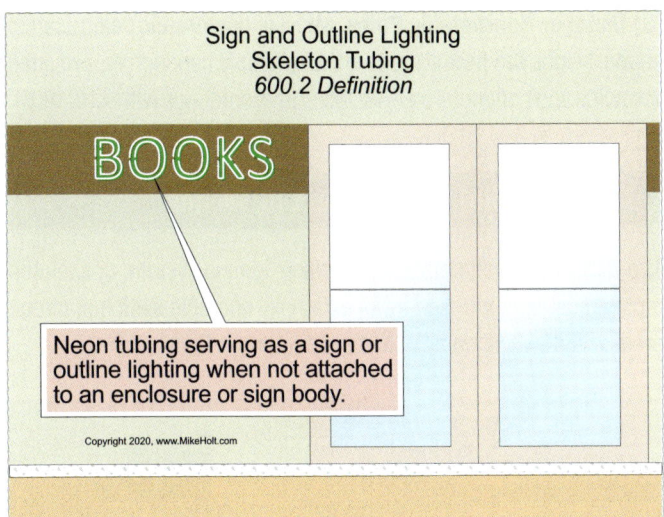
▶Figure 600-5

(A) **Field-Installed Skeleton Tubing.** Field-installed skeleton tubing is not required to be listed.

(B) **Outline Lighting.** Field-installed outline lighting is not required to be listed if it consists of listed luminaires wired in accordance with Chapter 3.

600.4 Markings

(A) **Signs and Outline Lighting Systems.** Signs and outline lighting systems must be listed, labeled, and marked with the manufacturer's name, trademark, voltage and current ratings, or other means of identification.

(B) **Signs with a Retrofitted Illumination System.** Signs with a retrofitted illumination system must contain the following:

(1) The sign must be marked that the illumination system has been replaced.

(2) The marking must include the kit provider's and installer's name, logo, or unique identifier.

(3) Signs equipped with tubular light-emitting diode lamps powered by the existing sign sockets must have an additional warning label(s) alerting personnel during relamping that the sign has been modified and that fluorescent lamps are not to be used.

(D) **Marking Visibility.** The markings required in 600.4(A) and listing labels must be visible after installation and be permanently applied in a location visible prior to servicing. The marking is permitted to be installed in a location not viewed by the public.

(E) **Durability.** Marking must be permanent, durable, and weatherproof when in a wet location.

600.5 Branch Circuits

(A) **Required Branch Circuit.** Each commercial building or occupancy accessible to pedestrians must have at least one accessible outlet located at the entrance of each tenant space that is supplied by a dedicated branch circuit rated at least 20A. ▶Figure 600-6

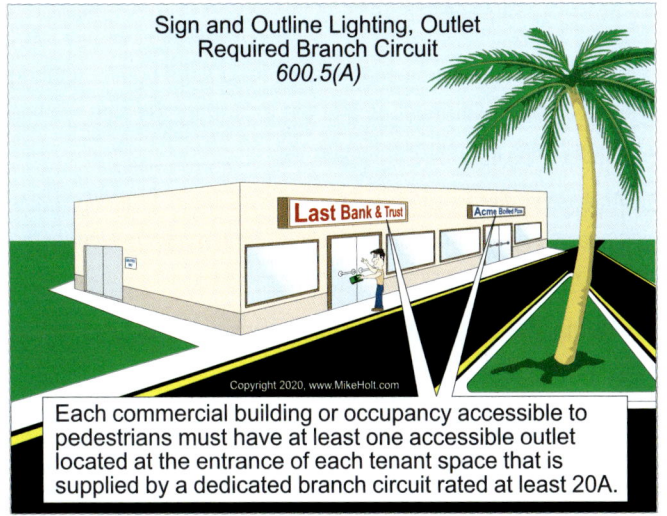
▶Figure 600-6

A sign or outline lighting outlet is not required at entrances for deliveries, service corridors, or service hallways that are intended to be used only by service personnel or employees. ▶Figure 600-7

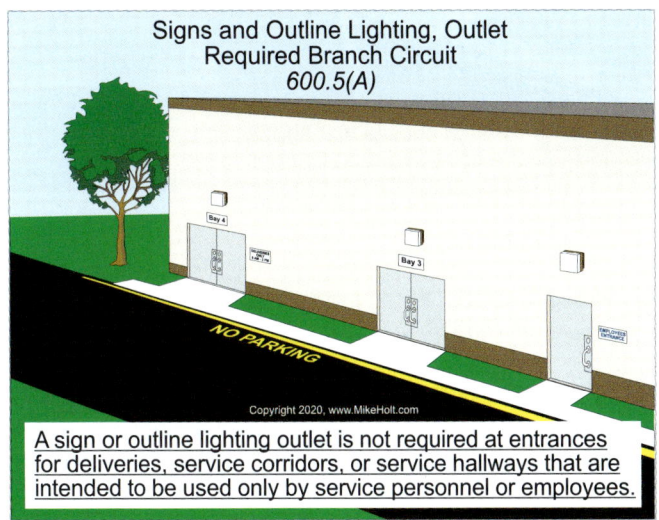
▶Figure 600-7

600.6 | Electric Signs and Outline Lighting

Author's Comment:

▸ Essentially, what this means is that each commercial building and each commercial occupancy accessible to pedestrians requires a minimum of one 20A branch circuit for the sign outlet. This requirement applies whether or not a sign will be installed. If it is supplying a neon sign [600.5(C)(1), that branch circuit can be rated up to 30A.

(B) Marking. A disconnecting means for a sign, outline lighting system, or controller must be marked to identity the sign, outline lighting system, or controller it controls.

Ex: An external disconnecting means that is mounted on the sign body, sign enclosure, sign pole, or controller is not required to identify the sign or outline lighting system it controls.

(C) Rating. Branch circuits that supply signs are considered continuous loads. ▸Figure 600–8

▸Figure 600–8

(D) Wiring Methods. Wiring methods used to supply signs must comply with 600.5(D)(1), (D)(2), and (D)(3).

(1) Supply. The wiring method used to supply signs and outline lighting systems must terminate within a sign, an outline lighting system enclosure, a suitable box, a conduit body, or panelboard.

(2) Enclosures as Pull Boxes. Transformer enclosures are permitted to be used as pull or junction boxes for conductors supplying other adjacent signs, outline lighting systems, or floodlights that are part of a sign, and are permitted to contain both branch- and secondary-circuit conductors, provided the sign disconnecting means de-energizes all current-carrying conductors in these enclosures.

(3) Metal or Nonmetallic Poles. Metal or nonmetallic poles used to support signs are permitted to enclose supply conductors, provided the poles and conductors are installed in accordance with 410.30(B).

600.6 Disconnecting Means

The circuit conductors to a sign, outline lighting system, or skeleton tubing must be controlled by an externally operable switch or circuit breaker that will open all phase conductors. ▸Figure 600–9

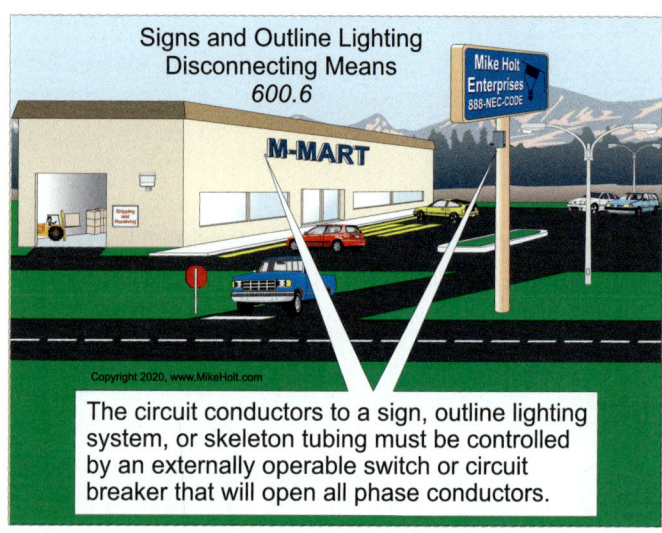

▸Figure 600–9

Note: The location of the disconnect is intended to allow service or maintenance personnel and first responders complete and local control of the disconnect.

Author's Comment:

▸ The disconnect for the sign is permitted to be located next to the sign [404.8(A) Ex 2]. In many cases, the sign disconnect is an integral part of the sign itself or simply field installed and conveniently secured to the outside of the sign.

(A) Disconnect Location. The sign disconnect is permitted to be located as follows:

(1) At the Point of Entry to a Sign. The sign disconnect must be located where the conductors enter a sign enclosure, sign body, or pole. ▸Figure 600–10

Ex 1: A sign disconnect is not required to be located at the point the conductors enter a sign enclosure or sign body for conductors that pass through a sign where not accessible and enclosed in a Chapter 3 raceway or metal-jacketed cable.

Electric Signs and Outline Lighting | 600.6

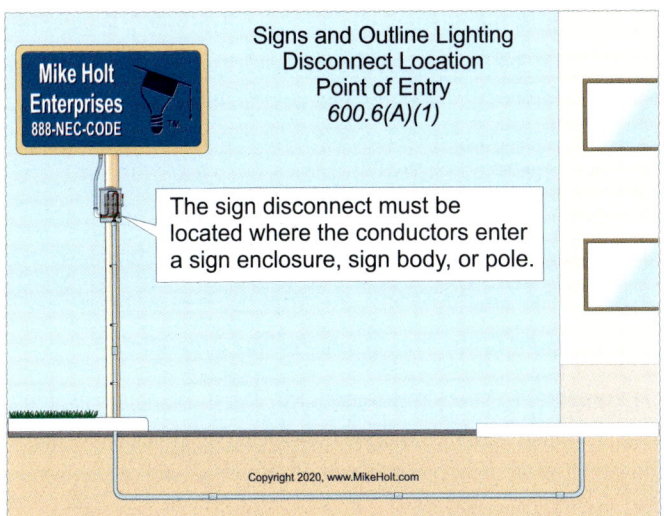
▶Figure 600-10

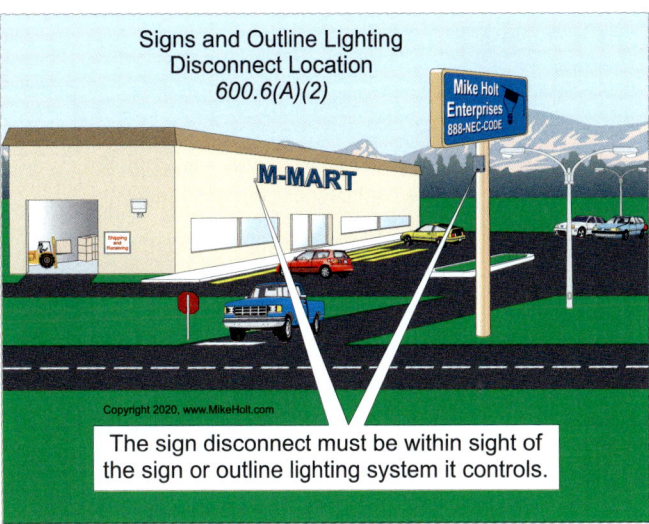
▶Figure 600-11

Ex 2: A sign disconnect is not required to be located at the point the conductors enter a sign enclosure or sign body for a feeder that supplies a panelboard located within the sign under the following conditions: The feeder conductors must be enclosed <u>where not accessible</u> in a Chapter 3 raceway or metal-jacketed cable, a permanent field-applied warning label having sufficient durability to withstand the environment involved, complying with 110.21(B), and visible during servicing is applied to the raceway or metal-clad cable at or near the point of the feeder circuit conductors' entry into the sign enclosure or sign body, and the warning label reads:

DANGER. THIS RACEWAY CONTAINS ENERGIZED CONDUCTORS

The warning label must identify the location of the sign disconnect and it must be capable of being locked in the open position with provisions for locking to remain in place whether the lock is installed or not [110.25].

(2) Within Sight of the Sign. The sign disconnect must be within sight of the sign or outline lighting system it controls. ▶Figure 600-11

If the sign disconnect is not within sight of the sign or outline lighting, the disconnect must be capable of being locked in the open position with provisions for locking to remain in place whether the lock is installed or not [110.25]. A permanent field-applied warning label, having sufficient durability to withstand the environment involved and complying with 110.21(B) that identifies the location of the sign disconnect, must be located on the sign where it will be visible during servicing. ▶Figure 600-12

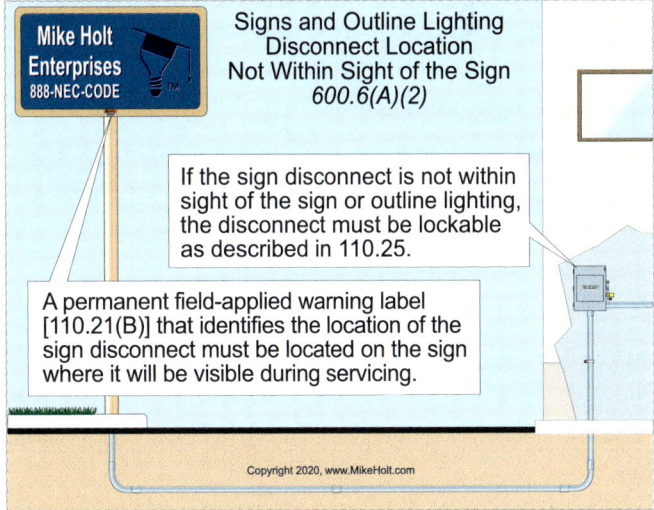
▶Figure 600-12

Author's Comment:

▸ According to Article 100, "Within Sight" means that it is visible and not more than 50 ft from the location of the equipment.

(3) Controller Disconnect as Sign Disconnect. Signs or outline lighting systems operated by controllers located external to the sign or outline lighting system must have a disconnect for the sign controller in accordance with the following:

(1) The controller disconnect must be located within sight of or within the controller enclosure.

(2) The controller disconnect must disconnect the sign or outline lighting and the controller from all phase conductors. ▶Figure 600-13

600.7 | Electric Signs and Outline Lighting

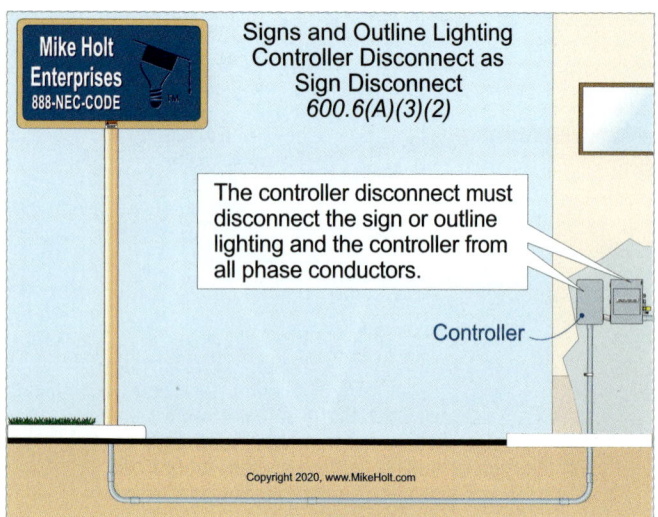
▶Figure 600-13

(3) The controller disconnect must be capable of being locked in the open position with provisions for locking to remain in place whether the lock is installed or not [110.25].

Ex: Where the controller disconnect is not within sight of the controller, a permanent field-applied warning label, having sufficient durability to withstand the environment involved and in accordance with 110.21(B) that identifies the location of the sign disconnect, must be located on the sign where it can be visible during servicing.

(4) Remote Location. The disconnecting means, if located remote from the sign, sign body, or pole, must be mounted at an accessible location available to first responders and service personnel. ▶Figure 600-14

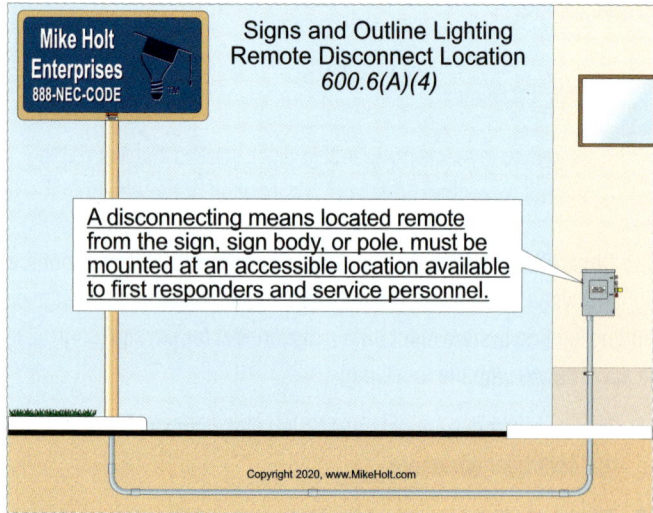
▶Figure 600-14

The location of the disconnect must be marked with a label at the sign location and marked as the disconnect for the sign or outline lighting system. The label must be permanent, field-applied, have sufficient durability to withstand the environment involved, and be in accordance with 110.21(B).

600.7 Grounding and Bonding

(A) Equipment Grounding Conductor and Grounding.

(1) Equipment Grounding Conductor. Metal equipment of signs, outline lighting systems, and skeleton tubing must be connected to the circuit equipment grounding conductor of a type recognized in 250.118. ▶Figure 600-15

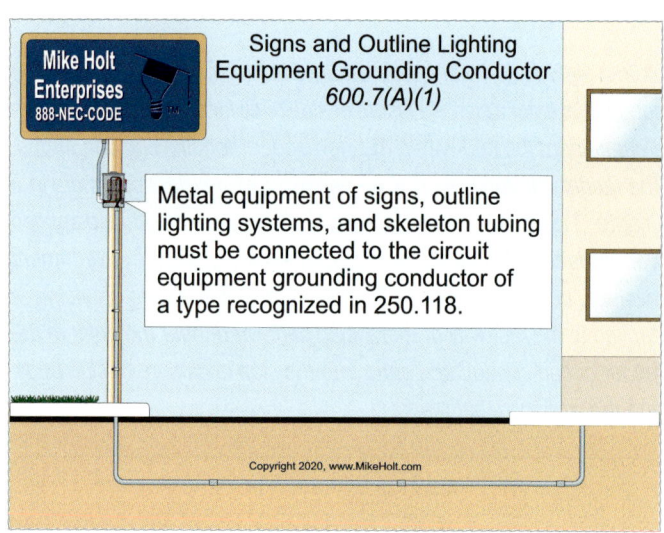
▶Figure 600-15

(2) Size of Equipment Grounding Conductor. If the equipment grounding conductor is of the wire type, it must be sized in accordance with 250.122.

(3) Connections. Equipment grounding conductor connections must be made in accordance with 250.130 in a method specified in 250.8.

> **Author's Comment:**
>
> ▸ According to 250.8, equipment grounding conductors of the wire type must terminate in any of the following methods:
>
> (1) Listed pressure connectors
>
> (2) Terminal bars
>
> (3) Pressure connectors listed for grounding and bonding
>
> (4) Exothermic welding

(5) Machine screws that engage at least two threads or are secured with a nut

(6) Self-tapping machine screws that engage at least two threads

(7) Connections that are part of a listed assembly

(8) Other listed means

(4) Auxiliary Grounding Electrode. Auxiliary grounding electrodes are not required for signs and outline lighting, but if installed, they must comply with 250.54. ▶Figure 600–16

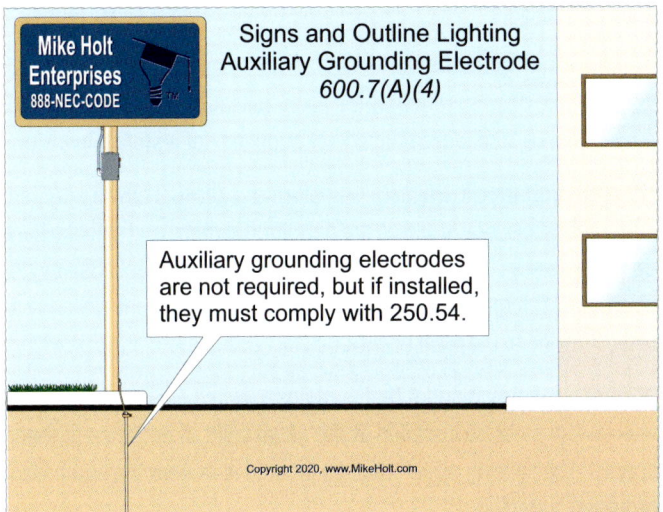

▶Figure 600–16

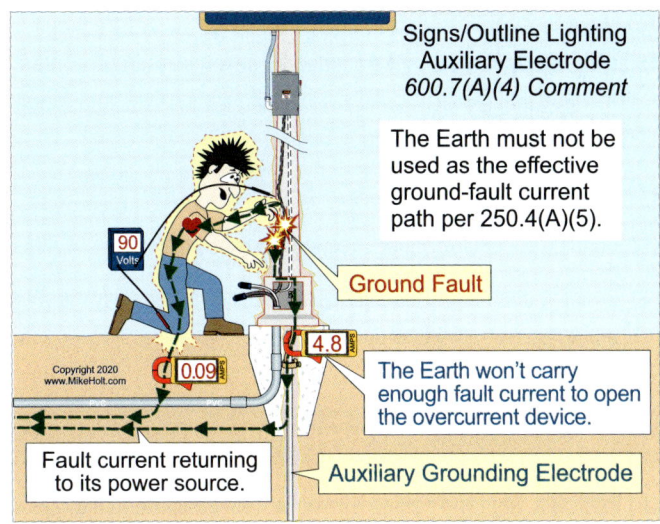

▶Figure 600–17

(B) Bonding.

(1) Metal Parts. Metal parts of signs and outline lighting systems must be bonded to the transformer or power-supply equipment grounding conductor.

Ex: The metal parts of a section sign or outline lighting system supplied by a remote Class 2 power supply are not required to be connected to an equipment grounding conductor.

(2) Bonding Connections. Bonding connections must be made in accordance with 250.8.

Author's Comment:

▶ According to 250.54, auxiliary electrodes need not be bonded to the building grounding electrode system, the grounding conductor to the electrode need not be sized in accordance with 250.66, and the contact resistance of the electrode to the Earth is not required to comply with the 25-ohm requirement of 250.53(A)(2) Ex.

▶ The Earth must not be used as the effective ground-fault current path required by 250.4(A)(4) and 250.4(A)(5). This is because the contact resistance of a grounding electrode to the Earth is high, and very little ground-fault current returns to the electrical supply source via the Earth. The result is the circuit overcurrent protective device will not open and clear a ground fault; therefore, metal parts will remain energized with dangerous step and touch voltage. ▶Figure 600–17

Author's Comment:

▶ According to 250.8, bonding conductors must terminate in any of the following methods:

(1) Listed pressure connectors

(2) Terminal bars

(3) Pressure connectors listed for grounding and bonding

(4) Exothermic welding

(5) Machine screws that engage at least two threads or are secured with a nut

(6) Self-tapping machine screws that engage at least two threads

(7) Connections that are part of a listed assembly

(8) Other listed means

(4) Flexible Metal Conduit Length. Listed flexible metal conduit or listed liquidtight flexible metal conduit for secondary circuit conductors for neon tubing can be used as a bonding means if the total length of the conduit does not exceed 100 ft.

(7) Bonding Conductors.

(1) Bonding conductors must be copper and not smaller than 14 AWG.

(2) Bonding conductors installed outside a sign or raceway must be protected from physical damage.

600.9 Location

(A) Vehicles. Sign and outline lighting system equipment must be at least 14 ft above areas accessible to vehicles unless protected from physical damage. ▶Figure 600-18

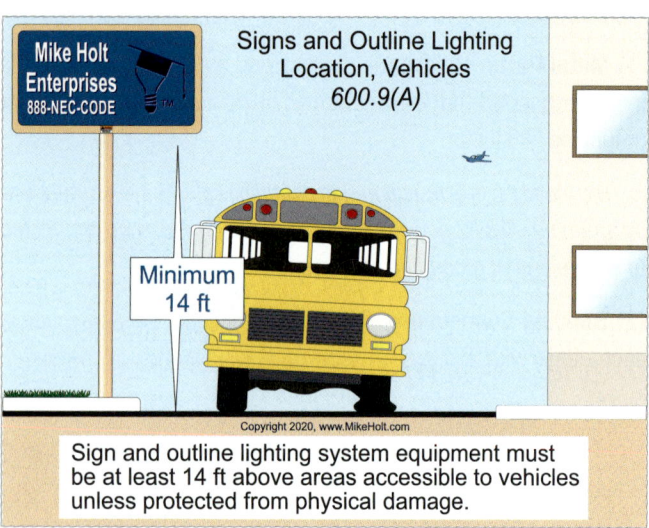

▶Figure 600-18

(B) Pedestrians. Neon tubing used for signs, decorative elements, skeleton tubing, or art forms must be protected from physical damage where readily accessible to pedestrians.

(C) Adjacent to Combustible Materials. Signs and outline lighting systems must be installed so that adjacent combustible materials are not subjected to temperatures that exceed 194°F.

(D) Wet Location. Signs and outline lighting systems installed in wet locations must be weatherproof and must have drain holes.

600.21 Ballasts, Transformers, Class 2 Power Sources, and Electronic Power Supplies

Ballasts, transformers, electronic power supplies, and Class 2 power sources must be self-contained or enclosed in a listed sign body or listed separate enclosure.

(A) Accessibility. Ballasts, transformers, Class 2 power sources, and electronic power supplies must be securely fastened in place.

(B) Location. The secondary conductors from ballasts, transformers, Class 2 power sources, and electronic power supplies must be as short as possible.

(D) Working Space. A working space not less than 3 ft high by 3 ft wide by 3 ft deep is required for each ballast, transformer, Class 2 power source, and electronic power supply if not installed in a sign.

(E) Attic Locations. Ballasts, transformers, Class 2 power sources, and electronic power supplies are permitted in attics and soffits where an access door (36 in. by 22.50 in. minimum) and a passageway not less than 3 ft high by 2 ft wide with a suitable permanent walkway at least 1 ft wide to the point of entrance for each component is provided.

At least one lighting outlet that contains a switch or is controlled by a wall switch must be installed at the usual point of entrance to these spaces. The lighting outlet must be located at or near the equipment requiring servicing.

(F) Suspended Ceilings. Ballasts, transformers, electronic power supplies, and Class 2 power sources can be located above a suspended ceiling, provided the enclosures are securely fastened in place and not connected to the suspended-ceiling grid for support.

Ballasts, transformers, and electronic power supplies installed above a suspended ceiling are not permitted to be connected to the branch-circuit wiring by a flexible cord. ▶Figure 600-19

600.24 Class 2 Power Sources

(A) Listing. Class 2 power supplies and power sources must be listed for use with electric signs and outline lighting systems or be a component in a listed sign.

(B) Grounding. Metal parts of Class 2 power sources must be connected to the circuit equipment grounding conductor supplying the power source.

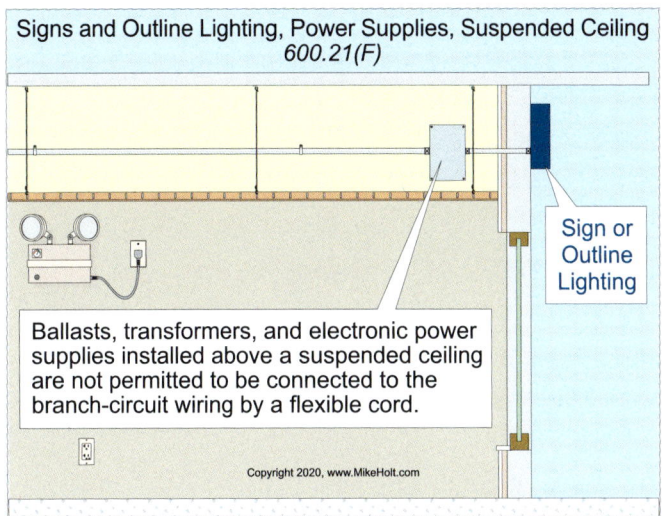

▶Figure 600–19

(C) **Flexible Cords.** Flexible cords must comply with Article 400, be identified as extra-hard usage, rated for outdoor use, and be water and sunlight resistant.

(D) **Grounding.** PV signs must be grounded in accordance with Article 690, Part V and 600.7.

(E) **Disconnecting Means.** The PV system disconnect must comply with Article 690, Part III and 600.6.

600.35 Retrofit Kits

(A) **General.** A general-use or sign-specific retrofit kit for a sign or outline lighting system must include installation instructions and requirements for field conversion of a host sign. The retrofit kit must be listed and labeled.

(B) **Installation.** The retrofit kit must be installed in accordance with the installation instructions.

(1) **Wiring Methods.** Wiring methods must be in accordance with Chapter 3.

Ex: If powered from a Class 2 source, wiring methods must be in accordance with 600.12(C)(1)(2) and (C) (2), 600.24, and 600.33.

(2) **Damaged Parts.** All parts not replaced by a retrofit kit must be inspected for damage. Any part found to be damaged or damaged during conversion of the sign must be replaced or repaired to maintain the sign or outline lighting system's dry, damp, or wet location rating.

(3) **Workmanship.** Field conversion workmanship must be in accordance with 110.12.

(4) **Marking.** The retrofitted sign must be marked in accordance with 600.4(B).

Part II. Field-Installed Skeleton Tubing, Outline Lightning, and Secondary Wiring

600.34 Photovoltaic (PV) Powered Sign

Field wiring of PV installations must be in accordance with Article 690, sign installation instructions, and the following:

(A) **Equipment.** PV components intended for use in PV powered sign systems must be listed for PV use.

(B) **Wiring.** Wiring external to the PV sign body must be:

(1) Listed, labeled, and suitable for photovoltaic applications.

(2) Routed to closely follow the sign body or enclosure.

(3) As short as possible and secured at intervals not exceeding 3 ft.

(4) Protected where subject to physical damage.

Notes

ARTICLE 604 — MANUFACTURED WIRING SYSTEMS

Introduction to Article 604—Manufactured Wiring Systems

Article 604 applies to field-installed manufactured wiring systems. These come with manufacturer's instructions, so *Code* compliance is almost automatic if you follow them.

The specific requirements contained in this article are not difficult to understand, but you should be familiar with them before installing manufactured wiring systems or wired partitions.

604.1 Scope

Article 604 applies to field-installed manufactured wiring systems.
▶Figure 604–1

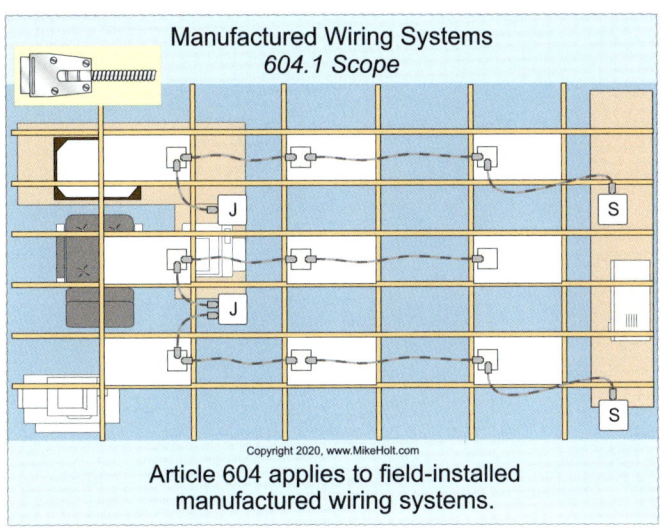
▶Figure 604–1

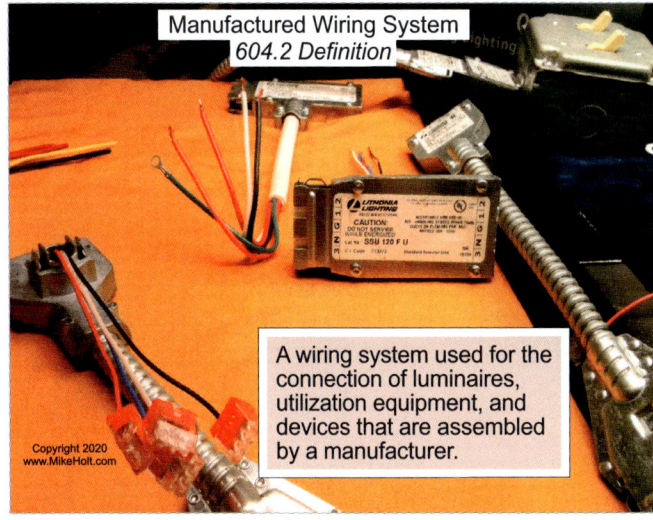
▶Figure 604–2

Author's Comment:

▶ Manufactured wiring systems are typically installed in commercial and institutional occupancies because of their ability to be easily installed and relocated as the need arises.

604.2 Definition

Manufactured Wiring System. A system used for the connection of luminaires, utilization equipment, and devices that are assembled by a manufacturer with components which cannot be inspected at the building site without damage to, or destruction of, the component. ▶Figure 604–2

604.6 Listing Requirements

Manufactured wiring systems and associated components must be listed.

604.7 | Manufactured Wiring Systems

604.7 Installation—Securing and Supporting

Type AC and Type MC cable used for manufactured wiring systems must be secured and supported according to the requirements of Article 320 for Type AC cable and Article 330 for Type MC cable. ▶Figure 604-3

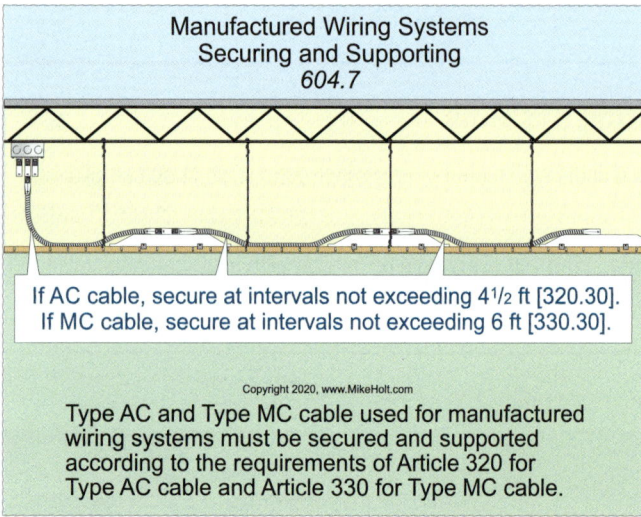

▶Figure 604-3

604.10 Uses Permitted

Manufactured wiring systems can be installed in accessible and dry locations, and in plenum spaces in accordance with 300.22(C). ▶Figure 604-4

▶Figure 604-4

Author's Comment:

▶ Type AC cable must be secured at intervals not exceeding 4½ ft [320.30], and Type MC cable must be secured at intervals not exceeding 6 ft [330.30].

ARTICLE 620 — ELEVATORS, ESCALATORS, AND MOVING WALKS

Introduction to Article 620—Elevators, Escalators, and Moving Walks

Except for dumbwaiters, the equipment covered by Article 620 moves people. Thus, a major concept in this article is that of keeping people separated from electrical power. That is why, for example, 620.3 requires live parts to be enclosed. This article consists of 10 parts:

- **Part I. General.** This part provides the scope of the article, definitions, and voltage limitations.
- **Part II. Conductors.** The single-line diagram of Figure 620.13 in the *NEC* illustrates how the requirements of Part II work together.
- **Part III. Wiring.** This addresses wiring methods and branch-circuit requirements for different equipment.
- **Part IV. Installation of Conductors.** Part IV covers conductor fill, supports, and related items.
- **Part V. Traveling Cables.** Installation, suspension, location, and protection of cables that move with the motion of the elevator or lift are all covered.
- **Part VI. Disconnecting Means and Control.** The requirements vary with the application.
- **Part VII. Overcurrent Protection.** While most of this part refers to Article 430, it does include additional requirements such as providing selective coordination.
- **Part VIII. Machine and Control Rooms and Spaces.** The primary goal here is the prevention of unauthorized access.
- **Part IX. Equipment Grounding Conductor.** While most of this part refers to Article 250, it includes additional requirements as well. For example, 15A and 20A, 125V receptacles in certain locations must be GFCI protected.
- **Part X. Emergency and Standby Systems.** This deals with regenerative power and with the need for a disconnecting means that can disconnect an elevator from both the normal power system and the emergency or standby system.

Part I. General

620.1 Scope

Article 620 contains the requirements for the installation of electrical equipment and wiring in connection with elevators, escalators, and moving walks. ▶Figure 620–1 and ▶Figure 620–2

620.6 GFCI-Protected Receptacles

Receptacles rated 15A and 20A, 125V located in pits, hoistways, on the cars of elevators, and in escalator and moving walk wellways must be of the GFCI type. ▶Figure 620–3

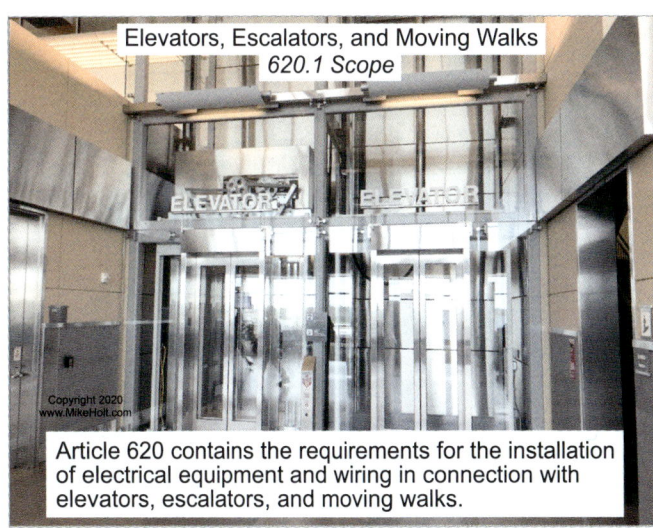

Article 620 contains the requirements for the installation of electrical equipment and wiring in connection with elevators, escalators, and moving walks.

▶Figure 620–1

620.13 | Elevators, Escalators, and Moving Walks

▶Figure 620–2

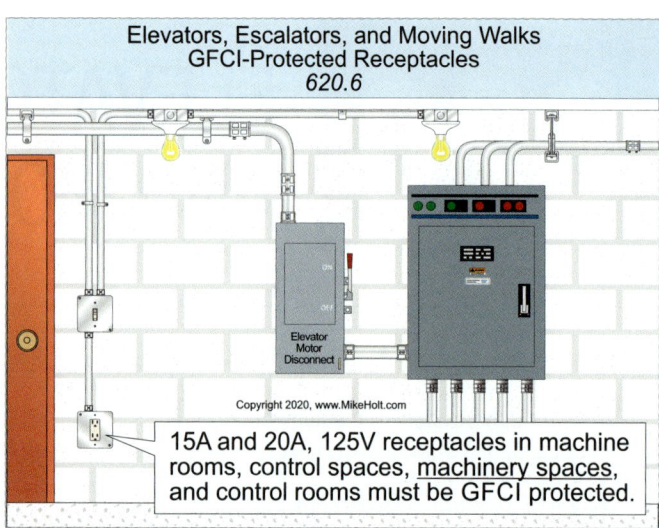
▶Figure 620–4

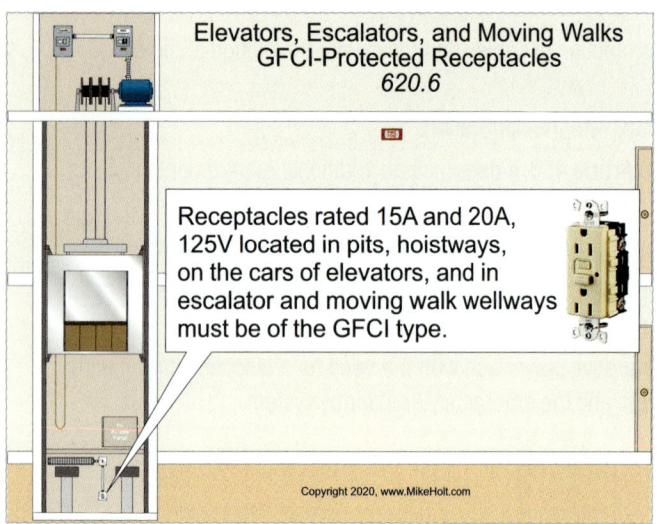
▶Figure 620–3

Receptacles rated 15A and 20A, 125V installed in machine rooms, control spaces, machinery spaces, and control rooms must be GFCI protected. ▶Figure 620–4

A permanently installed sump pump must be hard wired or be supplied by a single receptacle that is GFCI protected.

Part II. Conductors

620.13 Feeder and Branch-Circuit Conductors

(A) Conductor Supplying Single Motor. The ampacity of the branch circuit must not be less than the motor nameplate and 430.22(E).

(D) Conductor Supplying Multiple Motors. The ampacity of the feeder must not be less than the motor nameplate, 430.22(E), 430.24, and demanded by 620.14.

620.16 Short-Circuit Current Rating

(A) Marking. Elevator control panels must be marked with a short-circuit rating to be able to withstand the available fault current at the line terminals [110.10].

Part III. Wiring

620.22 Branch Circuits for Elevator Car(s)

(A) Car Light, Receptacles, Auxiliary Lighting, and Ventilation. A separate branch circuit must supply the car lights. The car lights branch circuit is permitted to supply receptacles, accessory equipment (alarm devices, alarm bells, and monitoring devices not part of the control system), auxiliary lighting power source, and ventilation on each elevator car or inside the operation controller.

Where there is no machine room, control room, machinery space, or control space outside the hoistway, the overcurrent device must be located outside the hoistway and accessible to qualified persons only.

(B) Air-Conditioning and Heating Source. Air-conditioning and heating units must be supplied by a separate branch circuit for each car.

Author's Comment:

▸ While the air-conditioning and heating must be served by an individual circuit for each elevator car, the branch circuit for the elevator car lights is permitted to serve more than one elevator car. Branch-circuit overcurrent protective devices for elevator cars must be located in the elevator machine room.

620.23 Branch Circuits for Machine Room/Machinery Space

(A) Separate Branch Circuits. The branch circuit(s) supplying lighting for machine rooms, control rooms, machinery spaces, and control spaces must be on a circuit separate from the one supplying receptacles. These circuits may not supply any other load(s). ▸Figure 620-5

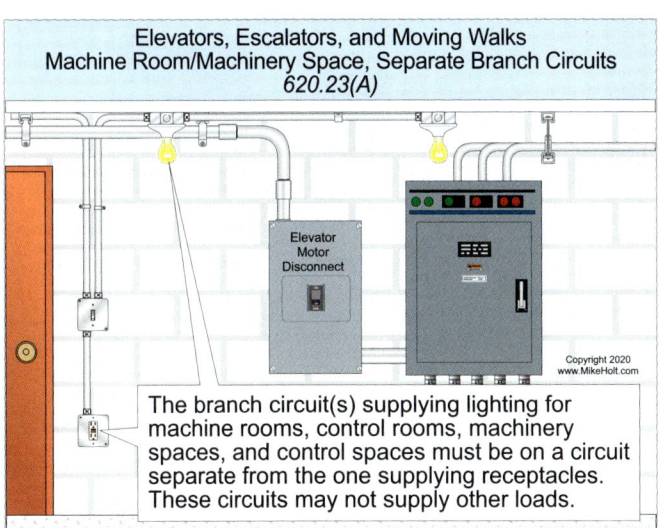
▸Figure 620-5

The required lighting in these spaces is not permitted to be connected to the load side of a GFCI.

(B) Light Switch. The switch for machine rooms, control rooms, and machinery space or control space lighting must be located at the point of entry for these areas.

(C) Duplex Receptacle. At least one 125V, single-phase, 15A or 20A duplex receptacle must be installed in each machine room or control room, and machinery space or control space [620.6]. ▸Figure 620-6

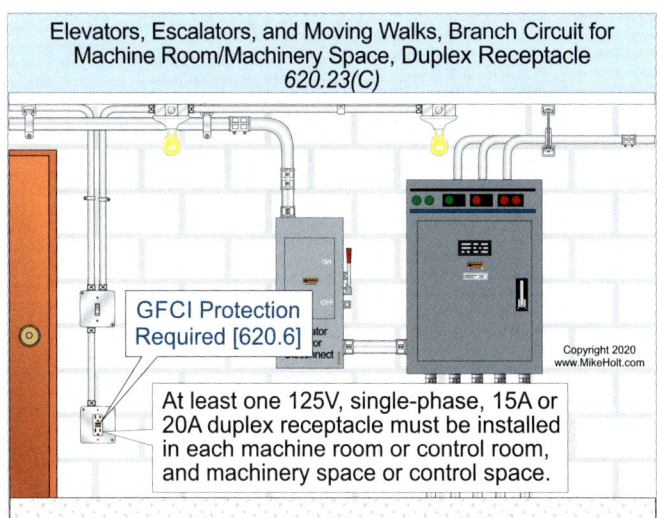
▸Figure 620-6

620.24 Branch Circuit for Hoistway Pit Lighting and Receptacles

(A) Separate Branch Circuits. Separate branch circuits must supply the hoistway pit lighting and receptacle(s), and the required lighting is not permitted to be connected to the load side of a GFCI [620.85].

(B) Light Switch. The switch for hoistway pit lighting must be readily accessible from the pit access door. ▸Figure 620-7

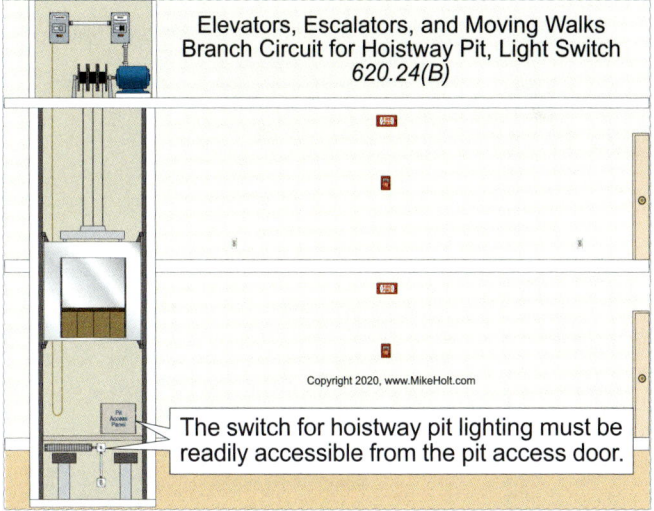
▸Figure 620-7

(C) Duplex Receptacle. At least one 15A or 20A, 125V duplex GFCI receptacle must be installed in a hoistway pit [620.6]. ▸Figure 620-8

Note 2: See 620.6 for GFCI requirements.

620.37 | Elevators, Escalators, and Moving Walks

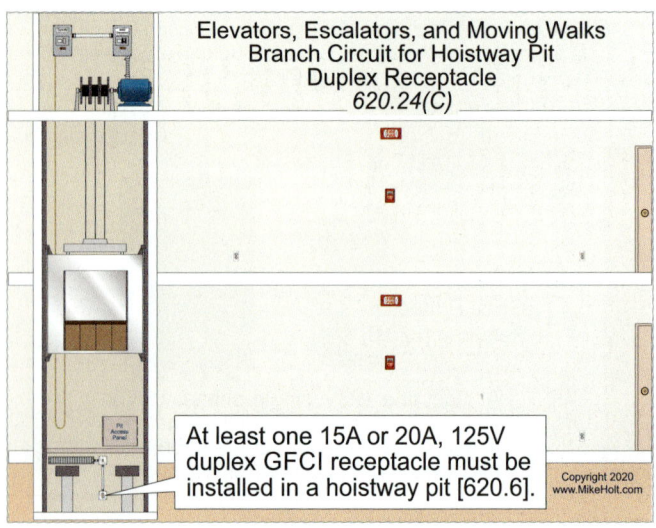
▶Figure 620–8

Part IV. Installation of Conductors

620.37 Wiring in Elevator Hoistways, Control, and Machine Rooms/Spaces

(A) Uses Permitted. Only wiring, raceways, and cables including communications, fire detection, power, lighting, heating, ventilating, and air-conditioning associated with the elevator are permitted inside the elevator hoistway, machine room, or control room. ▶Figure 620–9

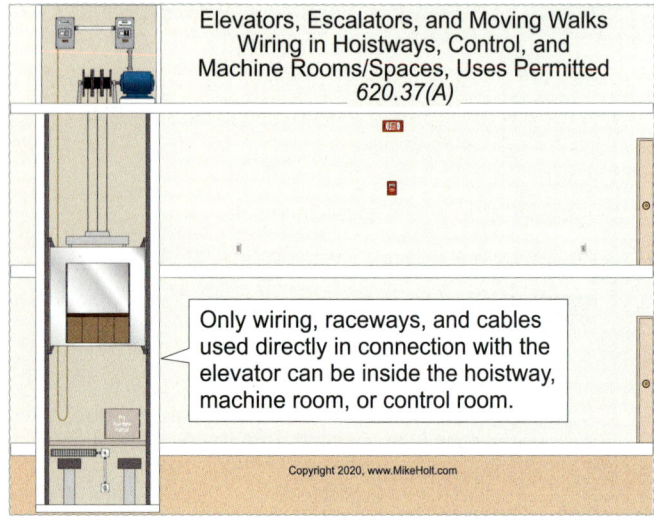
▶Figure 620–9

Part VI. Disconnecting Means and Control

620.51 Disconnecting Means

A disconnect that opens all phase conductors must be provided for each elevator, escalator, or moving walk. The disconnect for the main power supply conductors is not permitted to disconnect power to the branch circuits required in 620.22, 620.23, and 620.24.

(A) Type. The disconnect must be listed and be an enclosed externally operable fused motor-circuit switch or circuit breaker that is lockable only in the open position with provisions for locking to remain in place whether the lock is installed or not [110.25]. ▶Figure 620–10

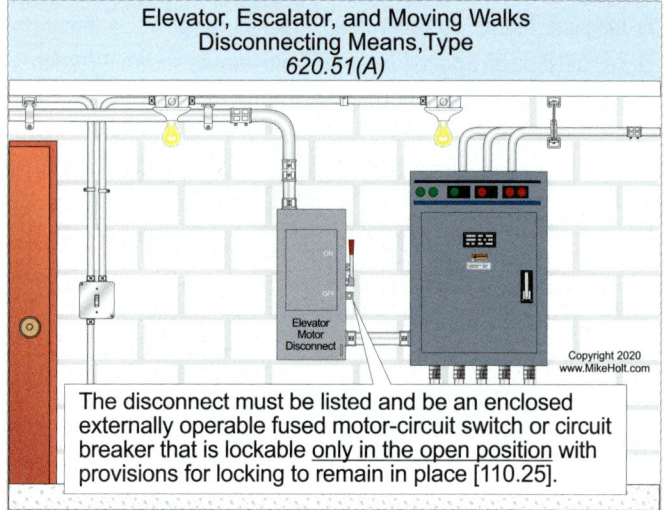
▶Figure 620–10

Note: See ASME A17.1/CSA B44, *Safety Code for Elevators and Escalators*, for additional information for the disconnect.

(C) Location. The disconnect must be readily accessible to qualified persons.

> **Author's Comment:**
> ▸ With advancements in technology, and in an effort to save space, many elevators without machine rooms are being installed. The disconnect is located on the elevator itself and is considered readily accessible to qualified persons.

(D) Identification and Signs.

(2) Available Fault Current Marking. Elevator control panels must be marked with the available fault current at the line terminal.

(E) Surge Protection. Where the disconnecting means is designated as part of an emergency or standby system, surge protection must be provided.

ARTICLE 625 — ELECTRIC VEHICLE POWER TRANSFER SYSTEM

Introduction to Article 625—Electric Vehicle Power Transfer System

Electric vehicles have been around for a long time. Anyone who has worked in a factory or warehouse, or visited a big box store, has probably encountered an electric lift truck. And, of course, we are all familiar with golf carts. These and other off-road vehicles have charging requirements that are easily accommodated by small charging systems.

But today, a new challenge has emerged and is becoming increasingly common. That challenge is the electrically powered passenger vehicle, bus, truck, and motorcycle. Such vehicles, especially an electric car or bus, can weigh considerably more than a golf cart and just moving one takes a proportionately larger motor. In fact, many designs use multiple drive motors.

Those motors are powered by batteries. Adding to the battery sizing requirement are other demands. For example, these vehicles:

- Must be able to travel at highway speeds over distances roughly comparable to those traveled by their internal combustion engine counterparts.
- Have powered accessories that you typically will not find on a golf cart, such as air conditioning, electric windows, stereo systems, windshield wipers, security systems, and window defrosters.
- Are expected to start in summer heat and in brutal winter cold.

The battery system for an electrically powered passenger vehicle is therefore considerably larger than that for a golf cart or other typical off-road electric vehicle. Consequently, the charging system must have the capability of delivering far more power than the one for a typical off-road electric vehicle.

An electrically powered passenger vehicle needs a dedicated charging circuit. Article 625 defines the requirements for the installation of the electrical equipment needed to charge automotive-type electric and hybrid vehicles including cars, motorcycles, and buses.

This article consists of three parts:

- **Part I. General.** This includes the scope of the article, definitions, voltages, and listing/labeling requirements.
- **Part II. Equipment Construction.** Most of this applies to the manufacturer, but there are a few requirements you need to know.
- **Part III. Installation.** This part covers overcurrent protection and the disconnect in addition to the different requirements for indoor and outdoor locations.

Part I. General

625.1 Scope

Article 625 covers the installation of conductors and equipment connecting an electric vehicle to premises wiring for the purposes of charging, power export, or bidirectional current flow. ▶Figure 625–1

625.2 Definitions

The following definitions only apply within this article.

Electric Vehicle Power Export Equipment (EVPE). The equipment, including the outlet on the vehicle, that is used to provide electrical power at voltages greater than 30V ac or 60V dc to loads external to the vehicle as the source of supply.

625.5 | Electric Vehicle Power Transfer System

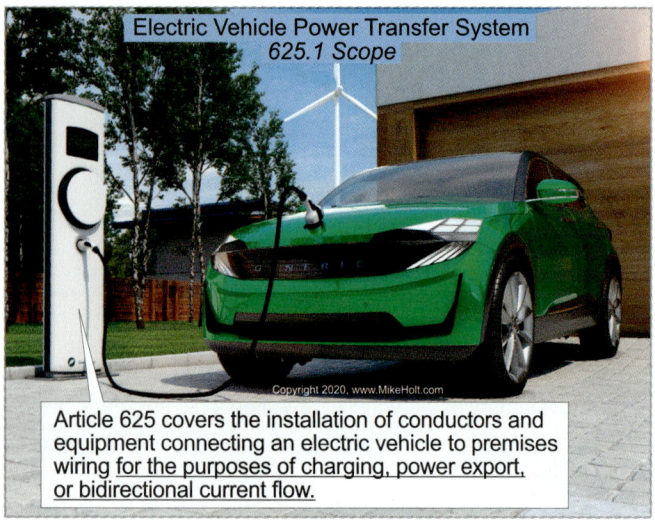

▶Figure 625-1

Note: Electric vehicle power export equipment and electric vehicle supply equipment are sometimes contained in one piece of equipment, referred to as a "bidirectional EVSE."

Electric Vehicle Supply Equipment (EVSE). Conductors, electric vehicle connectors, attachment plugs, personnel protection system, devices, and power outlets installed for the purpose of transferring energy between the premises wiring and the electric vehicle. ▶Figure 625-2

▶Figure 625-2

Note: Electric vehicle power export equipment and electric vehicle supply equipment are sometimes contained in one piece of equipment, sometimes referred to as a "bidirectional EVSE."

Wireless Power Transfer Equipment (WPTE). Equipment consisting of a charger power converter and a primary pad. The two devices are either separate units or they are contained within a single enclosure. ▶Figure 625-3

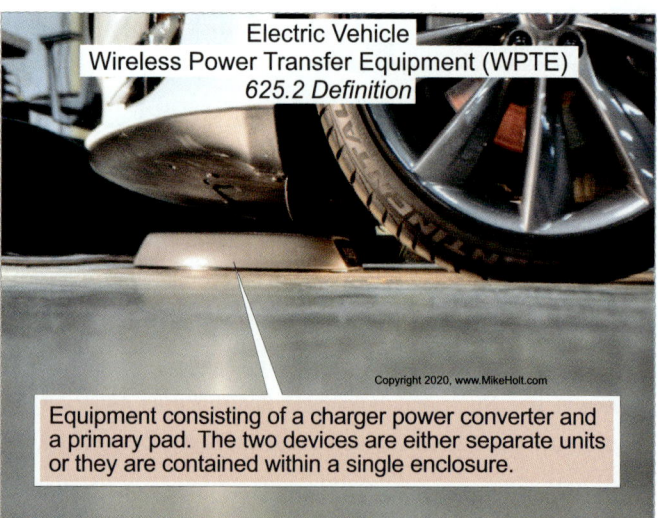

▶Figure 625-3

625.5 Listed

All electric vehicle power transfer equipment covered by this article must be listed.

Part III. Installation

625.40 Electric Vehicle Branch Circuit

Each outlet for electric vehicle supply equipment must be supplied by a dedicated branch circuit that serves no other outlets.

625.41 Overcurrent Protection

Overcurrent protection for circuits supplying electric vehicle supply equipment (EVSE), including bidirectional EVSE and wireless equipment (WPTE), must be sized no less than 125 percent of the maximum load of the electric vehicle supply equipment. ▶Figure 625-4

Author's Comment:

▶ Since the charging load for electric vehicle supply equipment is required to be sized no less than 125 percent of the load, then the conductors must be sized to be protected by the circuit overcurrent protective device in accordance with 240.4, including 110.14(C)(1) considerations, as well as 310.16.

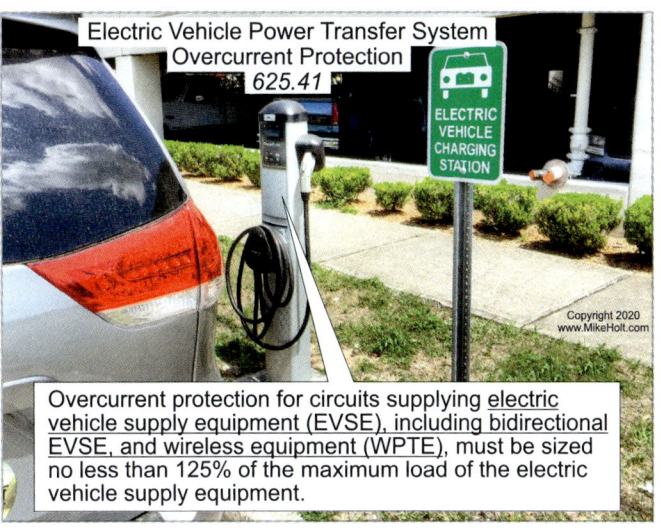
▶Figure 625-4

625.43 Disconnecting Means

Electric vehicle equipment rated more than 60A or over 150V to ground, must have a readily accessible disconnect that is capable of being locked in the open position with provisions for locking to remain in place whether the lock is installed or not [110.25].

625.48 Interactive Systems

Electric vehicle supply equipment (EVSE) that incorporates a power export function and is part of an interactive system that serves as an optional standby system, an electric power production source, or a bidirectional power feed must be listed and marked as suitable for that purpose. When used as an optional standby system, the requirements of Article 702 apply; when used as an electric power production source, the requirements of Article 705 apply.

Electric vehicle power export equipment (EVPE) that consists of a receptacle outlet only must be in accordance with 625.60.

Author's Comment:

▶ As an example of how technology has affected what falls within the scope of the *Code*, installations used to export electric power from vehicles to premises wiring or for bidirectional current flow are now covered [90.2].

625.50 Location

Electric vehicle supply equipment (EVSE) must be located to permit direct electrical coupling of the electric vehicle connector to the electric vehicle. ▶Figure 625-5

Unless specifically listed and marked otherwise, the coupling means of the electric vehicle supply equipment (EVSE) must be located at a height of not less than 18 in. above the floor level for indoor locations, and not less than 24 in. above grade level for outdoor locations.

625.52 Ventilation

The ventilation requirement for charging an electric vehicle in an indoor enclosed space is determined by any of the following:

(A) Ventilation Not Required. Mechanical ventilation is not required where the electric vehicle supply equipment is listed for charging electric vehicles indoors without ventilation.

625.42 Rating

The power transfer equipment must have sufficient rating to supply the load served. Electric vehicle charging loads are considered to be continuous loads for the purposes of this article. Services and feeders must be sized in accordance with the product ratings. Where an automatic load management system is used, the maximum equipment load on a service and feeder is the maximum load permitted by the automatic load management system.

Adjustable settings are allowed only on fixed-in-place equipment. If adjustments have an impact on the rating label, those changes must be in accordance with manufacturer's instructions, and the adjusted rating must appear with sufficient durability to withstand the environment involved on the rating label.

Electric vehicle supply equipment with restricted access to an ampere adjusting means is permitted to have an ampere rating(s) that is equal to the adjusted current setting. Sizing the service and feeder to match the adjusting means is allowed.

Restricted access must prevent the user from gaining access to the adjusting means. Restricted access must be accomplished by at least one of the following:

(1) A cover or door that requires the use of a tool to open.

(2) Locked doors accessible only to qualified personnel.

(3) Password protected commissioning software accessible only to qualified personnel.

625.54 | Electric Vehicle Power Transfer System

▶Figure 625–5

Author's Comment:

▸ GFCI breakers or receptacles typically used in dwelling units are not suitable for back feeding. That would prohibit their use for a bidirectional EVSE. This GFCI requirement only applies to cord-and-plug-connected EVSE, making hard wired EVSE the only type suitable for bidirectional use.

625.60 Alternating-Current Electric Vehicle Power Export (EVPE) Receptacles

Alternating-current receptacles installed in electric vehicles and intended to allow for connection of off-board utilization equipment must comply with:

(A) Type. The receptacle must be listed.

(B) Rating. The receptacle outlet must be rated a maximum of 50A, 250V, single-phase.

(C) Overcurrent Protection. The overcurrent protection must be integral to the power export system.

(D) GFCI Protection for Personnel. Ground-fault protection for personnel must be provided for all receptacles. The GFCI reset and indication must be in a readily accessible location.

Note: There are various methods available to achieve GFCI protection.

(B) Ventilation Required. Mechanical ventilation is required where the electric vehicle supply equipment is listed for charging electric vehicles with ventilation for indoor charging. The ventilation must include both supply and exhaust equipment permanently installed and located to intake and vent directly to the outdoors.

625.54 Ground-Fault Circuit-Interrupter Protection for Personnel

In addition to the GFCI protection requirements contained in 210.8, all receptacles installed for the connection of electric vehicle supply equipment must be GFCI protected. ▶Figure 625–6

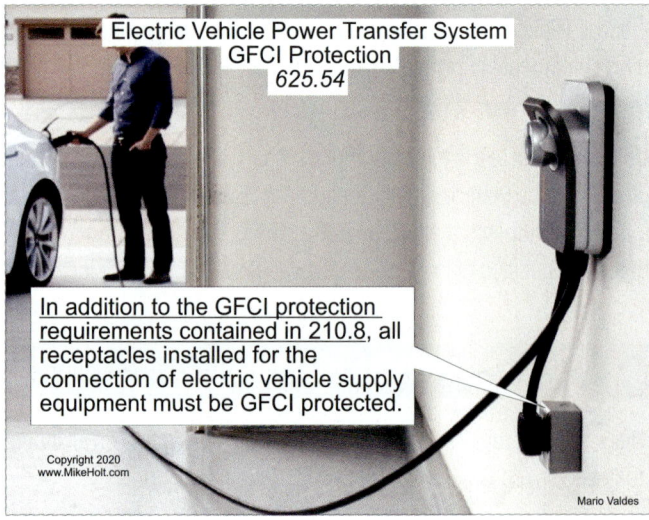

▶Figure 625–6

ARTICLE 630 ELECTRIC WELDERS

Introduction to Article 630—Electric Welders

Electric welding equipment does its job either by creating an electric arc between two surfaces or by heating a rod that melts from overcurrent. Either way results in a hefty momentary current draw. Welding machines come in many shapes and sizes. On the smaller end of the scale are portable welding units used for manual welding, such as in a fabrication shop. At the larger end are robotic welding machines the size of a house used for making everything from automobile bodies to refrigerator panels. All of these must comply with Article 630.

The primary concern of this article is adequately sizing the conductors and circuit protection to handle this type of load. Fortunately for the design engineer and the field electrician, Article 630 requires certain information to be provided on the nameplate of the equipment. This article explains how to use that information to properly size the conductor and circuit protection.

Part I. General

630.1 Scope

Article 630 covers electric arc welding and resistance welding apparatus, plasma cutting, and other similar welding and cutting equipment connected to an electric supply system. ▶Figure 630-1

Article 630 covers electric arc welding, and resistance welding apparatus, plasma cutting, and similar welding and cutting equipment connected to an electric supply system.

▶Figure 630-1

Author's Comment:

▶ There are two basic types of electric welding—arc welding and resistance welding. Arc welding uses a rod that melts when it touches the metal. Resistance welding, also called "spot welding," uses a pair of electrodes that fuse two pieces of metal together when a high current is applied. The resistance of the metal causes it to melt at the spot where the electrodes are placed and makes the weld.

630.6 Listing

Welding equipment must be listed.

Part II. Arc Welders

630.11 Ampacity of Supply Conductors

(A) Individual Arc Welders. The supply conductors for arc welders must have an ampacity of not less than the arc welder nameplate rating. If the nameplate rating is not available, the supply conductors must have an ampacity of not less than the rated primary current multiplied by the factor in Table 630.11(A) based on the duty cycle of the arc welder.

630.11 | Electric Welders

Table 630.11(A) Duty Cycle Multiplication Factors for Arc Welders

Duty Cycle	Multiplier for Arc Welders	
	Nonmotor-Generator	Motor-Generator
100	1.00	1.00
90	0.95	0.96
80	0.89	0.91
70	0.84	0.86
60	0.78	0.81
50	0.71	0.75
40	0.63	0.69
30	0.55	0.62
20 or less	0.45	0.55

Solution:

Demand Load = Primary Rating × Multiplier [Table 630.11(A)]

Demand Load = 30A × 55%

Demand Load = 16.50A

Use 12 AWG rated 20A at 60°C [110.14(C)(1)(a) and Table 310.16].

Answer: (a) 12 AWG

▶ **Individual Nonmotor-Generator Arc Welder Example 2**

Question: *A nonmotor-generator arc welder has a primary current rating of 40A with a duty cycle of 50 percent. What is the minimum size branch-circuit conductor permitted to be used for this welder?* ▶Figure 630–3

(a) 14 AWG   (b) 12 AWG   (c) 10 AWG   (d) 8 AWG

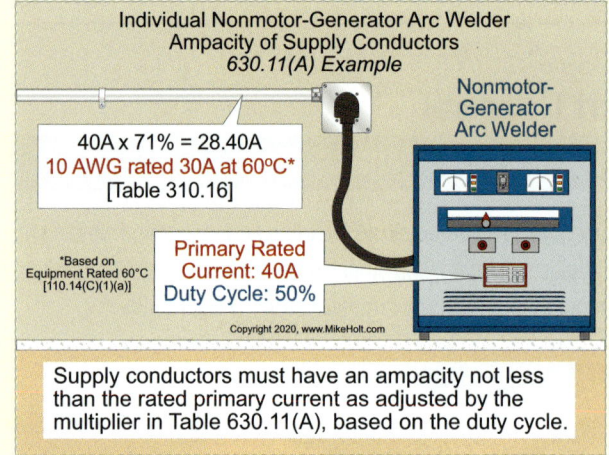

▶Figure 630–3

Solution:

Demand Load = Primary Rating × Multiplier [Table 630.11(A)]

Demand Load = 40A × 71%

Demand Load = 28.40A

Use 10 AWG rated 30A at 60°C [110.14(C)(1)(a) and Table 310.16].

Answer: (c) 10 AWG

▶ **Individual Nonmotor-Generator Arc Welder Example 1**

Question: *A nonmotor-generator arc welder has a primary current rating of 30A with a duty cycle of 30 percent. What is the minimum size branch-circuit conductor permitted to be used for this welder?* ▶Figure 630–2

(a) 12 AWG   (b) 10 AWG   (c) 8 AWG   (d) 6 AWG

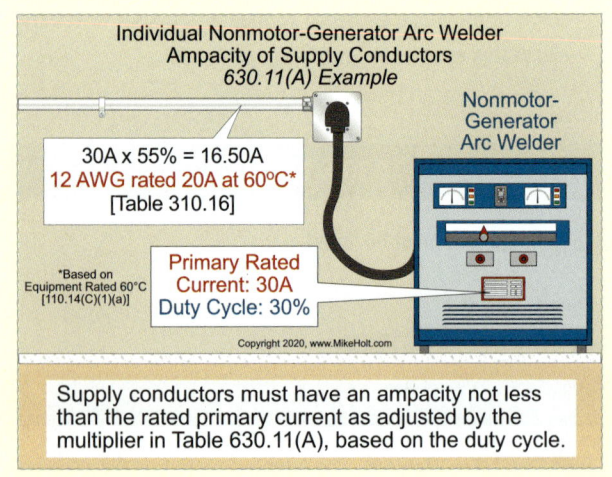

▶Figure 630–2

▶ Individual Motor-Generator Arc Welder Example 1

Question: A motor-generator arc welder has a primary current rating of 30A with a duty cycle of 30 percent. What is the minimum size branch-circuit conductor permitted to be used for this welder? ▶Figure 630–4

(a) 12 AWG (b) 10 AWG (c) 8 AWG (d) 6 AWG

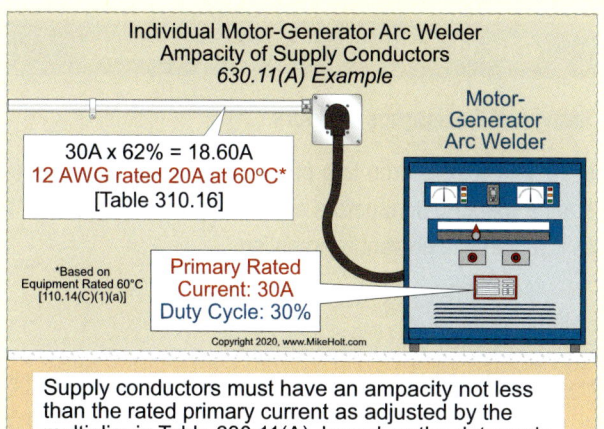

▶Figure 630–4

Solution:

Demand Load = Primary Rating × Multiplier [Table 630.11(A)]

Demand Load = 30A × 62%

Demand Load = 18.60A

Use 12 AWG rated 20A at 60°C [110.14(C)(1)(a) and Table 310.16].

Answer: (a) 12 AWG

▶ Individual Motor-Generator Arc Welder Example 2

Question: A motor-generator arc welder has a primary current rating of 40A with a duty cycle of 50 percent. What is the minimum size branch-circuit conductor permitted to be used for this welder? ▶Figure 630–5

(a) 14 AWG (b) 12 AWG (c) 10 AWG (d) 8 AWG

Solution:

Demand Load = Primary Rating × Multiplier [Table 630.11(A)]

Demand Load = 40A × 75%

Demand Load = 30A

Use 10 AWG rated 30A at 60°C [110.14(C)(1)(a) and Table 310.16].

Answer: (c) 10 AWG

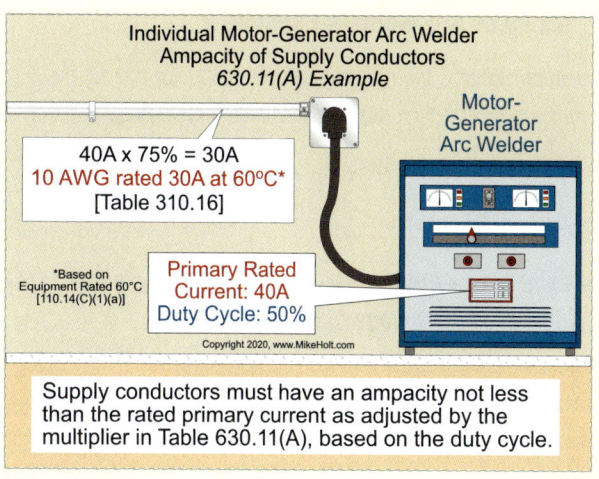

▶Figure 630–5

(B) Group of Welders. Feeder conductors that supply a group of arc welders must have a minimum ampacity of not less than the sum of the currents as determined in 630.11(A) based on 100 percent of the two largest arc welders, 85 percent for the third largest arc welder, 70 percent for the fourth largest arc welder, and 60 percent for all remaining arc welders.

Author's Comment:

▸ This calculation method provides an ample margin of safety under high-production conditions.

▶ Group of Arc Welders Example 1

Question: What is the minimum feeder conductor size for five 30A nonmotor-generator arc welders with a duty cycle of 30 percent?

(a) 4 AWG (b) 1 AWG (c) 1/0 AWG (d) 2/0 AWG

Solution:

Demand Load = Primary Rating × Multiplier [Table 630.11(A)] × Arc Welder Percentage [630.11(B)]

Welder 1	30A × 55% = 16.50A × 100%	16.50A
Welder 2	30A × 55% = 16.50A × 100%	16.50A
Welder 3	30A × 55% = 16.50A × 85%	14.03A
Welder 4	30A × 55% = 16.50A × 70%	11.55A
Welder 5	30A × 55% = 16.50A × 60%	+ 9.90A
Total Demand Load		68.61A

Minimum Conductor Size = 4 AWG rated 70A at 60°C [110.14(C)(1)(a) and Table 310.16]

Answer: (a) 4 AWG

630.12 | Electric Welders

▶ Group of Arc Welders Example 2

Question: What is the minimum feeder conductor size for five 50A nonmotor-generator arc welders with a duty cycle of 50 percent?

(a) 4 AWG (b) 3 AWG (c) 1/0 AWG (d) 2/0 AWG

Solution:

Demand Load = Primary Rating × Multiplier [Table 630.11(A)] × Arc Welder Percentage [630.11(B)]

Welder 1	50A × 71% = 35.50A × 100%	35.50A
Welder 2	50A × 71% = 35.50A × 100%	35.50A
Welder 3	50A × 71% = 35.50A × 85%	30.18A
Welder 4	50A × 71% = 35.50A × 70%	24.85A
Welder 5	50A × 71% = 35.50A × 60%	+21.30A
Total Demand Load		147.33A

Minimum Conductor Size = 1/0 AWG rated 150A at 75°C [110.14(C)(1)(b) and Table 310.16]

Answer: (c) 1/0 AWG

630.12 Overcurrent Protection

Where the calculated overcurrent protection value does not correspond to the standard protective device ratings in 240.6(A), the next higher standard rating is permitted.

(A) Welders. Each arc welder must have overcurrent protection rated at not more than 200 percent of the maximum rated supply current at the maximum rated output nameplate, or not more than 200 percent of the rated primary current of the arc welder.

(B) Conductors. The conductors must be protected by an overcurrent protective device rated at not more than 200 percent of the conductor ampacity rating.

▶ Overcurrent Protection Example

Question: What is the maximum overcurrent protection rating for 10 THHN conductors used for an arc welder branch circuit?

(a) 30A (b) 40A (c) 50A (d) 60A

Solution:

Overcurrent Protection = 30A × 200%
Overcurrent Protection = 60A

Answer: (d) 60A

630.13 Disconnecting Means

A disconnect is required for each arc welder that is not equipped with an integral disconnect.

Part III. Resistance Welders

630.31 Ampacity of Supply Conductor

(A) Individual Resistance Welders.

Note: To limit voltage drop to a permissible performance value for resistance welders, conductors are usually sized larger than that which is required to prevent overheating.

> **Author's Comment:**
>
> ▶ To avoid cold welds due to insufficient power, follow the equipment voltage ranges stated in the listing or labeling instructions [110.3(B)].

(1) The ampacity of the supply conductors for varied-duty cycle resistance welders must not be less than 70 percent of the rated primary current for seam and automatically fed resistance welders, and 50 percent of the rated primary current for manually operated resistance welders [630.31(A)(1)].

(2) The supply conductors for resistance welders with a specific duty cycle and nonvarying current levels must have an ampacity of not less than the rated primary current multiplied by the factors in Table 630.31(A)(2), based on the duty cycle of the resistance welder.

Table 630.31(A)(2) Duty Cycle Multiplication Factors for Resistance Welders	
Duty Cycle	Multiplier
30	0.55
25	0.50
20	0.45
15	0.39
10	0.32
7.50	0.27
5 or less	0.22
50	0.71
40	0.63

▶ Individual Resistance Welders Example 1

Question: What size branch-circuit conductors are required for a 50A resistance welder having a duty cycle of 50 percent? ▶Figure 630–6

(a) 8 AWG   (b) 6 AWG   (c) 4 AWG   (d) 2 AWG

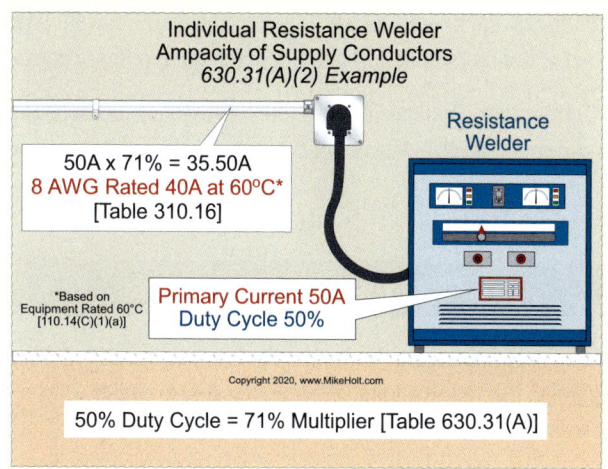

▶Figure 630–6

Solution:

Demand Load = Primary Rating × Multiplier [Table 630.31(A)(2)]
Demand Load = 50A × 71%
Demand Load = 35.50A

Use 8 AWG rated 40A at 60°C [110.14(C)(1)(a) and Table 310.16].

Answer: (a) 8 AWG

▶ Individual Resistance Welders Example 2

Question: What size branch-circuit conductors are required for a 30A resistance welder having a duty cycle of 30 percent? ▶Figure 630–7

(a) 12 AWG   (b) 10 AWG   (c) 8 AWG   (d) 6 AWG

Solution:

Demand Load = Primary Rating × Multiplier [Table 630.31(A)(2)]
Demand Load = 30A × 55%
Demand Load = 16.50A

Use 12 AWG rated 20A at 60°C [110.14(C)(1)(a) and Table 310.16].

Answer: (a) 12 AWG

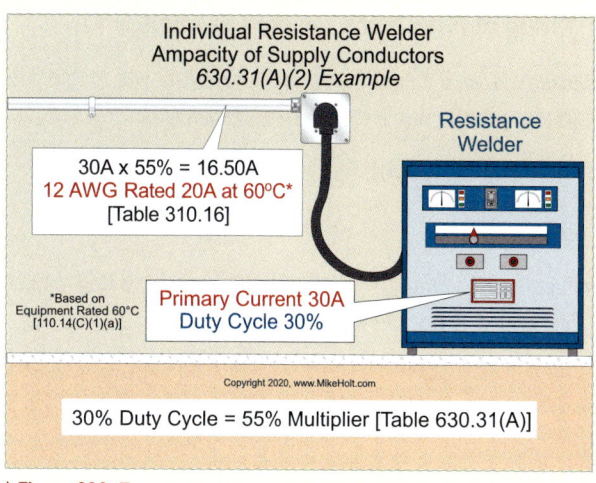

▶Figure 630–7

(B) Groups of Resistance Welders. Feeder conductors that supply a group of resistance welders must have an ampacity of not less than the sum of the value determined using 630.31(A)(2) for the largest resistance welder in the group, plus 60 percent of the values determined for all remaining resistance welders [630.31(B)].

▶ Group of Resistance Welders Example 1

Question: What is the minimum feeder conductor size for five 30A resistance welders with a duty cycle of 30 percent?

(a) 4 AWG   (b) 3 AWG   (c) 2 AWG   (d) 1 AWG

Solution:

Demand Load = Primary Rating × Multiplier [Table 630.31(A)(2)]
× Resistance Welder Percentage [630.31(B)]

Welder 1	30A × 55% = 16.50A × 100%	16.50A
Welder 2	30A × 55% = 16.50A × 60%	9.90A
Welder 3	30A × 55% = 16.50A × 60%	9.90A
Welder 4	30A × 55% = 16.50A × 60%	9.90A
Welder 5	30A × 55% = 16.50A × 60%	+ 9.90A
Total Demand Load		56.10A

Minimum Conductor Size = 4 AWG rated 70A at 60°C [110.14(C)(1)(a) and Table 310.16]

Answer: (a) 4 AWG

630.32 | Electric Welders

▶ Group of Resistance Welders Example 2

Question: What is the minimum feeder conductor size for five 50A resistance welders with a duty cycle of 50 percent?

(a) 4 AWG (b) 3 AWG (c) 2 AWG (d) 1 AWG

Solution:

Demand Load = Primary Rating × Multiplier [Table 630.31(A)(2)] × Resistance Welder Percentage [630.31(B)]

Welder 1	50A × 71% = 35.50A × 100%	35.50A
Welder 2	50A × 71% = 35.50A × 60%	21.30A
Welder 3	50A × 71% = 35.50A × 60%	21.30A
Welder 4	50A × 71% = 35.50A × 60%	21.30A
Welder 5	50A × 71% = 35.50A × 60%	+21.30A
Total Demand Load		120.70A

Minimum Conductor Size = 1 AWG rated 130A at 75°C [110.14(C)(1)(b) and Table 310.16]

Answer: (d) 1 AWG

630.32 Overcurrent Protection

Where the calculated overcurrent protection value does not correspond with the standard protective device ratings in 240.6(A), the next higher standard rating is permitted.

(A) Welders. Each resistance welder must have overcurrent protection set at not more than 300 percent of the rated primary current.

(B) Conductors. Branch-circuit conductors must be protected by an overcurrent protective device rated at not more than 300 percent of the conductor rating.

630.33 Disconnecting Means

A switch or circuit breaker is required to disconnect each resistance welder and its control equipment from the supply circuit.

ARTICLE 640 — AUDIO SIGNAL AMPLIFICATION AND REPRODUCTION EQUIPMENT

Introduction to Article 640—Audio Signal Amplification and Reproduction Equipment

If you understand the three major goals of Article 640 you will be able to better understand and apply its requirements. These three goals are to:

- Reduce the spread of fire and smoke.
- Comply with other articles.
- Prevent shock.

This article includes several rules, such as specifics in the mechanical execution of work, and requirements for audio equipment located near bodies of water to reduce shock hazards peculiar to audio equipment installations.

In addition, Article 640 distinguishes between permanent and temporary audio installations. Part II provides rules for permanent installations, and Part III provides requirements for portable and temporary installations.

Part I. General

640.1 Scope

(A) Covered. Article 640 covers equipment and wiring for permanent and temporary audio sound and public address system installations. ▶Figure 640-1

▶Figure 640-1

Note: Audio system locations include (but are not limited to) restaurants, hotels, business offices, commercial and retail sales environments, churches, schools, auditoriums, theaters, stadiums, and outdoor events such as fairs, festivals, circuses, public events, and concerts.

(B) Not Covered. This article does not cover audio systems for fire and burglary alarms.

640.2 Definitions

The following definitions only apply to this article.

Abandoned Cable. Installed audio distribution cable that is not terminated to equipment and not identified for future use with a tag.

Author's Comment:

- Section 640.6(B) requires the accessible portions of abandoned audio cables to be removed and 640.6(C) specifies the tagging for future use requirements.

Audio System. Within this article, the totality of all equipment and interconnecting wiring used to fabricate a fully functional audio signal processing, amplification, and reproduction system.

640.3 | Audio Signal Amplification and Reproduction Equipment

Loudspeaker. Equipment that converts an alternating-current electric signal into an acoustic signal.

640.3 Locations and Other Articles

(A) Spread of Fire or Products of Combustion. Audio circuits installed through fire-resistant-rated walls, partitions, floors, or ceilings must be firestopped to limit the possible spread of fire or products of combustion in accordance with the specific instructions supplied by the manufacturer for the specific type of cable and construction material (drywall, brick, and so on) in accordance with 300.21.

Author's Comment:

▸ Penetrations into or through fire-resistant-rated walls, floors, partitions, or ceilings must be firestopped using an approved method so the possible spread of fire or products of combustion will not be substantially increased [300.21]. ▶Figure 640-2

▸ Although boxes are not required for audio circuits, one is required for an audio device located in a fire-rated assembly.

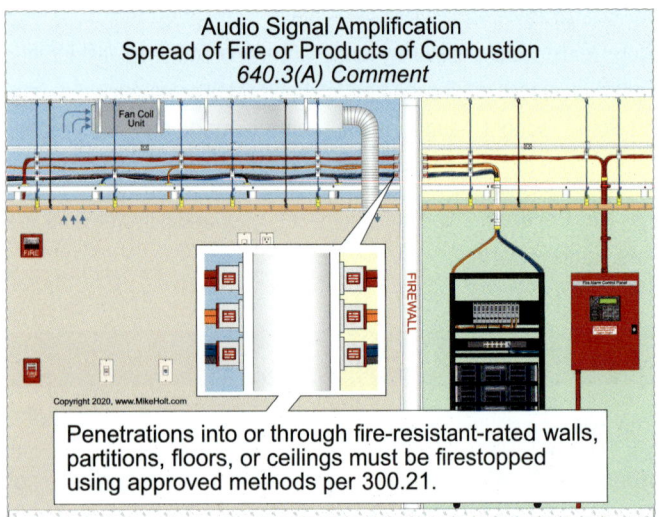

▶Figure 640-2

(B) Ducts and Plenum Spaces. Audio circuits installed in fabricated ducts for environmental air must comply with 300.22(B), and when installed in plenum spaces, audio circuits must comply with 300.22(C).

Ex 1: Class 2 plenum-rated cables installed in accordance with 725.135(B) and Table 725.154 can be installed in ducts specifically fabricated for environmental air.

Ex 2: Class 2 plenum-rated cables installed in accordance with 725.135(C) and Table 725.154 can be installed in plenum spaces.

640.4 Protection of Electrical Equipment

Amplifiers, loudspeakers, and other audio equipment must be located or protected against environmental exposure or physical damage that might cause a fire, shock, or personal hazard.

640.6 Mechanical Execution of Work

(A) Installation of Audio Cables. Exposed audio cables must be supported so the cable will not be damaged by normal building use. In addition, straps, staples, cable ties, hangers, or similar fittings must secure audio cables in a manner that will not damage the cable. ▶Figure 640-3

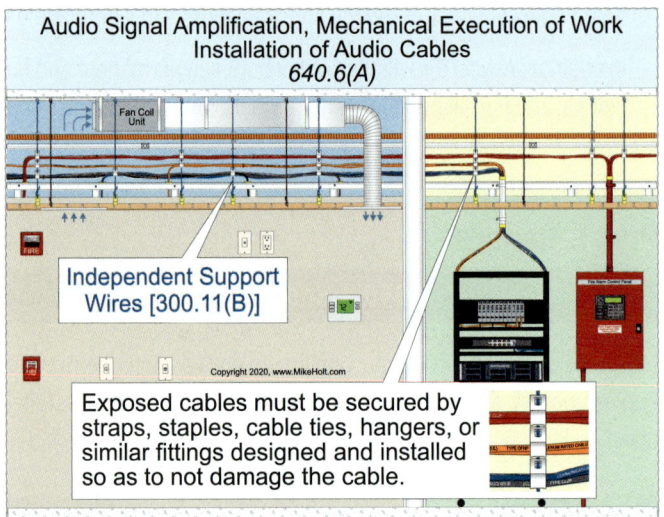

▶Figure 640-3

Audio cables installed parallel or perpendicular to framing members must be protected against damage from penetration by screws or nails by a 1¼ in. separation from the face of the framing member or by a suitable metal plate, in accordance with 300.4(D). ▶Figure 640-4

(B) Abandoned Audio Cables. The accessible portions of abandoned cables must be removed. ▶Figure 640-5

Audio Signal Amplification and Reproduction Equipment | 640.10

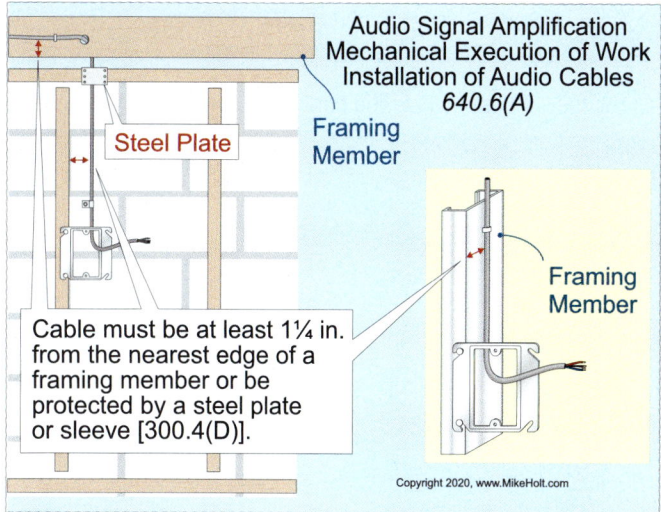
▶Figure 640-4

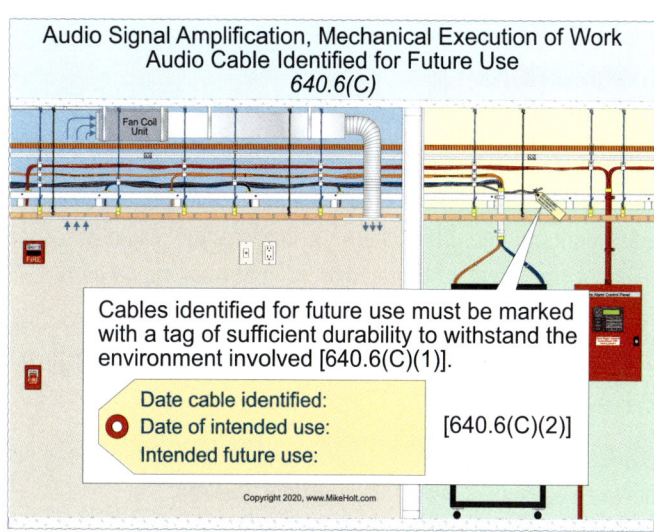
▶Figure 640-6

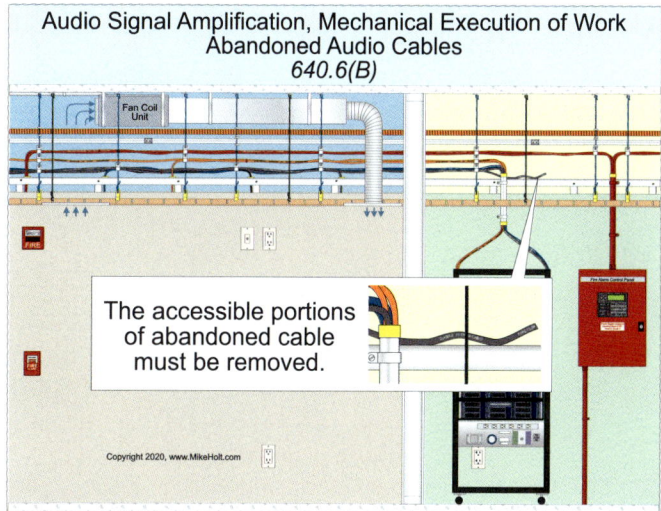
▶Figure 640-5

Author's Comment:

▸ An abandoned audio distribution cable is one that is not terminated to equipment and not identified for future use with a tag [640.2].

▸ This rule does not require the removal of concealed cables abandoned in place, which includes cables in raceways. According to Article 100, cables in raceways that are concealed are not considered accessible.

(C) Audio Cable Identified for Future Use. ▶Figure 640-6

(1) Cables identified for future use must be marked with a tag of sufficient durability to withstand the environment involved.

(2) Cable tags must include the following information:

(1) The date the cable was identified for future use.

(2) The date of expected use.

(3) The intended future use of the cable.

640.9 Wiring Methods

(A) Wiring to and Between Audio Equipment.

(1) Branch Circuit. Branch-circuit wiring for audio equipment must comply with Chapters 1 through 4.

(3) Audio Circuits Output Wiring. Audio output wiring must be installed in accordance with Article 725.

640.10 Audio Systems Near Bodies of Water

(A) Branch-Circuit Power. Audio equipment supplied by a branch circuit is not permitted to be placed within 5 ft horizontally of the inside wall of a pool, spa, hot tub, or fountain. In addition to the requirements in 210.8(B), the equipment must be supplied by a GFCI-protected branch circuit where required by other articles of the *Code*.

Note: See 680.27(A) for installation of underwater audio equipment.

(B) Class 2 Power Supply. Audio system equipment powered by a listed Class 2 power supply or an amplifier listed for use with Class 2 wiring, are restricted in their placement near bodies of water by the manufacturer's instructions.

Part II. Permanent Audio System Installations

640.21 Use of Flexible Cords and Flexible Cables

(A) Branch-Circuit Power. Power-supply cords for permanent audio equipment are permitted where the interchange, maintenance, or repair of equipment is facilitated by using a power-supply cord.

(B) Loudspeakers. Cables for loudspeakers must comply with Article 725, and the conductors for outdoor speakers must be identified for the environment.

(C) Between Equipment. Cables for distributing audio signals between equipment must comply with Article 725.

640.23 Conduit or Tubing

(A) Number of Conductors. The number of conductors in a conduit or tubing must not exceed percentage fill requirements of Chapter 9, Table 1.

ARTICLE 645 — INFORMATION TECHNOLOGY EQUIPMENT (ITE)

Introduction to Article 645—Information Technology Equipment (ITE)

One of the unique things about Article 645 is the requirement for a shutoff switch for information technology equipment rooms [645.10]. This requirement seems to be wrong on its face because it allows someone to shut off power to the IT room off from a single point. So, despite having a UPS and taking every precaution against a power outage, the IT system is still vulnerable to a shutdown from a readily accessible switch.

What about the rest of Article 645? The major goal is to reduce the spread of fire and smoke. The raised floors common in IT rooms pose additional challenges to achieving this goal, so this article devotes a fair percentage of its text to raised floor requirements. Fire-resistant walls, separate HVAC systems, and other requirements further help to achieve this goal.

645.1 Scope

Article 645 provides optional wiring methods and materials for information technology equipment (ITE) and systems in an information technology equipment room as an alternative to those required in other chapters of this *Code*. ▶Figure 645-1

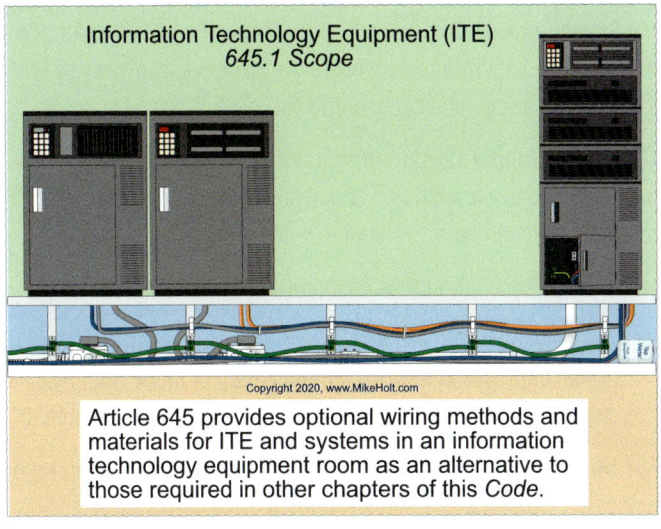

▶Figure 645-1

Article 645 provides optional wiring methods and materials for ITE and systems in an information technology equipment room as an alternative to those required in other chapters of this *Code*.

Note 1: An information technology equipment room is an enclosed area specifically designed to comply with the construction and fire protection provisions of NFPA 75, *Standard for the Fire Protection of Information Technology Equipment*.

645.2 Definitions

The following definitions only apply to this article.

Abandoned Cable. Installed supply circuits and interconnecting cables that are not terminated at equipment and not identified for future use with a tag.

645.3 Other Articles

Circuits and equipment must comply with 645.3(A) through (I) as applicable.

(A) Spread of Fire or Products of Combustion. Electrical circuits and equipment must be installed in such a way that the spread of fire or products of combustion will not be substantially increased. Openings into or through fire-rated walls, floors, and ceilings for electrical equipment must be firestopped using methods approved by the authority having jurisdiction to maintain the fire-resistance rating of the fire-rated assembly [300.21, 770.26, and 800.26].

645.4 | Information Technology Equipment (ITE)

(B) Plenum Spaces. The following apply to wiring and cabling in a plenum space above an information technology equipment room:

(1) Wiring must be in accordance with 300.22(C)(1).

(2) Class 2 plenum-rated cables must be installed in accordance with 725.135(C) and Table 725.154.

(3) Plenum-rated fire alarm cables must be installed in accordance with 760.53(B)(2), 760.135(C), and Table 725.154.

(4) Plenum-rated optical fiber cables must be installed in accordance with 770.113(C) and Table 770.154(a).

(5) Plenum-rated communications cables must be installed in accordance with 800.113 and Table 800.154(a).

(6) Plenum-rated coaxial cables must be installed in accordance with 800.113 and Table 800.154(a).

Author's Comment:

▸ Many of the wiring methods and cable types employed in the installation of signaling, communications, data transmission, audio, radio and television systems, and so on, are subject to the same requirements and restrictions. The majority of these requirements are consolidated in Article 800 of the *NEC*.

(D) Classification of Data Circuits. Data circuits for information technology systems are classified as Class 2 circuits in accordance with 725.121(A)(4) and must be installed in accordance with the requirements of Article 725 [725.1].

Class 2 circuit conductors installed in the same cable with communications circuits are reclassified as communications circuits and the cable must be listed as communications cable [725.139(D)(1) and 800.133(A)(1)(c)].

(E) Fire Alarm Cables and Equipment. Parts I, II, and III of Article 760 apply to fire alarm systems cables and equipment installed in an information technology equipment room. Only fire alarm cables listed in accordance with Part IV of Article 760 and listed fire alarm equipment are permitted to be installed in an information technology equipment room.

(H) Optical Fiber Cables. Only optical fiber cables listed in accordance with 770.179 are permitted to be installed in an information technology equipment room.

645.4 Special Requirements

The wiring methods permitted in 645.5 are only permitted where all the following conditions are met:

(1) A disconnect that complies with 645.10 is provided.

(2) A dedicated heating/ventilating/air-conditioning system is provided for the information technology equipment room and is separated from other areas of the occupancy.

(3) The information technology and communications equipment is listed.

(4) The room is occupied and accessible only to persons needed for the maintenance and operation of information technology equipment.

(5) The information technology equipment room is separated from other occupancies by fire-resistant-rated walls, floors, and ceilings with protected openings.

(6) Only electrical equipment and wiring associated with the operation of the information technology room is installed in the room.

Note: This includes HVAC systems, communications systems (twisted pair, antennas, and coaxial cable), fire alarm systems, security systems, water detection systems, and other related protective equipment.

645.5 Supply Circuits and Interconnecting Cables

(A) Branch-Circuit Conductors. Branch-circuit conductors for information technology equipment must have an ampacity of not less than 125 percent of the total connected load.

(B) Power-Supply Cords. Information technology equipment can be connected to a branch circuit by a power-supply cord meeting the following requirements: ▸Figure 645–2

(1) The power-supply cord is no longer than 15 ft.

(2) The power-supply cord and attachment plug must be listed for use on information technology equipment or made from flexible cord, plugs, and cord connectors listed for use on ITE equipment.

(C) Interconnecting Cables. Cables listed for information technology equipment can be used to interconnect information technology equipment without the 15-foot cable length limitation contained in 645.5(B)(1).

(D) Physical Damage. If exposed to physical damage, supply circuits and interconnecting cables must be protected.

Information Technology Equipment (ITE) | **645.5**

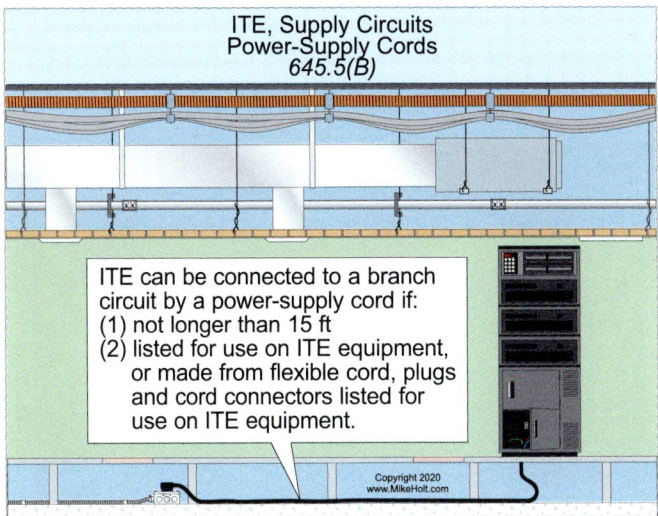

▶Figure 645–2

(2) PVC conduit

(3) Intermediate metal conduit

(4) Electrical metallic tubing

(5) Electrical nonmetallic tubing

(6) Metal wireway

(7) Nonmetallic wireway

(8) Surface metal raceway with metal cover

(9) Surface nonmetallic raceway

(10) Flexible metal conduit

(11) Liquidtight flexible metal conduit

(12) Liquidtight flexible nonmetallic conduit

(13) Type MI cable

(14) Type MC cable

(15) Type AC cable

(16) Associated metallic and nonmetallic boxes or enclosures

(17) Type TC power and control tray cable

(E) Under Raised Floors. Where the area under the raised floor is accessible and openings minimize the entrance of debris beneath the floor, power cables, communications cables, connecting cables, interconnecting cables, cord-and-plug connections, and receptacles associated with the information technology equipment can be installed under a raised floor. The installation requirement must comply with (1) through (3) as follows:

(1) Branch-Circuit Wiring Under a Raised Floor. ▶Figure 645–3

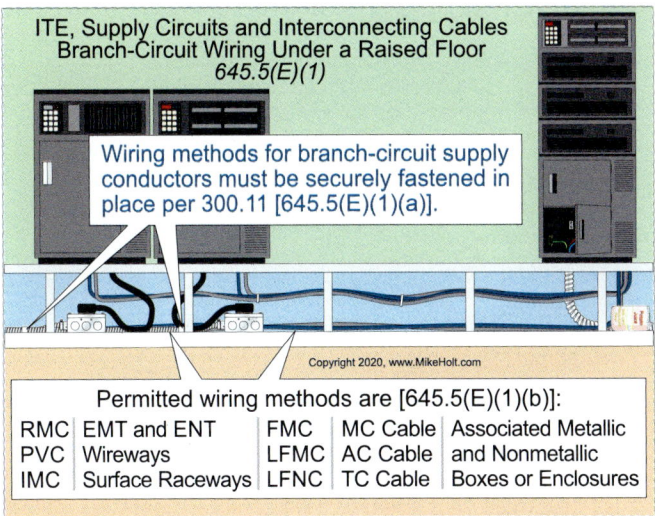

▶Figure 645–3

(a) Branch-circuit wiring under a raised floor must be securely fastened in place in accordance with 300.11.

(b) The following wiring methods are permitted under a raised floor:

(1) Rigid metal conduit

(2) Power-Supply Cords, Data Cables, Cables, and Conductors. The following power-supply cords, interconnecting cables, cables, and conductors are permitted under a raised floor:

(1) Power-supply cords of listed information technology equipment in accordance with 645.5(B)

(2) Interconnecting cables enclosed within a raceway

(3) Equipment grounding conductors

(4) Where the air space under a raised floor is protected by an automatic fire suppression system, in addition to wiring installed in accordance with 725.135(C), Types CL2R, CL3R, CL2, and CL3 and substitute cables including CMP, CMR, CM, and CMG installed in accordance with 725.154(A) are permitted under raised floors.

Note: Figure 725.154(A) in the *NEC* illustrates the cable substitution hierarchy for Class 2 cables.

(5) Where the air space under a raised floor is not protected by an automatic fire suppression system, in addition to wiring installed in accordance with 725.135(C), substitute Type CMP cable installed in accordance with 725.154(A) is permitted under raised floors.

(6) Listed Type DP cable

(3) Installation Requirements for Optical Fiber Cables Under a Raised Floor.

645.5 | Information Technology Equipment (ITE)

(1) Optical Fiber Cables Under a Raised Floor. Where the air space under a raised floor is protected by an automatic fire suppression system, optical fiber Types OFNR, OFCR, OFN, and OFC cables installed in accordance with 770.113(C) are permitted under raised floors. ▶Figure 645-4

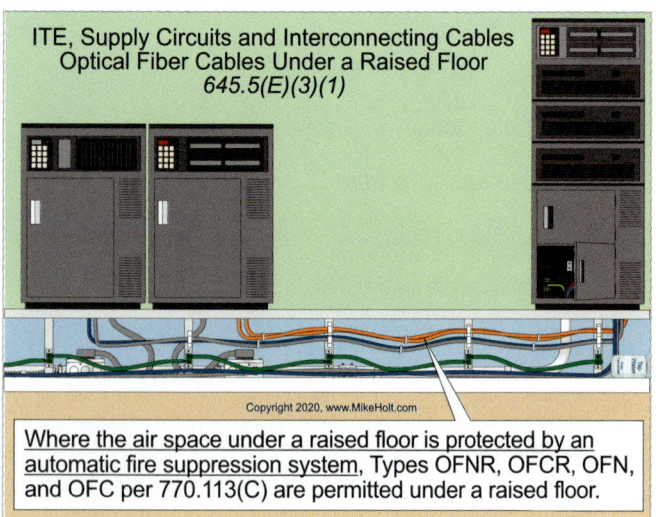

▶Figure 645-4

(2) Where the air space under a raised floor is not protected by an automatic fire suppression system, only optical fiber cables installed in accordance with 770.113(C) are permitted under raised floors.

(F) Securing in Place. Power cables, communications cables, connecting cables, interconnecting cables, and associated boxes, connectors, plugs, and receptacles that are listed as part of (or for) information technology equipment are not required to be secured in place where installed under raised floors. ▶Figure 645-5

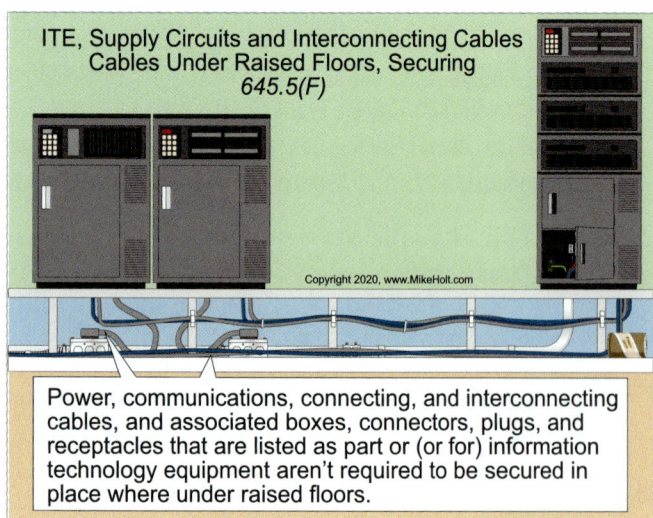

▶Figure 645-5

(G) Abandoned Supply Circuits and Interconnecting Cables. The accessible portion of abandoned supply circuits and interconnecting cables must be removed unless contained in a raceway. ▶Figure 645-6

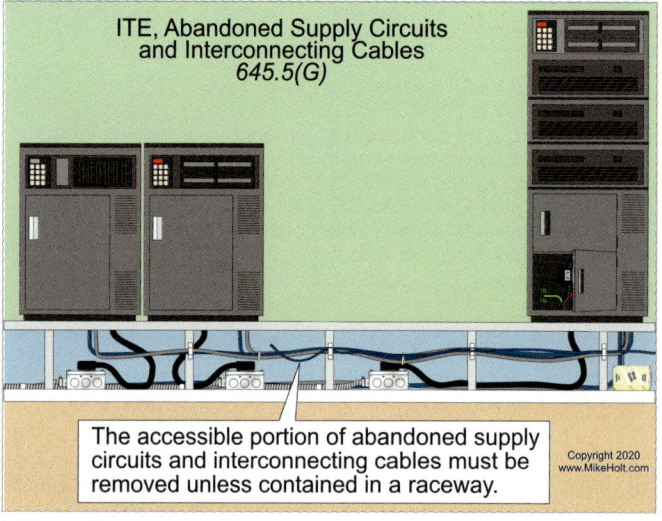

▶Figure 645-6

Author's Comment:

▶ An abandoned cable is one that is not terminated to equipment and not identified for future use with a tag [645.2].

(H) Installed Supply Circuits and Interconnecting Cables Identified for Future Use. ▶Figure 645-7

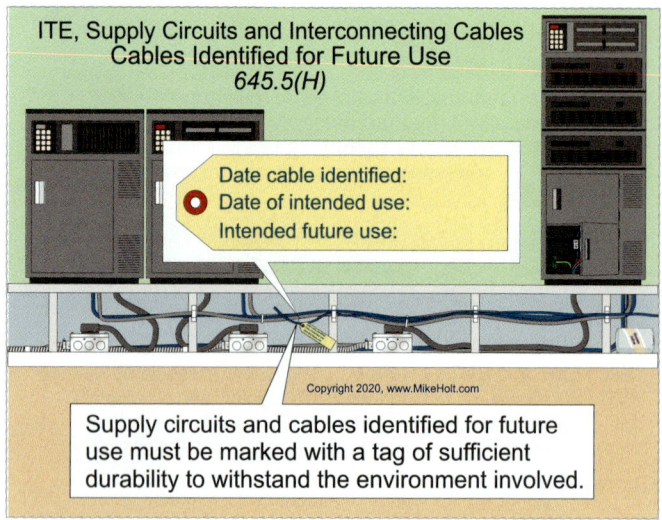

▶Figure 645-7

(1) Supply circuits and interconnecting cables identified for future use must be marked with a tag of sufficient durability to withstand the environment involved.

(2) Supply circuit tags and interconnecting cable tags must have the following information:

(1) Date identified for future use

(2) Date of intended use

(3) Information relating to the intended future use

645.10 Disconnecting Means

A disconnect is required for electronic equipment in the information technology equipment room and dedicated HVAC systems that serve the room or in designated zones within the room.

(A) Remote Disconnect Controls.

(1) Remote disconnect controls must be at an approved readily accessible location.

(2) The remote disconnect means for the control of electronic equipment power and HVAC systems must be grouped and identified. A single means to control both is permitted.

(4) Additional means to prevent unintentional operations of remote disconnect controls are permitted.

645.15 Equipment Grounding and Bonding

Exposed metal parts of an information technology system must be connected to the circuit equipment grounding conductor or be double insulated. ▶Figure 645–8

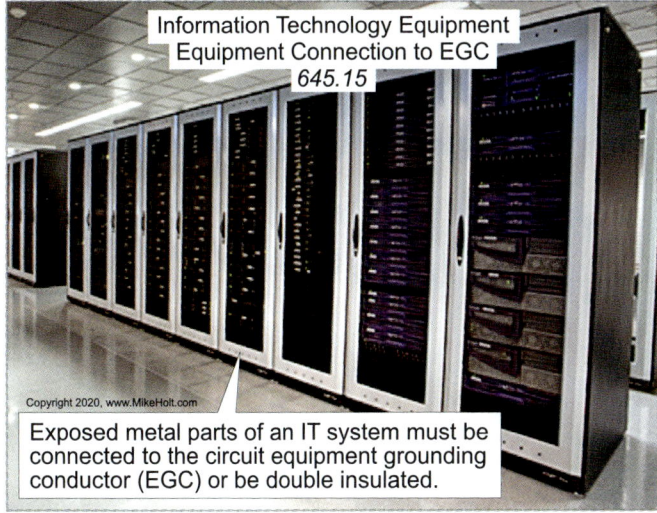

▶Figure 645–8

Where signal reference structures are installed, they must be bonded to the circuit equipment grounding conductor for the information technology equipment. ▶Figure 645–9 and ▶Figure 645–10

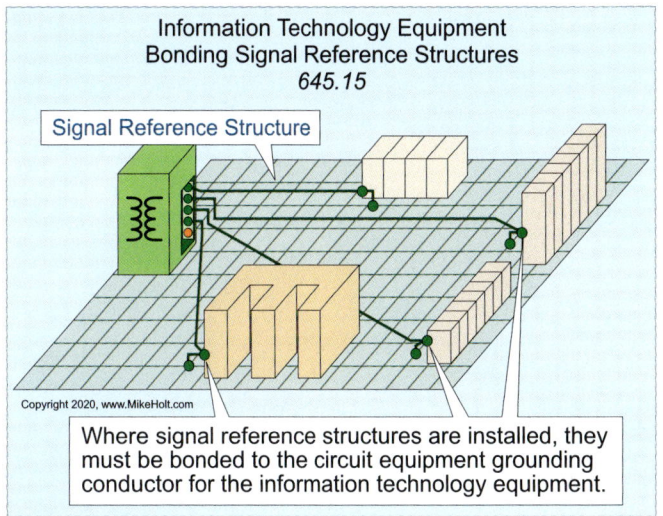

▶Figure 645–9

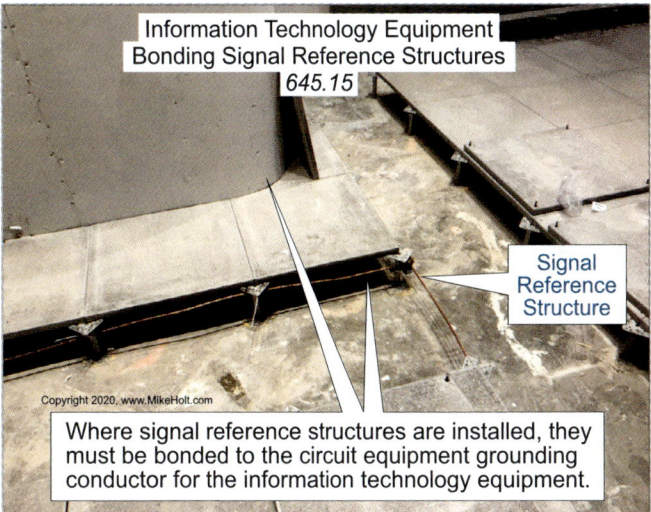

▶Figure 645–10

Note 2: If isolated ground receptacles are installed, they must be connected to an insulated equipment grounding conductor in accordance with 250.146(D) and 406.3(D).

Notes

ARTICLE 680 — SWIMMING POOLS, SPAS, HOT TUBS, FOUNTAINS, AND SIMILAR INSTALLATIONS

Introduction to Article 680—Swimming Pools, Spas, Hot Tubs, Fountains, and Similar Installations

The requirements contained in Article 680 apply to the installation of electrical wiring and equipment for swimming pools, spas, hot tubs, fountains, hydromassage bathtubs, and electrically powered pool lifts. The overriding concern of this article is to keep people and electricity separated.

This article is divided into eight parts. The various parts apply to certain types of installations, so be careful to determine which parts of this article apply to what and where. For instance, Part I and Part II apply to spas and hot tubs installed outdoors, except as modified in Part IV. In contrast, hydromassage bathtubs are only covered by Part VII. Read the details of Article 680 carefully so you will be able to provide a safe installation.

- ▶ Part I. General.
- ▶ Part II. Permanently Installed Pools. Installations at permanently installed pools must comply with both Parts I and II of this article.
- ▶ Part III. Storable Swimming Pools, Storable Spas, and Storable Hot Tubs. Installations of storable pools, storable spas, and storable hot tubs must comply with Parts I and III of Article 680.
- ▶ Part IV. Spas and Hot Tubs. Spas and hot tubs must comply with Parts I and IV of this article; outdoor spas and hot tubs must also comply with Part II in accordance with 680.42.
- ▶ Part V. Fountains. Parts I and V apply to permanently installed fountains. If they have water in common with a pool, Part II also applies. Self-contained, portable fountains are covered by Article 422, Parts II and III.
- ▶ Part VI. Pools and Tubs for Therapeutic Use. Parts I and VI apply to pools and tubs for therapeutic use in health care facilities, gymnasiums, athletic training rooms, and similar installations.
- ▶ Part VII. Hydromassage Bathtubs. Only Part VII of Article 680 applies to hydromassage bathtubs.
- ▶ Part VIII. Electrically Powered Pool Lifts. Parts I and II apply to electrically powered pool lifts only when referenced in Part VIII.

Part I. General Requirements for Pools, Spas, Hot Tubs, and Fountains

Author's Comment:

- ▶ The requirements contained in Part I of Article 680 apply to permanently installed pools [680.20], storable pools [680.30], spas and hot tubs [680.42 and 680.43], fountains [680.50], and pool lifts [680.80].

680.1 Scope

Article 680 applies to the installation of electric wiring and equipment for swimming pools, hot tubs, spas, fountains, hydromassage bathtubs, and pool lifts. ▶Figure 680–1

680.2 | Swimming Pools, Spas, Hot Tubs, Fountains, and Similar Installations

▶Figure 680–1

680.2 Definitions

The definitions in this section apply only within this article.

Corrosive Environment. Areas where pool sanitation chemicals are stored, handled, or dispensed; and confined areas under decks adjacent to such areas as well as areas with circulation pumps, automatic chlorinators, filters, open areas under decks adjacent to or abutting the pool structure, and similar locations. ▶Figure 680–2

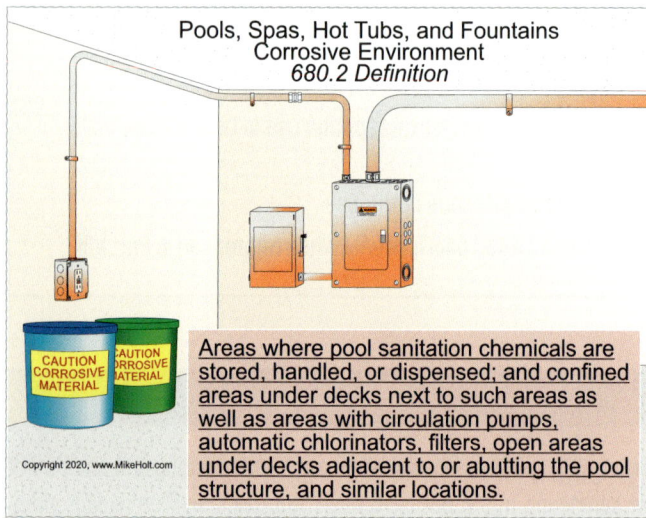

▶Figure 680–2

Note: Sanitation chemicals and pool water pose a risk of corrosion (gradually damaging or destroying materials) due to the presence of oxidizers (for example, calcium hypochlorite, sodium hypochlorite, bromine, and chlorinated isocyanurates) and chlorinating agents that release chlorine when dissolved in water. More information about swimming pool chemicals can be found on or in the following:

(1) Environmental Protection Agency website

(2) NFPA 400, *Hazardous Materials Code*

(3) *Advisory: Swimming Pool Chemicals: Chlorine, OSWER 90-008.1*, available from the EPA National Service Center for Environmental Publications (NSCEP)

Electrically Powered Pool Lift. An electrically powered lift that provides accessibility to and from a pool or spa for people with disabilities. ▶Figure 680–3

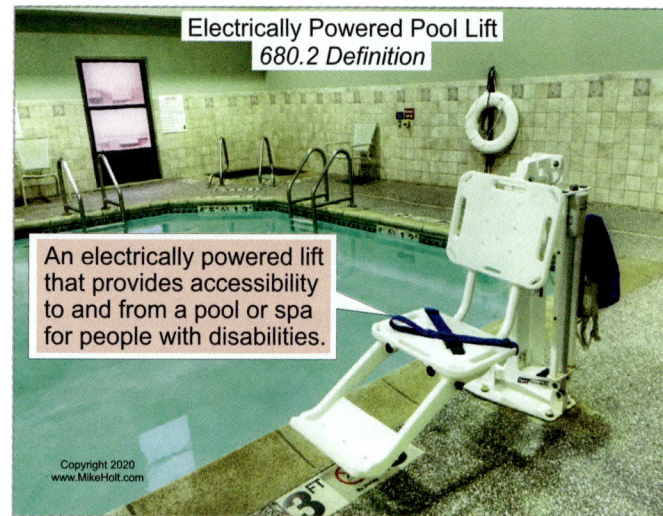

▶Figure 680–3

Forming Shell. A structure designed to support a wet-niche luminaire. ▶Figure 680–4

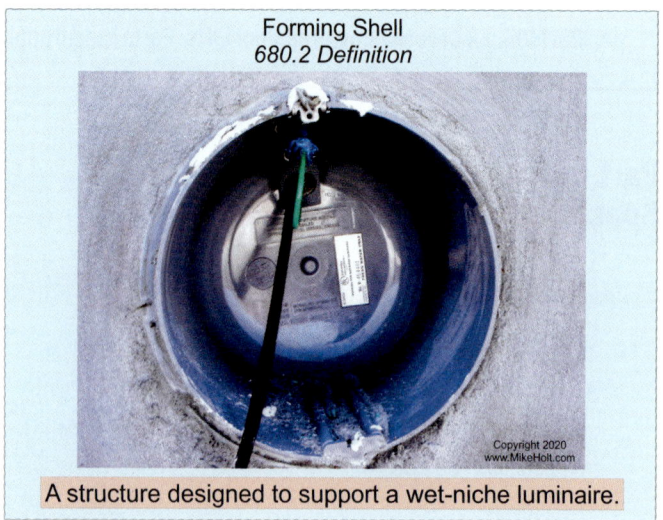

▶Figure 680–4

Swimming Pools, Spas, Hot Tubs, Fountains, and Similar Installations | 680.2

Fountain. An ornamental structure or recreational water feature from which one or more jets or streams of water are discharged into the air including splash pads, ornamental pools, display pools, and reflection pools. This definition does not include drinking water fountains or water coolers. ▶Figure 680-5

▶Figure 680-5

Hydromassage Bathtub. A permanently installed bathtub with a recirculating piping system designed to accept, circulate, and discharge water after each use. ▶Figure 680-6

▶Figure 680-6

Immersion Pool. A pool for the ceremonial or ritual immersion of users which is designed and intended to have its contents drained or discharged. ▶Figure 680-7

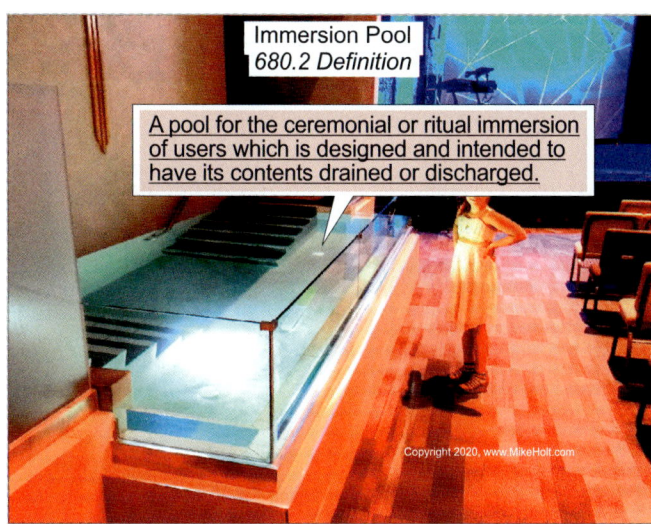
▶Figure 680-7

Low-Voltage Contact Limit. A voltage not exceeding the following values: ▶Figure 680-8

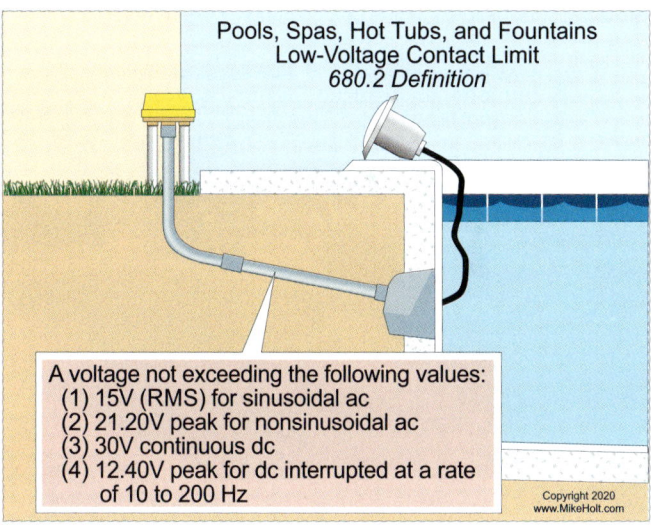
▶Figure 680-8

(1) 15V (RMS) for sinusoidal alternating current.

(2) 21.20V peak for nonsinusoidal alternating current.

(3) 30V for continuous direct current.

(4) 12.40V peak for direct current that is interrupted at a rate of 10 to 200 Hz.

Maximum Water Level. The highest level water reaches before it spills out. ▶Figure 680-9

680.2 | Swimming Pools, Spas, Hot Tubs, Fountains, and Similar Installations

▶Figure 680–9

Permanently Installed Swimming, Wading, Immersion, and Therapeutic Pools. Pools constructed in the ground or partially in the ground, pools capable of holding water of a depth greater than 42 in., and pools installed inside of a building. ▶Figure 680–10

▶Figure 680–10

Pool. Manufactured or field-constructed equipment designed to contain water on a permanent or semipermanent basis and used for swimming, wading, immersion, or other purposes.

> **Author's Comment:**
>
> ▸ The definition of a pool includes baptisteries (immersion pools) which must comply with the requirements of Article 680.
>
> ▸ An above ground pool having a maximum water depth greater than 42 in. is considered a permanent pool. See the definition of 'storable pool.'

Spa or Hot Tub. A hydromassage pool or tub designed for recreational or therapeutic use typically not drained after each use. ▶Figure 680–11

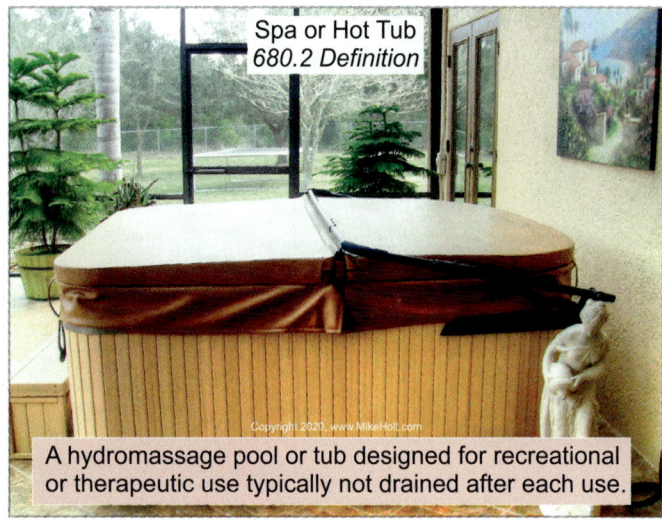

▶Figure 680–11

Splash Pad. A fountain with a water depth 1 in. or less intended for recreational use by pedestrians. This definition does not include showers intended for hygienic rinsing prior to use of a pool, spa, or other water feature. ▶Figure 680–12

▶Figure 680–12

Storable Swimming Pools. A pool that is intended to be stored when not in use, constructed on or above the ground, and is capable of holding water to a depth of 42 in., or a pool constructed with nonmetallic, molded polymeric walls or inflatable fabric walls regardless of dimension.

Wet-Niche Luminaire. A luminaire intended to be installed in a forming shell where it will be completely surrounded by water. ▶Figure 680–13

▶Figure 680-13

680.3 Approval of Equipment

Electrical equipment and products covered by this article are required to be listed and must be installed in compliance with this article.

680.4 Inspections After Installation

The authority having jurisdiction is permitted to require periodic inspection and testing.

680.5 Ground-Fault Circuit Interrupters

The GFCI requirements in Article 680, unless otherwise noted, are in addition to the requirements in 210.8.

680.6 Bonding and Equipment Grounding

Electrical equipment must be bonded in accordance with Part V of Article 250 and must be connected to the equipment grounding conductor requirements of Parts VI and VII of that article. Equipment must be connected by the wiring methods in Chapter 3 unless modified by this article. Equipment subject to these requirements include:

(1) Through-wall lighting assemblies and underwater luminaires except for listed low-voltage lighting.

(2) All electrical equipment within 5 ft of the inside wall of the specified body of water.

(3) All electrical equipment associated with the water recirculating system.

(4) Junction boxes.

(5) Transformer and power-supply enclosures.

(6) Ground-fault circuit interrupters.

(7) Subpanels that supply associated equipment.

680.7 Bonding and Equipment Grounding Terminals

Terminals used for bonding and equipment grounding must be identified as suitable for use in wet and corrosive environments. Field-installed terminals in damp, wet, and corrosive environments must be copper, copper alloy, or stainless steel and be listed for direct burial use. ▶Figure 680-14

▶Figure 680-14

680.9 Overhead Conductor Clearance

Overhead conductors must meet the clearance from the maximum water level requirements contained in Table 680.9(A).

(A) Overhead Power Conductors. Permanently installed pools, spas, hot tubs, fountains, diving structures, observation stands, towers, or platforms cannot be placed within the clearances contained in Table 680.9(A). ▶Figure 680-15 and ▶Figure 680-16

680.10 | Swimming Pools, Spas, Hot Tubs, Fountains, and Similar Installations

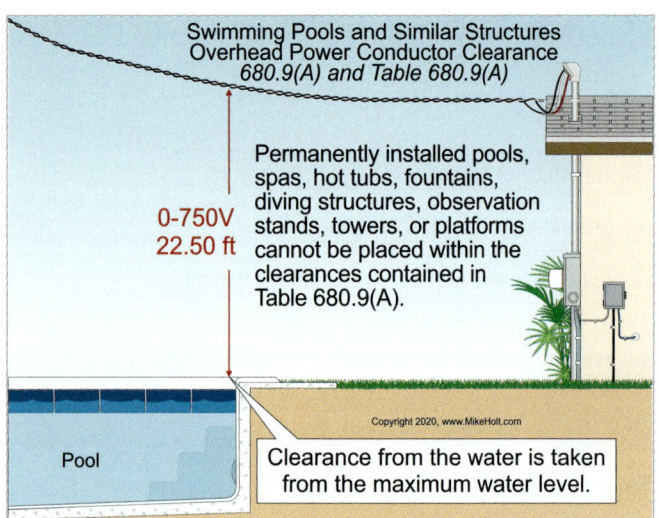

▶Figure 680–15

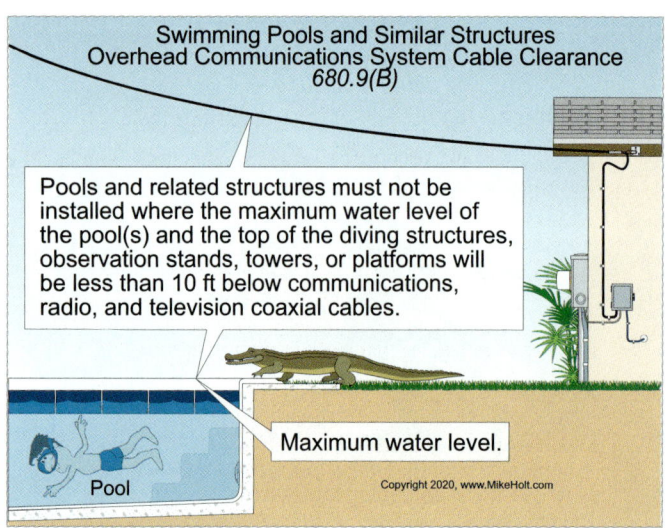

▶Figure 680–17

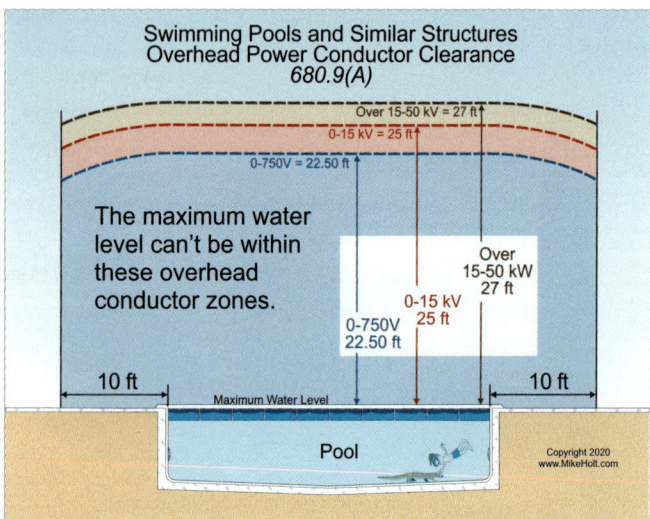

▶Figure 680–16

Author's Comment:

▸ This rule does not prohibit utility-owned overhead service-drop conductors from being installed over a pool, spa, hot tub, or fountain [90.2(B)(5)]. However, it does prohibit a pool, spa, hot tub, or fountain from being installed under an existing service drop that is not at least 22½ ft above the water.

(B) Communications Systems. Swimming and wading pools, and diving structures, observation stands, towers, or platforms must not be installed where the maximum water level of the pool(s) and the top of the diving structures, observation stands, towers, or platforms will be less than 10 ft below communications, radio, and television coaxial cables. ▶Figure 680–17

Author's Comment:

▸ This rule does not prohibit a utility-owned communications overhead cable from being installed over a pool, spa, hot tub, or fountain [90.2(B)(4)]. It does prohibit a pool, spa, hot tub, or fountain from being installed under an existing communications utility overhead supply that is not at least 10 ft above the water.

680.10 Electric Water Heaters

Branch-circuit conductors and overcurrent protection for pool, spa, and hot tub water heaters must be sized to carry no less than 125 percent of the nameplate current rating. ▶Figure 680–18

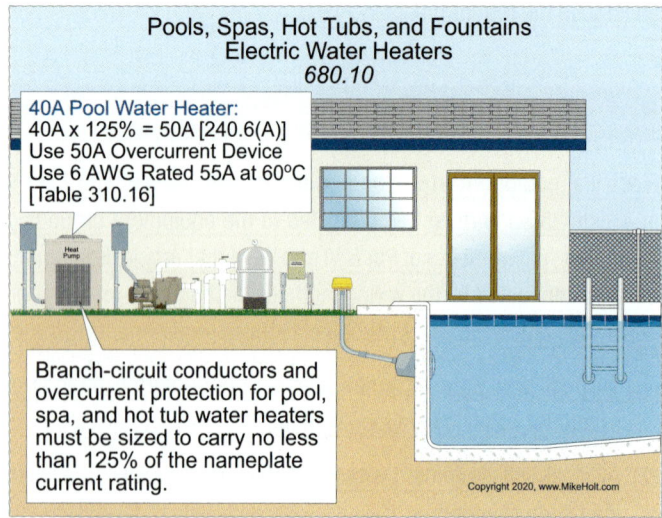

▶Figure 680–18

252 | Mike Holt's Illustrated Guide to Understanding the 2020 National Electrical Code, Volume 2

680.11 Underground Wiring

(A) Underground Wiring. Underground wiring located within 5 ft horizontally from the inside wall of the pool must be one of the following wiring methods. ▶Figure 680–19

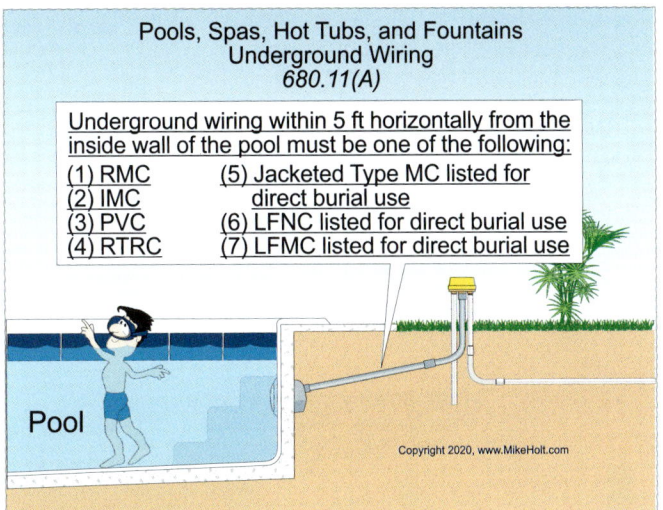
▶Figure 680–19

(1) Rigid metal conduit

(2) Intermediate metal conduit

(3) Rigid polyvinyl chloride conduit

(4) Reinforced thermosetting resin conduit

(5) Jacketed Type MC cable listed for direct burial use

(6) Liquidtight flexible nonmetallic conduit listed for direct burial use

(7) Liquidtight flexible metal conduit listed for direct burial use

(B) Wiring Under Pools. Underground wiring beneath pools is permitted for the supply of pool equipment permitted by this article and no other loads.

(C) Minimum Cover Requirements. Minimum cover depths contained in 300.5 apply.

680.12 Equipment Rooms and Pits

Permanently installed pools, storable pools, spas, hot tubs, or fountain equipment are not permitted to be located in rooms or pits that do not have drainage that prevents water accumulation during normal operation or filter maintenance. ▶Figure 680–20

Equipment must be suitable for the corrosive environment in accordance with 300.6.

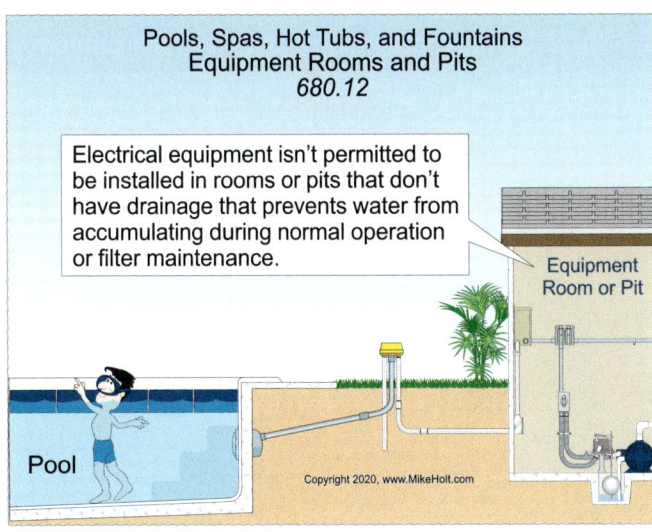
▶Figure 680–20

680.13 Maintenance Disconnecting Means

A maintenance disconnect is required for pool, spa, hot tub, or fountain equipment other than lighting. The maintenance disconnect must be readily accessible and located within sight and at least 5 ft from the pool, spa, hot tub, or fountain equipment unless separated from the open water by a permanently installed barrier. This horizontal distance is measured from the water's edge along the shortest path required to reach the disconnect. ▶Figure 680–21

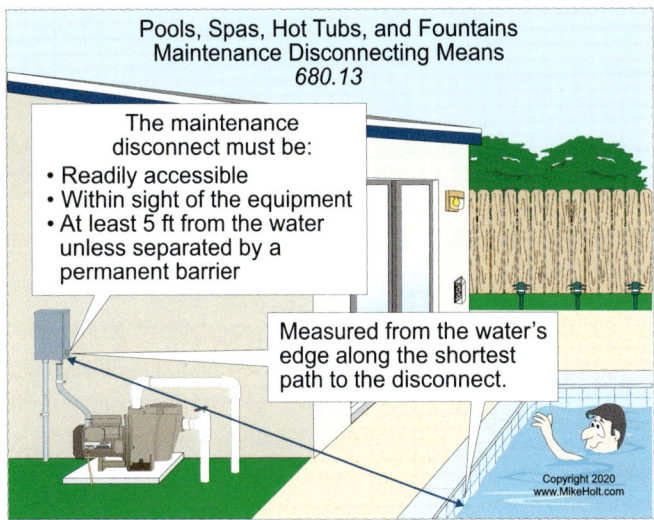
▶Figure 680–21

Author's Comment:

▶ According to Article 100, "Within Sight" means that it is visible and not more than 50 ft from the location of the equipment.

680.14 Wiring Methods in Corrosive Environment

Wiring methods in corrosive environments must be rigid metal conduit, intermediate metal conduit, rigid polyvinyl chloride conduit, or reinforced thermosetting resin conduit. ▶Figure 680-22

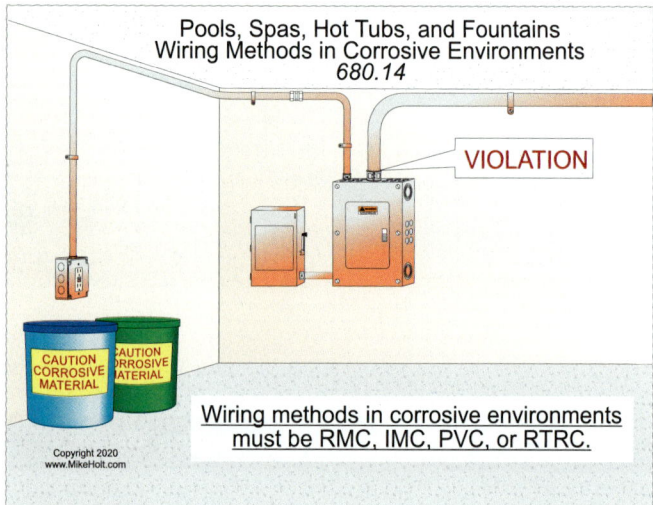

▶Figure 680-22

Part II. Permanently Installed Pools

680.20 General

The requirements contained in Part I and Part II apply to permanently installed pools as defined by 680.2 and aboveground pools having a water depth greater than 42 in.

680.21 Pool Motors

(A) Wiring Methods. The wiring to a pool-associated motor must comply with 680.21(A)(1) unless modified by (A)(2) or (A)(3).

(1) General. Branch-circuit wiring for pool-associated motors installed in corrosive locations must be rigid metal conduit, intermediate metal conduit, rigid polyvinyl chloride conduit, reinforced thermosetting resin conduit [680.14], or Type MC cable listed for the location. ▶Figure 680-23

The wiring methods must contain an insulated copper equipment grounding conductor sized in accordance with 250.122, but in no case can it be sized smaller than 12 AWG. ▶Figure 680-24

Where installed in noncorrosive environments, any Chapter 3 wiring method is permitted.

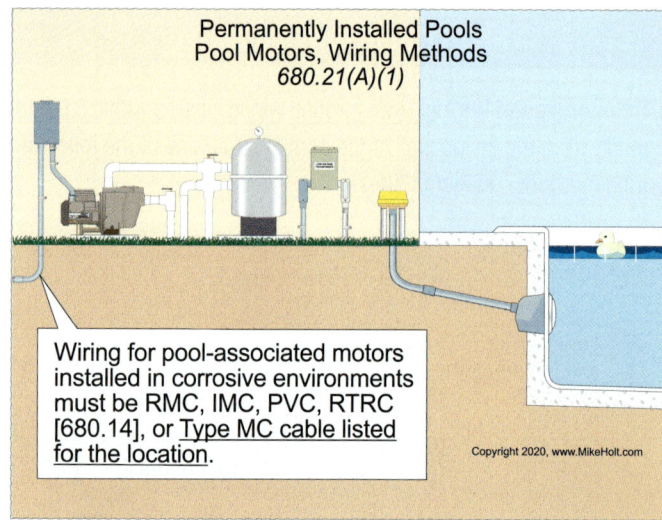

▶Figure 680-23

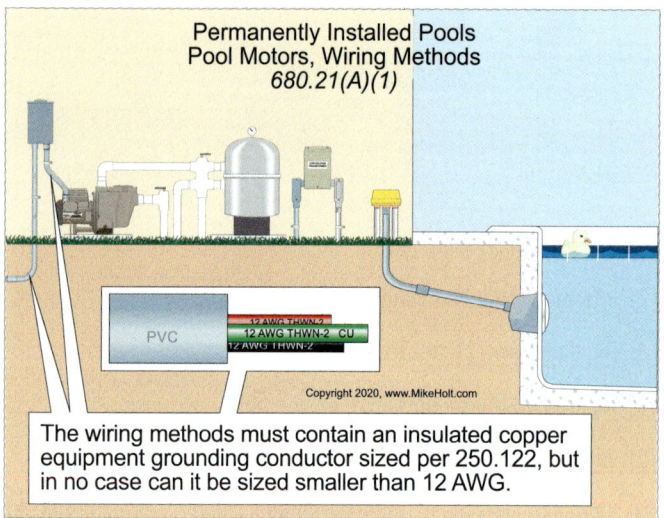

▶Figure 680-24

(2) Flexible Connections. Liquidtight flexible metal and liquidtight flexible nonmetallic conduit are permitted.

(C) GFCI Protection. GFCI protection is required for all pool motors rated 60A or less and not over 150V to ground, whether connected by receptacle or by direct connection. ▶Figure 680-25

Ex: Listed low-voltage motors not requiring grounding, with ratings not exceeding the low-voltage contact limit supplied by transformers or power supplies that comply with 680.23(A)(2), may be installed without GFCI protection.

(D) Pool Pump Motor Replacement. Where a pool pump motor is replaced, the replacement pump motor must be provided with GFCI protection. Figure 680-26

Swimming Pools, Spas, Hot Tubs, Fountains, and Similar Installations | 680.22

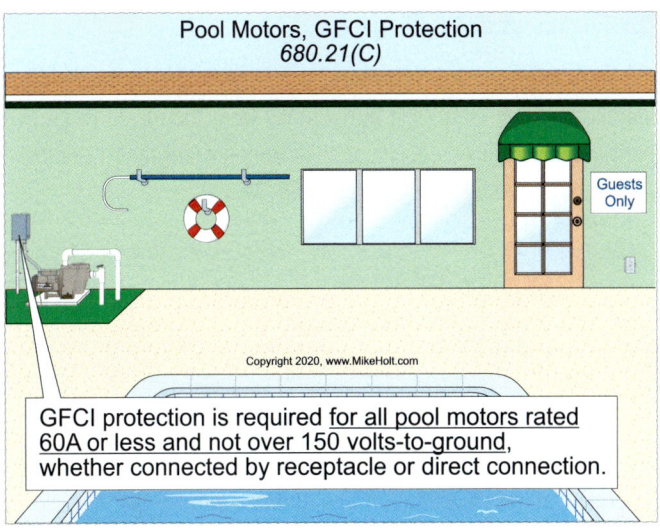
▶Figure 680–25

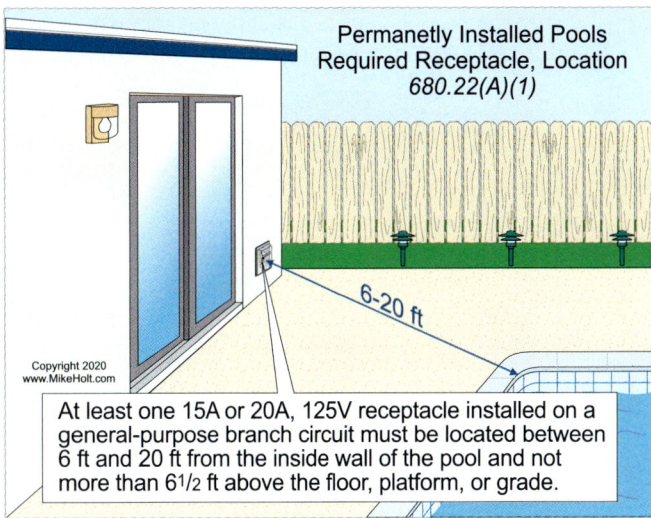
▶Figure 680–27

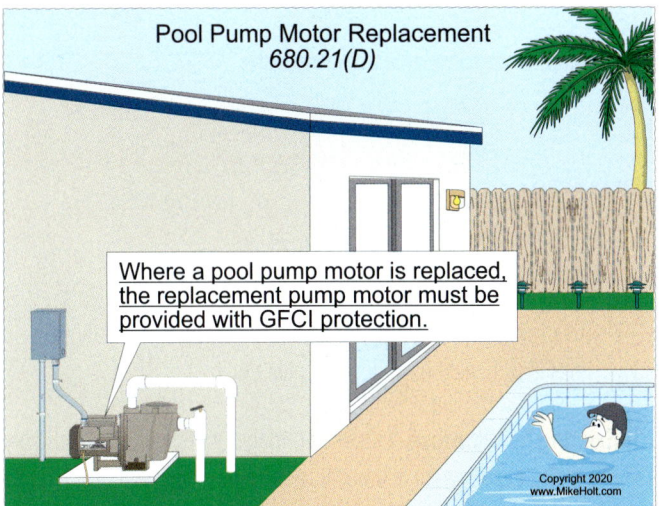
▶Figure 680–26

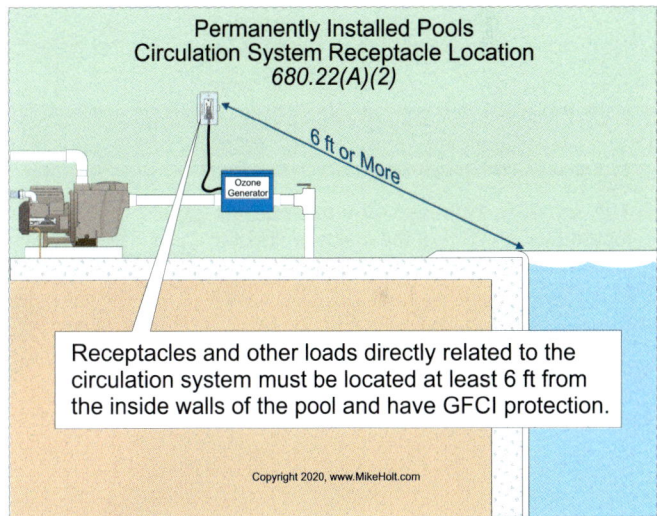
▶Figure 680–28

680.22 Receptacles, Luminaires, and Switches

(A) Receptacles.

(1) Required Receptacle, Location. At least one 15A or 20A, 125V receptacle installed on a general-purpose branch circuit must be located not less than 6 ft and not more than 20 ft from the inside wall of a permanently installed pool. This receptacle must be located not more than 6½ ft above the floor, platform, or grade level serving the pool. ▶Figure 680–27

(2) Circulation System. Receptacles for permanently installed pool motors, or other loads directly related to the circulation system, must be located at least 6 ft from the inside walls of the pool and have GFCI protection. ▶Figure 680–28

(3) Other Receptacles. Receptacles for loads not directly related to the circulation system must be located not less than 6 ft from the inside walls of a permanently installed pool. ▶Figure 680–29

(4) GFCI Protection. 15A and 20A, single-phase, 125V receptacles located within 20 ft of the inside walls of a pool must be GFCI protected. ▶Figure 680–30

(5) Pool Equipment Room. At least one GFCI-protected 15A or 20A, 125V receptacle must be located within a pool equipment room. Receptacles rated 150V or less to ground within the pool equipment room must be GFCI protected. ▶Figure 680–31

(6) Measurements. The receptacle distance is measured as the shortest path an appliance cord will follow without passing through a wall, doorway, or window.

680.22 | Swimming Pools, Spas, Hot Tubs, Fountains, and Similar Installations

▶Figure 680–29

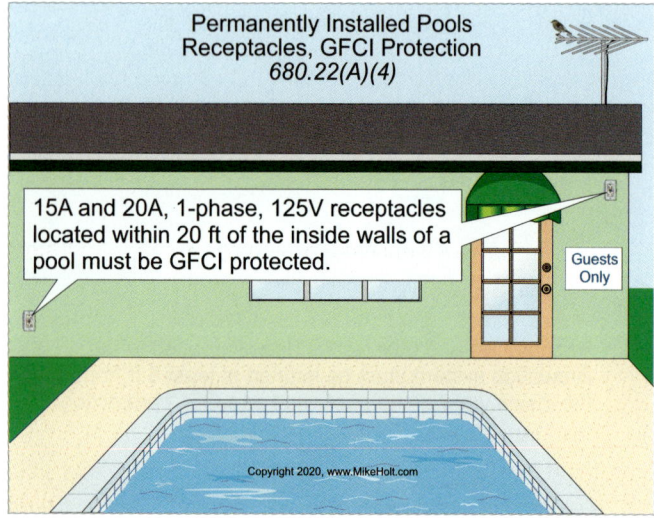

▶Figure 680–30

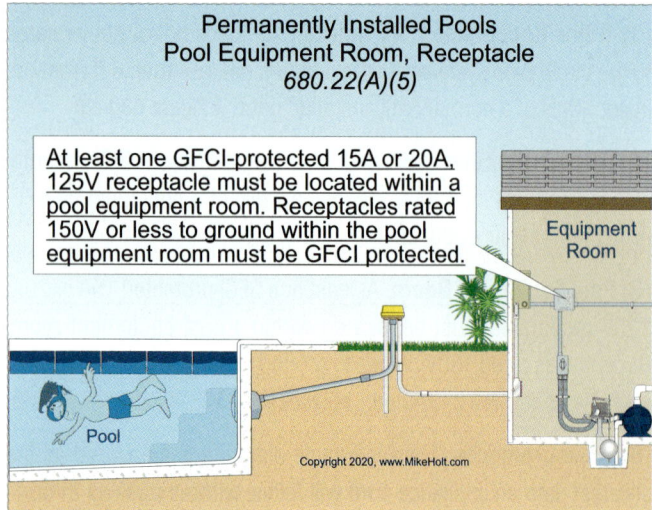

▶Figure 680–31

(B) Luminaires and Ceiling Fans.

(1) New Outdoor Installations. Luminaires and lighting outlets installed not less than 5 ft horizontally from the inside walls of a permanently installed pool must be located not less than 12 ft above the maximum water level. ▶Figure 680–32

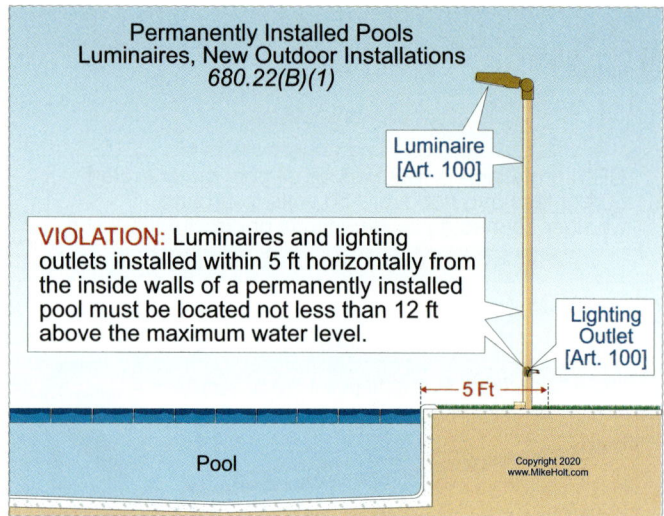

▶Figure 680–32

> **Author's Comment:**
>
> ▸ According to 680.2, the "Maximum Water Level" is the highest level water reaches before it spills out.

(3) Existing Installations. Existing lighting outlets within 5 ft horizontally from the inside walls of a permanently installed pool must not be less than 5 ft above the surface of the maximum water level, be rigidly attached to the existing structure, and be GFCI protected. ▶Figure 680–33

(4) GFCI Protection in Adjacent Areas. GFCI protection is required for lighting outlets located between 5 ft and 10 ft horizontally from the inside walls of a permanently installed pool and not less than 5 ft above the maximum water level.

(6) Low-Voltage Luminaires. Low-voltage lighting systems not exceeding low-voltage contact limits with a transformer or power supply that is listed, labeled, and identified for swimming pools or underwater luminaires can be installed without any distance limit to the water [680.23(A)(2)]. ▶Figure 680–34

All other low-voltage lighting must not be installed within 10 ft from the edge of the water in accordance with 411.5(B).

Swimming Pools, Spas, Hot Tubs, Fountains, and Similar Installations | 680.23

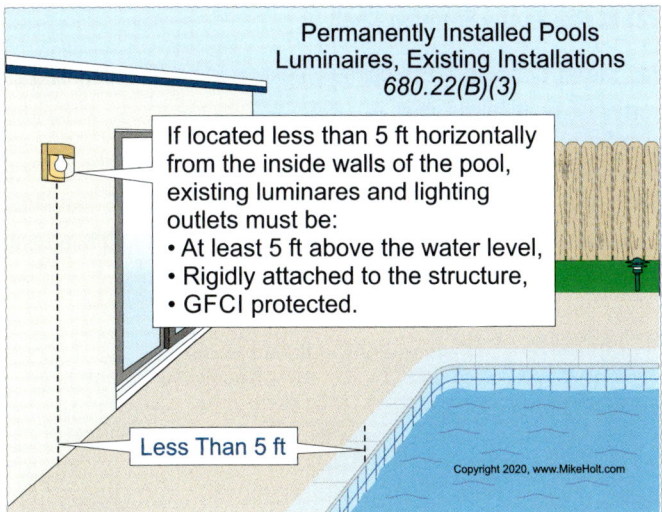
▶Figure 680-33

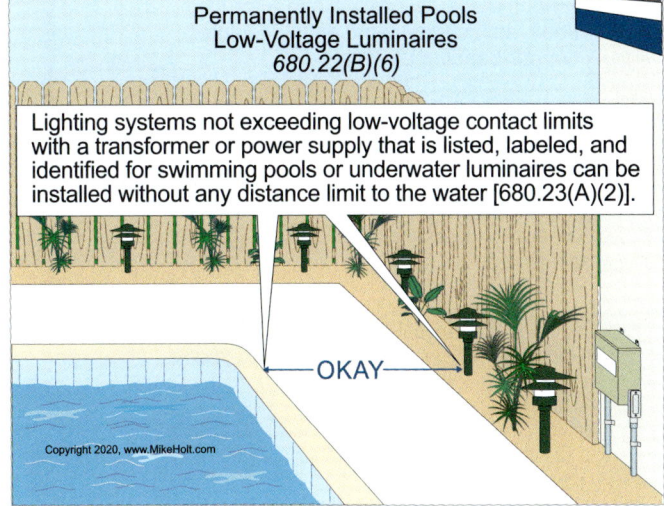
▶Figure 680-34

(7) Low-Voltage Gas-Fired Luminaires, Fireplaces, Fire Pits, and Similar Equipment. Listed gas-fired luminaires, fireplaces, fire pits, and similar equipment using low-voltage ignitors supplied by listed transformers or power supplies that comply with 680.23(A)(2) and do not exceed the low-voltage contact limit can be located less than 5 ft from the inside walls of the pool.

(8) Measurements. In determining the dimensions in this section addressing luminaires, the distance to be measured must be the shortest path an imaginary cord connected to the luminaire will follow without piercing a floor, wall, ceiling, doorway with a hinged or sliding door, window opening, or other effective permanent barrier.

(C) Switching Devices. Circuit breakers, time clocks, pool light switches, and other switching devices must be located not less than 5 ft horizontally from the inside walls of a permanently installed pool unless separated by a solid fence, wall, or other permanent barrier that provides at least a 5-foot reach distance. ▶Figure 680-35

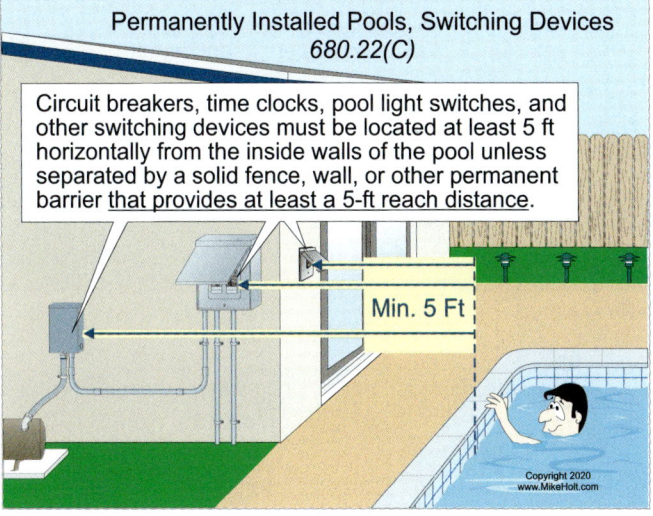
▶Figure 680-35

(D) Other Outlets. Other outlets must be not less than 10 ft from the inside walls of the pool.

Note: Other outlets may include (but are not limited to) remote-control, signaling, fire alarm, and communications circuits.

(E) Other Equipment. Other equipment with ratings exceeding the low-voltage contact limit must be located at least 5 ft horizontally from the inside walls of a pool unless separated from the pool by a solid fence, wall, or other permanent barrier. ▶Figure 680-36

680.23 Underwater Pool Luminaires

(A) General.

(2) Transformers and Power Supplies for Underwater Pool Luminaires. Transformers and power supplies for underwater pool luminaires must be listed, labeled, and identified for swimming pool use.

(3) GFCI Protection. Branch circuits supplying underwater pool luminaires at 120V must be GFCI protected. ▶Figure 680-37

(5) Wall-Mounted Luminaires. Underwater wall-mounted luminaires must be installed so the top of the luminaire lens is not less than 18 in. below the normal water level. ▶Figure 680-38

(B) Wet-Niche Luminaires.

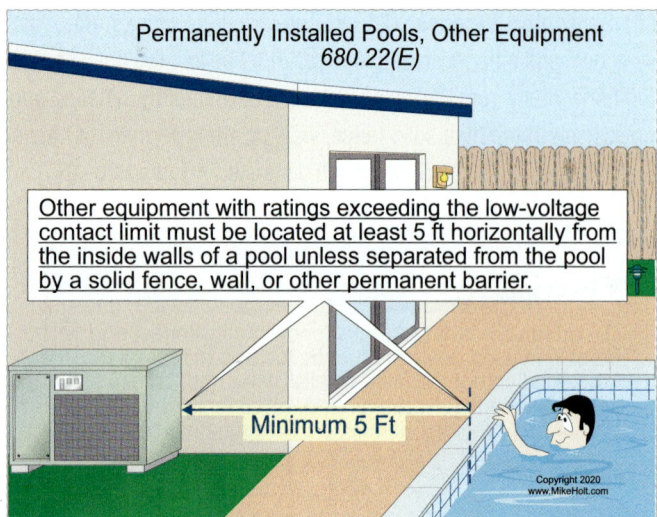
▶Figure 680–36

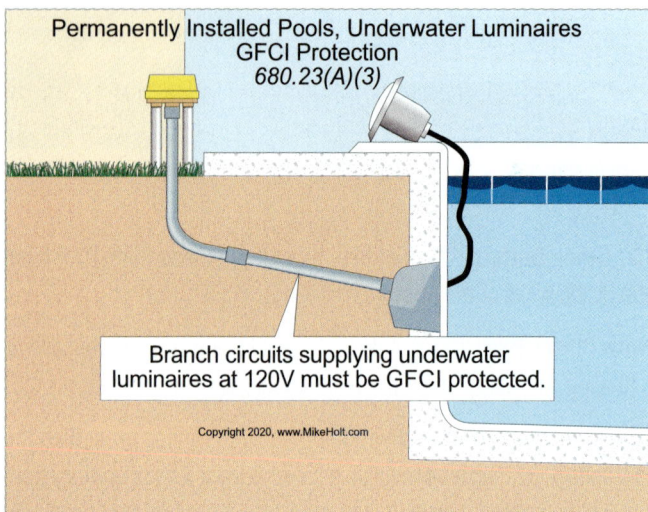
▶Figure 680–37

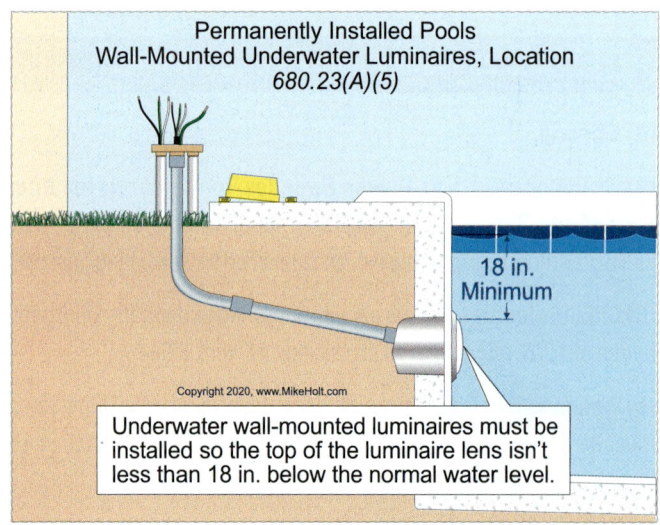
▶Figure 680–38

(2) Wiring to the Forming Shell.

(a) Metal Conduit. Metal conduit must be listed and identified as red brass or stainless steel.

(b) Nonmetallic Raceway. A nonmetallic raceway run to the forming shell of a wet-niche luminaire must contain an 8 AWG insulated (solid or stranded) copper conductor that terminates to the forming shell. ▶Figure 680–39 and ▶Figure 680–40

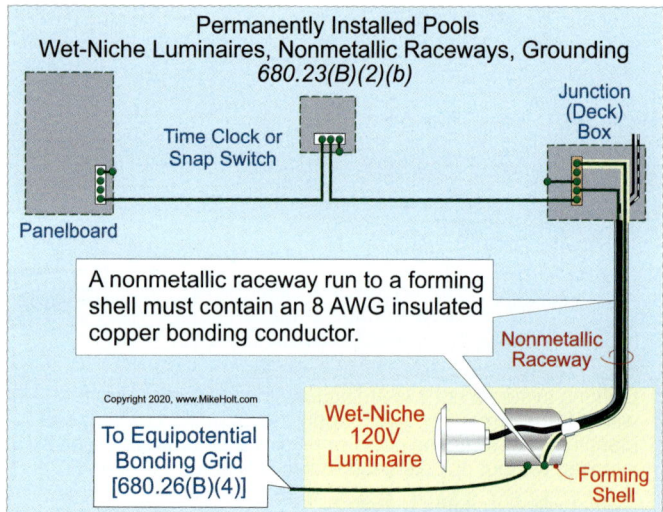
▶Figure 680–39

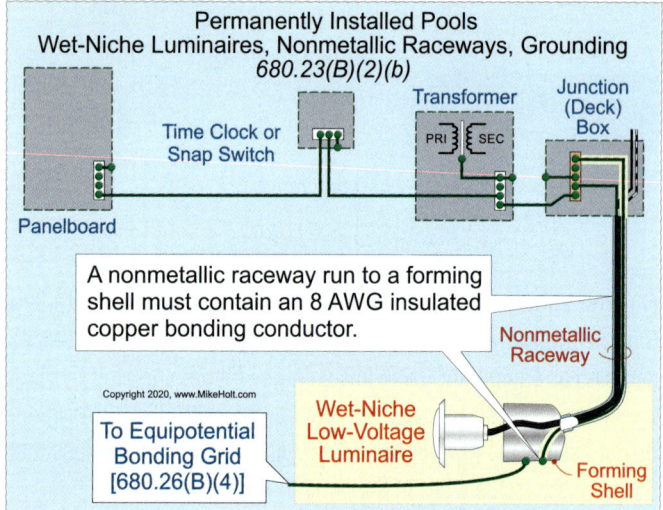
▶Figure 680–40

The termination of the 8 AWG bonding jumper in the forming shell must be covered with a listed potting compound to protect the connection from the possible deteriorating effects of pool water.

Author's Comment:

▸ According to 680.2, a "Wet-Niche Luminaire" is a luminaire intended to be installed in a forming shell where it will be completely surrounded by water. ▶Figure 680-41

▶Figure 680-41

Author's Comment:

▸ According to Article 680.2, a "Forming Shell" is a structure mounted in a pool or fountain to support a wet-niche luminaire. ▶Figure 680-42

▶Figure 680-42

(3) Equipment Grounding Provisions for Cords. The cord or cable supplying a low-voltage underwater luminaire that does not require grounding does not require an equipment grounding conductor. ▶Figure 680-43

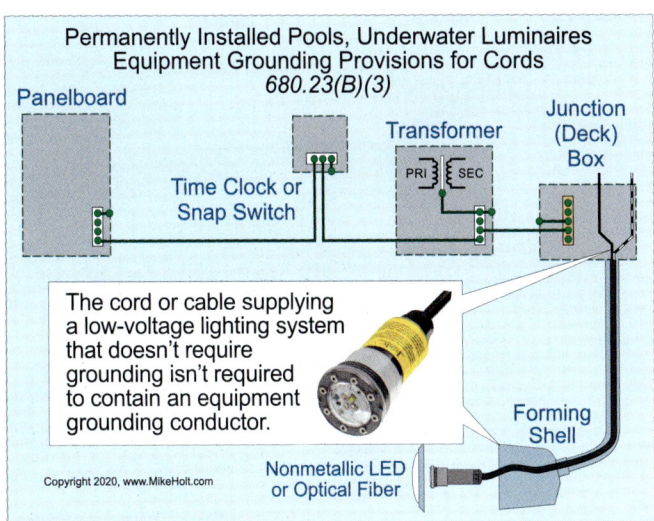
▶Figure 680-43

(6) Luminaire Servicing.

Pool. The location of the forming shell and length of flexible cord for wet-niche pool luminaires must allow for personnel to place the luminaire on the deck or other dry location for maintenance. ▶Figure 680-44

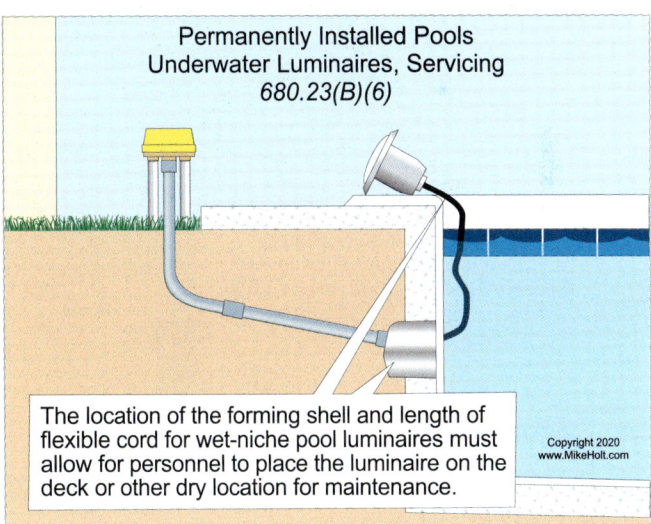
▶Figure 680-44

The luminaire maintenance location must be accessible without entering or going into the pool water.

Spa. In spa locations where wet-niche luminaires are installed in the foot well of the spa, the location of the forming shell and length of flexible cord for the underwater spa luminaire must allow for personnel to place the luminaire on the bench where the spa can be drained to make the bench location dry. ▶Figure 680-45

680.23 | Swimming Pools, Spas, Hot Tubs, Fountains, and Similar Installations

▶Figure 680–45

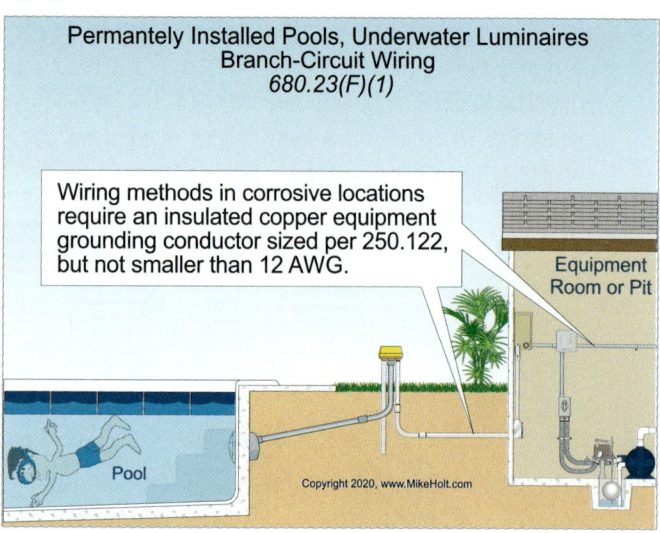

▶Figure 680–47

(F) Branch-Circuit Wiring.

(1) General. Branch-circuit wiring installed in corrosive locations must be in rigid metal conduit, intermediate metal conduit, rigid polyvinyl chloride conduit, reinforced thermosetting resin conduit [680.14], or liquidtight flexible nonmetallic conduit. ▶Figure 680–46

(2) Branch-Circuit Equipment Grounding Conductor. Branch-circuit conductors for all through-wall underwater pool luminaires must have insulated copper equipment grounding conductors without joint or splice except as permitted in 680.23(F)(2)(a) and (b), sized in accordance with 250.122, and not smaller than 12 AWG. ▶Figure 680–48

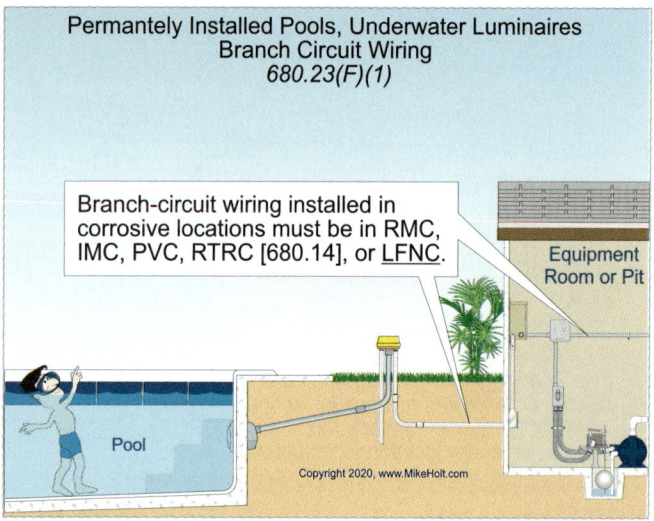

▶Figure 680–46

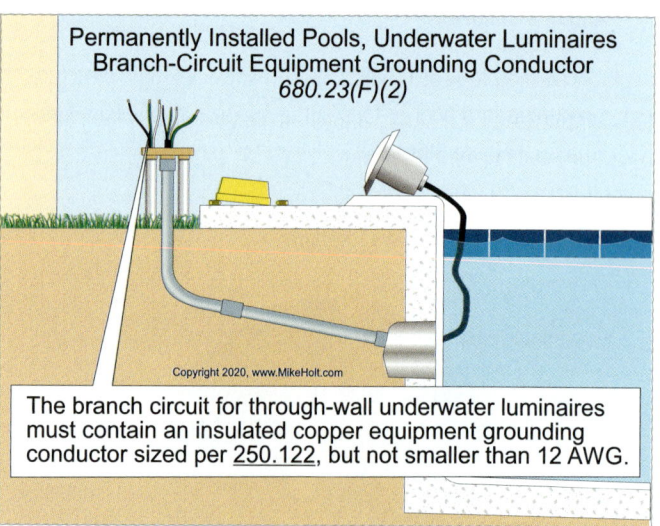

▶Figure 680–48

Wiring methods in corrosive environments must contain an insulated copper equipment grounding conductor sized in accordance with 250.122 but not smaller than 12 AWG. ▶Figure 680–47

Where installed in noncorrosive environments, any Chapter 3 wiring method is permitted.

The circuit equipment grounding conductor for the underwater pool luminaire is not permitted to be spliced, except for the following applications:

(a) If more than one underwater pool luminaire is supplied by the same branch circuit, the circuit equipment grounding conductor can terminate at a listed pool junction box meeting the requirements of 680.24(A).

(b) The circuit equipment grounding conductor can terminate at the grounding terminal of a listed pool transformer meeting the requirements of 680.23(A)(2). ▶Figure 680-49

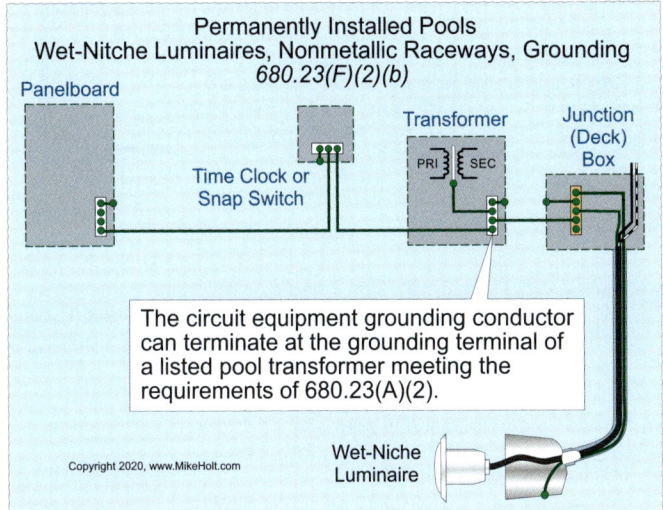

▶Figure 680-49

▶Figure 680-50

(2) Installation.

(a) Vertical Spacing. If the underwater pool luminaire operates at 120V, the junction box must be located not less than 4 in. above the ground or pool, or not less than 8 in. above the maximum water level, whichever provides the greater elevation. ▶Figure 680-51

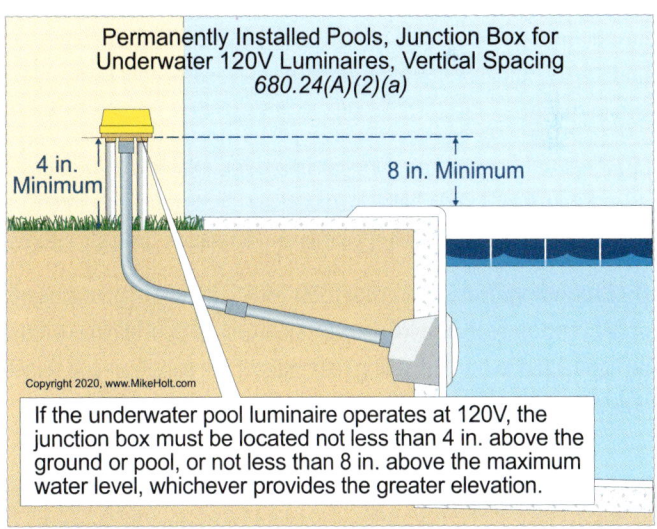

▶Figure 680-51

(3) Conductors. The branch-circuit conductors for the underwater pool luminaire on the load side of a GFCI or transformer used to comply with 680.23(A)(8) are not permitted to occupy raceways or enclosures with other conductors unless the other conductors are:

(1) GFCI protected or,

(2) Equipment grounding conductors and bonding jumpers as required by 680.23(B)(2)(b) or,

(3) Supply conductors to a feed-through-type GFCI.

680.24 Junction Box, Transformer, or GFCI Enclosure

(A) Junction Box. If a junction box is connected to a raceway that extends directly to an underwater pool luminaire forming shell, the junction box must comply with the following:

(1) Construction. The junction box must be listed, labeled, and identified as a swimming pool junction box. ▶Figure 680-50

(b) Horizontal Spacing. If the underwater pool luminaire operates at 120V, the junction box must be located not less than 4 ft from the inside wall of the pool unless separated by a solid fence, wall, or other permanent barrier. ▶Figure 680-52

680.25 | Swimming Pools, Spas, Hot Tubs, Fountains, and Similar Installations

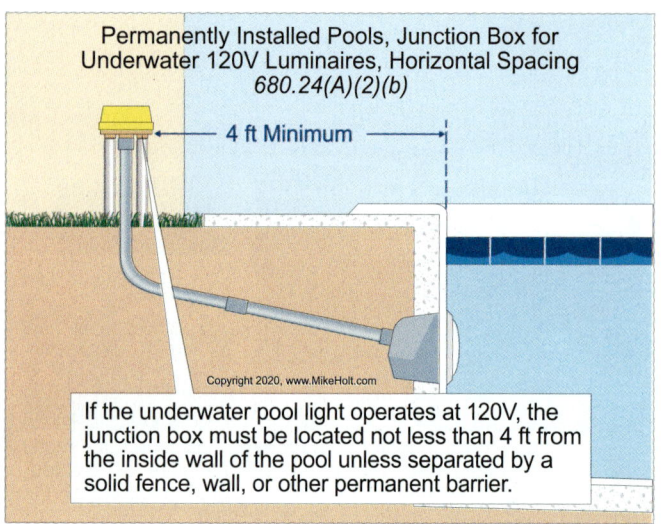

▶Figure 680-52

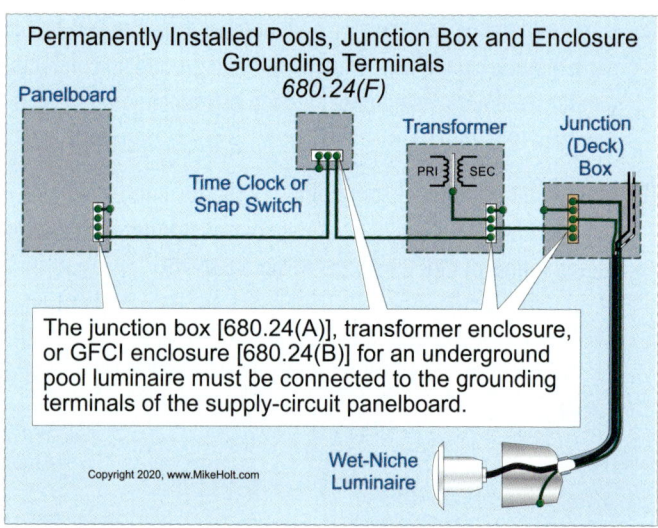

▶Figure 680-53

Author's Comment:

▸ The junction box must be supported by two metal conduits threaded wrenchtight into the enclosure according to 314.23(E).

(B) Transformer or GFCI Enclosure. If the enclosure for a transformer or GFCI is connected to a raceway that extends directly to an underwater luminaire forming shell, the enclosure must be listed for this purpose.

(C) Physical Protection. Junction boxes for underwater luminaires are not permitted to be located in a walkway unless afforded protection by being located under diving boards or adjacent to fixed structures.

(F) Grounding. The junction box [680.24(A)], transformer enclosure, or GFCI enclosure [680.24(B)] for an underground pool luminaire must be connected to the grounding terminals of the supply-circuit panelboard. ▶Figure 680-53

680.25 Feeders

(A) Wiring Methods. Where feeder wiring is installed in corrosive environments, the wiring methods must be rigid metal conduit, intermediate metal conduit, rigid polyvinyl chloride conduit, reinforced thermosetting resin conduit, or liquidtight flexible nonmetallic conduit [680.14].

The wiring methods in corrosive environments must have insulated copper equipment grounding conductors sized in accordance with Table 250.122, but not smaller than 12 AWG. ▶Figure 680-54

Where installed in noncorrosive environments, any Chapter 3 wiring method is permitted.

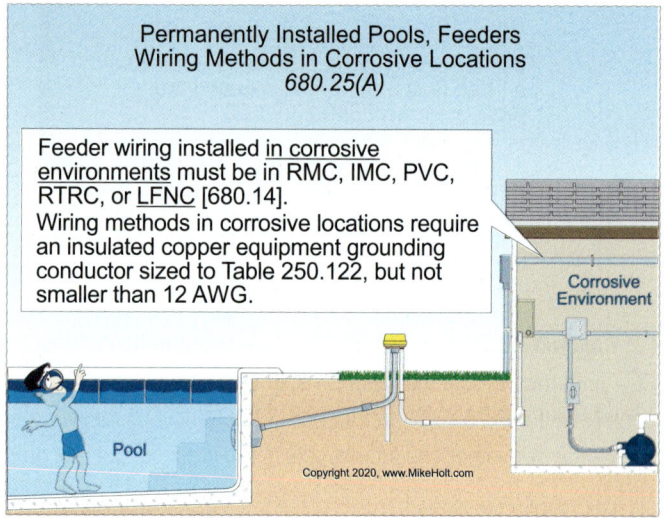

▶Figure 680-54

680.26 Equipotential Bonding

(A) Performance. Equipotential bonding is intended to reduce voltage gradients in the area around a permanently installed pool. ▶Figure 680-55

(B) Bonded Parts. The parts of a permanently installed pool listed in (B)(1) through (B)(7) must be bonded together with a solid insulated or bare copper conductor not smaller than 8 AWG using a listed pressure connector, terminal bar, or other listed means in accordance with 250.8(A). ▶Figure 680-56

Equipotential bonding is not required to extend (or be attached) to any panelboard, service disconnect, or grounding electrode.

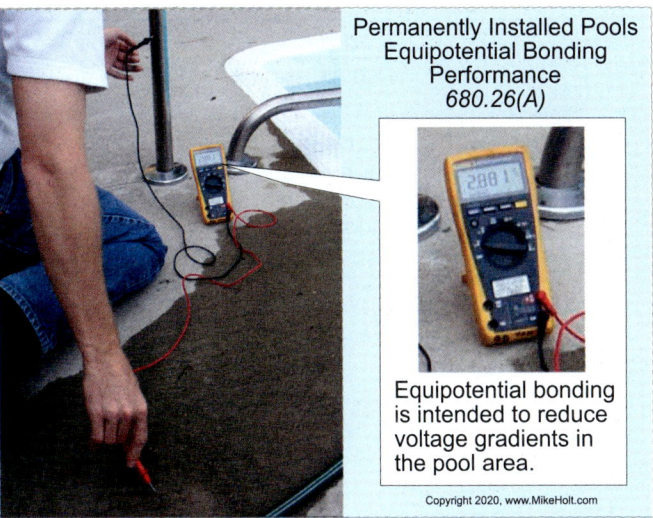
▶Figure 680-55

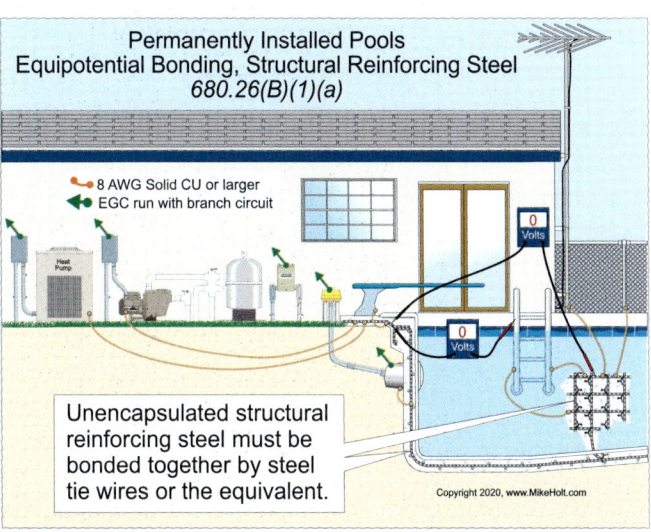
▶Figure 680-57

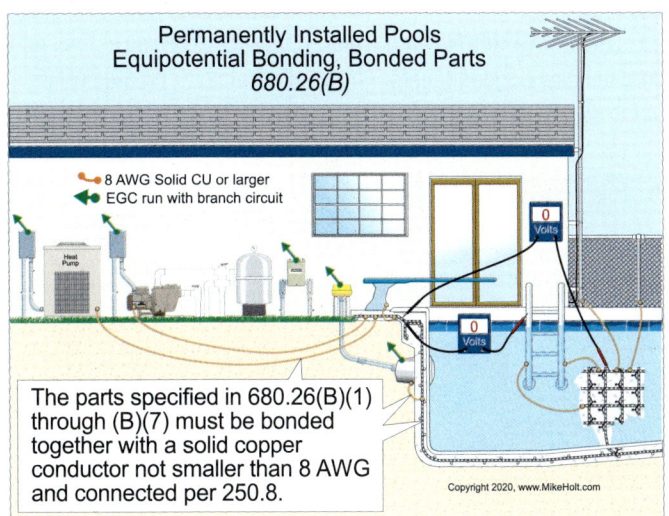
▶Figure 680-56

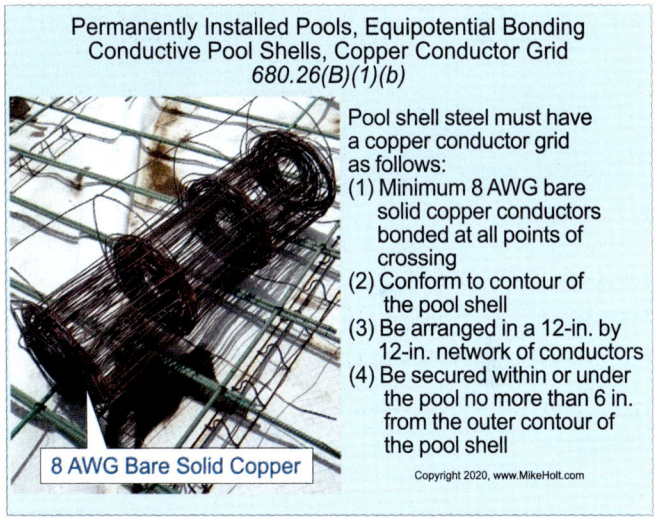
▶Figure 680-58

(1) Conductive Pool Shells. Cast-in-place concrete, pneumatically applied or sprayed concrete, and concrete block with painted or plastered coatings are considered conductive materials due to water permeability and porosity. Vinyl liners and fiberglass composite shells are considered nonconductive materials.

Reconstructed pool shells must also comply with this section.

(a) Structural Reinforcing Steel. Unencapsulated structural reinforcing steel must be bonded together by steel tie wires or the equivalent. ▶Figure 680-57

Where structural reinforcing steel is encapsulated in a nonconductive compound, a copper conductor grid must be installed in accordance with 680.26(B)(1)(b).

(b) Copper Conductor Grid. A copper conductor grid must comply with all of the following: ▶Figure 680-58

Author's Comment:

▸ Encapsulated structural reinforcing steel is used to prevent rebar corrosion and (if used) will make the pool shell insulated; therefore, a conductive copper grid is required in order to bond the pool shell.

(1) Be constructed of a minimum of 8 AWG bare solid copper conductors bonded to each other at all points of crossing in accordance with 250.8, or other approved means.

(2) Conform to the contour of the pool.

(3) Be arranged in a 12-in. by 12-in. network of conductors in a uniformly spaced perpendicular grid pattern with a tolerance of 4 in.

680.26 | Swimming Pools, Spas, Hot Tubs, Fountains, and Similar Installations

(4) Be secured within or under the pool no more than 6 in. from the outer contour of the pool shell.

(2) Perimeter Surfaces. Equipotential perimeter bonding must extend a minimum of 3 ft horizontally from the inside walls of a pool where not separated by a building or permanent wall 5 ft in height. ▶Figure 680-59

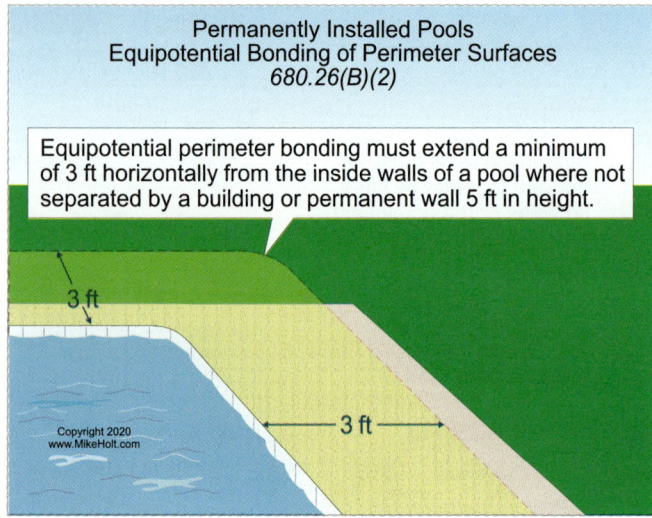

▶Figure 680-59

Perimeter surfaces less than 3 ft separated by a permanent wall or building 5 ft or more in height require equipotential bonding only on the pool side of the wall or building ▶Figure 680-60

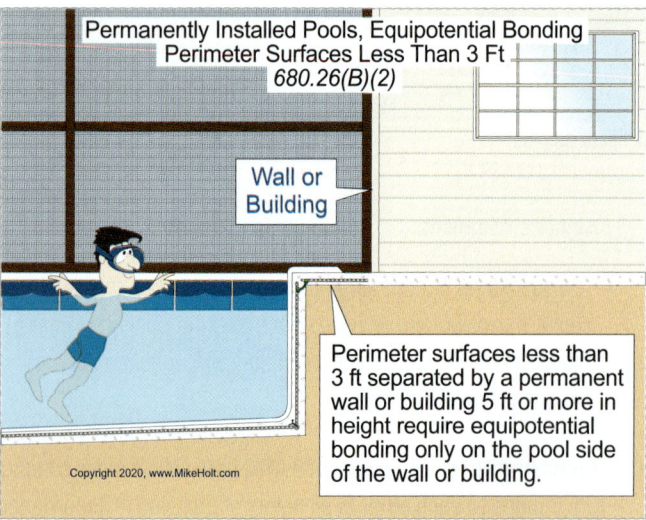

▶Figure 680-60

For conductive pool shells, equipotential bonding for perimeter surfaces must be attached to the concrete pool reinforcing steel or copper conductor grid at a minimum of four points uniformly spaced around the perimeter of the pool and be one of the following: ▶Figure 680-61

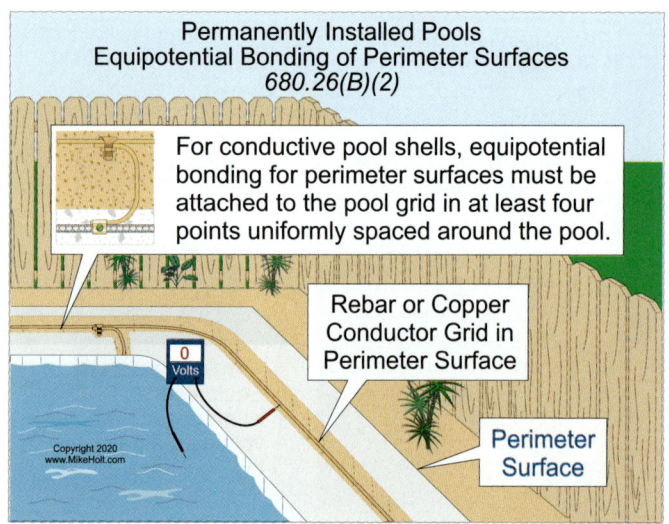

▶Figure 680-61

(a) Structural Reinforcing Steel. Unencapsulated structural reinforcing steel bonded together by steel tie wires or the equivalent in accordance with 680.26(B)(1)(a). ▶Figure 680-62

▶Figure 680-62

Author's Comment:

▶ The *NEC* does not provide any guidance on the installation requirements for structural reinforcing steel when used as a perimeter surface equipotential bonding method. ▶Figure 680-63

(b) Copper Ring. Where structural reinforcing steel is not available or is encapsulated in a nonconductive compound, a copper conductor can be used for equipotential perimeter bonding where the following requirements are met: ▶Figure 680-64

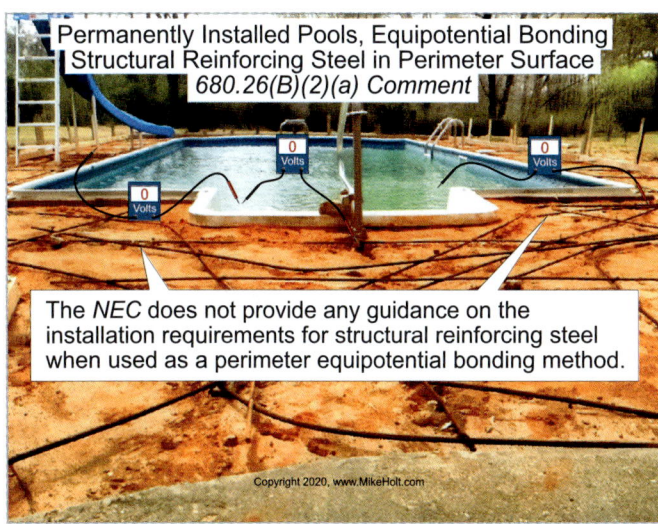

▶Figure 680-63

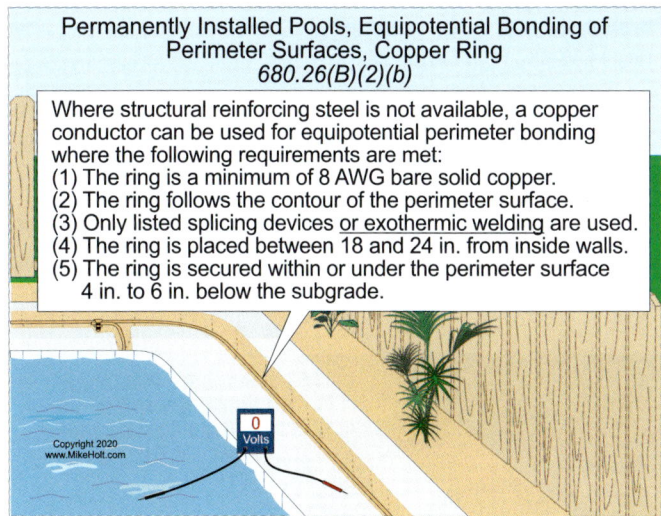

▶Figure 680-64

(1) The copper ring is constructed of 8 AWG bare solid copper or larger.

(2) The copper ring conductor follows the contour of the perimeter surface.

(3) Only listed splicing devices or exothermic welding are used.

(4) The copper ring conductor is placed between 18 in. and 24 in. from the inside walls of the pool.

(5) The copper ring conductor is secured within or under the perimeter surface 4 in. to 6 in. below the subgrade.

(c) Copper Grid. Where structural reinforcing steel is not available or is encapsulated in a nonconductive compound as an alternate method to a copper ring, a copper grid can be used for perimeter bonding where all the following requirements are met:

(1) The copper grid is constructed of 8 AWG solid bare copper and arranged in a 12-in. by 12-in. network of conductors in a uniformly spaced perpendicular grid pattern with a tolerance of 4 in. in accordance with 680.26(B)(1)(b)(3).

(2) The copper grid follows the contour of the perimeter surface extending 3 ft horizontally beyond the inside walls of the pool.

(3) Only listed splicing devices or exothermic welding are used.

(4) The copper grid is secured within or under the deck or unpaved surfaces between 4 in. and 6 in. below the subgrade.

(3) Metallic Components. Metallic parts of the pool structure must be bonded together.

(4) Underwater Lighting. All metal forming shells must be bonded.

Ex: Listed low-voltage lighting with nonmetallic forming shells are not required to be bonded.

(5) Metal Fittings. Metal fittings sized over 4 in. in any direction and located within or attached to the pool structure (such as ladders and handrails) must be connected to the swimming pool equipotential bonding means. ▶Figure 680-65

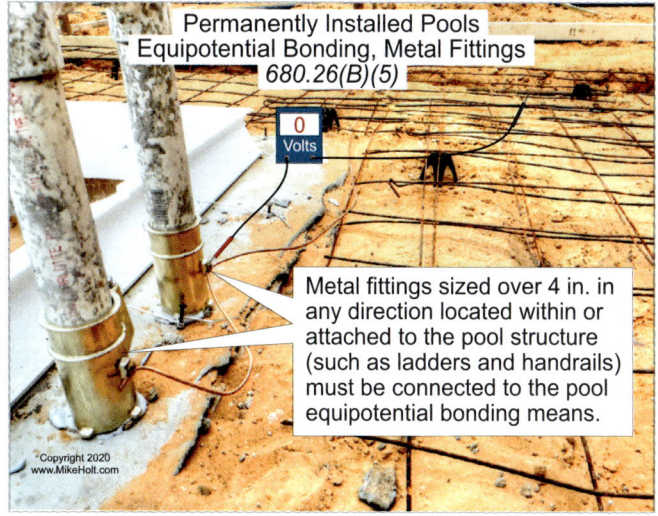

▶Figure 680-65

Metallic pool cover anchors 1 in. or less in any dimension and 2 in. or less in length are not required to be bonded to the equipotential bonding means.

(6) Electrical Equipment. Metal parts of electrical equipment associated with the pool water circulating system such as pool heaters, pump motors, and metal parts of pool covers must be connected to the swimming pool equipotential bonding means. ▶Figure 680-66

680.26 | Swimming Pools, Spas, Hot Tubs, Fountains, and Similar Installations

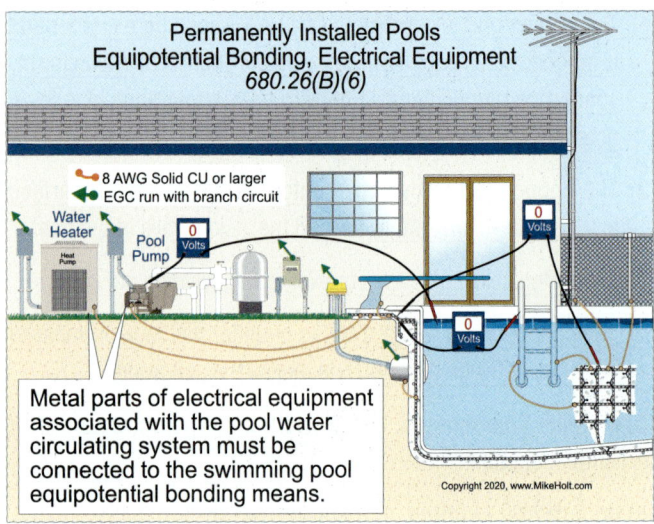

▶Figure 680-66

(a) Double-Insulated Water-Pump Motors. Where a double-insulated water-pump motor is installed, a solid 8 AWG copper conductor of sufficient length to make a bonding connection to a replacement motor from the swimming pool equipotential bonding means to an accessible point in the vicinity of the pool pump motor must be provided. ▶Figure 680-67

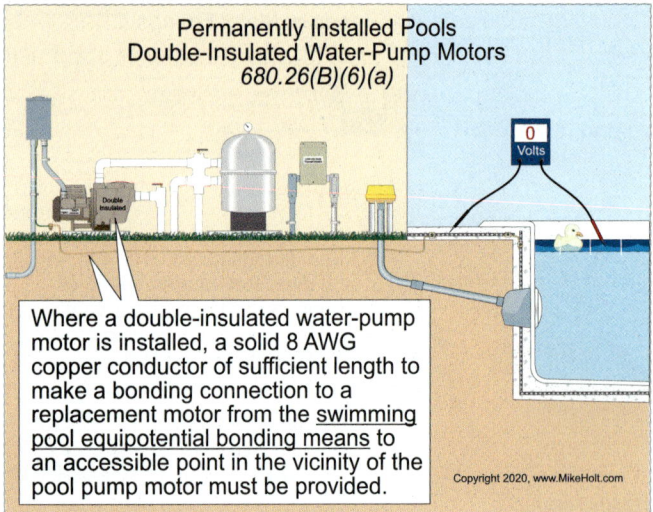

▶Figure 680-67

Where there is no connection between the swimming pool equipotential bonding means and the equipment grounding system for the premises, this bonding conductor must be connected to the equipment grounding conductor of the motor circuit.

(7) Fixed Metal Parts. Fixed metal parts such as metal-sheathed cables and raceways, metal piping, metal awnings, metal fences, and metal door and window frames located within 5 ft horizontally [680.26(B)(7) Ex 2] and 12 ft vertically [680.26(B)(7) Ex 3] from the inside wall of the pool, must be connected to the swimming pool equipotential bonding means. ▶Figure 680-68

▶Figure 680-68

Ex 1: Those separated from the pool by a permanent barrier that prevents contact by a person are not required to be bonded.

Ex 2: Those separated by a distance greater than 5 ft horizontally from the inside walls of the pool are not be required to be bonded. ▶Figure 680-69

▶Figure 680-69

(C) Pool Water. If the pool water in a nonconductive pool structure (vinyl or fiberglass) does not have a direct electrical connection to one of the bonded parts described in 680.26(B), an approved corrosion-resistant conductive surface that is at least 9 sq in. in contact with the water must be bonded in accordance with 680.26(B). ▶Figure 680-70

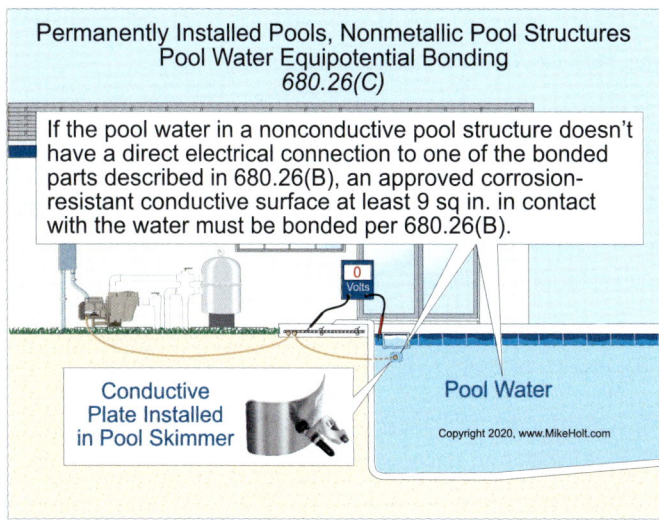

▶Figure 680-70

680.27 Specialized Equipment

(B) Electrically Operated Covers.

(1) Motors and Controllers. The electric motors, controllers, and wiring for an electrically operated cover must be located not less than 5 ft from the inside wall of a permanently installed pool unless separated by a permanent barrier.

(2) GFCI Protection. The branch circuit serving the electric motor and controller circuit must be GFCI protected.

680.28 Gas-Fired Water Heaters

Circuits serving gas-fired swimming pool water heaters operating at 120V must be GFCI protected.

Part III. Storable Pools, Spas, Hot Tubs, and Immersion Pools

680.30 General

Electrical installations for storable pools, storable spas, storable hot tubs, or storable immersion pools must comply with Part I as well as Part III of Article 680.

> **Author's Comment:**
>
> ▶ The requirements contained in Part I of Article 680 include definitions, cord-and-plug-connected equipment, overhead conductor clearances, and the locations of maintenance disconnects.

▶ The bonding requirements contained in 680.26 (Part II of Article 680) do not apply to storable pools, storable spas, storable hot tubs, or storable immersion pools. ▶Figure 680-71

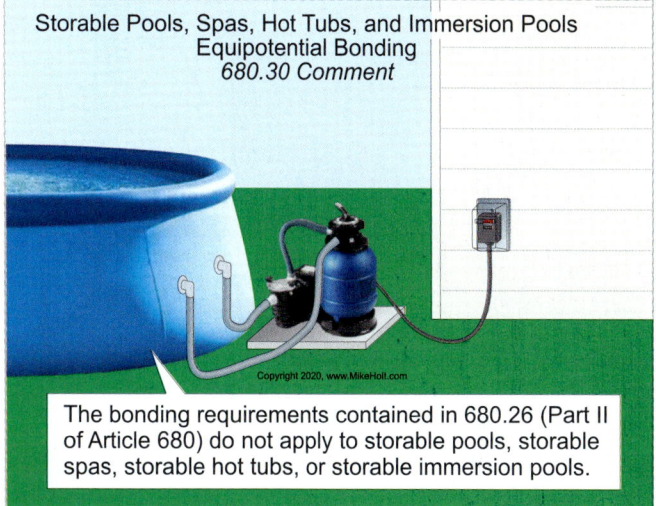

▶Figure 680-71

680.31 Pumps

A cord-connected pool filter pump must incorporate an approved system of double insulation or its equivalent and be provided with means for the termination of an equipment grounding conductor for the noncurrent-carrying metal parts of the pump.

An equipment grounding conductor must be run with the power-supply conductors in the flexible cord.

Cord-connected pool filter pumps must be provided with GFCI protection that is an integral part of the attachment plug or located in the power-supply cord within 12 in. of the attachment plug.

680.32 GFCI Protection

GFCI protection is required for electrical equipment associated with storable pools, and all 15A and 20A, 125V receptacles located within 20 ft from the inside walls of a storable pool, storable spa, or storable hot tub. ▶Figure 680-72

680.34 | Swimming Pools, Spas, Hot Tubs, Fountains, and Similar Installations

▶Figure 680-72

680.34 Receptacle Locations

Receptacles must not be located less than 6 ft from the inside walls of a storable pool, storable spa, or storable hot tub. The receptacle distance is measured as the shortest path a flexible cord will follow without passing through a wall, doorway, or window. ▶Figure 680-73

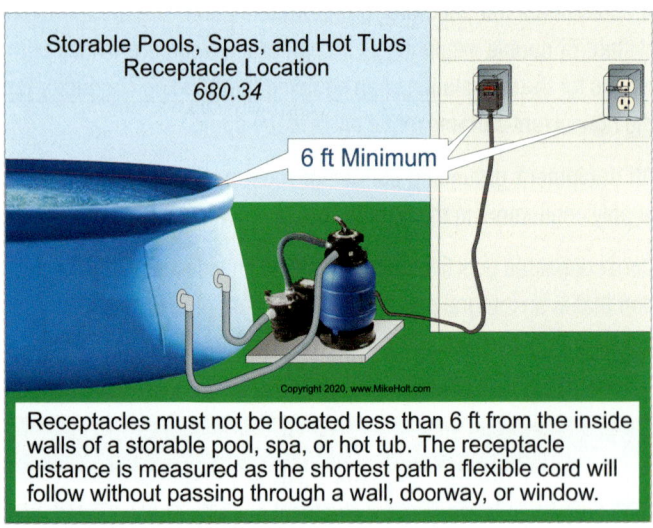

▶Figure 680-73

680.35 Storable and Portable Immersion Pools

Storable and portable immersion pools must comply with the additional requirements specified in 680.35(A) through (G) of the *Code*.

(A) Cord-Connected Storable and Portable Immersion Pools. Storable and portable immersion pools rated 20A, single-phase, 120V or less are permitted to be cord connected if they are GFCI protected.

(B) Pumps. A pump not built in the storable or portable immersion pool must be listed and labeled for swimming pool use.

(C) Heaters. If rated 20A and 30A, single-phase, 120V and 250V, the heater must be GFCI protected.

(E) Lighting Outlets. Unless within the low-voltage contact limit, lighting outlets must be located not less than 10 ft from the nearest point of an immersion pool.

(F) Switches. Switches, unless they are part of the unit, must be located not less than 5 feet from the immersion pool.

(G) Receptacles. All 50A, 250V or less receptacles within 20 ft of the inside wall of an immersion pool must be GFCI protected.

Part IV. Spas and Hot Tubs, and Permanently Installed Immersion Pools

680.40 General

Electrical installations for spas and hot tubs must comply with Part I as well as Part IV of Article 680.

680.41 Emergency Switch for Spas and Hot Tubs

In other than a one-family dwelling, a clearly labeled emergency spa or hot tub water recirculation and jet system shutoff is required. The emergency shutoff must be readily accessible to the users and located not less than 5 ft away, adjacent to, and within sight of the spa or hot tub. ▶Figure 680-74

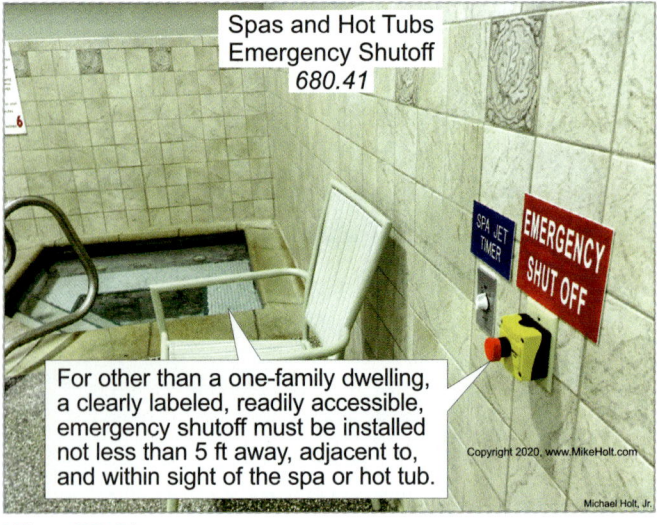

▶Figure 680-74

Author's Comment:

▸ Either the maintenance disconnect [680.13] or a push-button that controls a relay located in accordance with this section can be used to meet the emergency shutoff requirement. ▶Figure 680-75

▸ The purpose of the emergency shutoff is to protect users. Deaths and injuries have occurred in less than 3 ft of water because individuals became stuck to the water intake opening. This requirement applies to spas and hot tubs installed indoors as well as outdoors.

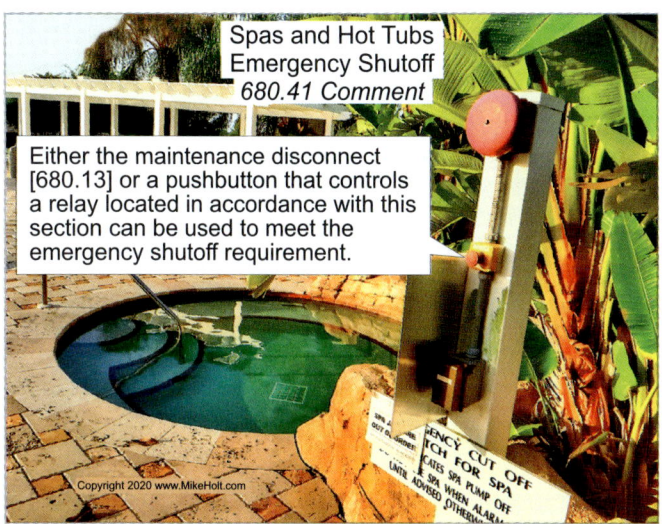

▶Figure 680-75

680.42 Outdoor Installations

(B) Equipotential Bonding. Equipotential bonding of perimeter surfaces for spas and hot tubs is not required if all the following conditions apply:

(1) The spa or hot tub is listed, labeled, and identified as a self-contained spa or hot tub for aboveground use. ▶Figure 680-76

(2) The spa or hot tub is not identified as suitable only for indoor use.

(3) The spa or hot tub is located on or above grade.

(4) The top rim of the spa or hot tub is at least 28 in. above any perimeter surface located within 30 in. of the spa or hot tub. Nonconductive external steps do not apply to the rim height measurement. ▶Figure 680-77

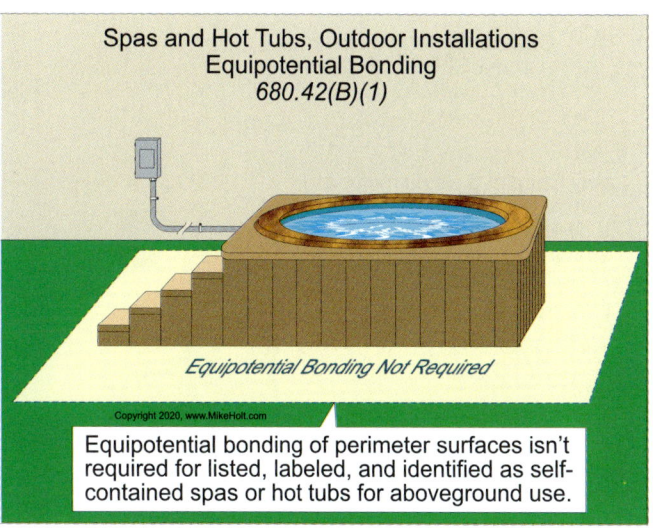

▶Figure 680-76

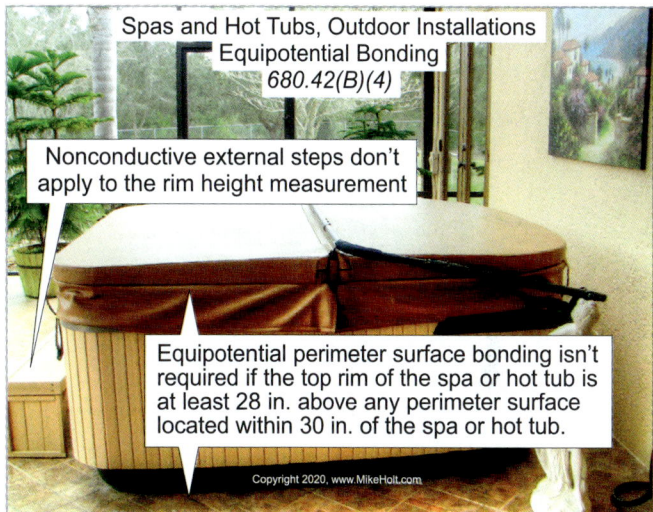

▶Figure 680-77

(C) Wiring. Any Chapter 3 wiring method is permitted in the interior of a dwelling unit for the connection to a spa and hot tub disconnect. ▶Figure 680-78

680.43 Indoor Installations

Electrical installations for an indoor spa or hot tub must comply with Parts I and II of Article 680 except as modified by this section.

Indoor installations of spas or hot tubs can be connected by any of the wiring methods contained in Chapter 3.

Ex 2: The equipotential bonding requirements for perimeter surfaces contained in 680.26(B)(2) do not apply to a listed self-contained spa or hot tub installed above an indoor finished floor.

680.44 | Swimming Pools, Spas, Hot Tubs, Fountains, and Similar Installations

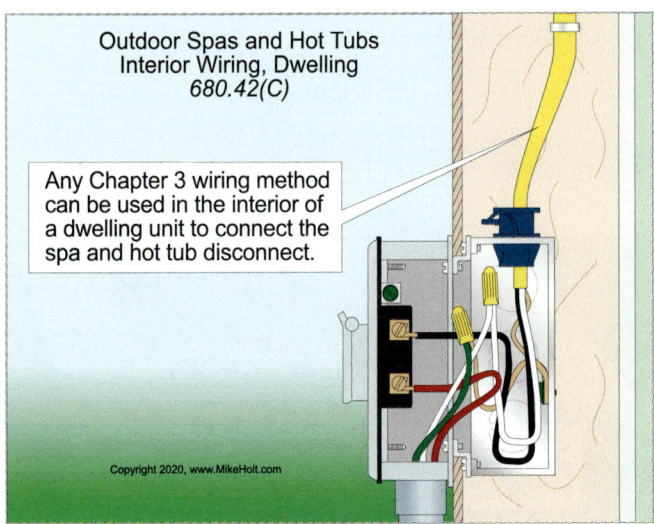

▶Figure 680-78

(4) Measurements. In determining the dimensions in this section, the distance to be measured is the shortest path a cord of an appliance connected to the receptacle will follow without piercing a floor, wall, ceiling, doorway with a hinged or sliding door, window opening, or other type of permanent barrier.

(C) Switches. Switches must be located at least 5 ft, measured horizontally, from the inside wall of the spa or hot tub. ▶Figure 680-80

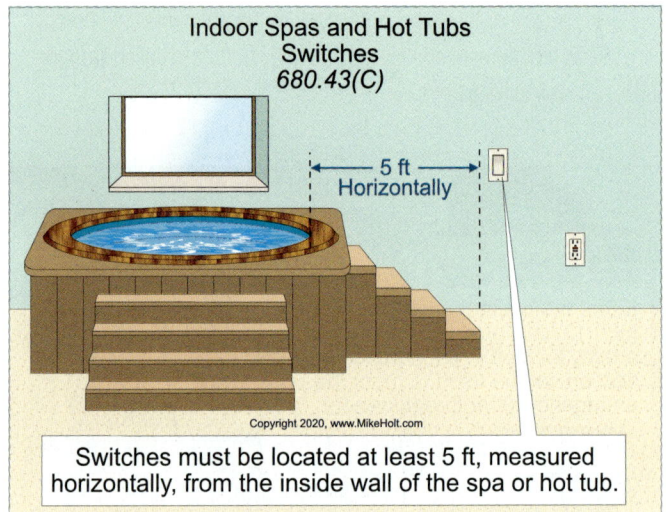

▶Figure 680-80

(A) Receptacles. At least one 15A or 20A, 125V receptacle on a general-purpose branch circuit must be located not less than 6 ft and not more than 10 ft from the inside wall of a spa or hot tub. ▶Figure 680-79

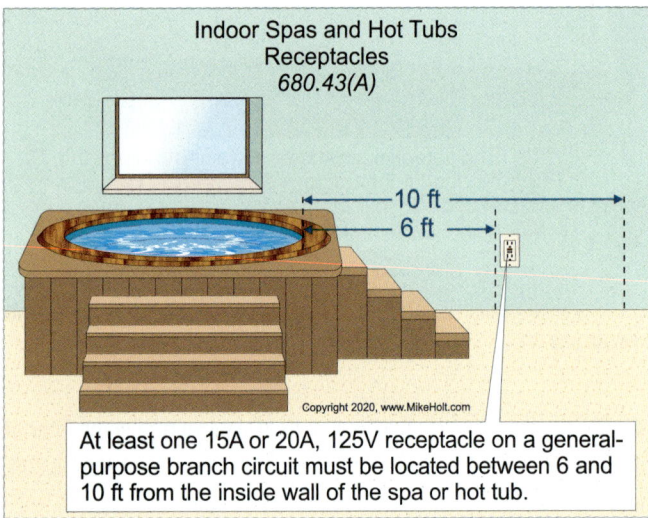

▶Figure 680-79

(1) Location. Receptacles must be located not less than 6 ft measured horizontally from the inside walls of the spa or hot tub.

(2) Protection, General. Receptacles rated 30A, 125V or less and located within 10 ft of the inside walls of a spa or hot tub must be GFCI protected.

(3) Protection, Spa or Hot Tub Supply Receptacle. Receptacles that provide power for spa or hot tub equipment must be GFCI protected.

680.44 GFCI Protection

Outlets that supply self-contained or packaged spa and hot tub assemblies must be GFCI protected, unless the spa or hot tub is listed, labeled, and identified to contain integral GFCI protection [680.44(A)]. ▶Figure 680-81

(A) Listed Units. If so marked, a listed, labeled, and identified self-contained spa or hot tub, or a listed, labeled, and identified packaged equipment assembly that includes integral GFCI protection for all electrical parts does not require additional GFCI protection. ▶Figure 680-82

680.45 Permanently Installed Immersion Pools

Electrical installations at permanently installed immersion pools, whether installed indoors or outdoors, must comply with Parts I, II, and IV of this article except as modified by section 680.45 and must be connected by the wiring methods of Chapter 3 of the *Code*. With regard to the provisions in Part IV of this article, an immersion pool is considered to be a spa or hot tub.

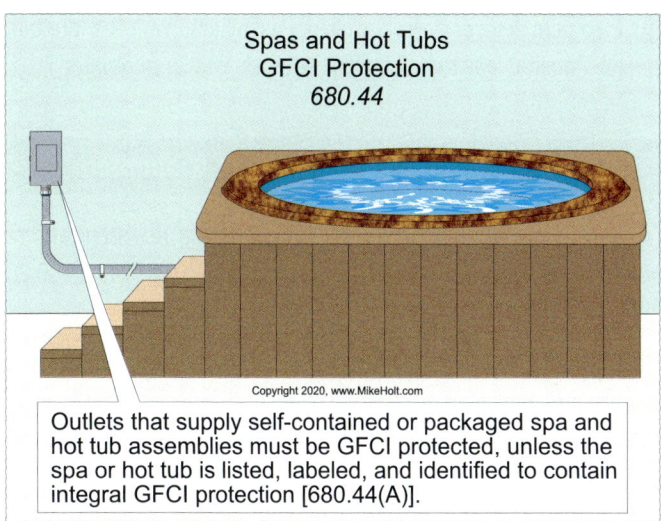

Outlets that supply self-contained or packaged spa and hot tub assemblies must be GFCI protected, unless the spa or hot tub is listed, labeled, and identified to contain integral GFCI protection [680.44(A)].

▶Figure 680-81

Author's Comment:

▶ According to 680.2, a "Fountain" is defined as an ornamental structure or recreational water feature from which one or more jets or streams of water are discharged into the air. They include splash pads, ornamental pools, display pools, and reflection pools.

680.51 Luminaires and Submersible Equipment

(A) GFCI Protection. GFCI protection is required for luminaires, submersible pumps, and other submersible equipment unless listed and supplied by a transformer or power supply that complies with 680.23(A)(2). ▶Figure 680-83

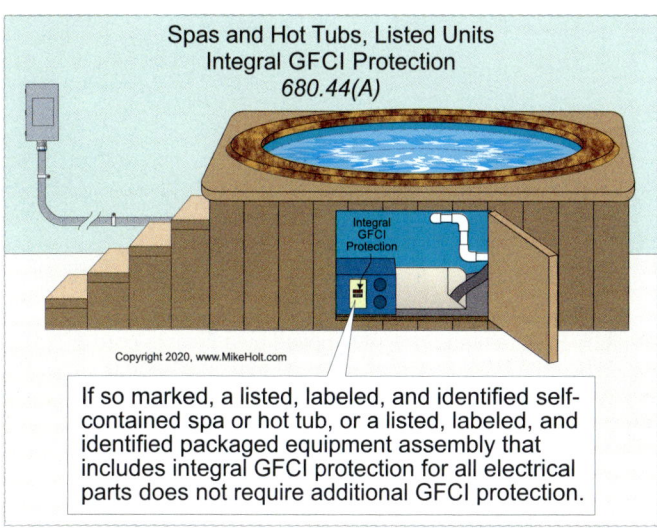

If so marked, a listed, labeled, and identified self-contained spa or hot tub, or a listed, labeled, and identified packaged equipment assembly that includes integral GFCI protection for all electrical parts does not require additional GFCI protection.

▶Figure 680-82

GFCI protection is required for luminaires, submersible pumps, and other submersible equipment unless listed and supplied by a transformer or power supply that complies with 680.23(A)(2).

▶Figure 680-83

Part V. Fountains

680.50 General

The general installation requirements contained in Part I apply to fountains (including splash pads) intended for recreational use by pedestrians, in addition to those requirements contained in Part V. Part II applies to fountains that have water common to pools.

(C) Luminaire Lenses. Luminaires must be installed so the top of the luminaire lens is below the normal water level unless listed for above-water use. ▶Figure 680-84

(E) Cords. The maximum length of each exposed flexible cord in a fountain is 10 ft. Power-supply cords that extend beyond the fountain perimeter must be enclosed in a wiring enclosure approved by the authority having jurisdiction.

(F) Servicing. Equipment must be capable of being removed from the water for relamping or for normal maintenance.

(G) Stability. Equipment must be inherently stable or be securely fastened in place.

680.54 | Swimming Pools, Spas, Hot Tubs, Fountains, and Similar Installations

▶Figure 680-84

680.54 Connection to an Equipment Grounding Conductor

(A) Connection to Equipment Grounding Conductor. The following equipment must be connected to the circuit equipment grounding conductor:

(1) Other than listed low-voltage luminaires not requiring grounding, all electrical equipment located within the fountain or within 5 ft of the inside wall of the fountain.

(2) All electrical equipment associated with the recirculating system of the fountain.

(3) Panelboards that are not part of the service equipment and supply any electrical equipment associated with the fountain.

Note: See 250.122 for the sizing of these conductors.

(B) Bonding. The following parts must be bonded together and connected to an equipment grounding conductor on a branch circuit supplying the fountain:

(1) All metal piping systems associated with the fountain

(2) All metal fittings within or attached to the fountain

(3) Metal parts of electrical equipment associated with the fountain water-circulating system including pump motors

(4) Metal raceways within 5 ft of the inside wall or perimeter of the fountain and not separated from it by a permanent barrier

(5) All metal surfaces within 5 ft of the inside wall or perimeter of the fountain and not separated from it by a permanent barrier

(6) Electrical devices and controls not associated with the fountain and located less than 5 ft from its inside wall or perimeter

680.55 Methods of Equipment Grounding

(A) Additional Requirements. The grounding requirements of 680.21(A), 680.23(B)(3), 680.23(F)(1) and (2), 680.24(F), and 680.25 apply to fountains.

(B) Supplied by Flexible Cord. Fountain equipment supplied by a flexible cord must have all exposed metal parts connected to an insulated copper equipment grounding conductor that is an integral part of the cord. ▶Figure 680-85

▶Figure 680-85

680.56 Cord-and-Plug-Connected Equipment

(A) Ground-Fault Circuit Interrupter. All electrical equipment, including power-supply cords, must be GFCI protected.

680.57 Electric Signs in or Adjacent to Fountains

Each branch circuit or feeder that supplies an electric sign installed within a fountain, or within 10 ft of the fountain edge, must be GFCI protected. ▶Figure 680-86

Swimming Pools, Spas, Hot Tubs, Fountains, and Similar Installations | 680.73

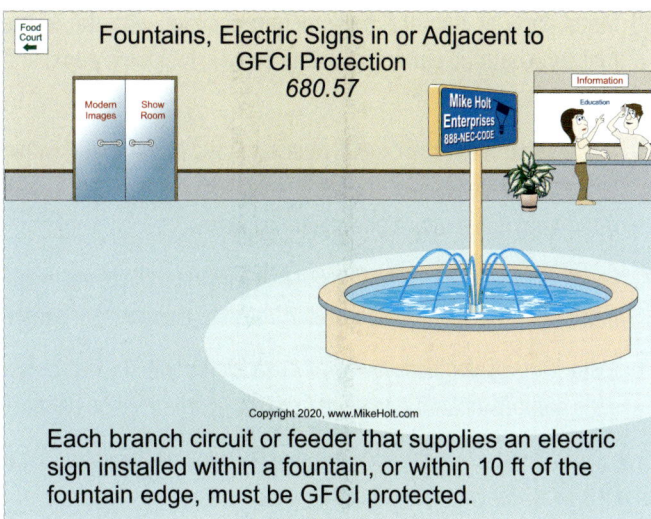
▶Figure 680–86

680.58 GFCI Protection for Adjacent Receptacles

GFCI protection is required for 15A and 20A, single-phase, 125V through 250V receptacles located within 20 ft of the fountain's edge. ▶Figure 680–87

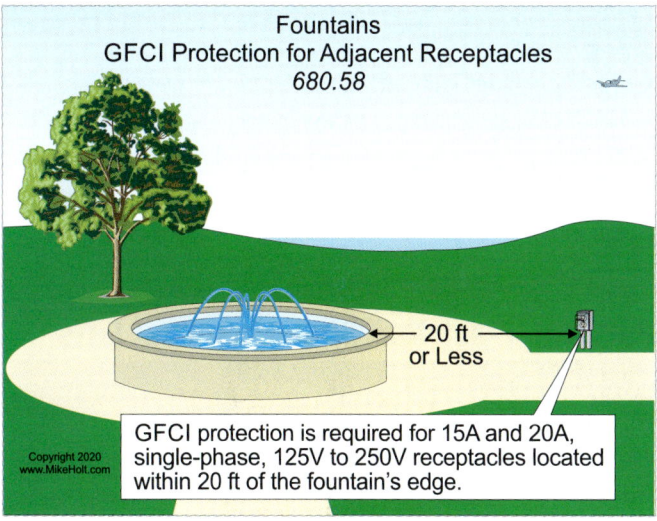
▶Figure 680–87

680.59 GFCI Protection for Permanently Installed Nonsubmersible Pumps

Outlets supplying permanently installed nonsubmersible pump motors rated 250V or less and 60A or less must be GFCI protected.

Part VII. Hydromassage Bathtubs

680.70 General

A hydromassage bathtub must only comply with the requirements of Part VII; it is not required to comply with the other parts of this article.

> **Author's Comment:**
>
> ▸ According to 680.2, a "Hydromassage Bathtub" is defined as a permanently installed bathtub with a recirculating piping system designed to accept, circulate, and discharge water after each use.

680.71 GFCI Protection

Hydromassage bathtubs and their associated electrical components must be on an individual branch circuit protected by a readily accessible GFCI device. ▶Figure 680–88

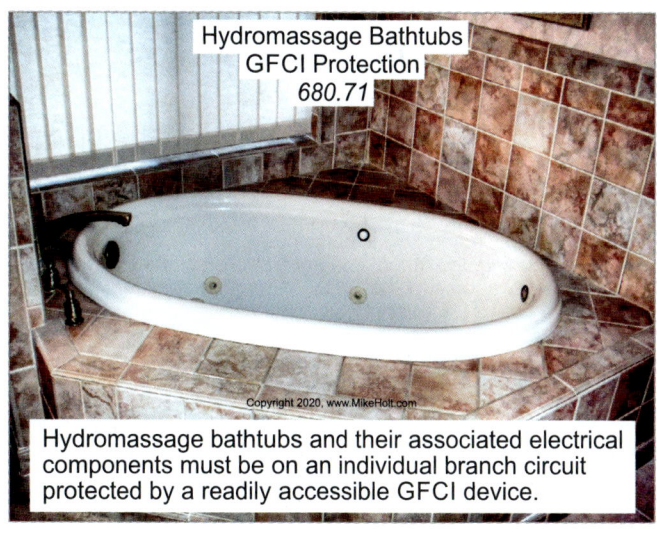
▶Figure 680–88

680.73 Accessibility

Electrical equipment for hydromassage bathtubs must be capable of being removed or exposed without damaging the building structure or finish. ▶Figure 680–89

680.74 | Swimming Pools, Spas, Hot Tubs, Fountains, and Similar Installations

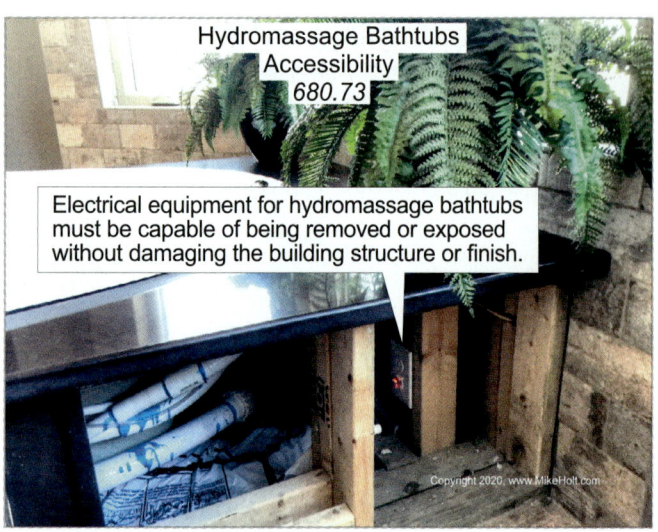

▶Figure 680–89

Where the hydromassage bathtub is cord-and-plug-connected and the supply receptacle is only accessible through a service access opening, the receptacle must be installed so its face is in direct view and be located within 1 ft of the opening. ▶Figure 680–90

▶Figure 680–90

680.74 Equipotential Bonding

(A) General. The following parts must be bonded together.

(1) Metal fittings within, or attached to, the hydromassage bathtub structure that are in contact with the circulating water.

(2) Metal parts of electrical equipment associated with the hydromassage bathtub water circulating system, including pump and blower motors.

(3) Metal-sheathed cables, metal raceways, and metal piping within 5 ft of the inside walls of the hydromassage bathtub and not separated from its area by a permanent barrier.

(4) Exposed metal surfaces within 5 ft of the inside walls of the hydromassage bathtub and not separated from it by a permanent barrier.

(5) Metal parts of electrical devices not associated with the hydromassage bathtub located within 5 ft from the hydromassage bathtub.

Ex 1: Small conductive surfaces not likely to become energized such as air and water jets, supply valve assemblies, drain fittings not connected to metallic piping, towel bars, mirror frames, and similar nonelectrical equipment not connected to metal framing are not required to be bonded.

Ex 2: Double-insulated motors and blowers are not required to be bonded.

(B) Bonding Conductor. Metal parts required to be bonded by 680.74(A) must be bonded together using an insulated or bare solid copper conductor not smaller than 8 AWG. Bonding jumpers are not required to be extended or attached to any remote panelboard, service disconnect, or any electrode.

A bonding jumper long enough to terminate on a replacement nondouble-insulated pump or blower motor must be provided, and it must terminate to the equipment grounding conductor of the branch circuit of the motor when a double-insulated circulating pump or blower motor is used.

Part VIII. Electrically Powered Pool Lifts

680.80 General

Electrically powered pool lifts as defined in 680.2 must comply with Part VIII of this article. Part VIII is not subject to the requirements of other parts of Article 680 except where the requirements are specifically referenced. ▶Figure 680–91

680.81 Equipment Approval

Electrically powered pool lifts must be listed, labeled, and identified for pool and spa use.

Swimming Pools, Spas, Hot Tubs, Fountains, and Similar Installations | 680.84

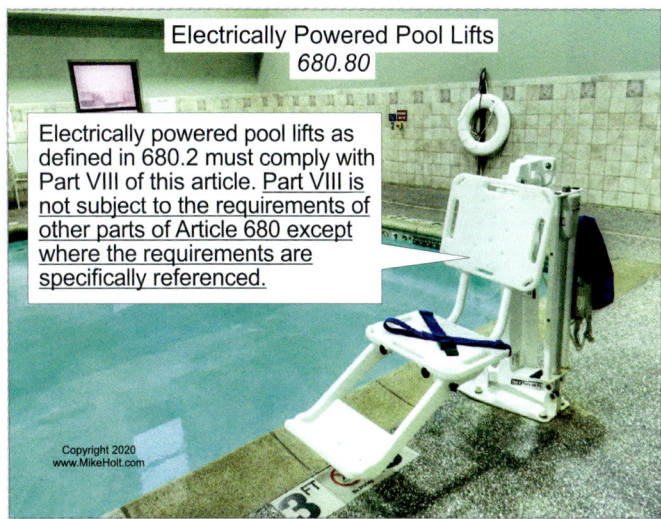

▶Figure 680–91

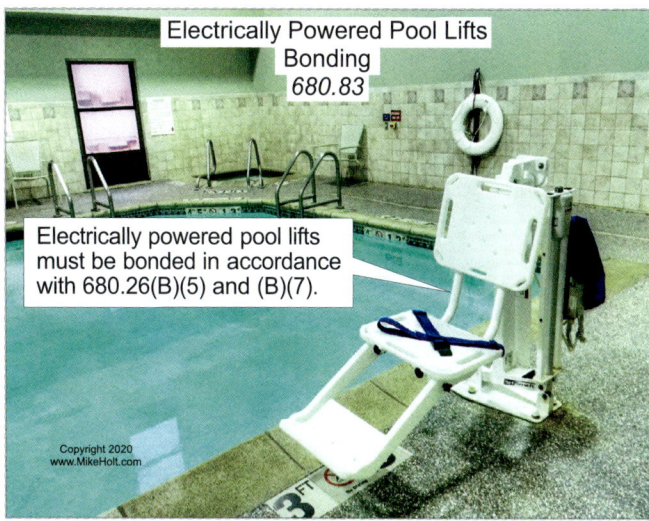

▶Figure 680–92

680.82 Protection

Electrically powered pool lifts must be GFCI protected and comply with 680.5.

680.83 Bonding

Electrically powered pool lifts must be bonded in accordance with 680.26(B)(5) and (B)(7). ▶Figure 680–92

680.84 Switching Devices and Receptacles

Switches and switching devices that operate above the low-voltage contact limit must comply with 680.22(C). Receptacles for electrically powered pool lifts that are operated above the low-voltage contact limit must comply with 680.22(A)(3) and (4).

Notes

ARTICLE 690 SOLAR PHOTOVOLTAIC (PV) SYSTEMS

Introduction to Article 690—Solar Photovoltaic (PV) Systems

You have seen, or maybe own, devices powered by photovoltaic cells, such as night lights, car coolers, and toys. These generally consist of a small solar module powering a small device running on a few volts and a fraction of an ampere. A solar PV system that powers a building or interconnects with an electric utility operates on the same principals but on a much larger scale.

Solar PV systems that provide electrical power to an electrical system are complex. There are many issues that require expert knowledge in electrical, structural, and architectural issues.

The purpose of the *NEC* is to safeguard persons and property from the hazards arising from the use of electricity [90.1(A)]. Article 690 is focused on the electrical hazards that may arise from installing and operating a PV system. It consists of eight parts.

The general *Code* requirements of Chapters 1 through 4 also apply to these installations, except as specifically modified by this article [90.3].

Part I. General

690.1 Scope

The requirements contained in Article 690 apply to solar photovoltaic systems other than those covered by Article 691. ▶Figure 690–1

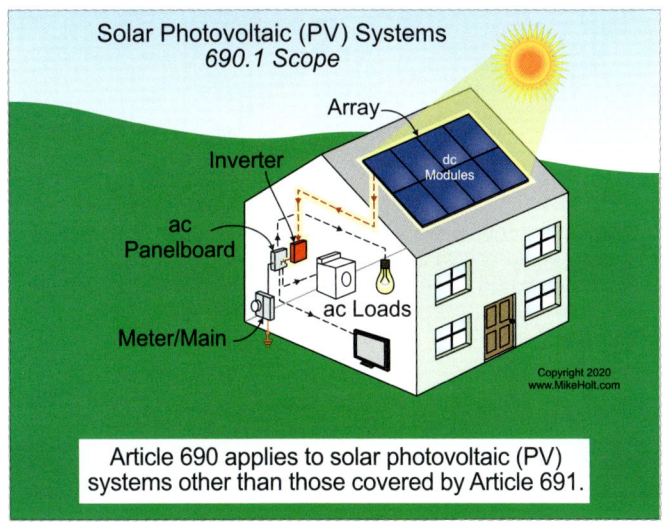

▶Figure 690–1

This article includes those PV systems that are interactive (operate in parallel with the electric utility), that are stand-alone systems, or are a combination of the two. PV systems can provide either ac or dc power.

Author's Comment:

▶ Energy storage systems are covered in Article 706 and are permitted to be connected to, but are not a part of, PV systems.

Review the details in ▶Figure 690–2, ▶Figure 690–3, ▶Figure 690–4, ▶Figure 690–5, and ▶Figure 690–6.

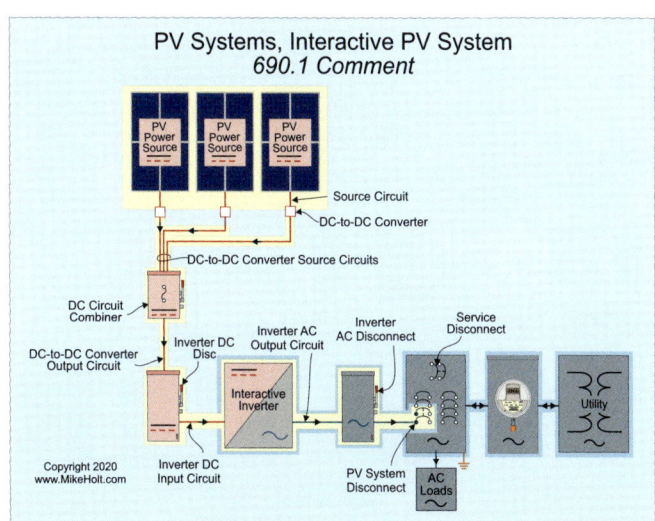

▶Figure 690–2

690.2 | Solar Photovoltaic (PV) Systems

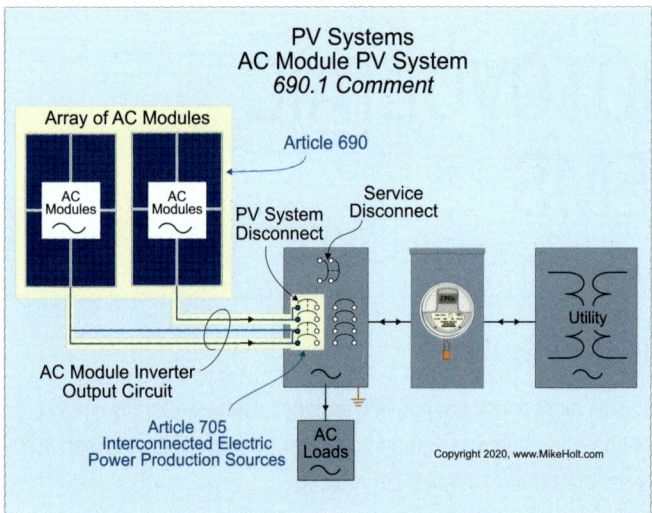
▶Figure 690-3

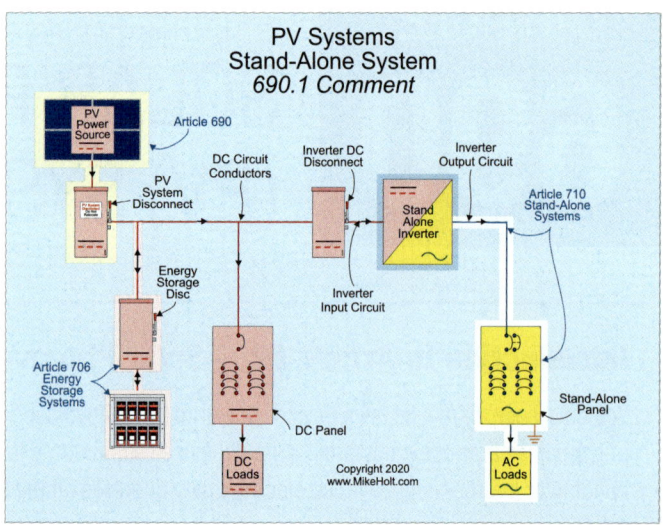
▶Figure 690-6

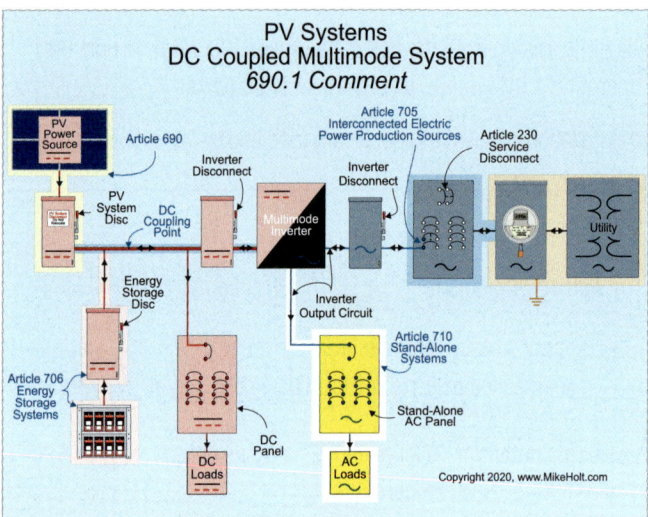
▶Figure 690-4

Note 2: Article 691 covers the installation of large-scale PV electric supply stations with an inverter generating capacity of not less than 5,000 kW, and not under the electric utility control. These facilities have specific design and safety features unique to large-scale PV supply stations and are for the sole purpose of providing electric supply to a system operated by a regulated utility. ▶Figure 690-7

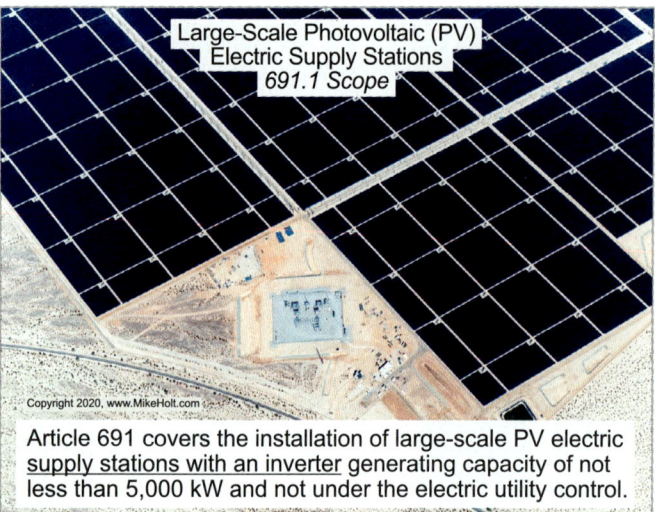
▶Figure 690-7

690.2 Definitions

The definitions in this section only apply within this article.

Alternating-Current Module System. An assembly of ac modules, wiring methods, materials, and subassemblies that are evaluated, identified, and defined as a system.

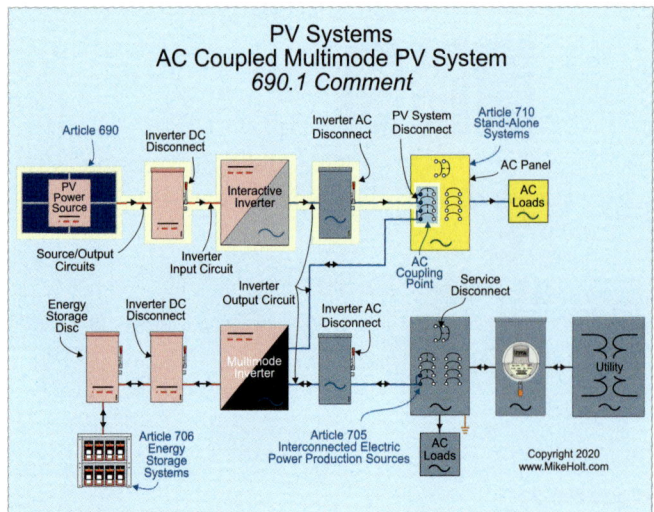
▶Figure 690-5

Solar Photovoltaic (PV) Systems | 690.2

Alternating-Current Module. An ac module is a complete, environmentally protected unit consisting of solar cells, inverter, and other components designed to produce alternating-current power. ▶Figure 690–8

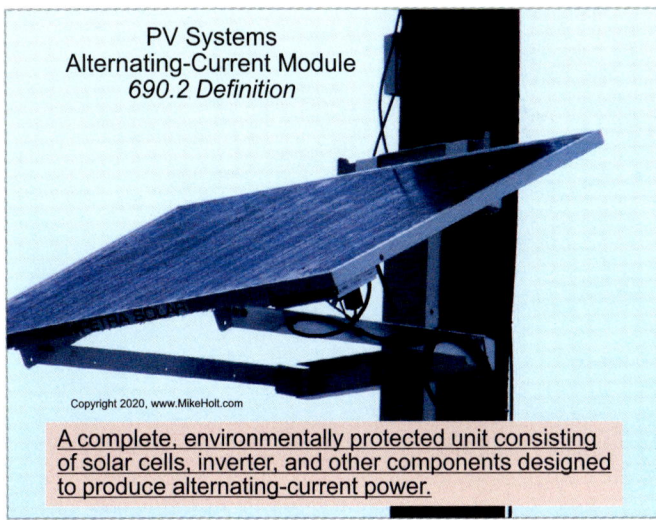
▶Figure 690–8

Author's Comment:

▸ Alternating-current modules are connected in parallel with each other and in parallel with the electric utility in an interactive mode. These modules operate interactively with the electric utility meaning that the ac output current from the ac module will cease exporting power upon sensing the loss of voltage from the electric utility.

▸ Manufacturers' instructions for ac modules will specify the size of the dedicated branch circuit on which they are to be connected and the maximum number of ac modules permitted on the branch circuit.

Array. An array is a mechanically and electrically integrated grouping of modules with a support system, including any attached system components such as inverter(s), dc-to-dc converter(s), and associated wiring. ▶Figure 690–9

DC-to-DC Converter Output Circuit. A dc-to-dc converter output circuit consists of the dc circuit conductors connected to the output of a dc combiner containing multiple dc-to-dc converter source circuits. ▶Figure 690–10

▶Figure 690–9

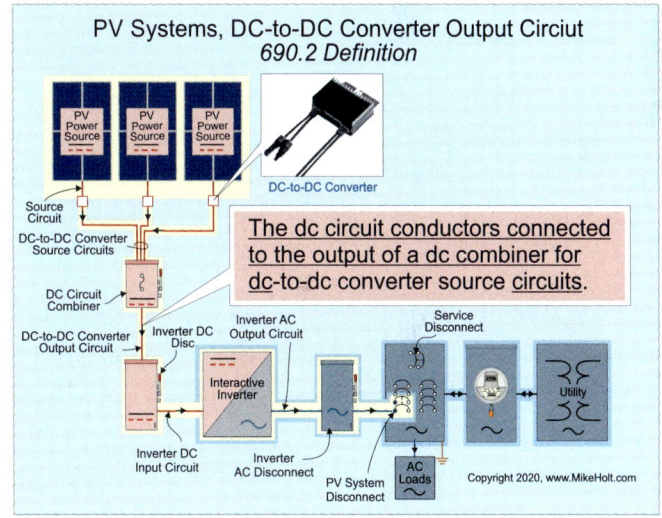
▶Figure 690–10

Author's Comment:

▸ According to Article 100, a "DC-to-DC Converter" is a device that can provide an output dc voltage and current at a higher or lower value than the input dc voltage and current. ▶Figure 690–11

▸ DC-to-DC converters are intended to maximize the power output of independent modules and reduce losses due to variances between the modules' outputs.

690.2 | Solar Photovoltaic (PV) Systems

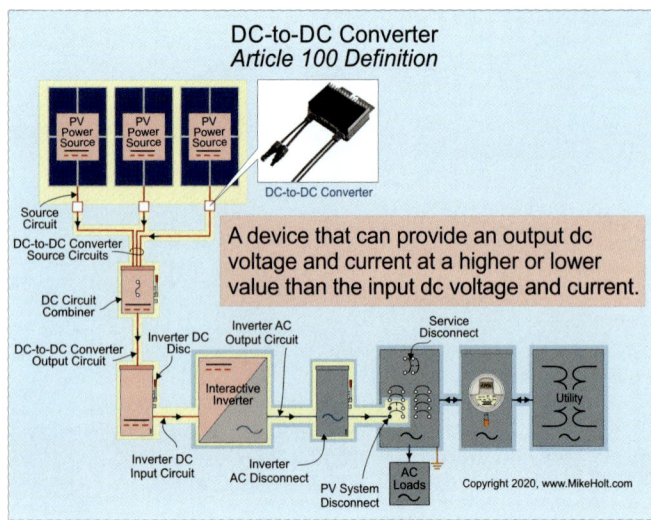

▶Figure 690–11

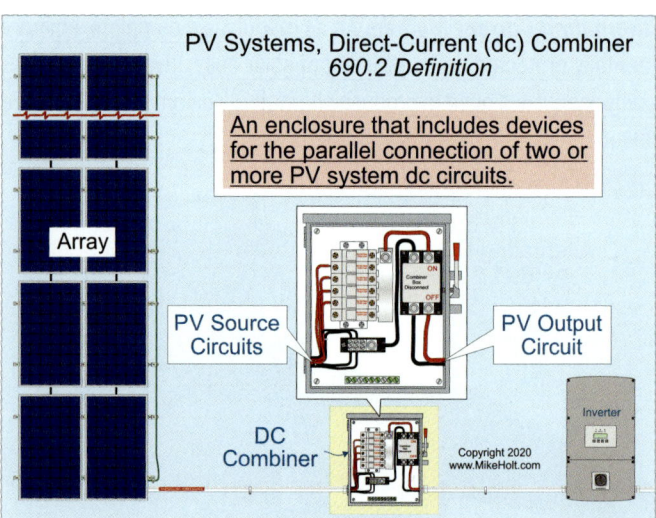

▶Figure 690–13

Author's Comment:

▶ A dc-to-dc converter enables the inverter to receive the circuit voltage that is maximized for direct-current and/or alternating-current power production by the inverter regardless of the circuit length, individual module performance, or variance in light exposure between modules.

DC-to-DC Converter Source Circuit. A dc-to-dc converter source circuit consists of the dc circuit conductors from the output of a dc-to-dc converter. ▶Figure 690–12

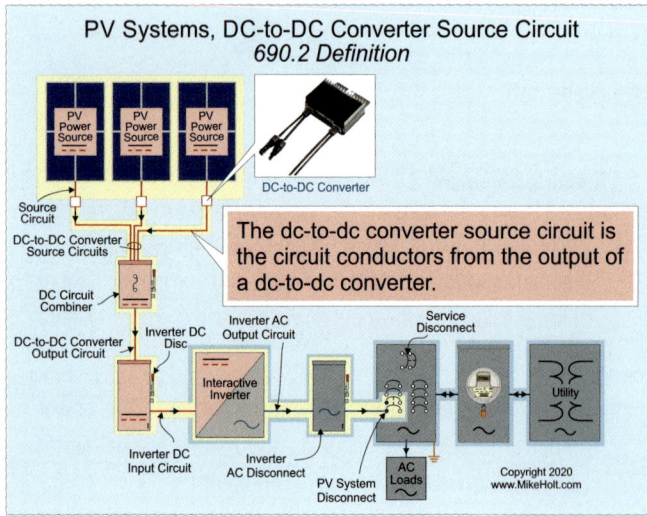

▶Figure 690–12

Direct-Current (dc) Combiner. A dc combiner is an enclosure that includes devices for the parallel connection of two or more PV system dc circuits. ▶Figure 690–13

Author's Comment:

▶ A dc combiner connects multiple PV source circuits and dc-to-dc converter source circuits in parallel with each other to create a PV output or dc-to-dc converter output circuit. Direct-current combiners can also recombine multiple PV output circuits and dc-to-dc converter output circuits with a larger two-wire PV output or dc-to-dc converter output circuit.

Electronic Power Converter. An electronic power converter is a device that uses electronics to convert one form of electrical power into another.

Note: Examples of electronic power converters include (but are not limited to) inverters, dc-to-dc converters, and electronic charge controllers. These devices have limited current capabilities based on the device ratings at continuous rated power.

Grounded, Functionally. A functionally grounded PV system is one that has an electrical ground reference for operational purposes that is not solidly grounded. ▶Figure 690–14

Note: A functionally grounded PV system is often connected to ground through an electronic means that is internal to an inverter or charge controller that provides ground-fault protection. Examples of operational purposes for functionally grounded systems include ground-fault detection and protection, as well as performance-related issues for some power sources.

Module. A PV module is a unit of environmentally protected solar cells and components designed to produce dc power. ▶Figure 690–15

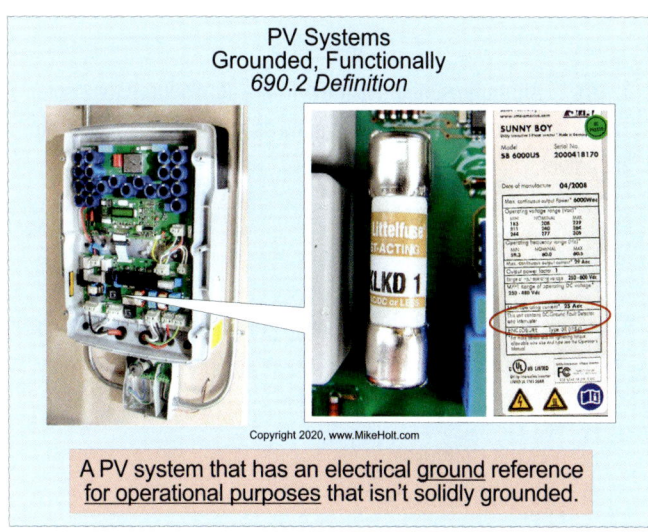
▶Figure 690–14

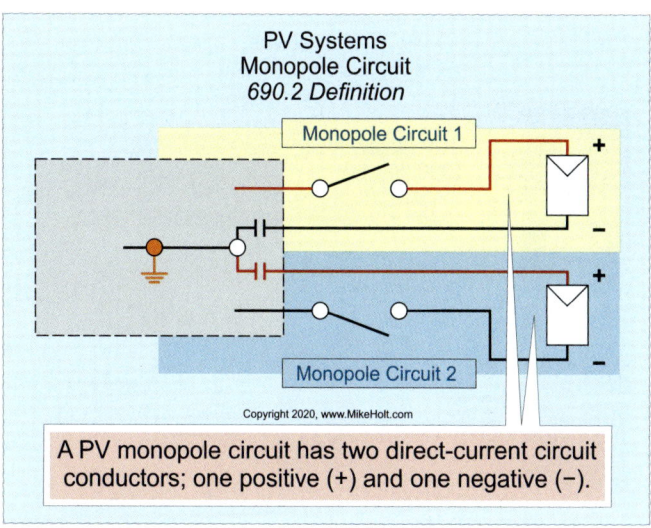
▶Figure 690–16

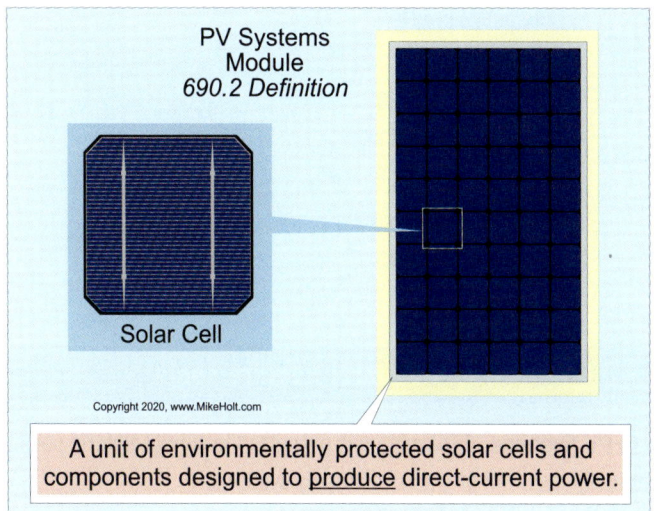
▶Figure 690–15

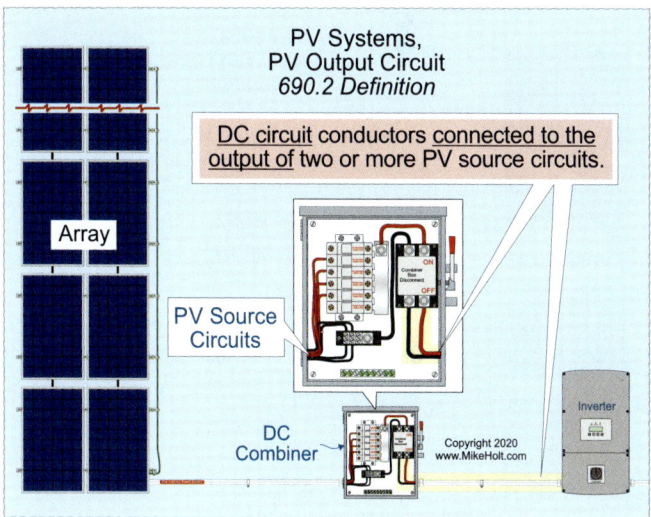
▶Figure 690–17

Author's Comment:

▸ PV modules use sunlight to generate direct-current (dc) electricity by using light (photons) to move electrons in a semiconductor. This is known as the "photovoltaic effect."

Monopole Circuit. A PV monopole circuit has two dc circuit conductors; one positive (+) and one negative (−). ▶Figure 690–16

PV Output Circuit. A PV output circuit consists of dc circuit conductors connected to the output of two or more PV source circuits. ▶Figure 690–17

PV Source Circuit. The PV source circuit consists of the dc circuit conductors between modules and from modules to dc combiners, electronic power converters, or the PV system disconnecting means.
▶Figure 690–18 and ▶Figure 690–19

PV System DC Circuit. The PV system dc circuit consists of any dc conductor in PV source circuits, PV output circuits, dc-to-dc converter source circuits, and dc-to-dc converter output circuits.

Solar Cell. The building block of a PV module that generates dc power when exposed to light. ▶Figure 690–20

690.4 | Solar Photovoltaic (PV) Systems

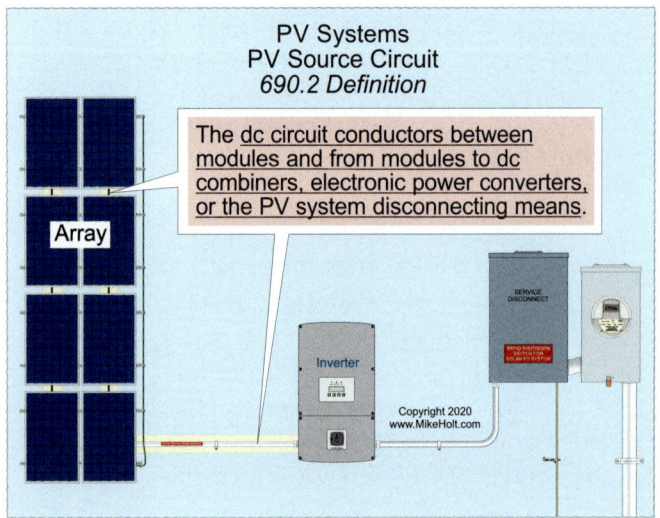
▶ Figure 690-18

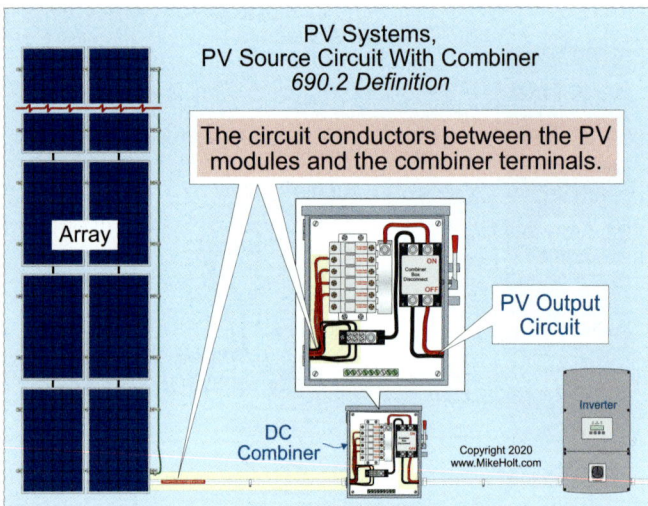
▶ Figure 690-19

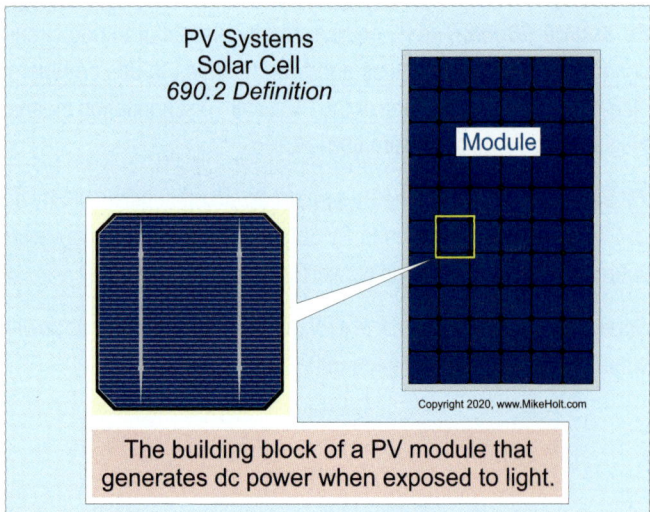
▶ Figure 690-20

Caution: Although sunlight is the primary light source for a solar cell, other light sources such as moonlight can generate dc power.

Author's Comment:

▸ All Article 100 definitions are important, but the following definitions located there are often components commonly found in PV systems:

  ▸ Charge Controller
  ▸ DC-to-DC Converter
  ▸ DC-to-DC Output Circuit
  ▸ Hybrid System
  ▸ Interactive Inverter
  ▸ Interactive System
  ▸ Inverter, Multimode
  ▸ Inverter Output Circuit
  ▸ Power Production System
  ▸ Photovoltaic (PV) System
  ▸ Stand-Alone System

690.4 General Requirements

(A) PV Systems. A PV system is permitted to supply electric power to buildings or other electrical supply systems.

(B) Listed or Field Labeled Equipment. Components of the PV system including inverters, PV modules, ac modules, ac module systems, dc combiners, dc-to-dc converters, rapid shutdown equipment, dc circuit controllers, and charge controllers must be listed or be evaluated for the application and have a field label applied. ▶ Figure 690-21

Author's Comment:

▸ "Listing" means the equipment is included in a list published by a testing laboratory acceptable to the authority having jurisdiction [Article 100].

▸ "Field Labeled" means the equipment or materials which have a label, symbol, or other identifying mark of a field evaluation body (FEB) indicates the equipment or material was evaluated and found to comply with the requirements described in the field body evaluation report [Article 100].

Solar Photovoltaic (PV) Systems | **690.6**

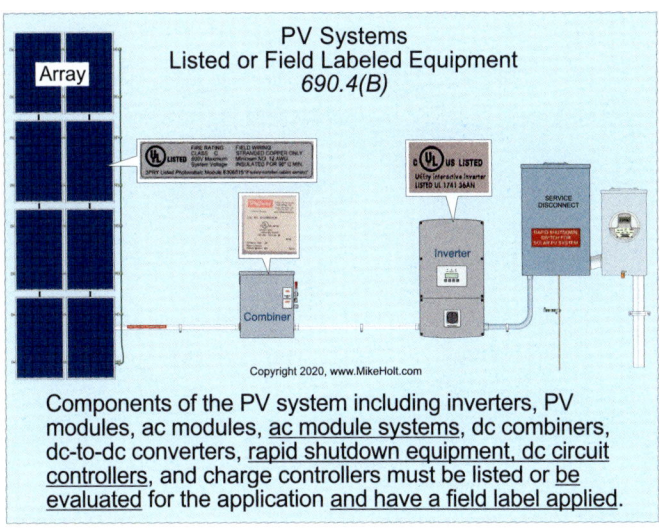
▶Figure 690–21

(C) Qualified Persons. The installation of PV systems must be performed by a qualified person.

Note: A qualified person has the knowledge related to the construction and operation of PV equipment and installations; along with safety training to recognize and avoid hazards to persons and property [Article 100]. ▶Figure 690–22

▶Figure 690–22

Author's Comment:

▸ NFPA 70E, *Standard for Electrical Safety in the Workplace*, provides information on the safety training requirements expected of a "qualified person."

▸ Examples of this safety training include (but are not limited to) training in the use of special precautionary techniques, personal protective equipment (PPE), insulating and shielding materials, and in the use of insulated tools and test equipment when working on or near exposed conductors or circuit parts that can become energized.

▸ In many parts of the United States, electricians, electrical contractors, electrical inspectors, and electrical engineers must complete an *NEC* review course each year as a requirement to maintain licensing. This, in and of itself, does not make one qualified to deal with the specific hazards involved with PV systems.

(D) Multiple PV Systems. Multiple PV systems are permitted on or in a building. Where PV systems are remotely located from each other a directory must be provided at each PV disconnect in accordance with 705.10.

(E) Where Not Permitted. No part of a PV system is permitted to be installed within a bathroom.

(F) Electronic Power Converters Not Readily Accessible. Electronic power converters (inverters and dc-to-dc converters) are not required to be readily accessible.

690.6 Alternating-Current Modules and Systems

(A) PV Source Circuits. The requirements of Article 690 do not apply to the source circuits for an ac module or ac module system. The source circuit, conductors, and the inverter(s) are considered internal components of a listed product. ▶Figure 690–23

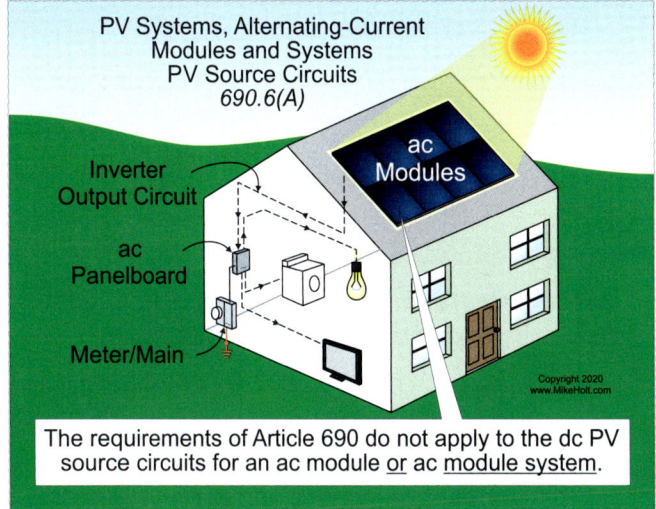
▶Figure 690–23

690.7 | Solar Photovoltaic (PV) Systems

Author's Comment:

▸ PV source circuits and inverters for ac modules or ac module systems are covered by the listing of the product. Listed factory-installed internal wiring of equipment that has been evaluated by a qualified testing laboratory does not require inspecting for *NEC* compliance [90.7].

(B) Output Circuit. The ac output circuit conductors for an ac module or ac module system are considered to be the "Inverter Output Circuit" as defined in Article 100. ▸Figure 690-24

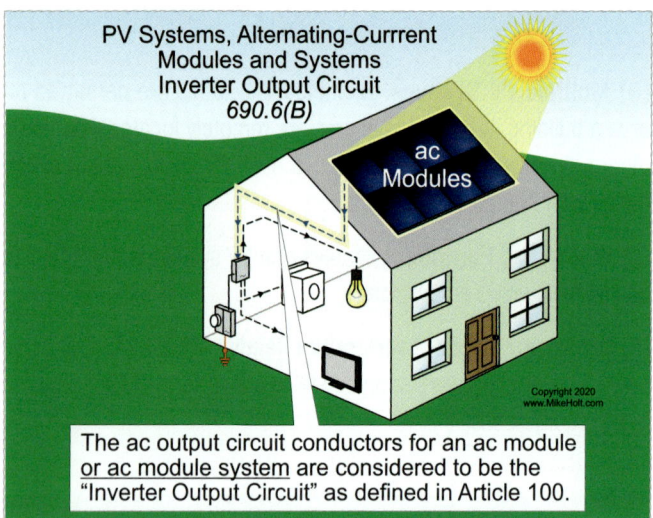

▸Figure 690-24

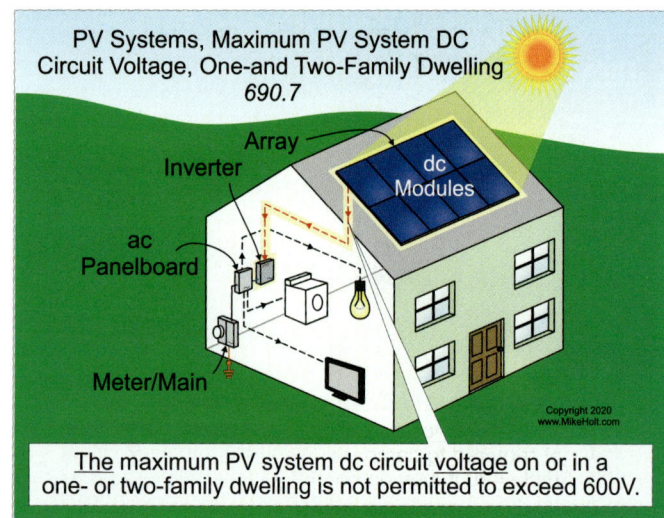

▸Figure 690-25

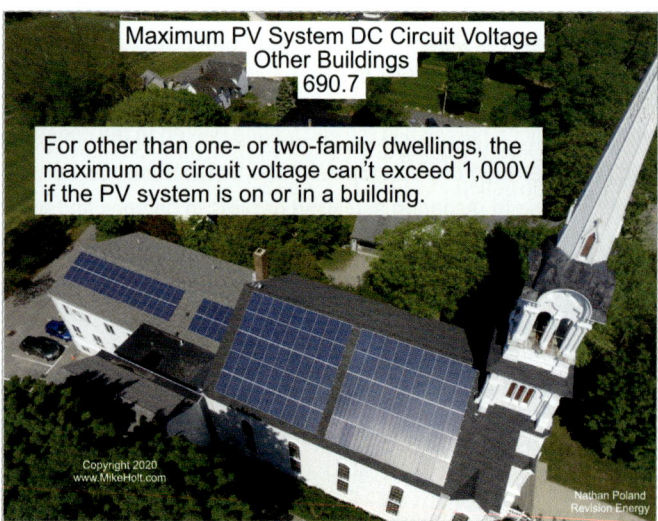

▸Figure 690-26

Part II. Circuit Requirements

690.7 Maximum PV System Direct-Current Circuit Voltage

For the purpose of Article 690, the maximum voltage of a circuit is defined as the highest voltage between any two conductors of a circuit.

The maximum voltage of a circuit value is used when selecting conductors, cables, equipment, determining working space, and other applications where circuit voltage ratings are used.

The maximum PV system dc circuit voltage on or in a one- or two-family dwelling is not permitted to exceed 600V. ▸Figure 690-25

For other than one- or two-family dwellings, the maximum PV system dc circuit voltage is not permitted to exceed 1,000V if the PV system is on or in a building. ▸Figure 690-26

PV systems not located on or in buildings with a maximum dc circuit voltage of not over 1,500V are not required to comply with Parts II and III of Article 490. ▸Figure 690-27

Author's Comment:

▸ The PV system dc circuit consists of PV source circuits, PV output circuits, dc-to-dc converter source circuits, and dc-to-dc converter output circuits [690.2].

(A) PV Source and Output Circuit Volts. The maximum PV source and output circuit dc voltage is determined by one of the following methods:

Solar Photovoltaic (PV) Systems | **690.7**

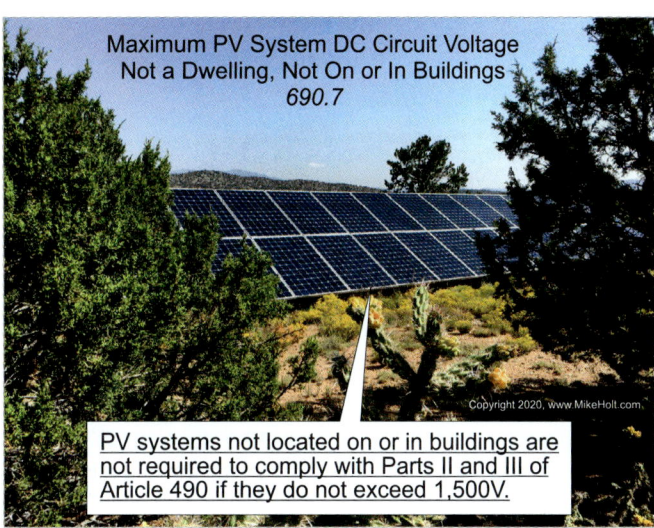

▶ Figure 690-27

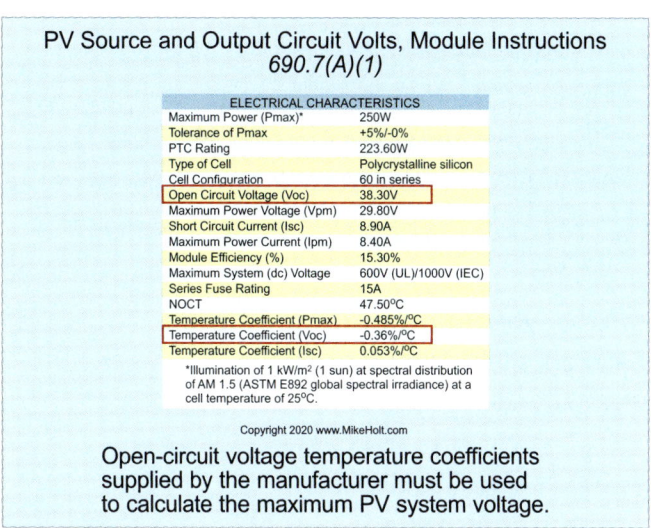

▶ Figure 690-29

(1) Module Instructions. The maximum PV source and output circuit dc voltage is equal to the sum of the dc module open-circuit voltage (Voc) of the series-connected modules as corrected for the lowest expected ambient temperature using the manufacturer's voltage temperature coefficient correction. ▶Figure 690-28 and ▶Figure 690-29

▶ **Maximum PV System Voltage, Based on Manufacturer Temperature Coefficient, %/°C Example**

Question: Using the manufacturer's temperature coefficient of −0.36%/°C, what is the maximum PV system source and output circuit dc voltage for twelve modules each rated 38.30 Voc at a temperature of −7°C? ▶Figure 690-30

(a) 493V (b) 513V (c) 529V (d) 541V

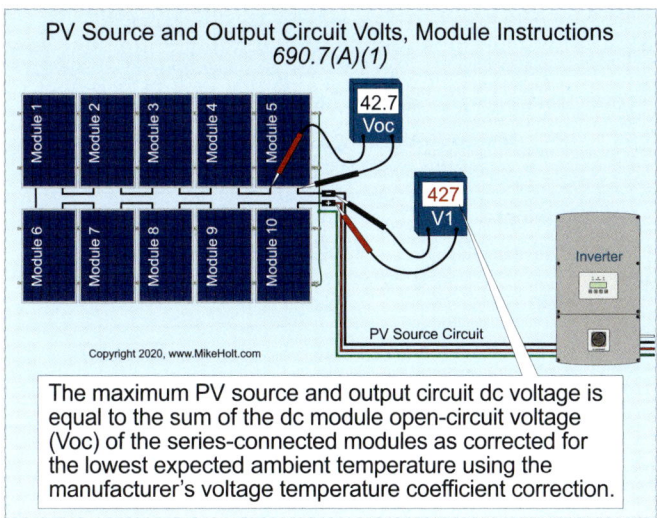

▶ Figure 690-28

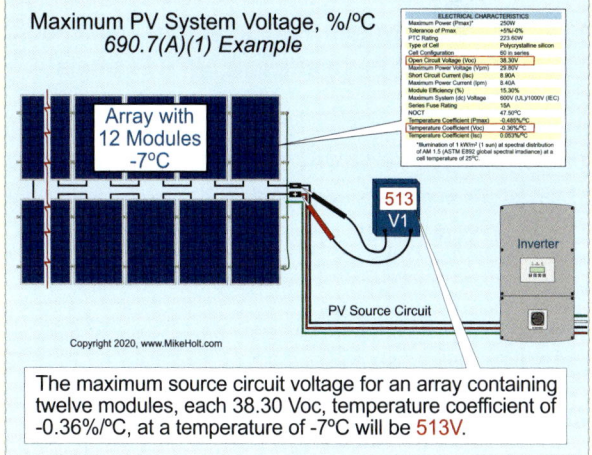

▶ Figure 690-30

Solution:

Four things are needed to calculate the maximum PV system circuit voltage:

1. The module Voc (open-circuit voltage) found on the manufacturer's label or datasheet.

•••

Author's Comment:

▸ A PV module's dc voltage has an inverse relationship with temperature, which means that at lower ambient temperatures, the module's dc output voltage increases and at higher ambient temperatures, the modules' dc voltage output decreases.

Mike Holt Enterprises • www.MikeHolt.com • 888.NEC.CODE (632.2633) | **285**

2. The module temperature coefficient of the Voc which is found on the manufacturer's label or datasheet.

3. The lowest expected ambient temperature. See the Solar America Board for Codes and Standards website (www.solarabcs.org).

4. The number of modules that are connected in series with each other.

PV Voc = Rated Voc × {1 + [(Temp. °C − 25°C) × Module Coefficient %/°C]} × # Modules

Voc of Module = 38.30 Voc
Temperature Coefficient of Voc of Module = −0.36%/°C
Lowest Temperature Expected = −7°C
Number of Series-Connected Modules = 12

PV Circuit Voltage = 38.30 Voc × {1+ [(−7°C − 25°C) × −0.36%/°C]} × 12 modules
PV Circuit Voltage = 38.30 Voc × [(1 + (-32°C × −0.36%/°C)] × 12 modules
PV Circuit Voltage = 38.30 Voc × (1 + 11.52%) × 12 modules
PV Circuit Voltage = 38.30 Voc × 111.52% × 12 modules
PV Circuit Voltage = 42.71V × 12 modules
PV Circuit Voltage = 513V

Answer: (b) 513V

▶ **Maximum PV System Voltage, Based on Manufacturer Temperature Coefficient, V/°C Example**

Question: Using the manufacturer's temperature coefficient of −0.137V/°C, what is the maximum PV source and output circuit dc voltage for twelve modules each rated 38.30 Voc at a temperature of −7°C? ▶Figure 690–31

(a) 493V   (b) 512V   (c) 524V   (d) 541V

Solution:

PV Voc (V/°C) = Rated Voc + [(Temp. °C − 25°C) × Module Coefficient V/°C] × # Modules

PV Circuit Voltage = {38.30V + [(−7°C − 25°C) × −0.137V/°C]} × 12 modules
PV Circuit Voltage = [38.30V + (-32°C × -0.137V/°C)] × 12 modules
PV Circuit Voltage = (38.30V + 4.384V) × 12 modules
PV Circuit Voltage = 42.684V × 12 modules
PV Circuit Voltage = 512V

Answer: (b) 512V

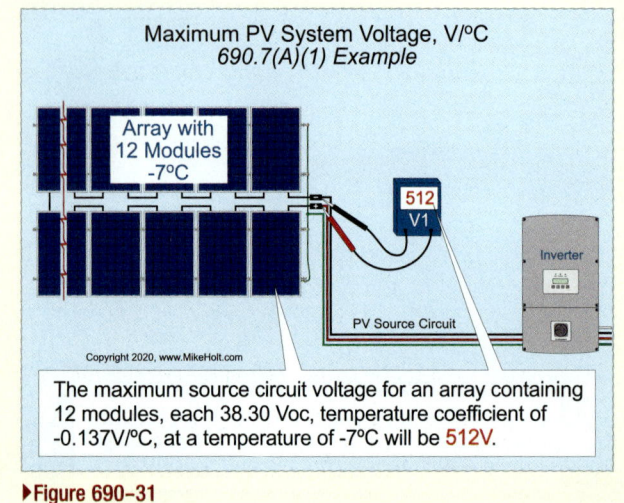

▶Figure 690–31

(2) Table of Crystalline and Multicrystalline Modules. The maximum PV source and output circuit voltage is equal to the sum of the dc module-rated open-circuit voltage (Voc) of the series-connected modules as corrected for the lowest expected ambient temperature in accordance with Table 690.7(A).

Table 690.7(A) Voltage Correction Factors for Crystalline and Multicrystalline Silicon Modules

Correction Factors for Ambient Temperatures Below 25°C (77°F).
(Multiply the rated open-circuit voltage by the appropriate correction factor shown below.)

Ambient Temperature (°C)	Factor	Ambient Temperature (°F)
24 to 20	1.02	76 to 68
19 to 15	1.04	67 to 59
14 to 10	1.06	58 to 50
9 to 5	1.08	49 to 41
4 to 0	1.10	40 to 32
−1 to -5	1.12	31 to 23
−6 to −10	1.14	22 to 14
−11 to −15	1.16	13 to 5
−16 to −20	1.18	4 to -4
−21 to −25	1.20	−5 to −13
−26 to -30	1.21	−14 to −22
−31 to −35	1.23	−23 to −31
−36 to −40	1.25	−32 to −40

> **Caution**
> ⚠ Illumination at dawn, dusk, when there is heavy overcast, and even on rainy days is sufficient to produce dangerous dc voltage. ▶Figure 690–32

▶Figure 690–32

▶ **Maximum PV System Voltage, Based on Table 690.7(A) Temperature Correction [690.7(A)(2)] Example**

Question: Using Table 690.7(A), what is the maximum PV system source and output circuit dc voltage for twelve crystalline modules each rated 38.30 Voc at a temperature of -7°C? ▶Figure 690–33

(a) 493V   (b) 513V   (c) 524V   (d) 541V

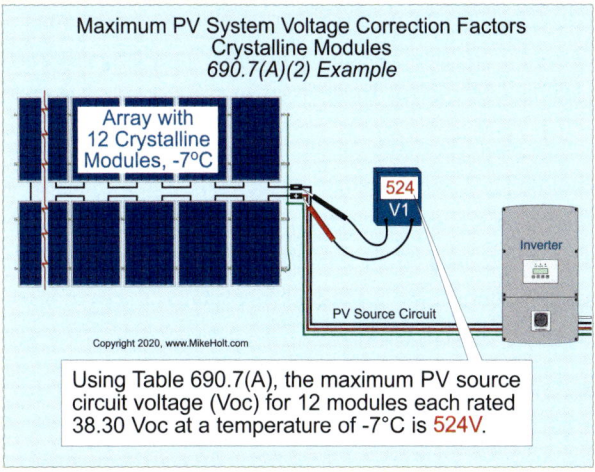
▶Figure 690–33

Solution:

PV Voc = Module Voc ×
Table 690.7 Correction Factor × # Modules
PV Circuit Voltage = 38.30 Voc × 1.14 × 12 modules
PV Circuit Voltage = 524V

Answer: (c) 524V

(3) Engineered Industry Standard Method. For PV systems with an inverter generating capacity of 100 kW or greater, the maximum PV source and output circuit dc voltage is permitted to be determined by a licensed professional electrical engineer providing documented and stamped PV system design using an industry standard method maximum dc voltage calculation.

Note 1: One source for lowest-expected, ambient temperature design data for various locations is the chapter titled "Extreme Annual Mean Minimum Design Dry Bulb Temperature" found in the *ASHRAE Handbook—Fundamentals.* This temperature data can be used to calculate maximum voltage.

Note 2: One industry standard method for calculating the maximum PV source and output circuit dc voltage is published by Sandia National Laboratories, reference SAND 2004-3535, *Photovoltaic Array Performance Model.*

(B) DC-to-DC Converter Source and Output Circuit Voltage. The maximum dc-to-dc converter dc voltage is determined by one of the following methods:

(1) Single DC-to-DC Converter. The maximum output dc voltage for a single dc-to-dc converter is based on the manufacturer's instructions for the dc-to-dc converter.

If the instructions do not provide a method to determine the maximum dc-to-dc converter output dc voltage, the maximum dc-to-dc output dc voltage will be equal to the rated output dc voltage of the dc-to-dc converter.

(2) Two or More Series-Connected DC-to-DC Converters. The maximum output circuit dc voltage for series-connected dc-to-dc converters is based on the manufacturer's instructions for the dc-to-dc converter.

If the instructions do not provide a method to determine the dc-to-dc converters' maximum output dc voltage, the maximum dc-to-dc output dc voltage for the series-connected dc-to-dc converters will be equal to the sum of the maximum rated output dc voltage of the dc-to-dc converters connected in series.

690.8 Circuit Current and Conductor Sizing

(A) Calculation of Maximum PV Circuit Current. The maximum PV system current is calculated in accordance with 690.8(A)(1) or (2):

(1) PV System Circuit Current. The maximum PV system dc circuit current is calculated in accordance with 690.8(A)(1)(a) through (e).

(a) PV Source Circuit Current Calculation.

(1) PV Systems Rated Less Than 100 kW. The maximum PV source circuit dc current is equal to the short-circuit current ratings marked on the modules connected in parallel multiplied by 125 percent. ▶Figure 690–34

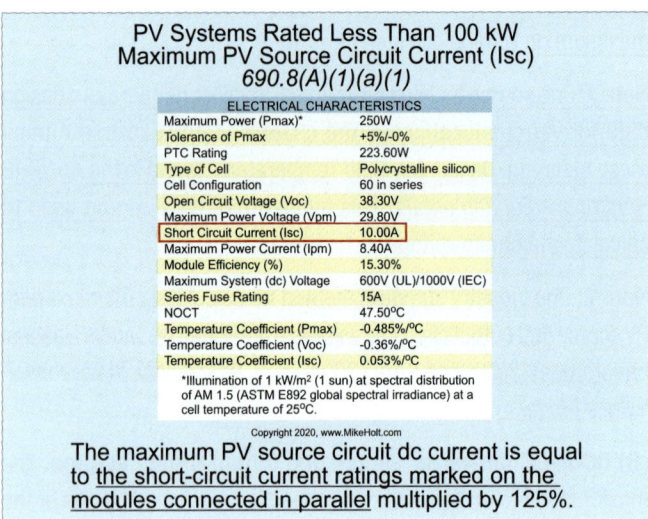

▶Figure 690–34

Author's Comment:

▸ The PV source circuit is defined as the two dc circuit conductors between modules, dc circuit conductors from the modules to dc-to-dc converters, dc circuit conductors from modules to dc combiners, and dc circuit conductors from modules to inverters [690.2].

▸ A module can produce more than the rated current when the intensity of the sunlight is greater than the standard used to determine the module's short-circuit rating. This happens when sunlight intensity is affected by altitude, reflection due to snow, refraction through clouds, or low humidity. For this reason, the PV system circuit current is calculated at 125 percent of the module's short-circuit current rating marked on the module's nameplate. This is commonly referred to as an "irradiance factor."

▶ **Maximum PV Source Circuit Current Example**

Question: What is the maximum PV source circuit dc current for 12 series-connected modules having a nameplate short-circuit current (Isc) of 10A? ▶Figure 690–35

(a) 12.50A   (b) 15A   (c) 20A   (d) 25A

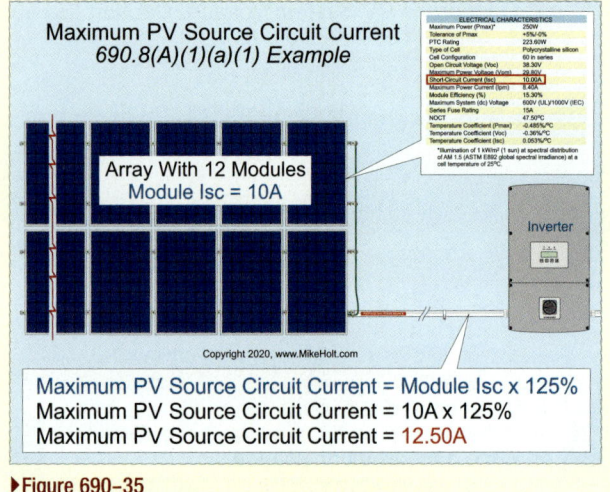

Maximum PV Source Circuit Current = Module Isc × 125%
Maximum PV Source Circuit Current = 10A × 125%
Maximum PV Source Circuit Current = 12.50A

▶Figure 690–35

Solution:

Source Circuit Current = Module Isc × 125%

Source Circuit Current = 10A × 125%

Source Circuit Current = 12.50A

Answer: (a) 12.50A

(2) PV System Rated 100 kW or Greater. The maximum PV source circuit dc current calculations for PV systems with an inverter with a generating capacity of 100 kW or greater can be determined by a licensed professional electrical engineer providing documented and stamped PV system design using an industry standard method.

The maximum PV source circuit dc current value is based on the highest 3-hour current average resulting from the simulated local irradiance on the array accounting for elevation and orientation. In no case is the maximum PV source circuit dc current permitted to be less than 70 percent of the maximum PV source circuit dc current as calculated in 690.8(A)(1)(a)(1).

Note: One industry standard method for calculating the maximum PV source current is available from Sandia National Laboratories, reference SAND 2004-3535, *Photovoltaic Array Performance Model*. This model is used by the System Advisor Model simulation program provided by the National Renewable Energy Laboratory.

(b) PV Output Circuit Current Calculation. The maximum PV output circuit dc current is equal to the sum of parallel PV source circuit dc currents as calculated in 690.8(A)(1)(a).

Author's Comment:

▸ The PV output circuit consists of the two dc circuit conductors connected to the output of a dc combiner.

▶ **Maximum PV Output Circuit Current Example**

Question: What is the maximum PV output circuit dc current for four source circuits where each source circuit contains 12 dc modules, each having a nameplate Isc of 10A? ▶Figure 690–36

(a) 25A (b) 35A (c) 40A (d) 50A

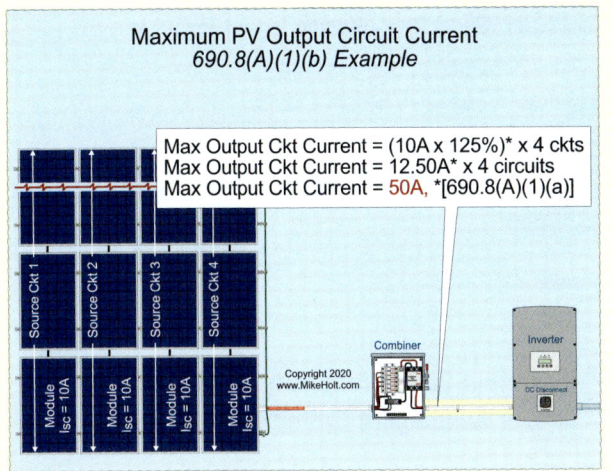
▶Figure 690–36

Solution:

PV Output Circuit Current = (Module Isc × 125%)* × Number of Source Circuits

PV Output Circuit Current = (10A × 125%)* × 4 circuits

PV Output Circuit Current = 12.50A × 4 circuits

PV Output Circuit Current = 50A
*[690.8(A)(1)(a)]

Answer: (d) 50A

(c) DC-to-DC Converter Source Circuit Current. The maximum dc-to-dc converter source circuit dc current is equal to the dc-to-dc converter's continuous output current rating marked on the converter.
▶Figure 690–37

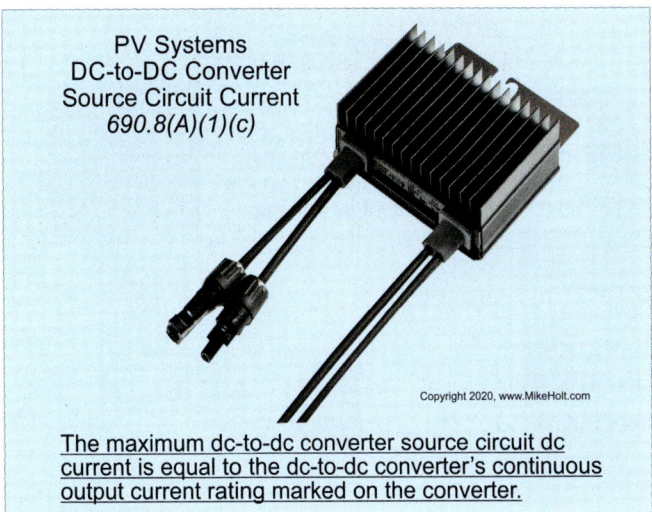
▶Figure 690–37

Author's Comment:

▸ A dc-to-dc converter source circuit is the two dc circuit conductors from the output of a dc-to-dc converter [690.2].

(d) DC-to-DC Converter Output Circuit Current. The maximum dc-to-dc output circuit dc current is equal to the sum of the parallel-connected dc-to-dc converter source circuit dc currents as calculated in 690.8(A)(1)(c).

Author's Comment:

▸ A dc-to-dc converter output circuit is the two dc circuit conductors connected to the output of the dc combiner containing multiple dc-to-dc converter source circuits [690.2].

(e) Inverter Output Circuit Current. The maximum inverter output circuit dc current is equal to the continuous output current rating marked on the inverter for the output ac voltage. ▶Figure 690–38

Author's Comment:

▸ The inverter output circuit is the circuit conductors connected to the alternating-current output of an inverter [Article 100].

(2) Input of Electronic Power Converters. Where a circuit is protected with an overcurrent device not exceeding the conductor ampacity, the maximum current can be the rated input current of the electronic power converter.

(B) Conductor Sizing. PV circuit conductors must be sized to carry the larger of 690.8(B)(1) or (B)(2).

690.8 | Solar Photovoltaic (PV) Systems

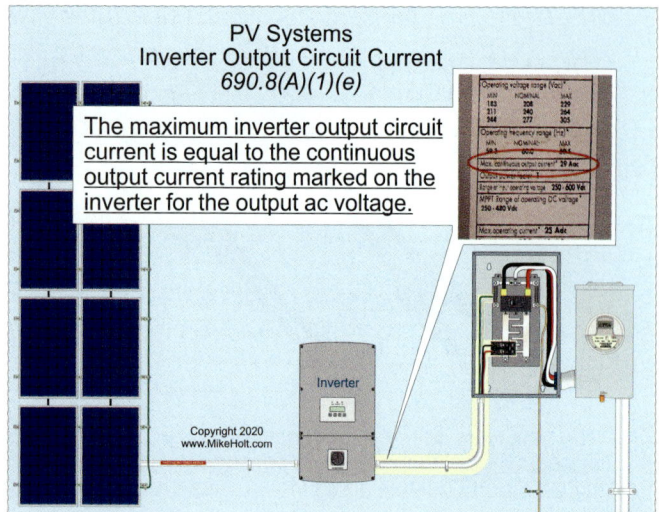
▶Figure 690-38

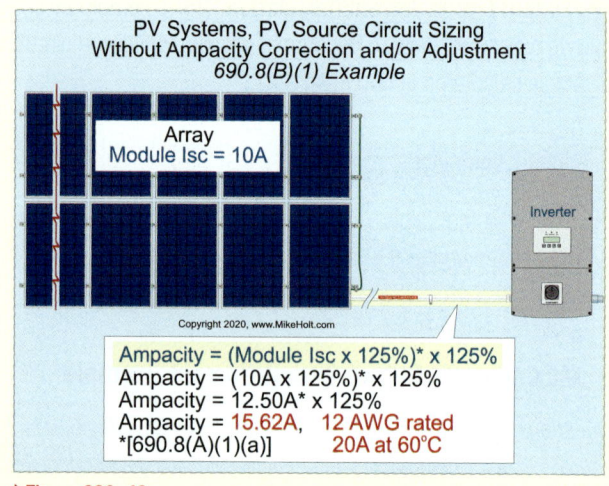
▶Figure 690-40

(1) Conductor Sizing, Without Ampacity Correction and/or Adjustment. PV circuit conductors within the scope of 690.8(A) must have an ampacity of not less than 125 percent of the current as determined by 690.8(A), without ampacity correction and/or adjustment.
▶Figure 690-39

Solution:

Conductor Ampacity = (Module Isc × 125%)* × 125%

Conductor Ampacity = (10A × 125%)* × 125%

Conductor Ampacity = 12.50A × 125%

Conductor Ampacity = 15.62A

Use 12 AWG rated 20A at 60°C [110.14(C)(1)(a) and Table 310.16]. *[690.8(A)(1)(a)]

Answer: *(b) 15.62A*

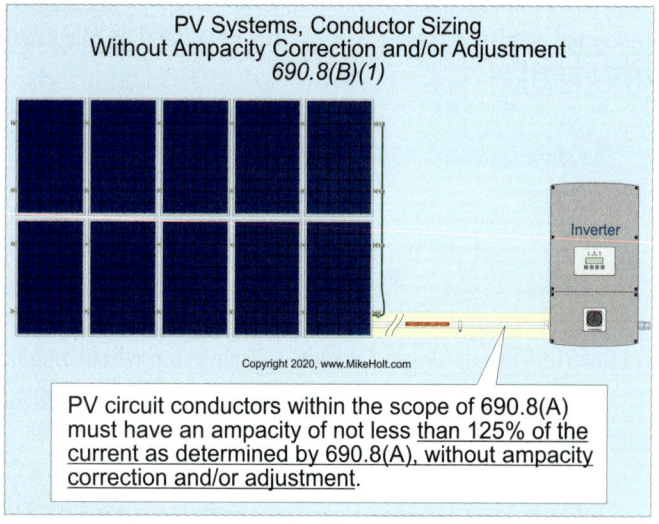
▶Figure 690-39

▶ **PV Output Circuit Ampacity Without Correction and/or Adjustment Example**

Question: What is the minimum dc PV output circuit conductor ampacity, without the application of conductor correction or adjustment, supplied by four source circuits each with a short-circuit current rating of 10A where the terminals are rated 75°C? ▶Figure 690-41

(a) 33A (b) 32A (c) 43A (d) 63A

Solution:

Conductor Ampacity = (Module Isc × 125% × Number of Source Circuits)* × 125%

Conductor Ampacity = (10A × 125% × 4 circuits)* × 125%

Conductor Ampacity = 50A × 125%

Conductor Ampacity = 62.50A

Use 6 AWG rated 65A at 75°C [110.14(C)(1)(a)(3) and Table 310.16]. *[690.8(A)(1)(a)]

Answer: *(d) 63A*

▶ **PV Source Circuit Without Ampacity Correction and/or Adjustment Example**

Question: What is the minimum dc source circuit conductor ampacity, without the application of conductor correction or adjustment, for source circuit conductors having a short-circuit current rating of 10A? ▶Figure 690-40

(a) 12.50A (b) 15.62A (c) 20.41A (d) 25.56A

Solar Photovoltaic (PV) Systems | **690.8**

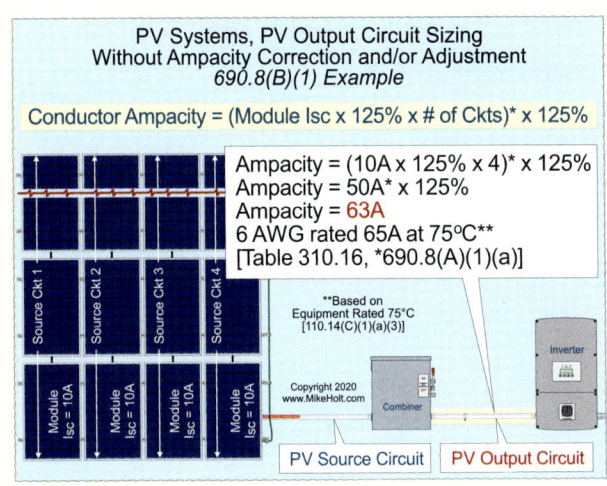
▶Figure 690-41

Ex: Where the assembly, including the overcurrent devices protecting the circuit(s), is listed for operation at 100 percent of its rating, the ampere rating of the overcurrent device can be sized to 100 percent of the continuous and noncontinuous loads.

(2) Conductor Sizing, With Ampacity Correction and/or Adjustment. PV circuit conductors within the scope of 690.8(A) must have an ampacity of not less than 100 percent of the current as determined by 690.8(A) after the application of conductor ampacity correction and adjustment in accordance with Table 310.15(B)(1) and Table 310.15(C)(1). ▶Figure 690-43

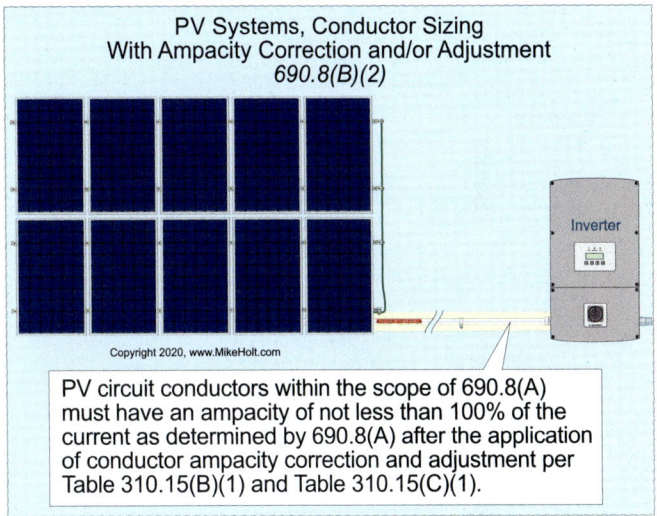
▶Figure 690-43

▶ **Inverter Output Circuit Ampacity Without Correction and/or Adjustment Example**

Question: What is the minimum inverter ac output circuit conductor ampacity, without the application of conductor ampacity correction and/or adjustment factors, if the maximum continuous nameplate rating of the inverter is 24A where the terminals are rated 75°C? ▶Figure 690-42

(a) 20A (b) 25A (c) 30A (d) 35A

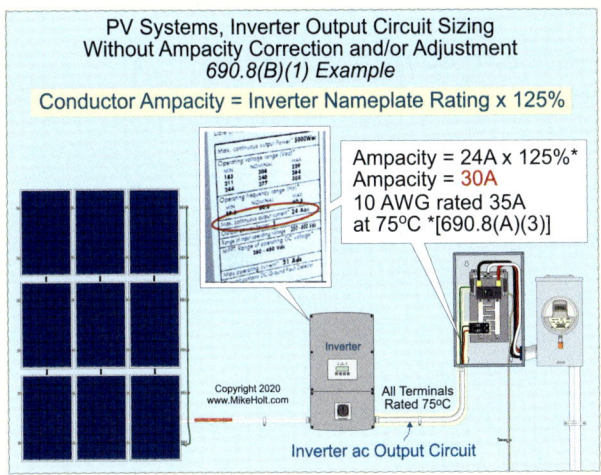
▶Figure 690-42

Solution:

Conductor Ampacity = Inverter Nameplate Rating [690.8(A)(1)(e)] × 125%

Conductor Ampacity = 24A × 125%

Conductor Ampacity = 30A

Use 10 AWG rated 35A at 75°C [310.16].

Answer: (c) 30A

Author's Comment:

▸ The Table 310.16 ampacity must be corrected when the ambient temperature is less than 77°F or greater than 86°F and adjusted when more than three current-carrying conductors are bundled together. The temperature correction [Table 310.15(B)(1)] and conductor bundling adjustment [Table 310.15(C)(1)] are applied to the conductor ampacity based on the temperature rating of the conductor insulation as contained in Table 310.16, typically in the 90°C column [310.15].

690.8 | Solar Photovoltaic (PV) Systems

▶ **PV Source Circuit Ampacity with Correction and Adjustment Example 1**

Question: What is the conductor ampacity with temperature correction for two current-carrying 12 AWG USE-2 or PV conductors rated 90°C within a raceway or cable located 1 in. above a roof where the ambient temperature is 94°F in accordance with 310.15(B)(1)? The modules have an Isc rating of 10A. ▶Figure 690-44

(a) 19A   (b) 29A   (c) 39A   (d) 49A

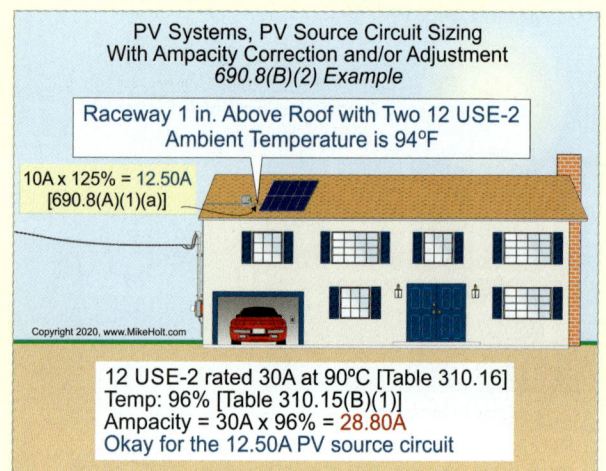

▶Figure 690-44

Solution:

Conductor Ampacity = Table 310.16 Ampacity at 90°C Column x Temperature Correction.

Temperature Correction = 0.96 based on a 94°F ambient temperature [Table 310.15(B)(1)].

12 AWG is rated 30A at 90°C [Table 310.16].

Conductor Corrected Ampacity = 30A x 96%
Conductor Corrected Ampacity = 28.80A

Note: 12 AWG with ampacity correction has sufficient ampacity to supply the source circuit dc current of 12.50A (10A x 125%) [690.8(A)(1)(a)].

Answer: (b) 29A

▶ **PV Source Circuit Ampacity with Correction and Adjustment Example 2**

Question: For an array with modules having a nameplate Isc rating of 10A for each source circuit, what is the conductor ampacity with temperature correction and adjustment for four current-carrying 12 AWG USE-2 conductors located 1 in. above a roof where the ambient temperature is 94°F? ▶Figure 690-45

(a) 23A   (b) 24A   (c) 25A   (d) 26A

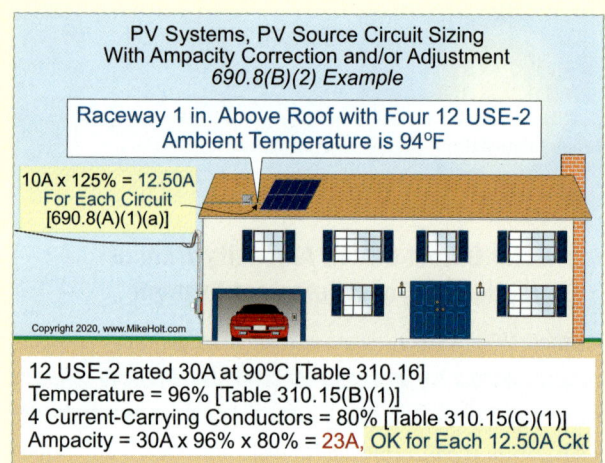

▶Figure 690-45

Solution:

Conductor Ampacity = Table 310.16 Ampacity at 90°C Column x Temperature Correction x Bundle Adjustment

Temperature Correction = 0.96 based on a 94°F ambient temperature [Table 310.15(B)(1)].

Bundle Adjustment = 80% based on four current-carrying conductors [Table 310.15(C)(1)].

12 AWG is rated 30A at 90°C [Table 310.16].

Conductor Corrected/Adjusted Ampacity = 30A x 96% x 80%
Conductor Corrected/Adjusted Ampacity = 23A

Note: 12 AWG has sufficient ampacity with correction and adjustment to supply the dc source circuits each with a current of 12.50A (10A × 125%) [690.8(A)(1)(a)].

Answer: (a) 23A

▶ **PV Output Circuit Ampacity with Correction Example**

Question: What is the dc PV output circuit conductor ampacity with conductor temperature correction for two 6 AWG USE-2 or PV output circuit conductors located 1 in. above a roof where the PV output circuit dc current is 40A and the ambient temperature is 94°F? ▶Figure 690–46

(a) 59A (b) 69A (c) 72A (d) 89A

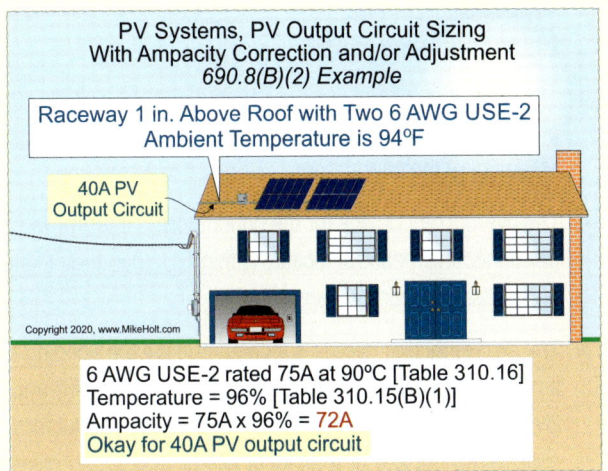

▶Figure 690–46

Solution:

Conductor Ampacity = Table 310.16 Ampacity at 90°C Column x Temperature Correction

Temperature Correction = 0.96 based on 94°F ambient temperature [Table 310.15(B)(1)].

6 AWG is rated 75A at 90°C [Table 310.16].

Conductor Corrected Ampacity = 75A x 96%
Conductor Corrected Ampacity = 72A

Note: 6 AWG with correction has sufficient ampacity to supply the PV output circuit dc current of 40A.

Answer: (c) 72A

▶ **Inverter Output Circuit Ampacity with Correction and Adjustment Example**

Question: What is the conductor ampacity with temperature correction for two current-carrying 10 AWG RHH/RHW-2/USE-2 or PV conductors rated 90°C supplying a 24A inverter output circuit and installed in a location where the ambient temperature is 94°F? ▶Figure 690–47

(a) 18.40A (b) 29.40A (c) 38.40A (d) 49.40A

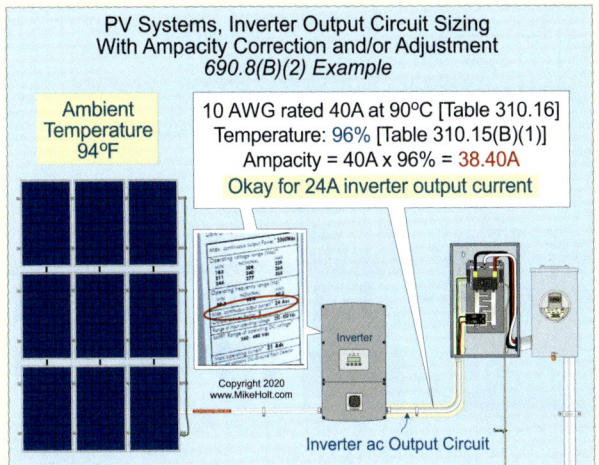

▶Figure 690–47

Solution:

Conductor Ampacity = Ampacity at 90°C Column [Table 310.16] x Temperature Correction.

Temperature Correction = 0.96 based on a 94°F ambient temperature [Table 310.15(B)(1)].

10 AWG is rated 40A at 90°C [Table 310.16].

Conductor Ampacity = 40A x 96%
Conductor Ampacity = 38.40A

Note: 10 AWG has sufficient ampacity with correction to supply the inverter output circuit dc current of 24A [690.8(A)(1)(e)].

Answer: (c) 38.40A

690.9 Overcurrent Protection

(A) General. PV system dc circuit and inverter output conductors and equipment must be protected against overcurrent. PV system dc circuit conductors sized in accordance with 690.8(A)(2) are required to be protected against overcurrent by one of the methods in 690.9(A)(1) through (A)(3).

690.9 | Solar Photovoltaic (PV) Systems

(1) Circuits Without Overcurrent Protection. Overcurrent protection is not required where both of the following conditions are met:

(1) The PV system dc circuit conductors have an ampacity equal to or greater than the maximum dc current calculated in accordance with 690.8(A).

(2) Where the currents from all PV sources do not exceed the maximum overcurrent protective device rating specified by the manufacturer for the PV module or electronic power converters (inverters, dc-to-dc converters, and charge controllers). ▶Figure 690–48

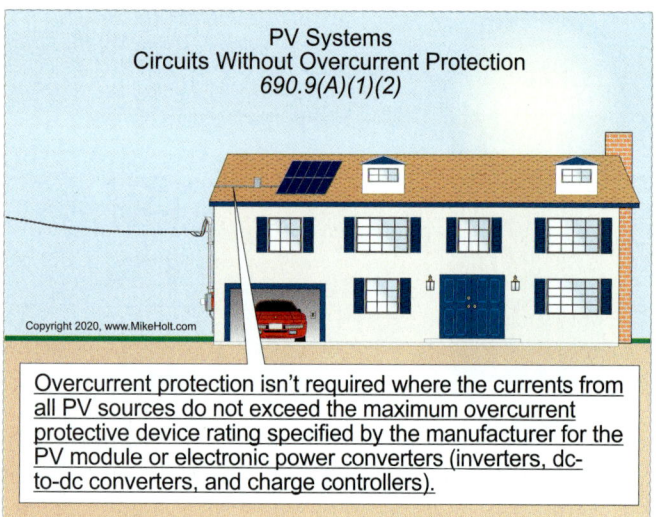

▶Figure 690–48

(2) Overcurrent Protection Required on One End. PV system circuit conductors connected to sources having an available maximum circuit current greater than the ampacity of the conductor must have overcurrent protection at the point of connection to the higher current source for circuit conductors connected at one end to a current-limited supply (PV modules, inverters, and dc-to-dc converters).

Note: PV system dc circuits and electronic power converter (inverters, dc-to-dc converters, and charge controllers) outputs are current-limited and in some cases do not need overcurrent protection. When these circuits are connected to higher current sources, such as parallel-connected PV system dc circuits or energy storage systems, the overcurrent device is often installed at the higher current source end of the circuit conductor.

(3) Other Circuits. PV circuits conductors that do not comply with 690.9(A)(1) or (A)(2) must be protected by one of the following methods:

(1) PV circuit conductors on (but not within) a building must not be longer than 10 ft in length and must have overcurrent protection at one end of the circuit.

(2) PV system circuit conductors within a building must not be longer than 10 ft in length, be within a raceway or metal-clad cable, and have overcurrent protection on one end of the circuit.

(3) PV circuit conductors protected from overcurrent on both ends.

(4) PV circuit conductors not installed on or within buildings having overcurrent protection at one end of the circuit must comply with all of the following conditions:

   a. The PV system circuit conductors are in metal raceways, metal-clad cables, enclosed metal cable trays, underground, or in pad-mounted enclosures.

   b. The PV system circuit conductors terminate to a single circuit breaker or a single set of fuses that limit the current to the ampacity of the conductors.

   c. The overcurrent device for the conductors is integral with the disconnecting means or located within 10 ft (conductor length) of the disconnecting means.

   d. The disconnecting means is located outside the building or at a readily accessible location nearest the point of entrance of the conductors inside the building. PV circuit conductors are considered outside of a building where they are encased or installed under not less than 2 in. of concrete or brick in accordance with 230.6.

(B) Overcurrent Device Ratings. Overcurrent devices for PV dc circuits must be listed for PV systems. ▶Figure 690–49

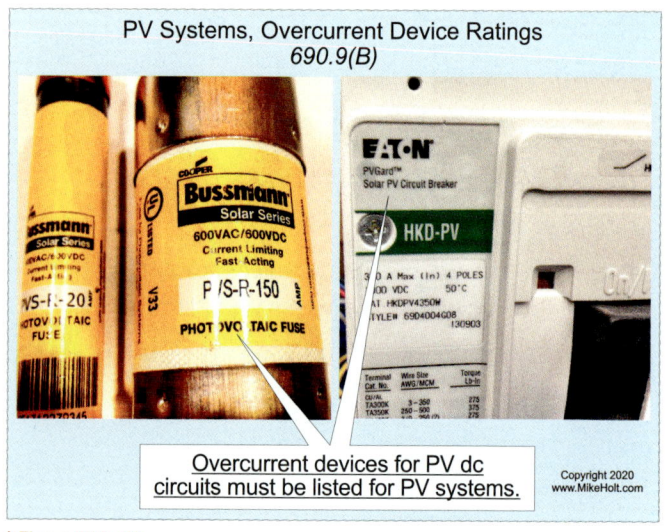

▶Figure 690–49

Electronic devices that are listed to prevent backfeed in PV dc circuits are permitted to prevent overcurrent of conductors on the PV array side of the electronic device.

Overcurrent protective devices required by 690.9(A)(2) must comply with one of the following. The next higher standard size overcurrent device in accordance with 240.4(B) is permitted.

(1) The overcurrent protective device must have a rating of not less than 125 percent of the maximum currents as calculated in 690.8(A).
▶Figure 690-50

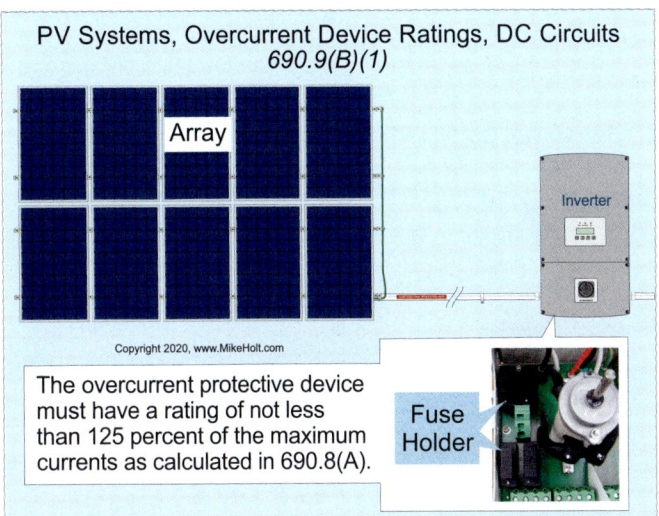
▶Figure 690-50

(2) Where the assembly, together with its overcurrent device(s), is listed for continuous operation at 100 percent of its rating, the overcurrent protective device can be sized at 100 percent of the maximum currents as calculated in 690.8(A).

Note: Some electronic devices prevent backfeed current, which in some cases is the only source of overcurrent in PV system dc circuits.

(C) Source and Output Circuits. A single overcurrent protective device can be used to protect PV modules, dc-to-dc converters, and source circuit and output circuit conductors. Where a single overcurrent protective device is used to protect source circuits or output circuits, it must be placed in the same polarity for all circuits within the PV system.

Note: A single overcurrent protective device in either the positive or negative conductors of a functionally grounded PV system provides adequate overcurrent protection.

690.10 Stand-Alone Systems

Wiring for stand-alone PV systems must be in accordance with 710.15.
▶Figure 690-51

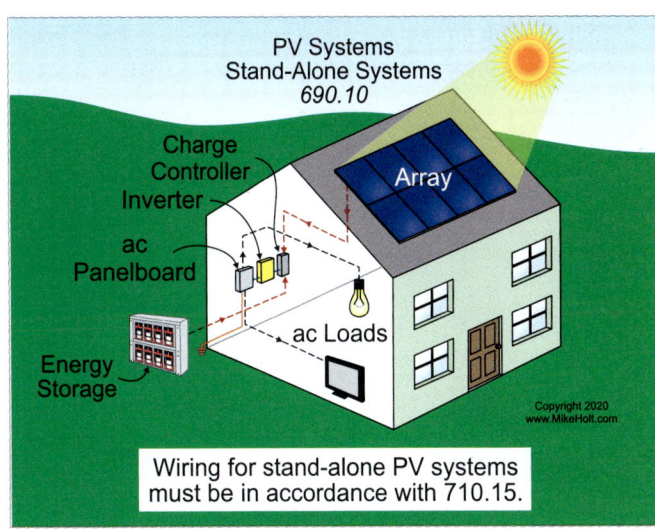
▶Figure 690-51

690.11 Arc-Fault Circuit Protection

PV system dc circuits operating at 80V dc or greater must be protected by a listed PV arc-fault circuit interrupter or other component listed to provide equivalent protection.

Ex: PV dc AFCI protection is not required for PV circuits not installed on or in buildings if the circuits are within metal raceways, metal-clad cables, enclosed cable trays, or underground. PV dc AFCI protection is not required for PV circuits installed in a detached building whose sole purpose is to house PV system equipment.

690.12 Rapid Shutdown

PV system conductors on or in a building must be controlled by a rapid shutdown system to reduce shock hazard for firefighters in accordance with 690.12(A) through (D). ▶Figure 690-52

Ex: A rapid shutdown system is not required for ground-mounted PV system conductors that enter buildings whose sole purpose is to house PV system equipment.

(A) Controlled Conductors. PV system conductors controlled by the rapid shutdown system include:

(1) PV system dc circuit conductors.

(2) Inverter output ac circuits originating from inverters located within the array boundary.

690.12 | Solar Photovoltaic (PV) Systems

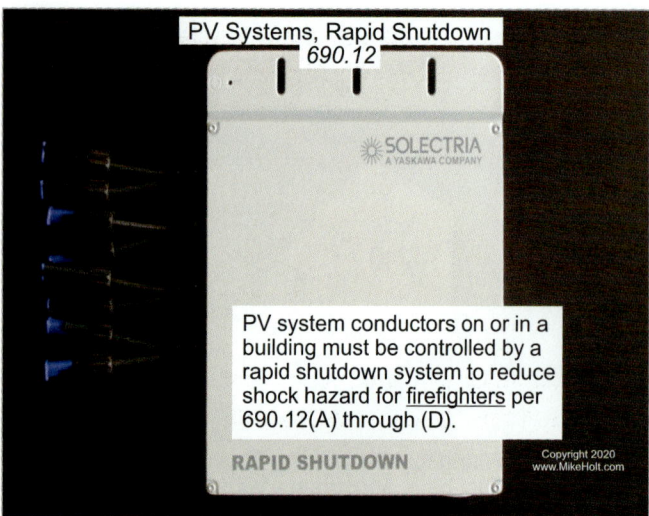

▶Figure 690-52

Note: The ac output conductors from PV systems will be either de-energized after shutdown initiation or remain energized if supplied by a utility service. To prevent PV systems with ac output conductors from remaining energized, they must be controlled by the rapid shutdown system after shutdown initiation.

(B) Controlled Limits. For the purpose of rapid shutdown, the array boundary is defined as the area 1 ft outside the perimeter of the PV array.

(1) Outside the Array Boundary. PV system circuit conductors located outside the PV array boundary or more than 3 ft from the point of entry inside a building must be limited to 30V within 30 seconds of rapid shutdown initiation.

(2) Inside the Array Boundary. The PV system rapid shutdown system must comply with one of the following:

(1) A PV hazard control system listed for the purpose must be installed in accordance with the manufacturer's installation instructions. Where a hazard control system requires initiation to transition to a controlled state, the rapid shutdown initiation device [690.12(C)] must perform this initiation.

Note: A listed or field-labeled hazard PV control system is comprised of either an individual piece of equipment that fulfills the necessary functions, or multiple pieces of equipment coordinated to perform the functions as described in the manufacturer's installation instructions.

(2) PV system circuit conductors located inside the PV array boundary must be limited to 80V within 30 seconds of rapid shutdown initiation.

(3) PV arrays must have no exposed wiring methods or exposed conductive parts and be installed more than 8 ft from exposed conductive parts.

(C) Initiation Device. A rapid shutdown initiation device is required to initiate the rapid shutdown function of the PV system. When the rapid shutdown initiation device is placed in the "off" position, this indicates that the rapid shutdown function has been initiated.

For one- and two-family dwellings, the rapid shutdown initiation device must be located outside the building at a readily accessible location.

For a single PV system, the rapid shutdown initiation must occur by the operation of any single device that must be at least one of the following types:

(1) The service disconnect. ▶Figure 690-53

▶Figure 690-53

(2) The PV system disconnect. ▶Figure 690-54

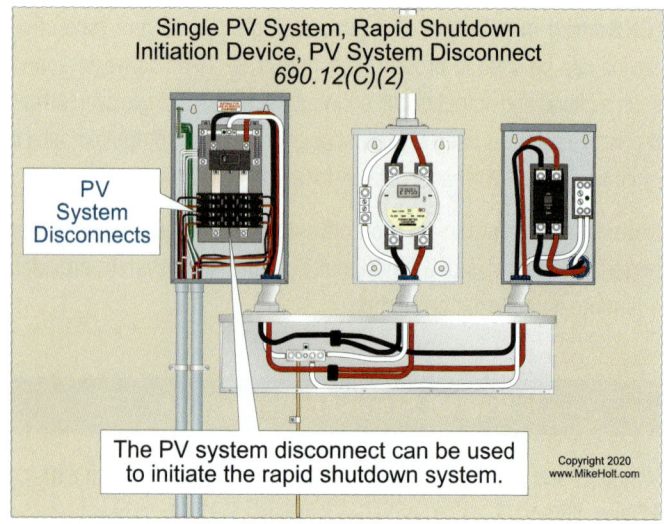

▶Figure 690-54

(3) A readily accessible switch that plainly indicates whether it is in the "off" or "on" position.

Note: An example of where a rapid shutdown initiation device that complies with 690.12(C)(3) would be used is where a PV system is connected to an optional standby or stand-alone system.

Where multiple PV systems are on a single service, the rapid shutdown initiation device(s) for the multiple PV systems must consist of not more than six switches or six sets of circuit breakers, or a combination of not more than six switches and sets of circuit breakers.

(D) Equipment. Equipment that performs the rapid shutdown function, other than initiation devices, must be listed for providing rapid shutdown protection.

Part III. Disconnect

690.13 PV System Disconnect

Means must be provided to disconnect the PV system conductors from power systems, energy storage systems, utilization equipment, and associated premises wiring.

(A) Location. The PV system disconnect must be readily accessible.

The door or hinged cover for the PV system disconnecting means must be locked or require a tool to open.

Note: Rapid shutdown systems installed in accordance with 690.12 address the concerns related to energized conductors entering a building.

(B) Marking. The PV system disconnect must indicate if it is in the open (off) or closed (on) position and be marked "PV SYSTEM DISCONNECT" or equivalent. ▶Figure 690-55

Where the line and load terminals of the PV system disconnect may be energized when the disconnect is in the open (off) position, the disconnect must be marked with the following or equivalent:

> **WARNING—ELECTRIC SHOCK HAZARD**
> **TERMINALS ON THE LINE AND LOAD SIDES**
> **MAY BE ENERGIZED IN THE OPEN POSITION**

The warning markings on the disconnect must be permanently affixed and have sufficient durability to withstand the environment involved [110.21(B)].

(C) Maximum Number of Disconnects. The disconnecting means for a PV system must consist of not more than six switches or six sets of circuit breakers, or a combination of not more than six switches and sets of circuit breakers. ▶Figure 690-56

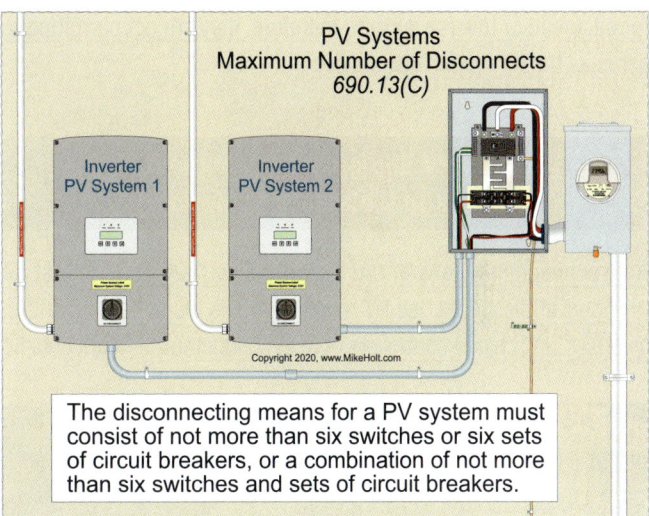

▶Figure 690-56

A single PV system disconnect is permitted for the combined ac output of one or more inverters or ac modules in an interactive system.

Note: This requirement of a maximum of six PV system disconnects does not limit the number of PV systems on a premises [690.4(D)]. The dedicated circuit breaker for an interactive inverter in accordance with 705.12(A) is an example of a single PV system disconnect.

(D) Ratings. The PV system disconnect must have a rating sufficient for the maximum circuit current, the available fault current, and the voltage at the terminals of the PV system disconnect.

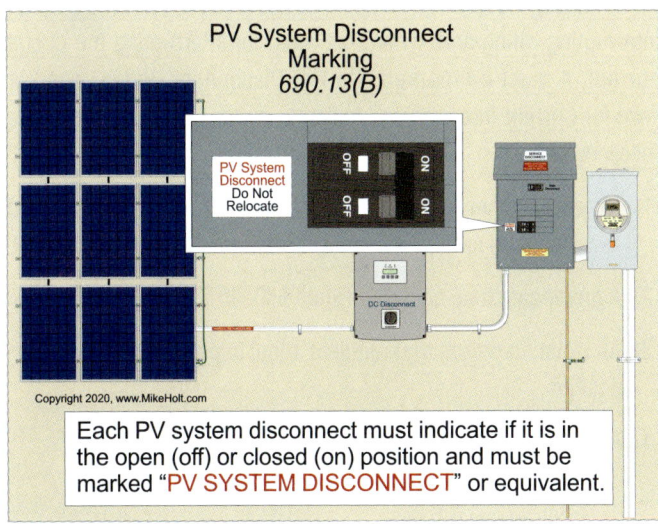

▶Figure 690-55

(E) Type of Disconnect. The PV system disconnect must simultaneously disconnect all PV system circuit conductors. The PV system disconnect, its remote operating device, or the enclosure providing access to the disconnect must be capable of being locked in the open position in accordance with 110.25. The PV system disconnect must be one of the following types:

(1) A manually operable switch or circuit breaker.

(2) A mating connector meeting the requirements of 690.33(D)(1) or (D)(3).

(3) A pull-out switch with sufficient interrupting rating.

(4) A remote-controlled switch or circuit breaker that is operable manually and is opened automatically when control power is interrupted.

(5) A device listed or approved for the intended application.

Note: Circuit breakers marked "line" and "load" may not be suitable for backfeed or reverse current; therefore, they are not permitted to serve as the PV system disconnect.

690.15 PV Equipment Disconnecting Means to Isolate PV Equipment

A disconnecting means of the required type [690.15(D)] must be provided to disconnect ac PV modules, fuses, dc-to-dc converters, inverters, and charge controllers from all conductors. ▶Figure 690–57

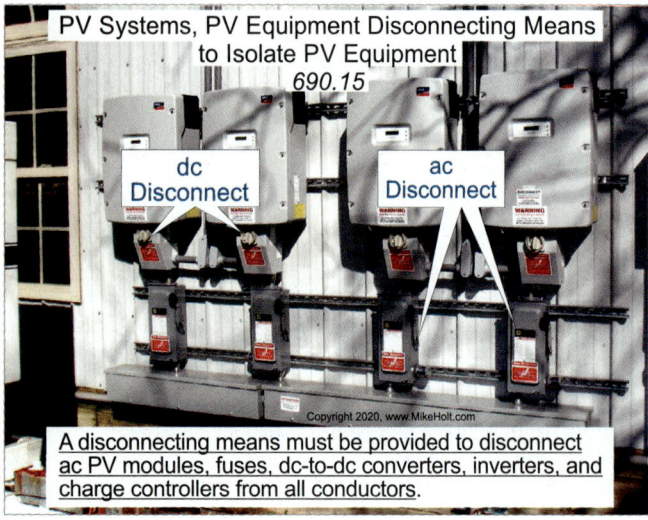

▶Figure 690–57

Author's Comment:

▸ The purpose of the PV disconnecting means is to ensure the safe and convenient replacement or maintenance of PV equipment without exposing qualified persons to energized conductors.

(A) Location. Isolating devices or disconnecting means must be placed either within the PV equipment or within sight and within 10 ft of the PV equipment. The PV equipment disconnect can be located further than 10 ft from the equipment if it can be remotely operated from within 10 ft of the equipment. ▶Figure 690–58

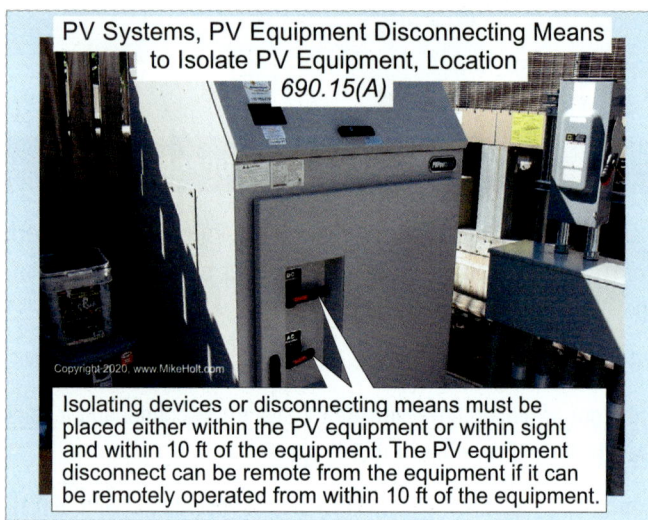

▶Figure 690–58

The door or hinged cover for the PV equipment disconnect must be locked or require a tool to open.

(B) Isolating Device. An isolating device is not required to have an interrupting rating and, where not rated for interrupting the circuit current, it must be marked "Do Not Disconnect Under Load" or "Not for Current Interrupting." Isolating devices must be one of the following types:

(1) A mating connector meeting the requirements of 690.33 and listed and identified for use with specific equipment. ▶Figure 690–59

(2) A finger-safe fuse holder. ▶Figure 690–60

(3) An isolating device that requires a tool to place in the open (off) position.

(4) An isolating device listed for the intended application.

Solar Photovoltaic (PV) Systems | 690.15

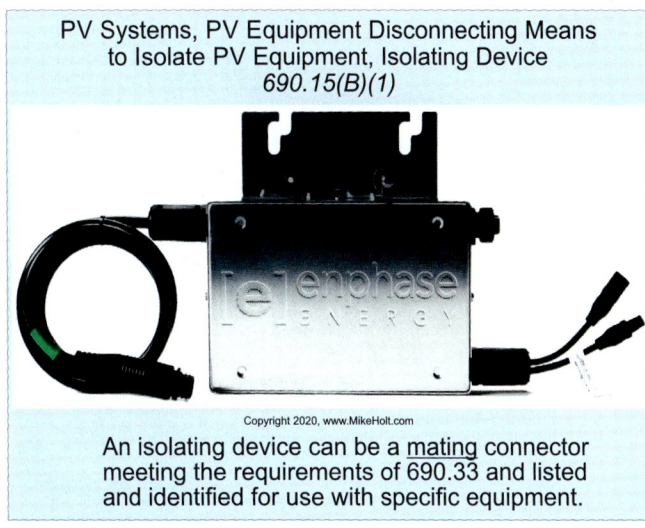
▶Figure 690-59

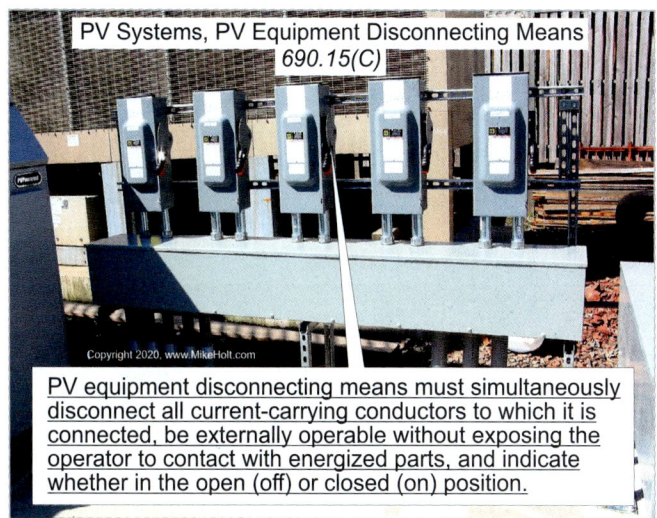
▶Figure 690-61

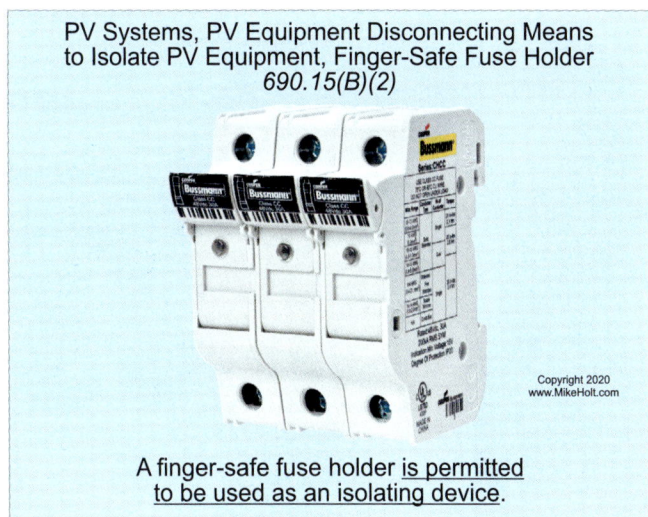
▶Figure 690-60

(C) Equipment Disconnecting Means. The PV equipment disconnecting means must have a rating sufficient for the maximum circuit current, available fault current, and the voltage at the terminals of the disconnect.

The PV equipment disconnecting means must simultaneously disconnect all current-carrying circuit conductors to which it is connected, must be externally operable without exposing the operator to contact with energized parts, and indicate whether it is in the open (off) or closed (on) position. ▶Figure 690-61

Where the PV equipment disconnect is not within sight and within 10 ft of the equipment, the PV equipment disconnect must be capable of being locked in the open position in accordance with 110.25.

The equipment disconnecting means must be of the same type as required in 690.13(E).

An equipment disconnecting means, other than those complying with 690.33, must be marked in accordance with the warning in 690.13(B) if the line and load terminals can be energized in the open position.

Author's Comment:

▸ According to 690.13(B), each PV system disconnect must indicate if it is in the open (off) or closed (on) position and the disconnect must be permanently marked "PV SYSTEM DISCONNECT" or equivalent. Where the line and load terminals of the PV system disconnect may be energized when the disconnect is in the open (off) position, the disconnect must be marked with the following words or equivalent:

**WARNING—ELECTRIC SHOCK HAZARD
TERMINALS ON THE LINE AND LOAD SIDES
MAY BE ENERGIZED IN THE OPEN POSITION**

The warning markings on the disconnect must be permanently affixed and have sufficient durability to withstand the environment involved [110.21(B)].

Note: A common installation practice is to terminate circuit conductors on the line side of a disconnect which will de-energize load-side terminals, blades, and fuses when the disconnect is in the open position.

(D) Type of Disconnecting Means. Where disconnects are required to isolate equipment, the disconnecting means must be one of the following types:

(1) Over 30A Circuit. A disconnecting means in accordance with 690.15(C).

(2) Not over 30A Circuit. An isolating device in accordance with 690.15(B).

Part IV. Wiring Methods

690.31 Wiring Methods

(A) Wiring Systems. Permitted methods include Chapter 3 wiring methods, wiring systems and fittings listed for PV arrays, and wiring that is part of a listed PV system. ▶Figure 690-62

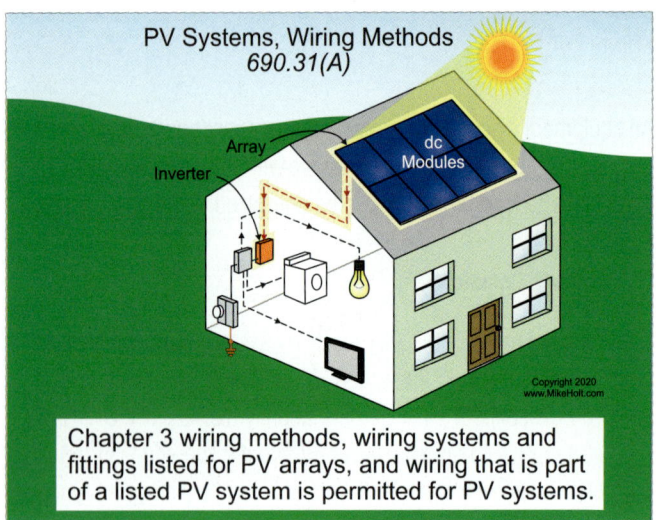

▶Figure 690-62

PV system dc circuit conductors operating at over 30V installed in a readily accessible location must be guarded or installed within a raceway or Type MC cable. ▶Figure 690-63 and ▶Figure 690-64

PV circuit conductors with insulation rated at 105°C and 125°C must have their ampacity [690.31(A)(b)] corrected by Table 690.31(A)(a).

Note: See 110.14(C) for conductor temperature limitations due to termination provisions.

(B) Identification and Grouping. PV system circuits are permitted in the same enclosure, cable, or raceway with each other and with Class 1 circuits associated with the PV system [725.48(B)(1)].

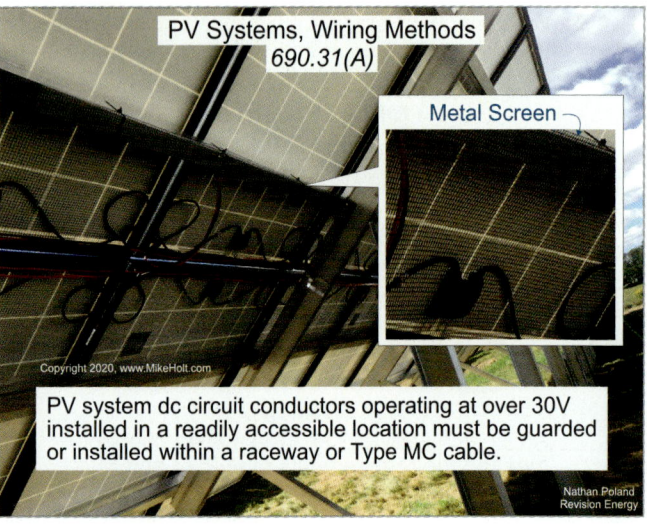

▶Figure 690-63

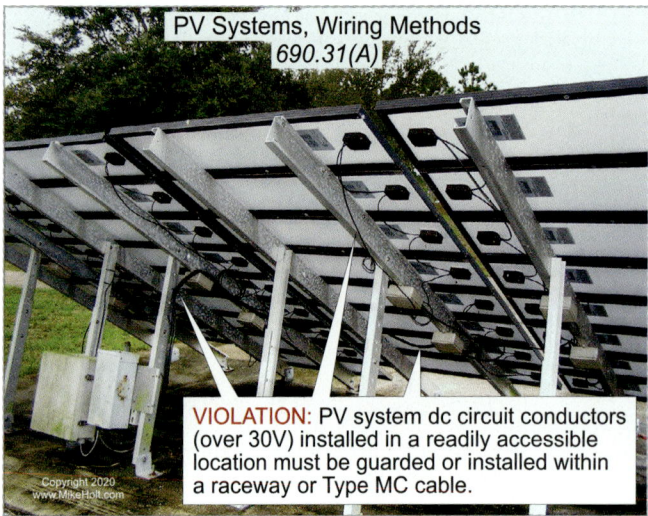

▶Figure 690-64

Table 690.31(A)(a) Correction Factors			
	Temperature Rating of Conductor		
Ambient Temperature (°C)	105°C (221°F)	125°C (257°F)	Ambient Temperature (°F)
31–35	0.97	0.97	87–95
36–40	0.93	0.95	96–104
41–45	0.89	0.92	105–113
46–50	0.86	0.89	114–122
51–55	0.82	0.86	123–131

Table 690.31(A)(a) Correction Factors (continued)

Ambient Temperature (°C)	Temperature Rating of Conductor		Ambient Temperature (°F)
	105°C (221°F)	125°C (257°F)	
56–60	0.77	0.83	132–140
61–65	0.73	0.79	141–149
66–70	0.68	0.76	150–158
71–75	0.63	0.73	159–167
76–80	0.58	0.69	168–176
81–85	0.52	0.65	177–185
86–90	0.45	0.61	186–194
91–95	0.37	0.56	195–203
96–100	0.26	0.51	204–212
101–105	–	0.46	213–221
106–110	–	0.4	222–230
111–115	–	0.32	231–239
116–120	–	0.23	240–248

Table 690.31(A)(b) Conductor Ampacity, Not More Than Three Current-Carrying Conductors in Raceway, Cable, or Earth, with Ambient Temperature of 30°C (86°F)

Wire Size AWG	PVC, CPE, XLPE 105°C	XLPE, EPDM 125°C
18	15	16
16	19	20
14	29	31
12	36	39
10	46	50
8	64	69
6	81	87
4	109	118
3	129	139
2	143	154
1	168	181
1/0	193	208
2/0	229	247
3/0	263	284
4/0	301	325

PV system dc circuit conductors are not permitted to be installed in the same enclosure, cable, or raceway with non-PV system circuit conductors or inverter output circuit conductors unless separated by a barrier or partition. ▶Figure 690-65

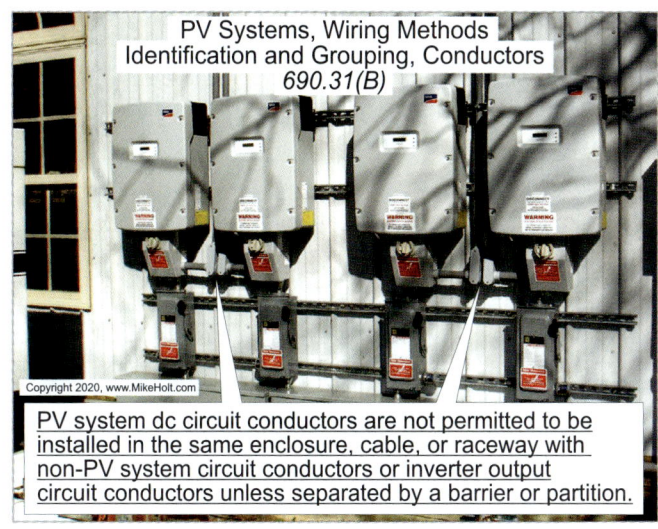

▶Figure 690-65

Ex: PV system dc circuits within multiconductor jacketed cable, Type MC cable, or listed wiring harnesses identified for the application can be installed in the same enclosure, cable, or raceway with non-PV system circuits. All conductors, harnesses, or assemblies must have an insulation rating equal to at least the maximum circuit dc voltage applied to any conductor within the enclosure, cable, or raceway.

PV system dc circuits must be identified and grouped as required by 690.31(B)(1) and (B)(2).

(1) Identification. PV system dc circuit conductors must have all termination, connection, and splice points permanently identified for polarity by color coding, marking tape, tagging, or other approved means. ▶Figure 690-66

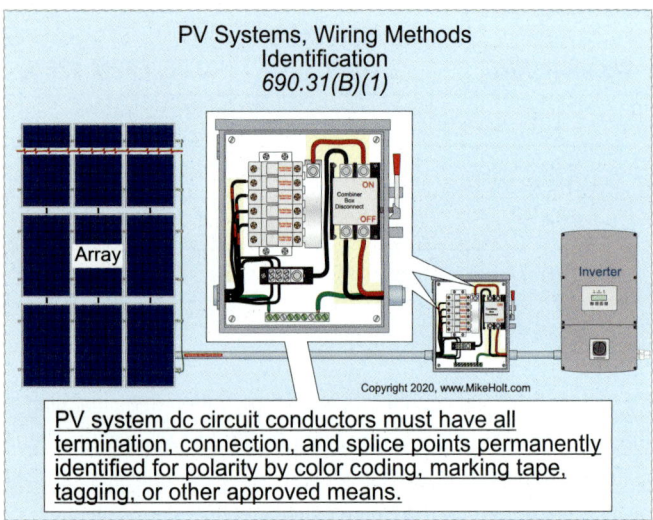

▶Figure 690-66

Conductors relying on marking tape, tagging, or other approved means for polarity identification must be by an approved permanent marking means such as labeling, sleeving, or shrink-tubing that is suitable for the conductor size.

The marking tape, tagging, or other approved means for polarity identification must include the positive sign (+) or the word "POSITIVE" or "POS" for the positive conductor, and the negative sign (−) or the word "NEGATIVE" or "NEG" for the negative conductor. Marking must be durable and be of a color other than green, white, gray, or red.

Ex: Identification is not required where the identification of the conductors is evident by spacing or arrangement.

(2) Grouping. Where PV system dc circuit conductors are in the same enclosure or wireway with other PV system dc circuit conductors, the PV system dc circuit conductors of each system must be grouped together by the use of cable ties or similar means at least once and at intervals not to exceed 6 ft.

Ex: Grouping is not required if the dc circuit enters from a cable or raceway unique to the circuit that makes the grouping obvious.

(C) Cables. Type PV wire, Type PV cable, and Type DG cable must be listed.

(1) Single-Conductor Cable. Single-conductor cable within the PV array must be one of the following types: ▶Figure 690-67

(1) Type PV wire or Type PV Cable.

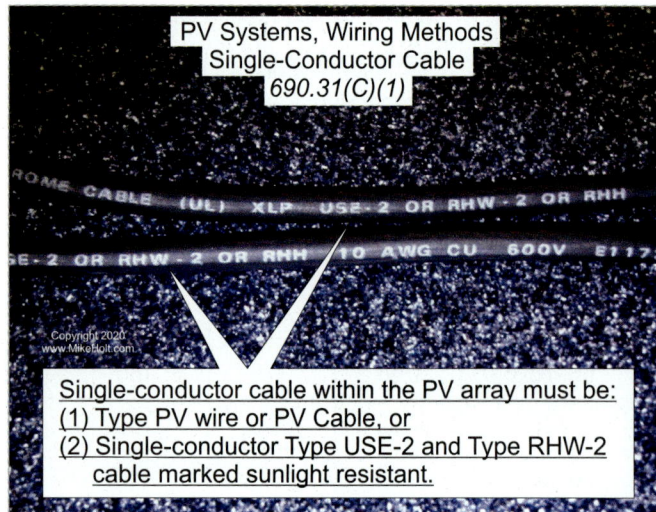

▶Figure 690-67

(2) Single-conductor Type USE-2 and Type RHW-2 cable marked sunlight resistant.

Exposed single-conductor cables must be supported and secured at intervals not to exceed 24 in. by cable ties, straps, hangers, or similar fittings listed and identified for securement and support in outdoor locations.

Type PV wire or Type PV cable is permitted to be installed in all locations where RHW-2 is permitted.

(2) Cable Tray. Single-conductor Type PV wire, Type PV cable, or Type DG cable can be installed in cable trays in outdoor locations, provided the cables are supported at intervals not to exceed 12 in. and secured at intervals not to exceed 4½ ft.

Note: Type PV wire, Type PV cable, and Type DG cable have nonstandard outer diameters. Chapter 9, Table 1 contains the allowable percent of cross section of conduit and tubing for conductors and cables. ▶Figure 690-68

(3) Multiconductor Jacketed Cable. Where a multiconductor jacketed cable is part of a listed PV assembly, the cable must be installed in accordance with the manufacturer's instructions.

Multiconductor jacketed cable that is not part of a listed assembly or not covered in this *Code* must be installed in accordance with the product listing instructions.

Multiconductor jacketed cable must be installed in accordance with the following requirements:

(1) In Raceways. Multiconductor jacketed cable on or in buildings must be installed in a raceway, except for rooftop installations.

Solar Photovoltaic (PV) Systems | **690.31**

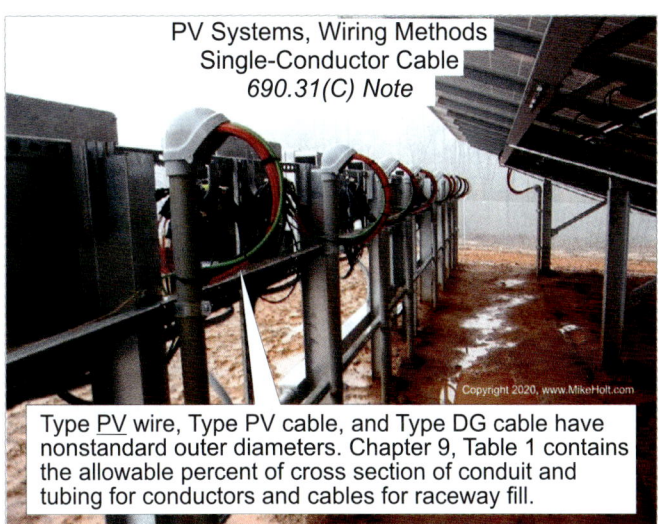

Type PV wire, Type PV cable, and Type DG cable have nonstandard outer diameters. Chapter 9, Table 1 contains the allowable percent of cross section of conduit and tubing for conductors and cables for raceway fill.

▶Figure 690-68

(2) Not Within Raceway. Where multiconductor jacketed cable is not installed within a raceway, the cable must:

   a. Be marked "Sunlight Resistant" in exposed outdoor locations.

   b. Be protected or guarded where subject to physical damage.
   ▶Figure 690-69

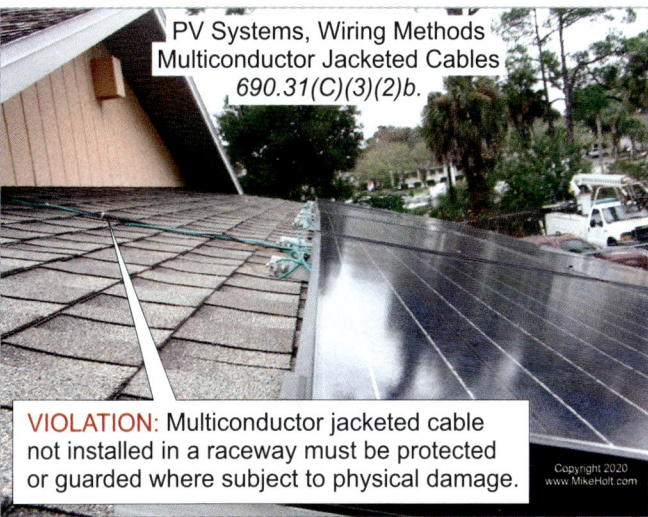

▶Figure 690-69

   c. Closely follow the surface of support structures.

   d. Be secured at intervals not exceeding 6 ft.

   e. Be secured within 24 in. of mating connectors or entering enclosures.

   f. Be marked "Direct Burial" where buried in the earth.

(4) Flexible Cords and Cables for Tracking PV Arrays. Flexible cords connected to moving parts of tracking PV arrays must be installed in accordance with Article 400, be identified as hard-service cord or portable power cable, be suitable for extra-hard usage, and be listed for outdoor use, water resistant, and sunlight resistant.

Stranded copper Type PV wire used for moving parts of tracking PV arrays must have a minimum number of strands as specified in Table 690.31(C)(4).

Table 690.31(C)(4) Minimum PV Wire Strands for Moving Parts of Tracking PV Arrays	
PV Wire AWG	Minimum Strands
18	17
16–10	19
8–4	49
2	130
1 AWG–1,000 MCM	259

(5) Flexible, Fine-Stranded Cables. Flexible, fine-stranded cables must terminate on terminals, lugs, devices, or connectors identified for the use of finely stranded conductors in accordance with 110.14. ▶Figure 690-70

▶Figure 690-70

(D) PV System Direct-Current Circuits On or In Buildings. When the PV system dc circuit is located inside a building, the PV system's dc circuit conductors must be installed in a metal raceway, Type MC cable, or a metal enclosure. ▶Figure 690-71

690.31 | Solar Photovoltaic (PV) Systems

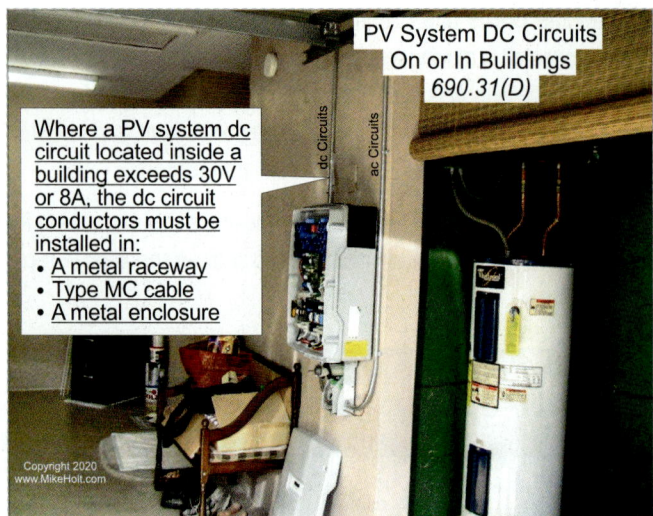
▶Figure 690–71

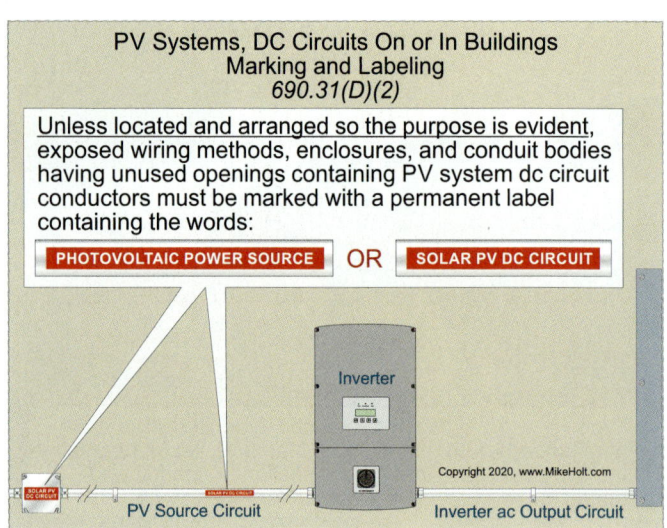
▶Figure 690–72

Ex: PV hazard control system conductors that are installed for a rapid shutdown application in accordance with 690.12(B)(2)(1) can be provided with (or listed for use with) nonmetallic enclosures, nonmetallic raceways, and permitted cable types other than Type MC cable, at the point of penetration of the building to the PV hazard control actuator.

Wiring methods for PV system dc circuits on or in buildings must comply with the following additional requirements:

(1) Flexible Wiring Methods. Where flexible metal conduit smaller than trade size ¾ or Type MC cable smaller than 1 in. in diameter containing PV system dc circuit conductors is run across ceilings or floor joists, the flexible metal conduit or Type MC cable must be protected by substantial guard strips that are at least as high as the flexible metal conduit or Type MC cable.

Where flexible metal conduit or Type MC cable containing PV system dc circuit conductors is run exposed further than 6 ft from their connection to equipment, the flexible metal conduit or Type MC cable must closely follow the building surface or be protected from physical damage by an approved means.

(2) Marking and Labeling. Unless located and arranged so the purpose is evident, the following wiring methods and enclosures containing PV system dc circuit conductors must be marked with a permanent label containing the words "PHOTOVOLTAIC POWER SOURCE" or "SOLAR PV DC CIRCUIT." ▶Figure 690–72

(1) Exposed raceways, cable trays, and other wiring methods.

(2) Covers or enclosures of pull boxes and junction boxes.

(3) Conduit bodies having unused openings.

The label must be visible after installation. The letters must be capitalized and be a minimum height of ⅜ in. in white on a red background.
▶Figure 690–73

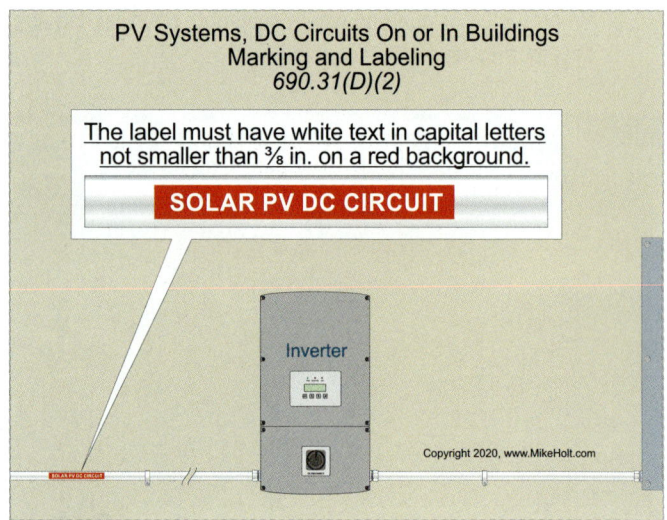
▶Figure 690–73

Labels must appear on every section of the wiring system that is separated by enclosures, walls, partitions, ceilings, or floors. Spacing between labels must not be more than 10 ft, and the label must be suitable for the environment. ▶Figure 690–74

(F) Wiring Methods and Mounting Systems. Roof-mounted PV array mounting systems are permitted to be held in place with an approved means other than those required by 110.13. The wiring methods must allow any expected movement of the array.

Note: Expected movement of unattached PV arrays is often included in structural calculations.

Solar Photovoltaic (PV) Systems | **690.33**

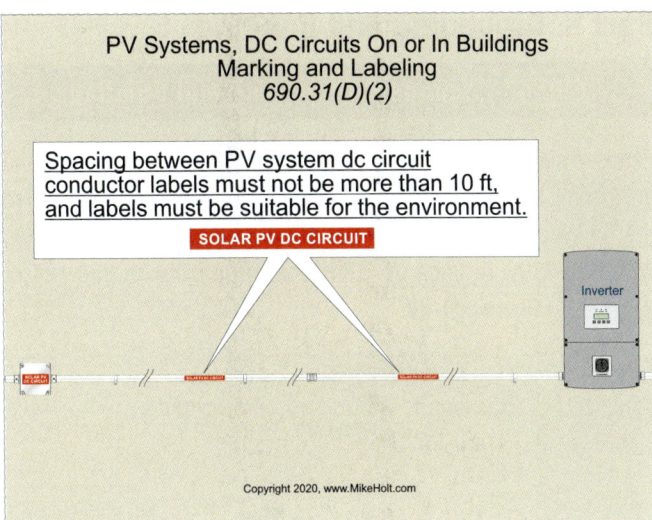
▶Figure 690-74

690.32 Component Interconnections

Fittings and connectors that are intended to be concealed at the time of on-site use for building-integrated PV systems must be listed for on-site interconnection of modules or other array components. ▶Figure 690-75

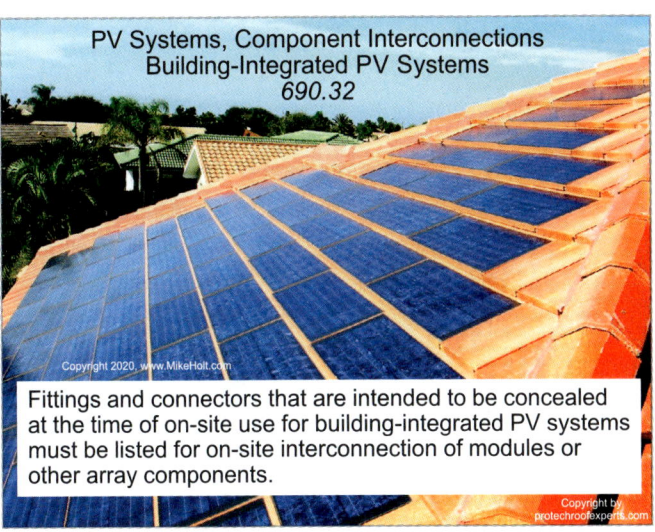
▶Figure 690-75

Author's Comment:

▶ Building-integrated PV systems have PV system dc circuit conductors embedded in built-up, laminate, or membrane roofing materials on roofs.

690.33 Connectors (Mating)

Mating connectors, other than listed connectors for building-integrated PV systems as covered in 690.32, must comply with the following:
▶Figure 690-76

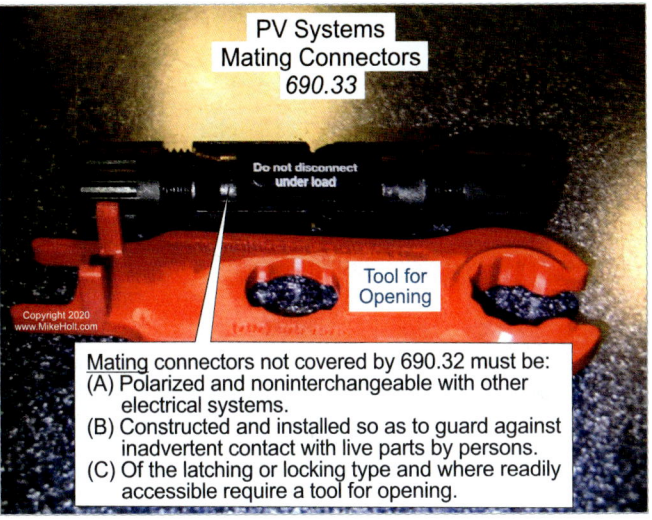
▶Figure 690-76

(A) Configuration. The mating connectors must be polarized and be noninterchangeable with other electrical systems on the premises.

(B) Guarding. The mating connectors must be constructed and installed so as to guard against inadvertent contact with live parts by persons.

(C) Type. Mating connectors must be of the latching or locking type and where readily accessible require a tool for opening. Where mating connectors are not of the identical type and brand, they must be listed and identified for intermatability as described in the manufacturer's instructions.

(D) Interruption of Circuit. Mating connectors must comply with one of the following requirements. ▶Figure 690-77

(1) Mating connectors must be rated to interrupt current without hazard to the operator.

(2) A tool must be required to open the mating connector and the mating connectors must be marked "Do Not Disconnect Under Load" or "Not for Current Interrupting."

(3) Mating connectors supplied as part of listed equipment must be used in accordance with instructions provided with the listed connected equipment.

690.34 | Solar Photovoltaic (PV) Systems

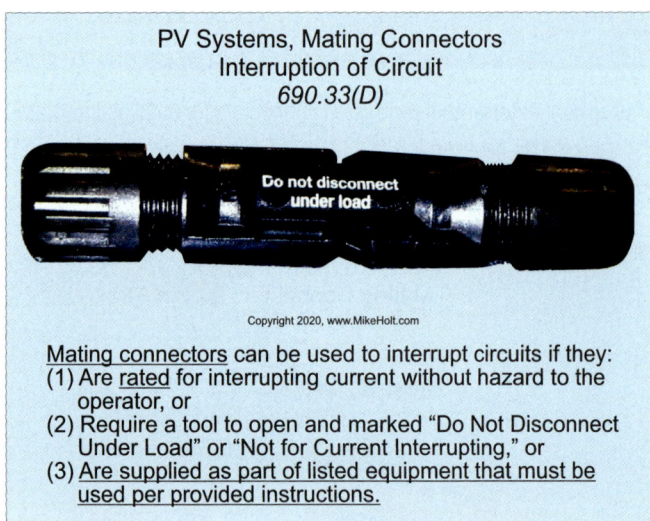
▶Figure 690–77

Note: Some listed equipment, such as micro inverters, are evaluated to make use of mating connectors as disconnect devices even though the mating connectors are marked as "Do Not Disconnect Under Load" or "Not for Current Interrupting."

690.34 Access to Boxes

Junction, pull, and outlet boxes are permitted to be located behind PV modules. ▶Figure 690–78

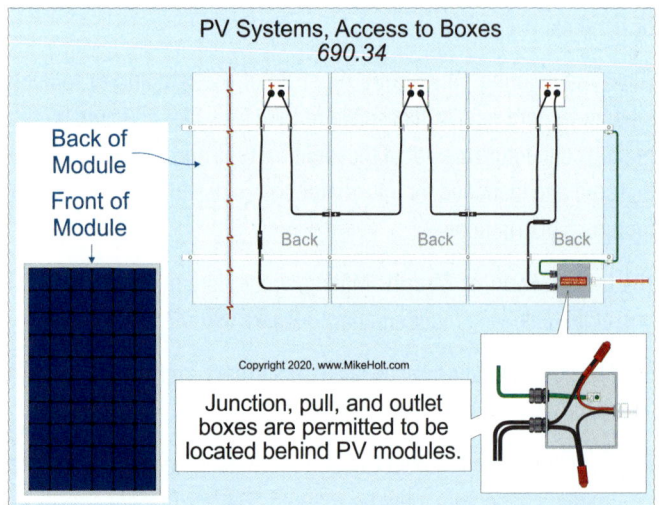
▶Figure 690–78

Part V. Grounding and Bonding

690.43 Equipment Grounding and Bonding

Exposed metal parts of PV module frames, electrical equipment, and enclosures containing PV system conductors must be connected to the PV system circuit equipment grounding conductor complying with 690.43(A) through (D) and in accordance with 250.134 or 250.136. ▶Figure 690–79

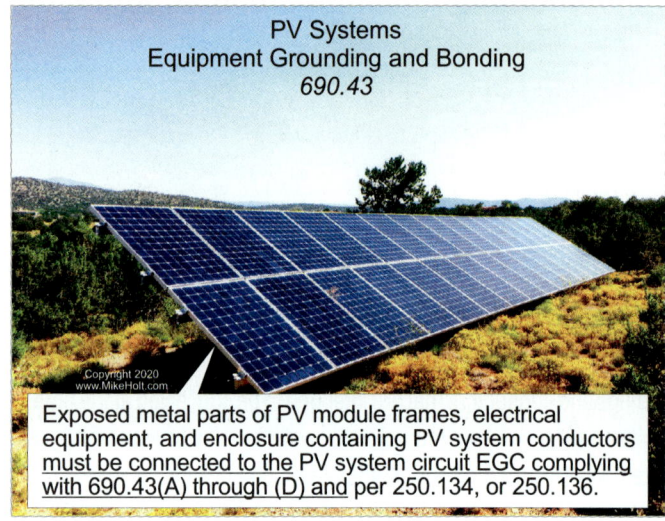
▶Figure 690–79

Author's Comment:

▶ According to 250.134, metal parts of equipment, raceways, and enclosures must be connected to one of the equipment grounding conductor types identified in 250.118. An equipment grounding conductor of the wire type for a dc circuit can be run separately from the circuit conductors when it is within the array [250.134 Ex 2].

(A) Photovoltaic Module Mounting Systems and Devices. Devices used to secure and bond PV module frames to metal support structures and adjacent PV modules must be listed, labeled, and identified for bonding. Devices that mount adjacent PV modules are permitted to bond adjacent PV modules.

(B) Equipment Secured to Grounded Metal Support Structure. Metallic support structures listed, labeled, and identified for bonding and grounding metal parts of PV systems can be used to bond PV equipment to the metal support structure.

Solar Photovoltaic (PV) Systems | **690.43**

Metallic support structures used as equipment grounding conductors must have identified bonding jumpers installed between separate metallic sections of the support structure or the support structure must be identified for equipment bonding purposes. The metallic support structure must be connected to the PV circuit equipment grounding conductor as required by 690.43. ▶Figure 690–80

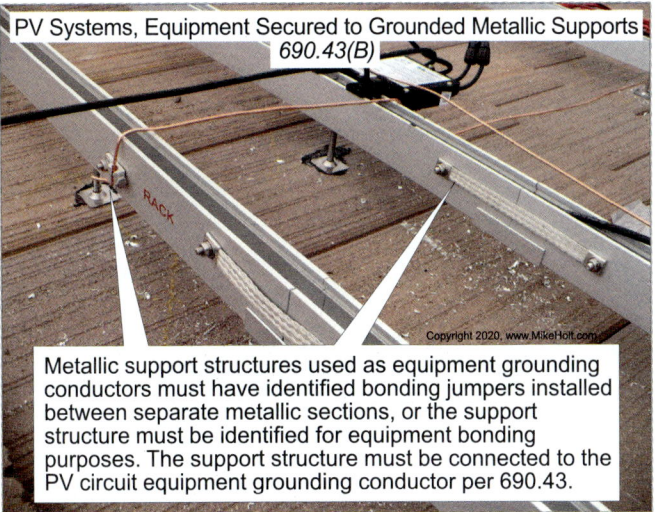
▶Figure 690–80

(C) With Circuit Conductors. When PV system circuit conductors leave the vicinity of the PV array, the equipment grounding conductors for the PV system and metal support structure must be contained within the same raceway, cable, or otherwise run with the PV circuit conductor. ▶Figure 690–81 and ▶Figure 690–82

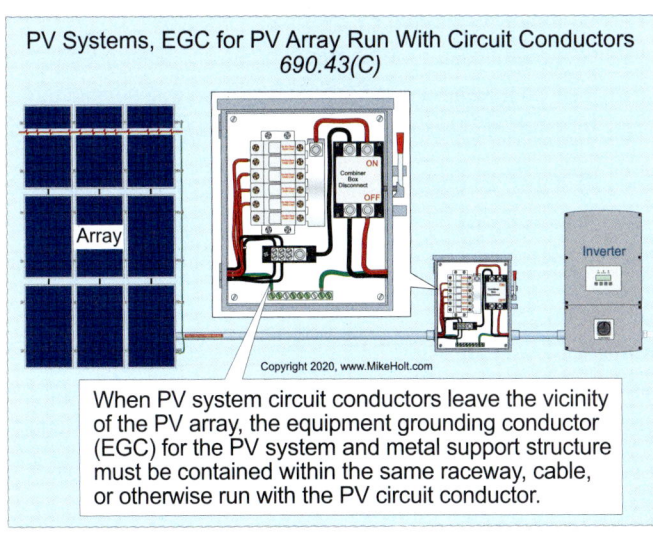
▶Figure 690–81

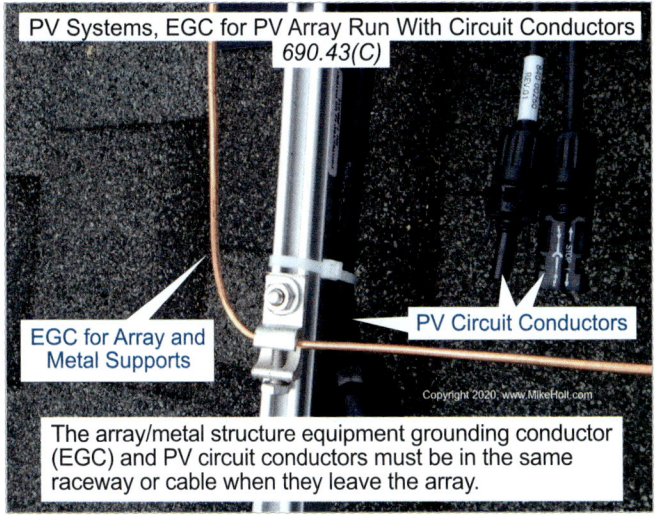
▶Figure 690–82

Author's Comment:

▸ Exposed equipment grounding conductors 8 AWG and smaller for dc circuits [250.134 Ex 2] are permitted to be run separately from the circuit conductors where not subject to physical damage [250.120(C)].

(D) Bonding Over 250V. The bonding requirements contained in 250.97 do not apply to functionally grounded PV system circuits operating at over 250V to ground. ▶Figure 690–83

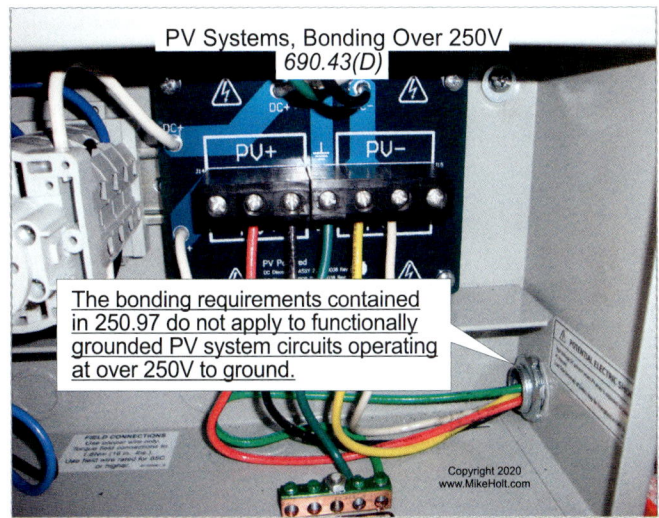
▶Figure 690–83

690.45 Size of Equipment Grounding Conductors

Equipment grounding conductors for PV system circuits must be sized in accordance with 250.122 based on the rating of the circuit overcurrent protective device. ▶Figure 690–84

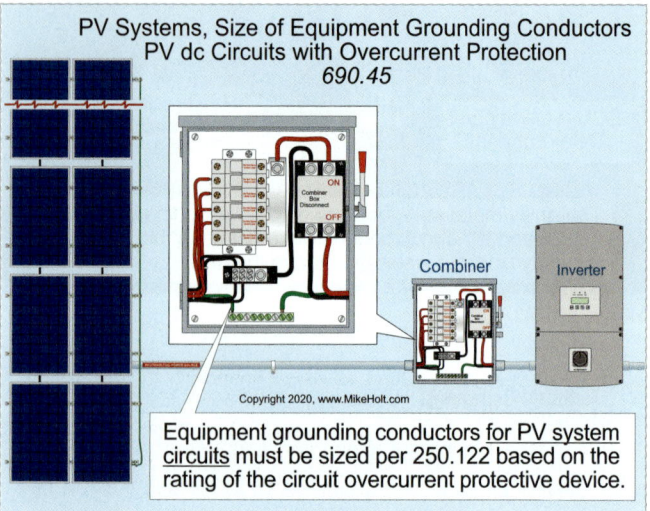

▶Figure 690–84

Where no overcurrent protective device is required [690.9(A)(1)], the equipment grounding conductor for the PV system dc circuit must be sized in accordance with Table 250.122 based on an assumed overcurrent device for the circuit sized in accordance with 690.9(B). Equipment grounding conductors are not required to be increased in size to address voltage-drop considerations. ▶Figure 690–85

▶Figure 690–85

690.47 Grounding Electrode System

(A) Required Grounding Electrode System. A building or structure supporting a PV system must utilize a grounding electrode system installed in accordance with Part III of Article 250. ▶Figure 690–86

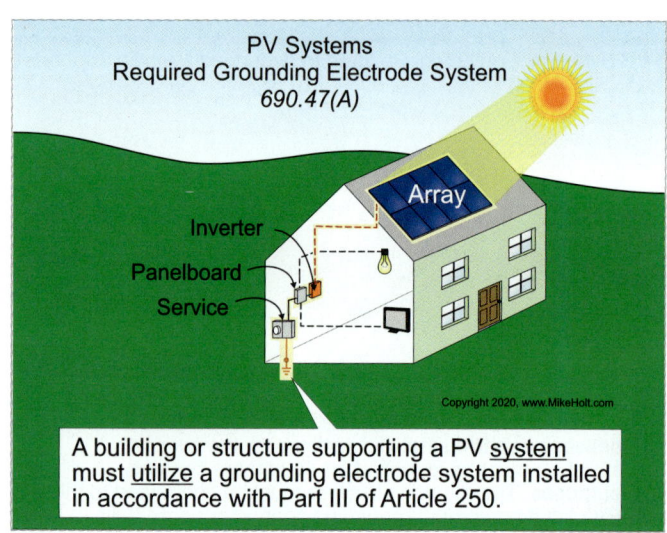

▶Figure 690–86

Author's Comment:

▸ Part III of Article 250 addresses the grounding electrode system, the grounding electrode types, and the grounding electrode installation requirements.

(1) Functionally Grounded PV Systems. Functionally grounded PV systems are grounded to the building grounding electrode system when the PV output ac circuit equipment grounding conductor terminates to distribution equipment. ▶Figure 690–87

The use of the PV output circuit equipment grounding conductor to serve as the required PV equipment grounding conductor connection to ground is the only connection to ground required for the functionally grounded PV system. ▶Figure 690–88

Note. Most PV systems are functionally grounded rather than solidly grounded. For functionally grounded systems, the inverter equipment grounding conductor is connected to the grounded distribution equipment. This connection is used for the ground-fault protection and equipment grounding of the PV array.

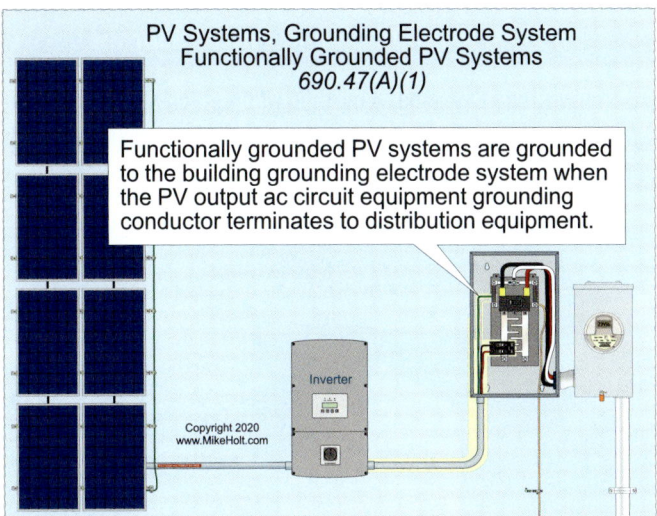
▶Figure 690-87

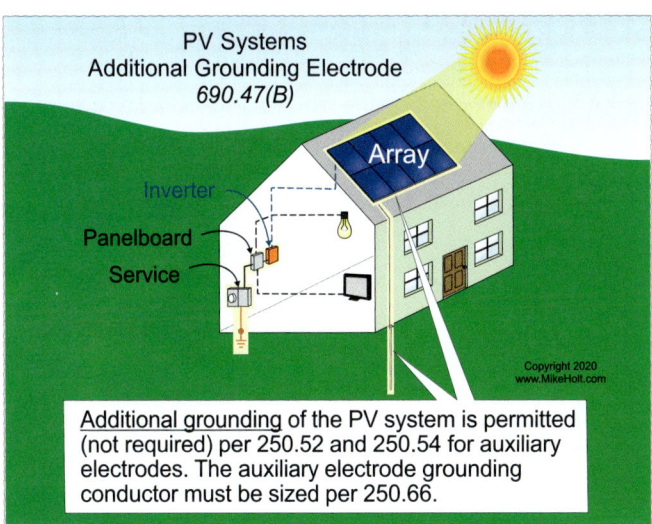
▶Figure 690-89

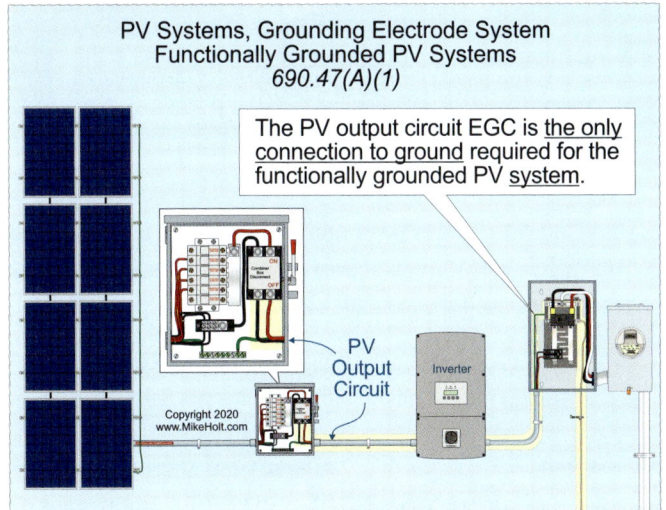
▶Figure 690-88

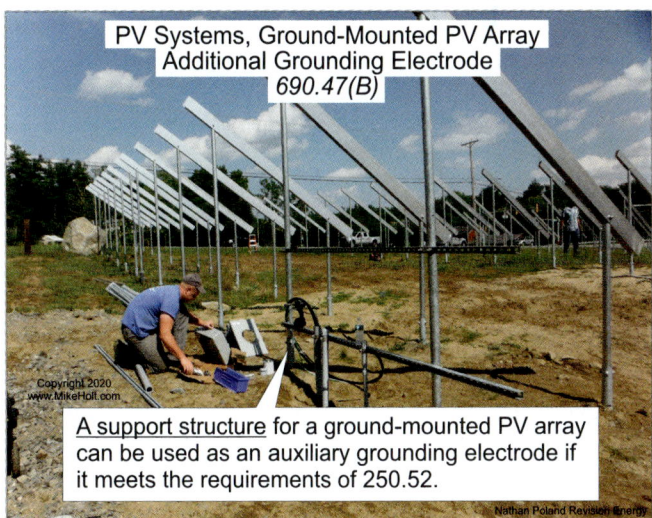
▶Figure 690-90

(B) Additional Grounding Electrode. Additional grounding of the PV system is permitted (but not required) in accordance with 250.52 and 250.54 for auxiliary electrodes. The auxiliary electrode grounding conductor must be sized in accordance with 250.66. ▶Figure 690-89

A support structure for a ground-mounted PV array can be used as an auxiliary grounding electrode if it meets the requirements of 250.52. ▶Figure 690-90

PV arrays mounted to buildings can use the metal frame of the building structure as a grounding electrode conductor where the requirements of 250.68(C)(2) are met.

Part VI. Markings and Labels

690.53 Direct-Current PV Circuit Label

A permanent readily visible label indicating the maximum PV system dc voltage as calculated in accordance with 690.7 must be installed at one of the following locations: ▶Figure 690-91

(1) PV system dc disconnect

(2) PV system electronic power conversion equipment

(3) Distribution equipment associated with the PV system

690.54 | Solar Photovoltaic (PV) Systems

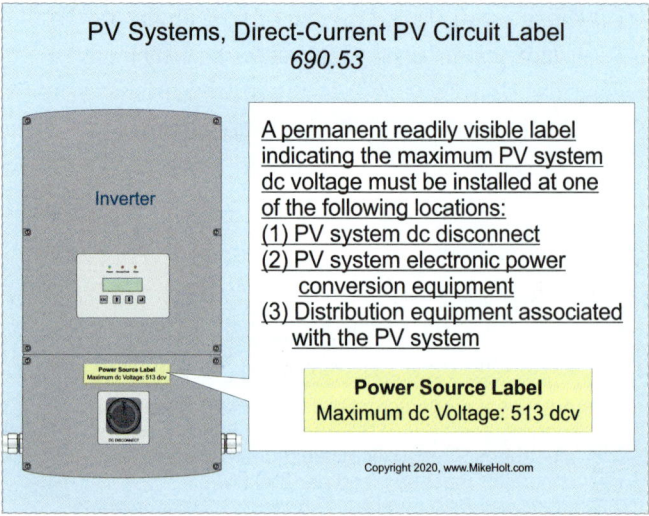

▶Figure 690–91

690.54 Interactive System Point of Interconnection

The point of interactive system interconnection with the electric utility must be marked at the PV system disconnecting means with the rated inverter ac output current and nominal ac voltage. ▶Figure 690–92

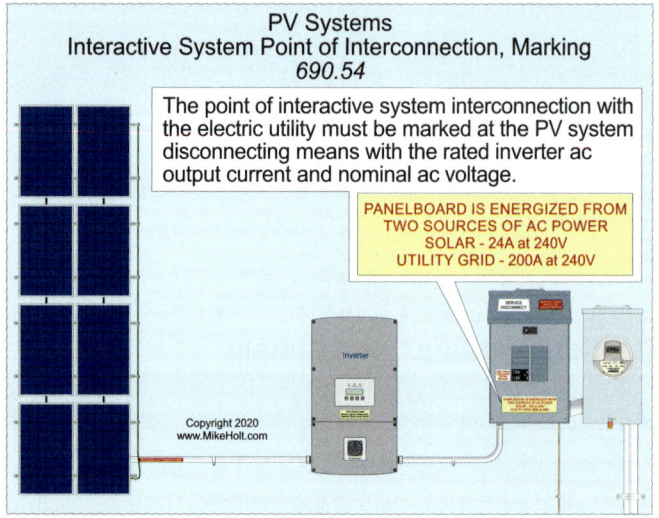

▶Figure 690–92

690.55 Energy Storage

PV system dc circuit conductors connected to energy storage systems must be marked for polarity in accordance with 690.31(B)(1).

690.56 Identification of Power Sources

(A) Stand-Alone Systems. A building with a stand-alone PV system must have a permanent plaque or directory installed in accordance with 710.10. ▶Figure 690–93

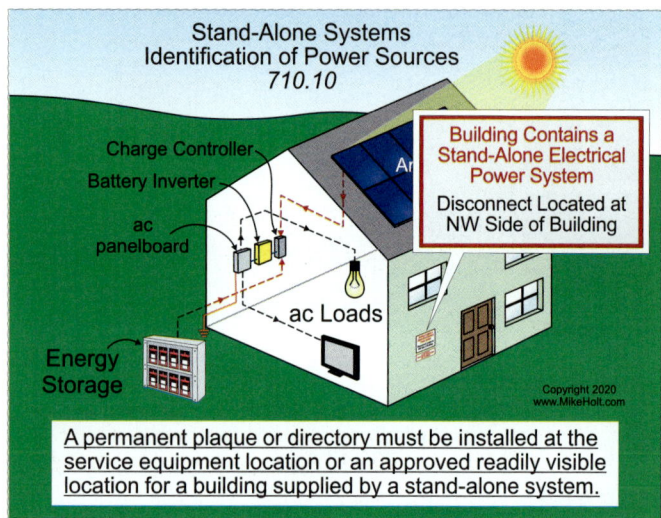

▶Figure 690–93

(B) Building with Utility Power and PV Systems. A building having both utility power and an interactive PV system(s) must have a plaque or directory installed in accordance with 705.10. ▶Figure 690–94

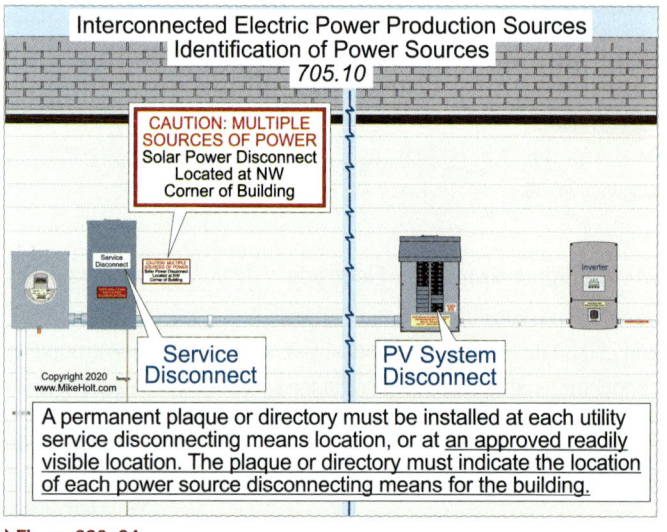

▶Figure 690–94

(C) Building with Rapid Shutdown System(s). A building with a rapid shutdown system [690.12] must have a permanent label indicating the location of all rapid shutdown initiation devices. The label must be located at each service equipment location or at an approved readily visible location and the label must include a diagram of a building with a roof with the following words: ▶Figure 690–95

Solar Photovoltaic (PV) Systems | **690.71**

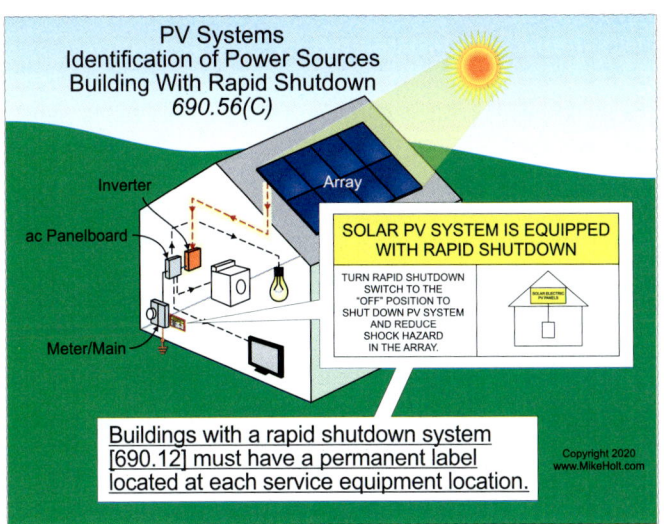
▶Figure 690-95

(1) Buildings with More Than One Rapid Shutdown Type. A building having more than one rapid shutdown system or a building without a rapid shutdown system must have a label with a detailed plan view diagram of the roof showing each PV system with a dotted line around areas that remain energized after the rapid shutdown has been initiated.

(2) Rapid Shutdown Switch. A rapid shutdown switch must have a label that includes the following wording located on or no more than 3 ft from the switch: "RAPID SHUTDOWN SWITCH FOR SOLAR PV SYSTEM." The rapid shutdown label must be reflective with all letters capitalized and having a minimum height of ⅜ in. in white on a red background. ▶Figure 690-97

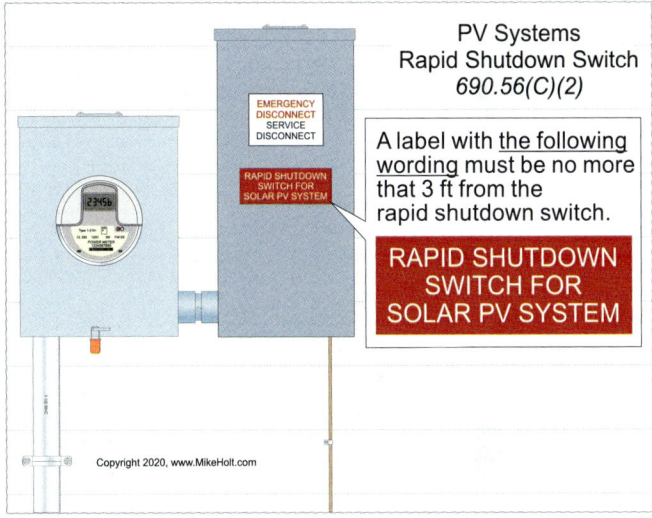
▶Figure 690-97

SOLAR PV SYSTEM IS EQUIPPED WITH RAPID SHUTDOWN
TURN RAPID SHUTDOWN SWITCH TO THE "OFF"
POSITION TO SHUT DOWN PV SYSTEM AND
REDUCE SHOCK HAZARD IN THE ARRAY

The title "SOLAR PV SYSTEM IS EQUIPPED WITH RAPID SHUTDOWN" must have capitalized characters with a minimum height of ⅜ in. in black on a yellow background. The remaining characters must be capitalized with a minimum height of 3/16 in. in black on white background.
▶Figure 690-96

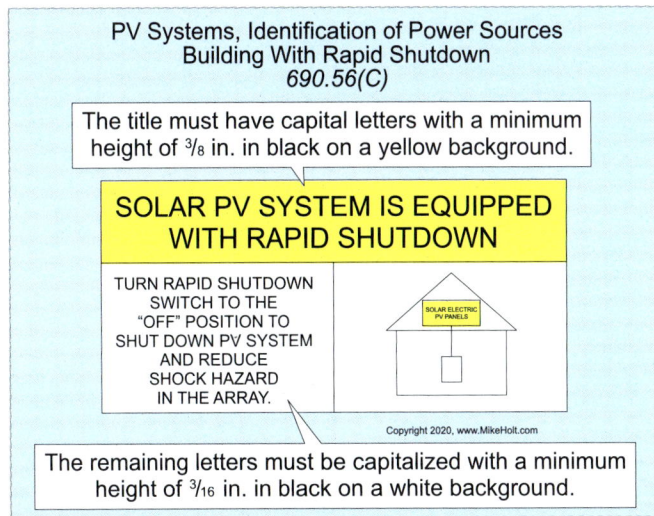
▶Figure 690-96

Note: See Note Figure 690.56(C) in the *NEC* for an example.

Part VII. Connections to Other Sources

690.59 Connection to Other Power Sources

PV systems connected in parallel with the electric utility must have the interconnection made in accordance with Parts I and II of Article 705 for the interconnection of electric utility and PV systems. ▶Figure 690-98

Part VIII. Energy Storage Systems

690.71 Energy Storage Systems

Energy storage systems connected to a PV system must be installed in accordance with Article 706.

690.72 | Solar Photovoltaic (PV) Systems

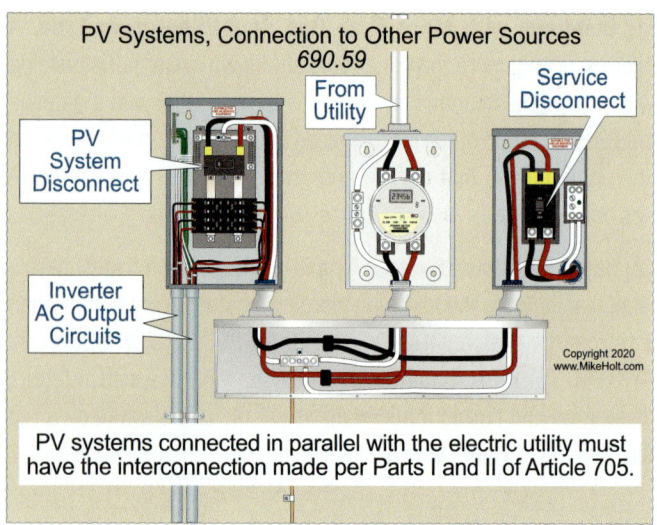

▶Figure 690-98

690.72 Self-Regulated PV Charge Control

The PV dc charge controller source circuit is considered to comply with 706.33 if:

(1) The PV source circuit is matched to the dc voltage rating and charge current requirements of the interconnected battery cells, and

(2) The maximum charging current multiplied by one hour is less than three percent of the rated battery capacity expressed in ampere-hours or as recommended by the battery manufacturer.

ARTICLE 691 — LARGE-SCALE PHOTOVOLTAIC (PV) ELECTRIC SUPPLY STATIONS

Introduction to Article 691—Large-Scale Photovoltaic (PV) Electric Supply Stations

The general requirements for solar photovoltaic (PV) systems are covered by Article 690. When a system is 5,000kW or larger, it becomes a large-scale PV electric supply station and is then covered by the requirements of Article 691. This article defines what a large-scale photovoltaic system is and the additional requirements that must be met to take advantage of the alternative design and safety features unique to large systems. Large-scale PV systems are privately owned PV systems that are operated solely to provide electricity to a regulated utility as compared to Article 690 systems that may be operated to provide power to the end user, utility, or a combination of both. They require a careful documented review of the design by an engineer to ensure safe operation and compliance with the applicable electrical standards and industry practices.

691.1 Scope

Article 691 covers the installation of large-scale PV electric supply stations with an inverter generating capacity of not less than 5,000 kW and not under the electric utility control. ▶Figure 691–1

Article 691 covers the installation of large-scale PV electric supply stations with an inverter generating capacity of not less than 5,000 kW and not under the electric utility control.

▶Figure 691–1

Note 1: Facilities covered by this article have specific design and safety features unique to large-scale PV facilities and are operated for the sole purpose of providing electric supply to a system operated by a regulated utility for the transfer of electric energy.

691.4 Special Requirements for Large-Scale PV Electric Supply Stations

Large-scale PV electric supply stations are only permitted to be accessible to authorized personnel and must comply with the following requirements:

(1) Electrical circuits and equipment must be maintained and operated by qualified personnel.

(2) PV electric supply stations must be restricted by fencing or other means in accordance with 110.31 and have field-applied hazard markings that are permanently affixed and have sufficient durability to withstand the environment involved [110.21(B)].

(3) The connection between the PV electric supply and the utility system must be through medium- or high-voltage switch gear, substation, switchyard, or similar methods whose sole purpose is to safely and effectively interconnect the two systems.

(4) Loads within the PV electric supply station must only be used to power auxiliary equipment for the generation of the PV power.

(5) Large-scale PV electric supply stations must not be installed on buildings.

691.5 Equipment

All electrical equipment must be approved for installation by one of the following:

(1) Listing and labeling.

(2) Be evaluated for the application and have a field label applied.

(3) Where products complying with 691.5(1) or (2) are not available, by engineering review validating that the electrical equipment is evaluated and tested to relevant standards or industry practice.

691.6 Engineered Design

Documentation of the electric supply station must be stamped by a licensed professional electrical engineer and provided upon request of the authority having jurisdiction. Additional stamped independent engineering reports by a licensed professional electrical engineer detailing compliance of the design with applicable electrical standards and industry practice must be provided upon request of the authority having jurisdiction.

This documentation must include details of the conformance of the design with Article 690 and any alternative methods to Article 690, or other articles of the *NEC*.

691.7 Conformance of Construction to Engineered Design

Documentation by a licensed professional electrical engineer that the construction of the electric supply station conforms to the electrical engineered design must be provided upon request of the authority having jurisdiction. Additional stamped independent engineering reports by a licensed professional electrical engineer detailing that the construction conforms with this *Code*, applicable standards, and industry practice must be provided upon request of the authority having jurisdiction. This independent engineer must be retained by the system owner or installer.

691.8 Direct-Current Operating Voltage

Large-scale PV electric supply station calculations must be included in the documentation required in 691.6.

691.9 Disconnect for Isolating Photovoltaic Equipment

Isolating devices are not required to be located within sight of equipment and may be located remotely from the equipment.

The engineered design required by 691.6 must document disconnection procedures and means of isolating equipment.

Note: For information on electrical system maintenance, see NFPA 70B, *Recommended Practice for Electrical Equipment Maintenance*. For information on written procedures and conditions of maintenance, including lockout/tagout procedures, see NFPA 70E, *Standard for Electrical Safety in the Workplace*.

Buildings whose sole purpose is to house and protect supply station equipment are not required to include a rapid shutdown function to reduce shock hazard for firefighters [690.12]. Written standard operating procedures must be available at the site detailing necessary shutdown procedures in the event of an emergency.

691.10 Arc-Fault Mitigation

PV systems that do not provide arc-fault protection as required by 690.11 must include details of fire mitigation plans to address dc arc faults in the documentation required in 691.6.

691.11 Fence Bonding and Grounding

Fence grounding requirements and details must be included in the documentation required in 691.6.

Note: See 250.194 for fence bonding and grounding requirements for PV systems that operate at more than 1,000V between conductors. Grounding requirements for other portions of electric supply station fencing are assessed based on the presence of overhead conductors, proximity to generation and distribution equipment, and associated step and touch potential.

ARTICLE 695 FIRE PUMPS

Introduction to Article 695—Fire Pumps

The general philosophy behind most *Code* requirements is to provide circuit overcurrent protection that will shut equipment down before allowing the supply conductors to overheat and become damaged from overload. Article 695 departs from this philosophy. The idea is that the fire pump motor must keep running no matter what! Since it supplies water to a facility's fire protection piping, which in turn supplies water to the sprinkler system and fire hoses, it is better to sacrifice the fire pump rather than the entire structure. This article contains many requirements to make certain an uninterrupted supply of water is maintained.

Some of these requirements are obvious. For example, locate the pump where its exposure to fire is minimized, which is usually in a separate space with fire-rated construction. It is important that the source of power is maintained for both the fire pump and its jockey (pressure maintenance) pump. Also, fire pump wiring must remain independent of all other wiring. Some of the requirements of Article 695 seem wrong at first glance, until you remember why that fire pump is there in the first place. For example, the disconnect must be designed to be lockable in the closed position. You would normally expect it to be lockable in the open position because other articles require that for the safety of maintenance personnel. But the fire pump runs to ensure the safety of an entire facility and everyone within. For the same reason, fire pump power circuits cannot have automatic overcurrent protection against overloads.

Remember, the fire pump must be kept in service, even if doing so damages or destroys the pump. It is better to sacrifice the fire pump than to save it and lose the facility. The intent of this article is to allow enough time for building occupants to escape and (if possible) to save the facility.

695.1 Scope

(A) Covered. Article 695 covers the installation of: ▶Figure 695–1

(1) Electric power sources and interconnecting circuits.

(2) Switching and control equipment dedicated to fire pump drivers.

(B) Not Covered. Article 695 does not cover:

(1) Performance, maintenance, testing, and the internal wiring of the components of the system.

(2) The installation of pressure maintenance (jockey or makeup) pumps.

Note: Article 430 governs the installation of pressure maintenance (jockey or makeup) pumps, whether or not they are supplied by the fire pump.

(3) Transfer equipment upstream of the fire pump transfer switch(es).

▶Figure 695–1

695.3 | Fire Pumps

Author's Comment:

▸ Fire pump installations should be designed by qualified experts in the field due to the critical importance of properly designed systems. Fire pump installations can interconnect with other systems such as backup power systems and sprinkler systems. Generally, the electrician or electrical contractor doing a fire pump installation will not be doing any calculations but following a set of specifications provided for the job.

695.3 Electric Power Source(s)

(A) Individual Sources. Power to fire pump motors must be supplied by a reliable source that has the capacity to carry the locked-rotor current of the fire pump motor(s), pressure maintenance pump motors, and the full-load current of any associated fire pump equipment. Specifically permitted reliable sources of power include:

Note: See 9.3.2 and A.9.3.2 from NFPA 20, *Standard for the Installation of Stationary Pumps for Fire Protection*, for guidance on the determination of electric power source reliability.

(1) Electric Utility Service Connection. A separate service located remotely from normal service to minimize unintentional interruption [230.72(B)] or a connection located ahead of but not within the service disconnect [230.82(5)]. ▸Figure 695–2

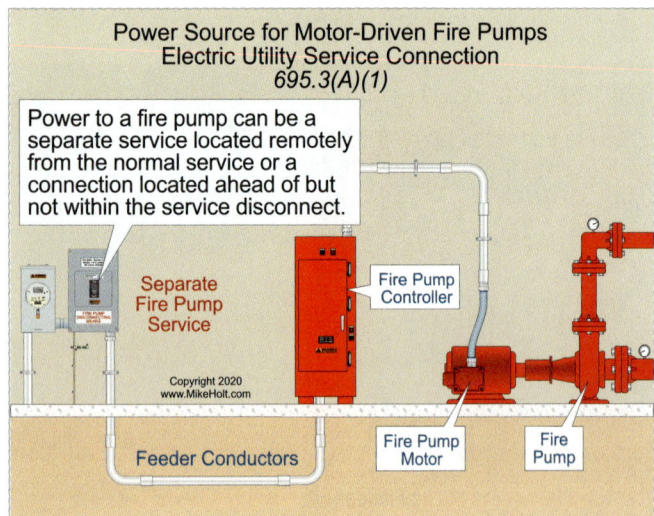

▸Figure 695–2

Author's Comment:

▸ To minimize unintentional interruption, the service disconnect for the fire pump system must be located remotely from the other power system service disconnect [230.72(B)]. Generally, the pump feeder tap termination point is situated ahead of the main service disconnect(s) and the fire pump disconnect is within sight of fire pump itself.

(2) On-Site Power. An on-site power generator located and protected to minimize damage by fire.

(B) Multiple Sources. If reliable power cannot be obtained from a source described in 695.3(A), power must be supplied by any of the following:

(1) Individual Sources. A combination of two or more of the individual sources from 695.3(A) approved by the authority having jurisdiction.

(2) Individual Source and On-Site Standby Generator. A combination of one of the sources in 695.3(A) and a generator complying with 695.3(D) approved by the authority having jurisdiction.

Ex to (1) and (2): An alternate source of power is not required where a backup, engine, steam turbine, or electric motor driven fire pump with an independent power source in accordance with 695.3(A) or (C) is installed.

(F) Transfer of Power. Transfer of power to the fire pump controller must take place within the pump room.

695.4 Continuity of Power

(B) Connection Through Disconnect and Overcurrent Device.

(1) Number of Disconnecting Means.

(a) A single means of disconnect is permitted to be installed between the fire pump electric supply and:

(1) A listed fire pump controller,

(2) A listed fire pump power transfer switch, or

(3) A listed combination fire pump controller/power transfer switch.

(2) Overcurrent Device Selection.

(a) Individual Sources. Overcurrent protection for individual sources must comply with the following:

(1) The overcurrent protective device(s) must be selected or set to carry indefinitely the sum of the locked-rotor current of the largest fire pump motor and 100 percent of the full-load current of the other pump motors and fire pump's accessory equipment. ▶Figure 695–3

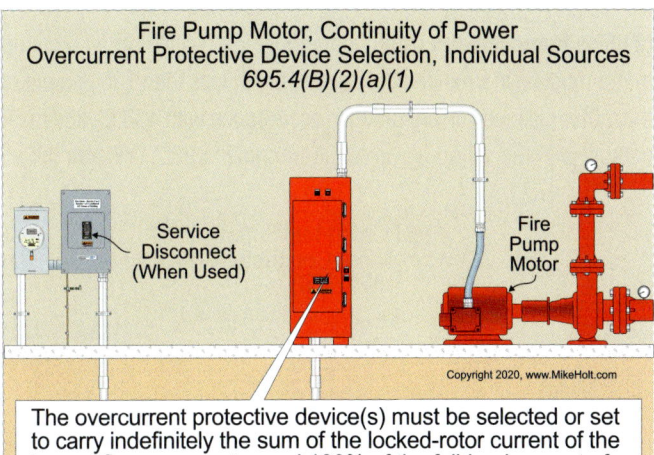

▶Figure 695–3

▶ Fire Pump Overcurrent Size Example

Question: What size overcurrent protective device and conductor is required for a 25 hp, 460V, three-phase fire pump motor that has a locked-rotor current rating of 183A? ▶Figure 695–4

(a) 100A, 8 AWG
(b) 200A, 8 AWG
(c) 400A, 8 AWG
(d) 450A, 8 AWG

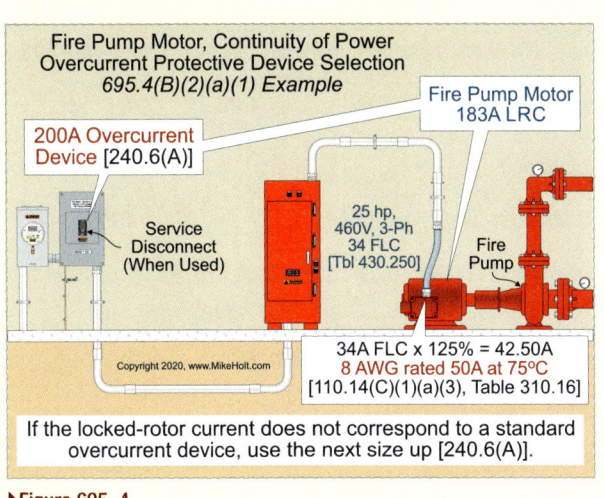

▶Figure 695–4

Solution:

Locked-Rotor Current = 183A
Protection Size = 200A [240.6(A) and 695.4(B)(2)(a)(1)]

Determine the branch-circuit conductor at 125 percent of the motor's FLC [Table 310.16, 430.22, and Table 430.250].

Branch-Circuit Conductor = 34A × 125%
Branch-Circuit Conductor = 42.50A

Use an 8 AWG conductor rated 50A at 75°C [110.14(C)(1)(a)(3) and Table 310.16].

Answer: (b) 200A, 8 AWG

If the locked-rotor current value does not correspond to a standard overcurrent device size, the next larger standard overcurrent device size must be used in accordance with 240.6.

(2) Overcurrent protection must be listed for fire pump service and must not:

a. open within 2 minutes at 600 percent of the full-load current of the pump motor(s).

b. open with a re-start locked-rotor current of 24 times the full-load current of the pump motor(s).

c. open within 10 minutes at 300 percent of the full-load current of the pump motor(s).

d. have a field adjustable trip setting.

(b) On-Site Standby Generators. Overcurrent protective devices between an on-site standby generator and a fire pump controller must be sized in accordance with 430.62, based on the largest rating or setting of the short-circuit and ground-fault device for the largest motor FLC and the sum of other motors on the feeder.

695.5 Transformers

(A) Size. If a transformer supplies an electric fire pump motor, it must be sized at no less than 125 percent of the sum of the fire pump motor(s) and pressure maintenance pump(s) motor loads, and 100 percent of the ampere rating of the fire pump's accessory equipment.

695.6 | Fire Pumps

(B) Overcurrent Protection. The primary overcurrent protective device(s) must be sized to carry indefinitely the sum of the locked-rotor current of the fire pump motor(s) and pressure maintenance pump motor(s), and 100 percent of the ampere rating of the fire pump's accessory equipment. Secondary overcurrent protection is not permitted. The requirement to carry the locked-rotor current indefinitely does not apply to fire pump motor conductors.

695.6 Power Wiring

(A) Supply Conductors.

(1) Services and On-Site Power Production Facilities. Service conductors and conductors supplied by on-site power production facilities must be physically routed outside buildings. Where supply conductors are run inside the building, they must be encased in 2 in. of concrete or brick [230.6].

Ex: Supply conductors within the fire pump room are not required to be encased in 2 in. of concrete or brick as required by 230.6(1) or (2).

Note: See 250.24(C) for routing the grounded conductor to the service equipment.

(2) Feeder Conductors. Fire pump supply conductors must comply with all the following:

(1) Independent Routing. The conductors must be kept entirely independent of all other wiring.

(2) Associated Fire Pump Loads. Conductors must only supply loads directly associated with the fire pump system.

(3) Protection from Potential Damage. Conductors must be protected from potential damage by fire, structural failure, or operational accident.

(4) Inside a Building. Fire pump conductors routed through a building must be protected from fire for two hours using any of the following methods:

(a) Encasing the cable or raceway in at least 2 in. of concrete.

(b) Using a cable or raceway that is a listed fire-resistive cable system.

(c) Using a cable or raceway that is a listed electrical circuit protective system.

Ex: The feeder conductors located between an electrical equipment room and fire pump room are not required to have two-hour fire protection unless otherwise required in 700.10(D).

(B) Conductor Size.

(1) Fire Pump Motors and Other Equipment. Conductors supplying a fire pump motor(s) pressure maintenance pumps, and associated fire pump accessory equipment, must have a minimum ampacity of not less than 125 percent of the sum of the fire pump motor(s) and pressure maintenance motor(s) full-load current(s), and 100 percent of the associated fire pump accessory equipment.

(2) Fire Pump Motors Only. Conductors supplying only a fire pump motor must have a minimum ampacity of not less than 125 percent of the motor full-load current rating in accordance with 430.22 and must comply with the voltage-drop requirements in 695.7. ▶Figure 695–5

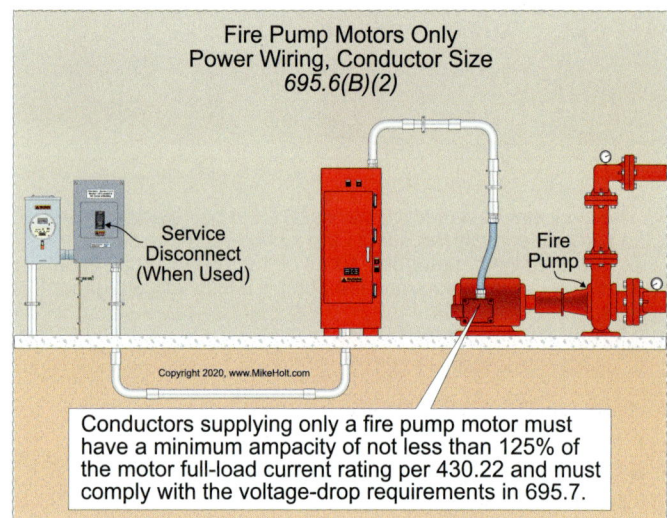

▶Figure 695–5

▶ Fire Pump Conductor Size Example

Question: What size conductor is required for a 25 hp, 460V, three-phase fire pump motor with terminals rated 75°C? ▶Figure 695–6

(a) 8 AWG (b) 6 AWG (c) 4 AWG (d) 3 AWG

Solution:

25 hp, 208V, Three-Phase Motor FLC = 34A [Table 430.250]

Determine the branch-circuit conductor at 125 percent of the motor's FLC [Table 310.16, 430.22, and Table 430.250].

Branch-Circuit Conductor = 34A × 125%

Branch-Circuit Conductor = 42.50A

Use an 8 AWG conductor rated 50A at 75°C [110.14(C)(1)(a)(3) and Table 310.16].

Answer: (a) 8 AWG

Fire Pumps | 695.7

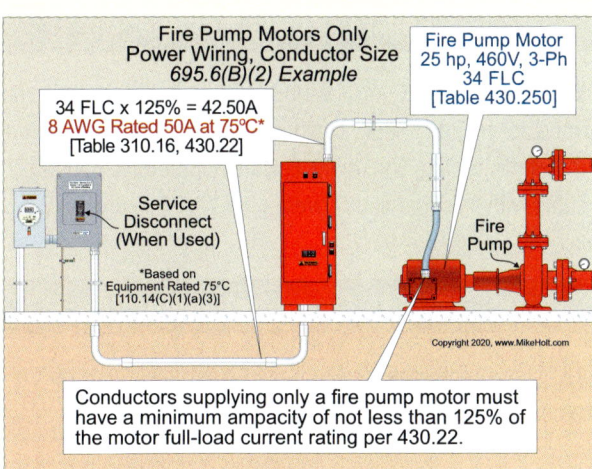
▶Figure 695-6

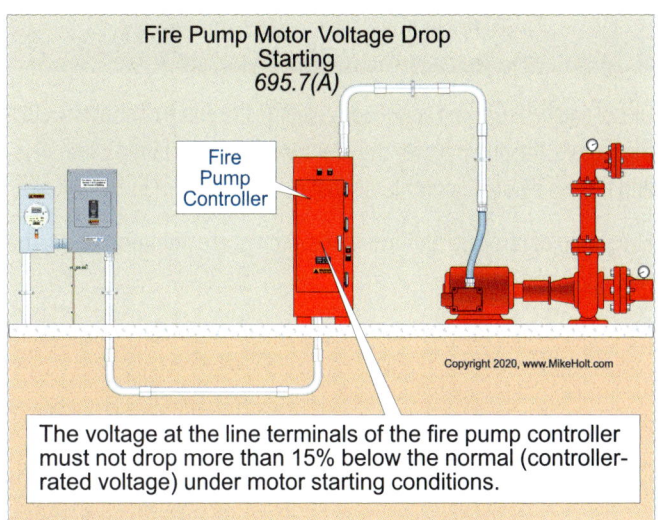
▶Figure 695-7

(D) Pump Wiring. Wiring from the fire pump controllers to the fire pump motors must be in rigid metal conduit, intermediate metal conduit, electrical metallic tubing, liquidtight flexible metal conduit, liquidtight flexible nonmetallic conduit, listed Type MC cable with an impervious covering, or Type MI cable. The connections in the motor terminal box must be made with a listed device. Twist-on, insulation-piercing type, and soldered wire connectors are not allowed.

(G) Ground-Fault Protection of Equipment. Ground-fault protection of equipment (GFPE) is not permitted in the fire pump power circuit.

(J) Terminations. Where raceways or cables terminated at a fire pump controller, the following requirements apply:

(1) Raceway or cable fittings must be listed and identified for use in wet locations.

(2) The enclosure type rating of the raceway or cable fittings must be at least equal to that of the fire pump controller.

(3) The installation instructions of the manufacturer of the fire pump controller must be followed.

(4) Alterations to the fire pump controller, other than raceway or cable terminations, must be approved by the authority having jurisdiction.

695.7 Voltage Drop

(A) Starting. The voltage at the line terminals of the fire pump controller is not permitted to drop more than 15 percent below the normal (controller-rated voltage) under motor starting conditions. ▶Figure 695-7

(B) Running. The voltage at the load terminals of the fire pump controller is not permitted to drop more than 5 percent below the voltage rating of the motor connected to those terminals when the motor operates at 115 percent of the fire pump motor full-load current rating.
▶Figure 695-8

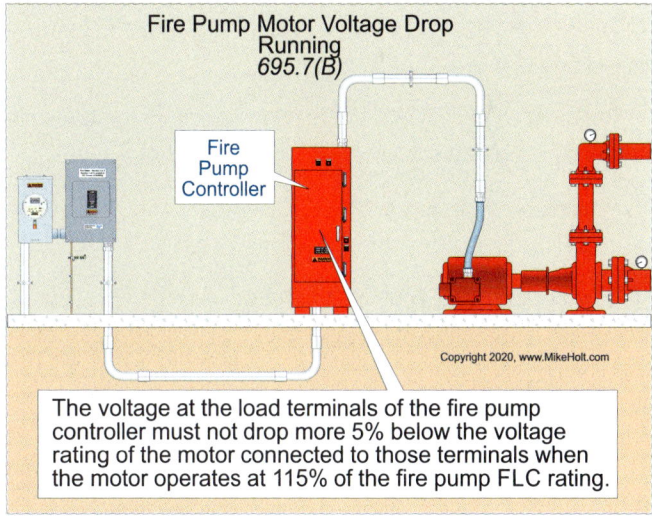
▶Figure 695-8

Author's Comment:

▸ Sizing conductors for fire pump circuits to account for start-up and running voltage drop because of low power factor during start-up must be performed by a qualified person; typically an electrical engineer.

695.10 Listed Equipment

Diesel engine fire pump controllers, electric fire pump controllers, electric motors, fire pump power transfer switches, foam pump controllers, and limited service controllers must be listed for fire pump service.

Fire pump controllers and transfer switches are not permitted to be reconditioned.

695.14 Control Wiring

(E) Wiring Methods. Control wiring must be in rigid metal conduit, intermediate metal conduit, liquidtight flexible metal conduit, electrical metallic tubing, liquidtight flexible nonmetallic conduit, Type MC cable with an impervious covering, or Type MI cable.

695.15 Surge Protection

A listed surge protective device must be installed in or on the fire pump controller.

CHAPTER 6 PRACTICE QUESTIONS

Please use the 2020 *Code* book to answer the following questions.

CHAPTER 6—SPECIAL EQUIPMENT

Article 600—Electric Signs and Outline Lighting

1. Article 600 covers the installation of conductors, equipment, and field wiring for _____, retrofit kits, and outline lighting, regardless of voltage.

    (a) electric signs
    (b) outline lighting
    (c) neon tubing
    (d) all of these

2. A kit consisting of primary parts, which does not include all the parts for a complete subassembly but includes a list of required parts and installation instructions to complete the subassembly in the field for a sign is called a "_____."

    (a) general use retrofit kit
    (b) reconditioning kit
    (c) maintenance kit
    (d) sign specific retrofit kit

3. A "section sign" is a sign or _____, shipped as subassemblies, that requires field-installed wiring between the subassemblies to complete the overall sign.

    (a) outline lighting system
    (b) skeleton tubing system
    (c) neon system
    (d) sign body

4. Fixed, mobile, or portable electric signs, section signs, outline lighting, photovoltaic (PV) powered signs, and retrofit kits shall be _____, unless otherwise approved by special permission.

    (a) marked
    (b) approved
    (c) identified for the location
    (d) listed and labeled

5. Field-installed skeleton tubing shall not be required to be _____ where installed in conformance with the *Code*.

    (a) listed
    (b) identified for the purpose
    (c) marked
    (d) approved

6. Signs and outline lighting systems shall be listed and labeled, and marked with the _____.

    (a) manufacturer's name, trademark, or other means of identification
    (b) input voltage
    (c) current rating
    (d) all of these

7. For signs with a retrofitted illumination system, the sign shall be marked that the illumination system has been _____.

    (a) replaced
    (b) modified
    (c) refurbished
    (d) updated

Article 600 | Practice Questions

8. Signs with a retrofitted illumination system equipped with tubular light-emitting diode lamps powered by the existing sign sockets shall include a label meeting the requirements of 110.21(B), includes a warning not to install _____ lamps, and be visible during relamping.

   (a) incandescent
   (b) fluorescent
   (c) LED
   (d) all of these

9. The markings required on signs and outline lighting systems in 600.4(A) shall be permanent, durable, and _____ when installed in wet locations.

   (a) weatherproof
   (b) laminated
   (c) rainproof
   (d) indelible

10. Each commercial occupancy accessible to pedestrians shall have at least one sign outlet in an accessible location at each entrance to each tenant space supplied by a branch circuit rated at least _____.

    (a) 15A
    (b) 20A
    (c) 30A
    (d) 40A

11. A sign or outline lighting outlet shall not be required at commercial occupancy entrances for _____ that are intended to be used only by service personnel or employees.

    (a) deliveries
    (b) service corridors
    (c) service hallways
    (d) any of these

12. A disconnecting means for a sign, outline lighting system, or controller shall be marked to identify the _____, outline lighting system, or controller it controls.

    (a) branch circuit
    (b) feeder
    (c) sign
    (d) all of these

13. Branch circuits that supply signs shall be considered to be _____ loads for the purposes of calculations.

    (a) continuous
    (b) separate
    (c) combined
    (d) dynamic

14. Each sign and outline lighting system, feeder conductor(s), or branch circuit(s) supplying a sign, outline lighting system, or skeleton tubing shall be controlled by an externally operable switch or circuit breaker that opens all _____ conductors and controls no other load.

    (a) ungrounded
    (b) grounded
    (c) equipment grounding
    (d) all of these

15. Each sign and outline lighting system shall be controlled by an externally operable switch or circuit breaker that opens all ungrounded conductors simultaneously on _____ branch circuits.

    (a) 15A
    (b) 20A
    (c) multiwire
    (d) outdoor

16. The location of the sign and outline lighting system feeder or branch-circuit disconnect is intended to allow service or maintenance personnel and _____ complete and local control of the disconnecting means.

    (a) security
    (b) emergency
    (c) first responders
    (d) local jurisdictional

17. The disconnecting means for a sign or outline lighting system shall be permitted to be located at the point of entry to a sign and the disconnect shall be located at the point the feeder circuit or branch circuit(s) supplying a sign or outline lighting system enters a _____.

    (a) sign enclosure
    (b) sign body
    (c) pole in accordance with 600.5(D)(3)
    (d) any of these

18. A disconnect shall not be required for branch circuit(s) or feeder conductor(s) passing through the sign where enclosed in a Chapter 3 _____ raceway or metal-jacketed cable identified for the location.

    (a) listed
    (b) labeled
    (c) identified
    (d) approved

19. A disconnect shall not be required at the point of entry to a sign enclosure or sign body for branch circuit(s) or feeder conductor(s) that supply an internal _____ in a sign enclosure or sign body.

    (a) switchboard(s)
    (b) switchgear(s)
    (c) panelboard(s)
    (d) any of these

20. Where the disconnecting means is out of the line of sight from any section of a sign or outline lighting able to be energized, the disconnecting means shall be _____ in the open position in accordance with 110.25.

    (a) secured
    (b) bolted
    (c) lockable
    (d) visible when

21. A permanent field-applied marking identifying the location of the disconnecting means shall be applied to the sign in a location visible during _____ and the warning label shall comply with 110.21(B).

    (a) installation
    (b) repair
    (c) retrofitting
    (d) servicing

22. Where the disconnecting means for a sign or outline lighting is not located within sight of the _____, a permanent field-applied marking identifying the location of the disconnecting means shall be applied to the controller in a location visible during servicing and the warning label shall comply with 110.21(B).

    (a) controller
    (b) branch circuit
    (c) feeder
    (d) photocell

23. Metal equipment of signs, outline lighting, and skeleton tubing systems shall be grounded by connection to the _____ of the supply branch circuit(s) or feeder using the types of equipment grounding conductors specified in 250.118.

    (a) grounding electrode conductor
    (b) equipment grounding conductor
    (c) neutral conductor
    (d) ground rod

24. Listed flexible metal conduit or listed liquidtight flexible metal conduit that encloses the secondary circuit conductor from a transformer or power supply for use with neon tubing shall be permitted as a bonding means if the total accumulative length of the conduit in the secondary circuit does not exceed _____ ft.

    (a) 6
    (b) 25
    (c) 50
    (d) 100

25. Bonding conductors used for the bonding connections of the noncurrent-carrying metal parts of signs shall not be smaller than _____ AWG.

    (a) 14
    (b) 12
    (c) 8
    (d) 6

26. The bottom of sign and outline lighting system equipment shall be at least _____ ft above areas accessible to vehicles unless protected from physical damage.

    (a) 12
    (b) 14
    (c) 16
    (d) 18

27. Neon tubing, other than _____, readily accessible to pedestrians shall be protected from physical damage.

    (a) Class I, Division 1 locations
    (b) listed dry-location, portable signs
    (c) fixed equipment
    (d) wet-location portable signs

Article 604 | Practice Questions

28. Signs and outline lighting systems shall be installed so that adjacent combustible materials are not subjected to temperatures in excess of _____.

    (a) 60°C
    (b) 75°C
    (c) 90°C
    (d) 105°C

29. A working space not less than 3 ft high by 3 ft wide by _____ ft deep is required for each ballast, transformer, electronic power supply, and Class 2 power source or at its enclosure where not installed in a sign.

    (a) 2
    (b) 3
    (c) 4
    (d) 6

30. At least one lighting outlet containing a switch or controlled by a wall switch shall be installed in attic spaces containing ballasts for electric signs. At least one _____ shall be at the usual point of entry to these spaces. The lighting outlet shall be provided at or near the equipment requiring servicing.

    (a) receptacle
    (b) switch
    (c) point of control
    (d) luminaire

31. Ballasts, transformers, electronic power supplies, and Class 2 power sources for signs shall be permitted to be located above suspended ceilings, provided that their enclosures are securely fastened in place and _____.

    (a) are effectively bonded
    (b) not dependent on the suspended-ceiling grid for support
    (c) are rated at not more than 300V
    (d) effectively grounded

Article 604—Manufactured Wiring Systems

1. A manufactured wiring system is a system assembled by a manufacturer, which cannot be inspected at the building site without _____.

    (a) a permit
    (b) a manufacturer's representative present
    (c) damage or destruction to the assembly
    (d) an engineer's supervision

2. Manufactured wiring systems and associated components shall be _____.

    (a) listed
    (b) labeled
    (c) identified
    (d) approved

3. Manufactured wiring systems shall be _____ in accordance with the applicable cable or conduit article for the cable or conduit type employed.

    (a) inspected and tested
    (b) relocated
    (c) secured and supported
    (d) reassembled

Article 620—Elevators, Escalators, and Moving Walks

1. Article 620 covers the installation of electrical equipment and wiring used in connection with elevators, dumbwaiters, escalators, moving walks, platform lifts, and _____.

    (a) stairway chairlifts
    (b) pool lifts
    (c) boat hoists
    (d) all of these

2. Each 15A and 20A, 125V, single-phase receptacle installed in pits, in hoistways, on the cars of elevators and dumbwaiters associated with wind turbine tower elevators, on the platforms or in the runways and machinery spaces of platform lifts and stairway chairlifts, and in escalator and moving walk wellways shall be _____.

    (a) on a GFCI-protected circuit
    (b) of the GFCI type
    (c) provided with GFPE protection
    (d) current-limiting

3. All 15A and 20A, 125V, single-phase receptacles installed in _____ for elevators, dumbwaiters, escalators, moving walks, lifts, and chairlifts shall have ground-fault circuit-interrupter protection for personnel.

    (a) machine rooms
    (b) control spaces and machine spaces
    (c) control rooms
    (d) all of these

4. A(an) _____ branch circuit shall supply the elevator car lights and shall be permitted to supply receptacles, accessory equipment (alarm devices, alarm bells, monitoring devices not part of the control system), auxiliary lighting power source, and ventilation on each elevator car or inside the operation controller.

   (a) GFCI-protected
   (b) AFCI-protected
   (c) multiwire
   (d) separate

5. The branch circuit(s) supplying the lighting for an elevator machine room/machinery space shall be separate from the branch circuit(s) supplying the receptacle(s). The required lighting shall not be connected to the load side of a(an) _____.

   (a) local subpanel
   (b) SWD-type circuit breaker
   (c) HID-type circuit breaker
   (d) GFCI

6. A(an) _____ shall be located at the point of entry to an elevator machine room.

   (a) directory
   (b) lighting switch
   (c) control circuit disconnecting means
   (d) emergency exit map

7. At least _____ 125V, single-phase, 15A or 20A, duplex receptacle(s) shall be provided in each elevator machine room and elevator machinery space.

   (a) one
   (b) two
   (c) three
   (d) four

8. Separate _____ shall supply the elevator hoistway pit lighting and receptacles and the required lighting shall not be connected to the load side of a ground-fault circuit interrupter.

   (a) feeders
   (b) subpanels
   (c) emergency systems
   (d) branch circuits

9. The lighting switch for hoistway pits shall be readily accessible from the _____.

   (a) pit access door
   (b) elevator car
   (c) floor of the pit
   (d) machinery room

10. At least _____ 125V, single-phase, 15A or 20A, duplex receptacle(s) shall be provided in the elevator hoistway pit.

    (a) one
    (b) two
    (c) three
    (d) four

11. Only wiring, raceways, and cables used directly in connection with an elevator shall be permitted inside the hoistway and the machine room.

    (a) True
    (b) False

12. A single means for disconnecting all ungrounded main power supply conductors for each _____ shall be provided and be designed so that no pole can be operated independently.

    (a) elevator or dumbwaiter
    (b) escalator or moving walk
    (c) platform lift or stairway chairlift
    (d) any of these

13. The disconnecting means for an elevator or escalator shall be an enclosed externally operable circuit breaker or fused motor circuit switch that is _____.

    (a) capable of interrupting six times the locked-rotor current
    (b) lockable
    (c) inherently protected
    (d) suitable for use as service equipment

14. The location of the disconnecting means for an elevator shall be located where it is _____ to qualified persons.

    (a) accessible
    (b) readily accessible
    (c) disclosed only
    (d) accessible only with a key

Article 625 | Practice Questions

Article 625—Electric Vehicle Power Transfer System

1. Article 625 covers the electrical conductors and equipment connecting an electric vehicle to premises wiring for the purposes of _____.

    (a) charging
    (b) power export
    (c) bidirectional current flow
    (d) all of these

2. "Electric vehicle supply equipment" includes the conductors and electric vehicle connectors, _____ installed specifically for the purpose of transferring energy between the premises wiring and the electric vehicle.

    (a) attachment plugs
    (b) fittings
    (c) power outlets
    (d) all of these

3. Electric vehicle power export equipment. and electric vehicle supply equipment are sometimes contained in one piece of equipment, sometimes referred to as a "_____ EVSE."

    (a) directional
    (b) supplemental
    (c) bi-directional
    (d) integrated

4. "Wireless power transfer equipment" (WPTE) is equipment consisting of a charger power converter and a primary pad that are _____.

    (a) integrated
    (b) contained within one enclosure
    (c) separate units or contained within one enclosure
    (d) bidirectional

5. All equipment covered by the scope of Article 625 shall be _____.

    (a) listed
    (b) labeled
    (c) identified
    (d) all of these

6. Each outlet installed for the purpose of charging electric vehicles shall be supplied by an individual _____ circuit that shall have no other outlets.

    (a) parallel branch
    (b) feeder
    (c) branch
    (d) GFCI-protected

7. Conductors that supply electric vehicle supply equipment shall be sized for continuous duty and have a rating of not less than 125 percent of the maximum load of the electric vehicle supply equipment.

    (a) True
    (b) False

8. For electric vehicle equipment rated more than _____ or more than 150 volts-to-ground, the disconnecting means shall be provided and installed in a readily accessible location.

    (a) 20A
    (b) 30A
    (c) 50A
    (d) 60A

9. The electric vehicle supply equipment located outdoors shall be located to permit direct electrical coupling of the EV connector (conductive or inductive) to the electric vehicle.

    (a) True
    (b) False

10. The _____ of electric vehicle supply equipment located indoors shall be located not less than 18 in. above the floor level.

    (a) attachment plugs
    (b) fittings
    (c) power outlets
    (d) coupling means

11. Where electric vehicle storage batteries are used or electric vehicle supply equipment is _____ for charging electric vehicles indoors without ventilation, mechanical ventilation shall not be required.

    (a) listed
    (b) labeled
    (c) identified
    (d) all of these

12. Where the electric vehicle supply equipment is listed for charging electric vehicles that require ventilation for indoor charging, mechanical ventilation shall include permanently installed supply and exhaust equipment located to intake from inside the building and vent outdoors.

    (a) True
    (b) False

13. In addition to the requirements in 210.8, all receptacles installed for the connection of electric vehicle charging shall have arc-fault circuit-interrupter protection.

    (a) True
    (b) False

Article 630—Electric Welders

1. Article _____ covers apparatus for electric arc welding, resistance welding, plasma cutting, and other similar welding and cutting process equipment that is connected to an electrical supply system.

    (a) 600
    (b) 620
    (c) 630
    (d) 680

2. All welding and cutting power equipment under the scope of Article 630 shall be _____.

    (a) identified
    (b) labeled
    (c) listed
    (d) approved

3. The ampacity of the supply conductors to an individual electric arc welder shall not be less than the effective current value on the rating plate.

    (a) True
    (b) False

4. Minimum conductor ampacity feeding a group of welders shall be based on the individual currents determined in 630.11(A) as the sum of _____ percent of the two largest welders, plus 85 percent of the third largest welder, plus 70 percent of the fourth largest welder, plus 60 percent of all remaining welders.

    (a) 100
    (b) 115
    (c) 125
    (d) 175

5. An arc welder shall have overcurrent protection rated or set at not more than _____ percent of the rated primary current of the welder.

    (a) 100
    (b) 125
    (c) 150
    (d) 200

6. A disconnecting means shall be provided in the supply circuit for each arc welder not equipped with _____, and the identity shall be marked in accordance with 110.22(A).

    (a) a governor
    (b) a shunt-trip device
    (c) an integral disconnect
    (d) GFCI protection

7. The required ampacity for the supply conductors for a resistance welder with a duty cycle of 15 percent and a primary current of 21A is _____.

    (a) 5.67A
    (b) 6.72A
    (c) 8.19A
    (d) 9.45A

8. Each resistance welder shall have an overcurrent device rated or set at not more than _____ percent of the rated primary current of the welder.

    (a) 80
    (b) 100
    (c) 125
    (d) 300

Article 640 | Practice Questions

9. Conductors that supply one or more resistance welders shall be protected by an overcurrent device rated or set at not more than _____ percent of the conductor ampacity.

   (a) 80
   (b) 100
   (c) 125
   (d) 300

10. A _____ shall be provided to disconnect each resistance welder and its control equipment from the supply circuit.

    (a) contactor
    (b) relay
    (c) magnetic starter
    (d) switch or circuit breaker

Article 640—Audio Signal Amplification and Reproduction Equipment

1. Electronic organs or other electronic musical instruments are included in the scope of Article 640.

   (a) True
   (b) False

2. Audio distribution cable not terminated at equipment and not identified for future use with a tag is considered abandoned.

   (a) True
   (b) False

3. For audio signal processing, amplification, and reproduction equipment, 300.22(B) shall apply to _____ installed in ducts specifically fabricated for environmental air.

   (a) speakers
   (b) Class 3 circuits
   (c) equipment and circuits
   (d) only power-limited circuits

4. Class 2 and Class 3 cables for audio signal processing, amplification, and reproduction equipment installed in accordance with 725.135(B) and Table 725.154 shall be permitted to be installed in ducts specifically fabricated for environmental air.

   (a) True
   (b) False

5. Class 2 and Class 3 cables for audio signal processing, amplification, and reproduction equipment installed in accordance with 725.135(C) and Table 725.154 shall not be permitted to be installed in other spaces used for environmental air (plenums).

   (a) True
   (b) False

6. Amplifiers, loudspeakers, and other equipment shall be located or protected so as to guard against environmental exposure or physical damage that might cause _____.

   (a) a fire
   (b) shock
   (c) personal hazard
   (d) any of these

7. Exposed audio cables shall be secured by _____ or similar fittings designed and installed so as not to damage the cable.

   (a) straps
   (b) staples
   (c) hangers
   (d) any of these

8. The accessible portion of abandoned audio distribution cables shall be removed.

   (a) True
   (b) False

9. Audio cables identified for future use shall be marked with a tag of sufficient durability to withstand _____.

   (a) moisture
   (b) humidity
   (c) the environment involved
   (d) temperature fluctuations

10. Audio system equipment supplied by branch-circuit power shall not be placed horizontally within _____ of the inside wall of a pool, spa, hot tub, fountain, or the prevailing or tidal high water mark.

    (a) 18 in.
    (b) 2 ft
    (c) 5 ft
    (d) 10 ft

Article 645—Information Technology Equipment (ITE)

1. Article 645 covers _____ of information technology equipment and systems in an information technology equipment room that meets the requirements of 645.4.

    (a) equipment
    (b) power-supply wiring
    (c) interconnecting wiring
    (d) all of these

2. For information technology equipment, supply circuits and interconnecting cables not terminated to equipment and not identified for future use with a tag are considered to be _____.

    (a) abandoned
    (b) unused
    (c) for future use
    (d) removed from service

3. Section(s) _____ shall apply to penetrations of the fire-resistant information technology room boundary.

    (a) 300.21
    (b) 770.26
    (c) 800.26
    (d) all of these

4. Which of the following sections and tables apply to wiring and cabling in other spaces used for environmental air (plenums) above an information technology equipment room?

    (a) Wiring methods: 300.22(C)(1)
    (b) Class 2, Class 3, and PLTC cables: 725.135(C) and Table 725.154
    (c) Fire alarm systems: 760.53(B)(2), 760.135(C), and Table 760.154
    (d) all of these

5. Which of the following sections and tables apply to wiring and cabling in other spaces used for environmental air (plenums) above an information technology equipment room?

    (a) Optical fiber cables: 770.113(C) and Table 770.154(a)
    (b) Communications circuits: 800.113 and Table 800.154(a)
    (c) CATV and radio distribution systems: 820.113 and Table 800.154(a)
    (d) all of these

6. Article 645 does not apply unless an information technology equipment room contains _____.

    (a) a disconnecting means complying with 645.10
    (b) a separate heating/ventilating/air-conditioning (HVAC) system
    (c) separation by fire-resistance-rated walls, floors, and ceilings
    (d) all of these

7. Ventilation in the underfloor area of an information technology equipment room shall be used in that room only, unless provided with fire/smoke dampers at the point of penetration of the room boundary.

    (a) True
    (b) False

8. Only electrical equipment and wiring associated with the operation of the information technology room is allowed to be installed in the room. Examples include HVAC systems, communications systems, telephone, fire alarm systems, security systems, water detection systems, and other related protective equipment.

    (a) True
    (b) False

9. Branch-circuit conductors for data processing equipment in information technology equipment rooms shall have an ampacity not less than _____ of the total connected load.

    (a) 80 percent
    (b) 100 percent
    (c) 125 percent
    (d) the sum

10. Where supply cords of listed information technology equipment are installed under a raised floor, they shall not be longer than _____ ft.

    (a) 10
    (b) 12
    (c) 15
    (d) 16

11. Separate information technology equipment units shall be permitted to be interconnected by means of listed cables and cable assemblies. Where exposed to physical damage, supply circuits and interconnecting cables shall be protected.

    (a) True
    (b) False

Article 645 | Practice Questions

12. Where the area under the floor is accessible and openings minimize the entrance of debris beneath the floor, _____, and receptacles associated with the information technology equipment shall be permitted.

    (a) power and communication cables
    (b) connecting and interconnecting cables
    (c) cord-and-plug connections
    (d) all of these

13. Information technology equipment branch circuit supply conductors under a raised floor shall be permitted to be installed only in an electrical metallic tubing (EMT) raceway.

    (a) True
    (b) False

14. Nonmetallic raceways for branch circuit supply conductors can be installed in the area under raised floors of approved construction of information technology equipment rooms.

    (a) True
    (b) False

15. Which of the following are permitted under raised floors of information technology equipment rooms for information technology equipment?

    (a) supply cords of listed information technology equipment in accordance with 645.5(B)
    (b) interconnecting cables enclosed in a raceway
    (c) equipment grounding conductors
    (d) all of these

16. Types CL2, CM, and CMG cables are permitted within the raised floor area of an information technology equipment room if installed in accordance with 725.154(A).

    (a) True
    (b) False

17. Interconnecting cables under raised floors that support information technology equipment shall be permitted to be listed Type _____ cable having adequate fire-resistant characteristics suitable for use under raised floors of an information technology equipment room.

    (a) RF
    (b) UF
    (c) LS
    (d) DP

18. In addition to optical fiber cables installed in accordance with 770.113(C), Types OFNR, OFCR, OFN, and OFC shall be permitted under raised floors of an information technology equipment room.

    (a) True
    (b) False

19. Power cables, communications cables, connecting cables, interconnecting cables, and associated boxes, connectors, plugs, and receptacles that are listed as part of, or for, information technology equipment shall not be required to be secured in place where installed _____.

    (a) above suspended ceilings
    (b) exposed on interior walls
    (c) under raised floors
    (d) exposed on exterior walls

20. The accessible portion of abandoned interconnecting cables under an information technology room raised floor shall be removed unless the cables are contained within a _____.

    (a) raceway
    (b) restricted area
    (c) junction box
    (d) cable tray

21. Installed supply circuits and interconnecting cables identified for future use in information technology equipment rooms shall be marked with a tag of sufficient durability to withstand the environment involved which shall include the _____.

    (a) date the cable was identified for future use
    (b) date of intended use
    (c) intended future use of the cable
    (d) all of these

22. An approved means shall be provided to disconnect power to all electronic equipment in the information technology equipment room or in designated zones within the room. There shall also be a similar approved means to disconnect the power to all _____ serving the room or designated zones.

    (a) dedicated HVAC systems
    (b) lighting circuits
    (c) audio systems
    (d) all of these

23. Remote disconnect controls provided to disconnect power to all electronic equipment in the information technology equipment room, shall be located at an approved _____ location.

    (a) accessible
    (b) readily accessible
    (c) secured
    (d) restricted

24. The remote disconnect means for the control of electronic equipment power and HVAC systems shall be grouped and identified. A single means to control both shall be permitted.

    (a) True
    (b) False

25. Exposed noncurrent-carrying metal parts of an information technology system shall be _____.

    (a) GFPE protected
    (b) inaccessible to non-qualified personnel
    (c) GFCI protected
    (d) bonded to an equipment grounding conductor or double insulated

Article 680—Swimming Pools, Spas, Hot Tubs, Fountains, and Similar Installations

1. The construction and installation of electrical wiring for, and equipment in or adjacent to, all swimming, wading, therapeutic, and decorative pools is covered in Article _____.

    (a) 555
    (b) 600
    (c) 680
    (d) 690

2. An electrically powered lift that provides accessibility to and from a pool or spa for people with disabilities is known as an "electrically powered _____ lift."

    (a) spa
    (b) disability
    (c) pool
    (d) tub

3. In accordance with Article 680, the definition of a "fountain" includes drinking water coolers.

    (a) True
    (b) False

4. For pools, fountains, and similar installations, "the low-voltage contact limit" is a voltage not exceeding _____.

    (a) 15V (RMS) for sinusoidal ac or 21.20V peak for nonsinusoidal ac
    (b) 30V for continuous dc
    (c) 12.40V peak for dc that is interrupted at a rate of 10 to 200 Hz
    (d) all of these

5. A "spa" or "hot tub" is a hydromassage pool or tub and is generally not designed to have the contents drained or discharged after each use.

    (a) True
    (b) False

6. A "wet-niche luminaire" is intended to be installed in a _____.

    (a) transformer
    (b) forming shell
    (c) hydromassage bathtub
    (d) all of these

7. After the completion of permanently installed swimming pools, the authority having jurisdiction shall be permitted to require _____ inspection and testing.

    (a) seasonal
    (b) monthly
    (c) periodic
    (d) annual

8. Insulated overhead service conductors that are cabled together with a bare messenger and operate at not over 750 volts-to-ground shall maintain a _____ ft clearance in any direction to the water level of swimming pools, fountains, and similar installations.

    (a) 14
    (b) 16
    (c) 20
    (d) 22½

9. All electric pool water heaters shall have the heating elements subdivided into loads not exceeding _____.

    (a) 20A
    (b) 35A
    (c) 48A
    (d) 60A

Article 680 | Practice Questions

10. Underground wiring shall not be permitted under a pool unless this wiring is necessary to supply pool equipment permitted by Article 680, and the _____ cover depths shall be as given in Table 300.5.

    (a) maximum
    (b) permissible
    (c) minimum
    (d) any of these

11. The maintenance disconnecting means required for swimming pool equipment shall be _____ and at least 5 ft from the water's edge, unless separated by a permanently installed barrier.

    (a) secured
    (b) at least 24 in. above the highest water level of the pool
    (c) capable of being locked in the open position
    (d) readily accessible and within sight of its equipment

12. Wiring methods described in 680.14 shall be _____ for use in corrosive environments.

    (a) listed
    (b) labeled
    (c) identified
    (d) listed and identified

13. Wiring methods installed in a corrosive environment for pool-associated motors for permanently installed pools shall comply with 680.14 or shall include an insulated copper equipment grounding conductor sized in accordance with Table 250.122, but not smaller than _____ AWG.

    (a) 18
    (b) 16
    (c) 14
    (d) 12

14. Outlets supplying all pool motors on branch circuits rated 150V or less to ground and _____ or less, single- or three-phase, shall be provided with Class A ground-fault circuit-interrupter protection.

    (a) 20A
    (b) 30A
    (c) 50A
    (d) 60A

15. Grounding-type GFCI-protected receptacles that provide power for water-pump motors related to the circulation and sanitation system of a pool shall be located not less than _____ ft from the inside walls of the pool.

    (a) 3
    (b) 6
    (c) 8
    (d) 12

16. All receptacles supplied by branch circuits rated _____ or less to ground within a pool equipment room shall be GFCI protected.

    (a) 110V
    (b) 125V
    (c) 150V
    (d) 250V

17. Luminaires installed above new outdoor pools or the area extending _____ ft horizontally from the inside walls of the pool shall be installed at a height not less than 12 ft above the maximum water level of the pool.

    (a) 3
    (b) 5
    (c) 10
    (d) 12

18. Metallic low-voltage gas-fired luminaires, decorative fireplaces, fire pits, and similar equipment in permanently installed pool areas shall be bonded in accordance with the requirements in 680.26(B).

    (a) True
    (b) False

19. Outlets in or around pool areas shall be not less than _____ ft from the inside walls of the pool.

    (a) 5
    (b) 8
    (c) 10
    (d) 20

20. Wet-niche luminaires shall be installed with the top of the luminaire lens not less than _____ in. below the normal water level of the pool.

    (a) 6
    (b) 12
    (c) 18
    (d) 24

21. Wet-niche luminaires shall be connected to an equipment grounding conductor not smaller than _____ AWG.

    (a) 12
    (b) 10
    (c) 8
    (d) 6

22. The junction box connected to a conduit that extends to the forming shell of a luminaire that operates at over 15V shall be located not less than _____ in. above the ground level or pool deck.

    (a) 4
    (b) 6
    (c) 8
    (d) 12

23. Junction boxes for pool lighting shall be located not less than _____ ft from the inside wall of a pool unless separated by a fence or wall.

    (a) 3
    (b) 4
    (c) 6
    (d) 8

24. The _____ terminals of a junction box, transformer enclosure, or other enclosure in the supply circuit to a wet-niche or no-niche luminaire and the field-wiring chamber of a dry-niche luminaire shall be connected to the equipment grounding terminal of the panelboard.

    (a) equipment grounding
    (b) grounded
    (c) grounding terminals
    (d) ungrounded

25. An 8 AWG or larger solid copper equipotential bonding conductor shall be extended to service equipment to eliminate voltage gradients in the pool area.

    (a) True
    (b) False

26. For equipotential bonding, the perimeter surface to be bonded shall be considered to extend for _____ ft horizontally beyond the inside walls of the pool and shall include unpaved surfaces and other types of paving.

    (a) 3
    (b) 5
    (c) 10
    (d) 12

27. Metallic pool cover anchors intended for insertion in a concrete or masonry deck surface, 1 in. or less in any dimension and 2 in. or less in length shall require bonding.

    (a) True
    (b) False

28. Where a double-insulated water pool pump motor is installed where there is no connection between the swimming pool equipotential bonding means and the equipment grounding system for the premises, a solid 8 AWG copper bonding conductor shall be connected to _____.

    (a) a ground rod
    (b) the equipment grounding conductor of the motor circuit
    (c) an 8 AWG bonding grid
    (d) any of these

29. The electric motors, controllers, and wiring for an electrically operated pool cover shall be located at least _____ ft from the inside wall of the pool or separated from the pool by a permanent barrier.

    (a) 5
    (b) 6
    (c) 10
    (d) 20

30. Circuits serving gas-fired swimming pool and spa water heaters operating at voltages above the low-voltage contact limit shall be provided with _____ protection for personnel.

    (a) GFCI
    (b) AFCI
    (c) combined AFCI/GFCI
    (d) a gas valve emergency shut-off

Article 690 | Practice Questions

31. All 15A and 20A, 125V receptacles located within _____ ft of the inside walls of a storable pool, storable spa, or storable hot tub shall be GFCI protected.

    (a) 8
    (b) 10
    (c) 15
    (d) 20

32. In spas or hot tubs, a clearly labeled emergency shutoff or control switch shall be _____, not less than 5 ft away, adjacent to, and within sight of the spa or hot tub.

    (a) accessible
    (b) readily accessible
    (c) available
    (d) of the pneumatic type

33. The equipotential bonding requirements for perimeter surfaces contained in 680.26(B)(2) do not apply to a listed self-contained spa or hot tub installed above a finished floor.

    (a) True
    (b) False

34. Receptacles rated 30A or less, 125V located within 10 ft of the inside walls of an indoor spa or hot tub, shall be _____.

    (a) GFCI protected
    (b) AFCI protected
    (c) of the twist-locking type
    (d) readily accessible

35. The branch circuit supplying submersible fountain equipment shall be _____ unless the equipment is listed for operation at not more than 15V.

    (a) not greater than 240V nominal
    (b) GFCI protected
    (c) not less than 20A
    (d) rated at least 30V

36. Metal piping systems associated with a fountain shall be bonded to the equipment grounding conductor of the _____.

    (a) branch circuit supplying the fountain
    (b) bonding grid
    (c) equipotential plane
    (d) grounding electrode system

37. Fountain electrical equipment that is supplied by a flexible cord shall have all exposed noncurrent-carrying metal parts grounded by an insulated copper equipment grounding conductor that is an integral part of this _____.

    (a) cord
    (b) feeder circuit
    (c) branch circuit
    (d) fountain

38. Electric signs installed within a fountain or within _____ ft of the fountain edge, shall have ground-fault circuit-interrupter protection for personnel.

    (a) 2
    (b) 5
    (c) 6
    (d) 10

39. Outlets supplying all permanently installed nonsubmersible fountain pump motors rated 250V or less and _____ or less, single- or three-phase, shall be provided with ground-fault circuit-interrupter protection.

    (a) 20A
    (b) 30A
    (c) 50A
    (d) 60A

40. Where installed for hydromassage bathtubs, double-insulated _____ shall not be bonded.

    (a) motors and blowers
    (b) cords
    (c) cables
    (d) fittings

Article 690—Solar Photovoltaic (PV) Systems

1. Article 690 applies to solar PV systems, including _____.

    (a) array circuit(s), inverter(s), and controller(s) for such PV systems
    (b) those interactive with other electrical power production sources or stand-alone, or both
    (c) PV systems with ac or dc output for utilization
    (d) all of these

2. In accordance with Article 690, an "ac module system" is an assembly or subassembly of _____ that are evaluated, identified, and defined as a system.

    (a) ac modules
    (b) wiring methods
    (c) material
    (d) all of these

3. In accordance with Article 690, a "dc-to-dc _____ circuit" is the dc circuit conductors connected to the output of a dc combiner for dc-to-dc converter source circuits.

    (a) converter output
    (b) converter control
    (c) inverter output
    (d) inverter control

4. In accordance with Article 690, a "dc combiner" is an enclosure that includes devices used to connect two or more PV system dc circuits in _____.

    (a) series
    (b) series-parallel
    (c) parallel
    (d) parallel-series

5. In accordance with Article 690, a solidly grounded PV system is often connected to ground through an electronic means internal to an inverter or charge controller that provides ground-fault protection.

    (a) True
    (b) False

6. In PV systems, a "_____ circuit" is an electrical subset of a PV system that has two conductors in the output circuit, one positive (+) and one negative (-).

    (a) bipolar
    (b) monopole
    (c) double-pole
    (d) module

7. In accordance with Article 690, a "PV system dc circuit" includes any dc conductor(s) in PV source circuits, PV output circuits, _____ converter source circuits, and dc-to-dc converter output circuits.

    (a) ac-to-dc
    (b) dc-to-ac
    (c) dc-to-dc
    (d) any of these

8. PV systems are permitted to supply a building or other structure in addition to any other _____ supply system(s).

    (a) electrical
    (b) telephone
    (c) data
    (d) communications

9. The installation of PV equipment and all associated wiring and interconnections shall be performed only by _____.

    (a) licensed electricians
    (b) qualified personnel
    (c) master electricians
    (d) journeyman electricians

10. PV system equipment and disconnecting means are permitted to be installed in a bathroom when listed for the application.

    (a) True
    (b) False

11. Article 690 requirements pertaining to dc PV source circuits do not apply to ac PV modules since the PV source circuit, conductors, and inverters are considered as internal wiring of the ac module.

    (a) True
    (b) False

12. For one- and two-family dwellings, the maximum voltage for PV system dc circuits is limited to _____.

    (a) 30V
    (b) 50V
    (c) 600V
    (d) 1,000V

Article 690 | Practice Questions

13. In a dc PV source circuit or output circuit, the maximum voltage, corrected for the lowest expected ambient temperature for that circuit, is permitted to be calculated in accordance with the listing or labelling instructions of the module.

    (a) True
    (b) False

14. For PV system source circuit or output circuits with a generating capacity of _____ kW or greater, the maximum voltage may be calculated using a documented and stamped PV system design, using an industry standard method maximum voltage calculation provided by a licensed professional electrical engineer.

    (a) 25
    (b) 50
    (c) 75
    (d) 100

15. For PV dc circuits connected to the output of a single dc-to-dc converter, the _____ shall be determined in accordance with the instructions included in the listing or labeling of the dc-to-dc converter.

    (a) minimum voltage
    (b) minimum current
    (c) maximum voltage
    (d) maximum current

16. To prevent PV system overvoltage of bipolar circuits in the event of a ground fault or arc fault, each monopole subarray circuit shall be _____ from ground.

    (a) grounded
    (b) connected to earth
    (c) isolated
    (d) shielded

17. The PV maximum output circuit current shall be the sum of parallel PV source circuit maximum currents as calculated in _____.

    (a) 690.8(A)(1)(a)
    (b) 690.8(A)(2)
    (c) 690.8(A)(3)
    (d) Article 220

18. In PV systems, where a single overcurrent device is used to protect a set of two or more parallel-connected module circuits, the ampacity of each of the module interconnection conductors shall not be less than the sum of the rating of the single overcurrent device plus _____ percent of the short-circuit current from the other parallel-connected modules.

    (a) 100
    (b) 115
    (c) 125
    (d) 150

19. In PV systems, when a circuit conductor is connected to a current-limited supply at one end, and also connected to a source having an available maximum current greater than the ampacity of the circuit conductor, the circuit conductors shall be protected from overcurrent at the point of connection to _____ current source(s).

    (a) the lower
    (b) the higher
    (c) either
    (d) both

20. Fuses or circuit breakers for PV dc circuits shall be _____ for use in PV systems.

    (a) identified
    (b) approved
    (c) recognized
    (d) listed

21. Overcurrent devices for PV source and output circuits shall be readily accessible.

    (a) True
    (b) False

22. Ground mounted PV system circuits that enter buildings, of which the sole purpose is to house PV system equipment, shall include a rapid shutdown function to reduce shock hazard for firefighters.

    (a) True
    (b) False

23. PV system circuits installed on or in buildings shall include a rapid shutdown function to reduce the risk of electrical shock for _____.

    (a) personnel
    (b) employees
    (c) firefighters
    (d) installers

24. For PV system rapid shutdown systems, controlled conductors located outside the array boundary or more than 3 ft from the point of entry inside a building shall be limited to not more than _____ within 30 seconds of rapid shutdown initiation.

    (a) 15V
    (b) 30V
    (c) 50V
    (d) 80V

25. For a single PV system, the rapid shutdown initiation shall occur by the operation of at least one or more of which of the following devices?

    (a) service disconnecting means
    (b) PV system disconnecting means
    (c) readily accessible switch that plainly indicates whether it is in the "off" or "on" position
    (d) any of these

26. A means is required to disconnect the PV system from all wiring systems including power systems, energy storage systems, and utilization equipment and its associated premises wiring.

    (a) True
    (b) False

27. Where PV system disconnecting means of systems above _____ are readily accessible to unqualified persons, any enclosure door or hinged cover that exposes live parts when open shall be locked or require a tool to open.

    (a) 30V
    (b) 120V
    (c) 240V
    (d) 600V

28. The maximum number of disconnects for each PV system shall consist of not more than _____ switches or _____ sets of circuit breakers, or a combination of not more than _____ switches and sets of circuit breakers, mounted in a single enclosure, or in a group of separate enclosures.

    (a) one
    (b) six
    (c) no limit
    (d) a total of twelve

29. The PV system disconnecting means shall have ratings sufficient for the _____ that is available at the terminals of the PV system disconnect.

    (a) maximum circuit current
    (b) available fault current
    (c) voltage
    (d) all of these

30. Isolating devices or equipment disconnecting means for PV system equipment shall be installed within the equipment or within sight and within _____ ft of the equipment.

    (a) 3
    (b) 10
    (c) 25
    (d) 50

31. An isolating device for PV system equipment shall be which of the following?

    (a) A mating connector meeting the requirements of 690.33 and listed and identified for use with specific equipment.
    (b) A finger-safe fuse holder or an isolating switch that requires a tool to place the device in the open (off) position.
    (c) An isolating device listed for the intended application.
    (d) any of these

32. The conductors of PV output circuits and inverter input and output circuits shall be identified at all points of termination, connection, and splices.

    (a) True
    (b) False

Article 690 | Practice Questions

33. Where the conductors of more than one PV system occupy the same junction box or raceway with removable cover(s), the ac and dc conductors of each system shall be grouped separately by cable ties or similar means at least once, and then shall be grouped at intervals not to exceed _____ ft.

    (a) 1
    (b) 3
    (c) 6
    (d) 10

34. Single-conductor cable _____ sunlight resistant and Type USE-2 and RHW-2 cable can be run exposed at outdoor locations for PV source circuits within the PV array.

    (a) approved
    (b) listed or labeled
    (c) marked
    (d) manufacturer certified

35. Where inside buildings, PV system dc circuits that exceed 30V or 8A installed where Type MC cable smaller than _____ in. in diameter containing PV power circuit conductors is installed across ceilings or floor joists, the raceway or cable shall be protected by substantial guard strips that are at least as high as the raceway or cable.

    (a) 3/8
    (b) 1/2
    (c) 3/4
    (d) 1

36. Labels or markings of PV system raceways and enclosures shall be suitable for the environment and be placed with a maximum of _____ ft of spacing.

    (a) 5
    (b) 10
    (c) 20
    (d) 25

37. Fittings and connectors that are intended to be concealed at the time of on-site assembly, where _____ for such use, shall be permitted for on-site interconnection of modules or other array components.

    (a) approved
    (b) identified
    (c) marked
    (d) listed

38. PV systems that exceed 30V or 8A shall be provided with direct-current _____ to reduce fire hazards.

    (a) arc-fault protection
    (b) rectifier protection
    (c) ground-fault monitors
    (d) ground-fault protection

39. Ground-fault protection of PV system equipment shall provide indication of ground faults at a readily accessible location. Examples of indication include but are not limited to _____.

    (a) a remote indicator light
    (b) alarm system monitoring
    (c) web-based services
    (d) any of these

40. Devices and systems used for mounting PV modules that are also used for bonding module frames shall be _____ for bonding PV modules. Devices that mount adjacent PV modules shall be permitted for bonding adjacent PV modules.

    (a) listed
    (b) labeled
    (c) identified
    (d) all of these

41. Where no overcurrent protection is provided for the PV circuit, an assumed overcurrent device rated in accordance with 690.9(B) shall be used to size the equipment grounding conductor in accordance with _____.

    (a) 250.66
    (b) 250.102(C)(1)
    (c) 250.122
    (d) Table 250.122

42. For PV systems that are not solidly grounded, the equipment grounding conductor for the output of the PV system, where connected to associated distribution equipment connected to a grounding electrode system, shall be permitted to be the only connection to ground for the system.

    (a) True
    (b) False

43. Facilities with stand-alone systems shall have _____ installed in accordance with 710.10.

    (a) plaques
    (b) directories
    (c) plaques and directories
    (d) plaques or directories

44. Buildings with PV systems shall have a permanent label located at each _____ location to which the PV systems are connected or at an approved readily visible location and shall indicate the location of rapid shutdown initiation devices.

    (a) service equipment
    (b) PV system disconnect
    (c) PV equipment disconnect
    (d) all of these

45. For buildings with rapid shutdown, the rapid shutdown switch shall have a label that reads "RAPID SHUTDOWN SWITCH FOR SOLAR PV SYSTEM" installed within _____ ft of the switch.

    (a) 3
    (b) 6
    (c) 10
    (d) 25

Article 691—Large-Scale Photovoltaic (PV) Electric Supply Stations

1. Article _____ covers the installation of large-scale PV electric supply stations with a generating capacity of not less than 5,000 kW and not under the electric utility control.

    (a) 690
    (b) 691
    (c) 705
    (d) 711

2. Facilities covered by Article 691 have specific design and safety features unique to large-scale _____ facilities and are operated for the sole purpose of providing electric supply to a system operated by a regulated utility for the transfer of electric energy.

    (a) industrial
    (b) electrical
    (c) distribution
    (d) PV

3. Large-scale PV electric supply stations are only permitted to be accessible to authorized personnel and, electrical circuits and equipment shall be maintained and operated by qualified personnel.

    (a) True
    (b) False

4. Electrical equipment for large-scale PV electric supply stations shall only be approved for installation by _____.

    (a) listing and labeling
    (b) being evaluated for the application and having a field label applied
    (c) qualified personnel
    (d) listing and labeling, or being evaluated for the application and having a field label applied

5. Engineering documentation of large-scale electric supply stations shall include details of conformance of the design with Article _____.

    (a) 250
    (b) 690
    (c) 702
    (d) 710

Article 695—Fire Pumps

1. Article 695 covers the installation of the electric power sources and interconnecting circuits, and the switching and control equipment dedicated to drivers for _____.

    (a) generators
    (b) fire pumps
    (c) alarm systems
    (d) large scale solar arrays

2. Power to fire pump motors shall be supplied by a reliable source of power that has the capacity to carry the _____.

    (a) sum of locked-rotor current of the fire pump motor(s)
    (b) locked-rotor current of the pressure maintenance pump motors
    (c) full-load current of any associated fire pump equipment
    (d) all of these

Article 695 | Practice Questions

3. When a fire pump is supplied by an individual source, the _____ shall be rated to carry indefinitely the sum of the locked-rotor current of the largest fire pump motor and pressure maintenance pump motor(s), and the full-load current of all of the other motors and associated fire pump accessory equipment.

    (a) overcurrent protective device(s)
    (b) pump motor conductors
    (c) pump motor controllers
    (d) source supply conductors

4. Transformers that supply a fire pump motor shall be sized no less than _____ percent of the sum of the fire pump motor(s) and pressure maintenance pump motors, and 100 percent of associated fire pump accessory equipment.

    (a) 100
    (b) 125
    (c) 250
    (d) 300

5. The primary overcurrent protective device for a transformer supplying a fire pump shall carry the sum of the locked-rotor current of the fire pump motor(s), pressure maintenance pump motor(s), and the full-load current of associated fire pump accessory equipment _____.

    (a) for 15 minutes
    (b) for 45 minutes
    (c) for 3 hours
    (d) indefinitely

6. Fire pump supply conductors on the load side of the final disconnecting means and overcurrent device(s) can be routed through a building where the conductors are protected from fire for two hours by _____.

    (a) encasing the cable or raceway in a minimum 2 in. of concrete
    (b) utilizing a cable or raceway that is a listed fire-resistive cable system
    (c) utilizing a cable or raceway that is a listed electrical circuit protective system
    (d) any of these

7. Feeder conductors supplying fire pump motors and accessory equipment shall be sized no less than _____ percent of the sum of the fire pump motor(s) and pressure maintenance motor(s) full-load currents, plus 100 percent of the ampere rating of the fire pump accessory equipment.

    (a) 100
    (b) 125
    (c) 250
    (d) 600

8. All wiring from the controllers to the fire pump motors shall be in _____, listed Type MC cable with an impervious covering, or Type MI cable.

    (a) rigid or intermediate metal conduit
    (b) electrical metallic tubing (EMT)
    (c) liquidtight flexible metallic or nonmetallic conduit
    (d) any of these

9. Ground-fault protection of equipment shall _____ in any fire pump power circuit.

    (a) not be installed
    (b) be provided
    (c) be permitted
    (d) be listed

10. The voltage at the line terminals of a fire pump motor controller shall not drop more than _____ percent below the controller's normal rated voltage under motor-starting conditions.

    (a) 5
    (b) 10
    (c) 15
    (d) 20

11. When a fire pump motor operates at 115 percent of its full-load current rating, the supply voltage at the load terminals of the fire pump controller shall not drop more than _____ percent below the voltage rating of the motor connected to those terminals.

    (a) 5
    (b) 10
    (c) 15
    (d) 20

12. All electric motor-driven fire pump control wiring shall be in _____.

    (a) rigid metal conduit or intermediate metal conduit
    (b) liquidtight flexible metal conduit, electrical metallic tubing, or liquidtight flexible nonmetallic conduit
    (c) listed Type MC cable with an impervious covering or Type MI cable
    (d) any of these

13. A(an) _____ surge protection device shall be installed in or on the fire pump controller.

    (a) listed
    (b) labeled
    (c) identified
    (d) approved

Notes

CHAPTER 7

SPECIAL CONDITIONS

Introduction to Chapter 7—Special Conditions

Chapter 7, which covers special conditions, is the third of the *NEC* chapters that deal with special topics. Chapters 5 and 6 cover special occupancies, and special equipment, respectively. Remember, the first four chapters of the *Code* are sequential and form a foundation for each of the subsequent three. Chapter 8 covers communications systems (twisted pair and coaxial cable) and is not subject to the requirements of Chapters 1 through 7 except where the requirements are specifically referenced there.

What exactly is a "Special Condition"? It is a situation that does not fall under the category of special occupancies or special equipment but creates a need for additional measures to ensure the "safeguarding of people and property" mission of the *NEC* as stated in 90.1(A).

▶ **Article 700—Emergency Systems.** The requirements of Article 700 apply only to the wiring methods for "Emergency Systems" that are essential for safety to human life and required by federal, state, municipal, or other regulatory codes. When normal power is lost, emergency systems must be capable of supplying emergency power in 10 seconds or less and be able to run loads for at least 2 hours on gasoline and 90 minutes on a battery.

▶ **Article 701—Legally Required Standby Systems.** Legally required standby systems provide electrical power to aid in firefighting, rescue operations, control of health hazards, and similar operations, and are required by federal, state, municipal, or other regulatory codes. When normal power is lost, legally required standby systems must be capable of automatically supplying standby power in 60 seconds or less and be able to run loads for at least 2 hours on gasoline and 90 minutes on a battery.

▶ **Article 702—Optional Standby Systems.** Optional standby systems are intended to protect public or private facilities or property where life safety does not depend on the performance of the system. These systems are typically installed to provide an alternate source of electrical power for such facilities as industrial and commercial buildings, farms, and residences, and to serve loads that, when stopped during any power outage, can cause discomfort, serious interruption of a process, or damage to a product or process. Optional standby systems are intended to supply on-site generated power, either automatically or manually, to loads selected by the customer.

▶ **Article 705—Interconnected Electric Power Production Sources.** It used to be that a premises having more than one electric power source was a unique situation, but as more and more facilities supplement their utility electric supply with alternate sources of energy it's become more commonplace. Alternate power sources such as solar or wind turbine that run in parallel with a primary utility source require particular consideration an requirements. Article 705 provides the guidance necessary to ensure a safe installation.

▶ **Article 706—Energy Storage Systems.** Energy storage systems can be (and usually are) connected to other energy sources, such as the local utility distribution system. There can be more than one source of power connected to an ESS and the connection to other energy sources is required to comply with the requirements of Article 705 which covers installation of one or more electric power production sources operating in parallel with a utility source of electricity. It might also be a good idea to be mindful of how this article correlates with other articles in the *Code* such as Articles 480, 690, 692, and 694.

•••

Chapter 7 | Special Conditions

▶ **Article 710—Stand Alone Systems.** A "stand alone system" is an electrical system that is self-sufficient and a completely "off the grid" source of electrical energy such as solar or wind. However, it still may be connected to a utility supply as part of an interconnected system but the fact that it can be self-sustaining is why Article 710 specifically addresses these systems.

▶ **Article 725—Remote-Control, Signaling, and Power-Limited Circuits.** Article 725 contains the requirements for remote-control, signaling, and power-limited circuits that are not an integral part of a device or appliance.

   ▶ *Remote-Control Circuit.* A circuit that controls others through a relay or solid-state device. For example, a circuit that controls the coil of a motor starter or lighting contactor is one type of remote-control circuit.

   ▶ *Signaling Circuit.* A circuit that supplies energy to an appliance or device that gives a visual and/or audible signal. Circuits for doorbells, buzzers, code-calling systems, signal lights, annunciators, burglar alarms, and other indication or alarm devices are examples of signaling circuits.

▶ **Article 760—Fire Alarm Systems.** This article covers the installation of wiring and equipment for fire alarm systems. They include fire detection and alarm notification, voice communications, guard's tour, sprinkler waterflow, and sprinkler supervisory systems.

▶ **Article 770—Optical Fiber Cables.** Article 770 covers the installation of optical fiber cables which transmit signals using light for control, signaling, and communications. It also contains the installation requirements for raceways that contain optical fiber cables, and rules for composite cables (often called "hybrid" cables in the field) that combine optical fibers with current-carrying metallic conductors.

ARTICLE 700 — EMERGENCY SYSTEMS

Introduction to Article 700—Emergency Systems

Emergency systems are often required as a condition of an operating permit for a given facility. According to NFPA 101, *Life Safety Code*, emergency power systems are generally installed where artificial illumination is required for safe exiting and for panic control in buildings subject to occupancy by large numbers of people such as high-rise buildings, jails, sports arenas, schools, health care facilities, and similar structures.

The authority having jurisdiction makes the determination as to whether such a system is necessary for a given facility and what it must entail. Sometimes an emergency system simply provides power for exit lighting and exit signs upon loss of the main power or in the case of fire. Its purpose is not to provide power for normal business operations, but rather to provide lighting and controls essential for human life safety.

The general goal is to keep the emergency operation as reliable as possible. The emergency system must be able to supply all emergency loads simultaneously. When the emergency supply also supplies power for other nonemergency loads, the emergency loads take priority over the others, and those other loads must be subject to automatic load pickup and load shedding to support the emergency loads if the emergency system does not have adequate capacity and rating for all loads simultaneously.

As you study Article 700, keep in mind that emergency systems are essentially lifelines for people. The entire article is based on keeping those lifelines from breaking.

Part I. General

700.1 Scope

Article 700 applies to the electrical safety of the installation, operation, and maintenance of emergency power systems. These consist of circuits and equipment intended to supply illumination, power (or both) within 10 seconds [700.12] when the normal electrical supply is interrupted. ▶Figure 700–1

Some examples of circuits for which emergency power is required are those supplying egress lighting, exit signs, fire alarms, fire pumps, and voice evacuation.

Note 3: For specific locations of emergency lighting requirements, see NFPA 101, *Life Safety Code*.

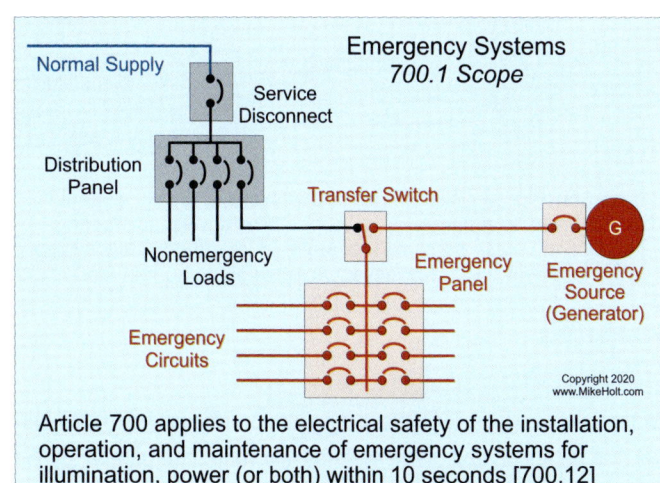

Article 700 applies to the electrical safety of the installation, operation, and maintenance of emergency systems for illumination, power (or both) within 10 seconds [700.12] when the normal electrical supply is interrupted.

▶Figure 700–1

700.2 | Emergency Systems

Author's Comment:

▸ According to NFPA 101, *Life Safety Code*, emergency power systems are generally installed where artificial illumination is required for safe exiting and for panic control in buildings subject to occupancy by large numbers of people. Some examples are high-rise buildings, jails, sports arenas, schools, health care facilities, and similar structures.

Note 4: For specific performance requirements of emergency power systems, see NFPA 110, *Standard for Emergency and Standby Power Systems*.

700.2 Definitions

This definition applies within this article and throughout the *Code*.

Emergency Systems. Emergency power systems are those systems legally required and classed as emergency by a governmental agency having jurisdiction. These systems are intended to automatically supply illumination and/or power essential for safety to human life. ▸Figure 700–2

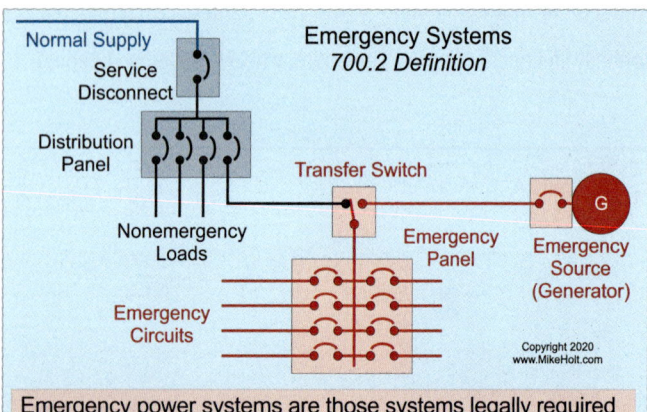

▸Figure 700–2

Note: Emergency power systems may also provide power to maintain life, fire detection and alarm systems, elevators, fire pumps, public safety communications systems (twisted pair, antennas, and coaxial cable), industrial processes where current interruption would produce serious life safety or health hazards, and similar functions.

700.3 Tests and Maintenance

(A) Conduct or Witness Test. To ensure that the emergency power system meets or exceeds the original installation specifications, the authority having jurisdiction must conduct or witness an acceptance test of the emergency power system upon completion.

(B) Periodic Testing. Emergency power systems must be periodically tested on a schedule approved by the authority having jurisdiction to ensure adequate maintenance has been performed and the systems are in proper operating condition.

Author's Comment:

▸ Running the emergency power system under its maximum anticipated load and making sure power is transferred within 10 seconds is often considered an acceptable method of operational testing.

(C) Maintenance. Emergency system equipment must be maintained in accordance with manufacturer instructions and industry standards.

(D) Written Record. A written record of the acceptance test, periodic testing, and maintenance must be kept.

Author's Comment:

▸ The *NEC* does not specify the required record retention period.

700.4 Capacity and Rating

(A) Rating. An emergency power system must be suitable for the available fault current at its terminals.

(B) Capacity. An emergency power system must have adequate capacity in accordance with Article 220 or by another approved method.

700.5 Transfer Equipment

(A) General. Transfer equipment must be automatic, listed, and marked for emergency use, and approved by the authority having jurisdiction. The equipment must be automatic to prevent the inadvertent interconnection of emergency and other power systems. ▸Figure 700–3

Emergency Systems | 700.8

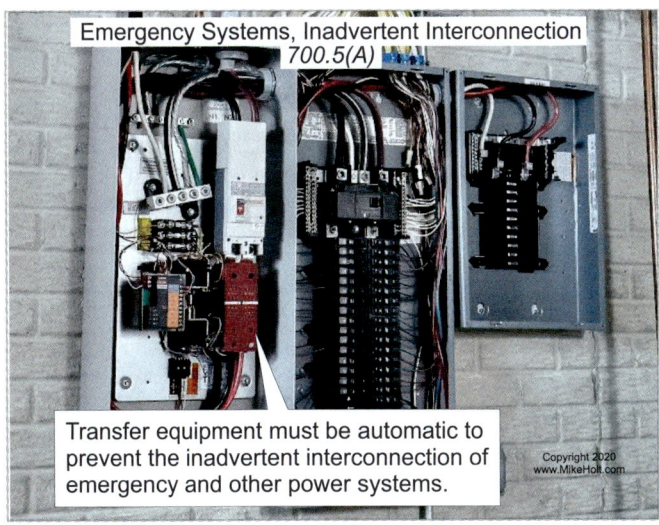
▶Figure 700-3

Meter-mounted transfer switches are not permitted for emergency system use.

(C) Automatic Transfer Switches. Automatic transfer switches must be able to be electrically operated and mechanically held. They are not permitted to be reconditioned.

(D) Use. Transfer equipment must supply only emergency loads. ▶Figure 700-4

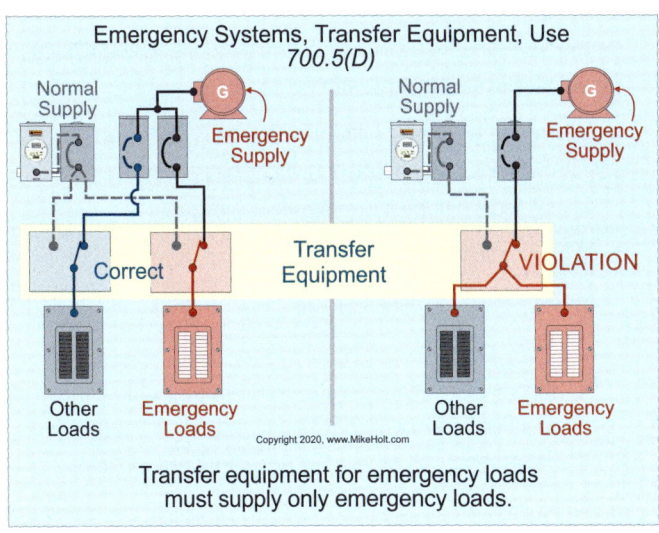
▶Figure 700-4

Author's Comment:

▶ Multiple transfer switches are required where a single generator is used to supply emergency loads, legally required standby loads, and optional loads.

(E) Documentation. The short-circuit current rating of the transfer equipment must be field marked on the exterior of the transfer equipment.

700.7 Signs

(A) Emergency Sources. A sign must be placed at service-entrance equipment indicating the type and location of each on-site emergency power source. ▶Figure 700-5

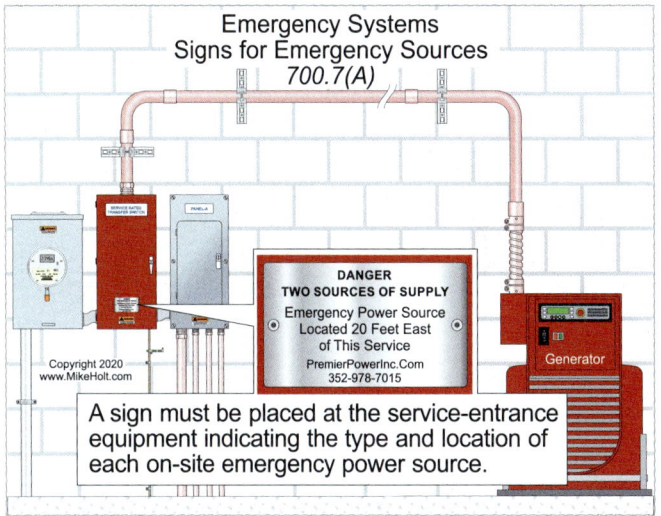
▶Figure 700-5

700.8 Surge Protection

A listed surge protective device must be installed for all emergency system panelboards and switchboards. ▶Figure 700-6

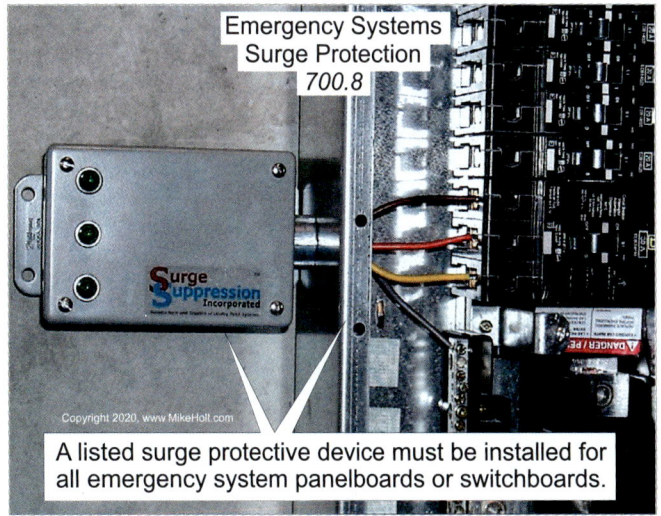
▶Figure 700-6

Part II. Circuit Wiring

700.10 Wiring

(A) Identification. Components of the emergency system must be permanently marked so they are easily identified as part of the emergency system.

(1) Boxes and enclosures, transfer switches, generators, and power panels for emergency circuits must be permanently marked as a component of an emergency circuit or system. ▶Figure 700-7

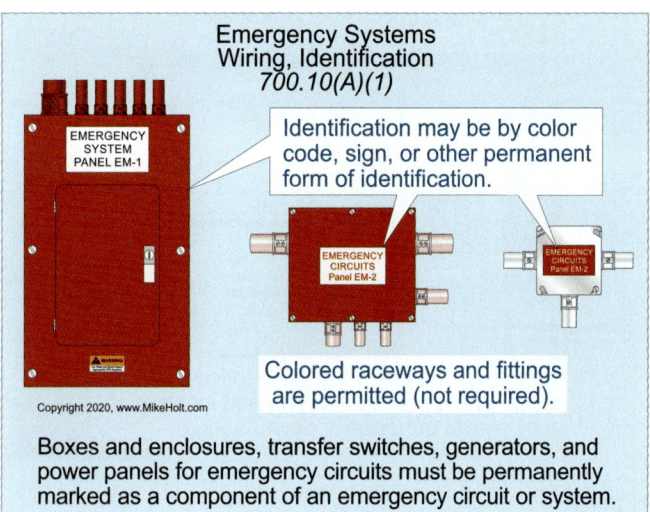

▶Figure 700-7

> **Author's Comment:**
>
> ▸ The marking required by this section for enclosures, cables, and raceways can be by any approved method that identifies the component(s) as part of the emergency system, such as the words "Emergency System," "Emergency Circuits," or by color code such as the use of a red raceway or box cover. Colored raceways and fittings are permitted but not required.

(2) Cable and raceway systems must be permanently marked as part of the emergency system at intervals not exceeding 25 ft.

Receptacles connected to the emergency power system must be identified by having a distinctive color or marking on either the receptacle or receptacle cover plate.

(B) Wiring. Emergency system conductors cannot be installed within any enclosure, raceway, cable, or luminaire with nonemergency loads, except for the following:

(1) Wiring in transfer equipment. ▶Figure 700-8

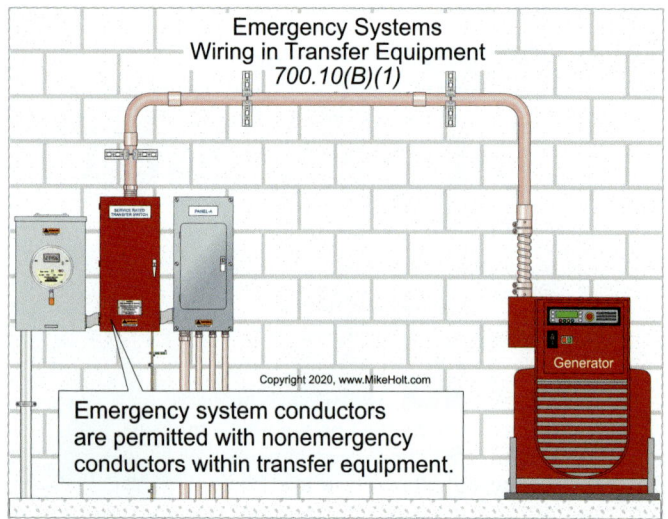

▶Figure 700-8

(2) Luminaires and exit signs supplied from emergency and other sources of power.

(3) Wiring from two sources in a listed load control relay supplying exit or emergency luminaires, or in a common junction box, attached to exit or emergency luminaires

(4) Wiring within a common junction box attached to unit equipment, containing only the branch circuit supplying the unit equipment and the emergency circuit supplied by the unit equipment

(5) Wiring from an emergency system can supply emergency and other loads in accordance with the following:

  a. Where the emergency and nonemergency loads are in separate vertical switchboard or switchgear sections or individual disconnects mounted in separate enclosures.

  b. Where the bus is:

   (i) Supplied by a feeder without overcurrent protection at the source.

   (ii) Supplied by a feeder with overcurrent protection that is selectively coordinated with the next downstream overcurrent protective device in the nonemergency system.

  c. Emergency circuits are not permitted to originate from the same vertical switchgear section, vertical switchboard section, panelboard enclosure, or individual disconnect enclosure as other circuits.

  d. It is permitted to utilize single or multiple feeders to supply distribution equipment between an emergency source and the point where the emergency loads are separated from all other loads.

Note: See *NEC* Note Figure 700.10(B)(5)(b)(1) and Note Figure 700.10(B)(5)(b)(2) for additional information.

Author's Comment:

▸ Separation of the circuits served by a generator source for emergency, legally required, and optional standby circuits may be accomplished by running feeders from a single generator to individual overcurrent protective devices, or to a distribution switchboard that separates emergency circuits in different vertical sections from other loads.

(C) Wiring Design and Location. Emergency wiring circuits must be designed and located to minimize the hazards that might cause failure due to flooding, fire, icing, vandalism, and other adverse conditions.

Part III. Sources of Power

700.12 General Requirements

In the event of failure of the normal supply to the building, emergency power must be available within 10 seconds. Emergency equipment must be energized from different sources in case of normal power failure. The emergency power supply must be any of the following:

(A) Power Source Considerations. In selecting an emergency source of power, consideration must be given to the occupancy and the type of service to be rendered, whether of minimum duration, as for evacuation of a theater, or longer duration, as for supplying emergency power and lighting due to an indefinite period of current failure from trouble either inside or outside the building.

(B) Equipment Design and Location. Equipment must be designed and located so as to minimize the hazards that might cause complete failure due to flooding, fires, icing, and vandalism.

(C) Storage Battery. Storage batteries are permitted as the emergency power source if of suitable rating and capacity to supply and maintain the total load for a period of at least 90 minutes, without the voltage applied to the load falling below 87½ percent of normal. Automotive-type batteries are not permitted for this purpose. Automatic battery charging means must be provided.

(D) Generator Set.

(1) Prime Mover-Driven. A generator approved by the authority having jurisdiction and sized in accordance with 700.4 is permitted as the emergency power source if it has means to automatically start the prime mover when the normal service fails.

(2) Internal Combustion Engines as Prime Movers.

(a) On-Site Fuel Supply. Where internal combustion engines are used as the prime mover, an on-site fuel supply must be provided with an on-premises fuel supply sufficient for not less than two hours' operation of the system. ▸Figure 700-9

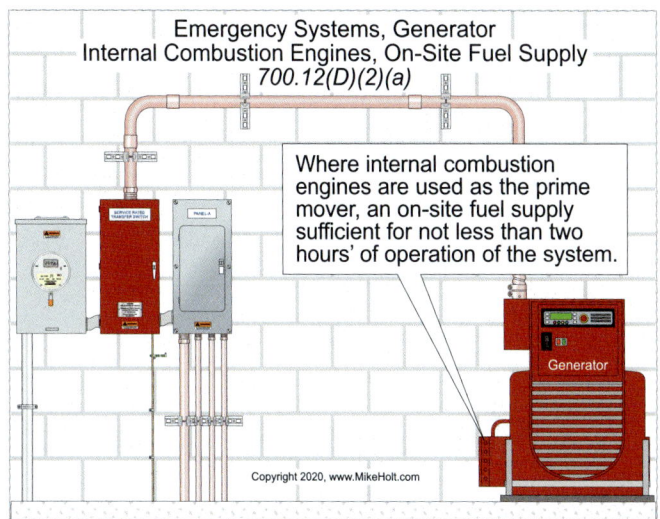

▸Figure 700-9

(b) Fuel Transfer Pumps. Where power is needed for the operation of the fuel transfer pumps to deliver fuel to a generator set day tank, this pump must be connected to the emergency power system.

(c) Public Gas System, Municipal Water Supply. Prime movers must not be solely dependent on a public utility gas system for their fuel supply or municipal water supply for their cooling systems.

Ex: Where approved by the authority having jurisdiction, the use of other than on-site fuels is permitted where there is a low probability of a simultaneous failure of both the off-site fuel delivery system and power from the outside electrical utility company.

(d) Automatic Fuel Transfer. Where dual fuel supplies are used, means must be provided for automatically transferring from one fuel supply to another.

(5) Outdoor Generator Sets. If the generator is equipped with a readily accessible disconnecting means located within sight of the building, an additional disconnecting means is not required at the building or structure. ▸Figure 700-10

(E) Uninterruptible Power Supplies. Uninterruptible power supplies are permitted as the emergency power source if they comply with the applicable requirements of 700.12(B) and (C).

(F) Separate Service. An additional service is permitted as the emergency power source where approved by the authority having jurisdiction [230.2(A)] and the following: ▸Figure 700-11

700.12 | Emergency Systems

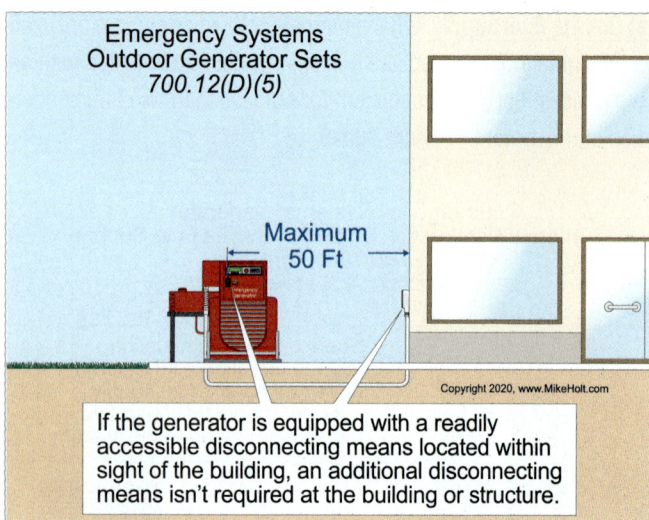

▶Figure 700–10

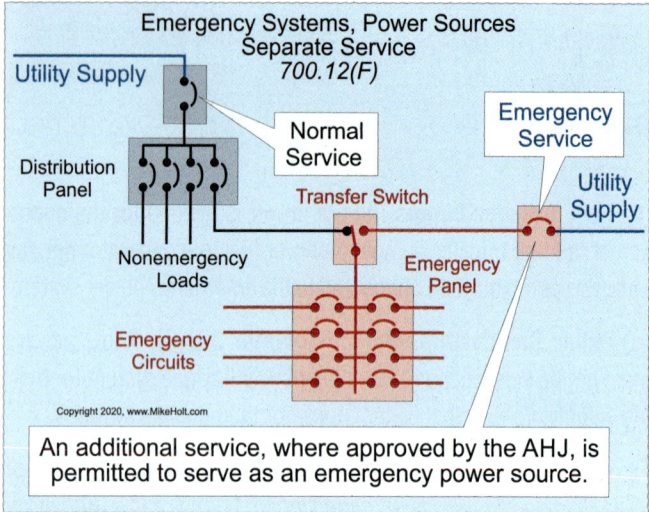

▶Figure 700–11

(1) Separate service conductors are installed from the utility.

(2) The emergency service conductors are electrically and physically remote from other service conductors to minimize the possibility of simultaneous interruption of supply.

Author's Comment:

▶ To minimize the possibility of simultaneous interruption, the service disconnect for the emergency system must be located remotely from the other power system's service disconnect [230.72(B)].

(H) Direct-Current Microgrid Systems. Sources connected to a dc microgrid system are permitted where the system is capable of being isolated from all nonemergency sources. Direct-current microgrid systems used as a source of power for emergency systems must be of suitable rating and capacity to supply and maintain the total emergency load for not less than 2 hours of full-demand operation. Where a dc microgrid system source serves as the normal supply for the building or group of buildings concerned, it must not serve as the sole source of power for the emergency standby system.

(I) Emergency Battery Pack Unit Equipment.

(1) Components of Unit Equipment. Individual emergency lighting battery pack unit equipment is permitted as the emergency power source.

(2) Installation of Unit Equipment. Unit equipment must be permanently fixed in place with any Chapter 3 wiring method, or a cord-and-plug connection with a flexible cord not longer than 3 ft in length.

(3) The branch-circuit wiring that supplies emergency battery pack equipment must be one of the following:

a. The same branch circuit serving the normal lighting in the area, with a connection ahead of any local switches. ▶Figure 700–12

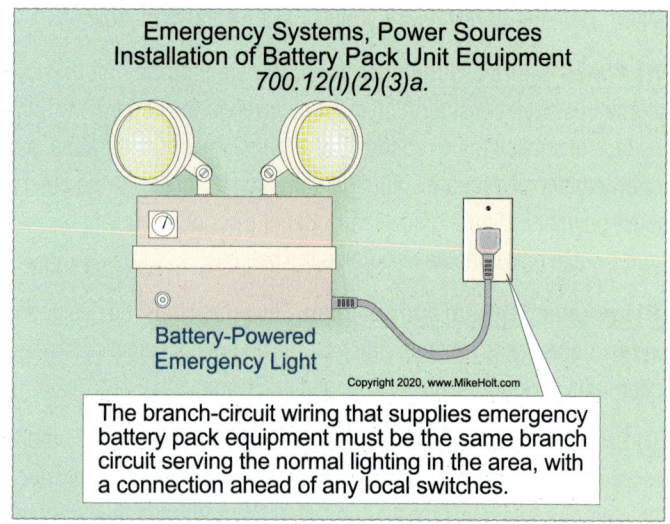

▶Figure 700–12

Author's Comment:

▶ There are two reasons why the emergency battery pack unit equipment must be connected ahead of the switch controlling the normal area lighting: (1) in the event of a power loss to the lighting circuit, the emergency battery lighting packs will activate and provide emergency lighting for people to exit the building, and (2) the emergency lighting battery packs will not turn on when the switch controlling normal lighting is turned off.

b. Where the normal lighting circuit is served by one or more branch circuits, a separate branch circuit, provided with a lock-on feature, that originates from the same panelboard as the normal lighting circuits. The branch-circuit disconnecting means for this branch circuit must be provided with a lock-on feature.

(4) The branch circuit that feeds the emergency battery pack unit equipment must be clearly identified at the distribution panel.

Author's Comment:

- Identification and marking must be in accordance with 110.22(A) and 408.4(A).

(6) Power for remote heads providing the exterior lighting of an exit door can be supplied by the emergency battery pack unit equipment serving the area immediately inside the exit door.

Part IV. Emergency System Circuits for Lighting and Power

700.15 Loads on Emergency Branch Circuits

Emergency circuits must only supply emergency loads.

700.16 Emergency Illumination

(A) General. Emergency illumination must include means of egress lighting, illuminated exit signs, and all other luminaires specified as necessary to provide the required illumination.

(B) System Reliability. Emergency lighting systems must be designed and installed so that the failure of any illumination source will not leave in total darkness any space that requires emergency illumination. ▶Figure 700–13

Author's Comment:

- This means that a single remote head is never sufficient for an area. A minimum of two lighting heads is always required. This is the reason individual emergency battery pack unit equipment (sometimes called "Bugeyes" in the field) always has two lighting heads.

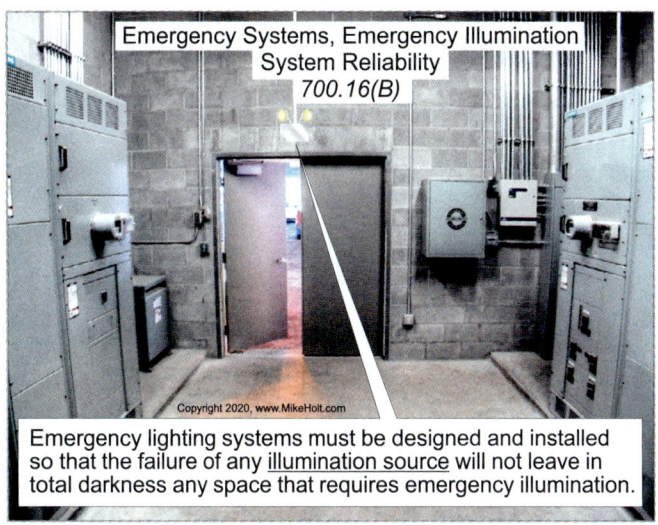
▶Figure 700–13

Control devices installed in emergency lighting systems must be listed for use in those systems. See 700.12(F).

Note: 700.23 through 700.26 provides requirements for applications for emergency system control devices.

(D) Disconnecting Means. When an emergency system is installed, emergency illumination is required for an indoor service disconnect.
▶Figure 700–14

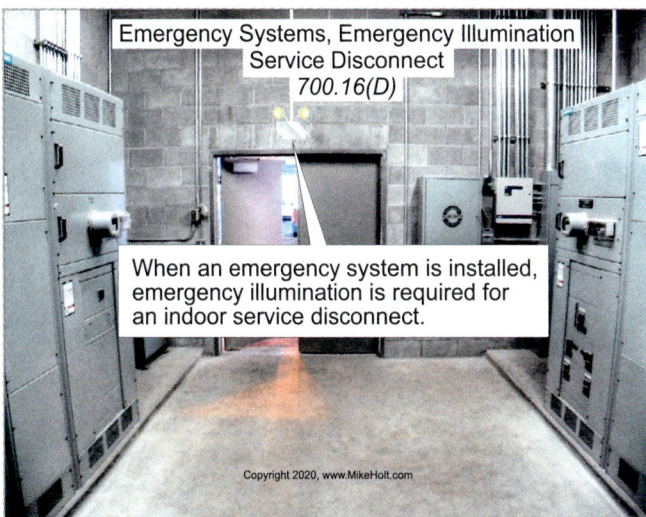
▶Figure 700–14

700.19 | Emergency Systems

700.19 Multiwire Branch Circuits

Multiwire branch circuits are not permitted to supply emergency system circuits. ▶Figure 700–15

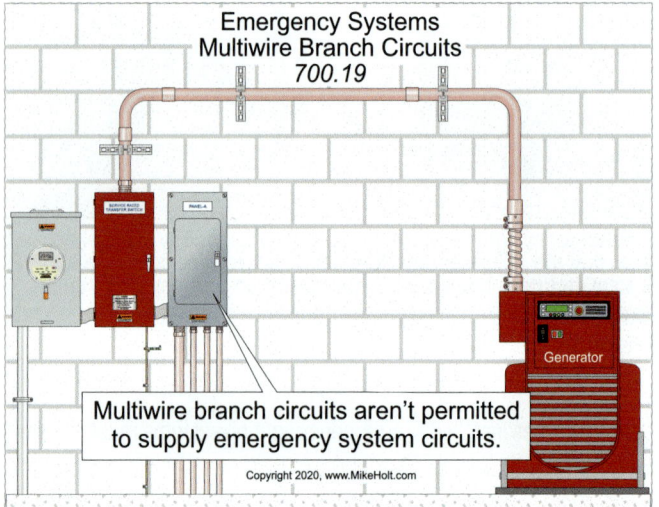

▶Figure 700–15

Part VI. Overcurrent Protection

700.30 Accessibility

The branch-circuit overcurrent devices for emergency circuits must be accessible to authorized persons only.

700.32 Selective Coordination

Overcurrent devices for emergency power systems must be selectively coordinated with all supply-side overcurrent protective devices. The design must be made by an engineer or similarly qualified person and it must be documented and made available to those authorized to design, install, inspect, maintain, and operate the system.

> **Author's Comment:**
>
> ▸ According to Article 100, "Selective Coordination" means the overcurrent protection scheme confines the interruption to a specific area rather than to the whole system. For example, if a short circuit or ground fault occurs with selective coordination, the only breaker/fuse that will open is the one protecting just the branch circuit involved. Without selective coordination, an entire floor of a building can go dark.

Note: See the *NEC* Note Figure 700.32 for an example of how emergency system overcurrent protective devices (OCPDs) selectively coordinate with all supply-side OCPDs.

NEC Note Figure 700.32 Emergency System Selective Coordination

▸ OCPD D selectively coordinates with OCPDs C, F, E, B, and A.
▸ OCPD C selectively coordinates with OCPDs F, E, B, and A.
▸ OCPD F selectively coordinates with OCPD E.
▸ OCPD B is not required to selectively coordinate with OCPD A because OCPD B is not an emergency system OCPD.

ARTICLE 701 — LEGALLY REQUIRED STANDBY SYSTEMS

Introduction to Article 701—Legally Required Standby Systems

In the hierarchy of electrical systems, Article 700 Emergency Systems receives top priority. Taking the number two spot is Legally Required Standby Systems, which fall under Article 701. Legally required standby systems must supply standby power in 60 seconds or less after a power loss. Some examples of required standby circuits are those supplying fire command center power and lighting, ventilation and automatic fire detection, and egress elevators.

Article 700 basically applies to systems or equipment required to protect people who are in an emergency and trying to get out, while Article 701 addresses systems or equipment needed to help people responding to the emergency.

Part I. General

701.1 Scope

Article 701 applies to the installation, operation, and maintenance of legally required standby systems consisting of circuits and equipment intended to supply illumination or power when the normal electrical supply or system is interrupted. ▶Figure 701–1

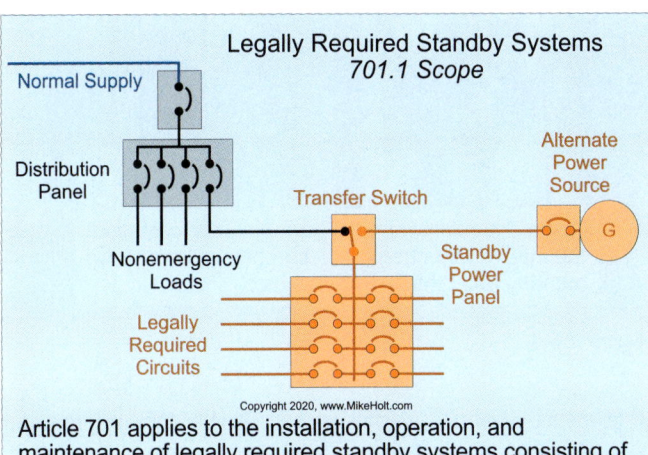

Article 701 applies to the installation, operation, and maintenance of legally required standby systems consisting of circuits and equipment intended to supply illumination or power when the normal electrical supply or system is interrupted.

▶Figure 701–1

Author's Comment:

▸ Legally required standby systems provide electric power to aid in firefighting, rescue operations, control of health hazards, and similar operations.

701.2 Definition

The definition in this section applies throughout the *Code*.

Legally Required Standby Systems. Legally required standby systems are those systems classified as legally required by any governmental agency having jurisdiction. These systems are intended to automatically supply power to selected loads (other than those classed as emergency loads) in the event of failure of the normal power source. ▶Figure 701–2

Note: Legally required standby systems typically supply loads such as heating and refrigeration systems, communications systems (twisted pair, antennas, and coaxial cable), ventilation and smoke removal systems, sewage disposal, lighting systems, and industrial processes that, when stopped, could create hazards or hamper rescue or firefighting operations.

701.3 | Legally Required Standby Systems

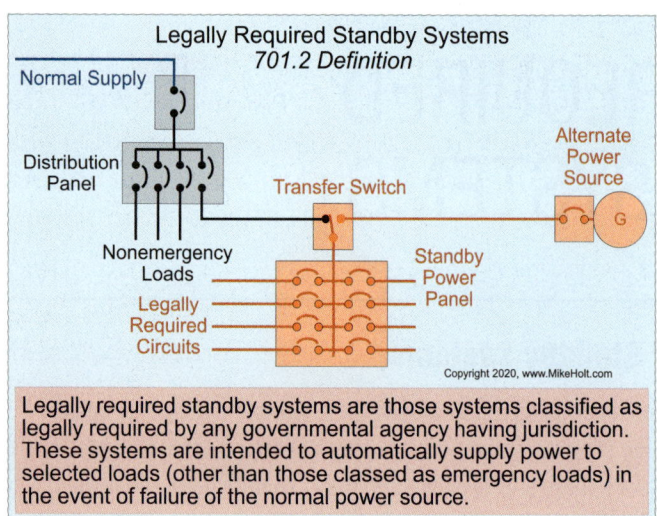

▶Figure 701-2

701.3 Tests and Maintenance

(A) Conduct or Witness Test. To ensure that the legally required standby system meets or exceeds the original installation specifications, the authority having jurisdiction must conduct or witness an acceptance test of the legally required system upon completion of the installation.

(B) Periodic Testing. Legally required standby systems must be periodically tested in a manner approved by the authority having jurisdiction to ensure adequate maintenance has been performed and the systems are in proper operating condition.

> **Author's Comment:**
>
> ▶ Running the legally required standby system under the loads of the facility to make sure power transfers within 60 seconds is often considered an acceptable method of operational testing.

(C) Maintenance. Legally required standby system equipment must be maintained in accordance with the manufacturer's instructions and industry standards.

(D) Written Record. A written record must be kept of all required tests and maintenance.

> **Author's Comment:**
>
> ▶ The *NEC* does not specify the required record retention period.

701.4 Capacity and Rating

(A) Rating. Equipment for a legally required standby system must be suitable for the available fault current at its terminals.

(B) Capacity. The alternate power supply must have adequate capacity in accordance with Article 220 or by another approved method.

(C) Load Pickup, Load Shedding, and Peak Load Shaving. The legally required standby alternate power supply can supply legally required standby and optional standby system loads if there is adequate capacity or where automatic selective load pickup and load shedding are provided that will ensure adequate power to the legally required standby system circuits.

701.5 Transfer Equipment

(A) General. Transfer equipment must be automatic, listed, and marked for emergency system or legally required standby system use, and approved by the authority having jurisdiction. Transfer equipment must prevent the inadvertent interconnection of legally required standby and other power systems. ▶Figure 701-3

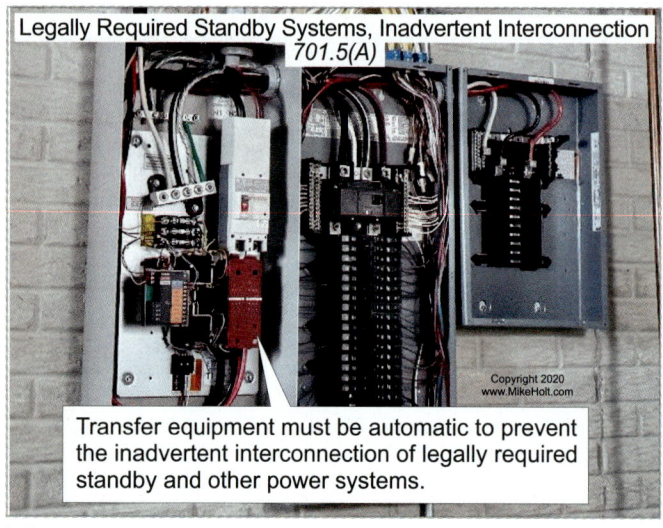

▶Figure 701-3

Meter-mounted transfer switches are not permitted for legally required standby system use.

(C) Automatic Transfer Switch. Automatic transfer switches must able to be electrically operated and mechanically held, and they are not permitted to be reconditioned.

(D) Documentation. The short-circuit current rating of the transfer equipment must be field marked on the exterior of the transfer equipment.

701.6 Signals

Audible and visual signal devices must be installed where practicable for the purposes of:

(A) Malfunction. To indicate a malfunction of the standby source of power.

(B) Carrying Load. To indicate that the standby source is carrying load.

(C) Not Functioning. To indicate that the battery charger is not functioning.

(D) Ground Fault. To indicate a ground fault in solidly grounded wye, legally required standby systems of more than 150V to ground and circuit protective devices rated 1,000A or more.

701.7 Signs

(A) Mandated Standby. A sign must be placed at the service-entrance equipment indicating the type and location of on-site legally required standby power systems. ▶Figure 701-4

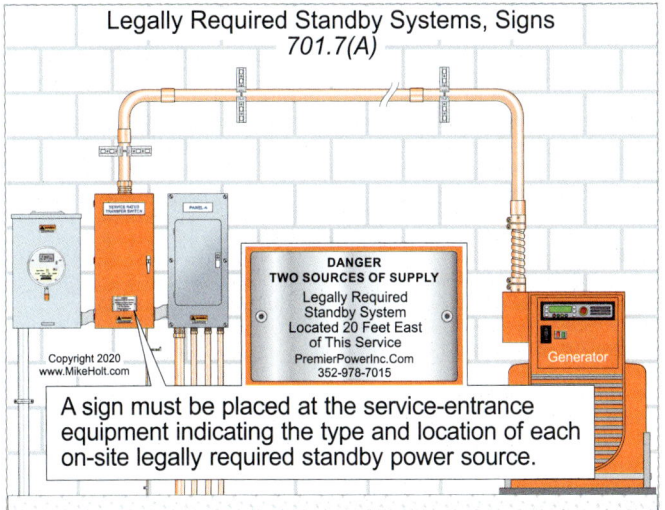

▶Figure 701-4

Part II. Circuit Wiring

701.10 Wiring

Legally required standby system wiring is permitted to be in the same raceways, boxes, and cabinets with other general wiring.

Part III. Sources of Power

701.12 General Requirements

If the normal supply fails, legally required standby power must be available within 60 seconds. The supply system for the legally required standby power supply is permitted to be one or more of the following:

(A) Power Source Considerations. In selecting a legally required standby source of power, consideration must be given to the type of service to be rendered, whether of short-time duration or long duration.

(B) Equipment Design and Location. Consideration must be given to the location or design, or both, of all equipment to minimize the hazards that might cause complete failure due to floods, fires, icing, and vandalism.

Note: For further information, see ANSI/IEEE 493, *Recommended Practice for the Design of Reliable Industrial and Commercial Power Systems*.

(C) Storage Battery. Storage batteries must be of suitable rating and capacity to supply and maintain the total load for a minimum period of 90 minutes without the voltage applied to the load falling below 87½ percent of normal. Automotive-type batteries are not permitted. Automatic battery charging means must be provided.

(D) Generator Set.

(1) Prime Mover-Driven. A generator approved by the authority having jurisdiction and sized in accordance with 701.4 is permitted as the legally required power source if it has the means to automatically start the prime mover on failure of the normal service.

(2) Internal Combustion Engines as Prime Mover. Where internal combustion engines are used as the prime mover, an on-site fuel supply must be provided for not less than two hours of operation of the system. ▶Figure 701-5

(5) Outdoor Generator Sets. If the generator is equipped with a readily accessible disconnecting means located within sight of the building, an additional disconnecting means is not required at the building or structure. ▶Figure 701-6

(E) Uninterruptible Power Supplies. Uninterruptible power supplies are permitted as the legally required power source and must comply with 701.12(B) and (C).

(F) Separate Service. An additional service is permitted as the legally required power source where approved by the authority having jurisdiction [230.2(A)] and separate service conductors are installed from the utility. ▶Figure 701-7

701.30 | Legally Required Standby Systems

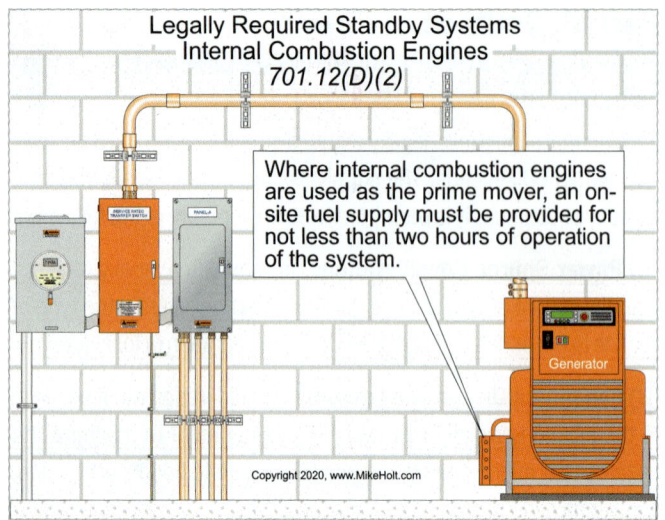

▶Figure 701-5

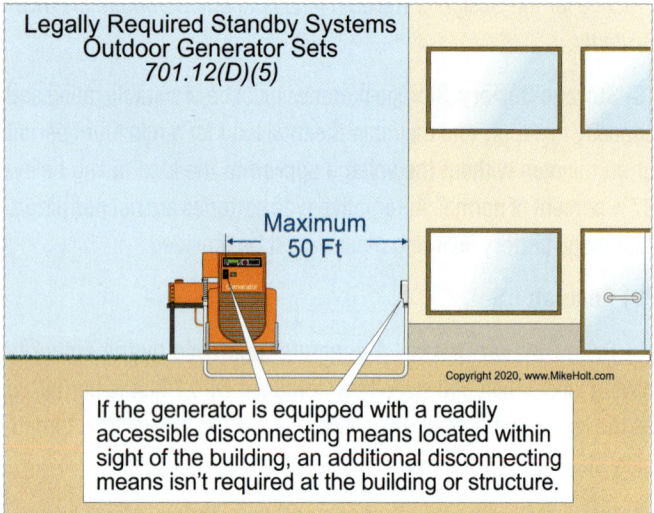

▶Figure 701-6

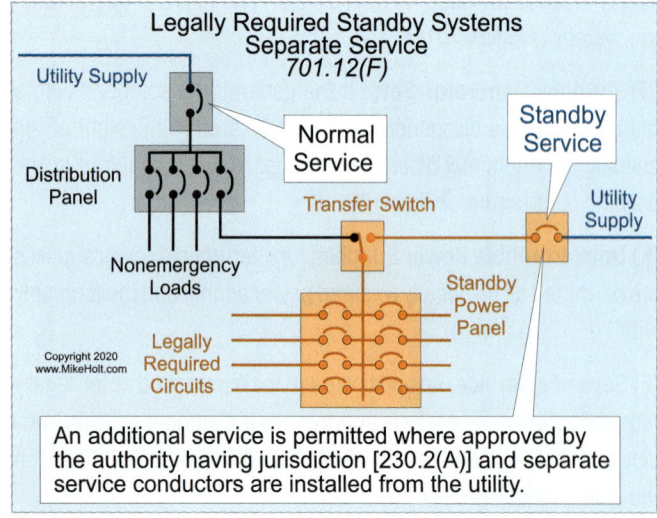

▶Figure 701-7

The legally required service conductors must be electrically and physically remote from other service conductors to minimize the possibility of simultaneous interruption of supply.

> **Author's Comment:**
>
> ▸ To minimize the possibility of simultaneous interruption, the service disconnect for the legally required power system must be located remotely from the other power system's service disconnect [230.72(B)].

(G) Connection Ahead of Service Disconnecting Means. If approved by the authority having jurisdiction, connection ahead of, but not within, the same cabinet, enclosure, or vertical switchboard or switchgear section is permitted as the legally required power source. See 230.82(5) for additional information. ▶Figure 701-8

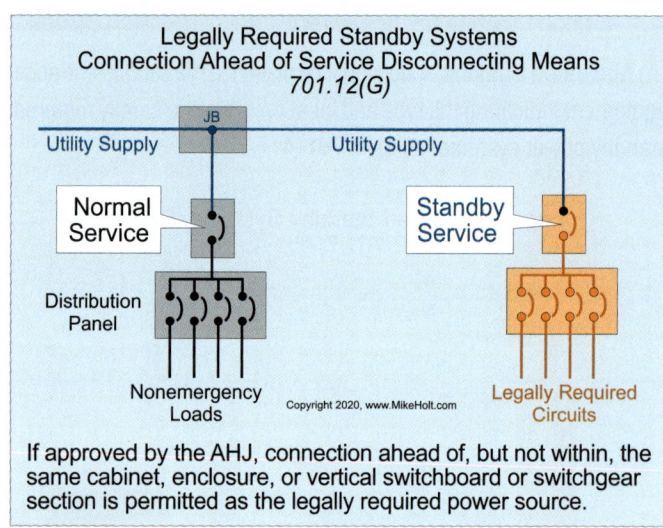

▶Figure 701-8

To minimize the possibility of simultaneous interruption, the disconnect for the legally required power system must be located remotely from other power system service disconnects.

Part IV. Overcurrent Protection

701.30 Accessibility

The branch-circuit overcurrent devices for legally required standby circuits must be accessible to authorized persons only.

701.32 Selective Coordination

Overcurrent devices for legally required standby systems must be selectively coordinated with all supply-side overcurrent protective devices. The design must be made by an engineer or similarly qualified person and it must be documented and made available to those authorized to design, install, inspect, maintain, and operate the system.

Author's Comment:

▶ According to Article 100, "Selective Coordination" means the overcurrent protection scheme confines the interruption to a specific area rather than to the whole system. For example, if a short circuit or ground fault occurs with selective coordination, the only breaker/fuse that will open is the one protecting just the branch circuit involved. Without selective coordination, an entire floor of a building can go dark.

Note: See the *NEC* Note Figure 701.32 for an example of how legally required standby system overcurrent protective devices (OCPDs) selectively coordinate with all supply-side OCPDs.

NEC Note Figure 701.32 Emergency System Selective Coordination

▶ OCPD D selectively coordinates with OCPDs C, F, E, B, and A.
▶ OCPD C selectively coordinates with OCPDs F, E, B, and A.
▶ OCPD F selectively coordinates with OCPD E.
▶ OCPD B is not required to selectively coordinate with OCPD A because OCPD B is not a legally required standby system OCPD.

Notes

ARTICLE 702 — OPTIONAL STANDBY SYSTEMS

Introduction to Article 702—Optional Standby Systems

Taking third priority after Emergency and Legally Required Systems, Optional Standby Systems protect public or private facilities or property where life safety does not depend on the performance of the system. These systems are not required for rescue operations.

Suppose a glass plant loses power. Once glass hardens in the equipment (which it will do when process heat is lost) the plant is going to suffer a great deal of downtime and expense before it can resume operations. An optional standby system can prevent this loss.

You will see these systems in facilities where loss of power can cause economic loss or business interruptions. Data centers can lose millions of dollars from a single minute of lost power. A chemical or pharmaceutical plant can lose an entire batch from a single momentary power glitch. In many cases, the lost revenue cannot be recouped.

This article also applies to the installation of optional standby generators in homes, farms, small businesses, and many other applications where standby power is not legally required.

Part I. General

702.1 Scope

The systems covered by Article 702 consist of those permanently installed, including prime movers, and those arranged for connection to a premises wiring system from a portable alternate power supply. ▶Figure 702–1

Author's Comment:

▸ Article 702 covers portable alternate power supplies such as trailer- and vehicle-mounted generators, and small units that might be used for a small premises such as a dwelling. ▶Figure 702–2

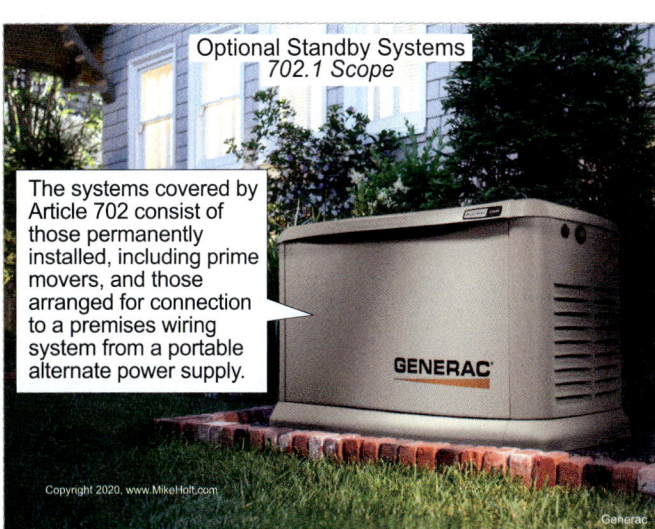

▶Figure 702–1

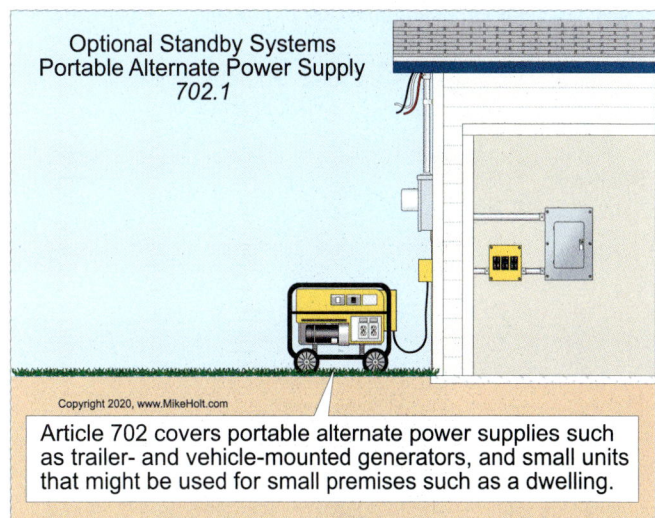

▶Figure 702–2

702.2 | Optional Standby Systems

Author's Comment:

▸ Portable generators for temporary power are not covered by Article 702 if they are not connected to the premises wiring. ▸Figure 702–3

▸Figure 702–3

702.2 Definition

The definition in this section applies throughout the *Code*.

Optional Standby Systems. Optional standby systems are intended to supply power to public or private facilities, or to property where life safety does not depend on the performance of the system. These systems are intended to supply on-site generated or stored power to selected loads either automatically or manually. ▸Figure 702–4

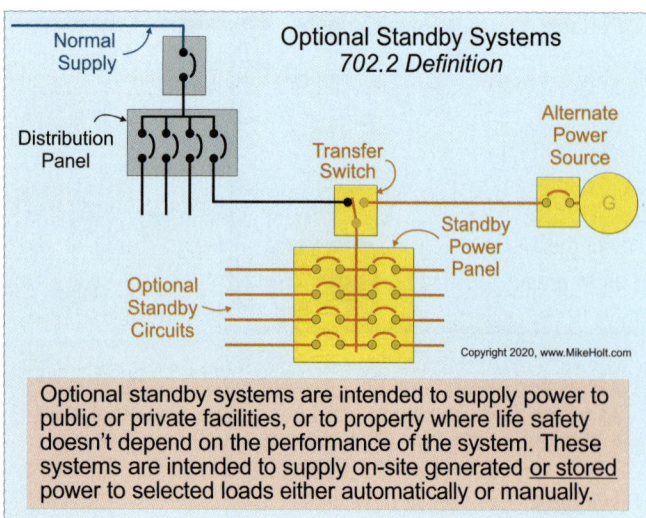

▸Figure 702–4

Note: Optional standby systems are typically installed to provide an alternate source of electric power for such facilities as industrial and commercial buildings, farms, and residences and to serve loads such as heating and refrigeration systems, data processing and communications systems (twisted pair and coaxial cable), and industrial processes that, when stopped during any power outage, can cause discomfort, economic loss, serious interruption of the process, damage to the product or process, or the like.

702.4 Capacity and Rating

(A) Available Fault Current. Optional standby system equipment must be suitable for the available fault current at its terminals.

(B) System Capacity.

(1) Manual Transfer Equipment. Where manual transfer equipment is used, an optional standby system must be capable of supplying all of the equipment intended to be operated at one time. The user of the optional standby system is permitted to select the load connected to the system.

Author's Comment:

▸ When a manual transfer switch is used, the user of the optional standby system selects the loads to be connected to the system, which determines the system's kVA/kW rating.

(2) Automatic Transfer Equipment. An optional standby generator must be sized to the calculated load in accordance with Article 220 or by another approved method. ▸Figure 702–5

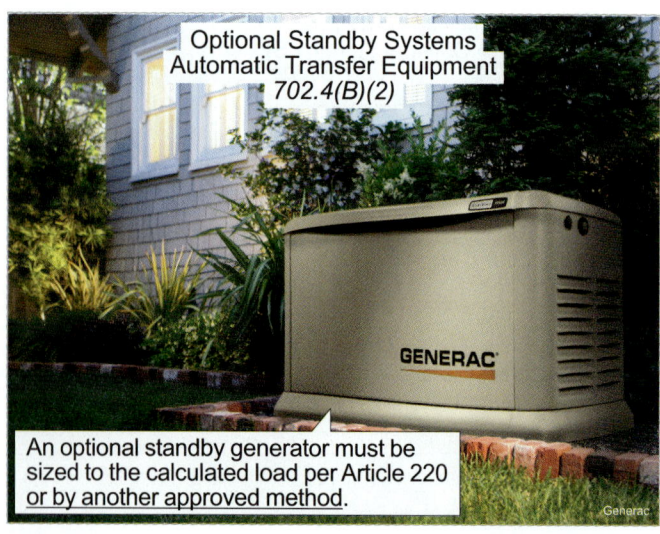

▸Figure 702–5

(a) Full Load. The standby source must be capable of supplying the full load upon automatic transfer.

(b) Load Management. Where an automatic load management system is employed, the standby system must be capable of supplying the full load that will be connected.

> **Author's Comment:**
>
> ▸ For existing facilities, the maximum demand data for one year or the average power demand for a 15-minute period over a minimum of 30 days can be used to size the electric power source [220.87]. ▶Figure 702–6

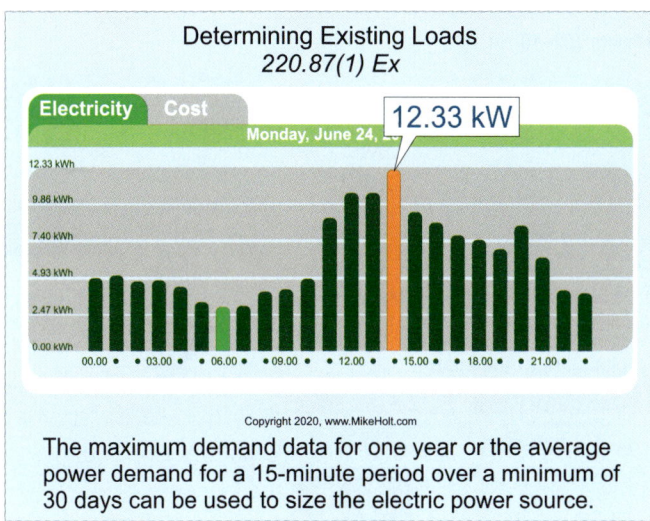

▶Figure 702–6

▶Figure 702–7

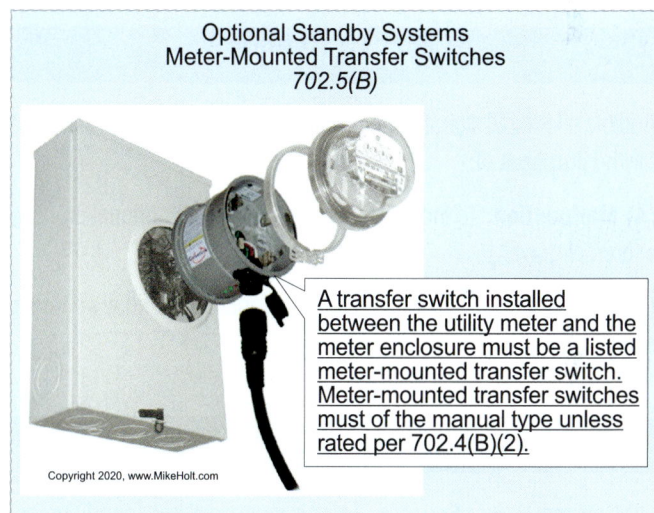

▶Figure 702–8

702.5 Transfer Equipment

(A) General. Transfer equipment (manual or automatic) is required for the connection of an optional power supply. ▶Figure 702–7

Ex: Temporary connection of a portable generator without transfer equipment is permitted where conditions of maintenance and supervision ensure that only qualified persons will service the installation, and where the normal supply is physically isolated by a lockable disconnect or by the disconnection of the normal supply conductors.

(B) Meter-Mounted Transfer Switches. A transfer switch installed between the utility meter and the meter enclosure must be a listed meter-mounted transfer switch. Meter-mounted transfer switches must be of the manual type unless rated in accordance with 702.4(B)(2). ▶Figure 702–8

(C) Documentation. In other than dwelling units, the short-circuit current rating of the transfer equipment must be field marked on the exterior of the transfer equipment.

(D) Inadvertent Interconnection. Transfer equipment must be suitable for the intended use and must be listed, designed, and installed so as to prevent the inadvertent interconnection of all sources of supply in any operation of the transfer equipment. ▶Figure 702–9

(E) Parallel Installation. Transfer equipment and electric power production systems installed to permit operation in parallel with the normal source must also meet the requirements of Article 705.

702.6 | Optional Standby Systems

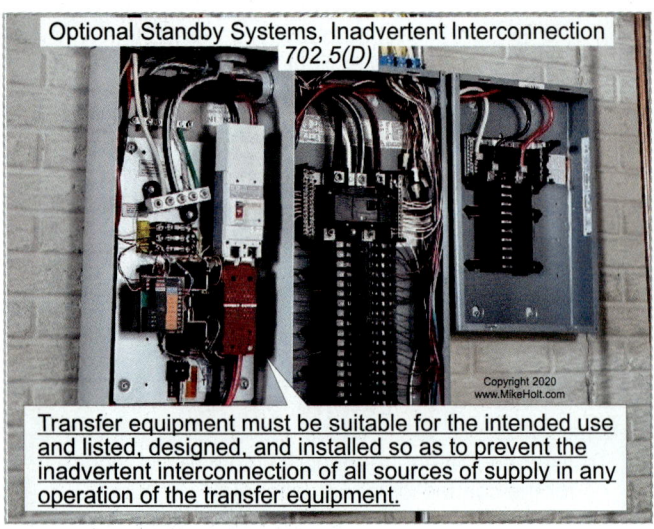
▶Figure 702-9

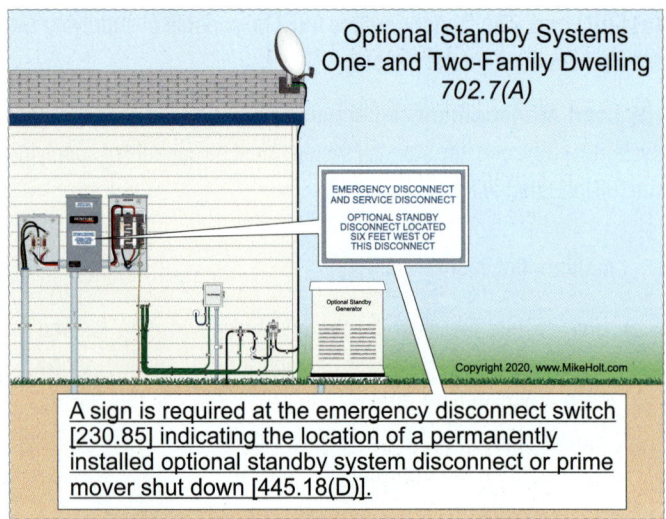
▶Figure 702-10

702.6 Signals

Audible and visual signal devices must be installed where practicable for the purposes of:

(A) Malfunction. To indicate a malfunction of the optional standby source of power.

(B) Carrying Load. To indicate that the optional standby source is carrying load.

702.7 Signs

(A) Optional Power Sources. A sign is required at service equipment for commercial and industrial installations that indicates the type and location of each on-site optional standby power source.

For one- and two-family dwelling units, a sign is required at the emergency disconnect switch mandated in 230.85 that indicates the location of each permanently installed on-site optional standby power source disconnect or means to shut down the prime mover as required in 445.18(D). ▶Figure 702-10

(C) Power Inlet. Where a power inlet is used for a temporary connection to a portable generator, a warning sign must be placed near the inlet to indicate the type of transformer permitted to be connected to the inlet stating: ▶Figure 702-11

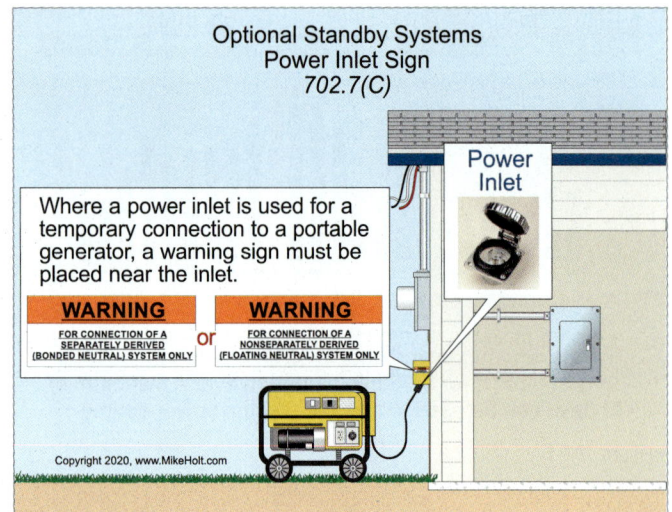
▶Figure 702-11

WARNING—FOR CONNECTION OF A SEPARATELY DERIVED (BONDED NEUTRAL) SYSTEM ONLY
OR
WARNING—FOR CONNECTION OF A NONSEPARATELY DERIVED (FLOATING NEUTRAL) SYSTEM ONLY

Part II. Circuit Wiring

702.10 Wiring

Optional standby system wiring can occupy the same raceways, cables, boxes, and cabinets with other wiring.

Optional Standby Systems | **702.12**

702.11 Portable Generator Grounding

(A) Separately Derived System. Where a portable generator has the neutral conductor bonded to the equipment grounding conductor (separately derived system), it must be grounded in accordance with 250.30. ▶Figure 702-12

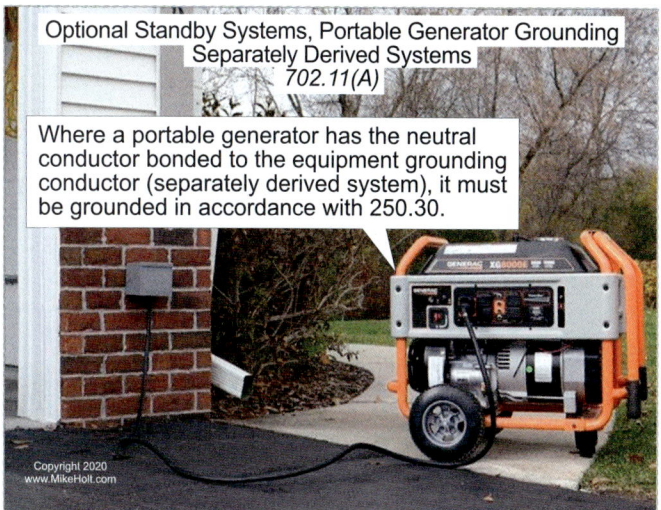

▶Figure 702-12

(B) Nonseparately Derived System. Where a portable generator does not have the neutral conductor bonded to the equipment grounding conductor, the generator must be grounded in accordance with 250.34(A).

702.12 Outdoor Generator Sets

(A) Portable Generators Greater Than 15 kW and Permanently Installed Generators. Where an outdoor generator set is equipped with a readily accessible disconnecting means located within sight of the building or structure supplied, an additional disconnecting means is not required for the building. ▶Figure 702-13

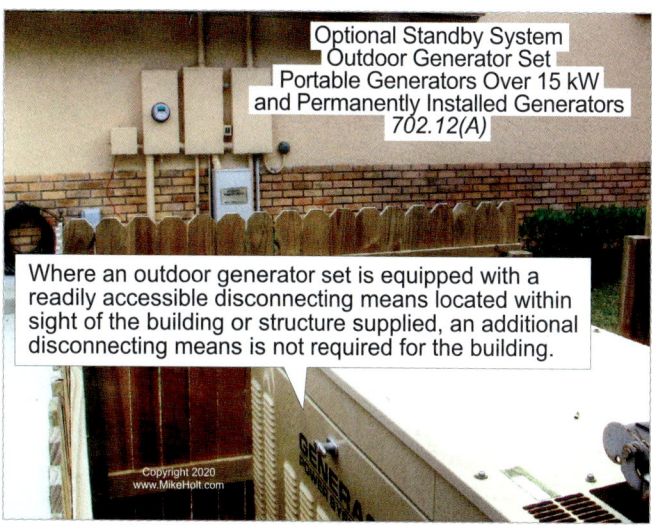

▶Figure 702-13

(B) Portable Generators 15 kW or Less. Where a portable generator rated 15 kW or less is installed using a flanged inlet, a disconnecting means is not required.

Notes

ARTICLE 705
INTERCONNECTED ELECTRIC POWER PRODUCTION SOURCES

Introduction to Article 705—Interconnected Electric Power Production Sources

Anytime there is more than one source of power supplying a building, safety concerns arise. In cases where a source such as a generator is used strictly for backup power, Articles 700, 701, or 702 require transfer switches and other safety measures to be implemented. When interconnected electrical power production sources, such as wind powered generators, solar PV systems, or fuel cells are connected in parallel with utility power, there is no transfer switch. In fact, there will often be multiple sources of electrical supply connected simultaneously.

Article 705 covers the requirements for the interconnection of electric power sources that operate in parallel with a primary source. The primary source is typically the electric utility power source, but it can be an on-site source.

Part I. General

705.1 Scope

This article covers the installation of electric power production sources operating in parallel with the primary source of electricity. ▶Figure 705–1

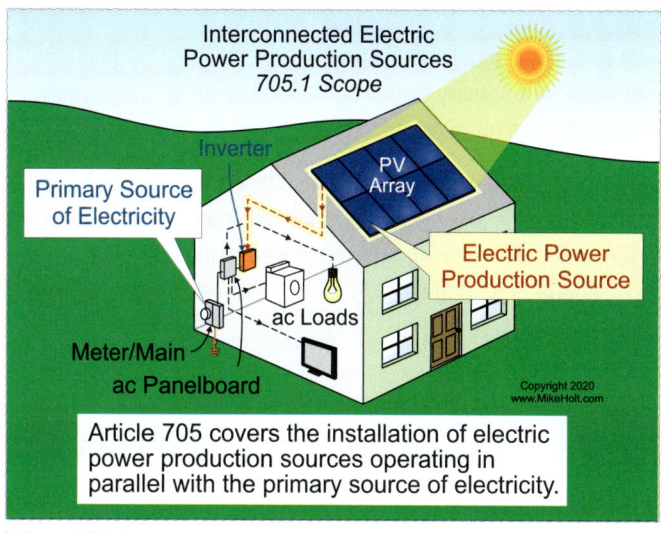

▶Figure 705–1

Note: The primary source of electricity typically includes the electric utility or it can be an on-site power source(s).

Author's Comment:

▸ Other on-site sources include:

   ▸ Energy storage systems, Article 706.
   ▸ Fuel cells, Article 692.
   ▸ Generators, Article 445.
   ▸ Solar PV systems, Article 690.
   ▸ Large-scale PV electric power production facilities, Article 691.
   ▸ Storage batteries, Article 480.
   ▸ Wind electric systems, Article 694.

705.2 Definitions

The definitions in this section apply within this article and throughout the *Code*.

Microgrid Interconnect Device. A device that enables a microgrid system to separate from and reconnect to operate in parallel with a primary power source. ▶Figure 705–2

Note: Microgrid controllers typically are used to measure and evaluate electrical parameters and provide the logic for the signal to initiate and complete transition processes.

705.6 | Interconnected Electric Power Production Sources

▶Figure 705–2

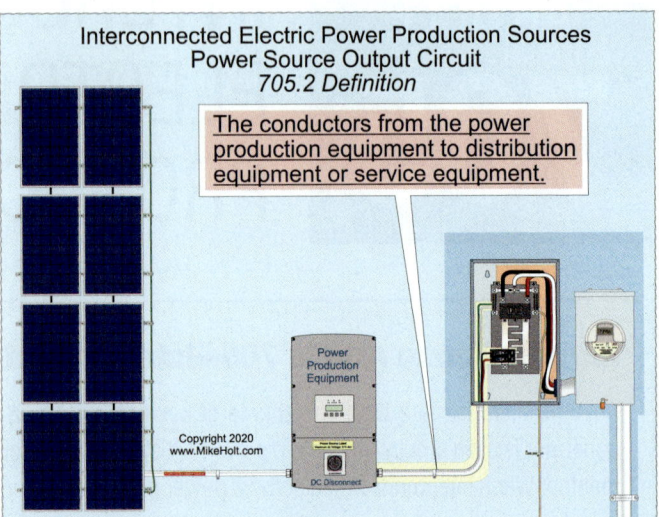
▶Figure 705–4

Microgrid System. A premises wiring system that has generation, energy storage, and load(s), or any combination of them, that includes the ability to disconnect from and operate in parallel with the primary source. ▶Figure 705–3

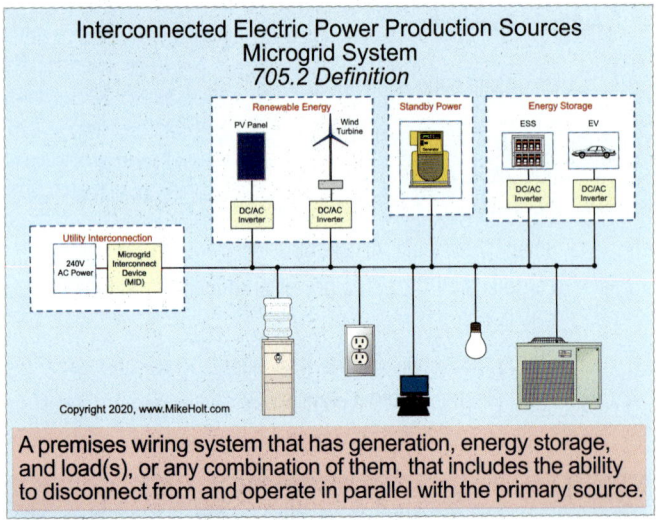
▶Figure 705–3

Power Source Output Circuit. The conductors from the power production equipment to distribution equipment or service equipment. ▶Figure 705–4

705.6 Equipment Approval

Interactive equipment intended to operate in parallel with electric power production sources including (but not limited to) interactive inverters, engine generators, energy storage equipment, and wind turbines must be approved for interactive function and be listed or be evaluated for interactive function and have a field label applied, or both.

705.8 System Installation

The installation of electrical power production sources operating in parallel with a primary source of electricity (electric utility) must be performed by a qualified person.

Note: A qualified person is one who has the knowledge related to the construction and operation of the interconnection of electrical power production sources and installations; along with safety training to recognize and avoid hazards to persons and property relating to those systems [Article 100]. ▶Figure 705–5

705.10 Identification of Power Sources

A permanent plaque or directory must be installed at each utility service disconnecting means location, or at an approved readily visible location. The plaque or directory must indicate the location of all building power source disconnecting means and be grouped with other plaques or directories for other on-site sources of power. ▶Figure 705–6

Interconnected Electric Power Production Sources | 705.11

▶Figure 705-5

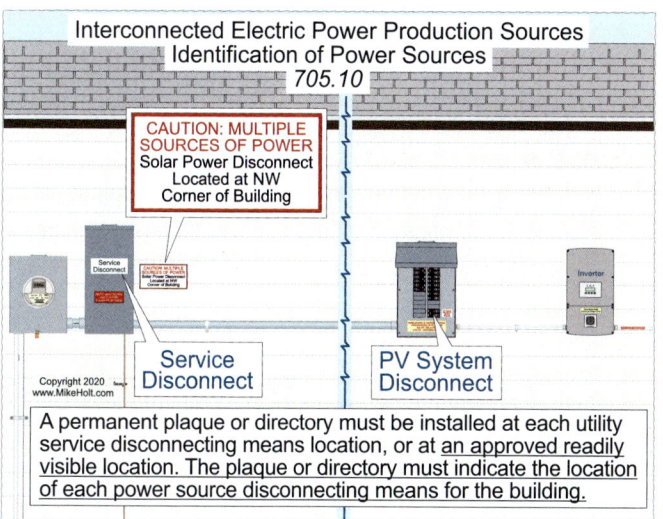

▶Figure 705-6

The plaque or directory must be marked with the wording "CAUTION: MULTIPLE SOURCES OF POWER." Any posted diagrams must be correctly oriented with respect to the diagram's location.

The marking must be permanently affixed and have sufficient durability to withstand the environment involved [110.21(B)].

Ex: Plaques or directories for installations having multiple co-located power production sources are permitted to be identified as a group(s). A plaque or directory is not required for each power source.

Author's Comment:

▸ The exception to 705.10 infers that since there is typically only one utility supply location that if there are other alternative power sources at remote locations, only one plaque or directory is required at the utility source indicating the location of the other remote power sources.

705.11 Supply-Side Source Connections

An electric power production source connected on the supply side of the electric utility service disconnecting means as permitted in 230.82(6) must comply with (A) through (E): ▶Figure 705-7

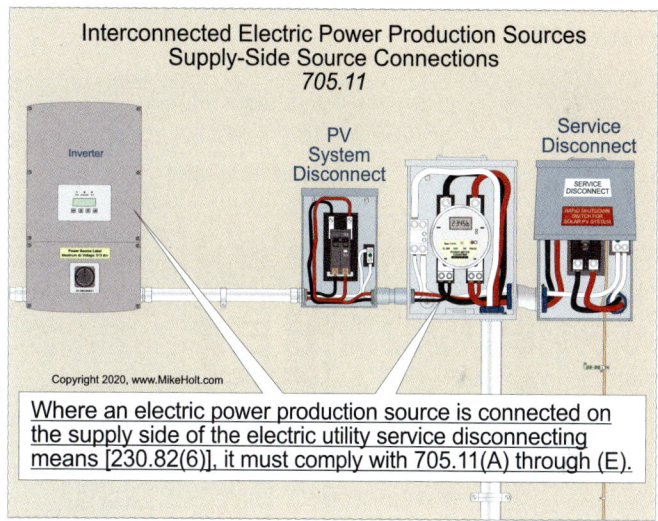

▶Figure 705-7

(A) Output Rating. The sum of the supply-side power source output current ratings, other than those controlled by a power control system in accordance with 705.13, are not permitted to exceed the ampacity of the service conductors. ▶Figure 705-8

Note: See Article 100 for the definition of "Service Conductors."

Author's Comment:

▸ Service conductors are the conductors from the load side of the electric utility service point to the service disconnect [Article 100]. ▶Figure 705-9

▸ Service conductors (load side of service point) include overhead service conductors, overhead service-entrance conductors, and underground service conductors. These conductors are not under the exclusive control of the serving electric utility, which means they are owned by the customer and fall within the requirements of Article 230.

705.11 | Interconnected Electric Power Production Sources

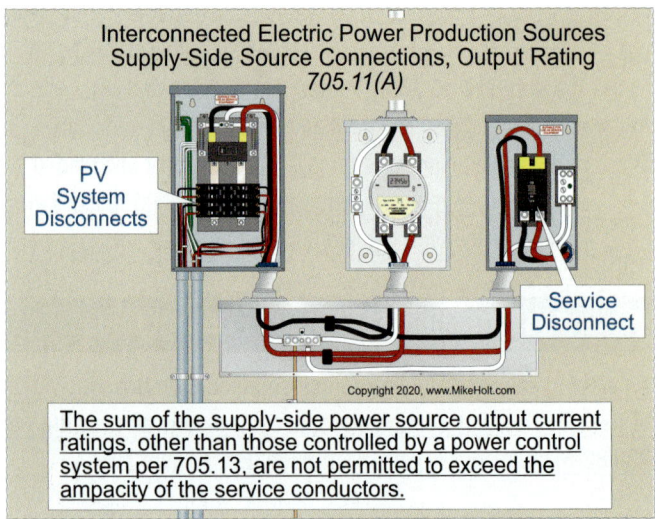

▶Figure 705-8

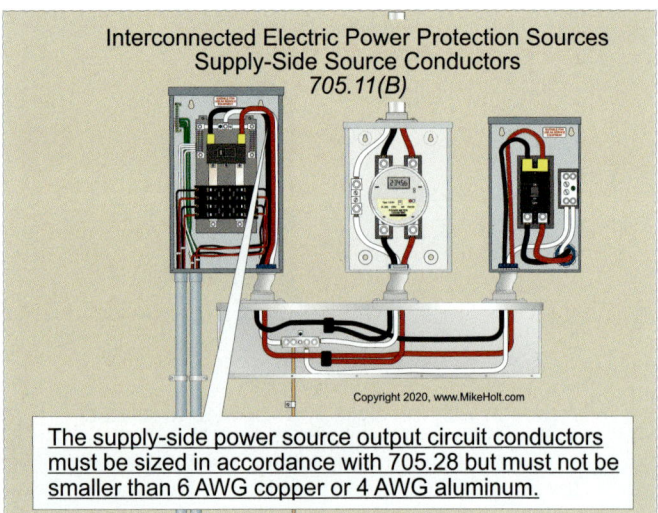

▶Figure 705-10

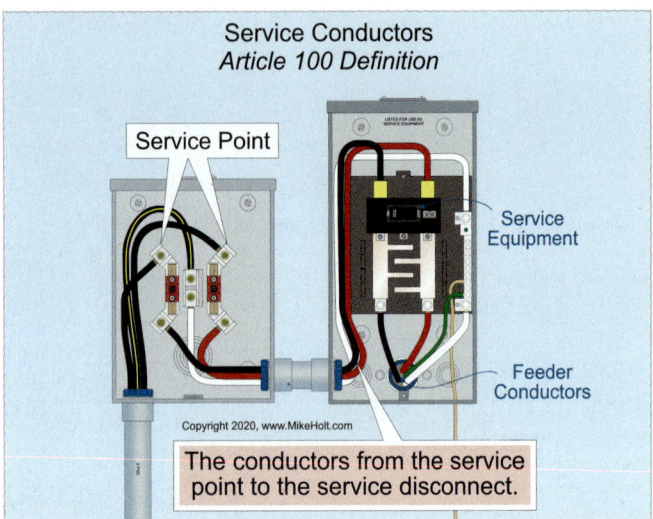

▶Figure 705-9

(B) Conductors. The supply-side power source output circuit conductors must be sized in accordance with 705.28 but must not be smaller than 6 AWG copper or 4 AWG aluminum. ▶Figure 705-10

Supply-side power source output circuit conductors must be installed within a wiring method in accordance with 230.30 for underground installations and 230.43 for aboveground installations.

(C) Overcurrent Protection. Supply-side power source output circuit conductors must have overcurrent protection in accordance with 705.30.

Outside. Where supply-side power source output circuit conductors make their supply-side connection to service conductors outside a building, the overcurrent protective device for the supply-side power source output circuit conductors must be located at a readily accessible location outside the building or at the first readily accessible location where the supply-side power source output circuit conductors enter the building.

Inside. Where the supply-side power source output circuit conductors make their connection to service conductors inside a building, the length of supply-side power source output circuit conductors must comply with one of the following requirements:

(1) For dwelling units, the length of supply-side power source output circuit conductors must not exceed 10 ft from the point of the supply-side connection to the overcurrent protection [705.30]. ▶Figure 705-11

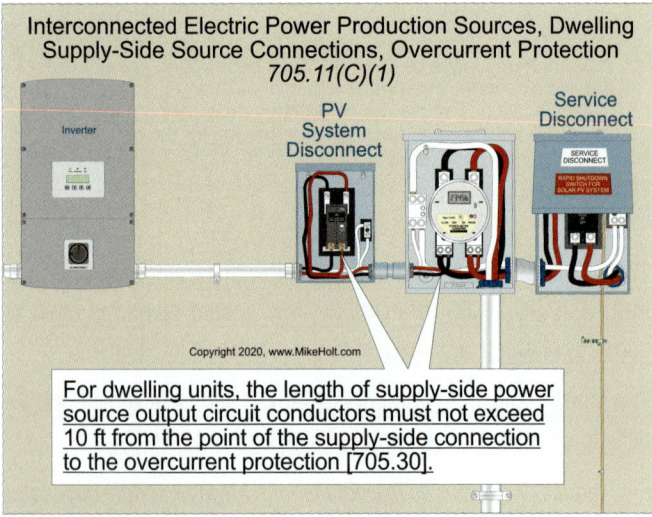

▶Figure 705-11

For other than dwelling units, the length of the supply-side power source output circuit conductors must not exceed 16.50 ft from the point of the supply-side connection to the overcurrent protection [705.30].

(2) In other than dwelling units, where cable limiters are located within 16.50 ft from the point of the supply-side connection, overcurrent protection of supply-side conductors is required within 71 ft from the point of the supply-side connection [705.30].

(D) Connections. Supply-side connections must be made with listed connectors that comply with 110.14.

Modifications to equipment to accommodate the supply-side connection must be in accordance with the manufacturer's instructions or the equipment modification must be evaluated for the application and have a field label applied.

Supply-side connections within meter socket enclosures under the exclusive control of the electric utility are only permitted where approved by the electric utility.

(E) Ground-Fault Protection. Ground-fault protection of equipment meeting the requirements of 230.95 must be provided for power source output circuit current rated 1,000A or more from a solidly grounded wye system where the voltage-to-ground exceeds 150V and the phase-to-phase voltage does not exceed 1,000V.

705.12 Load-Side Source Connections

Electric power source output circuit conductors are permitted to be connected to the load side of service equipment. ▶Figure 705-12

Where distribution equipment or feeders are capable of supplying branch circuits and/or feeders, or are supplied with a primary source of electricity and other power production sources, the interconnection of power production source equipment to the primary source of electricity must be in accordance with one of the following methods:

(A) Dedicated Overcurrent and Disconnect. The power production source terminates to a dedicated circuit breaker or fusible disconnect.

(B) Bus or Conductor Ampere Rating. The interconnection of each power production source to a bus or conductor must be in accordance with one of the following methods:

(1) Feeder Ampacity. Where a power source connection is made to the feeder primary source overcurrent device, the feeder conductor must have an ampacity of no less than 125 percent of the source output circuit current.

Where a power source output connection is made to a feeder at a location that is not at the opposite end of the feeder primary source overcurrent device, the feeder ampacity on the load side of the power source output connection must be as follows:

(a) The feeder ampacity on the load side of the power source connection must not be less than the sum of the rating of the primary source overcurrent device plus 125 percent of the power source output circuit current rating. ▶Figure 705-13

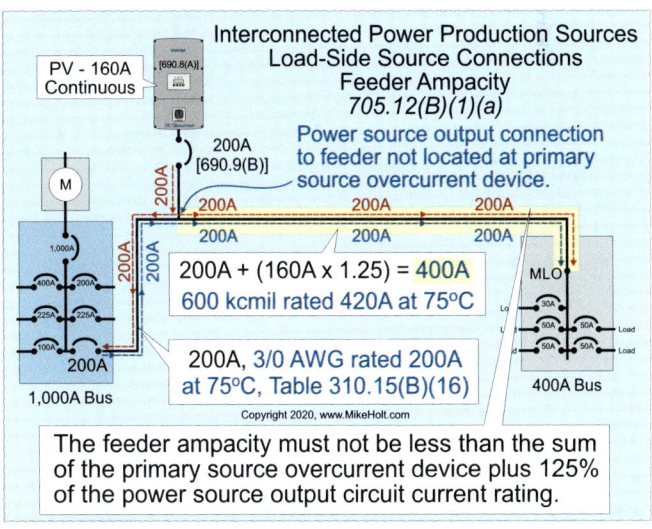

▶Figure 705-13

(b) Where an overcurrent protective device is placed at the load side of the power source connection to the feeder conductor, the feeder ampacity must not be less than the rating of the overcurrent protective device. ▶Figure 705-14

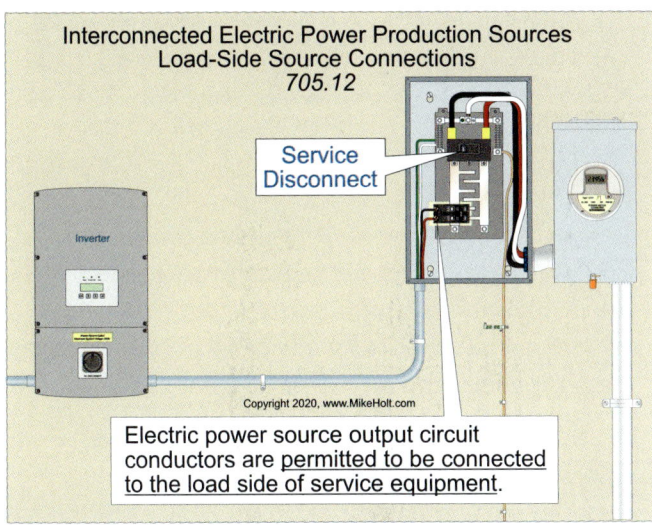

▶Figure 705-12

705.12 | Interconnected Electric Power Production Sources

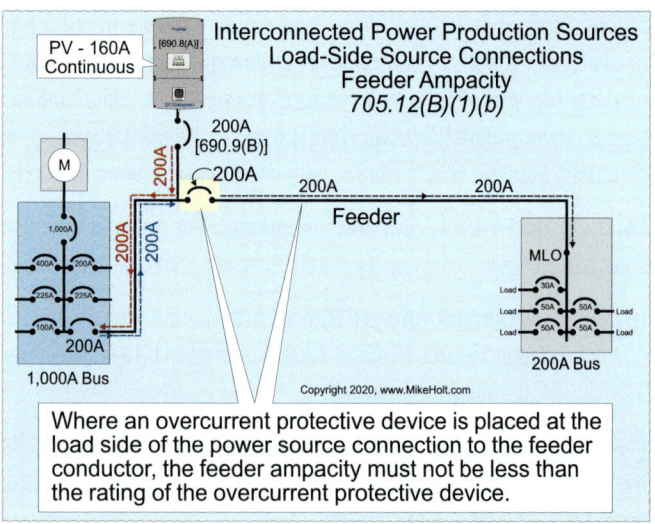

▶Figure 705-14

(2) Taps. Where a tap connection is made to a feeder that is supplied with both a primary source of power and an additional power source, the tap conductors in accordance with 240.21(B) must be sized based on the sum of the feeder protective device plus 125 percent of the PV system rated output circuit current.

Author's Comment:

▸ **10-Foot Tap.** PV system taps not longer than 10 ft must have an ampacity of not less than ten percent of the sum of the feeder protective device plus 125 percent of the PV system rated output circuit current. In no case can it be less than the rating of the terminating overcurrent device [240.21(B)(1)]. ▶Figure 705-15

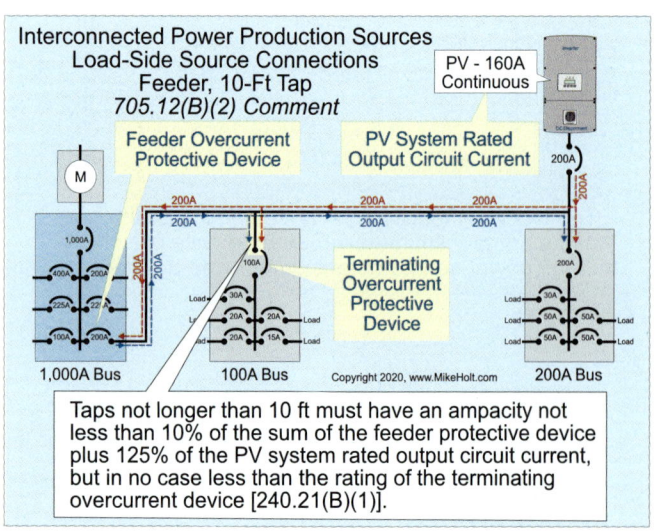

▶Figure 705-15

Author's Comment:

▸ **25-Foot Tap.** PV system taps not longer than 25 ft must have an ampacity of not less than 33 percent of the sum of the feeder protective device plus 125 percent of the PV system rated output circuit current. In no case can it be less than the rating of the terminating overcurrent protective device [240.21(B)(2)].

▶ Feeder Tap—10-Foot Example

Question: What size tap conductor (not over 10 ft long) made from a 200A-protected feeder supplied with an inverter having an ac output current rating of 160A is required to a 100A overcurrent protective device? ▶Figure 705-16

(a) 3 AWG   (b) 2 AWG   (c) 1 AWG   (d) 3/0 AWG

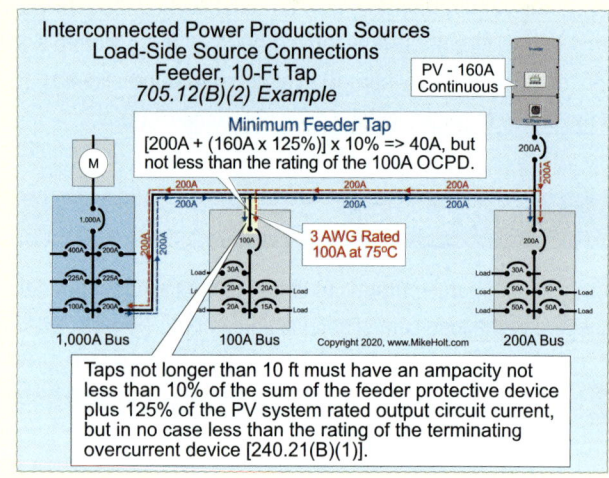

▶Figure 705-16

Solution:

PV system taps not longer than 10 ft must have an ampacity of not less than ten percent of the sum of the feeder protective device (200A) plus 125 percent of the PV system rated output circuit current (160A); but, in no case can the tap be less than the rating of the terminating overcurrent protective device (100A) [240.21(B)(1)].

Feeder Tap Conductor Ampacity => [200A + (160A x 125%)] x 10%, but not less than 100A

Feeder Tap Conductor Ampacity => (200A + 200A) x 10%, but not less than 100A

Feeder Tap Conductor Ampacity => 400A x 10%, but not less than 100A

Feeder Tap Conductor Ampacity => 40A, but not less than 100A

Feeder Contactor Size = 3 AWG rated 100A at 75°C [Table 310.16]

Answer: (a) 3 AWG

▶ **Feeder Tap—25-Foot Example**

Question: What size tap conductor, more than 10 ft but not more than 25 ft long made from a 200A-protected feeder supplied with an inverter having an ac output current rating of 160A is required to a 100A overcurrent protective device? ▶Figure 705-17

(a) 3 AWG (b) 2 AWG (c) 1 AWG (d) 1/0 AWG

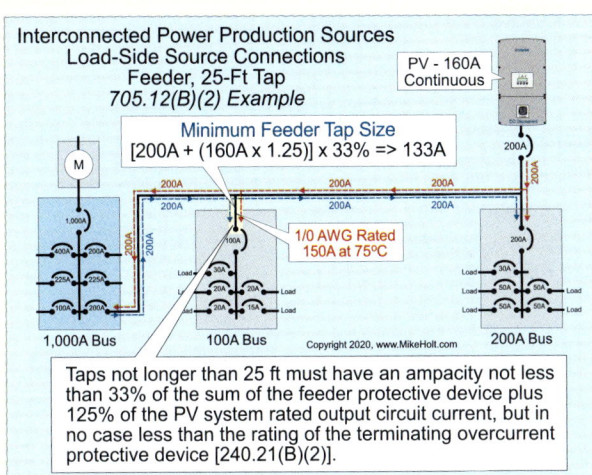

▶Figure 705-17

Solution:

PV system taps not longer than 25 ft must have an ampacity of not less than 33 percent of the sum of the feeder protective device (200A) plus 125 percent of the PV system rated output circuit current (160A); but, in no case less than the rating of the terminating overcurrent protective device (100A) [240.21(B)(2)].

Feeder Tap Conductor Ampacity => [200A + (160A x 125%)] x 33%, but not less than 100A

Feeder Tap Conductor Ampacity => (200A + 200A) x 33%, but not less than 100A

Feeder Tap Conductor Ampacity => 400A x 33%, but not less than 100A

Feeder Tap Conductor Ampacity => 133A, but no less than 100A

Feeder Contactor Size = 1/0 AWG rated 150A at 75°C [Table 310.16]

Answer: (d) 1/0 AWG

(3) Busbars. Power source connections to panelboard busbars must be by one of the following methods:

(1) Busbars at 100%. Termination of power source conductors to an overcurrent protective device placed at any point of the panelboard requires the busbar to have an ampacity rating of not less than the sum of the rating of the overcurrent protective device protecting the panelboard busbar plus 125 percent of the power source(s) output circuit current. ▶Figure 705-18

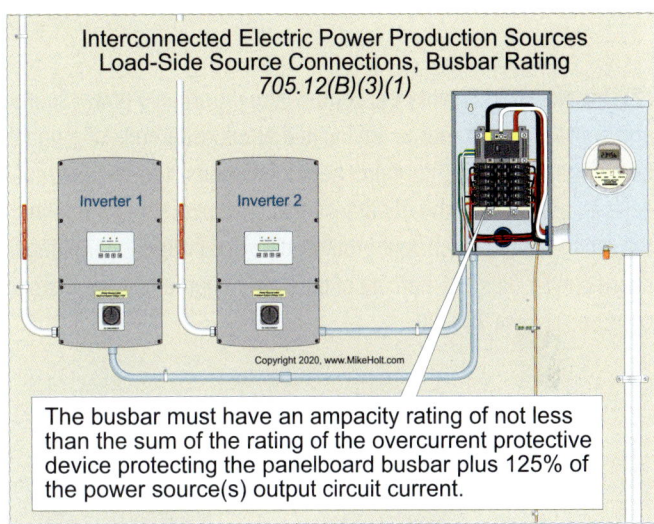

▶Figure 705-18

▶ **Panelboard Busbar Ampere Rating—Example**

Question: What is the minimum busbar ampere rating for a panelboard protected by a 150A overcurrent protective device if it is supplied by two interactive inverters each having an output ac current rating of 20A? ▶Figure 705-19

(a) 200A (b) 250A (c) 260A (d) 300A

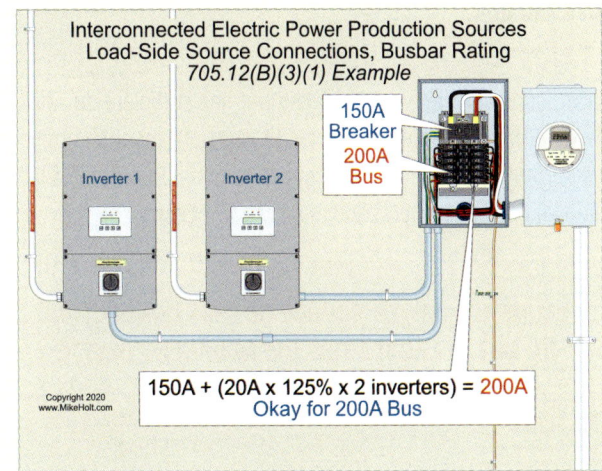

▶Figure 705-19

705.12 | Interconnected Electric Power Production Sources

Solution:

Minimum Busbar Ampere Rating => 150A + (20A x 125% x 2 interactive inverters)

Minimum Busbar Ampere Rating => 150A + 50A

Minimum Busbar Ampere Rating => 200A

Answer: (a) 200A

(2) One Hundred Twenty Percent. Where the primary power source and another power source are located at opposite ends of a panelboard (backfed) that contains additional loads, the busbar must have an ampacity rating of not less than 120 percent of the sum of the rating of the overcurrent protective device protecting the panelboard busbar plus 125 percent of the power source(s) output circuit current. ▶Figure 705-20

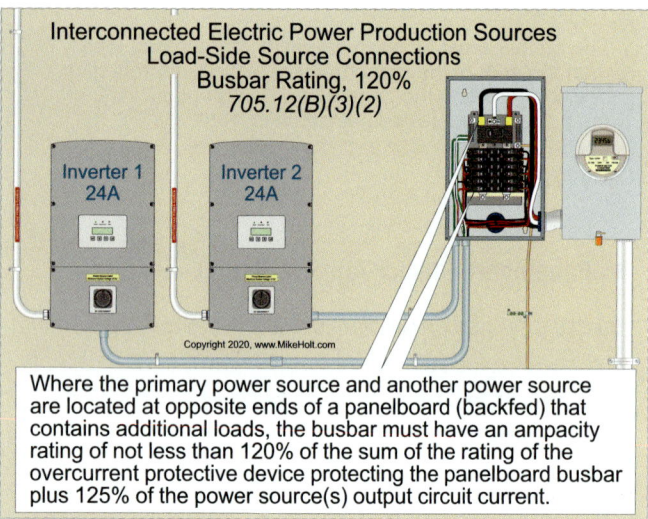

▶Figure 705-20

A permanently affixed warning label that has sufficient durability to withstand the environment involved [110.21(B)] must be applied to the distribution equipment adjacent to the backfed breaker for the additional power source(s) and must read: ▶Figure 705-21

**WARNING—POWER SOURCE OUTPUT CONNECTION
DO NOT RELOCATE THIS OVERCURRENT DEVICE**

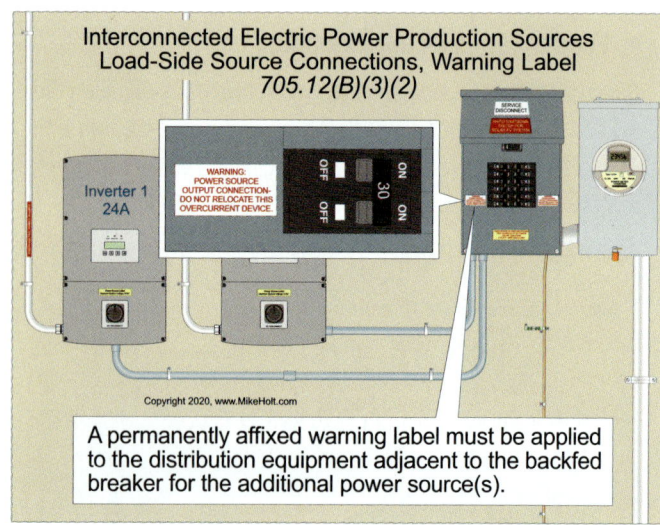

▶Figure 705-21

▶ **Panelboard Busbar Ampere Rating—Opposite Feeder Termination Example**

Question: Can a 200A rated panelboard protected by a 175A overcurrent device be supplied by two interactive inverters where each has an output ac current rating of 24A and are located opposite the feeder termination? ▶Figure 705-22

(a) Yes   (b) No

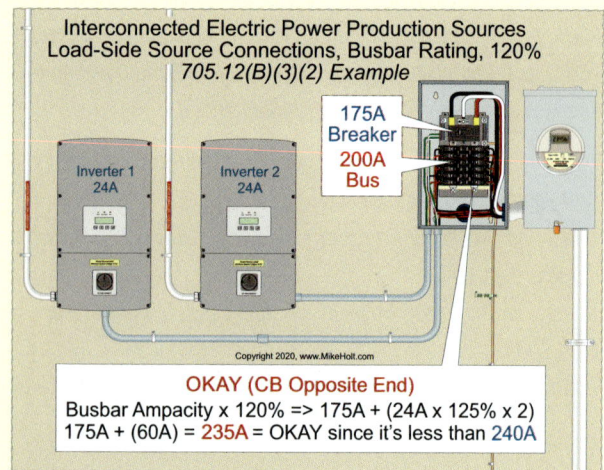

▶Figure 705-22

Solution:

The panelboard busbar ampacity must have an ampacity of not less than 120 percent of the sum of the rating of the overcurrent protective device protecting the panelboard busbar plus 125 percent of the power source(s) output circuit current.

Panelboard Ampacity x 120% => 175A + (24A x 125% x 2 inter-active inverters)
200A x 120% => 175A + 60A
240A =>235A

Answer: (a) Yes

(3) Sum of Breakers. Where the primary power source and another power source are not located at opposite ends of a panelboard, the busbar must have an ampacity of not less than the sum of the ampere ratings of all the overcurrent protective devices, exclusive of the overcurrent device protecting the panelboard busbar. ▶Figure 705–23

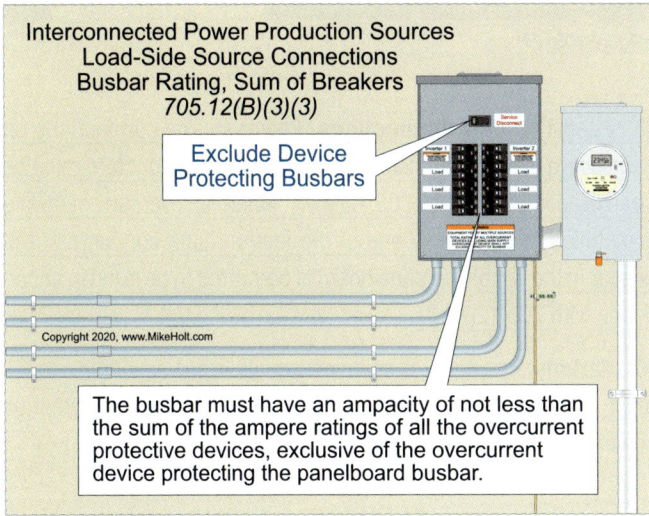
▶Figure 705–23

▶ **Panelboard Busbar Ampere Rating—Sum of Breakers Not to Exceed Busbar Ampere Rating Example 1**

Question: What is the minimum busbar ampere rating for a panelboard containing two 30A, two-pole circuit breakers and six 20A, two-pole circuit breakers? ▶Figure 705–24

(a) 12A   (b) 140A   (c) 180A   (d) 210A

Solution:

The panelboard busbar ampacity must have an ampacity of not less than the sum of the ampere ratings of all the overcurrent protective devices, exclusive of the overcurrent device protecting the panelboard busbar.

Panelboard Busbar => (30A x 2) + (20A x 6)
Panelboard Busbar => 60A + 120A
Panelboard Busbar = 180A

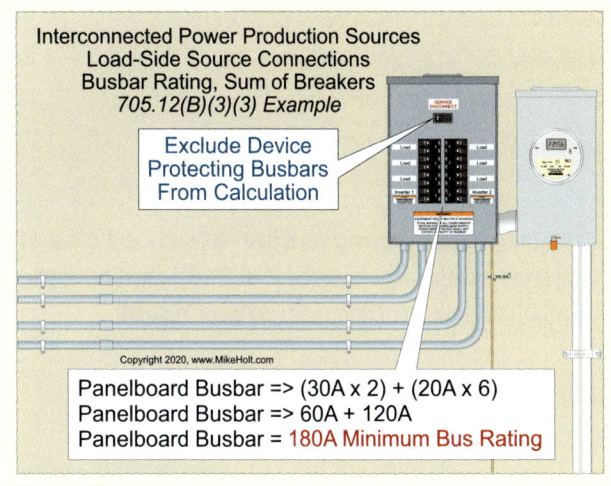
▶Figure 705–24

Answer: (c) 180A

▶ **Panelboard Busbar Ampere Rating—Sum of Breakers Not to Exceed Busbar Ampere Rating Example 2**

Question: What is the minimum busbar ampere rating for a panelboard containing six 30A, two-pole circuit breakers and one 20A, one-pole circuit breaker? ▶Figure 705–25

(a) 125A   (b) 150A   (c) 175A   (d) 200A

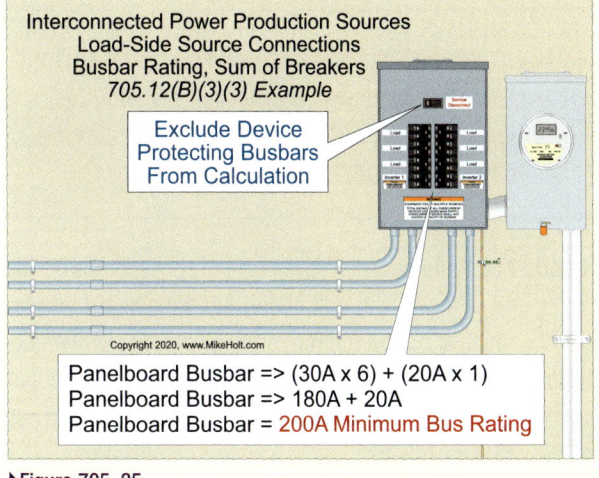
▶Figure 705–25

Solution:

The panelboard busbar ampacity must be equal to or greater than the sum of the ampere ratings of all the overcurrent protective devices on the panelboard busbar.

•••

705.12 | Interconnected Electric Power Production Sources

Panelboard Busbar => (30A x 6) + (20A x 1)
Panelboard Busbar => 180A + 20A
Panelboard Busbar = 200A

Answer: (d) 200A

A permanently affixed warning label that has sufficient durability to withstand the environment involved [110.21(B)] must be applied to the distribution equipment and read: ▶Figure 705-26

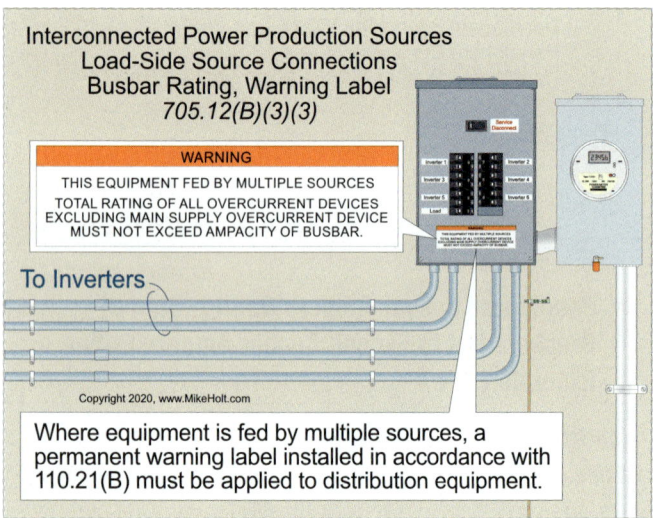

▶Figure 705-26

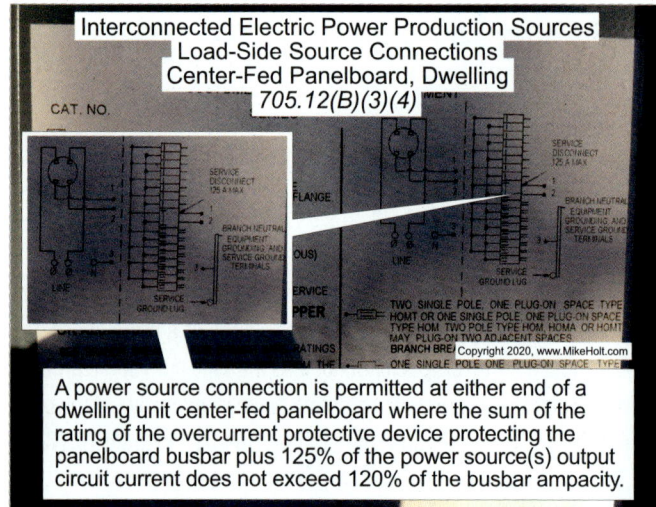

▶Figure 705-27

WARNING—THIS EQUIPMENT FED BY MULTIPLE SOURCES. TOTAL RATING OF ALL OVERCURRENT DEVICES EXCLUDING MAIN SUPPLY OVERCURRENT DEVICE MUST NOT EXCEED AMPACITY OF BUSBAR.

(4) Center-Fed Panelboard. A power source connection is permitted at either end of a dwelling unit center-fed panelboard where the sum of the rating of the overcurrent protective device protecting the panelboard busbar plus 125 percent of the power source(s) output circuit current does not exceed 120 percent of the panelboard busbar ampacity. ▶Figure 705-27

(5) Engineering Supervisions. Switchgear, switchboards, and panelboards designed under engineering supervision that includes available fault current and busbar load calculations for a power source connection.

(6) Feed-Through Connections. Power source connections on panelboard busbars connected to feed-through conductors must be sized in accordance with 705.12(B)(1). Where an overcurrent device is installed at the supply end of the feed-through conductors, the busbar in the supplying panelboard is permitted to be sized in accordance with 705.12(B)(3).

(C) Marking. Panelboards containing multiple power source circuits must be field marked to indicate the presence of all sources of all power source circuits. ▶Figure 705-28

▶Figure 705-28

(D) Suitable for Backfeed. Fused disconnects and circuit breakers not marked "line" and "load" are suitable for backfeed. Circuit breakers marked "line" and "load" can be suitable for backfeed or reverse current if specifically rated for this application. ▶Figure 705-29

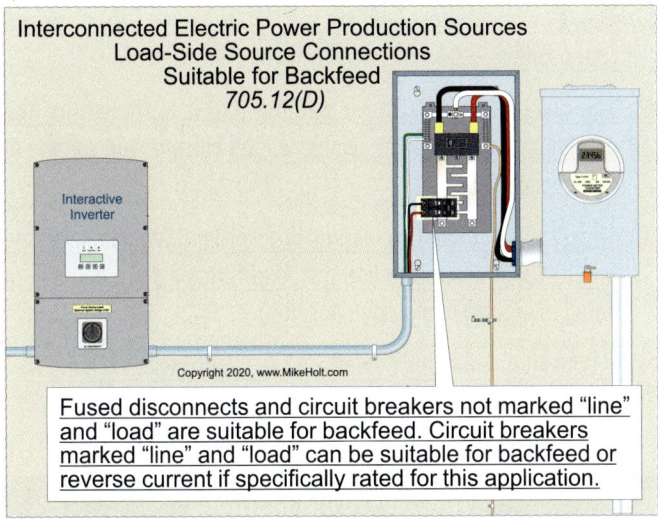

▶Figure 705-29

(E) Fastening. Backfed circuit breakers for electric power sources that are listed and identified as interactive are not required to be secured in place by an additional fastener as required by 408.36(D). ▶Figure 705-30

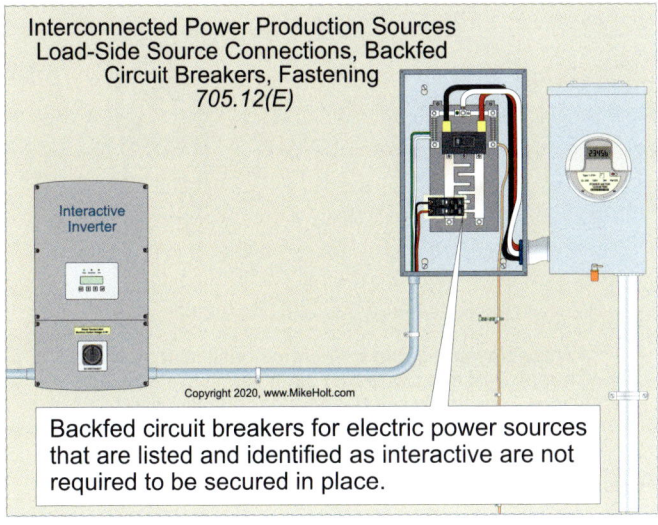

▶Figure 705-30

Author's Comment:

▶ PV ac inverter circuit breakers are not required to be fastened in place because the PV interactive inverter automatically ceases to export ac current when the breaker is removed.

705.13 Power Control Systems

Power control systems that control the output of power production sources, energy storage systems, and other equipment must be listed. The power control system must limit the current to the ampacity of the conductors or the ratings of the busbars to which it is connected in accordance with 705.13(A) through (E).

(A) Monitoring. The power control system controller must monitor all current within the power control system.

A busbar or conductor on the load side of the service disconnect that is not monitored by the power control system must be sized in accordance with 705.12.

Where the power control system is connected to the supply side of service equipment as permitted by 705.11, the power control system must monitor the current on the service conductors and prevent overload of those conductors.

(B) Settings. The sum of the power control system currents plus all monitored currents from other sources of supply must not exceed the ampacity of any busbar or conductor ampacity supplied by the power production sources.

Where the power control system is connected to an overcurrent device protecting busbars or conductors not monitored by the power control system, the setting of the power control system must be set to the ratings of that overcurrent device.

(C) Overcurrent Protection. The power control system must provide overcurrent protection either by overcurrent devices or the functionality as an overcurrent device in the product listing.

Note: Some power control systems are listed to provide overcurrent protection.

(D) Single Power Source Rating. The rating of the overcurrent device for any single power source controlled by the power control system is not permitted to exceed the rating of the busbar or the ampacity of the conductors to which it is connected.

(E) Access to Settings. The access to settings of the power control system must be restricted to qualified personnel in accordance with the requirements of 240.6(C).

705.16 | Interconnected Electric Power Production Sources

Author's Comment:

▸ According to 240.6(C), restricted access is achieved by one of the following methods:

▸ Locating behind removable and sealable covers over the adjusting means.

▸ Locating behind bolted equipment enclosure doors.

▸ Locating behind locked doors accessible only to qualified personnel.

▸ Password protection, with the password accessible only to qualified personnel.

705.16 Interrupting and Short-Circuit Current Rating

Consideration should be given to the contribution of fault currents from all interconnected power sources for the interrupting and short-circuit current ratings of equipment on interactive systems.

705.20 Disconnect

Means must be provided to disconnect the power source output circuit conductors from conductors of other systems. The supply-side power source disconnecting means must comply with the following:

(1) The disconnect must be one of the following types:

(a) A manually operable switch or circuit breaker.

(b) A load-break-rated pull-out switch.

(c) A remote-controlled switch or circuit breaker that is capable of being operated manually and can be opened automatically when control power is interrupted.

(d) A device listed or approved for the intended application.

(2) The disconnect must simultaneously disconnect all phase conductors of the circuit.

(3) The disconnect must be readily accessible from a readily accessible location.

(4) The disconnect must be externally operable without exposed live parts.

(5) Enclosures with doors or hinged covers with exposed live parts when open must require a tool to open or must be lockable where readily accessible to unqualified persons.

(6) The disconnect must indicate if it is in the open (off) or closed (on) position.

(7) The disconnect must have a rating that is sufficient for the maximum circuit current, available fault current, and voltage at the terminals.

(8) The disconnect must be marked in accordance with the warning in 690.13(B) where the line and load terminals are capable of being energized in the open position.

Note: With interconnected power sources, some switches and fuses are likely to be energized from both directions. See 240.40.

705.25 Wiring Methods

(A) General. All raceway and cable wiring methods included in Chapter 3 of this *Code* and other wiring systems and fittings specifically listed, intended, and identified for use with power production equipment are permitted. ▸Figure 705–31

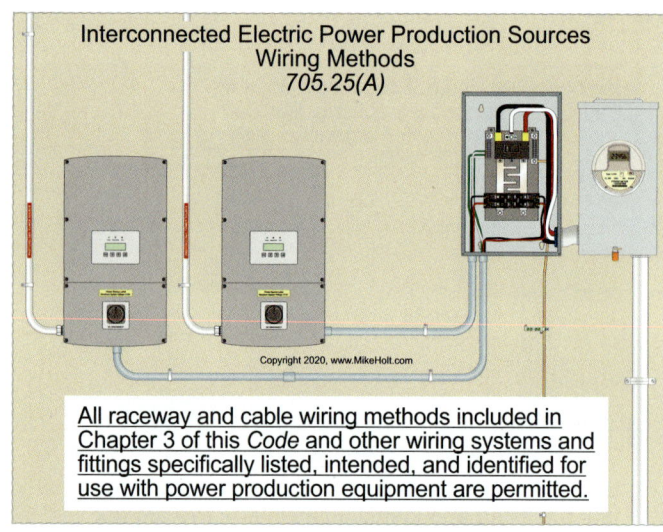

All raceway and cable wiring methods included in Chapter 3 of this *Code* and other wiring systems and fittings specifically listed, intended, and identified for use with power production equipment are permitted.

▸Figure 705–31

(B) Flexible Cords and Cables. Flexible cords and cables used to connect moving parts of a power production system, or where used for ready removal for maintenance and repair, must be in accordance with the requirements contained in Article 400. The flexible cord or cable must be listed and identified as Type DG cable, hard service cord or portable power cable, be suitable for extra-hard usage, and be listed for outdoor use and water resistant. Cables exposed to sunlight must be sunlight resistant. Flexible, fine-stranded cables must terminate on terminals, lugs, devices, or connectors identified for the use of finely stranded conductors in accordance with 110.14(A).

(C) Multiconductor Cable Assemblies. Multiconductor cable assemblies used in accordance with their listings are permitted.

Note: An ac module harness is one example of a multiconductor cable assembly.

705.28 Circuit Sizing and Current

(A) Calculation of Maximum Circuit Current. The maximum power source output circuit current is equal to the continuous output current rating of the power production equipment. ▶Figure 705-32

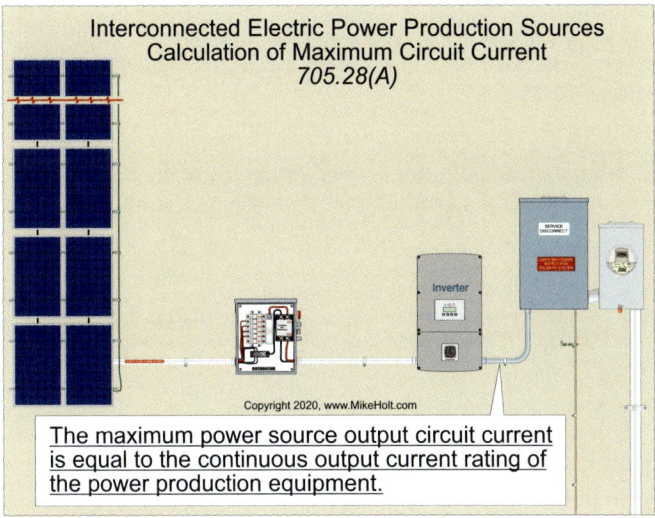

▶Figure 705-32

(B) Conductor Ampacity. Circuit conductors must be sized to the largest of the following:

(1) One hundred twenty-five percent of the maximum continuous output current rating of the power production equipment [705.28(A)] without conductor ampacity correction and/or adjustment.

(2) One hundred percent of the maximum continuous output current rating of the power production equipment [705.28(A)] after conductor ampacity correction and/or adjustment.

(3) Where circuit conductors are tapped to feeders, the tap conductors must have an ampacity as calculated in accordance with 240.21(B) [705.12(B)(2)]. ▶Figure 705-33

(C) Neutral Conductors. Neutral conductors may be sized in accordance with either of the following:

(1) Single-Phase Line-to-Neutral Power Sources. The ampacity of a neutral conductor to which a single-phase line-to-neutral power source is connected is not permitted to be less than the ampacity calculation in accordance with 705.28(B).

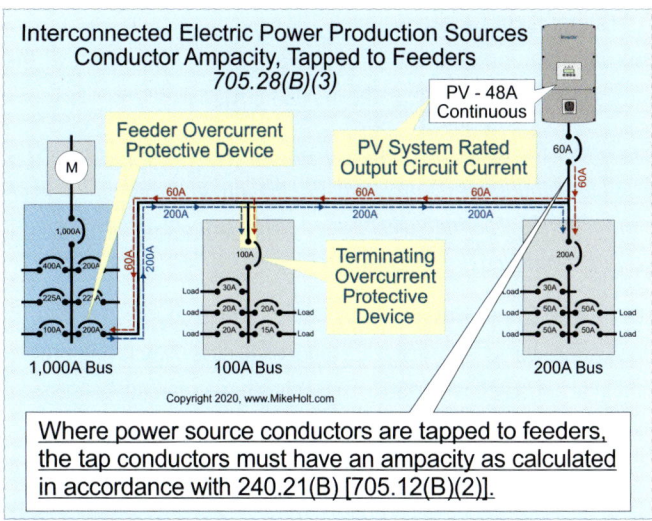

▶Figure 705-33

(2) Neutral Conductor for Instrumentation, Voltage Detection, or Phase Detection. A neutral conductor to power production equipment that is used solely for instrumentation, voltage detection, or phase detection is permitted to be sized in accordance with Table 250.102(C)(1).

705.30 Overcurrent Protection

(A) Circuits and Equipment. Power source output circuit conductors must be provided with overcurrent protection. Circuits connected to more than one electrical power source must have overcurrent protection located so as to provide overcurrent protection from all sources of power. ▶Figure 705-34

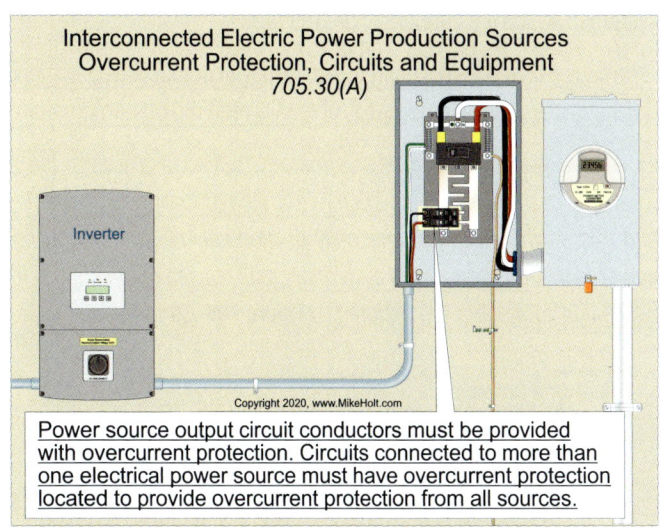

▶Figure 705-34

705.32 | Interconnected Electric Power Production Sources

(B) Overcurrent Device Ratings. The overcurrent protective device must have an ampere rating of not less than 125 percent of the maximum current as calculated in 705.28(A).

Ex: Where the assembly, together with its overcurrent device(s) is listed for continuous operation at 100 percent of its rating, the overcurrent device is permitted to be sized at 100 percent of the maximum current calculated in 705.28(A).

(C) Power Transformers. Transformers with a source of power on each side (inverter and utility) are required to have overcurrent protection in accordance with 450.3(B) by considering the utility-powered side of the transformer as the primary.

705.32 Ground-Fault Protection

Where a ground-fault protection of equipment (GFPE) device is installed in accordance with 230.95, the output of an interactive system must be connected to the supply side of the GFPE device.

Ex: The output connection of an interactive system is permitted to be made to the load side of the ground-fault protection, if ground-fault protection for equipment from all ground-fault current sources is provided.

705.40 Loss of Utility Power

The output of power production equipment must automatically disconnect from all phase conductors of the interconnected systems when one or more of the primary source (utility) phases opens. The power production equipment is not permitted to be reconnected to the primary source of power until all the phases of the interconnected system to which it's connected are restored.

This requirement does not apply to electric power production equipment providing power to an emergency or legally required standby system.

Ex: A listed interactive inverter is permitted to automatically disconnect when one or more phase conductors from the primary source opens, and it is permitted to automatically or manually resume exporting power to the interconnected system once all phases of the source to which it is connected are restored. ▶Figure 705–35

> **Author's Comment:**
>
> ▶ If the utility (primary source) loses power, an interactive inverter stops exporting power. During the power loss, an interactive inverter will remain de-energized until the utility power is restored. ▶Figure 705–36

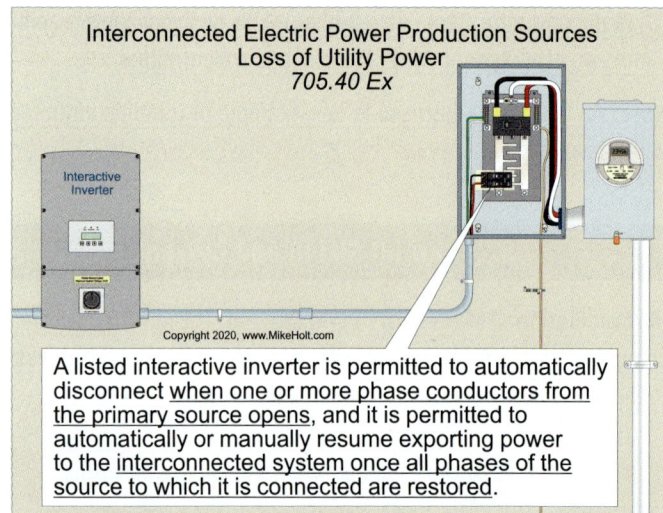

▶Figure 705–35

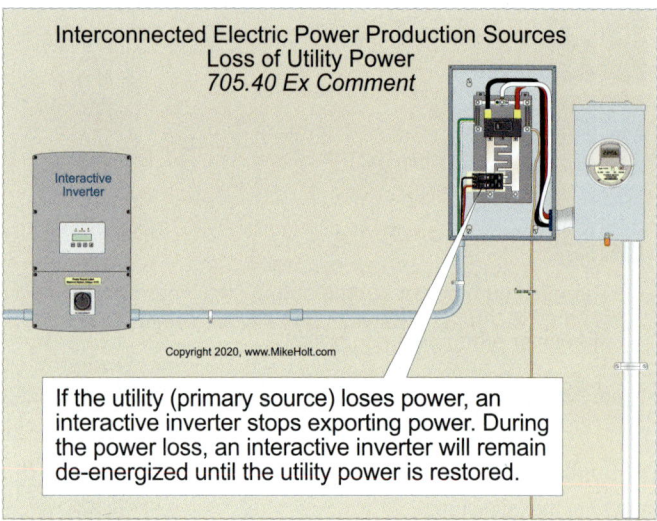

▶Figure 705–36

Note 1: Risks to personnel and equipment associated with the primary source could occur if an interactive electric power production source is set to operate as an intentional island. Special detection methods are required to determine that a primary source supply system outage has occurred and whether there should be automatic disconnection. When the primary source supply system is restored, special detection methods are typically required to limit exposure of power production sources to out-of-phase reconnection.

Interactive power production equipment is permitted to operate in island mode to supply loads that are disconnected from the electric power production and distribution network.

705.45 Unbalanced Interconnections

(A) Single-Phase. Single-phase inverters must be placed on the system so that unbalanced system voltage at the utility service disconnect is not more than three percent.

Note: For interactive power sources, unbalanced voltages can be minimized by the same methods that are used for single-phase loads on a three-phase power system. See ANSI/C84.1, *Electric Power Systems and Equipment—Voltage Ratings (60 Hertz)*.

Author's Comment:

▸ ANSI C84.1, *Electric Power Systems and Equipment—Voltage Ratings (60 Hertz)* recommends that "electric supply systems should be designed to limit the maximum voltage unbalance to three percent when measured at the electric-utility revenue meter under no-load conditions." Connecting multiple single-phase inverters to a three-phase system can result in an increase in unbalanced system voltage.

▸ The formula to determine the maximum unbalanced voltage is: **Maximum Unbalanced Voltage = Maximum Deviation from Average Voltage/Average Voltage x 100%**.

▸ Existing Installation Example

Question: If two single-phase PV systems are connected to lines B–C and this causes the B–C voltage to increase from 200V to 202V because of a decrease in loading, the maximum unbalanced system voltage for the following line voltages: A–B 206V, B–C 202V, and A–C 204V will be _____ percent.

(a) 1   (b) 1.50   (c) 2.04   (d) 3

Solution:

Maximum Unbalanced Voltage = Maximum Deviation Volts from Average Voltage/Average Voltage x 100%

Average Voltage = (206V + 202V + 204V)/3 lines
Average Voltage = 612V/3 lines
Average Voltage = 204V

Maximum Deviation from Average = 206V–204V
Maximum Deviation from Average = 2V

Maximum Unbalanced Voltage = 2V/204V x 100%
Maximum Unbalanced Voltage = .0098 x 100%
Maximum Unbalanced Voltage = 1%

Answer: (a) 1

▸ Unbalanced System Voltage—Two Inverters Example 1

Question: If two single-phase PV systems are connected to lines B–C and this results in the B–C voltage increasing from 200V to 201V because of a decrease in loading, the maximum unbalanced system voltage for the following line voltages: A–B 206V, B–C 201V, and A–C 204V will be _____ percent.

(a) 1   (b) 1.15   (c) 1.50   (d) 2.06

Solution:

Maximum Unbalanced Voltage = Maximum Deviation from Average Voltage/Average Voltage x 100%.

Average Voltage = (206V + 201V + 204V)/3 lines
Average Voltage = 611V/3 lines
Average Voltage = 203.67V

Maximum Deviation from Average = 206V–203.67V
Maximum Deviation from Average = 2.33V

Maximum Unbalanced Voltage = 2.33V/203.66V x 100%
Maximum Unbalanced Voltage = .0114 x 100%
Maximum Unbalanced Voltage = 1.15%

Answer: (b) 1.15

▸ Unbalanced System Voltage—Two Inverters Example 2

Question: If two single-phase PV systems are connected to lines A–B and this causes the A–B voltage to increase from 206V to 208V because of a decrease in loading, the maximum unbalanced system voltage for the following line voltages: A–B 208V, B–C 200V, and A–C 204V will be _____ percent.

(a) 1   (b) 1.15   (c) 1.50   (d) 1.96

Solution:

Maximum Unbalanced Voltage = Maximum Deviation from Average Voltage/Average Voltage x 100% (for Percent).

Average Voltage = (208V + 200V + 204V)/3 lines
Average Voltage = 612V/3 lines
Average Voltage = 204V

Maximum Deviation from Average = 208V–204V
Maximum Deviation from Average = 4V

Maximum Unbalanced Voltage = 4V/204V x 100%
Maximum Unbalanced Voltage = .0196 x 100%
Maximum Unbalanced Voltage = 1.96%

Answer: (d) 1.96

705.50 | Interconnected Electric Power Production Sources

(B) Three-Phase. Three-phase inverters must have all phases automatically de-energized upon loss of, or unbalanced, voltage in one or more phases unless the inverter is designed so that significant unbalanced voltages will not result.

Part II. Microgrid Systems

705.50 System Operation

Microgrid systems are permitted to disconnect from the primary source of power or other interconnected electric power production sources and operate as an isolated microgrid system operating in island mode.

705.60 Primary Power Source Connection

Connections to primary power sources that are external to the microgrid system must comply with the requirements of 705.11, 705.12, or 705.13.

Power source conductors connecting to a microgrid system, including conductors supplying distribution equipment, are considered power source output conductors.

ARTICLE 706 — ENERGY STORAGE SYSTEMS

Introduction to Article 706—Energy Storage Systems

The addition of Article 706 to the *Code* during the 2017 revision cycle recognized the important role that energy storage would play to manage the massive amounts of grid-connected energy production from alternative sources such as wind and solar. Because of the need to store this energy, the *NEC* Correlating Committee formed a 79-member task group (along with input from many other sources) to develop the requirements contained within this article.

It is important to understand what Article 706 does and does not apply to. The scope says it applies to all permanently installed energy storage systems (ESS) "having a capacity greater than 1 kWh." They may be stand-alone or interactive with other electric power production sources. Although much of the original language used to create Article 706 came from deleted sections of Article 690 Solar Photovoltaic (PV) Systems, an ESS can store energy from any power source; there are no restrictions.

An energy storage system consists of one or more components that (when assembled together) is capable of storing electrical energy for future use. An energy storage system (ESS) might include (but is not limited to) batteries, capacitors, and kinetic energy devices (such as flywheels and compressed air). Some of these systems will have either ac or dc output available. They may also include inverters and converters to change stored energy into electrical energy. An ESS might directly power loads such as in a stand-alone system, or it might provide another energy management function like buffering energy produced by an intermittent source such as a wind or PV system.

Energy storage systems can be (and usually are) connected to other energy sources, such as the local utility distribution system. There can be more than one source of power connected to these systems and their connection to other energy sources must comply with the requirements of Article 705 which provides the rules for installations of one or more electric power production source operating in parallel with a primary source of electricity, such as a utility.

It is important to note that Article 480 (Storage Batteries) has not been removed. While this may create confusion for some struggling to understand the difference between an ESS and a battery system, the easiest way to identify the two at this point is to look for the system listing. Updates to the 2020 *NEC* now require that any ESS be listed as a system and will most often be based on the requirements of UL 9540, Standard for Energy Storage Systems and Equipment. There is no system listing requirement for battery systems in 480, and all lead-acid batteries are exempt from any listing. Unlike battery systems, an ESS often also includes other equipment such as inverters or other electronic power converters.

Part I. General

706.1 Scope

This article applies to all energy storage systems having a capacity greater than 1 kWh that may be stand-alone or interactive with the electric utility supply. Energy storage systems are primarily intended to store and provide energy during normal operating conditions. ▶Figure 706–1

Note 1: For batteries rated in ampere hours, kWh is equal to the battery nominal rated voltage times the battery ampere-hour rating, divided by 1,000.

706.2 | Energy Storage Systems

▶Figure 706-1

▶Figure 706-2

Author's Comment:

▸ To better understand ampere hours relative to kilo-watt hours think of your cellphone. Many cellphone batteries are rated at 3,000 mAh (milli-amp hours) which, when divided by 1,000, equal be 3 ampere hours. Lithium-ion batteries, prominent in cell phones, have a voltage of 3.70V so when multiplied by 3 ampere hours result in 11.10 watt-hours. As you probably now realize, calculating the amount of power available in a battery is simply an exercise in Ohm's Law but on a larger scale.

706.2 Definitions

The definitions in this section only apply to this article.

Energy Storage System (ESS). One or more components assembled together capable of storing energy and providing electrical energy into the premises wiring system or the electric utility supply. ▶Figure 706-2

Note 1: Energy storage systems can include (but are not limited to) batteries, capacitors, and kinetic energy devices such as flywheels and compressed air. Energy storage systems can include inverters or converters to change voltage levels or to make a change between an alternating-current or a direct-current system.

Note 2: Energy storage systems differ from other storage systems such as a UPS system, which is a power supply that provides alternating-current power for loads for some period of time in the event of a power failure.

Flow Battery. An energy storage component similar to a fuel cell that stores its active materials in the form of two electrolytes external to the reactor interface.

Note: Two commercially available flow battery technologies are zinc bromine and vanadium redox, sometimes referred to as a pumped electrolyte energy storage system.

706.3 Qualified Personnel

The installation and maintenance of energy storage system equipment and all associated wiring and interconnections must be performed only by qualified persons.

Note: See Article 100 for the definition of "Qualified Person."

706.4 System Requirements

Each energy storage system must have a nameplate plainly visible after installation and marked with the following:

(1) Manufacturer's name, trademark, or other descriptive marking by which the organization responsible for supplying the energy storage system can be identified.

(2) Rated frequency.

(3) Number of phases if alternating current.

(4) Rating (kW or kVA).

(5) Available fault current derived by the energy storage system (ESS) at the output terminals.

(6) Maximum output and input current of the energy storage system (ESS) at the output terminals.

(7) Maximum output and input voltage of the energy storage system (ESS) at the output terminals.

(8) Utility-interactive capability if applicable.

706.5 Listing

Energy storage systems must be listed.

Author's Comment:

▸ Although the *Code* does not specify the specific standard used to list ESSs, updated building and fire codes are more specific and now increasingly require a UL 9540, *Standard for Energy Storage Systems and Equipment* listing for these systems. Annex A of the *NEC* provides references to product safety standards that the Code-Making Panels believe are generally relevant to each article.

706.6 Multiple Systems

Multiple energy storage systems are permitted in or on a single building.

Author's Comment:

▸ As with PV systems, energy storage systems may be multiple pieces of equipment assembled into a single system, or each piece of equipment may be considered an ESS on its own. The best way to identify an ESS is to look for a nameplate and review the instructions, both of which are part of the equipment's listing.

706.8 Storage Batteries

Storage batteries not associated with an energy storage system (ESS) must comply with Article 480.

Author's Comment:

▸ The difference between a storage battery as addressed in Article 480 and an ESS covered in Article 706 is not completely clear in the *NEC*. We expect this differentiation will improve in future *Code* revisions. From a practical perspective, storage batteries in Article 480 will be more limited to commercial or industrial applications for purposes such as starting generators or backing up exit lighting. The popularity of packaged and listed ESS systems utilizing new battery chemistries such as lithium-ion will continue to rise so Article 706 will be increasingly utilized for future battery storage applications. Also note that unlike Article 480, Article 706 is not just limited to battery-based energy storage.

706.9 Maximum Voltage

The maximum voltage of an energy storage system must be the rated energy storage system input and output voltage(s) indicated on the energy storage system nameplate(s) or system listing.

Part II. Disconnect

706.15 Disconnect

(A) ESS Disconnecting Means. A disconnecting means must be provided for all phase conductors derived from an energy storage system (ESS) and is permitted to be integral to listed ESS equipment. The disconnecting means must be readily accessible and located within sight of the ESS. The disconnecting means must comply with all of the following:

(1) The disconnecting means must be readily accessible.

(2) The disconnecting means must be located within sight of the ESS. Where it is impractical to install the disconnecting means within sight of the ESS, the disconnect is permitted to be installed as close as practicable, and the location of the disconnecting means must be field marked on (or immediately adjacent to) the ESS. The marking must be of sufficient durability to withstand the environment involved and must not be handwritten.

(3) The disconnecting means must be lockable in the open position in accordance with 110.25. For dwelling unit(s), the disconnect must be located at a readily accessible location outside the building.

Author's Comment:

▸ It is important to note that the requirements in 706.15(A) can be met with disconnects that are integral to the listed ESS equipment. Since an ESS application may have multiple individual ESS units, each may require a disconnecting means, but this does not necessarily mean each will require a separate disconnect switch adjacent to the units. Many ESS manufacturers will choose to incorporate a means of disconnect into their ESS units. These disconnects will be evaluated during the system's listing.

(B) Remote Actuation. Where controls to activate the disconnect of an energy storage system are not located within sight of the system, the location of the controls must be field marked on the disconnect.

(C) Notification and Marking. Each energy storage system disconnect must plainly indicate whether it is in the open (off) or closed (on) position and be permanently marked:

ENERGY STORAGE SYSTEM DISCONNECT

The disconnect must be legibly marked in the field to indicate the following:

(1) The nominal energy storage system alternating-current voltage and maximum energy storage system direct-current voltage.

(2) The available fault current derived from the energy storage system.

(3) An arc-flash label applied in accordance with acceptable industry practice.

(4) The date the available fault current calculation was performed.

Ex: List items (2), (3), and (4) do not apply to one- and two-family dwellings.

Note 1: Industry practices for equipment labeling are described in NFPA 70E, *Standard for Electrical Safety in the Workplace*. This standard provides specific criteria for developing arc-flash labels for equipment that provides nominal system voltage, incident energy levels, arc-flash boundaries, minimum required levels of personal protective equipment, and so forth.

Note 2: Battery equipment suppliers can provide available fault current on any particular battery model.

Where the line and load terminals within the energy storage system disconnect may be energized in the open position, the disconnect must be marked with the following words or equivalent:

**WARNING ELECTRIC SHOCK HAZARD
TERMINALS ON THE LINE AND LOAD
SIDES MAY BE ENERGIZED IN THE OPEN POSITION**

The notification(s) and marking(s) must be permanently affixed and have sufficient durability to withstand the environment involved [110.21(B)].

(D) Partitions Between Components. Where circuits from the input or output terminals of energy storage components pass through a wall, floor, or ceiling, a readily accessible disconnect must be provided within sight of the energy storage component. Fused disconnects or circuit breakers are permitted to serve as the required disconnect.

Author's Comment:

▸ It is important to note that 706.15(D) will not apply to every ESS application where circuit conductors travel through walls, floors, or ceilings. This section is for those applications (typically large ones) where the battery is in one room and other equipment that is part of the ESS is in another. In those cases, a disconnect must be located in the room containing the battery. This does not apply to situations where the entire ESS is in one room and the output circuit from the ESS connects to other systems in other rooms. In those cases, the disconnect location requirements in 706.15(A) are all that apply.

Part III. Installation Requirements

706.20 General

(A) Ventilation. Provisions appropriate to the energy storage technology must be made for sufficient diffusion and ventilation of any possible gases from the storage device (if present) to prevent the accumulation of an explosive mixture. A pre-engineered or self-contained energy storage system is permitted to provide ventilation in accordance with the manufacturer's recommendations and listing for the system.

Note 1: See NFPA 1, *Fire Code*, Chapter 52, for ventilation considerations for specific battery chemistries.

Note 2: Some storage technologies do not require ventilation.

Note 3: Sources for the design of ventilation of battery systems are IEEE 1635-2012/ASHRAE Guideline 21, *Guide for the Ventilation and Thermal Management of Batteries for Stationary Applications*, and the UBC.

Note 4: Fire protection considerations are addressed in NFPA 1, *Fire Code*.

Author's Comment:

▸ To meet unique requirements such as ventilation of an ESS, the manufacturer's instructions included in the product's listing must be used. Requiring energy storage systems to be listed means installers will not be asked to calculate things such as proper ventilation. They will simply comply with the installation instructions, much like they do with other electrical equipment.

(B) Dwelling Units. Energy storage systems for one- and two-family dwelling units are not permitted to have a direct-current voltage greater than 100V between conductors or to ground.

Ex: Where live parts are not accessible during routine energy storage system maintenance, a maximum energy storage system voltage of 600V dc is permitted.

Author's Comment:

▸ Since an ESS may have alternating-current output, there will be many cases where the voltage limits in 706.20(B) will not even be considered by installers or inspectors since the dc voltages will be internal to the equipment and therefore covered under the equipment's listing.

(C) Spaces About Energy Storage System Components.

(1) General. Working spaces for energy storage systems must be in accordance with 110.26.

(2) Space Between Components. Energy storage systems are permitted to have space between components in accordance with the manufacturer's instructions and listing.

Note: Additional space may be needed to accommodate energy storage system hoisting equipment, tray removal, or spill containment.

706.21 Directory (Identification of Power Sources)

Energy storage systems must be identified by markings or labels that are permanently affixed with sufficient durability to withstand the environment involved [110.21(B)].

(A) Facilities with Utility Services and Energy Storage Systems. Plaques or directories must be installed in accordance with 705.10.

Part IV. Circuit Requirements

706.30 Circuit Sizing and Current

(A) Maximum Rated Current for a Specific Circuit. The maximum current for a specific circuit must be calculated in accordance with the following.

(1) Nameplate-Rated Circuit Current. Circuit current must be the rated current indicated on the energy storage system nameplate(s) or system listing. Where the energy storage system has separate input (charge) and output (discharge) circuits or ratings, they must be considered individually. Where the same terminals on the energy storage system are used for charging and discharging, the rated current must be the greater of the two.

(2) Inverter Output Circuit Current. The maximum current must be the inverter's continuous output current rating.

(3) Inverter Input Circuit Current. The maximum current must be the continuous inverter input current rating when the inverter is producing its rated power at the lowest input voltage.

(4) Inverter Utilization Output Circuit Current. The maximum current must be the continuous alternating-current output current rating of the inverter when the inverter is producing its rated power.

(5) DC-to-DC Converter Output Current. The maximum current must be the dc-to-dc converter's continuous output current rating.

(B) Conductor Ampacity. The ampacity of the feeder circuit conductors from the energy storage system(s) to the wiring system serving the loads to be serviced by the system must not be less than the greater of the (1) nameplate(s)-rated circuit current as determined in accordance with 706.30(A)(1), or (2) the rating of the energy storage system's overcurrent protective device(s).

(C) Ampacity of Grounded or Neutral Conductor. If the output of a single-phase, 2-wire energy storage system output(s) is connected to the grounded or neutral conductor and a single-phase conductor of a 3-wire system or of a three-phase, 4-wire, wye-connected system, the maximum unbalanced neutral load current plus the energy storage system(s) output rating must not exceed the ampacity of the grounded or neutral conductor.

706.31 Overcurrent Protection

(A) Circuits and Equipment. Energy storage system circuit conductors must be protected in accordance with the requirements of Article 240. Protective devices for energy storage system circuits must be in accordance with the requirements of 706.31(B) through (F), and circuits must be protected at the source from overcurrent.

(B) Overcurrent Device Ampere Ratings. Overcurrent protective devices, where required, must be rated in accordance with Article 240 and the rating provided on systems serving the energy storage system and must be not less than 125 percent of the maximum currents calculated in 706.30(A).

Ex: Where the assembly (including the overcurrent protective devices) is listed for operation at 100 percent of its rating, the ampere rating of the overcurrent devices is permitted to be not less than the maximum currents calculated in 706.30(B).

(C) Direct-Current Rating. Overcurrent protective devices, either fuses or circuit breakers, used in any direct-current portion of an energy storage system must be listed for direct current and have the appropriate voltage, current, and interrupting ratings for the application.

(D) Current Limiting. A listed and labeled current-limiting overcurrent protective device must be installed adjacent to the energy storage system for each direct-current output circuit. ▶Figure 706–3

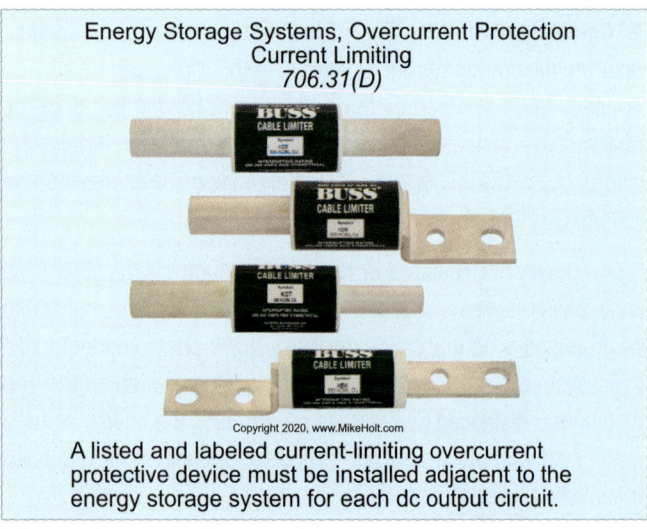

▶Figure 706–3

Ex: Where current-limiting overcurrent protection is provided for the direct-current output circuits of a listed energy storage system, additional current-limiting overcurrent devices are not required.

(E) Fuses. Means must be provided to disconnect any fuses associated with energy storage system equipment and components when the fuse is energized from both directions and is accessible to other than qualified persons. Switches, pullouts, or similar devices that are rated for the application are permitted to serve as a means to disconnect fuses from all sources of supply.

(F) Location. Where circuits from the input or output terminals of energy storage components in an energy storage system pass through a wall, floor, or ceiling, overcurrent protection must be provided at the energy storage component of the circuit.

Author's Comment:

▸ As with 706.15(D), this one will not apply to every ESS application where circuit conductors travel through walls, floors, or ceilings. This section is for those applications (typically large ones) where the battery is in one room and other equipment that is part of that ESS system is located in another.

706.33 Charge Control

(A) General. Provisions must be provided to control the charging process of the energy storage system. All adjustable means for control of the charging process must be accessible only to qualified persons.

(B) Diversion Charge Controller.

(1) Sole Means of Regulating Charging. An energy storage system employing a diversion charge controller as the sole means of regulating charging must be equipped with a second independent means to prevent overcharging of the storage device.

(2) Circuits with Diversion Charge Controller and Diversion Load. Circuits containing a diversion charge controller and a diversion load must comply with the following:

(1) The current rating of the diversion load must be less than or equal to the current rating of the diversion load charge controller. The voltage rating of the diversion load must be greater than the maximum energy storage system voltage. The power rating of the diversion load must be at least 150 percent of the power rating of the charging source.

(2) The conductor ampacity and the rating of the overcurrent device for this circuit must be at least 150 percent of the maximum current rating of the diversion charge controller.

(3) Energy Storage System Using Interactive Inverters. Systems using interactive inverters to control energy storage state-of-charge by diverting excess power into an alternate electric power production and distribution system, such as utility, must comply with 706.33(B)(3)(a) and (b).

(a) These systems are not required to comply with 706.33(B)(2).

(b) These systems must have a second, independent means of controlling the energy storage system charging process for use when the alternate system is not available, or when the primary charge controller fails or is disabled.

(C) Charge Controllers and DC-to-DC Converters. Where charge controllers and other dc-to-dc power converters that increase or decrease the output current or output voltage with respect to the input current or input voltage are installed, all of the following apply:

(1) The ampacity of the conductors in output circuits must be based on the maximum rated continuous output current of the charge controller or converter for the selected output voltage range.

(2) The voltage rating of the output circuits must be based on the maximum voltage output of the charge controller or converter for the selected output voltage range.

Part V. Flow Battery Energy Storage Systems

Part V applies to energy storage systems composed of, or containing, flow batteries.

Note: Due to the unique design features and difference in operating characteristics of flow batteries as compared with that of storage batteries such as lead acid or lithium ion batteries, the requirements for flow batteries have been included here rather than in Article 480.

Notes

ARTICLE 710 STAND-ALONE SYSTEMS

Introduction to Article 710—Stand-Alone Systems

Stand-alone power production sources are what the name implies; they are not connected to the utility power grid or any other power production/distribution network.

The wiring for stand-alone systems must comply with Chapters 1 through 4 of the *NEC*. Depending on the purpose and design of a particular stand-alone source, the wiring might need to comply with Chapter 6 and other articles in Chapter 7.

Occupying about half a page, this article is one of the shortest in the *Code*, but its brevity does not imply insignificance. In fact, it will take on increasing significance as the growth in stand-alone system installations continues. Many of these are systems that use solar or other "alternative energy" sources, but fossil fuel sources are also in the mix.

710.1 Scope

This article covers electric power production systems that operate in island mode and are not connected to an electric utility supply. ▶Figure 710-1

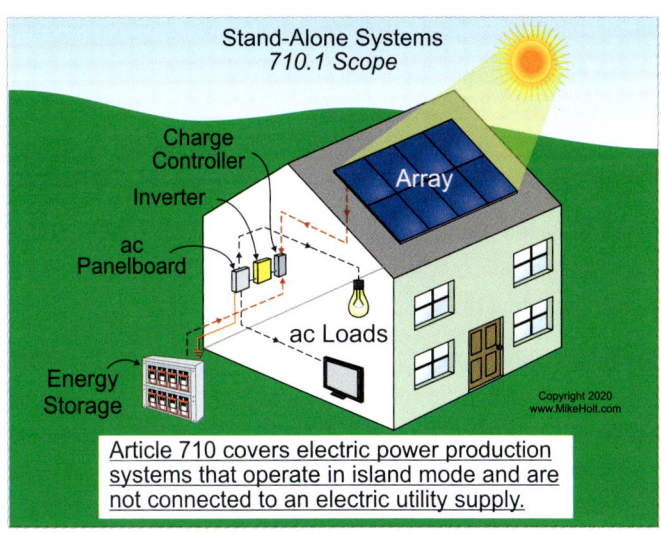

▶Figure 710-1

Note: Stand-alone systems are capable of operating in island mode, independent from the electric utility, and include isolated microgrid systems or they can be interactive with other power sources. Stand-alone systems often include a single or a compatible interconnection of sources such as engine generators, solar PV, wind, an energy storage system, or batteries.

Author's Comment:

▸ According to Article 100, "Island Mode" is the operational mode for stand-alone power production equipment, an isolated microgrid, multimode inverter, or an interconnected microgrid that is disconnected from the electric utility supply.

710.6 Equipment Approval

Stand-alone equipment must be approved for the intended use in accordance with one of the following: ▶Figure 710-2

(1) Be listed for the application.

(2) Be evaluated for the application and have a field label applied.

Note: Inverters identified as "multimode" and "stand-alone" are specifically identified and certified to operate in this application. Stand-alone inverters operate only in island mode. Multimode inverters operate in either island mode or interactive mode setting. A multimode inverter operates in island mode when it is not connected to an electric utility supply. Stand-alone inverters are not evaluated and are not intended for connection to export power in parallel with an electric utility.

710.10 | Stand-Alone Systems

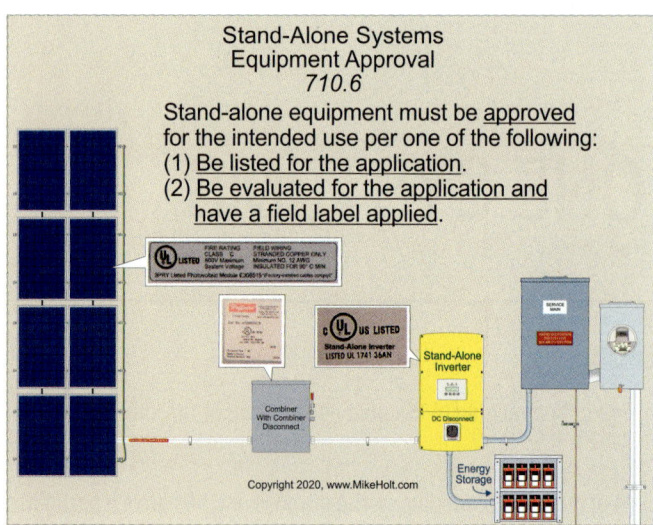
▶Figure 710-2

Author's Comment:

▸ According to Article 100, a "Multimode Inverter" is equipment having the capabilities of both interactive and stand-alone inverters. ▶Figure 710-3

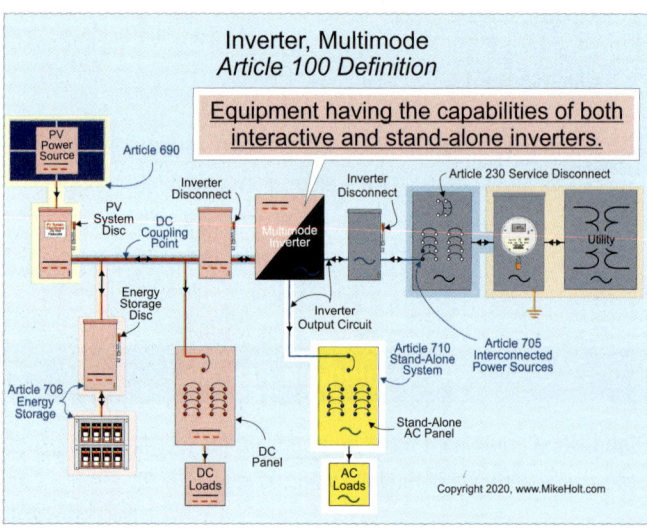
▶Figure 710-3

710.10 Identification of Power Sources

A permanent plaque or directory must be installed at the service equipment location or an approved readily visible location for a building supplied by a stand-alone system. The plaque or directory must identify the location of each power source disconnect or be grouped with other plaques or directories for other on-site sources.

Where multiple sources supply the building, the plaque or directory must be marked with the wording "CAUTION: MULTIPLE SOURCES OF POWER." The marking must be permanently affixed with sufficient durability to withstand the environment involved [110.21(B)].

Ex: Installations with multiple co-located power production sources can be identified as a group(s). The plaque or directory is not required to identify each power source individually.

710.12 Stand-Alone Inverter Input Circuit Current

The maximum inverter input current is the continuous inverter input current rating when the inverter is producing its rated power at the lowest input voltage.

710.15 General

The wiring on the supply side of the building disconnect must comply with the following:

(A) Supply Output. The power supply to premises wiring systems fed by stand-alone or isolated microgrid power sources can have a capacity that is less than the calculated load, but it must not be less than the largest single utilization equipment connected to the stand-alone system.

Note: For general-use loads, the stand-alone system capacity is based on the sum of the capacity of all firm sources such as generators and energy storage system inverters. For specialty loads intended to be powered directly from a variable source, the stand-alone capacity is calculated using the sum of the variable sources, such as PV or wind inverters, or the combined capacity of both firm and variable sources.

(B) Sizing and Protection. The circuit conductors between a stand-alone source and a building disconnect must be sized based on the sum of the output ratings of the stand-alone source(s).

(C) Single 120V Supply. Stand-alone and isolated microgrid systems can supply 2-wire, single-phase, 120V or 3-wire, 120/240V service equipment or distribution panels where there are no 240V outlets and no multiwire circuits. Service equipment or distribution panels must be marked with the following words or equivalent:

> **WARNING: SINGLE 120-VOLT SUPPLY. DO NOT CONNECT MULTIWIRE BRANCH CIRCUITS!**

Stand-Alone Systems | **710.15**

(E) Energy Storage or Backup Power System Requirements. Stand-alone system are not required to have energy storage or backup power.

(F) Backfed Circuit Breakers. Plug-in type backfed circuit breakers must be secured in accordance with 408.36(D). **Figure 710–4**

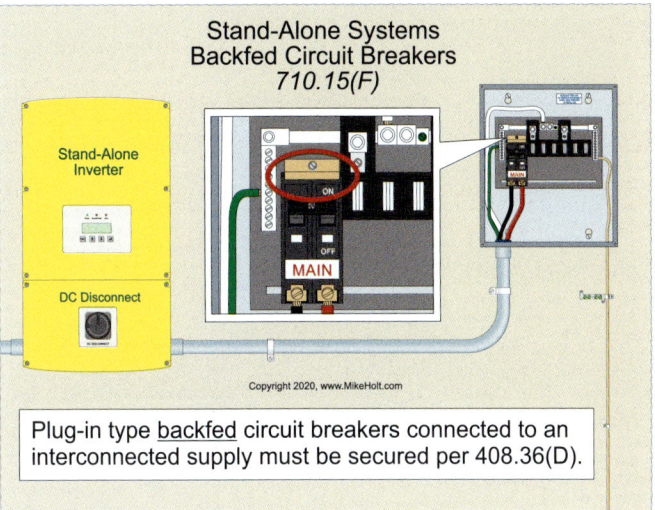

▶Figure 710–4

Notes

ARTICLE 725 — REMOTE-CONTROL, SIGNALING, AND POWER-LIMITED CIRCUITS

Introduction to Article 725—Remote-Control, Signaling, and Power-Limited Circuits

Circuits covered by Article 725 are remote-control, signaling, and power-limited circuits that are not an integral part of a device or appliance. This article includes circuits for burglar alarms, access control, sound, nurse call, intercoms, some computer networks, some lighting dimmer controls, and some low-voltage industrial controls.

Here is a quick look at the types of circuits:

- A remote-control circuit controls other circuits through a relay or solid-state device, such as a motion-activated security lighting circuit.
- A signaling circuit provides output that is a signal or indicator such as a buzzer, flashing light, or annunciator.
- A power-limited circuit is a circuit supplied by a transformer or other electric power source that limits the amount of power to provide safety from electrical shock and/or fire ignition.

The purpose of Article 725 is to allow for the fact that these circuits "are characterized by usage and power limitations that differentiate them from electrical power circuits" [725.1 Note]. This article provides alternative requirements for minimum conductor sizes, overcurrent protection, insulation requirements, wiring methods, and materials.

Article 725 consists of four parts. Part I provides general information, Part II pertains to Class 1 circuits, Part III addresses Class 2 circuits, and Part IV focuses on listing requirements. The key to understanding and applying each of these parts is in knowing the voltage and energy levels of the circuits, the wiring method involved, and the purpose(s) of the circuit.

Part I. General

725.1 Scope

Article 725 contains the requirements for remote-control, signaling, and power-limited circuits that are not an integral part of a device or utilization equipment. ▶Figure 725-1

Note: These circuits have electrical power and voltage limitations that differentiate them from electrical power circuits. Alternative requirements are given regarding minimum conductor sizes, overcurrent protection, insulation requirements, and wiring methods and materials.

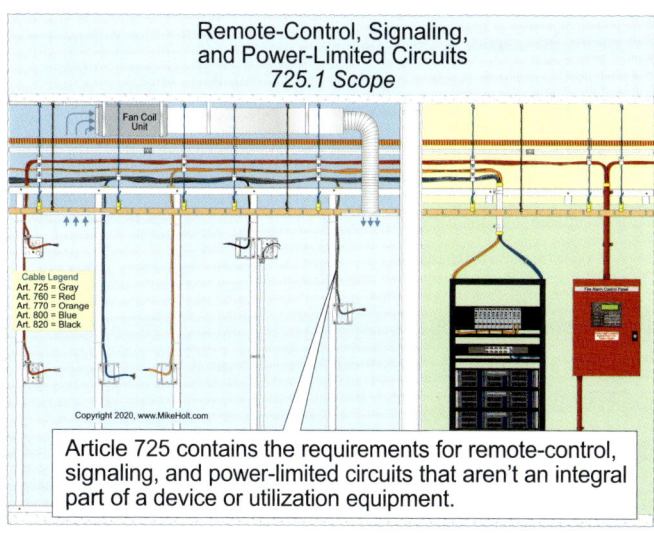

▶Figure 725-1

725.2 | Remote-Control, Signaling, and Power-Limited Circuits

Author's Comment:

▸ To understand when to apply the requirements of Article 725 for remote-control and signaling circuits, you must understand the following Article 100 Definitions:

- ▸ **Remote-Control Circuit.** Any electrical circuit that controls another circuit through a relay or equivalent device is a remote-control circuit. An example is the 120V branch circuit that operates the coil of a motor starter or lighting contactor, or the 24V circuit for a garage door opener.

- ▸ **Signaling Circuit.** Any electrical circuit that energizes signaling equipment is a signaling circuit. Examples include doorbells, buzzers, signal lights, annunciators, burglar alarms, and other detection indication or alarm devices.

- ▸ **Class 1 Circuit.** The wiring system between the load side of a Class 1 circuit overcurrent protective device and the connected equipment. See 725.41 for the voltage and power limitations of Class 1 circuits.

- ▸ **Class 2 Circuit.** The portion of the wiring system between the load side of a Class 2 power supply and the connected Class 2 equipment. Due to power the limitations of its power supply, a Class 2 circuit is considered safe from a fire initiation standpoint and provides acceptable electric shock protection.

725.2 Definitions

The definitions in this section only apply to this article.

Abandoned Cable. A cable that is not terminated to equipment and not identified for future use with a tag. ▸Figure 725-2

▸Figure 725-2

Author's Comment:

▸ Section 725.25 requires the accessible portion of abandoned cables to be removed.

Cable Bundle. A group of cables that are tied together or in contact with one another in a closely packed configuration for at least 40 in. ▸Figure 725-3

Note: Separation of individual cables can result in less heating. Combing of the cables can result in less heat dissipation and more signal cross talk between cables.

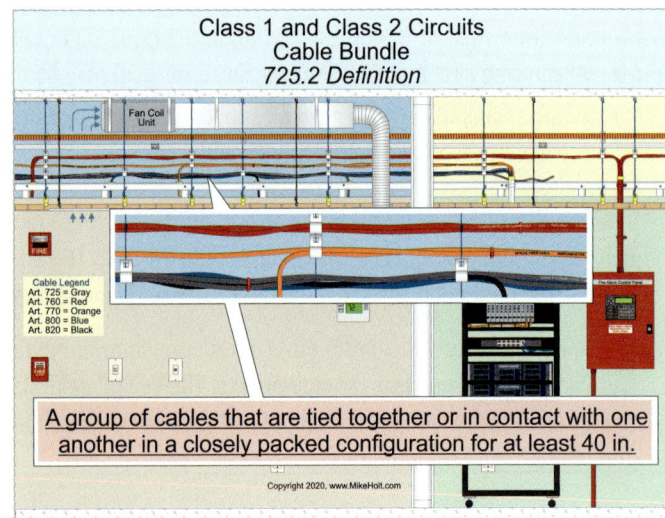
▸Figure 725-3

725.3 Other Articles

In addition to the requirements of this article, circuits and equipment must comply with the articles or sections listed in 725.3(A) through (P). Only those sections contained in Article 300 specifically referenced below apply to Class 1, 2, and 3 circuits.

Author's Comment:

▸ Boxes or other enclosures are not required for Class 2 splices or terminations because Article 725 does not reference 300.15, which contains those requirements. ▸Figure 725-4

Remote-Control, Signaling, and Power-Limited Circuits | 725.3

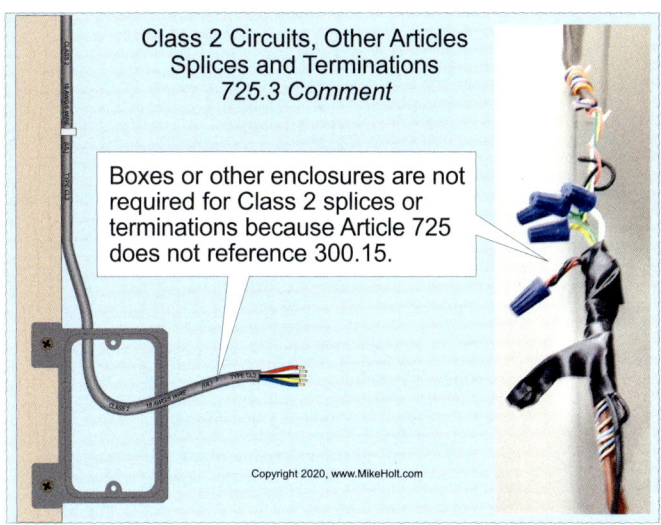
▶Figure 725-4

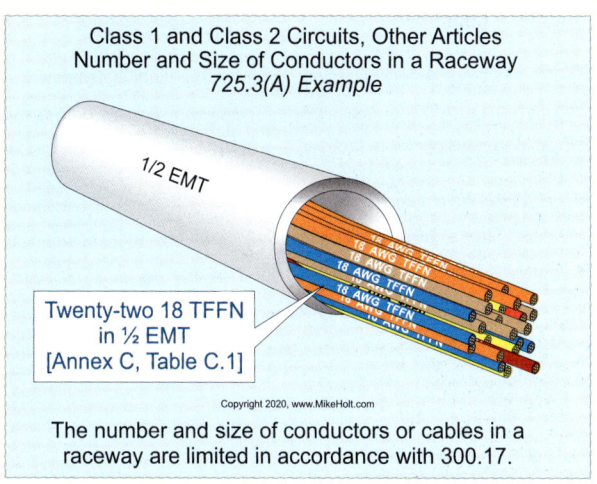
▶Figure 725-5

(A) Number and Size of Conductors in a Raceway. The number and size of conductors or cables within a raceway are limited in accordance with 300.17.

Author's Comment:

▸ Raceways must be large enough to permit the installation and removal of conductors without damaging conductor insulation [300.17].

▸ When all conductors within a raceway are the same size and insulation, the number of conductors permitted can be found in Annex C for the raceway type [Chapter 9, Notes to Tables, Note 1].

▸ For conductors not included in Chapter 9 (such as multiconductor cable) the actual dimensions must be used, and if one multiconductor cable is used inside a raceway the single conductor percentage fill area must be used [Chapter 9, Notes to Table, Notes 5 and 9].

▶ **Example**

Question: How many 18 TFFN fixture wires can be installed in trade size ½ electrical metallic tubing? ▶Figure 725-5

(a) 16   (b) 18   (c) 22   (d) 38

Answer: (c) 22 [Annex C, Table C.1]

(B) Spread of Fire or Products of Combustion. Installation of Class 1 and Class 2 circuits must comply with 300.21.

Author's Comment:

▸ Electrical circuits and equipment must be installed in such a way that the spread of fire or products of combustion will not be substantially increased. Openings into or through fire-resistive walls, floors, and ceilings for electrical equipment must be firestopped using methods approved by the authority having jurisdiction to maintain the fire-resistance rating of the fire-resistive assembly [300.21]. ▶Figure 725-6

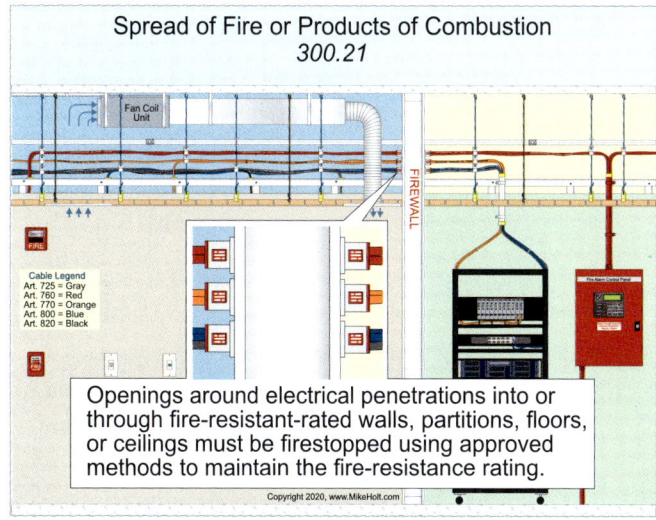
▶Figure 725-6

725.3 | Remote-Control, Signaling, and Power-Limited Circuits

Author's Comment:

▸ Firestopping materials are listed for the specific types of wiring methods and the construction of the assembly they penetrate.
▸Figure 725-7

▸ Visit International Firestop Council's website (www.firestop.org) for additional information on firestop system training complying with ASTM E2174, *Standard Practice for On-Site Inspection of Installed Firestops* and ASTM E2393, *Standard Practice for On-Site Inspection of Installed Fire Resistive Joint Systems and Perimeter Fire Barriers*.

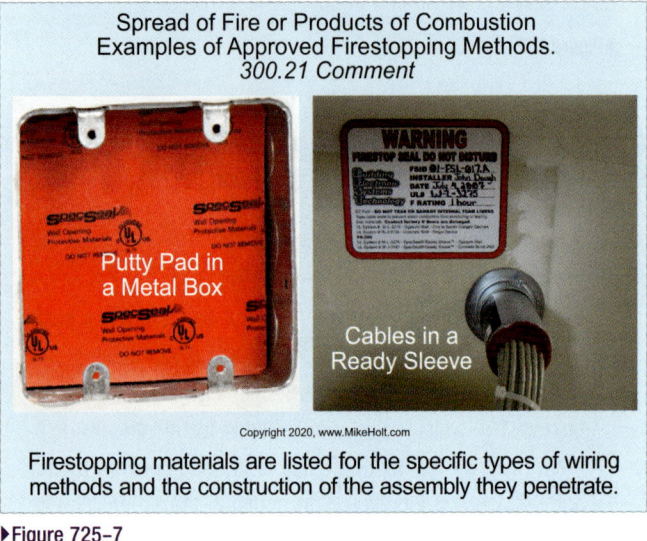
▸Figure 725-7

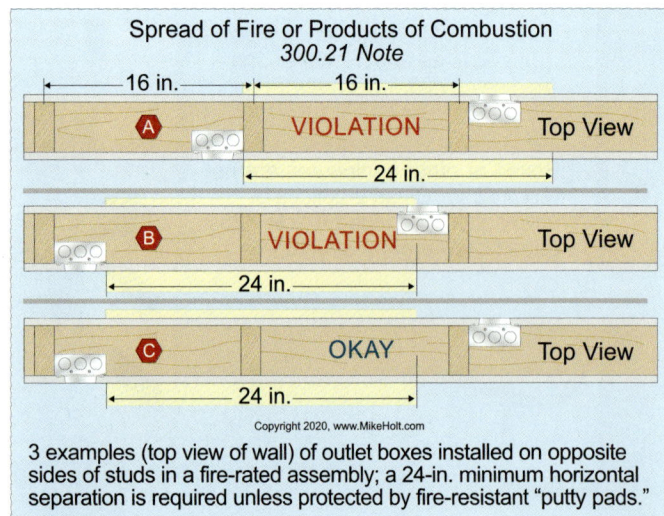
▸Figure 725-8

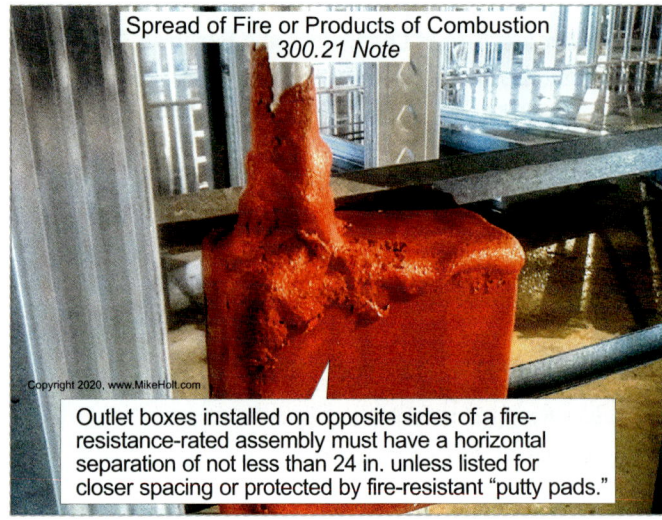
▸Figure 725-9

Author's Comment:

▸ Directories of electrical construction materials published by qualified testing laboratories contain listing and installation restrictions necessary to maintain the fire-resistive rating of assemblies. Building codes also have restrictions on penetrations on opposite sides of a fire-resistive wall.

▸ Outlet boxes must have a horizontal separation of not less than 24 in. when installed on opposites sides in a fire-resistive assembly, unless an outlet box is listed for closer spacing or protected by fire-resistant "putty pads" in accordance with manufacturer's instructions. ▸Figure 725-8 and ▸Figure 725-9

Author's Comment:

▸ Boxes installed in fire-resistive assemblies must be listed for the purpose. If steel boxes are used, they must be secured to the framing member, so cut-in type boxes are not permitted (UL White Book, *Guide Information for Electrical Equipment*).

▸ "Putty pads" are typically installed on the exterior of the box, but many manufactures have listed inserts for box interiors.

(C) Ducts and Plenum Spaces. Class 1 and Class 2 circuits installed in ducts or plenums must comply with 300.22. ▸Figure 725-10

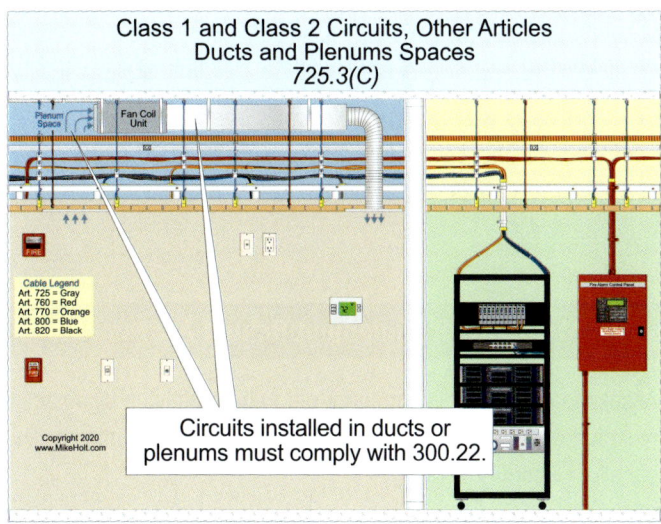
▶Figure 725-10

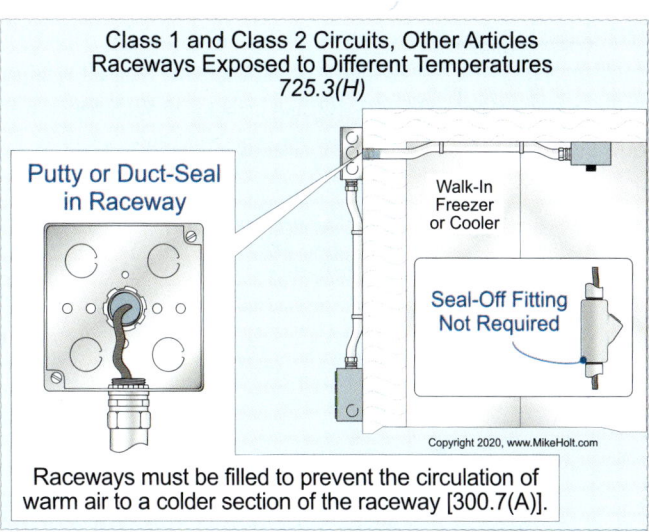
▶Figure 725-11

Ex 1: Class 2 cables selected in accordance with Table 725.154 and installed in accordance with 725.135(B) and 300.22(B) Ex, are permitted to be installed in ducts specifically fabricated for environmental air.

Ex 2: Class 2 cables selected in accordance with Table 725.154 and installed in accordance with 725.135(C) are permitted to be installed in plenum spaces.

(D) Hazardous Locations. Class 1 and Class 2 circuits installed in hazardous (classified) locations must comply with 501.10(B)(1), 501.150, 502.10(B)(1), 502.150, 503.10(A)(1), 503.150, 506.15(A), 506.15(C), 511.7(B)(1), 515.7(A), and Article 517, Part IV.

(E) Cable Trays. Class 1, 2, and 3 circuits in cable trays must be installed in accordance with Parts I and II of Article 392.

(H) Raceways Exposed to Different Temperatures. If a raceway is subjected to different temperatures, and where condensation is known to be a problem, the raceway must be filled with a material approved by the authority having jurisdiction that will prevent the circulation of warm air to a colder section of the raceway. [300.7(A)]. ▶Figure 725-11

Author's Comment:

▶ This raceway seal is one that is approved by the authority having jurisdiction to prevent the circulation of warm air to a cooler section of the raceway and is not the same thing as an explosionproof seal.

(J) Bushing. When a raceway is used for the support or protection of cables, a fitting is required to reduce the potential for abrasion and must be placed at the location the cables enter the raceway in accordance with 300.15(C). ▶Figure 725-12

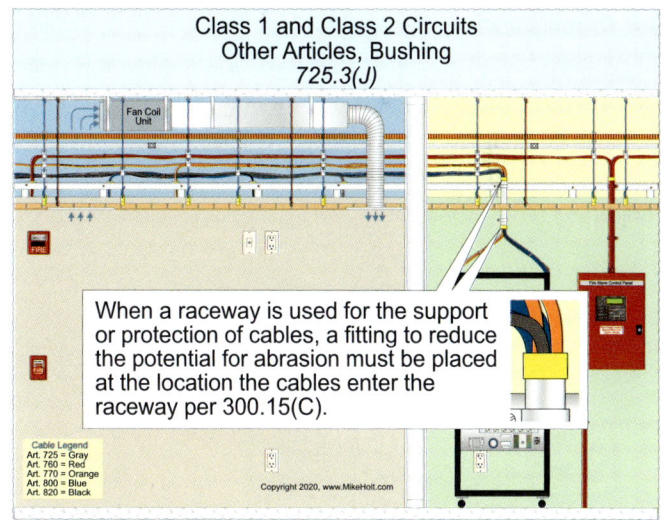
▶Figure 725-12

(L) Corrosive, Damp, or Wet Locations. Where installed in corrosive, damp, or wet locations, Class 2 cables must be identified for the location in accordance with 110.11 and 310.10(F). Conductors and cables installed in underground raceways [300.5(B)], or in raceways aboveground in wet locations [300.9], must also be identified for wet locations. Where corrosion may occur, the requirements of 300.6 must be used.

(M) Cable Routing Assemblies. Class 2 cables can be installed in cable routing assemblies selected in accordance with Table 800.154(c), listed in accordance with 800.182, and installed in accordance with 800.110(C) and 800.113. ▶Figure 725-13

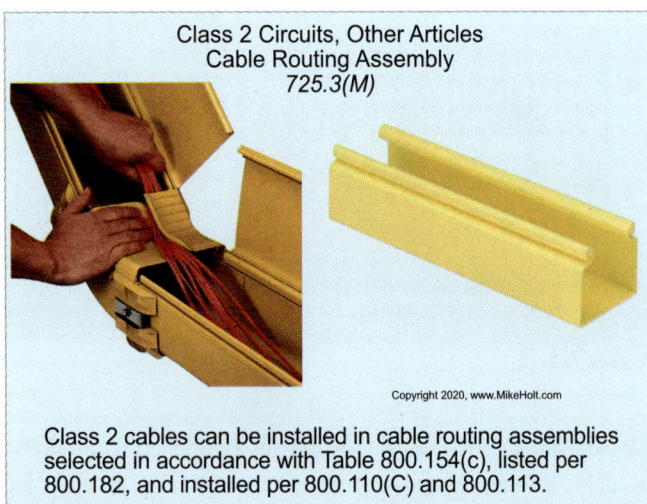

▶Figure 725-13

(N) Communications Raceways. Class 2 cables can be installed in communications raceways selected in accordance with Table 800.154(b), listed in accordance with 800.182, and installed in accordance with 800.113 and 362.24 through 362.56, where the requirements applicable to electrical nonmetallic tubing apply. ▶Figure 725-14

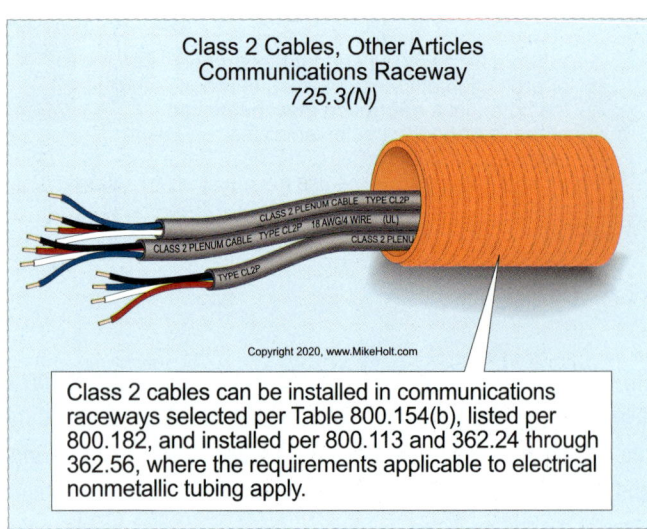

▶Figure 725-14

(O) Temperature Limitation of Class 2 Cables. The requirements of 310.14(A)(3) for the temperature limitation of conductors applies to Class 2 cables.

(P) Identification of Equipment Grounding Conductors. Equipment grounding conductors must be identified in accordance with 250.119.

Ex: Conductors with green insulation is permitted to be used as ungrounded signal conductors for Types CL3P, CL2P, CL3R, CL2R, CL3, CL2, CL3X, CL2X, and substitute cables installed in accordance with 725.154(A).

725.21 Electrical Equipment Behind Access Panels

Access to equipment is not permitted to be prohibited by an accumulation of cables that prevents the removal of suspended-ceiling panels. ▶Figure 725-15

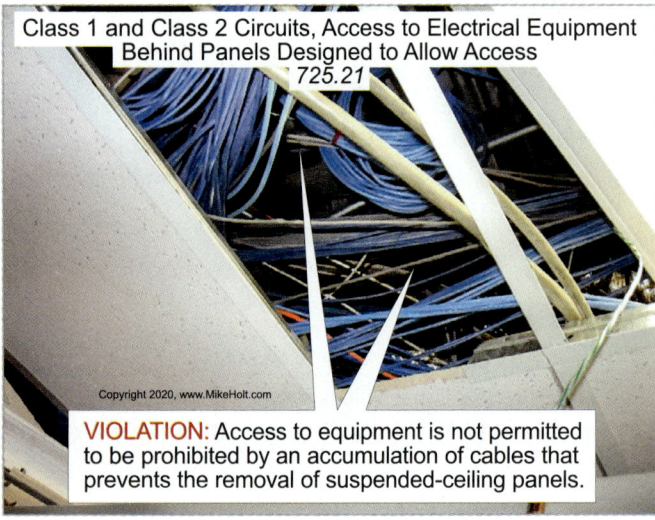

▶Figure 725-15

725.24 Mechanical Execution of Work

Equipment and cabling must be installed in a neat and workmanlike manner. ▶Figure 725-16

Exposed cables must be supported by the structural components of the building so the cable will not be damaged by normal building use. Support must be by straps, staples, hangers, cable ties, or similar fittings designed and installed in a manner that will not damage the cable. ▶Figure 725-17

Note: Paint, plaster, cleaners, abrasives, corrosive residues, or other contaminants can result in an undetermined alteration of Class 2 cable properties.

Remote-Control, Signaling, and Power-Limited Circuits | 725.25

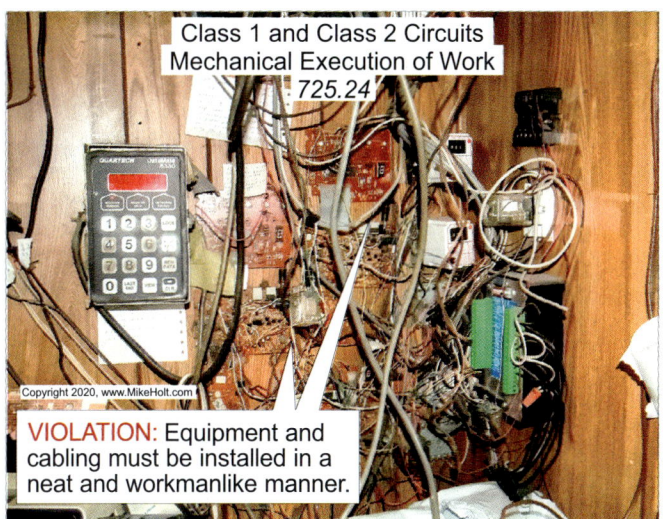
▶Figure 725-16

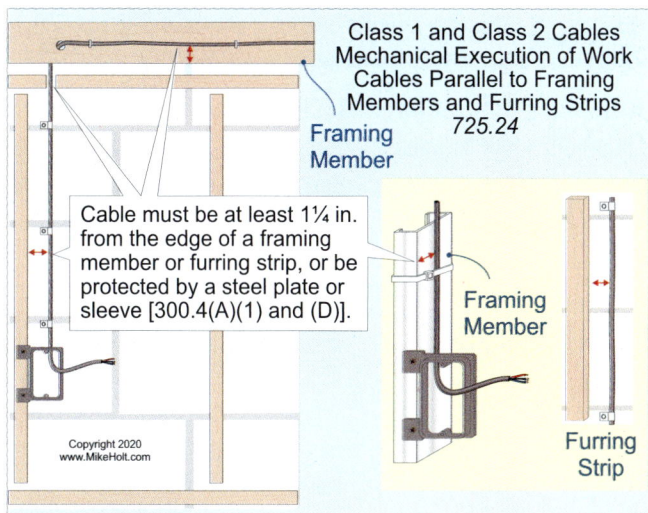
▶Figure 725-18

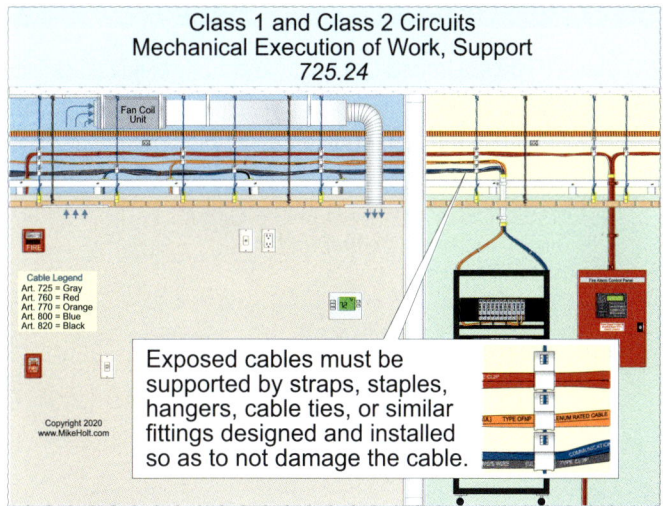
▶Figure 725-17

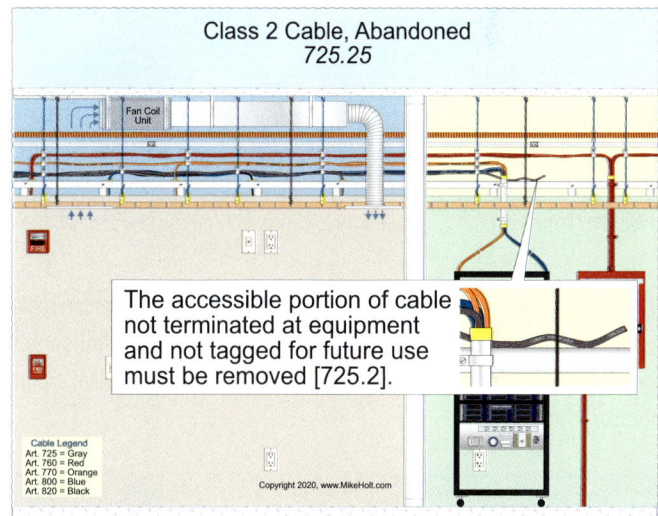
▶Figure 725-19

Cables installed through or parallel to framing members or furring strips must be protected where they are likely to be penetrated by nails or screws by installing the wiring method so it is not less than 1¼ in. from the nearest edge of the framing member or furring strips, or by protecting it with a ¹⁄₁₆ in. thick steel plate or equivalent [300.4(A) and (D)]. ▶Figure 725-18

725.25 Abandoned Cable

To limit the spread of fire or products of combustion within a building, the accessible portion of Class 2 cables not terminated at equipment or tagged for future use must be removed [725.2]. ▶Figure 725-19

Tags identifying cables for future use must be able to withstand the environment involved.

Author's Comment:

▶ Cables installed in concealed raceways are not considered accessible; therefore, they are not required to be removed. See the definition of "Abandoned Cable" in 725.2.

Mike Holt Enterprises • www.MikeHolt.com • 888.NEC.CODE (632.2633) | 399

725.31 Safety-Control Equipment

(A) Remote-Control Circuits. Circuits used for safety-control equipment must be classified as Class 1 if the failure of the remote-control circuit or equipment introduces a direct fire or life hazard.
▶Figure 725-20

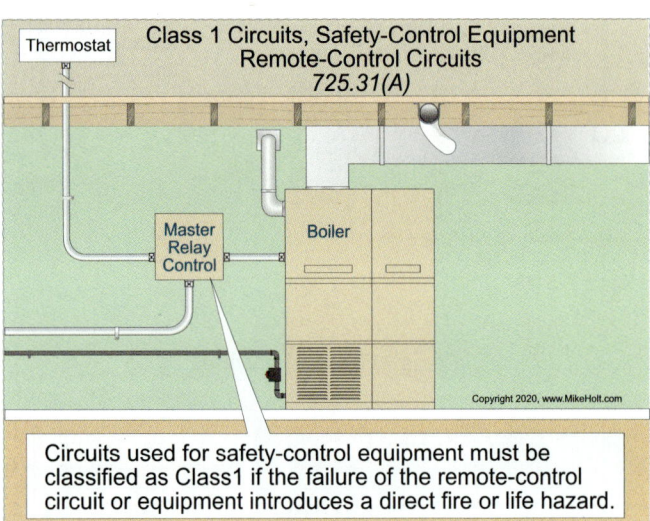
▶Figure 725-20

Room thermostats, water temperature regulating devices, and similar controls used in conjunction with electrically controlled household heating and air-conditioning are not considered safety-control equipment. ▶Figure 725-21

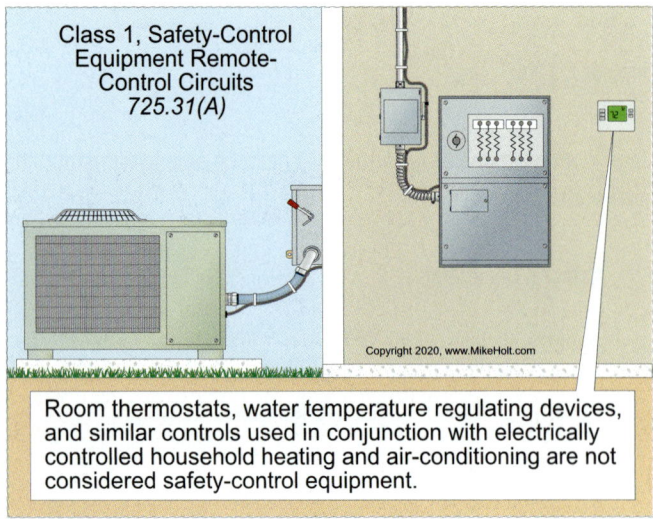
▶Figure 725-21

(B) Physical Protection. If damage to remote-control circuits of safety-control equipment would introduce a hazard [725.31(A)], conductors must be installed in rigid metal conduit, intermediate metal conduit, PVC conduit, electrical metallic tubing, Type MI cable, Type MC cable, or be otherwise suitably protected from physical damage.

725.35 Circuit Requirements

(1) Class 1 circuits must comply with Parts I and II of Article 725.

(2) Class 2 circuits must comply with Parts I and III of Article 725.

Part II. Class 1 Circuit Requirements

725.41 Class 1 Circuit Classifications and Requirements

(A) Class 1 Power-Limited Circuits. Class 1 power-limited circuits must be supplied from a power supply that limits the output to 30V and no more than 1,000 VA. ▶Figure 725-22

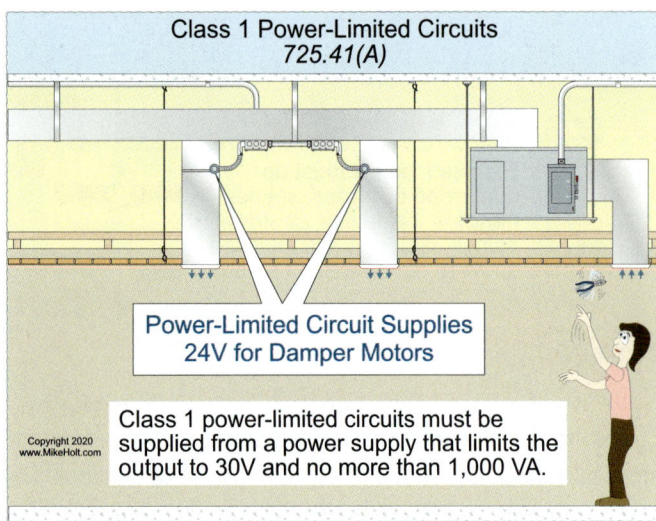
▶Figure 725-22

Author's Comment:

▶ Class 1 power-limited circuits are not that common. They are used when the voltage must be less than 30V (safe from electric shock in dry locations), and where the power demands exceed the 100 VA energy limitations of Class 2 circuits, such as for motorized loads like remote-controlled window blinds [Chapter 9, Table 11(A)].

Remote-Control, Signaling, and Power-Limited Circuits | **725.48**

(B) Class 1 Remote-Control and Signaling Circuits. Class 1 remote-control and signaling circuits must not exceed 600V. The power output of the source is not required to be power limited. ▶Figure 725–23

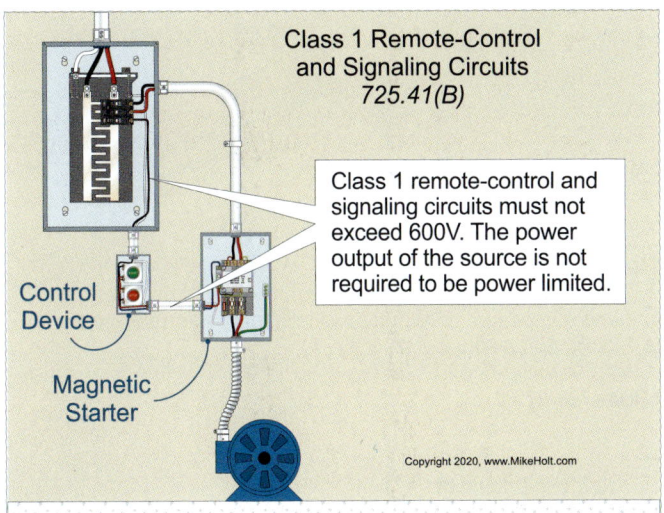

▶Figure 725–23

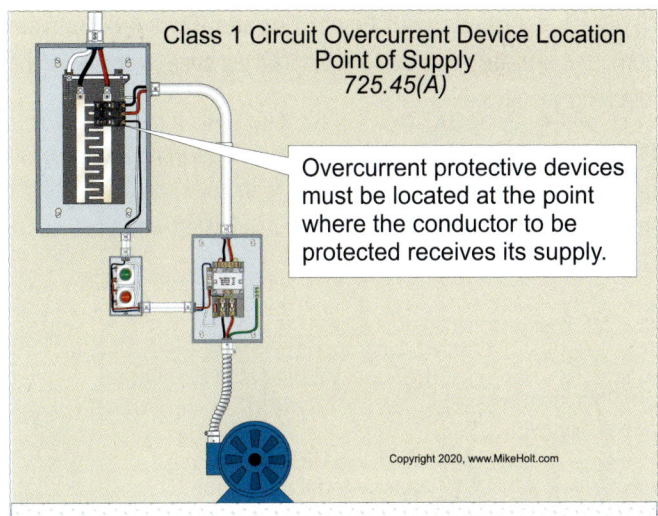

▶Figure 725–24

725.43 Class 1 Circuit Overcurrent Protection

Overcurrent protection for conductors 14 AWG and larger must be in accordance with the conductor ampacity in accordance with 110.14(C)(1) and Table 310.16. Overcurrent protection for 18 AWG conductors is not permitted to exceed 7A; and for 16 AWG conductors, overcurrent protection is not permitted to exceed 10A.

725.45 Class 1 Circuit Overcurrent Protective Device Location

(A) Point of Supply. Overcurrent protective devices must be located at the point where the conductor to be protected receives its supply. ▶Figure 725–24

(D) Primary Side of Transformer. Class 1 circuit conductors supplied by a transformer having only a 2-wire secondary can be protected by the primary overcurrent protective device in accordance with 450.3(B), provided the primary overcurrent protective device does not exceed the value determined by multiplying the secondary conductor ampacity by the secondary-to-primary transformer voltage ratio. ▶Figure 725–25

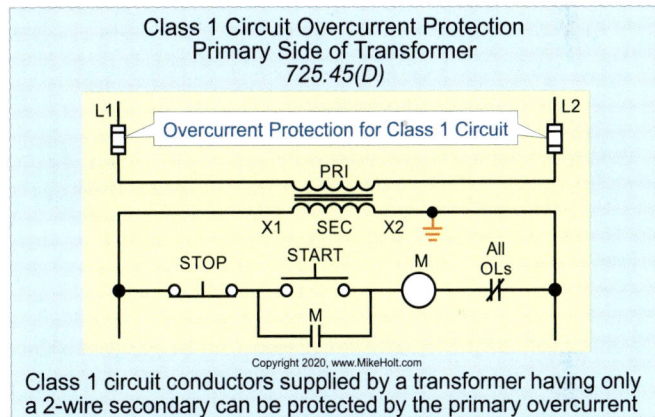

▶Figure 725–25

725.46 Class 1 Circuit Wiring Methods

Class 1 circuits must be installed in accordance with Part I of Article 300, and Class 1 wiring must be installed in a suitable Chapter 3 wiring method.

725.48 Conductors of Different Circuits in Same Cable, Cable Tray, Enclosure, or Raceway

(A) Class 1 Circuits with Other Class 1 Circuits. Two or more Class 1 circuits can be installed in the same cable, enclosure, or raceway provided all conductors are insulated for the maximum voltage of any conductor.

725.49 | Remote-Control, Signaling, and Power-Limited Circuits

(B) Class 1 Circuits with Power Circuits. Class 1 circuits are permitted to be installed with electrical power conductors under the following conditions:

(1) In a Cable, Enclosure, or Raceway. Class 1 circuits can be in the same cable, enclosure, or raceway with power-supply circuits if the equipment powered is functionally associated with the Class 1 circuit. ▶Figure 725-26

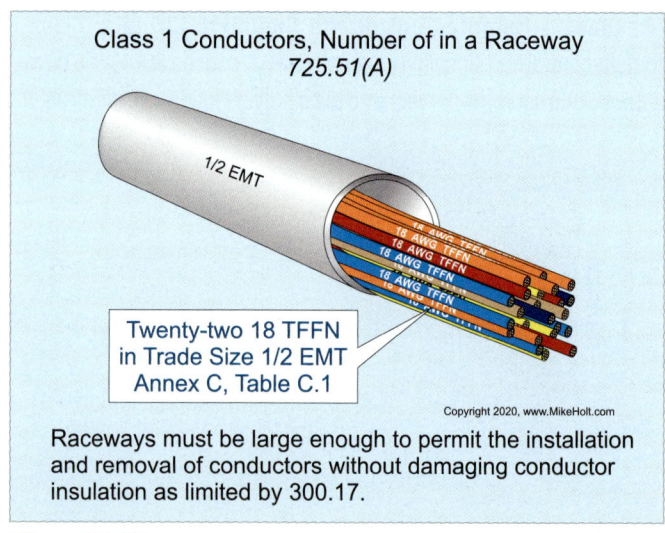

▶Figure 725-27

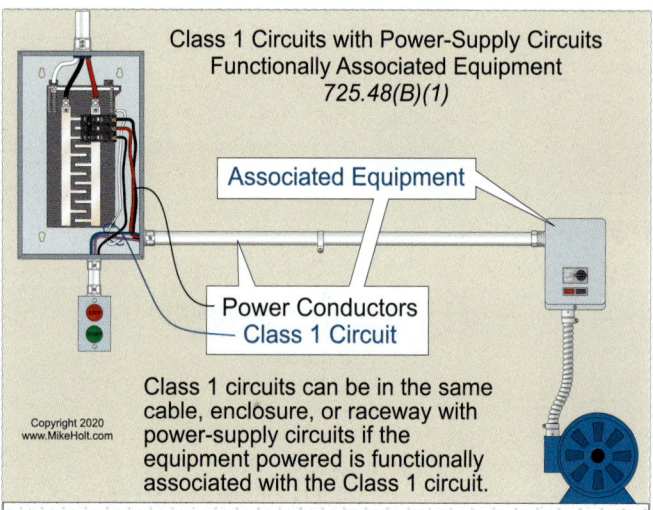

▶Figure 725-26

Class 1 circuits are permitted to be installed together with the conductors of electric light, power, nonpower-limited fire alarm, and medium power network-powered broadband communications circuits where separated by a barrier.

725.49 Class 1 Circuit Conductors

(A) Size and Use. Conductors of sizes 18 AWG and 16 AWG installed within a raceway, enclosure, or listed cable are permitted if they do not supply a load that exceeds the ampacities given in Table 402.5. Conductors 14 AWG and larger must meet the ampacities given in Table 310.16.

(B) Insulation. Class 1 circuit conductors must have at least a 600V insulation rating.

725.51 Number of Conductors in a Raceway

(A) Class 1 Circuit Conductors. Raceways must be large enough to permit the installation and removal of conductors without damaging conductor insulation as limited by 300.17. ▶Figure 725-27

Author's Comment:

▶ When all conductors within a raceway are the same size and insulation, the number of conductors permitted can be found in Annex C for the raceway type [Chapter 9, Notes to Tables, Note 1].

▶ For conductors not included in Chapter 9 (such as multiconductor cable), the actual dimensions must be used. If one multiconductor cable is used inside a raceway, the single conductor percentage fill area must be used [Chapter 9, Notes to Tables, Note 5 and 9].

▶ These conductors are subject to the ampacity adjustment factors in 310.15(C)(1) only if they carry continuous loads in excess of 10 percent of the conductor(s) ampacity.

Part III. Class 2 Circuit Requirements

725.121 Power Sources for Class 2 Circuits

(A) Power Source. The power supply for a Class 2 circuit must be as follows:

(1) A listed Class 2 transformer. ▶Figure 725-28

(2) A listed Class 2 power supply.

(3) Equipment listed as a Class 2 power source.

▶Figure 725-28

Ex 2: Where a circuit has an energy level at or below the limits established in Chapter 9, Table 11(A) and 11(B), the equipment is not required to be listed as a Class 2 power transformer, power supply, or power source.

(4) Listed audio/video information technology equipment (computers), communications, and industrial equipment limited-power circuits. ▶Figure 725-29

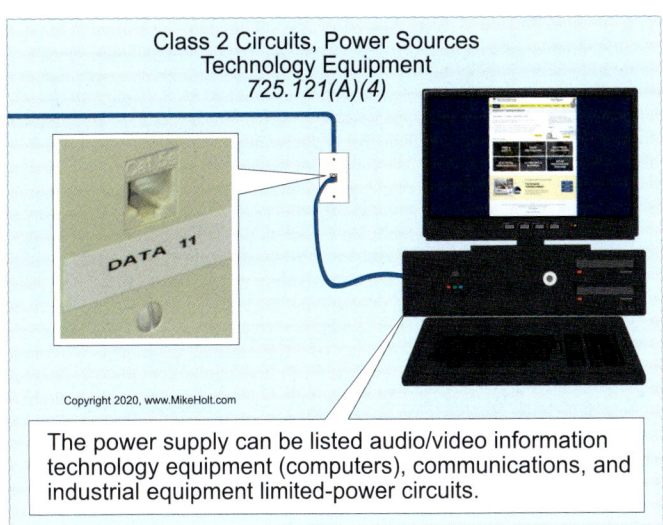
▶Figure 725-29

(5) A battery source or battery source system that is listed and identified as Class 2.

(C) Marking. The power sources for power-limited circuits in 725.121(A)(3) and power-limited circuits for listed audio/video equipment, listed information technology equipment, listed communications equipment, and listed industrial equipment in 725.121(A)(4) must have a label indicating the maximum voltage and rated current output per conductor for each connection point on the power source. Where multiple connection points have the same rating, a single label is permitted to be used.

Note 1: The rated current for power sources covered in 725.144 is the output current per conductor the power source is designed to deliver to an operational load at normal operating conditions, as declared by the manufacturer.

725.124 Circuit Marking

Equipment supplying Class 2 circuits must be durably marked to indicate each circuit that is a Class 2 circuit.

725.127 Wiring Methods on Supply Side of the Class 2 Power Source

Conductors and equipment on the supply side of the Class 2 power supply must be installed in accordance with Chapters 1 through 4. The overcurrent protection for Class 2 transformers or power supplies must not exceed 20A. ▶Figure 725-30

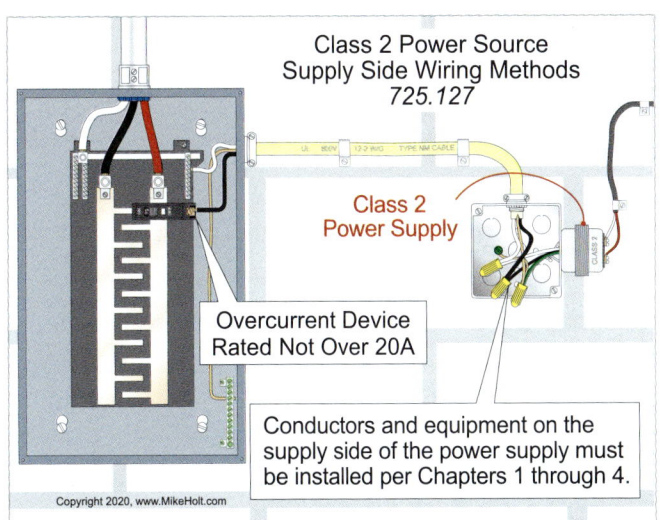
▶Figure 725-30

725.130 | Remote-Control, Signaling, and Power-Limited Circuits

725.130 Wiring Methods on Load Side of the Class 2 Power Source

(A) Class 1 Wiring Methods. Class 2 circuits are permitted to use a Class 1 wiring method in accordance with 725.46.

Ex 2: Class 2 circuits can be reclassified as a Class 1 circuit if the Class 2 equipment markings are eliminated and the circuit is installed using a Chapter 3 wiring method in accordance with 725.46. ▶Figure 725–31

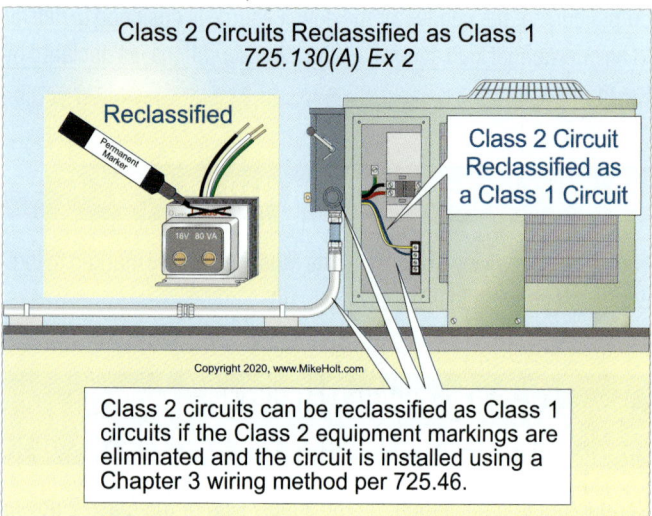

▶Figure 725–31

Author's Comment:

▶ Where a Class 2 circuit is reclassified as a Class 1 circuit, it can be run in the same raceway, cable, or enclosure with power conductors of functionally associated equipment [725.48(B)]. ▶Figure 725–32

Note: Class 2 circuits reclassified and installed as Class 1 circuits are no longer Class 2 circuits, regardless of their continued connection to a Class 2 power source.

(B) Class 2 Wiring Methods. Class 2 circuits are permitted to use Class 2 wiring of the type in 725.179 if installed in accordance with 725.133 and 725.154.

725.135 Installation of Class 2 Cables

Installation of Class 2 cables must comply with 725.135(A) through (M).

(A) Listing. Class 2 cables installed in buildings must be listed.

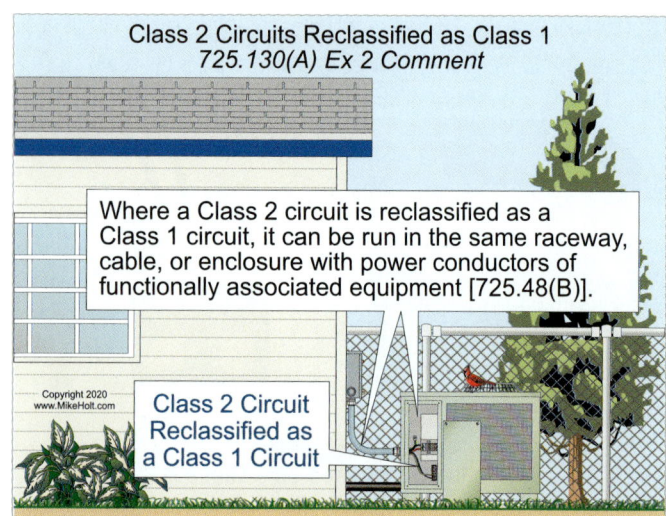

▶Figure 725–32

(B) Ducts Specifically Fabricated for Environmental Air Spaces. Plenum rated Class 2 cables are permitted to be installed within ducts specifically fabricated for environmental air spaces in accordance with 725.3(C) Ex 1 if the cable is directly associated with the air distribution system and complies with (1) or (2): ▶Figure 725–33

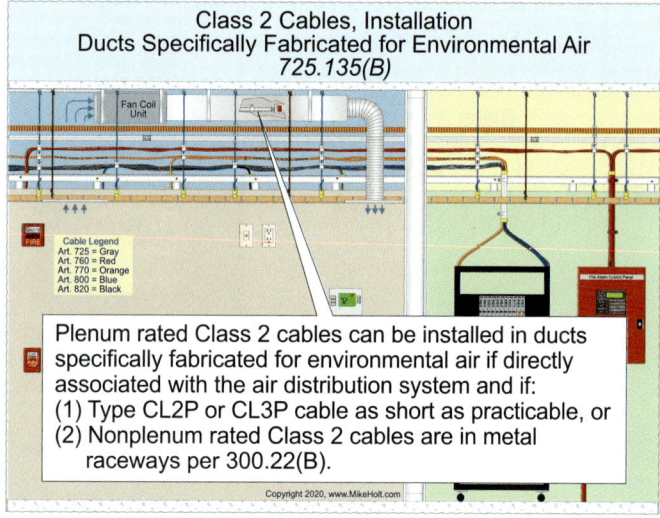

▶Figure 725–33

(1) Types CL2P or CL3P cable (without a raceway) are permitted where the length is as short as practicable to perform the required function.

(2) Nonplenum rated Class 2 cables installed in metal raceways in accordance with 300.22(B).

(C) Plenum Spaces. Plenum rated Class 2 cables are permitted to be installed within plenum air spaces in accordance with 725.3(C) Ex 2 if the Class 2 cables are plenum rated, except where installed in a metallic raceway in accordance with 300.22(C). ▶Figure 725-34

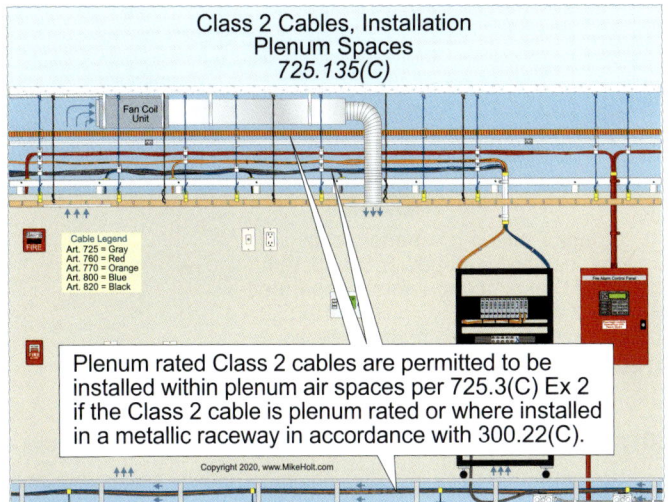

▶Figure 725-34

(H) Cable Trays. Cables installed in cable trays outdoors must be Type PLTC. The following cables are permitted in cable trays inside buildings:

(1) Types CM, CL2P, CL3P, CL2R, CL3R, CL2, CL3, and PLTC cables.

(2) Types CL2P, CL3P, CL2R, CL3R, CL2, CL3, and PLTC cables installed in:
   a. Plenum communications raceways.
   b. Riser communications raceways.
   c. General-purpose communications raceways.

(K) Other Building Locations. The following cables are permitted in building locations other than the locations covered in 725.135(B) through (I):

(1) Types CL2P, CL3P, CL2R, CL3R, CL2, CL3, and PLTC cables.

(2) A maximum of 10 ft of exposed Type CL2X in nonconcealed spaces.

(3) A maximum of 10 ft of exposed Type CL3X in nonconcealed spaces.

(4) Types CL2P, CL3P, CL2R, CL3R, CL2, CL3, and PLTC cables installed in:
   a. Plenum communications raceways.
   b. Plenum cable routing assemblies.
   c. Riser communications raceways.
   d. Riser cable routing assemblies.
   e. General-purpose communications raceways.
   f. General-purpose cable routing assemblies.

(5) Types CL2P, CL3P, CL2R, CL3R, CL2, CL3, CL2X, CL3X, and PLTC cables installed in raceways recognized in Chapter 3.

(M) One- and Two-Family Dwelling Units. The following cables are permitted in dwelling units:

(1) Types CL2P, CL3P, CL2R, CL3R, CL2, CL3, and PLTC cables.

(2) Type CL2X less than ¼ in. in diameter.

(3) Type CL3X less than ¼ in. in diameter.

(4) Types CL2P, CL3P, CL2R, CL3R, CL2, CL3, and PLTC cables installed in:
   a. Plenum communications raceways.
   b. Plenum cable routing assemblies.
   c. Riser communications raceways.
   d. Riser cable routing assemblies.
   e. General-purpose communications raceways.
   f. General-purpose cable routing assemblies.

(5) Types CL2P, CL3P, CL2R, CL3R, CL2, CL3, CL2X, CL3X, and PLTC cables installed in raceways recognized in Chapter 3.

(6) Type CMUC under-carpet communications cables.

725.136 Separation from Power Conductors

(A) Enclosures, Raceways, or Cables. Class 2 cables are not permitted in any enclosure or raceway with power and Class 1 circuits, except as permitted in (B) through (I). ▶Figure 725-35

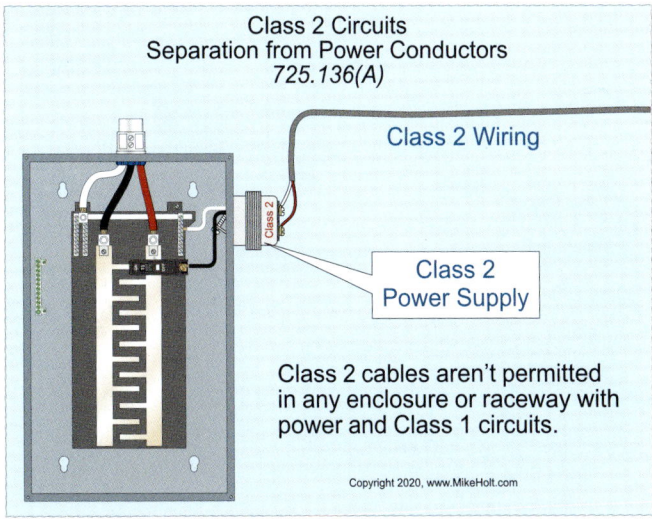

▶Figure 725-35

725.136 | Remote-Control, Signaling, and Power-Limited Circuits

Author's Comment:

▸ Class 2 wiring must be separated from power, lighting, and Class 1 circuits so the higher-voltage conductors do not accidentally energize the Class 2 conductors. ▸Figure 725-36

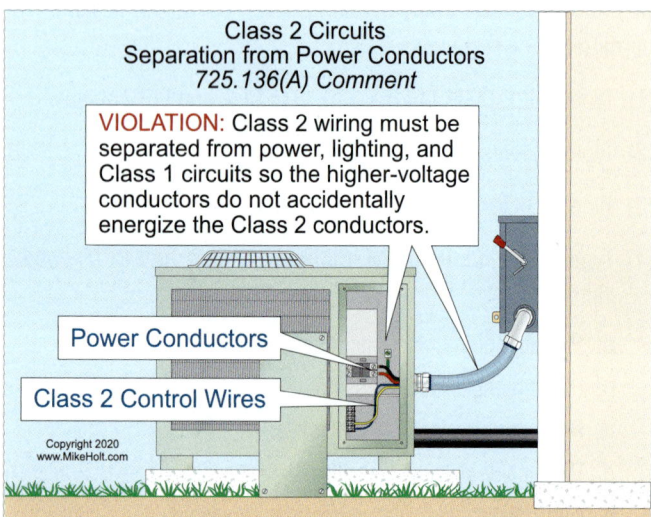

▸Figure 725-36

(B) Separated by Barriers. Class 2 circuit conductors can be installed with power conductors and Class 1 conductors if separated by a barrier. ▸Figure 725-37 and ▸Figure 725-38

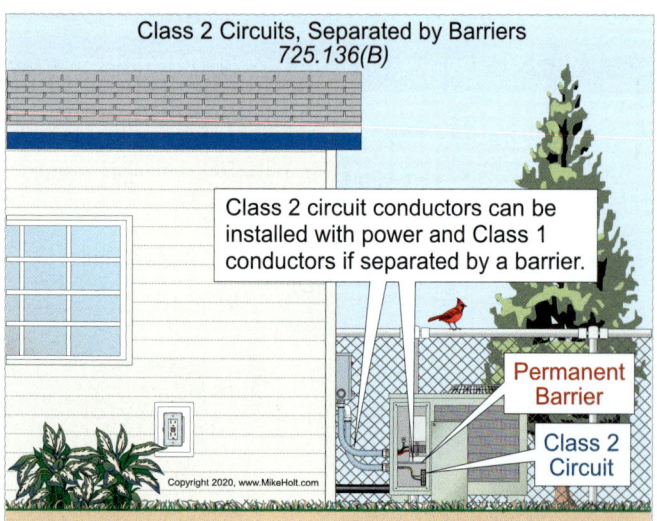

▸Figure 725-37

Author's Comment:

▸ Separation is required to prevent a fire or shock hazard that can occur from a short between the Class 2 circuits and the higher-voltage circuits.

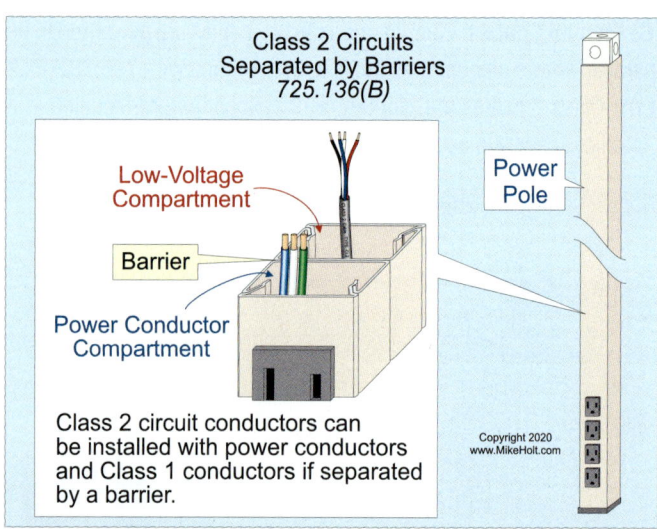

▸Figure 725-38

(D) Associated Systems Within Enclosures. Class 2 circuit conductors are permitted to be installed in compartments, enclosures, and outlet boxes with electric light and power circuits where (1) or (2) applies:

(1) Class 2 circuit conductors are permitted to be installed with power, Class 1, and nonpower-limited fire alarm circuit conductors where routed to maintain a minimum of ¼ in. separation. ▸Figure 725-39

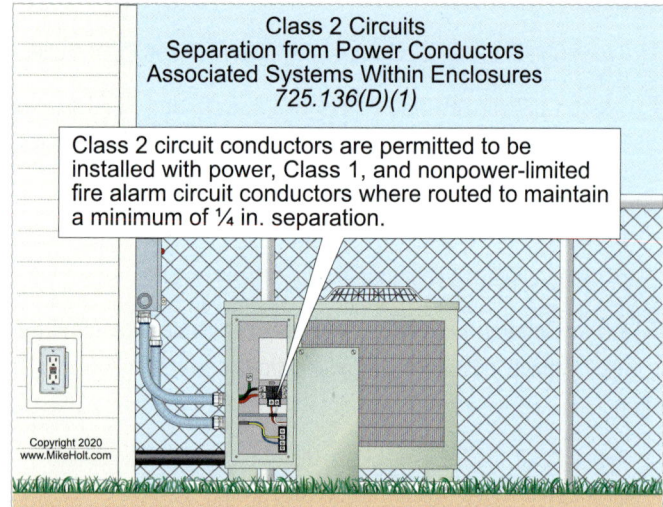

▸Figure 725-39

(2) Class 2 circuit conductors are permitted to be installed with power conductors where introduced solely to connect to equipment associated with power circuit conductors that operate at not over 150V to ground if the Class 2 circuits are contained in a Class 3 cable, and the Class 2 circuit conductors extending beyond the Class 3 cable maintain a minimum of ¼ in. separation from the power conductors. ▸Figure 725-40

Remote-Control, Signaling, and Power-Limited Circuits | 725.139

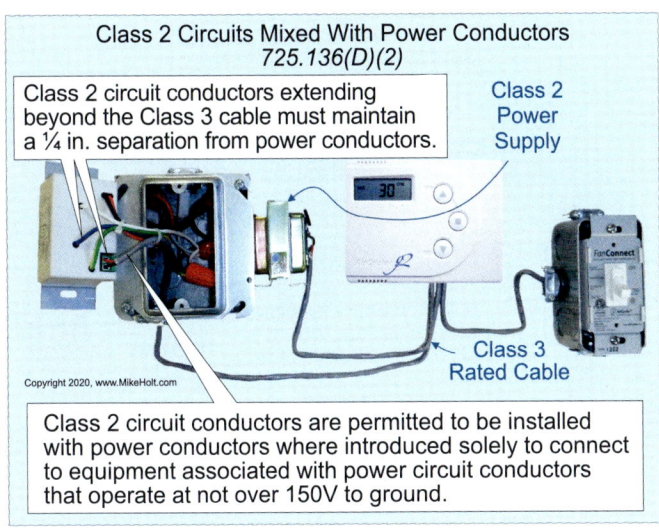
▶Figure 725-40

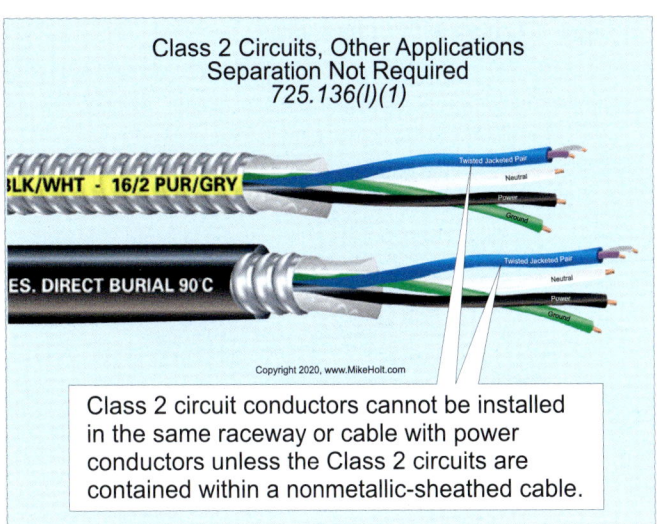
▶Figure 725-42

(G) Cable Trays. Class 2 circuit conductors can be installed with power conductors and Class 1 conductors if separated by a barrier or where the Class 2 circuits are installed in Type MC cable. ▶Figure 725-41

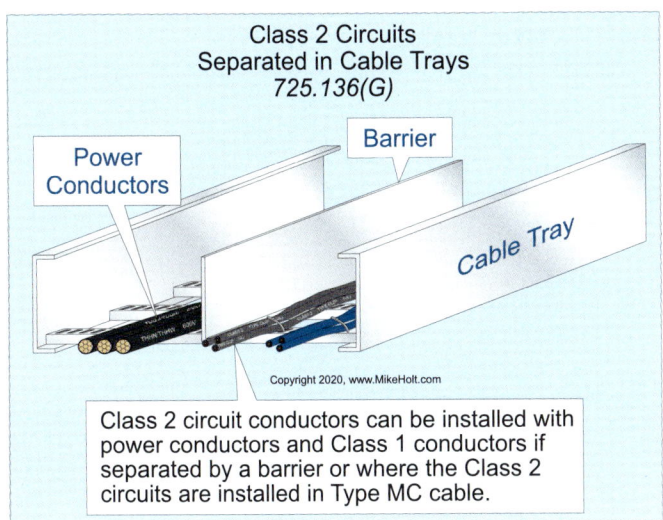
▶Figure 725-41

(I) Other Applications. Class 2 circuit conductors cannot be installed in the same raceway or cable with power conductors unless:

(1) The Class 2 circuits are contained within a nonmetallic-sheathed cable. ▶Figure 725-42

725.139 Conductors of Different Circuits in Same Cable, Enclosure, Cable Tray, Raceway, or Cable Routing Assembly

(A) Class 2 Conductors. Class 2 circuit conductors can be in the same cable, cable routing assembly, enclosure, or raceway with other Class 2 circuit conductors.

(D) Class 2 Circuits with Communications Circuits.

(1) Classified as Communications Circuits. Class 2 circuits are permitted within the same cables with conductors of communications circuits if the cable is listed communications cable that has been installed in accordance with Part V of Article 805. ▶Figure 725-43

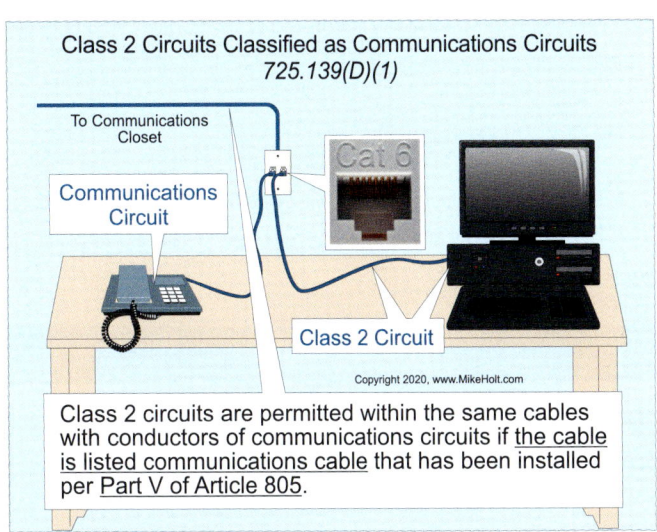
▶Figure 725-43

Mike Holt Enterprises • www.MikeHolt.com • 888.NEC.CODE (632.2633) | 407

(E) Class 2 Cables with Other Cables. Jacketed Class 2 cables can be in the same enclosure, cable tray, raceway, or cable routing assembly as jacketed cables of any of the following: ▶Figure 725-44

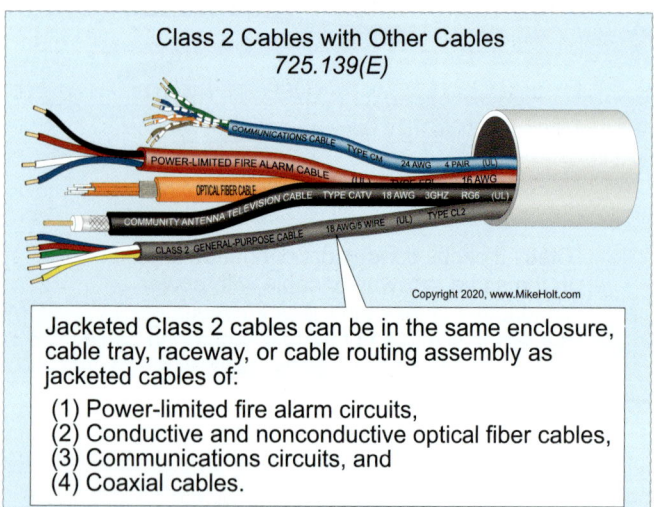
▶Figure 725-44

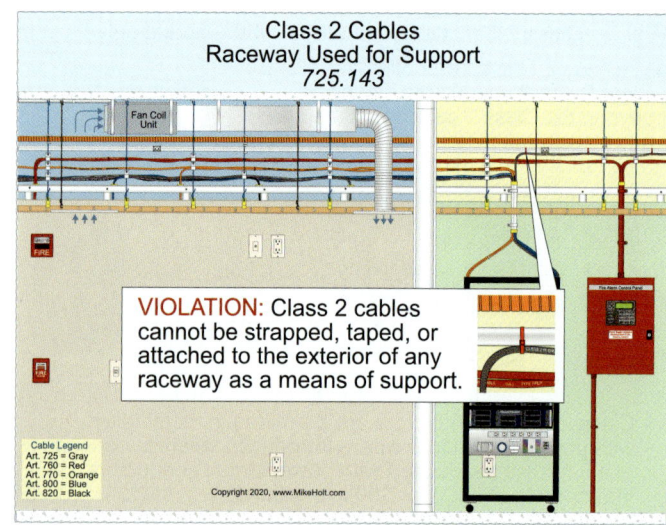
▶Figure 725-45

(1) Power-limited fire alarm circuits in accordance with Parts I and III of Article 760.

(2) Nonconductive and conductive optical fiber cables in accordance with Parts I and IV of Article 770.

(3) Communications circuits in accordance with Parts I and IV of Article 805.

(4) Coaxial cables in accordance with Parts I and IV of Article 820.

(F) Class 2 Circuits with Audio System Circuits. Audio output circuits [640.9(C)] using Class 2 wiring methods in accordance with 725.133 and 725.154 are not permitted to be installed in any cable routing assembly, raceway, or cable with Class 2 cables.

> **Author's Comment:**
> ▸ Audio circuits must use a Class 2 wiring method when required by 640.9(C); however, these circuits are not Class 2 circuits!

725.143 Support

Class 2 cables cannot be strapped, taped, or attached to the exterior of any raceway as a means of support. ▶Figure 725-45

Class 2 control cables can be supported by the raceway that supplies power to the equipment controlled by the Class 2 cable [300.11(C)(2)]. ▶Figure 725-46

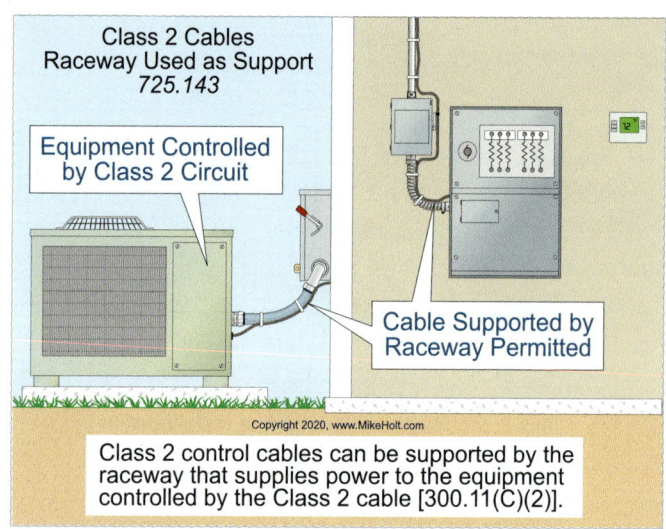
▶Figure 725-46

725.144 Transmission of Power and Data

This section applies to Class 2 circuits that transmit power and data to a powered device. Section 300.11 and Parts I and III of Article 725 apply to Class 2 circuits that transmit power and data.

Conductors that carry power and data must be copper and the current is not permitted to exceed the current limitation of the connectors.

Note 1: An example of cables that transmit power and data include closed-circuit TV cameras (CCTV).

Note 2: The 8P8C connector is in widespread use with powered communications systems. IEC 60603-7, *Connectors for Electronic Equipment—Part 7-1: Detail specification for 8-way, unshielded, free and fixed connectors*, specifies these connectors to have a current-carrying capacity per contact of 1A maximum at 60°C. See IEC 60603-7 for more information on current-carrying capacity at higher and lower temperatures.

Note 3: The requirements of Table 725.144 were derived for carrying power and data over 4-pair copper balanced twisted-pair cabling. This type of cabling is described in ANSI/TIA 568-C.2, *Commercial Building Telecommunications Cabling Standard—Part 2: Balanced Twisted-Pair Telecommunications Cabling and Components.*

Note 4: See TIA-TSB-184-A, *Guidelines for Supporting Power Delivery Over Balanced Twisted-Pair Cabling*, for information on installation and management of balanced twisted-pair cabling supporting power delivery.

Note 5: See ANSI/NEMA C137.3, *American National Standard for Lighting Systems—Minimum Requirements for Installation of Energy Efficient Power over Ethernet (PoE) Lighting Systems*, for information on installation of cables for PoE lighting systems.

Note 6: The rated current for power sources covered in 725.144 is the output current per conductor the power source is designed to deliver to an operational load at normal operating conditions, as declared by the manufacturer. In the design of these systems, the actual current in a given conductor might vary from the rated current per conductor by as much as 20 percent. An increase in current in one conductor is offset by a corresponding decrease in current in one or more conductors of the same cable.

Table 725.144 Copper Conductor Ampacity in 4-Pair Class 2 Power/Data Cables with All Conductors Carrying Current

See *NEC* Table 725.144 for details.

Table 725.144 Note 1: For bundle sizes over 192 cables, or for conductor sizes smaller than 26 AWG, ampacities are permitted to be determined by qualified personnel under engineering supervision.

Table 725.144 Note 2: Where only half of the conductors in each cable are carrying current, the values in the table are permitted to be increased by a factor of 1.40.

Note 1 to Table 725.144: Elevated cable temperatures can reduce a cable's data transmission performance. For information on practices for 4-pair balanced twisted-pair cabling, see TIA-TSB-184-A and 6.4.7, 6.6.3, and Annex G of ANSI/TIA-568-C.2, which provide guidance on adjustments for operating temperatures between 20°C and 60°C.

Note 2 to Table 725.144: The per-contact current rating of connectors can limit the maximum current below the ampacity shown in Table 725.144.

(A) Use of Class 2 Cables to Transmit Power and Data. Where Types CL3P, CL2P, CL3R, CL2R, CL3, or CL2 transmit power and data, the rated current per conductor of the power source is not permitted to exceed the ampacities in Table 725.144 at an ambient temperature of 30°C. For ambient temperatures above 30°C, the correction factors in Table 310.15(B)(1) must be applied.

Ex: Compliance with Table 725.144 is not required for conductors 24 AWG or larger and the rated current per conductor of the power source does not exceed 0.30A.

Note: One example of the use of Class 2 cables is a network of closed-circuit TV cameras using 24 AWG, 60°C rated, Type CL2R, Category 5e balanced twisted-pair cabling.

(B) Use of Class 2-LP Cables to Transmit Power and Data. Cable Types CL3P-LP, CL2P-LP, CL3R-LP, CL2R-LP, CL3-LP, or CL2-LP are permitted to supply power to equipment from a power source with a rated current per conductor up to the marked current limit located immediately following the suffix "-LP" and are permitted to transmit data to the equipment. Where the number of bundled LP cables is 192 or less and the selected ampacity of the cables in accordance with Table 725.144 exceeds the marked current limit of the cable, the ampacity determined from the table is permitted to be used. For ambient temperatures above 30°C, the correction factors of Table 310.15(B)(1) or Equation 310.15(B)(2) must apply. The Class 2-LP cables must comply with the following, as applicable:

(1) Cables with the suffix "-LP" are permitted to be installed in bundles, raceways, cable trays, communications raceways, and cable routing assemblies.

(2) Cables with the suffix "-LP" and a marked current limit must follow the substitution hierarchy of Table 725.154 and Figure 725.154(A) in the *NEC* for the cable type without the suffix "-LP" and without the marked current limit.

(3) System design is permitted by qualified persons under engineering supervision.

Note: An example of a limited power (LP) cable is a cable marked Type CL2-LP (0.5A), 23 AWG.

725.154 Applications of Class 2 Cables

Class 2 cables must comply with any requirements in 725.154(A) through (C) and in Table 725.154. ▶Figure 725–47

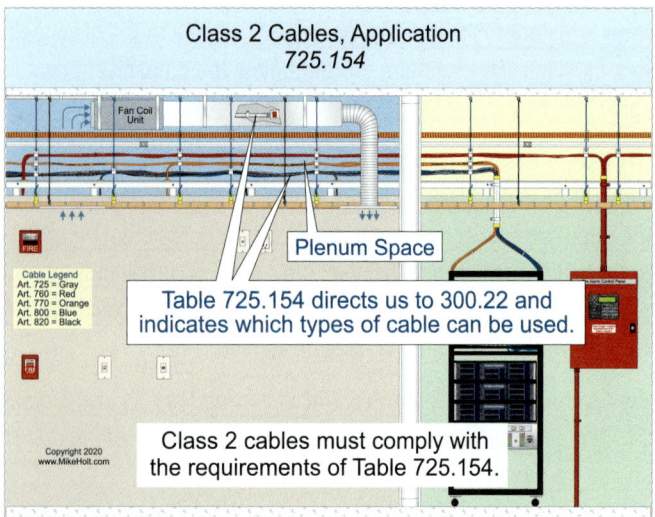

▶Figure 725–47

(A) Class 2 Cable Substitutions. Cable substitutions can be made in accordance with Table 725.145(A) and *NEC* Figure 725.154(A) Cable Substitution Hierarchy.

Part IV. Listing Requirements

725.170 Listing and Marking of Equipment for Power and Data Transmission

Listed power sources for circuits intended to provide power and data over Class 2 cables to remote equipment must comply with 725.121, and the marking of equipment output connections must be in accordance with 725.121(C).

725.179 Listing and Marking of Class 2 Cables

Class 2 cables, nonmetallic plenum raceways, and cable routing assemblies installed within buildings must be listed and marked in accordance with 725.179(J). ▶Figure 725–48

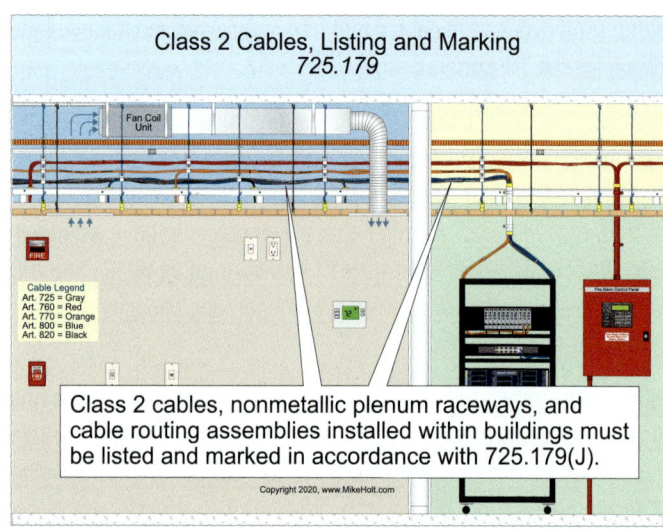

▶Figure 725–48

Author's Comment:

▶ Where installed in corrosive, damp, or wet locations, Class 2 cables must be identified for the location in accordance with 110.11 and 310.10(F). Conductors and cables installed in underground raceways [300.5(B)], or in raceways aboveground in wet locations [300.9], must also be identified for wet locations. Where corrosion may occur, the requirements of 300.6 must be used [725.3(L).

(A) Types CL2P and CL3P. Types CL2P and CL3P cable must be listed as suitable for use in plenum spaces. ▶Figure 725–49

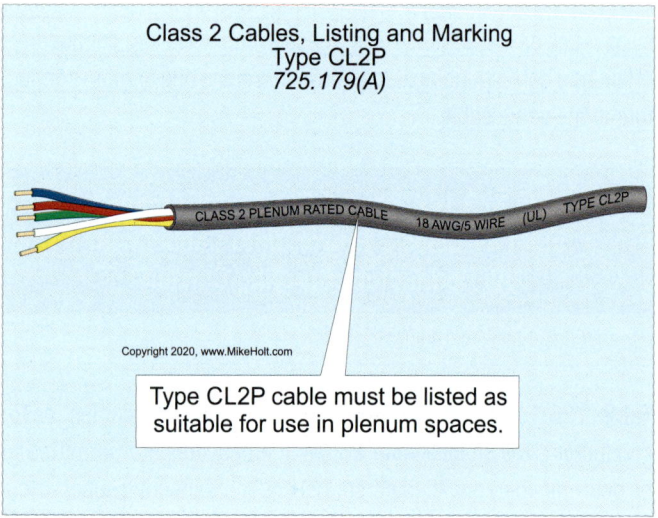

▶Figure 725–49

(G) Cable Voltage Rating. Class 2 cables must have a voltage rating of not less than 150V, and Class 3 cables must have a voltage rating of not less than 300V.

(I) Limited Power (LP) Cables. Limited power (LP) cables must be listed as suitable for carrying power and data circuits up to a specified current for each conductor. The cables must be marked with the suffix "-LP (XXA)" where "XXA" designates that current limit is amperes per conductor.

Note: An example of the marking on a Class 2 cable with an LP rating is "CL2-LP. (75°C) 23 AWG 4-pair," which indicates that it is a 4-pair plenum cable with 23 AWG conductors, a temperature rating of 75°C, and a current limit of 0.60A per conductor.

(J) Marking. Class 2 cables must be marked in accordance with Table 715.179(J) and voltage ratings are not permitted to be marked on the cable.

Note: Voltage markings on cables may suggest that the cables are suitable for Class 1 or electric power and light applications, which they are not.

Table 725.179(J) Cable Marking

Cable Marking	Type
CL3P	Class 3 plenum cable
CL2P	Class 2 plenum cable
CL3R	Class 3 riser cable
CL2R	Class 2 riser cable
PLTC	Power-limited tray cable
CL3	Class 3 cable
CL2	Class 2 cable
CL3X	Class 3 cable, limited use
CL2X	Class 2 cable, limited use

Note: Class 2 cable types are listed in descending order of fire-resistance rating; Class 3 cables are listed above Class 2 cables because Class 3 cables can be substituted for Class 2 cables.

Notes

ARTICLE 760 — FIRE ALARM SYSTEMS

Introduction to Article 760—Fire Alarm Systems

Article 760 covers the installation of wiring and equipment for fire alarm systems including circuits controlled and powered by the fire alarm. These systems include fire detection and alarm notification, guard's tour, sprinkler waterflow, and sprinkler supervisory systems. NFPA 72, *National Fire Alarm and Signaling Code,* provides the requirements for the selection, installation, performance, use, testing, and maintenance of fire alarm systems.

Part I. General

760.1 Scope

Article 760 covers the installation of wiring and equipment for fire alarm systems, including circuits controlled and powered by the fire alarm system. ▶Figure 760–1

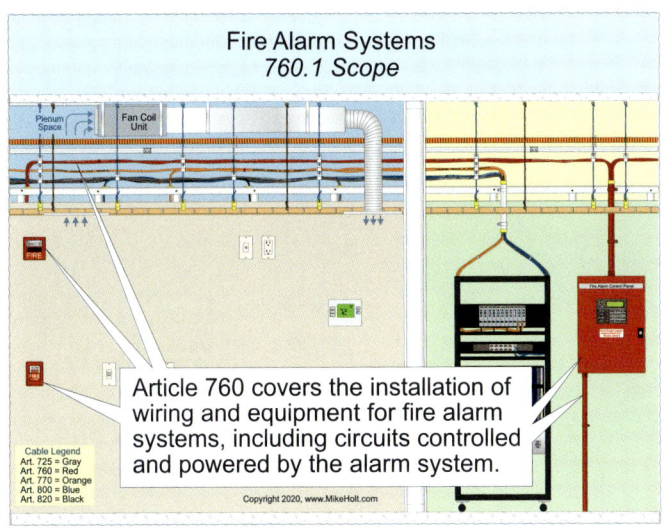

▶Figure 760–1

Author's Comment:

▶ Residential smoke alarm systems, including interconnecting wiring, are not covered by Article 760 because they are not powered by a fire alarm system as defined in NFPA 72, *National Fire Alarm and Signaling Code.*

Note 1: Fire alarm systems include fire detection and alarm notification, guard's tour, sprinkler waterflow, and sprinkler supervisory systems. Other circuits that might be controlled or powered by the fire alarm system include elevator capture, elevator shutdown, door release, smoke doors and damper control, fire doors and damper control, and fan shutdown. NFPA 72, *National Fire Alarm and Signaling Code,* provides the requirements for the selection, installation, performance, use, testing, and maintenance of fire alarm systems.

Author's Comment:

▶ Building control circuits associated with the fire alarm system, such as elevator capture and fan shutdown, must comply with Article 725 [760.3(E)]. Article 760 applies if these components are powered and directly controlled by the fire alarm system.

▶ NFPA 101, *Life Safety Code*, or the local building code specifies when and where a fire alarm system is required.

760.2 Definitions

The definitions in this section only apply to this article.

Abandoned Fire Alarm Cable. A cable that is not terminated to equipment and not identified for future use with a tag. ▶Figure 760–2

760.3 | Fire Alarm Systems

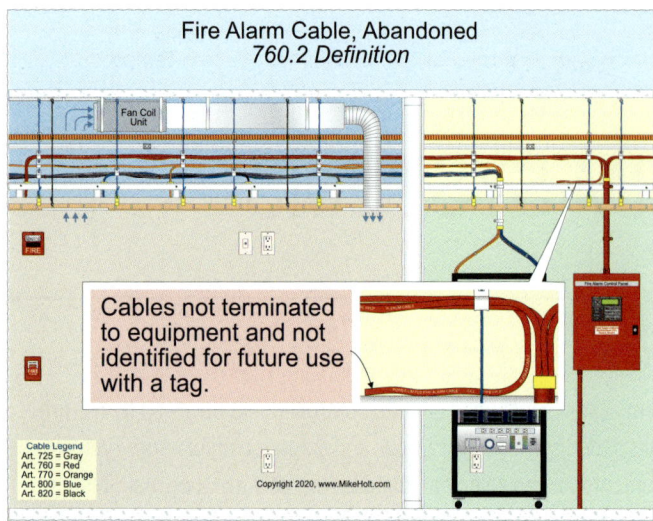
▶Figure 760-2

Author's Comment:

▸ Section 760.25 requires the accessible portion of abandoned cables to be removed.

Fire Alarm Circuit. The portion of the wiring system and connected equipment powered and controlled by the fire alarm system. ▶Figure 760-3

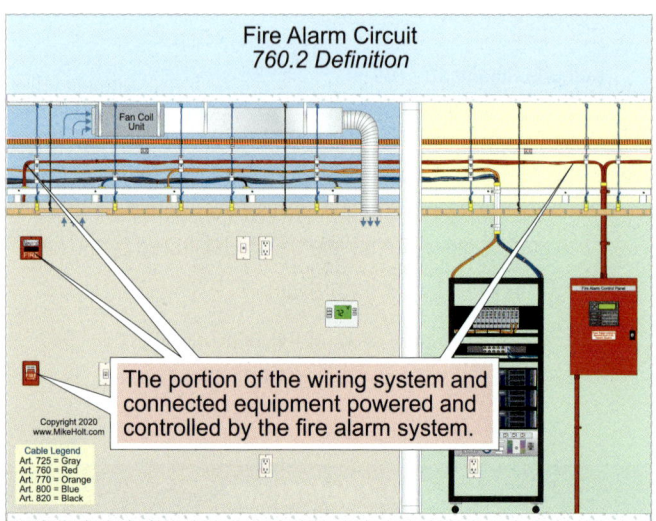
▶Figure 760-3

Power-Limited Fire Alarm Circuit (PLFA). A power-limited fire alarm circuit must have the voltage and power limited by a listed power supply that complies with 760.121. ▶Figure 760-4

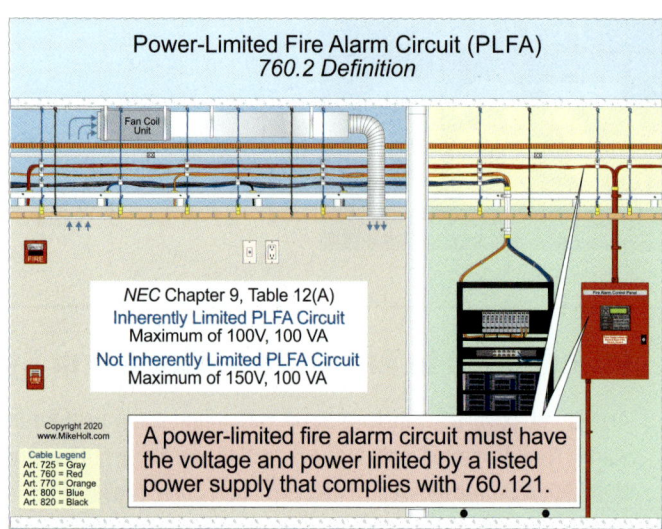
▶Figure 760-4

760.3 Other Articles

Fire alarm circuits and equipment must comply with 760.3(A) through (O). Only those sections contained in Article 300 specifically referenced below apply to fire alarm systems.

(A) Spread of Fire or Products of Combustion. Installation of fire alarm circuits must comply with 300.21. ▶Figure 760-5

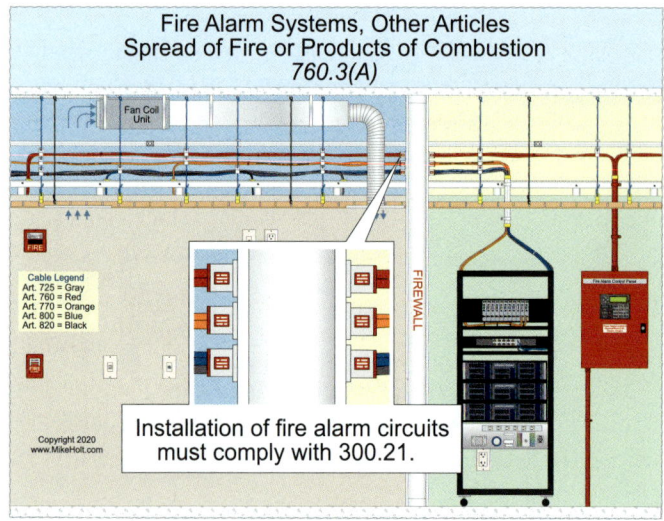
▶Figure 760-5

(B) Ducts and Plenum Spaces. Fire alarm cables installed in ducts or plenum spaces must comply with 300.22. ▶Figure 760-6

Ex 1: Power-limited fire alarm cables selected in accordance with Table 760.154 and installed in accordance with 760.135(B) and 300.22(B) Ex are permitted to be installed in ducts specifically fabricated for environmental air.

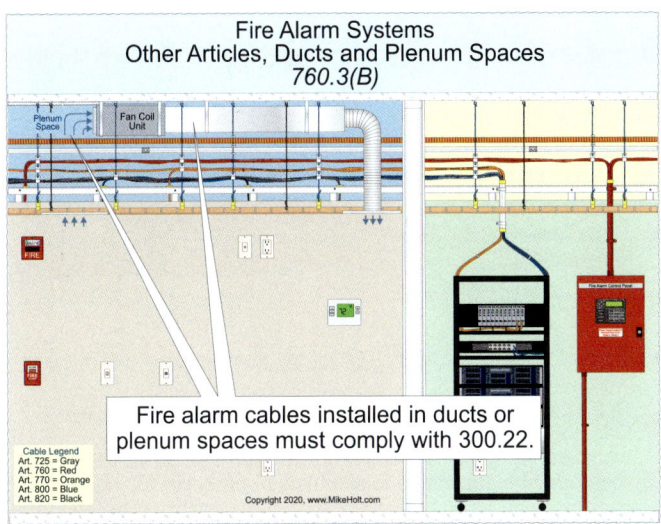
▶Figure 760-6

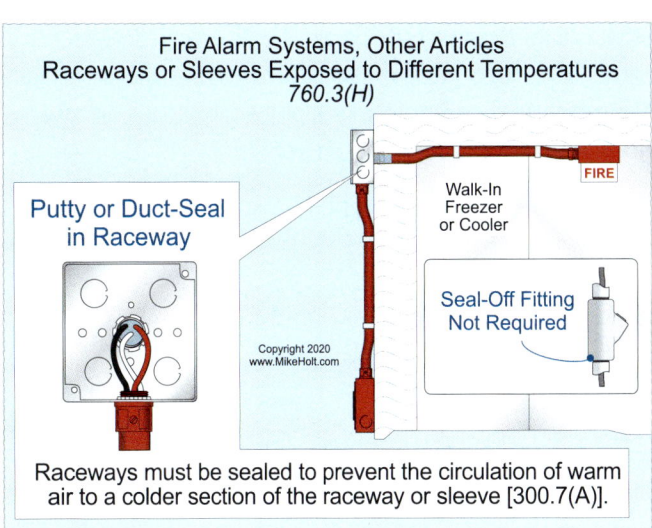
▶Figure 760-7

Ex 2: Power-limited fire alarm cables selected in accordance with Table 760.154 and installed in accordance with 760.135(C) are permitted to be installed in plenum spaces.

(D) Corrosive, Damp, or Wet Locations. Fire alarm circuits installed in corrosive, damp, or wet locations must be identified for use in the operating environment [110.11], must be of materials suitable for the environment in which they are to be installed, and must be of a type suitable for the application [300.5(B), 300.6, 300.9, and 310.10(F)].

(E) Building Control Circuits. Class 1, 2, and 3 circuits used for building controls (elevator capture, fan shutdown, and so on) associated with the fire alarm system, but not controlled and powered by the fire alarm system, must be installed in accordance with Article 725.

(F) Optical Fiber Cables. Optical fiber cables utilized for fire alarm circuits must be installed in accordance with Article 770.

(H) Raceways or Sleeves Exposed to Different Temperatures. If a raceway or sleeve is subjected to different temperatures, and where condensation is known to be a problem, the raceway or sleeve must be filled with a material approved by the authority having jurisdiction that will prevent the circulation of warm air to a colder section of the raceway in accordance with 300.7(A). ▶Figure 760-7

(J) Number and Size of Conductors in a Raceway. Raceways must be large enough to permit the installation and removal of conductors without damaging conductor insulation [300.17].

Author's Comment:

▶ When all conductors within a raceway are the same size and insulation, the number of conductors permitted can be found in Annex C for the raceway type.

Author's Comment:

▶ For conductors not included in Chapter 9 (such as multiconductor cable), the actual dimensions must be used. If one multiconductor cable is used inside a raceway the single conductor percentage fill area must be used [Chapter 9, Notes to Tables, Note 5 and 9].

▶ **Example**

Question: How many 18 TFFN fixture wires can be installed in trade size ½ electrical metallic tubing? ▶Figure 760-8

(a) 16   (b) 18   (c) 22   (d) 38

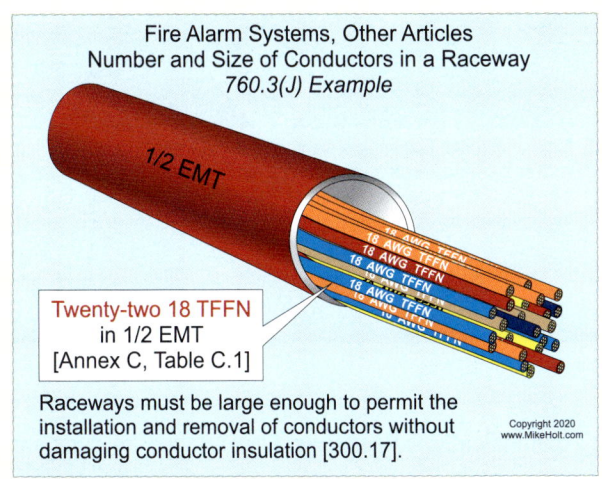
▶Figure 760-8

Answer: (c) 22
[Annex C, Table C.1]

(K) Bushing. When a raceway is used for the support or protection of cables, a bushing or fitting is required to reduce the potential for abrasion and must be placed at the location the cables enter the raceway in accordance with 300.15(C). ▶Figure 760–9

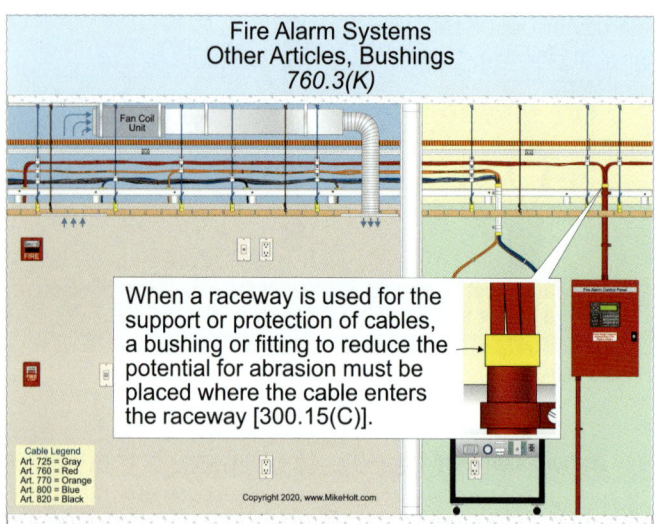

▶Figure 760–9

(L) Cable Routing Assemblies. Power-limited fire alarm cables can be installed in cable routing assemblies selected in accordance with Table 800.154(c), listed in accordance with 800.182, and installed in accordance with 800.110(C) and 800.113. ▶Figure 760–10

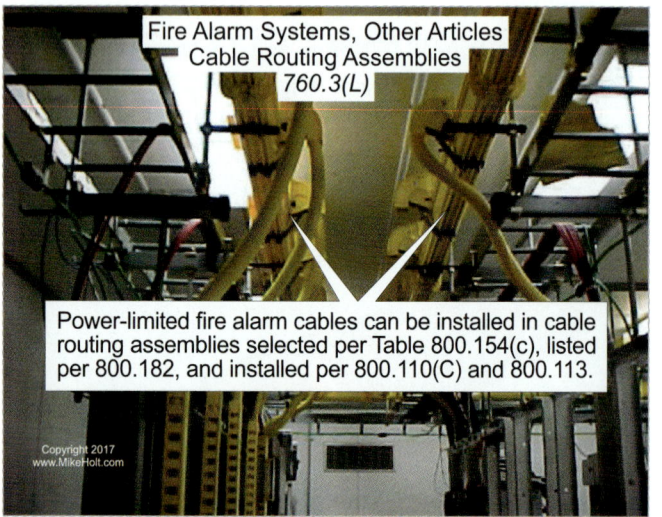

▶Figure 760–10

(M) Communications Raceways. Power-limited fire alarm cables can be installed in communications raceways selected in accordance with Table 800.154(b), listed in accordance with 800.182, and installed in accordance with 800.113 and 362.24 through 362.56 where the requirements applicable to electrical nonmetallic tubing apply. ▶Figure 760–11

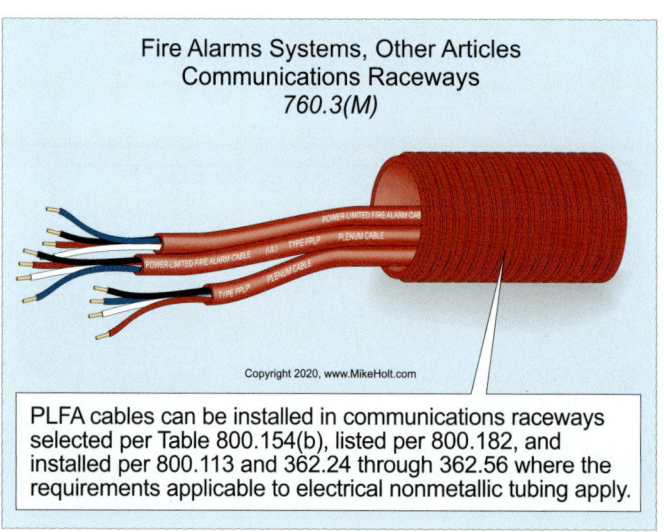

▶Figure 760–11

(N) Temperature Limitations. The requirements of 310.14(A)(3) on the temperature limitation of conductors apply to power-limited fire alarm cables and nonpower-limited fire alarm cables.

(O) Identification of Equipment Grounding Conductors. Equipment grounding conductors must be identified in accordance with 250.119.

Ex: Conductors with green insulation are permitted to be used as ungrounded signal conductors for Types FPLP, FPLR, FPL, and substitute cables installed in accordance with 760.154(A).

760.21 Access to Electrical Equipment Behind Panels Designed to Allow Access

Access to equipment is not permitted to be prohibited by an accumulation of cables that prevents the removal of suspended-ceiling panels.

Author's Comment:

▶ Cables must be located so suspended-ceiling panels can be moved to provide access to electrical equipment.

760.24 Mechanical Execution of Work

(A) General. Equipment and cabling must be installed in a neat and workmanlike manner.

Exposed cables must be supported by the structural components of the building so the cable(s) will not be damaged by normal building use. Support must be by straps, staples, hangers, cable ties, or similar fittings designed and installed in a manner that will not damage the cable. Installations must comply with 300.4. ▶Figure 760–12

Fire Alarm Systems | 760.25

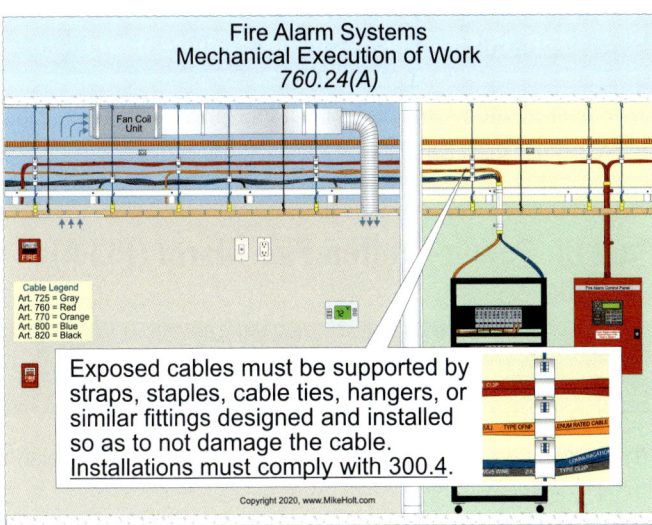

▶Figure 760–12

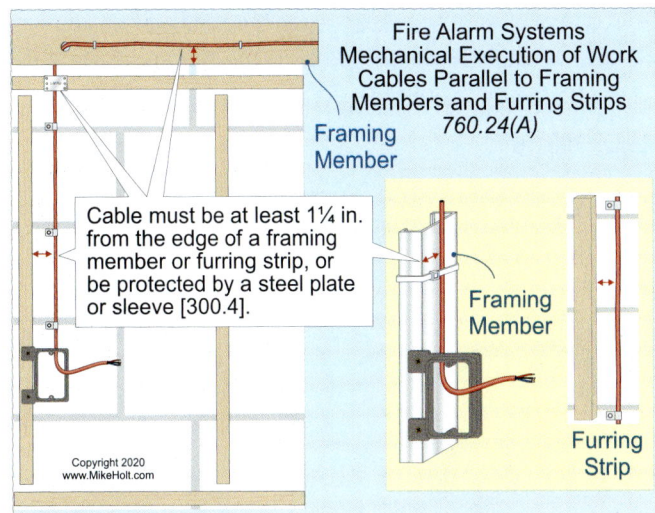

▶Figure 760–14

Author's Comment:

▸ Raceways and cables can be supported by independent support wires attached to the suspended ceiling in accordance with 300.11(B) [760.130(B)]. ▶Figure 760–13

760.25 Abandoned Cables

To limit the spread of fire or products of combustion within a building, the accessible portion of cable that is not terminated at equipment and not tagged for future use must be removed. ▶Figure 760–15

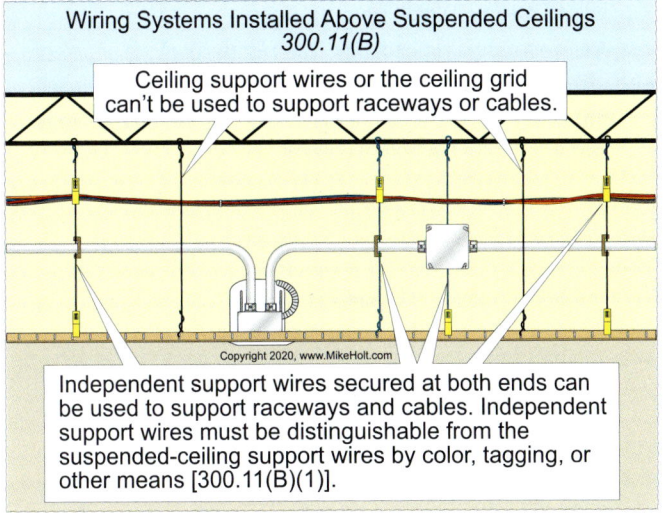

▶Figure 760–13

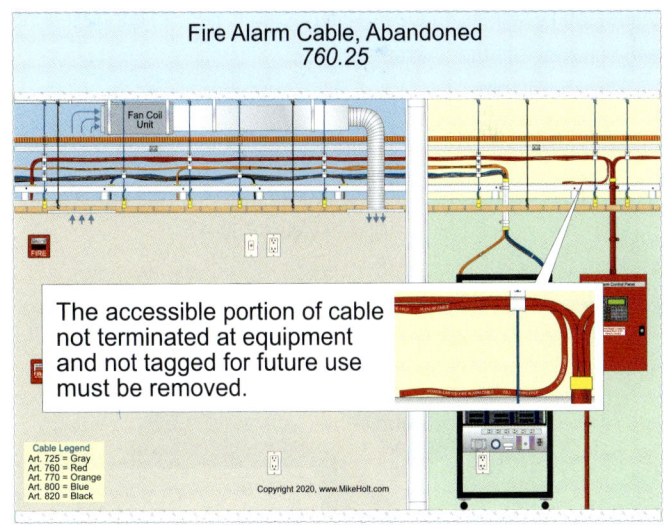

▶Figure 760–15

Note: Paint, plaster, cleaners, abrasives, corrosive residues, or other contaminants might result in an undetermined alteration of PLFA and NPLFA cable properties.

Cables installed through or parallel to framing members or furring strips must be protected where they are likely to be penetrated by nails or screws by installing the wiring method so it is not less than 1¼ in. from the nearest edge of the framing member or furring strips, or by protecting them with a ¹⁄₁₆ in. thick steel plate or the equivalent [300.4]. ▶Figure 760–14

Tags identifying cables for future use must be able to withstand the environment involved.

Author's Comment:

▸ Cables installed in concealed raceways are not considered accessible; therefore, they are not required to be removed. See the definition of "Abandoned Fire Alarm Cable" in 760.2.

760.30 Fire Alarm Circuit Identification

Fire alarm circuits must be identified at terminal and junction locations.
▶Figure 760-16

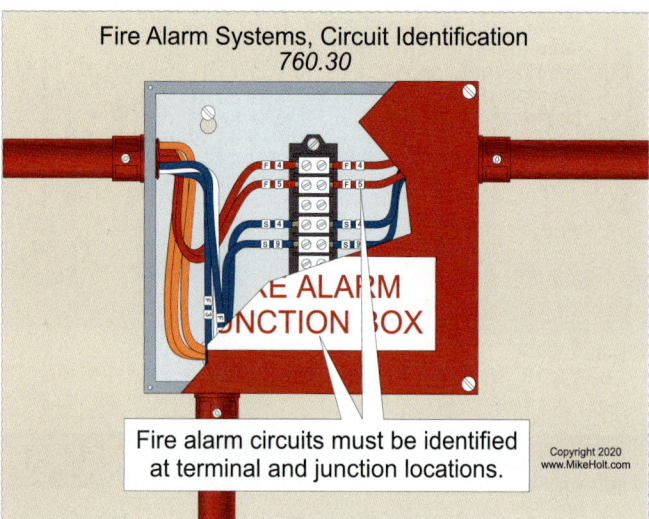
▶Figure 760-16

The identification must be in such a manner that will help to prevent unintentional signals on the fire alarm system circuits during testing and servicing of other systems.

Author's Comment:

▸ Red raceways and fittings are sometimes used, but that color is not required by the *NEC*. ▶Figure 760-17

▶Figure 760-17

760.35 Fire Alarm Circuit Requirements

(B) Power-Limited Fire Alarm Circuits. Power-limited fire alarm (PLFA) circuits must comply with Parts I and III of this article.

Part III. Power-Limited Fire Alarm (PLFA) Circuits

760.121 Power Sources for Power-Limited Fire Alarm Circuits

(A) Power Source. The power source for a power-limited fire alarm circuit must be:

(1) A listed PLFA transformer, or

(2) A listed PLFA power supply, or

(3) Listed equipment marked to identify the PLFA power source.

Note: Examples of listed equipment are:

▸ A fire alarm control panel with integral power source.

▸ A circuit card listed for use as a PLFA source, where used as part of a listed assembly.

▸ A current-limiting impedance, listed for the purpose or part of a listed product, used in conjunction with a nonpower-limited transformer or a stored energy source, for example, storage battery, to limit the output current.

(B) Branch Circuit. Power-limited fire alarm equipment must be supplied by a branch circuit that supplies no other load and is not GFCI or AFCI protected. ▶Figure 760-18

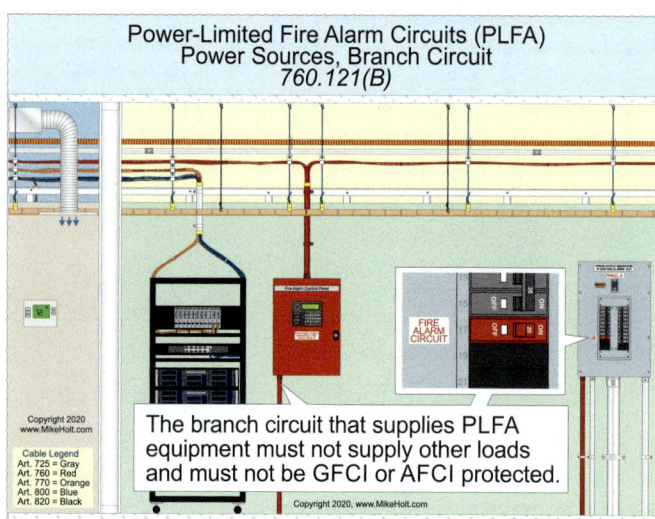
▶Figure 760-18

Fire Alarm Systems | 760.130

The location of the branch-circuit overcurrent protective device for the power-limited fire alarm equipment must be permanently identified at the fire alarm control unit. ▶Figure 760–19

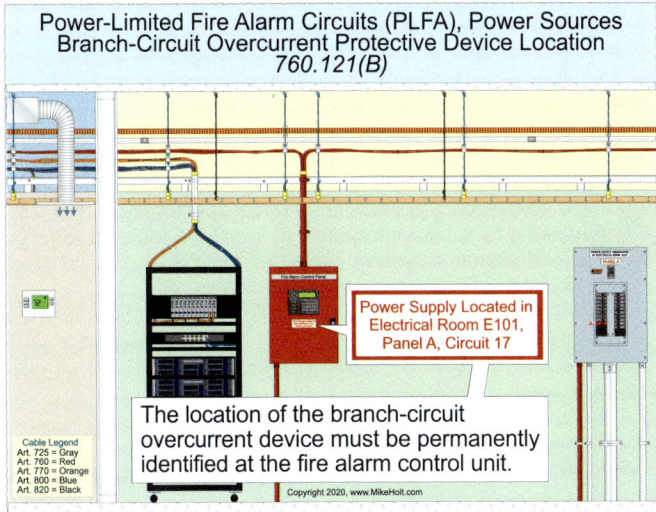

▶Figure 760–19

The branch-circuit overcurrent protective device must be identified in red, be accessible only to qualified personnel, and be identified as the "FIRE ALARM CIRCUIT." The red identification must not damage the overcurrent protective device or obscure any manufacturer's markings. The fire alarm branch-circuit disconnecting means is permitted to be secured in the closed (on) position. ▶Figure 760–20

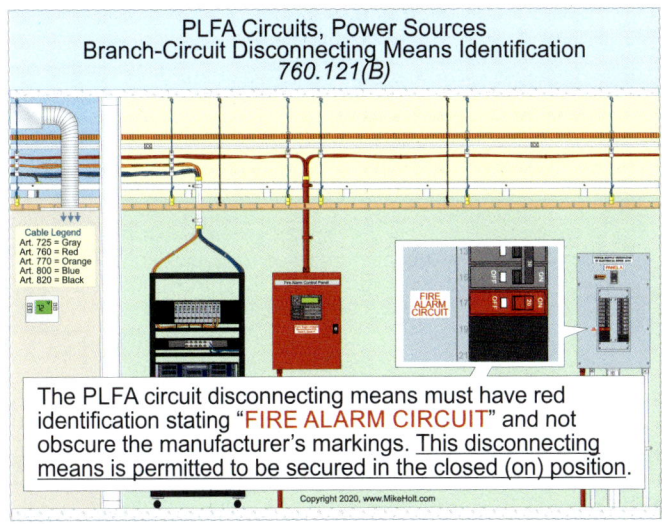

▶Figure 760–20

760.124 Marking

Fire alarm equipment supplying power-limited fire alarm cable circuits must be durably marked to indicate each circuit that is a power-limited fire alarm circuit.

760.127 Wiring Methods on Supply Side of the Power-Limited Fire Alarm Source

Conductors and equipment on the supply side of the power-limited fire alarm power supply must be installed in accordance with Chapters 1 through 4. ▶Figure 760–21

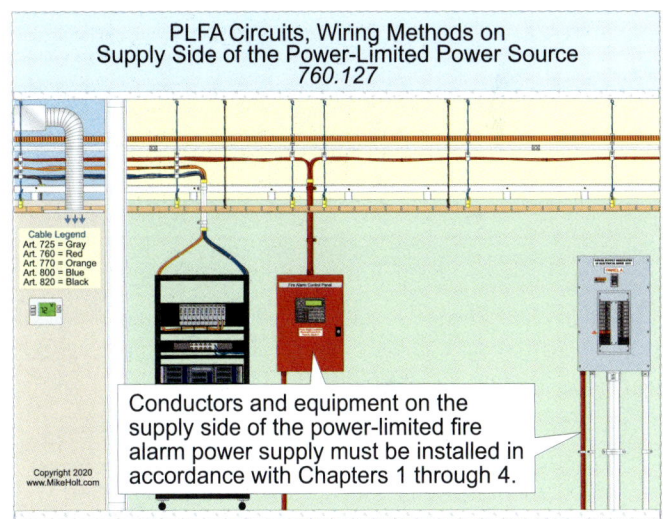

▶Figure 760–21

760.130 Wiring Methods on Load Side of the Power-Limited Fire Alarm Power Source

(B) PLFA Wiring Methods and Materials.

(1) Cable splices and terminations of power-limited fire alarm conductors must be made in listed fittings, boxes, enclosures, fire alarm devices, or utilization equipment [110.3(B) and 300.15]. ▶Figure 760–22 Exposed power-limited fire alarm cable(s) must be adequately supported and protected against physical damage [300.11(A)]. ▶Figure 760–23

760.135 | Fire Alarm Systems

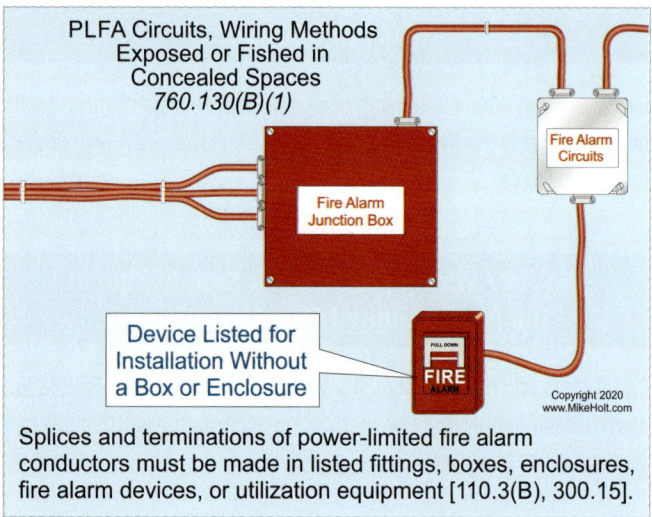

▶Figure 760-22

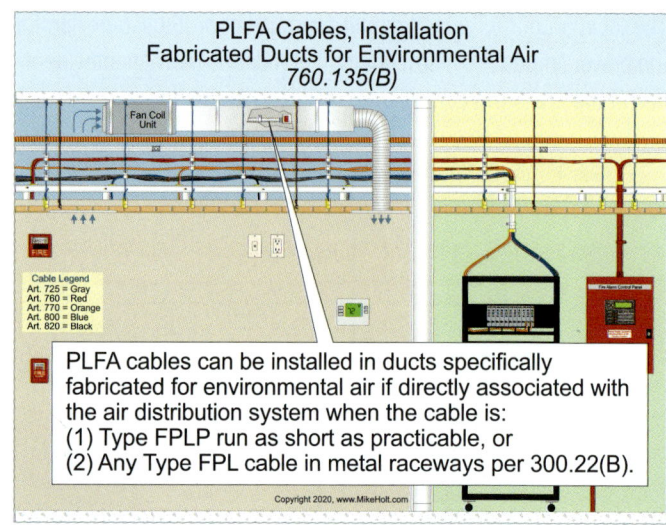

▶Figure 760-24

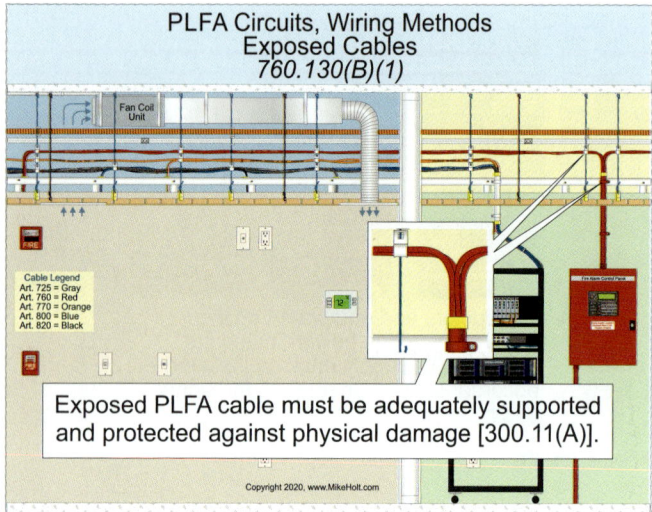

▶Figure 760-23

760.135 Installation of PLFA Cables in Buildings

Installation of power-limited fire alarm cables in buildings must comply with 760.135(A) through (J).

(A) Listing. Power-limited fire alarm (PLFA) cables installed in buildings must be listed.

(B) Ducts Specifically Fabricated for Environmental Air Spaces. Plenum rated power-limited fire alarm (PLFA) cables are permitted to be installed within ducts specifically fabricated for environmental air spaces in accordance with 760.3(B) Ex 1 if the cable is directly associated with the air distribution system and complies with (1) or (2): ▶Figure 760-24

(1) Type FPLP cables are permitted where the length is as short as practicable to perform the required function.

(2) Any Type FPL cable installed in metal raceways in compliance with 300.22(B).

(C) Plenum Spaces. Plenum-rated cables, plenum-rated raceways containing plenum-rated cables, and Types FPLP, FPLR, and FPL cables in accordance with 300.22(C) are permitted in plenum spaces. ▶Figure 760-25

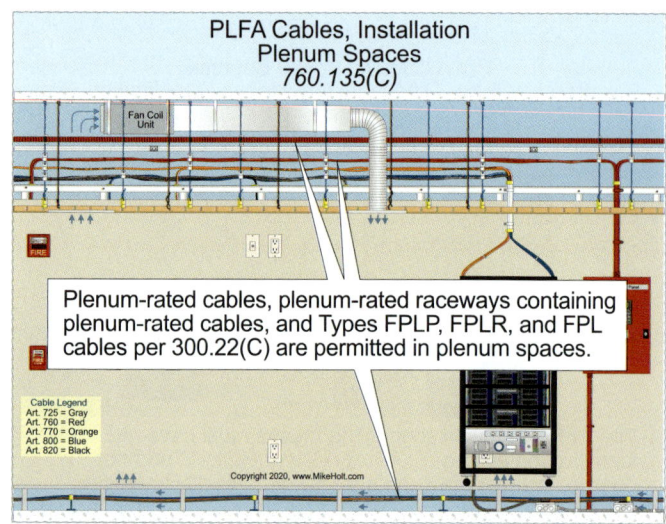

▶Figure 760-25

(H) Other Building Locations. The following power-limited fire alarm cables are permitted to be installed in building locations:

(1) Types FPLP, FPLR, and FPL cables.

(2) Types FPLP, FPLR, and FPL cables installed in:

a. Plenum communications raceways.
b. Plenum cable routing assemblies.
c. Riser communications raceways.
d. Riser cable routing assemblies.
e. General-purpose communications raceways.
f. General-purpose cable routing assemblies.

(3) Types FPLP, FPLR, and FPL cables installed within a raceway of a type recognized in Chapter 3.

760.136 Separation from Power Conductors

(A) General. Power-limited fire alarm conductors are not permitted to be placed in any enclosure, raceway, or cable with power conductors.

(B) Separated by Barriers. If separated by a barrier, power-limited fire alarm circuits are permitted with electric power conductors.

> **Author's Comment:**
>
> ▸ Separation is required to prevent a fire or shock hazard that can occur from a short between the fire alarm circuit and the higher-voltage circuits.

(D) Associated Systems. Power-limited fire alarm conductors are permitted to be installed with power conductors where introduced solely to connect to equipment associated with power circuit conductors, and:

(1) A minimum of ¼ in. separation is maintained from the power-limited fire alarm conductors to the power conductors.

(G) Other Applications. In other applications, power-limited fire alarm circuit conductors must be separated by not less than 2 in. from power conductors unless:

(1) The power and power-limited fire alarm conductors are within separate Chapter 3 wiring methods. ▸Figure 760-26

760.143 Support of PLFA Cables

Power-limited fire alarm cables are not permitted to be strapped, taped, or attached to the exterior of any raceway as a means of support.
▸Figure 760-27

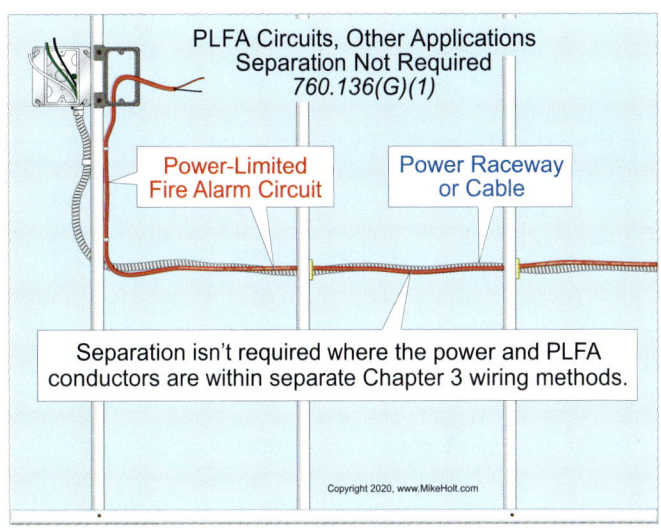

▸Figure 760-26

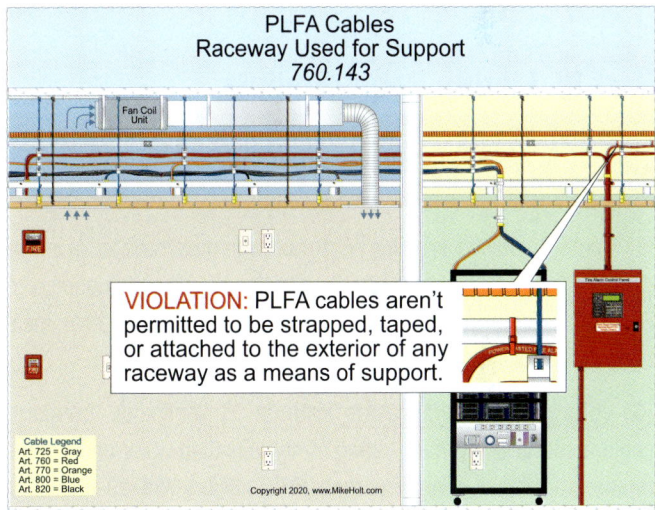

▸Figure 760-27

760.154 Applications of Power-Limited Fire Alarm Cables (PLFA)

PLFA cables must comply with the requirements in Table 760.154 or for cable substitutions in Table 760.154(A). ▸Figure 760-28

(A) Fire Alarm Cable Substitutions. Cable substitutions shown in Table 760.154(A) and in *NEC* Figure 760.154(A) *Cable Substitution Hierarchy* are permitted.

760.179 | Fire Alarm Systems

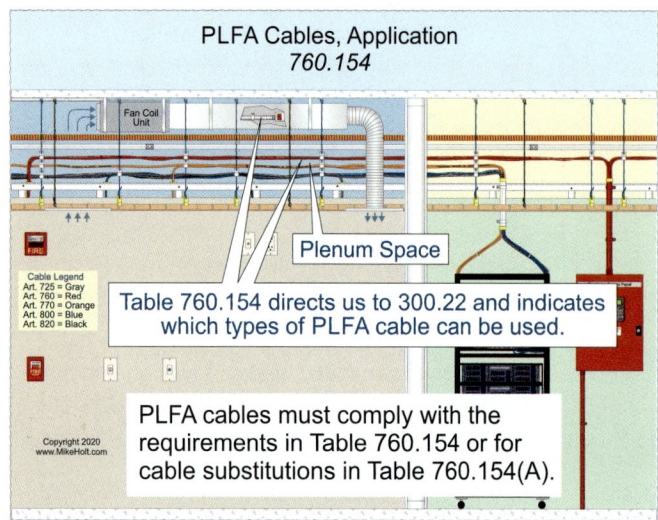
▶Figure 760–28

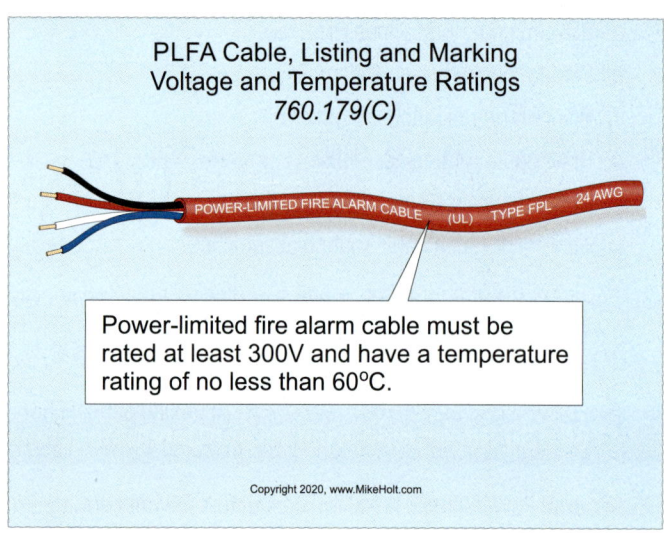
▶Figure 760–29

Part IV. Listing Requirements

760.179 Listing and Marking of Power-Limited Fire Alarm Cables (PLFA)

PLFA cables installed as wiring within buildings must be listed in accordance with 760.179(A) through (H) and be marked in accordance with 760.179(I). Cable in a wet location must be listed for use in wet locations or have a moisture-impervious metal sheath.

(C) Voltage and Temperature Ratings. Power-limited fire alarm cable must have a voltage rating of not less than 300V and have a temperature rating of not less than 60°C. ▶Figure 760–29

(I) Marking. Cables must be marked in accordance with Table 760.179(I) and are listed in order of fire performance starting with best cable type.

Table 760.179(I) Cable Markings	
Cable Marking	Type
FPLP	Power-limited fire alarm plenum cable
FPLR	Power-limited fire alarm riser cable
FPL	Power-limited fire alarm cable

ARTICLE 770 OPTICAL FIBER CABLES

Introduction to Article 770—Optical Fiber Cables

Article 770 provides the requirements for installing optical fiber cables and special raceways for optical fiber cables. It also contains the requirements for composite cables (often called "hybrid") that combine optical fibers with current-carrying conductors.

While we normally think of Article 300 in connection with wiring methods, you only need to use Article 770 for optical fiber cables, except where it makes specific references to Article 300 [770.3]. For instance, in 770.113 reference is made to 300.22, which applies when installing optical fiber cables and optical fiber raceways in ducts and plenum spaces.

Article 90 states that the *NEC* is not a design guide or installation manual. Thus, Article 770 does not deal with the performance of optical fiber systems. For example, it does not mention the bending radius for cables. It does not explain how to install and test cable safely either, but that does not mean you should look into an optical fiber cable, even if you cannot see any light coming through it. Light used in these circuits is usually not visible, but it can still damage your eyes.

Part I. General

770.1 Scope

Article 770 covers the installation of optical fiber cables which transmit light for control, signaling, and communications. This article does not cover the construction of optical fiber cables. ▶Figure 770–1

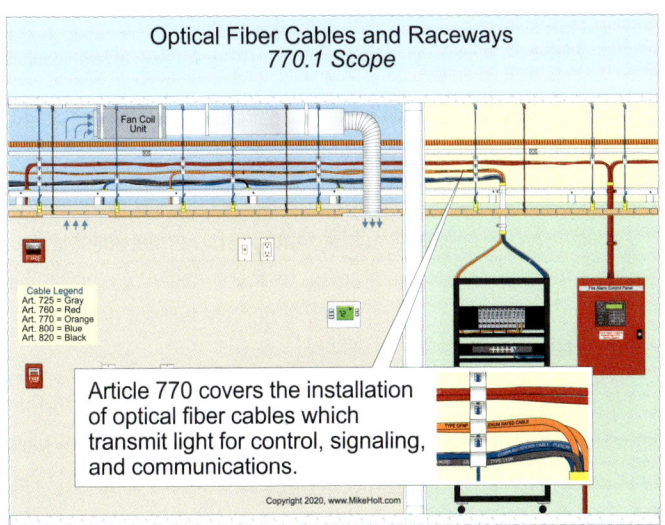

▶Figure 770–1

Author's Comment:

▶ The growth of high-tech applications and significant technological development of optical fibers and the equipment used to send and receive light pulses has increased the use of optical fibers. Since optical fiber cable is not affected by electromagnetic interference, there has been a large growth in its uses in communications for voice, data transfer, data processing, and computer control of machines and processes.

770.2 Definitions

See Part 1 of Article 100 for common item definitions. The definitions in this section only apply within Article 770.

Abandoned Optical Fiber Cable. A cable that is not terminated to equipment and not identified for future use with a tag. ▶Figure 770–2

Author's Comment:

▶ Section 770.25 requires the accessible portion of abandoned cables to be removed.

770.3 | Optical Fiber Cables

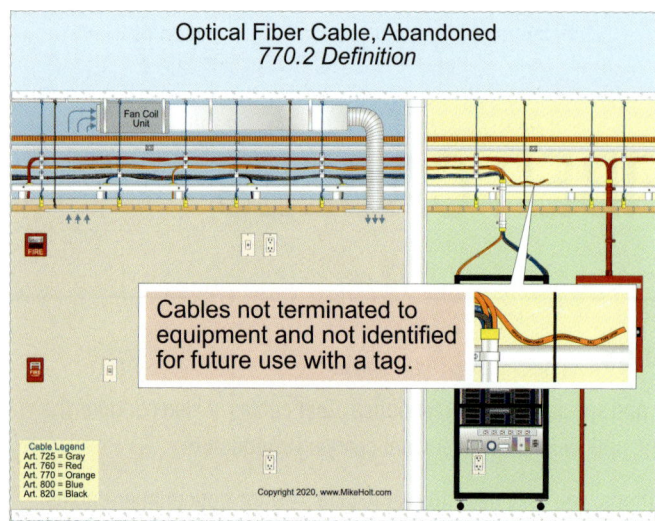
▶Figure 770–2

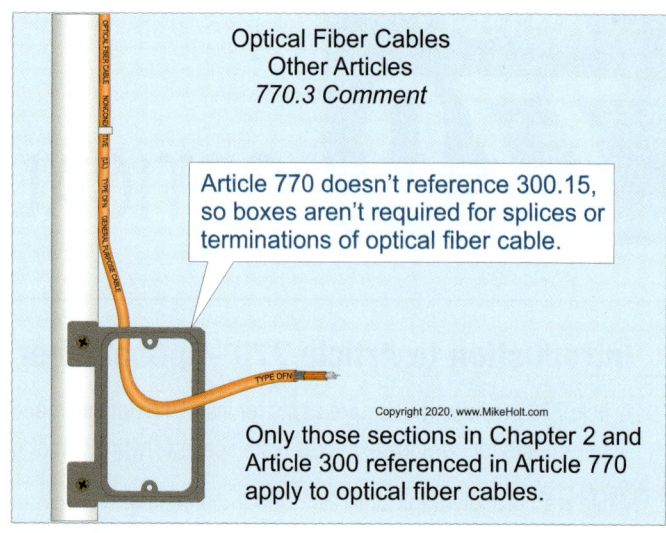
▶Figure 770–3

Exposed (to Accidental Contact). A conductive optical fiber cable that, in the case of failure of supports or insulation, the cable's noncurrent-carrying conductive members can come into contact with an electrical circuit.

Note: See Article 100 for other definitions of "Exposed (as applied to live parts)" and "Exposed (as applied to wiring methods)."

Author's Comment:
▸ Also see Article 100 for the definitions of "Cable, Optical Fiber," "Cable, Optical Fiber, Composite," "Cable, Optical Fiber, Conductive," "Cable, Optical Fiber, Nonconductive," and "Optical Fiber Cable."

770.3 Other Articles

Only those sections in Chapter 2 and Article 300 referenced in Article 770 apply to optical fiber cables.

Author's Comment:
▸ Article 770 does not reference 300.15, so boxes are not required for splices or terminations of optical fiber cable. ▶Figure 770–3

770.21 Access to Electrical Equipment Behind Panels Designed to Allow Access

Access to equipment is not permitted to be denied by an accumulation of optical fiber cables that prevents the removal of suspended-ceiling panels.

Author's Comment:
▸ Cables must be located so suspended-ceiling panels can be moved to provide access to electrical equipment.

770.24 Mechanical Execution of Work

Equipment and cabling must be installed in a neat and workmanlike manner and comply with 300.4 and 300.11.

Exposed cables must be supported by the structural components of the building so the cable will not be damaged by normal building use. Support must be by straps, staples, hangers, cable ties, or similar fittings designed and installed in a manner that will not damage the cable. ▶Figure 770–4

Cables installed through or parallel to framing members or furring strips must be protected where they are likely to be penetrated by nails or screws by installing the wiring method so it is not less than 1¼ in. from the nearest edge of the framing member or furring strips, or by protecting it with a ¹⁄₁₆ in. thick steel plate or equivalent [300.4(A)(1) and (D)]. ▶Figure 770–5

Optical Fiber Cables | 770.25

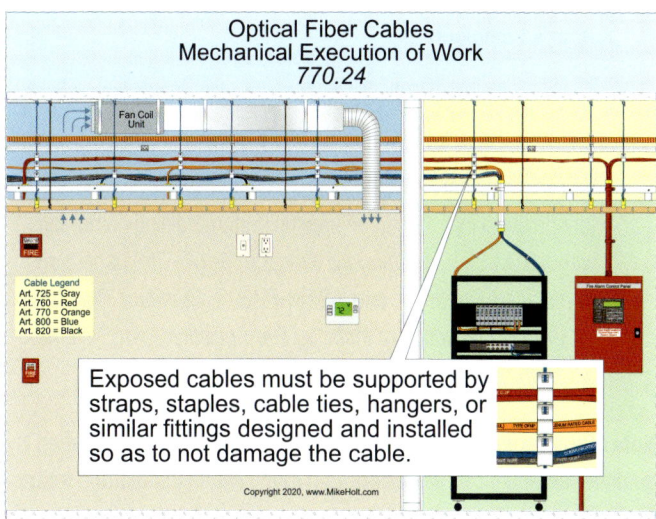
▶Figure 770-4

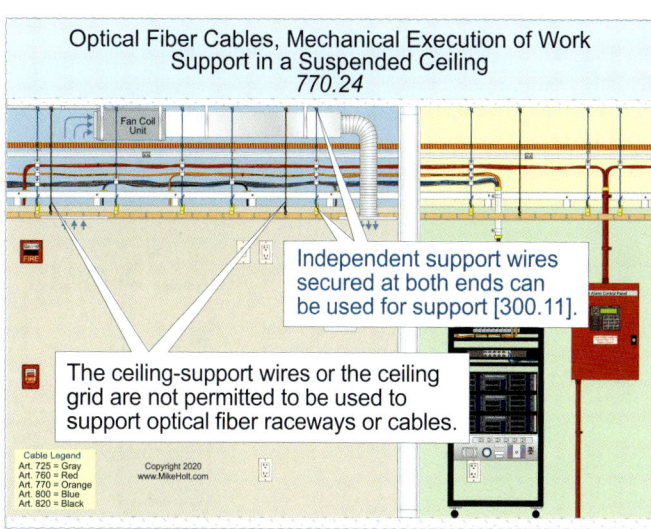
▶Figure 770-6

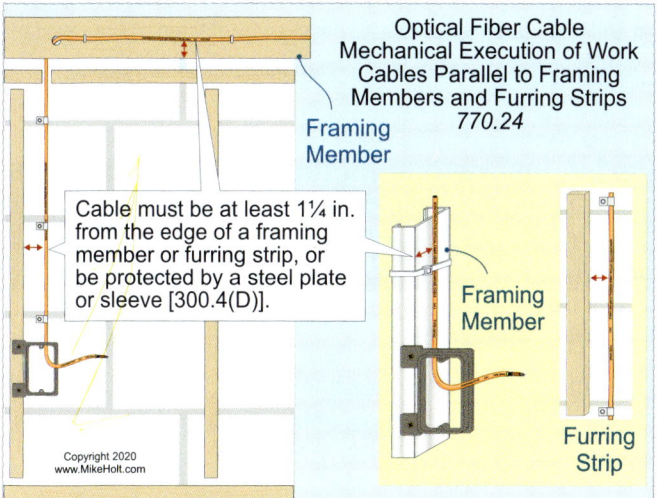
▶Figure 770-5

Communications raceways and cable assemblies must be securely fastened in place. The ceiling-support wires or the ceiling grid are not permitted to be used to support optical fiber raceways or cables [300.11(B)]. ▶Figure 770-6

Cable ties used to secure or support optical fiber cables in plenums must be listed for use in a plenum space in accordance with 300.22(C).

Note 1: Industry practices are described in ANSI/NECA/FOA 301, *Standard for Installing and Testing Fiber Optic Cables;* ANSI/TIA-568.0-D, *Generic Telecommunications Cabling for Customer Premises;* and ANSI/TIA 568.3-D, *Optical Fiber Cabling and Components Standard*.

Note 3: Paint, plaster, cleaners, abrasives, corrosive residues, or other contaminants can result in an undetermined alteration of optical fiber cable properties.

770.25 Abandoned Cable

To limit the spread of fire or products of combustion within a building, the accessible portion of cable that is not terminated at equipment and not identified for future use with a tag must be removed [770.2]. ▶Figure 770-7

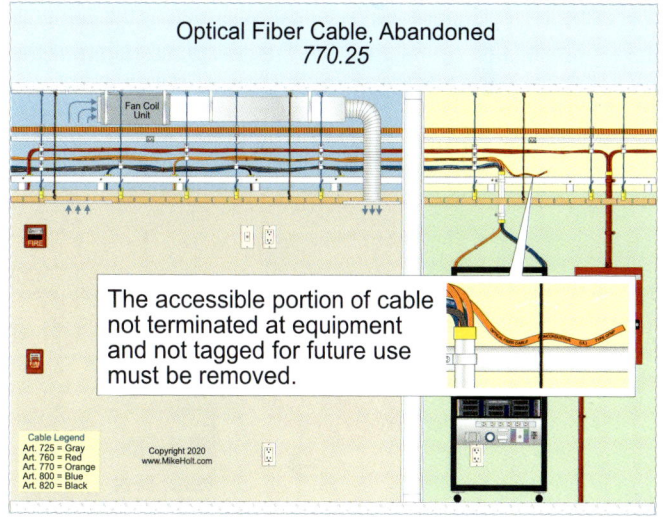
▶Figure 770-7

Tags identifying cables for future use must be able to withstand the environment involved. ▶Figure 770-8

Author's Comment:

▸ Cables installed in concealed raceways are not considered accessible; therefore, they are not required to be removed.

770.26 | Optical Fiber Cables

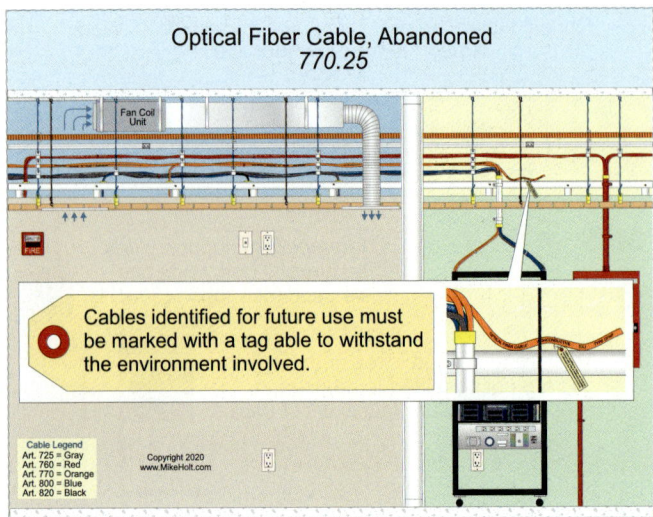
▶Figure 770–8

Author's Comment:

▸ Firestop material is listed for the specific types of wiring methods and construction structures.

▸ Visit International Firestop Council's website (www.firestop.org) for additional information on firestop system training complying with ASTM E2174, *Standard Practice for On-Site Inspection of Installed Firestops*, and ASTM E2393, *Standard Practice for On-Site Inspection of Installed Fire Resistive Joint Systems and Perimeter Fire Barriers*.

Note: Directories of electrical construction materials published by qualified testing laboratories contain many listing installation restrictions necessary to maintain the fire-resistive rating of assemblies. Outlet boxes must have a horizontal separation of not less than 24 in. when installed on opposites sides in a fire-resistive assembly, unless an outlet box is listed for closer spacing or protected by fire-resistant "putty pads" in accordance with manufacturer's instructions.

770.26 Spread of Fire or Products of Combustion

Optical fiber cables and communications raceways must be installed in such a way that the spread of fire or products of combustion will not be substantially increased. Openings in fire-resistant-rated walls, floors, and ceilings for optical fiber cables and communications raceways must be firestopped using methods approved by the authority having jurisdiction to maintain the fire-resistance rating of the fire-resistive assembly. ▶Figure 770–9

Part V. Installation Methods Within Buildings

770.110 Raceways and Cable Routing Assemblies, and Cable Trays for Optical Fiber Cables

(A) Types of Raceways.

(1) Chapter 3 Raceways. Optical fiber cables can be installed in any Chapter 3 raceway that is installed in accordance with the requirements of Chapter 3.

(2) Communications Raceways. Optical fiber cables can be installed in listed communications raceways in accordance with Table 800.154(b). ▶Figure 770–10

(B) Raceway Fill for Optical Fiber Cables.

(1) Without Electric Light or Power Conductors. If optical fiber cables are installed within a raceway without current-carrying conductors, the raceway fill tables of Chapters 3 and 9 do not apply.

(2) Nonconductive Optical Fiber Cables with Electric Light or Power Conductors. Where nonconductive optical fiber cables are installed with electric light or power conductors in a raceway, the raceway fill requirements of Chapters 3 and 9 apply.

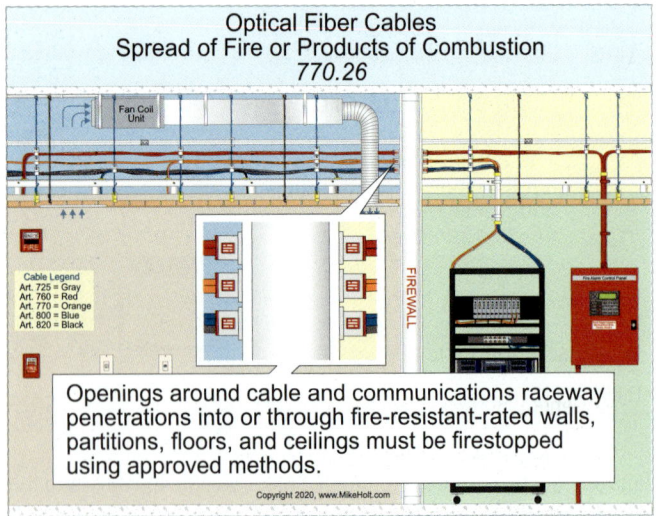
▶Figure 770–9

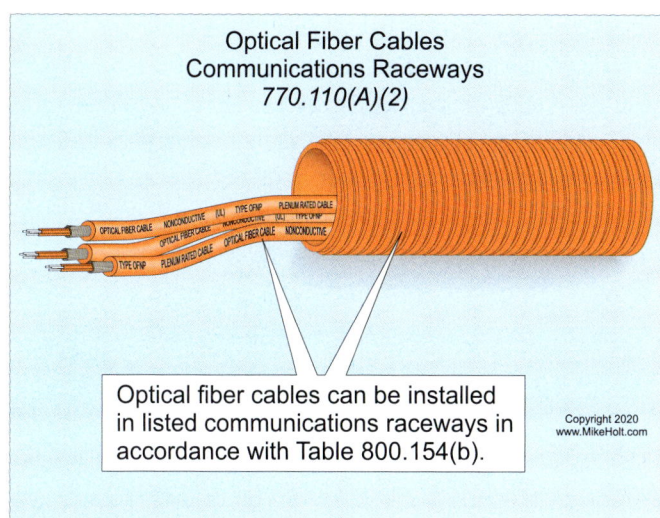
▶Figure 770-10

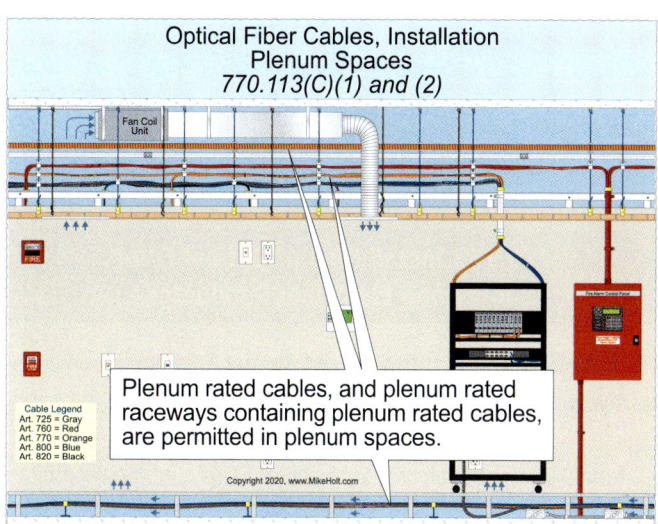
▶Figure 770-11

770.113 Installation of Optical Fiber Cables

(A) Listing. Optical fiber cables installed within buildings must be listed in accordance with 770.179 <u>and installed within the limitations of the listing</u>.

Ex: Optical fiber cables installed in compliance with 770.48 are not required to be listed.

(B) Ducts Specifically Fabricated for Environmental Air Spaces. Plenum rated optical fiber cables are permitted to be installed within ducts specifically fabricated for environmental air spaces in accordance with 300.22(B) if the cable is directly associated with the air distribution system and complies with (1) and (2):

(1) The cable is plenum rated with a length up to four feet.

(2) The cable is installed within a metal raceway or plenum rated raceway in compliance with 300.22(B).

(C) Plenum Spaces. The following optical fiber cables are permitted in plenum spaces as described in 300.22(C): ▶Figure 770-11

(1) Plenum rated optical fiber cables.

(2) Plenum rated optical fiber cables installed in plenum rated communications raceways.

(3) Plenum rated optical fiber cables installed in plenum rated cable routing assemblies.

(4) Plenum optical fiber cables supported by open metal cable tray systems.

(5) Any type of optical fiber cables installed in metal raceways in accordance with 300.22(C).

(H) Cable Trays. The following cables can be installed in cable trays:

(1) Types OFNP, OFCP, OFNR, OFCR, OFNG, OFCG, OFN, and OFC cables.

(2) Types OFNP, OFCP, OFNR, OFCR, OFNG, OFCG, OFN, and OFC cables installed in:

   a. Plenum communications raceways.

   b. Riser communications raceways.

   c. General-purpose communications raceways.

(J) Other Building Locations. The following cables are permitted in the spaces not described in 770.113(B) through (I):

(1) Types OFNP, OFCP, OFNR, OFCR, OFNG, OFCG, OFN, and OFC cables.

(2) Types OFNP, OFCP, OFNR, OFCR, OFNG, OFCG, OFN, and OFC cables installed in:

   a. Plenum communications raceways.

   b. Plenum cable routing assemblies.

   c. Riser communications raceways.

   d. Riser cable routing assemblies.

   e. General-purpose communications raceways.

   f. General-purpose cable routing assemblies.

(3) Types OFNP, OFCP, OFNR, OFCR, OFNG, OFCG, OFN, and OFC cables installed in a Chapter 3 type raceway.

770.114 | Optical Fiber Cables

770.114 Grounding

Noncurrent-carrying conductive members of optical fiber cables must be bonded to an intersystem bonding termination [250.94(A)].

770.133 Installation of Optical Fiber Cables and Electrical Conductors

(B) In Cabinets, Outlet Boxes, and Similar Enclosures. Nonconductive optical fiber cables are not permitted to occupy the same cabinet, outlet box, panel, or similar enclosure housing the electrical terminations of an electric light, power, Class 1, nonpower-limited fire alarm, or medium-power network-powered broadband communications circuit unless one or more of the following conditions exist:

(1) The nonconductive optical fiber cables are functionally associated with the electric light, power, Class 1, nonpower-limited fire alarm, or medium-power network-powered broadband communications circuit.

(2) The conductors for electric light, power, Class 1, nonpower-limited fire alarm, Type ITC, or medium-power network-powered broadband communications circuits operate at 1,000V or less.

(3) The nonconductive optical fiber cables and the electrical terminations of electric light, power, Class 1, nonpower-limited fire alarm, or medium-power network-powered broadband communications circuit are installed in factory- or field-assembled control centers.

(4) The nonconductive optical fiber cables are installed in an industrial establishment where conditions of maintenance and supervision ensure that only qualified persons service the installation.

When optical fibers are within the same composite cable for electric light, power, Class 1, nonpower-limited fire alarm, or medium-power network-powered broadband communications circuits operating at 1,000V or less, they are permitted to be installed only where the functions of the optical fibers and the electrical conductors are associated.

Optical fibers in composite optical fiber cables containing only current-carrying conductors for electric light, power, or Class 1 circuits rated 1,000V or less are permitted to occupy the same cabinet, cable tray, outlet box, panel, raceway, or other termination enclosure with conductors for electric light, power, or Class 1 circuits operating at 1,000V or less.

Optical fibers in composite optical fiber cables containing current-carrying conductors for electric light, power, or Class 1 circuits rated over 1,000V are permitted to occupy the same cabinet, cable tray, outlet box, panel, raceway, or other termination enclosure with conductors for electric light, power, or Class 1 circuits in industrial establishments where conditions of maintenance and supervision ensure that only qualified persons service the installation.

770.154 Applications of Listed Optical Fiber Cables

Listed optical fiber cables must be installed as indicated in Table 770.154(a), as limited by 770.110 and 770.113. Cable substitutions in accordance with Table 770.154(b) and *NEC* Figure 725.154 are permitted. ▶Figure 770–12

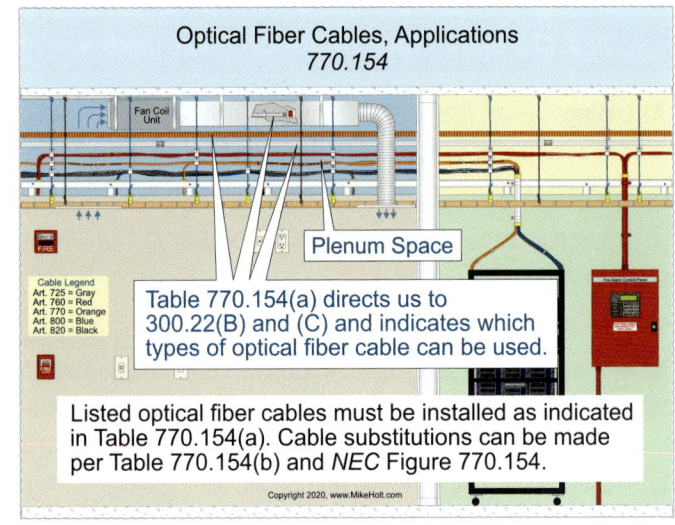

▶Figure 770–12

CHAPTER 7 PRACTICE QUESTIONS

Please use the 2020 *Code* book to answer the following questions.

CHAPTER 7—SPECIAL CONDITIONS
Article 700—Emergency Systems

1. Article _____ applies to the electrical safety of the installation, operation, and maintenance of emergency systems intended to supply, distribute, and control electricity for illumination, power, or both, to required facilities when the normal electrical supply or system is interrupted.

   (a) 500
   (b) 600
   (c) 700
   (d) 800

2. "Emergency systems" are those systems legally required and classed as emergency by a governmental agency having jurisdiction. These systems are intended to automatically supply illumination and/or power essential for _____.

   (a) community activity
   (b) safety to human life
   (c) public recreation
   (d) police and emergency services exclusively

3. Emergency systems are generally installed where artificial illumination is required for safe exiting and for panic control in buildings occupied by large numbers of persons, such as _____ and similar institutions.

   (a) hotels
   (b) theaters and sports arenas
   (c) health care facilities
   (d) all of these

4. Emergency systems may provide power for ventilation where essential to maintain life, fire detection and alarm systems, elevators, fire pumps, public safety communications systems, industrial processes where current interruption would produce serious _____.

   (a) production slowdowns
   (b) life safety or health hazards
   (c) equipment failure
   (d) structural damage

5. The _____ shall conduct or witness a test of the complete emergency system upon installation and periodically afterward.

   (a) electrical engineer
   (b) authority having jurisdiction
   (c) qualified person
   (d) manufacturer's representative

6. Emergency system equipment shall be maintained in accordance with _____.

   (a) the authority having jurisdiction
   (b) UL listing(s)
   (c) manufacturer instructions and industry standards
   (d) OSHA regulations

7. A written record shall be kept of required tests and maintenance on emergency systems.

   (a) True
   (b) False

Article 700 | Practice Questions

8. The emergency system equipment shall be suitable for the _____ current at its terminals.

    (a) demand load
    (b) available fault
    (c) peak-demand
    (d) shaved-load

9. An emergency system shall have adequate _____ in accordance with Article 220 or by another approved method.

    (a) lighting
    (b) capacity
    (c) water flow
    (d) ambient temperature

10. For emergency systems, transfer equipment shall be _____ for emergency use and approved by the authority having jurisdiction.

    (a) automatic
    (b) listed
    (c) marked
    (d) all of these

11. Automatic transfer switches for emergency systems shall be _____.

    (a) able to be remotely operated
    (b) able to be locked in the "closed' position
    (c) permitted to be reconditioned
    (d) electrically operated and mechanically held

12. An emergency transfer switch for emergency systems shall supply only _____.

    (a) emergency loads
    (b) computer equipment
    (c) UPS equipment
    (d) all of these

13. Where used for emergency systems, the short-circuit current rating of the transfer equipment, based on the specific overcurrent protective device type and settings protecting the transfer equipment, shall be field marked on the _____ of the transfer equipment.

    (a) exterior
    (b) top
    (c) interior
    (d) underside

14. In locations containing an emergency system, a sign shall be placed at the service-entrance equipment indicating the type and location of each on-site emergency power source.

    (a) True
    (b) False

15. A listed surge protective device shall be installed in or on all emergency systems switchboards and panelboards.

    (a) True
    (b) False

16. Emergency circuits shall be permanently marked so they will be readily identified as a _____ of an emergency circuit or system.

    (a) segment
    (b) section
    (c) component
    (d) critical branch

17. Emergency circuits shall be permanently marked so they will be readily identified as a component of an emergency circuit or system and receptacles supplied from the emergency system shall have a(an) _____ color or marking on the receptacle cover plates or the receptacles.

    (a) approved
    (b) distinctive
    (c) legible
    (d) luminescent

18. Wiring from an emergency source or emergency source distribution overcurrent protection to emergency loads shall be kept entirely independent of all other wiring and equipment unless wiring _____.

    (a) from the normal power source is located in transfer equipment enclosures
    (b) is supplied from two sources in exit or emergency luminaires
    (c) is from two sources in a listed load control relay supplying exit or emergency luminaires, or in a common junction box, attached to exit or emergency luminaires
    (d) all of these

19. If wiring from an emergency source is used to supply emergency and other loads, then _____ switchgear sections or switchboard sections, with or without a common bus, or individual disconnects mounted in separate enclosures shall be used to separate emergency loads from all other loads.

    (a) separate vertical
    (b) separate horizontal
    (c) combined vertical and horizontal
    (d) identified

20. Wiring from an emergency source to supply emergency and other (nonemergency) loads shall be permitted if the common bus of separate sections of the switchgear, separate sections of the switchboard, or the individual enclosures are supplied by single or multiple feeders with or without _____.

    (a) overcurrent protection at the source
    (b) ground-fault protection at the source
    (c) a current-limiting device at the source
    (d) load-shaving monitoring

21. Emergency systems circuit wiring shall be designed and located to minimize the hazards that might cause failure because of _____.

    (a) flooding
    (b) fire
    (c) icing
    (d) all of these

22. In the event of failure of the normal supply to the building/structure, emergency power shall be available within _____ seconds.

    (a) 5
    (b) 10
    (c) 30
    (d) 60

23. Emergency equipment for emergency systems shall be _____ and located so as to minimize the hazards that might cause complete failure due to flooding, fires, icing, and vandalism.

    (a) approved
    (b) listed
    (c) installed
    (d) designed

24. Emergency systems equipment shall be designed and located so as to minimize the hazards that might cause complete failure due to _____ and vandalism.

    (a) flooding
    (b) fires
    (c) icing
    (d) all of these

25. A storage battery supplying emergency lighting and power for emergency systems shall maintain not less than 87½ percent of normal voltage at total load for a period of at least _____ hour(s).

    (a) 1
    (b) 1½
    (c) 2
    (d) 2½

26. Unit equipment for emergency systems shall be on the same branch circuit that serves the normal lighting in the area and connected _____ any local switches.

    (a) with
    (b) ahead of
    (c) after
    (d) downstream of

27. In emergency systems, only appliances and lamps required for emergency use shall be supplied by _____.

    (a) emergency lighting circuits
    (b) multiwire branch circuits
    (c) HID-rated circuit breakers
    (d) only load-shaved circuits

28. Emergency lighting systems shall be designed and installed so that the failure of any individual lighting element, such as the burning out of a lamp, cannot leave in total darkness any space that requires emergency illumination.

    (a) True
    (b) False

29. The branch circuit serving emergency lighting and power circuits shall be permitted to be part of a multiwire branch circuit.

    (a) True
    (b) False

Article 701 | Practice Questions

30. Emergency system(s) overcurrent devices shall be selectively coordinated with all _____ overcurrent protective devices.

    (a) supply-side
    (b) load-side
    (c) downstream
    (d) reconditioned

Article 701—Legally Required Standby Systems

1. Article 701 applies to the electrical safety of the installation, operation, and maintenance of _____ intended to supply, distribute, and control electricity to required facilities for illumination or power, or both, when the normal electrical supply or system is interrupted.

    (a) emergency systems
    (b) legally required standby systems
    (c) optional standby systems
    (d) dwelling standby systems

2. A "legally required standby system" is intended to automatically supply power to _____ in the event of failure of the normal source.

    (a) those systems classed as emergency systems
    (b) selected loads
    (c) critical branch circuits
    (d) essential circuits

3. The _____ shall conduct or witness a test of the complete legally required standby system upon installation.

    (a) electrical engineer
    (b) authority having jurisdiction
    (c) qualified person
    (d) manufacturer's representative

4. Legally required standby systems shall be tested _____ on a schedule and in a manner approved by the authority having jurisdiction to ensure the systems are maintained in proper operating condition.

    (a) monthly
    (b) quarterly
    (c) annually
    (d) periodically

5. Legally required standby system equipment shall be maintained in accordance with _____.

    (a) UL listing(s)
    (b) local emergency services requirements
    (c) manufacturer instructions and industry standards
    (d) local jurisdictional requirements

6. A written record shall be kept of required tests and maintenance on legally required standby systems.

    (a) True
    (b) False

7. Legally required standby system equipment shall be suitable for _____ at its terminals.

    (a) the available fault current
    (b) the maximum overload current only
    (c) the minimum fault current
    (d) a one-hour rating

8. A legally required standby system shall have adequate capacity in accordance with Article _____ or by another approved method.

    (a) 210
    (b) 220
    (c) 230
    (d) 700

9. Transfer equipment for legally required standby systems, including automatic transfer switches, shall be _____.

    (a) automatic
    (b) listed and marked for standby use
    (c) approved by the authority having jurisdiction
    (d) all of these

10. Automatic transfer switches on legally required standby systems shall be electrically operated and _____ held.

    (a) electrically
    (b) mechanically
    (c) gravity
    (d) any of these

11. Where used for legally required standby systems, the short-circuit current rating of the transfer equipment, based on the specific overcurrent protective device type and settings protecting the transfer equipment, shall be field marked on the _____ of the transfer equipment.

    (a) exterior
    (b) top
    (c) interior
    (d) underside

12. Audible and visual signal devices shall be provided, where practicable, for legally required standby systems to indicate _____.

    (a) a malfunction of the emergency source
    (b) that the emergency source is carrying load
    (c) that the battery charger is not functioning
    (d) all of these

13. A sign shall be placed at the service entrance indicating the _____ of each on-site legally required standby power source.

    (a) capacity
    (b) date of last testing
    (c) manufacturer
    (d) type and location

14. Legally required standby system wiring shall be permitted to occupy the same raceways, cables, boxes, and cabinets with other general wiring.

    (a) True
    (b) False

15. Where approved by the authority having jurisdiction, connections ahead of and not within the same cabinet, enclosure, vertical switchgear section, or vertical switchboard section as the service disconnecting means shall be permitted for _____ standby service.

    (a) emergency
    (b) legally required
    (c) optional
    (d) all of these

16. The branch-circuit overcurrent devices for legally required standby systems shall be accessible only to _____.

    (a) the authority having jurisdiction
    (b) authorized persons
    (c) the general public
    (d) qualified persons

17. Overcurrent devices for legally required standby systems shall be _____ with all supply-side overcurrent devices.

    (a) series rated
    (b) selectively coordinated
    (c) installed in parallel
    (d) labeled

Article 702—Optional Standby Systems

1. Optional standby systems are typically installed to provide an alternate source of power for _____.

    (a) data processing and communication systems
    (b) emergency systems for health care facilities
    (c) emergency systems for hospitals
    (d) emergency systems for fire houses

2. Where manual transfer equipment is used, an optional standby system shall have adequate _____ for the supply of all equipment intended to be operated at one time.

    (a) ventilation
    (b) supervision
    (c) fuel supply
    (d) capacity and rating

3. Where manual transfer equipment is used, an optional standby system shall have adequate capacity and rating for the supply of all _____.

    (a) equipment intended to be operated at the same time
    (b) equipment where life safety is dependent
    (c) emergency and egress lighting
    (d) fire and security systems

4. Where manual transfer equipment is used in an optional standby system, the _____ of the optional standby system shall be permitted to select the load connected to the system.

    (a) installer
    (b) designer
    (c) user
    (d) inspector

Article 702 | Practice Questions

5. Where automatic transfer equipment is used, an optional standby system shall be capable of supplying _____.

   (a) the full load that is transferred by the automatic transfer equipment
   (b) all equipment upon which life safety is dependent
   (c) all emergency and egress lighting
   (d) all fire and security systems

6. Where a load management system is employed that will automatically manage the connected load of an optional standby system, the standby source shall have a capacity sufficient to supply _____ load that will be connected by the load management system.

   (a) 80 percent of the
   (b) 115 percent of the
   (c) 125 percent of the
   (d) the maximum

7. Transfer equipment shall be required for all optional standby systems subject to the requirements of _____ and for which an electric utility supply is either the normal or standby source.

   (a) the authority having jurisdiction
   (b) Article 702
   (c) the equipment manufacturer
   (d) the owner of the facility

8. For optional standby systems, the temporary connection of a portable generator without transfer equipment shall be permitted where conditions of maintenance and supervision ensure that only qualified persons will service the installation, and where the normal supply is physically isolated by _____.

   (a) a lockable disconnecting means
   (b) the disconnection of the normal supply conductors
   (c) an extended power outage
   (d) a lockable disconnecting means, or the disconnection of the normal supply conductors

9. Optional standby system transfer switches installed between the _____ and the meter enclosure shall be listed meter-mounted transfer switches.

   (a) service connection point
   (b) utility meter
   (c) utility transformer
   (d) cold sequence disconnect

10. Meter-mounted transfer switches shall be of the _____ type unless rated as determined by 702.4(B)(2).

    (a) automatic
    (b) manual
    (c) monitoring
    (d) remote

11. Where used for optional standby systems in other than dwelling units, the short-circuit current rating of the transfer equipment, based on the specific overcurrent protective device type and settings protecting the transfer equipment, shall be field marked on the _____ of the transfer equipment.

    (a) exterior
    (b) top
    (c) interior
    (d) underside

12. Optional standby system transfer equipment shall be suitable for the intended use and shall be _____ so as to prevent the inadvertent interconnection of all sources of supply in any operation of the transfer equipment.

    (a) listed
    (b) designed
    (c) installed
    (d) all of these

13. Optional standby system transfer equipment and electric power production systems installed to permit operation in parallel with the _____ shall also meet the requirements of Article 705.

    (a) PV system
    (b) generator
    (c) normal source
    (d) battery storage system

14. Audible and visual signal devices shall be provided, where practicable, for optional standby systems to indicate a malfunction of the emergency power source and _____.

    (a) that the emergency source is carrying load
    (b) that the battery charger is not functioning
    (c) a ground fault has occurred
    (d) all of these

15. A sign shall be placed at the service-entrance equipment for commercial and industrial installations indicating the _____ of each on-site optional standby power source.

    (a) type
    (b) date of installation
    (c) date of last testing
    (d) type and location

16. For _____, a sign shall be placed at the disconnecting means required in 230.85 that indicates the location of each permanently installed on-site optional standby power source disconnect or means to shut down the prime mover as required in 445.18(D).

    (a) schools
    (b) hospitals
    (c) hotels
    (d) one- and two-family dwellings

17. For one- and two-family dwellings, a sign shall be placed at the disconnecting means required in 230.85 that indicates the location of each permanently installed on-site optional standby power source disconnect or means to shut down the _____ as required in 445.18(D).

    (a) prime mover
    (b) utility supply
    (c) secondary source
    (d) primary source

Article 705—Interconnected Electric Power Production Sources

1. Article 705 covers installations of one or more electric power production sources operating in parallel with a _____ source(s) of electricity.

    (a) secondary
    (b) alternate
    (c) primary
    (d) stand-alone

2. The definitions in Article 705 shall apply only within Article 705.

    (a) True
    (b) False

3. In accordance with Article 705, a premises wiring system that has generation, energy storage, and load(s), or any combination thereof, that includes the ability to disconnect from and parallel with the primary source is known as a "_____ system."

    (a) tandem
    (b) primary
    (c) microgrid
    (d) dual function

4. Interactive equipment intended to operate in parallel with electric power production sources shall be listed for interactive function or be _____ for interactive function and have a field label applied, or both.

    (a) tested
    (b) evaluated
    (c) approved
    (d) licensed

5. For interconnected power production source(s), installation of one or more electrical power production sources operating in parallel with a primary source(s) of electricity shall be performed only by _____.

    (a) qualified persons
    (b) utility company persons
    (c) the authority having jurisdiction
    (d) utility company persons or the authority having jurisdiction

6. Interconnected power production installations with multiple co-located power production sources shall be permitted to be identified as a group(s).

    (a) True
    (b) False

7. Interconnected power production source(s) are permitted to be connected to the supply side of the service disconnecting means when in compliance with 705.11.

    (a) True
    (b) False

Article 705 | Practice Questions

8. For supply-side connected interconnected power production source(s), the sum of the interconnected power source continuous current output ratings on a service, other than those controlled in accordance with 705.13, shall not exceed the ampacity of the _____.

   (a) service conductors
   (b) power production source output current
   (c) service disconnect rating
   (d) sum of all overcurrent protective devices

9. Where supply-side power source output circuit conductors make their connection to the service outside of a building, they shall be protected by overcurrent devices in a(an) _____ outside the building or at the first readily accessible location where the power source conductors enter the building.

   (a) location
   (b) readily accessible location
   (c) accessible location
   (d) secured location

10. For supply-side connected interconnected power production source(s), all metal enclosures, metal wiring methods, and metal parts associated with supply-side power source output conductors shall be _____ in accordance with 250.92(B).

    (a) bonded
    (b) grounded
    (c) bonded and grounded
    (d) bonded or grounded

11. For supply-side connected interconnected power production source(s), the grounding terminal or bus for the supply-side disconnecting means shall be connected to a(an) _____ sized in accordance with 250.102, based on the size of the conductors in 705.11(B).

    (a) supply-side bonding jumper
    (b) equipment grounding conductor
    (c) grounded service conductor
    (d) grounding electrode

12. For supply-side connected interconnected power production source(s), if the power production equipment requires a grounded conductor, a connection shall be made between the supply-side bonding jumper and the grounded conductor at the supply-side disconnecting means in accordance with 705.11(F).

    (a) True
    (b) False

13. For supply-side connected interconnected power production source(s), the connection of power source output circuit conductors to the service conductors shall be made using _____ connectors as described in 110.14 and comply with all enclosure fill requirements.

    (a) listed
    (b) marked
    (c) identified
    (d) all of these

14. Interconnected power production source(s) are permitted to be connected to the load side of the service disconnecting means at any distribution equipment on the premises.

    (a) True
    (b) False

15. Where an interconnected power source connection is made to a feeder, the feeder shall have an ampacity _____ percent of the power source output circuit current.

    (a) equal to 125
    (b) greater than 125
    (c) not greater than 125
    (d) equal to 125 percent of the power source output circuit current, or greater than 125

16. Where interconnected power production source output connections are made at feeders, all taps shall be sized based on the sum of _____ percent of all power source(s) output circuit current(s) and the rating of the overcurrent device protecting the feeder conductors for sizing tap conductors using the calculations in 240.21(B).

    (a) 100
    (b) 115
    (c) 125
    (d) 175

17. Where interconnected power production source output connections are made at busbars, and there are two sources (one a primary power source and the other another power source) located at opposite ends of a busbar that contains loads, the sum of 125 percent of the power source(s) output circuit current and the rating of the overcurrent device protecting the busbar shall not exceed _____ percent of the ampacity of the busbar.

    (a) 110
    (b) 120
    (c) 125
    (d) 150

18. Where interconnected power production source output connections are made at busbars (one a primary power source and the other another power source) are not located at opposite ends of a busbar that contains loads, the sum of the ampere ratings of all overcurrent devices on interconnected power production source(s) panelboards, both load and supply devices, excluding the rating of the overcurrent device protecting the busbar, shall not exceed _____ percent of the ampacity of the busbar.

    (a) 80
    (b) 100
    (c) 120
    (d) 125

19. Where interconnected power production source output connections are made at either end of busbars of a center-fed panelboard in a dwelling unit, the sum of 125 percent of the power source(s) output circuit current and the rating of the overcurrent device protecting the busbar shall not exceed _____ percent of the current rating of the busbar.

    (a) 110
    (b) 115
    (c) 120
    (d) 125

20. Where interconnected power production source output connections are made to circuit breakers not marked "line" and "load," the circuit breaker is considered suitable for backfeed.

    (a) True
    (b) False

21. Where interconnected power production source output connections are made to circuit breakers _____ "line" and "load," the circuit breaker is considered suitable for backfeed if specifically rated for backfeed.

    (a) not marked
    (b) marked
    (c) identified as
    (d) listed for

22. Listed plug-in-type circuit breakers backfed for interconnected power production sources that are listed and identified as _____ shall not require a fastener as required by 408.36(D).

    (a) interactive
    (b) active
    (c) reactive
    (d) interactive or active

23. In accordance with Article 705, the sum of all interconnected power production system-controlled currents, plus all monitored currents from other sources of supply, shall not exceed _____ percent of the ampacity of any busbar or conductor supplied by the power production sources.

    (a) 100
    (b) 115
    (c) 125
    (d) 150

24. In accordance with Article 705, the contribution of _____ currents from all interconnected power production source(s) shall not exceed the interrupting and short-circuit current ratings of equipment on interactive systems.

    (a) demand
    (b) load
    (c) monitored
    (d) limited

25. Means shall be provided to disconnect power source output circuit conductors of interconnected electric power production equipment from conductors of other systems. The disconnecting means shall be a _____.

    (a) manually operable switch or circuit breaker
    (b) load-break-rated pull-out switch
    (c) device listed or approved for the intended application
    (d) any of these

Article 705 | Practice Questions

26. All raceway and cable wiring methods included in Chapter _____ of this *Code* and other wiring systems and fittings specifically listed, intended, and identified for used with interconnected electric power production systems and equipment shall be permitted.

    (a) 1
    (b) 2
    (c) 3
    (d) 4

27. Circuit conductors for interconnected power production systems shall _____.

    (a) be sized to carry the maximum currents in 705.28(A) multiplied by 125 percent without adjustment or correction factors
    (b) be sized to carry the maximum currents in 705.28(A) with adjustment and correction factors
    (c) where connected to feeders if smaller than the feeder conductors (feeder tap), the conductor ampacity shall be calculated in accordance with 240.21(B) based on the overcurrent device protecting the feeder
    (d) all of these

28. Neutral conductors for interconnected power production systems used solely for instrumentation, voltage detection, or phase detection can be sized in accordance with _____.

    (a) 250.66
    (b) 250.102
    (c) 250.122
    (d) 310.16

29. In accordance with Article 705, transformers with power sources on each side (primary and secondary) of the transformer shall be provided with primary overcurrent protection in accordance with 450.3. The primary shall be the side of the transformer connected to the largest source of _____ current.

    (a) available fault
    (b) short-circuit
    (c) output power source
    (d) available fault current or short-circuit

30. For interconnected power production systems, risks to personnel and equipment associated with the _____ could occur if an interactive electric power production source can operate as an intentional island.

    (a) primary source of power
    (b) power production system
    (c) primary source of power or power production system
    (d) possibility of a lightning strike

31. For interconnected power production systems, when the primary source supply system is restored, special detection methods are typically required to limit exposure of power production sources to _____ reconnection.

    (a) out-of-phase
    (b) primary power
    (c) secondary power
    (d) utility

32. For interconnected power production systems, single-phase power sources in interactive systems shall be connected to three-phase power systems in order to limit unbalanced voltages at the point of interconnection to not more than _____ percent.

    (a) 2
    (b) 3
    (c) 5
    (d) 10

33. In accordance with Article 705, microgrid systems shall be permitted to disconnect from the primary source of power or other interconnected power production source(s) and operate as an isolated microgrid system operating in _____ mode.

    (a) isolated
    (b) island
    (c) standby
    (d) shutdown

34. In accordance with Article 705, microgrid interconnect devices shall _____.

    (a) be required for any connection between a microgrid system and a primary power source
    (b) be listed or field labeled for the application
    (c) have a sufficient number of overcurrent devices located to provide protection from all sources
    (d) all of these

Article 706—Energy Storage Systems

1. Energy storage systems can include inverters or converters to change current levels, or to make a change between an alternating-current or a direct-current system.

    (a) True
    (b) False

2. A disconnecting means must be provided for all _____ derived from an energy storage system (ESS).

    (a) branch circuits
    (b) phase conductors
    (c) supply circuits
    (d) combiners

3. Provisions appropriate to the energy storage technology must be made for sufficient diffusion and ventilation of any possible gases from the storage device (if present) to prevent the accumulation of _____.

    (a) noxious gases
    (b) toxic gases
    (c) an explosive mixture
    (d) fumes

4. Energy storage systems for one- and two-family dwelling units are not permitted to have a direct-current voltage greater than _____ between conductors or to ground.

    (a) 100V
    (b) 120V
    (c) 240V
    (d) 300V

Article 710—Stand-Alone Systems

1. Article 710 covers electric power production systems that operate in _____ mode and installations not connected to an electric power production and distribution network.

    (a) island
    (b) standby
    (c) tandem
    (d) generating

2. Stand-alone systems are capable of operating in _____ with other power sources.

    (a) island mode, independent from the electric utility
    (b) isolated microgrid systems
    (c) interactive mode
    (d) all of these

3. All stand-alone system equipment shall be approved for the intended use by being _____.

    (a) listed for the application
    (b) evaluated for the application and having a field label applied
    (c) listed for the application, or being evaluated for the application and having a field label applied
    (d) listed for the application, and being evaluated for the application and having a field label applied

4. A permanent _____ shall be installed at a building supplied by a stand-alone system at each service equipment location or at an approved readily visible location. The _____ shall denote the location of each power source disconnect for the building or be grouped with other plaques or directories for other on-site sources.

    (a) plaque
    (b) directory
    (c) marking
    (d) plaque or directory

5. For stand-alone systems, where multiple sources supply the building, the plaque or directory must _____.

    (a) be marked with the wording "CAUTION: MULTIPLE SOURCES OF POWER"
    (b) have the marking permanently affixed
    (c) have markings with sufficient durability to withstand the environment involved
    (d) all of these

6. The supply output of the power supply to premises wiring systems fed by stand-alone or isolated microgrid power sources shall be permitted to have less capacity than the calculated load.

    (a) True
    (b) False

Article 725 | Practice Questions

7. The supply output capacity of the sum of all sources of the stand-alone supply shall be _____ the load posed by the largest single utilization equipment connected to the stand-alone system.

   (a) less than
   (b) the lowest demand load on
   (c) equal to or greater than
   (d) the highest demand on

8. In consideration of the supply output for general-use loads, the stand-alone system capacity can be calculated using the sum of the capacity of the firm sources, such as _____.

   (a) generators
   (b) energy storage system inverters
   (c) generators and energy storage system inverters
   (d) PV combiners

9. The sizing and protection of the circuit conductors between a stand-alone system source and a building or structure disconnecting means shall be based on the sum of the output ratings of the stand-alone source(s).

   (a) True
   (b) False

10. Stand-alone and isolated microgrid systems can supply 120V to single-phase, 3-wire, 120/240V service disconnects of distribution panels if there are no 240V outlets and no multiwire circuits.

    (a) True
    (b) False

11. Stand-alone systems require either energy storage or backup power supplies.

    (a) True
    (b) False

12. Stand-alone system plug-in type backfed circuit breakers connected to an interconnected supply shall be secured in accordance with 408.36(D).

    (a) True
    (b) False

Article 725—Remote-Control, Signaling, and Power-Limited Circuits

1. Article 725 covers _____ circuits that are not an integral part of a device or of utilization equipment.

   (a) remote-control
   (b) signaling
   (c) power-limited
   (d) all of these

2. Class 2, Class 3, and PLTC cable that is not terminated at equipment and not identified for future use with a tag is considered _____.

   (a) reconditioned
   (b) abandoned
   (c) demolished
   (d) reusable

3. Class 1, 2, and 3 circuits installed through fire-resistant-rated walls, partitions, floors, or ceilings shall be firestopped to limit the possible spread of fire or products of combustion.

   (a) True
   (b) False

4. If remote-control, signaling, and power-limited circuits are installed in a raceway that is subjected to different temperatures, and where condensation is known to be a problem, the raceway shall be filled with an approved material that will prevent the circulation of warm air to a colder section of the raceway. An explosionproof seal _____.

   (a) is required for this purpose
   (b) that has been proven effective for this purpose is not required
   (c) is not required for this purpose
   (d) is the only method of doing this

5. When a raceway is used for the support or protection of cables for remote-control, signaling, and power-limited circuits, a bushing to reduce the potential for abrasion shall be placed at the location the cables emerge from the raceway.

   (a) True
   (b) False

6. Class 2, Class 3, and Type PLTC cables shall be permitted to be installed in plenum cable routing assemblies, riser cable routing assemblies, and general-purpose cable routing assemblies when _____.

    (a) selected in accordance with Table 800.154(C)
    (b) listed in accordance with the provisions of 800.182
    (c) installed in accordance with 800.110(D) and 800.113
    (d) all of these

7. Class 2, Class 3, and Type PLTC cables shall be permitted to be installed in plenum communications raceways, riser communications raceways, and general-purpose communications raceways when _____, where the requirements applicable to electrical nonmetallic tubing (ENT) apply.

    (a) selected in accordance with the provisions of Table 800.154(B)
    (b) listed in accordance with 800.182
    (c) installed in accordance with 800.113 and 362.24 through 362.56
    (d) all of these

8. The requirements of 310.14(A)(3) on the temperature limitation of conductors shall apply to Class 1, Class 2, and Class 3 cables.

    (a) True
    (b) False

9. Class 1, Class 2, and Class 3 cables _____ conductors shall be identified in accordance with 250.119

    (a) ungrounded
    (b) grounded
    (c) equipment grounding
    (d) shielded

10. Access to electrical equipment shall not be denied by an accumulation of remote-control, signaling, or power-limited wire and cables that prevent removal of panels, including suspended-ceiling panels.

    (a) True
    (b) False

11. Class 1, Class 2, and Class 3 circuits installed _____ on the surface of ceilings and walls shall be supported by the building structure in such a manner that the cable will not be damaged by normal building use.

    (a) exposed
    (b) concealed
    (c) hidden
    (d) in raceways

12. Exposed Class 1, Class 2, and Class 3 cables shall be supported by straps, staples, hangers, or similar fittings designed and installed so as not to damage the cable.

    (a) True
    (b) False

13. _____ or other contaminants can result in an undetermined alteration of Class 1, 2, and 3 cable properties.

    (a) Paint and plaster
    (b) Cleaners and abrasives
    (c) Corrosive residues
    (d) all of these

14. Accessible portions of abandoned Class 2 and Class 3 cables shall be removed.

    (a) True
    (b) False

15. Class 2 cables identified for future use shall be marked with a tag of sufficient durability to withstand _____.

    (a) moisture
    (b) humidity
    (c) the environment involved
    (d) temperature fluctuations

16. Remote-control circuits for safety-control equipment shall be classified as _____ if the failure of the equipment to operate introduces a direct fire or life hazard.

    (a) Class 1
    (b) Class 2
    (c) Class 3
    (d) Class I, Division 1

Article 725 | Practice Questions

17. Class 1 circuits shall be classified as Class 1 power-limited circuits where they are supplied from a source that has a rated output of not more than _____ and 1,000 VA.

    (a) 12V
    (b) 24V
    (c) 30V
    (d) 50V

18. Class 1 circuits shall be classified Class 1 remote-control and signaling circuits where they are used for remote-control or signaling purposes and do not exceed _____.

    (a) 30V
    (b) 125V
    (c) 250V
    (d) 600V

19. Class 1 circuits shall be installed in accordance with Part I of Article 300 and are exempt from the wiring methods from the remaining articles in Chapter 3.

    (a) True
    (b) False

20. Class 1 circuits and power-supply circuits shall be permitted to occupy the same cable, enclosure, or raceway without a barrier _____.

    (a) only where the equipment powered is functionally associated
    (b) where the circuits involved are not a mixture of ac and dc
    (c) under no circumstances
    (d) only where the equipment is essential for life safety

21. Class 1 circuits shall be permitted to be installed together with the conductors of _____ and medium power network-powered broadband communications circuits where separated by a barrier

    (a) electric light
    (b) power
    (c) nonpower-limited fire alarm
    (d) all of these

22. The power source for a Class 2 circuit shall be _____.

    (a) a listed Class 2 transformer
    (b) a listed Class 2 power supply
    (c) other listed equipment marked to identify the Class 2 power source
    (d) any of these

23. _____ audio/video information technology (computer), communications, and industrial equipment limited-power circuits are permitted to be used as the power source for a Class 2 or a Class 3 circuit.

    (a) Listed
    (b) Labeled
    (c) Identified
    (d) Approved

24. The power sources for limited-power circuits in 725.121(A)(3) and limited-power circuits for listed audio/video information technology (equipment) and listed industrial equipment in 725.121(A)(4) shall have a label indicating the maximum voltage and _____ output for each connection point.

    (a) fault current
    (b) rated current
    (c) overcurrent
    (d) running current

25. Rated current for Class 2 and Class 3 power sources for conductors that transmit _____, is the output current per conductor the power source is designed to deliver to an operational load at normal operating conditions, as declared by the manufacturer.

    (a) power and data
    (b) emergency signaling
    (c) fire signaling
    (d) alarm signaling

26. Rated current for _____ power sources for conductors covered in 725.144 is the output current per conductor the power source is designed to deliver to an operational load at normal operating conditions, as declared by the manufacturer.

    (a) Class 1
    (b) Class 2
    (c) Class 3
    (d) Class 2 and Class 3

27. Equipment supplying Class 2 or Class 3 circuits shall be durably marked where plainly visible to indicate _____.

    (a) each circuit that is a Class 2 or Class 3 circuit
    (b) the circuit VA rating
    (c) the size of conductors serving each circuit
    (d) all of these

28. Class 2 and Class 3 circuits reclassified and installed as Class 1 circuits are no longer Class 2 or Class 3 circuits, unless there is a continued connection to a Class 2 or Class 3 power source.

    (a) True
    (b) False

29. Cables and conductors of Class 2 and Class 3 circuits _____ be placed with conductors of electric light, power, Class 1, nonpower-limited fire alarm circuits, and medium power network-powered broadband communications circuits.

    (a) shall be permitted to
    (b) shall not
    (c) shall
    (d) shall be required to

30. Conductors of Class 2 and Class 3 circuits shall not be placed in any enclosure, raceway, cable, or similar fittings with conductors of Class 1 or electric light or power conductors, unless _____.

    (a) insulated for the maximum voltage present
    (b) totally comprised of aluminum conductors
    (c) separated by a barrier
    (d) all of these

31. Audio system circuits using Class 2 or Class 3 wiring methods are not permitted in the same cable, raceway, or cable routing assembly with _____.

    (a) other audio system circuits
    (b) Class 1 conductors or cables
    (c) Class 3 conductors or cables
    (d) Class 2 conductors or Class 3 conductors or cables

32. The exterior portion of raceways shall not be used as a means of support for Class 2 or Class 3 cables.

    (a) True
    (b) False

33. Sections 725.144(B) and (B) shall apply to _____ that transmit power and data to a powered device.

    (a) all circuits
    (b) Class 1, 2, and 3 circuits
    (c) Class 2 and 3 circuits
    (d) low voltage circuits

34. The requirements of Parts I and III of Article 725 and 300.11 shall apply to Class 2 and Class 3 circuits that transmit power and data.

    (a) True
    (b) False

35. The conductors for Class 2 and Class 3 circuits that carry power for the data circuits shall be copper and the current in the power circuit shall not exceed the current limitation of the _____.

    (a) conductors
    (b) connectors
    (c) wiring method
    (d) equipment served

36. One example of the use of cables for Class 2 or Class 3 circuits that transmit power and data is the connection of closed-circuit TV cameras (CCTV).

    (a) True
    (b) False

37. The 8P8C connector is in widespread use with powered communications systems using Class 2 or Class 3 circuits and these connectors are typically rated at _____ maximum.

    (a) 0.50A
    (b) 1.00A
    (c) 1.20A
    (d) 1.30A

38. When using Table 725.144, bundle sizes over _____ cables, or conductor sizes smaller than 26 AWG, ampacities shall be permitted to be determined by qualified personnel under engineering supervision.

    (a) 129
    (b) 178
    (c) 187
    (d) 192

39. Where only half of the conductors in each cable are carrying current, the values in Table 725.144 shall be permitted to be increased by a factor of _____.

    (a) 1.00
    (b) 1.20
    (c) 1.40
    (d) 1.60

40. Where Types CL3P, CL2P, CL3R, CL2R, CL3, or CL2 transmit power and data, the rated current per conductor of the power source shall not exceed the ampacities in Table 725.144 at an ambient temperature of _____.

    (a) 30°C
    (b) 60°C
    (c) 75°C
    (d) 90°C

41. One example of the use of Class 2 cables is a network of closed-circuit TV cameras using 24 AWG, 60°C rated, Type CL2R, Category 5e balanced twisted-pair cabling

    (a) True
    (b) False

42. Where Types CL3P-LP, CL2P-LP, CL3R-LP, CL2R-LP, CL3-LP, or CL2-LP transmit power and data, the rated current per conductor of the power source installed at temperatures above 86°F, the correction factors in Table _____ shall apply to the ampacities in Table 725.144.

    (a) 310.15(B)(3)(a)
    (b) 310.15(B)(7)
    (c) 310.15(B)(1)
    (d) 310.16

43. Class 2-LP and Class 3-LP cables shall comply with which of the following, as applicable?

    (a) Cables with the suffix "-LP" shall be permitted to be installed in bundles, raceways, cable trays, communications raceways, and cable routing assemblies.
    (b) Cables with the suffix "-LP" and a marked ampere level shall follow the substitution hierarchy of Table 725.154 and NEC Figure 725.154(a) for the cable type without the suffix "-LP" and without the marked ampere level.
    (c) System design shall be permitted by qualified persons under engineering supervision.
    (d) any of these

44. Class 2, Class 3, and Type PLTC cables, installed as wiring methods within buildings, shall be _____ as resistant to the spread of fire and other criteria in accordance with 725.179(A) through (I) and shall be marked in accordance with 725.179(J).

    (a) listed
    (b) labeled
    (c) identified
    (d) approved

45. Types CL2P and CL3P plenum cable shall be _____ as suitable for use in ducts, plenums, and other space for environmental air and shall be listed as having adequate fire-resistant and low-smoke producing characteristics.

    (a) marked
    (b) labeled
    (c) listed
    (d) approved

46. Class 2 and Class 3 plenum cables listed as suitable for use in ducts, plenums, and other spaces used for environmental air shall be Type _____.

    (a) CL2P and CL3P
    (b) CL2R and CL3R
    (c) CL2 and CL3
    (d) PLTC

Article 760—Fire Alarm Systems

1. Article 760 covers the requirements for the installation of wiring and equipment of _____.

    (a) communications systems
    (b) antennas
    (c) fire alarm systems
    (d) fiber optics

2. Fire alarm systems include _____.

    (a) fire detection and alarm notification
    (b) guard's tour
    (c) sprinkler waterflow
    (d) all of these

3. Fire alarm cables that are not terminated at equipment other than a connector and not identified for future use with a tag are considered abandoned.

    (a) True
    (b) False

4. _____ fire alarm cables installed in ducts, plenums, or other spaces used for environmental air shall comply with 300.22.

    (a) Fire rated
    (b) Metal-clad
    (c) Power-limited and nonpower limited
    (d) Line-voltage

5. _____ fire alarm cables selected in accordance with Table 760.154 and installed in accordance with 760.135(B) and 300.22(B) Ex shall be permitted to be installed in ducts specifically fabricated for environmental air.

   (a) Power-limited
   (b) Nonpower-limited
   (c) Power-limited and nonpower-limited
   (d) Line-voltage

6. _____ fire alarm cables selected in accordance with Table 760.154 and installed in accordance with 760.135(C) shall be permitted to be installed in other spaces used for environmental air (plenums).

   (a) Fire-rated
   (b) Metal-clad
   (c) Power-limited and nonpower-limited
   (d) Line-voltage

7. Where _____ cables are utilized for fire alarm circuits, the cables shall be installed in accordance with Article 770.

   (a) Class 1
   (b) Class 2
   (c) Class 3
   (d) optical fiber

8. If fire alarm conductors are installed in a raceway that is subjected to different temperatures, and where condensation is known to be a problem, the raceway shall be filled with a material approved by the authority having jurisdiction that will prevent the circulation of warm air to a colder section of the raceway. An explosionproof seal _____.

   (a) is required for this purpose
   (b) has been proven effective for this purpose
   (c) is not required for this purpose
   (d) is the only method of doing this

9. Raceways enclosing cables and conductors for fire alarm systems shall be large enough to permit the _____ of conductors without damaging conductor insulation as limited by 300.17.

   (a) concealment
   (b) bending space
   (c) splicing
   (d) installation and removal

10. When a raceway is used for the support or protection of cables for fire alarm circuits, a bushing to reduce the potential for abrasion shall be placed at the location the cables emerge from the raceway.

    (a) True
    (b) False

11. Power-limited fire alarm cables shall be permitted to be installed in plenum cable routing assemblies, riser cable routing assemblies, and general-purpose cable routing assemblies where _____.

    (a) selected in accordance with Table 800.154(c)
    (b) listed in accordance with the provisions of 800.182
    (c) installed in accordance with 800.110(C) and 800.113
    (d) all of these

12. Power-limited fire alarm cables shall be permitted to be installed in plenum communications raceways, riser communications raceways, and general-purpose communications raceways where _____, and where the requirements applicable to electrical nonmetallic tubing apply.

    (a) selected in accordance with Table 800.154(B)
    (b) listed in accordance with the provisions of 800.182
    (c) installed in accordance with 800.113 and 362.24 through 362.56
    (d) all of these

13. The requirements of 310.14(A)(3) on the temperature limitation of conductors shall apply to nonpower-limited fire alarm cables only.

    (a) True
    (b) False

14. Power-limited and nonpower-limited fire alarm cables with green insulation shall be permitted to be used as ungrounded signal conductors.

    (a) True
    (b) False

15. Fire alarm circuit cables and conductors installed exposed on the surface of ceilings and sidewalls shall be supported by _____, hangers, or similar fittings designed and installed so as not to damage the cable.

    (a) straps
    (b) staples
    (c) cable ties
    (d) any of these

Article 760 | Practice Questions

16. Accessible portions of abandoned fire alarm cable shall be removed.

    (a) True
    (b) False

17. Fire alarm cables identified for future use shall be marked with a tag of sufficient durability to withstand _____.

    (a) moisture
    (b) humidity
    (c) the environment involved
    (d) temperature fluctuations

18. Fire alarm circuits shall be identified at all terminal and junction locations in a manner that helps prevent unintentional signals on fire alarm system circuits during _____ of other systems.

    (a) installation
    (b) testing and servicing
    (c) renovations
    (d) all of these

19. The fire alarm circuit disconnecting means for a power-limited fire alarm system shall _____.

    (a) have red identification
    (b) be accessible only to qualified personnel
    (c) be identified as "FIRE ALARM CIRCUIT"
    (d) all of these

20. The power source for a power-limited fire alarm circuit can be supplied through a ground-fault circuit interrupter or an arc-fault circuit interrupter.

    (a) True
    (b) False

21. The fire alarm branch-circuit disconnecting means shall be permitted to be secured in the "on" position.

    (a) True
    (b) False

22. Fire alarm equipment supplying power-limited fire alarm circuits shall be durably marked where plainly visible to indicate each circuit that is _____.

    (a) supplied by a nonpower-limited fire alarm circuit
    (b) a power-limited fire alarm circuit
    (c) a fire alarm circuit
    (d) supervised

23. Cable splices or terminations in power-limited fire alarm systems shall be made in listed _____ or utilization equipment.

    (a) fittings
    (b) boxes or enclosures
    (c) fire alarm devices
    (d) any of these

24. Power-limited fire alarm circuit cables and conductors shall not be placed in any cable, cable tray, compartment, enclosure, manhole, _____, or similar fitting with conductors of electric light, power, Class 1, nonpower-limited fire alarm circuits, and medium-powered network-powered broadband communications circuits unless permitted by 760.136(B) through (G).

    (a) outlet box
    (b) device box
    (c) raceway
    (d) any of these

25. Generally speaking, conductors for lighting or power may occupy the same enclosure or raceway with conductors of power-limited fire alarm circuits.

    (a) True
    (b) False

26. Power-limited fire alarm cables can be supported by strapping, taping, or attaching to the exterior of a conduit or raceway.

    (a) True
    (b) False

27. Power-limited fire alarm cables installed within buildings shall be _____ as being resistant to the spread of fire.

    (a) marked FR
    (b) listed
    (c) identified
    (d) color coded

28. Power-limited fire alarm cable used in a _____ location shall be listed for use in _____ locations or have a moisture-impervious metal sheath.

    (a) dry
    (b) damp
    (c) wet
    (d) hazardous

29. Cables used in power-limited fire alarm systems shall have a voltage rating of not less than _____.

    (a) 100V
    (b) 300V
    (c) 600V
    (d) 1,000V

30. Cables used in power-limited fire alarm systems shall have a temperature rating of not less than _____.

    (a) 60°C
    (b) 75°C
    (c) 90°C
    (d) 100°C

Article 770—Optical Fiber Cables

1. Article 770 covers the installation of optical fiber cables. This article does not cover the construction of _____.

    (a) coaxial cables
    (b) tray cables
    (c) optical fiber cables
    (d) industrial trolley cables

2. Optical fiber cables not terminated at equipment other than a connector, and not identified for future use with a tag are considered abandoned.

    (a) True
    (b) False

3. Access to electrical equipment shall not be denied by an accumulation of optical fiber cables that _____ removal of panels, including suspended-ceiling panels.

    (a) prevents
    (b) hinders
    (c) blocks
    (d) requires

4. Optical fiber cables installed _____ on the surface of ceilings and walls shall be supported by the building structure in such a manner that the cable will not be damaged by normal building use.

    (a) exposed
    (b) in raceways
    (c) hidden
    (d) exposed and concealed

5. Accepted industry practices for optical fiber installations are described in _____.

    (a) ANSI/NECA/BICSI 568, *Standard for Installing Commercial Building Telecommunications Cabling*
    (b) ANSI/NECA/FOA 301, *Standard for Installing and Testing Fiber Optic Cables*
    (c) other ANSI-approved installation standards
    (d) all of these

6. Paint, plaster, cleaners, abrasives, corrosive residues, or other contaminants may result in an undetermined alteration of optical fiber cable _____.

    (a) usefulness
    (b) voltage
    (c) properties
    (d) reliability

7. Accessible portions of abandoned optical fiber cable shall be removed.

    (a) True
    (b) False

8. Openings around penetrations of optical fiber cables and communications raceways through fire-resistant-rated walls, partitions, floors, or ceilings shall be _____ using approved methods to maintain the fire-resistance rating.

    (a) closed
    (b) opened
    (c) draft stopped
    (d) firestopped

9. When optical fiber cable is installed in a Chapter 3 raceway, the raceway shall be installed in accordance with Chapter 3 requirements.

    (a) True
    (b) False

10. Optical fibers shall be permitted within the same composite cable as electric light, power, and Class 1 circuits operating at 1,000V or less where the functions of the optical fibers and the electrical conductors are associated.

    (a) True
    (b) False

Article 770 | Practice Questions

11. Nonconductive optical fiber cables shall not be permitted to occupy the same cabinet, outlet box, panel, or similar enclosure unless the nonconductive optical fiber cables are functionally associated with the electric circuits.

    (a) True
    (b) False

CHAPTER 8

COMMUNICATIONS SYSTEMS

Introduction to Chapter 8—Communications Systems

Chapter 8 of the *National Electrical Code* covers the wiring requirements for communications systems such as telephones, radio and TV antennas, satellite dishes, closed-circuit television (CCTV), coaxial cable systems, and network- and premises-powered broadband systems for use of voice, audio, video and data. ▶Figure 1

Communications systems are not subject to the general requirements contained in Chapters 1 through 4 or the special requirements of Chapters 5 through 7, except where a Chapter 8 rule specifically refers to one of those chapters [90.3]. Also, installations of communications equipment under the exclusive control of communications utilities located outdoors, or in building spaces used exclusively for such installations, are exempt from the *NEC* [90.2(B)(4)].

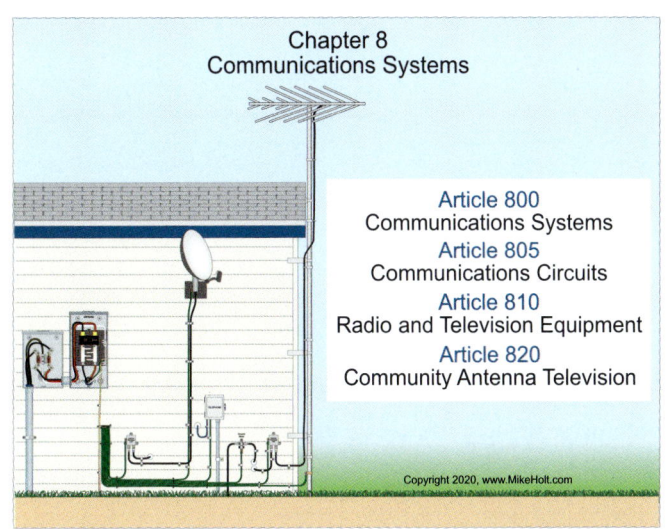

▶Figure 1

▶ **Article 800—General Requirements for Communications Systems.** This article covers general requirements for the installation of communications circuits, community antenna television and radio distribution systems, network-powered broadband communications systems, and premises-powered broadband communications systems, unless modified by Articles 805 or 820.

▶ **Article 805—General Requirements for Communications Circuits.** Article 805 covers the installation requirements for circuits and equipment related to telephone wiring and other telecommunications purposes such as computer local area networks (LANs), and outside wiring for fire and burglar alarm systems connected to central monitoring stations.

▶ **Article 810—Radio and Television Antenna Equipment.** This article covers antenna systems for radio and television receiving equipment, amateur radio transmitting and receiving equipment, and certain features of transmitter safety. It also includes antennas such as multi-element, vertical rod and dish, and the wiring and cabling that connects them to the equipment.

▶ **Article 820—Community Antenna Television (CATV) and Radio Distribution Systems (Coaxial Cable).** Article 820 covers the installation of coaxial cables to distribute limited-energy high-frequency signals for television, cable TV, and closed-circuit television (CCTV) which is often used for security purposes. It also covers the premises wiring of satellite TV systems where the dish antenna is outside and covered by Article 810.

ARTICLE 800 — GENERAL REQUIREMENTS FOR COMMUNICATIONS SYSTEMS

Introduction to Article 800—General Requirements for Communications Systems

Article 800 contains the general rules for, and apply to, installations of those systems covered by Articles 805 and 820. Note that the scope of this article does not include Article 810, Radio and Television Equipment. That article still stands alone from the rest of the *Code*, including the Chapter 8 Articles. The specific rules in Articles 805, 820, 830, and 840 supplement or modify the requirements in Article 800. This is similar to the language in 90.3 that says the general rules in Chapters 1 through 4 may be modified by the specific rules in Chapters 5 through 7.

Part I. General

800.1 Scope

Article 800 covers general requirements for communications systems. They apply to communications circuits, community antenna television and radio distribution systems, and network- and premises-powered broadband communications systems, unless modified by Articles 805 or 820. ▶Figure 800–1

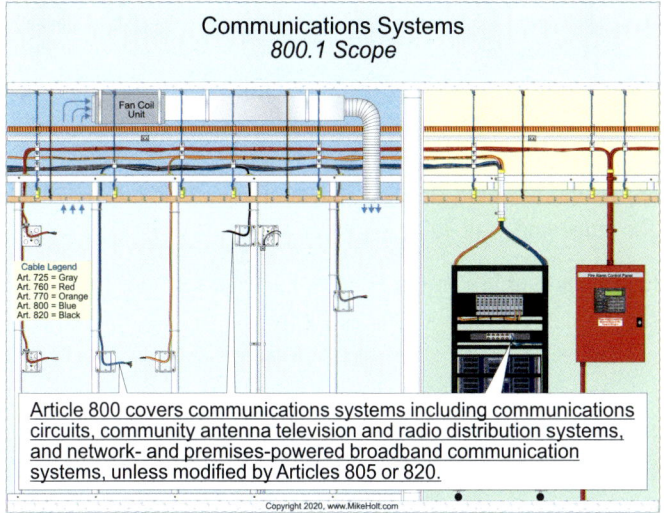

▶Figure 800–1

800.2 Definitions

The definitions for more common items that appear in Article 100 and those that are contained here in 800.2 apply throughout Chapter 8.

Author's Comment:

▸ Throughout articles in the *NEC*, definitions specific to that article generally appear in the xxx.2 section of the individual article. What is unique about Chapter 8 is that definitions applicable throughout all of the articles in that chapter are listed in section 800.2.

▸ Another unique feature of Chapter 8 is that common wiring methods, bonding methods, and other installation requirements that apply throughout the chapter are also consolidated in Article 800.

Abandoned Cable. Cable that is not terminated to equipment or not identified for future use with a tag. ▶Figure 800–2

Author's Comment:

▸ Section 800.25 requires the accessible portion of abandoned cables to be removed.

Communications Circuit. The circuit that extends service from the communications utility or service provider up to and including the customer's communications equipment. ▶Figure 800–3

800.3 | General Requirements for Communications Systems

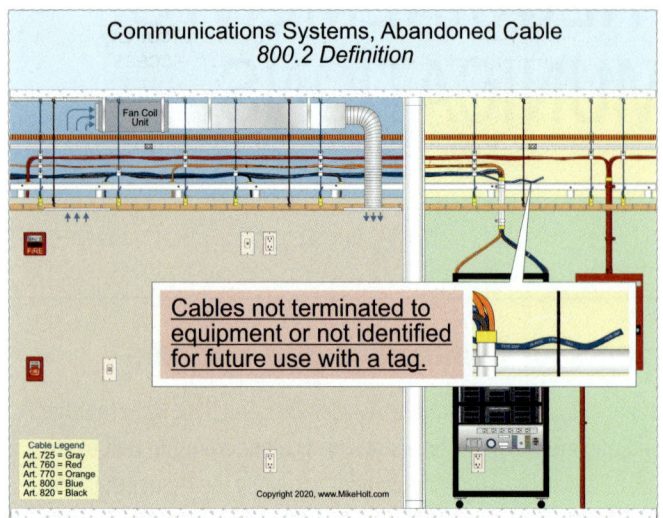
▶Figure 800-2

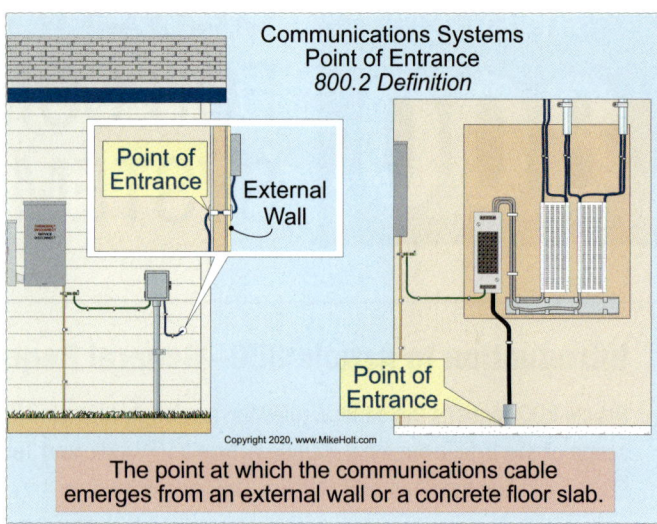
▶Figure 800-4

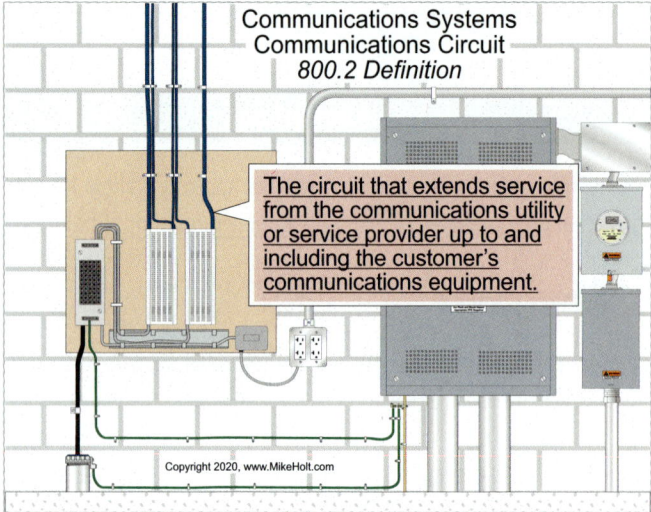
▶Figure 800-3

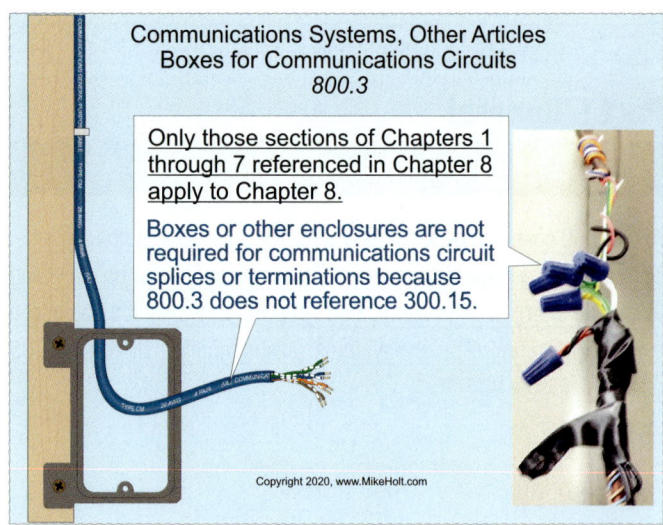
▶Figure 800-5

Exposed (to Accidental Contact). A condition where failure of support or insulation can result in the circuit contacting another circuit.

Point of Entrance. The point within a building at which the cable emerges from an external wall or concrete floor slab. ▶Figure 800-4

800.3 Other Articles

Only those sections of Chapters 1 through 7 referenced in Chapter 8 apply to Chapter 8. ▶Figure 800-5

(A) Hazardous (Classified) Locations. For circuits and equipment installed in a location that is classified in accordance with 500.5 and 505.5, the applicable requirements of Chapter 5 apply.

(B) Wiring in Ducts for Dust, Loose Stock, or Vapor Removal. The requirements of 300.22(A) apply.

(C) Equipment in Plenum Spaces. Equipment installed in plenum spaces must comply with 300.22(C)(3).

> **Author's Comment:**
>
> ▸ According to 300.22(C)(3), electrical equipment with a metal enclosure, or a nonmetallic enclosure listed for use in an air-handling space, can be installed in a plenum space. ▶Figure 800-6

(D) Installation and Use. Communications equipment must be installed and used according to manufacturers' instructions in accordance with 110.3(B).

General Requirements for Communications Systems | 800.24

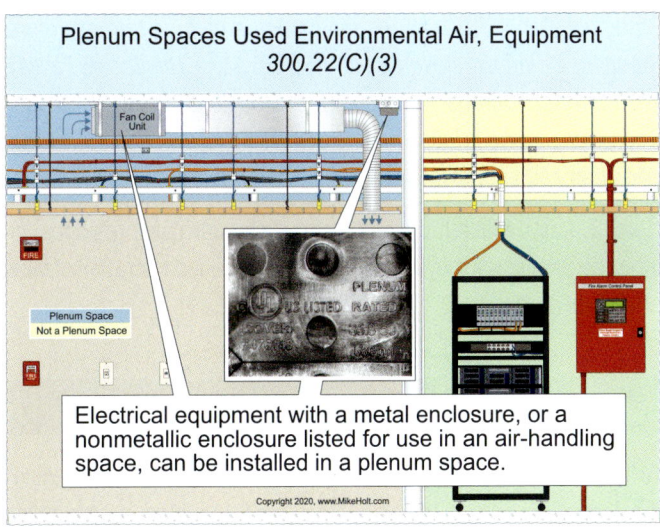
▶Figure 800-6

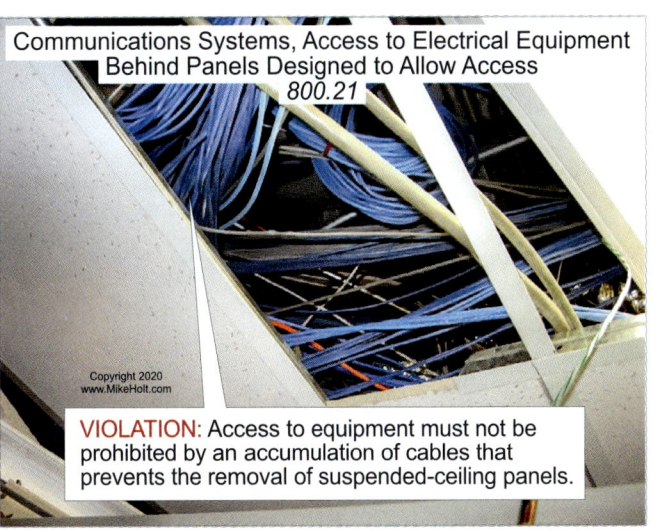
▶Figure 800-7

(E) Optical Fiber Cable. Where optical fiber cable is used to provide a communications circuit within a building, Article 770 applies.

(F) Other Communications Systems. Communications systems must comply with the following requirements:

(1) Communications Circuits—Article 805

(2) Antennas—Article 810

(3) Coaxial Cable Systems—Article 820

800.21 Access to Electrical Equipment Behind Panels Designed to Allow Access

Access to equipment must not be prohibited by an accumulation of cables that prevents the removal of suspended-ceiling panels. ▶Figure 800-7

800.24 Mechanical Execution of Work

Equipment and cabling must be installed in a neat and workmanlike manner. ▶Figure 800-8

Exposed cables must be supported by the structural components of the building so the cable will not be damaged by normal building use. Support must be by straps, staples, hangers, cable ties, or similar fittings designed and installed in a manner that will not damage the cable. ▶Figure 800-9

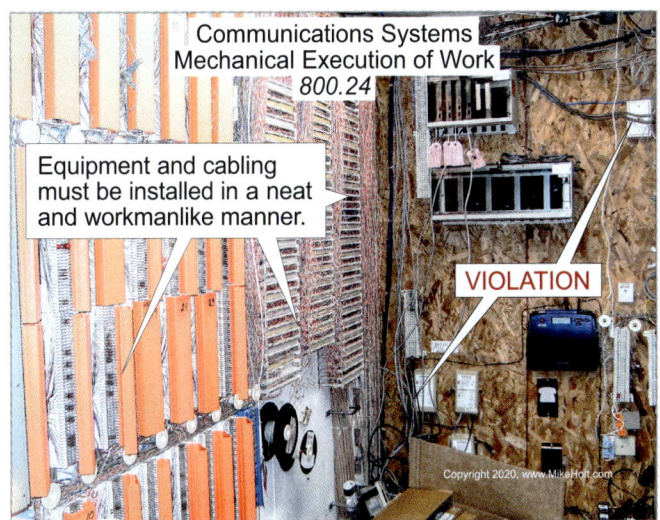
▶Figure 800-8

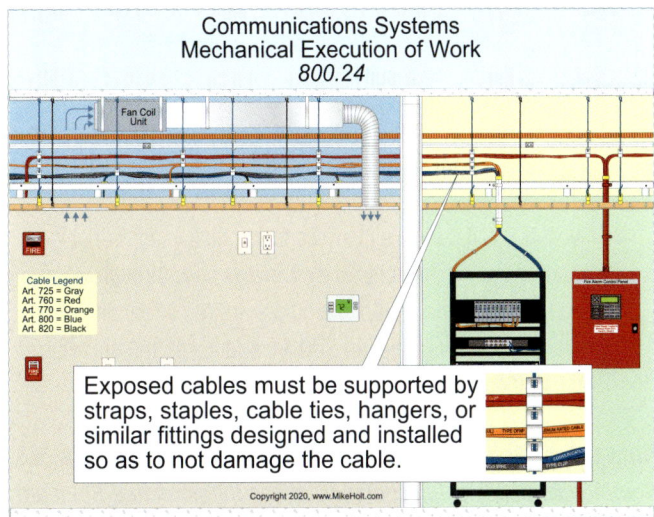
▶Figure 800-9

800.25 | General Requirements for Communications Systems

Exposed cables must comply with 300.4 and 300.11. Nonmetallic cable ties in plenum spaces must comply with 805.170(C). ▶Figure 800-10 and ▶Figure 800-11

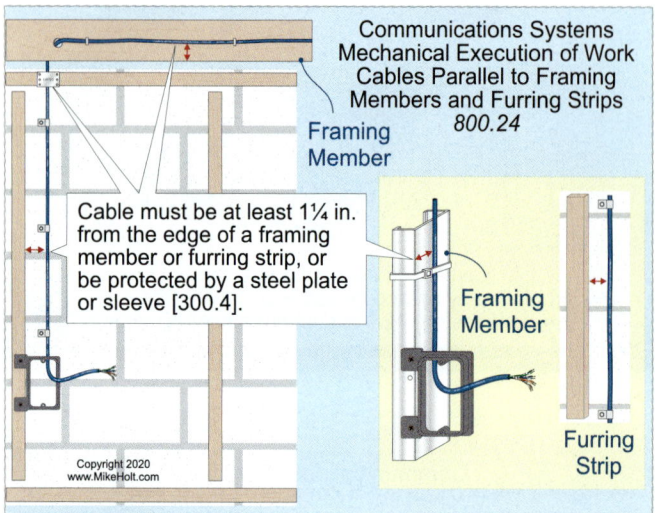

▶Figure 800-10

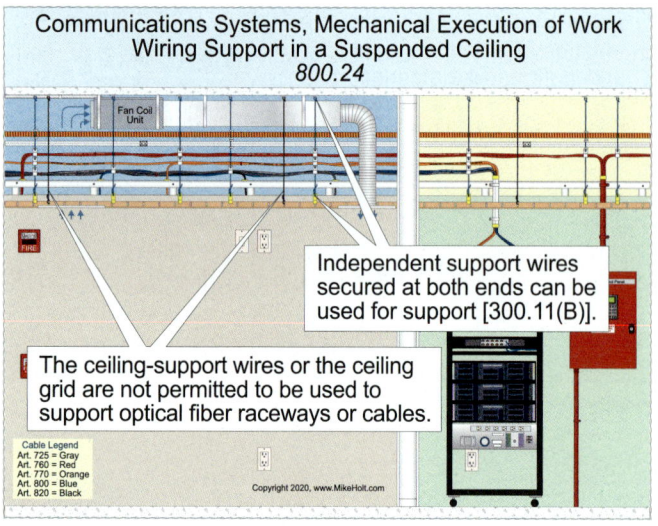

▶Figure 800-11

Author's Comment:

▶ Section 300.4 contains the rules for protection against physical damage when cables and raceways pass through wood and metal members, and when they are run in parallel with framing members. Section 300.11 addresses the securing and supporting requirements of wiring methods.

Note 1: Accepted industry practices are described in ANSI/TIA-568, *Commercial Building Telecommunications Infrastructure Standard*; ANSI/TIA-569-D, *Telecommunications Pathways and Spaces*; ANSI/TIA-570-C, *Residential Telecommunications Infrastructure*

Standard; ANSI/TIA-1005-A, *Telecommunications Infrastructure Standard for Industrial Premises*; ANSI/TIA-1179, *Healthcare Facility Telecommunications Infrastructure Standard*; ANSI/TIA-4966, *Telecommunications Infrastructure Standard for Educational Facilities*; and other ANSI-approved installation standards.

Note 3: Paint, plaster, cleaners, abrasives, corrosive residues, or other contaminants may result in an undetermined alteration of wire and cable properties.

800.25 Abandoned Cable

To limit the spread of fire or products of combustion within a building, the accessible portion of cable that is not terminated at equipment and not identified for future use with a tag must be removed [800.2]. Tags identifying cables for future use must be able to withstand the environment involved. ▶Figure 800-12

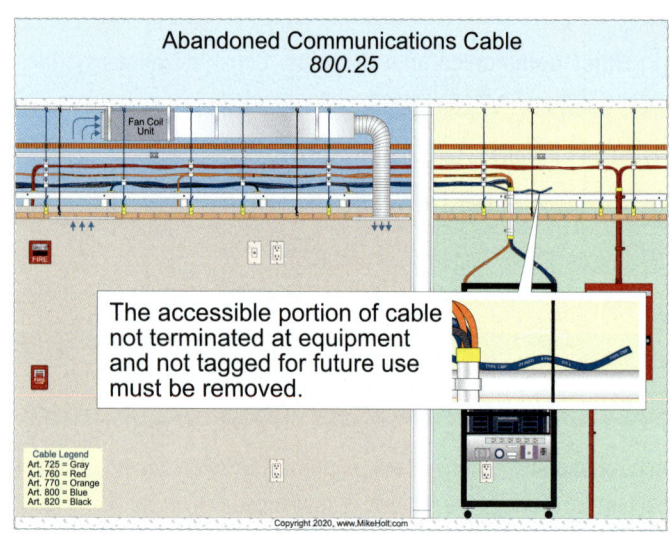

▶Figure 800-12

800.26 Spread of Fire or Products of Combustion

Communications circuits and equipment must be installed in such a way that the spread of fire or products of combustion will not be substantially increased. Openings into or through fire-resistant-rated walls, floors, and ceilings for electrical equipment must be firestopped using methods approved by the authority having jurisdiction to maintain the fire-resistance rating of the fire-rated assembly. ▶Figure 800-13 and ▶Figure 800-14

General Requirements for Communications Systems | 800.26

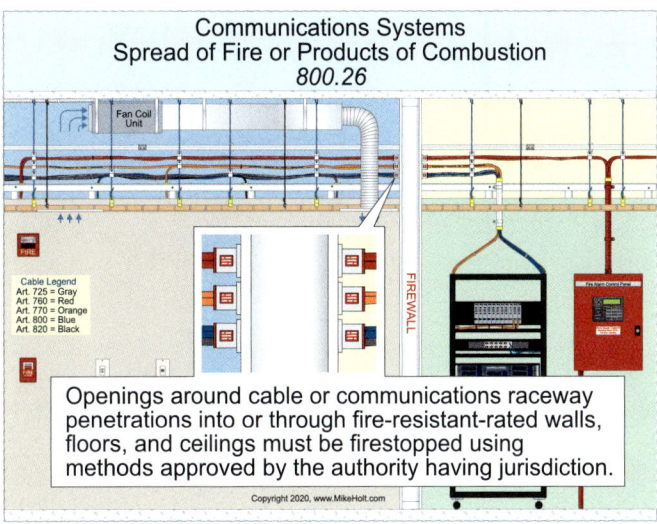

▶Figure 800-13

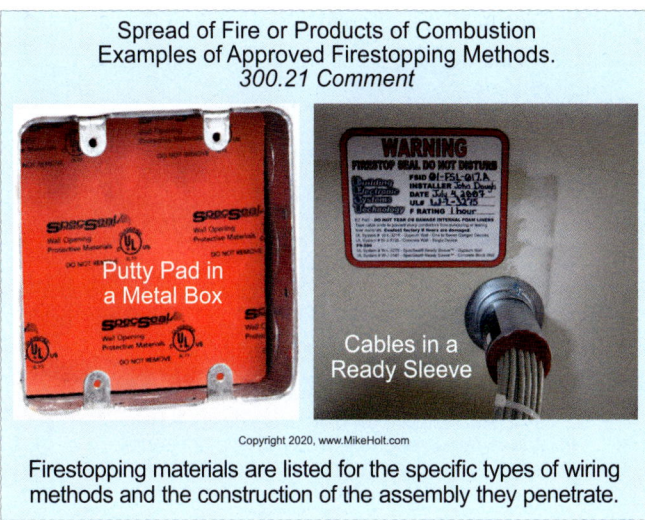

▶Figure 800-15

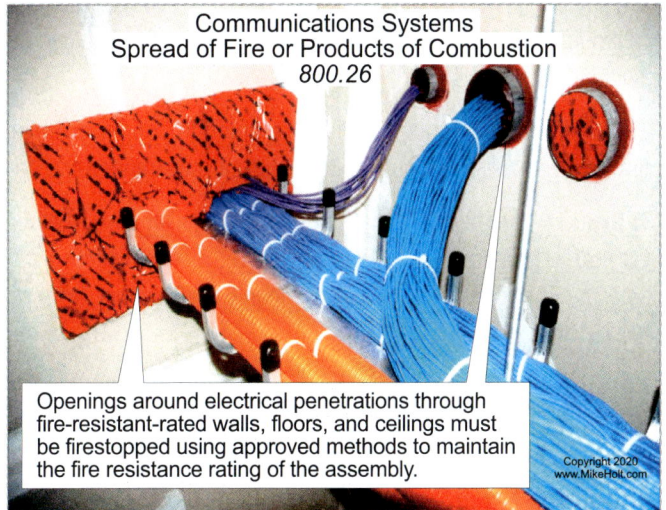

▶Figure 800-14

Author's Comment:

▸ Firestopping materials are listed for the specific types of wiring methods and the construction of the assembly they penetrate.
▶Figure 800-15

Note: Directories of electrical construction materials published by recognized testing laboratories contain listing and installation restrictions necessary to maintain the fire-resistive rating of assemblies. Building codes also have restrictions on penetrations on opposite sides of a fire-resistance-rated wall. Outlet boxes must have a horizontal separation of not less than 24 in. when installed on opposite sides in a fire-rated assembly, unless an outlet box is listed for closer spacing or protected by fire-resistant "putty pads" in accordance with manufacturer's instructions. ▶Figure 800-16 and ▶Figure 800-17

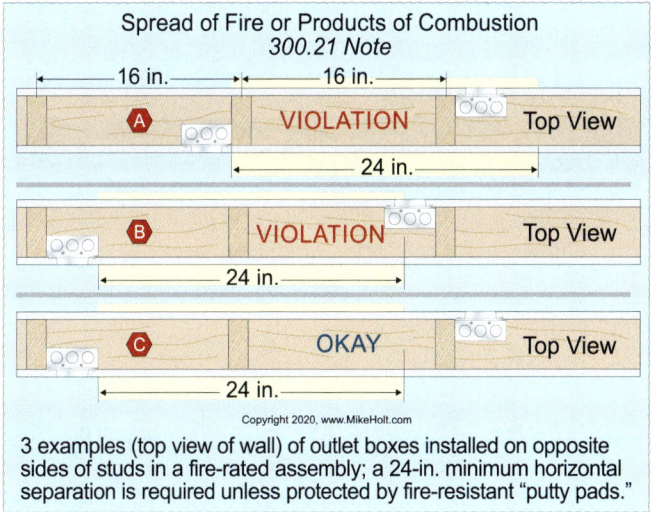

▶Figure 800-16

800.49 | General Requirements for Communications Systems

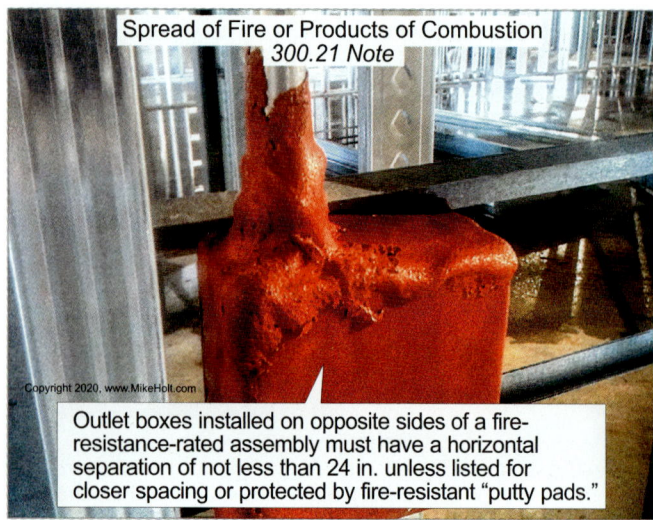

▶Figure 800–17

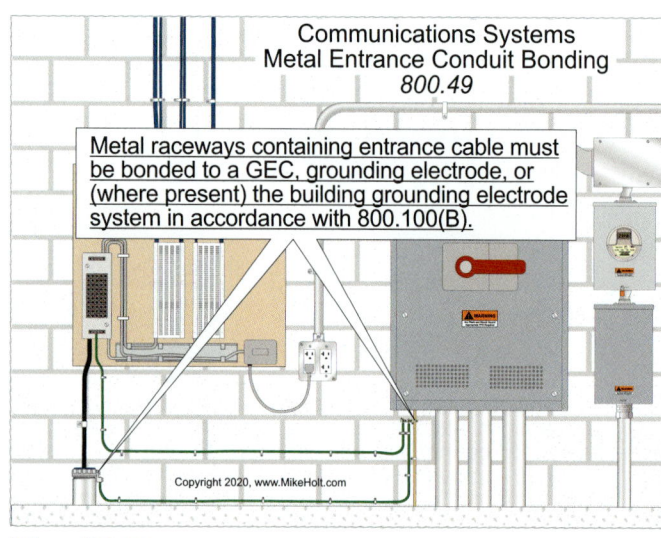

▶Figure 800–18

Author's Comment:

▸ Boxes installed in fire-resistance rated assemblies must be listed for the purpose. If steel boxes are used, they must be secured to the framing member, so cut-in type boxes are not permitted (UL White Book, *Guide Information for Electrical Equipment*). "Putty pads" are typically installed on the exterior of the box, but many manufactures have listed inserts for the interior of the box.

Part II. Wires and Cables Outside and Entering Buildings

800.49 Metal Entrance Conduit Bonding

Metal raceways containing entrance cable must be bonded to a grounding electrode conductor, grounding electrode, or (where present) the building grounding electrode system in accordance with 800.100(B). ▶Figure 800–18

800.53 Separation from Lightning Conductors

Where practicable, a separation of at least 6 ft must be maintained between communications circuits and lightning protection conductors.

Part III. Bonding Methods

800.100 Cable and Primary Protector Bonding

(A) Bonding Conductor.

(1) Insulation. The bonding conductor must be listed and can be insulated, covered, or bare.

(2) Material. The bonding conductor must be copper or other corrosion-resistant conductive material and can be stranded or solid.

(3) Size. The bonding conductor must not be smaller than 14 AWG, have current-carrying capacity not less than the metallic sheath of the cable, and is not required to be larger than 6 AWG copper. ▶Figure 800–19

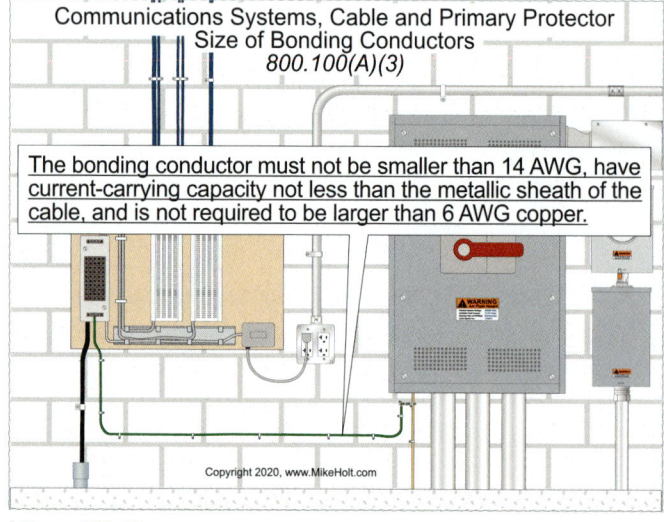

▶Figure 800–19

(4) Length. The bonding conductor must be as short as practicable. For one- and two-family dwellings, the bonding conductor is not permitted to exceed 20 ft in length. ▶Figure 800–20

General Requirements for Communications Systems | 800.100

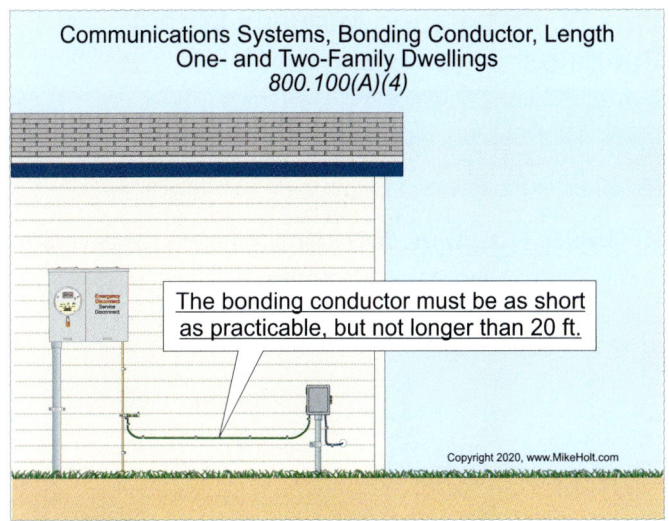
▶Figure 800–20

Author's Comment:

▸ Lightning does not like to travel around corners or through loops, which is why the bonding jumper must be run as straight as practicable.

(6) Physical Protection. The bonding conductor is not permitted to be subject to physical damage. If installed in a metal raceway, both ends of the raceway must be bonded to the bonding conductor or connected to the same terminal or electrode to which the bonding conductor is connected.

Author's Comment:

▸ Installing the bonding conductor in PVC conduit is a better practice.

Note: Limiting the length of the bonding conductor helps limit induced voltage differences between the building's power and communications systems during lightning events.

Ex: If the bonding conductor is over 20 ft in length for one- and two-family dwellings, a separate ground rod not less than 5 ft long [800.100(B)(3)(3)] with fittings suitable for the application [800.100(C)] must be installed. The additional ground rod must be bonded to the power grounding electrode system with a minimum 6 AWG [800.100(D)]. ▶Figure 800–21

(B) Electrode. The bonding conductor must be connected in accordance with (B)(1), (B)(2), or (B)(3).

(1) Buildings with an Intersystem Bonding Termination. The bonding conductor must terminate to the intersystem bonding termination as required by 250.94. ▶Figure 800–22

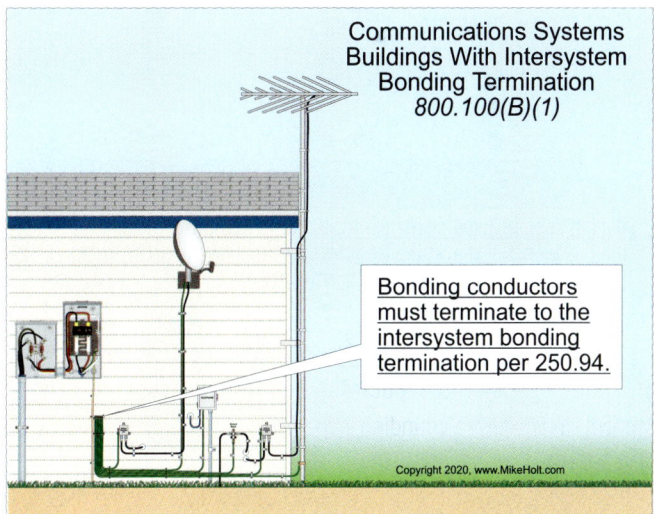
▶Figure 800–22

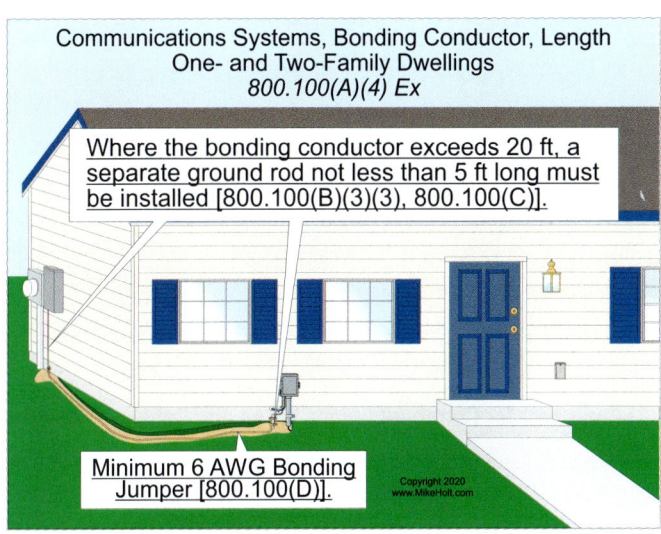
▶Figure 800–21

(5) Run in Straight Line. The bonding conductor must be run in as straight a line as practicable.

Author's Comment:

▸ According to the Article 100 definition, an "Intersystem Bonding Termination" is a device that provides a means to connect intersystem bonding conductors for communications systems to the grounding electrode system. ▶Figure 800–23

800.110 | General Requirements for Communications Systems

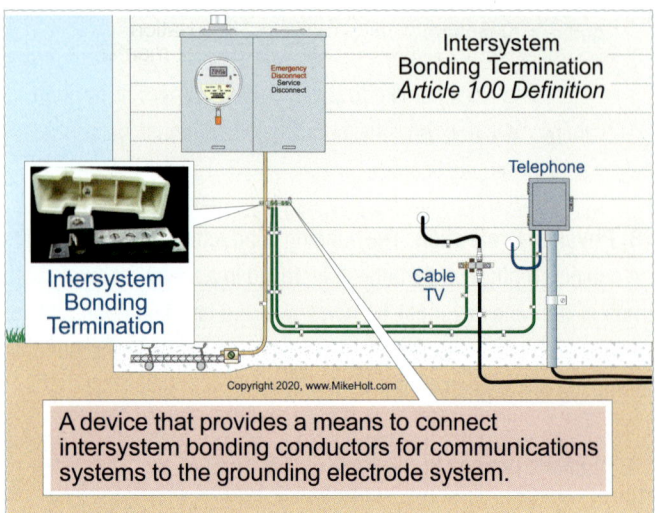

▶Figure 800-23

Note: Figure 800.100(B)(1) in the *NEC* illustrates the connection of the bonding conductor in buildings or structures equipped with an intersystem bonding termination.

(D) Bonding of Electrodes. If a separate grounding electrode (such as a rod) is installed for a communications system, it must be bonded to the building's power grounding electrode system with a minimum 6 AWG copper conductor. ▶Figure 800-24

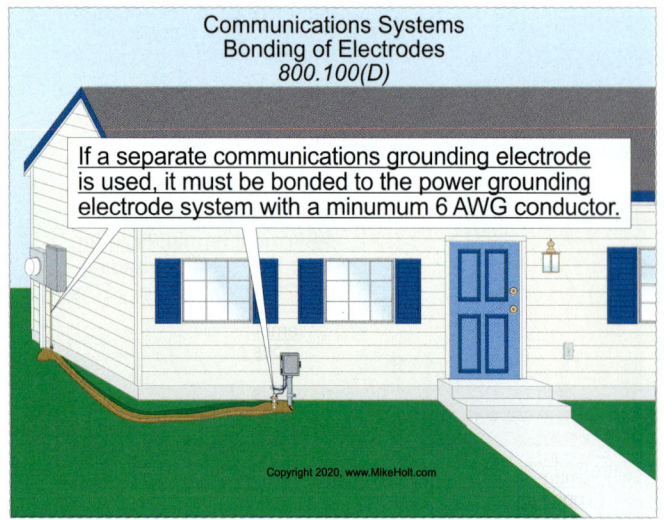

▶Figure 800-24

Note 2: Bonding separate electrodes together helps reduce induced voltage differences between the power and communications systems during lightning events.

Part IV. Installation Methods Within Buildings

800.110 Raceways and Cable Routing Assemblies

(A) Types of Raceways.

(1) Chapter 3 Raceways. Communications cables can be installed in any Chapter 3 raceway in accordance with the requirements of Chapter 3. ▶Figure 800-25

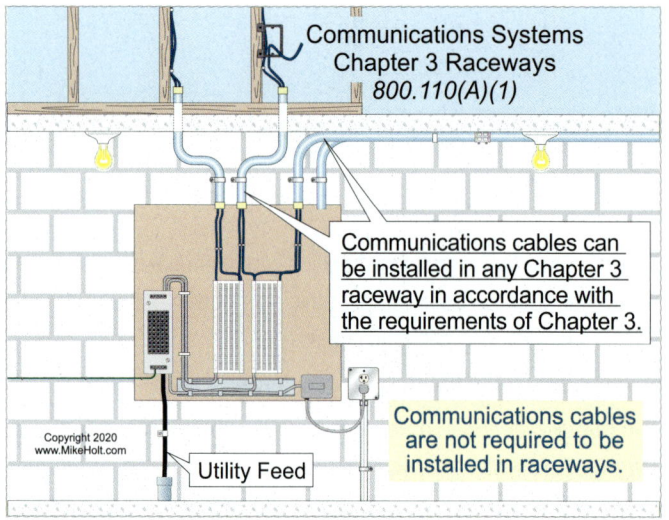

▶Figure 800-25

Author's Comment:

▶ Communications cable is not required to be installed in a Chapter 3 raceway, but when it is, it must be installed in accordance with the Chapter 3 requirements for that raceway.

(2) Communications Raceways. Communications cables can be installed in communications raceways selected using Table 800.154(b), listed in accordance with 800.182, and installed in accordance with 800.113 and 362.24 through 362.56 where the requirements for electrical nonmetallic tubing (ENT) apply. ▶Figure 800-26

(3) Innerduct for Communications Wires and Cables, or Coaxial Cables. Listed plenum communications raceways, listed riser communications raceways, and listed general-purpose communications raceways selected in accordance with Table 800.154(b) are permitted to be installed as innerduct in any type of listed raceway permitted in Chapter 3.

(B) Raceway Fill for Communications Wires and Cables. The raceway fill limitations of 300.17 do not apply to communications cables installed within a raceway.

General Requirements for Communications Systems | 800.113

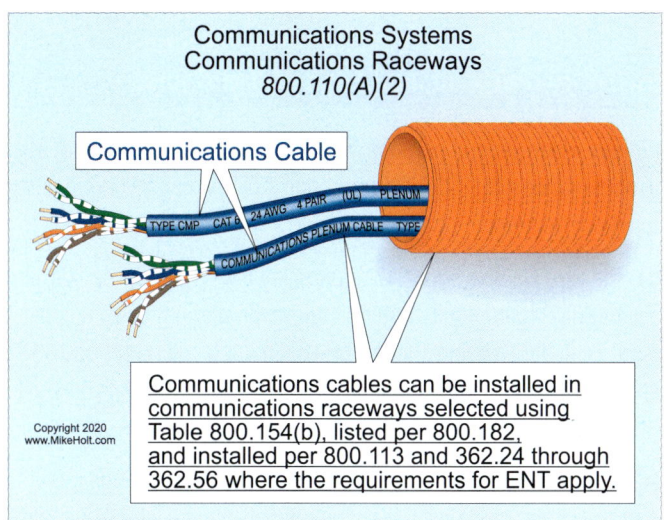

▶Figure 800-26

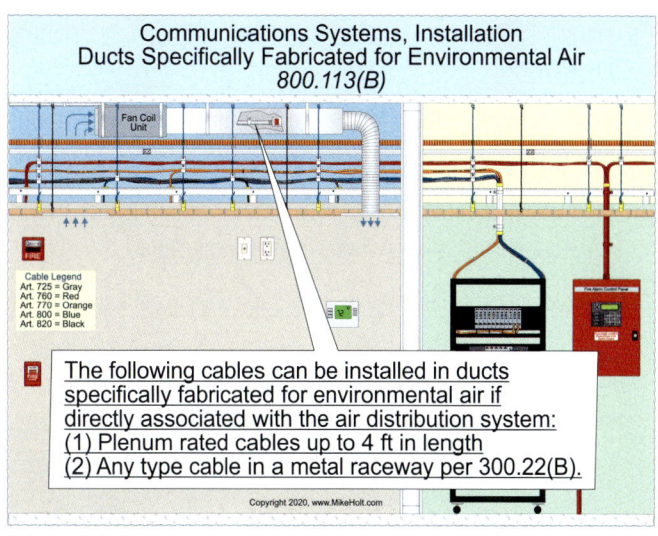

▶Figure 800-27

(C) Cable Routing Assemblies. Communications cables can be installed in cable routing assemblies selected in accordance with Table 800.154(c), listed in accordance with 800.182, and installed in accordance with 800.110(C)(1) and (C)(2), and 800.113.

(1) Horizontal Support. Where installed horizontally, cable routing assemblies must be supported every 3 ft and at each end or joint, unless listed otherwise. The distance between supports can never exceed 10 ft.

(2) Vertical Support. Where installed vertically, cable routing assemblies must be supported every 4 ft, unless listed otherwise, and are not permitted to have more than one joint between supports.

800.113 Installation of Communications Wires, Cables, Raceways, and Cable Routing Assemblies

The installation of cables, cable routing assemblies, and communications raceways must comply with 800.110 and the following:

(A) Listing. Cables, cable routing assemblies, and communications raceways installed in buildings must be listed.

Ex: Outside plant cables installed per 805.48 and 820.48 are not be required to be listed.

(B) Ducts Specifically Fabricated for Environmental Air. The following cables are permitted in ducts specifically fabricated for environmental air as described in 300.22(B) if they are directly associated with the air distribution system: ▶Figure 800-27

(1) Plenum-rated cables up to 4 ft in length

(2) Any type of cable in a metal raceway in accordance with 300.22(B)

Note: For information on fire protection of wiring installed in fabricated ducts, see NFPA 90A, *Standard for the Installation of Air-Conditioning and Ventilating Systems*.

(C) Plenum Spaces. The following cables, cable routing assemblies, and communications raceways can be installed in plenum spaces as described in 300.22(C): ▶Figure 800-28

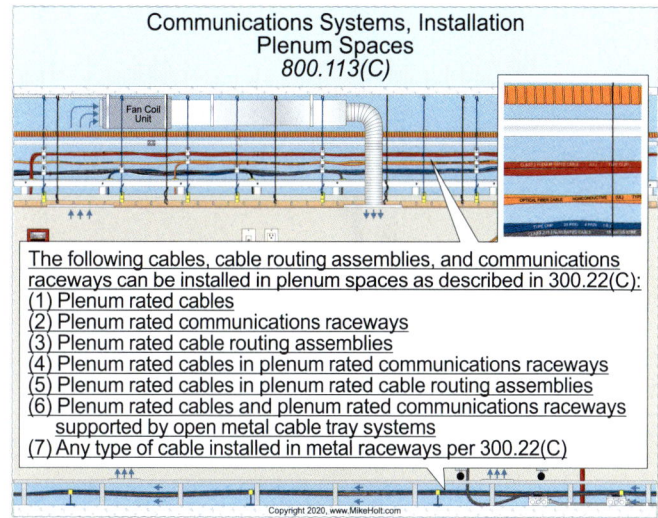

▶Figure 800-28

(1) Plenum-rated cables

(2) Plenum-rated communications raceways

(3) Plenum-rated cable routing assemblies

800.154 | General Requirements for Communications Systems

(4) Plenum-rated cables installed in plenum-rated communications raceways

(5) Plenum-rated cables installed in plenum-rated cable routing assemblies

(6) Plenum-rated cables and plenum-rated communications raceways supported by open metal cable tray systems

(7) Any type of cable installed in metal raceways in compliance with 300.22(C)

800.154 Applications of Listed Communications Wires, Cables, and Raceways, and Listed Cable Routing Assemblies

Permitted and nonpermitted applications of listed communications wires, cables, coaxial cables and raceways, and listed cable routing assemblies must be in accordance with one of the following:

(1) Listed communications wires and cables as indicated in Table 800.154(a)

(2) Listed communications raceways as indicated in Table 800.154(b)

(3) Listed cable routing assemblies as indicated in Table 800.154(c)

The permitted applications are subject to the installation requirements of 800.110 and 800.113.

800.179 Plenum, Riser, General-Purpose, and Limited-Use Cables

Plenum, riser, general-purpose, and limited-use cables must be listed in accordance with 800.179(A) through (D). The cable voltage rating must not be marked on the cable.

(A) Plenum Cables. Type CMP (communications plenum cables) and Type CATVP (community antenna television plenum coaxial cables) must be listed as being suitable for use in ducts, plenums, and other spaces used for environmental air and also be listed as having adequate fire-resistant and low smoke-producing characteristics.

(C) General-Purpose Cables. Type CM (communications general-purpose cables) and Type CATV (community antenna television coaxial general-purpose cables) must be listed as being suitable for general-purpose use, with the exception of risers and plenums, and also be listed as being resistant to the spread of fire.

ARTICLE 805 — GENERAL REQUIREMENTS FOR COMMUNICATIONS CIRCUITS

Introduction to Article 805—General Requirements for Communications Circuits

The general rules for Chapter 8 installations, other than Article 810 installations, are consolidated within Article 800 while the specific requirements for communications circuits are found here in Article 805. These rules supplement or modify the requirements in Article 800. This is similar to the language in 90.3 that says the general rules in Chapters 1 through 4 may be modified by the specific rules in Chapters 5 through 7.

Article 805 has its roots in telephone technology. Consequently, it addresses telephone, fax, voice, and related systems. Here are a few key points to remember about Article 805:

- Do not attach incoming communications cables to the service-entrance power mast.
- Keep the bonding conductor for the primary protector as straight and as short as possible.
- If you locate communications cables above a suspended ceiling, route and support them to allow access via ceiling panel removal.
- Keep these cables separated from lightning protection circuits.
- If you install communications cables in a Chapter 3 raceway, you must do so in accordance with the *NEC* requirements for the raceway system.
- Special labeling and marking provisions apply—follow them carefully.

Part I. General

805.1 Scope

Article 805 covers communications circuits and equipment. ▶Figure 805–1

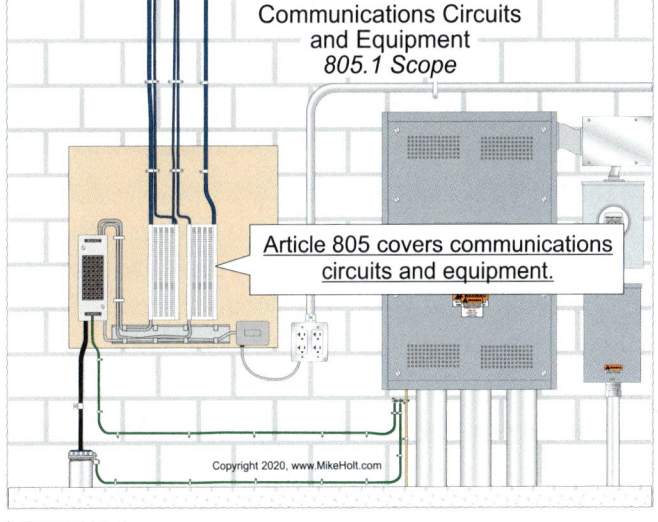

▶Figure 805–1

805.2 Definitions

This definition applies only to Article 805.

Communications Circuit Integrity (CI) Cable. Cable used in communications systems to ensure continued operation of critical circuits during a specified time under fire conditions.

805.18 Installation of Equipment

Communications equipment must be listed in accordance with 805.170.

Part III. Protection

805.90 Primary Protection

(A) Application. A listed primary protector installed in accordance with 110.3(B) is required for each circuit. ▶Figure 805–2

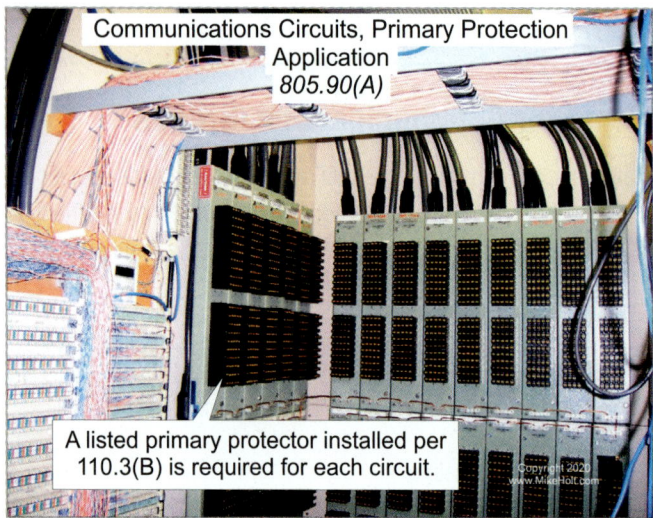

▶Figure 805–2

Author's Comment:

▶ Select a location for the primary protector so the shortest bonding conductor can be used. Doing so will reduce differences in voltage between circuits and other metallic systems during lightning events.

805.93 Bonding or Interruption

(A) Entering Buildings. In installations where the communications cable enters a building, the metallic sheath members of the cable must be bonded as specified in 800.100 or interrupted by an insulating joint or equivalent device. The bonding or interruption must be as close as practicable to the point of entrance.

(B) Terminating on the Outside of Buildings. In installations where the communications cable is terminated on the outside of the building, the metallic sheath members of the cable must be bonded as specified in 800.100 or interrupted by an insulating joint or equivalent device. The bonding or interruption must be as close as practicable to the point of termination of the cable. ▶Figure 805–3

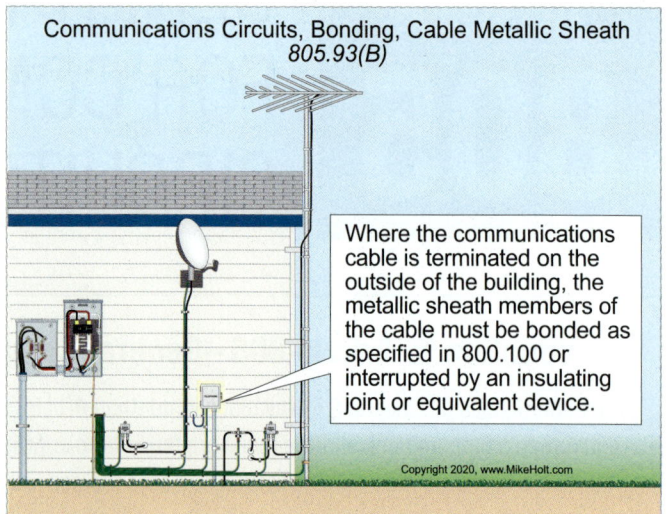

▶Figure 805–3

Part IV. Installation Methods Within Buildings

805.133 Installation of Communications Wires, Cables, and Equipment

(A) Separation from Power Conductors.

(1) In Raceways, Cable Trays, Boxes, Enclosures, and Cable Routing Assemblies.

(a) With Other Circuits. Communications cables can be in the same raceway, cable tray, cable routing assembly, box, or enclosure with cables of any of the following: ▶Figure 805–4

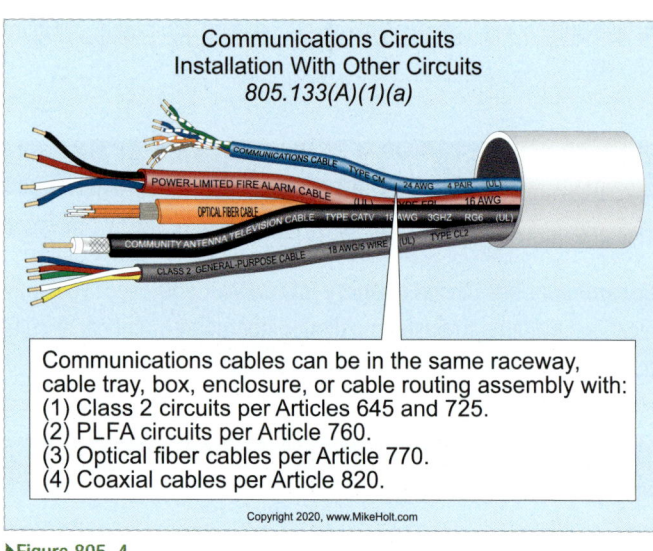

▶Figure 805–4

General Requirements for Communications Circuits | 805.156

(1) Class 2 circuits in accordance with Articles 645 and 725.

(2) Power-limited fire alarm circuits in accordance with Article 760.

(3) Optical fiber cables in accordance with Article 770.

(4) Coaxial cables in accordance with Article 820.

(b) Class 2 Circuits. Class 2 conductors can be within the same listed communications cable with communications conductors [725.139(D)(1)]. ▶Figure 805-5

(B) Support of Communications Cables. Communications cables are not permitted to be strapped, taped, or attached to the exterior of any raceway as a means of support. ▶Figure 805-6

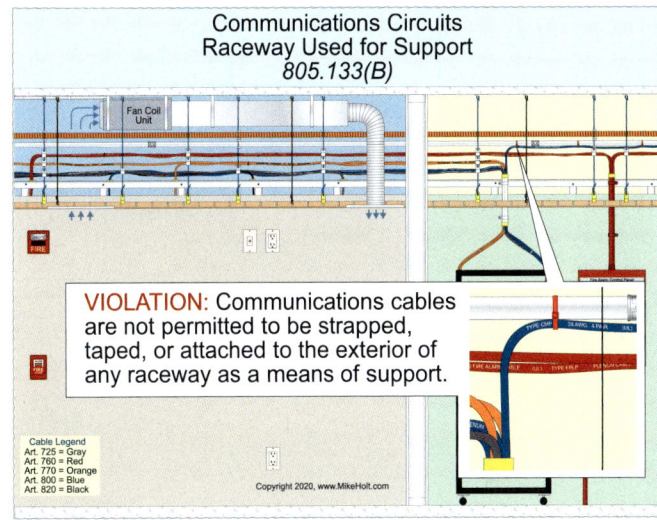

▶Figure 805-6

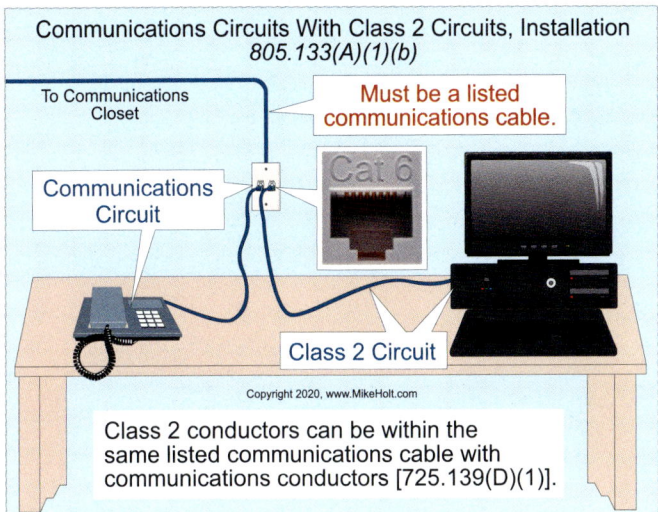

▶Figure 805-5

Author's Comment:

▶ A common application of this requirement is when a single cable is used for both voice communications and data.

▶ Listed Class 2 cables have a voltage rating of not less than 150V [725.179(G)], whereas communications cables have a voltage rating of at least 300V [800.179].

(c) With Power Conductors in Same Raceway or Enclosure. Communications conductors are not permitted to be placed in any raceway, compartment, outlet box, junction box, or similar fitting with conductors of electric power or Class 1 circuits.

Ex 1: Power conductors can be in the same enclosure with communications conductors if separated by a barrier.

Ex 2: Power conductors that supply communications equipment must maintain a ¼ in. separation from communications conductors within the enclosure.

Author's Comment:

▶ Exposed cables must be supported by the structural components of the building so the cable will not be damaged by normal building use. The cables must be secured by straps, staples, cable ties, hangers, or similar fittings designed and installed in a manner that will not damage the cable [800.24].

805.154 Communications Cable(s) Substitutions

Cable substitutions are permitted provided that the substitute is more fire resistant than the original as indicated in the Cable Substitution Hierarchy in *NEC* figure 805.154.

805.156 Dwelling Unit Communications Outlet

For new construction, at least one communications outlet must be installed in a readily accessible area within each dwelling unit and cabled to the service provider's demarcation point. ▶Figure 805-7

Mike Holt Enterprises • www.MikeHolt.com • 888.NEC.CODE (632.2633) | 463

805.156 | General Requirements for Communications Circuits

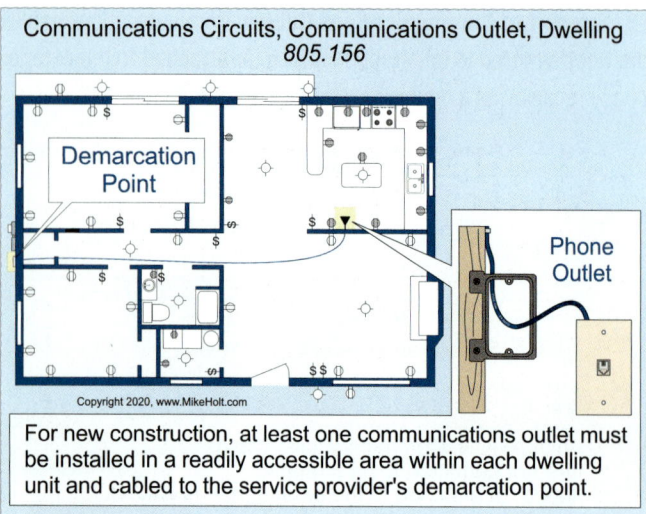

▶Figure 805-7

ARTICLE 810 — RADIO AND TELEVISION ANTENNA EQUIPMENT

Introduction to Article 810—Radio and Television Antenna Equipment

Unlike other articles in this chapter, Article 810 is not covered by the general rules in Article 800; as a result, it stands completely alone in the *Code* unless a rule in 810 references a specific rule elsewhere in the *NEC*.

This article covers transmitter and receiver (satellite dish and antenna) equipment, and the wiring and cabling associated with that equipment. Here are a few key points to remember about Article 810:

- Avoid contact with conductors of other systems.
- Do not attach satellite dishes, antennas, or other equipment to the service-entrance power mast.
- Keep the bonding conductor as straight as practicable and protect it from physical damage.
- If the mast is not bonded properly, you risk flashovers and possible electrocution.
- Remember that the purpose of bonding is to prevent a difference of voltage between metallic objects and other conductive items, such as swimming pools.
- Clearances are critical, and Article 810 contains detailed clearance requirements. For example, it provides separate clearance requirements for indoor and outdoor locations.

See Figure 800.100(B)(1) and Figure 800.100(B)(2) in the *NEC* for examples of bonding conductors and grounding electrode conductors.

Part I. General

810.1 Scope

Article 810 contains the installation requirements for television and radio receiving (antenna) equipment such as satellite dishes and amateur/citizen band radio antennas. ▶Figure 810–1

Author's Comment:

- Article 810 covers:
  - Antennas that receive local television signals.
  - Satellite antennas, which are often referred to as satellite dishes.
  - Roof-mounted antennas for AM/FM/XM radio reception.
  - Amateur radio transmitting and receiving equipment, including HAM radio equipment (a noncommercial [amateur] communications system). ▶Figure 810–2

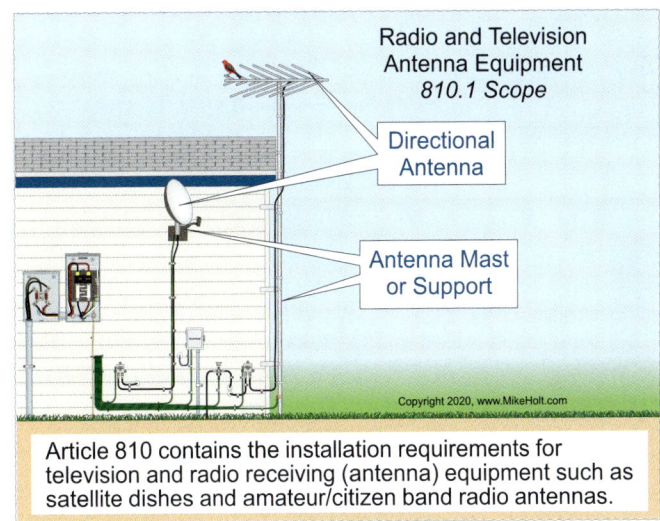

Article 810 contains the installation requirements for television and radio receiving (antenna) equipment such as satellite dishes and amateur/citizen band radio antennas.

▶Figure 810–1

810.4 | Radio and Television Antenna Equipment

▶Figure 810-2

810.4 Community Television Antenna

The antenna for community television systems must be installed in accordance with this article, but the coaxial cable beyond the point of entrance must be installed in accordance with Article 820. ▶Figure 810-3

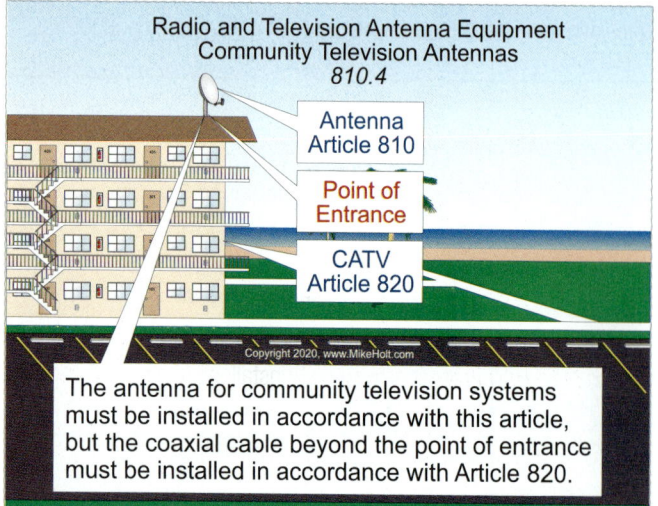
▶Figure 810-3

Author's Comment:

▸ A community TV antenna is used for multiple-occupancy facilities such as apartments, condominiums, motels, and hotels.

Part II. Receiving Equipment—Antenna Systems

810.12 Supports

Outdoor antennas and lead-in conductors must be securely supported, and the lead-in conductors must be securely attached to the antenna. The antennas or lead-in conductors are not permitted to be attached to the electric service mast. ▶Figure 810-4

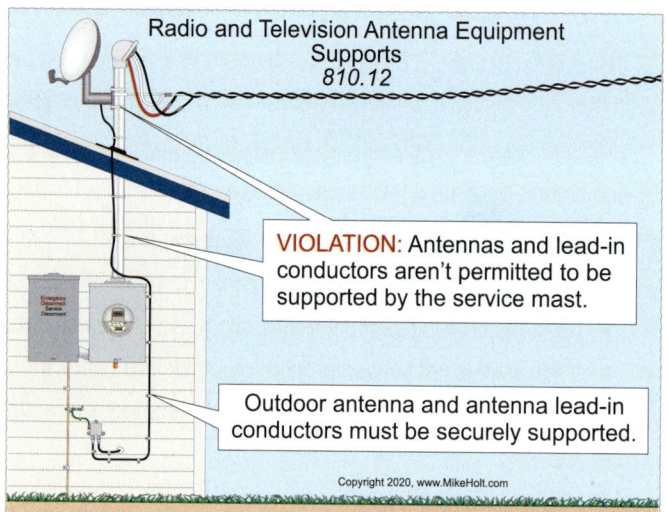
▶Figure 810-4

810.13 Avoid Contact with Conductors of Other Systems

Outdoor antennas and lead-in conductors must be kept at least 2 ft away from exposed electric power conductors to avoid the possibility of accidental contact.

Author's Comment:

▸ According to the *National Electrical Code Handbook*, "One of the leading causes of electrical shock and electrocution is the accidental contact of radio, television, and amateur radio transmitting and receiving antennas, and equipment with light or power conductors. Extreme caution should therefore be exercised during this type of installation, and periodic visual inspections should be conducted thereafter."

810.15 Metal Antenna Supports—Bonding

Outdoor masts and metal structures that support antennas must be bonded in accordance with 810.21, unless the antenna and its related supporting mast or structure are within a zone of protection defined by a 150-ft radius rolling sphere. ▶Figure 810-5

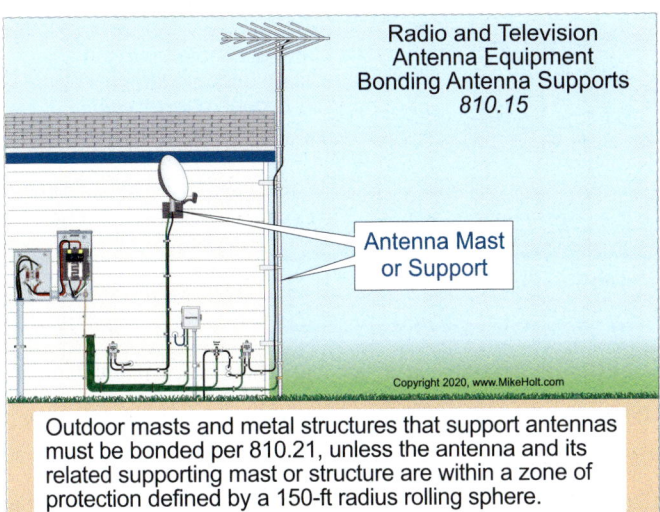

▶Figure 810-5

Note: See NFPA 780, *Standard for the Installation of Lightning Protection Systems* [4.8.3.1], for the application of the term "Rolling Sphere."

810.18 Clearances

(A) Outside of Buildings. Lead-in conductors attached to buildings must be installed so they cannot swing closer than 2 ft to the conductors of circuits of 250V or less, or closer than 10 ft to the conductors of circuits of over 250V.

Lead-in conductors must be kept at least 6 ft from the lightning protection system, and underground antenna lead-in conductors must maintain a separation not less than 12 in. from electric power conductors. ▶Figure 810-6

Ex: Separation is not required where the underground antenna lead-in conductors or the electric power conductors are installed in raceways or metal cable armor. ▶Figure 810-7

(B) Indoors. Indoor antenna and lead-in conductors are not permitted to be less than 2 in. from electric power conductors.

Ex 1: Separation is not required if the antenna lead-in conductors or the electric power conductors are installed within a metal raceway or metal cable armor.

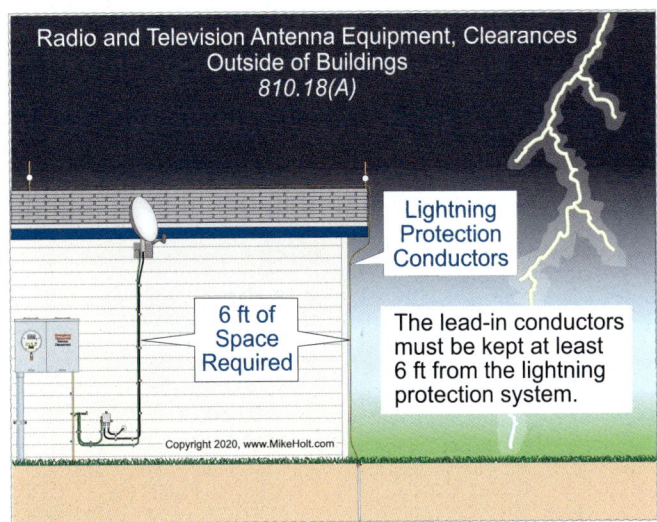

▶Figure 810-6

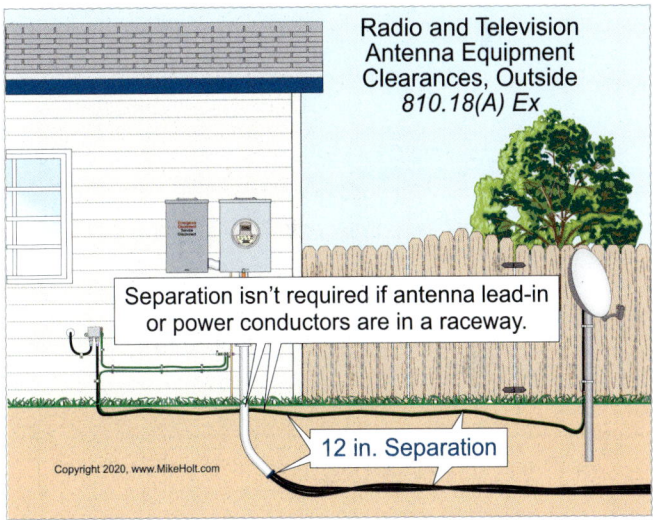

▶Figure 810-7

(C) Boxes and Enclosures. Indoor antenna lead-in conductors can be in the same box or enclosure with electric power conductors where separated by an effective, permanently installed barrier. ▶Figure 810-8

810.20 Antenna Discharge Unit

(A) Listed. Each lead-in conductor from an outdoor antenna must be provided with a listed antenna discharge unit. ▶Figure 810-9

(B) Location. The antenna discharge unit must be located outside or inside the building, nearest the point of entrance, but not near combustible material or in a hazardous (classified) location as defined in Article 500.

810.21 Radio and Television Antenna Equipment

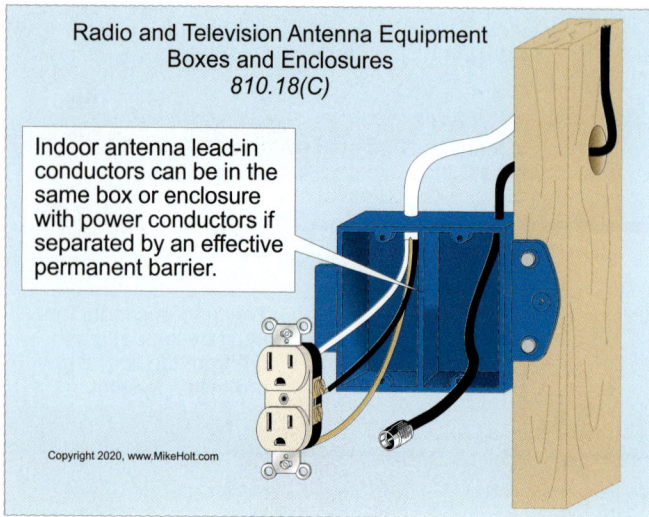
▶Figure 810–8

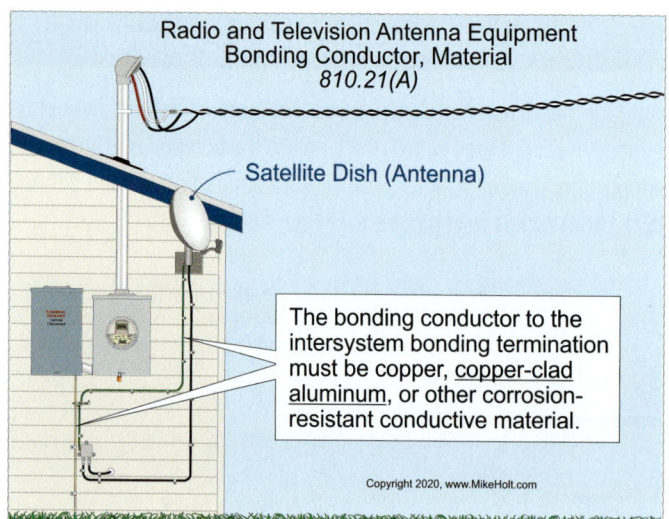
▶Figure 810–10

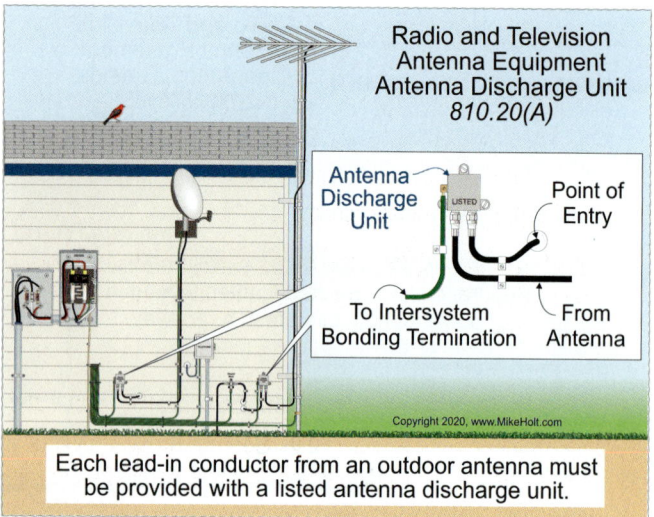
▶Figure 810–9

(B) Insulation. Insulation on bonding conductors is not required.

(C) Supports. The bonding conductor must be securely fastened in place.

(D) Physical Protection. Bonding conductors must be mechanically protected where subject to physical damage; and where installed in a metal raceway, both ends of the raceway must be bonded to the bonding conductor.

> **Author's Comment:**
> ▸ Installing the bonding conductor in PVC conduit is a better practice.

(E) Run in Straight Line. The bonding conductor must be run in as straight a line as practicable.

> **Author's Comment:**
> ▸ Lightning does not like to travel around corners or through loops, which is why the bonding conductor must be run as straight as practicable.

(F) Electrode. The bonding conductor must terminate in accordance with (1), (2), or (3).

(1) Buildings with an Intersystem Bonding Termination. The bonding conductor for the antenna mast and antenna discharge unit must terminate to the intersystem bonding termination [Article 100] as required by 250.94. ▶Figure 810–11

(G) Inside or Outside Building. The bonding conductor can be installed either inside or outside the building.

(C) Bonding. The antenna discharge unit must be bonded in accordance with 810.21.

810.21 Bonding Conductors and Grounding Electrode Conductors

Bonding conductors must meet the following requirements:

(A) Material. The bonding conductor to the intersystem bonding termination must be copper, copper-clad aluminum, copper-clad steel, aluminum, bronze, or other corrosion-resistant conductive material. ▶Figure 810–10

Where aluminum or copper-clad aluminum is used, it must not be installed outside within 18 in. from the Earth or where subject to corrosive conditions.

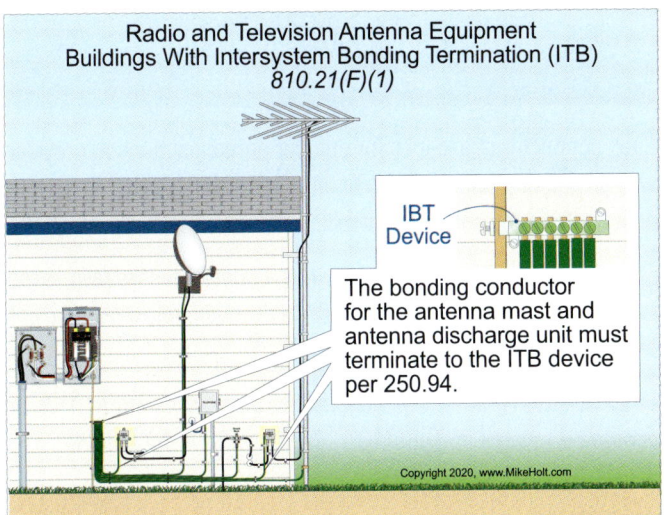
▶Figure 810-11

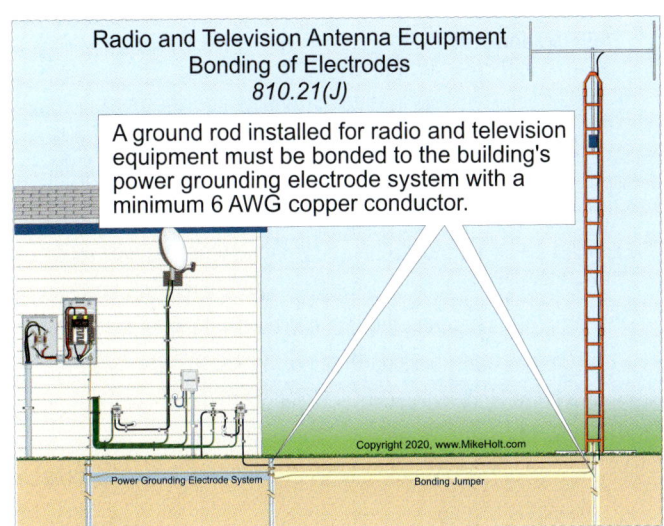
▶Figure 810-13

(H) Size. The bonding conductor is not permitted to be smaller than 10 AWG copper, 8 AWG aluminum, or 17 AWG copper-clad steel or bronze. ▶Figure 810-12

▶Figure 810-12

(J) Bonding of Electrodes. A ground rod installed for the radio and television equipment must be bonded to the building's power grounding electrode system with a minimum 6 AWG copper conductor. ▶Figure 810-13

Author's Comment:

▸ A separate grounding electrode is not required for radio and TV equipment, but if it is installed, then it must be bonded to the building's power grounding electrode system with a minimum 6 AWG copper conductor.

▸ Bonding of electrodes helps reduce induced voltage differences between the power and communications systems during lightning events.

(K) Electrode Connection. Termination of the bonding conductor must be by exothermic welding, listed lugs, listed pressure connectors, or listed clamps. Grounding fittings that are concrete-encased or buried in the Earth must be listed for direct burial in accordance with 250.70. ▶Figure 810-14

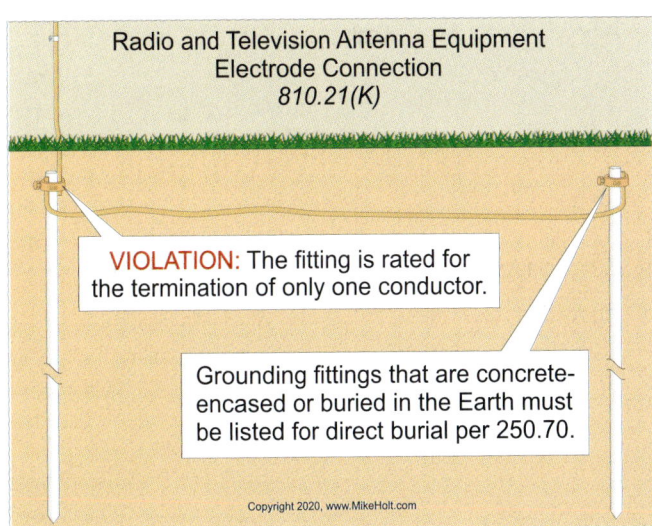
▶Figure 810-14

810.51 | Radio and Television Antenna Equipment

Author's Comment:

▸ Grounding the lead-in antenna cables and the mast helps prevent voltage surges caused by static discharge or nearby lightning strikes from reaching the center conductor of the lead-in coaxial cable. Because the satellite dish sits outdoors, wind creates a static charge on the antenna as well as on the cable to which it is attached. This charge can build up on both the antenna and the cable until it jumps across an air space, often passing through the electronics inside the low noise block down converter feedhorn (LNBF) or receiver. Connecting the antenna and/or satellite dish to the building's grounding electrode system (grounding) helps dissipate this static charge.

▸ Nothing can prevent damage from a direct lightning strike, but grounding with proper surge protection can help reduce damage to the satellite dish and other equipment from nearby lightning strikes.

Part III. Amateur and Citizen Band Transmitting and Receiving Stations—Antenna Systems

810.51 Other Sections

In addition to complying with Part III, antenna systems for amateur and citizen band transmitting and receiving stations must comply with 810.11 through 810.15.

810.57 Antenna Discharge Units—Transmitting Stations

Each conductor of a lead-in for outdoor antennas must be provided with an antenna discharge unit or other suitable means to drain static charges from the antenna system.

Ex 1: Where the lead-in is protected by a continuous metallic shield that is bonded in accordance with 810.58, an antenna discharge unit or other suitable means is not required.

Ex 2: Where the antenna is bonded in accordance with 810.58, an antenna discharge unit or other suitable means is not required.

810.58 Bonding Conductors and Grounding Electrode Conductors—Amateur and Citizen Band Transmitting and Receiving Stations

Bonding conductors must comply with 810.58(A) through 810.58(C).

(A) Other Sections. Bonding conductors for amateur and citizen band transmitting and receiving stations must comply with 810.21(A) through 810.21(C).

(B) Size of Protective Bonding Conductor. The protective bonding conductor for transmitting stations must be as large as the lead-in but not smaller than 10 AWG copper, bronze, or copper-clad steel.

ARTICLE 820 — COMMUNITY ANTENNA TELEVISION (CATV) AND RADIO DISTRIBUTION SYSTEMS (COAXIAL CABLE)

Introduction to Article 820—Community Antenna Television (CATV) and Radio Distribution Systems (Coaxial Cable)

This article focuses on the distribution of television and radio signals within a facility or on a property via cable rather than their transmission or reception via antenna. These signals are limited energy, but they are high frequency.

- Article 800 defines the "Point of Entrance" for these circuits and the general requirements regarding installation methods of all types of communications wiring.
- Ground the incoming coaxial cable as close as practicable to the point of entrance.
- If coaxial cables are located above a suspended ceiling, route and support them to allow access via ceiling panel removal.
- Clearances are critical, and Article 800 contains detailed clearance requirements. For example, it requires at least 6 ft of clearance between coaxial cable and lightning conductors.
- The bonding conductor must be connected to the intersystem bonding termination if there is one in (or at) the building.
- If you use a separate grounding electrode, you must run a bonding jumper to the power grounding system.

Part I. General

820.1 Scope

Article 820 covers the installation of coaxial cables for distributing high-frequency signals typically employed in community antenna television systems (CATV). ▶Figure 820–1

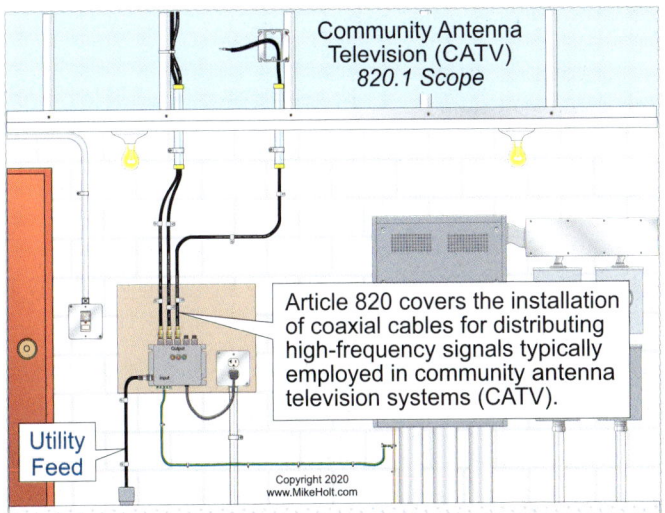

▶Figure 820–1

Author's Comment:

- Article 820 covers the installation of coaxial cable for cable television, closed-circuit television, security cameras, and radio and television receiving equipment.
- Coaxial cables that connect antennas to television and radio receiving equipment [810.3] and community television systems [810.4] must be installed in accordance with this article. ▶Figure 820–2

Part III. Protection

820.93 Grounding of the Outer Conductive Shield of Coaxial Cables

(A) Coaxial Cables Entering Building. Coaxial cables supplied to a building must have the metallic sheath members bonded as close as practicable to the point of entrance in accordance with 820.100. ▶Figure 820–3

820.100 | Community Antenna Television (CATV) and Radio Distribution Systems (Coaxial Cable)

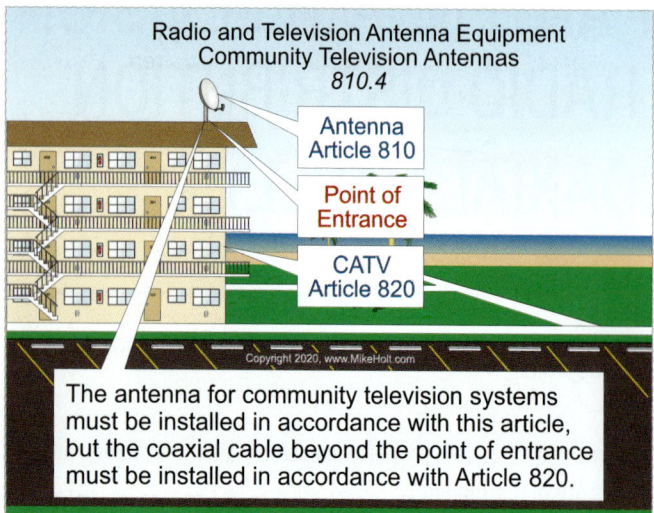
▶Figure 820-2

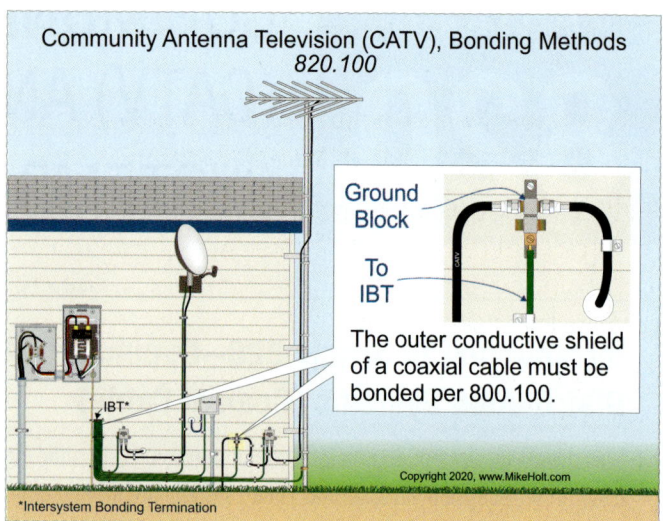
▶Figure 820-4

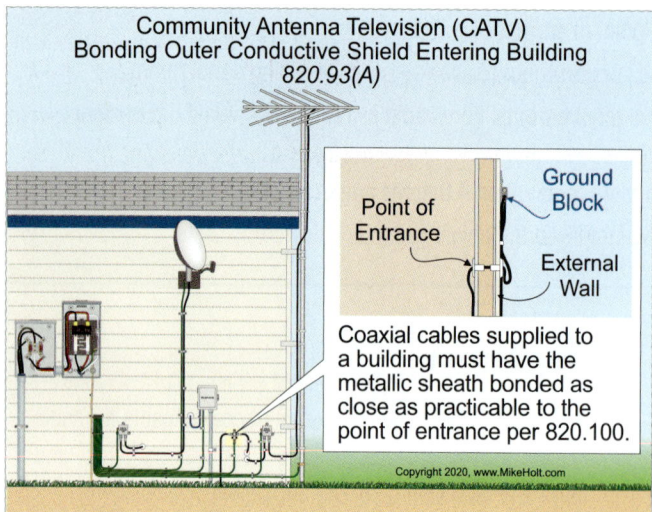
▶Figure 820-3

Part IV. Grounding Methods

820.100 Bonding and Grounding Methods

The outer conductive shield of a coaxial cable must be bonded in accordance with 800.100. ▶Figure 820-4

Part V. Installation Methods Within Buildings

820.133 Installation of Coaxial Cables and Equipment

(A) Separation from Power Conductors.

(1) In Raceways, Cable Trays, Boxes, Enclosures, and Cable Routing Assemblies.

(a) Other Circuits. Coaxial cables are permitted in the same raceway, cable tray, box, enclosure, or cable routing assembly with jacketed cables of any of the following: ▶Figure 820-5

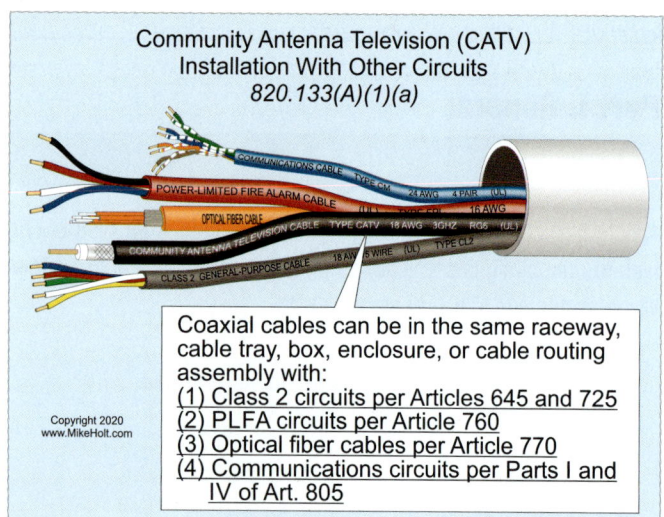
▶Figure 820-5

(1) Class 2 remote control, signaling, and power-limited circuits in compliance with Article 645 or Parts I and III of Article 725

(2) Power-limited fire alarm systems in compliance with Parts I and III of Article 760

(3) Nonconductive and conductive optical fiber cables in compliance with Parts I and V of Article 770

(4) Communications circuits in compliance with Parts I and IV of Article 805

(5) Low-power network-powered broadband communications circuits in compliance with Parts I and V of Article 830

(b) With Power Conductors in Same Raceway or Enclosure. Coaxial cables are not permitted to be placed in any raceway, compartment, outlet box, junction box, or similar fitting with conductors of electric power or Class 1 circuits.

Ex 1: Power conductors are permitted in the same enclosure with coaxial cables if separated by a barrier.

Ex 2: Power conductors that supply coaxial cable distribution equipment must maintain ¼ in. separation from coaxial cables within the enclosure.

(2) Other Applications. Coaxial cable must be separated at least 2 in. from conductors of any electric light, power, Class 1, nonpower-limited fire alarm, or medium-power network-powered broadband communications circuits.

Ex 1: Separation is not required where either (1) all of the conductors of electric light, power, Class 1, nonpower-limited fire alarm, and medium-power network-powered broadband communications circuits are in a raceway, or in metal-sheathed, metal-clad, nonmetallic-sheathed, Type AC or Type UF cables, or (2) all of the coaxial cables are encased in a raceway. ▶Figure 820–6

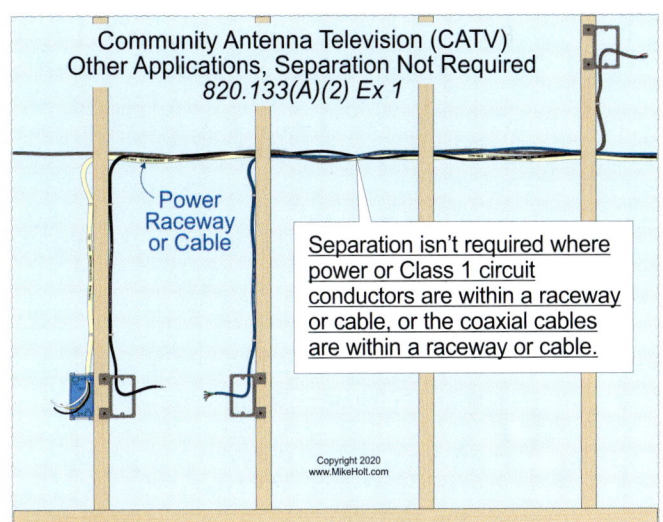

▶Figure 820–6

Ex 2: Separation is not required where the coaxial cables are permanently separated from the conductors of electric light, power, Class 1, nonpower-limited fire alarm, and medium-power network-powered broadband communications circuits by a continuous and firmly fixed nonconductor, such as porcelain tubes or flexible tubing, in addition to the insulation on the wire.

CHAPTER 8

PRACTICE QUESTIONS

Please use the 2020 *Code* book to answer the following questions.

CHAPTER 8—COMMUNICATIONS SYSTEMS

Article 800—General Requirements for Communications Systems

1. The Article 800 general requirements for communications systems apply to communications circuits, community antenna television and radio distribution systems, network-powered broadband communications systems, and premises-powered broadband communications systems, unless modified by Articles 805 or _____.

    (a) 820
    (b) 830
    (c) 840
    (d) any of these

2. The definitions in Part I of Article 100 shall apply throughout Chapter 8. The definitions in 800.2 shall apply only within Chapter 8.

    (a) True
    (b) False

3. Communications cables not terminated at equipment or not identified for future use with a tag are considered _____.

    (a) deserted
    (b) abandoned
    (c) reconditioned
    (d) reusable

4. Communications cables such as CATV cable not terminated at equipment other than a coaxial cable connector and not identified for future use with a tag are considered abandoned.

    (a) True
    (b) False

5. A "_____ circuit" is one that extends service from the communications utility or service provider up to and including the customer's communications equipment.

    (a) limited-energy
    (b) remote-signaling
    (c) power-limited
    (d) communications

6. "Communications circuits" are circuits that extend _____ and outside wiring for fire alarms and burglar alarms from the communications utility to the customer's communications equipment up to and including equipment such as a telephone, fax machine, or answering machine.

    (a) voice
    (b) audio and video
    (c) interactive services
    (d) all of these

7. A communications circuit that is in such a position that, in case of failure of supports or _____, contact with another circuit may result, and is considered to be exposed to accidental contact.

    (a) insulation
    (b) shielding
    (c) fittings
    (d) the grounding conductor

Article 800 | Practice Questions

8. The point of entrance of a communications circuit is the point _____ a building at which the communications wire or cable emerges from an external wall or from a concrete floor slab.

   (a) outside
   (b) within
   (c) on
   (d) penetrating

9. The point of entrance of a communications cable such as CATV coaxial cable is the point _____ a building at which the coaxial cable emerges from an external wall or from a concrete floor slab.

   (a) outside
   (b) within
   (c) on
   (d) under

10. Only those sections of _____ referenced in Chapter 8 shall apply to Chapter 8.

    (a) Chapters 1 through 4
    (b) Chapters 2 and 3
    (c) Chapters 1 through 7
    (d) the Annexes

11. For communications circuit wiring in _____, the requirements of 300.22(A) shall apply.

    (a) underfloor spaces
    (b) suspended ceiling spaces
    (c) plenums
    (d) ducts for dust, loose stock, or vapor removal

12. For communications circuit wiring in _____, the requirements of 300.22(C)(3) shall apply.

    (a) spaces for environmental air
    (b) ducts for dust
    (c) ducts for loose stock
    (d) ducts for vapor removal

13. Where _____ cable is used to provide a communications circuit within a building, Article 770 shall apply.

    (a) coaxial
    (b) fire alarm
    (c) low-voltage
    (d) optical fiber

14. Access to electrical equipment shall not be denied by an accumulation of communications _____ that prevents the removal of suspended-ceiling panels.

    (a) routers
    (b) amplifiers
    (c) ductwork
    (d) wires and cables

15. Communications cables installed _____ on the surface of ceilings and walls shall be supported by the building structure in such a manner that the cable will not be damaged by normal building use.

    (a) in raceways
    (b) in conduit
    (c) hidden
    (d) exposed and concealed

16. _____ may result in an undetermined alteration of communications wire and cable properties.

    (a) Paint or plaster
    (b) Cleaners or abrasives
    (c) Corrosive residues or other contaminants
    (d) any of these

17. Accessible portions of abandoned communications cable shall be removed.

    (a) True
    (b) False

18. Openings around penetrations of communications cables, communications raceways, and cable routing assemblies through fire-resistant-rated walls, partitions, floors, or ceilings shall be _____ using approved methods to maintain the fire resistance rating.

    (a) closed
    (b) opened
    (c) draft stopped
    (d) firestopped

19. Metal conduit containing communications entrance wire or cable shall be connected by a _____ to a grounding electrode or, where present, the building grounding electrode system in accordance with 800.100(B).

    (a) copper conductor
    (b) steel structure
    (c) metal water pipe
    (d) bonding or grounding electrode conductor

20. Where practicable, a separation of at least _____ ft shall be maintained between lightning conductors and all communication wires and cables and CATV type coaxial cables on buildings.

    (a) 1
    (b) 2
    (c) 3
    (d) 6

21. In one- and two-family dwellings, the primary protector bonding conductor or grounding electrode conductor for communications systems shall be as short as practicable, not to exceed _____ ft in length.

    (a) 5
    (b) 8
    (c) 10
    (d) 20

22. Limiting the length of the primary protector grounding conductors for communications circuits helps to reduce voltage between the building's _____ and communications systems during lightning events.

    (a) power
    (b) fire alarm
    (c) lighting
    (d) lightning protection

23. In one- and two-family dwellings where it is not practicable to achieve an overall maximum primary protector grounding electrode conductor length of _____ ft, a separate ground rod meeting the minimum dimensional criteria of 800.100(B)(3)(2) or (B)(3)(3) shall be driven, the grounding electrode conductor shall be connected to the ground rod in accordance with 800.100(C), and the ground rod shall be connected to the power grounding electrode system in accordance with 800.100(D).

    (a) 5
    (b) 8
    (c) 10
    (d) 20

24. Communications systems bonding conductors and grounding electrode conductors shall be protected where exposed to _____.

    (a) line voltage conductors
    (b) soil
    (c) physical damage
    (d) all of these

25. Communications grounding electrodes shall be bonded to the power grounding electrode system at the building or structure served using a minimum _____ AWG copper bonding jumper.

    (a) 10
    (b) 8
    (c) 6
    (d) 4

26. Where communications wires and cables are installed in a Chapter 3 raceway, the raceway shall be installed in accordance with Chapter 3 requirements.

    (a) True
    (b) False

27. The raceway fill requirements of Chapters 3 and 9 shall apply to _____-power network-powered broadband communications cables.

    (a) low
    (b) medium
    (c) high
    (d) multiconductor

28. Communications systems _____ installed in buildings shall be listed.

    (a) wires and cables
    (b) cable routing assemblies
    (c) raceways
    (d) all of these

29. Communications systems wires, cables, cable routing assemblies, and communications raceways shall not be permitted in other spaces used for environmental air.

    (a) True
    (b) False

Article 805 | Practice Questions

30. Communications systems wires, cables, cable routing assemblies, and communications raceways shall be permitted in plenum risers for one- and two-family dwellings.

    (a) True
    (b) False

31. Communications plenum cable shall be _____ as being suitable for use in other spaces used for environmental air.

    (a) marked
    (b) identified
    (c) approved
    (d) listed

Article 805—General Requirements for Communications Circuits

1. For communications circuits, equipment electrically connected to a communications network shall be _____ in accordance with 805.170.

    (a) labeled
    (b) approved
    (c) field-marked
    (d) labeled

2. In installations where the communications cable is terminated on the outside of the building, the metallic sheath members of the cable shall be _____ as specified in 800.100 or interrupted by an insulating joint or equivalent device.

    (a) grounded or bonded
    (b) approved and connected
    (c) spliced and terminated
    (d) copper or aluminum

3. To accommodate communications circuits in new construction, a minimum of _____ communications outlet shall be installed within the dwelling in a readily accessible area and cabled to the service provider demarcation point.

    (a) zero
    (b) one
    (c) two
    (d) three

Article 810—Radio and Television Antenna Equipment

1. Article _____ covers antenna systems for television receiving equipment, amateur and citizen band radio transmitting and receiving equipment, and certain features of transmitter safety.

    (a) 680
    (b) 700
    (c) 810
    (d) 840

2. Outdoor antennas and lead-in conductors shall be securely supported. Lead-in conductors shall be securely attached to the antenna, but they shall not be attached to the electric service mast.

    (a) True
    (b) False

3. Masts and metal structures supporting antennas shall be grounded in accordance with 810.21 unless the antenna and its related supporting mast or structure are within a zone of protection defined by a _____-ft radius rolling sphere.

    (a) 75
    (b) 100
    (c) 125
    (d) 150

4. NFPA 780, *Standard for the Installation of Lightning Protection Systems*, provides information for the application of the term "rolling sphere" as used in 810.15.

    (a) True
    (b) False

5. Underground antenna conductors for radio and television receiving equipment shall be separated at least _____ from any light, power, or Class 1 circuit conductors.

    (a) 12 in.
    (b) 18 in.
    (c) 5 ft
    (d) 6 ft

6. Indoor antenna and lead-in conductors for radio and television receiving equipment shall be separated by at least _____ from conductors of any electric light, power, or Class 1 circuit conductors, unless otherwise permitted.

    (a) 2 in.
    (b) 12 in.
    (c) 18 in.
    (d) 6 ft

7. Indoor antenna lead-in conductors for radio and television receiving equipment can be in the same enclosure with conductors of other wiring systems where separated by an effective permanently installed barrier.

    (a) True
    (b) False

8. Antenna discharge units shall be located outside the building only.

    (a) True
    (b) False

9. Radio and television receiving antenna systems shall have bonding or grounding electrode conductors that are _____.

    (a) copper or other corrosion-resistant conductive material
    (b) insulated, covered, or bare
    (c) securely fastened in place and protected where subject to physical damage
    (d) all of these

10. The grounding electrode conductor for an antenna mast shall be _____ where subject to physical damage.

    (a) electrically protected
    (b) protected
    (c) connected
    (d) disconnected

11. The bonding conductor or grounding electrode conductor for a radio/television antenna system shall be protected where subject to physical damage, and where installed in a metal raceway, both ends of the raceway shall be bonded to the _____ conductor.

    (a) contained
    (b) grounded
    (c) ungrounded
    (d) largest

12. The bonding conductor or grounding electrode conductor for an antenna mast or antenna discharge unit shall be run to the grounding electrode in as straight a line as practicable.

    (a) True
    (b) False

13. If the building or structure served has an intersystem bonding termination, the bonding conductor for an antenna mast shall be connected to the intersystem bonding termination.

    (a) True
    (b) False

14. If the building or structure served has no radio and television equipment intersystem bonding termination, the _____ conductor or grounding electrode conductor shall be connected to the nearest accessible location on the building or structure grounding electrode system as covered in 250.50.

    (a) grounded
    (b) neutral
    (c) service equipment enclosure
    (d) bonding

15. The grounding electrode conductor for an antenna mast or antenna discharge unit, if copper, shall not be smaller than 10 AWG.

    (a) True
    (b) False

16. If a separate grounding electrode is installed for the radio and television equipment, it shall be bonded to the building's electrical power grounding electrode system with a bonding jumper not smaller than _____ AWG.

    (a) 10
    (b) 8
    (c) 6
    (d) 1/0

Article 820—Community Antenna Television (CATV) and Radio Distribution Systems (Coaxial Cable)

1. Article _____ covers the installation of coaxial cables for distributing radio frequency signals typically employed in community antenna television (CATV) systems.

    (a) 300
    (b) 430
    (c) 800
    (d) 820

Article 820 | Practice Questions

2. The outer conductive shield of a CATV coaxial cable entering a building shall be grounded as close to the point of entrance as practicable.

    (a) True
    (b) False

FINAL EXAM A

STRAIGHT ORDER

Please use the 2020 *Code* book to answer the following questions.

1. Which of the following systems shall be installed and removed in accordance with the *NEC* requirements?

    (a) Signaling conductors, equipment, and raceways
    (b) Communications conductors, equipment, and raceways
    (c) Electrical conductors, equipment, and raceways
    (d) all of these

2. The *Code* covers underground mine installations and self-propelled mobile surface mining machinery and its attendant electrical trailing cable.

    (a) True
    (b) False

3. Installations shall comply with the material located in the *NEC* Annexes because they are part of the requirements of the *Code*.

    (a) True
    (b) False

4. Nonmandatory Informative Annexes contained in the back of the *Code* book are _____.

    (a) for information only
    (b) not enforceable as a requirement of the *Code*
    (c) enforceable as a requirement of the *Code*
    (d) for information only and not enforceable as a requirement of the *Code*

5. All _____ shall be covered with an insulation equivalent to that of the conductors or with an identified insulating device.

    (a) splices
    (b) joints
    (c) free ends of conductors
    (d) all of these

6. The required working space for access to live parts of equipment operating at 300 volts-to-ground, where there are exposed live parts on one side and grounded parts on the other side, is _____ ft.

    (a) 3
    (b) 3½
    (c) 4
    (d) 4½

7. When determining a Class I, Division 2 location, the _____ is a factor that should be considered in determining the classification and extent of the location.

    (a) quantity of flammable material that might escape in case of an accident
    (b) adequacy of ventilating equipment
    (c) record of the industry or business with respect to explosions or fires
    (d) all of these

Straight Order | Final Exam A

8. Electrical and electronic equipment in hazardous (classified) locations shall be protected by a(an) _____ technique.

   (a) explosionproof
   (b) dust-ignitionproof
   (c) dusttight
   (d) any of these

9. Wiring methods and materials permitted in Class I, Division 1 locations include _____.

   (a) threaded rigid metal or threaded steel IMC
   (b) flexible fittings listed for Class I, Division 1 locations
   (c) boxes approved for Class I, Division 1 locations
   (d) all of these

10. Wiring methods permitted in Class I, Division 1 locations are permitted in Class I, Division 2 locations.

    (a) True
    (b) False

11. General-purpose enclosures and fittings are permitted in Class I, Division 2 locations unless the enclosure contains make-and-break contacts for _____ as required by 501.105(B)(1), 501.115(B)(1), and 501.150(B)(1).

    (a) meters, instruments, and relays
    (b) circuit breakers or motor controllers
    (c) signaling, alarm, remote-control, and communications systems
    (d) all of these

12. A sealing fitting shall be permitted to be installed within _____ ft of either side of the boundary where a conduit leaves a Class I, Division 1 location.

    (a) 5
    (b) 6
    (c) 8
    (d) 10

13. In Class I, Division 1 locations, seals for cables at all terminations, shall be installed within _____ in. of the enclosure or as required by the enclosure marking.

    (a) 6
    (b) 12
    (c) 18
    (d) 20

14. Circuit breakers in Class I, Division 2 locations that are not hermetically sealed or oil-immersed shall be installed in a Class I, Division 1 enclosure.

    (a) True
    (b) False

15. Luminaires installed in Class I, Division 2 locations shall be protected from physical damage by a suitable _____.

    (a) warning label
    (b) pendant
    (c) guard or by location
    (d) all of these

16. In Class I, Division 1 locations, all apparatus and equipment of signaling, alarm, remote-control, and communications systems _____ shall be identified for Class I, Division 1 locations.

    (a) over 50V
    (b) over 100 volts-to-ground
    (c) regardless of voltage
    (d) except those operating at less than 24V

17. In Class II, Division 2 locations, where provision must be made for flexibility, _____ shall apply.

    (a) 502.10(A)(2)
    (b) 502.10(A)(3)
    (c) 502.10(B)(1)
    (d) 502.10(B)(4)

18. In Class II, Division 1 locations, motors, generators, and other rotating electrical machinery shall be _____.

    (a) listed for the environment
    (b) explosionproof
    (c) general duty
    (d) identified for the location or totally enclosed pipe-ventilated

19. In Class II, Division 2 locations, flexible cord can serve as the supporting means for a pendant luminaire.

    (a) True
    (b) False

20. In Class III locations, locknut-bushing and double-locknut types of fittings may be depended on for bonding purposes.

    (a) True
    (b) False

21. In Class III locations, portable lighting equipment shall be equipped with handles and protected with substantial guards. Lampholders shall be of the unswitched type with no provision for _____.

    (a) receiving attachment plugs
    (b) grounding connections
    (c) lamp installation
    (d) hooks or hangers

22. In major repair garages where ventilation is not provided, any pit or depression below floor level shall be a Class I, Division _____ location.

    (a) 1
    (b) 2
    (c) 1 or Division 2
    (d) 1 and Division 2

23. Type NM cable can be installed above a Class I location in a commercial garage.

    (a) True
    (b) False

24. In patient care spaces, metal faceplates shall be directly connected to an insulated copper equipment grounding conductor by means of _____ securing the faceplate to a metal yoke or strap of a receptacle or to a metal outlet box.

    (a) ground clips
    (b) rivets
    (c) metal mounting screws
    (d) a spot weld

25. In assembly occupancies, Type NM cable, ENT, and PVC conduit shall be permitted to be installed in those portions of buildings not required to be of _____ construction by the applicable building code.

    (a) Class I, Division 1
    (b) fire-rated
    (c) occupancy-rated
    (d) aboveground

26. When installed indoors for carnivals, circuses, and fairs, flexible cords and flexible cables shall be listed for wet locations and shall be sunlight resistant.

    (a) True
    (b) False

27. For carnivals and fairs, receptacles of the locking type not accessible from grade level that only facilitate quick disconnecting and reconnecting of electrical equipment shall not be required to be provided with GFCI protection.

    (a) True
    (b) False

28. An "equipotential plane" is an area where wire mesh or other conductive elements are embedded in or placed under concrete and bonded to _____.

    (a) all metal structures
    (b) fixed nonelectrical equipment that could become energized
    (c) the electrical grounding system
    (d) all of these

29. Luminaires used in agricultural buildings shall _____.

    (a) minimize the entrance of dust, foreign matter, moisture, and corrosive material
    (b) be protected by a suitable guard if exposed to physical damage
    (c) be listed for use in wet locations when exposed to water
    (d) all of these

30. GFCI protection in a mobile home shall be provided for _____.

    (a) receptacle outlets installed outdoors and in compartments accessible from outside
    (b) receptacles within 6 ft of a wet bar sink, dishwasher outlets, and where installed to serve countertop surfaces
    (c) all receptacles in bathrooms including receptacles in luminaires
    (d) all of these

31. Article 555 covers marinas, boatyards, docking facilities but not floating buildings.

    (a) True
    (b) False

32. In land areas not subject to tidal fluctuation, the electrical datum plane shall be a horizontal plane that is _____ ft above the highest tide level for the area occurring under normal circumstances, based on the highest high tide.

    (a) 1
    (b) 1½
    (c) 2
    (d) 2½

33. Electrical connections shall be located at least _____ in. above the deck of a floating pier.

    (a) 12
    (b) 18
    (c) 24
    (d) 30

34. Shore power receptacles installed in accordance with 555.33(A) shall have individual GFPE set to open at currents not exceeding _____ milliamperes.

    (a) 6
    (b) 30
    (c) 75
    (d) 100

35. A _____ shall be used to serve as the required shore power receptacle disconnecting means, and it shall be identified as to which receptacle it controls.

    (a) circuit breaker
    (b) switch
    (c) circuit breaker or fused knife switch
    (d) circuit breaker, switch, or both

36. The provisions of Article _____ apply to temporary electric power and lighting installations.

    (a) 480
    (b) 555
    (c) 590
    (d) 600

37. Types NM, NMC, and SE cables can be used for branch circuits for temporary installations without height limitation and without concealment.

    (a) True
    (b) False

38. Vegetation shall not be used to support overhead conductor spans of _____ for temporary installations.

    (a) luminaires
    (b) receptacles
    (c) branch circuits or feeders
    (d) lighting conductors

39. Where overcurrent protective devices that have been previously used are installed in a temporary installation, these overcurrent protective devices shall be examined to ensure these devices _____.

    (a) have been properly installed
    (b) have been properly maintained
    (c) show no evidence of impending failure
    (d) all of these

40. Each commercial occupancy accessible to pedestrians shall have at least one sign outlet in an accessible location at each entrance to each tenant space supplied by a branch circuit rated at least _____.

    (a) 15A
    (b) 20A
    (c) 30A
    (d) 40A

41. The disconnecting means for a sign or outline lighting system shall be permitted to be located at the point of entry to a sign and the disconnect shall be located at the point the feeder circuit or branch circuit(s) supplying a sign or outline lighting system enters a _____.

    (a) sign enclosure
    (b) sign body
    (c) pole in accordance with 600.5(D)(3)
    (d) any of these

42. Listed flexible metal conduit or listed liquidtight flexible metal conduit that encloses the secondary circuit conductor from a transformer or power supply for use with neon tubing shall be permitted as a bonding means if the total accumulative length of the conduit in the secondary circuit does not exceed _____ ft.

    (a) 6
    (b) 25
    (c) 50
    (d) 100

43. Ballasts, transformers, electronic power supplies, and Class 2 power sources for signs shall be permitted to be located above suspended ceilings, provided that their enclosures are securely fastened in place and _____.

    (a) are effectively bonded
    (b) not dependent on the suspended-ceiling grid for support
    (c) are rated at not more than 300V
    (d) effectively grounded

44. Each 15A and 20A, 125V, single-phase receptacle installed in pits, in hoistways, on the cars of elevators and dumbwaiters associated with wind turbine tower elevators, on the platforms or in the runways and machinery spaces of platform lifts and stairway chairlifts, and in escalator and moving walk wellways shall be _____.

    (a) on a GFCI-protected circuit
    (b) of the GFCI type
    (c) provided with GFPE protection
    (d) current-limiting

45. The lighting switch for hoistway pits shall be readily accessible from the _____.

    (a) pit access door
    (b) elevator car
    (c) floor of the pit
    (d) machinery room

46. Article 625 covers the electrical conductors and equipment connecting an electric vehicle to premises wiring for the purposes of _____.

    (a) charging
    (b) power export
    (c) bidirectional current flow
    (d) all of these

47. For electric vehicle equipment rated more than _____ or more than 150 volts-to-ground, the disconnecting means shall be provided and installed in a readily accessible location.

    (a) 20A
    (b) 30A
    (c) 50A
    (d) 60A

48. Article _____ covers apparatus for electric arc welding, resistance welding, plasma cutting, and other similar welding and cutting process equipment that is connected to an electrical supply system.

    (a) 600
    (b) 620
    (c) 630
    (d) 680

49. Each resistance welder shall have an overcurrent device rated or set at not more than _____ percent of the rated primary current of the welder.

    (a) 80
    (b) 100
    (c) 125
    (d) 300

50. Class 2 and Class 3 cables for audio signal processing, amplification, and reproduction equipment installed in accordance with 725.135(B) and Table 725.154 shall be permitted to be installed in ducts specifically fabricated for environmental air.

    (a) True
    (b) False

51. Ventilation in the underfloor area of an information technology equipment room shall be used in that room only, unless provided with fire/smoke dampers at the point of penetration of the room boundary.

    (a) True
    (b) False

52. Nonmetallic raceways for branch circuit supply conductors can be installed in the area under raised floors of approved construction of information technology equipment rooms.

    (a) True
    (b) False

53. Installed supply circuits and interconnecting cables identified for future use in information technology equipment rooms shall be marked with a tag of sufficient durability to withstand the environment involved which shall include the _____.

    (a) date the cable was identified for future use
    (b) date of intended use
    (c) intended future use of the cable
    (d) all of these

54. All electric pool water heaters shall have the heating elements subdivided into loads not exceeding _____.

    (a) 20A
    (b) 35A
    (c) 48A
    (d) 60A

55. All receptacles supplied by branch circuits rated _____ or less to ground within a pool equipment room shall be GFCI protected.

    (a) 110V
    (b) 125V
    (c) 150V
    (d) 250V

56. Junction boxes for pool lighting shall be located not less than _____ ft from the inside wall of a pool unless separated by a fence or wall.

    (a) 3
    (b) 4
    (c) 6
    (d) 8

57. Circuits serving gas-fired swimming pool and spa water heaters operating at voltages above the low-voltage contact limit shall be provided with _____ protection for personnel.

    (a) GFCI
    (b) AFCI
    (c) combined AFCI/GFCI
    (d) a gas valve emergency shut-off

58. Fountain electrical equipment that is supplied by a flexible cord shall have all exposed noncurrent-carrying metal parts grounded by an insulated copper equipment grounding conductor that is an integral part of this _____.

    (a) cord
    (b) feeder circuit
    (c) branch circuit
    (d) fountain

59. PV system equipment and disconnecting means are permitted to be installed in a bathroom when listed for the application.

    (a) True
    (b) False

60. The PV maximum output circuit current shall be the sum of parallel PV source circuit maximum currents as calculated in _____.

    (a) 690.8(A)(1)(a)
    (b) 690.8(A)(2)
    (c) 690.8(A)(3)
    (d) Article 220

61. For PV system rapid shutdown systems, controlled conductors located outside the array boundary or more than 3 ft from the point of entry inside a building shall be limited to not more than _____ within 30 seconds of rapid shutdown initiation.

    (a) 15V
    (b) 30V
    (c) 50V
    (d) 80V

62. An isolating device for PV system equipment shall be which of the following?

    (a) a mating connector meeting the requirements of 690.33 and listed and identified for use with specific equipment
    (b) a finger-safe fuse holder or an isolating switch that requires a tool to place the device in the open (off) position
    (c) an isolating device listed for the intended application
    (d) any of these

63. PV systems that exceed 30V or 8A shall be provided with direct-current _____ to reduce fire hazards.

    (a) arc-fault protection
    (b) rectifier protection
    (c) ground-fault monitors
    (d) ground-fault protection

64. For buildings with rapid shutdown, the rapid shutdown switch shall have a label that reads "RAPID SHUTDOWN SWITCH FOR SOLAR PV SYSTEM" installed within _____ ft of the switch.

    (a) 3
    (b) 6
    (c) 10
    (d) 25

65. Feeder conductors supplying fire pump motors and accessory equipment shall be sized no less than _____ percent of the sum of the fire pump motor(s) and pressure maintenance motor(s) full-load currents, plus 100 percent of the ampere rating of the fire pump accessory equipment.

    (a) 100
    (b) 125
    (c) 250
    (d) 600

66. Emergency system equipment shall be maintained in accordance with _____.

    (a) the authority having jurisdiction
    (b) UL listing(s)
    (c) manufacturer instructions and industry standards
    (d) OSHA regulations

67. Where used for emergency systems, the short-circuit current rating of the transfer equipment, based on the specific overcurrent protective device type and settings protecting the transfer equipment, shall be field marked on the _____ of the transfer equipment.

    (a) exterior
    (b) top
    (c) interior
    (d) underside

68. Wiring from an emergency source to supply emergency and other (nonemergency) loads shall be permitted if the common bus of separate sections of the switchgear, separate sections of the switchboard, or the individual enclosures are supplied by single or multiple feeders with or without _____.

    (a) overcurrent protection at the source
    (b) ground-fault protection at the source
    (c) a current-limiting device at the source
    (d) load-shaving monitoring

69. In emergency systems, only appliances and lamps required for emergency use shall be supplied by _____.

    (a) emergency lighting circuits
    (b) multiwire branch circuits
    (c) HID-rated circuit breakers
    (d) only load-shaved circuits

70. The _____ shall conduct or witness a test of the complete legally required standby system upon installation.

    (a) electrical engineer
    (b) authority having jurisdiction
    (c) qualified person
    (d) manufacturer's representative

71. Automatic transfer switches on legally required standby systems shall be electrically operated and _____ held.

    (a) electrically
    (b) mechanically
    (c) gravity
    (d) any of these

72. Overcurrent devices for legally required standby systems shall be _____ with all supply-side overcurrent devices.

    (a) series rated
    (b) selectively coordinated
    (c) installed in parallel
    (d) labeled

73. Where a load management system is employed that will automatically manage the connected load of an optional standby system, the standby source shall have a capacity sufficient to supply _____ load that will be connected by the load management system.

    (a) 80 percent of the
    (b) 115 percent of the
    (c) 125 percent of the
    (d) the maximum

74. Optional standby system transfer equipment and electric power production systems installed to permit operation in parallel with the _____ shall also meet the requirements of Article 705.

    (a) PV system
    (b) generator
    (c) normal source
    (d) battery storage system

75. Where supply-side power source output circuit conductors make their connection to the service outside of a building, they shall be protected by overcurrent devices in a(an) _____ outside the building or at the first readily accessible location where the power source conductors enter the building.

    (a) location
    (b) readily accessible location
    (c) accessible location
    (d) secured location

Straight Order | Final Exam A

76. Where interconnected power production source output connections are made at feeders, all taps shall be sized based on the sum of _____ percent of all power source(s) output circuit current(s) and the rating of the overcurrent device protecting the feeder conductors for sizing tap conductors using the calculations in 240.21(B).

    (a) 100
    (b) 115
    (c) 125
    (d) 175

77. In accordance with Article 705, the sum of all interconnected power production system-controlled currents, plus all monitored currents from other sources of supply, shall not exceed _____ percent of the ampacity of any busbar or conductor supplied by the power production sources.

    (a) 100
    (b) 115
    (c) 125
    (d) 150

78. For interconnected power production systems, risks to personnel and equipment associated with the _____ could occur if an interactive electric power production source can operate as an intentional island.

    (a) primary source of power
    (b) power production system
    (c) primary source of power or power production system
    (d) possibility of a lightning strike

79. A disconnecting means must be provided for all _____ derived from an energy storage system (ESS).

    (a) branch circuits
    (b) phase conductors
    (c) supply circuits
    (d) combiners

80. A permanent _____ shall be installed at a building supplied by a stand-alone system at each service equipment location or at an approved readily visible location. The _____ shall denote the location of each power source disconnect for the building or be grouped with other plaques or directories for other on-site sources.

    (a) plaque
    (b) directory
    (c) marking
    (d) plaque or directory

81. Stand-alone systems require either energy storage or backup power supplies.

    (a) True
    (b) False

82. When a raceway is used for the support or protection of cables for remote-control, signaling, and power-limited circuits, a bushing to reduce the potential for abrasion shall be placed at the location the cables emerge from the raceway.

    (a) True
    (b) False

83. Exposed Class 1, Class 2, and Class 3 cables shall be supported by straps, staples, hangers, or similar fittings designed and installed so as not to damage the cable.

    (a) True
    (b) False

84. Class 1 circuits shall be installed in accordance with Part I of Article 300 and are exempt from the wiring methods from the remaining articles in Chapter 3.

    (a) True
    (b) False

85. Rated current for _____ power sources for conductors covered in 725.144 is the output current per conductor the power source is designed to deliver to an operational load at normal operating conditions, as declared by the manufacturer.

    (a) Class 1
    (b) Class 2
    (c) Class 3
    (d) Class 2 and Class 3

86. Sections 725.144(B) and (B) shall apply to _____ that transmit power and data to a powered device.

    (a) all circuits
    (b) Class 1, 2, and 3 circuits
    (c) Class 2 and 3 circuits
    (d) low voltage circuits

87. Where Types CL3P, CL2P, CL3R, CL2R, CL3, or CL2 transmit power and data, the rated current per conductor of the power source shall not exceed the ampacities in Table 725.144 at an ambient temperature of _____.

    (a) 30°C
    (b) 60°C
    (c) 75°C
    (d) 90°C

88. Where _____ cables are utilized for fire alarm circuits, the cables shall be installed in accordance with Article 770.

    (a) Class 1
    (b) Class 2
    (c) Class 3
    (d) optical fiber

89. Power-limited and nonpower-limited fire alarm cables with green insulation shall be permitted to be used as ungrounded signal conductors.

    (a) True
    (b) False

90. The fire alarm branch-circuit disconnecting means shall be permitted to be secured in the "on" position.

    (a) True
    (b) False

91. Power-limited fire alarm cable used in a _____ location shall be listed for use in _____ locations or have a moisture-impervious metal sheath.

    (a) dry
    (b) damp
    (c) wet
    (d) hazardous

92. Optical fiber cables installed _____ on the surface of ceilings and walls shall be supported by the building structure in such a manner that the cable will not be damaged by normal building use.

    (a) exposed
    (b) in raceways
    (c) hidden
    (d) exposed and concealed

93. Nonconductive optical fiber cables shall not be permitted to occupy the same cabinet, outlet box, panel, or similar enclosure unless the nonconductive optical fiber cables are functionally associated with the electric circuits.

    (a) True
    (b) False

94. For communications circuit wiring in _____, the requirements of 300.22(C)(3) shall apply.

    (a) spaces for environmental air
    (b) ducts for dust
    (c) ducts for loose stock
    (d) ducts for vapor removal

95. Metal conduit containing communications entrance wire or cable shall be connected by a _____ to a grounding electrode or, where present, the building grounding electrode system in accordance with 800.100(B).

    (a) copper conductor
    (b) steel structure
    (c) metal water pipe
    (d) bonding or grounding electrode conductor

96. Where communications wires and cables are installed in a Chapter 3 raceway, the raceway shall be installed in accordance with Chapter 3 requirements.

    (a) True
    (b) False

97. For communications circuits, equipment electrically connected to a communications network shall be _____ in accordance with 805.170.

    (a) labeled
    (b) approved
    (c) field-marked
    (d) labeled

98. NFPA 780, *Standard for the Installation of Lightning Protection Systems*, provides information for the application of the term "rolling sphere" as used in 810.15.

    (a) True
    (b) False

99. The bonding conductor or grounding electrode conductor for a radio/television antenna system shall be protected where subject to physical damage, and where installed in a metal raceway, both ends of the raceway shall be bonded to the _____ conductor.

    (a) contained
    (b) grounded
    (c) ungrounded
    (d) largest

100. Article _____ covers the installation of coaxial cables for distributing radio frequency signals typically employed in community antenna television (CATV) systems.

    (a) 300
    (b) 430
    (c) 800
    (d) 820

FINAL EXAM B

RANDOM ORDER

Please use the 2020 *Code* book to answer the following questions.

1. The grounding electrode conductor for an antenna mast shall be _____ where subject to physical damage.

   (a) electrically protected
   (b) protected
   (c) connected
   (d) disconnected

2. Isolating devices or equipment disconnecting means for PV system equipment shall be installed within the equipment or within sight and within _____ ft of the equipment.

   (a) 3
   (b) 10
   (c) 25
   (d) 50

3. In Class III locations, switches, circuit breakers, motor controllers, and fuses, including pushbuttons, relays, and similar devices, shall be provided with _____.

   (a) Class I enclosures
   (b) general duty enclosures
   (c) dusttight enclosures
   (d) seals at each enclosure

4. Permanent safety signs shall be installed to give notice of electrical shock hazard risks to persons using or swimming near a boat dock or marina and shall _____.

   (a) comply with 110.21(B)(1) and be of sufficient durability to withstand the environment
   (b) be clearly visible from all approaches to a marina, docking facility, or boatyard facility
   (c) state "WARNING—POTENTIAL SHOCK HAZARD—ELECTRICAL CURRENTS MAY BE PRESENT IN THE WATER"
   (d) all of these

5. A(an) _____ surge protection device shall be installed in or on the fire pump controller.

   (a) listed
   (b) labeled
   (c) identified
   (d) approved

6. The _____ of electric vehicle supply equipment located indoors shall be located not less than 18 in. above the floor level.

   (a) attachment plugs
   (b) fittings
   (c) power outlets
   (d) coupling means

7. Accessible portions of abandoned fire alarm cable shall be removed.

   (a) True
   (b) False

8. Only those sections of _____ referenced in Chapter 8 shall apply to Chapter 8.

    (a) Chapters 1 through 4
    (b) Chapters 2 and 3
    (c) Chapters 1 through 7
    (d) the Annexes

9. Meter-mounted transfer switches shall be of the _____ type unless rated as determined by 702.4(B)(2).

    (a) automatic
    (b) manual
    (c) monitoring
    (d) remote

10. The electrical datum plane for floating piers and boat landing stages shall be a horizontal plane 30 in. above the water level at the floating pier or boat landing stage and a minimum of _____ in. above the level of the deck.

    (a) 12
    (b) 18
    (c) 24
    (d) 30

11. Except for the assembly occupancies explicitly covered by 520.1, Article 518 covers all buildings or portions of buildings or structures designed or intended for the gathering together of _____ or more persons.

    (a) 16
    (b) 50
    (c) 100
    (d) 125

12. Article 690 applies to solar PV systems, including _____.

    (a) array circuit(s), inverter(s), and controller(s) for such PV systems
    (b) those interactive with other electrical power production sources or stand-alone, or both
    (c) PV systems with ac or dc output for utilization
    (d) all of these

13. The point of entrance of a communications circuit is the point _____ a building at which the communications wire or cable emerges from an external wall or from a concrete floor slab.

    (a) outside
    (b) within
    (c) on
    (d) penetrating

14. Hazardous (classified) locations shall be classified depending on the properties of the _____ that could be present, and the likelihood that a flammable or combustible concentration or quantity is present.

    (a) flammable liquid-produced vapors
    (b) flammable gases
    (c) combustible dusts
    (d) all of these

15. An emergency system shall have adequate _____ in accordance with Article 220 or by another approved method.

    (a) lighting
    (b) capacity
    (c) water flow
    (d) ambient temperature

16. A "_____ circuit" is one that extends service from the communications utility or service provider up to and including the customer's communications equipment.

    (a) limited-energy
    (b) remote-signaling
    (c) power-limited
    (d) communications

17. Signs and outline lighting systems shall be installed so that adjacent combustible materials are not subjected to temperatures in excess of _____.

    (a) 60°C
    (b) 75°C
    (c) 90°C
    (d) 105°C

18. A storage battery supplying emergency lighting and power for emergency systems shall maintain not less than 87½ percent of normal voltage at total load for a period of at least _____ hour(s).

    (a) 1
    (b) 1½
    (c) 2
    (d) 2½

19. Electric signs installed within a fountain or within _____ ft of the fountain edge, shall have ground-fault circuit-interrupter protection for personnel.

    (a) 2
    (b) 5
    (c) 6
    (d) 10

20. Manufactured wiring systems shall be _____ in accordance with the applicable cable or conduit article for the cable or conduit type employed.

    (a) inspected and tested
    (b) relocated
    (c) secured and supported
    (d) reassembled

21. An "equipotential plane" is an area where wire mesh or other conductive elements are embedded in or placed under concrete and bonded to _____.

    (a) all metal structures
    (b) fixed nonelectrical equipment that could become energized
    (c) the electrical grounding system
    (d) all of these

22. For temporary power outlets existing or installed as permanent wiring, GFCI protection can be incorporated into a listed _____.

    (a) circuit breaker
    (b) receptacle
    (c) cord set
    (d) any of these

23. Optional standby system transfer equipment shall be suitable for the intended use and shall be _____ so as to prevent the inadvertent interconnection of all sources of supply in any operation of the transfer equipment.

    (a) listed
    (b) designed
    (c) installed
    (d) all of these

24. In motor fuel dispensing facilities, all metal raceways, the metal armor or metallic sheath on cables, and all noncurrent-carrying metal parts of fixed and portable electrical equipment _____ shall be grounded and bonded.

    (a) operating at under 600V
    (b) regardless of voltage
    (c) over 300V
    (d) under 50V

25. Threaded conduits or fittings installed in hazardous (classified) locations shall be made wrenchtight to _____.

    (a) prevent sparking when fault current flows through the conduit system
    (b) prevent seepage of gases or fumes
    (c) prevent sag in the conduit runs
    (d) maintain a workmanship like installation

26. Power-limited fire alarm cables can be supported by strapping, taping, or attaching to the exterior of a conduit or raceway.

    (a) True
    (b) False

27. Optical fiber cables not terminated at equipment other than a connector, and not identified for future use with a tag are considered abandoned.

    (a) True
    (b) False

28. For one- and two-family dwellings, a sign shall be placed at the disconnecting means required in 230.85 that indicates the location of each permanently installed on-site optional standby power source disconnect or means to shut down the _____ as required in 445.18(D).

    (a) prime mover
    (b) utility supply
    (c) secondary source
    (d) primary source

29. This *Code* covers the installation of ____ for public and private premises, including buildings, structures, mobile homes, recreational vehicles, and floating buildings.

    (a) optical fiber cables
    (b) electrical equipment
    (c) raceways
    (d) all of these

30. Factory-installed ____ wiring of listed equipment need not be inspected at the time of installation of the equipment, except to detect alterations or damage.

    (a) external
    (b) associated
    (c) internal
    (d) all of these

31. Raceways enclosing cables and conductors for fire alarm systems shall be large enough to permit the ____ of conductors without damaging conductor insulation as limited by 300.17.

    (a) concealment
    (b) bending space
    (c) splicing
    (d) installation and removal

32. The branch-circuit overcurrent devices for legally required standby systems shall be accessible only to ____.

    (a) the authority having jurisdiction
    (b) authorized persons
    (c) the general public
    (d) qualified persons

33. Cord connectors for carnivals, circuses, and fairs can be laid on the ground when the connectors are ____ for a wet location.

    (a) listed
    (b) labeled
    (c) approved
    (d) identified

34. "Communications circuits" are circuits that extend ____ and outside wiring for fire alarms and burglar alarms from the communications utility to the customer's communications equipment up to and including equipment such as a telephone, fax machine, or answering machine.

    (a) voice
    (b) audio and video
    (c) interactive services
    (d) all of these

35. Each multiconductor cable installed in conduit in a Class I, Division 1 location shall be considered as a single conductor if the cable is incapable of transmitting ____ through the cable core.

    (a) gases or vapors
    (b) dust
    (c) flyings
    (d) any of these

36. For communications circuit wiring in ____, the requirements of 300.22(C)(3) shall apply.

    (a) spaces for environmental air
    (b) ducts for dust
    (c) ducts for loose stock
    (d) ducts for vapor removal

37. Interconnected power production source(s) are permitted to be connected to the load side of the service disconnecting means at any distribution equipment on the premises.

    (a) True
    (b) False

38. The electrical datum plane for floating piers and boat landing stages, shall be a horizontal plane ____ in. above the water level at the floating pier or boat landing stage and a minimum of 12 in. above the level of the deck.

    (a) 12
    (b) 18
    (c) 24
    (d) 30

39. Power-limited fire alarm cables shall be permitted to be installed in plenum communications raceways, riser communications raceways, and general-purpose communications raceways where _____, and where the requirements applicable to electrical nonmetallic tubing apply.

    (a) selected in accordance with Table 800.154(B)
    (b) listed in accordance with the provisions of 800.182
    (c) installed in accordance with 800.113 and 362.24 through 362.56
    (d) all of these

40. When installed indoors for carnivals, circuses, and fairs, flexible cords and flexible cables shall be listed for wet locations and shall be sunlight resistant.

    (a) True
    (b) False

41. Communications systems bonding conductors and grounding electrode conductors shall be protected where exposed to _____.

    (a) line voltage conductors
    (b) soil
    (c) physical damage
    (d) all of these

42. Article 517 applies to electrical construction and installation criteria in health care facilities that provide services to _____.

    (a) human beings
    (b) animals
    (c) children only
    (d) intellectually challenged persons

43. In locations containing an emergency system, a sign shall be placed at the service-entrance equipment indicating the type and location of each on-site emergency power source.

    (a) True
    (b) False

44. If wiring from an emergency source is used to supply emergency and other loads, then _____ switchgear sections or switchboard sections, with or without a common bus, or individual disconnects mounted in separate enclosures shall be used to separate emergency loads from all other loads.

    (a) separate vertical
    (b) separate horizontal
    (c) combined vertical and horizontal
    (d) identified

45. Where Types CL3P-LP, CL2P-LP, CL3R-LP, CL2R-LP, CL3-LP, or CL2-LP transmit power and data, the rated current per conductor of the power source installed at temperatures above 86°F, the correction factors in Table _____ shall apply to the ampacities in Table 725.144.

    (a) 310.15(B)(3)(a)
    (b) 310.15(B)(7)
    (c) 310.15(B)(1)
    (d) 310.16

46. Class 1, 2, and 3 circuits installed through fire-resistant-rated walls, partitions, floors, or ceilings shall be firestopped to limit the possible spread of fire or products of combustion.

    (a) True
    (b) False

47. A conduit run between a conduit seal and the point at which the conduit leaves a Class I, Division 1 location shall contain no union, coupling, box, or other fitting except for a listed _____ reducer installed at the conduit seal.

    (a) explosionproof
    (b) fireproof
    (c) vaportight
    (d) dusttight

48. A single means for disconnecting all ungrounded main power supply conductors for each _____ shall be provided and be designed so that no pole can be operated independently.

    (a) elevator or dumbwaiter
    (b) escalator or moving walk
    (c) platform lift or stairway chairlift
    (d) any of these

49. In Class I, Division 1 or Division 2 locations where the boxes, fittings, or enclosures are required to be explosionproof, if a flexible cord is used it shall terminate with a cord connector or attachment plug listed for the location, or a listed cord connector installed with a seal that is listed for the location. In Division 2 locations where explosionproof equipment is not required, the cord shall terminate _____.

    (a) with irreversible connections
    (b) with a listed receptacle
    (c) in a splice of any manner
    (d) with a listed cord connector or listed attachment plug

Random Order | Final Exam B

50. Vegetation shall not be used to support overhead conductor spans of _____ for temporary installations.

    (a) luminaires
    (b) receptacles
    (c) branch circuits or feeders
    (d) lighting conductors

51. Temporary electrical power and lighting shall be permitted during emergencies and for _____.

    (a) tests
    (b) experiments
    (c) developmental work
    (d) all of these

52. Wiring methods permitted in Class I, Division 1 locations are permitted in Class I, Division 2 locations.

    (a) True
    (b) False

53. Article _____ covers the electrical conductors and equipment installed within or on mobile and manufactured homes and the conductors that connect mobile and manufactured homes to a supply of electricity.

    (a) 550
    (b) 551
    (c) 555
    (d) 590

54. Accessible portions of abandoned optical fiber cable shall be removed.

    (a) True
    (b) False

55. Amplifiers, loudspeakers, and other equipment shall be located or protected so as to guard against environmental exposure or physical damage that might cause _____.

    (a) a fire
    (b) shock
    (c) personal hazard
    (d) any of these

56. A permanent _____ shall be installed at a building supplied by a stand-alone system at each service equipment location or at an approved readily visible location. The _____ shall denote the location of each power source disconnect for the building or be grouped with other plaques or directories for other on-site sources.

    (a) plaque
    (b) directory
    (c) marking
    (d) plaque or directory

57. Types CL2, CM, and CMG cables are permitted within the raised floor area of an information technology equipment room if installed in accordance with 725.154(A).

    (a) True
    (b) False

58. Wiring for lighting located inside tents and concession areas at carnivals, circuses, and fairs, where subject to physical damage shall be provided with mechanical protection.

    (a) True
    (b) False

59. Wiring methods installed in a corrosive environment for pool-associated motors for permanently installed pools shall comply with 680.14 or shall include an insulated copper equipment grounding conductor sized in accordance with Table 250.122, but not smaller than _____ AWG.

    (a) 18
    (b) 16
    (c) 14
    (d) 12

60. Where supply-side power source output circuit conductors make their connection to the service outside of a building, they shall be protected by overcurrent devices in a(an) _____ outside the building or at the first readily accessible location where the power source conductors enter the building.

    (a) location
    (b) readily accessible location
    (c) accessible location
    (d) secured location

61. In a Class I, Division 2 location, switches and circuit breakers shall be installed in explosionproof enclosures meeting the requirements for Class I, Division 1 locations.

    (a) True
    (b) False

62. Types NM, NMC, and SE cables can be used for branch circuits for temporary installations without height limitation and without concealment.

    (a) True
    (b) False

63. The maintenance disconnecting means required for swimming pool equipment shall be _____ and at least 5 ft from the water's edge, unless separated by a permanently installed barrier.

    (a) secured
    (b) at least 24 in. above the highest water level of the pool
    (c) capable of being locked in the open position
    (d) readily accessible and within sight of its equipment

64. Stand-alone and isolated microgrid systems can supply 120V to single-phase, 3-wire, 120/240V service disconnects of distribution panels if there are no 240V outlets and no multiwire circuits.

    (a) True
    (b) False

65. Legally required standby system equipment shall be maintained in accordance with _____.

    (a) UL listing(s)
    (b) local emergency services requirements
    (c) manufacturer instructions and industry standards
    (d) local jurisdictional requirements

66. An overload is the same as a short circuit or ground fault.

    (a) True
    (b) False

67. Seals in Class II hazardous (classified) locations shall be explosionproof.

    (a) True
    (b) False

68. All receptacles installed for other than shore power shall be protected in accordance with _____.

    (a) 110.11
    (b) 200.3
    (c) 210.8
    (d) 250.62

69. Where manual transfer equipment is used, an optional standby system shall have adequate _____ for the supply of all equipment intended to be operated at one time.

    (a) ventilation
    (b) supervision
    (c) fuel supply
    (d) capacity and rating

70. All 15A and 20A, 125V, single-phase receptacles installed _____ of agricultural buildings shall be GFCI protected.

    (a) in areas having an equipotential plane
    (b) outdoors
    (c) in dirt confinement areas for livestock
    (d) any of these

71. Separate information technology equipment units shall be permitted to be interconnected by means of listed cables and cable assemblies. Where exposed to physical damage, supply circuits and interconnecting cables shall be protected.

    (a) True
    (b) False

72. After the completion of permanently installed swimming pools, the authority having jurisdiction shall be permitted to require _____ inspection and testing.

    (a) seasonal
    (b) monthly
    (c) periodic
    (d) annual

73. GFCI protection is required for 15A, 20A, and 30A, 125V receptacle outlets that are installed or existing as part of the permanent wiring of the building/structure when used during construction or remodeling. Listed cord sets or adapters that incorporate listed GFCI protection for portable use can be used to meet this requirement.

    (a) True
    (b) False

74. Automatic transfer switches on legally required standby systems shall be electrically operated and _____ held.

    (a) electrically
    (b) mechanically
    (c) gravity
    (d) any of these

75. A conductor used to connect the system grounded conductor, or the equipment to a grounding electrode or to a point on the grounding electrode system, is called the "_____ conductor."

    (a) main grounding
    (b) common main
    (c) equipment grounding
    (d) grounding electrode

76. Types CL2P and CL3P plenum cable shall be _____ as suitable for use in ducts, plenums, and other space for environmental air and shall be listed as having adequate fire-resistant and low-smoke producing characteristics.

    (a) marked
    (b) labeled
    (c) listed
    (d) approved

77. Type _____ cable shall be permitted to be installed in a branch-circuit raceway in a temporary underground installation.

    (a) NM
    (b) NMC
    (c) SE
    (d) any of these

78. The disconnecting means for an elevator or escalator shall be an enclosed externally operable circuit breaker or fused motor circuit switch that is _____.

    (a) capable of interrupting six times the locked-rotor current
    (b) lockable
    (c) inherently protected
    (d) suitable for use as service equipment

79. Installations supplying _____ power to ships and watercraft in marinas and boatyards are covered by the *NEC*.

    (a) shore
    (b) primary
    (c) secondary
    (d) auxiliary

80. An arc welder shall have overcurrent protection rated or set at not more than _____ percent of the rated primary current of the welder.

    (a) 100
    (b) 125
    (c) 150
    (d) 200

81. Paint, plaster, cleaners, abrasives, corrosive residues, or other contaminants may result in an undetermined alteration of optical fiber cable _____.

    (a) usefulness
    (b) voltage
    (c) properties
    (d) reliability

82. Rigid metal conduit and IMC shall not be required to be threaded when used in Class II, Division 2 locations.

    (a) True
    (b) False

83. In accordance with Article 705, the sum of all interconnected power production system-controlled currents, plus all monitored currents from other sources of supply, shall not exceed _____ percent of the ampacity of any busbar or conductor supplied by the power production sources.

    (a) 100
    (b) 115
    (c) 125
    (d) 150

84. When a fire pump motor operates at 115 percent of its full-load current rating, the supply voltage at the load terminals of the fire pump controller shall not drop more than _____ percent below the voltage rating of the motor connected to those terminals.

    (a) 5
    (b) 10
    (c) 15
    (d) 20

85. If the *NEC* requires new products that are not yet available at the time a new edition is adopted, the _____ may permit the use of the products that comply with the most recent previous edition of the *Code* adopted by that jurisdiction.

    (a) electrical engineer
    (b) master electrician
    (c) authority having jurisdiction
    (d) permit holder

86. In patient care spaces, luminaires more than _____ ft above the floor and switches located outside of the patient care vicinity shall be permitted to be connected to an equipment grounding return path complying with 517.13(A) or (B).

    (a) 7
    (b) 7½
    (c) 7¾
    (d) 8

87. Insulated overhead service conductors that are cabled together with a bare messenger and operate at not over 750 volts-to-ground shall maintain a _____ ft clearance in any direction to the water level of swimming pools, fountains, and similar installations.

    (a) 14
    (b) 16
    (c) 20
    (d) 22½

88. Stand-alone systems require either energy storage or backup power supplies.

    (a) True
    (b) False

89. Mobile home and manufactured home feeder circuit conductors shall have a capacity not less than the loads supplied and have an ampacity of not less than _____.

    (a) 50A
    (b) 60A
    (c) 100A
    (d) 200A

90. In Class III locations, locknut-bushing and double-locknut types of fittings may be depended on for bonding purposes.

    (a) True
    (b) False

91. Section(s) _____ shall apply to penetrations of the fire-resistant information technology room boundary.

    (a) 300.21
    (b) 770.26
    (c) 800.26
    (d) all of these

92. Each sign and outline lighting system shall be controlled by an externally operable switch or circuit breaker that opens all ungrounded conductors simultaneously on _____ branch circuits.

    (a) 15A
    (b) 20A
    (c) multiwire
    (d) outdoor

93. In spas or hot tubs, a clearly labeled emergency shutoff or control switch shall be _____, not less than 5 ft away, adjacent to, and within sight of the spa or hot tub.

    (a) accessible
    (b) readily accessible
    (c) available
    (d) of the pneumatic type

94. Each resistance welder shall have an overcurrent device rated or set at not more than _____ percent of the rated primary current of the welder.

    (a) 80
    (b) 100
    (c) 125
    (d) 300

95. In one- and two-family dwellings, the primary protector bonding conductor or grounding electrode conductor for communications systems shall be as short as practicable, not to exceed _____ ft in length.

    (a) 5
    (b) 8
    (c) 10
    (d) 20

96. Audio system equipment supplied by branch-circuit power shall not be placed horizontally within _____ of the inside wall of a pool, spa, hot tub, fountain, or the prevailing or tidal high water mark.

    (a) 18 in.
    (b) 2 ft
    (c) 5 ft
    (d) 10 ft

97. In land areas subject to tidal fluctuation, the electrical datum plane shall be a horizontal plane that is _____ ft above the highest tide level for the area occurring under normal circumstances, based on the highest high tide.

    (a) 1
    (b) 1½
    (c) 2
    (d) 2½

98. Transfer equipment shall be required for all optional standby systems subject to the requirements of _____ and for which an electric utility supply is either the normal or standby source.

    (a) the authority having jurisdiction
    (b) Article 702
    (c) the equipment manufacturer
    (d) the owner of the facility

99. The bottom of sign and outline lighting system equipment shall be at least _____ ft above areas accessible to vehicles unless protected from physical damage.

    (a) 12
    (b) 14
    (c) 16
    (d) 18

100. For supply-side connected interconnected power production source(s), the grounding terminal or bus for the supply-side disconnecting means shall be connected to a(an) _____ sized in accordance with 250.102, based on the size of the conductors in 705.11(B).

    (a) supply-side bonding jumper
    (b) equipment grounding conductor
    (c) grounded service conductor
    (d) grounding electrode

INDEX

Description	Rule	Page

A

Agricultural Buildings
Definitions	547.2	161
Equipotential Planes	547.10	163
Luminaires	547.8	163
Scope	547.1	161
Wiring Methods	547.5	162

Amateur and Citizen Band Transmitting and Receiving Stations—Antenna Systems
Antenna Discharge Units—Transmitting Stations	810.57	470
Bonding Conductors and Grounding Electrode	810.58	470
Other Sections	810.51	470

Arc Welders
Ampacity of Supply Conductors	630.11	231
Disconnecting Means	630.13	234
Overcurrent Protection	630.12	234

Assembly Occupancies
General Classifications	518.2	153
Illumination	518.6	154
Other Articles	518.3	154
Scope	518.1	153
Wiring Methods	518.4	154

Audio Signal Amplification and Reproduction Equipment
Audio Systems Near Bodies of Water	640.10	239
Conduit or Tubing	640.23	240
Definitions	640.2	237
Locations and Other Articles	640.3	238
Mechanical Execution of Work	640.6	238
Protection of Electrical Equipment	640.4	238
Scope	640.1	237
Use of Flexible Cords and Flexible Cables	640.21	240
Wiring Methods	640.9	239

C

Carnivals, Circuses, Fairs, and Similar Events
Definitions	525.2	157
Equipment Grounding	525.31	160
GFCI-Protected Receptacles and Equipment	525.23	160
Outdoor Portable Distribution or Termination Boxes	525.22	159
Overhead Conductor Clearances	525.5	157
Portable Equipment Grounding Conductor Continuity	525.32	160
Protection of Electrical Equipment	525.6	158
Rides, Tents, and Concessions	525.21	159
Scope	525.1	157
Wiring Methods	525.20	158

Class I Hazardous (Classified) Locations
Enclosures Containing Make-and-Break Contact Devices	501.115	120
Flexible Cords, Class I, Divisions 1 and 2	501.140	122
Grounding and Bonding	501.30	119
Limited-Energy and Communications Systems	501.150	124
Luminaires	501.130	121
Motors and Generators	501.125	121
Raceway and Cable Seals	501.15	113
Receptacles and Attachment Plugs	501.145	123
Scope	501.1	111
Utilization Equipment	501.135	122
Wiring Methods	501.10	111

Class II Hazardous (Classified) Locations
Enclosures Containing Make-and-Break Contacts	502.115	129
Explosionproof Equipment	502.5	125
Flexible Cords	502.140	131
Grounding and Bonding	502.30	128
Limited-Energy and Communications Systems	502.150	132
Luminaires	502.130	130
Motors and Generators	502.125	130
Receptacles and Attachment Plugs	502.145	132
Scope	502.1	125
Sealing	502.15	127
Wiring Methods	502.10	125

Description	Rule	Page
C (continued)		
Class III Hazardous (Classified) Locations		
Enclosures Containing Make-and-Break Contacts	503.115	135
Flexible Cords	503.140	136
Grounding and Bonding	503.30	134
Limited-Energy and Communications Systems	503.150	136
Luminaires	503.130	135
Motors and Generators	503.125	135
Receptacles and Attachment plugs	503.145	136
Scope	503.1	133
Wiring Methods	503.10	133
Commercial Garages, Repair and Storage		
Classification of Hazardous Areas	511.3	137
GFCI-Protected Receptacles	511.12	140
Scope	511.1	137
Seals	511.9	139
Special Equipment	511.10	140
Underground Wiring Below Class I Locations	511.8	139
Wiring and Equipment Above Hazardous (Classified) Locations	511.7	138
Community Antenna Television (CATV) and Radio Distribution Systems (Coaxial Cable)		
Bonding and Grounding Methods	820.100	472
Grounding of the Outer Conductive Shield of Coaxial Cables	820.93	471
Installation of Coaxial Cables and Equipment	820.133	472

D

Description	Rule	Page
Definitions		
Definitions	100	21

E

Description	Rule	Page
Electric Signs and Outline Lighting		
Ballasts, Transformers, Class 2 Power Sources, and Electronic Power Supplies	600.21	218
Branch Circuits	600.5	213
Class 2 Power Sources	600.24	218
Definitions	600.2	212
Disconnecting Means	600.6	214
Grounding and Bonding	600.7	216
Listing	600.3	212
Location	600.9	218
Markings	600.4	213
Photovoltaic (PV) Powered Sign	600.34	219
Retrofit Kits	600.35	219
Scope	600.1	211

Description	Rule	Page
Electric Vehicle Power Transfer System		
Alternating-Current Electric Vehicle Power Export (EVPE) Receptacles	625.60	230
Definitions	625.2	227
Disconnecting Means	625.43	229
Electric Vehicle Branch Circuit	625.40	228
Ground-Fault Circuit-Interrupter Protection for Personnel	625.54	230
Interactive Systems	625.48	229
Listed	625.5	228
Location	625.50	229
Overcurrent Protection	625.41	228
Rating	625.42	229
Scope	625.1	227
Ventilation	625.52	229
Elevators, Escalators, and Moving Walks		
Branch Circuit for Hoistway Pit Lighting and Receptacles	620.24	225
Branch Circuits for Elevator Car(s)	620.22	224
Branch Circuits for Machine Room/Machinery Space	620.23	225
Disconnecting Means	620.51	226
Feeder and Branch-Circuit Conductors	620.13	224
GFCI-Protected Receptacles	620.6	223
Scope	620.1	223
Short-Circuit Current Rating	620.16	224
Wiring in Elevator Hoistways, Control, and Machine Rooms/Spaces	620.37	226
Emergency Systems		
Capacity and Rating	700.4	346
Definitions	700.2	346
Emergency Illumination	700.16	351
General Requirements	700.12	349
Loads on Emergency Branch Circuits	700.15	351
Multiwire Branch Circuits	700.19	352
Scope	700.1	345
Selective Coordination	700.32	352
Signs	700.7	347
Surge Protection	700.8	347
Tests and Maintenance	700.3	346
Transfer Equipment	700.5	346
Wiring	700.10	348
Energy Storage Systems		
Charge Control	706.33	386
Circuit Sizing and Current	706.30	385
Definitions	706.2	382
Directory (Identification of Power Sources)	706.21	385
Disconnect	706.15	383

Description	Rule	Page
General	706.20	384
Listing	706.5	383
Maximum Voltage	706.9	383
Multiple Systems	706.6	383
Overcurrent Protection	706.31	386
Qualified Personnel	706.3	382
Scope	706.1	381
Storage Batteries	706.8	383
System Requirements	706.4	382

F

Fire Alarm Systems

Description	Rule	Page
Abandoned Cables	760.25	417
Access to Electrical Equipment Behind Panels Designed to Allow Access	760.21	416
Applications of Power-Limited Fire Alarm Cables (PLFA)	760.154	421
Definitions	760.2	413
Fire Alarm Circuit Identification	760.30	418
Fire Alarm Circuit Requirements	760.35	418
Installation of PLFA Cables in Buildings	760.135	420
Listing and Marking of Power-Limited Fire Alarm Cables (PLFA)	760.179	422
Marking	760.124	419
Mechanical Execution of Work	760.24	416
Other Articles	760.3	414
Power Sources for Power-Limited Fire Alarm Circuits	760.121	418
Scope	760.1	413
Separation from Power Conductors	760.136	421
Support of PLFA Cables	760.143	421
Wiring Methods on Load Side of the Power-Limited Fire Alarm Power Source	760.130	419
Wiring Methods on Supply Side of the Power-Limited Fire Alarm Source	760.127	419

Fire Pumps

Description	Rule	Page
Continuity of Power	695.4	316
Control Wiring	695.14	320
Electric Power Source(s)	695.3	316
Listed Equipment	695.10	320
Power Wiring	695.6	318
Scope	695.1	315
Surge Protection	695.15	320
Transformers	695.5	317
Voltage Drop	695.7	319

G

General Requirements

Description	Rule	Page
Approval of Conductors and Equipment	110.2	65
Arc Flash Hazard Warning	110.16	80
Available Fault Current	110.24	83
Conductor Material	110.5	66
Conductor Sizes	110.6	67
Conductor Termination and Splicing	110.14	72
Deteriorating Agents	110.11	69
Enclosure Types	110.28	92
Equipment Short-Circuit Current Rating	110.10	68
High-Leg Conductor Identification	110.15	79
Identification of Disconnecting Means	110.22	82
Interrupting Rating (Overcurrent Protective Devices)	110.9	68
Lockable Disconnecting Means	110.25	83
Markings	110.21	81
Mechanical Execution of Work	110.12	70
Mounting and Cooling of Equipment	110.13	72
Scope	110.1	65
Spaces About Electrical Equipment	110.26	84
Suitable Wiring Methods	110.8	67
Use and Product Listing (Certification) of Equipment	110.3	66
Voltage Rating of Electrical Equipment	110.4	66
Wiring Integrity	110.7	67

General Requirements for Communications Circuits

Description	Rule	Page
Bonding or Interruption	805.93	462
Communications Cable(s) Substitutions	805.154	463
Definitions	805.2	461
Dwelling Unit Communications Outlet	805.156	463
Installation of Communications Wires, Cables, and Equipment	805.133	462
Installation of Equipment	805.18	461
Primary Protection	805.90	462
Scope	805.1	461

General Requirements for Communications Systems

Description	Rule	Page
Abandoned Cable	800.25	454
Access to Electrical Equipment Behind Panels Designed to Allow Access	800.21	453
Applications of Listed Communications Wires, Cables, and Raceways, and Listed Cable Routing Assemblies	800.154	460
Cable and Primary Protector Bonding	800.100	456
Definitions	800.2	451
Installation of Communications Wires, Cables, Raceways, and Cable Routing Assemblies	800.113	459
Mechanical Execution of Work	800.24	453
Metal Entrance Conduit Bonding	800.49	456

Description	Rule	Page

G (continued)

General Requirements for Communications Systems (continued)

Other Articles	800.3	452
Plenum, Riser, General-Purpose, and Limited Use Cables	800.179	460
Raceways and Cable Routing Assemblies	800.110	458
Scope	800.1	451
Separation from Lightning Conductors	800.53	456
Spread of Fire or Products of Combustion	800.26	454

H

Hazardous (Classified) Locations

Classifications of Hazardous Locations	500.5	105
Documentation	500.4	104
Equipment	500.8	109
Material Groups	500.6	107
Other Articles	500.3	104
Protection Techniques	500.7	107
Scope—Articles 500 Through 503	500.1	104

Health Care Facilities

Definitions	517.2	145
Equipment Grounding Conductor for Receptacles and Fixed Electrical Equipment in Patient Care Spaces	517.13	147
General Care Spaces	517.18	151
Isolated Ground Receptacles	517.16	150
Scope	517.1	145
Wiring Methods	517.12	147

I

Information Technology Equipment (ITE)

Definitions	645.2	241
Disconnecting Means	645.10	245
Equipment Grounding and Bonding	645.15	245
Other Articles	645.3	241
Scope	645.1	241
Special Requirements	645.4	242
Supply Circuits and Interconnecting Cables	645.5	242

Interconnected Electric Power Production Sources

Circuit Sizing and Current	705.28	377
Definitions	705.2	365
Disconnect	705.20	376
Equipment Approval	705.6	366
Ground-Fault Protection	705.32	378
Identification of Power Sources	705.10	366
Interrupting and Short-Circuit Current Rating	705.16	376

Description	Rule	Page
Load-Side Source Connections	705.12	369
Loss of Utility Power	705.40	378
Overcurrent Protection	705.30	377
Power Control Systems	705.13	375
Scope	705.1	365
Supply-Side Source Connections	705.11	367
System Installation	705.8	366
Unbalanced Interconnections	705.45	379
Wiring Methods	705.25	376

L

Large-Scale Photovoltaic (PV) Electric Supply Stations

Arc-Fault Mitigation	691.10	314
Conformance of Construction to Engineered Design	691.7	314
Direct-Current Operating Voltage	691.8	314
Disconnect for Isolating Photovoltaic Equipment	691.9	314
Engineered Design	691.6	314
Equipment	691.5	314
Fence Bonding and Grounding	691.11	314
Scope	691.1	313
Special Requirements for Large-Scale PV Electric Supply Stations	691.4	313

Legally Required Standby Systems

Capacity and Rating	701.4	354
Definition	701.2	353
General Requirements	701.12	355
Scope	701.1	353
Selective Coordination	701.32	357
Signals	701.6	355
Signs	701.7	355
Tests and Maintenance	701.3	354
Transfer Equipment	701.5	354
Wiring	701.10	355

M

Manufactured Wiring Systems

Definition	604.2	221
Installation—Securing and Supporting	604.7	222
Listing Requirements	604.6	221
Scope	604.1	221
Uses Permitted	604.10	222

Marinas, Boatyards, and Docking Facilities

Boat Hoists	555.9	173
Boat Receptacle Disconnecting Means	555.36	177
Bonding of Noncurrent-Carrying Metal Parts	555.13	174
Definitions	555.2	169
Electric Shock Hazard Signage	555.10	173

Description	Rule	Page
Electrical Connections	555.30	174
Electrical Datum Plane Distances	555.3	171
Equipment Grounding Conductor	555.37	177
Ground-Fault Protection of Equipment (GFPE) and Ground-Fault Circuit-Interrupter (GFCI) Protection	555.35	176
Load Calculations for Service and Feeder Conductors	555.6	172
Location of Service Equipment	555.4	172
Maximum Voltage	555.5	172
Motor Fuel Dispensing Stations—Hazardous (Classified) Locations	555.11	173
Receptacles	555.33	175
Repair Facilities—Hazardous (Classified) Locations	555.12	174
Scope	555.1	169
Transformers	555.7	172
Wiring Methods and Installation	555.34	175

Mobile Homes, Manufactured Homes, and Mobile Home Parks

Description	Rule	Page
AFCI Protection	550.25	167
Definitions	550.2	165
Feeder	550.33	167
General Requirements	550.4	166
Mobile and Manufactured Home Service Disconnect	550.32	167
Receptacle Outlets	550.13	166
Scope	550.1	165
Wiring Methods and Materials	550.15	166

Motor Fuel Dispensing Facilities

Description	Rule	Page
Classification of Locations	514.3	141
Conduit Seal	514.9	143
Grounding and Bonding	514.16	144
Scope	514.1	141
Underground Wiring	514.8	142
Wiring and Equipment Above Class I Locations	514.7	142
Wiring and Equipment Within Class I Locations	514.4	142

N

NEC Introduction

Description	Rule	Page
Code Arrangement	90.3	10
Enforcement	90.4	11
Examination of Equipment for Product Safety	90.7	13
Mandatory Requirements and Explanatory Material	90.5	13
Purpose of the *NEC*	90.1	7
Scope of the *NEC*	90.2	8

O

Optical Fiber Cables

Description	Rule	Page
Abandoned Cable	770.25	425
Access to Electrical Equipment Behind Panels Designed to Allow Access	770.21	424
Applications of Listed Optical Fiber Cables	770.154	428
Definitions	770.2	423
Grounding	770.114	428
Installation of Optical Fiber Cables	770.113	427
Installation of Optical Fiber Cables and Electrical Conductors	770.133	428
Mechanical Execution of Work	770.24	424
Other Articles	770.3	424
Raceways and Cable Routing Assemblies, and Cable Trays for Optical Fiber Cables	770.110	426
Scope	770.1	423
Spread of Fire or Products of Combustion	770.26	426

Optional Standby Systems

Description	Rule	Page
Capacity and Rating	702.4	360
Definition	702.2	360
Outdoor Generator Sets	702.12	363
Portable Generator Grounding	702.11	363
Scope	702.1	359
Signals	702.6	362
Signs	702.7	362
Transfer Equipment	702.5	361
Wiring	702.10	362

R

Receiving Equipment—Antenna Systems

Description	Rule	Page
Antenna Discharge Unit	810.20	467
Avoid Contact with Conductors of Other Systems	810.13	466
Bonding Conductors and Grounding Electrode Conductors	810.21	468
Clearances	810.18	467
Metal Antenna Supports—Bonding	810.15	467
Supports	810.12	466

Remote-Control, Signaling, and Power-Limited Circuits

Class 1 Circuit Requirements

Description	Rule	Page
Class 1 Circuit Classifications and Requirements	725.41	400
Class 1 Circuit Conductors	725.49	402
Class 1 Circuit Overcurrent Protection	725.43	401
Class 1 Circuit Overcurrent Protective Device Location	725.45	401
Class 1 Circuit Wiring Methods	725.46	401
Conductors of Different Circuits in Same Cable, Cable Tray, Enclosure, or Raceway	725.48	401
Number of Conductors in a Raceway	725.51	402

Index

Description	Rule	Page
R (continued)		
Class 2 Circuit Requirements		
Applications of Class 2 Cables	725.154	410
Circuit Marking	725.124	403
Conductors of Different Circuits in Same Cable, Enclosure, Cable Tray, Raceway, or Cable Routing Assembly	725.139	407
Installation of Class 2 Cables	725.135	404
Power Sources for Class 2 Circuits	725.121	402
Separation from Power Conductors	725.136	405
Support	725.143	408
Transmission of Power and Data	725.144	408
Wiring Methods on Load Side of the Class 2 Power Source	725.130	404
Wiring Methods on Supply Side of the Class 2 Power Source	725.127	403
General		
Abandoned Cable	725.25	399
Circuit Requirements	725.35	400
Definitions	725.2	394
Electrical Equipment Behind Access Panels	725.21	398
Mechanical Execution of Work	725.24	398
Other Articles	725.3	394
Safety-Control Equipment	725.31	400
Scope	725.1	393
Resistance Welders		
Ampacity of Supply Conductor	630.31	234
Disconnecting Means	630.33	236
Overcurrent Protection	630.32	236

S

Description	Rule	Page
Solar Photovoltaic (PV)		
Systems Access to Boxes	690.34	306
Alternating-Current Modules and Systems	690.6	283
Arc-Fault Circuit Protection	690.11	295
Circuit Current and Conductor Sizing	690.8	288
Component Interconnections	690.32	305
Connection to Other Power Sources	690.59	311
Connectors (Mating)	690.33	305
Definitions	690.2	278
Direct-Current PV Circuit Label	690.53	309
Energy Storage	690.55	310
Energy Storage Systems	690.71	311
Equipment Grounding and Bonding	690.43	306
General Requirements	690.4	282
Grounding Electrode System	690.47	308
Identification of Power Sources	690.56	310

Description	Rule	Page
Interactive System Point of Interconnection	690.54	310
Maximum PV System Direct-Current Circuit Voltage	690.7	284
Overcurrent Protection	690.9	293
PV Equipment Disconnecting Means to Isolate PV Equipment	690.15	298
PV System Disconnect	690.13	297
Rapid Shutdown	690.12	295
Scope	690.1	277
Self-Regulated PV Charge Control	690.72	312
Size of Equipment Grounding Conductors	690.45	308
Stand-Alone Systems	690.10	295
Wiring Methods	690.31	300
Stand-Alone Systems		
Equipment Approval	710.6	389
General	710.15	390
Identification of Power Sources	710.10	390
Scope	710.1	389
Stand-Alone Inverter Input Circuit Current	710.12	390
Swimming Pools, Spas, Hot Tubs, Fountains, and Similar Installations		
Electrically Powered Pool Lifts		
Bonding	680.83	275
Equipment Approval	680.81	274
General	680.80	274
Protection	680.82	275
Switching Devices and Receptacles	680.84	275
Fountains		
Connection to an Equipment Grounding Conductor	680.54	272
Cord-and-Plug-Connected Equipment	680.56	272
Electric Signs in or Adjacent to Fountains	680.57	272
General	680.50	271
GFCI Protection for Adjacent Receptacles	680.58	273
GFCI Protection for Permanently Installed Nonsubmersible Pumps	680.59	273
Luminaires and Submersible Equipment	680.51	271
Methods of Equipment Grounding	680.55	272
General Requirements		
Approval of Equipment	680.3	251
Bonding and Equipment Grounding	680.6	251
Bonding and Equipment Grounding Terminals	680.7	251
Definitions	680.2	248
Electric Water Heaters	680.10	252
Equipment Rooms and Pits	680.12	253
Ground-Fault Circuit Interrupters	680.5	251
Inspections After Installation	680.4	251
Maintenance Disconnecting Means	680.13	253
Overhead Conductor Clearance	680.9	251

Description	Rule	Page
Scope	680.1	247
Underground Wiring	680.11	253
Wiring Methods in Corrosive Environment	680.14	254
Hydromassage Bathtubs		
Accessibility	680.73	273
Equipotential Bonding	680.74	274
General	680.70	273
GFCI Protection	680.71	273
Permanently Installed Pools		
Equipotential Bonding	680.26	262
Feeders	680.25	262
Gas-Fired Water Heaters	680.28	267
General	680.20	254
Junction Box, Transformer, or GFCI Enclosure	680.24	261
Pool Motors	680.21	254
Receptacles, Luminaires, and Switches	680.22	255
Specialized Equipment	680.27	267
Underwater Pool Luminaires	680.23	257
Spas and Hot Tubs, and Permanently Installed Immersion Pools		
Emergency Switch for Spas and Hot Tubs	680.41	268
General	680.40	268
GFCI Protection	680.44	270
Indoor Installations	680.43	269
Outdoor Installations	680.42	269
Permanently Installed Immersion Pools	680.45	270

Description	Rule	Page
Storable Pools, Spas, Hot Tubs, and Immersion Pools		
General	680.30	267
GFCI Protection	680.32	267
Pumps	680.31	267
Receptacle Locations	680.34	268
Storable and Portable Immersion Pools	680.35	268

T

Temporary Installations

	Rule	Page
All Wiring Installations	590.2	179
General	590.4	180
GFCI Protection for Personnel	590.6	182
Listing of Decorative Lighting	590.5	182
Overcurrent Protective Devices	590.8	183
Scope	590.1	179
Time Constraints	590.3	179

Notes

ABOUT THE AUTHOR

Mike Holt—Author

Founder and President
Mike Holt Enterprises
Groveland, Florida

Mike Holt is an author, businessman, educator, speaker, publisher and *National Electrical Code* expert. He has written hundreds of electrical training books and articles, founded three successful businesses, and has taught thousands of electrical *Code* seminars across the US and internationally. His electrical training courses have set the standard for trade education, enabling electrical professionals across the country to take their careers to the next level.

Mike's approach to electrical training is based on his own experience as an electrician, contractor, inspector and teacher. Because of his struggles in his early education, he's never lost sight of how hard it can be for students who are intimidated by school, by their own feelings towards learning, or by the complexity of the *NEC*. As a result of that, he's mastered the art of explaining complicated concepts in a straightforward and direct style. He's always felt a responsibility to his students and to the electrical industry to provide education beyond the scope of just passing an exam. This commitment, coupled with the lessons he learned at the University of Miami's MBA program, have helped him build one of the largest electrical training and publishing companies in the United States.

Mike's one-of-a-kind presentation style and his ability to simplify and clarify technical concepts explain his unique position as one of the premier educators and *Code* experts in the country. In addition to the materials he's produced, and the extensive list of companies around the world for whom he's provided training, Mike has written articles that have been seen in numerous industry magazines including, *Electrical Construction & Maintenance (EC&M), CEE News, Electrical Design and Installation (EDI), Electrical Contractor (EC), International Association of Electrical Inspectors (IAEI News), The Electrical Distributor (TED), Power Quality (PQ),* and *Solar Pro.*

Mike's ultimate goal has always been to increase electrical safety and improve lives and he is always looking for the best ways for his students to learn and teach the *Code* and pass electrical exams. His passion for the electrical field continues to grow and today he is more committed than ever to serve this industry.

His commitment to pushing boundaries and setting high standards extends into his personal life. Mike's an eight-time Overall National Barefoot Waterski Champion with more than 20 gold medals, and many national records, and he has competed in three World Barefoot Tournaments. In 2015, at the tender age of 64, he started a new adventure—competitive mountain bike racing. Every day he continues to find ways to motivate himself, both mentally and physically.

Mike and his wife, Linda, reside in New Mexico and Florida, and are the parents of seven children and six grandchildren. As his life has changed over the years, a few things have remained constant: his commitment to God, his love for his family, and doing what he can to change the lives of others through his products and seminars.

Special Acknowledgments

My Family. First, I want to thank God for my godly wife who's always by my side and also for my children.

My Staff. A personal thank you goes to my team at Mike Holt Enterprises for all the work they do to help me with my mission of changing peoples' lives through education. They work tirelessly to ensure that in addition to our products meeting and exceeding the educational needs of our customers, we stay committed to building life-long relationships with them throughout their electrical careers.

The National Fire Protection Association. A special thank you must be given to the staff at the National Fire Protection Association (NFPA), publishers of the *NEC*—in particular, Jeff Sargent for his assistance in answering my many *Code* questions over the years. Jeff, you're a "first class" guy, and I admire your dedication and commitment to helping others understand the *NEC*. Other former NFPA staff members I would like to thank include John Caloggero, Joe Ross, and Dick Murray for their help in the past.

ABOUT THE ILLUSTRATOR

Mike Culbreath—Illustrator

Mike Culbreath
Graphic Illustrator
Alden, Michigan

Mike Culbreath has devoted his career to the electrical industry and worked his way up from apprentice electrician to master electrician. He started working in the electrical field doing residential and light commercial construction, and later did service work and custom electrical installations. While working as a journeyman electrician, he suffered a serious on-the-job knee injury. As part of his rehabilitation, Mike completed courses at Mike Holt Enterprises, and then passed the exam to receive his Master Electrician's license. In 1986, with a keen interest in continuing education for electricians, he joined the staff to update material and began illustrating Mike Holt's textbooks and magazine articles.

Mike started with simple hand-drawn diagrams and cut-and-paste graphics. Frustrated by the limitations of that style of illustrating, he took a company computer home to learn how to operate some basic computer graphics software. Realizing that computer graphics offered a lot of flexibility for creating illustrations, Mike took every computer graphics class and seminar he could to help develop his skills. He's worked as an illustrator and editor with the company for over 30 years and, as Mike Holt has proudly acknowledged, has helped to transform his words and visions into lifelike graphics.

Originally from south Florida, Mike now lives in northern lower Michigan where he enjoys hiking, kayaking, photography, gardening, and cooking; but his real passion is his horses. He also loves spending time with his children Dawn and Mac and his grandchildren Jonah, Kieley, and Scarlet.

Mike Culbreath-Special Acknowledgments

I would like to thank Eric Stromberg, an electrical engineer and super geek (and I mean that in the most complimentary manner, this guy is brilliant), for helping me keep our graphics as technically correct as possible. I would also like to thank all our students for the wonderful feedback to help improve our graphics.

A special thank you goes to Cathleen Kwas for making me look good with her outstanding layout design and typesetting skills; to Toni Culbreath who proofreads all of my material; and to Dawn Babbitt who has assisted me in the production and editing of our graphics. I would also like to acknowledge Belynda Holt Pinto, our Executive Vice-President, Brian House for his input (another really brilliant guy), and the rest of the outstanding staff at Mike Holt Enterprises, for all the hard work they do to help produce and distribute these outstanding products.

And last but not least, I need to give a special thank you to Mike Holt for not firing me over 30 years ago when I "borrowed" one of his computers and took it home to begin the process of learning how to do computer illustrations. He gave me the opportunity and time needed to develop my computer graphics skills. He's been an amazing friend and mentor since I met him as a student many years ago. Thanks for believing in me and allowing me to be part of the Mike Holt Enterprises family.

ABOUT THE MIKE HOLT TEAM

There are many people who played a role in the production of this textbook. Their efforts are reflected in the quality and organization of the information contained in this textbook, and in its technical accuracy, completeness, and usability.

Technical Writing

Brian House is Vice President of Digital and Technical Training at Mike Holt Enterprises and a permanent member of the video teams. He played a key role in editing this textbook, coordinating the content, and researching to assure the technical accuracy and flow of the information and illustrations presented.

Editorial and Production

A special thanks goes to **Toni Culbreath** for her outstanding contribution to this project. She worked tirelessly to proofread and edit this publication. Her attention to detail and her dedication is irreplaceable.

Dan Haruch is the newest member of our technical team. His skillset and general knowledge of the *NEC*, combined with his work ethic and ability to work with other members of the production team, were a major part of the successful publication of this textbook.

Many thanks to **Cathleen Kwas** who did the design, layout, and production of this textbook. Her desire to create the best possible product for our customers is greatly appreciated.

Also, thanks to **Paula Birchfield** who was the Production Coordinator for this product. She helped keep everything flowing and tied up all the loose ends. She, **Jeff Crandall** and **Kirsten Shea** did a great job proofing the final files prior to printing.

Video Team

The following special people provided technical advice in the development of this textbook as they served on the video team along with author **Mike Holt** and graphic illustrator **Mike Culbreath**.

Daniel Brian House
Master Electrician, Instructor
Ocala, Florida

Brian House is Vice President of Digital and Technical Training at Mike Holt Enterprises, and a Certified Mike Holt Instructor. Starting in the 1990s Brian owned and ran a contracting firm that did everything from service work to designing energy-efficient lighting retrofits, exploring "green" biomass generators, and partnering with residential PV companies. He began teaching seminars in 2000 after joining the elite group of instructors who attended Mike Holt's Train the Trainer boot camp. Brian was personally selected for development by Mike Holt after being named as one of the top presenters in that class. He now travels around the country to teach Mike Holt seminars to groups that include electricians, instructors, the military, and engineers. His first-hand experience as an electrical contractor, along with Mike Holt's instructor training, gave him a teaching style that is practical, straightforward, and refreshing.

Brian is high-energy, with a passion for doing business the right way. He expresses his commitment to the industry and his love for its people whether he's teaching, working on books, or developing instructional programs. Brian also leads the Mike Holt Enterprises apprenticeship and digital products teams. They're creating cutting-edge training tools and partnering with apprenticeship programs nation-wide to help them take their curriculum to the next level.

Brian and his wife Carissa have shared the joy of their four children and many foster children during 22 years of marriage. When not mentoring youth at work or church, he can be found racing mountain bikes with his kids or fly fishing on Florida's Intracoastal Waterway. He's passionate about helping others and regularly engages with the youth of his community to motivate them into exploring their future.

Video Team | About the Mike Holt Team

Eric Stromberg, P.E.
Electrical Engineer/Instructor
Los Alamos, New Mexico

Eric Stromberg has a bachelor's degree in electrical engineering and is a professional engineer. He started in the electrical industry when he was a teenager helping the neighborhood electrician. After high school, and a year of college, Eric worked for a couple of different audio companies, installing sound systems in a variety of locations from small buildings to baseball stadiums. After returning to college he worked as a journeyman wireman for an electrical contractor.

After graduating from the University of Houston, Eric took a job as an electronic technician and installed and serviced life safety systems in high-rise buildings. After seven years he went to work for Dow Chemical as a power distribution engineer. His work with audio systems had made him very sensitive to grounding issues and he took this experience with him into power distribution. Because of this expertise, Eric became one of Dow's grounding subject matter experts. This is also how Eric met Mike Holt, as Mike was looking for grounding experts for his 2002 Grounding vs. Bonding video.

Eric taught the *National Electrical Code* for professional engineering exam preparation for over 20 years, and has held continuing education teacher certificates for the states of Texas and New Mexico. He was on the electrical licensing and advisory board for the State of Texas, as well as on their electrician licensing exam board. Eric now works for a Department of Energy research laboratory in New Mexico, where he's responsible for the electrical standards as well as being a part of the laboratory's AHJ.

Eric's oldest daughter lives with her husband in Zurich, Switzerland, where she teaches for an international school. His son served in the Air Force, has a degree in Aviation logistics, and is a pilot and owner of an aerial photography business. His youngest daughter is a singer/songwriter in Los Angeles.

Mario Valdes, Jr.
Electrical Inspector, Plans Examiner
Pembroke Pines, Florida

Mario Valdes Jr. is an electrical inspector and plans examiner for an engineering firm that does private provider and municipal support services. He started his career at 16 years old with his father, who owns an electrical contracting company and worked himself up to a master electrician. Once he received his Florida state contractor's license, he ran his father's company as a project manager and estimator. Mario's passion for the *National Electrical Code* led him to obtain his inspector and plan review certifications to embark on a new journey as an electrical professional in the *Code*-compliance industry.

Mario is a goal setter and plans to become a certified instructor within a year. He's worked in very complex projects such as hospitals, casinos, hotels, and multi-family high-rise buildings bringing him diverse experience in the electrical field. He is a member of the IAEI, NFPA, & ICC and believes that by staying active in these organizations he'll be ahead of the game, with cutting-edge knowledge pertaining to safety codes. He enjoys participating in meetings and giving his input on certain topics.

When not immersed in the electrical world he enjoys fitness training because a healthy mind requires a healthy body.

Mario resides in Miami, Florida with his beautiful family which includes his wife and his two sons, and they enjoy family getaways to Disney World and other amusement parks.